READINGS IN AMERICAN
EDUCATIONAL HISTORY

READINGS IN AMERICAN EDUCATIONAL HISTORY

BY

Edgar W. Knight, Ph. D.

Kenan Professor of Educational History
University of North Carolina

AND

Clifton L. Hall, Ph. D.

Associate Professor of Education
George Peabody College for Teachers

GREENWOOD PRESS, PUBLISHERS
NEW YORK

Preface

«««««««««««««««««««««««««««««««««««<◇>»»»»»»»»»»»»»»»»»»»»»»»»»»»»»»»

The purpose of this collection of documents of American education is to make easily available to students and teachers of the subject carefully selected original sources of the educational and social history of the United States. The documents here brought together begin with those on Henrico College and East India School in Virginia in the early part of the seventeenth century—the first educational efforts in English North America—and continue into 1950.

Interpretations of history are likely to vary, according to the interpreters. The late Charles A. Beard referred to written history as "the historian's act of faith," but it is generally recognized that faiths differ widely from one another. One result of this condition is that few teachers of educational and social history would say that they are entirely satisfied with the conventional textbooks. Nor are students today, particularly at the collegiate level, as ready and as willing as they once seemed to be to accept at face value all the statements found in their prescribed textbooks, however eminent the writers of these may be. In recent years, particularly with the influx of students under the G.I. Bill of Rights, collegiate classrooms have become pervaded more than formerly by a critical and sometimes even a skeptical attitude.

For many reasons an increasing number of teachers of educational and social history should like to provide their students with primary sources in the subject rather than to have them confine their reading to one or more textbooks. Moreover, acquaintance with original sources is encouragingly becoming properly recognized as the foundation of all sound historical knowledge; and nowadays good practice in teaching history, whether educational and social, political, economic, or of other aspects, requires that students of the subject have access to and acquaintance with the original sources. One difficulty in providing for such acquaintance in educational and social history has generally been the inaccessibility of such material. In an effort partially to remove this difficulty, the present volume has been prepared.

When George H. Martin in 1894 published the *Evolution of the Massachusetts Public School System* he said in the preface that a complete history of education in that state could never be prepared until the source materials,

v

which were very abundant but widely scattered, were made available and properly used. That complaint, made more than a half century ago in Massachusetts, which has always been careful to preserve its records, has often been heard in and of other states. Moreover, a complete history of American education will be difficult if not impossible to write, until more attention has been given to the original sources in the subject.

It is encouraging to students and teachers of the subject to observe the recent increase of interest in the educational and social history of the United States. This increase of interest has appeared in the large number of textbooks published in the field in the past few years as well as by the recent appearance of the *History of Education Journal*. In an effort further to stimulate this interest, it seemed that the time was ripe for the publication of a carefully selected collection of documents of American education, and more particularly so since there appeared to be none in print.

Every effort has been made in this collection to make it representative of education in the various historical periods and in its various phases. Here the teacher and the student of the subject will find documents which throw light on the "battles" which have been waged around the so-called principles of American education and in the struggles of the American people to have these principles established in actual practice. Among these principles are those of public support and control, the education of teachers, the extension of education upward from the elementary school, and free and universal and compulsory education. The documents here included illustrate the persistence of so-called "problems" whose roots run back far into the past. This volume should therefore be helpful to students and teachers of almost all aspects of American education: students and teachers of educational administration and supervision; elementary, secondary, and higher education; the education of teachers; educational practices; educational issues between Church and State in education; Federal relations in education; and many other issues which are so acute in the current American educational scene.

The editors are fully conscious that the choice of documents by other editors and compilers might have resulted in a different collection. Although they had competent advice from teachers and students of history throughout the United States, the editors alone must be held responsible for the selection here made. The abundance of material which demanded consideration for inclusion in the volume presented their chief difficulty. From this abundance choices had to be made, in an effort to prepare a volume not too bulky for ready use but at the same time sufficiently inclusive to provide the teacher and student of the subject with a representative collection of the most important documents of American education. These have been experimented with and tested in classes in educational and social history at the University of North Carolina, Columbia University, George Peabody College for Teachers, and the University of Michigan. Except for brief previews of each section and occasional explanatory notes, the documents are intended to speak for themselves.

These documents bear on "the colonial climate" and its apprenticeship theories and practices, the colonial teacher, philanthropy and education, advertisements of schools, teachers and tutors, tutorial practices, and varied educational interests and activities. There are documents on opposition to the education of Americans abroad; early proposals for a national university and the removal of the College of Geneva to Virginia; early movements for religious freedom and the separation of the Church and State; early copyright laws and efforts to protect literary property. Also included are original materials on Lancasterian schools, the Lyceum, the early labor movement and its educational interests, manual labor and agricultural schools, and significant letters by Horace Mann and Henry Barnard and other antebellum educational leaders; on elementary, secondary, higher education and the education of teachers, collegiate rules, on efforts to gain public support and public control of education and compulsory-attendance legislation; on teachers and teaching and educational practices; on court decisions effecting education; reports of national educational committees; the education and other rights of women and of Negroes; loyalty oaths for teachers; Federal aid to education and educational activities of the Federal government; issues in graduate work; interest in international educational relations and the work of UNESCO; and many other phases of education. It is believed that these documents will stimulate intelligent study of contemporary problems and issues in American education.

Grateful acknowledgment is made to Isaac Copeland, Carolyn A. Daniel, Thomas L. Patrick, Elaine von Oesen, and Minna Pickard for intelligent research assistance in locating some of the documents, and to Mrs. Mabel T. Hill, Mrs. Sibyl Georch Powe and Mrs. Dorothy Lyon, for invaluable help in transcribing and verifying the materials.

E. W. K.
C. L. H.

Table of Contents

«««««« «««««««««««««««««««««««««««««««««««<>»»»»»»»»»»»»»»»»»»»»»»»»»»»»»»»»»»

PAGE

PREFACE v

I

THE COLONIAL CLIMATE

1. Henrico College and the East India School

A Letter from "Dust and Ashes" Is Presented to the Company, 1621 . . . 4
Passengers and Crew of Royal James Make Contribution to School in Virginia, 1621 5
Report of the Indian Massacre Which Destroyed the Prospects of the College, 1622 5
The Virginia Company of London Is Ready to Assist the East India School, 1625 7

2. Apprenticeship Theories and Practices

Extract from the English Act of 1601 8
Apprenticeship Legislation in Virginia, 1642 9
Initial Legislation on Apprenticeship in Massachusetts, 1642 10
Some Apprenticeship Indentures in Virginia in the Seventeenth Century . . 10
Some Apprenticeship Indentures in New England in the Seventeenth Century . 12
Indenture of John Campbell to a Schoolmaster in New York, 1722 . . . 13
Andrew Johnson is Apprenticed to a Tailor, 1822 14
Andrew Johnson's Master Offers a Reward of Ten Dollars for the Return of the Apprentice, 1824 15
Indentured Schoolmasters for Disposal in Baltimore, 1786 15

3. The Colonial Teacher

Instructions from the Classis of Amsterdam to Schoolmasters in the Dutch Possessions, 1636 16
Instructions to Evert Pietersen, a Teacher in New Amsterdam, 1661 . . . 16
John Shutte is Licensed to Teach in Albany, New York, 1665 17
Contract with a Dutch Schoolmaster in Flatbush, New York, 1682 . . . 17
The General Assembly of Virginia Requests Change in the Method of Licensing Schoolmasters in That Colony and the Reply of the Governor, 1686 . . 19
Ezekiel Cheever, Famed New England Schoolmaster, Asks to Keep His Position and Pay, c. 1687 20
Governor Edward Cornbury Grants License to James Jeffray to Teach in the City of New York, 1706 21
Instructions for the Clergy Employed by the Society for the Propagation of the Gospel in Foreign Parts, 1706 21
Instructions for Schoolmasters Employed by the Society, 1706 26

ix

PAGE

Qualifications Required of Schoolmasters of the Society, 1711 27
Membership in the Established Church Required of the Master of a School in
    Charleston, South Carolina, 1712 29
England's Oath Required of Teachers and Others, 1714 29
A Presbyterian Schoolmaster in South Carolina Promises to Conform to the
    Rites of the Established Church, 1747 29
Agreement Between the Congregation of the Reformed Church, Lancaster,
    Pennsylvania, and John Hoffman, Teacher, 1747 30
Contract Between a Schoolmaster and the Congregation of New Providence,
    Montgomery County, Pennsylvania, c. 1750 30
One Purpose of Benjamin Franklin's Academy in Philadelphia Was to Prepare
    Teachers, 1750 31
Christopher Dock Tells How Children Should Be Received and Treated in
    School, 1750 31
Schoolmasters in New Jersey Must Hold License from the Bishop of London,
    1758 35
Qualifications Required of Teachers in New Jersey, 1760 35
Membership in the Established Church Required of the Master of a School in
    Newbern, North Carolina, 1766 36
Massachusetts Enacts a Loyalty Oath for Teachers, 1776 36
New Jersey Requires Schoolmasters to Take Oaths of Abjuration and Allegiance,
    1777 37
Pennsylvania Requires Loyalty Oath for Teachers, 1778 37
An Early Protest Against a Loyalty Oath for Teachers, 1779 38
Joshua Bennett's Fine Is Remitted, 1779 40

4. *Advertisements of Schools, Teachers and Tutors; Tutorial Practices*

Many Subjects Are Offered in Charleston, South Carolina, 1733, 1744 . . . 41
French and Spanish Languages Are Taught in New York, 1735 42
Andrew Lamb Qualifies Youth for Business in Philadelphia, 1751 42
Advertisement of John Walker, 1752 43
Advertisement of Reverend B. Booth's Academy Near Liverpool, England, 1766   44
Advertisement of an Academy in County York, England, 1769 44
Philip Vickers Fithian Tells John Peck How to Behave as a Tutor in Virginia,
    1774 45
John Davis, Tutor from England, Has a Lively Interview with a South Carolina
    Planter and His Wife, 1797 54

5. *Varied Educational Interests and Activities*

The Will of Benjamin Syms (Virginia), 1634 58
"The Laws, Liberties and Orders of Harvard College," 1642-1646 60
Initial Educational Legislation in Massachusetts, 1647 62
Rules of Harvard College, 1650 63
President Henry Dunster is Dismissed from Harvard Because of His Views on
    Infant Baptism, 1653 64
On Fines and Corporal Punishment at Harvard, 1656 67
The Need for a College in Virginia, 1660-1662 67
Sir William Berkeley's Report on Virginia, 1671 68
Thomas Budd's Views on Educational Provisions Needed in Pennsylvania and
    New Jersey, 1685 69
Remonstrance Against Locating the Collegiate School at New Haven, 1717 . 71
Notice of John Peter Zenger to the Subscribers to His Paper, November 25, 1734   72
Subjects and Questions Discussed by Candidates for the Degree of Master of
    Arts at Harvard, July 6, 1743 72
Benjamin Franklin's "Proposals Relating to the Education of Youth in Pen-
    silvania," 1749 74

PAGE

List of Pecuniary Mulcts (Fines) at Harvard, c. 1750 80
Advertisement Announcing the Opening of King's (Now Columbia) College, 1754 81
Lottery for King's College in New York, 1754 83
The College of William and Mary Confers Honorary Degree of Master of Arts on Benjamin Franklin, 1756 84
The Overseers of Harvard Remonstrate Against Another College in Massachusetts, 1762 84
Thomas Jefferson to John Page About Conditions at the College of William and Mary, 1763 87
George Washington Receives the Degree of LL.D. from Harvard, 1776 . . 87

II

TOWARD EDUCATIONAL INDEPENDENCE

1. Opposition to the Education of Americans in Europe

A Benefit Expected from Benjamin Franklin's Academy in Philadelphia, 1750 91
Thomas Jefferson on Education in Europe, 1785 91
The Legislature of Georgia Makes Aliens of Georgians Who Study in Europe, 1785 93
Noah Webster Criticizes the Education of Americans in Europe, 1788 . . . 93
Resolution of the Virginia House of Delegates on Education in Europe, December 1, 1795 96
George Washington on Education in Europe, 1795 97

2. Early Proposals for a National University and for the Removal of the College of Geneva to Virginia

Samuel Blodget's Account of a Conversation with General Washington on a National University, 1775 98
The Legislature of Virginia Vests in George Washington Shares of Stock in Navigation Companies, 1784 99
George Washington to the Commissioners of the Federal District on the National University, 1795 100
George Washington to John Adams on the Removal of the College of Geneva to Virginia, 1794 101
George Washington to Congress on a National University, 1796 102
George Washington Gives His Shares in the Potomac Company for the National University, 1799 103
Jefferson to Congress on National University, 1806 103
A Bill for the Establishment of a National University, 1816 104
The Secretary of the Treasury to the President of the Senate on the Shares of Stock Which Washington Left for the National University, 1905 . . . 105

3. Early Movement for Religious Freedom: Separation of Church and State

Constitutional Provisions in North Carolina, 1776 107
Jefferson's Bill for Establishing Religious Freedom in Virginia, 1779 . . . 108
Extracts from the Massachusetts Bill of Rights, 1780 110
Benjamin Franklin to "Messrs. Weems and Gant, Citizens of the United States in London," July 18, 1784 110
Massachusetts Establishes Complete Religious Freedom, 1833 112

4. Early Constitutional Provisions for Schools

PAGE

Pennsylvania, 1776 113
North Carolina, 1776; Continued Unchanged in the Constitution of 1835 . . 113
Georgia, 1777 114
Vermont, 1777 114
Massachusetts, 1780 114
New Hampshire, 1784, 1792 116
Extract from the Ordinance of 1787 116
Vermont, 1787 116
Pennsylvania, 1790, 1838 117
Delaware, 1792; Continued Unchanged in the Constitution of 1831 117
Georgia, 1798 117
Ohio, 1803 117
Indiana, 1816 118

5. Literary Property Begins to Receive Protection; Copyright Laws

Connecticut Enacts First American Law on Copyright, 1783 120
Copyright Law of Massachusetts, 1783 122
First Copyright Law Enacted by Congress, May 31, 1790 123

*6. Chevalier Quesnay de Beaurepaire's Academy of Arts and Sciences
in Richmond, Virginia*

Sara Bache to Benjamin Franklin on Quesnay's Academy, 1783 127
Announcement of Quesnay's Academy of Arts and Sciences, 1786 128
Quesnay to the Royal Academy of Sciences, Paris, 1788 128
Official Approval of Quesnay's Academy by the Royal Censor, 1788 . . . 129
Prospectus of Quesnay's Academy, July 1, 1788 129

III

NEW FORCES AND THE AWAKENING

An Academy on the Lancasterian Plan is Established in North Carolina, 1814 135
Early Lancasterian Schools in Philadelphia, 1817 135
James Stevenson of Virginia to Joseph Lancaster, 1819 136
Joseph C. Cabell of Virginia to Joseph Lancaster, 1819 137
Joseph Lancaster to His Daughter, 1819 139
John C. Calhoun to Joseph Lancaster, 1820 141
Board of Regents of New York May Charter Lancasterian Schools, 1821 . . 142
The Pennsylvania Society for the Promotion of Public Schools Declares Its
    Purposes, 1828 143
Josiah Holbrook Proposes a Constitution for the Lyceum, 1828 145
Questions Addressed by the Working Men of Philadelphia to Candidates for the
    Legislature, 1829 146
Platform of the Boston Working Men's Party, 1830 147
Public Schools Not a Province of Government, 1830 148
An Argument Against Public Schools, 1830 149
Stephen Girard Provides in His Will for a Lancasterian School in Philadelphia,
    1831 150
A Meeting Is Held in Washington to Promote Interest in Sunday Schools, 1831 150
The American Lyceum Is Organized, 1831 151
Some Questions Proposed for Discussion at the Fifth Annual Convention of the
    American Lyceum, 1835 153
The Program of an Educational Convention in Michigan, 1838 153

PAGE

Dorothea Dix Memorializes the Legislature of Massachusetts on the Horrible
    Conditions of Prisons and Asylums, 1843 155
The Secretary of a Virginia Educational Convention Requests Advice from
    Horace Mann, 1845 157
Mann Replies to the Request of Mr. Gooch, 1845 158
A Mississippian Asks Mann's Advice About Education, 1846 160
The Grand Lodge of the Independent Order of Odd Fellows of North Carolina
    Asks Horace Mann's Advice on Its Educational Activities, 1840's . . . 160
Horace Mann on "The Ground of the Free School System," 1846 . . . 163
Horace Mann on the Relation Between Education and Prosperity, 1848 . . 165
The Masonic Lodge of Selma, Alabama, Asks Mann to Recommend Teachers
    for Its School, 1848 166
The Office of Indian Affairs Asks Mann's Advice, 1848 167
John B. Minor to Mann, 1849 169
An Argument in Massachusetts Against the Poll Tax as a Requirement for
    Voting, 1853 172
William H. Stiles of Georgia to Henry Barnard, 1856 173
Ashbel Smith to Barnard, 1858 175
Henry Barnard on the Influence of the Lyceum, 1864 176

IV

EXTENDING THE SCHOOLS UPWARD BEFORE 1860

The Opening of Newark Academy in New Jersey Is Announced, 1775 . . . 181
Charter of Liberty Hall Academy, North Carolina, 1777 182
Jefferson's Bill for Amending the Constitution of the College of William and
    Mary, 1779 186
Phillips Andover Academy, Massachusetts, Is Chartered, 1780 192
The First State University Is Chartered, 1785 192
Agricultural and Manual Labor Schools Are Recommended, 1787 . . . 196
Act Providing for the Support of the University of North Carolina, 1789 . . 200
Some Rules of Cokesbury College, Abingdon, Maryland, 1792 201
The Senatus Academicus Reports a Plan of Education for the University of
    Georgia, November 27, 1800 202
The Legislature of North Carolina Repeals the Law Appropriating Escheats for
    the Support of the University, 1800 204
Collegiate Degrees Conferred at Commencement, 1802 205
Proposal for Establishing a University in Virginia by Subscriptions, Lottery and
    a Luxury Tax, 1805 206
North Carolina's "Dartmouth College Case," 1805 209
The Legislature of North Carolina Reënacts the Law Providing for the Support
    of the University of that State by Escheats, 1805 211
Thomas Jefferson Declines to Sell Lottery Tickets for the Benefit of East
    Tennessee College and Gives Its Trustees Some Counsel, 1810 . . . 212
Jefferson's Reply to Governor Plumer on the Dartmouth College Case, 1816 . 213
The Catholepistemiad or University of Michigania Is Established, 1817 . . 214
Report of the Rockfish Gap Commission (Thomas Jefferson, Chairman) to
    Locate the Site of the University of Virginia, 1818 216
Daniel Webster Cites the North Carolina Case of 1805 to Support His Argument
    in the Dartmouth College Case 228
The Trustees of Dartmouth College v. Woodward, 1819 229
Congressional Objections to the Proposal to Grant Public Lands for the
    Endowment of State Universities, 1819 233
A Comparison of Collegiate Rules at Harvard, the University of Virginia and
    the University of South Carolina, 1820's 235
Professor George Ticknor on Harvard, 1821 237

PAGE

Advertisement for the Opening of Indiana State Seminary Which Developed
  into Indiana University, 1824 237
Captain Alden Partridge's Arguments for Military Education, c. 1825 . . . 238
The First Public High School Law in the United States, 1827 247
Stephen Girard Provides for a College in Philadelphia for "Poor Male White
  Orphans," 1830 247
Evidence of Interest in Manual Labor Schools, 1831 255
The Legislature of Tennessee Opposes Appropriations to the United States
  Military Academy, 1833 256
The Committee on Education of the Legislature of Pennsylvania Recommends
  Manual Labor Schools, 1833 257
The Founding of Oberlin College, Ohio, 1834 257
J. Marion Sims Reports a Duel in South Carolina College, 1835 258
President Francis Wayland of Brown University on Some Aspects of the
  Collegiate System in the United States, 1842 260
To Dissolve Prejudices, Northern Students Should Go South and Southern
  Students North, 1843 263
Program of Studies at the University of Michigan, 1843 264
A Student in the University of North Carolina to a Friend in Virginia, 1845 . 265
Defense of the Classics and Criticisms of the Elective System, 1852 . . . 267
The Legislature of Illinois Recommends that Congress Provide for Industrial
  Universities, 1853 270
Henry Harrisse on the Powers and Duties of Collegiate Trustees, 1854 . . 271
A Senator in the Legislature of Texas Opposed the Bill for a University, 1856 272
Williams College in 1856 274
A Sketch of Woodward High School in Cincinnati, 1856 277
An Act to Establish the University of Texas, 1858 279
The Veto Message of President James Buchanan on the Morrill Bill, 1859 . . 282
Chancellor F. A. P. Barnard Is Tried and Exonerated by the Board of Trustees
  of the University of Mississippi, 1860 289
Governor Sam Houston's Message to the Legislature of Texas on the University
  and on Giving Aid to Other Institutions, 1860 295

V

GAINING PUBLIC SUPPORT AND CONTROL; COMPULSORY
ATTENDANCE LEGISLATION

Non-residents of Boston Must Pay for the Instruction of Their Children, 1711 299
Boston Finds Its Schools Expensive, 1750 299
Thomas Jefferson's Bill "For the More General Diffusion of Knowledge"
  Introduced into the Legislature of Virginia, 1779 299
Dr. Benjamin Rush to the Legislature of Pennsylvania on a System of Public
  Education, 1786 306
Report of a Committee of the House of Representatives of Pennsylvania on a
  School System, 1794 308
New York's Act for the "Encouragement of Schools," 1795 309
Connecticut Establishes the First Permanent Public School Fund in the
  United States, 1795 316
Pennsylvania Makes Provision for "The Education of the Poor Gratis," 1802 . 318
An Address to the Public in Behalf of Public Schools in New York City, 1805 319
Virginia Establishes a Literary Fund for the Encouragement of Learning, 1810 321
The State of New York Provides for Common Schools and for a State Super-
  intendent, 1812 321
James G. Carter on "This Wretched Mockery" of Education in Massachusetts,
  1824 330

PAGE

An Early Educational "Survey," by the Faculty of the College (Now University)
of South Carolina, 1825 331
An Open Letter Against Schools and Internal Improvements, 1829 340
The Workingmen of Philadelphia on Education at Public Expense, 1830 . . 342
An Argument Against State Support of Education, 1830 343
Messages of Governors of States on Education, 1831 343
Extracts from the Message of Governor Wolf to the Legislature of Pennsylvania,
1833 344
A Melancholy Picture of Schools in New Jersey, 1835 345
The Able Speech by Thaddeus Stevens on Behalf of Free Schools in Penn-
sylvania, 1835 346
Tennessee Creates an *Ex Officio* State Board of Education and Provides for a
Chief State School Officer, 1836 355
Governor Edward Everett Recommends a State Board of Education for
Massachusetts, 1837 359
Massachusetts Creates the First State Board of Education in the United States,
1837 360
Horace Mann Replies to the Boston Schoolmasters, 1845 362
A Subscriber to His Paper Writes Horace Greeley in Opposition to Free Schools
in New York, 1849 363
An Editorial in Favor of Free Schools, 1849 364
The First Compulsory School Law in the United States, 1852 365
Compulsory School Attendance Legislation, 1852-1918 366
Names of County Superintendents in Pennsylvania, With Their Salaries, 1854 366
Compulsory-Attendance Legislation Is Urged for New York, 1867 367
New York Abolishes the Rate Bill, 1867 368
Secretary B. G. Northorp, of the Connecticut State Board of Education,
Answers the Opponents of Compulsory Educational Legislation, 1872 . . 368
New York's First Compulsory School Attendance Legislation, 1874 370
Proposed Amendment to the Constitution of the United States Prohibiting the
States from Using Public School Funds or Public Lands for the Benefit
of Religious Groups, 1876 373
Enactment of Compulsory-Attendance Laws Favored, 1897 373
Tennessee's Compulsory School Law, 1905 373
Opposition to Compulsory Educational Legislation, 1914 377
Mississippi's Initial Law on Compulsory Attendance at School, 1918 . . . 377
Children of Compulsory School Age Cannot Be Compelled to Attend Public
Schools, 1925 380
Ralph Bradford, General Manager of the Chamber of Commerce of the
United States, on the Need for Closer Relations Between Business and
Education, 1944 383
"Alas, the Poor School Superintendent," 1946 384
Average Salaries of Public School Teachers in the United States, 1946-1947 . 385
The United States Chamber of Commerce Presents the Arguments For and
Against Federal Aid to General Education, 1948 386

VI

TEACHERS AND TEACHING

Dr. Benjamin Rush on the Occupation of the Teacher, 1790 403
James G. Carter on Teachers in Massachusetts, 1824 403
A Teacher's Contract in Texas, 1825 405
Superintendent A. G. Flagg of the Common Schools of New York on Lack of
Good Salaries of Teachers, 1828 406
Samuel Read Hall on "The Requisite Qualifications of an Instructor," 1829 . 406
The Origin and Early Years of the American Institute of Instruction, 1830 . . 409

PAGE

Wages of Teachers in Connecticut, 1832 412
The Committee on Education of the Legislature of Pennsylvania on Teachers
    in the Common Schools, 1833 413
Phillips Andover Academy (Massachusetts) Undertakes the Education of
    Teachers, 1834 413
Henry Barnard on Teachers in the German Schools, 1835 414
Calvin E. Stowe Says Women Should Be Employed in the Elementary Schools,
    1837 414
Horace Mann Reports Private Gift of $10,000 to Promote Instruction in
    Normal Schools in Massachusetts, 1838 415
The Legislature of Massachusetts Accepts the Gift and Resolves to Provide for
    the Education of Teachers, 1838 416
Admission Requirements and Course of Study in the Early Normal Schools
    of Massachusetts, 1839 416
Henry Barnard on the Heavy "Turnover" Among Teachers in Connecticut, 1839 418
Henry Barnard on Women as Teachers, 1839 418
Superintendent Francis R. Shunk of Pennsylvania on the Need for Improved
    Methods of Teaching and Managing Schools, 1841 420
On the Need for the Education of Teachers in Texas, 1846 420
Advice of David P. Page to Prospective Teachers, 1847 422
Fifty Students at the University of Virginia Are Educated at the Expense of
    the State on Condition That They Teach Two Years, 1857 422
President James B. Angell Recommends Courses in Pedagogy at the University
    of Michigan, 1874 423
The University of Michigan Establishes a Chair of the "History, Theory, and
    Art of Education," 1879 423
The National Educational Association Commends the Practice of the Study of
    Pedagogy in Colleges and Universities, 1880 424
William James on "Psychology and the Teaching Art," 1892 424
The Committee of Ten on Teachers and Teaching, 1893 429
The Committee of Fifteen on the Training Secondary School Teachers, 1895 . 431
Average Monthly Salaries of Rural Teachers in Thirty-four States, 1897 . . 435
Defects and Remedies in the Certification of Teachers, 1906 436
Normal Schools Are Transformed into Colleges, 1912 438
Teachers in High Schools Deficient in English, 1913 441
The Need for Professionally Prepared Teachers, 1914 441
The Need of Loyalty Oaths for Teachers, 1920 443
Governor Alfred E. Smith Vetoes Teachers' Oath Bill in New York, 1920 . . 443
Governor Dixon of Montana Vetoes Measure for Loyalty Oath, 1921 . . . 444
Governor Franklin D. Roosevelt Warns of Excess Supply of Teachers, 1930 . 444
How Much Schooling Did American Teachers Have in 1930-31? 444
California's Teachers' Oath, 1931 446
New York's Teachers' Oath, 1934 446
Congress Enacts Legislation for "Loyalty Oath" for Teachers in the District
    of Columbia, 1935 447
Some Arguments For and Against Teachers' Oaths, 1935 447
Teachers' Oath in Massachusetts, 1935 448
Carl Becker of Cornell University on Loyalty Oaths for Teachers, 1935 . . 449
The American Association of University Professors Opposes Loyalty Oaths for
    Teachers, 1937 451
Congress Repeals the Provision Relating to the Teaching or Advocating of
    Communism, 1937 452
Illness of Teachers Causes the Annual Loss of Two Million School Days, 1938 452
Abraham Flexner on the Importance of Humor in Teachers and Teaching, 1938 454
"Leading Issues and Promising Trends" in Teacher Education, 1946 . . . 456
Average Annual Salaries of Teachers, Principals and Other Instructional
    Personnel in Public Elementary and Secondary Schools, 1948 . . . 460
New York Requires Loyalty Oath for Teachers, 1949 460

PAGE

The University of California Requires Loyalty Oath of Its Faculty, 1949 . . 462
The National Education Association Opposes Members of the Communist
Party as Teachers in American Schools, 1949 462
The National Education Association Resolves on Professional Standards for
Teachers, 1949 463
Phi Beta Kappa on Freedom of Teaching, 1949 464
The American Association of School Administrators Oppose Loyalty Oaths for
Teachers and Communists as Teachers, 1950 464

VII

SOME EDUCATIONAL PRACTICES

Boston Requests the Selectmen to Recommend "Suitable Persons" for Masters
in "The Grammar School at ye North," 1712 467
The Ministers of Boston Are Consulted About a Master for the North Grammar
School, 1718 467
Rowland Jones, Schoolmaster in Pennsylvania, Gives an Account of His
Method of Teaching, 1730 467
Curriculum Is Announced for Franklin's Academy of Philadelphia, 1750 . . 468
The Selectmen of Boston Induct a Master of the North Writing School, 1761 469
An Account of School Life at Phillips Andover Academy, 1780 469
Jedidiah Morse, Pioneer American Geographer, on Imperfections in Geog-
raphies Dealing with America, 1789 470
Dr. Benjamin Rush on Proper Amusements and Punishments for Schools, 1790 471
How the Day in School in Middlesex County, Connecticut, Was Spent, 1799 . 476
"Peter Parley" (Samuel G. Goodrich) Describes a Typical Rural School in
New England Around 1800 477
Some Fly-Leaf Scribblings of Children in the School-Books in the Early Days 478
J. Marion Sims, Famous American Surgeon and Gynecologist, Tells of His
Early Education in South Carolina, 1819 480
Regulations for the Schools of Providence, Rhode Island, 1820 484
Rules and Contract for Governing a School in South Carolina, 1820 . . 485
Horace Greeley on "Turning Out" the Teacher in New England About 1820 . 487
Pestalozzian Department in a Kentucky School, 1830 487
How to Prevent the Evils of Whispering Among Pupils and Their Leaving
Their Seats, 1833 488
Henry Barnard on the Practice of "Boarding Around," 1840 491
Books in Use in the Common Schools of Virginia in 1844 491
Horace Mann on the Value of Written Examinations in the Schools, 1845 . . 493
Textbooks Purchased for the Schools of Arkansas, 1846 499
Description of a School in New York State, 1847 500
David P. Page on Public Examinations, 1847 501
Braxton Craven of Union Institute (North Carolina) on Proper Practices in
the School, 1849 503
An Account of the Old Practice of "Boarding Around" the Teacher, c. 1850 . 506
The Struggle for the Mastery in Indiana, c. 1850 507
Geography Is Taught by Singing, 1852 510
Herbert Quick on the Influence of McGuffey's Readers, c. 1870 516
The Committee of Fifteen on the Correlation of Studies in Elementary
Education, 1895 517
Resolutions of the National Educational Association, 1897 519
The Carnegie Foundation's Definition of Educational "Units," 1906 . . . 520
A District Superintendent of Schools of Brooklyn, New York, on Sex Hygiene
in the Schools, 1914 522
Superintendent Thomas A. Mott, Seymour, Indiana, on Sex Hygiene in the
Schools, 1914 523

PAGE

National Manufacturers' Association on the Plight of the Public Schools, 1914   524
Charles W. Eliot on Educational Defects in the United States, 1919   .   .   .   524
Hamlin Garland Describes "Friday Exercises" at the Seminary Which He
    Attended in the Middle West, 1923   525
Hamlin Garland Testifies to the Influence of the McGuffey's *Readers,* 1923   .   527
A Statement of the Principles of Progressive Education, 1924   528
Charles W. Eliot Congratulates *Progressive Education* on its First Issue, 1924   .   530
The Status of Latin and Greek in the American Schools, 1923-1924   530
Pope Pius XI Opposes "Progressive Education," 1929   531
A Plea for Common Sense in Education, 1932   531
W. J. Cameron on the McGuffey's *Readers,* 1935   533
John Dewey States the Aims of "Progressives," 1938   535

VIII

EXTENDING THE SCHOOLS UPWARD AFTER 1860

The Morrill (Land-Grant College) Act, 1862   541
The Supreme Court of Michigan Establishes the Legality of Taxes for
    Secondary Education, 1874   544
Editorial Protest Against the Ph.D. as an Honorary Degree, 1892   .   .   .   554
Charles W. Super of Ohio University (Athens) on "So-Called Honorary
    Degrees," 1892   554
The Committee of Ten Proposes a Program for Secondary Schools, 1893   .   .   555
The Committee of Ten on Requirements for Admission to College, 1893   .   .   557
The Committee on College Entrance Requirements Approves the Elective
    System in High Schools, 1899   559
The Association of American Universities Is Formed, 1900   561
William James on the Ph.D. Octopus, 1903   563
Charter of General Education Board, 1903   569
The Right Honorable James Bryce, M.P., on Higher Education in the United
    States, 1905   571
Andrew Carnegie Establishes the Carnegie Foundation for the Advancement
    of Teaching, 1905   575
A Committee of the N.E.A. Advises "Economy of Time in Education," 1913   .   577
Charter of The Rockefeller Foundation, 1913   578
Call for Meeting for the Organization of the American Association of University
    Professors, 1914   579
President Alexander Meiklejohn of Amherst College on the Purpose of the
    Liberal College, 1914   580
Stephen Leacock on the American System of Graduate Instruction, 1916   .   .   582
The Seven Cardinal Principles of Secondary Education, 1918   586
Thorstein Veblen on Academic Administration and Policy, 1918   .   .   .   590
Thorstein Veblen on the Influence of Business Upon Higher Education, 1918   .   594
On Competition in the Colleges, 1920   597
Some "Defects and Excesses of Present-Day Athletic Contests," 1929   .   .   598
Inter-Collegiate Horse-Racing Is Proposed for Inter-Collegiate Football, 1932   601
Alfred E. Smith Receives an Honorary Degree from Harvard, 1933   604
Bliss Perry on Complicated Educational Administration, 1935   605
Stephen Leacock on Higher Education, 1935   605
Robert M. Hutchins on Higher Education, 1938   606
President F. P. Keppel of Carnegie Corporation of New York on the "Prepos-
    terous" Increase in the Creation of Academic Degrees, 1939   .   .   .   608
Extracts from the "G.I. Bill of Rights," the Education of Veterans, 1944   .   .   609
The President's Commission on Higher Education Recommends National
    Scholarship and Fellowship Programs, 1947   612
The Rôle of the Federal Government in Higher Education, 1947   .   .   .   617

PAGE

Two Members of the President's Commission on Higher Education Dissent from Its Recommendations on Financing Higher Education, 1947 . . . 620
Harold J. Laski on the Graduate System of Education in The United States, 1948 624
Trends in Costs of Higher Education, 1948 630
Can the Private Schools Survive? 1948 631
Charter of the Regional Council for Education, 1948 633
General Conclusions of the Temporary Commission on the Need for a State University in New York, 1948 635
Governor Thomas E. Dewey Approves the Bill About Complaints Against Educational Institutions for Alleged Discrimination of Applicants, 1948 . 640
An Act in Relation to Complaints Against Educational Institutions for Alleged Discrimination in the Admission of Applicants, 1948 641
Some Standards of the New England Association of Colleges and Secondary Schools, 1949 644
Standards for Independent Secondary Schools (Amended December 6, 1946) 648
Standards for Public Secondary Schools (Adopted December 6, 1946) . . . 649
Policies, Regulations, and Criteria of the North Central Association for the Approval of Secondary Schools, 1949 651
An International University Is Proposed in Congress, 1949 654
The Indiana Association of Church Related Independent Colleges Opposes Federal Aid to Higher Education, 1949 657

IX

UP FROM SLAVERY: EDUCATIONAL AND OTHER RIGHTS OF NEGROES

South Carolina Prohibits the Teaching of Slaves to Write, 1740 661
The Presbytery of Lexington (Virginia) Licenses John Chavis as Preacher, 1800 661
John Chavis, Negro, Is Engaged as Missionary by the General Assembly of the Presbyterian Church, 1801 662
The Court of Quarter Sessions of Rockbridge County, Virginia, Certifies to the Freedom of John Chavis, 1802 662
Joseph Gales, Whig Editor of a Raleigh Newspaper, Praises Chavis and His School, 1830 663
The Importation of Slaves Is Prohibited, 1808 663
A Methodist Minister of Charleston Is "Pumped" for Teaching Negroes, 1823 664
The General Assembly of Virginia Prohibits the Teaching of Slaves, Free Negroes, or Mulattoes to Read or Write, 1831 664
North Carolina Forbids Slaves or Free Negroes to Preach, 1831 665
Alabama Forbids the Teaching of Slaves to Read or Write, 1832 666
The Religious Instruction of Slaves in South Carolina, 1834 666
The General Assembly of South Carolina Prohibits Slaves from Being Taught to Read or Write, 1834 666
Provision for Schools for Colored Children in New York, 1841 667
The Legislature of Virginia Provides for a Young Slave To Be Taught, 1842 . 668
Religious Instruction of Negroes in South Carolina, 1847 669
Mrs. Margaret Douglass Is Arrested, Tried, and Convicted of Teaching Negro Children to Read in Norfolk, Virginia, 1853 669
Hinton Rowan Helper on the Baneful Influences of Slavery, 1857 670
"Southerner at School with Negroes!" 1863 673
The Emancipation Proclamation, 1863 673
The Freedmen's Bureau Is Established, 1865 674
The Capacity of the Negro for Education, 1865 675
The Northern Teacher in the South after 1865 676

PAGE

A Virginia Editor Objects to Northern Teachers, 1866 677
The Ku Klux Klan Warns a Northern Teacher, 1868 677
The Civil Rights Act, 1875 678
Threat to a White Teacher of a Negro School in Pike County, Alabama, 1875 679
Booker T. Washington Receives an Honorary Master's Degree from Harvard, 1896 679
John Spencer Bassett of Trinity College Describes Booker T. Washington the Greatest Man Born in the South in a Century, with the Exception of Robert E. Lee, and Starts Violent Controversy, 1903 682
President Kilgo Resigns in Defense of Bassett, 1903 683
The Legislature of Kentucky Prohibits Mixed Schools, 1904 685
Berea College v. *Commonwealth of Kentucky,* 1908 685
Court Cases Face Tests in Southern Universities, 1935 689
Negro Teachers in Maryland Seek Salaries Equal to Those Paid White Teachers, 1937 690
Missouri's Position on the Teaching of Negroes from 1847 to 1865 Is Reported, 1938 691
Missouri ex rel. Gaines v. *Canada, Registrar of the University of Missouri, et al.,* 1938 691
A Newspaper Account of "The Gaines Decision," 1938 693
Editorial Comment on "The Gaines Decision," 1938 694
Sixteen States Are Affected by "The Gaines Case," 1938 694
Alston et al. v. *School Board of the City of Norfolk* (Virginia) *et al.,* 1940 . 695
The University of Texas Must Admit Negroes, 1950 696
The University of Oklahoma Must Not Segregate White and Negro Students, 1950 698

X

EDUCATIONAL AND OTHER RIGHTS OF WOMEN; CO-EDUCATION

Mary Wollstonecraft on Education and Other Rights of Women, 1792 . . . 703
Dr. Benjamin Rush on the Education of Women, 1798 705
Thomas Jefferson on the Education of Women, 1818 706
Mary Lyon on the Purposes of Mount Holyoke Seminary, 1835 . . . 707
A College for Women in Kentucky, 1835 710
Some Activities at Wesleyan College, Macon, Georgia, 1837 711
The First Convention on the Rights of Women Declares Its Sentiments and Resolutions, 1848 713
Placing a Daughter at School, 1853 717
Interest in the South in the Education of Women, 1857 717
President Charles W. Eliot of Harvard University on the Subject, 1869 . . 718
Rules at Mount Holyoke in the Eighteen Seventies 718
President F. A. P. Barnard of Columbia University on the Subject, 1878 . 721
The National Educational Association Resolves on the Higher Education of Women, 1879 721
President James B. Angell of the University of Michigan on the Subject, 1883 722
President Nicholas Murray Butler of Columbia University Says Co-Education Is a Dead Issue, 1902 722
President G. Stanley Hall of Clark University on the Subject, 1904 . . . 722
President John F. Goucher of Baltimore Woman's College on the Subject, 1904 722
President M. Carey Thomas of Bryn Mawr College on the Subject, 1908 . 723
President Emeritus C. A. Richmond of Union College on the Subject, 1934 . 723

XI

SOME LATER EDUCATIONAL DEVELOPMENTS

PAGE

Henry Huxley Rebukes Bishop Wilberforce Over Darwinism, 1860 727
The Hoar Bill to Provide for a System of National Education, 1870 . . . 728
The Blair Bill to Aid in the Establishment and Temporary Support of Common
    Schools, 1881 732
Sentiment on the Blair Bill Changes, 1886 736
Federal Aid for Education in the South Is Urged, 1887 736
The Culture-Epoch Theory in Education, 1899 736
The Kindergarten Should Be an Integral Part of the Public School System, 1913 740
Discussion of the Report of the Committee on Tests and Standards of Efficiency
    of the National Council of Education, 1913 741
Leonard P. Ayres on the History and Present Status of Educational Measure-
    ments, 1918 744
A Bill to Create a Department of Education and for Federal Aid to Education,
    1918 749
Pope Pius XI Opposes Sex Education and Co-education, 1929 757
A New Educational Program for the State of New York, 1938 758
Evaluation of the Contributions of the National Youth Administration, 1939 . 762
Children May Be Expelled from School for Refusing to Salute the National
    Flag, 1940 766
New Jersey Provides for the Transportation of Children to Non-Public Schools,
    1941 767
Children May Not Be Expelled from School for Refusing to Salute the National
    Flag, 1943 768
The Supreme Court Sustains the Practice of Public Transportation of Non-
    Public School Children, 1947 771
Extracts from the Constitution of the United Nations Educational, Scientific
    and Cultural Organization, 1948 773
The Supreme Court Holds That Religious Instruction Cannot Be Given in
    Public School Buildings, 1948 775
Practice and Usage in Aid to Sectarian Schools and Sectarianism in Public
    Schools, 1949 778
President Truman on the Rôle of Education and Research in Our Democratic
    Society, 1950 779

INDEX 783

READINGS IN AMERICAN EDUCATIONAL HISTORY

«« I »»

THE COLONIAL CLIMATE

《《《》》》》》》》》》》》》》》》》》》》》》》》》》》》》

Education in the American colonies was a direct inheritance from Europe. All the thirteen colonies except Georgia were established in the seventeenth century; and in the early years of colonization the stream of migration to this country was chiefly English and the essential forms of American colonial culture were English. A voyage of a few weeks across the ocean could not greatly alter the theory or practice of education which the colonists had known in their old homes. England had her universities of Cambridge and Oxford and by the end of the seventeenth century the colonists had their Harvard, the College of William and Mary, and Yale; and by 1769 six other colleges: Princeton and Rutgers in New Jersey; King's (now Columbia) in New York; Academy and College of Philadelphia (now the University of Pennsylvania); Brown in Rhode Island and Dartmouth in New Hampshire. England had her Latin grammar schools and so did all the colonies except perhaps Georgia, and these served in the New the same purposes for which they had been established in the Old World—preparation of the sons of the well-to-do for college.

Documents in this chapter deal with Henrico College and East India School in Virginia, the first educational efforts in English North America; apprenticeship theories and practices; advertisements of schools and for teachers and tutors, and extracts from the diary of Philip Fithian, tutor in the Carter family in Virginia; educational provisions in wills; philanthropic societies; colonial teachers; charters and rules of colonial colleges; miscellaneous interests and activities, including the honorary diplomas in Latin of Benjamin Franklin (College of William and Mary) and of George Washington (Harvard).

The first steps toward educational efforts in English North America were taken for the colony of Virginia under the auspices of the Virginia Company of London in plans for Henrico College and East India School. The original charter of Virginia in 1606 referred to the need for "propagating of Christian religion to such people, as yet live in darkness and miserable ignorance of the true knowledge and worship of God, and may in time bring the infidels and savages . . . to human civility and quiet government . . .," and the second charter of 1609 made reference to the same need. The documents that follow reveal much

1

interest in these educational efforts, from the message of King James the First to his Archbishops in 1617 to the Indian massacre in 1622; and three years later the Virginia Company of London seemed willing to continue its assistance. These materials are drawn largely from the excellent work of Susan Myra Kingsbury, *The Records of the Virginia Company of London,* published in four stout volumes by the Library of Congress between 1906 and 1935. The best secondary account of this abortive educational undertaking is by R. H. Land, "Henrico and Its College," *William and Mary College Quarterly Historical Magazine,* Second Series, Vol. 18, No. 4 (October, 1938). The spelling in the documents here given as edited by Kingsbury is preserved with no attempt to modernize the text of the extracts drawn from that source.

« 1 »

Henrico College
and the East India School

《《》》》》》》》》》》》》》》》》》》》》》》》》》》》》》》》》》》

The Treasurer Reports on Funds for the College
at Henrico, 1619 *

It was also by mr Trer propounded to the Cort as a thing most worthy to be taken into consideracon both for the glory of God, and honor of the Company, that forasmuch as the King in his most gracious fauor hath graunted his Lres to the seuerall Bishops of this Kingdome for the collecting of monies to erect and build a Colledge in Virginia for the trayning and bringing vp of Infidells children to the true knowledge of God & vnderstanding of righteousnes. And considering what publique notice may be taken in foreslowing to sett forward the accon, especially of all those Wch hath contributed to the same, that therefore to begin that pious worke, there is allready towards it—1500li,—or thereabouts, whereof remayning in cash 800li, the rest is to be answered out of the Stock of the Generall Company for so much Wch they borrowed, besides the likelihood of more to come in; ffor mr Treasuror hauing some conference Wth the Bishop of Lichfield, he hath not heard of any Colleccon that hath beene for that busines in his Diocese; but promiseth when he hath a warrt therevnto he will Wthall dilligence further the enterprize; Wherevpon he conceaued it the fittest; that as yet they should not build the Colledge, but rather forebeare a while; and begin first with the meanes they haue to provide and settle an Annuall revennue, and out of that to begin the ereccon of the said Colledge: And for the performance hereof also moued, that a certaine peece of Land be Laid out at Henrico being the place formerly resolued of Wch should be called the Colledge Land, and for the planting of the same send presently ffifty good persons to be seated thereon and to occupy the same according to order, and to haue halfe the benefitt of their Labor and the other halfe to goe in setting forward the worke, and for mayntenance of the Tutors & Schollers.

* Susan M. Kingsbury, *The Records of the Virginia Company of London* (Library of Congress), I, p. 220 (May 26, 1619).

3

A Letter from "Dust and Ashes" Is Presented
to the Company, 1621 *

The Letter subscribed D and A was brought to the former Court by an vnknowne messenger was nowe againe presented to be read the Content whereof are followeth.[1]

Ianuary 28th 1621

Most worthie Companie

Whereas I sent the Treasuror and yor selues a letter subscribed Dust and Ashes wch promised 550li to such vses therein expressed, and did soone afterward, accordinge to my promise send the said money to Sr Edwin Sandys to be deliuered to the Companie, In wch letter I did not strictly order the bestowinge of the said money but shewed my intent for the conversion of Infidell Children, as it will appeare by that letter wch I desire may be read in open Court wherein I chiefely comended the orderinge thereof to the wisdome of you the Honoble Companie, And whereas the gentlement of the Southampton Hundred haue vndertaken the disposinge of the said 550li I haue longe attended to see the erectinge of some Schoole or other waye whereby some of the Children of the Virginians might haue bin taught and brought vp in Christian religion and good manners wch not beinge donne accordinge to my intent but the money deteyned by a priuate hundred all this while contrary to my minde, though I iudje verie charitably of that honoble Society, And as already you haue receaued a great and the most painefully gained part of my estate toward the layinge of the foundacon of Christian religion and helpinge forward of this pious worke in that Heathen nowe Christian land, So nowe I require of the whole Body of yor Honoble and worthie Companie (whome I entrusted with the dispose of the said moneyes,) to see the same speedily and faithfully converted to the worke intended: And I do further propound to you the honoble Companie that if you will procure that some of the male Children of ye Virginians (though but a fewe) be brought ouer into England here to be educated and taught, and to weare a habbit as the Children of Christ Hospitall do, and that you wilbe pleased to see the said 550li converted to this vse then I do faithfully promise that when eight or ten of the Virginians Children are brought ouer, and placed in London either in Christ Hospitall or el in the Virginian Schoole or Hospitall (as it may be called and by the will and guift of good men may be yearely augmented) where the Companie may haue an ey ouer them and be (as it were) nursinge ffathers vnto them then I say I faithfully promise to add 450li more to make the Sume 1000li wch if God permitt I will cheerfully send you only I desire to nominate the first Tutor or Gouernor who shall take charge to nurse and instruct them: But

---

* *Ibid.*, pp. 585-87.
[1] This document was copied into the manuscript at a later date. (Kingsbury's note.)

if you in yor Wisedomes like not of this mocon then my humble Suite
vnto ye whole body of yor Honoble Companie is that my former guift
of 50li be wholly imployed & bestowed vpon a free Schoole to be erected
in Southampton Hundred (so it be presently imployed) or such other
place as I or my freind shall well like of wherein both English and Virginians may be taught together and that the said Schoole be endowed
with such priuiledges as you in yor wisdomes shall thinke fitt: The Mr
of wch Schoole I humbly craue may not be allowed to goe ouer except
he first bringe in to the Companie sound testimony of his sufficiency in
learning and sincerity of life The Lord giue you wise and vnderstandinge
hart that his worke herein be not negligently performed.

D and A

Passengers and Crew of Royal James Make Contribution to School in Virginia, 1621 *

There is one thinge likewise that hath lately hapned vnto us, not great
in itself but of great good hope; the gentlemen and Mariners of the Royall
James belonging to the East India Company, being mett at Cap Bona
Speranza by some English Shipps outward bound, and certified of the
prosperitie of Virginia, did there (vppon the exhortation of Mr Copland
theire Minister) bestowe the sume of 70li towardes the buildinge of a free
schoole in Virginia: wch pious guift hath lately received an addiccon of
30li by an vnknowne person. The maner of employeinge the mony wch
the Company hath resolued vppon, we send you here inclosed, desiringe
that you would likewise take it into yor considerations.

Report of the Indian Massacre Which Destroyed the Prospects of the College, 1622 †

The country being in this estate, an occasion was ministered of sending
to *Opachankano* the King of these Sauages, about the middle of *March*
last, what time the Messenger returned backe with these words from him,
That he held the peace concluded so firme, as the Skie should sooner
fall then it dissolue; yea, such was the treacherous dissimulation of that
people who then had contriued our destruction, that euen two dayes
before the Massacre, some of our men were guided thorow the woods
by them in safety: and one *Browne,* who then to learne the language
liued among the *Warrascoyacks* (a Prouince of that King) was in friendly
manner sent backe by them to Captaine *Hamor* his Master, and many
the like passages, rather increasing our former confidence, then any wise
in the world ministering the least suspition of the breach of the peace,

* *Ibid.,* III, p. 531 (December 5, 1621).
† *Ibid.,* III, pp. 550-51, 564-65; 566 (1622).

or of what instantly ensued; yea, they borrowed our owne Boates to conuey themselues crosse the Riuer (on the bankes of both sides whereof all our Plantations were) to consult of the diuellish murder that ensued, and of our vtter extirpation, which God of his mercy (by the meanes of some of themselues conuerted to Christianitie) preuented; and as well on the Friday morning (the fatal day) the 22 of *March,* as also in the euening, as in other dayes before, they came vnarmed into our houses, without Bowes or arrowes, or other weapons, with Deere, Turkies, Fish, Furres, and other prouisions, to sell, and trucke with vs, for glasse, beades, and other trifles: yea in some places, sate downe at Breakfast with our people at their tables, whom immediately with their owne tooles and weapons, eyther laid downe, or standing in their houses, they basely and barbarously murthered, not sparing eyther age or sexe, man, woman or childe; so sodaine in their cruell execution, that few or none discerned the weapon or blow that brought them to destruction. In which manner they also slew many of our people then at their seuerall workes and husbandries in the fields, and without their houses, some in planting Corne and Tobacco, some in gardening, some in making Bricke, building, saw-ing, and other kindes of husbandry, they well knowing in what places and quarters each of our men were, in regard of their daily familiarity, and resort to vs for trading and other negotiations, which the more willingly was by vs continued and cherished for the desire we had of effecting that great master-peece of workes, their conuersion. And by this means that fatall Friday morning, there fell vnder the bloudy and barbarous hands of that perfidious and inhumane people, contrary to all lawes of God and men, of Nature & Nations, three hundred forty seuen men, women, and children, most by their owne weapons; and not being content with taking away life alone, they fell after againe vpon the dead, making as well as they could, a fresh murder, defacing, dragging, and mangling the dead carkasses into many pieces, and carrying some parts away in derision, with base and brutish triumph. . . .

Here following is set downe a true list of the names of all those that were massacred by the treachery of the Sauages in VIRGINIA, the 22 *March* last, To the end that their lawfull heyres may take speedy order for the inheriting of their lands and estates there: For which the Honour-able *Company of Virginia* are ready to doe them all right and fauour. . . .

Slaine of the Colledge People, about two miles from Henrico-Citie.

Samuel Stringer.	Thomas Cooke.
George Soldan.	Iohn Clements.
William Basset.	Iames Faulkoner.
Iohn Perry.	Christopher Henley.
Edward Ember.	William Iordan.
Iarrat Moore.	Robert Dauis.

Thomas Xerles.   Thomas Hobson.
Thomas Freeman.   William Baily.
Iohn Allen.

The Virginia Company of London Is Ready to Assist
the East India School, 1625 *

We should be redie wth our vtmost endevors to asiste yt pious worke
of ye East India freescoole, but we must not dissemble, that besides theire
vnseasonable arivall, we doupt yt the age of mr Careleff will over ballance
all his other sufficyency, though exceedinge good, and the number soe few,
as little wilbe expected from them, They were not liable to subsist of them
selves vppon certen Cleered grounde wch they might have had in Martins
hundred, and cam in so late as they could hardlie haue howsed themselves,
But what Accomodations they could possiblely give them, was offered by
mr Horwood and mr Emersone, but mr Careleff vtterly refused to seate
there, though we advised him to it, he pretending yt many of you disliked
of that place, and yt the charge of disposinge ye men lay vppon him, The
accoumpt of ye people and goodes formerly sent for the Easte India scoole,
we heerwith send you, We desire yt theire zeale who haue traduced us in
that business may heerafter be ioyned wth some better knowledge, and yt
casuall faylings by mortalitie and otherwise, may not be charged uppon us.

* *Ibid.*, IV, pp. 565-66 (June 15, 1625). Land notes (pp. 496-97): "Possibly a greater blow
to Henrico College than the massacre was the revocation of the charter of the Virginia Company.... The company had attempted to revive Henrico College after the massacre; but
when the colony became a royal province, nothing more was done for it...."

« 2 »

Apprenticeship Theories and Practices

«««««««««««««««««««««««««««««««««««««<>»»»»»»»»»»»»»»»»»»»»»»»»»»»»»»»»

Extract from the English Act of 1601 *

And be it further enacted, That it shall be lawful for the said church-wardens and overseers, or the greater part of them, by the assent of any two justices of the peace aforesaid, to bind any such children, as aforesaid, to be apprentices, where they shall see convenient, till such man-child shall come to the age of four and twenty years, and such woman-child to the age of one and twenty years, or the time of her marriage; the same to be as effectual to all purposes, as if such child were of full age, and by indenture of covenant bound him or herself....

* *The Statutes at Large, from the Thirty-ninth Year of Q. Elizabeth, to the Twelfth Year of K. Charles II, Inclusive....* VII, beginning on page 30. The statute runs to twenty-two sections and may be found in full in Edgar W. Knight, *Documentary History of Education in the South Before 1860.* (Chapel Hill, University of North Carolina Press, 1949), I, pp. 37-45. Practices of apprenticeship for poor, orphan, and illegitimate children were common in all the colonies and extended far into the nineteenth century until movements for orphanages, juvenile courts, children's home societies, and public welfare legislation and agencies displaced the practice of "binding out" underprivileged children. The English act of 1601 was the statutory foundation of the theories and practices of apprenticeship in this country, some traces of which appeared before colonial legislation on the subject was enacted. The system applied to Negro and mulatto children, although indentures for them, especially in the South, did not always make it obligatory on the master to teach a Negro or mulatto apprentice to read and write. After the Nat Turner insurrection in Virginia in 1831, which "started a wave of contagious fear in the slave-holding states," legal prohibitions against teaching Negroes to read and write became extensive. Prior to that insurrection, however, there were cases of apprenticing free Negro children under indentures that promised the benefits of the usual educational features of the system which required instruction in a trade, in religion and morals, and later in the elements of the arts of language and of calculation to the "rule of three" (proportion: single rule of three, simple; double rule of three, compound proportion). See M. W. Jernegan, *Laboring and Dependent Classes in Colonial America, 1607-1783* (Chicago, University of Chicago Press, 1931); Edgar W. Knight, "The Evolution of Public Education in Virginia," *Sewanee Review,* January, 1916, and "Public Education of Dependents: The Apprenticeship System," in his *Public Education in the South* (Boston, Ginn & Co., 1922); A. E. Smith, *Colonists in Bondage: White Servitude and Convict Labor in America* (Chapel Hill, University of North Carolina Press, 1947); R. B. Morris, *Government and Labor in Early America* (New York, Columbia University Press, 1946). Additional light on this topic is given by Jernegan in his "Compulsory Education in the American Colonies," "The Educational Development of the Southern Colonies," and "Compulsory Education in the Southern Colonies," in *School Review,* XXVII (January, May, and June), 1919.

Apprenticeship Legislation in Virginia, 1642 *

WHEREAS sundry laws and statues by act of parliament established, have with great wisdome ordained, for the better educateing of youth in honest and profitable trades and manufactures, as also to avoyd sloath and idlnesse wherewith such young children are easily corrupted, as also for releife of such parents whose poverty extends not to give them breeding. That the justices of the peace should at their discretion, bind out children to trades-men or husbandmen to be brought vp in some good and lawfull calling, And whereas God Almighty, among many his other blessings, hath vouch-safed increase of children to this collony, who now are multiplied to a considerable number, who if instructed in good and lawfull trades may much improve the honor and reputation of the country, and noe lesse their owne good and theire parents comfort: But forasmuch as for the most part the parents, either through fond indulgence or perverse obstinacy, are most averse and unwilling to parte with theire children, *Be it therefore inacted by authoritie of this Grand Assembly,* according to the aforesayd laudable custom in the kingdom of England, That the comissioners of the severall countyes respectively do, at theire discretion, make choice of two children in each county of the age of eight or seaven years at the least, either male or female, which are to be sent vp to James Citty between this and June next to be imployed in the public flax houses vnder such master and mistresse as shall be there appointed, In carding, knitting and spin-ning, &c. And that the said children be furnished from the said county with six barrels of corne, two coverletts, or one rugg and one blankett: One bed, one wooden bowle or tray, two pewter spoones, a sow shote of six months old, two laying hens, with convenient apparell both linen and woollen, with hose and shooes, And for the better provision of howseing for the said children, *It is inacted,* That there be two houses built by the first of April next of forty foot long a peece with good and substantial timber, The houses to be twenty foot broad apeece, eight foot high in the pitche and a stack of brick chimneys standing in the midst of each house, and that they be lofted with sawne boardes and made with convenient partitions, And it is further thought fitt that the commissioners have caution not to take vp any children but from such parents who by reason of their poverty are disabled to maintaine and educate them, *Be it likewise agreed,* That the Governour hath agreed with the Assembly for the sume of 10000 lb. of tob'o. to be paid him the next crop, to build and finish the said howses in manner and form before expressed.

* Hening, *Statutes at Large of Virginia,* I, pp. 336-37 (1642).

Initial Legislation on Apprenticeship in Massachusetts, 1642 *

This Cort, taking into consideration the great neglect of many parents & masters in training up their children in learning, & labor, & other implyments which may be proffitable to the common wealth, do hereupon order and decree, that in euery towne ye chosen men appointed for managing the prudentiall affajres of the same shall henceforth stand charged with the care of the redresse of this evill, so as they shallbee sufficiently punished by fines for the neglect thereof, upon presentment of the grand jury, or other information or complaint in any Court within this jurisdiction; and for this end they, or the greater number of them, shall have power to take account from time to time of all parents and masters, and of their children, concerning their calling and implyment of their children, especially of their ability to read & understand the principles of religion & the capitall lawes of this country, and to impose fines upon such as shall refuse to render such accounts to them when they shall be required; and they shall have power, with consent of any Court or the magistrate, to put forth apprentices the children of such as they shall [find] not to be able & fitt to imploy and bring them up. They shall take . . . that boyes and girles be not suffered to converse together, so as may occasion any wanton, dishonest, or immodest behavior; & for their better performance of this trust committed to them, they may divide the towne amongst them, appointing to every of the said townesmen a certaine number of families to have special oversight of. They are also to provide that a sufficient quantity of materialls, as hemp, flaxe, ecra, may be raised in their severall townes, & tooles & implements provided for working out the same; & for their assistance in this so needfull and beneficiall imploymt, if they meete wth any difficulty or opposition wch they cannot well master by their own power, they may have recorse to some of the matrats, who shall take such course for their help & incuragmt as the occasion shall require according to iustice; & the said townesmen, at the next Cort in those limits, after the end of their year, shall give a breife account in writing of their proceedings herein, provided that they have bene so required by some Cort or magistrate a month at least before; & this order to continew for two yeares, & till the Cort shall take further order.

Some Apprenticeship Indentures in Virginia in the Seventeenth Century †

York Court, 20 Oct., 1646.—It is ordered, with the consent of Mr. Edmund Chisman, father-in-law to John Lilly, orphant; William Barber,

---

* *Records of the Company of Massachusetts Bay*, II, pp. 6, 7. Similar legislation was enacted in other New England colonies. See M. W. Jernegan, *op. cit.*, Part II.
† *William and Mary College Quarterly Historical Magazine*, V, pp. 221-23.

father-in-law to the orphans of John Dennett, vizt.: Thomas Dennett, Margaret Dennett, and Sarah Dennett; & Daniel ffoxe, father-in-law to the orphants of Clark & Munday, that the estates belonging to the sd sevrall orphants, wch this day they have filed an accot of to this cort, shall henceforward with all there increase freely come & belong unto the said orphants wth out any charges for the future subsistance or education of the sd orphants, or for there care, paines, or charge in prserving & looking to ye sd sevrall orphants estates, as long as they or any of them shall remaine under the tuition of ye above sd Edmund Chisman, William Barber, & Daniel ffoxe, &c.

YORK COUNTY.—Orphants Cort held August 24th, 1648.
Present: Capt Nicholas Martin, Capt John Chisman, Mr Hugh Gwyn, Mr ffrancis Willis, Mr ffrancis Morgan.
Whereas John foster, orphant to John foster, late of Hampton pish, deceased, whoe is left without any mentaynance or estate whatsoever, and Stephen Gill, godfather to ye sd foster, haveing made humble suite to this court that the sd John foster, whoe hath by him beene already provided for and kept about a yeare, that he may have the tuition and bringing upp of ye sd John foster, and that he may be put wth him for some certayne tyme by this cort. It is therefore ordered that the sd John foster shall live & remaine under tuition & bringing upp of ye sd Stephen Gill, for ye space of nine yeares from ye date hereof. Dureing which tyme ye sd Gill is hereby injoined to p'vide sufficiently for ye sd foster, & to take care that he bee brought upp in ye feare of God and taught to Reade.

LANCASTER COUNTY, Jan'y 6, 1655.—The court hath ordered Jno, ye base child of Thomas Mannan, borne of Eliza: Tomlin, shall, according to ye will of ye mother, bee kept by Roger Harris & his wife until he arrive at ye Age of 18 years, he, ye sd Harris providing yt ye sd child be taught to write & reade. And yt ye sd Harris have all of ye tobacco due from Jno Robinson pd him at ye crop on ye 10th of November next, the same being 600 & caske.

SURRY COUNTY, June 15, 1681.—Wm. Rogers bound apprentice to Thomas Bage to serve till 21—his master to teach him his trade of blacksmith, and to read & wright, &c.
April 15, 1701. Sarah, the daughter of John Allen, deced, is bound to Thomas Bentley until she shall arrive at the age of eighteen years—the said Bentley obligeing himselfe to instruct her in the rudiments of the Christian Religion, to learne or cause her to be learnt to reade perfectly, and at the expiration of the said tearm to provide and give her a decent suit of Apparell, and ordered that Indentures be drawne accordingly.
Similar order in reference to her brother John.

May 4, 1697. Ordered that unless Jno Clements do put John High to school to learne to reade & write, he do appeare at the next court, and bring ye said John with him, that the court may then do therein as shall be found fitt.

ELIZABETH CITY COUNTY, July 18, 1698.—Ann Chandler, orphan of Daniel Chandler, bound apprentice to Phyllemon Miller till 18 or day of marriage, to be taught to read a chapter in the Bible, ye Lord's prayer, and ten commandments, and sempstress work.

ISLE OF WIGHT COUNTY.—At an Orphan's Court held on the 1st May, Anno 1694.
Prsent: Col. Arthur Smith, Capt. Henry Applewhait, Mr. Hen. Baker, Mr. Thos. Giles, Mr. Antho. Holladay, justices.
Charles Edwards having exhibited a peticon to this Court for Grace Griswood, an Orphan Girl, that she might live with him, ye sd Charles, till eighteen years old or marryed. It is thereupon ordered yt the sd Orphan doe live & abide with the sd Edwards till age or marryage as aforesaid, & ye sd Charles doth hereby oblige himselfe to mainteyn her decently & see yt she be taught to read, sew, spinn & knitt, & at the expiration of the tyme to have sufficient cloathing as shall be thought well by the court.

YORK COURT, May ye 26th 1690.—Whereas Thomas Thorpe and Ellinor his wife sued Robt Green to this court, and in their peticon declare that they did binde Richard Gilbert there son An Apprentice to ye Defent for the space of nine yeares by one Indenture under hand and seale to bee Instructed and taught in ye Arts and Mistery of a taylor and to teach or cause him to be taught to reade & to write a Leagable hand, and not to Imploye him to Labour in the Grownd, Excepting in helping to make corne for the Defendts ffamely, but ye defendt without regard to ye said Indenture Dayley keeps the said Apprentice to Labour in the Ground from year to year and omitts giveing him Learning or teach him his trade which is to ye said Apprentice utter Rewing and undoing. Therefore itt is ordered that ye said Robt Green doe at ye next court Enter into a Bond of 4000 lb tobacco & cash, with good and sufficient security for the true pformance of ye said Indenture and to fulfill every clause and Artickle therein expressed, according to ye true Interest and meaning ye same.

Some Apprenticeship Indentures in New England
in the Seventeenth Century

These are to show, that Elizabeth Brailbrook widow of Watertown, hath put her daughter (with the consent of the selectmen) into the hands of Simont Tomson & his wife of Ipswich ropemaker to be as an apprentice, untill she comes to the age of eighteen years, in which time the said Sarah is to serve them in all lawful Comands, and the said Simont is to teach her to reade the English Tongue, and to instruct her in the knowledge of God and his Ways.*

It is agreed between the Selectmen and br. Tolman that hee shall take Henry lakes child to keepe it untill it com to 21 years of age etc. and therefore to haue 26 pounds and to give security to the towne and to teach it to reade and wright and when it is capable if he lives the said br Tolman to teach it his trade.†

At a generall towne meeteing Nov. 7, 1670. Ordered that John Edy seit shall goe to John Fisk his house and to George Lorance and Willyam preist houseis to inquir a bought their Children wither they be Lerned to read the english tong and in case they be defective to warne in the said John George and Willyam to the next meeting of the selectmen. ‡

Willyam priest John Fisk and George Lorance being warned to a meeting of the select men at John Bigulah his house they makeing their a peerance: and being found defecttive weer admonished for not Learning their Children to read the english toung; weer convinced did acknowledg their neglect and did promise a mendment. §

Nathan fisk John whitney and Isaak mickstur meaking return of thear inquiry aftur childrens edduccation finde that John fisks children ear naythur taught o read nor yet thear caticise. ||

Charlestowne Selectmen being presented for not observing the Law conc'ning the Katechiseing of Children, and Keeping them to imployment. The Court comended it to ye selectmen, that they attend their duty there in as the law directed, and make returne thereof to the next Court, and to pay costs—2s.6d.¶

Indenture of John Campbell to a Schoolmaster in New York, 1722 **

This Indenture Wittnesseth that John Campbel Son of Robert Campbell of the City of New York with the Consent of his father and mother hath

* *Watertown Records* (Massachusetts), I, p. 47 (1656). Given in Jernegan, *op. cit.*, p. 119.
† *Dorchester Town Records* (Massachusetts), 306 (1651). Given in Jernegan, *op. cit.*, p. 120.
‡ *Watertown Records* (Massachusetts), I, p. 102. Given in Jernegan, *op. cit.*, p. 122.
§ *Ibid.* (December 13, 1670). Given in Jernegan, *op. cit.*
|| *Ibid.* (November 25, 1672). Given in Jernegan, *op. cit.*
¶ MSS. Records of the County Court of Middlesex, Mass., 1649-1693, I, p. 194. Given in Jernegan, *op. cit.*, p. 123.
** Citty of N. Yorke Indentures, February 19, 1694 to January 29, 1707, pp. 145-47 (MS. folio in City Hall of New York City). Given in Robert F. Seybolt, *Source Studies in American Colonial Education* (Urbana, Illinois, University of Illinois, 1925), pp. 85, 86.

put himself and by these presents doth Voluntarily put and bind himself Apprentice to George Brownell of the Same City Schoolmaster to learn the Art Trade or Mystery and with the Said George Brownell to Serve from the twenty ninth day of May one thousand seven hundred and twenty one for and during the Term of ten years and three Months to be Compleat and Ended During all which term the said Apprentice his said Master and Mistress faithfully Shall Serve their Secrets keep and Lawfull Commands gladly everywhere obey he Shall do no damage to his said Master or Mistress nor suffer it to be done by others without Letting or Giving Notice thereof to his said Master or Mistress he shall not Waste his said Master or Mistress Goods or Lend them Unlawfully to any he shall not Committ fornication nor Contract Matrimony within the Said Term at Cards Dice or any other unlawfull Game he shall not Play: he Shall not absent himself by Day or by Night from his Said Master or Mistress Service without their Leave; nor haunt Alehouses Taverns or Playhouses but in all things behave himself as a faithfull Apprentice ought to Do towards his said Master or Mistress during the Said Term. And the said George Brownell Doth hereby Covenant and Promise to teach and Instruct or Cause the said Apprentice to be taught and Instructed in the Art Trade or Calling of a Schoolmaster by the best way or means he or his wife may or can if the Said Apprentice be Capable to Learn and to find and Provide unto the Said Apprentice sufficient meat Drink Apparel Lodging and washing fitting for an Apprentice during the Said Term: and at the Expiration thereof to give unto the Said Apprentice one Suit of Cloth new Consisting of a coatvest coat and Breeches also one New hatt Six New Shirts Three pair of Stockings one pair of New Shoes Suitable for his said Apprentice. In Testimony Whereof the Parties to these Presents have hereunto Interchangeably Sett their hands and Seals the third day of August in the Eighth year of the Reign of our Sovereign Lord George King of Great Brittain &c. Anno Domini One thousand seven hundred and Twenty One. John Campbel. Signed Sealed and Delivered in the presence of Mary Smith Cornelius Kiersted Memorandum Appeared before me John Cruger Esq. Alderman and One of his Majesties Justices of the Peace for this City and County. John Campbell and Acknowledged the within Indenture to be his Voluntary Act and Deed New York the 9th Aprill 1722.

Andrew Johnson Is Apprenticed to a Tailor, 1822 *

At a court of Pleas and Quarterly Sessions begun and held at the Court House in Raleigh on the 3rd Monday of February, 1822 being the forty-sixth year of American Independence (and the 18th day of February).

Ordered that A. Johnson,† an orphan boy and son of Jacob Johnson,

---

* Records of Wake County.
† Johnson became the seventeenth President of the United States.

deceased, 14 years of age, be bound to Jas. J. Selby till he arrive at lawful age to learn the trade of a Tailor.

Andrew Johnson's Master Offers a Reward of Ten Dollars for the Return of the Apprentice, 1824 *

TEN DOLLARS REWARD

Ran away from the Subscriber, on the night of the 15th instant, two apprentice boys, legally bound, named William and Andrew Johnson. The former is of a dark complexion, black hair, eyes, and habit. They are much of a height, about 5 feet 4 or 5 inches. The latter is very fleshy, freckled face, light hair, and fair complexion. They went off with two other apprentices, advertised by Messrs. Wm. & Chas. Fowler. When they went away, they were well clad—blue cloth coats, light colored homespun coats, and new hats, the maker's name in the crown of the hats, is Theodore Clark. I will pay the above Reward to any person who will deliver said apprentices to me in Raleigh, or I will give the above Reward for Andrew Johnson alone.

All persons are cautioned against harboring or employing said apprentices on pain of being prosecuted.

JAMES J. SELBY, *Tailor.*

RALEIGH, N. C. June 24, 1824.

Indentured Schoolmasters for Disposal in Baltimore, 1786 †

Men and Women Servants

JUST ARRIVED

In the Ship Paca, Robert Caulfield, Master, in five Weeks from Belfast and Cork, a number of healthy Men and Women SERVANTS.

Among them are several valuable tradesmen, viz.

Carpenters, Shoemakers, Coopers, Blacksmiths, Staymakers, Bookbinders, Clothiers, Diers, Butchers, Schoolmasters, Millwrights, and Labourers.

Their indentures are to be disposed of by the Subscribers,

BROWN, and MARIS,

WILLIAM WILSON.

BALTIMORE, May 29, 1786.

---

* *The Raleigh Gazette,* June 24, 1824.

† *Maryland Gazette or Baltimore Advertiser,* May 30, June 6 and 13, 1786. Given in Seybolt, *op. cit.,* p. 84.

« 3 »

The Colonial Teacher

《《《《《《《《《《《《《《《《《《《《《《《《《《《《《《《《《《《《《《《》》》》》》》》》》》》》》》》》》》》》》》》》》》》》

Instructions from the Classis of Amsterdam to Schoolmasters
in the Dutch Possessions, 1636 *

He is to instruct the youth both on shipboard and on land, in reading, writing, ciphering, and arithmetic, with all zeal and diligence; he is also to implant the fundamental principles of true Christian religion and salvation, by means of catechizing; he is to teach them the customary forms of prayers and also to accustom them to pray; he is to give heed to their manners, and bring these as far as possible to modesty and propriety, and to this end he is to maintain good discipline and order, and further to do all that is required of a good, diligent and faithful schoolmaster.

Instructions to Evert Pietersen, a Teacher
in New Amsterdam, 1661 †

1. He shall take good care, that the children, coming to his school, do so at the usual hour, namely at eight in the morning and one in the afternoon.

2. He must keep good discipline among his pupils.

3. He shall teach the children and pupils the Christian prayers, commandments baptism, Lord's supper, and the questions with answers of the catechism, which are taught here on every Sunday afternoon in the church.

---

* Given in Thomas E. Finegan, *Free Schools: A Documentary History of the Free School Movement in New York State* (Albany, University of the State of New York, 1921), p. 16. The story of the teacher in the colonial period is not always the most encouraging chapter in American educational history. He was not often an inspiring figure or a person of high repute. Too often he was a man of questionable probity in his private life, of inferior education, shiftless and itinerant in habits, poorly paid and as poorly esteemed by the public, as the records seem to show. Ichabod Crane, the timorous schoolmaster who was chased at night by his Dutch rival in love masquerading as a headless horseman to drive Ichabod from his job, is perhaps not a fiction of American educational literature. See Willard S. Elsbree, *The American Teacher* (New York, American Book Co., 1939), chapter I, "The Colonial Schoolmaster."

† Given in Finegan, *op. cit.*, pp. 16, 17.

16

4. Before school closes he shall let the pupils sing some verses and a psalm.

5. Besides his yearly salary he shall be allowed to demand and receive from every pupil quarterly as follows: For each child, whom he teaches the a b c, spelling, and reading, 30 st.; for teaching to read and write, 50 st.; for teaching to read, write and cipher, 60 st.; from those who come in the evening and between times pro rata a fair sum. The poor and needy, who ask to be taught for God's sake, he shall teach for nothing.

6. He shall be allowed to demand and receive from everybody, who makes arrangements to come to his school and comes before the first half of the quarter preceding the first of December next, the school dues for the quarter, but nothing from those, who come after the first half of the quarter.

7. He shall not take from anybody, more than is herein stated. Thus done and decided by the Burgomasters of the City of Amsterdam, in N. N., November 4, 1661.

John Shutte Is Licensed to Teach in Albany, New York, 1665 *

Whereas, the teaching of the English tongue is necessary in this government; I have, therefore, thought fitt to give license to John Shutte to be the English Schoolmaster at Albany; And, upon condition that the said John Shutte shall not demand any more wages from each Schollar than is given by the Dutch to their Dutch Schoolmasters, I have further granted to the said John Shutte that hee shall bee the onely English Schoolmaster at Albany.

Given under my hand, at Fort James in New York, the 12th day of October, 1665.

RICH'RD NICOLLS.

Contract with a Dutch Schoolmaster in Flatbush, New York, 1682 †

School Service. I. The School shall begin at eight o'clock, and go out at eleven; and in the afternoon shall begin at one o'clock and end at four. The bell shall be rung when the school commences.

II. When the school begins, one of the children shall read the morning prayer, as it stands in the catechism, and close with the prayer before dinner; in the afternoon it shall begin with the prayer after dinner, and end with the evening prayer. The evening school shall begin with the Lord's prayer, and close by singing a psalm.

III. He shall instruct the children on every Wednesday and Saturday,

---

* Daniel J. Pratt, *Annals of Public Education in the State of New York from 1626 to 1746* (Albany, The Argus Co., 1872), p. 57.
† *Ibid.,* pp. 65-67.

in the common prayers, and the questions and answers in the catechism, to enable them to repeat them the better on Sunday before the afternoon service, or on Monday, when they shall be catechised before the congregation. Upon all such occasions, the schoolmaster shall be present, and shall require the children to be friendly in their appearance and encourage them to answer freely and distinctly.

IV. He shall be required to keep his school nine months in succession, from September to June, in each year, in case it should be concluded upon to retain his services for a year or more, or without limitation; and he shall then be required to be regulated by these articles, and to perform the same duties which his predecessor, Jan Thibaud, above named, was required to perform. In every particular therefore, he shall be required to keep school, according to this seven months agreement, and shall always be present himself.

Church Service. I. He shall keep the church clean, and ring the bell three times before the people assemble to attend the preaching and catechism. Also before the sermon is commenced, he shall read a chapter out of the Holy Scriptures, and that, between the second and third ringing of the bell. After the third ringing he shall read the ten commandments, and the twelve articles of our faith, and then take the lead in singing. In the afternoon after the third ringing of the bell, he shall read a short chapter, or one of the Psalms of David, as the congregation are assembling; and before divine service commences, shall introduce it, by the singing of a Psalm or Hymn.

II. When the minister shall preach at Brooklyn, or New-Utrecht, he shall be required to read twice before the congregation, from the book commonly used for that purpose. In the afternoon he shall also read a sermon on the explanation of the catechism, according to the usage and practice approved of by the minister. The children as usual, shall recite their questions and answers out of the catechism, on Sunday, and he shall instruct them therein. He, as chorister, shall not be required to perform these duties, whenever divine service shall be performed in Flatlands, as it would be unsuitable, and prevent many from attending there.

III. For the administration of Holy Baptism, he shall provide a basin with water, for which he shall be entitled to receive from the parents, or witnesses, twelve styvers. He shall, at the expense of the church, provide bread and wine, for the celebration of the Holy Supper; He shall be in duty bound promptly to furnish the minister with the name of the child to be baptized, and with the names of the parents and witnesses. And he shall also serve as messenger for the consistory.

IV. He shall give the funeral invitations, dig the grave, and toll the bell, for which service he shall receive for a person of fifteen years and upwards, twelve guilders, and for one under that age, eight guilders. If he should be required to give invitations beyond the limits of the town, he shall be entitled to three additional guilders, for the invitation of every other town, and if he should be required to cross the river, and go to New York, he shall receive four guilders.

School Money. He shall receive from those who attend the day school, for a speller or reader, three guilders a quarter, and for a writer four guilders. From those who attend evening school, for a speller or reader, four guilders, and for a writer, six guilders shall be given.

Salary. In addition to the above, his salary shall consist of four hundred guilders, in grain, valued in Seewant, to be delivered at Brooklyn Ferry, and for his services from October to May, as above stated, a sum of two hundred and thirty-four guilders, in the same kind, with the dwelling-house, barn, pasture lot and meadows, to the school appertaining. The same to take effect from the first day of October, instant.

Done and agreed upon in Consistory, under the inspection of the Honorable Constable and Overseers, the 8th, of October, 1682.

Constable and Overseers	*The Consistory*
CORNELIUS BARRIAN,	CASPARUS VAN ZUREN, *Minister,*
RYNIER AERTSEN,	ADRIAEN REYERSE,
JAN REMSEN,	CORNELIS BARENT VANDWYCK.

I agree to the above articles, and promise to perform them according to the best of my ability.

JOHANNES VAN ECKKELEN

The General Assembly of Virginia Requests Change in the Method of Licensing Schoolmasters in That Colony and the Reply of the Governor, 1686 *

To *his Excellencie* ffrancis *Lord* Howard *Baron* of Effingham *his Majesties Lt & Governor Genl* of Virginia.

The house of Burgesses now assembled, humbly present.

That whereas your Excellencie has been pleased by your late precept to command that all Schoolmasters should make their personall appearance at *James City,* there to receive your Excellencies License & approbation to teach & that none Shall be admitted to that Office before they haue there taken out such a qualification and whereas this house doe too Sencibly vnderstand from their Respective Counties, that severall knowing skilfull Schoolmasters leave of their imploy because they are vnable out of such small allowance as they yearly have to endure the charge they are now necessarily exposed to, for the procuring of their Licenses to teach. This house doe therefore in the Name of themselves and all the inhabitants of

* H. R. McIlwaine (Ed.), *Journals of the House of Burgesses of Virginia,* 1659/60-1693, pp. 270, 274.

this Countrey, humbly pray that for the greater ease of such as are willing to employ themselves in so necessary an vndertakeing, your Excellencie would please to appoint in every Countie, some One of such person or persons as to your Excellencie shall seem most fit, for the due examination of them, & that such persons vpon their well approueing their Capacities, may likewise haue power from your Excellency to grant them a license for so moderate & reasonable a fee, as in the like cases is vsuall & Customary to be paid in *England*.

Mr Speaker *and Gentlemen.*

I haue recd from you an Address relateing to Schoolmasters in that as in all other matters, I shall give you all reasonable satisfaction and therefore am to tell you, that what Comands to me I have giuen therein are pursueant to his Majesties Speciall Comands to me, as by the Instruction herewith sent vnto you, you may observe, in which not being so forward, as it was expected I should haue been, my memory was therein refreshed by the Lord Bishop of *London,* and as I am Comanded to haue it performed, so I am desireous to have it done with as much ease & encouragement to the inhabitants, as possible may be and as testimonies thereof I will direct, that Examination shall be taken of the fitness & abilities of persons presented for Schoolmasters by the next of his Majesties Councell of this Colonie, & vpon his approueing of the persons they shall be accordingly lycenced for Schoolmasters, with whom I shall cause to be left blanke lycenses vnder my hand & seale to be filled up with the name & names of such person & persons approued of, for which shall be required no more than a Small fee to my Clerke for the writeing the same. Signed

By his Excellencies Comand.
E Chilton C Genl Assmbly

Ezekiel Cheever, Famed New England Schoolmaster, Asks to Keep His Position and Pay, c. 1687 *

To his Excellency Sr. Edmund Andros Knight, Governour & Capt. Generall of his Majesties Territories & Dominions in New England.

The humble peticon of Ezekiel Cheever of Boston Schoolmr. Sheweth, that your poor peticoner hath neer fifty yeares been employed in ye work & office of a publick Grammar-Schoolmr. in severall places in this Countrey, With wt. acceptance & success I submit to the judgment of those, that are able to testify. Now seeing God is pleased mercifully yet to continue my wonted abilities in mind, health of body, vivacity of spirit, delight in my work, which alone I am in anyway fit for, & capable of, & whereby I have my outward subsistence. I almost humly entreat your

---

* *Hutchison Papers,* III, p. 343. Given in H. F. Jenk's *Catalogue of the Boston Public Latin School* (Boston, 1886), p. 268.

Excellency, yt according to your former kindness often manifested, I may by your Excellencies favour, allowance, & encouragement still be continued in my present place. And whereas there is due to me about fifty five pounds for my labours past & ye former way of that part of my maintenance usually raised by a rate is thought good to be altered. I with all submission beseech your Excellency, that you would be pleased to give order for my due satisfaction, ye want of which would fall heavy upon me in my old age, & my children also who are otherwise poor enough.

And you poor peticonr. shall ever pray &c.

Your Excellencies most humble servt.

EZEKIEL CHEEVER

Governor Edward Cornbury Grants License to James Jeffray to Teach in the City of New York, 1706 *

To MR. JAMES JEFFRAY Greeting.

I do hereby authorize and Impower You to Keep and Teach School within the city of New York and to Instruct all children with whom you Shall be intrusted in the art of Writing and Arithmetick for and During my Pleasure.

Given under my hand and Seal at ffort Anne in New York this Seventeenth day of Aprill—in the fifth Year of the Reign of our Sovereign Lady Anne, by the Grace of God of England, Scotland, ffrance and Ireland Queen Defender of the faith, etc.—Annoque Domini 1706.

CORNBURY.

Instructions for the Clergy Employed by the Society for the Propagation of the Gospel in Foreign Parts, 1706 †

Upon their Admission to the Society.

I. That, from the Time of their Admission, they lodge not in any Publick House; but at some Bookseller's, or in other private and reputable Families, till they shall be otherwise accommodated by the Society.

II. That till they can have a convenient Passage, they employ their

* Given in Pratt, *op. cit.,* p. 92.

† Given in C. F. Pascoe, *Two Hundred Years of the S. P. G., 1701-1900,* pp. 837-40.

This Society, often referred to as the S. P. G., received charter in England in 1701 "for the purpose of providing the ministrations of religion for our countrymen in the Colonies, and of bringing the surrounding heathen to the Knowledge of the truth." Useful accounts of the work of the Society appear in C. F. Pascoe, *Two Hundred Years of the S. P. G., 1701-1900,* "Published at the Society's Office" (1901); Ernest Hawkins, *Historical Notices of the Missions to the Church of England in the North American Colonies, Previous to the Independence of the United States* (London, 1845); James S. M. Anderson, *History of the Church of England in the Colonies and Foreign Dependencies of the British Empire* (London, 1845). The charter of the Society appears in Pascoe, *op. cit.,* pp. 932-45; in Hawkins, *op. cit.,* pp. 415-21; and in Edgar W. Knight, *A Documentary History of Education in the South Before 1860* (Chapel Hill, University of North Carolina Press, 1949), I, pp. 64-70.

Time usefully; in Reading Prayers, and Preaching, as they have Opportunity; in hearing others Read and Preach; or in such Studies as may tend to fit them for their Employment.

III. That they constantly attend the Standing Committee of this Society, at the Secretary's, and observe their Directions.

IV. That before their Departure they wait upon his Grace the Lord Archbishop of *Canterbury,* their Metropolitan, and upon the Lord Bishop of *London,* their Diocesan, to receive their Paternal Benediction and Instructions.

Upon their going on Board the Ship designed for their Passage.

I. That they demean themselves not only inoffensively and prudently, but so as to become remarkable Examples of Piety and Virtue to the Ship's Company.

II. That whether they be Chaplains in the Ship's, or only Passengers, they endeavor to prevail with the Captain or Commander, to have Morning and Evening Prayer said daily; as also Preaching and Catechizing every Lord's Day.

III. That throughout their Passage they Instruct, Exhort, Admonish, and Reprove, as they have occasion and opportunity, with such Seriousness and Prudence, as may gain them Reputation and Authority.

Upon their Arrival in the Country whither they shall be sent.
First, *With Respect to themselves.*

I. That they always keep in their View the great Design of their Undertaking, *viz.* To promote the Glory of Almighty God, and the Salvation of Men, by Propagating the Gospel of our Lord and Saviour.

II. That they often consider the Qualifications requisite for those who would effectually promote this Design, *viz.* A sound Knowledge and hearty Belief of the Christian Religion; an Apostolical Zeal, tempered with Prudence, Humility, Meekness and Patience; a fervent Charity towards the Souls of Men; and finally, that Temperance, Fortitude, and Constancy, which become good Soldiers of Jesus Christ.

III. That in order to the obtaining and preserving the said Qualifications, they do very frequently in their Retirements offer up fervent Prayers to Almighty God for his Direction and Assistance; converse much with the Holy Scriptures; seriously reflect upon their Ordination Vows; and consider the Account which they are to render to the Great Shepherd and Bishop of our Souls at the last Day.

IV. That they acquaint themselves thoroughly with the Doctrine of the Church of *England,* as contained in the Articles and Homilies; its Worship and Discipline, and Rules for Behaviour of the Clergy, as contained in the Liturgy and Canons; and that they approve themselves accordingly, as genuine Missionaries from this Church.

V. That they endeavour to make themselves Masters in those Controversies which are necessary to be understood, in order to the Preserving their Flock from the Attempts of such Gainsayers as are mixed among them.

VI. That in their outward Behaviour they be circumspect and unblameable, giving no Offence either in Word or Deed; that their ordinary Discourse be grave and edifying; their Apparel decent, and proper for Clergymen; and that in their whole Conversation they be Instances and Patterns of the Christian Life.

VII. That they do not board in, or frequent Publick-houses, or lodge in Families of evil Fame; that they wholly abstain from Gaming, and all such Pastimes; and converse not familiarly with lewd or prophane Persons, otherwise than to order to reprove, admonish, and reclaim them.

VIII. That in whatsoever Family they shall lodge, they persuade them to join with them in daily Prayer Morning and Evening.

IX. That they be not nice about Meats and Drinks, nor immoderately careful about their Entertainment in the Places where they shall sojourn; but contented with what Health requires, and the Place easily affords.

X. That as they be frugal, in Opposition to Luxury, so they avoid all Appearance of Covetousness, and recommend themselves, according to their Abilities, by the prudent Exercise of Liberality and Charity.

XI. That they take special Care to give no offence to the Civil Government, by intermeddling in Affairs not relating to their own Calling and Function.

XII. That, avoiding all Names of Distinction, they endeavour to preserve a Christian Agreement and Union one with another, as a Body of Brethren of one and the same Church, united under the Superior Episcopal Order, and all engaged in the same great Design of Propagating the Gospel; and to this End, keeping up a Brotherly Correspondence, by meeting together at certain Times, as shall be most convenient, for mutual Advice and Assistance.

Secondly, *With respect to their Parochial Cure.*

I. That they conscientiously observe the Rules of our Liturgy, in the Performance of all the Offices of their Ministry.

II. That, besides the stated Service appointed for Sundays and Holidays, they do, as far as they shall find it practicable, publickly read the daily Morning and Evening Service, and decline no fair Opportunity of Preaching to such as may be occasionally met together from remote and distant Parts.

III. That they perfom every Part of Divine Service with that Seriousness and Decency, that may recommend their Ministrations to their Flock, and excite a Spirt of Devotion in them.

IV. That the chief Subjects of their Sermons be the great Fundamental

Principles of Christianity, and the Duties of a sober, righteous, and godly Life, as resulting from those Principles.

V. That they particularly preach against those Vices which they shall observe to be most predominant in the Places of their Residence.

VI. That they carefully instruct the People concerning the Nature and Use of the Sacraments of Baptism and the Lord's Supper, as the peculiar Institutions of Christ, Pledges of Communion with Him, and Means of deriving Grace from Him.

VII. That they duly consider the Qualifications of those adult Persons to whom they administer Baptism; and of those likewise whom they admit to the Lord's Supper; according to the Directions of the Rubricks in our Liturgy.

VIII. That they take special Care to lay a good Foundation for all their other Ministrations, by Catechizing those under their Care, whether Children, or other ignorant Persons, explaining the Catechism to them in the most easy and familiar Manner.

IX. That in their instructing *Heathens* and *Infidels,* they begin with the Principles of Natural Religion, appealing to their Reason and Conscience; and thence proceed to shew them the Necessity of Revelation, and the Certainty of that contained in the Holy Scriptures, by the plainest and most obvious Arguments.

X. That they frequently visit their respective Parishioners; those of our own Communion, to keep them steady in the Profession and Practice of Religion, as taught in the Church of *England;* those that oppose us, or dissent from us, to convince and reclaim them with a Spirit of Meekness and Gentleness.

XI. That those, whose Parishes shall be of large Extent, shall, as they have Opportunity and Convenience, officiate in the several Parts thereof, so that all the Inhabitants may by Turns partake of their Ministrations; and that such as shall be appointed to officiate in several Places shall reside sometimes at one, sometimes at another of those Places, as the Necessities of the People shall require.

XII. That they shall, to the best of their Judgments, distribute those small Tracts given by the Society for that Purpose, amongst such of their Parishioners as shall want them most, and appear likely to make the best Use of them; and that such useful Books, of which they have not a sufficient Number to give, they be ready to lend to those who will be most careful in reading and restoring them.

XIII. That they encourage the setting up of Schools for the teaching of Children; and particularly by the Widows of such Clergymen as shall die in those Countries, if they be found capable of that Employment.

XIV. That each of them keep a Register of his Parishioners' Names, Profession of Religion, Baptism, &c. according to the Scheme annexed, No. I. for his own Satisfaction, and the Benefit of the People.

Thirdly, *With respect to the Society.*

I. That each of them keep a constant and regular Correspondence with the Society, by their Secretary.

II. That they send every six Months an Account of the State of their respective Parishes, according to the Scheme annexed, No. II.

III. That they communicate what shall be done at the Meetings of the Clergy, when settled, and whatsoever else may concern the Society.

Notitia Parochialis; to be made by each Minister soon after his Acquaintance with his People, and kept by him for his own Ease and Comfort, as well as the Benefit of his Parishioners.

I. Names of Parishioners	II. Profession of Religion	III. Which of them baptized	IV. When baptized	V. Which of them Communicants	VI. When they first communicated	VII. What Obstructions they meet with in their Ministration

No. II.

Notitia Parochialis; or an Account to be sent Home every six Months to the Society by each Minister, concerning the spiritual State of their respective Parishes.

I. *Number of Inhabitants.*	
II. *No. of the Baptized.*	
III. *No. of Adult Persons baptized this Half-year.*	
IV. *No. of actual Communicants of the* Church of England.	
V. *No. of those who profess themselves of the* Church of England.	
VI. *No. of Dissenters of all Sorts, particularly Papists.*	
VII. *No. of Heathens and Infidels.*	
VIII. *No. of Converts from a prophane, disorderly and unchristian Course, to a Life of Christian Purity, Meekness, and Charity.*	

Instructions for Schoolmasters Employed by the Society, 1706 *

I. That they will consider the End for which they are employed by the Society, *viz.* The instructing and disposing Children to believe and live as Christians.

II. In order to this End, that they teach them to read truly and distinctly, that they may be capable of reading the Holy Scriptures, and other pious and useful Books, for informing their Understandings, and regulating their Manners.

III. That they instruct them thoroughly in the Church-Catechism; teach them first to read it distinctly and exactly, then to learn it perfectly by Heart; endeavouring to make them understand the Sense and Meaning of it, by the help of such Expositions as the Society shall send over.

IV. That they teach them to write a plain and legible Hand, in order to the fitting them for useful Employment; with as much Arithmetick as shall be necessary to the same Purpose.

V. That they be industrious, and give constant Attendance at proper School-Hours.

VI. That they daily use, Morning and Evening, the Prayers composed for their Use in this Collection, with their Scholars in the School, and teach them the Prayers and Graces composed for their Use at Home.

VII. That they oblige their Scholars to be constant at Church on the Lord's Day, Morning and Afternoon, and at all other Times of Publick Worship; that they cause them to carry their Bibles and Prayer Books with them, instructing them how to use them there, and how to demean themselves in the several Parts of Worship; that they be there present with them, taking Care of their reverent and decent Behaviour, and examine them afterwards, as to what they have heard and learned.

VIII. That when any of their Scholars are fit for it, they recommend them to the Minister of the Parish, to be publickly Catechized in the Church.

IX. That they take especial Care of their Manners, both in their Schools and out of them; warning them seriously of those Vices to which Children are most liable; teaching them to abhor Lying and Falsehood, and to avoid all sorts of Evil-speaking; to love Truth and Honesty; to be modest, gentle, well-behaved, just and affable, and courteous to all their Companions; respectful to their Superiors, particularly towards all that minister in holy Things, and especially to the Minister of their Parish; and all this from a Sense and Fear of Almighty God; endeavouring to bring them in their tender Years to that Sense of Religion, which may render it the constant Principle of their Lives and Actions.

X. That they use all kind and gentle Methods in the Government of their Scholars, that they may be loved as well as feared by them; and that

* *Ibid.*, pp. 844-45.

when Correction is necessary, they make the Children to understand, that it is given them out of kindness, for their Good, bringing them to a Sense of their Fault, as well as of their Punishment.

XI. That they frequently consult with the Minister of the Parish, in which they dwell, about the Methods of managing their Schools, and be ready to be advised by him.

XII. That they do in their whole Conversation shew themselves Examples of Piety and Virtue to their Scholars, and to all with whom they shall converse.

XIII. That they be ready, as they have Opportunity, to teach and instruct the *Indians* and *Negroes* and their Children.

XIV. That they send to the Secretary of the Society, once in every six Months, an Account of the State of their respective Schools, the Number of their Scholars, with the Methods and Success of their Teaching.

[The following form appears in the "Standing Orders" of the later edition]:

Notitia Scholastica; *or an Account to be sent every Six Months to the* Society *by each* Schoolmaster, *concerning the State of their respective Schools.*

1. Attendance daily given.	
2. Number of Children taught in the School.	
3. Number of Children baptized in the Church of *England*.	
4. Number of *Indian* and Negroe Children.	
5. Number of Children born of Dissenting Parents.	
6. Other Schools in or near the Place.	
7. Of what Denomination.	
8. Other Employments of the Schoolmaster.	

Qualifications Required of Schoolmasters of the Society, 1711 *

8th Febry 1711/12

The Secretary reported from the Comee that they had, according to order, Consider'd of Rules & orders for the qualification & Conduct of Schoolmasters, and having Inspected the Society's Collection of Papers, had adapted these following for that purpose, wch they agreed to lay before the Society vizt.

* Gertrude Foster (Comp.), "Documentary History of Education in South Carolina" (typescript doctoral dissertation, University of South Carolina, 1932), VI, pp. 16-19.

1. That no person be admitted as Schoolmaster till he bring Certificates of the following particulars
   1. his age
   2. his condition of life whether Single or mary'd
   3. his temper
   4. his prudence
   5. his Learning
   6. his Sober & pious Conversation
   7. his Zeal and the Xtian Religion & diligence in his calling
   8. his affection to the present government
   9. his conformity to the doctrine & discipline of the Church of England

2. That no person Shall be employ's as a Schoolmaster by the Society till he has been tryed and approved by three members appointed by the Society or Committee who Shall testify by word or writing his ability to teach reading, writing and the Catechism of the Church of England and Such exposition thereof as the Society Shall order.

3. That they obServe the Instructions given to the School masters by the Society, Set down page 33.34.35. of the Said *Collection of papers*.

4. That no Testimonyal Shall be allowed of, but Such as are Signed by the respective minister of the parish; and where that is not practicable, by Some other persons of Credit and note, three at least of the Communion of the Church of England, whereof one Shall be a Clergyman, and Such as Shall be well known to some of the members of the Society.

5. That all Schoolmasters, in matters which they desire Shou'd be Laid before ye Society do Correspond only with the Secretary of this Society.

6. That if any Schoolmaster, in the Service of the Society, Shall return from the Plantations, without leave first had from the Society, Such School master Shall receive no farther allowance from the time he Shall leave his Service there.

7. That all School masters sent over to the plantations by the Society, being Marryed men, be obliged to take their wives with them, unless they can offer such reasons as Shall induce ye Society to dispense there with.

8. That the Salary of every Schoolmaster who is not dismis'd the Service for Some misdemeanour Shall continue one year, and no longer, after the Society have resolved at their bord to dismiss Such Persons from their Service.

The above Report of the Committee being Read and consider'd was Agreed to be laid before the Society anniversary meeting in order to be confirm'd at that time if it Shall be thou't fit.

15 Febry 1711/12.

The Report of the Comee for Rules and Orders for the qualifications and conduct of Schoolmasters being consider'd, ye Same was read and approv'd wth these Alterations vizt in the second Rule That no Schoolmaster be Sent instead of Employ'd—In the 4th to ye word (Parish) be added the words Where he last liv'd. In the 5th before the Word Secretary be inserted (President or)

Order'd that there be added to ye said Orders, That no Schoolmaster be sent in ye Societys Service till he be espiscopally Ordain'd Deacon, and that he have a Sallary not under Thirty pounds p ann.

Agreed that the Rules, and Orders aforemention'd relating to Schoolmaster be made Standing Orders and that ye Title of the Instructions be Instructions for Schoolmasters Sent by ye Society &c.

Membership in the Established Church Required of the Master of a School in Charleston, South Carolina, 1712 *

. . . That the person to be master of the said school shall be of the religion of the Church of England, and conform to the same, and shall be capable to teach the learned languages, that is to say, Latin and Greek tongues, and to catechise and instruct the youth in the principles of the Christian religion, as professed in the Church of England.

England's Oath Required of Teachers and Others, 1714 †

I do sincerely promise and swear, That I will be faithful, and bear true allegiance to his majesty King George. So help me God.

I do swear, that I do from my heart abhor, detest and abjure, as impious and heretical, that damnable doctrine and position, That princes excommunicated or deprived by the Pope, or any authority by the see of Rome, may be deposed or murthered by their subjects, or any other whatsoever. And I do declare, that no foreign prince, person, prelate, state or potentate, hath or ought to have any jurisdiction, power, superiority, pre-eminence or authority, ecclesiastical or spiritual, within this realm. So help me God.

A Presbyterian Schoolmaster in South Carolina Promises to Conform to the Rites of the Established Church, 1747 ‡

. . . We have the Other Day got a Presbyterian Schoolmaster Mackenzie by Name, Who after some Cavils and Objections, has promised in every thing to conform exactly to the Rites of the Establish'd Church, and has ever Since been very Urgent wth me about the salary, which the Honourable Society are pleased to Appoint the Cathechist and Schoolmaster of these Islands. I assured him it did not depend on Me, tho possibly it might

---

* Cooper, *The Statutes at Large of South Carolina*, II, p. 393. Given in Elsbree, *op. cit.*, p. 48.

† *The Statutes at Large, from the Twelfth Year of Queen Anne, to the Fifth Year of King George I*, XIII, pp. 187, 189.

‡ Given in Foster, *op. cit.*, V, p. 752.

on his own Behaviour; Which he might depend on my laying faithfully before the Society.

Agreement Between the Congregation of the Reformed Church, Lancaster, Pennsylvania, and John Hoffman, Teacher, 1747 *

On this day, May 4th, 1747, I, the undersigned, John Hoffman, parochial teacher of the church at Lancaster, have promised in the presence of the congregation to serve as chorister, and as long as we have no pastor, to read sermons on Sunday. In summer, I promise to hold catechetical instruction with the young, as becomes a faithful teacher, and also to lead them in singing; and to attend to the clock. On the other hand, the congregation promises me an annual salary consisting of voluntary offerings from all the members of the church, to be written in a special register and arranged according to the amounts contributed, so that the teacher may be adequately compensated for his labor.

Furthermore, I have firmly and irrevocably agreed with the congregation on the aforesaid date that I will keep school on every working day during the entire year, as is the usual custom, and in such a manner as becomes a faithful teacher. In consideration thereof they promise me a free dwelling and four cords of wood, and have granted me the privilege of charging for each child that may come to school the sum of five shillings (I say 5 sh.) for three months, and for the whole year one pound (I write £1). I promise to enter upon my duties without fail, if alive and well, on the 24th of November, 1747.

Contract Between a Schoolmaster and the Congregation at New Providence, Montgomery County, Pennsylvania, c. 1750 †

That the schoolhouse shall always be in charge of a faithful Evangelical Lutheran schoolmaster, whose competency to teach Reading, Writing, Arithmetic, as also to play the organ (*Orgelschlagen*) and to use the English language, has been proved by the pastor; special regard being had at the same time, to the purity of his doctrine and his life. He shall be required to treat all his pupils with impartial fidelity, and to instruct the children of other denominations, and of the neighborhood generally. He shall not allow the children to use profane language either in or out of school; but shall carefully teach them how, both in church and in school, and in the presence of others and upon the highway, to conduct themselves in a Christian and upright manner, and "not like the Indians." He shall never

---

* Given in J. P. Wickersham, *A History of Education in Pennsylvania* (Lancaster, Inquirer Publishing Co., 1886), p. 140.
† *Ibid.*, pp. 140, 141.

permit either parents or employers to quarrel with him in the presence of the children; persons having complaints to make shall be referred, at once, to the pastor and vestry. He shall be allowed seven shillings and sixpence, and one-half bushel of grain every six months, for each scholar; in addition, he shall live in the schoolhouse free of rent, to which a piece of ground shall be attached, have the collections taken in the church on two of the chief festivals of the year, together with other occasional perquisites. It shall be his duty also to enter a record of the baptized children in the books of the church.

One Purpose of Benjamin Franklin's Academy in Philadelphia Was to Prepare Teachers, 1750 *

That a number of the poorer Sort will be hereby qualified to act as Schoolmasters in the Country, to teach Children Reading, Writing, Arithmetic, and the Grammar of their Mother Tongue, and being of good morals and known character, may be recommended from the Academy to Country Schools for that purpose; The Country suffering at present very much for want of good Schoolmasters, and obliged to employ in their Schools, vicious imported Servants, or concealed Papists, who by their bad Examples and Instructions often deprave the Morals or corrupt the Principles of the Children under their Care.

Christopher Dock Tells How Children Should Be Received and Treated in School, 1750 †

The children arrive as they do because some have a great distance to school, others a short distance, so that the children cannot assemble as punctually as they can in a city. Therefore, when a few children are present, those who can read their Testament sit together on one bench; but the boys and girls occupy separate benches. They are given a chapter which they read at sight consecutively. Meanwhile I write copies for them. Those who

* Minutes of the Common Council of Philadelphia, July 31, 1750, when that body made a donation to the academy. Given in F. N. Thorpe, *Benjamin Franklin and the University of Pennsylvania* (Washington, Bureau of Education, Circular of Information No. 2, 1892), pp. 245-46. The quotation has often been attributed to Franklin who was a member of the Common Council, but it stated one of four benefits that the Common Council expected from the institution. E. E. Brown, in *The Making of Our Middle Schools* (p. 250, note) says that perhaps the word *poorer* referred to lack of economic "means rather than lack of brains."

† *Schulordnung.* Given in Martin G. Brumbaugh, *The Life and Works of Christopher Dock* (Philadelphia, J. B. Lippincott Co., 1908). Dock is said to have published the first professional book in this country on education and teaching. (The first book on the subject in English was by Samuel R. Hall, *Lectures on School-Keeping,* 1829). A German, Dock came to Pennsylvania in the early part of the eighteenth century, got interested in the education of the children of his German neighbors, and opened a school in what is now Montgomery County in that state. In 1750 he wrote his *Schulordnung,* which was published in 1770. The first English translation of the treatise was made by Governor Samuel Pennypacker of Pennsylvania.

have read their passage of Scripture without error take their places at the table and write. Those who fail have to sit at the end of the bench, and each new arrival the same; as each one is thus released in order he takes up his slate. This process continues until they have all assembled. The last one left on the bench is a "lazy pupil."

When all are together, and examined, whether they are washed and combed, they sing a psalm or a morning hymn, and I sing and pray with them. As much as they can understand of the Lord's Prayer and the ten commandments (according to the gift God has given them), I exhort and admonish them accordingly. This much concerning the assembling of pupils. But regarding prayer I will add this additional explanation. Children say the prayers taught them at home half articulately, and too fast, especially the "Our Father" which the Lord Himself taught His disciples and which contains all that we need. I therefore make a practice of saying it for them kneeling, and they kneeling repeat it after me. After these devotional exercises those who can write resume their work. Those who cannot read the Testament have had time during the assemblage to study their lesson. These are heard recite immediately after prayer. Those who know their lesson receive an O on the hand, traced with crayon. This is a mark of excellence. Those who fail more than three times are sent back to study their lesson again. When all the little ones have recited, these are asked again, and any one having failed in more than three trials a second time, is called "Lazy" by the entire class and his name is written down. Whether such a child fear the rod or not, I know from experience that this denunciation of the children hurts more than if I were constantly to wield and flourish the rod. If then such a child has friends in school who are able to instruct him and desire to do so, he will visit more frequently than before. For this reason: if the pupil's name has not been erased before dismissal the pupils are at liberty to write down the names of those who have been lazy, and take them along home. But if the child learns his lesson well in the future, his name is again presented to the other pupils, and they are told that he knew his lesson well and failed in no respect. Then all the pupils call "Diligent" to him. When this has taken place his name is erased from the slate of lazy pupils, and the former transgression is forgiven.

The children who are in the spelling class are daily examined in pronunciation. In spelling, when a word has more than one syllable, they must repeat the whole word, but some, while they can say the letters, cannot pronounce the word, and so cannot be put to reading. For improvement a child must repeat the lesson, and in this way: The child gives me the book, I spell the word and he pronounces it. If he is slow, another pupil pronounces it for him, and in this way he hears how it should be done, and knows that he must follow the letters and not his own fancy.

Concerning A B C pupils, it would be best, having but one child, to let it learn one row of letters at a time, to say forward and backward. But with many, I let them learn the alphabet first, and then ask a child to point out a letter that I name. If a child is backward or ignorant, I ask another, or the whole class, and the first one that points to the right letter, I grasp his finger and hold it until I have put a mark opposite his name. I then ask for another letter, &c. Whichever child has during the day received the greatest number of marks, has pointed out the greatest number of letters. To him I owe something—a flower drawn on paper or a bird. But if several have the same number, we draw lots; this causes less annoyance. In this way not only are the very timid cured of their shyness (which is a great hindrance in learning), but a fondness for school is increased. Thus much in answer to his question, how I take the children into school, how school proceeds before and after prayers, and how the inattentive and careless are made attentive and careful, and how the timid are assisted.

Further I will state that when the little ones have recited for the first time, I give the Testament pupils a verse to learn. Those reading newspapers and letters sit separately, and those doing sums sit separately. But when I find that the little ones are good enough at their reading to be fit to read the Testament, I offer them to good Testament readers for instruction. The willing teacher takes the pupil by the hand and leads him to his seat. I give them two verses to try upon. But if I find that another exercise is necessary after this (such as finding a passage in Scripture, or learning a passage, in which case each reads a verse), I give only one verse, which is not too hard for those trying to read in the Testament. If pupils are diligent and able, they are given a week's trial, in which time they must learn their lesson in the speller with the small pupils and also their lesson with the Testament pupil. If they stand the test they are advanced the next week from the spelling to the Testament class, and they are also allowed to write. But those who fail in the Testament remain a stated time in the A B C class before they are tested again. After the Testament pupils have recited, the little ones are taken again. This done they are reminded of the chapter read them, and asked to consider the teaching therein. As it is the case that this thought is also expressed in other passages of Holy Writ, these are found and read, and then a hymn is given containing the same teaching. If time remains, all are given a short passage of Scripture to learn. This done, they must show their writing exercises. These are examined and numbered, and then the first in turn is given a hard word to spell. If he fails the next must spell it and so on. The one to spell correctly receives his exercise. Then the first is given another hard word, and so each receives his exercise by spelling a word correctly.

As the children carry their dinner, an hour's liberty is given them after dinner. But as they are usually inclined to misapply their time if one is not constantly with them, one or two of them must read a story of the Old Testament (either from Moses and the Prophets, or from Solomon's or

Sirach's Proverbs), while I write copies for them. This exercise continues during the noon hour.

It is also to be noted that children find it necessary to ask to leave the room, and one must permit them to do this, not wishing the uncleanness and odor in the school. But the clamor to go out would continue all day, and sometimes without need, so that occasionally two or three are out at the same time, playing. To prevent this I have driven a nail in the doorpost, on which hangs a wooden tag. Any one needing to leave the room looks for the tag. If it is on the nail, this is his permit to go out without asking. He takes the tag out with him. If another wishes to leave, he does not ask either, but stands by the door until the first returns, from whom he takes the tag and goes. If the tag is out too long, the one wishing to go inquires who was out last, and from him it can be ascertained to whom he gave the tag, so that none can remain out too long. . . .

Now regarding his second question: How different children need different treatment, and how according to the greatness of the offense punishment must be increased or lessened.

I should gladly tell my friend all of this truly, but as the subject is such a broad one, I really do not know where to begin or end. This is because the wickedness of youth exhibits itself in so many ways, and the offenses which are taught them by those older than themselves are so various, and as God himself declares . . . Corruption is so great, and increases daily in so many ways, that I am convinced that it is impossible to do anything of one's own power. Where the Lord does not help build, all that build work in vain. The slap of the hand, hazel branch and birch rod are means of preventing wicked outburst, but they cannot change the stubborn heart, which hold us all in such sway since the fall, that we are all inclined more to the bad than to the good, so long as the heart is unchanged and not renewed by the spirit of God. But while the seed of wickedness is present, to remove it, not only from ourselves, but from our fellow man and from our youth. As this old evil and serpent's sting is the same in all, we all are enabled to seek earnestly the same surgeon and apply the means of recovery which He prescribes for such evil, to ourselves and our youth. For without recovery we cannot reach peace, for the worm that forever gnaws our conscience through the serpent's sting leads to eternal damnation. May God mercifully assist us all, that we may not neglect the promise to enter into His rest, and none of us remain behind. Amen.

Because, as has been said, it would take too long to enumerate all cases, I shall give my friend only a few, together with the means that I have sought to apply. But these means cannot cure the damage. The Lord of Lords, who holds all in His hand, and for whose help we need much to pray in such cases, deserves all the praise if we see improvement.

First, among many children swearing or cursing is so common, expressing itself variously in so many wicked words. If this evil is not warded off, such sour "leaven leavens the whole lump," therefore such children are carefully examined, whether they understand what they are saying. As it is frequently very evident that they do not, they are asked whether they have thought of the words themselves or have heard them; they usually reply that they heard them from So and So. If asked why they say it also, the answer is usually again, because So and So said it. Thus often ignorance is shown. They do not know why they are saying it. To such it must be explained that they must guard against such words; that they are against God's will and command. If they hear So and So use them, they shall tell that person that he or she is doubly sinning, for they got into trouble in school by repeating the words. If such children then promise not to use the words again, they go free the first time. But if after being warned they persist in the bad habit, after being certain that the accusation is true, they are put upon the punishment seat, with the yoke on their neck, as a sign of punishment. On promising to be good in the future they escape with a few slaps. If they again offend, the punishment is increased, and they must furnish surety. The oftener the offense, the more bondsmen. These bondsmen's business is to warn and remind the offender and prevent repetition. This is the rein and the bit to be put into their mouths for such offense, but the change of heart must come from a higher hand, and must be sought with diligent prayer. The import of God's word must also be explained to the offender and the other pupils. What great weight is in all this (if one persist and is found guilty to the end) and that man must render an account of himself, on the judgment day, of every idle word spoken. Such passages they must look up and read, and for their further instruction they are given a song or a psalm to learn. . . .

Schoolmasters in New Jersey Must Hold License
from the Bishop of London, 1758 *

We do further direct that . . . no Schoolmaster be henceforth permitted to come from England and to keep School in the said province without the License of the said Bishop of London, and that no other person now there or that shall come from other parts, shall be admitted to keep School in that Our said province of New Jersey, without your License first obtained.

Qualifications Required of Teachers in New Jersey, 1760 †

NEW YORK, November 5. On the 21st Instant, his Excellency Thomas Boone, Esq., Governor of New Jersey, issued a proclamation setting forth, that whereas the Education of Youth is a Matter of great Consequence, and

---

* Instructions to the Governor of New Jersey from England, *New Jersey Archives* (First Series), IX, p. 68. Given in Elsbree, *op. cit.*, p. 47.
† *New York Mercury*, November 4, 1760. Given in Elsbree, *op. cit.*, p. 42.

ought not to be trusted but to Persons of good Character, and loyal Principles, and professed Protestants; therefore he requires all Magistrates to inform themselves sufficiently of the Character of the School-Masters in the Province; to administer the Oaths to them, and give them, under the Hands of two, a Certificate of Approbation, by which they may obtain a License; and forbidding all Persons, after the 31st of December, to execute the Office of a Schoolmaster without such License first obtain'd.

Membership in the Established Church Required of the Master of a School in Newbern, North Carolina, 1766 *

. . . That no Person shall be admitted to be Master of the said School, but who is of the established Church of *England;* and who, at the Recommendation of the Trustees or Directors, or the Majority of them, shall be duly licensed by the Governor, or Commander in Chief for the Time being.

Massachusetts Enacts a Loyalty Oath for Teachers, 1776 †

. . . And no settled Minister or Grammar-school Master who shall refuse or neglect to sign said Declaration [of allegiance], shall be entitled by the laws of this Colony, to demand or recover any Salary or Reward for any Time or Service spent or performed in their Respective Offices, from and after such Refusal or Neglect until they shall Subscribe such Declaration; and if any of the Governors of Harvard College shall Refuse to sign the Declaration aforesaid, they shall be thereby disqualified to receive any salaries or Grants of the General Assembly for Services done after their refusal as aforesaid. ‡

* *Complete Revisal of All the Acts of the Assembly, of the Province of North Carolina,* 1773, p. 359.
† *Laws of Massachusetts,* 1775-1780, p. 161. For classification and analysis of the "test" laws enacted in this country during the Revolutionary War, see C. H. Van Tyne, *The Loyalists in the American Revolution.* There may be found quotations from "loyalist poetry," such as:

> "When penal laws were passed by vote
> I thought the test a grievance,
> Yet sooner than I'd lose a groat,
> I swore the state allegiance."

> "The imposer of the oath 'tis breaks it;
> Not he who for convenience takes it." Van Tyne, *op. cit.,* p. 134.

‡ It appears that in times of military and economic crises and in other periods of social and political confusion, legislative efforts to restrain teachers from engaging in "subversive activities" are attempted. Such efforts in this country reach back to the eighteenth century, and appeared during the Revolutionary War, the Civil War, during each of the two World Wars and in the 1930's. Between 1917 and 1930 about a dozen states enacted such legislation and in 1950 more than twenty states and the District of Columbia had requirements of loyalty oaths for teachers. Some higher educational institutions also had regulations on loyalty oaths. But in August, 1949, Circuit Court Judge Joseph Sherbow of Maryland held that a loyalty oath statute of that state violated the basic freedoms guaranteed by the Constitution of the United States and by the Constitution and Declaration of Rights of Maryland, and similar decision was given on a statute in New York.

New Jersey Requires Schoolmasters to Take Oaths
of Abjuration and Allegiance, 1777 *

2. AND WHEREAS it is of the last Moment to a free and independent State, that the rising Generation should be early instructed in the Principles of publick Virtue, and duly impressed with the amiable Ideas of Liberty and Patriotism, and at the same Time inspired with the keenest Abhorrence of despotick and arbitrary Power: AND WHEREAS publick Teachers and Instructors may be greatly instrumental in tincturing the youthful Mind with such Impressions, either in Favour of a just and equal Administration, or of a slavish Submission to lawless Rule, as in their riper Years are not easily obliterated, and are, for that Reason, important Objects of legislative Attention, BE IT THEREFORE ENACTED *by the Authority aforesaid,* That every Schoolmaster or Usher in this State, who shall not, within two Months after the Publication of this Act, take and subscribe the said Oaths, or, if one of the People called *Quakers,* the Affirmations of Abjuration and Allegiance, before some proper Officer herein after mentioned, shall, for every Week after the Expiration of the said two Months that he continues to keep School, or teach as an Usher, until he shall take and subscribe the said Oaths or Affirmations, forfeit the Sum of *Six Pounds;* to be recovered by Action of Debt or otherwise, before any Justice of the Peace, with Costs of Suit, by any Person who will sue for the same; and applied one Half to the Use of the Person who shall sue for the same, and the other Half to be paid to the Overseer of the Poor, for the Use of the Poor of the District where the Offence was committed.

Pennsylvania Requires Loyalty Oath for Teachers, 1778 †

And be it further enacted that all trustees, provosts, rectors, professors, masters and tutors of any college or academy and all schoolmasters and ushers . . . who shall at any time after the first day of June next, be admitted unto or enter upon any of the above mentioned preferments, offices, or places, or shall take upon him or them any such practice, employment or business, as aforesaid, without having first taken and subscribed the before mentioned oath or affirmation, he or they shall be ipso facto adjudged incapable and disabled in law, to all intents and purposes whatsoever, to have occupancy or enjoy the said preferment or preferments, office or offices, employment or employments or any part of them, or any matter or thing aforesaid, or any profit or advantage appertaining to them, or any of them; and every such office or place of trust shall be void; and is hereby adjudged void; and any person that shall be lawfully convicted of the

---

* *Acts passed II Independence,* A.D. *1777,* pp. 28, 29.
† *The Acts of the General Assembly of the Commonwealth of Pennsylvania,* 1775-1780, p. 232.

premises, or any of them, in or upon any presentment or indictment in any court of record in this state, shall also forfeit any sum, not exceeding five hundred pounds, which the court shall adjudge together with costs, one-half of which said fine shall go to the use of the state, and the other half to him, her or them who shall commence and carry on such prosecution with effect.

An Early Protest Against a Loyalty Oath for Teachers, 1779 *

To the General Assembly of Pennsylvania: The memorial and address of the religious Society called Quakers respectfully sheweth:

That divers laws have been lately enacted which are very injurious in their nature, oppressive in the manner of execution, and greatly affect us in our religious and civil liberties and privileges, particularly a law passed by the last Assembly entitled "A further supplement to the test laws of this State," in the operation whereof the present and succeeding generations are materially interested. We therefore apprehend it a duty owing to ourselves and our posterity to lay before you the grievances to which we are subjected by these laws.

Our predecessors on their early settlement in this part of America, being piously concerned for the posterity of the colony and the real welfare of their posterity, among other salutory institutions promoted at their own expense the establishment of schools for the instruction of their Youth in useful and necessary learning and their education in piety and virtue, the practice of which forms the most sure basis for perpetuating the enjoyment of Christian liberty and essential happiness.

By the voluntary contributions by the members of our religious Society, schools were set up in which not only their children were taught but their liberality hath been extended to poor children of other religious denominations generally, great numbers of whom have partaken thereof; and these schools have been in like manner continued and maintained for a long course of years.

Duty to Almighty God made known in the consciences of men and confirmed by the holy Scriptures is an invariable rule which should govern their judgment and actions. He is the only Lord and Sovereign of Conscience, and to him we are accountable for our conduct, as by him all men are to be finally judged. By conscience we mean the apprehension and persuasion a man has of his duty to God and the liberty of conscience we plead for is a free open profession and unmolested exercise of that duty, such a conscience as under the influence of divine grace keeps within the

---

* Given in Isaac Sharpless, *A History of the Quaker Government in Pennsylvania* (Philadelphia, T. S. Leach and Co., 1899), II, pp. 184-87. This protest arose out of the case of Joshua Bennett, a Quaker schoolmaster of Lancaster who had not taken the oath required of teachers under a statute of Pennsylvania of 1778, above. Bennett was fined 100 pounds and upon inability to pay was put in jail, but the fine was later remitted.

bounds of morality in all the affairs of human life and teacheth to live soberly righteously and godly in the world.

As a religious Society, we have ever held forth the Gospel dispensation was introduced for completing the happiness of mankind by taking away the occasion of strife contention and bloodshed and therefore we all conscientiously restrained from promoting or joining in wars and fightings: and when laws have been made to enforce our compliance contrary to the convictions of our consciences, we have thought it our duty patiently to suffer though we have often been grievously oppressed. Principle we hold in this respect requires us to be a peaceable people and through the various changes and revolutions which have occurred since our religious Society has existed, we have never been concerned in promoting or abetting any combinations insurrections or parties to endanger the public peace or by violence to oppose the authority of government apprehending it our duty quietly to admit and peaceably to demeanor ourselves under every government which Divine Providence in his unerring wisdom may permit to be placed over us; so that no government can have just occasion for entertaining fears or jealousies of disturbance or danger from us. But if any professing with us deviate from this peaceable principle into a contrary conduct and foment discords, feuds or animosities, giving just occasion of uneasiness and disquiet, we think it our duty, to declare against their proceeding.

By the same divine principle, we are restrained from complying with the injunctions and requisitions made on us of tests and declarations of fidelity to either party who are engaged in actual war lest we contradict by our conduct the profession of our faith.

It is obvious that in these days of depravity, as in former times, because of oaths the land mourns and the multiplying the use of them and such solemn engagements renders them familiar, debases the mind of the people and adds to the number of those gross evils already lamentably prevalent which have drawn down the chastisement of heaven on our guilty country.

We are not actuated by political or party motives; we are real friends to our country, who wish its prosperity and think a solicitude for the enjoyments of our equitable rights, and that invaluable privilege, Liberty of Conscience, free from coercion, cannot be justly deemed unreasonable. Many of us and other industrious inhabitants being exposed to heavy penalties and sufferings, which are abundantly encreased by the rigour of mistaken and unreasonable men under the sanction of law, whereby many are already reduced to great straits and threatened with total ruin, the effects of whose imprisonment must at length be very sensibly felt by the community at large through the decline of cultivation and the necessary employments.

We have been much abused and villified by many anonymous publications and our conduct greatly perverted and misrepresented by groundless reports and the errors of individuals charged upon us as a body in order to render us odious to the people and prepossess the minds of persons in power against us; being conscious of our innocence and "submitting our cause to the Lord who judgeth righteously" we have preferred patience in bearing the reproach to public contest, not doubting that as the minds of the people become more settled and composed, our peaceable demeanor would manifest the injustice we suffered, and being persuaded that on a cool dispassionate hearing we should be able to invalidate or remove the mistaken suggestions and reports prevailing to our prejudice.

The matters we have now freely laid before you are serious and important, which we wish you to consider wisely as men and religiously as Christians manifesting yourselves friends to true liberty and enemies to persecution, by repealing the several penal laws affecting tender consciences and restoring to us our equitable rights that the means of education and instruction of our youth which we conceive to be our reasonable and religious duty, may not be obstructed and that the oppressed may be relieved. In your consideration whereof, we sincerely desire that you may seek for and be directed by that supreme "wisdom which is pure, peaceable, gentle and easy to be entreated, full of mercy and good fruits" and are your real friends.

Signed on behalf of a meeting of the Representatives of the said people held in Philadelphia the 4th day of the 11th mo 1779.

Joshua Bennett's Fine Is Remitted, 1779 *

The Council, taking into consideration the case of the schoolmaster now confined in the gaol of the County of Lancaster, he having been convicted of keeping a school, not having taken the oath of allegiance according to law; & fined by the Court of Quarter Sessions of the Peace for the County of Lancaster, in the sum of one hundred pounds.

Ordered that the fine of one hundred pounds, adjudged by the Court of Quarter Sessions of the Peace for the County of Lancaster to be paid by Joshua Bennett (he having been convicted in the said Court of having kept a school, not having taken the oath of affirmation of allegiance, according to the law) be remitted.

* *Colonial Records of Pennsylvania* (1776-1779), II, p. 652. Bennett was a Quaker. See Donald F. Shaughnessy, "Teachers' Loyalty-Oath Laws and Joshua Bennett," *School and Society*, Vol. 71 (April 8, 1950), pp. 209-11.

« 4 »

Advertisements of Schools,
Teachers, and Tutors;
Tutorial Practices

«««««««««««««««««««««««««««««««««« »»»»»»»»»»»»»»»»»»»»»»»»»»»»»»»

John Walton Offers to Teach Many Subjects in New York, 1723 *

There is a School in New York, in the Broad Street, near the Exchange where Mr. John Walton, late of Yale-Colledge, Teacheth Reading, Writing, Arethmatick, whole Numbers and Fractions, Vulgar and Decimal, The Mariners Art, Plain and Mercators Way; Also Geometry, Surveying, the Latin Tongue, and Greek and Hebrew Grammars, Ethicks, Rhetorick, Logick, Natural Philosophy and Metaphysicks, all or any of them for a Reasonable Price. The School from the first of October till the first of March will be tended in the Evening. If any Gentlemen in the Country are disposed to send their Sons to the said School, if they apply themselves to the Master he will immediately procure suitable Entertainment for them, very cheap. Also if any Young Gentleman of the City will please to come in the Evening and make some Tryal of the Liberal Arts, they may have opportunity of Learning the same Things which are commonly Taught in Colledges.

Many Subjects Are Offered in Charleston, South Carolina, 1733, 1744

At the house of Mrs. Delaweare on Broad Street is taught these sciences

Arithmetic	Surveying	Astronomy
Algebra	Dialling	Gauging
Geometry	Navigation	Fortification
Trigonometry		

* Given in Robert F. Seybolt, *Source Studies in American Colonial Education: The Private School* (Urbana, University of Illinois, Bulletin No. 28, Bureau of Educational Research, 1925), p. 99. Many of the colonial newspapers contained numerous advertisements of schools and for teachers and tutors. Excellent examples of these advertisements appear in Charles L. Coon, *North Carolina Schools and Academies, 1790-1840: A Documentary History* (Raleigh, Edwards and Broughton Printing Co., 1915). See also Robert F. Seybolt, *The Private Schools of Colonial Boston* (Cambridge, Harvard University Press, 1935); E. W. G. Boogher, *Secondary Education in Georgia, 1732-1858* (Philadelphia, [No publisher given], 1933: doctoral dissertation at the University of Pennsylvania); Edgar W. Knight, *A Documentary History of Education in the South Before 1860* (Chapel Hill, University of North Carolina Press, 1949), I, pp. 571-664.

The STEREOGRAPHIC or ORTHOGRAPHIC Projection of the Sphere. The use of the Globe and the Italian method of Bookkeeping by

JOHN MILLER.*

Reading, Writing, Arithmetick vulgar and decimal, Geometry, Trigonometry plain and spherical, Mensuration of solid and superficial Bodies, Navigation, Surveying, Gaging, and many other useful Branches of the Mathematicks, Euclid's Elements, Italian, bookkeeping, and Grammar, &c: explain'd and taught in the clearest manner by *Archibald Hamilton,* who may be heard of at Mr. *Coon's* Taylor in *Church-street.* N.B. He attends at any time and Place requir'd to teach, or to keep Books; and is willing upon a reasonable and speedy Encouragement to undertake a School in Town or Country for teaching all or any Part of what is above specified, otherwise to go off the country.†

WHITE POINT

Reading, Writing in all the Hands us'd in Great Britain, Arithmetick in whole Numbers, and Fractions vulgar and decimal, Merchants Accompts, in the true Italian Method of double Entry, by Debtor and Creditor, and Dancing are taught at the House of Mrs. Fisher on White Point, by

GEORGE BROWNELL and JOHN PRATT ‡

French and Spanish Languages Are Taught in New York, 1735 §

This is to give Notice that over against the Sign of the black Horse in Smith-street, near the Old Dutch Church, is carefully taught the French and Spanish Languages, after the best Method that is now practised in Great Britain, which for the encouragement of those who intend to learn the same is taught for 20s per Quarter.

Andrew Lamb Qualifies Youth for Business, in Philadelphia, 1751 ||

ANDREW LAMB

Is removed to Mr. Abraham Taylor's Alley, near Second-street, which was formerly a school with good conveniences, and continues to qualify youth for business, &c. viz.

Writing, arithmetick, vulgar and decimal, merchants accompts, the Italian method, by double entry, Dr. and Cr. the only true way that is now

---

* *The South Carolina Gazette,* May 12, 1733.
† *The South-Carolina Gazette,* February 12 to February 19, 1737. Also February 19 to 26 and February 26 to March 5, 1737.
‡ *The South-Carolina Gazette,* Sept. 3, 10, 17, 1744.
§ *New York Gazette,* July 14, 21, 28, and August 4 and 11, 1735. Given in Seybolt, *op. cit.,* p. 33.
|| *Pennsylvania Gazette,* February 19, March 19, April 4 and 18, June 20, 1751. Given in Seybolt, *op. cit.,* pp. 39, 40.

used; Navigation in all its parts, both theory and practice, viz. Geometry, Trigonometry, and Plain-sailing; Traverse, Mercator, and Parallel Sailing; Coasting, Bearing and Distance of Land, and Current Sailing. All these are geometrically, logarithmetrically, and instrumentally performed. Next the practice, which is the main thing intended; and here I shall give you a complete journal from the Lizard to the Rock of Lisbon, with lee-way and variation allowed each course, and rules to apply them, and an amplitude at sun rising and setting, and applied to the east and west variation; this is one of the journals that I kept to Lisbon, and is therefore recommended to all ingenious artists, as a pattern for any other voyage; and I can shew several journals of my own works to the American plantations, and one from England to Cape Henlopen, in 20 days, 1748. And to make mercator charts, a new and easy method, and to work any journal in them, which makes a traverse in the mercator charts, and is proved so exact as the proportions in mercator's sailing, by the latitudes and longitudes every day at noon; and sheweth the plain tract which the ship made the whole voyage, and a true method to correct all journals, and to bring the ship safe to the desired port, which is the only thing intended by a good journal. Also Surveying, Gauging, Dialling, and Spherical Geometry, Trigonometry in all its various cases, and Great-Circle Sailing, applied in several problems, which proves the meridional parts in mercators sailing to a fair demonstration; and the application of all the most useful and necessary problems in great variety of astronomy. All these are carefully taught and diligently attended, by

ANDREW LAMB

N.B. I teach in their own houses at certain hours, when desired, with due attendance and diligence. I have above 30 years experience in teaching both the theory and practice of navigation.

Sailors, take a friend's advice, be not cheated by land-men that pretend to navigation, for they know nothing of a sea journal, which is the principal thing you want to know, and the use of sea-charts: My Scholars are qualified to go mates the first voyage, and bring me a good account of their journals.

Advertisement of John Walker, 1752

JOHN WALKER

LATELY arriv'd in *Williamsburg* from *London,* and who for ten Years past has been engag'd in the Education of Youth, undertakes to instruct young Gentlemen in Reading, Writing, Arithmetick, the most material Branches of Classical Learning, and ancient and modern Geography and History; but, as the noblest End of Erudition and Human Attainments, he will exert his principal Endeavours to improve their Morals, in Proportion to their Progress in Learning, that no Parent may repent his Choice in trusting him with the Education of his Children.

Mrs. *Walker,* likewise, teaches young Ladies all Kinds of Needle Work; makes Capuchins, Shades, Hats, and Bonnets; and will endeavour to give Satisfaction to those who shall honour her with their Custom.

The above-mentioned *John Walker,* and his Wife, live at Mr. *Cobb*'s new House, next to Mr. *Coke*'s, near the Road going down to the Capitol Landing; where there is also to be sold, Mens Shoes and Pumps, *Turkey* Coffee, Edging and Lace for Ladies Caps, and some Gold Rings.*

Advertisement of Reverend B. Booth's Academy
Near Liverpool, England, 1766 †

At the Rev. B. BOOTH's ACADEMY, *the seat of the late Lady* MOLLINEAUX's *at* Woolton, *five miles from* Liverpool, *young* GENTLEMEN *are educated on the following terms:*

	£	s.	d.
FOR Board, and learning English, Latin, Greek, Writing, Arithmetick, Merchants Accounts, Geography, Navigation, Astronomy, Surveying, Mathematicks in general, Drawing and Perspective,	21	0 *per Ann.*	0
Entrance for do	1	1	0
Musick, per quarter,	1	1	0
Entrance for do	0	10	6
Dancing, per quarter,	0	15	0
Entrance for do	0	5	0
Fencing, per quarter,	1	1	0
Entrance for do	0	10	6
Fire, per annum,	0	5	0

Washing, according to their age, from 7 s. 6 d. to 10 s. per quarter.

Particulars relating to those who do not board in the Academy, may be had from the master.

Advertisement of an Academy in County York, England, 1769 ‡

At the ACADEMY *in* LEEDS,
Which is pleasantly situated in the county of
York, *in England,*

YOUNG Gentlemen are genteely boarded, and diligently instructed in *English,* the Classicks, Modern Languages, Penmanship, Arithmetick, Mer-

---

* *The Virginia Gazette* (Williamsburg, William Hunter), November 17, 1752, p. 2; also November 24, 1752, p. 3; December 1, 1752, p. 3.

† *The Virginia Gazette* (Williamsburg, Alex. Purdie, and John Dixon), November 27, 1766, p. 2; also December 4, 1766, p. 3.

‡ *Ibid.,* November 2, 1769, p. 3; also November 9, 1769, p. 3; November 16, 1769, p. 3.

chants Accounts, Mathematicks, Modern Geography, Experimental Philosophy, and Astronomy, for twenty guineas *per annum,* if under twelve years of age, by Mr. AARON GRIMSHAW, and able masters. Drawing, Musick, and Dancing, are extra charges. Due regard is paid to the young Gentlemens health, morals, and behaviour.

Philip Vickers Fithian Tells John Peck How to Behave as a Tutor in Virginia, 1774 *

NOMINI HALL August 12th 1774.

SIR.

I never reflect, but with secret, and peculiar pleasure, on the time when I studied in *Deerfield* with you,† & several other pleasant companions, under our common, & much respected instructor, Mr. *Green.*
And I acknowledge now, with a thankful heart, the many favours, which I received from your family while I was a member of it. This sense of obligation to your Family, And personal friendship for you, have excited me, when it was in my power, to introduce you to the business which I now occupy; into a family, where, if you be prudent and industrious, I am confident you will speedily acquire to yourself both Honour & Profit—But

* Probably no contemporary account now available gives a more interesting and vivid view of life on a plantation in the late eighteenth century than these materials, first published in 1900 by the Princeton Historical Association, edited by John Rogers Williams (Princeton, N. J., The University Library). Williams also edited and published some of the selections in *The American Historical Review,* January, 1900, pp. 290-319. At that time the Philip Fithian papers were the property of Mrs. Edward W. Hitchcock, of Philadelphia, who was a descendant of the Fithian family. She died in 1900, while the book, which bore the title *Philip Vickers Fithian, Journal and Letters, 1767-1774,* was in press. In 1943 Colonial Williamsburg, Inc., reprinted the work which was edited, with an introduction, by Hunter Dickinson Farish, under the title *Journal & Letters of Philip Vickers Fithian, 1773-1774: A Plantation Tutor of the Old Dominion,* from which Fithian's letter to Peck is taken, with the permission of the publishers. The Williamsburg edition includes some materials omitted from the Princeton edition. Copious extracts from the Williamsburg edition are given in Edgar W. Knight, *A Documentary History of Education in the South Before 1860* (Chapel Hill, University of North Carolina Press, 1949), I, pp. 573-623. The Fithian manuscripts now are the property of the Princeton University Library. Peck and Fithian were classmates at Princeton. Peck married Anne Tasker ("Nancy") Carter and settled in Virginia.

† The tutorial system was very popular in the Southern Colonies, especially in Virginia and South Carolina which also sent many young people to Europe for their education. Perhaps the best-known account of tutorial practices is that by young Fithian, tutor of the children of Robert Carter, at Nomini Hall in Westmoreland County, Virginia, a member of one of the wealthiest and most influential families in that colony. Fithian was born in New Jersey in 1747, was admitted to the junior class in Princeton in 1770, was graduated two years later, then studied theology for the Presbyterian ministry. In the fall of 1773 he was offered a position as tutor in the Carter family through a letter from President Witherspoon of Princeton. Dr. Witherspoon advised young Fithian to take the position in Virginia, if only for a short time, although it appears that the staunch Calvinist warned the young man against the moral and physical dangers he would likely face in the conditions many people believed to exist among the wealthy and regal families of the Old Dominion. The young man seems to have been agreeably surprised when he found at Nomini Hall so many evidences of culture, refinement, and elegance of life instead of the alleged revelry and riotous and loose living. The master of Nomini Hall, grandson of "King Carter," was a man of wide culture, of studious habits, and preferred the quietude of his family estate to the "gayeties of the Governor's court at Williamsburg," although he was a member of the King's Council which sat in that town.

inasmuch as you are wholly a stranger to this Province; & have had little or no Experience in the business which you ar shortly to enter upon; & lest, from common Fame, which is often erroneous, you shall have entertained other notions of the manners of the People here, & of your business as a Tutor, than you will find, when you come, to be actually true; I hope you will not think it *vain* or *untimely,* if I venture to lay before you some Rules for your direction which I have collected from a year's observation. I shall class what I have to say in the following order. First. I shall attempt to give you some direction for the plan of your Conduct among your neighbours, & the People in General here, so long as you sustain the character of a Tutor. Then I shall advise you concerning the rules which I think will be most profitable & convenient in the management of your little lovely charge, the School. Last of all. I shall mention several Rules for your personal conduct. I choose to proceed in the order I have laid down, as well that you may more fully & speedily recieve my mind, as that you may also the more readily select out and apply what you shall find to be most necessary.

First. When you have thought of removinging, for a Time, out of the Colony in which you was born, & in which you have hitherto constantly resided, I make no doubt but you have at the same time expected to find a very considerable alteration of manners, among your new acquaintances, & some peculiarities toto Caelo different, from any you have before been accustomed to. Such a thought is natural; And you will if you come into Virginia, in much shorter time than a year be convinced that it is just. In New-Jersey Government throughout, but especially in the Counties where you have any personal acquaintance, Gentlemen in the first rank of Dignity & Quality, of the Council, general Assembly, inferior Magistrates, Clergy-Men, or independent Gentlemen, without the smallest fear of bringing any manner of reproach either on their office, or their high-born, long recorded Families associate freely & commonly with Farmers & Mechanicks tho' they be poor & industrious. Ingenuity & industry are the Strongest, & most approved recommendations to a Man in that Colony. The manners of the People seem to me, (probably I am overborn by the force of prejudice in favour of my native Soil), to bear some considerable resemblance of the manners in the ancient Spartan Common-Wealth—The Valour of its In-habitants—was the best, & only security of that State against the enemy; & the wise laws of its renowned Legislator were the powerful Cement which kept them firm & invincible—In our Government, the laborious part of Men, who are commonly ranked in the midling or lower Class, are accounted the strenth & Honor of the Colony; & the encouragement they receive from Gentlemen in the highest stations is the spring of Industry, next to their private advantage. The Level which is admired in New-Jersey Government, among People of every rank, arises, no doubt, from the very great division of the lands in that Province, & consequently from the near approach to an equality of Wealth amongst the Inhabitants, since it is not famous for trade. You know very well that the Lands in a small township are divided, & then again subdivided into two & three Hundred Separate, proper, creditable estates; for example *Deerfield & Fairfield* two Townships, or Precincts, in which you & I are tolerably well acquainted, in the former of which, are the Seats of two Judges of the Sessions; & in the latter resides one of the representatives in General Assembly for the County; But if 16000 £ would purchase the whole landed estates of these three Gentlemen, who are supposed to be the most wealthy in the County, if we rate their Land at the Low Consideration of 4L p acre, with all conveniences, each would have 4000 Acres. Now you may suppose how small a quantity many must have when two or three hundred Landholders reside in each of these small Precincts; Hence we see Gentlemen, when they are not actually engaged in the publick Service, on their farms, setting a laborious example to their Domesticks, & on the other hand we see labourers at the Tables & in the Parlours of their Betters enjoying the advantage, & honor of their society and Conversation—I do not call it an objection to this, that some few, who have no substance but work like Slaves as necessity drives them for a few Months in the year; with the price of this Labour they visit Philadelphia; & having there acquired a fashionable Coat, & a Stock of Impudence, return home to spend the remainder of the year, in idleness & disgrace!—But you will find the tables turned the moment you enter this Colony. The very Slaves, in some families here, could not be bought under 30000 £. Such amazing property, no matter how deep it is involved, blows up the owners to an imagination, which is visible in all, but in various degrees according to their respective virtue, that they are exalted as much above other Men in worth & precedency, as blind stupid fortune has made a difference in their property; excepting always the value they put upon posts of honour, & menial acquirements—For example, if you should travel through this Colony, with a well-confirmed testimonial of your having finished with Credit a Course of studies at Nassau-Hall; you would be rated, without any more questions asked, either about your family, your Estate, your business, or your intention, at 10,000 £; and you might come, & go, & converse, & keep company, according to this value; & you would be dispised & slighted if yo(u) rated yourself a farthing cheaper. But when I am giving directions to you, from an expectation that you will be shortly a resident here, altho you have gone through a College Course, & for any thing I know, have never written a Libel, nor stolen a Turkey, yet I think myself in duty bound to advise you, lest some powdered Coxcomb should reproach your education, to cheapen your price about 5000 £; because any young Gentleman travelling through the Colony, as I said before, is presum'd to be acquainted with Dancing, Boxing, playing the Fiddle, & Small-Sword, & Cards. Several of which you was only entering upon, when I left New-Jersey; towards the Close of last year; and if you stay here any time your Barrenness in these must be detected. I will however allow, that in the Family where you act as tutor you place yourself, according to your most accute Calculation, at a perfect equidistance between the father & the eldest Son. Or let the same distance be observed in every article of behaviour between you & the eldest Son, as there ought to be, by the latest & most approved precepts of Moral-Philosophy, between the eldest Son, & his next youngest Brother. But whenever you go from Home, where you are to act on your own footing, either to a Ball; or to a *Horse-Race,* or to a *Cock-Fight,* or to a *Fish-Feast,* I advise that you rate yourself very low, & if you bett at all, remember that 10,000 £ in Reputation & learning does not amount to a handfull of Shillings in ready Cash!—One considerable advantage which you promise yourself by coming to this Colony is to extend the Limits of your acquaintance; this is laudable, & if you have enough of prudence & firmness, it will be of singular advantage— Yet attempt slowly & with the most Jealous Circumspection—If you fix your familiarity wrong in a single instance, you are in danger of total, if not immediate ruin—You come here, it is true, with an intention to teach, but you ought likewise to have an inclination to learn. At any rate I solemnly injoin it upon you, that you never suffer the spirit of a Pedagogue to attend you without the walls of your little Seminary. In all promiscuous Company be as silent & attentive as Decency will allow you, for you have nothing to communicate, which such company, will hear with pleasure, but you may learn many things which, in after life, will do you singular service.— In regard to Company in general, if you think it worth the while to attend to my example, I can easily instruct you in the manner of my Conduct in this respect. I commonly attend Church; and often, at the request of Gentle-men, after Service according to the custom, dine abroad on Sunday— I seldom fail, when invited by Mr or Mrs *Carter,* of going out with them; but I make it a point, however strongly solicited to the contrary, to return home with them too—Except in one of these cases, I seldom go out, but with a valuable variety of books I live according to Horace's direction, & love "Secretum Iter et fallentis Semita Vitae." Close retirement and a life by Stealth. The last direction I shall venture to mention on this head, is, that you abstain totally from Women. What I would have you understand from this, is, that by a train of faultless conduct in the whole course of your tutorship, you make every Lady within the Sphere of your acquaint-ance, who is between twelve & forty years of age, so much pleased with your person, & so fully satisfied as to your abilities in the capacity of— a Teacher; & in short, fully convinced, that, from a principle of Duty, you have, both by night & by day endeavoured to acquit yourself honourably, in the Character of a Tutor; & that, on this account, you have their free & hearty consent, without making any manner of demand upon you, either to stay longer in the County with them, which they would choose, or when-ever your business calls you away, that they may not have it in their Power either by charms or Justice to detain you, & when you must leave them, have their sincere wishes & constant prayrs for Length of days & much prosperity, I therefore beg that you will attend literally to this advice, & abstain totally from Women. But this last precaution, which I have been at some pains to dress in the plainest language, I am much inclined to think, will be wholly useless in regard to you, notwithstanding it is founded in that *Honour* and *Equity* which is on all hands allow'd to be due from one Sex to the other, & to many of your *age, & Standing* no doubt would be entirely salutary. Because the necessary connections which you have had with the Fair, from your Puberty upwards have been so unfavourable & ill-fated, that instead of apprehending any danger on the score of over fondness, I am fearful your rancour has grown so inveterate at length, as, not only to preserve you, in thought & practice, pure of every Fleshly foible, but has carried you so far towards the other extream, as that you will need many persuasions, when your circumstances shall seem to require it, to bring you back to a rational & manly habit of thinking & acting with respect to the Sex; which yet, after all (& eternally will continue to be, tho it is much courted & whined after) if considered in the fullest manner, & set forth to the best advantage, never rises above its divine definition Viz "The weaker Vessel." But without detaining you any longer with a matter merely depending on accident or Circumstance I pass on to the second General Head; in which "Ludis atque Jocis amotis" I shall offer to your consideration & recommend for your practice several Rules concerning the management of the School.

2. You will act wisely, if, from the beginning, you convince all your Scholars which you may easily do, of your abilities in the several branches, which you shall profess to teach; you are not to tell them, totidem Verbis, "that you understand, perhaps as well as any man on the Continent both the Latin & Greek Classicks"; "& have gone through the usual Course in the noted College of New-Jersey, under Dr Witherspoon, so universally known & admired, where you have studied Criticism, Oratory, History, not to mention Mathematical & philosophical Studies, & dipt a good way into the French-Language, & that you have learn 'd a smattering of Dancing, Cards, &c. &c. &c." For Dun-p or Hack--n or the most profound dunce in your College or School would have too much sense to pass such impudence by, & not despise and reproach it; but you may speedily & certainly make them think you a "Clever Fellow" (which is a phrase in use here for a good Scholar) if you never mention any thing before them, only what you seem to be wholly master of—This will teach them never to dispute your determination, & always to rely upon your Judgment; two things which are most essential for your peace, & their advantage. That you may avoid yourself of this with certainty I shall recommend for your practice the following method, as useful at least, if not intirely necessary. Read over carefully, the lessons in Latin & Greek, in your leisure hours, that the story & Language be fresh in your memory, when you are hearing the respective

lessons; for your memory is treacherous, & I am pretty certain it would confound you if you should be accosted by a pert School-Boy, in the midst of a blunder, with "Physician heal thyself"!—You ought likewise to do this with those who are working Figures; probably you may think that because the highest Cypher is only in decimal arithmetic, it is not there fore worth your critical attention to be looking previously into the several Sums. But you are to consider that a sum in the Square-Root, or even in the Single Rule of three direct, is to your Pupils of as great importance, as the most abstruse problem in the Mathematicks to an able artist; & you may lay this down for a Maxim, that they will reckon upon your abilities, according as they find you acquainted & expert in what they themselves are studying. If therefore you have resolution (as I do not question your ability) to carry this plan which I have laid down into execution; you will thereby convince them of the propriety of their Subordination to you, & obedience to your instructions, so that you may lead them, without any resistance, and fix them to the Study of whatever Science you think proper, in which they will rise according to their respective Capacities. I have said that you ought to strive "from the beginning" in fixing this very material article in the minds of your Scholars, Viz a Sense of your authority; for one error of Judgment, or false determination will diminish your Ability with them more than doing forty things with truth would increase your authority—They act in this case as you would do in the company of a number of Strangers— A whole evenings conversation, if it was tolerable good Sense, would perhaps make little or no impression on you; But if through hast in speaking, or inattention, any one should let fall a sentence either remarkably foolish, or grossly wicked, it would be difficult if not impossible to persuade you presently that the author was not either a *thick-Scull,* or a *Villain!*— The education of children requires constant unremitting attention. The meanest qualification you can mention in a useful teacher is *diligence* And without diligence no possible abilities or qualifications can bring children on either with speed or profit. There must be a Combination of qualifications which must all operate strongly & uniformly. In short, give this said Pedagogizing the softest name you will, it is still a "difficult Task." You will meet with numberless difficulties, in your new imployment, which you never dreamt had yet existence. All these you must endeavor to resist & Subdue. This I have seen compared to a Man swimming against a current of Water. But I am mistaken if you will agree, after having six months practice, that the comparison be strong as the truth: You will add to the figure, I am certain, & throw into the Current sharp fragments of *Ice & Blocks,* which would make swimming not only difficult but dangerous! I am not urging these things to discourage you; they are hints for your direction, which, if you will attend to, tho' at first the practice seem rough & unpleasant, shall yet make the remainder of your task pleasing, & the whole of it useful. I will mention several of these Obstacles that you may the more easily guard against them. You will, in the first place, be often solicited, probably oftner than you would wish, to ride abroad; this, however, if you do it moderately, & in seasonable time, & go to proper company, I recommend as conducive to health to one in your sedentary manner of living. But if you go much into company, you will find it extremely difficult to break away with any manner of credit till very late at night or in most cases several days, & if you are wanting to your School, you do manifest injury to your Imployer. In this case, I advise you to copy Mr *Carter*. Whenever he invites you, ride. You may *stay,* and talk, & drink, & ride to as great excess as he: & may with safety associate yourself with those whom you find to be his intimates. In all other Cases, except when you ride to Church, at least till you are very intimate in the Colony, you had better ride to a certain Stump, or to some noted plantation, or pretty landscape; you will have in this every advantage of exercise, the additional advantage of undisturbed Meditation, & you will be under no Jealous apprehension in point of behaviour, nor any restraint as to the time of your return.

Another current difficulty will be petitions for holidays. You must have good deal of steadiness if you are able to evade cleverly this practice which has grown so habitual to your little charge from a false method in their early education that they absolutely claim it as a necessary right.

You must also as much as you can, avoid visible partiality. At least you must never suffer your fondness for one Scholar to grow so manifest, as that all your School shall see you look over a fault in him or her which same fault, if commited by another, you severely chastise. This will certainly produce in the others hatred & contempt. A fourth difficulty, and the last I shall mention, consists in knowing when, & in what measure to give the Boys Liberty to go from Home. The two younger Boys are wholly under your inspection; so that not only the progress they make in learning, but their moral Conduct (for both of these are critically observed & examined) either justifies or condemns your management to the World. If you keep them much at home, & close to business, they themselves will call you unfeeling and cruel; & refuse to be industrious; if you suffer them to go much abroad they are certainly out of the way of improvement by study, probably, by discovering their gross Ignorance, they will expose to ridicule both themselves & all their former instructors, & possibly they may commit actual Crimes so as very much to injure themselves; & scandalize their family; but in each of these you will have a large share of blame, perhaps more than the parents, or even the Boys themselves— It will be said that the parents gave them no licence relying wholly on your Judgment & prudence, this will in good measure Justify them to the world. And as to the Boys they are full of youthful impetuosity & vigour, & these compel them, when they are free of restraint, to commit actions which with proper management they had surely avoided. I say, when you lay these things together, & view them on every side you will find so many perplexities arising in your mind, from a sense of ignorance of your duty, that you will proceed with caution & moderation, & will be careful to examine with some precision into the circumstances of *time, company, & Business* when you license them to go out entirely at the risk of your Reputation—But the practice of three or four Weeks will give you a more full notion of these & many other incidents than I am able now either to recollect or express; I shall have gained my End if these hints prevent you from setting off wrong, & doing inadvertantly at first what your Scholars will assert to be precedents for your after conduct. I go on, therefore, in the third place as I proposed,

3. To mention several Rules for your personal conduct. The happy Education which you have had in point of religion, you ought to consider as an important and distinguishing Blessing of Heaven. That train of useful *Instruction, Advice & Example* to which you have been accustomed from your infancy is a more perfect, & will be a safer guide in your future walk, than any directions I am able to give you. You have taken notice of a method for Assistance in Composition, which Longinus recommends.

Place, says he, in imagination, several eminent ancient Authors before your Eyes, & suppose that they inspect your Work, a Sense of Inferiority would make you diligent, & your composition accurate. Perhaps the same advice when transferr'd to Morality, would be equally salutary. Unless it be objected that a Belief of Gods presence at all times in every place is the strongest possible restraint against committing Sin. This I constantly admit; but when I consider how easily our minds are put in motion, & how strongly they are sometimes agitated merely by the senses, & that the senses are affected most by things which fall under their immediate notice, I am fully convinced that if some such plan as I have just mentioned should be fallen upon, & practised, it would make a visible and useful change in our behaviour—In this place I think it needful to caution you against hasty & ill founded prejudices. When you enter among a people, & find that their manner of living, their *Eating, Drinking,* Diversions, Exercise &c., are in many respects different from any thing you have been accustomed to, you will be apt to fix your opinion in an instant, & (as some divines deal with poor Sinners) you will condemn all before you without any meaning or distinction what seems in your Judgment disagreeable at first view, when you are smitten with the novelty. You will be making ten thousand Comparisons. The face of the Country, The *Soil,* the *Buildings,* the *Slaves,* the *Tobacco,* the method of spending *Sunday* among Christians; *Ditto* among the Negroes; the three grand divisions of time at the Church on Sundays, Viz. before Service giving & receiving letters of business, reading Advertisements, consulting about the price of Tobacco, Grain &c., & settling either the lineage, Age, or qualities of favourite Horses 2. In the Church at Service, prayrs read over in haste, a Sermon seldom under & never over twenty minutes, but always made up of sound morality, or deep studied Metaphysicks. 3. After Service is over three quarters of an hour spent in strolling round the Church among the Crowd, in which time you will be invited by several different Gentlemen home with them to dinner. The Balls, the Fish-Feasts, the Dancing-Schools, the Christnings, the Cock fights, the Horse-Races, the Chariots, the Ladies Masked, for it is a custom among the Westmorland Ladies whenever they go from home, to muffle up their heads, & Necks, leaving only a narrow passage for the Eyes, in Cotton or silk handker-chiefs; I was in distress for them when I first came into the Colony, for every Woman that I saw abroad, I looked upon as ill either with the *Mumps* or Tooth-Ach!—I say, you will be often observing & comparing these things which I have enumerated, & many more that now escape me, with the manner of spending Money time & credit at Cohansie: You are young, &, (you will allow me the Expression) in the morning of Life. But I hope you have plann'd off, and entered upon the work which is necessary to be performed in the course of your Day; if not, I think it my duty to acquaint you, that a combination of the amusements which I have just now mentioned, being always before your Eyes, & inviting your Compliance will have a strong tendency to keep you doubtful & unsetled, in your notions of Morality & Religion, or else will fix you in a false & dangerous habit of *thinking* & *acting,* which must terminate at length in Sorrow & despair. You are therefore, if you count any thing upon the value of my advice, to fix the plan in which you would spend your life; let this be done with deliberation, Candour, & precission, looking to him for direction, by fervent Prayr, who is the "Wonderful Counsellor"; & when you have done this, let no importunity of whatever kind prevail over you, & cause you to transgress your own Limitations. I have already exceeded the usual bounds of an Epistle. But you will easily pardon a little prolixity, when I assure you it flows from a heart deeply impressed with a sense of the many difficulties which you must encounter, & the dangers which will surround you when you come first out from the peaceful recess of Contemplation, & enter, young and unexperienced, into the tumultuous undiscerning World. I submit these hints to your con-sideration, & have nothing more than sincere & ardent wishes for your present & perpetual Felicity.

I am, Sir,
yours.
PHILIP V. FITHIAN

To MR JOHN PECK.
on going to Virginia in
Character of a Tutor.

John Davis, Tutor from England, Has a Lively Interview with a South Carolina Planter and His Wife, 1797 *

I landed at *Charleston*† with Doctor *De Bow,* who had clad himself in his black suit, and though a young man, wore a monstrous pair of spectacles on his nose. Adieu jollity! adieu laughter! the Doctor was without an acquaintance on a strange shore, and he had no other friend but his Solemnity to recommend him. It was to no purpose that I endeavoured to provoke him to laughter by my remarks; the Physician would not even relax his risible muscles into a smile.

The Doctor was right. In a few days he contrived to hire part of a house in Union-street; obtained credit for a considerable quantity of drugs; and only wanted a chariot to equal the best Physician in *Charleston.*

The Doctor was in possession of a voluble tongue; and I furnished him with a few *Latin* phrases, which he dealt out to his hearers with an air of profound learning. He generally concluded his speeches with *Nullius addictus jurare in verba magistri!*

Wishing for some daily pursuit, I advertised in one of the papers for the place of Tutor in a respectable family; not omitting to observe that the advertiser was the translator of *Buonaparte's* Campaign in *Italy.* The editor of the Gazette assured me of an hundred applications; and that early the next morning I should not be without some. His predictions were verified; for the following day, on calling at the office, I found a note left from a Planter who lived a mile from the town, desiring me to visit him that afternoon at his house. I went thither accordingly. Every thing indicated opulence and ease. Mr. H————— received me with the insolence of prosperity. You are, said he, the person who advertised for the place of Tutor in a respectable family? I answered with a bow.

Planter. What, Sir, are your qualifications?

Tutor. I am competently skilled, Sir, in the *Latin* and *French* languages, not unacquainted with *Greek,* conversant with Geography, and accustomed to composition in my vernacular idiom.

---

* *Travels of Four Years and A Half in the United States of America* (Morrison Edition), pp. 51-58.

† Among the many unofficial "inspectors" who visited the United States in the latter part of the eighteenth century was John Davis, who was born in England in 1776 and "reared in the lap of opulence," was a man of good education and cultivation and of wide reading, and a traveler "who was professionally literary, who cared little for the political aspects of what he saw. . . ." He numbered among his American friends many men of high political and social station and was able to gratify his eagerness to travel and at the same time "to subsist comfortably." He had a post for a time in the College of Charleston and later as teacher on a plantation in Virginia where the people of the neighborhood assured him that if he would continue with them for seven years they would build for him a "brick seminary" that would rival the College of William and Mary. "I now opened what some called an academy but others an Old Field School." In 1805 he published in England his *Travels of Four Years and A Half in the United States of America,* which was reprinted in New York in 1909 by Henry Holt and Co., Inc., with an introduction by A. J. Morrison.

Planter. But if you possess all *that there* learning, how comes it you could not get into some College, or School.

Tutor. Why, Sir, it is found even in Colleges that dunces triumph, and men of letters are disregarded by a general combination in favour of dulness.

Planter. Can you *drive* well, Sir?[1]

Tutor. Drive, Sir, did you say? I really do not comprehend you.

Planter. I mean, Sir, can you keep your scholars in order?

Tutor. Yes, Sir, if they are left entirely to my direction.

Planter. Ah! that would not be. Mrs. H———, who is a woman of extensive learning, (she lost a fine opportunity once of learning *French,* and only a few years ago could write the best hand of any lady in *Charleston,*) Mrs. H——— would superintend your management of the school.

Tutor. Mrs. ———, Sir, would do me honour.

Planter. Mrs. H———, Sir, is in the real sense of the word, a woman of literature; and her eldest daughter is a prodigy for her age. She could tell at nine years old whether a pudding was boiled enough; and, now, though only eleven, can repeat *Pope's* Ode on Solitude by heart. Ah! *Pope* was a *pretty* poet; my wife is very fond of *Pope.* You have read him, I make no doubt, Sir. What is your opinion of his works?

Tutor. In his Rape of the Lock, Sir, he exhibits most of the *vis imaginandi* that constitutes the poet; his Essay on Criticism is scarcely inferior to *Horace's* Epistle to the Pisoes; his Satires———

Planter. But I am surprised, Sir, you bestow no praise on his Ode on Solitude. Mrs. H———, who is quite a critic in those matters, allows the Ode on Solitude to be his best, his noblest, his sublimest production.

Tutor. Persuaded, Sir, of the critical acuteness of Mrs. H———, it is not safe to depart from her in opinion;—and if Mrs. H——— affirms the Ode on Solitude to be the sublimest of Mr. *Pope's* productions, it would be rather painful than pleasant to undeceive her in opinion.

Planter. That is right, Sir, I like to see young men modest. What spelling-book do you use?

Tutor. What spelling-book, Sir? Indeed—really—upon my word Sir,—any—oh! *Noah Webster's,* Sir.

Planter. Ah! I perceive you are a New England man, by giving the preference to *Noah Webster.*

Tutor. Sir, I beg your pardon; I am from Old England.

[1] The term *drive,* requires some little note explanatory to the *English* reader. No man forgets his original trade. An Overseer on a Plantation, who preserves subordination among the negroes, is said to *drive well;* and Mr. H——— *having once been an Overseer himself,* the phrase very naturally predominated in his mind.

Planter. Well, no matter for that,—but Mrs. H————, who is an excellent speller, never makes use of any other but *Matthew Carey's* spelling-book. It is a valuable work, the copyright is secured. But here comes Mrs. H———— herself.

Mrs. H———— now entered, followed by a negro girl, who held a peacock's feather in her hand. Mrs. H———— received my bow with a mutilated curtesy, and throwing herself on a sopha, called peremptorily to *Prudence* to brush the flies from her face. There was a striking contrast between the dress of the lady and her maid; the one was tricked out in all the finery of fashion; while the black skin of the other peeped through her garments.

Well, my dear, said Mr. H————, this young man is the person who advertised for the place of tutor in a respectable family. A little conversation with him will enable you to judge, whether he is qualified to instruct our children in the branches of a liberal education.

Mrs. H————. Why independent of his literary attainments, it will be necessary for him to produce certificates of his conduct. I am not easily satisfied in my choice of a tutor; *a body* should be very cautious in admitting a stranger to her family. This gentleman is young, and young men are very frequently addicted to bad habits. Some are prone to late hours; some to hard drinking; and some to Negur girls: the last propensity I could never forgive.

Mr. H. Yes, my dear, you discharged Mr. *Spondee,* our last tutor, for his intimacy with the Negur girls:—*Prudence* had a little one by him. *Prudence* looked reproachfully at her master; the child was in reality the offspring of Mr. H————, who fearing the inquiries of the world on the subject, fathered it upon the last tutor. But they must have been blind who could not discover that the child was sprung from Mr. H————; for it had the same vulgar forehead, the same vacant eye, and the same idiot laugh.

Mr. H. Do, my dear, examine the young man a little on literary matters. He seems to have read *Pope.*

Mrs. H. What, Sir, is your opinion of Mr. *Pope's* Ode on Solitude?

Tutor. It is a tolerable production, madam, for a child.

Mrs. H. A tolerable production for a child! Mercy on us! It is the *most sublimest* of his productions. But tastes differ. Have you read the works of *Dr. Johnson?* Which do you approve the most.

Tutor. Why, Madam, if you allude to his poems, I should, in conformity with your judgment, give a decided preference to his Epitaph on a Duck, written, if I mistake not, when he was four years old. It need scarcely fear competition with *Pope's* Ode on Solitude. At this moment the eldest daughter of this learned lady, of this unsexed female, tripped into the room on light, fantastic toe. Come, my daughter, said the lady, let this gentleman hear you repeat the Ode on Solitude.

Excuse me, Madam, cried I, taking up my hat and bowing.

Do you hear the child, Bawled Mr. H————. I pray you, sir, to excuse me, rejoined I.

Mrs. H. It will not take the child ten minutes.

Tutor. Ten minutes, Madam, are the sixth part of an hour that will never return!

Mr. H. Politeness dictates it.

Tutor. Excuse me, I entreat you, Sir.

Mr. H. I cannot excuse you, I shall hire you as tutor, and I have a right to expect from you submission. I may perhaps give you the sum of fifty pounds a year.

Don't mention it, Sir, said I. There again you will have the goodness to excuse me. Madam, your most obedient. Miss, your very obsequious. Sir, your humble servant.[2]

My walk back to *Charleston* was along the shore of the *Atlantic,* whose waves naturally associated the idea of a home I despaired ever again to behold. . . .

---

[2] It has been my object in this scene to soften the condition of private tutors in America, by putting up Mr. H———— *in signum terroris et Memoriae* to other purse-proud planters. I write not from personal pique, but a desire to benefit society. Happy shall I think myself should this page hold the mirror up to the inflation of pride, and the insolence of prosperity.

« 5 »

Varied Educational Interests and Activities*

《《 》》》》》》》》》》》》》》》》》》》》》》》》》》》》》》》》

The Will of Benjamin Syms (Virginia), 1634 †

In the name of God Amen this Twelfth day of Febry Anno Domini one thousand Six hundred and thirty four I Benjamin Syms being of perfect health, & memory praised by God make & ordain this my last Will and textament in manner & forme following Viz

* The documents in this section do not lend themselves to easy classification as in preceding sections but are important for their reflection of significant if miscellaneous educational interests. Two interesting experiments in philanthropy and education in the colonial period were Bethesda Orphan House in Georgia and the Winyaw Indigo Society in South Carolina. The idea of Bethesda Orphan House, the oldest orphan school in the United States and still in existence, was suggested to the Reverend George Whitefield by Reverend John Wesley, and with the aid of his friend, James Habersham, the institution was established somewhat on the pattern of the remarkable educational and charitable institution which had been founded at Halle in 1695 by August Hermann Francke (1663-1727), the German Lutheran religious leader and educational reformer. Shortly after Whitefield's death in Massachusetts in 1770 Bethesda Orphan House, "the most prominent institution of learning in the colony prior to the Revolution," was destroyed by fire. It was later rebuilt only to suffer a second destruction by hurricane and fire. In 1808 the legislature of Georgia authorized the trustees to dispose of the property and after paying its debts to distribute the remainder of the proceeds to charitable institutions in Savannah. For Benjamin Franklin's appraisal of Whitefield see Jared Sparks (Ed.), *The Works of Benjamin Franklin*, I, pp. 136-40. The Winyaw Indigo Society was formed in 1740 largely as a convivial club of planters who met in Georgetown monthly to discuss the latest London News, "to hold high discourse over the growth and prosperity of the indigo plant, and to refresh the inner man, and so to keep up to a proper standard the endearing ties of social life by imbibing freely of the inevitable bowl of punch." A school was founded by the society in 1756 and had a successful career until 1861. The Civil War practically destroyed the value of the Society's endowment, the building was occupied for more than a year by Federal troops and the library was scattered. When the organization was allowed possession of the building again, funds were raised for a new endowment. The school continued its work from 1866 to 1886 when it was incorporated as one of the public graded schools of the state. During the past five decades the Society has engaged in no educational work but still retains its organization and library. For documents on Bethesda Orphan House and Winyaw Indigo Society see Edgar W. Knight, *A Documentary History of Education in the South Before 1860* (Chapel Hill, University of North Carolina Press, 1949), I, pp. 235-95.

† The Will Book for Elizabeth City County, Virginia, in which the will of Syms should be recorded is lacking, but the Virginia State Library has a certified copy of it and photocopy of that copy is in the Southern Historical Collection of the University of North Carolina. This is believed to be the first endowment for education in English North America. It was combined with funds provided by Thomas Eaton's will (1659) for educational purposes and the school conducted under these endowments had a long and successful history,

I commend my soul into the hands of God my Creator and Redeemer and my body to the Earth from whence it came to have Christian burial whereas there is due to me two hundred acres of land lying in the old Poquoson River and Eight Milch cows—I bequeath it as followth Viz The use of the said land with the milk and Increase Male of the said cattle to be for the mantayance of an honest & learned man to keep upon the said Ground a free School to Educate & teach the Children of the adjoining Parishes of Elizb City & Poquoton from Mary's Mount downwards to the Poquoson River.

Item My Will and desire is that the Worshipful the Commander and ye rest of the Commissioners of this liberty with the ministers and Church Wardens of the said Parish where the said School is founded to see it from time to time justly & truly performed.

Item My Will and Desire is that when it please God there is sufficient Increase of the said cattle yt some part of them be saved for the erecting a very sufficient School house and the Rest of the Increase that arc left to be disposed of before nominated and in Repairing the said School.

Item My Will is that the Increase of the said Cattle after the said School Master is sufficiently stocked for his maintaynance shall be spent according to the directions of the said Commander & Commitions with the rest of them to manteyne poor children, or decayed or maimed persons of the said parish.

Item I give and bequeath unto George Thompson the Soun of Roger Thompson, late of Barstable in the County of Duenshire decd one thousand, pos weight of Tobacco in leafe.

Item Whereas there is due unto me one bond of one hundred pounds from Thomas Worth in the County of Cornewall, which said bond is now in the hands of Wassell Webbing of Baching in the County of Essen I Doe also give & bequeath to the said George Thompson.

Item My Will and desire is that if the said George Thompson or Angell Thompson should decease that then whatever I have bequeath In this my Will & testament to Remaine to the surviver.

Item I Doe further will and desire that if should please God to take away both the Said George & Angell Thompson that then whatever I have bequeath them in this my will to Return to the use and benifit of the said School for want of Heirs of Either of their bodys lawfully begotten.

Item I give and bequeath unto Angell Thompson son of the said Roger

---

becoming the Syms-Eaton Academy in 1902. In 1940 the General Assembly of Virginia enacted a bill to restore the school, perhaps as a sort of "museum piece," but the governor of the state disapproved the measure by a "pocket veto." The amount of these early endowments was at that time reported to be about $10,000, invested in government bonds. For the wide practice of providing for education in the South by means of wills, see Edgar W. Knight, *op. cit.*, I, pp. 202-34; 296-334.

Thompson decd three thousand pounds of Tobacco in leaf with twelve young Cattle with all the Increase of those cattle which belongs unto me unto this my Will be   with all such goods, hoggs Poultry and household stuffe as are or shall be found belonging unto me with twelve barrels of corn.

Item I give and bequeath unto the said Angle Thompson two hundred and fifty acres of land which is due unto me for transportations, of five Servants in the Peter & John of London in the year our Lord one thousand Six hundred twenty Six Capt. John being the commander of the said ship.

Item I give and bequeath five hundr Pounds of Toba to be imployed to the use of the Church of the old Poquoson.

Item I give and bequeath to the minister of the said Parish which shall beat the time when this my will shall be   two hundd pounds of Tobacco.

Item I request my well beloved friends Mr Thomas Oldis and John Snode to be Overseers to see those legacies Performed according, to the full Intent and meaning of my last will and Testament. To whom I give as a rememberance of my love three hundd Pounds of Toba and one Ewe goate being at the house of John Branch at Back River.

In witness whereof I have hereunto set my hand and seal the day and year first above written

his mark
BENJAMIN SYMS

"The Laws, Liberties and Orders of Harvard College," 1642-1646 *

1. When any scholar is able to read Tully, or such like classical Latin author *extempore,* and make and speak true Latin in verse and prose *suo (ut aiunt) Marte,* and decline perfectly the paradigms of nouns and verbs in the Greek tongue, then may he be admitted into the College, nor shall any claim admission before such qualifications.

2. Every one shall consider the main end of his life and studies, to know God and Jesus Christ, which is eternal life; John xvii. 3.

3. Seeing the Lord giveth wisdom, every one shall seriously, by prayer in secret, seek wisdom of Him; Proverbs ii. 2, 3, &c.

4. Every one shall so exercise himself in reading the Scriptures twice a day, that they be ready to give an account of their proficiency therein, both in theoretical observations of language and logic, and in practical and spiritual truths, as their Tutor shall require, according to their several abilities respectively, seeing the entrance of the word giveth light, &c.; Psalm cxix. 130.

* Josiah Quincy, *The History of Harvard University* (Cambridge, published by John Owen, 1840), I, pp. 515-17.

5. In the public church assembly, they shall carefully shun all gestures that show any contempt or neglect of God's ordinances, and be ready to give an account to their Tutors of their profiting, and to use the helps of storing themselves with knowledge, as their Tutors shall direct them. And all Sophisters and Bachelors (until themselves make common place) shall publicly repeat sermons in the Hall, whenever they are called forth.

6. They shall eschew all profanation of God's holy name, attributes, word, ordinances, and times of worship; and study, with reverence and love, carefully to retain God and his truth in their minds.

7. They shall honor as their parents, magistrates, elders, tutors, and aged persons, by being silent in their presence (except they be called on to answer), not gainsaying; showing all those laudable expressions of honor and reverence in their presence that are in use, as bowing before them, standing uncovered, or the like.

8. They shall be slow to speak, and eschew not only oaths, lies, and uncertain rumors, but likewise all idle, foolish, bitter scoffing, frothy, wanton words, and offensive gestures.

9. None shall pragmatically intrude or intermeddle in other men's affairs.

10. During their residence they shall studiously redeem their time, observe the general hours appointed for all the scholars, and the special hour for their own lecture, and then diligently attend the lectures, without any disturbance by word or gesture; and, if of any thing they doubt, they shall inquire of their fellows, or in case of non-resolution, modestly of their Tutors.

11. None shall, under any pretence whatsoever, frequent the company and society of such men as lead an ungirt and dissolute life. Neither shall any, without license of the Overseers of the College, be of the artillery or trainband. Nor shall any, without the license of the Overseers of the College, his Tutor's leave, or, in his absence, the call of parents or guardians, go out to another town.

12. No scholar shall buy, sell, or exchange any thing, to the value of sixpence, without the allowance of his parents, guardians, or Tutors; and whosoever is found to have sold or bought any such things without acquainting their tutors or parents, shall forfeit the value of the commodity, or the restoring of it, according to the discretion of the President.

13. The scholars shall never use their mother tongue, except that in public exercises of oratory, or such like, they be called to make them in English.

14. If any scholar, being in health, shall be absent from prayers or lectures, except in case of urgent necessity, or by the leave of his Tutor, he shall be liable to admonition (or such punishment as the President shall think meet), if he offend above once a week.

15. Every scholar shall be called by his surname only, till he be

invested with his first degree, except he be a fellow commoner, or knight's eldest son, or of superior nobility.

16. No scholar shall, under any pretence of recreation or other cause whatever (unless foreshowed and allowed by the President or his Tutor), be absent from his studies or appointed exercises, above an hour at morning bever, half an hour at afternoon bever, an hour and a half at dinner, and so long at supper.

17. If any scholar shall transgress any of the laws of God, or the House, out of perverseness, or apparent negligence, after twice admonition, he shall be liable, if not *adultus,* to correction; if *adultus,* his name shall be given up to the Overseers of the College, that he may be publicly dealt with after the desert of his fault; but in greater offences such gradual proceeding shall not be exercised.

18. Every scholar, that on proof is found able to read the original of the Old and New Testament into the Latin tongue, and to resolve them logically, withal being of honest life and conversation, and at any public act hath the approbation of the Overseers and Master of the College, may be invested with his first degree.

19. Every scholar, that giveth up in writing a synopsis or summary of Logic, Natural and Moral Philosophy, Arithmetic, Geometry, and Astronomy, and is ready to defend his theses or positions, withal skilled in the originals as aforesaid, and still continues honest and studious, at any public act after trial he shall be capable of the second degree, of Master of Arts.

Initial Educational Legislation in Massachusetts, 1647 *

It being one cheife proiect of ye ould deluder, Satan, to keepe men from the knowledge of ye Scriptures, as in formr times by keeping ym in an unknowne tongue, so in these latter times by perswading from ye use of tongues, yt so at least ye true sence & meaning of ye originall might be clouded by false glosses of saint seeming deceivers, yt learning may not be buried in ye grave of or fathrs in ye church and commonwealth, the Lord assisting or endeavors,—

It is therefore ordred, yt evry towneship in this iurisdiction, aftr ye Lord hath increased ym number to 50 householdrs, shall then forthwth appoint one wth in their towne to teach all such children as shall resort to him to write & reade, whose wages shall be paid eithr by ye parents or mstrs of such childen, or by ye inhabitants in genrall, by way of supply, as ye maior part of those yet ordr ye prudentials of ye towne shall appoint; provided, those yt send their children be not oppressed by paying much

* *Records of the Company of Massachusetts Bay,* II, p. 203. Often referred to as the "old deluder" act, this law seems to have had influence on similar legislation in other New England colonies.

more yn they can have ym taught for in othr townes; & it is furthr ordered, yt where any towne shall increase to ye numbr of 100 families or house-holdrs, they shall set up a grammar schoole, ye mr thereof being able to instruct youth so farr as they shall be fited for ye university, provided yt if any towne neglect ye performance hereof above one yeare, yt every such towne shall pay 5£ to ye next schoole till they shall performe this order.

Rules of Harvard College, 1650 *

No scholar whatever, without the foreacquaintance and leave of the President and his Tutor, or in the absence of either of them, two of the Fellows, shall be present at or in any of the public civil meetings, or concourse of people, as courts of justice, elections, fairs, or at military exercise, in the time or hours of the College exercise, public or private. Neither shall any scholar exercise himself in any military band, unless of known gravity, and of approved sober and virtuous conversation, and that with the leave of the President and his Tutor.

No scholar shall take tobacco, unless permitted by the President, with the consent of their parents or guardians, and on good reason first given by a physician, and then in a sober and private manner.

To the intent that no scholar may misspend his time to the dishonor of God and the society, or the grief and disappointment of his friends, but that the yearly progress and sufficiency of scholars may be manifest, it is therefore ordered, that henceforth there shall be three weeks of visitation yearly, foresignified publicly by the President of the College, between the 10th of June and the Commencement, wherein from nine o'clock to eleven in the forenoon, and from one to three in the afternoon, of the second and third day of the week, all scholars of two years' standing and upwards, shall sit in the Hall to be examined by all comers, in the Latin, Greek, and Hebrew tongues, and in Rhetoric, Logic, and Physics; and they that expect to proceed Bachelors that year, to be examined of their sufficiency according to the laws of the College; and such that expect to proceed Masters of Arts, to exhibit their synopsis of acts required by the laws of the College. And, in case any of the Sophisters, Questionists, or Inceptors, fail in the premises required at their hands, according to their standings respectively, or be found insufficient for their time and standing in the judgment of any three of the visitors, being Overseers of the College, they shall be deferred to the following year. But they, that are approved sufficient for their degrees, shall proceed, and the Sophisters publicly approved shall have their names publicly set up in the Hall.

Whereas by experience we have found it prejudicial to the promoting

---

* Quincy, *op. cit.*, I, pp. 517-19. The rules governing the conduct of students were similar in all the nine colonial colleges and reflected the Calvinistic severity of that period. Collegiate rules were important aspects of the "colonial climate."

of learning and good manners in the College, to admit such young scholars who have been negligent in their studies, and disobedient to their masters in the schools, and so by an evil custom or habit become utterly unfit to improve, for their own benefit according to their friends' expectation, the liberty of students in the College; it is therefore ordered by the President and Fellows of Harvard College, that no scholar whatsoever, where these be published, shall henceforth be admitted from any such school, unless having the testimony of the master of such school, of his obedience and submission to all godly school discipline, and of his studiousness and diligence, at leastwise for one quarter of a year last before his coming thence; or, in case of discontinuance from school, then it is expected he shall bring the testimony of his sober and studious conversation, under the hand of a magistrate or elder, or two or three competent and pious witnesses.

President Henry Dunster Is Dismissed from Harvard Because of His Views on Infant Baptism, 1653 *

Among the early friends of the College, no one deserves more distinct notice than Henry Dunster. He united in himself the character of both patron and President; for, poor as he was, he contributed, at a time of its utmost need, one hundred acres of land towards its support; besides rendering to it, for a succession of years, a series of official services, well directed, unwearied, and altogether inestimable.

Under his administration, the first code of laws was formed; rules of admission, and the principles on which degrees should be granted, were established; and scholastic forms, similar to those customary in the English Universities, were adopted; many of which continue, with little variation, to be used at the present time.† The charter of 1642 was probably, and that of 1650 was avowedly, obtained on his petition. By solicitations among his friends, and by personal sacrifices, he built a President's house. He was instant in the relief of the College in its extreme wants. The Commissioners of the United Colonies stood to the people of New England, in that day, somewhat in the relation in which Congress now stands to the people of the United States. They had, however, only the power to recommend measures, not to enforce them. Dunster formed the plan of concentrating upon the College the patronage of all the Colonies. Under his auspices, a memorial was addressed by Mr. Shepard, pastor of the church in Cambridge, to those Commissioners, for a general

---

* *Ibid.*, I, pp. 15-20. This is believed to be the first case involving in this country what has come to be known as "academic freedom." Samuel Eliot Morison says: "The news that the President of Harvard had gone 'antipaedobaptist' aroused as much consternation in the community as if President Conant should announce his adherence to the Third International." *Three Centuries of Harvard*, p. 19.

† 1840.

contribution for the maintenance of poor scholars at the College, to the end, that "the Commonwealth may be furnished with knowing and uderstanding men, and the churches with an able ministry." The tenor of this memorial strikingly illustrates the simplicity and the poverty of the times. It entreats the Commissioners to recommend "to every family throughout the plantations (which is able and willing to give) to contribute a fourth part of a bushel of corn, or something equivalent thereto, which, it declares, would be "a blessed means of comfortable provision, for the diet of such students, as stand in need of support." The Commissioners approved the plan, and made the recommendation requested. . . .

Dunster's usefulness, however, was deemed to be at an end, and his services no longer desirable, in consequence of his falling, in 1653, as Cotton Mather expresses it, "into the briers of Antipaedobaptism," and of his having borne "public testimony, in the church at Cambridge, against the administration of baptism to any infant whatsoever."

It was time, in the opinion of our worthy ancestors, for them to bestir themselves, when the pious Mitchel himself declared, that his own faith in the orthodox doctrine of Paedobaptism had been so shaken, and such "scruples and suggestions," in respect to it, "had been injected into him by Mr. Dunster's discourses," that he did not dare to trust himself within reach of their "venom and poison," it being "not hard to discern that they came from the *Evil One.*"

Indicted by the grand jury for disturbing the ordinance of infant baptism in the Cambridge church, convicted by the court, sentenced to a public admonition on lecture day, and laid under bonds for good behaviour, Dunster's martyrdom was consummated by being compelled, in October, 1654, to resign his office of President, and to throw himself on the tender mercies of the General Court.

There is a simple, touching pathos, in the following "Considerations," he submitted to that body in the ensuing November, showing why he should not be compelled at once, for the convenience of his successor, to quit the President's house.

"1st. The time of the year is unseasonable, being now very near the shortest day, and the depth of winter.

"2d. The place unto which I go, is unknown to me and my family, and the ways and means of subsistence, to one of my talents and parts, or for the containing or conserving my goods, or disposing of my cattle, accustomed to my place of residence.

"3d. The place from which I go, hath fire, fuel, and all provisions for man and beast, laid in for the winter. To remove some things will be to destroy them; to remove others, as books and household goods, to hazard them greatly. The house I have builded, upon very damageful conditions to myself, out of love for the College, taking country pay in lieu of bills of exchange on England, or the house would not have been built; and a considerable part of it was given me, at my request, out of respect to myself, albeit for the College.

"4th. The persons, all besides myself, are women and children, on whom little help, now their minds lie under the actual stroke of affliction and grief. My wife is sick, and my youngest child extremely so, and hath been for months, so that we dare not carry him out of doors, yet much worse now than before. However, if a place be found, that may be comfortable for them, and reasonably answer the obstacles above mentioned, myself will willingly bow my neck to any yoke of personal denial, for I know for what and for whom, by grace, I suffer.

"The whole transaction of this business is such, which in process of time, when all things come to mature consideration, may very probably create grief on all sides; yours subsequent, as mine antecedent. I am not the man you take me to be. Neither if ye knew what, should, and why, can I persuade myself that you would act, as I am at least tempted to think you do. But our times are in God's hands, with whom all sides hope, by grace in Christ, to find favor, which shall be my prayer for you, as for myself,

"Who am, honored Gentlemen, yours to serve,

"HENRY DUNSTER."

An appeal of this kind was irresistible; and, notwithstanding "the venom" of his heresy, and the detected coöperation with him of the *"Evil One,"* the General Court consented that he should remain in the President's house till the March following.

Although the Court granted him this indulgence, their treatment of him, in other respects, was neither kind nor just. He found the seminary a school. It rose, under his auspices, to the dignity of a College. No man ever questioned his talents, learning, exemplary fidelity, and usefulness. His scanty salary had been paid, not in cash, nor in kind, but by transfers of town rates; thereby vesting him with the character of tax-gatherer, and exposing him to all the vexations, delays, complaints, losses, and abatements incident to that office. In 1643, he complained bitterly to Governor Winthrop, of the injuries he sustained by this practice. Every year he had been subjected to depreciation, delay, and loss, which he prays may be made up to him. He concludes his petition with this characteristic declaration; "Considering the poverty of the country, I am willing to descend to the lowest step; and, if nothing can comfortably be allowed, I sit still appeased; desiring nothing more than to supply me and mine with food and raiment."

Neither his modesty, humility, nor virtues stood him in any stead amidst the prevailing prejudices and poverty of the time. After his resignation, the Corporation, in May, 1655, interested themselves in his behalf, and stated to the General Court, that, "notwithstanding they have paid Mr. Dunster all that they have been able, there is still due to him nearly forty pounds, which justice and equity require should be paid; and, besides what is due in strict account, they think an hundred pounds ought to be allowed Mr. Dunster, in consideration of his extraordinary pains in raising up and carrying on the College for so many years past, and desire it may be seriously considered, and hope it may make much for the country's honorable discharge in the hearts of all, and perpetual encouragement of their servants in such public works, if it be attended."

The attempt was without success; and a committee of the Deputies treat his appeal to their humanity and justice in the following heartless way. "What extraordinary labor in, about, and concerning the weal of the College, for the space of fourteen years, we know of none, except what was the President's duty, belonging to his place; unless he can show the particulars of these labors, which were extraordinary." The result of the whole affair was, that he obtained nothing from the General Court; and that the Corporation, after his death, paid to his widow twenty pounds, in full of the balance due to his estate. . . .

On Fines and Corporal Punishment at Harvard, 1656 *

It is hereby ordered that the President and Fellows of Harvard College, for the time being, or the major part of them, are hereby empowered, according to their best discretion, to punish all misdemeanors of the youth in their society, either by fine, or whipping in the Hall openly, as the nature of the offence shall require, not exceeding ten shillings or ten stripes for one offence; and this law to continue in force until this Court or the Overseers of the College provide some other order to punish such offences. The magistrates have past this with reference to the consent of their brethren, the deputies, thereunto.

Voted in the affirmative 21st of October, 1656.

EDWARD RAWSON, *Secretary.*

Consented to by the Deputies.

WILLIAM TORREY.

The Need for a College in Virginia, 1660-1662 †

Bee itt enacted that there bee a petition drawn up by this grand assembly to the king's most excellent majestie for his letters pattents to collect and gather the charity of well disposed people in England for the erecting of colledges and schooles in this countrye and alsoe for his majesties letters to both universities of Oxford and Cambridge to furnish the

---

* *Ibid.,* pp. 513-14.
† Hening, *Statutes at Large of Virginia,* II, pp. 30-31, 37, 56.

church here with ministers for the present and this petition to be recommended to the right honourable governor Sir William Berkeley. (March, 1660/61).

Whereas for the advancement of learning, promoteing piety & provision of an able & successive ministry in this country, it hath been thought fitt that a colledge of students of the liberall arts and sciences be erected and maintayned In pursuance whereof the right honourable his majesties governour, council of state, and burgesses of the present grand assembly have severally subscribed severall considerable sumes of money and quantityes of tobacco (out of their charity and devotion) to be paid to the honourable Grand Assembly or such treasurer or treasurers as they shall now or their successors hereafter at any time appoint upon demand after a place is provided and built upon for that intent and purpose, *It is ordered* that the commissioners of the severall county courts do att the next followinge court in their severall countys subscribe such sumes of money & tobaccoe towards the furthering and promoteing the said persons and necessary worke to be paid by them or their heires, as they shall think fitt, and that they alsoe take the subscriptions of such other persons at their said courts who shall be willing to contribute towards the same And that after such subscriptions taken they send orders to the vestryes of the severall parishes in their severall countys for the subscriptions of such inhabitants and others who have not already subscribed and that the same be returned to Francis Morrison Esquire. (March 1660/61).

Whereas the want of able and faithful ministers in this countrey deprives us of those great blessings and mercies that always attend upon the service of God; which want, by reason of our great distance from our native country, cannot in probability be always supplied from thence: Bee it enacted, that for the advance of learning, education of youth, supply of the ministry, and promotion of piety, there be land taken up or purchased for a college and free school: And that there be with as much speed as may be convenient houseing erected thereon, for entertainment of students and scholars. (March, 1661/62).

Sir William Berkeley's Report on Virginia, 1671 *

The questions from the Commissioners of Trade and Plantations in 1670 and the replies the following year from Sir William Berkeley, governor of Virginia, throw interesting light on conditions in that colony at that time. Hening says of this material: "A more correct statistical account of Virginia, at that period, cannot, perhaps, anywhere be found. The answers appear to have been given with great candor, and were from a man well versed in every thing relating to the country, having been for

* *Ibid.,* pp. 511-17. Here may be found all the questions from the Commissioners of Trade and Plantations and Berkeley's answers.

many years governor. As it respects the *inhabitants* of Virginia, *Sir William Berkeley* seems to have been well qualified to rear them up as food for despots, since, in his answer to the last enquiry, he thanks God that there are no *'free-schools* or *printing,'* and 'hopes' that we shall have none these hundred yeares." Berkeley's historic exclamation in his answer to the last question has often been misquoted or misunderstood. There had been in Virginia for a long time foundations for English "free" schools and the governor himself had approved an act of 1642 which incorporated the school established in Elizabeth City County on the will of Benjamin Syms who provided the first educational endowment in English North America. Only the question on education and Berkeley's answer are given here:

What course is taken about the instructing the people, within your government in the christian religion; and what provision is there made for the paying of your ministry?

Answer: The same course that is taken in England out of towns; every man according to his ability instructing his children. We have fforty eight parishes, and our ministers are well paid, and by my consent should be better *if they would pray oftener and preach less.* But of all other commodities, so of this, *the worst are sent us,* and we had few that we could boast of, since the persicution in *Cromwell's* tiranny drove divers worthy men hither. But I thank God, *there are no free schools* nor *printing,* and I hope we shall not have these hundred years, for *learning* has brought disobedience, and heresy, and sects into the world, and *printing* has divulged them, and libels against the best government. God keep us from both!

Thomas Budd's Views on Educational Provisions Needed in Pennsylvania and New Jersey, 1685 *

1. Now it might be well if a law was made by the Governors and General Assemblies of Pennsylvania and New Jersey, that all persons inhabiting in the said Provinces, do put their children seven years to the public school, or longer, if the parents please.

2. That schools be provided in all towns and cities, and persons of known honesty, skill and understanding be yearly chosen by the Governor and General Assembly, to teach and instruct boys and girls in all the most useful arts and sciences that they in their youthful capacities may be capable to understand, as the learning to read and write true English, Latin, and other useful speeches and languages, and fair writing, arith-

---

* *Good Order Established in Pennsylvania and New Jersey* (London, 1685). Given in J. P. Wickersham, *A History of Education in Pennsylvania* (Lancaster, Inquirer Publishing Co., 1886), p. 51. According to Wickersham, Budd was a Quaker, became a Proprietor and an early settler in New Jersey and for a time served as a member of the General Assembly of that colony. He died in Philadelphia toward the end of the eighteenth century.

metic and book-keeping; and the boys to be taught and instructed in some mystery or trade, as the making of mathematical instruments, joinery, twinery, the making of clocks and watches, weaving, shoe-making, or any other useful trade or mystery that the school is capable of teaching; and the girls to be taught and instructed in the spinning of flax and wool, the knitting of gloves and stockings, sewing and making of all sorts of useful needle-work, and the making of straw-work as hats, baskets &c., or any other useful art or mystery that the school is capable of teaching.

3. That the scholars be kept in the morning two hours at reading, writing, book-keeping &c., and other two hours at work in that art, mystery or trade that he or she most delighteth in, and then let them have two hours to dine and for recreation; and in the afternoon two hours at work at their several employments.

4. The Seventh day of the week, the scholars may come to school only in the forenoon; and at a certain time in the afternoon, let a meeting be kept by the schoolmasters and their scholars, where after good instruction and admonition is given by the masters to the scholars, and thanks returned to the Lord for his mercies and blessings that are daily received from Him, then, let a strict examination be made by the masters, of the conversation of the scholars in the week past, and let reproof, admonition and correction be given to the offenders, according to the quantity and quality of their faults.

5. Let the like meetings be kept by the school mistresses, and the girls apart from the boys. By strictly observing this good order, our children will be hindered of running into that excess of riot and wickedness that youth is incident to, and they will be a comfort to their tender parents.

6. Let one thousand acres of land be given and laid out in a good place, to every public school that shall be set up, and the rent or income of it go towards defraying of the charge of the school.

7. And to the end that the children of poor people and the children of Indians may have the like good learning with the children of rich people, let them be maintained free of charge to their parents, out of the profits of the school, arising by the work of the scholars, by which the poor and the Indians, as well as the rich, will have their children taught, and the remainder of the profits, if any be, to be disposed of in the building of schoolhouses and improvements on the thousand acres of land which belongs to the school.

Remonstrance Against Locating the Collegiate School
at New Haven, 1717 *

The Genll. Assembly of this Collony having some time given power to certain Trustees to Erect a Collegiate School in this Colony and to Determine the place of its Settlement, & having also Contributed to its yearly Maintainance & given a very Considerable Summe of Money to the building an House for Entertaining of Schollars. And whereas the Counties of N London & Hartford being more in Numbers than the rest of ye Government & paying the Greatest part of the Money given for the Subsisting the Collegiate School, & having furnished the sd. School with the greatest Number of Schollars, had reason to Expect that in apointing the place of the School Good respect should have been had to them therein. But finding it quite Otherwise, & that the Settling thereof at N Haven is attended with great Difficulty, such as cant be easily overcome, it being so very remote & the Transporting any thing by Water so uncertain, & there being so little Communication between these Counties & N Haven. & Understanding that at a Meeting of ye Major part of the Trustees at Hartford (which Major part by the Charter given to the Trustees have full power to act) did then determine that if they Could not Universally Agree to the Settlement of sd. School when they should meet at next Commencement at Saybrook, then they should refer the Nomination of the place to the Meeting of ye Genll. Assembly next October following. Those of the Trustees that Dissented from the Settling the Collegiate School at N Haven were under a Necessity in faithfullness to those Counties for whose Conveniency they were Concerned to inform the Genll. Assembly of the Same, but there being Nothing Issued: We do for or. selves declare our Dissatisfaction with the Settling of ye School at N Haven, by only an Equal part of the Trustees, & hereby Remonstrate against the same & desire that the Genll. Assembly that shall be in May next, may be moved that by an Act they may make a full Settlement thereof, & yt. it be part of the Instructions of yr. Deputies at the sd. Genll. Assembly, to offer ys. our remonstrance & Endeavour yt. the School be settled in a place, that shall be judged by them most Convenient & where it may be best subsisted & most accomodable to the greatest part of the Government.

* Given in Franklin B. Dexter, *Documentary History of Yale University* (New Haven, Yale University Press, 1916), pp. 81-82. Arthur T. Hadley, who became president of Yale in 1899 (the first layman to hold that post), is reported to have said that the institution "was founded after a fashion, at the beginning of the eighteenth century, along the north shore of Long Island Sound. For many years it was difficult to say where it was and where it belonged."

Notice of John Peter Zenger to the Subscribers to His Paper, November 25, 1734 *

To all my Subscribers and Benefactors who take my weekly Journall. *Gentlemen, Ladies and Others;*

As you last week were Disappointed of my Journall, I think it Incumbent upon me, to publish my Apoligy which is this. On the Lords Day, the Seventeenth of this Instant I was Arrested, taken and Imprisoned in the common Gaol of this City, by Virtue of a Warrant from the *Governour,* and the Honorable *Francis Harrison,* Esq; and others in Council of which (God willing) Yo'l have a Coppy whereupon I was put under such Restraint that I had not the Liberty of Pen, Ink, or Paper, or to see, or speak with People, till upon my Complaint to the Honourable the Chief Justice, at my appearing before him upon my *Habias Corpus* on the *Wednesday* following. Who discountenanced that Proceeding, and therefore I have had since that time the Liberty of Speaking through the Hole of the Door, to my Wife and Servants by which I doubt not yo'l think me sufficiently Excused for not sending my last weeks *Journall,* and I hope for the future by the Liberty of Speaking to my servants thro' the Hole of the Door of the Prison, to entertain you with my weekly *Journall* as formerly. *And am your obliged Humble Servant.*

Subjects and Questions Discussed by Candidates for the Degree of Master of Arts at Harvard, July 6, 1743 †

Quaestiones pro modulo discutiendae, sub Reverendo D. Edvardo Holyoke, Collegii Harvardini, quod est, Divina Providentia, Cantabrigiae Nov-Anglorum, Praeside. In comitiis publicis a Laureae Magistralis Candidatis: Pridie nonarum quintilis, MDCCXLIII.

Questions methodically to be discussed by the Candidates for the Degree of Master of Arts, in Public Assembly, under the Reverend Mr. Edward Holyoke, President of Harvard College, by divine Providence, at Cambridge in New England; on the 6th of July, A.D. 1743.

* Livingston Rutherford, *John Peter Zenger, His Press, His Trial and A Bibliography of Zenger Reprints* (New York, Dodd, Mead & Co., 1904), pp. 46, 47. See also Charles F. Heartman, *John Peter Zenger and His Fight for the Freedom of the Press* (Highland Park, New Jersey, 1934, printed for Harry B. Weiss), p. 26. The case of John Peter Zenger marks the first step toward freedom of the press and one of the first steps toward the independence of the judiciary in this country. The case grew out of some articles published in *The New York Weekly Journal* which had been established under the direction of Zenger in 1733. James Alexander and William Smith, attorneys, were disbarred from the famous libel case for taking exceptions to the commissions of the judge. Friends of Zenger went to Philadelphia and got the eminent lawyer Andrew Hamilton interested in the case, the outcome of which was the significant departure from the English principle of libel, that the greater the truth the greater the libel. The case is important in educational history because of the close relation between freedom of the press and academic freedom and education.

† Benjamin Peirce, *A History of Harvard University . . . to the Period of the American Revolution* (Cambridge, Brown, Shattuck, and Co., 1833), pp. 111-13. For an account of debating activities in higher education in the early days, see David Potter, *Debating in the Colonial Chartered Colleges* (New York, Teachers College, Columbia University, 1944).

I. An Fidei Confessio verbis merê humanis declaranda sit.
Affirmat respondens
Thomas Prince.

II. *An omnis Simulatio sit Vitium.*
Negat respondens
Benjamin Stevens.

III. An Solidorum Dissolutio in Menstruis per Attractionem perficiatur.
Affirmat respondens
Samuel Gay.

IV. An privata Utilitas, ultimus Actionum Moralium Finis esse debeat.
Negat respondens
Georgius Bethune.

V. An supremo Magistratui resistere liceat, si aliter servari Respublica nequit.
Affirmat respondens
Samuel Adams.

VI. An omnis Motio et Sensatio animalis Nervorum Motu peragantur.
Affirmat respondens
Johannes Gibbins.

VII. An Imperium Civile ex Pactis oriatur.
Affirmat respondens
Samuel Downe.

VIII. *An ex Operibus, Sanctificationi comitantibus, optime exquiratur Justificatio.*
Affirmat respondens
Samuel White.

IX. An Obligatio ad Virtutem in abstractis Rerum Relationibus fundetur.
Affirmat respondens
Samuel Orne.

X. An quaelibet Cultûs Divini Forma, Reipublicae nullo modo incommoda, sit omnino toleranda.
Affirmat respondens
Johannes Newman.

XI. An haec Regula [*Quod dubitas ne feceris*] sit, in rebus moralibus, admittenda.
Affirmat respondens
Samuel Hendley.

I. Whether a Confession of Faith may be declared in words merely humane?
Affirmed by Thomas Prince.

II. Whether every Dissimulation be a Vice?
Deny'd by Benjamin Stevens.

III. Whether the Dissolution of Solids in corrosive Liquors be performed by Attraction?
Affirmed by Samuel Gay.

IV. Whether Private Profit ought to be the chief End of Moral Actions?
Deny'd by George Bethune.

V. Whether it be lawful to resist the Supream Magistrate, if the Common Wealth cannot otherwise be preserved?
Affirmed by Samuel Adams.

VI. Whether all Animal Motion and Sensation be performed by the Motion of the Nerves?
Affirmed by John Gibbins.

VII. Whether Civil Government ariseth out of Contract?
Affirmed by Samuel Downe.

VIII. Whether Justification be best discovered by Works attending Sanctification?
Affirmed by Samuel White.

IX. Whether the Obligation to Virtue be founded in the Abstract Relations of Things?
Affirmed by Samuel Orne.

X. Whether every Form of Divine Worship may be universally tolerated, in no manner incommoding the public good?
Affirmed by John Newman.

XI. Whether this Rule [What thou doubtest do not] may be admitted in Morality?
Affirmed by Samuel Hendley.

XII. An Intellectus humanus Divinae Fidei Mensura sit.
Negat respondens
Jonathan Hoar.

XII. Whether the Humane Intellect be the Measure of Divine Faith?
Deny'd by Jonathan Hoar.

XIII. An Voluntas Dei sit sola et adaequata moralium Actionum Norma.
Affirmat respondens
Samuel Hale.

XIII. Whether the Will of God be the only and adequate Rule of Moral Actions?
Affirmed by Samuel Hale.

XIV. An Conscientia invincibiliter erronea sit inculpabilis.
Affirmat respondens
Nathaniel Snell.

XIV. Whether a Conscience invincibly erroneous may be blameless?
Affirmed by Nathaniel Snell.

XV. *An Scriptura credendi et agendi sit Norma perfecta et sola.*
Affirmat respondens
Samuel Langdon.

XV. Whether the Scriptures be the perfect and only Rule of Believing and Acting?
Affirmed by Samuel Langdon.

XVI. An Religio Christiana Vi et Armis propaganda sit.
Negat respondens
Jacobus Hovey.

XVI. Whether the Christian Religion may be propagated by Force and Arms?
Deny'd by James Hovey.

XVII. An detur Jus Gentium a Jure Naturae distinctum.
Affirmat respondens
Josephus Davis.

XVII. Whether the Law of Nations be distinct from the Law of Nature?
Affirmed by Joseph Davis.

XVIII. An Peccata praeterita et futura simul remittantur.
Negat respondens
Amarias Frost.

XVIII. Whether Past and Future Sins are forgiven at the same time?
Deny'd by Amarias Frost.

XIX. An Spiritus Sancti Operatio in Mente sit Causa naturalis impropria Erroris.
Affirmat respondens
Sylvanus Conant.

XIX. Whether the Operations of the Holy Spirit in the Mind may be the improper Cause of Natural Errors?
Affirmed by Sylvanus Conant.

Benjamin Franklin's "Proposals Relating to the Education of Youth in Pensilvania," 1749 *

ADVERTISEMENT TO THE READER

It has long been regretted as a Misfortune to the Youth of this Province, that we have no Academy, in which they might receive the Accomplishments of a regular Education. The following Paper of Hints towards forming a Plan for that Purpose, is so far approv'd by some publick-

---

* *Proposals Relating to the Education of Youth in Pensilvania.* By Benjamin Franklin, Facsimile Reprint with an introduction by William Pepper (Philadelphia, University of Pennsylvania Press, 1931). Franklin's voluminous notes and quotations from earlier writers on education are omitted and only the text is given here. See also Jared Sparks, *The Works of Benjamin Franklin,* I, pp. 569-76. Franklin's own account of his "Proposals" appears in his biography which is given in Sparks, *op. cit.,* I, pp. 158-61.

spirited Gentlemen, to whom it has been privately communicated, that they have directed a Number of Copies to be made by the Press, and properly distributed, in order to obtain the Sentiments and Advice of Men of Learning, Understanding, and Experience in these Matters; and have determined to use their Interest and best Endeavours, to have the Scheme, when compleated, carried gradually into Execution; in which they have Reason to believe they shall have the hearty Concurrence and Assistance of many who are Wellwishers to their Country. Those who incline to favour the Design with their Advice, either as to the Parts of Learning to be taught, the Order of Study, the Method of Teaching, the Economy of the School, or any other Matter of Importance to the Success of the Undertaking, are desired to communicate their Sentiments as soon as may be, by Letter directed to B. Franklin, *Printer,* in Philadelphia.

PROPOSALS, &C.

The good Education of Youth has been esteemed by wise Men in all Ages, as the surest Foundation of the Happiness both of private Families and of Common-wealths. Almost all Governments have therefore made ia a principal Object of their Attention, to establish and endow with proper Revenues, such Seminaries of Learning, as might supply the succeeding Age with Men qualified to serve the Publick with Honour to themselves, and to their Country.

Many of the first Settlers of these Provinces, were Men who had received a good Education in *Europe,* and to their Wisdom and good Management we owe much of our present Prosperity. But their Hands were full, and they could not do all Things. The present Race are not thought to be generally of equal Ability: For though the *American* Youth are allow'd not to want Capacity; yet the best Capacities require Cultivation, it being truly with them, as with the best Ground, which unless well tilled and sowed with profitable Seed, produces only ranker Weeds.

That we may obtain the Advantages arising from an Increase of Knowledge, and prevent as much as may be the mischievous Consequences that would attend a general Ignorance among us, the following *Hints* are offered towards forming a Plan for the Education of the Youth of *Pennsylvania,* viz.

It is propos'd,

THAT some Persons of Leisure and publick Spirit, apply for a CHARTER, by which they may be incorporated, with Power to erect an ACADEMY for the Education of Youth, to govern the same, provide Masters, make Rules, receive Donations, purchase Lands, &c. and to add to their Number, from Time to Time such other Persons as they shall judge suitable.

That the Members of the Corporation make it their pleasure, and in some Degree their Business, to visit the Academy often, encourage and countenance the Youth, countenance and assist the Masters, and by all

Means in their Power advance the Usefulness and Reputation of the Design; that they look on the Students as in some Sort their Children, treat them with Familiarity and Affection, and when they have behav'd well, and gone through their Studies, and are to enter the World, zealously unite, and make all the Interest that can be made to establish them, whether in Business, Offices, Marriages, or any other Thing for their Advantage, preferably to all other Persons whatsoever even of equal Merit.

And if Men may, and frequently do, catch such a Taste for cultivating Flowers, for Planting, Grafting, Inoculating, and the like, as to despise all other Amusements for their Sake, why may not we expect they should acquire a Relish for that *more useful* Culture of young Minds. *Thompson says,*

> *'Tis Joy to see the human Blossoms blow,*
> *When infant Reason grows apace, and calls*
> *For the kind Hand of an assiduous Care;*
> *Delightful Task! to rear the tender Thought,*
> *To teach the young Idea how to shoot,*
> *To pour the fresh Instruction o'er the Mind,*
> *To breathe th' enliv'ning Spirit, and to fix*
> *The generous Purpose in the glowing Breast.*

That a House be provided for the ACADEMY, if not in the Town, not many Miles from it; the Situation high and dry, and if it may be, not far from a River, having a Garden, Orchard, Meadow, and a Field or two.

That the House be furnished with a Library (if in the Country, if in the Town, the Town Libraries may serve) with Maps of all Countries, Globes, some mathematical Instruments, an Apparatus for Experiments in Natural Philosophy, and for Mechanics; Prints, of all Kinds, Prospects, Buildings, Machines, Ec.

That the Rector be a Man of good Understanding, good Morals, diligent and patient; learn'd in the Languages and Sciences, and a correct pure Speaker and Writer of the *English* Tongue; to have such Tutors under him as shall be necessary.

That the boarding Scholars diet together, plainly, temperately, and frugally.

That to keep them in Health, and to strengthen and render active their Bodies, they be frequently exercis'd in Running, Leaping, Wrestling, and Swimming, Ec.

That they have peculiar Habits to distinguish them from other Youth, if the Academy be in or near the Town; for this, among other Reasons, that their Behaviour may be the better observed.

As to their Studies, it would be well if they could be taught *every thing* that is useful, and *every thing* that is ornamental; But Art is long, and their Time is short. It is therefore propos'd that they learn those Things that are likely to be *most useful* and *most ornamental.* Regard being had to the several Professions for which they are intended.

All should be taught to write a *fair Hand,* and swift, as that is useful to All. And with it may be learnt something of *Drawing,* by Imitation of Prints, and some of the first Principles of Perspective.

Arithmetick, Accounts, and some of the first Principles of *Geometry* and *Astronomy.*

The *English* Language might be taught by Grammar; in which some of our best Writers, as *Tillotson, Addison, Pope, Algernoon Sidney, Cato's* Letters, &c. should be Classicks: The *Stiles* principally to be cultivated, being the *clear* and the *concise.* Reading should also be taught, and pronouncing, properly, distinctly, emphatically; not with an even Tone, which *under-does,* nor a theatrical, which *over-does* Nature.

To form their Stile, they should be put on Writing Letters to each other, making Abstracts of what they read; or writing the same Things in their own Words; telling or writing Stories lately read, in their own Expressions. All to be revis'd and corrected by the Tutor, who should give his Reasons, explain the Force and Import of Words, &c.

To form their Pronunciation, they may be put on making Declamations, repeating Speeches, delivering Orations, &c. The Tutor assisting at the Rehearsals, teaching, advising, correcting their Accent, &c.

But if History be made a constant Part of their Reading, such as the Translations of the *Greek* and *Roman* Historians, and the modern Histories of antient *Greece* and *Rome,* &c. may not almost all Kinds of useful Knowledge be that Way introduc'd to Advantage, and with Pleasure to the Student? As Geography, by reading with Maps, and being required to point out the Places *where* the greatest Actions were done, to give their old and New Names, with the Bounds, Situation, Extent of the Countries concern'd, &c.

Chronology, by the Help of *Helvicus* or some other Writer of the Kind, who will enable them to tell *when* those Events happened; what Princes were Contemporaries, what States or famous Men flourish'd about that Time, &c. The several principal Epochas to be first well fix'd in their Memories.

Antient Customs, religious and civil, being frequently mentioned in History, will give Occasion for explaining them; in which the Prints of Medals, Basso Relievo's, and antient Monuments will greatly assist.

Morality, by descanting and making continual Observations on the Causes of the Rise or Fall of any Man's Character, Fortune, Power, &c. mention'd in History; the Advantages of Temperance, Order, Frugality, Industry, Perseverance, &c. &c. Indeed the general natural Tendency of Reading good History, must be, to fix in the Minds of Youth deep Impressions of the Beauty and Usefulness of Virtue of all Kinds, Publick Spirit, Fortitude, &c.

History will show the wonderful Effects of Oratory, in governing, turning and leading great Bodies of Mankind, Armies, Cities, Nations. When the Minds of Youth are struck with Admiration at this, then is the Time to give them the Principles of that Art, which they will study with Taste and Application. Then they may be made acquainted with the best Models among the Antients, their Beauties being particularly pointed out to them. Modern Political Oratory being chiefly performed by the Pen and Press, its Advantages over the Antient in some Respects are to be shown; as that its Effects are more extensive, more lasting, &c.

History will also afford frequent Opportunities of showing the Necessity of a *Publick Religion,* from its Usefulness to the Publick; the Advantage of a Religious Character among private Persons; the Mischiefs of Superstition, &c. and the Excellency of the Christian Religion above all others antient or modern.

History will also give Occasion to expatiate on the Advantage of Civil Orders and Constitutions, how Men and their Properties are protected by joining in Societies and establishing Government; their Industry encouraged and rewarded, Arts invented, and Life made more comfortable: The Advantages of *Liberty,* Mischiefs of *Licentiousness,* Benefits arising from good Laws and a due Execution of Justice, &c. Thus may the first Principles of sound *Politicks* be fix'd in the Minds of Youth.

On *Historical* Occasions, Questions of Right and Wrong, Justice and Injustice, will naturally arise, and may be put to Youth, which they may debate in Conversation and in Writing. When they ardently desire Victory, for the Sake of the Praise attending it, they will begin to feel the Want, and be sensible of the Use of *Logic,* or the Art of Reasoning to *discover* Truth, and of Arguing to *defend* it, and *convince* Adversaries. This would be the Time to acquaint them with the Principles of that Art. *Grotius, Puffendorff,* and some other Writers of the same Kind, may be used on these Occasions to decide their Disputes. Public Disputes warm the Imagination, whet the Industry, and strengthen the natural Abilities.

When Youth are told, that the Great Men whose Lives and Actions they read in History, spoke two of the best Languages that ever were, the most expressive, copious, beautiful; and that the finest Writings, the most correct Compositions, the most perfect Productions of Human Wit and Wisdom, are in those Languages, which have endured Ages, and will endure while there are Men; that no Translation can do them Justice, or give the Pleasure found in Reading the Originals; that those Languages contain all Science; that one of them is become almost universal, being the Language of Learned Men in all Countries; that to understand them is a distinguishing Ornament, &c. they may be thereby made desirous of learning those Languages, and their Industry sharpen'd in the Acquisition of them. All intended for Divinity should be taught the *Latin* and *Greek;* for Physick, the *Latin, Greek* and *French;* for Law, the *Latin* and *French;* Merchants, the *French, German,* and *Spanish:* And though all should not be compell'd to learn *Latin, Greek,* or the modern foreign Languages; yet none that have an ardent Desire to learn them should be refused; their *English,* Arithmetick, and other Studies absolutely necessary, being at the same Time not neglected.

If the new *Universal History* were also read, it would give a *connected* Idea of human Affairs, so far as it goes, which should be follow'd by the best modern Histories, particularly of our Mother Country; then of these Colonies; which should be accompanied with Observations on their Rise, Encrease, Use to *Great-Britain,* Encouragements, Discouragements, &c. the Means to make them flourish, secure their Liberties, &c.

With the History of Men, Times and Nations, should be read at proper Hours or Days, some of the best *Histories of Nature,* which would not only be delightful to Youth, and furnish them with Matter for their Letters, &c. as well as other History; but afterwards of great Use to them, whether they are Merchants, Handicrafts, or Divines; enabling the first the better to understand many Commodities, Drugs, &c. the second to improve his Trade or Handicraft by new Mixtures, Materials, &c. and the last to adorn his Discourses by beautiful Comparisons, and strengthen them by new Proofs of Divine Providence. The Conversation of all will be improved by it, as Occasions frequently occur of making Natural Observations, which are instructive, agreeable, and entertaining in almost all Companies. *Natural History* will also afford Opportunities of introducing many Observations, relating to the Preservation of Health, which may be afterwards of great Use. *Arbuthnot* on Air and *Aliment, Sanctorius* on Perspiration, *Lemery* on Foods, and some others, may now be read, and a very little Explanation will make them sufficiently intelligible to Youth.

While they are reading Natural History, might not a little *Gardening, Planting, Grafting, Inoculating,* &c. be taught and practised; and now and then Excursions made to the neighbouring Plantations of the best Farmers, their Methods observ'd and reason'd upon for the Information of Youth. The Improvement of Agriculture being useful to all, and Skill in it no Disparagement to any.

The History of *Commerce,* of the Invention of Arts, Rise of Manufactures, Progress of Trade, Change of its Seats, with the Reasons, Causes, &c. may also be made entertaining to Youth, and will be useful to all. And this, with the Accounts in other History of the prodigious Force and Effect of Engines and Machines used in War, will naturally introduce a Desire to be instructed in *Mechanicks,* and to be inform'd of the Principles of that Art by which weak Men perform such Wonders, Labour is sav'd, Manufacture expedited, &c. &c. This will be the Time to show them Prints of antient and modern Machines, to explain them, to let them be copied, and to give Lectures in Mechanical Philosophy.

With the whole should be constantly inculcated and cultivated, that *Benignity of Mind,* which shows itself in *searching for* and *seizing* every

Opportunity *to serve* and *to oblige;* and is the Foundation of what is called Good Breeding; highly useful to the Possessor, and most agreeable to all.

The Idea of what is *true Merit,* should also be often presented to Youth, explain'd and impress'd on their Minds, as consisting in an *Inclination* join'd with an *Ability* to serve Mankind, one's Country, Friends and Family; which *Ability* is (with the Blessing of God) to be acquir'd or greatly encreas'd by *true Learning;* and should indeed be the great *Aim* and *End* of all Learning.

List of Pecuniary Mulcts (Fines) at Harvard, c. 1750 *

Absence from prayers,	£0	0	2
Tardiness at prayers,	0	0	1
Absence from Professor's public lecture,	0	0	4
Tardiness at do.	0	0	2
Profanation of Lord's Day, not exceeding	0	3	0
Absence from public worship,	0	0	9
Tardiness at do.	0	0	3
Ill behaviour at public worship, not exceeding	0	1	6
Going to meeting before bell-ringing,	0	0	6
Neglecting to repeat the sermon,	0	0	9
Irreverent behaviour at prayers, or public divinity lectures,	0	1	6
Absence from chambers, &c., not exceeding	0	0	6
Not declaiming, not exceeding	0	1	6
Not giving up a declamation, not exceeding	0	1	6
Absence from recitation, not exceeding	0	1	6
Neglecting analysing, not exceeding	0	3	0
Bachelors neglecting disputations, not exceeding	0	1	6
Respondents neglecting do. from 1*s.* 6*d.* to	0	3	0
Undergraduates out of town without leave, not exceeding	0	2	6
Undergraduates tarrying out of town without leave, not exceeding *per diem,*	0	1	3
Undergraduates tarrying out of town one week without leave, not exceeding	0	10	0
Undergraduates tarrying out of town one month without leave, not exceeding	2	10	0
Lodging strangers without leave, not exceeding	0	1	6
Entertaining persons of ill character, not exceeding	0	1	6
Going out of College without proper garb, not exceeding	0	0	6
Frequenting taverns, not exceeding	0	1	6
Profane cursing, not exceeding	0	2	6
Graduates playing cards, not exceeding	0	5	0
Undergraduates playing cards, not exceeding	0	2	6
Undergraduates playing any game for money, not exceeding	0	1	6
Selling and exchanging without leave, not exceeding	0	1	6
Lying, not exceeding	0	1	6
Opening door by pick-locks, not exceeding	0	5	0
Drunkenness, not exceeding	0	1	6
Liquors prohibited under penalty, not exceeding	0	1	6

* Quincy, *op. cit.,* II, pp. 499-500.

Offence	£	s	d
Second offence, not exceeding	0	3	0
Keeping prohibited liquors, not exceeding	0	1	6
Sending for do.	0	0	6
Fetching do.	0	1	6
Going upon the top of the College,	0	1	6
Cutting off the lead,	0	1	6
Concealing the transgression of the 19th Law,	0	1	6
Tumultuous noises,	0	1	6
Second offence,	0	3	0
Refusing to give evidence,	0	3	0
Rudeness at meals,	0	1	0
Butler and cook to keep utensils clean, not exceeding	0	5	0
Not lodging at their chambers, not exceeding	0	1	6
Sending freshmen in studying time,	0	0	9
Keeping guns, and going on skating,	0	1	0
Firing guns or pistols in College yard,	0	2	6
Fighting or hurting any person, not exceeding	0	1	6

Advertisement Announcing the Opening of King's (Now Columbia) College, 1754 *

To such Parents as have now (or expect to have) Children prepared to be educated in the COLLEGE *of* New York.

As the Gentlemen who are appointed by the Assembly, to be Trustees of the intended Seminary, or College, of *New-York,* have thought fit to appoint me to take the Charge of it, and have concluded to set up a Course of Tuition in the learned Languages, and in the liberal Arts and Sciences; they have judged it adviseable that I should publish this *Advertisement,* to inform such as have Children ready for a College Education, that it is proposed to begin Tuition upon the first Day of *July,* next, at the Vestry Room in the new *School-House,* adjoining to *Trinity-Church* in *New-York,* which the Gentlemen of the Vestry are so good as to favour them with the Use of, in the Interim, 'till a convenient Place may be built.

II. The lowest Qualifications they have judged requisite in order to Admission into the said College, are as follow, *viz.* That they be able to read well, and write a good legible Hand, and that they be well versed in the five first Rules in *Arithmetick, i.e.* as far as *Division* and *Reduction:* And as to *Latin* and *Greek,* that they have a good Knowledge in the *Grammars,* and be able to make Grammatical *Latin;* and both in constructing and parsing, to give a good . . . of *Tully,* and of the first Books of *Virgil's Aeneid,* and some of the first Chapters of the *Gospel* of *St. John,* in *Greek.* —In these Books therefore, they may expect to be examined; but higher Qualifications must hereafter be expected.—And if there be any of the higher Classes in any College, or under private Instruction, that incline to

* *The New York Mercury,* May 31, 1754. The college began instruction in July of that year in a small room in the rear of Trinity Church, opposite Wall Street. There were eight students and Dr. Samuel Johnson was the president and faculty.

come hither, they may expect Admission to proportionably higher Classes here.

III. And that People may be the better satisfied in sending their Children for Education to this College, it is to be understood, That as to Religion, there is no Intention to impose on the Scholars the peculiar Tenets of any particular Sect of Christians, but to inculcate upon their tender Minds, the great Principles of Christianity and Morality, in which, true Christians of each Denomination are generally agreed.—And as to the daily Worship in the College, Morning and Evening, it is proposed that it would ordinarily consist of such a Collection of Lessons, Prayers and Praises of the Liturgy of the Church, as are for the most Part taken out of the Holy Scriptures, and such as are agreed on by the Trustees, to be in the best Manner expressive of our common Christianity.—And, as to any peculiar Tenets, every one is left to judge freely for himself, and to be required only to attend constantly at such Places of Worship on the Lord's Day, as their Parents or Guardians shall think fit to order or permit.

IV. The chief Thing that is aimed at in this College, is, to teach and engage the Children to *know God in Jesus Christ,* and to love and serve him in all *Sobriety, Godliness* and *Righteousness* of Life, *with a perfect Heart and a willing Mind;* and to train them up in all virtuous Habits, and all such useful Knowledge, as may render them creditable to their Families and Friends, Ornaments to their country, and useful to the publick Weal in their generations.—To which good Purposes, it is earnestly desired that their Parents, Guardians, and Masters, would train them up from their Cradles, under strict Government, and in all Seriousness, Virtue and Industry, that they may be qualified to make orderly and tractable Members of this Society.—And above all that, in order hereunto, they be very careful themselves to set them good Examples of true Piety and Virtue in their own Conduct.—For, as Examples have a very powerful Influence over young Minds, and especially those of their Parents; in vain are they solicitous for a good Education for their Children, if they themselves set before them Examples of Impiety and Profaneness, or of any Sort of Vice whatsoever.

Vth and Lastly, A *serious, virtuous* and *industrious* Course of Life being first provided for, it is further the Design of this College, to instruct and perfect the Youth in the learned Languages, and in the Arts of *Reasoning* exactly, of *Writing* correctly, and *Speaking* eloquently: And in the Arts of *Numbering* and *Measuring,* of *Surveying* and *Navigation,* of *Geography* and *History,* of *Husbandry, Commerce* and *Government;* and in the Knowledge of *all Nature* in the *Heavens* above us, and in the *Air, Water* and *Earth* around us, and the various Kinds of *Meteors, Stones, Mines* and *Minerals, Plants* and *Animals,* and of every Thing *useful* for the Comfort, the Convenience, and Elegance of Life, in the chief *Manufactures* relating to any of these Things—And finally, to lead them from the Study of Nature, to the Knowledge of themselves, and of the God of Nature, and their Duty to him, themselves, and one another; and every Thing that can contribute to their Happiness both here and hereafter.

Thus much, *Gentlemen,* it is thought proper to advertise you of, concerning the nature of Design of this College. And I pray God, it may be attended with all the Success you can wish, for the best Good of the rising Generations; to which, while I continue here, I shall willingly contribute my Endeavours to the utmost of my Power; who am,

Your real friend
and most humble Servant,
SAMUEL JOHNSON.

N.B. The Charge of the Tuition is establish'd by the Trustees to be only *Twenty-five Shillings* for each Quarter.

Lottery for King's College in New York, 1754 *

By a Law passed in November last, a public Lottery is directed for a further Provision towards founding a College for the Advancement of Learning within this Colony, to consist of 5000 Tickets, at Thirty Shillings each, 832 of which to be fortunate, viz.

Number of Prizes		Value of each		Total Value
1	of	£ 1000	is	£ 1000
1	of	500	is	500
1	of	300	is	300
1	of	200	is	200
3	of	100	are	300
15	of	50	are	750
15	of	25	are	375
20	of	10	are	200
775	of	5	are	3875

832 Prizes $\begin{cases} \text{5000 Tickets at Thirty} \\ \text{Shillings each, makes} \end{cases}$ £7500
4168 Blanks

15 per Cent. to be deducted from the Prizes. The Drawing was ordered to commence on the first Tuesday in June following; but as it was likely a considerable quantity of Tickets would then remain unsold, a further Provision was made to prolong the Time of Drawing, 'till the Remainder were sold; which are to be had at the Dwelling-houses of the Managers appointed, Abraham Van Wyck & Abraham Lynsen; and as the greatest Part are disposed of, and the Sale continuing daily, the Managers are in Hopes soon to be ready for drawing, of which the Public will have timely Notice, as directed in said Act.

* *Ibid.,* June 3, 1754.

The College of William and Mary Confers Honorary Degree of Master of Arts on Benjamin Franklin, 1756 *

At a meeting of ye President & Masters of W. & M. College,
Present.

Ye Revd T. Dawson, A.M., president; T. Robinson, A.M., W. Preston, A.M., R. Graham, A.M., J. Camm, A.M., and Em. Jones, A.B.

Ys Day, Ben. Franklin, Esquire, favored ye Society with his company, and had ye Degree of A.M. conferred upon him by ye Revd T. Dawson, A.M. president to wm he was in publick presented by the Revd W. Preston, A.M. A Copy of ye Diploma:

Praeses et Magistri Collegii Guil: & Mar: in Virginia omnibus, ad quos hoc praesens Scriptum pervenerit, salutem in Domino Septiternam.

Quum in Charta Regia nobis concessum & confirmatum fuit, ut eos qui se Literis & Studiis praecipue ornarunt, gradibus Academicis decoremus; Quum volumus in hujus modi Honorem imprimis Evehi virum inclytissimum quo nobis & Juventuti Virginiensi Exemplum valde egregium proponamus; Quumque Benjaminum Franklin Armigerum nobis commendarunt Gradus Artium Magistri a diversis Collegiis Americanis in eum collatus, quinetiam Honores a Rege Christianissimo, a regia Scientarum apud Parisios Academia, a regia Societate Londinensi ei accumulati, nec non ejusdem Celebritas & Gloria, ob miras in Philosophia naturali Patefactiones excogitatas, per totam Literarum Rempublicam evulgatae; idcirco in frequenti Senatu Die Secundo mensis Aprilis Anno Domini 1756 habito, conspirantibus omnibus Suffragiis, praefatum Benjaminum Franklin Armigerum, virum omni Laude dignum, Artium magistrum renunciavimus & constituimus. In cujus Rei Testimonium huic Diplomati Sigillum Collegii Gulielmi & Mariae commune apponi fecimus.

Dat Die men: & An: praedict:

THOMAS DAWSON, *President.*

The Overseers of Harvard Remonstrate Against Another College in Massachusetts, 1762 †

The tender concern on many occasions expressed by the respectable gentlemen of the Deputation of Dissenters in England, for the general interests of their brethren on this side the water, leaves us no room to apprehend that this address will be unfavorably received; or that the subject of it will not engage some share of their attention.

You in particular, Sir, will permit us to hope for your favor. What we

---

* *William and Mary College Quarterly Historical Papers,* II, pp. 208-09.

† Quincy, *op. cit.,* II, pp. 475-78. A more lengthy protest appears on pp. 464-75. This is an early example of the fear of competition, which remains one of deadliest afflictions in higher education in this country, perhaps outranking imitativeness with which it is so closely related.

are to inform you of at present, is, that an attempt was made about two years ago, and we find is now prosecuting, for establishing a new college in this Province; which, if carried into execution, will not only greatly prejudice Harvard College, but be a real disservice to literature in New England.

We shall here give a short detail of the rise and progress of this attempt; and what we apprehend is now in hand for bringing it to effect.

A number of persons in one of the western counties of the Province, viz. the County of Hampshire, petitioned the General Court in January, 1762, for a charter for the establishing a college in that county.

The petition was so far supported as to allow the petitioners to bring a bill for that purpose; and it was first presented to the Council, who assigned a time to act upon it, at the distance of several days from its presentment, in order that the board should be as full as might be, and that the members of it might have sufficient opportunity to consider it thoroughly. At the time assigned, the bill was taken in hand, and a long debate had thereon; and, it appearing to the board, that the establishment of another college would not only prejudice Harvard College, but be a great detriment to the learning of the Province, they rejected the bill by a great majority. The next day the bill was sent for by the House of Representatives; among whom all the members belonging to the western counties were zealous advocates for the bill; and a vote in favor of it passed by a small majority. Many of the House (who in reality were against the bill, and who relied upon the Council for its rejection,) voted for it notwithstanding, in order to bring the members of the said western counties to favor an application made by the Overseers of Harvard College to the General Court, for building a new Hall at Cambridge, which at that time was under consideration of the House; and many of the House were influenced by its being declared, that the intended college would not occasion any public charge to the government, and a clause of that kind, to make it the more palatable, was inserted in the bill. As soon as it had passed the House, it was sent to the Council for concurrence. A time was assigned to take the bill again into consideration; and, the same reasons still influencing, it was again rejected. The advocates of the bill, before they knew the fate of it, had given out, that in case they failed in it, they should be able to accomplish their design in another way. And, when the bill was finally rejected, some of them said they had the promise of a charter from Governor Bernard; and a few days after his Excellency acquainted the Council, that, upon application made to him, he had signed a charter for establishing a college in the County of Hampshire. Alarmed at this, a number of the Overseers of Harvard College waited upon the Governor, to request that he would not grant the charter till the Overseers should have a meeting upon that important affair. His Excellency having granted the request, a meeting was called, and held, at which the Governor was present; and, after a large debate, a vote was passed, requesting that his Excellency would not grant said charter. At the same meeting, on the Governor's declaring that he should put this affair of the charter out of his own hands, to be determined upon by those who had authority to direct him, and on his proposing that a committee should be appointed to draw up the reasons against the granting the charter (which reasons he said, should accompany his representation of the affair to the ministry), a committee was appointed for that purpose, who were to make report at the next meeting of the Overseers. Upon this, the meeting was adjourned, and at the adjournment, the reasons were reported, and unanimously accepted; and a committee appointed to wait upon the Governor with a fair draft of them.

Thus have we given you a short account of every thing material that has passed here upon the affair of the charter;[1] and, as it is probable, that further measures have been or will be taken to obtain a charter, viz. by procuring an order from his Majesty to the Governor here, to grant said charter, (in which case, the Governor has said, it would not be in his power to refuse it,) we think it our indispensable duty, in pursuance of a vote of the Overseers aforesaid, to take every lawful method to prevent the grant of the said charter; or for any charter for establishing another college in this Province: and the first and most likely method that occurred to us (and which we are persuaded will prove effectual, if they will please to afford their influence in the affair,) was to apply to the President and Board of Deputation aforesaid.

And in order that they may be informed of the reasons, upon which the opposition to such a charter is grounded, we take the liberty to send you herewith a copy of the reasons presented to Governor Bernard, referred to above. And we cannot but hope they will have weight enough with you, Sir, and the other gentlemen of the Deputation, to engage you to use your joint interest with the ministry and the several public boards, that no such charter be granted by his Majesty, nor any order or mandamus sent to Governor Bernard for granting such an one.

You will observe, that, in the reasons aforesaid, it is not questioned (though it is hinted that it might be) whether the Governor had a power of granting such a charter: yet, as there seems to be great room to question that power, not only as it respects the particular charter mentioned, but charters in general, we have procured the opinion of a gentleman of the law on that subject, and send it herewith; by which you will see what ground there is for our present opinion, that the Governor has no such power. But whether he has or can have such a power or not; or whether it reside indelegably in the King or not; or whether the Province charter, granted by King William and Queen Mary, in 1691, has abridged the

---

[1] That the governors of Harvard College neglect to propagate orthodox principles of religion and vital piety, and that a principal end proposed in founding another seminary is to remedy this supposed defect in the present method of education,—this insinuation we think very injurious, not only to the immediate governors and Corporation of our College, but to the board of Overseers.

Crown (so far as relates to the Province) of such a power or not; it is of great importance, that no such charter should be granted. For though the charter, if obtained, should finally prove not good in law, yet for a while, and perhaps a considerable while too, it would have effect; and such effect as might gain a solid establishment for the intended college: which would be equally hurtful, whether the charter was originally good in law, or not. As the Overseers aforesaid, and, indeed, all well-wishers to literature in the Province, (except those who are immediately concerned in the intended new college,) have this matter greatly at heart; and as the prevention of the charter aforesaid may prevent an establishment that will be greatly prejudicial to the interests of learning here, we persuade ourselves, Sir, that the President and the other worthy gentlemen of the Deputation, from their known regard to the welfare of New England, will do their endeavour to put an effectual stop to the granting of such a charter.

In the name of the Overseers of Harvard College, we are, with the most profound respect for the President and members of the Deputation, Sir,

Your most obedient humble servants.

At a meeting of the Overseers of Harvard College, by adjournment, at the Council Chamber in Boston, April 1st, 1762.

Voted, That Captain Erving, General Brattle, Mr. Bowdoin, Mr. Treasurer, Dr. Chauncy, Dr. Mayhew, Mr. Pemberton, Mr. Eliot, and Mr. Cooper, be a committee to guard against the influence of any application that may be made at home by the Hampshire petitioners, for a charter from home or elsewhere, in such ways as they may judge most effectual; particularly by transmitting to some suitable person or persons at home, a copy of the reasons presented to his Excellency, against the expediency of his granting such a charter.

Thomas Jefferson to John Page About Conditions at the College of William and Mary, 1763 *

Affairs at W. and M. are in the greatest confusion. Walker, M'Clurg and Wat Jones are expelled *pro tempore,* or, as Horrox softens it, rusticated † for a month. Lewis Burwell, Warner Lewis, and one Thompson have fled to escape flagellation. . . .

George Washington Receives the Degree of LL.D. from Harvard, 1776 ‡

April 3d, 1776.—At a meeting of the President and Fellows at Watertown, *Voted,* that the following Diploma be presented to his Excellency

* Ford, *The Writings of Thomas Jefferson,* I, p. 353.

† Rustication was an old form of collegiate discipline or punishment under which some students delinquent in their academic duties were required to leave the campus and go to the country, sometimes perhaps with a tutor, to catch up with their work.

‡ Quincy, *op. cit.,* II, pp. 506-07.

General Washington, as an expression of the gratitude of this College for his eminent services in the cause of his country and to this Society.

Senatus Academiae Cantabrigiensis in Nov-Anglia omnibus in Christo fidelibus, ad quos literae praesentes pervenerint, salutem in Domino sempiternam.

Cum eum in finem Gradus Academici instituti fuerint, ut Viri scientia, sapientia, et virtute insignes, qui de De literaria et de Re Publica optime meruerint, honoribus hisce laureatis remunerarentur; maxime decet ut honore tali afficiatur Vir illustrissimus Georgius Washington, Armiger, Exercitus Coloniarum in America Foederatarum Imperator praeclarus, cujus scientia et amor patriae undique patent: qui, propter eximias virtutes tam civiles quam militares, primum, a civibus suis Legatus electus, in Consessu celeberrimo Americano de Libertate, ad extremum periclitata, et de Salute publica, fideliter et peritissime consuluit; deinde, postulante Patria, sedem in Virginia amoenissimam et res proprias perlubenter reliquit, ut per omnes castrorum labores et pericula, nulla mercede accepta, Nov-Angliam ab armis Britannorum iniquis et crudelibus liberaret, et Colonias caeteras tuereter; et qui, sub Auspiciis Divinis maxime spectandis, ab Urbe Bostonia, per undecim menses clausa, munita, et plusquam septem millium militum praesidio firmata, naves et copias hostium in fugam praecipitem et probrosam deturbavit; adeo ut cives, plurmis duritiis et saevitiis oppressi, tandem salvi laetentur, villae vicinae quiescant, atque sedibus suis Academia nostra restituatur.

Sciatis igitur, quod nos Praeses et Socii Collegii Harvardini in Cantabrigia Nov-Anglorum (consentientibus Honorandis admodum et reverendis Academiae nostrae Inspectoribus) Dominum supradictum, summo honore dignum, Georgium Washington, Doctorem Utriusque Juris, tum Naturae et Gentium, tum Civilis, statuimus et creavimus, eique simul dedimus et concessimus omnia jura, privilegia, et honores ad istum gradum pertinentia.

In cujus rei testimonium nos, communi sigillo Universitatis hisce literis affixo, chirographa apposuimus die terito Aprilis, anno salutis millesimo septingentesimo septuagesimo sexto.

SAMUEL LANGDON, S. T. D., *Praeses.*
NATHANIEL APPLETON, S. T. D.,
JOHANNES WINTHROP, LL. D., *Mat. et Phil. P. Hol.,*
(L. S.) ANDREAS ELIOT, S. T. D.,   } *Socii.*
SAMUEL COOPER, S. T. D.,
JOHANNES WADSWORTH, *Log. et Eth. Praec.,*
——————————, *Thesaurar.*

«« II »»

TOWARD EDUCATIONAL
INDEPENDENCE

«««««««««««««««««««««««««««««««««««««»»»»»»»»»»»»»»»»»»»»»»»»»»»»»»»

Opposition to the cultural and educational dependence of this country upon Europe began as early as 1699, when a student at the College of William and Mary protested against the practice of sending Virginians to Europe for their education, and increased as the warnings of the Revolution became more and more numerous. The documents that follow deal with this subject and with the proposals for a national university and for the removal of the College of Geneva to Virginia; the movement for religious freedom and the separation of the church and state; early constitutional provisions for education; and the movement to give protection to literary property. For additional documents on these subjects see Edgar W. Knight, *A Documentary History of Education in the South Before 1860* (Chapel Hill, University of North Carolina Press, 1950), II, pp. 1-134.

« 1 »

Opposition to the Education of
Americans in Europe

«««««««««««««««««««««««««««««««««‹›»»»»»»»»»»»»»»»»»»»»»»»»»»»»»»»»»

A Benefit Expected from Benjamin Franklin's Academy
in Philadelphia, 1750 *

That the Youth of Pensilvania may have an opportunity of receiving a good Education at home, and be under no necessity of going abroad for it; Whereby not only considerable Expense may be saved to the Country, but a stricter Eye may be had over their morals by their Friends and Relations.

Thomas Jefferson on Education in Europe, 1785 †

PARIS, October 15, 1785.

... But why send an American youth to Europe for education? What are the objects of an useful American education? Classical knowledge, modern languages, chiefly French, Spanish and Italian; Mathematics, Natural philosophy, Natural history, Civil history, and Ethics. In Natural philosophy, I mean to include Chemistry and Agriculture, and in Natural history, to include Botany, as well as the other branches of those departments. It is true that the habit of speaking the modern languages cannot be so well acquired in America; but every other article can be as well acquired at William and Mary College, as at any place in Europe. When college education is done with, and a young man is to prepare himself for public life, he must cast his eyes (for America) either on Law or Physics. For the former, where can he apply so advantageously as to Mr. Wythe? For the latter, he must come to Europe: the medical class of students, therefore, is the only one which need come to Europe. To enumerate them all would require a volume. I will select a few. If he goes to England, he learns drinking, horse racing and boxing. These are the peculiarities of English education. The

---

* Minutes of the Common Council of Philadelphia, June 31, 1750, when that body made a donation to the academy. Given in F. N. Thorpe, *Benjamin Franklin and the University of Pennsylvania* (Washington, Bureau of Education, Circular of Information No. 2, 1892), p. 245.
† Letter to J. Bannister, Jr. Philip S. Foner, *Basic Writings of Thomas Jefferson*, pp. 532-33.

following circumstances are common to education in that and the other countries of Europe. He acquires a fondness for European luxury and dissipation, and a contempt for the simplicity of his own country; he is fascinated with the privileges of the European aristocrats, and sees, with abhorrence, the lovely equality which the poor enjoy with the rich, in his own country; he contracts a partiality for aristocracy or monarchy; he forms foreign friendships which will never be useful to him, and loses the seasons of life for forming, in his own country, those friendships which, of all others, are the most faithful and permanent; he is led, by the strongest of all human passions, into a spirit for female intrigue, destructive of his own and others' happiness, or a passion for whores, destructive of his health, and, in both cases, learns to consider fidelity to the marriage bed as an ungentlemanly practice, and inconsistent with happiness; he recollects the voluptary dress and arts of the European women, and pities and despises the chaste affections and simplicity of those of his own country; he retains, through life, a fond recollection, and a hankering after those places, which were the scenes of his first pleasures and of his first connections; he returns to his own country, a foreigner, unacquainted with the practices of domestic economy, necessary to preserve him from ruin, speaking and writing his native tongue as a foreigner, and therefore, unqualified to obtain those distinctions, which eloquence of the pen and tongue ensures in a free country; for I would observe to you, that what is called style in writing or speaking is formed very early in life, while the imagination is warm, and impressions are permanent. I am of opinion, that there never was an instance of a man's writing or speaking his native tongue with elegance, who passed from fifteen to twenty years of age out of the country where it was spoken. Thus, no instance exists of a person's writing two languages perfectly. That will always appear to be his native language, which was most familiar to him in his youth. It appears to me, then, that an American, coming to Europe for education, loses in his knowledge, in his morals, in his health, in his habits, and in his happiness. I had entertained only doubts on this head before I came to Europe: what I see and hear, since I came here, proves more than I had even suspected. Cast your eye over America: who are the men of most learning, of most eloquence, most beloved by their countrymen and most trusted and promoted by them? They are those who have been educated among them, and whose manners, morals, and habits are perfectly homogeneous with those of the country.

Did you expect by so short a question, to draw such a sermon on yourself? I dare say you did not. But the consequences of foreign education are alarming to me as an American. I sin, therefore, through zeal, whenever I enter on the subject.

The Legislature of Georgia Makes Aliens of Georgians
Who Study in Europe, 1785 *

AND BE IT ENACTED, by the authority aforesaid that if any Person or persons under the age of sixteen years shall after the passing of this Act be sent abroad without the limits of the United States and reside there three years for the purpose of receiving an education under a foreign power. Such person or persons after their return to this State shall for three Years be considered and treated as aliens in so far as not to be eligible to a Seat in the Legislature or Executive authority or to hold any office civil or military in the State for that term and so in proportion for any greater number of years as he or they shall be absent as aforesaid, but shall not be injured or disqualified in any other respect.

Noah Webster Criticizes the Education of Americans
in Europe, 1788 †

. . . Before I quit this subject, I beg leave to make some remarks on a practice which appears to be attended with important consequences; I mean that of sending boys to Europe for an education, or sending to Europe for teachers. That this was right before the revolution will not be disputed; at least so far as national attachments were concerned; but the propriety of it ceased with our political relation to Great Britain.

In the first place, our honor as an independent nation is concerned in the establishment of literary institutions, adequate to all our own purposes; without sending our youth abroad, or depending on other nations for books and instructors. It is very little to the reputation of America to have it said abroad, that after the heroic achievements of the late war, this independent people are obliged to send to Europe for men and books to teach their children A B C.

But in another point of view, a foreign education is directly opposite to our political interests and ought to be discountenanced, if not prohibited.

Every person of common observation will grant, that most men prefer the manners and the government of that country where they are educated. Let ten American youths be sent, each to a different European kingdom, and live there from the age of twelve to twenty, & each will give the preference to the country where he has resided.

The period from twelve to twenty is the most important in life. The impressions made before that period are commonly effaced; those that are made during that period *always* remain for many years, and *generally* thro' life.

* Allen D. Candler (Comp.), *The Colonial Records of the State of Georgia*, XIX, Part II, p. 378.
† *The American Magazine*, May, 1788, pp. 370-73.

Ninety-nine persons of a hundred, who pass that period in England or France, will prefer the people, their manners, their laws, and their government to those of their native country. Such attachments are injurious, both to the happiness of the men, and to the political interests of their own country. As to private happiness, it is universally known how much pain a man suffers by a change of habits in living. The customs of Europe are and ought to be different from ours; but when a man has been bred in one country, his attachments to its manners make them in a great measure, necessary to his happiness; on changing his residence, he must therefore break his former habits, which is always a painful sacrifice; or the discordance between the manners of his own country and his habits, must give him incessant uneasiness; or he must introduce, into a circle of his friends, the manners in which he was educated. All these consequences may follow at the same time, and the last, which is inevitable, is a public injury. The refinement of manners in every country should keep pace exactly with the increase of its wealth—and perhaps the greatest evil American now feels is, an improvement of taste and manners which its wealth cannot support.

A foreign education is the very source of this evil—it gives young gentlemen of fortune a relish for manners and amusements which are not suited to this country; which, however, when introduced by this class of people, will always become fashionable.

But a corruption of manners is not the sole objection to a foreign education; An attachment to a *foreign* government, or rather a want of attachment to our *own,* is the natural effect of a residence abroad, during the period of youth. It is recorded of one of the Greek cities, that in a treaty with their conquerors, it was required that they should give a certain number of *male children* as hostages for the fulfilment of their engagements. The Greeks absolutely refused, on the principle that these children would imbibe the ideas and embrace the manners of foreigners, or lose their love for their own country: But they offered the same number of *old* men, without hesitation. This anecdote is full of good sense. A man should always form his habits and attachments in the country where he is to reside for life. When these habits are formed, young men may travel without danger of losing their patriotism. A boy who lives in England from twelve to twenty, will be an *Englishman* in his manners and his feelings; but let him remain at home till he is twenty, and form his attachments, he may then be several years abroad, and still be an *American.*[1] There may be exceptions to this observation; but living examples may be mentioned, to prove the truth of the general principle here advanced, respecting the influence of habit.

It may be said that foreign universities furnish much better opportunities of improvement in the sciences than the American. This may be true, and

[1] Cicero was twenty-eight years old when he left Italy to travel into Greece and Asia. "He did not stir abroad," sayd Dr. Middleton, "till he had completed his education at home; for nothing can be more pernicious to a nation, than the necessity of a foreign one." Life of Cicero—Vol. 1, p. 48.

yet will not justify the practice of sending young lads from their own country. There are some branches of science which may be studied to much greater advantage in Europe than in America, particularly chymistry. When these are to be acquired, young gentlemen ought to spare no pains to attend the best professors. It may, therefore, be useful, in some cases, for students to cross the atlantic to *complete* a course of studies; but it is not necessary for them to go early in life, nor to continue a long time. Such instances need not be frequent even now; and the necessity for them will diminish in proportion to the future advancement of literature in America.

It is, however, much questioned whether, in the ordinary course a study, a young man can enjoy greater advantages in Europe than in America. Experience inclines me to raise a doubt, whether the danger to which a youth must be exposed among the sons of dissipation abroad, will not turn the scale in favor of our American colleges. Certain it is, that four fifths of the great literary characters in America never crossed the Atlantic.

But if our universities and schools are not so good as the English or Scotch, it is the business of our rulers to improve them—not to endow them merely; for endowments alone will never make a flourishing seminary—but to furnish them with professors of the first abilities and most assiduous application, and with a complete apparatus for establishing theories by experiments. Nature has been profuse to the Americans, in genius, and in the advantages of climate and soil. If this country, therefore, should long be indebted to Europe for opportunities of acquiring any branch of science in perfection, it must be by means of a criminal neglect of its inhabitants.

The difference in the nature of the American and European governments, is another objection to a foreign education. Men form modes of reasoning or habits of thinking on political subjects, in the country where they are bred—these modes of reasoning may be founded on fact in all countries—but the same principles will not apply in all governments, because of the infinite variety of national opinions and habits. Before a man can be a good Legislator, he must be intimately acquainted with the temper of the people to be governed. No man can be thus acquainted with a people, without residing amongst them and mingling with all companies. For want of this acquaintance, a Turgot and a Price * may reason most absurdly upon the constitutions of the American states; and when any person has been long accustomed to believe in the propriety or impropriety of certain maxims or regulations of government, it is very difficult to change his opinions, or to persuade him to adapt this reasoning to new and different circumstances . . .

It is therefore of infinite importance that those who direct the councils

* Richard Price (1723-1791), English political and moral philosopher, was a close friend of Benjamin Franklin, and "corresponded with Turgot." In 1776 Price published a pamphlet with the title "Observations on Civil Liberty and Justice and Policy of the War with America."

of a nation, should be educated in that nation. Not that they should restrict their personal acquaintance to their own country, but their first ideas, attachments and habits should be acquired in the country which they are to govern and defend. When a knowledge of their own country is obtained, and an attachment to its laws and interests deeply fixed in their hearts, then young gentlemen may travel with infinite advantage and perfect safety. I wish not therefore to discourage travelling, but, if possible, to render it more useful to individuals and to the community. My meaning is, that *men* should travel, and not *boys.*

But it is time for the Americans to change their usual route, and travel thro a country which they never think of, or think beneath their notice.— I mean the United States.

While these States were a part of the British Empire, our interest, our feelings, were those of English men—our dependence led us to respect and imitate their manners—and to look up to them for our opinions. We little thought of any national interest in America—and while our commerce and government were in the hands of our parent country, and we had no common interest, we little thought of improving our acquaintance with each other or of removing prejudices, and reconciling the discordant feelings of the inhabitants of the different Provinces. But independence and union render it necessary that the citizens of different States should know each others characters and circumstances—that all jealousies should be removed —that mutual respect and confidence should succeed—and a harmony of views and interests be cultivated by a friendly intercourse. . . .

Americans, unshackle your minds, and act like independent beings. You have been children long enough, subject to the control, and subservient to the interest of a haughty parent. You have now an interest of your own to augment and defend—you have an empire to raise and support by your exertions—and a national character to establish and extend by your wisdom and virtues. To effect these great objects, it is necessary to frame a liberal plan of policy, and to build it on a broad system of education. Before this system can be formed and embraced, the Americans must *believe* and *act* from the belief, that it is dishonorable to waste life in mimicking the follies of other nations, and basking in the sunshine of foreign glory.

Resolution of the Virginia House of Delegates on Education in Europe, December 1, 1795 *

Whereas the migration of American youth to foreign countries, for the completion of their education, exposes them to the danger of imbibing

* *Journal of the House of Delegates, of the Commonwealth of Virginia,* 1795, pp. 63-64. This resolution appears also in Sparks, *The Writings of George Washington,* XI, pp. 24-25, note.

political prejudices disadvantageous to their own republican forms of government, and ought therefore to be rendered unnecessary and avoided.

1. *Resolved,* That the plan contemplated for erecting an University at the Federal City where the youth of the several states may be assembled, and their course of education finished, deserves the countenance and support of each state.

George Washington on Education in Europe, 1795 *

It is with indescribable regret, that I have seen the youth of the United States migrating to foreign countries, in order to acquire the higher branches of erudition, and to obtain a knowledge of the Sciences. Altho' it would be injustice to many to pronounce the certainty of their imbibing maxims, not congenial with republicanism; it must nevertheless be admitted, that a serious danger is encountered, by sending abroad among other political systems those, who have not well learned the value of their own.

The time is therefore come, when a plan of Universal education ought to be adopted in the United States. . . .

* John C. Fitzpatrick (Ed.), *The Writings of George Washington* (Washington, Government Printing Office, 1940), Vol. 34, pp. 149-50.

« 2 »

Early Proposals for a National University and for the Removal of the College of Geneva to Virginia

《《《《《《《《《《《《《《《《《《《《《《《《《《《《《《《《《《《《《》》》》》》》》》》》》》》》》》》》》》》》》》》》》》》

Samuel Blodget's Account of a Conversation with General Washington on a National University, 1775 *

As the most minute circumstances are sometimes interesting for their relation to great events,† we relate the first we ever heard of a national

---

* Samuel Blodget, *Economica: A Statistical Manual for the United States* (Washington, 1806), pp. 22-23; Appendix, i, iii-x. See also G. Brown Goode, "The Origin of the National Scientific and Educational Institutions of the United States," in *Papers of the American Historical Association,* IV (April, 1890), p. 19, footnote.

† Beginning in the latter part of the eighteenth and continuing into the present century many proposals were made for a national university. Since 1787 when the first definite proposal for such an institution was made "there has been with the exception of one period, scarcely a year that has failed to bring forth articles, proposals, or bills pertaining to a national university." But the story of these many attempts is not continuous. During some periods the idea of a national university "seems to have been quite dormant," for example, from the close of the administration of John Quincy Adams in 1829 to the meeting of the National Educational Association in 1869. During those years "no president recommended the establishment of a national university; no congressman introduced a bill to effect it; and no leader of national importance sponsored the idea," which was not, however, wholly dead. (Edgar B. Wesley, *Proposed: The University of the United States* [Minneapolis, University of Minnesota Press, 1936], pp. v, 3, 13. See also James W. Hill, "The Movement to Establish a National University Prior to 1860: A Documentary History" [typescript master's thesis at the University of North Carolina, 1946].) From 1872 to 1933 sixty bills for the establishment of a national university were introduced into Congress, about two-thirds of them in the Senate. At the meeting of the National Educational Association in 1873 President Charles W. Eliot of Harvard voiced vigorous opposition to the proposal of a Senate bill then before Congress and in 1874 President Andrew D. White of Cornell University made an energetic speech for a national university and sharply answered President Eliot. Apparently no bill has been introduced in Congress on the subject since 1936, but in April of 1948 a bill was introduced to create an international university.

The arguments for a national university included: the necessity for educating American youth at home; for the fostering of a common spirit of nationalism; for the promotion of scholarship and research; for coöperation with other institutions of higher learning and for raising their standards. The arguments against such an institution included the lack of necessity for it; the impracticability for people distant from Washington to go there for their education; institutions already established would meet the needs of the people; higher education was not a responsibility of the federal government; the high cost of such an institution; lack of authority by Congress to establish a national university; and the unfairness for a national university to be in competition with higher educational institutions already in existence.

university: it was in the camp at Cambridge, in October 1775, when major William Blodget went to the quarters of general *Washington,* to complain of the ruinous state of the colleges, from the conduct of the militia quartered therein. The writer of this being in company with his friend and relation, and hearing general Greene join in lamenting the then ruinous state of the eldest seminary of Massachusetts, observed, *merely to console the company of friends,* that to make amends for these injuries, after our war, he hoped, we should erect a noble national university, at which the youth of all the world might be proud to receive instruction. What was thus pleasantly said, Washington immediately replied to, with that inimitably expressive and truly interesting look, for which he was sometimes so remarkable: *"Young man you are a prophet! inspired to speak, what I feel confident will one day be realized."* He then detailed to the company his impressions, that all North America would one day become united; he said, that a colonel Byrd, of Virginia, he believed, was the first man who had pointed out the best central seat, *near to the present spot,* or about the falls of Potomack. General Washington further said, that a Mr. Evans had expressed the same opinion, with many other gentlemen, who from a cursory view of a chart of North America, received this natural and truly correct impression. The look of general Washington, the energy of his mind, his noble and irresistable eloquence, all conspired, so far to impress *the writer* with these subjects, that if ever he should unfortunately become insane, it will be from his anxiety for the *federal city* and National University. . . .

The Legislature of Virginia Vests in George Washington Shares of Stock in Navigation Companies, 1784 *

I. WHEREAS it is the desire of the representatives of this commonwealth to embrace every suitable occasion of testifying their sense of the unexampled merits of George Washington, esquire, towards his country; and it is their wish in particular that those great works for its improvement, which, both as springing from the liberty which he has been so instrumental in establishing, and as encouraged by his patronage, will be durable monuments of his glory, may be made monuments also of the gratitude of his country:

II. *Be it enacted by the General Assembly,* That the treasurer be directed, in addition to the subscriptions he is already authorized to make to the respective undertakers for opening the navigations of Potowmack

---

* Hening, *Statutes at Large of Virginia,* XI, pp. 525-26. Washington was reluctant to accept the shares for his own personal profit and this act was amended and read in part: "That the said shares with the tolls and profits hereafter accruing therefrom, shall stand appropriated to such objects of a public nature, in such manner, and under such distributions, as the said George Washington, esq. by deed during his life, or by his last will and testament, shall direct and appoint." *Ibid.,* pp. 42-44.

and James rivers, to subscribe to the amount of fifty shares to the former, and a hundred shares to the latter, to be paid in like manner with the subscriptions above-mentioned; and that the shares so subscribed, be, and the same are hereby vested in George Washington, esq. his heirs and assigns, forever, in as effectual a manner as if the subscriptions had been made by himself or by his attorney.

George Washington to John Adams on the Removal of the College of Geneva to Virginia, 1794 *

I have not been able to give the papers herewith enclosed more than a hasty reading, returning them without delay, that you may offer the perusal of them to whomsoever you shall think proper. The picture, drawn in them, of the Genevese is really interesting and affecting. The proposition of transplanting the members entire of the university of that place to America, with the requisition of means to establish the same, and to be accompanied by a considerable emigration, is important, requiring more consideration than under the circumstances of the moment I am able to bestow upon it.

That a national university in this country is a thing to be desired, has always been my decided opinion; and the appropriation of ground and funds for it in the Federal City has long been contemplated and talked of; but how far matured, or how far the transporting of an entire seminary of foreigners, who may not understand our language, can be assimilated therein, is more than I am prepared to give an opinion upon; or, indeed, how far funds in either case are attainable.

My opinion, with respect to emigration, is, that except of useful mechanics, and some particular descriptions of men or professions, there is no need of encouragement; while the policy or advantage of its taking place in a body (I mean the settling of them in a body) may be much questioned; for by so doing they retain the language, habits, and principles, good or bad, which they bring with them. Whereas, by an intermixture with our people, they or their descendants get assimilated to our customs, measures, and laws; in a word, soon become one people.

I shall, at any leisure hour after the session is fairly opened, take pleasure in a full and free conversation with you on this subject.

George Washington to the Commissioners of the Federal District on the National University, 1795 †

A plan for the establishment of a university in the Federal city has frequently been the subject of conversation; but in what manner it is proposed to commence this important institution, on how extensive a scale, the

---

* Jared Sparks (Ed.), The Writings of George Washington, XI, pp. 1-2.
† Ibid., pp. 14-16.

means by which it is to be effected, how it is to be supported, or what progress is made in it, are matters altogether unknown to me. It has always been a source of serious reflection and sincere regret with me that the youth of the United States should be sent to foreign countries for the purpose of education. Although there are doubtless many, under these circumstances, who escape the danger of contracting principles unfavorable to republican government, yet we ought to deprecate the hazard attending ardent and susceptible minds, from being too strongly and too early prepossessed in favor of other political systems before they are capable of appreciating their own.

For this reason I have greatly wished to see a plan adopted by which the arts, sciences, and belles-lettres could be taught in their fullest extent, thereby embracing all the advantages of European tuition, with the means of acquiring the liberal knowledge which is necessary to qualify our citizens for the exigencies of public as well as private life; and (which with me is a consideration of great magnitude) by assembling the youth from the different parts of this rising Republic, contributing from their intercourse and interchange of information to the removal of prejudices which might perhaps sometimes arise from local circumstances.

The Federal city, from its centrality and the advantages which in other respects it must have over any other place in the United States, ought to be preferred as a proper site for such a university. And if a plan can be adopted upon a scale as extensive as I have described, and the execution of it should commence under favorable auspices in a reasonable time, with a fair prospect of success, I will grant in perpetuity 50 shares in the navigation of the Potomac River towards the endowment of it.

What annuity will arise from these 50 shares when the navigation is in full operation can at this time be only conjectured; and those who are acquainted with it can form as good a judgment as myself.

As the design of this university has assumed no form with which I am acquainted, and as I am equally ignorant who the persons are who have taken or are disposed to take the maturing of the plan upon themselves, I have been at a loss to whom I should make this communication of my intentions. If the commissioners of the Federal city have any particular agency in bringing the matter forward, then the information which I now give to them is in its proper course. If, on the other hand, they have no more to do in it than others who may be desirous of seeing so important a measure carried into effect, they will be so good as to excuse my using them as the medium for disclosing these my intentions; because it appears necessary that the funds for the establishment and support of the institution should be known to the promoters of it, and I see no mode more eligible for announcing my purpose. . . .

George Washington to Congress on a National University, 1796 *

I have heretofore proposed to the consideration of Congress the expediency of establishing a National University, and also a Military Academy. The desirability of both these institutions has so constantly increased with every new view I have taken of the subject, that I cannot omit the opportunity of one for all recalling your attention to them.

The assembly to which I address myself, is too enlightened not to be fully sensible how much a flourishing state of the arts and sciences contributes to national prosperity and reputation. True it is, that our country, much to its honor, contains many seminaries of learning highly respectable and useful; but the funds upon which they rest are too narrow to command the ablest professors, in the different departments of liberal knowledge, for the institution contemplated, though they would be excellent auxiliaries.

Amongst the motives to such an institution, the assimilation of the principles, opinions, and manners of our countrymen, by the common education of a portion of our youth from every quarter, well deserves attention. The more homogeneous our citizens can be made in these particulars, the greater will be our prospect of permanent union; and a primary object of such a national institution should be, the education of our youth in the science of government. In a republic, what species of knowledge can be equally important, and what duty more pressing on its legislature, than to patronize a plan for communicating it to those, who are to be the future guardians of the liberties of the country?

The institution of a military academy is also recommended by cogent reasons. However pacific the general policy of a nation may be, it ought never to be without an adequate stock of military knowledge for emergencies. The first would impair the energy of its character, and both would hazard its safety, or expose it to greater evils when war could not be avoided. Besides that war might often not depend upon its own choice. In proportion as the observance of pacific maxims might exempt a nation from the necessity of practising the rules of the military art, ought to be its care in preserving and transmitting, by proper establishments, the knowledge of that art. Whatever argument may be drawn from particular examples, superficially viewed, a thorough examination of the subject will evince, that the art of war is at once comprehensive and complicated; that it demands much previous study; and that the possession of it, in its most improved and perfect state, is always of great moment to the security of a nation. This, therefore, ought to be a serious care of every government; and for this purpose, an academy, where a regular course of instruction is

---

* *Ibid.,* XII, pp. 71-72. For Benjamin Rush's views on the national university, see D. D. Runes (Ed.), *The Selected Writings of Benjamin Rush* (New York, Philosophical Library, Inc., 1947), pp. 101-05. This seems to have appeared first in *The Pennsylvania Gazette,* November 29, 1788.

given, is an obvious expedient, which different nations have successfully employed.

George Washington Gives His Shares in the Potomac Company
for the National University, 1799 *

I give and bequeath, in perpetuity, the 50 shares which I hold in the Potomac Company (under the aforesaid acts of the legislature of Virginia), toward the endowment of a university, to be established within the limits of the District of Columbia, under the auspices of the General Government, if that Government should incline to extend a fostering hand toward it; and, until such a seminary is established, and the funds arising on these shares shall be required for its support, my further will and desire is, that the profit accruing therefrom shall, whenever dividends are made, be laid out in purchasing stock in the Bank of Columbia, or some other bank, at the discretion of my executors, or by the Treasurer of the United States for the time being, under the direction of Congress; provided that honorable body should patronize the measure; and the dividends proceeding from the purchase of such stock are to be vested in more stock, and so on, until a sum adequate to the accomplishment of the object is obtained; of which I have not the smallest doubt before many years pass away, even if no aid or encouragement is given by legislative authority, or from any other source.

Jefferson to Congress on National University, 1806 †

... There will still, ere long, be an accumulation of moneys in the Treasury beyond the instalments of public debt which we are permitted by contract to pay. They cannot, then, without a modification, assented to by the public creditors, be applied to the extinguishment of this debt, and the complete liberation of our revenues, the most desirable of all objects; nor, if our peace continues, will they be wanting for any other existing purpose. The question, therefore now comes forward: To what other objects shall these surplusses be appropriated, and the whole surplus of impost, after the entire discharge of the public debt, and during those in-

* From the Will of George Washington. Sparks, *op. cit.*, I, p. 572. By his will Washington left to Liberty Hall Academy, which changed its name to Washington College and became Washington and Lee University, those shares which he held in the James River Navigation Company. From this gift that institution has received about $400,000, "about eight times the capital fund itself" and still has the capital fund. Letter from President Francis P. Gaines to Edgar W. Knight, January 30, 1946. What happened to the shares for the national university remains unsolved. Wesley says (*op. cit.*, p. 8) that guesses about the subject include: the stock was not turned in when the navigation company was reorganized; that it became worthless; was destroyed by the fire of 1814; was never legally accepted by Congress and never transferred to the United States. Of these he thinks the fourth may seem "most probable." See below the letter from the Secretary of the Treasury on the subject, February 15, 1905.

† *Annals of Congress*, 9th Congress, 2d Session, pp. 14-15.

tervals when the purposes of war shall not call for them? Shall we suppress the impost, and give that advantage to foreign over domestic
manufactures? On a few articles, of more general and necessary use, the
suppression, in due season, will doubtless be right, but the great mass of
the articles on which impost is paid is foreign luxuries, purchased by
those only who are rich enough to afford themselves the use of them.
Their patriotism would certainly prefer its continuance and application
to the great purposes of the public education, roads, rivers, canals, and
such other objects of public improvement as it may be thought proper to
add to the Constitutional enumeration of federal powers. By these operations new channels of communication will be opened between the States;
the lines of separation will disappear; their interests will be identified and
their Union cemented by new and indissoluble ties. Education is here
placed among the articles of public care, not that it would be proposed
to take its ordinary branches out of the hands of private enterprise, which
manages so much better all the concerns to which it is equal; but a public
institution can alone supply those sciences which, though rarely called for,
are yet necessary to complete the circle, all the parts of which contribute
to the improvement of the country, and some of them to its preservation.
The subject is now proposed for the consideration of Congress, because,
if approved by the time the State Legislatures shall have deliberated on
this extension of the federal trusts, and the laws shall be passed and other
arrangements made for their execution, the necessary funds will be on
hand, and without employment. I suppose an amendment to the Constitution, by consent of the States, necessary, because the objects now recommended are not among those enumerated in the Constitution, and to which
it permits the public moneys to be applied.

The present consideration of a national establishment, for education
particularly, is rendered proper by this circumstance; also that, if Congress, approving the proposition, shall yet think it more eligible to found
it on a donation of lands, they have now in their power to endow it with
those which will be among the earliest to produce the necessary income.
This foundation would have the advantage of being independent on war,
which may suspend other improvements, by requiring for its own purpose
the resources destined for them.

A Bill for the Establishment of a National University, 1816 *

*Be it enacted, by the Senate and House of Representatives of the
United States of America in Congress assembled,* That the President of
the United States be, and he is hereby, authorized to cause to be erected,
on such site within the District of Columbia as he shall select, the build-

* *Annals of Congress,* 14th Congress, 1st Session, pp. 1031-32. This bill differed not greatly
from other bills on the same subject and introduced into Congress from time to time.

ings necessary for a National University; and, for defraying the expense thereof, the sum of ———— thousand dollars is hereby appropriated, to be paid out of any money in the Treasury of the United States not otherwise appropriated by law.

Sec. 2. And be it further enacted, That the President of the United States be, and he is hereby, authorized and required to cause to be surveyed and laid into building lots the whole, or such parts as he may think proper, of the ground reserved for the use of the United States, in the City of Washington; and to cause the same to be sold, at such times and places, and in such proportions, and under such regulations as he shall prescribe; and the proceeds thereof, after defraying the charges of survey and sale, to be invested in such stocks or public securities as shall by him be deemed most advisable; and the same, when so invested, and the dividends thereon arising, shall constitute a fund for the support of a National University.

Sec. 3. And be it further enacted, That the President of the United States be, and he is hereby, requested to cause to be prepared and laid before Congress, at its next session, a plan for the regulation and government of the said university.

The Secretary of the Treasury to the President of the Senate on the Shares of Stock Which Washington Left for the National University, 1905 *

TREASURY DEPARTMENT,
OFFICE OF THE SECRETARY,
WASHINGTON, *February 15, 1905.*

SIR: I have the honor to acknowledge the receipt of Senate resolution of the 14th instant—

That the Secretary of the Treasury be directed to inform the Senate what was the amount of the bequest made by George Washington to the United States for the foundation of the university and what appropriation was made of it.

In reply thereto I have the honor to state that in the will of General George Washington (see Sparks's Writings of Washington, Vol. 1, pp. 571 and 572) a bequest of 50 shares of the Potomac Company of the value of £100 is made for the establishment of a university in the District of Columbia, but there is no record in the Treasury Department showing that the shares thus bequeathed or any moneys arising therefrom were ever received by the General Government.

Mr. Worthington C. Ford, formerly Chief of the Bureau of Statistics,

* *Senate Documents* (Serial No. 4766), Vol. 4, 58th Congress, 3d Session, 1904-1905, Document 164, pp. 1-2.

this Department, published a volume in 1891 containing the will of General George Washington, and in connection therewith states that the object of this bequest was never carried out (Wills of George Washington and his Ancestors, by W. C. Ford, Brooklyn, 1891) pp. 91 and 92.

In a treatise entitled "Authenticated copy of the last will and testament of George Washington, of Mount Vernon," published by A. Jackson, of Washington, D. C., in 1868, Appendix, pages 10 and 11, referring to General Washington's wish that a university be established in the District of Columbia, it is stated "This desire was never carried into effect, and the fifty shares thus donated reverted to the estate."

The two publications above mentioned are to be found in the Library of Congress,

Respectfully,

L. M. SHAW,
Secretary.

The President of the Senate.

« 3 »

Early Movement for Religious Freedom:
Separation of Church and State

«««««««««««««««««««««««««««««««««»»»»»»»»»»»»»»»»»»»»»»»»»»»»»»

Constitutional Provisions in North Carolina, 1776

That all men have a natural and unalienable right to worship Almighty God according to the dictates of their own conscience.*

That there shall be no establishment of any one religious church or denomination in this State, in preference to any other; neither shall any person, on any pretense whatsoever, be compelled to attend any place of worship contrary to his own faith or judgment, nor be obliged to pay for the purchase of any glebe, or the building of any house of worship, or for the maintenance of any minister or ministry, contrary to what he believes

* Article 19, Declaration of Rights of North Carolina, 1776. Given in Henry G. Connor and Joseph B. Cheshire, Jr., *The Constitution of North Carolina Annotated*, p. lxviii. The movement for religious liberty, through separation of the church and state, began almost simultaneously in Virginia, Pennsylvania, and New York soon after the Declaration of Independence in 1776 and several years before the Federal Constitution was framed. That famous charter of American liberty, which was framed in 1787 and with ten amendments was adopted in 1791, abolished religious tests and prevented Congress from making any law establishing a state church or prohibiting the free exercise of religion. The Constitution of the United States protects the state against interference from the church and the church against interference from the state and establishes an arrangement of friendly independence—a free church and a free state.

At the outbreak of the American Revolution most of the thirteen colonies had established churches. In Massachusetts, Connecticut, and New Hampshire the Congregational Church was established. Attempts at establishing a state church were not made in Rhode Island, Delaware, or Pennsylvania and such attempts were not successful in New Jersey. In Virginia, the Carolinas, Georgia, and Maryland and in a few counties in New York the Anglican Church was by law established and its ministers paid as other officers of the state. Teachers in those colonies were required to hold appropriate certification from the Church through the permission of the Bishop of London or other ecclesiastical authority in England or his representative in America. Without separation of church and state neither complete religious freedom nor freedom of educational enterprise could be enjoyed.

Attacks upon ecclesiastical establishments and the movement for religious freedom and the separation of the church and the state were strengthened by Jefferson's famous bill for religious freedom for Virginia which was introduced into the General Assembly of that state in 1779 and was enacted into law in 1785. In the five states where the clergy of the Anglican Church possessed legal privileges and immunities, dissenters were early victorious in their efforts to break down ecclesiastical establishments and separate the church and the state. This separation was finally completed in the various states when disestablishment was made in New Hampshire in 1817, in Connecticut in 1818, and in Massachusetts in 1833. See Philip Schaff, "Church and State in the United States," *Papers of the American Historical Association*, II, No. 4 (New York, G. P. Putnam's Sons, 1888).

right, or has voluntarily engaged to perform; but all persons shall be at liberty to exercise their own mode of worship: Provided, that nothing herein contained shall be construed to exempt preachers of treasonable or seditious discourses, from legal trial and punishment.*

Jefferson's Bill for Establishing Religious Freedom in Virginia, 1779 †

Section I. Well aware ‡ that the opinions and belief of men depend not on their own will, but follow involuntarily the evidence proposed to their minds; that Almighty God hath created the mind free, and manifested his supreme will that free it shall remain by making it altogether insusceptible of restraint; that all attempts to influence it by temporal punishments, or burthens, or by civil incapacitations, tend only to beget habits of hypocrisy and meanness, and are a departure from the plan of the holy author of our religion, who being lord both of body and mind, yet choose not to propagate it by coercions on either, as was in his Almighty power to do, but to exalt it by its influence on reason alone; that the impious presumption of legislature and ruler, civil as well as ecclesiastical, who, being themselves but fallible and uninspired men, have assumed dominion over the faith of others, setting up their own opinions and modes of thinking as the only true and infallible, and as such endeavoring to impose them on others, hath established and maintained false religions over the greatest part of the world and through all time: That to compel a man to furnish contributions of money for the propagation of opinions which he disbelieves and abhors, is sinful and tyrannical; that even the forcing him to support this or that teacher of his own religious persuasion, is depriving him of the comfortable liberty of giving his contributions to the particular pastor whose morals he would make his pattern, and whose powers he feels most persuasive to righteousness; and is withdrawing from the ministry those temporary rewards, which proceeding from an approbation of their personal conduct, are an additional incitement to earnest and unremitting labours for the

---

* Section 34, Constitution of North Carolina, 1776. Given in Connor and Cheshire, *op. cit.*, pp. lxxiii, lxxiv.

† P. L. Ford, *The Writings of Thomas Jefferson*, II, pp. 237-39.

‡ On June 13, 1776, Jefferson introduced into the General Assembly a bill to create a committee to revise and codify the laws of Virginia. The committee, composed of Jefferson, George Wythe, George Mason, Edmund Pendleton, and Thomas L. Mann, met the following January and apportioned the work among the revisers. The result was 126 bills, the titles of which were set out in the committee's report. For some reason or reasons, the General Assembly seems to have given little attention to the report until 1784 when James Madison was able to have it printed (500 copies); and during the next two years fifty-six of the bills, with some amendment, were enacted into law. Among the most significant of the bills prepared by Jefferson were "A Bill for the More General Diffusion of Knowledge"; "A Bill for Amending the Constitution of the College of William and Mary"; and "A Bill for Establishing Religious Freedom," which Jefferson himself ranked in importance next to the Declaration of Independence. This bill was introduced into the General Assembly, June 13, 1779, and immediately became a heated issue with much memorializing for and against the proposed measure, which was passed over from session to session and did not become law until 1785.

instruction of mankind; that our civil rights have no dependence on our religious opinions, any more than our opinions in physics or geometry; and therefore the proscribing any citizen as unworthy the public confidence by laying upon him an incapacity of being called to offices of trust or emolument, unless he profess or renounce this or that religious opinion, is depriving him injudiciously of those privileges and advantages to which, in common with his fellow-citizens, he has a natural right; that it tends also to corrupt the principles of that very religion it is meant to encourage, by bribing with a monopoly of worldly honours and emoluments, those who will externally profess and conform to it; that though indeed these are criminals who do not withstand such temptation, yet neither are those innocent who lay the bait in their way; that the opinions of men are not the object of civil government, nor under its jurisdiction; that to suffer the civil magistrate to intrude his powers into the field of opinion and to restrain the profession or propagation of principles on supposition of their ill tendency is a dangerous fallacy, which at once destroys all religious liberty, because he being of course judge of that tendency will make his opinions the rule of judgment, and approve or condemn the sentiments of others only as they shall square with or suffer from his own; that it is time enough for the rightful purposes of civil government for its officers to interfere when principles break out into overt acts against peace and good order; and finally, that truth is great and will prevail if let to herself; that she is the proper and sufficient antagonist to error, and has nothing to fear from the conflict unless by human interposition disarmed of her natural weapons, free argument and debate; errors ceasing to be dangerous when it is permitted freely to contradict them.

Sect. II. We the General Assembly of Virginia do enact that no man shall be compelled to frequent or support any religious worship, place, or ministry whatsoever, nor shall be enforced, restrained, molested, or burthened in his body or goods, or shall otherwise suffer, on account of his religious opinions or belief; but that all men shall be free to profess, and by argument to maintain, their opinions in matters of religions, and that the same shall in no wise diminish, enlarge, or affect their civil capacities.

Sect. III. And though we well know that this Assembly, elected by the people for their ordinary purposes of legislation only, have no power to restrain the acts of succeeding Assemblies, constituted with powers equal to our own, and that therefore to declare this act to be irrevocable would be of no effect in law; yet we are free to declare, and do declare, that the rights hereby asserted are of the natural rights of mankind, and that if any act shall be hereafter passed to repeal the present or to narrow its operations, such act will be an infringement of natural right.

Extracts from the Massachusetts Bill of Rights, 1780 *

ARTICLE I. All men are born free and equal, and have certain natural, essential, and unalienable rights; among which may be reckoned the right of enjoying and defending their lives and liberties; that of acquiring, possessing, and protecting property; in fine, that of seeking and obtaining their safety and happiness.

II. It is the right as well as the duty of all men in society, publicly, and at stated seasons, to worship the Supreme Being, the great Creator and Preserver of the universe. And no subject shall be hurt, molested, or restrained, in his person, liberty, or estate, for worshipping God in the manner and season most agreeable to the dictates of his own conscience; or for his religious profession of sentiments; provided he doth not disturb the public peace, or obstruct others in their religious worship. . . .

As the happiness of a people and the good order and preservation of civil government essentially depend upon piety, religion, and morality, and as these cannot be generally diffused through a community but by the institution of the public worship of God and of public instructions, in piety, religion, and morality. Therefore to promote their happiness and secure the good order and preservation of their government, the people of this commonwealth have a right to invest their legislature with power to authorize and require, and the legislature shall from time to time authorize and require, the several towns . . . and other bodies—politic or religious societies, to make suitable provision, at their own expense, for the institution of the public worship of God and the support and maintenance of public Protestant teachers of piety, religion, and morality. . . .

And the people of this commonwealth . . . do invest their legislature with authority to enjoin upon all the subjects an attendance upon the instructions of the public teachers aforesaid. . . .

And every denomination of Christians, demeaning themselves peaceably and as good subjects of the commonwealth, shall be equally under the protection of the law; and no subordination of any one sect or denomination to another shall ever be established by law. . . .

Benjamin Franklin to "Messrs. Weems and Gant, Citizens of the
United States in London," July 18, 1784 †

GENTLEMEN,

On receipt of your letter, acquainting me that the Archbishop of Canterbury would not permit you to be ordained, unless you took the oath of allegiance, I applied to a clergyman of my acquaintance for information on

* B. F. Poore (Ed.), *The Federal and State Constitutions* (Washington, Government Printing Office, 1877), Part I, p. 956.
† Jared Sparks (Ed.), *The Works of Benjamin Franklin*, X, pp. 109-11.

the subject of your obtaining ordination here. His opinion was, that it could not be done; and that, if it were done, you would be required to vow obedience to the Archbishop of Paris. I next inquired of the Pope's Nuncio, whether you might not be ordained by their Bishop in America, powers being sent him for that purpose, if he has them not already. The answer was, "The thing is impossible, unless the gentlemen become Catholics."

This is an affair of which I know very little, and therefore I may ask questions and propose means that are improper or impracticable. But what is the necessity of your being connected with the Church of England? Would it not be as well, if you were of the Church of Ireland? The religion is the same, though there is a different set of bishops and archbishops. Perhaps if you were to apply to the Bishop of Derry, who is a man of liberal sentiments, he might give you orders as of that Church. If both Britain and Ireland refuse you, (and I am not sure that the Bishops of Denmark or Sweden would ordain you, unless you become Lutherans,) what is then to be done? Next to becoming Presbyterians, the Episcopalian clergy of America, in my humble opinion, cannot do better than to follow the example of the first clergy of Scotland, soon after the conversion of that country to Christianity. When their King had built the Cathedral of St. Andrews's, and requested the King of Northumberland to lend his bishops to ordain one for them, that their clergy might not as heretofore be obliged to go to Northumberland for orders, and their request was refused; they assembled in the Cathedral; and, the mitre, crosier, and robes of a bishop being laid upon the altar, they, after earnest prayers for direction in their choice, elected one of their own number; when the King said to him, *"Arise, go to the altar, and receive your office at the hand of God."* His brethren led him to the altar, robed him, put the crosier in his hand, and the mitre on his head, and he became the first Bishop of Scotland.

If the British Islands were sunk in the sea (and the surface of this globe has suffered greater changes), you would probably take some such method as this; and, if they persist in denying you ordination, it is the same thing. A hundred years hence, when people are more enlightened, it will be wondered at, that men in America, qualified by their learning and piety to pray for and instruct their neighbours, should not be permitted to do it till they had made a voyage of six thousand miles out and home, to ask leave of a cross old gentleman at Canterbury; who seems, by your account, to have as little regard for the souls of the people of Maryland, as King William's Attorney-General, Seymour, had for those of Virginia. The Reverend Commissary Blair, who projected the College of that Province, and was in England to solicit benefactions and a charter, relates, that, the Queen, in the King's absence, having ordered Seymour to draw up the charter, which was to be given, with two thousand pounds in money, he opposed the grant; saying that the nation was engaged in an expensive war, that the money was wanted for better purposes, and he did not see the least occasion for a college in Virginia. Blair represented to him that its intention was to educate and qualify young men to be ministers of the Gospel, much wanted there; and begged Mr. Attorney would consider, that the people of Virginia had souls to be saved, as well as the people of England. "Souls!" said he, *"damn your souls. Make tobacco."* I have the honor to be, Gentlemen, &c.

Massachusetts Establishes Complete Religious Freedom, 1833 *

ART. XI. Instead of the third article of the bill of rights, the following modification and amendment thereof is substituted.

"As the public worship of GOD and instructions in piety, religion and morality, promote the happiness and prosperity of a people and the security of a republican government;—therefore, the several religious societies of this commonwealth, whether corporate or unincorporate, at any meeting legally warned and holden for that purpose, shall ever have the right to elect their pastors or religious teachers, to contract with them for their support, to raise money for erecting and repairing houses for public worship, for the maintenance of religious instruction, and for the payment of necessary expenses: and all persons belonging to any religious society shall be taken and held to be members, until they shall file with the clerk of such society, a written notice, declaring the dissolution of their membership, and thenceforth shall not be liable for any grant or contract which may be thereafter made, or entered into by such society:—and all religious sects and denominations, demeaning themselves peaceably, and as good citizens of the commonwealth, shall be equally under the protection of the law; and no subordination of any one sect or denomination to another shall ever be established by law."

* Constitution of Massachusetts. Given in *The General Laws of the Commonwealth of Massachusetts*, 1921, I, p. xc.

« 4 »

Early Constitutional Provisions for Schools

«««»»

Pennsylvania, 1776 *

Sec. 44. A school or schools shall be established in every county by the legislature, for the convenient instruction of youth, with such salaries to the masters, paid by the public, as may enable them to instruct youth at low prices; and all useful learning shall be duly encouraged and promoted in one or more universities.

Sec. 45. Laws for the encouragement of virtue, and prevention of vice and immorality, shall be made and constantly kept in force, and provision shall be made for their due execution; and all religious societies or bodies of men heretofore united or incorporated for the advancement of religion or learning, or for other pious and charitable purposes, shall be encouraged and protected in the enjoyment of the privileges, immunities, and estates which they were accustomed to enjoy, or could of right have enjoyed, under the laws and former constitution of this State.

North Carolina, 1776; Continued Unchanged in the Constitution of 1835 †

41. That a school or schools shall be established by the legislature, for the convenient instruction of youth, with such salaries to the masters, paid

---

* These and the selections that follow appear in B. F. Poore, *The Federal and State Constitutions, Colonial Charters, and Other Organic Laws of the United States,* two volumes (Washington, Government Printing Office, 1877). Education was not mentioned in the Federal Constitution but its Tenth Amendment says: "The powers not delegated to the United States by the Constitution, nor prohibited by it to the States, are reserved to the States respectively, or to the people." Between 1776 and 1800 all of the states adopted new constitutions, except Connecticut and Rhode Island which apparently considered their colonial charters adequate; and some states revised or amended their constitutions. The constitutions of New Hampshire, New Jersey, Delaware, Maryland, Virginia, and South Carolina (in 1776); New York (in 1777); South Carolina (in 1778 and 1790); and Kentucky (in 1792 and 1799) had nothing to say about education. Connecticut had no state constitution until 1818 and Rhode Island none until 1842, but both were silent on the subject of education. The constitutions of Maryland and of some other states were amended one or more times without mentioning education. Of the sixteen states in the Union before 1800 half had something to say about education. Seven of the original states and Vermont, which was admitted in 1791, considered education so important that constitutional statements were made on the subject.

† Note the striking similarity between the provision in this constitution and that in the constitution of Pennsylvania, above. Pennsylvania's provision was adopted in September and North Carolina's in December, 1776.

by the public, as may enable them to instruct at low prices; and all useful learning shall be duly encouraged, and promoted, in one or more universities.

Georgia, 1777

ART. 54. Schools shall be erected in each county, and supported at the general expense of the State, as the Legislature shall hereafter point out.

Vermont, 1777

Sec. XL. A school or schools shall be established in every town, by the legislature, for the convenient instruction of youth, with such salaries to the masters, paid by each town; making proper use of school lands in each town, thereby to enable them to instruct youth at low prices. One grammar school in each county, and one university in this State, ought to be established by direction of the General Assembly.

Sec. XLI. Laws for the encouragement of virtue and prevention of vice and immorality, shall be made and constantly kept in force; and provision shall be made for their due execution; and all religious societies or bodies of men, that have or may be hereafter united and incorporated, for the advancement of religion and learning, or for other pious and charitable purposes, shall be encouraged and protected in the enjoyment of the privileges, immunities and estates which they, in justice ought to enjoy, under such regulations, as the General Assembly of this State shall direct.

Massachusetts, 1780

Section I. The University

ART. I. Whereas our wise and pious ancestors, so early as the year 1636, laid the foundation of Harvard College, in which university many persons of great eminence have, by the blessing of God, been initiated in those arts and sciences which qualified them for public employments, both in church and state; and whereas the encouragement of arts and sciences and all good literature, tends to the honor of God, the advantage of the Christian religion, and the great benefit of this and the other United States of America, it is declared, that the president and fellows of Harvard College, in their corporate capacity, and their successors in their capacity, their officers and servants, shall have, hold, use, exercise, and enjoy all the powers, authorities, rights, liberties, privileges, immunities, and franchises which they now have, or are entitled to have, hold, use, exercise, and enjoy; and the same are hereby ratified and confirmed unto them, the said president and fellows of Harvard College, and to their successors, and to their officers and servants respectively, forever.

ART. 2. And whereas there have been, at sundry times, by divers persons, gifts, grants, devises of houses, lands, tenements, goods, chattels, legacies, and conveyances heretofore made, either to Harvard College, in Cambridge, in New England, or to the president and fellows of Harvard College, or to the said college by some other description, under several charters successively, it is declared that all the said gifts, grants, devises, legacies, and conveyances are hereby forever confirmed unto the president and fellows of Harvard College, and to their successors, in the capacity aforesaid, according to the true intent and meaning of the donor or donors, grantor or grantors, devisor or devisors.

ART. 3. And whereas by an act of the general court of the colony of Massachusetts Bay, passed in the year of 1642, the governor and deputy governor, for the time being, and all the magistrates of that jurisdiction, were, with the president, and a number of the clergy, in the said act described, constituted the overseers of Harvard College, and it being necessary, in this new constitution of government, to ascertain who shall be deemed successors to the said governor, deputy governor, and magistrates, it is declared that the governor, lieutenant-governor, council, and senate of this commonwealth, are, and shall be deemed, their successors; who, with the president of Harvard College, for the time being, together with the ministers of the Congregational churches in the towns of Cambridge, Watertown, Charlestown, Boston, Roxbury, and Dorchester, mentioned in the said act, shall be, and hereby are, vested with all the powers and authority belonging or in anyway appertaining to the overseers of Harvard College: *Provided,* That nothing herein shall be construed to prevent the legislature of this Commonwealth from making such alterations in the government of the said university as shall be conducive to its advantage and the interest of the republic of letters, in as full a manner as might have been done by the legislature of the late province of the Massachusetts Bay.

Section 2. The Encouragement of Literature

Chap. V, Sec. 2. Wisdom and knowledge, as well as virtue, diffused generally among the body of the people, being necessary for the preservation of their rights and liberties; and as these depend on spreading the opportunities and advantages of education in the various parts of the country, and among the different orders of the people, it shall be the duty of the legislatures and magistrates, in all future periods of this Commonwealth, to cherish the interests of literature and the sciences, and all seminaries of them; especially the university at Cambridge, public schools, and grammar-schools in the towns; to encourage private societies and public institutions, by rewards and trades, manufactures, and a natural history of the country; to countenance and inculcate the principles of humanity and general benevolence, public and private charity, industry and frugality, honesty and punctuality in their dealings; sincerity, good humor, and all social affections and generous sentiments among the people.

New Hampshire, 1784, 1792

Sec. 83. Knowledge and learning generally diffused through a community being essential to the preservation of a free government, spreading the opportunities and advantages of education through the various parts of the country being highly conducive to promote this end, it shall be the duty of the legislatures and magistrates, in all future periods of this government, to cherish the interest of literature and the sciences, and all seminaries and public schools; to encourage private and public institutions, rewards and immunities for the promotion of agriculture, arts, sciences, commerce, trade, manufactures, and natural history of the country; to countenance and inculcate the principles of humanity and general benevolence, public and private charity, industry and economy, honesty and punctuality, sincerity, sobriety, and all social affections and generous sentiments among the people.

Extract from the Ordinance of 1787 *

Religion, morality, and knowledge being necessary to good government and the happiness of mankind, schools and the means of education shall forever be encouraged.

Vermont, 1787

Sec. 38. Laws for the encouragement of virtue, and prevention of vice and immorality, ought to be constantly kept in force, and duly executed; and a competent number of schools ought to be maintained in each town for the convenient instruction of youth; and one or more grammar schools be incorporated, and properly supported in each county in this State. And all religious societies, or bodies of men, that may be hereafter united or incorporated, for the advancement of religion and learning, or for other pious and charitable purposes, shall be encouraged and protected in the enjoyment of the privileges, immunities, and estates, which they in justice ought to enjoy under such regulations as the General Assembly of this State shall direct.

This section was also incorporated in the constitution of 1793 unchanged, and is still in force.

* Ordinance of 1787, Article III.

Pennsylvania, 1790, 1838

Sec. 1. The legislature shall, as soon as conveniently may be, provide, by law, for the establishment of schools throughout the State, in such manner that the poor may be taught *gratis.*

Sec. 2. The arts and sciences shall be promoted in one or more seminaries of learning.

Delaware, 1792. Continued Unchanged in the Constitution of 1831

Art. VIII, *Sec. 12.* The Legislature shall, as soon as conveniently may be, provide by law for . . . establishing schools, and promoting arts and sciences.

Georgia, 1798

Art. IV, *Sec. 13.* The arts and sciences shall be promoted, in one or more seminaries of learning; and the legislature shall, as soon as conveniently may be, give such further donations and privileges to those already established as may be necessary to secure the objects of their institution; and it shall be the duty of the general assembly, at their next session, to provide effectual measures for the improvement and permanent security of the funds and endowments of such institutions.

Ohio, 1803

Article VIII

That the general, great, and essential principles of liberty and free government may be recognized, and forever unalterably established, we declare—

Sec. 3. That all men have a natural and indefeasible right to worship Almighty God according to the dictates of their conscience; that no human authority can, in any case whatever, control or interfere with the rights of conscience; that no man shall be compelled to attend, erect, or support any place of worship, or to maintain any ministry, against his consent; and that no preference shall ever be given by law to any religious society or mode of worship; and no religious test shall be required as a qualification to any office of trust or profit. But religion, morality, and knowledge being essentially necessary to the good government and the happiness of mankind, schools and the means of instruction shall forever be encouraged by legislative provision, not inconsistent with the rights of conscience.

Sec. 25. That no law shall be passed to prevent the poor in the several counties and townships within this State, from an equal participation in the schools, academies, colleges, and universities within this State, which are endowed, in whole or in part, from the revenues arising from the donations made by the United States for the support of schools and colleges; and the doors of the said schools, academies, and universities shall be open for the reception of scholars, students, and teachers of every grade, without any distinction of preference whatever, contrary to the intent for which the said donations were made.

Indiana, 1816

Section I. Knowledge and learning generally diffused through a community being essential to the preservation of a free government, and spreading the opportunities and advantages of education through the various parts of the country being highly conducive to this end, it shall be the duty of the general assembly to provide by law for the improvement of such lands as are, or hereafter may be, granted by the United States to this State for the use of schools, and to apply any funds which may be raised from such lands, or from any other quarter, to the accomplishment of the grand object for which they are or may be intended. But no lands granted for the use of schools or seminaries of learning shall be sold, by authority of this State, prior to the year eighteen hundred and twenty; and the moneys which may be raised out of the sale of any such lands, or otherwise obtained for the purposes aforesaid, shall be and remain a fund for the exclusive purpose of promoting the interest of literature and the sciences, and for the support of seminaries and the public schools. The general assembly shall, from time to time, pass such laws as shall be calculated to encourage intellectual, scientific, and agricultural improvement by allowing rewards and immunities for the promotion and improvement of arts, sciences, commerce, manufactures, and natural history; and to countenance and encourage the principles of humanity, industry, and morality.

Sec. 2. It shall be the duty of the general assembly, as soon as circumstances will permit, to provide by law for a general system of education, ascending in a regular graduation from township schools to a State university, wherein tuition shall be gratis, and equally open to all.

Sec. 3. And for the promotion of such salutary end, the money which shall be paid as an equivalent by persons exempt from military duty, except in times of war, shall be exclusively, and in equal proportions, applied to the support of county seminaries; also, all fines assessed for any breach of the penal laws shall be applied to said seminaries, in the counties wherein they shall be assessed.

Sec. 4. It shall be the duty of the general assembly, as soon as circumstances will permit, to form a penal code, founded on the principles of reformation, and not of vindictive justice; and also to provide one or more farms to be an asylum for such persons who, by reason of age, infirmity, or other misfortunes, may have a claim upon the aid and beneficence of society, on such principles that such persons may therein find employment and every reasonable comfort, and lose by their usefulnness the degrading sense of dependence.

Sec. 5. The general assembly, at the time they lay off a new county, shall cause at least 10 per cent to be reserved out of the proceeds of the sale of town-lots in the seat of justice of such county for the use of a public library for such county; and at the same session they shall incorporate a library company, under such rules and regulations as will best secure its permanence and extend its benefits.

« 5 »

Literary Property Begins to Receive
Protection; Copyright Laws

«««««««««««««««««««««««««««««««««««»»»»»»»»»»»»»»»»»»»»»»»»»»»»»

Connecticut Enacts First American Law on Copyright, 1783 *

WHEREAS *it is perfectly agreeable to the Principles of natural Equity and Justice, that every Author should be secured in receiving the Profits that may arise from the Sale of his Works,†and such Security may encourage Men of Learning and Genius to publish their Writings; which may do Honor to their Country, and Service to Mankind.*

Be it enacted by the Governor, Council and Representatives, in General Court assembled, and by the Authority of the same, That the Author of any Book or Pamphlet not yet printed, or of any Map or Chart, being an Inhabitant or Resident in these United States, and his Heirs and Assigns, shall have the sole Liberty of printing, publishing and vending the same within this State, for the Term of fourteen Years, to commence from the

---

* *Acts and Laws of the State of Connecticut in America* (New-London, Timothy Green, 1784), pp. 133-34. This was the first act passed in this country on the subject of copyright.

† Legislation for the protection of literary property and for the encouragement of the arts and sciences bears a close relation to education. Laws on copyright were enacted by some of the states and by Congress through the vigorous leadership of Noah Webster, regarded as the "father" of the copyright in this country, Connecticut leading in providing this protection in January, 1783. Massachusetts followed in March, Maryland in April, New Jersey in May, and New Hampshire and Rhode Island in December of the same year. Pennsylvania and South Carolina enacted such legislation in March, 1784; Virginia in October and North Carolina in December, 1785; Georgia in February, 1786; and New York the same year. Under Article I, Section 8, the Constitution of the United States empowered Congress to "promote the progress of science and the useful arts, by securing for limited times, to authors and inventors the exclusive right to their respective writings and discoveries." And in 1790 Congress enacted the first national statute on the subject, making state legislation on copyright thereafter unnecessary. For a very good account of copyright see R. R. Bowker, *Copyright: Its History and Its Law* (Boston, Houghton Mifflin Co., 1912). One of the earliest suits at law involving copyright was brought by Jedidiah Morse through his counsel James (later Chancellor) Kent of New York and Alexander Hamilton against one Winterbothan who, while serving a political prison term in Newgate, had copied verbatim several hundred pages from Morse's geography. Morse felt it a duty to test the effectiveness of the Congressional statute on copyright and the case was finally decided in 1798 to his entire satisfaction. For Noah Webster's own account of the origin of copyright legislation in this country, see Noah Webster, *A Collection of Papers on Political, Literary and Moral Subjects* (New York, Webster and Clark, 1843), pp. 173-78. Consult Ervin C. Shoemaker, *Noah Webster: Pioneer of Learning* (New York, Columbia University Press, 1936); and Harry R. Warfel, *Noah Webster: Schoolmaster to America* (New York, The Macmillan Co., 1936).

Day of its first Publication in this State. And if any Person or Persons within said Term of fourteen years as aforesaid, shall presume to print or re-print any such Book, Pamphlet, Map or Chart within this State, or to import or introduce into this State for Sale, any Copies thereof, re-printed beyond the Limits of this State, or shall knowingly publish, vend and utter, or distribute the same without the Consent of the Proprietor thereof in Writing, signed in the Presence of two credible Witnesses, every such Person or Persons shall forfeit and pay to the Proprietor of such Book, Pamphlet, Map or Chart double the Value of all the Copies thereof, so printed, imported, distributed, vended, or exposed for Sale; to be recovered by such Proprietor in any Court of Law in this State, proper to try the same.

Provided nevertheless, That no Author, Assignee or Proprietor of any such Book, Pamphlet, Map or Chart shall be entitled to take the Benefit of this Statute, until he shall duly register his Name as Author, Assignee, or Proprietor, with the Title thereof, in the Office of the Secretary of this State, who is hereby impowered and directed to enter the same on Record.

And be it further enacted by the Authority aforesaid, That at the Expiration of said Term of fourteen Years, in the Cases above mentioned, the sole Right of printing and disposing of any such Book, Pamphlet, Map or Chart in this State, shall return to the Author thereof, if then living, and his Heirs and Assigns, for the Term of fourteen Years more, to commence at the End of said first Term; and that all and every Person or Persons, who shall re-print, import, vend, utter or distribute in this State, any Copies thereof without the Consent of such Proprietor, obtained as aforesaid, during said second Term of fourteen Years, shall be liable to the same Penalties, recoverable in the same Manner as is herein before enacted and provided.

And whereas it is equally necessary, for the Encouragement of Learning, that the Inhabitants of this State be furnished with useful Books, &c. at reaable Prices.

Be it further enacted, That when ever any such Author or Proprietor of such Book, Pamphlet, Map or Chart, shall neglect to furnish the Public with sufficient Editions thereof, or shall sell the same at a Price unreasonable, and beyond what may be adjudged a sufficient Compensation for his Labour, Time, Expence and Risque of Sale, the Judge of the Superior Court in this State, on Complaint thereof made to him in Writing, is hereby authorized and impowered to summon such Author or Proprietor to appear before the next Superior Court, to be holden in that County where such Author or Proprietor dwells, if a Resident in this State, if not, in that County where such Complainant dwells; and said Court are hereby authorized and impowered to enquire into the Justice of said Complaint, and if the same be found true, to take sufficient Recognizance and Security of such Author or Proprietor, conditioned that he shall within such reasonable Time, as said Court shall direct, publish and offer for Sale in this

State, a sufficient Number of Copies of such Book, Pamphlet, Map or Chart, at such reasonable Price as said Court shall, on due Consideration affix: And if such Author or Proprietor shall, before said Court, neglect or refuse to give such Security as aforesaid, the said Court are hereby authorized and impowered to give to such Complainant, a full and ample License to reprint and publish such Book, Pamphlet, Map or Chart, in such Numbers and for such Term as said Court shall judge just and reasonable: Provided said Complainant shall give sufficient Security before said Court, to afford said reprinted Edition at such reasonable Price as said Court shall thereto affix.

And be it further enacted, That any Person or Persons who shall procure and print any unpublished Manuscript, without the Consent and Approbation of the Author or Proprietor thereof, first had and obtained, (if such Author or Proprietor be living, and resident in, or Inhabitant of these United States) shall be liable to suffer and pay to the said Author or Proprietor his just Damages for such Injury; to be recovered by Action brought on this Statute, in any Court of Law in this State, proper to try the same.

Provided always, That nothing in this Act shall extend to affect, prejudice or confirm the Rights which any Person may have to the printing or publishing of any Book, Pamphlet, Map or Chart, at Common Law, in Cases not mentioned in this Act, or to screen from legal Punishment any Person or Persons who may be guilty of printing or publishing any Book, Pamphlet or Paper that may be prophane, treasonable, defamatory, or injurious to Government, Morals or Religion.

Provided also, That this Act shall not extend, or be construed to extend in Favour, or for the Benefit of any Author or Persons residing in, or Inhabitants of any other of the United States, until the State or States, in which such Person or Persons reside or dwell, shall have passed similar Laws in Favour of the Authors of new Publications, and their Heirs and Assigns.

Copyright Law of Massachusetts, 1783 *

An Act for the Purpose of securing to Authors the exclusive Right and Benefit of publishing their Literary Productions, for twenty-one Years.

Whereas the improvement of knowledge, the progress of civilization, the publick weal of the community, and the advancement of human happiness, greatly depend on the efforts of learned and ingenious persons in the various arts and sciences: as the principal encouragement such persons can have to make great and beneficial exertions of this nature must exist in the legal security of the fruits of their study and industry to themselves: and as such security is one of the natural rights of all men, there being no prop-

* *The Laws of the Commonwealth of Massachusetts, from November 28, 1780, to February 28, 1807,* I, pp. 94-95.

erty more peculiarly a man's own than that which is produced by the labour of his mind;

Therefore, to encourage learned and ingenious persons to write useful
books for the benefit of mankind,

Sect. 1. Be it enacted by the Senate and House of Representatives in
General Court assembled, and by authority of the same,

That all books, treatises, and other literary works, having the name or
names of the author or authors thereof printed and published with the
same, shall be the sole property of the said author or authors being subjects of the United States of America, their heirs and assigns, for the full
and complete term of twenty-one years, from the date of their first publication.

Sect. 2. And be it further enacted by the authority aforesaid,

That if any person or persons shall print, reprint, publish, sell or expose
to sale, or shall cause to be printed, reprinted, published, sold, or exposed
to sale, any book, treatise, or other literary work not yet printed, written
by any subject of the United States of America, whose name, as author,
shall have been thereto prefixed, without consent of the author or authors,
or their assigns, during said term, shall forfeit and pay a sum not exceeding
Three Thousand Pounds, nor less than *Five Pounds,* to the use of such
author or authors, or their assigns; to be recovered by action of debt in any
court of record proper to try the same. *Provided always,* That every author
of such book, treatise, or other literary work, shall, in order to his holding
such sole property in them, present two printed copies of each and every
of them to the library of the University at Cambridge for the use of the
said University; and prior to his recovery of the said forfeiture, or any
part thereof, shall produce, in open court where such action shall be tried,
a receipt of such book, treatise, or other literary work, from the Librarian
of the said University for the time being. *Provided also,* That this act shall
not be construed to extend in favour or for the benefit of any author or
authors, subject or subjects of any other of the United States, until the
State or States of which such authors are subjects, shall have passed similar
laws, for the securing to authors the exclusive right and benefit of publishing their literary productions.

(This Act passed March 17, 1783.)

First Copyright Law Enacted by Congress, May 31, 1790 *

An Act for the encouragement of learning, by securing the copies of maps,
charts, and books, to the authors and proprietors of such copies, during the
times therein mentioned.

Section 1. Be it enacted by the Senate and House of Representatives of

---

* Richard Peters (Ed.), *The Public Statutes at Large of the United States of America*
(Boston, Charles C. Little and James Brown, 1850), Vol. I, pp. 124-26.

the United States of America in Congress assembled, That from and after the passing of this act, the author and authors of any map, chart, book or books already printed within these United States, being a citizen or citizens thereof, or resident within the same, his or their executors, administrators or assigns, who hath or have not transferred to any other person the copyright of such map, chart, book or books, share or shares thereof; and any other person or persons, being a citizen or citizens of these United States, or residents therein, his or their executors, administrators or assigns, who hath or have purchased or legally acquired the copyright of any such map, chart, book or books, in order to print, reprint, publish or vend the same, shall have the sole right and liberty of printing, reprinting, publishing and vending such map, chart, book or books, for the term of fourteen years from the recording the title thereof in the clerk's office, as is herein after directed: And that the author and authors of any map, chart, book or books already made and composed, and not printed or published, or that shall hereafter be made and composed, being a citizen or citizens of these United States, or resident therein, and his or their executors, administrators or assigns, shall have the sole right and liberty of printing, reprinting, publishing and vending such map, chart, book or books, for the like term of fourteen years from the time of recording the title thereof in the clerk's office as aforesaid. And if, at the expiration of the said term, the author or authors, or any of them, be living, and a citizen or citizens of these United States, or resident therein, the same exclusive right shall be continued to him or them, his or their executors, administrators or assigns, for the further term of fourteen years: *Provided,* he or they shall cause the title thereof to be a second time recorded and published in the same manner as is herein after directed, and that within six months before the expiration of the first term of fourteen years aforesaid.

Sec. 2. And be it further enacted, That if any other person or persons, from and after the recording the title of any map, chart, book or books, and publishing the same as aforesaid, and within the times limited and granted by this act, shall print, reprint, publish, or import, or cause to be printed, reprinted, published, or imported from any foreign kingdom or state, any copy or copies of such map, chart, book or books, without the consent of the author or proprietor thereof, first had and obtained in writing, signed in the presence of two or more credible witnesses; or knowing the same to be so printed, reprinted, or imported, shall publish, sell, or expose to sale, or cause to be published, sold, or exposed to sale, any copy of such map, chart, book or books, without such consent first had and obtained in writing as aforesaid, then such offender or offenders shall forfeit all and every copy and copies of such map, chart, book or books, and all and every sheet and sheets, being part of the same, or either of them, to the author or proprietor of such map, chart, book or books, who shall forthwith destroy the same: And every such offender and offenders shall also forfeit and pay the sum of fifty cents for every sheet which shall be found in his or their possession, either printed or printing, published, imported or exposed to sale, contrary to the true intent and meaning of this act, the one moiety thereof to the author or proprietor of such map, chart, book or books who shall sue for the same, and the other moiety thereof to and for the use of the United States, to be recovered by action of debt in any court of record in the United States, wherein the same is cognizable. *Provided always,* That such action be commenced within one year after the cause of action shall arise, and not afterwards.

Sec. 3. And be it further enacted, That no person shall be entitled to the benefit of this act, in cases where any map, chart, book or books, hath or have been already printed and published, unless he shall first deposit, and in all other cases, unless he shall before publication deposit a printed copy of the title of such map, chart, book or books, in the clerk's office of the district court where the author or proprietor shall reside: And the clerk of such court is hereby directed and required to record the same forthwith, in a book to be kept by him for that purpose, in the words following, (giving a copy thereof to the said author or proprietor, under the seal of the court, if he shall require the same). "District of   to wit: *Be it remembered,* That on the day of   in the   year of the independence of the United States of America, A.B. of the said district, hath deposited in this office the title of a map, chart, book or books, (as the case may be) the right whereof he claims as author or proprietor, (as the case may be) in the words following, to wit: [here insert the title] in conformity to the act of the Congress of the United States, intituled 'An act for the encouragement of learning, by securing the copies of maps, charts, and books, to the authors and proprietors of such copies, during the times therein mentioned.' C.D. clerk of the district of   ." For which the said clerk shall be entitled to receive sixty cents from the said author or proprietor, and sixty cents for every copy under seal actually given to such author or proprietor as aforesaid. And such author or proprietor shall, within two months from the date thereof, cause a copy of the said record to be published in one or more of the newspapers printed in the United States, for the space of four weeks.

Sec. 4. And be it further enacted, That the author or proprietor of any such map, chart, book or books, shall, within six months after the publishing thereof, deliver, or cause to be delivered to the Secretary of State a copy of the same, to be preserved in his office.

Sec. 5. And be it further enacted, That nothing in this act shall be construed to extend to prohibit the importation or vending, reprinting or publishing within the United States, of any map, chart, book or books, written, printed, or published by any person not a citizen of the United States, in foreign parts or places without the jurisdiction of the United States.

Sec. 6. And be it further enacted, That any person or persons who shall print or publish any manuscript, without the consent and approbation of the author or proprietor thereof, first had and obtained as aforesaid, (if such author or proprietor be a citizen of or resident in these United States) shall be liable to suffer and pay to the said author or proprietor all damages occasioned by such injury to be recovered by a special action on the case founded upon this act, in any court having cognizance thereof.

Sec. 7. And be it further enacted, That if any person or persons shall be sued or prosecuted for any matter, act or thing done under or by virtue of this act, he or they may plead the general issue, and give the special matter in evidence.

Approved, May 31, 1790.

« 6 »

Chevalier Quesnay de Beaurepaire's Academy of Arts and Sciences in Richmond, Virginia

《《》》》》》》》》》》》》》》》》》》》》》》》》》》》》》》》》》》》》

Sara Bache to Benjamin Franklin on Quesnay's Academy, 1783 *

PHILA, *February 27, 1783.*

MY DEAR AND HONORED FATHER:

With this letter you will receive a project for a French Academy † which is to be established here. It is a very extensive plan and will do honor to the gentleman who has designed it as well as to America. If it can be executed, it will in no way interfere with the plans of the colleges; it will be solely for the completion of the education of young men after they have graduated from college. Monsieur Quesnay regards you as the father of science in this country, and appreciates the advice and instruction which you have never failed to give those whose talents are worthy of recognition. Money is the one thing needful, but you will be informed how you can be most serviceable. I can conceive how occupied you must be in this important crisis; but as a mother who desires to give to her children a use-

---

* Given in H. B. Adams, *Thomas Jefferson and the University of Virginia* (Washington, Government Printing Office, 1888), p. 24.

† The effort to establish in Richmond, Virginia, "a kind of French Academy of arts and sciences, with branch academies in Baltimore, Philadelphia, and New York," shows something of the influence which grew out of the French alliance with this country. It was an extraordinary effort, the idea of which Quesnay said was suggested to him in 1778 by John Page, lieutenant governor of Virginia. There was wide interest among Virginians in the project for which Quesnay raised by subscriptions a considerable sum of money. The list of the original subscribers in Virginia, which cannot be included here, appears in the work which Quesnay published in Paris in 1788, *Mémoire, status et prospectus, concernant L'Académie des sciences et beaux-arts . . . à Richmond,* from which some of the documents that follow are taken. These documents show that the Academy was founded, but circumstances were not favorable for its success. Herbert B. Adams wrote that if Quesnay's undertaking had been successful "it is probable that the University of Virginia would never have been founded. There would have been no need of it. The Academy of the United States of America, established at Richmond, would have become the centre of higher education not only for Virginia, but for the whole South and possibly for a large part of the North, if the Academy had been extended, as proposed, to the cities of Baltimore, Philadelphia, and New York." The building in which the Academy had its home was destroyed by fire in 1811 and the plan of Quesnay failed.

127

ful and polite education and who will be especially proud to have them trained in her own country and under her own eyes, I pray you to give M. Quesnay all the assistance that may lie in your power. I will only add the love and respect of the family.

Your affectionate daughter,

SARA BACHE.

Announcement of Quesnay's Academy of Arts and Sciences, 1786 *

On *Monday* the 4th of *September* (the hot Season Vacancy being over) Notice is hereby given, that from that Day the different Schools of Mr. *Quesnay's* Academy shall be regularly attended until the 1st of *July,* 1787.

As the Hall of the Academy will be for a short Time occupied by Mess. *Hallam & Henry,* as a THEATRE, during their Residence in this City, the Scholars shall be attended to as usual in the same private House now occupied for that Purpose. And the same Decorum will be kept, until the Wings of the Academy shall be built, in Order that the Scholars have no Communication with the Theatre—and to keep that Decency requisite for such a public School.

According to the Trustees' approbation, Mr. *Richard Morris* is accepted and appointed Master, to teach the young Ladies TAMBOUR, EMBROIDERIES, and PATTERNS, and all Kind of NEEDLE WORK, also VOCAL MUSIC—The Ladies will be attended by him as convenient as possible to them.

Proper Ushers for foreign Languages, Geography, Writing, Arithmetic, and Music, are daily expected; and if the schools should be properly encouraged, there are Masters engaged, and will receive orders to set off immediately from Europe.

In order that the Scholars of the Suburbs of this City might avoid boarding in Town, for the only Purpose of learning to dance, it will be at their Option to follow the ancient Rules, *viz.*—to engage for the Year, attend three Days running every Month, beginning the first *Monday* of each, at 51, 10s. *per* Year, and eight Dollars Entrance.

A. M. QUESNAY.

RICHMOND, Aug. 28, 1786.

Quesnay to the Royal Academy of Sciences, Paris, 1788 †

GENTLEMEN:

The project which I have had the honor of submitting could receive no more flattering sanction than yours, nor appear under auspices more ca-

---

* *Virginia Independent Chronicle,* August 30, 1786.

† This document, and the two that follow, are translations from Quesnay de Beaurepaire, *Mémoire, status et prospectus, concernant L'Académie des sciences et beaux-arts . . . à Richmond* (Paris, 1788). Copy is in the Library of the University of Virginia; microcopy is in the Southern Historical Collection, University of North Carolina. For a brief secondary account of this remarkable effort in the late eighteenth century to establish "higher education in this country upon a grand scale" see H. B. Adams, *op. cit.,* pp. 21-30.

pable of winning all suffrages. You constitute, Sirs, a focus of light which helps to illuminate both hemispheres, a centre about which revolve the efforts of all who strive for the progress of the sciences and public education.

The United States of America, Sirs, will see with very lively satisfaction, perpetuated under your auspices, an establishment which should tend to increase their intercourse with France; and Americans will share in the tribute of appreciation which I owe you personally for the welcome with which you have honored me.

I have owed it, no doubt, to that celebrated grandfather whom you adopted; but it is sufficient in other respects to show you my interest, to experience yours, which has already spread, as have your deeds and your renown, over the whole face of the earth.

I am with profound respect,

Sirs,

Your very humble and very
obedient servant

QUESNAY DE BEAUREPAIRE.

Official Approval of Quesnay's Academy by the Royal Censor, 1788

APPROBATION

We have read, by order of Monseigneur, the Keeper of the Seals, the present manuscript. The plan which it contains appears to us very ingenious and very suitable for achieving its object, and consequently deserves the approbation and support of governments, as well as of all distinguished persons in position to advance its success. This establishment (praiseworthy in every respect) is undertaken with a courage and constancy which display notable character in its Author, grandson of Doctor Quesnay, that illustrious philosopher to whom Europe owes the discovery of the principles which constitute that form of government most advantageous to the human race.

PARIS, the 27th of February, 1788.

Signed, DE HESSELN, *Royal Censor.*

Prospectus of Quesnay's Academy, July 1, 1788

ARTICLE I.

The subscription shall be composed of four hundred shares of the value of twelve hundred pounds (of Tours) each. They shall be divided according to the pleasure of the subscribers into half-shares of six hundred pounds, and into quarter shares of three hundred pounds. Each coupon shall bear the number of the share of which it forms a part.

Art. II.

Three hundred and fifty of these shares shall be disposed of in America, in England, Holland, France, Germany and Poland. The other fifty shall belong without cost to the Founder-President to be disposed of at his pleasure.[1]

Art. III.

The shares or coupons shall be stamped with the seal of the Academy, signed by the founder-president, the only personal obligor to the stockholders, and countersigned by the general treasurer in Paris. Upon delivery which he shall make of them to each of those interested, they shall pay price of said shares into his hands.

Art. IV.

For the convenience of the French stockholders and others, there shall be established correspondents in the principal cities of the kingdom and abroad. These correspondents, charged with authority, empowered by the same signatures, shall be authorized to deliver temporary receipts for the value of stock or coupons for which they shall receive the amount, and upon payment these correspondents shall deliver the same to the general depository in Paris, and there shall be delivered to them the amount of shares or of coupons necessary to make the redistribution to each of those interested.

Art. V.

The proceeds of these shares shall be employed, under the care of commissioners appointed for the purpose, in securing objects absolutely necessary, which are, for the most part, lacking in America, such as utensils pertaining to the arts and trades, books, models, machines, printing presses in type and copper-plate, instruments for astronomy, chemistry, and experimental physics; furthermore, for advances to professors, masters and artists, before their departure as well as after their arrival in Virginia; for expenses of transportation, insurance, &c.

Art. VI.

Those of the articles above named which may be furnished by any subscribers shall be taken on account, after agreement with the commissioners, and upon a proper estimate of their worth according to article 23 of the Statutes and Regulations.

Art. VII.

Annually in January upon the statement of the condition of receipts and disbursements, approved beforehand by the administrative council of

---

[1] The proceeds of these fifty shares shall be employed mainly for the reimbursement of the first American subscribers of 1786.

the Academy, the dividend to be paid the stockholders shall be determined in the general assembly held in Richmond and called for this purpose. The first declaration of dividend shall be for the six months of the year 1791, and the others for the same period following.

Art. VIII.

After seven, ten, thirteen, and fifteen years, beyond his share of dividends, the stockholder shall receive the repayment of his capital in four equal installments of three hundred pounds each.

Art. IX.

Although paid in part during the first period, the stockholders shall remain interested during the whole time, and shall annually draw out on each share their four-hundredth (quatre-centieme) in the profits reserved for them, and the additions hereinafter mentioned up to and including the fifteenth year.

Art. X.

Upon reaching the last period for payment, the holder shall send the stock to the treasurer for payment. The coupons for annual or additional interest, or even for repayment of capital, which have not been presented, until past due, in the course of five years after that above fixed for the time of the full payment, shall remain, as the share, itself, null and void.

Art. XI.

That part of the dividend applicable to unsold shares, and to those which by consent of the stockholder should have been redeemed before maturity, shall belong to the founder-president and be added to his annual receipts.

Art. XII.

The stockholders resident in America shall receive at will, on maturity, the amount of their interest coupons and amounts due them from the depository of the general treasurer in Richmond, or from the special treasurers in the different States; the European stockholders, at the depository of the treasurer general in Paris, or from the agency of the correspondents established in the different countries of Europe.

Art. XIII.

Independently of the special liability of the property which belongs or shall belong to the Academy, of the general mortgage upon the existing funds, upon the buildings already completed, or which may be built in future, the founder-president, as a guarantee of repayment at the dates fixed above, agrees to leave each year on deposit in the depository of the general treasurer of the Academy in Richmond one-fourth of the sum which shall belong to him as his share of the profits, to be divided with the shareholders.

ART. XIV.

Beyond his share in the annual dividend, the holder of a share shall receive gratuitously a copy of the catalogue of the Academy (containing the names of the academicians, of the subscribers and students), the catalogue of the botanical garden, and the announcement of the work undertaken, and, in addition, a volume of observations and memoirs of the Academy, and a selected copy of all the new engravings, such as prints, geographical charts and music, which shall issue from the presses of the Academy during the year.

ART. XV AND LAST.

The articles gratuitously given according to the previous Article will only be granted to the owner of a full share. The holders of coupons will only have a right to their proportionate part in the division of the dividend and in the return of the capital, according to the dates which have been fixed.

FORM OF SHARES

To which will be attached the coupons for annual interest, and accessories, and four coupons for repayment of three hundred pounds each.

No. (   ) Academy
of the United States of America
Established in Richmond, the Capital of Virginia.
Share of twelve hundred pounds (of Tours).

The bearer of the present share, according to the conditions of the Prospectus issued, of which a copy has been sent him, and under the mortgages and conditions therein announced, payable in four equal payments, is entitled to one four-hundredth in the dividend declared annually to the shareholders, payable at the bank of the general treasurer in Paris, or at the hands of the various correspondents who shall be named for the purpose in several cities of Europe; and in America, at the depository of the general treasurer in Richmond, or from the special American treasurers; and shall have the right to the free and additional issues.

PARIS, July 1st, 1788.

Founder-President.

Countersigned.
General Treasurer
PARIS.

Subscriptions may be obtained also from the Chevalier de Beaurepaire, *Grand-Hotel of Toulouse, Rue du Jardinet.*

And from M. Bassuel du Vignois, Advocate of Parliament, Councellor of the King, Recorder of the Roman Court and of the Legations, Perpetual Corresponding Secretary, and Grand Treasurer. *Rue des Grands-Augustins, No. 30, Paris.*

NEW FORCES AND THE AWAKENING

«««««««‹«««««««««««««««««««««««««««««««»»»»»»»»»»»»»»»»»»»»»»»»»»»»»»»»»

Interest in education as a function of government developed slowly in this country. Some forces that stimulated that interest were set out in Chapter II, "Toward Educational Independence." In the early part of the nineteenth century other forces appeared which increased that interest. Among these were the monitorial system of instruction, the secular Sunday School, the lyceum, educational journalism, educational conventions, and memorials to legislatures. Forces that tended to awaken a social consciousness included the growth of the means of transportation and communication, the awakening of a class consciousness among the laboring people in the industrial centers, the removal of property qualifications for voting and the extension of the suffrage, the abolition of imprisonment for debt and other humanitarian movements. Other very important forces appeared in the work of energetic and influential *antebellum* educational leaders such as James G. Carter, Horace Mann, Henry Barnard, Calvin Wiley, Caleb Mills, and others. See Edgar W. Knight, *Education in the United States,* third revised edition (Boston, Ginn & Co., 1951), chapters VII and VIII; Newton Edwards and Herman G. Richey, *The School in the American Social Order* (Boston, Houghton Mifflin Co., 1947), Part Two.

Interest in the monitorial system of instruction was wide in this country in the early part of the nineteenth century and is believed to have stimulated interest in public education. This system, which Joseph Lancaster, English Quaker, claimed to have invented, was one of many educational novelties which have attracted the attention of the American people but whose fair promises were unfulfilled. This one made wide appeal chiefly because it promised a royal road to learning through inexpensive methods of teaching. Lancaster is said to have lost himself in "dreamy calculations" of the time required to educate all the people in the world by his system; and Alexander Bell, Anglican divine who contested Lancaster's claim to priority in the invention or discovery of the "mutual tuition" of pupils (those knowing little teaching those who knew less), is reported to have claimed: "Give me 24 pupils today and I will give you back 24 teachers tomorrow." Lancaster claimed in his advertising that under his plan one teacher, "often a lad from fourteen to eighteen years of age, can be rendered competent to the government of a school containing from 200 to 1000 scholars. The expense of Education for each individual will also diminish in proportion as the Number under the care of the master increases. The System of Order and Tuition serves in lieu of experience and discretion in the Teacher, whose qualifications consist only of a small degree of Elementary Knowledge. . . ." Governor Clinton of New York, Governor Wolcott of Connecticut, Archibald D. Murphey, "father of the public schools of North Carolina" and President Joseph Caldwell of the University of that state, and many other intelligent people advocated the system. In 1826 Maryland established a state system of Lancasterian schools but soon abandoned the undertaking. As public opinion became aroused on the subject of public education, as the material prosperity of the people increased and they recognized a need for schools and developed a willingness to provide for them by taxation, the Lancasterian system disappeared.

After Lancaster fell out with the British and Foreign School Society, which had been established in 1808, he came to this country in 1818, visited and lectured in the principal cities in Virginia where he seems to have been warmly received, and while here wrote and received many letters on his plan of education and seems to have aroused enthusiasm among people hitherto indifferent. In the library of the American Antiquarian Society, Worcester, Massachusetts, are "at least a dozen large folio boxes" containing the papers of Joseph Lancaster. The originals of the letters that appear in this chapter are the property of that Society and are here used by its permission. Microcopies are in the Southern Historical Collection, the University of North Carolina. See Edgar W. Knight, "Interest in the South in Lancasterian Methods," The North Carolina Historical Review, XXV (July, 1948), pp. 377-402.

《《《《《《《 《《《《《《《《《《《《《《《《《《《《《《《《《《《《《《《《《〇》》》》》》》》》》》》》》》》》》》》》》》》》》》》》》》》》

An Academy on the Lancasterian Plan Is Established
in North Carolina, 1814 *

We congratulate our fellow-citizens on the prospect of establishing in the Preparatory School of our Academy, the highly approved mode of teaching children the first rudiments of Learning, invented by the celebrated Joseph Lancaster of London, by which one man can superintend the instruction of any number of scholars from 50 to 1000. At the monthly meeting of the trustees of the Academy on Saturday last, a favorable Report was made by a committee who had been appointed to consider this subject, from which it appeared, that when this plan shall be introduced, the children of all such parents in the city and neighborhood as are unable to pay their tuition, may be taught without additional expense, so that this institution will answer all the purposes of a free school.

The Report was unanimously concurred with, and a subscription immediately opened for effecting the object, which Mr. Glendenning generously headed with $50. Nearly $200. were subscribed by the Trustees present; and there is no doubt but a sufficient fund will be immediately raised for sending a fit person to the District of Columbia (where there is a school of this kind in operation under the direction of one of Mr. Lancaster's pupils),† to receive the necessary instruction, and return hither for the purpose of undertaking the contemplated School, which it is proposed shall open with the ensuing year. Benevolent individuals who are willing to give aid to this plan for disseminating the benefits of education amongst the poorer classes of the community, are requested to place their names to the subscription paper, which is in the hands of Wm. Peace, Esq., Treasurer of the Academy.

Early Lancasterian Schools in Philadelphia, 1817 ‡

IN THE PRESS
And will be published in a few days,
By Benjamin Warner, No. 147 High Street
(For the Philadelphia Society
For the establishment and Support
Of Charity Schools)

* Editorial in *The Raleigh Register*, April 1, 1814.
† Robert Ould.
‡ *Aurora General Advertiser* (Philadelphia), August 21, 1817.

135

A Manual
of the
System of Teaching
Reading, Writing, Arithmetic, and Needle-Work
In the Elementary Schools of the British
and Foreign School Society
Also
Lessons
Adapted to the Lancastrian System of Education

When the rapid increase of our population is compared with the means of procuring Education, it is much to be feared, that at no distant period, a large proportion of the people, in many sections of the United States, will be destitute of this important blessing, unless private benevolence or public provision should apply the remedy. The Lancastrian System, as detailed in the above Manual, presents the best mode yet discovered of spreading the benefits of Education, either in the hands of individual Tutors or School Societies: under these impressions, the Philadelphia Society believe they cannot better fulfill the purpose of their Association, than by extending the knowledge of the System, and offering the means which the Lessons afford of carrying it into complete operation.

The views of the Society, however, in their publication, are not confined to Charity Schools: every citizen is interested; because the effects of the general introduction of this System will be the same as the creation or gift of a vast capital to be expended in Education: Its economy brings it within reach of the poor man's means; and to parents in moderate circumstances it will prove a saving of money, as well as a saving of time to their children. Nor are the most wealthy above the benefits which will flow from the general introduction of this System; its morality and the peculiar and happy fitness of all its details, to the capacities and feelings of children, no less than its economy, entitle it to the approbation and support of everyone who is interested in the welfare of the rising generation.

James Stevenson of Virginia to Joseph Lancaster, 1819 *

WELLSBURGH, Va 13 February 1819.

Dear Sir

My object in writing this letter is to know if I could by going to that place, (or any other,) be instructed by you on your System of Education and if so on what terms and how long it would take to acquire a knowledge of the systems. What branches of education are taught and if a knowledge

---

* This and the following seven letters are used by permission of the American Antiquarian Society, Worcester, Mass.

of the languages is necessary? What the probable expense to furnish a school room for two hundred or two hundred and fifty schollars &c.

I have been engaged for nearly two years in teaching and with tolerable success. My desire is to be usefull as a teacher. and from what I have heard of your system I am led to believe that to be able to teach it well is the way to become most usefull.

I have to regret that my circumstances at present will not allow me to spend much time or money perhaps not enough to acquire a compotent knowledge of the system.

I had thought of going to Cincinnate (from whence I have encouragement) where a school has been established said to on your System by a Mr. Dawson; but seeing your publication respecting a Mr. Edwards I have given up the thoughts of going there lest I should be imposed on.

Should the terms be such that I can comply with I will endeavour to be there or wereever I could get the necessary instruction some time in May perhaps April. Another Person expects to go with me on the same errand Your answer will be a favour conferred on

Yours &c
JAMES STEVENSON

MR. LANCASTER

Joseph C. Cabell of Virginia to Joseph Lancaster, 1819

WARMINISTER, VIRGINIA, 1st July. 1819.

SIR.

There was scarcely any one in this country more gratified by the intelligence of your arrival in America than the stranger who now has the honor to address you. The perusal of various articles in the Edinburgh Review, & some of your own writings had inspired me with a high respect for the Author of a system of elementary instruction by which one man is competent to teach a thousand pupils more rapidly than the smallest number can be advanced in the ordinary method. As I understand your object in coming to the United States is to be useful thro the means of the diffusion of your new plan of education I hope I shall not trespass too far on your valuable time in addressing you a letter of enquiry in respect to it. That your system is immensely valuable in large towns where great numbers can be brought together into one school, no doubt can be entertained. But as we have but few of these in the United States, and as the greater part of the population, especially in the Southern section is thinly scattered over a vast extent of territory, the value of the system to this nation, will depend essentially upon its applicability to small Country Schools. Upon this point it is that I am particularly desirous of information. The Edinburgh Review states that "the Essence of the new method consists in economizing the expence of education by teaching very large numbers at once. Beautiful & useful as it is, when applied to schools of a certain size, it is wholly inapplicable to small seminaries; at least it loses all its advantages. One teacher now superintends a school of 1000 or 1200 children. Yet in pa: 137 of your work entitled improvements in education you say "The System of tuition & rewards which are described in the former part of this work, will be found well adapted to initiatory schools," and in pa: 135 you observe that "the number of children that attend a school of this class is very fluctuating, and seldom exceeds thirty." I have no recollection of anything in the context either of the Edinburgh Review or of your works, which would put this subject in a different point of view. There seems to me to be a plain difference of opinion between yourself and the Editor of the Review: and I hope you will be found to be correct, because upon this question depends almost the whole value of your system to the American people. Of this you will be satisfied when I inform you that of the Rural initiatory schools in Virginia hardly one in a hundred consists of more than thirty scholars. I am of the opinion they would not average more than twenty: yet I believe that schools of thirty children, male & female, could be made up generally over the country if the introduction of an improved method depended on the presence of that number. Altho' in such small seminaries the economy of the system would in a great degree be lost, yet I hope the rapidity might be retained. If your present vocations allow you time to answer this enquiry, I should be exceedingly happy to hear from you: & should you give me the information I expect & desire, you may enable me to be of service to my country.

I am, Sir, with great respect, your obt. servt.

JOSEPH C. CABELL †

MR. JOSEPH LANCASTER

† Cabell was a close and faithful friend and worker with Jefferson on plans for education in Virginia. He was also greatly interested in Pestalozzian methods of teaching. In the interest of his health he was in Europe from 1803 to 1806 and visited Pestalozzi's famous school at Yverdun in company with William McClure who brought Joseph Neef, once an assistant to Pestalozzi, to Philadelphia where he opened a school on Pestalozzian principles. As secretary of the board of school commissioners of Nelson County, Virginia, Cabell reported in 1824 that the teachers of that mountain county were acquainted with the Pestalozzian system about which Cabell was himself enthusiastic. In that report he said that in Pestalozzianism was a "sure cure for the miserable conditions most of our schools have fallen into. . . . The new system has been adopted by the WHOLE of our public schools, and from present indications, it promises in the course of another year to become the exclusive and universal method." In 1830 the board of school commissioners of Washington County, Virginia, recommended in its report that the General Assembly of that State provide for the establishment of a school on the Pestalozzian plan in each county "for the education of young men as teachers." Widespread interest in Pestalozzianism, however, did not develop in the United States until after 1860.

Joseph Lancaster to His Daughter, 1819 *

FREDERICKSBURGH 10mo 26 1819

DEAR ELIZABETH,

I arrived here this morning—visited School today—lecture here *tonight,* and tomorrow pass on to Richmond Virginia—address there. I find that Robert Ould has made *200$* in *fees* for training *teachers*—Yet to borrow a dollar of him would be little better than attempting to bleed a stone. I have found a friend whose heart is open, and his hand stretched out. I have no doubt of *the Rent* being received *by ye 31* (I mean one quarter)—if I can command both, which I think likely will.

And now, my dear Darling, write to me and cheer up; I work for One who has never left or forsaken me, and *I believe never will. Confidence in Him in gloomy times,* has always been my consolation and my Crown. May it be thine! and may'st thou learn it early, for in this wild and wicked world, Sin and ingratitude require that our Souls should find shelter from their efforts, *in the Rock of Ages.* Remember that all we can ever suffer *here,* is *short* of what we merit from Omniptence: and that our great afflictions are *light* compared with the *awfulness* of our final change—which *future* hope alone can make easy, and render our career triumphant over the Grave in His faith which hath said, *"Oh Death I will be thy Death"*— My heart has been touched by Divine Love— Oh for *early* dedication and *lasting* faithfulness! I had the God of thy Father, and they Father's Father, bless-comfort and keep they by night and by day! I implore His blessing on thy head, and never cease to love thee *all the day long.*

Be assured I shall not travel long—I feel that I *must* settle; the Lord direct me! and *may I never succeed* but in the *right place!*—that, I believe, is somewhere in this country, perhaps *in* Virginia. *Ere long I shall know.* My love to my Brother and the young men, tell them to dismiss alarms-fear God and take *courage,* and all will be well. Tomorrow I shall write again with some of the needful.*

Tell R. Jones, *Cook* is a *noble fellow*—he will see it; but *Ould* is a selfish contemptible *miser,* I have found him out completely.

*I shall then give further directions. Give my love to thy Mother—remember me affectionately to Robinson. I shall now be at work, *lecturing,* which will cheer my heart, and, I hope, fill thy pocket, my dar Lady Treasurer, after *all* and in *all,* everything I have known to be done by my beloved child, in my absence, has met my approbation. I was delighted to see thee again,—to see thee *so much* lika a woman. I bless the Lord *for* the

---

* This letter and the three letters that follow seem to disclose Lancaster's affection for his daughter but also his visionary and improvident if not mercenary traits. Robert Ould, from whom he could not borrow money, was an American disciple and personal representative of Lancaster and had an approved school at Georgetown in the District of Columbia for the training of teachers in Lancasterian methods.

firmness of thy *mind.* May He be thy support and bless thee, is the prayer of thy affectionate father

Jos Lancaster

Richmond/Virginia, 10 mo 28—1819

My Dear Child,

I lectured twice at Fredericksburgh—*only 84 people* attended, *but the produce was 42* dollars—at 50 cents each person: of which I remit 15— Jones will be able to get them changed at 3 or 4 cents discount, as they are very good Notes and in high repute—I have not time to get them exchanged for United States money—but will do so with my next.

There is a place *here* called the Capitol (in allusion to the Capitol in which the *Senate* of ancient Rome used to meet) where the Legislature of this State usually meet. Formerly, it was not uncommon for Lectures to be given it—latterly, it has been forbidden; but the Governor and Council have unanimously granted it in my favour—an *honour unexpected,* and *one* which will have its *due* effect in *Richmond.* Tomorrow (7th day evening) *2nd day* and *3rd day are fixed for Lectures here,* and 4th day, I trust, *at Petersburgh.*

The *Legislature* does not meet here for a month, when I hope to be among them—and afterwards (the next week to my being here) in Washington. *The people here are not like the Bostonians;* they do not put in *buttons*—bad silver and copper—*forged* notes and *bits of tin;* but they pay their *50 cents* each and *call* it *cheap.* I am told, that at Charleston in Carolina they think nothing of *a dollar* for *a Lecture,* but I am not yet disposed to try Charleston.

Respecting the *Rent,* I have no doubt that the Landlord will be easy a *few days,* for his own credit sake.

The next Post, or perhaps two, I expect you will receive from two friends of mine, 50$, and as much more from myself, which will meet the Rent: the present is for my house and family.

I can have little doubt (from my Lectures in the Town of *Fredericksburgh* and the expectation here) *but that* the Scene is changed, and you may all hope for the best. Expect to hear from me every Post, and believe me with Love *to all* and true affection

thy loving Father
Joseph Lancaster.

Direct to me
 Post Office Norfolk, Virginia

Richmond 11 mo 2 1819

My dear Elizabeth,

The enclosed will shew thee that the door of hope is opening bright— tomorro's post will bring as much more. It is to thee I send my money, *it* being part of my plan of education, to *accustom thee to the use of it;* and I *shall be very uneasy* if I do not *receive letters from thee in thy own hand.* I hope thou will always write thy letters to me without allowing *any* one to take them—and put them into the Post Office thyself—write me along letter and tell me thy heart. *Remember,* I have given thy uncle no *authority* over *thee*—he has no power to exact obedience—thou art mine, and I allow none to control thee but myself; thou knowest I love thee; and do not let the fear of grieving me add *to my troubles,* by keeping thee silent. I know that thou wast—unhappy at the thought of thy uncle coming to the house—be assured I shall very soon be in Philadelphia if anything unpleasant occur—that I would be *near* thee and not allow of separation, but there seems a bright prospect here.

My lectures have produced within a week above 90$—the enclosed makes 45$ I have sent home; I hope to send more tomorrow. Do write to me and tell me how thou art.

I have requested Friend Robinson to burn *the deed*—see it done if needful; I apprehend it is not legal and may do harm—*I see* we must trust in God and not in man for our prosperity—*we shall prosper* but not by that means.

I hope 'ere long to assist thee in a Girls School in this place. Thou knows how to treat thy Uncle with proper respect—but thy *obedience* to him is thy own pleasure, for I have full confidence in thee.
direct Post Office Norfolk Virginia if write immly.

[No signature]

PETERSBURGH, VIRGINIA 11 mo 4, 1819

DEAR CHILD,

I wish thee to write to me at length, and *put* the letter in the P. Office *thyself.* Give my love to thy mother and tell *her* to write to me *also,* and to entrust the letter *only* to thy care to put in the Post Office. I am quite uneasy that I had no letter from thee at *Washington or Richmond,* do let me have letters by Return of Post P. O. Norfolk.

Enclosed are 20$—more will come after my next lecture tonight. . . .

John C. Calhoun to Joseph Lancaster, 1820

DEPARTMENT OF WAR 13th March 1820

SIR,

I havent been able to examine your letter of the 21st. Ult. containing proposals to compile and publish a book for the use of Indian Schools, wch you handed to me, until very recently, and I find there is no information as to the plan of the book, to enable me to judge of its usefulness in the way contemplated, and of the propriety of affording its publication the encouragement which it is asked for. If you will furnish me with an outline of the book, an early answer upon the subject will be given.

I have the honor to be, your mo obt. Sert.

J. C. CALHOUN.

DEPARTMENT OF WAR, 16 May 1820—

SIR

Your letter of the 1st has been received. I am satisfied that the book which you propose to publish could be found very useful in the schools for the education of Indian children, and there is no objection to subscribing for the number of copies you propose, but they will be useless to the Department unless the Societies under whose patronage these schools are, or may be, established, could be induced to adopt your method of teaching in them. The School at Brainard, in the Cherokee Nation, is the only one now established on the Lancasterian plan, and judging from the success which has attended it, I have no doubt, if it were more generally introduced, that it would be found, not only the most agreeable to the Scholars, making their progress more easy, and rapid, but highly advantageous for the interests of the institutions themselves. The Department has no control over these benevolent societies as to the mode of teaching which they shall adopt in their schools, but it would be much gratified if they would cooperate with you so far as to adopt your plan in them generally, and in that case it would have no hesitation in taking any number of copies of your book that could be usefully disposed of among them; and it is very probable, if you were to open a correspondence with them, they would have no objection to acceding to your views. Should you be inclined to commence a correspondence with them upon this subject,—to give you an opportunity, I annex a list of the societies the most actively engaged in the cause of civilization.* An early communication of your success will be received with pleasure. . . . I have the honor to be your obt. Sert.

J. C. CALHOUN

Board of Regents of New York May Charter
Lancasterian Schools, 1821 †

The founders and benefactors of any school established, or to be established for the instruction of youth, on the system of Lancaster or Bell, or any other system approved by the board of regents, or as many of such founders as shall have contributed more than one half of the property col-

---

* The Societies listed by Calhoun were The American Board of Commissioners for Foreign Missions, Worcester and Salem, Massachusetts; The Missionary Society of New York; The United Foreign Missionary Society of New York; The American Baptist Board of Foreign Missions; The Society of United Brethren, Salem, North Carolina.

† *Statutes at Large of the State of New York*, I, p. 411.

lected or appropriated for the use of such school, may make to the regents of the university, an application in writing, under their hands, requesting that such school may be incorporated, nominating the first trustees, and specifying the name by which the incorporation is to be called.

The Pennsylvania Society for the Promotion of Public Schools Declares Its Purposes, 1828 *

Whilst some maintain that the cause of education may flourish when trusted to the efforts of individuals, unassisted by legislative enactments on the bounty of the public treasury, another large and respectable class, whose experience has convinced them of the fallacy of this opinion, are ardently desirous to introduce into the Commonwealth some system, sanctioned by law, of more efficacy, and more comprehensive than the plan which is now in operation. Many efforts have been made to effect this highly desirable object by zealous and patriotic citizens in different parts of the State. With a firmness of purpose, which a want of success has never relaxed, these efforts have been perseveringly continued. Although the Legislature has repeatedly rejected the petitions contained in their memorials, and disregarded the advice as repeatedly given in the annual messages of the Executive, recommending education to their fostering care—still their labors have not been entirely in vain: the public attention has been awakened, much valuable information has been published, and a manifest increase of the friends of a system for the promotion of public education has been effected. Nevertheless, a cooperation in effort, as well as unity of design, is essential to success, which cannot be expected from the unconnected and even contradictory labors which have heretofore so frequently proved abortive. To accomplish the important purposes which we have previously mentioned, a more promising, and we venture to hope, a more efficient plan has been adopted. An Association has been formed in Philadelphia, with branches in every part of the State, for the sole and express purpose of concentrating the efforts of the friends of public schools, and thus jointly endeavoring to effect what individual exertions have hitherto failed to accomplish. This Society is at present composed of about two hundred and fifty members, and a correspondence has been commenced with one hundred and twenty members, who reside in every district in the State. It is intended to direct the continual attention of the public to the importance of the subject: to collect and diffuse all information which may be deemed valuable, and to persevere in their labors until they shall be crowned with success. . . .

In Philadelphia and Lancaster, public schools, supported by public taxes, and accessible to the poor gratuitously, have been established by

* Given in J. P. Wickersham, *A History of Education in Pennsylvania* (Lancaster, Inquirer Publishing Co., 1886), pp. 296-98.

law, and the blessings of education conferred on thousands who might otherwise have continued in ignorance. For the successful introduction of this plan, our citizens are indebted to the patriotic, intelligent and persevering efforts of a few individuals, who were compelled to combat with ignorance, the prejudices and the pecuniary interests of numerous active and hostile opponents; their benevolent designs were but partially supported by public opinion, and consequently have not been carried into execution in any other towns of Pennsylvania.

Although repeated applications have been made to our Legislature by memorials signed by numerous and respectable citizens, and supported by many of the members of both Houses of our Assembly, and although the cause of education is a never-failing topic recommended in the annual messages of our Governors, every effort to establish a school fund, or any general plan for promoting common elementary schools similar to those which have been introduced into the districts above mentioned, or to those which have so long and so usefully flourished in several of our sister States, has proved abortive.

With the exceptions which we have mentioned, we are indebted for the establishment of those elementary schools in which the children of our citizens at present receive the rudiments of instruction, almost exclusively to the efforts of those individuals who depend on them for the means of support: the character of these schools consequently depends on the individuals who administer their concerns. Although, doubtless, many schools exist which justify the high reputation which they enjoy, the Committee are compelled to state that the great majority of these institutions are unworthy of the State in which they are permitted to continue. From the circumstance of their being the absolute property of individuals, no supervision or effectual control can be exercised over them; it is therefore almost unnecessary to state that many abuses prevail in the management of these irresponsible institutions.

Individuals, sometimes destitute of character, and frequently of the requisite abilities and attainments, establish these seminaries more from a desire of private speculation than for the important and legitimate end which they ostensibly announce to the public. Hence the ignorance, the inattention, and even the immorality of the teachers of our common schools, have long been subjects of regret to the reflecting and benevolent class of our fellow citizens. Frequent efforts have been made by some of the more intelligent and public spirited to diminish, if not entirely to prevent, these evils in their respective districts, by organizing associations for the purpose of procuring suitable instructors for their children. This plan, when zealously pursued, has been attended by the most beneficial results; but it is necessarily limited and generally transient in its effects, depending for its success, as well as its establishment and continuance, on the zeal and intelligence of a few individuals. It is a common, but a very true re-

mark, that the performance of duties relating equally to the common interests of society, is too frequently neglected when the performance of
these duties is not specifically assigned to particular persons; hence the
general inattention to the character of schoolmasters, in consequence of
which individuals are frequently permitted to usurp this important station,
who are entirely incapable of filling many of even the humblest occupations of society. In accepting the very small salaries with which many of
them are contented, they at once gratify the unwise parsimony of the parents of their pupils, and attach at least a modest valuation to their own
services. Even these apologies for schools have not been universally established throughout our Commonwealth. *In some districts no schools of
any description exist!* No means whatever of acquiring education are resorted to. Teachers are unwilling to incur the expense of establishing seminaries, unless some probability exists of obtaining a sufficient number of
pupils to afford them the means of maintenance. The differences of opinion, and the jarring interests of the inhabitants, in relation to suitable sites
for schoolhouses, and sometimes the culpable apathy of the population,
occasion whole districts to remain destitute of these all-important institutions. It is almost unnecessary to state that ignorance, and its never-failing
consequence, crime, prevail in these neglected spots to a greater extent
than in other more favored portions of the State. . . .

Josiah Holbrook Proposes a Constitution for the Lyceum, 1828 *

American Lyceum. The undersigned agree to associate under the name
——————, Branch of the American Lyceum, and adopt the following
articles for their constitution.

Article 1. The objects of the lyceum are the improvement of its members
in useful knowledge, and the advancement of popular education, by introducing uniformity and improvements in common schools, by becoming
auxiliary to a board of education.

Article 2. To effect these objects, they will procure a cabinet, consisting
of books, apparatus for illustrating the sciences, and a collection of minerals, and will hold meetings for discussions, dissertations, illustrating the
sciences, or other exercises which shall be thought expedient.

Article 3. Any person may be a member of the lyceum, by paying into
the treasury annually, 2 dollars; and 20 dollars paid at any one time will
entitle a person, his or her heirs, or assigns, to membership forever. Persons under 18 years of age will be entitled to all the privileges of the society, except of voting, for one-half of the annual sum above named.

Article 4. The officers of this branch of the lyceum shall be a president,
vice-president, treasurer, recording and corresponding secretaries, 3 or 5

* *American Journal of Education,* III, p. 503.

curators, and 3 delegates, to be appointed by ballot on the first Wednesday of September annually.

Article 5. The president, vice-president, treasurer, and secretaries will perform the duties usually implied in those offices. The curators will have charge of the cabinet and all other property of the lyceum not appertaining to the treasury, and will be the general agents to do any business for the society under their direction. The delegates will meet delegates from branches of the lyceum in this county semiannually, to adopt regulations for their general and mutual benefit, or to take measures to introduce uniformity and improvements into common schools, and to diffuse useful and practical knowledge generally through the community, particularly to form and aid a board of education.

Article 6. To raise the standard of common education, and to benefit the juvenile members of the lyceum, a portion of the books procured shall be fitted to young minds; and teachers of schools may be permitted to use for the benefit of their pupils who are members of the lyceum, the apparatus and minerals under such restrictions as the association shall prescribe.

Article 7. The president or any five members will have power at any time to call a special meeting, which meeting shall be legal, if notice shall be given according to the direction in the By-Laws.

Article 8. The lyceum will have power to adopt such regulations and by-laws as shall be necessary for the management and use of the cabinet, for holding meetings, or otherwise for their interest.

Article 9. The foregoing articles may be altered or amended by vote of two-thirds present, at any legal meeting; said alteration or amendment having been proposed at a meeting, not less than four weeks previous to the one at which it is acted upon.

Questions Addressed by the Working Men of Philadelphia to Candidates for the Legislature, 1829 *

Sir: The Delegates of the Working Men for the city, having placed your name in the list of fourteen, (from which seven will be chosen) as a candidate for the State Legislature; they are desirous (through the medium of the undersigned committee) to obtain your views in relation to the following subjects:

First. An equal and general system of Education.

Second. The banking system, and all other exclusive monopolies, considered with regard to the good or ill effects produced upon the productive classes by their operations.

Third. Lotteries, whether a total abolishment of them is not essential to the moral as well as pecuniary interest of society. Upon the important

* *New York Free Enquirer*, October 7, 1829. Given in Commons and others (Eds.), *A Documentary History of American Industrial Society*, V, pp. 93, 94.

subject of Education we wish most distinctly to understand whether you do, or do not consider it essential to the welfare of the rising generation, "That an open school and competent teachers for every child in the state, from the lowest branch of an infant school to the lecture rooms of practical science, should be established, and those who superintend them to be chosen by the people."

Our object in soliciting your views, sir, upon these several important points, is to enable us in the discharge of our duty, as delegates, to select such men for the Legislature, as are willing as well as competent, to legislate upon subjects which the Working Men of the city consider of the greatest importance, not only to themselves but the community at large. If your views should be in accordance with the interests of those we have the honor to represent, we request you to allow us to place your name on our Ticket. We are very respectfully, Sir, your obedient servants, JOHN THOMASON, THOMAS TAYLOR, WILLIAM ENGLISH, JOHN ASHTON, JR., BENJ. MIFFLIN, *Committee.*

N.B. An immediate answer is particularly requested.

Platform of the Boston Working Men's Party, 1830 *

1. That we are determined by all fair and honorable means, to exalt the character, and promote the cause, of those who, by their productive industry, add riches to the state, and strength to our political institutions.

2. That we exclude from our association none, who, by their honest industry, render an equivalent to society for the means of subsistence which they draw therefrom.

3. That we regard all attempts to degrade the working classes as so many blows aimed at the destruction of popular virtue—without which no human government can long subsist.

4. That we view with abhorrence every attempt to disturb the public peace by uniting with political doctrines any question of religion or anti-religion.

5. That the establishment of a liberal system of education, attainable by all, should be among the first efforts of every lawgiver who desires the continuance of our national independence.

6. That provision ought to be made by law for the more extensive diffusion of knowledge, particularly in the elements of those sciences which pertain to mechanical employments, and to the politics of our common country.

7. That, as we hold to the natural and political equality of all men, we have a right to ask for laws which shall protect every good citizen from oppression, contumely and degradation.

* *Boston Courier*, August 28, 1830. Given in Commons and others (Eds.), *op. cit.,* V, pp. 188-89.

8. That we are opposed to monopolies, under whatever guise they may be imposed on the community—whether in the shape of chartered institutions for private gain; or in that of taxes, levied, nominally for the public good, on the many for the advantage of the few.

9. That we regard the multiplication of statutes, and the mysterious phraseology in which they are ordinarily involved, as actual evils, loudly demanding correction.

10. That the people have a right to understand every law made for their government, without paying enormous fees for having them expounded by attorneys—by those perhaps who were instrumental in their construction, and in rendering them incomprehensible, even to themselves.

11. That every representative chosen to declare the sentiments of the people, is bound to obey the popular voice, and to express it, or resign his trust forthwith.

12. That we are resolved to advocate, as one of our leading objects, the entire abrogation of all laws authorizing the imprisonment of the body for debt—at least until poverty shall be rendered criminal by law.

13. That we will endeavor by all practicable means to obtain a reform in our militia system.

14. That for the purpose of securing these objects, we will adopt a system of social discipline: hereby organizing ourselves under the title of Working Men of Boston.

15. That, for the furtherance of this plan, we recommend that a general meeting of our brethren and friends in the city, be held at an early day, for the purpose of selecting two delegates from each Ward, and two from South Boston, in order to constitute a General Executive Committee.

Public Schools Not a Province of Government, 1830 *

It is an old and sound remark, that government cannot provide for the necessities of the People; that it is they who maintain the government, and not the latter the People. Education may be among their necessities; but it is one of that description which the state or national councils cannot supply, except partially and in a limited degree. They may endow public schools for the indigent, and colleges for the most comprehensive and costly scheme of instruction. To create or sustain seminaries for the tuition of all classes—to digest and regulate systems; to adjust and manage details, to render a multitude of schools effective, is beyond their province and power. Education in general must be the work of the intelligence, need, and enterprise of individuals and associations. At present, in nearly all the most populous parts of the United States, it is attainable for nearly all the inhabitants; it is comparatively cheap, and if not the best possible, it is sus-

* *Philadelphia National Gazette,* July 12, 1830. Given in Commons and others (Eds.), *op. cit.,* V, pp. 108-09.

ceptible of improvement and likely to be advanced. Its progress and wider diffusion will depend, not upon government, but on the public spirit, information, liberality and training of the citizens themselves, who may appreciate duly the value of the object as a national good, and as a personal benefit for their children. Some of the writers about universal public instruction and discipline, seem to forget the constitution of modern society, and declaim as if our communities could receive institutions or habits like those of Sparta. The dream embraces grand Republican female academies, to make Roman matrons!

An Argument Against Public Schools, 1830 *

We remark the following toast in one of the lists which nearly fill the papers at this season.

"Education and general information—these must indeed constitute our only true National Bulwark. May the day soon come when in point of literary acquirements the poorest peasant shall stand on a level with his more wealthy neighbors."

It is our strong inclination and our obvious interest that literary acquirements should be universal; but we should be guilty of imposture, if we professed to believe in the possibility of that consummation. Literature cannot be acquired without leisure, and wealth gives leisure. Universal opulence, or even competency, is a chimera, as man and society are constituted. There will ever be distinctions of conditions of capacity, of knowledge and ignorance, in spite of all the fond conceits which may be indulged, or the wild projects which may be tried, to the contrary. The "peasant" must labor during those hours of the day, which his wealthy neighbor can give to the abstract culture of his mind; otherwise, the earth would not yield enough for the subsistence of all: the mechanic cannot abandon the operations of his trade, for general studies; if he should, most of the conveniences of life and objects of exchange would be wanting; languor, decay, poverty, discontent would soon be visible among all classes. No government, no statesman, no philanthropist, can furnish what is incompatible with the very organization and being of civil society. Education, the most comprehensive, should be, and is, open to the whole community; but it must cost to every one, time and money; and those are means which every one cannot possess simultaneously. Doubtless, more of education and of information is attainable for all in this republic, than can be had any where else by the poor or the operatives, so called.

* *Philadelphia National Gazette,* July 10, 1830. Given in Commons and others (Eds.), *op. cit.,* V, pp. 107-08.

Stephen Girard Provides in His Will for a Lancasterian School in Philadelphia, 1831 *

IV. I give and bequeath to "The Comptrollers of the Public Schools for the City and County of Philadelphia," the sum of *Ten Thousand Dollars,* for the use of the schools upon the Lancaster system, in the first section of the first school district of Pennsylvania.

A Meeting Is Held in Washington to Promote Interest in Sunday Schools, 1831 †

A meeting was held in the city of Washington, on the 16*th* of February to consider the object proposed by the American Sunday School Union, of supplying the Valley of the Mississippi with Sunday Schools. It was very numerously attended, and conducted, apparently with great unanimity, by leading gentlemen of every political party.

The Hon. Felix Grundy, of Tennessee, was called to the chair, and Matthew St. Clair Clark, Clerk of the House of Representatives, was appointed Secretary.

The President of the United States sent an apology for not being able to attend the meeting, with his best wishes for the success of the institution. Mr. Wirt also, the late Attorney General of the United States, sent a letter assigning the reason which detained him, and enclosing a donation of fifty dollars.

A number of resolutions, approving of the project, were proposed, and accompanied with addresses by the following gentlemen of the Congress of the United States: Mr. Whittlesey and Mr. Crane of Ohio, Mr. Coleman of Kentucky, Mr. Hayne of South Carolina, Mr. Frelinghuysen of New Jersey, Mr. Wickliffe of Kentucky, and Mr. Webster of Massachusetts; and also by F. S. Key, Esq. of Georgetown, and the Rev. J. W. Danforth and Walter Lowrie, Esq. of Washington.

The most perfect harmony pervaded the meeting, which was eloquently addressed by most of the gentlemen who moved resolutions. Mr. Whittlesey spoke for some time on the benefits of Sabbath Schools in the West. Mr. Coleman went at large into the importance of Sunday School instruction in the Valley of the Mississippi, and answered objections to Sunday Schools in general. Mr. Hayne briefly advocated the truth and power of Divine Revelation, and declared the Bible to be the basis of our country's happiness and prosperity. Mr. Wickliffe bore his testimony to the excellent effects of Sunday Schools which he had witnessed. He deprecated the idea, advanced either in ignorance or malice, of a union of Church and State being the aim or the consequence of these pious exertions. On the same

---

* *Stephen Girard Will.* Reprinted by Girard College from the Girard Will Case, 1947, p. 2.
† *American Annals of Education,* I, p. 178.

ground, we might object to most or all of the literary institutions of the country, as having this object. Messrs Key, Frelinghuysen, and Webster addressed the meeting at length, in favor of this plan of benevolence.

Mr. Webster spoke of the legal provision made for the mind even by heathen legislators; but of "the far superior value and efficacy of a system of instruction founded on the Bible, that grand textbook for universal commentary."

It is highly interesting to see gentlemen so absolutely and warmly opposed to each other in political sentiments, meeting on the subject of bible education as on common ground; and cordially promoting its extension as a means of national improvement and happiness; and it shows in what light the American Sunday School Union is viewed by some of our most distinguished statesmen.

The American Lyceum Is Organized, 1831 *

At the request of the New York State Lyceum, delegates and other friends of education assembled in the City of New York, on the 4th of May last, to organize a National Lyceum. By the politeness of the corporation of the City, the Convention assembled in City Hall. . . .

Soon after the Convention was organized, a committee on arrangements was appointed, consisting of Messrs. Griscom, Holbrook, Yates, Olmsted, and Sargent, who, after a short time, reported a constitution for the American Lyceum, and several subjects for discussion during their session.

The fundamental principle in the constitution, and the one which called forth much animated discussion and some difference of opinion, is the representative feature. The object of this principle in the constitution is to secure a representation from every section of the Union, and with it a collection of *facts* relating to the condition and wants of schools, and to provide and execute measures by which their wants may be supplied, and a uniform and improved system of education be introduced and extended throughout the country.

For the facts which are expected, as well as for all the operations of the

---

* *Ibid.*, pp. 373-76. The lyceum is believed to have originated in this country through the efforts of Josiah Holbrook (1788-1854), who was graduated from Yale in 1810 and began in 1826 "to establish on a uniform plan, in every town and village, a society for mutual improvement and the improvement of schools." This organization appeared in many states and served to stimulate interest in public education. For a list of some of the subjects discussed at meetings of the national organization, see *American Journal of Education*, XVI, p. 312. As early as 1835 there were, in addition to the national organization, many state, more than one hundred county and more than three thousand town and village organizations throughout the United States. Among names conspicuous in the movement as leaders and lecturers were Edward Everett, William C. Woodbridge, Thomas H. Gallaudet, John Griscom, Denison Olmsted, Philip Lindsley, Henry Ward Beecher, Wendell Phillips, Thomas S. Grimké, Ralph Waldo Emerson, Oliver Wendell Holmes, Horace Greeley, Abraham Lincoln and others. See also Cecil B. Hayes, *The American Lyceum: Its History and Contribution to Education*, Bulletin 12, 1932, United States Office of Education. The lyceum was succeeded by the Chautauqua movement and summer sessions of colleges and universities.

system, designed for direct instruction or utility, the principal dependence is on town Lyceums, which, it is hoped, will soon be universally established throughout the country. All the necessary facts relating to education can be collected with great ease by all the town Lyceums, and in a great measure from teachers, who are in many cases members, ex officio, of these societies. From the town Lyceums the facts are sent to county societies, where they are embodied, and again reported to state Lyceums, and thence to the National Society.

When the defects, wants, improvements, facilities, etc., of our schools, and of all literary institutions, are placed before the enlightened congress of teachers and other friends of education and of their country, they will be prepared to propose and recommend measures, for general adoption, still leaving them to be received or rejected by all to whom they relate.

Although the Lyceum, in all its departments, is a *voluntary* association, or an advisory body, and resorts to no law, nor to any other power but *evidence,* and the power of *motives;*—yet by enlightening and elevating *public sentiment,* before which legislatures, kings, and despots must bow, it may exert *power,* and the only power worthy to be exerted or acknowledged by intellectual and moral beings.

Constitution of the American Lyceum

Art. I. The Society shall be called the American Lyceum.

Art. II. The objects of the Lyceum shall be the advancement of Education, especially in Common Schools, and the general diffusion of knowledge.

Art. III. The members of the American Lyceum shall consist as follows: —*1st* Of Delegates from State, Territory, and District Lyceums. (Members equal to one half number congressmen from each State, etc., not less than three.) *2d* Persons appointed by executive committee. *3rd* Invited members.

Art. IV. Officers, and Executive Committee.

Art. V. Annual Meeting in May of each year, in New York.

Art. VI. Quorum.

Art. VII. Amending the Constitution.

Subjects for Discussion

After the adoption of the above outlined constitution, the following subjects were then presented to the Lyceum for discussion.

1. What are the greatest desiderata in relation to the improvement of common schools?

2. What are the most eligible and practical means of advancing and perfecting the science of instruction?

3. To what extent is the monitorial system advisable and practicable in common schools?

4. What is the most eligible plan of promoting education, by legislative enactments?

5. Ought manual labor schools to be encouraged, and upon what general plan?

6. Should every boy who can devote his whole time to study until the age of 16 be put to the study of Latin and Greek, and if not, to what class should these languages be restricted?

7. To what extent may lectures be useful in common schools?

8. To what extent can the natural sciences be advantageously introduced into common schools?

9. The object and usefulness of town and district Lyceums?

10. What should be the object of county and state Lyceums, and how should they be formed?

Some Questions Proposed for Discussion at the Fifth Annual Convention of the American Lyceum, 1835 *

1. Should natural history be taught in common schools?
2. Ought the principles of the Christian religion to be made a regular part of common instruction?
3. By what means may a taste for the fine arts be generally cultivated among all classes?
4. What improvements are necessary in the laws of the State of New York, in relation to common schools?
5. How may our thinly settled districts be best supplied with means of education?
6. Ought more female teachers to be employed in our common schools?
7. Ought corporal punishments to form a regular part of common-school discipline?
8. How may the application of science to the arts of life be best taught in common schools?
9. Ought political economy to be taught as a branch of common education?

The Program of an Educational Convention in Michigan, 1838 †

An important and interesting meeting of the friends of education, and especially the teachers of Michigan, was held at the city of Detroit, January 3-5. The meeting was addressed by Rev. J. D. Pierce, the State Superintendent of Public Instruction, and others, and the following "bill of fare" was provided in the papers and discussions. It has interested us so

* *Ibid.*, V, p. 267.
† *Ibid.*, VIII, pp. 136-42.

much that we have resolved to insert it. Perhaps it may afford hints to those of our neighbors who need a little prompting on these occasions.

1. The necessity of general education, as a safeguard of liberty, and as conducive especially to the stability of a republican form of government.

2. The influence of the practical spirit of this age upon good education, and upon the proper development of the mind.

3. The influence of periodical literature, and the political press in forming the taste, the tone of feeling, and general character of the American people.

4. The best methods of improving the character of primary schools, and enlarging, by additional branches, the field of elementary instruction.

5. Would the interests of general education be promoted by legislative provisions adequate to the *entire support* of common schools?

6. In what way can the most efficient system of inspecting common school teachers be secured?

7. Is it expedient or practicable to have entire uniformity in the class books for common schools or academies?

8. Have the late attempts to simplify the books used in elementary instruction been productive of any great advantage?

9. The utility of models in mechanism, and of demonstrative apparatus for schools.

10. The benefit of libraries for common schools.

11. The influence of studies, which are too general, upon the minds of the young.

12. The best construction of school houses, with reference to size, internal arrangement, warmth, and ventilation.

13. Vocal music as a branch of common education.

14. In what way can the study of grammar be more conducive than it is, to the end of "speaking and writing the English language with propriety"?

15. The system of instruction pursued at the Rensselaer Institution, requiring the pupils to lecture in recitation before their classes.

16. The importance of a higher standard in female education. The capacity of females for acquiring the highest branches of science, and the advantages to them of the study of Mathematics.

17. To what extent can the monitorial method of instruction be incorporated with the common system?

18. How far ought the catechetical form of instruction to be introduced into school books?

19. Is the method of communicating instruction by lectures adapted to develop and exercise the mental powers?

20. The best method of teaching the several branches of common education.

21. Ought the principle of education to be appealed to and fostered, as an incentive to proficiency and good conduct in school?

22. How far can an appeal to the sense of honor, and to the moral sentiments, be made the substitute for corporal punishment in the government of youth?

23. How far ought the theory of our republican form of government, and the history of its administration, to be made a subject of study in schools?

24. The comparative efficiency of the classics and the natural sciences, in disciplining the mind.

25. The moral discipline of schools, including the best methods of correcting vicious disposition, and of impressing a sense of moral obligation.

26. The importance of making the business of common school teaching a profession, by affording to that employment more adequate compensation.

27. How far should religious instruction be introduced into schools and academies?

28. In directing the studies of the young, how far should reference be had to the *practical utilities* of life?

Dorothea Dix Memorializes the Legislature of Massachusetts on the Horrible Conditions of Prisons and Asylums, 1843 *

GENTLEMEN,—I respectfully ask to present this Memorial, believing that the *cause,* which actuates to and sanctions so unusual a movement, presents no equivocal claim to public consideration and sympathy. Surrendering to calm and deep convictions of duty my habitual views of what is womanly and becoming, I proceed briefly to explain what has conducted me before you unsolicited and unsustained, trusting, while I do so, that the memorialist will be speedily forgotten in the memorial.

About two years since leisure afforded opportunity and duty prompted me to visit several prisons and almshouses in the vicinity of this metropolis. I found, near Boston, in the jails and asylums for the poor, a numerous class brought into unsuitable connection with criminals and the general mass of paupers. I refer to idiots and insane persons, dwelling in circumstances not only adverse to their own physical and moral improvement, but productive of extreme disadvantages to all other persons brought into association with them. I applied myself diligently to trace the causes of these evils, and sought to supply remedies. As one obstacle was surmounted, fresh difficulties appeared. Every new investigation has given depth to the conviction that it is only by decided, prompt, and vigorous legislation the evils to which I refer, and which I shall proceed more fully to illustrate, can be remedied. I shall be obliged to speak with great plainness, and to

* *Old South Leaflets,* VI, No. 148, pp. 489-91.

reveal many things revolting to the taste, and from which my woman's nature shrinks with peculiar sensitiveness. But truth is the highest consideration. *I tell what I have seen*—painful and shocking as the details often are —that from them you may feel more deeply the imperative obligation which lies upon you to prevent the possibility of a repetition or continuance of such outrages from humanity. If I inflict pain upon you, and move you to horror, it is to acquaint you with sufferings which you have the power to alleviate, and make you hasten to the relief of the victims of legalized barbarity.

I come to present the strong claims of suffering humanity. I come to place before the Legislature of Massachusetts the condition of the miserable, the desolate, the outcast. I come as the advocate of helpless, forgotten, insane, and idiotic men and women; of beings sunk to a condition from which the most unconcerned would start with real horror; of beings wretched in our prisons, and more wretched in our almshouses. And I cannot suppose it needful to employ earnest persuasion, or stubborn argument, in order to arrest and fix attention upon a subject only the more strongly pressing in its claims because it is revolting and disgusting in its details.

I must confine myself to few examples, but am ready to furnish other and more complete details, if required. If my pictures are displeasing, coarse, and severe, my subjects, it must be recollected, offer no tranquil, refined, or composing features. The condition of human beings, reduced to the extremest states of degradation and misery, cannot be exhibited in softened language, or adorn a polished page.

I proceed, gentlemen, briefly to call your attention to the *present* state of insane persons confined within this Commonwealth, in *cages, closets, cellars, stalls, pens! Chained, naked, beaten with rods,* and *lashed* into obedience.

As I state cold, severe *facts,* I feel obliged to refer to persons, and definitely to indicate localities. But it is upon my subject, not upon localities or individuals, I desire to fix attention; and I would speak as kindly as possible of all wardens, keepers, and other responsible officers, believing that *most* of these have erred not through hardness of heart and wilful cruelty so much as want of skill and knowledge, and want of consideration. Familiarity with suffering, it is said, blunts the sensibilities, and where neglect once finds a footing other injuries are multiplied. This is not all, for it may justly and strongly be added that from the deficiency of adequate means to meet the wants of these cases, it has been an absolute impossibility to do justice in this matter. Prisons are not constructed in view of being converted into county hospitals, and almshouses are not founded as receptacles for the insane. And yet, in the face of justice and common sense, wardens are by law compelled to receive, and the masters of almshouses not to refuse, insane and idiotic subjects in all stages of mental disease and privation.

It is the Commonwealth, not its integral parts, that is accountable for most of the abuses which have lately and do still exist. I repeat it, it is defective legislation which perpetuates and multiplies these abuses. . . .

The Secretary of a Virginia Educational Convention Requests Advice from Horace Mann, 1845 *

RICHMOND November 8th 1845.

SIR,

I am desirous of obtaining some hints from you on the subject of popular education, to be laid before a Convention which will meet in the city of Richmond on the 10th of December next.

Your own fame, as connected with this subject, which reached me on the other side of the Atlantic, where I first heard your name pronounced, must constitute my apology for addressing you in this manner.

There are a large number of persons in this state who are deeply solicitous of doing something to remedy the evils under which our population are suffering from a want of general instruction. They have determined to meet together in a deliberative assembly contemporaneously with the meeting of the State Legislature, in order to consult upon some system which may meet the favor of that body. They have many opponents and much apathy to contend with, besides the natural obstacles presented by the sparseness of population in our state and there are conflicting views among them as to the best mode of effecting the object they have in view. Some are in favor of raising the necessary means by state taxation and others by county levies; some for and some against the District school system; some are for adopting a general system operating everywhere whilst others are for submitting the question to the vote of the people in the counties and establishing the system or not according to their decision; some are for primary schools as the first object of importance and others for further endowing the Colleges and academies. No tangible scheme has yet been presented by the Central committee of Richmond (of which I am a member) for fear of dividing the friends of education in its discussion. The present system, if system it can be called, merely provides for the education of as many poor children as the school commissioners will find out and the fund, of $70,000 per annum, pays for *teaching* (?) at 4 cents per day.

* Letters to Mann came from almost every Southern state, more from Mississippi than any other state except Virginia. Unfortunately, only a few of Mann's replies to his Southern admirers have been located. If these could be had it would be possible to note whether the people in the West and in the South were more or were less interested in the work of the eminent educator than the people of his own section. But if contemporary records can be believed, few if any educational leaders of his generation were ever so arrogantly scorned and so stubbornly resisted as was Horace Mann either by the proud schoolmasters of Boston because of his educational views or by the supercilious and intolerant clergymen of Massachusetts because of his forthright defense of religious toleration. The originals of this letter and those that follow now are the property of the Massachusetts Historical Society, Boston, and are here used by its permission. Photocopies are in the Southern Historical Collection, the University of North Carolina. See Edgar W. Knight, "More Evidence of Horace Mann's Influence in the South," *The Educational Forum*, XII (January, 1948), pp. 167-84.

The Executive officer charged with its administration, is a worthy sep-
tenegarian [sic] of business habits, but no scholarship; and he is wedded
to it.

Such are some of the obstacles to be encountered in this work.

Now, sir, will you not afford us some suggestions in aid of our beginning
a radical reform of the state of things in which we are placed? I have no
hesitation in saying that anything from your pen, whether of argument or
of fact, will receive the attentive ear of the convention. I should also be
glad to hear what has been the success which has attended the publication
of your Common School journal, in a pecuniary point of view; in order
that some estimate may be formed of the success of a similar journal in this
State.

Should you find it convenient to comply with the request I have made,
the favor will be highly appreciated.

I am very respectfully
yr obt st

R. B. GOOCH

HORACE MANN ESQ.
BOSTON

Mann Replies to the Request of Mr. Gooch, 1845

BOSTON, Nov. 15, 1845.

R. B. GOOCH, ESQ.
DEAR SIR,

Within the last two or three months I have received several letters of
enquiry respecting our school system, its mode of administration, &c., from
gentlemen in Virginia, who are members of the Richmond committee, or
delegates to the convention * to be held at that place. Having replied to
those enquiries with as much particularity as could conveniently be done
by letter, I deem it unnecessary to go over the same ground in answer to
yours.

I certainly should not volunteer an opinion on the questions you present,
nor should I even express one very confidently, where the circumstances to
which it applies are so imperfectly known; but unless very strong reasons
can be shewn to the contrary, I should urge the measure of *state,* rather
than *county* taxation, for the support of schools. If left to the counties, I
should fear that those which need an improved system least, would be the
only ones which would adopt it, while with those who need it most, their
indifference would be proportionate to their need. As in the body, if the
healthy parts do not aid the diseased, the latter will soon run to corruption.

It seems to me, that your counties should be divided into districts, but

---

* The report of that convention appears in the *Journal of the House of Delegates* of Virginia, 1845-46, Document 16, where Mann's letter to Gooch also appears.

the general administration of all the districts in each county should be lodged in the same hands, and all the schools be supported, and the school-houses built by the same funds, otherwise, you may have a good school and a good schoolhouse in one place, while all which surround it are poor. If schools and schoolhouses are maintained from a *common* fund, each will insist on having as good a one as its neighbor, and all the selfish feelings will be enlisted on the side of improvement. If each one is to support its own, all selfish considerations of a pecuniary nature will be arrayed against improvement.

Although your next question has been substantially answered above, yet I say again, that if you submit it to the option of each county to adopt the system or not, it will be rejected by the counties that most require it. Some places may be so ignorant that they have already ceased to be alarmed at their ignorance. How will they ever be raised but by the aid of others? You may say, the continuation of their ignorance is a just punishment for their indifference; but is not this punishment inflicted upon the innocent quite as much as upon the guilty? What you want to put an end to, is both the offence and the punishment.

As to the relative importance of primary schools on the one hand, and colleges and academies on the other, you may depend upon it as upon a law of nature, that colleges and academies never will act *downwards* to raise the mass of the people by education; but on the contrary, common schools will feed and sustain the academies and colleges. Heat ascends, and it will warm upwards, but it will not warm downwards.

Permit me to say that you need an agent who shall devote his whole time to the subject; who shall visit all parts of the state, collect statistics, call conventions, address the people, send abroad circulars, maintain correspondence, &c. &c.

Another thing which you must have, before you will ever make any system flourish, is a Normal school. All the money in the world, without a higher grade of teachers than you can now command, will never raise your schools to any elevated standards.

A periodical devoted to education will be a highly important auxiliary, if you can find an able editor in the first place, and subscribers who will pay for it and read it in the second. But unless your prospects are better in this respect than mine ever have been, I can give you no encouragement. My common school journal makes an annual octavo volume of about 400 very large pages. I have edited it for now seven years as a labour of love— that is, for nothing; and it has hardly defrayed the printer's bills. I wish I could afford to send you a complete copy of it; for it contains all our laws, reports, accounts of the Normal school, &c. which are no where else to be found, but I should have to buy it for the purpose, and therefore you must excuse me.

If I had any private means of conveyance, I should like to send you a volume or two of our school abstracts, which are too bulky and heavy to be sent by mail.

I am unable, my dear sir, to write you further at this time, for I am only in the city for a few hours at present. I have been absent for several weeks, attending what we call "Teachers' Institutes"—that is, meetings of the teachers, who assemble and spend a fortnight or more together in reviewing, under more experienced instructors, all the common school studies, and in hearing lectures, oral communications, &c. on the art and science of teaching and governing, and I am obliged to start off again on the same errand in a few hours.

Wishing you all possible success in the noble enterprise you have in view, and being always ready, should I be so happy as to have the ability to furnish you with any aid.

I subscribe myself, very truly, yours &c. &c.

HORACE MANN.

A Mississippian Asks Mann's Advice About Education, 1846

JACKSON MISSISSIPPI
April 17,   /46

HORACE MANN ESQ
DEAR SIR

The distinction you have acquired on the subject of common schools induced me to believe you will attend to the following request although I have not the pleasure of a personal acquaintance with you.

We have paper laws in this State preparatory to going into the common school system. I am a commissioner in one of the counties to superinted [sic] &c &c—I enclose you Five dollars and wish you to send to me at this office all the Essays, pamphlets & reports that you may think interesting to me. I would be glad also to have an Essay or Two on Female Education —The amount I send I hope will enable you to get them together through a news-boy (those you may not have on hand) without much trouble.

Any suggestions you may take the trouble to suggest to me relative to the subject of common schools will be thankfully recd May I take the liberty hereafter should I find it necessary to correspond with you on the subject?

Very respectfully

HECTOR R. WEST

The Grand Lodge of the Independent Order of Odd Fellows of North Carolina Asks Horace Mann's Advice on Its Educational Activities, 1840's

Whereas, The subject of education is one of deep and abiding interest to this Grand Lodge, and whereas Cape Fear Lodge, No. 2, has now a male

NEW FORCES AND THE AWAKENINGNEW FORCES AND THE AWAKENING 161

and female school in operation in this town, in which has been adopted (the) Prussian System, with a view of informing ourselves as to its merits and prospect of success.

Resolved, That the Grand Lodge as a body visit said school.

Resolved, That this Grand Lodge is highly gratified with the examination of the scholars, and that the capacity and aptness of the teachers in the various departments has given entire satisfaction; and from the result of the examination made, the Lodge is fully satisfied that the system upon which the school is taught, is well calculated to impart a thorough knowledge of the various branches of study, to the scholars, on the cheapest plan and in the most practicable and useful manner, and would therefor earnestly recommend to the Subordinate Lodges the propriety of extending this system of education, by establishing schools on this system whenever their resources will admit of their doing so. And whereas the great difficulty at present appears to be the obtaining of competent teachers, they recommend that each of the Subordinate Lodges, either send a teacher or scholars to this or some other school, taught on the same plan for the purpose of becoming qualified to teach on this system.

Although the progress of Odd Fellowship has not been distinguished by that extraordinary increase, within the jurisdiction of this Grand Lodge, which has marked its course in other states, yet in no part of our wide extended country are its benign precepts and principles more warmly cherished, nor does it anywhere exercise more healthful moral influence, not only among its members, but in the communities where it has taken hold, than it does in the Old North State.

After discharging the duties required of us by the principles of our Order, there is none which has a higher claim to our attention than the promotion of Education, by establishing good Schools, for which purpose the organization of our Society peculiarly fits it; a subject, with the importance of which this Grand Lodge, at its last Communication, was so fully impressed that it passed resolutions recommending the Lodges under its jurisdiction to establish Schools after the model of the Prussian School established by Cape Fear Lodge, No. 2. The Subordinate Lodges, with praiseworthy zeal, endeavored to carry the views of the Grand Lodge into effect, but have been unable to do so, because of the great difficulty, or rather impossibility, of procuring English Teachers who thoroughly understand the principles and systems of instructing in the schools of Prussia—a system, the best, *beyond comparison,* yet adopted in our country to impart, at a *cheap rate, a thorough and practical education.* As the Subordinate Lodges, in their efforts to carry into effect the recommendation of the Grand Lodge, have encountered, to them, an insurmountable difficulty, the Grand Lodge seems called on to come to their aid. With a view of doing so, I would respectfully recommend for your consideration, the expediency of opening a correspondence with other State Grand Lodges, for the purpose of raising a fund, if necessary, to defray the expenses of sending some suitable and competent persons to examine the Schools of Prussia, and if their system should be approved of, to thoroughly learn it, so as to establish a Gymnasium or Normal School, for the instruction of Teachers on that plan in this country. If this can be accomplished, although the process would be slow, it would in the end be sure to confer a lasting benefit, not only on our Order, but upon the cause of Education in our country.

The suggestion of the M. W. Grand Master, in regard to the establishment of a School or Gymnasium for the education of Teachers upon the Prussian plan, the Committee think good; and recommend that the R. W. Grand Secretary be requested to open a correspondence with the Grand Secretaries of the various Grand Lodges in the United States, with the view of bringing the subject before their respective bodies at as early a period as practicable; and that he report the result of such correspondence at our next Annual Communication.

All of which is respectfully submitted.

(Signed) J. B. NEWBY, *Chairman.*

3rd School System. We are at a loss to determine here what to recommend, but from all we can gather would suggest, that in view of the infantile state of the Order within the jurisdiction of this Grand Lodge, we are incapable of sustaining a College; and could we do so still we think it would be far more in accordance with the principles of Odd Fellowship to afford the means of a good Common School Education to a large number of youth, than to give a Collegiate one to a few individuals. We say a few, because we see not where the funds are to come from to advance a number in this particular. Your committee would therefore conclude this Report by recommending the Normal System of Education as suggested by P.G.M., John McRae, Sen., and in order to the accomplishment of this great object, your Committee would offer the following Resolution:

Resolved, That the Grand Secretary be instructed to address a communication to Horace Mann, Esq., of Boston, Mass., he having made this subject the object of a mission to Prussia, and while there no doubt obtained all possible information with respect to their system of teaching, and and the principles upon which are based the Normal Schools of that Nation.

All of which is respectfully submitted.

A. PAUL REPITON, *Chairman.*

FAYETTEVILLE, N. C.
October 1, 1846.

SIR:

At the last Annual Communication of the R. W. Grand Lodge of North Carolina (I.O.O.F) a Report was adopted recommending the Normal System of Education as most deserving the patronage of "the Order" in this State. In that Report (which you will find on pages 8 and 9 of the "Proceedings" I herewith transmit to you), the following Resolution is embraced:

"Resolved, That the Grand Secretary be instructed to address a communication to Horace Mann, Esq., of Boston, Mass., he having made the subject the object of a mission to Prussia, and while there no doubt obtained all possible information with respect to their system of teaching, and the principles upon which are based the Normal Schools of that Nation."

In compliance with the above resolution, I have taken the liberty of addressing you—hoping that you will be pleased to communicate such information on the subject of Normal Schools as will enable the Grand Lodge to act understandingly in carrying out any scheme it may choose to adopt relative thereto.

This system of Education is yet in its infancy in this State, but as far as it has been tried, has fully met the most sanguine expectations of its friends. A large Male and Female School is now in the "full tide of successful experiment" in Wilmington; and a Female School upon the same plan was opened in this place (Fayetteville), in January last, which has thus far fully realized the expectations of its founders.

Be pleased to accept assurances of my sincere regard.

Yours, very respectfully,

J. B. Newby,

Gr. Sec'ry. Grand Lodge of N. C., I.O.O.F.

Horace Mann on "The Ground of the Free School System," 1846 *

The Pilgrim Fathers amid all their privations and dangers conceived the magnificent idea, not only of a universal, but of a free education for the whole people. To find the time and the means to reduce this grand conception to practice, they stinted themselves, amid all their poverty, to a still scantier pittance; amid all their toils, they imposed upon themselves still more burdensome labors; and, amid all their perils, they braved still greater dangers. Two divine ideas filled their great hearts,—their duty to God and to posterity. For the one they built the church, for the other they opened the school. Religion and knowledge,—two attributes of the same glorious and eternal truth, and that truth the only one on which immortal or mortal happiness can be securely founded!

It is impossible for us adequately to conceive the boldness of the measure which aimed at universal education through the establishment of free schools. As a fact, it had no precedent in the world's history; and, as a theory, it could have been refuted and silenced by a more formidable array of argument and experience than was ever marshalled against any

---

* Extracts from Horace Mann's *Tenth Annual Report* to the Massachusetts State Board of Education, 1846. Given also in *Old South Leaflets*, V, No. 109, pp. 177-79, 180.

other institution of human origin. But time has ratified its soundness. Two centuries of successful operation now proclaim it to be as wise as it was courageous, and as beneficent as it was disinterested. Every community in the civilized world awards it the meed of praise; and states at home and nations abroad, in the order of their intelligence, are copying the bright example. What we call the enlightened nations of Christendom are approaching, by slow degrees, to the moral elevation which our ancestors reached at a single bound. . . .

The alleged ground upon which the founders of our free-school system proceeded when adopting it did not embrace the whole argument by which it may be defended and sustained. Their insight was better than their reason. They assumed a ground, indeed, satisfactory and convincing to Protestants; but at that time only a small portion of Christendom was Protestant, and even now only a minority of it is so. The very ground on which our free schools were founded, therefore, if it were the only one, would have been a reason with more than half of Christendom for their immediate abolition.

In later times, and since the achievement of American independence, the universal and ever-repeated argument in favor of free schools has been that the general intelligence which they are capable of diffusing, and which can be imparted by no other human instrumentality, is indispensable to the continuance of a republican government. This argument, it is obvious, assumes, as a *postulatum*, the superiority of a republican over all other forms of government; and, as a people, we religiously believe in the soundness both of the assumption and of the argument founded upon it. But, if this be all, then a sincere monarchist, or a defender of arbitrary power, or a believer in the divine right of kings, would oppose free schools for the identical reasons we offer in their behalf. . . .

Again, the expediency of free schools is sometimes advocated on grounds of political economy. An educated people is always a more industrious and productive people. Intelligence is a primary ingredient in the wealth of nations. . . . The moralist, too, takes up the argument of the economist. He demonstrates that vice and crime are not only prodigals and spendthrifts of their own, but defrauders and plunderers of the means of others, that they would seize upon all the gains of honest industry and exhaust the bounties of Heaven itself without satiating their rapacity; and that often in the history of the world whole generations might have been trained to industry and virtue by the wealth which one enemy to his race has destroyed.

And yet, notwithstanding these views have been presented a thousand times with irrefutable logic, and with a divine eloquence of truth which it would seem that nothing but combined stolidity and depravity could resist, there is not at the present time, [1846] with the exception of the States of New England and a few small communities elsewhere, a country or a state in Christendom which maintains a system of free schools for the education of its children. . . .

I believe in the existence of a great, immortal, immutable principle of natural law, or natural ethics,—a principle antecedent to all human institutions, and incapable of being abrogated by any ordinance of man,—a principle of divine origin, clearly legible in the ways of Providence as those ways are manifested in the order of nature and in the history of the race, which proves the *absolute right* to an education of every human being that comes into the world, and which, of course, proves the correlative duty of every government to see that the means of that education are provided for all. . . .

Horace Mann on the Relation Between Education and Prosperity, 1848 *

. . . Now two or three things will doubtless be admitted to be true, beyond all controversy, in regard to Massachusetts. By its industrial condition, and its business operations, it is exposed, far beyond any other State in the Union, to the fatal extremes of overgrown wealth and desperate poverty. Its population is far more dense than that of any other State. It is four or five times more dense than the average of all the other States taken together; and density of population has always been one of the proximate causes of social inequality. According to population and territorial extent there is far more capital in Massachusetts—capital which is movable, and instantaneously available—than in any other State in the Union; and probably both these qualifications respecting population and territory could be omitted without endangering the truth of the assertion. It has been recently stated in a very respectable public journal, on the authority of a writer conversant with the subject, that from the last of June, 1846, to the first of August, 1848, the amount of money invested by the citizens of Massachusetts "in manufacturing cities, railroads, and other improvements," is "fifty-seven millions of dollars, of which more than fifty has been paid in and expended." The dividends to be received by citizens of Massachusetts from June, 1848, to April, 1849, are estimated by the same writer at ten millions, and the annual increase of capital at "little short of twenty-two millions." If this be so, are we not in danger of naturalizing and domesticating among ourselves those hideous evils which are always engendered between capital and labor, when all the capital is in the hands of one class and all the labor is thrown upon another?

Now surely nothing but universal education can counterwork this tendency to the domination of capital and the servility of labor. If one class possesses all the wealth and the education, while the residue of society is ignorant and poor, it matters not by what name the relation between them

* Extracts from Horace Mann's *Twelfth Annual Report* to the Massachusetts State Board of Education, 1848. Given also in *Old South Leaflets*, VI, No. 144, pp. 409-11.

may be called: the latter, in fact and in truth, will be the servile dependants and subjects of the former. But, if education be equably diffused, it will draw property after it by the strongest of all attractions; for such a thing never did happen, and never can happen, as that an intelligent and practical body of men should be permanently poor. Property and labor in different classes are essentially antagonistic; but property and labor in the same class are essentially fraternal. The people of Massachusetts have, in some degree, appreciated the truth that the unexampled prosperity of the State—its comfort, its competence, its general intelligence and virtue—is attributable to the education, more or less perfect, which all its people have received; but are they sensible of a fact equally important,—namely, that it is to this same education that two-thirds of the people are indebted for not being to-day the vassals of as severe a tyranny, in the form of capital, as the lower classes of Europe are bound to in the form of brute force?

Education, then, beyond all other devices of human origin, is the great equalizer of the conditions of men,—the balance-wheel of the social machinery. I do not here mean that it so elevates the moral nature as to make men disdain and abhor the oppression of their fellow-men. This idea pertains to another of its attributes. But I mean that it gives each man the independence and the means by which he can resist the selfishness of other men. It does better than to disarm the poor of their hostility towards the rich: it prevents being poor. Agrarianism is the revenge of poverty against wealth. The wanton destruction of the property of others—the burning of hay-ricks and corn-ricks, the demolition of machinery because it supersedes hand-labor, the sprinkling of vitriol on rich dresses—is only agrarianism run mad. Education prevents both the revenge and the madness. On the other hand, a fellow-feeling for one's class or caste is the common instinct of hearts not wholly sunk in selfish regards for person or for family. The spread of education, by enlarging the cultivated class or caste, will open a wider area over which the social feelings will expand; and, if this education should be universal and complete, it would do more than all things else to obliterate factitious distinctions in society. . . .

The Masonic Lodge of Selma, Alabama, Asks Mann to Recommend Teachers for Its School, 1848

SELMA, ALABAMA July 21, 1848

HON HORACE MANN

SIR,

The Masonic Lodge of this place, have just finished the execution of a large 3 story brick building intended for purposes of Education. The Institution was chartered at the last session of the Legislature of this State and the Board of Trustees wish to open it for the reception of pupils on the 1st Oct. next. There will be but one session of nine months—commencing in Oct. and ending in July—and they escaping the three months of the year, when our climate is most subject to fever. Though the Institute will embrace both a Male & Female Department yet it is not disposed to open the Male Department except for very small boys for the first session. We desire to make the Female Department of the very first character.

As one of the Committee approved by the Board of Trustees to correspond in the procurement of suitable Teachers, I take the liberty of addressing you as an individual whose name is extensively & favorably associated with the cause of Education, to aid the Board of Trustees in obtaining Teachers—

We want a male President—& three assistant Female Teachers in the Literary Department—the President, we would prefer, should be of middle age—of pleasing manners and married—We would require as *indispensible* [sic] qualification that he should be a finished scholar; have experience in teaching—be industrious and energetic, have a good temper, the above all exception in his *moral character*. We would prefer that he was a member of our Fraternity—though that we do not insist upon—as the school will have no connection with Masonry only to receive its support & patronage, & educate free of charge the indigent children of deceased worthy Masons —as far as our means will go.

Will you do the cause of Education in our State, the great service to correspond with me, & let me know upon what terms—for such teachers as I have described the President to be—(except that we do not wish our Female Teachers to be *married*) can be obtained—to commence on the 1st Oct. next? We should rely entirely upon your recommendation—provided the salaries would suit us—. Selma is situated upon the Alabama River in the heart of a rich country—60 miles below Montgomery, & within 36 hours by Steamboat from Mobile—The place has a good deal of trade, and is pleasantly situated for society,—

I flatter myself that having devoted so much of your time to the subject of Education, you will excuse the liberty which I have taken in asking this trouble of you—

With high respect.

Yr obdt sevat

WM. SEWELL

The Office of Indian Affairs Asks Mann's Advice, 1848

WAR DEPARTMENT,

OFFICE INDIAN AFFAIRS,

July 31, 1848.

SIR:

The Chickasaw tribe of Indians have determined to place at schools within the United States, a number of their youth, some of whom have been at the Choctaw Academy in Kentucky, and will leave that institution for the East on the first of August. It is therefore desirable to select proper schools for them as early as possible.

These Indians have set apart a portion of their own funds to carry this object into effect, and have placed the management of the fund as well the arrangements for the education of their boys, in the United States, and it is therefore all important that the strictest economy shall be used consistent with a due regard to the interests and improvement of the boys.

With this view, I have thought it would be desirable to place some of these boys, if not the whole of them, at preparatory schools in the Eastern States, and I have therefore taken the liberty to ask your advice and assistance in enabling me to accomplish the object in the best and most economical manner.

There will be 13 or 14 boys to be educated but it is not thought best to place them all at one institution. I think that not more than three or four should be together.

The system of education will be such as is in practice at the common schools, embracing all the branches of a thorough English education; and if any, or all the boys should exhibit the proper talents and qualifications to fit them for colleges, it is then the intention to put them there, so as to place them on a footing with the most privileged whites in the country.

It is my wish and intention that every expense of education, boarding, clothing, washing, books, stationery, medicine and medical attendance, and all other expenses whatsoever, shall be borne by the institution in which the boys are placed, and that a specific sum, not to be exceeded, be agreed upon, to be paid quarterly or otherwise as the school may desire. I will therefore take it as a great favor if you will interest yourself in furthering the views of these unfortunate but interesting people, by giving me the names and address of such schools as you may deem proper ones, so that I may write and ascertain the lowest terms upon which the boys can be educated.

With regard to the clothing, it may be proper to remark that nothing extravagant is desired, but it is expected that the boys will be clothed in a manner similar to those with whom they are associated.

Respectfully,
Your Obt Servt

W. Medill

Hon.
Horace Mann
House of Reps.

John B. Minor to Mann, 1849

UNIVERSITY OF VA.
Feb. 13. 1849

DEAR SIR,

I venture upon a very great liberty in addressing this letter to you, but I persuade myself that the indefatigable friend of popular education in Massachusetts cannot be indifferent to its progress in Virginia. I apply to you, therefore, with confidence, chastened only by the apprehension that the information and advice I ask may occasion you more trouble than, amidst your present duties, it is reasonable to expect you to bestow. If it should be so, I beg that you will select those topics only which seem most immediately, and practically useful, and pass the rest by.

You are probably aware that until a very few years ago, *free-schools* were unknown in Virginia, even to our dreams. Now, however, they exist, with various modifications, in ten or twelve counties, and the number is increasing. Our general system of public education *contemplates* the *indigent* alone as its subjects, and expends upon them not as much as is needed, but so much as the 'Literary Fund' * annually yields, which at present is something over $70,000, nothing being raised for the purpose by taxation.

The cause of popular education has made great progress amongst us, recently, and the public mind is uneasy and sensitive upon the subject. Its claims have universal homage paid to them with the lips,—homage wherein the mind and heart much more decidedly concur than formerly. By degrees the idea is dawning upon us that popular intelligence cannot be called into being by holiday harangues, picturing its importance, and that there is no legislative sleight of hand, whereby the great boon of universal education can be bestowed, without heavy burdens in the shape of taxes, and a great deal of long and painful travail amongst the people themselves in perfecting and controlling the system which is to fling the elements of knowledge broad-cast over the land. Our legislature, not unwisely, has left the leaven to pervade the popular masses without interference, contenting itself with clothing with the form and effect of law whatever plan may be acceptable to the people of the several counties. Although there has resulted, and will result, hence, an inconvenient diversity of systems, the policy leads to much and eager discussion in the primary assemblies of the people, which is invaluable in a community so utterly unprepared as we were, at first, to appreciate the appliances of general instruction, and at a future period, it will not be difficult to assimilate the various systems, and consolidate them finally, into one.

In this County (Albemarle) one of the central counties of the state, and

* This had been established in 1810.

not the least intelligent, we have at this moment a plan of free-school education pending, intended to operate in this county alone, and which is to be submitted for adoption or rejection, to the votes of the people. In common with many friends of the cause, I am intensely anxious that it should not be rejected, and by that solicitude am urged to beg from you whatever will illustrate to my countrymen the value and advantages of general primary instruction.

Perhaps, in order to put you fully in possession of our position, I ought to state the general principles of the system proposed. It rests upon two grounds—1st. That primary schools ought to be maintained at the *common* charge, for the *common* benefit;—2nd That the schools ought to be rigorously, & frequently inspected by a competent & responsible authority. It proposes

1. To divide the county (we have no townships)—where area is about 700 square miles, & population about 23,000,—into districts of such size that a child of proper age for school may attend from his home, daily.

2. To place the whole conduct of the system under charge of a board of commissioners, one elected, biennially, from each district, by the people thereof.

3. To entrust the Executive functions, & especially that of supervision to the commissioners, each in his own district, and to a County Superintendent elected, biennially, by the board of commissioners,—which latter officer, having a competent salary, is the regulator, & motive power of the whole, & is *ex officio,* a member, & president of the board.

4. To provide for the expenses of the system, mainly, by taxes on persons, & property equitably disposed;—allowing any district at its pleasure, to increase the amount of taxation therein, in order to provide better schools than the average.

5. To admit all white persons between the ages of five and twenty-one to the schools, without fee.

I now proceed to name the topics upon which, as I conceive, direct and authentic information would exert the most persuasive influence upon our people, but I am far from insisting that you touch upon them all, and shall be obliged to you for deviating, at your discretion, from the category, to other topics which you may think likely to tell with greater effect.

1. The gross amount expended in Massachusetts, on *primary* schools, discriminating teacher's wages & other expenses.

2. The mode of raising the funds,—discriminating what is derived from permanent capital, & what is annually levied in taxes,—State, County, town, & district respectively,—and what is contributed by individuals,—if anything,—in fees and donations.

3. The subjects of taxation,—showing somewhat, if possible, of the proportion of each.

4. The authentic valuation of property, in the State, distinguishing what is real from what is personal.

5. The proportion of the *tax* to the aggregate valuation of property, discriminating realty & personalty.

6. The cost of *ordinary* school-houses,—adapted to 30, 50, 70 and more pupils,—and the *minimum* cost of such houses;—their materials, cost of workmanship, per thousand of brick &c, and cost of annual repairs.

7. The methods of Superintendence, and the cost thereof.

8. The wages usually paid *competent* teachers.

9. The cost of maintaining a single school, in an average situation for a year, including a proper allowance for rent & repairs of house, fuel &c,—stating the items severally.

10. The ordinary duration of the schools, as free, and at individual expense, if so maintained at all.

11. The number of pupils usually in each school, & the *maximum* number, in policy allowable with one or more teachers.

12. The branches taught in the schools, & with what success.

13. The difficulty, if any, arising from the possible introduction into the schools of vicious children of corrupting influence, and the mode of obviating it; and the difficulty, if any, from the mingling of the sexes, & how obviated.

14. The satisfaction of the people with the burdens of the system, and with its general working;—and how their temper is authentically manifested.

15. The relative efficiency of *free-schools* open to all without distinction, and of schools to which the poor have free access, whilst the rich pay fees.

16. The relative efficiency of public free-schools, at a system established and maintained by law, and of a system of private schools, in no wise subjected to the surveillance of public authority, in respect to the actual pupils at such schools.

17. The effect of school, or district libraries.

18. The relation between the prevalence of popular education, and crime, as actually observed in Massachusetts, and New England generally, and as reported elsewhere.

19. The relation between the prevalence of popular education, and the value of property, as actually observed in Massachusetts, & New England, and as reported elsewhere.

20. The sources of most direct and practical information upon the subject of public primary education,—having reference to the origination, and first rough working of the system, rather than to refinements in the structure of School-houses, apparatus, methods of instruction &c, which are to us the ruffles, whilst yet we are without the shirt.

I cannot conclude without praying indulgence for thus intruding upon you. I trust to find an apologist in your own persevering zeal upon this subject, which has so long made your name familiar, that I do not merely use the language of formal compliment, when I assure you that I am,

With very high & sincere respect.
Your Rd & Obt st

JOHN B. MINOR *

An Argument in Massachusetts Against the Poll Tax as a Requirement for Voting, 1853 †

Many years ago, Sir, there was an illustration of this argument, made I believe by Benjamin Franklin, which settled this question at that time, and which ought to settle it in the mind of every man who knows the difference between a man and a piece of property; for I do not care whether the amount you require to make a voter is a dollar or a thousand dollars, the principle is the same. The moment you say that a man shall not vote unless he has money to purchase the right, you declare your right to put a rule upon him that he shall not vote unless he is worth a million, and that principle takes the power from the many, and puts it into the hands of the few, and just as few as the power the ruler or rulers have to make it. Now as to this argument of Dr. Franklin, who had the faculty of saying in ten words, more than most men say in ten hours. He says you require that a man shall have sixty dollars of property or he shall not vote. Very well, take an illustration. Here is a man to-day who owns a jackass, and the jackass is worth sixty dollars. Today the man is a voter, and he goes up to the polls with his jackass and deposits his vote. To-morrow the jackass dies. The next day the man comes to vote without the jackass and he cannot vote at all. Now tell me which was the voter, the man or the jackass? (Laughter.)

Well, Mr. Chairman, the jackass was the voter and not the man, for as long as the jackass lived he voted, but when the jackass died, he no longer voted!

Will you keep the jackass in the Constitution as the voter? True, you have made some progress, for as it now stands you reduce the value of your jackass from sixty dollars to $1.50. But when a man goes up to the polls to vote, he must have that amount in ready money, and if he had it one day and voted and lost it the next, then he can't vote at all. Now it is the poll-tax that votes and not the man.

---

* Minor was professor of law in the University of Virginia and became one of the authors of Virginia's first real state-wide public school law in 1870. Mann must have replied promptly. On February 24, 1849, Minor wrote and thanked Mann for his reply.

† Official Report of the Debates and Proceedings of the Convention Assembled to Revise and Amend the Constitution of the Commonwealth of Massachusetts (Boston, White and Potter, 1853), p. 565.

William H. Stiles of Georgia to Henry Barnard, 1856 *

SAVANNAH, GEO
January 1st 1856.

MY DEAR SIR

Your communication covering the Circular of the "American Journal of Education" is just received. In reply to the enquiry can I help you by my "pen subscription or influence", I answer in relation to the two latter points unhesitatingly in the affirmative and to the former conditionally so, should any thing of interest strike me as worthy of the pages of your Journal.

I have already the first number of your Journal as published in connection with the College Review in August last. I am much pleased with it & should like if possible to receive the second number. If No 3. is published on or before the 1st of March please forward that number to Milledgeville Geo but all others to Savannah.

Our legislature is now in session; we have before us the important subject of adopting a system of Common schools for this State, and as there is great interest evinced in that body on the subject of Education it is quite likely that I may succeed in obtaining for you a number of subscribers in this State.

At all events you shall have the benefit of what little influence I may possess, either personally or officially as Speaker of the House.

Your communication found me poring over the pages of Barnards "National Education in Europe" & "Normal Schools" "Report relating to the Public Schools of Rhode Island" "Annual Report of the Superintendent of Common Schools in Connecticut" "Principles of School Architecture" & "Journal of Education", and I can not refrain from saying that I would give almost anything if I only had Mr. Barnard himself, by my side for a half hour to aid me in preparing a bill for the adoption of a system of Common Schools adapted to our most extensive but for the greater part sparsely settled country—

Your systems at the North are doubtless most admirably adapted to your thickly settled & enlightened population—but for our thinly settled & unenlightened region they *seem* too complicated & my effort has been if possible to simplify them—Can I do this & have an efficient system? A superintendent or Commissioner for the State appointed by the Governor —A school committee of three from each county to be elected by the legal

---

* The original of this letter and of the one that follows to Barnard are the property of Washington Square Library of New York University. Microcopies are in the Southern Historical Collection, the University of North Carolina. In the Washington Square Library most of the Barnard papers may be found, more than 13,000 items. About 2,500 more or less miscellaneous pieces are in the Wadsworth Atheneum, Hartford, Connecticut. See Edgar W. Knight, "Some Evidence of Henry Barnard's Influence in the South," *Educational Forum*, XIII (March, 1949), pp. 301-12.

voters—three trustees for each school District—a superintendent for each county a clerk collector & treasurer either appointed by the school Committee for the County or elected by the voters of the respective Districts— I hold to be indispensible—Can I get along with these *alone* and can I dispense with any of them? As our people are entirely without experience we shall have to give great power & latitude to the Superintendent or Commissioner which might simplify the machinery whilst it would enhance greatly his labors—all the rules & regulations as to the division of the District—apportionment of the taxes, government of the school, &c he might lay down as rules which would obviate the necessity of a whole code of law on the subject—if it would not increase his difficulties & labors too seriously. What think you of these matters?

The laying out of the School Districts I apprehend will be a most difficult undertaking with us. It is to be done not geographically only but according to the number of scholars & the ability of their parents to respond to taxation I believe! Can you furnish me with any suggestions which may tend to facilitate this matter?

We shall probably devote about $100,000 of the proceeds of our State Rail Road to Education but the balance will have to be obtained by taxation—It occurred to me at first that I would propose a bill simply for the Appointment of a Superintendent for the State, & let him go thro the State lecturing on the subject of Education while he ascertained the condition of the population the number of children—& the advantages they possessed or the disadvantages they labored under as to education & to report not only this information but suggest a system of school to a future legislature —but I have subsequently thought that as this labor would occupy the Superintendent several years & he might not furnish much more information that we now have, we might as well set the system in operation at once & amend or add to afterwards as necessities might require. What do you think on this point?

(I think of recommending also a Normal school. How many teachers would be requisite for such an one as we should have & what the annual expense of the establishment, independent of the building?)

I hope you will excuse the very great liberty I have taken in propounding all these inquiries, I have ventured to do so only upon the very deep interest you feel in the cause of education & which is not I know limited to any State bounds—

You perceive from my inquiries we are groping in the dark here and any light which your enlarged experience will enable you to throw upon the same will be most gratefully received. We have now a recess of the legislature until the 14th of this month—if you write immediately please direct to this place—if so as to reach me after the 14th at Milledgeville. I shall deem it however an especial favor if you can write at once—as our bill on education is assigned to the 16th Inst & it will of course be necessary for me to have the information before.

Truly Yours
WILLIAM H STILES

HENRY BARNARD ESQ

If you will send me two or three more of your circulars it will aid me in calling attention to your Journal. W.H.S.

Ashbel Smith to Barnard, 1858 *

EVERGREEN, HARRIS CT. TEXAS
July 6, 1858

MY DEAR HENRY,

An hour or two of talk with you at this time would be of special satisfaction to me; it would help me solve a matter of great perplexity, on which I must come to a decision in the course of the present week.

We have built a school house in the city of Houston. It is an excellent building; large, substantial, being of good brick; and I think commodious, being fashioned in a measure after some of your model schoolhouses. By estimate it will seat between 300 and 400 pupils, and is provided with the necessary additional rooms. The cost has been about $25,000 which sum has been mostly spent on the edifice. It is indeed a noble structure.

Next comes the business of its furniture. I have given the Trustees your School architecture and some nos. of your Journal of Education. Some of our merchants, who are also trustees of the school will go to the North in a short time, and will there I presume make the purchases of the furniture.

Lastly comes the great difficulty of the whole matter; it is in the selection of the *personnel* of the government and instruction. There are among us persons qualified for the office of Head Master, or they could easily so make themselves; but they have other engrossing and lucrative pursuits. There is yet no surplus among us of accomplished scholars seeking imployment. In former times we should have turned probably to your section of the Union and sought there for some capable scholar for the Head Mastership; but the miserable abolition fanaticism renders it advisable for us not to apply to that quarter, but restricts us to the slave-holding states. In this conjuncture the Trustees have elected me as Superintendent to organize the Instruction, contrary to my expressed wishes; my management for a longer or shorter period is of course contemplated. What, my dear Barnard ought I to do?

* Smith was born in Hartford, Conn., and was graduated from Yale in 1824 where he was acquainted with Barnard. He taught school in Salisbury, N. C., from 1824 to 1826, studied medicine and returned to Salisbury to practice. He went to Texas in 1837 and as a member of the Legislature of that State in 1855 and later was regarded as an energetic leader in the cause of public education. He was president of the Board of Regents of the University of Texas in 1881 and had much to do with the organization of the institution.

July 17. The above was written several days ago as you may see from the date. I declined the appointment absolutely, definitively. On the very urgent request of several members of the Board of Trustees, I withdrew my letter and have accepted the office of Superintendent for a year. It has been deemed highly important—and in this opinion I coincide—that the Superintendent should be taken from among ourselves. He ought to be acclimated to the physical climate of Texas and also to our social and political institutions. I can remember when the preference would have been given to a teacher from the North; now full confidence could scarcely be felt in any Superintendent recently from that section. My dear Barnard, how deeply to be regretted is the state of feeling that has been engendered by the fanaticism of political antislavery. I beheld with admiration when last at New Haven the facilities now afforded at our old mother Yale, for the acquisition of knowledge, so greatly superior to what you and I enjoyed in our day. But the pest of abolitionism excludes the hundreds, yes the thousands of students from the South, who but for this demon would gladly resort thither for instruction. Why the University of Va numbers its 600 or 700—and Chapel Hill N.C. its 400 or 500 students. Had Yale preserved its catholic national faith, it would have had clustering around it thousands when other institutions have their hundreds.—But, I will not weary you with these ungracious topics;—nor do I expect to find you holding the same opinions as myself on these matters.—

I revert to myself and the Houston Academy. The Superintendence or Head Mastership has been accepted by me at a great sacrifice of pecuniary interest and of personal convenience and comfort. I am living at home on my plantation, surrounded by my colts, sheep, pigs, geese, etc, etc, and lastly and chiefly by my servants, in the receipt of an independent income from my crops, receiving and enjoying a good deal of company—yet so far as real care is concerned, I rival the gods of Epicurus *omnium vacatione munerum.* (freedom from all duties) I enjoy this repose—nevertheless I have put myself into the circumscription and confines of a literary institution. You will believe me, Henry, when I tell you it is from a love of the cause of education and a desire to do some good in the world.—

Henry Barnard on the Influence of the Lyceum, 1864 *

The first quarter of the present century was marked by a constantly increasing energy in the working of the leaven of educational improvement. Toward the end of that period and during the succeeding decade the ferment wrought so actively as to generate a numerous, heterogeneous brood of systems, plans, and institutions—many crude and rudely organized; many that never reached an organization; many that did their work quickly and well; few that have survived to the present time. Of all these, whether

* *American Journal of Education*, XIV, p. 535.

under the names of school systems (infant, free, monitorial, manual labor, agricultural, etc.), or of mechanics' institutions, lyceums, societies for the diffusion of useful knowledge, mercantile associations, teachers' seminaries, school agents' societies, library associations, book clubs, reading associations, educational journals, etc., none created so immediate and general interest, or excited for a time an influence so great or beneficent, as the American Lyceum.

« IV »

EXTENDING THE SCHOOLS
UPWARD BEFORE 1860

«««««««««««««««««««««««««««««««««««««««<>»»»»»»»»»»»»»»»»»»»»»»»»»»»»»»»»»»»

Some documents on secondary and higher education during the colonial period appear in Chapter I. By the Revolutionary War nine colleges that have survived were established. After the Dartmouth College Case in 1819 denominational efforts led to the chartering of many colleges and academies, the Presbyterians leading in the number established, followed by the Methodists, Baptists, Congregationalists, Catholics, and Episcopalians and then by denominations of smaller numerical strength. These energetic efforts to establish academic and collegiate institutions led to some sharp criticism as competition developed among them. In 1829 President Philip Lindsley of Nashville University said that colleges were rising like mushrooms and after being "duly lauded and puffed for a day . . . they sink to be heard no more." The mortality of these institutions was very high. D. G. Tewksbury estimated that of 516 colleges established before 1860 in sixteen states only 104 became permanent institutions. (*The Founding of American Colleges and Universities Before the Civil War* [New York, Teachers College, Columbia University, Bureau of Publications, 1932], pp. 24-28.) Among the causes of death were financial difficulties, unfavorable location, denominational competition, epidemics, natural disasters, and internal dissensions. Henry Tappan, later president of the University of Michigan, said in 1850 that higher education was being cheapened by trying to put it in reach of everybody and "fitting our colleges to the temper of the multitude"; and President F. A. P. Barnard of the University of Mississippi, later president of Columbia University, said in 1856 that colleges as creations of denominations divided the people. In organization and administration, curriculum, and regulations of students most of the higher educational institutions were very similar.

The Opening of Newark Academy in New Jersey
Is Announced, 1775 *

The Academy lately erected in a healthy part of the pleasant town of Newark in New Jersey, about eight miles from the city of New York, will on the third day of April next, be fit for the reception of the masters proper for the instruction of youth, and such children as can with conveniency lodge and board therein. They will be taught the learned languages and several branches of Mathemathicks. There will also be an English School for the teaching of Reading, Writing, Arithmetick, and Bookkeeping in the usual and Italian methods. Different rooms will be made use of for each branch of instruction; and such as choose may have their children taught the English tongue grammatically. The boys are separated from the girls in the English School. Those who can't board in the Academy, may have good lodging near the same in private families. The regulation and general direction of the instruction of the scholars will be under the auspices of the Governors of the Academy, who will from time to time inspect the conduct of the several masters, and examine the improvement of their pupils in learning.

Mr. William Haddon, one long experienced by several of the governors to be well qualified to teach the learned Languages and the Mathematicks, will have the superintendency of the youth to be taught in those branches of learning, and Robert Allan and Son to have the care and keeping of the schools for the instruction of Reading, Writing, Arithmetick, and Book-

* *Rivington's New York Gazetteer*, March 23, 1775.

Following the opening about the middle of the eighteenth century of Benjamin Franklin's academy in Philadelphia which grew into the University of Pennsylvania, academies appeared widely, particularly between 1775 and 1860. Private and denominational effort led to the establishment of most of these schools. E. W. G. Boogher (*Secondary Education in Georgia,* doctoral dissertation at the University of Pennsylvania, 1933, p. 85) reported more than 580 academies chartered in Georgia between 1783 and 1860; William H. Weathersby (*A History of Educational Legislation in Mississippi from 1798 to 1860* [Chicago, University of Chicago Press, 1921], pp. 66-70) reported 179 in Mississippi between 1807 and 1860; and Charles L. Coon (*North Carolina Schools and Academies, 1790-1840* [Raleigh, Edwards and Broughton Printing Co., 1915]) listed materials on 118 academies in North Carolina between 1790 and 1840. Although academies were very popular in the Southern states in the early period of their development and continued longer there perhaps than elsewhere because of the slow growth of the public high school, these institutions developed rapidly in other parts of the country as well. Variants of the academy were manual labor schools and military schools, the latter particularly popular in the South, in part because of slavery and the patrol system and also perhaps because of the natural fondness of Southerners for things military. The curriculum of the academy showed a range of subjects much broader than that of the colonial Latin-grammar schools; and out of many of the academies colleges were developed. Some of them were forerunners of normal schools.

keeping, who have discharged their trusts to the great satisfaction of their employers. As the intention of the benefactors and builders of this stately edifice, is for preparing youth to be useful members of the community, the greatest care will be taken to have them not only instructed in the branches of learning which their parents respectively order, but also in the paths of virtue and morality. Care also will be taken that they attend public worship at the usual times of holding the same at the churches to which they belong, there being in the said town two churches, one of the Church of England, and the other the Presbyterian; the ministers of which, for the time being, are always to be of the number of said Governors, and it is hoped that they, with the other Governors, will give that attendance to the trust they have undertaken, as will answer the laudable end proposed, and give ample satisfaction to the parents and the guardians of the children sent to the said Academy.

NEWARK 10th March, 1775

Charter of Liberty Hall Academy, North Carolina, 1777 *

I. Whereas the proper Education of Youth in this infant Country is highly necessary, and would answer the most valuable and beneficial Purposes to this State, and the good People thereof; and whereas a very promising Experiment hath been made at a Seminary † in the County of Mecklenburg, and a Number of Youths there taught have made great Advancements in the Knowledge of Learned Languages, and in the Rudiments of the Arts and Sciences, in the Course of a regular and finished Education, which they have since compleated at various Colleges in distant Parts of America; and whereas the Seminary aforesaid, and the several Teachers who have successively taught and presided therein, have hitherto been almost wholly supported by private Subscriptions: In order therefore that the said Subscriptions and other Gratuities may be legally possessed and duly applied, and the said Seminary, by the Name of Liberty Hall, may become more extensively and generally useful, for the Encouragement of

* Walter Clark (Ed.), *The State Records of North Carolina*, XXIV, pp. 30-32.
† The General Assembly of North Carolina in 1771 had chartered Queen's College at Charlotte, North Carolina, with power to confer degrees, and had provided for its support by a tax on liquors sold in Mecklenburg County for a period of ten years. But the Commissioners of Trade and Plantations disallowed the charter and asked whether the Crown should encourage "toleration by giving Royal Assent to an Establishment, which in all its consequences, promises great and permanent Advantages to a sect of Dissenters from the Established Church who have already extended themselves over the Province in very considerable numbers." Royal disallowance was proclaimed in 1773. Meantime, however, Queen's College had been opened to students and had operated without charter. In 1777 the General Assembly of the new state granted another charter and changed the name to Liberty Hall Academy. On his Southern tour Washington referred to the school in his diary, May 28, 1791: "...Charlotte is a trifling place, though the Court of Mecklenburg is held in it. There is a School (called a College) in it at which, at times there has been 50 to 60 boys." John G. Fitzgerald (Ed.), *The Diaries of George Washington, 1748-1799*, IV, p. 185. The question has been raised by some historians whether the disallowance of the charter of Queen's College did not turn in part on the British mercantile policy of the time.

liberal Knowledge in Languages, Arts and Sciences, and for diffusing the great Advantages of Education upon more liberal, easy, and generous Terms:

II. Be it Enacted, by the General Assembly of the State of North Carolina, and by the Authority of the same, That the said Seminary shall be, and it is hereby declared to be an Academy, by the Name of Liberty Hall.

III. And be it further Enacted, by the Authority aforesaid, That Isaac Alexander, President, and Messrs. Thomas Polk, Thomas Neal, Abrham Alexander, Waightstill Avery, Ephraim Brevard, David Caldwell, James Edmonds, John Simpson, Thomas Rees, Adlai Osborn, Samuel McCorkle, John McKnit Alexander, Thomas McCall, and James Hall, be, and they are hereby formed and incorporated into a Body politick and corporate, by the Name of President and Trustees of Liberty Hall, and by that Name shall have perpetual Succession, and a common Seal; and that they the said President and Trustees, and their Successors, by the Name aforesaid, or a Majority of them, shall be able and capable in Law to take, demand, receive and possess, all Monies, Goods and Chattels, that shall be given them for the Use of the said Academy, and the same apply according to the Will of the Donors: and by Gift, Purchase or Devise, to take, have, receive, possess, enjoy and retain, to them and their Successors for ever, any Lands, Rents, Tenements and Hereditaments, of what Kind, Nature, or Quality soever the same may be, in special Trust and Confidence that the same, or the Profits thereof, shall be applied to and for the Uses and Purposes of establishing and endowing the said Academy of Liberty Hall, in the County of Mecklenburg, building or purchasing suitable and convenient Houses for the same, providing a philosophical Apparatus and public Library, and supporting and paying Salaries to the President, and such Number of Professors and Tutors thereof, as shall be necessary to instruct the Students, and they shall be able to pay out of the public Funds that shall be in their Hands.

IV. And be it Enacted, by the Authority aforesaid, That the said President and Trustees, and their Successors, or a Majority of them, by the Name aforesaid, shall be able and capable in Law to bargain, sell, grant, demise, alien or dispose of, and convey and assure to the Purchasers, any such Lands, Rents, Tenements or Hereditaments aforesaid, when the Condition of the Grant to them, or the Will of the Devisor, does not forbid it. And further, that the said President and Trustees, and their Successors, for ever, or a Majority of them, shall be able and capable in Law, by the Name aforesaid, to sue and implead, be sued and impleaded, answer and be answered, in all Courts of Record whatsoever.

V. And be it further Enacted, by the Authority aforesaid, That the said President and Trustees be, and they are hereby impowered, authorized and required, to convene at the Town of Charlotte on the Third Tuesday of October next after passing this Act, and then and there elect and constitute,

by Commission in Writing under their Hands, and sealed with the common
Seal of the Corporation, such and so many Professors or Tutors as they
may think expedient; and then and there, and at all other Times for ever
hereafter, when the said President and Trustees, their Successors, or a
Majority of them, shall be convened and met together in the said County
of Mecklenburg, they shall have full Power and lawful Authority to elect
and constitute one or more Professors or Tutors; and also to make and ordain such Laws, Rules and Ordinances, not repugnant to the Laws of this
State, for the well ordering and governing the Students, their Morals Studies, and Academical Exercises, as to them shall seem meet; and to give
Certificates to such Students as shall leave the said Academy, certifying
their literary Merit, and the Progress they shall have made in useful Knowledge, whether it be in learned Languages, Arts or Sciences, or all of them.

VI. Be it further Enacted, by the Authority aforesaid, That the said
President and Tutors, before they enter upon the Execution of the Trust
reposed in them by this Act, shall take the Oath appointed for Public
Officers, and also the following Oath, viz:

I, A. B., do swear, that I will duly and faithfully, to the best of my Skill
and Ability, execute and discharge the several Trusts, Powers and Authorities, wherewith I am invested by an Act of the General Assembly, intituled,
An Act for incorporating the President and Trustees of Liberty Hall, in the
County of Mecklenburg; and that I will endeavour that all Monies, Goods,
Chattels, and the Profits of Lands, belonging to this Corporation, shall be
duly applied to the Use of the Academy, for the Advancement of Learning,
and as near as may be agreeable to the Will of the Donor. So HELP ME GOD.

And if any President or Trustee of said Academy shall enter upon the
Execution of the Trust reposed in him by this Act before taking the said
Oaths as above required, he shall forfeit and pay the Sum of Twenty
Pounds. Proclamation Money: to be recovered by Action of Debt, in the
Name of the Governor of the State for the Time being, and applied to pur-
chase Books for the Use of the said Academy.

VII. And be it further Enacted, by the Authority aforesaid, That the
President and Trustees shall annually in the Month of October, elect and
commissionate some Person to be Treasurer for the said Academy, during
the Term of one Year; which Treasurer shall enter into Bond, with sufficient Security, to the Governor for the Time being, in the Sum of Five
Thousand Pounds, conditioned for the faithful Discharge of his Office, and
the Trust reposed in him; and that all Monies and Chattels belonging to
the said Corporation, that shall be in his Hands at the Expiration of his
Office, shall then be immediately paid, and delivered into the Hands of the
Succeeding Treasurer. And every Treasurer shall receive all Monies, Donations, Gifts, Bequests, and Charities whatsoever, that may belong or
accrue to the said Academy during his Office, and at the Expiration thereof
shall account with the Trustees for the same, and the same pay and deliver

over to the succeeding Treasurer; and on his Neglect or Refusal to pay and deliver as aforesaid, the same Method of Recovery may be had against him, as is or may be provided for the Recovery of Monies from Sheriffs or other Persons chargeable with Public Monies.

VIII. And whereas it is necessary to make Provision for the Appointment of succeeding Presidents and succeeding Trustees, in order to keep up a perpetual Succession; Be it therefore Enacted, by the Authority aforesaid, That on the Death, Refusal to qualify, Resignation, or Removal out of the State, of the President or any of the Trustees for the Time being, it shall be lawful for the remaining Trustees, in the Room and Stead of such President, Trustee, or Trustees, or a Majority of them, and they are hereby authorized and required, to convene and meet together in the said County of Mecklenburg, and there elect and appoint another President, or one or more Trustees, dead, refusing to qualify, resigned, or removed out of the State; which President and Trustees so elected and appointed, shall be vested with the same Trusts, Powers and Authorities, as other Fellows and Trustees are invested with by Virtue of this Act, he or they having first taken the Oaths by this Act required.

IX. And be it further Enacted, by the Authority aforesaid, That the said Trustees and their Successors, or a Majority of them, at their Meeting in October annually, and at any other Meeting called for that Purpose (after due Notice given to at least Nine of the Trustees, signifying the Occasion of such Meeting) shall have full Power and Authority to hear any Complaint against the President, or any Professor or Tutor, and for Misbehaviour or Neglect to suspend, or wholly remove him or them from Office, and appoint others to fill the same Office or Offices respectively; and any President so removed from Office, shall from thenceforth cease to be a Member of the Corporation, and the President appointed in his Room and Stead shall be vested with all the Authority and Privileges with which the President by this Act appointed is invested.

X. Provided nevertheless, and be it further Enacted, That this Act, or any Thing therein contained, shall not extend, or be understood to make this Academy one of those Seminaries, mentioned in the Constitution, to oblige this State to support any President, Professor or Tutor, of said Academy, or other Charge or Expence thereof whatsoever; this Act of Incorporation having been obtained at the earnest Prayer and Intreaty of the said Trustees and others, who were desirous to contribute towards the Support thereof.

Read three Times and Ratified in General Assembly, the Ninth Day of May, Anno Dom. 1777.

Jefferson's Bill for Amending the Constitution of the College of William and Mary, 1779 *

A Bill for Amending the constitution of William and Mary, and substituting more certain revenues for its support; proposed by the committee of revisors of the laws of Virginia, appointed by the General Assembly in the year, 1776

Section 1. WHEREAS, a scheme for cultivating and disseminating useful knowledge in this country, which had been proposed by some of its liberal minded inhabitants, before the year 1690 of the Christian epocha, was approved, adopted, and cherished, by the General Assembly, upon whose petition King William and Queen Mary of England, to the crown whereof the people here at that time acknowledged themselves, as a colony, to be subject, by their charter, bearing date the seventh day of February, in the fourth year of their reign, gave license, in due form to Francis Nicholson, Esq. lieutenant governor of the colony, and seventeen other trustees, particularly named, to found a place of universal study, or perpetual college, in such part of the country as the general assembly should think fit, consisting of a president, six professors, and an hundred scholars, more or less; enabled the trustees, and their survivors, to take and hold lands, tenements, and hereditaments, to the yearly value of two thousand pounds, with intention, and in confidence, that, after application of the profits thereof, with such donation as by themselves and others might be made for that purpose, to the erecting, founding, and adorning the college, they should transfer the same to the president and professors; appointed James Blair, clerk, the first president; and empowered the trustees, and their successors,

* *Sundry Documents on the Subject of A System of Public Education for the State of Virginia* (Richmond, 1817), pp. 53-60. This bill appears also in Paul Leicester Ford's *The Writings of Thomas Jefferson*, II, pp. 229-35.

There is not yet available a comprehensive history of higher education or of graduate work in the United States. Charles F. Thwing's *A History of Higher Education in America* (New York, D. Appleton-Century Co., 1906) while old is about the best single account available. Donald G. Tewksbury's *The Founding of American Colleges and Universities Before the Civil War* (New York, Teachers College, Columbia University, Bureau of Publications, 1932) is an excellent study of a limited period and contains a very good bibliography. R. F. Butts' *The College Charts Its Course* (New York, McGraw-Hill Book Co., Inc., 1939) is a scholarly interpretation of some of the major historical conceptions that guided higher education in this country in the past and contains a superb annotated bibliography. For the numerous responsibilities and activities of important figures in higher education in the early days, see George P. Schmidt's *The Old Time College President* (New York, Columbia University Press, 1930); for the important part food played in the life of one institution see A. M. Bevis, *Diets and Riots* (Boston, Marshall Jones Co., 1936), a breezy account of "Harvard's three hundred years of hunger for food and knowledge" with a chuckle on every page. The late President James L. McConaughy of Wesleyan University (Connecticut) said in 1938: "A college president often stands or falls in his handling of two problems, chapel and food."

There are many histories of individual colleges and universities, but too many of these were written by people untrained in historical research and writing. The authors or compilers of most of them have been presidents, professors, or librarians *emeriti*, some of whom tended to be reminiscent. Happily, however, this condition is changing and the history of higher educational institutions is now more and more gaining the attention of competent historians who see in such effort opportunity for substantial research and publication.

to elect the succeeding presidents and the professors; willed the college, after it should be founded, to be called the College of William and Mary in Virginia; and incorporated the president and masters, enabling them and their successors to take and hold lands, tenements, hereditaments, goods and chattels, to the yearly value of two thousand pounds, of lawful money of England; appointed the trustees and their successors, to be elected in the manner therein prescribed, so as not to be less than eighteen, visitors of the college, with power to nominate one of themselves a rector annually, and to ordain statutes for the government of the college, not contrary to the royal prerogative, the laws of England or Virginia, or the canons of the church of England; willed that the president and professors should have a chancellor, to be nominated, every seventh year, in the manner therein prescribed; granted to the trustees a sum of money, than in the hands of William Byrd, Esq. the auditor, received for quitrents, to be applied towards erecting, founding, and adorning the college; and also granted to the trustees, to be transferred to the president and professors, in like manner as before directed, part of the then royal revenue, arising from the duty upon tobacco exported; and also granted to the said trustees the office of surveyor general of Virginia, with intention, and in confidence, that they and their successors, or the longest livers of them, should receive the profits thereof, until the foundation of the college; and when that should be effected, account for and pay the same or the surplus, above what should have been expended in that work, to the president and professors; and that thereafter the said office should be held by the said president and professors. And the said King and Queen, by their said charter, granted to the said trustees ten thousand acres of land on the south side of the Blackwater swamp, and also other ten thousand acres of land in Pamunkey neck, between the forks or branches of York river, with this intention, and in confidence, that the said trustees, or the longest livers of them, should transfer the said twenty thousand acres of land, after the foundation of the college, to the president and professors; as by the said charter, among other things, relation being thereunto had, may more fully appear. And whereas, voluntary contributions towards forwarding this beneficial scheme, the sum whereof exceeded two thousand pounds sterling, were received by the said trustees, with one thousand pounds sterling out of the money arising from the quitrents granted to the use of the said college by Queen Anne, part whereof was applied to the purchase of three hundred and thirty acres of land at the middle plantation, being the same place at which the general assembly, by their act passed in the year 1693, had directed the said college to be built, and whereon the same was accordingly built; and the general assembly, by one other act passed in the year 1693, entitled an act for laying an imposition upon skins and furs, for the better support of the college of William and Mary in Virginia, endowed the said college with certain duties on skins and furs therein specified, which duties were afterwards enlarged and confirmed to the use of the said college, and made payable to the president and professors by divers other acts of the general assembly. And by one other act passed in the year 1718, the said college was further endowed by the general assembly with the sum of one thousand pounds, out of the public funds, in the hands of the treasurer, which was directed to be laid out for the maintaining and educating scholars, and to be accounted for to the general assembly, from time to time, when required: which sum was accordingly paid to the said visitors, and by them invested in the purchase of two thousand one hundred and nineteen acres of land, on both sides of Nottoway river, in the counties of Prince George, Surry, and Brunswick, and seventeen negro slaves, to be employed in tilling and manuring the same; and certain scholarships were accordingly established on the said funds; and the general assembly, by their act, passed in the year 1726, and entitled an act for laying a duty on liquors, further endowed the said college with an annual revenue of two hundred pounds for twenty one years, to be paid out of certain duties thereon imposed on liquors; and by one other act, passed in the year 1734, endowed it with the whole of the said duties, during the residue of the said term then unexpired, a part or the whole thereof to be expended in purchasing a library for the said college: And by divers other acts, passed at subsequent times, the assemblies, for the times being, having continued to the said college the whole of the annual revenues, arising from the said duties, until the first of June, which shall be in the year 1780, to be applied to the funding scholarships, and other good uses, for the support of the said college, and to be accounted for to the general assembly; and the said general assembly by   of   in the year   gave a further donation to the said college, of   to be laid out in purchasing a mathematical apparatus for the said college, which was accordingly purchased. And the said trustees, in pursuance of the trust reposed in them, proceeded to erect the said college, and established one school of sacred theology, with two professorships therein, *to wit,* one for teaching the Hebrew tongue, and expounding the holy scriptures; the other for explaining the common places of divinity, and the controversies with heretics; one other school for philosophy, with two professorships therein, *to wit,* one for the study of rhetoric, logic, and ethics, and the other of physics, metaphysics, and mathematics; one other school for teaching the Latin and Greek tongues; and one other for teaching Indian boys reading, writing, vulgar arithmetic, the catechism and the principles of the christian religion; which last school was founded on the private donation of the honorable Robert Boyle, of the kingdom of England, and, by authority from his executors, submitted to the direction of the Earl of Burlington, one of the said executors of the bishop of London, for the time being and in default thereof, to the said trustees; and over the whole they appointed one president as supervisor:

Sect. 2. And, whereas the experience of near an hundred years hath proved, that the said college, thus amply endowed by the public, hath not answered their expectations, and there is reason to hope, that it would become more useful, if certain articles in its constitution were altered and amended, which being fixed, as before recited, by the original charter, cannot be reformed by the said trustees, whose powers are created and circumscribed by the said charter; and the said college being erected and constituted on the requisition of the general assembly, by the chief magistrate of the state their legal fiduciary for such purposes, being founded and endowed with the lands and revenues of the public, and intended for the sole use and improvement, and no wise in nature of a private grant, the same is of right subject to the public direction, and may by them be altered and amended, until such form be devised as will render the institution publicly advantageous, in proportion as it is publicly expensive; and the late change in the form of our government, as well as the contest of arms in which we are at present engaged, calling for extraordinary abilities both in council and field, it becomes the peculiar duty of the legislature, at this time, to aid and improve that seminary, in which those who are to be the future guardians of the rights and liberties of their country may be endowed with science and virtue, to watch and preserve the sacred deposit: *Be it therefore enacted by the General Assembly,* That, instead of eighteen visitors, or governors of the said college, there shall in future be five only, who shall be appointed by joint ballot of both houses of assembly, annually, to enter on the duties of their office on the new year's day ensuing their appointment, having previously given assurance of fidelity to the commonwealth, before any justice of the peace; and to continue in office until those next appointed shall be qualified; but those who shall be first appointed, after the passing of this act, and all others appointed during the course of any year to fill up vacancies happening by death, resignation, or removal out of the commonwealth, shall enter on duty immediately on such appointment. Any four of the said visitors may proceed to business; they shall choose their own rector, at their first meeting, in every year, and shall be deemed the lawful successors of the first trustees, and invested with all the rights, powers, and capacities given to them, save only so far as the same shall be abridged by this act; nor shall they be restrained in their legislation, by the royal prerogative, or the laws of the kingdom of England, or the canons or constitution of the English church, as enjoined in the said charter. There shall be three chancellors, in like manner apointed by joint ballot of both houses, from among the judges of the high court of chancery, or of the general court, to enter on their office immediately on such appointment, and to continue therein so long as they may remain in either of the said courts; any two of whom may proceed to business: to them shall belong solely the power of removing the professors, for breach or neglect of duty, immorality, severity, contumacy, or other good cause, and the judiciary powers in all disputes which shall arise on the statutes of the college, being called on for that purpose by the rector, or by the corporation of president and professors: a copy of their sentence of deprivation being delivered to the sheriff of the county wherein the college is, he shall forthwith cause the professor deprived to be ousted of his chambers and other freehold appertaining to the said college, and the remaining professors to be re-seized thereof, in like manner and form, and subject, on failure, to the like fines by the said chancellors, as in cases of writs of *habere facias seisinam* issued from courts of record. But no person shall be capable of being both visitor and chancellor at the same time; nor shall any professor be capable of being at the same time either visitor or chancellor. Instead of the president and six professors, licensed by the said charter, and established by the former visitors, there shall be eight professors, one of whom shall also be appointed president, with an additional salary of one hundred pounds a year; before they enter on the execution of their office, they shall give assurance of fidelity to the commonwealth, before some justice of the peace.—These shall be deemed the lawful successors of the president and professors appointed under the said charter, and shall have all their rights, powers and capacities, not otherwise disposed of by this act; to them shall belong the ordinary government of the college, and administration of its revenues, taking the advice of the visitors on all matters of great concern. There shall, in like manner, be eight professorships; *to wit,* one of moral philosophy, the laws of nature and of nations, and of the fine arts; one of law and police; one of history, civil and ecclesiastical; one of mathematics; one of anatomy and medicine; one of natural philosophy and natural history; one of the ancient languages, oriental and northern; and one of modern languages. The said professors shall likewise appoint, from time to time, a missionary, of approved veracity, to the several tribes of Indians, whose business shall be to investigate their laws, customs, religions, traditions, and more particularly their languages, constructing grammars thereof, as well as may be, and copious vocabularies, and, on oath, to communicate, from time to time, to the said president and professors, the materials he collects, to be by them laid up and preserved in their library; for which trouble the said missionary shall be allowed a salary, at the discretion of the vistors, out of the revenues of the college. And forasmuch as the revenue, arising from the duties on skins and furs, and those on liquors, with which the said college was endowed, by several acts of the general assembly, is subject to great fluctuations, from circumstances unforseen, insomuch that no calculation or foresight can enable the said visitors or professors to square thereto the expenditures of the said college, which being regular and permanent should depend on stable funds: *Be it therefore enacted,* That the revenue arising from the said duties shall be henceforth transferred to the use of the public, to be applied towards supporting the contingent charges of government; and that, in lieu thereof, the said college shall be endowed with an impost of five pounds of tobacco, on every hogshead of tobacco to be exported from this commonwealth, by land, or by water, to be paid to the inspectors, if such tobacco be carried to any public ware-house, by the person receiving the said tobacco from them, and by the said inspectors accounted for, on oath, to the said president and professors, on or before the 10th day of October, in every year, with an allowance of six per centum for their trouble; and if the said tobacco be not carried to any public ware-house, then the said impost shall be paid, collected, and accounted for to the said president and professors, by the same persons, at the same times, in and under the like manner, penalties and conditions, as prescribed by the laws, which shall be in force at the time, for collecting the duties imposed on exported tobacco, towards raising supplies of money for the public exigencies.—And that this commonwealth may not be without so great an ornament, nor its youth such an help towards attaining astronomical science, as the mechanical representation, or model of the solar system, conceived and executed by the greatest of astronomers, David Ryttenhouse: *Be it further enacted,* That the visitors, first appointed under this act, and their successors, shall be authorised to engage the said David Ryttenhouse, on the part of this commonwealth, to make and erect in the said college of William and Mary, and for its use, one of the said models, to be called by the name of the Ryttenhouse: the cost and expense of making, transporting and erecting whereof shall, according to the agreement or allowance of the said visitors, be paid by the treasurer of this commonwealth, on warrant from the auditors.

APPENDIX

First.—ETHICS . . . Moral Philosophy. Law of Nature. Law of Nations. —FINE ARTS . . . Sculpture. Painting. Gardening. Music. Architecture. Poetry. Oratory. Criticism.

Second.—LAW—Municipal . . . Common Law. Equity. Law Merchant. Law Maritime. Law Ecclesiastical.—Economical . . . Politics. Commerce.

Third.—HISTORY . . . Civil. Ecclesiastical.

Fourth.—MATHEMATICS—Pure . . . Arithmetic. Geometry.—Mixed . . . Mechanics. Optics. Acoustics. Astronomy.

Fifth.—Anatomy. Medicine.

Sixth.—NATURAL PHILOSOPHY . . . Chymistry. Statics. Hydrostatics. Pneumatics. Agriculture.—NATURAL HISTORY . . . Animals—Zoology. Vegetables—Botany. Minerals—Mineralogy.

Seventh.—ANCIENT LANGUAGES.—Oriental . . . Hebrew. Chaldee. Sy, riac.—Northern . . . Moeso-Gothic. Anglo Saxon. Old Icelandic.

Eighth.—MODERN LANGUAGES . . . French. Italian. German.
Missionary for Indian History, &c.

Phillips Andover Academy, Massachusetts, Is Chartered, 1780 *

Whereas, the education of youth has ever been considered by the wise and good, as an object of the highest consequence to the safety and happiness of a people; as at that period the mind easily receives and retains impressions, is formed with peculiar advantage to piety and virtue, and directed to the pursuit of the most useful knowledge; and, whereas the Honorable Samuel Phillips of Andover, in the County of Essex, Esq., and the Honorable John Phillips of Exeter, in the County of Rockingham, and State of New Hampshire, Esq., on the first day of April, in the year of our Lord one thousand seven hundred and seventy eight, by a legal instrument of that date, gave, granted, and assigned to the Honorable William Phillips, Esquire, and others, therein named, and to their heirs, divers lots and parcels of land, in said Instrument described, as well as certain other estate, to the use and upon the trust following, namely, that the rents, profits, and interest thereof, be forever laid out and expended by the Trustees in the said Instrument named, for the support of a Public Free School or Academy, in the town of Andover:—and, whereas the execution of the generous and important design of the grantors aforesaid will be attended with very great embarrassments, unless, by an act of incorporation, the Trustees, mentioned in the said Instrument, and their successors, shall be authorized to commence and prosecute actions at law, and transact such other matters in their corporate capacity, as the interest of the said Academy shall require.

Academy Established

1. Be it therefore enacted by the Council and the House of Representatives in General Court assembled, and by the authorship of the same; that there be and hereby is established in the Town of Andover, and County of Essex, an Academy, by the name of *Phillips Academy,* for the purpose of promoting piety and virtue, and for the education of youth, in the English, Latin, and Greek languages, together with Writing, Arithmetic, Music, and the Art of Speaking; also practical Geometry, Logic and Geography, and such other of the liberal Arts and Sciences, or Languages, as opportunity may hereafter permit, and as the Trustees, herein after provided, shall direct.

The First State University Is Chartered, 1785 †

An act for the more full and complete establishment of a public seat of learning in this State.

As it is the distinguishing happiness of free governments, that civil order should be the result of choice, and not necessity, and the common wishes

---

* *Acts and Laws of Massachusetts,* 1780, pp. 327-29.
† Watkins, *A Digest of the Laws of the State of Georgia,* pp. 299-302. This was the first state university to be chartered in this country, but several years passed before the institution

of the people become the laws of the land, their public prosperity, and even existence, very much depends upon suitably forming the minds and morals of their citizens. Where the minds of the people in general are viciously disposed and unprincipled, and their conduct disorderly, a free government will be attended with greater confusions, and with evils more horrid than the wild uncultivated state of nature: It can only be happy where the public principles and opinions are properly directed, and their manners regulated. This is an influence beyond the sketch of laws and punishments, and can be claimed only by religion and education. It should therefore be among the first objects of those who wish well to the national prosperity, to encourage and support the principles of religion and morality, and early to place the youth under the forming hand of society, that by instruction they may be moulded to the love of virtue and good order. Sending them abroad to other countries for their education will not answer these purposes, is too humiliating an acknowledgment of the ignorance or inferiority of our own, and will always be the cause of so great foreign attachments, that upon principles of policy it is not admissible.

This country, in the times of our common danger and distress, found such security in the principles and abilities which wise regulations had before established in the minds of our countrymen, that our present happiness, joined to pleasing prospects, should conspire to make us feel ourselves under the strongest obligation to form the youth, the rising hope of our land, to render the like glorious and essential services to our country.

And whereas, for the great purpose of internal education, divers allotments of land have, at different times, been made, particularly by the legislature at their sessions in July, one thousand seven hundred and eighty-three; and February, one thousand seven hundred and eighty-four all of which may be comprehended and made the basis of one general and complete establishment: THEREFORE *the representatives of the freemen of the State of Georgia, in General assembly met, this twenty-seventh day of January, in the year of our Lord one thousand seven hundred and eighty-five, enact, ordain, and declare, and by these presents it is* ENACTED, ORDAINED, AND DECLARED,

1st. The general superintendance and regulation of the literature of this State, and in particular of the public seat of learning, shall be committed and intrusted to the governor and council, the speaker of the house of assembly, and the chief justice of the State, for the time being, who shall, *ex officio,* compose one board, denominated the *Board of Visitors,* hereby vested with all the powers of visitation, to see that the intent of this institution is carried into effect, and John Houstoun, James Nathan Brownson, John Habersham, Abiel Holmes, Jenkin Davies, Hugh Lawson,

---

opened. The University of North Carolina was chartered in 1789 and opened in 1795. Georgia was the first state university to be chartered; North Carolina the first to be opened. The American state university had its origin in the South.

William Glascock, and Benjamin Taliaferro, esquires, who shall compose another board, denominated the *Board of Trustees.* These two boards united, or a majority of each of them, shall compose the SENATUS ACADEMICUS of the University of Georgia.

2d. All statutes, laws and ordinances, for the government of the university shall be made and enacted by the two boards united or a majority of each of them, subject always to be laid before the general assembly, as often as required, and to be repealed or disallowed, as the general assembly shall think proper.

3d. Property vested in the university, shall never be sold without the joint concurrence of the two boards, and by act of the legislature; but the leasing, farming, and managing of the property of the university for its constant support, shall be the business of the board of trustees. For this purpose they are hereby constituted a body corporate and politic, by the name of *Trustees of the University of Georgia,* by which they shall have perpetual succession, and shall and may be a person in law, capable to plead, and be impleaded, defend, and be defended, answer, and be answered unto, also to have, take, possess, acquire, purchase, or otherwise receive lands, tenements, hereditaments, goods, chattels, or other estates, and the same to lease, use, manage or improve, for the good and benefit of said university, and all property given or granted to or by the government of this State for the advancement of learning in general, is hereby vested in such trustees in trust as herein described.

4th. As the appointment of a person to be the president and head of the university is one of the first and most important concerns, on which its respect and usefulness greatly depend, the board of trustees shall first examine and nominate, but the appointment of the president shall be by the two boards jointly, who shall also have the power of removing him from office for misdemeanor, unfaithfulness, or incapacity.

5th. There shall be a stated annual meeting of the *Senatus Academicus* at the university, or at any other place or time to be appointed by themselves, at which the governor of the State, or in his absence, the president of the council shall preside; their records to be kept by the secretary of the university.

6th. As the affairs and business of the university may make more frequent meetings of the trustees necessary, the president and two of the members are empowered to appoint a meeting of the board, notice always to be given to the rest, or letters left at the usual places of their abode at least fourteen days before the said meeting, seven of the trustees thus convened shall be a legal meeting: In case of the death, absence or incapacity of the president, the senior trustee shall preside; the majority of the members present shall be considered a vote of the whole, and where the members are divided, the president shall have a casting vote.

Provided always, That nothing done at these special meetings, shall have any force or efficacy after the rising of the then next annual meeting of the trustees.

7th. The trustees shall have the power of filling up all vacancies of their own board, and appointing professors, tutors, secretary, treasurers, steward, or any other officers which they may think necessary, and the same to discontinue or remove, as they may think fit; but not without seven of their number, at least, concurring in such act.

8th. The trustees shall prescribe the course of public studies, appoint the salaries of the different officers, form and use a public seal, adjust and determine the expenses, and adopt such regulations, not otherwise provided for, which the good of the university may render necessary.

9th. All officers appointed to the instruction and government of the university, shall be of the christian religion; and within three months after they enter upon the execution of their trust, shall publicly take the oath of allegiance and fidelity, and the oaths of office prescribed in the statutes of the university; the president before the governor or president of council, and all other officers before the president of the university.

10th. The president, professors, tutors, students, and all officers and servants of the university whose office require their constant attendance, shall be, and they are hereby excused from military duty, and from all other such like duties and services; and all lands and other property of the university is hereby exempted from taxation.

11th. The trustees shall not exclude any person of any religious denomination whatsoever, from free and equal liberty and advantages of education, or from any of the liberties, privileges, and immunities of the university in his education, on account of his or their speculative sentiments in religion, or being of a different religious profession.

12th. The president of the university, with consent of the trustees, shall have power to give and confer all such honors, degrees and licenses as are usually conferred in colleges or universities, and shall always preside at the meeting of the trustees, and at all the public exercises of the university.

13th. The *Senatus Academicus* at their stated annual meetings shall consult and advise, not only upon the affairs of the university, but also to remedy the defects, and advance the interest of literature through the State in general. For this purpose it shall be the business of the members, previous to their meeting, to obtain an acquaintance with the State, and regulations of the schools and places of education in their respective counties, that they may be thus possessed of the whole, and have it lie before them for mutual assistance and deliberation. Upon this information they shall recommend what kind of schools and academies shall be instituted, agreeable to the constitution, in the several parts of the State, and prescribe what branches of instruction shall be taught and inculcated in each: They shall also examine and recommend the instructors to be employed in them, or appoint persons for that purpose. The president of the university, as often as the duties of his station will permit, and some of the members, at least once in a year, shall visit them, and examine into their order and performances.

14th. All public schools, instituted or to be supported by funds or public monies in this State, shall be considered as parts of members of the university, and shall be under the foregoing directions and regulations.

15th. Whatsoever public measures are necessary to be adopted for accomplishing these great and important designs, the trustees shall, from time to time, represent and lay before the general assembly.

16th. All laws and ordinances heretofore passed in any wise contrary to the true intent and meaning of the premises, are hereby repealed, and declared to be null and void.

17th. In full testimony and confirmation of this charter, ordinance and constitution, and all the articles therein contained, *The representatives of the freemen of the State of Georgia in general assembly, hereby order,* That this act shall be signed by the honorable Joseph Habersham, Esquire, speaker of the house of assembly, and sealed with the public seal of this State and the same, or the enrollment thereof in the records of this State, shall be good and effectual in law, to have and to hold the powers, privileges, and immunities, and all and singular the premises herein given, or which are meant, mentioned, or intended to be hereby given to the said *Board of Visitors,* and *Trustees,* and to their successors in office for ever.

JOSEPH HABERSHAM, *Speaker.*

SAVANNAH, January 27, 1785

Agricultural and Manual Labor Schools Are Recommended, 1787 *

Plan for establishing Schools in a new country, where the inhabitants are thinly settled, and whose children are to be educated with a special reference to a country life.

Take any number of settlers, we will suppose sixty families, collected in a village, and they will be able to support a schoolmaster, and easily maintain their children at school: for twenty shillings a year, paid by each family, will make up a competent salary for the master, and the children will be cloathed and fed at home.

But if sixty families are dispersed over a large tract of country, from twenty to forty miles in extent, how shall their children receive the benefits of education? The master's salary, it is true, can be paid as in the former case; but few parents will be disposed to incur the heavy expense of sending their children from home, and boarding them at a distant school.

---

* *The Columbia Magazine, or Monthly Miscellany,* April, 1787, pp. 356-59. It was this article which suggested to Dr. John de la Howe of South Carolina a plan, set out in his will of 1796, for a manual labor school which is believed to have been the first school of that kind set up in the United States. The school is still in operation.

Hence, in such a scattered settlement, general ignorance will ensue; and the people consequently degenerate into vice, irreligion and barbarism. —To remedy evils of such magnitude will be difficult; perhaps it will be thought impracticable: to attempt it, however, will be laudable; and all those who have the dearest interests of society at heart, will give the measure their support.

If by charitable donations, or by grants of the state, adequate funds could be formed, to defray the expenses of the board and tuition of such children, the evils before mentioned would be remedied: but such funds are not to be hoped for: and if they could be obtained, it might well be doubted whether that would be the best mode of educating children destined for a laborious country life. There the boys are to be the future farmers, and the girls the farmers' wives. If both could, in early life, be well instructed in the various branches of their future employments, they would make better husbands, better wives, and more useful citizens. And if the mode of communicating such instruction could at the same time enable them largely to contribute to their own support, another important advantages would be gained.—These reflections have given rise to the following PLAN of EDUCATION for a Country Life.

1. Let three or four hundred acres of land be appropriated for the use of a school: let it consist of a meadow, tillage and wood land, in convenient proportions.

2. Let a skilful and industrious manager be provided, who shall himself be a complete farmer, and have two labourers, one acquainted with farming, the other with gardening, to assist him.

3. Let the farm be completely stocked, and all the requisite carriages and husbandry utensils provided: such tools as are designed for boys, to be made of sizes suited to their strength.

4. Let the necessary buildings be erected for a school, a boarding house, a barn and work-shop. These may be very plain and cheap, and at the same time very comfortable. The necessary furniture and tools must also be provided.

5. A school master and a schoolmistress must be chosen with much circumspection. The latter will be the housekeeper.

6. A cook will be necessary; and she should know how to dress the plain, wholesome food of the country, in the best manner.

7. The childrens' beds and bedding, cloaths and materials for cloathing must be provided by their parents.

The necessary foundations being thus laid, the school and farm may be conducted agreeably to the following regulations.

1. No boy or girl under eight years of age should be admitted.

2. Both boys and girls should be taught to read, write and cypher. The boys should also be instructed in every useful branch of husbandry and

gardening, and the girls in every kind of work necessary for farmers' wives to know and practice.

3. For the purpose of working, let the boys be divided into such a number of classes as shall be judged convenient, distributing equal proportions of the larger and smaller boys to each class. Whenever the nature of the work to be done will admit of it; let equal portions of it be assigned to the several classes, in order to excite their emulation, to excel in industry and skill: and for this reason each portion of land should be cultivated, through a whole season, by the same class to which it was first allotted.—It will be obvious to direct the several boys in the same class, to perform such parts of the general labours required of it, as shall be adapted to their several capacities and strength.

4. All the boys may be taught the methods of making and rearing nurseries of the most useful kind of fruit trees, shrubs and bushes, and of improving the former by grafting and budding. Each boy should have an equal portion of land allotted to him, on which he should raise a nursery; and when he has finished his course of education, should be allowed to take home with him all the trees, shrubs and bushes he has reared and cultivated; excepting only such a proportion as shall be requisite for supplying the school-farm. In like manner he should be allowed to take home with him a collection of useful garden seeds. In this way the most valuable fruits and plants would in a few years be spread and cultivated through the whole settlement.

5. When orchards shall be grown, they may be instructed in the art of making and fermenting cyder, so as to produce a soft and pleasant liquor.

6. A small brewery may be erected on the farm, and all the boys taught to malt barley and oats; and both boys and girls may be taught the art of brewing, so far, at least, as the same might be practiced in every farmer's family.—Perhaps by extending the plan of the malthouse and brewery, they might be able to supply that wholesome and nourishing liquor, good beer, to a great part of the settlement; and thus the use of pernicious, distilled liquors be superseded. Malt, at least, might thus be furnished, and yield a small revenue towards supporting the school.

7. The management of cattle will make a necessary branch of their education; and the modern method of managing bees will well deserve their attention.

8. Tending the cattle, and providing fuel and fencing stuff, will be the principal employments of the winter. But the boys may also make the wood-work of all those utensils of husbandry which will be requisite for the ensuing session. The elder boys will be capable of handling axes, and all the other tools used in those employments.

9. The girls will be taught to sew, to knit, to spin, to cook, to make beds, to clean house, to make and mend their own cloaths, to make the

boys cloaths when cut out, and to mend them—to milk cows, and to make butter and cheese.

10. That they may learn to cook and perform all other houshold work, they should be divided into classes, in the same manner in which the boys were classed, and assist the house keeper and cook, a week at a time, in rotation.

11. A collection of children, from eight to fourteen or fifteen years of age, thus regularly employed, on a good farm, would be nearly able to maintain themselves; and if the expences of their schooling can thus be reduced as low, or nearly as low, as when, in ordinary cases, they live at home, the great obstacle to their education will be removed.

12. The winter will be the season most favourable for the literary instruction of the children; as then they will have but few necessary avocations; perhaps no more than will occasion that degree of exercise which the preservation of their health may require. But their learning need not be wholly interrupted in the summer. Every morning the boys may spend two hours at school, and be ready to go in the field to work by eight or nine o'clock. And when they go out, the girls may enter, and also spend two hours at school. Again at one o'clock (if they dine at noon) the boys may attend the school, continuing there an hour and an half, or two hours; and the girls may succeed them, as in the forenoon, attending the school a like length of time. Thus the same master might every day teach both girls and boys; and yet, in the whole, not to be confined above seven or eight hours in a day.—An hour every evening might be allowed the children, to amuse themselves in innocent sports.

13. The employments of a country life are so congenial to the human heart, the master of this rural academy could hardly forbear to engage in them, in the intervals between school hours. He would naturally be led to read the best authors on agriculture and rural affairs, and to get some acquaintance with botany. He would study theories, tracing useful practices back to their principles; and thus be able to communicate to the elder boys, or youth, a degree of scientific knowledge of the very important art of which, in the field, they daily learned the practice.

14. I hardly need mention, what ought to be an indispensable part of education in every literary institution, That the children at this rural academy would be taught the plainest and most important principles of religion and morality.

15. It is to be presumed that the abler farmers would continue their children at school till they should be fourteen or fifteen years old. These children of both sexes, might make further advances in learning. They might study geography, and read some instructive histories, particularly the history of the United States, and a few of the best English moral writers, in prose and verse. At the same time they might learn so much of

book-keeping as would be useful in the country; and the boys might be taught geometry, practical surveying, and the principles of mechanics.

16. Perhaps some useful manufactories might be established, in which the children, both male and female, might be very serviceable.

Such an institution as that here sketched out, need not be confined to frontier settlements; tho' the first idea of it was suggested by a reflection on their situation. Rural schools, or academies, upon such a plan, would perhaps be the most useful that could be established in the country towns and counties of this and every other state in America. Numerous advantages would result from them. I will hint at a few.

1. The children would be taught the plainest and most useful principles and rules of religion and morality.

2. They would be well and uniformly educated in the most necessary learning, and in the most important arts of civil life, *husbandry* and *domestic economy*.

3. They would acquire habits of industry.

4. Their manners and behaviour would be formed, and rendered mild and agreeable.

5. A few successive sets of scholars thus educated, returning to their several homes, would quite change the face of the country, in point of cultivation, and introduce a pleasing change in the knowledge, manners of the people, and abolish the invidious distinction of citizens and clowns.

Act Providing for the Support of the University of North Carolina, 1789 *

Whereas, the General Assembly by their Act, entitled "An Act to establish a University in this state," passed on the eleventh day of December instant, have declared that a University shall be established and erected in this state, which shall be called and known by the name of The University of North Carolina: And whereas, adequate funds will be found to be the means which will most effectually ensure to the state the advantages to be hoped and expected from such an institution.

I. Be it therefore enacted by the General Assembly of the State of North Carolina, and it is hereby enacted by the authority of the same, That a gift of all monies due and owing to the public of North Carolina, either for arrearages under the former or present government, up to the first day of January, one thousand seven hundred and eighty-three, inclusive, (monies or certificates due for confiscated property purchased excepted) shall be and is hereby declared to be fully and absolutely made, for the purpose of erecting the necessary bulidings, employing professors and

* Walter Clark (Ed.),*The State Records of North Carolina*, XXV, pp. 24-25. Repeal of this act in 1800 was the basis of North Carolina's "Dartmouth College Case" in 1805. See below, pp. 204, 209-211.

tutors, and carrying into complete effect the act before recited: And the Treasurer is hereby directed and required to commence suits, and to prosecute all persons owing as above mentioned, and the monies recovered in consequence thereof to pay into the hands of the Trustees named in said act, or their successors, to be applied to the purposes aforesaid. Provided, That nothing herein contained shall be construed to prevent the Treasurer or Comptroller from settling with and collecting from the executors of Robert Lanier, deceased, late Treasurer of Salisbury district, such sums in cash or certificates as may on a final settlement of his accounts be found to be due to the public; nor shall it extend to prevent their collecting from the Sheriffs of that district, their arrearages of taxes which became due under the present government, and which ought to have been paid into the office of the said Lanier as Treasurer aforesaid; provided they make such collection within the space of two years, after which time the arrearages of that district also shall be considered as being included in this gift.

II. And be it enacted, That all the property that has heretofore or shall hereafter escheat to the state, shall be and hereby is vested in the said Trustees, for the use and benefit of the said University.

III. And be it further enacted by the authority, aforesaid, That the lands and other property belonging to the University aforesaid, shall be, and the same is hereby exempt from all kind of public taxation.

Some Rules of Cokesbury College, Abingdon, Maryland, 1792 *

It is also our particular desire, that all who shall be educated in our College, may be kept at the utmost distance as from vice in general, so in particular from softness and effeminacy of manners.

We shall therefore inflexibly insist on their rising early in the morning; and we are convinced by constant observation and experience, that this is of vast importance both to mind and body. It is of admirable use either for preserving a good, or improving a bad constitution. . . .

On the same principle we prohibit *play* in the strongest terms: and in this we have the two greatest writers on the subject that perhaps any age has produced (Mr. *Locke* and Mr. *Rousseau*) of our sentiments: . . .

The students shall rise at five o'clock in the morning, summer and winter, at the ringing of the College-bell.

All the students . . . shall assemble together in the College at six o'clock, for public prayer, . . . From morning-prayer till seven, they shall be allowed to recreate themselves as is hereafter directed. At seven they shall have breakfast.

From eight to twelve, they are to be closely kept to their studies. From

* *The Doctrines and Discipline of the Methodist Episcopal Church in America* (Philadelphia, Printed by Parry Hall, 1792), pp. 60-69, *passim.* Cokesbury College had been founded in 1788.

twelve to three, they are to employ themselves in recreation and dining Dinner to be ready at one o'clock. From three till six, they are again to be kept closely to their studies. At six they shall sup. At seven there shall be public prayer. From evening-prayer till bed-time, they shall be allowed recreation. They shall all be in by nine o'clock, without fail.

Their recreation shall be gardening, walking, riding, and bathing, without doors, and the carpenter's, joiner's, cabinetmaker's or turner's business within doors. . . . A person skilled in gardening shall be appointed to overlook the students . . . in this recreation. . . . A master . . . shall always be present at the time of bathing. Only one shall bathe at a time; and no one shall remain in the water above a minute. No student shall be allowed to bathe in the river. A *Taberna Lignaria* [carpenter's shop] shall be provided . . . with all proper instruments and materials, and a skillful person . . . to overlook the students at this recreation. . . . The students shall be indulged with nothing which the world calls *play*. Let this rule be observed with the strictest nicety; for those who play when they are young, will play when they are old.

The Bishops shall examine by themselves or their delegates, into the progress of all the students in their studies, every half year, or oftener if possible.

The Senatus Academicus Reports a Plan of Education for the University of Georgia, November 27, 1800 *

Your Committee with deference report the following plan of education to be taught in six years, subject to the revision and alteration of the Professor to be appointed as above with the consent of the board of trustees.

In the first and second years Latin and Greek shall be taught, and English read occasionally at the discretion of the Tutor.

In the third year, Latin, Greek and Kennet's Antiquities; English grammar, Arithmetic, and Geography; two or more of the pupils should deliver pieces committed to memory each day in rotation.

In the fourth year, Greek and Latin occasionally, English grammar to be reviewed weekly, Arithmetic to be continued; Euclid's elements or some other treatise on Geometry, at the option of the Tutor. And the students in this year should once in each week be required to write a letter or some piece of simple composition for the inspection of the Tutor and pieces should be pronounced as in the last year.

In the fifth year Latin and Greek authors and English grammar to be occasionally reviewed; Trigonometry, Surveying and other practical branches of the Mathematics, with Algebra should be taught; composition and public speaking should be attended to as in the last year.

* Minutes of the *Senatus Academicus* of the University of Georgia. Verified typescript copy in the Library of that institution, Vol. I, 1799-1803, pp. 16-19. Typescript copy of that copy is in the Southern Historical Collection, University of North Carolina.

In the sixth year natural and moral philosophy, and the Belles Lettres should be taught, and compositions written weekly as in the preceding years. If either of the tutors should be acquainted with the French language, that may be taught in addition to, or instead of, the Latin and Greek, as Parents and Guardians may choose.

Your committee report that the following apparatus and books be purchased for the use of the institution, to wit,

A pair of globes of about twenty inches diameter supposed to be
worth about $130.00
Mathematical instruments including such as are usually used in
surveying $170.00

School Books

Rudimen's Rudiments 12	Copies	
Cordery 12	do	
Aesops fables 12	do	
Corneilius Nepos 12	do	
Caesar's Commentaries 12	do	Del. Ed.
Ovid's Metamorphoses 12	do	
Virgil 12	do	
Horace 12	do	
Caesar's Orations 12	do	
Terence 6	do	
Wittendal's Greek Grammar 6	do	
Greek Testament 6	do	
Lucian 4	do	
Xenophon 4	do	
Guthrie's Geography 12	do	Cary's Ed.
Cary's Atlas 2	do	
Ainsworth's Dictionary		large edit.
. . . do . . . . . . do 4	do	small
Johnson's Dictionary		folio
Young Man's best Companion 4	do	
Sheridan's Art of Speaking 4	do	
Do's Pronouncing grammar 2	do	
Lowth's english grammar 6	do	
Euclid's Elements 2	do	
Petour's Navigation 2	Copies	
Robinson's do 1	do	
Marten's Natural Philosophy 2	do	
Enfield's do 2	do	
Blair's Lectures 4	do	
Rollin's Belles lettres	do	
Hutchinson's Moral Philosophy		
Paley's do		

Books for the use of the Students at intervals when not engaged in the Academical Studies, to wit, Rollin's Ancient History; Vertot's Rome; Ferguson's Roman History; Gibbon's decline and fall of the Roman Empire; Antient and Modern Europe; Gordon's Tacitus; Livy in english; Gillies' history of Greece; Anacharses's travels; Humes history of England with the continuations; Robinson's Works including his history of Charles the fifth, of Scotland, of America, and his India; Doctor Adam Smith's Works; Watson's history of the low Countries; History of France by ; De Ritz Memoirs; Sully's Memoirs; Voltaires Age of Louis the 14th & 15th in english; Do: Charles the 12th do; Abbe Raynal's history of the East and West Indies in english; Ferguson's history of Civil society; Montesquieu's spirit of Laws; Vattel's law of Nations; Blackstone's Commentaries; De Lolme on the Constitution of England; Civil Law; Pope's, Swift's, Addison's, Temple's, and Locke's Works; Bolingbroke's Political works; Moore's travels; Blair's Atterbury's Seed's, Didderidge's Jorbin's and Witherspoon's sermons; Tiltotson's Works entire; Newton on the Prophecies; Letters of John Newton; Scougal's life of God in the Soul of Man; Dignity of Human Nature; Paley's evidences; Burnett's discources; Milton's paradise lost and regained; Pope's Iliad and Odyssey; Young's night thoughts; Gay's, Parnell's and Grey's poems; Dryden's works; including his Virgil; Quintilian in English; Longinus on the Sublime, in english; Demosthenes's Orations in english, and the American edition of the Encyclopedia.

Your Committee gave notice in one of the public Newspapers of Savannah, one of Augusta, and one of Louisville, that they would receive lists of subscriptions for Money, to be advanced in aid of the establishment of this institution.

The Legislature of North Car ꜱlina Repeals the Law Appropriating Escheats for the Support of the University, 1800 *

I. *Be it enacted by the General Assembly of the state of North-Carolina, and it is hereby enacted by the authority of the same,* That from and after the passing of this act, all acts or clauses of acts, which have heretofore granted power to the Trustees of the University of North-Carolina to seize and possess any escheated or confiscated property, real or personal, shall be, and the same is hereby repealed and made void.

II. *And be it further enacted,* That all escheated or confiscated property which the said Trustees, their Agents or Attornies, have not legally sold, by virtue of the said Laws, shall from hence revert to the State, and henceforth be considered as the property of the same, as though such laws had never been passed.

---

* Iredell, *The Public Acts of the General Assembly of North Carolina*, II, p. 150 (1800). This act led to North Carolina's case which Webster used in the Dartmouth College Case, 1819.

Collegiate Degrees Conferred at Commencement, 1802 *

At the Commencements in 1802 in the following Colleges, Degrees were conferred on the annexed number of persons.

Columbia College, New York

Bachelor of Arts	20
Master of Arts	5
Doctor of Divinity	1

Harvard University, Massachusetts

Bachelor of Arts	58
Master of Arts	29
Bachelor of Physic	4
Doctor of Physic	1
Doctor of Divinity	3

Dartmouth College, New Hampshire

Bachelor of Arts	22
Master of Arts	16
Bachelor of Physic	3
Doctor of Laws	2

Yale College, Connecticutt

Bachelor of Arts	61
Master of Arts	11
Doctor of Divinity	1
Doctor of Laws	2

Princeton College, New Jersey

Bachelor of Arts	26
Master of Arts	10
Doctor of Divinity	4
Doctor of Laws	2

University of North Carolina

Bachelor of Arts	3
Master of Arts	4

We intend to publish annually the number of the Graduates in all the Colleges from which we can obtain information to shew the progress of Education in each of the states; and we hope and trust ere long to find that North Carolina which exceeds most of them in population, and equals any of them in native genius, will produce annually an equal or greater number of young men of education. Our University possesses advantages equal to any. The situation is in high degree healthful and pleasant; its retirement is happily calculated for study; it is furnished with able professors; and the expences of board and education are much lower than at any other College in America.

These advantages beging to be duly appreciated. There were a hundred students at the last session and during this it is expected the number will be considerably increased. The want of the new College building which

* *Minerva; or Anti-Jacobin* (Raleigh, N. C.), August 29, 1803.

stands with the walls half raised, is beginning to be felt and the necessity of it will soon become very urgent. At present the trustees are unable to proceed further with it for want of funds.

Proposal for Establishing a University in Virginia by Subscriptions, Lottery and a Luxury Tax, 1805 *

Your petitioners approach the legislature, with hopes of awakening its attention, because one sustains & the other sweetens human life; and because one is the tutelar interest of the state, and the other its political soul.

A single fact will demonstrate their intimate connexion, and close affinity. By the official returns of the exports of the two countries, those of the United States appear to haxe exceeded those of Great Britain in the year 1803, in relation to the numbers of people; even allowing to Britain a re-exportation due to her foreign possessions, and confining the United States to native commodities. It is republicanism, which, within twenty years, has enabled us to overtake a start of centuries, in the arts of industry.

By saving her, agriculture will flourish. She was never saved by factitious wealth or exclusive knowledge; by the quackery of oracle, or the patriotism of privilege.

Some diffusion of knowledge, is admitted to be necessary for her existence; and in Virginia, the government diffuses none.

Hence, about five hundred of our children, at an expense of four hundred dollars each, are annually sent to other countries, to find, what they cannot find at home; and many return, fraught with the most pernicious prejudices. This annual drain of cash is equal to a capital of four millions. Yet half a million would save it. By laying out that sum in an university, the whole expense would be reimbursed to the state, in somewhat above two years, if extraneous educations should not increase; but as these daily accumulate, the annual loss will presently amount to the whole sum sufficient to establish an university. By investing half a million once, in providing for the education of our children at home, we shall therefore save an accumulating capital of half a million annually, to invigorate agriculture and industry.

If institutions for education, patronized by governments, are errors, why are our children forced abroad to such? Is it not better to erect them at home, and instil into our children our own principles, than to send them abroad, to bring back such as other governments may instill?

Your petitioners, pleased with the theory of equalizing knowledge by the education of a whole nation, have delayed to remind the legislature of the subject, from a hope of seeing this theory carried into practice. But it has not been effected in the United States, or in any other part of the world.

An impracticable design, can no longer be a good reason for defeating

* *The Richmond Enquirer*, December 6, 1805.

what is practicable. At least, a refusal to place a good education within the reach of a considerable portion of the people, for the purpose of giving a bad one to all, would be unjust, unless that purpose was fulfilled. Will the legislature do nothing for republicanism, under pretense of doing every thing? The same theory inculcates a community of knowledge, and a community of property. Is one part of it attainable without the other? Can we equalize knowledge without equalizing wealth? Moral machines are like physical. A wheel may work well in one, which would shatter another. If ballancing knowledge by sharing it equally, should not be a project exactly as speculative as an Agrarian law, it could yet be easily proved, that an Agrarian law, & an equal division of knowledge, are moral wheels constructed upon principles so similar, that neither could work well without the other; nor in union with the inequalities of knowledge or wealth, produced by fair commerce or honest industry.

Not a theoretical, but an attainable diffusion and balance of knowledge and wealth, should guide patriots. The wealth out of the hands of a government, is the balance against the wealth within them. Such also is the attainable balance of knowledge; and it becomes more necessary, as governments are enriched by charter patronage. Not bad, but the best educations, can create a balance on the side of the people, against the talents collected into governments, and rich corporations. Such only are safe centinels to watch power and alarm nations. They ought to be too wise to be deceived, and too numerous to be corrupted. By an intercourse with men but thus educated, the people will require more wisdom than from any system for bestowing narrow educations; because a cheap university, by pouring into society a far greater body of learned men, furnishes a band of patriots, who must teach the ignorant to defend their rights, for the sake of preserving their own. Neither this, nor a balance of knowledge in relation to other states, so important to Virginia, is attainable, by making learned men rare, or teaching all the people to read and write.

Our present policy splits real estates by laws of inheritance; accumulates factitious wealth by charters; and makes the best educations dear and rare, by a necessity for seeking them abroad. Thus, in a short time, a monopoly of wealth and knowledge, will be opposed to a scattered, unchartered, needy and ignorant landed interest. On the contrary, the best educations ought to be cheapened for agriculture, as the laws by dividing inheritances, diminish its ability to buy them; to sustain her against charter accumulations of privilege and wealth and to preserve the most faithful ally of republican government by making a right to keep a gun, dear in England, the rich became sole proprietors of the game. So they will monopolize good educations here from the same course.

The dereliction of education by the legislature, will expose it to the occupancy of some adventurer. Will it be seized by a monied aristocracy, from its costliness; or by an ambitious religious sect, as a medium for sow-ing with missionaries (in imitation of the Jesuits) its designs throughout the union? Or will such factions unite? Can a dereliction constitute the freedom of education, when an university, governed by the legislature, would be opened to all parties; and a dereliction, will condemn knowledge to become the test of one?

The ingenious theory before attended to, contends that governments ought not to meddle with education; but it does not approve and unite with this opinion, modes of gratifying avarice and ambition by law. It does not advise us to swallow the poison and neglect the antidote. This is inevitable death. To feed avarice and ambition by artificial accumulations, to leave education dear, and thus to weave knowledge into a wreath for the brow of monopoly, is a system, immeasurably distant from the theory, whence an enemy has been drawn, against cherishing knowledge by law.

Education is an instrument which will be used to sustain or to destroy governments, of the most powerful nature. If free governments throw it away, it will be seized and used by some tyrannical principle. In their custody, it is secured against misapplication, by the same responsibility which secures life and property.

A mode of government will probably cause a school to flourish, which causes a nation to flourish. Can a school flourish without government, whilst no other community can; or can aristocratical form, which are bad for nations, be good for colleges? Will irresponsibility, which paralyzes duty in one case, invigorate it in the other? personal genius and virtue may bestow temporary success upon bad principles, but good principles only can produce permanent good effects.

Your petitioners therefore implore the legislature, to set about the establishment of a college, by law and by example; upon a scale sufficiently plentiful and liberal, to educate the children of the state at home, in the most perfect manner.

Half a million of dollars will probably suffice. It is far less than Virginia pays for funding, for banking, or for Louisiana; and it will save her annual cent: per cent: in money, besides the returns in science and republican principles, with all their effects; to neither of which any of these pecuniary expenditures pretend.

To raise a fifth of this sum, it is proposed that the legislature open a subscription by law; that they resort in addition to an annual lottery, excluding lotteries for any other purpose; and that they provide for a deficiency by a tax upon pleasure horses, carriages, or other subjects.

Thus the poor will have secured to them the blessing of a moderate government without cost; and the contributions of the rich, for the sake of their own liberty and property, and the happiness of their children, will even bring back to them pecuniary profit. By making the subscriptions payable when one hundred thousand dollars are subscribed, even this mode of contribution may become very general, and tolerably equal among the wealthy.

If the government of the university is made accountable to the Legislature, an annual election of governors, will create an honorary degree; the discharge of which will be invigorated, as being a road to public favor, so as to prepare candidates for office, by habits of virtue and patriotism.

A site may be selected in one of the middle counties, near to fuel, wood, limestone and provisions, as far from the vices of towns; which may be kept at a distance by law, and by the purchase of a large tract of land; and the necessary professions and trades, as tenants, may be made subservient to collegiate morals.

Your petitioners, conscious that neither can flourish without the other; that agriculture will become a slave, if republicanism should perish; and that republicanism will perish, divided by charter interests; unless a vast accession of knowledge is infused into the agricultural interest, to regulate and check the vast accession of wealth bestowed upon exclusive privilege; the enemy of republicanism; doubt not of the same care of their welfare, which has often excited, and would upon this occasion kindle, the gratitude and filial piety for the Legislature of Virginia.

The writer of this essay, knows of about fifty youths sent out of the state for education. He solicits those who are willing to patronize an university by subscription, to communicate the sums they will subscribe to the editor of the Enquirer. On this part, he will subscribe two thousand dollars, and personally claim this engagement, if the undertaking is set on foot. For this purpose, a law empowering those, who will, to form themselves into a society, to appoint commissioners for soliciting subscriptions, and to provide a mode of bringing them into the treasury, when they shall amount to a certain sum, will be necessary.

North Carolina's "Dartmouth College Case," 1805 *

Section 41 of the Constitution declares that "schools shall be established by the Legislature for the convenient instruction of youth, with such salaries to the masters, paid by the public, as may enable them to instruct at low prices, and all useful learning shall be duly encouraged and promoted in one or more universities." In obedience to this injunction of the Constitution, the Legislature established an university, and in 1789 granted to the Trustees of the University "all the property that had heretofore or should hereafter escheat to the State." In 1800 the Legislature repealed this grant. This repealing act is void, it being in violation of section 10 of the Bill of Rights, which is a part of the Constitution. . . .

* *Trustees of the University of North Carolina* v. *Foy and Bishop*, in *North Carolina Reports of the Court of Conference*, Vol. 5, pp. 57 ff. See Edgar W. Knight, "North Carolina's 'Dartmouth College Case,' " *Journal of Higher Education*, XIX (March, 1948), pp. 116-22.

This was an action of ejectment brought to recover the posession of certain escheated lands in the district of Wilmington. The defendants pleaded in bar of the act of 1800, ch. 5, entitled "An act to repeal so much of the several laws now in force in this State as grants power to the Trustees of the University of North Carolina to seize and possess for the use of the said university any escheated or confiscated property." To this plea the plaintiff demurred, and the defendants have joined in demurrer, the case was sent to this Court for the opinion of the judges.

Haywood for plaintiff.

Duffey and *Jocelyn* for defendants.

Locke, J., delivered the opinion of the Court. The Legislature of North Carolina in 1789 granted to the Trustees of the University "all the property that has heretofore or shall hereafter escheat to the State." Ch. 21, sec. 2. And by another act, passed in 1794, they also granted "the confiscated property then unsold." Ch. 3, sec. 1. By an act passed in 1800 they declared, "that from and after the passing of this act, all acts and clauses of acts which have heretofore granted power to the Trustees of the University to seize and possess any escheated or confiscated property, real or personal, shall be and the same is hereby repealed and made void.

"*And be it further enacted,* That all escheated or confiscated property which the said trustees, their agents or attorneys, have not legally sold by virtue of the said laws shall from hence revert to the State, and henceforth be considered as the property of the same, as though such laws had never been passed." Chapter 5.

The Trustees of the University in pursuance of the powers vested in them by the act of 1789, have brought this suit to recover the possession of a tract of land escheated to the State before the passing of the repealing act in the year 1800. The defendants have pleaded this repealing act in bar, by which they allege the power of the trustees to support this action is entirely destroyed. It is therefore now to be considered how far the trustees have title under the act of 1789, and, in the next place, how far they are divested of that title by the repealing act of 1800. . . . The Constitution directed the General Assembly to establish this institution and endow it; then it would seem from the principle upon which all this doctrine is predicated, that the Constitution and not the Legislature had erected this corporation; the Legislature being only the agent or instrument, whose acts are valid and binding when they do not contravene any of the provisions of the Constitution. We view this corporation as standing on higher grounds than any other aggregate corporation; it is not only protected by the common law, but sanctioned by the Constitution. It cannot be considered that the Legislature would have complied with this constitutional requisition, by establishing a school for a month or any determinate number of years, and then abolishing the institution; because the people evidently intended this university to be as permanent as the Government itself. It would not be competent for the Legislature to declare that there should be no public school in the State, because such an act would directly oppose that important clause in the Constitution before mentioned. But if the Legislature can deprive the university of the appropriated and vested funds, they can do that which will produce the same consequences; for, deprive the institution of funds already vested and refuse to make any additional appropriations, and there never can exist in the State a public school or schools; and thus the Legislature may indirectly effect that purpose which, if expressed in the words before mentioned, they could not do. Besides, when the Legislature have established an university, appointed trustees and vested them with property which they were to hold in trust for the benefit of the institution, have they not discharged their duty as the agents of the people and transferred property, which is afterwards beyond their control? ... Although the trustees are a corporation established for public purposes, yet their property is as completely beyond the control of the Legislature as the property of individuals or that of any other corporation. Indeed, it seems difficult to conceive of a corporation established for merely private purposes. In every institution of that kind the ground of the establishment is some public good or purpose intended to be promoted; but in many the members thereof have a private interest, coupled with the public object. In this case, the trustees have no private interest beyond the general good; yet we conceive that circumstances will not make the property of the trustees subject to the arbitrary will of the Legislature. The property vested in the trustees must remain for the uses intended for the university, until the judiciary of the country in the usual and common form pronounce them guilty of such acts as will, in law, amount to a forfeiture of their rights or a dissolution of their body. The demurrer must therefore be allowed, and the plea in bar overruled.

The Legislature of North Carolina Reënacts the Law Providing for the Support of the University of that State by Escheats, 1805 *

Be it enacted by the General Assembly of the State of North Carolina, and it is hereby enacted by the authority of the same, That an act entitled "An act to repeal so much of the several laws now in force in this state as grants powers to the Trustees of the University of North Carolina to seize and possess for the use of the said university any escheated and confiscated property," so far as relates to the escheated property, be and the same is hereby repealed and made void.

* *Laws of North Carolina*, 1805, p. 2. The act restored the law of 1789, which had provided for the support of the University of North Carolina by escheats, following decision of the Court of Conference in North Carolina's "Dartmouth College Case," given above.

Thomas Jefferson Declines to Sell Lottery Tickets for the Benefit
of East Tennessee College and Gives Its Trustees
Some Counsel, 1810 *

To Messrs. Hugh L. White, Thomas M'Corry, James Campbell, Robert Craighead, John N. Gamble, Trustees for the lottery of East Tennessee College.

MONTICELLO, May 6, 1810.

GENTLEMEN,—I received, some time ago, your letter of February 28th, covering a printed scheme of a lottery for the benefit of the East Tennessee College, and proposing to send tickets to me to be disposed of. It would be impossible for them to come to a more inefficient hand. I rarely go from home, and consequently see but a few neighbors and friends, who occasionally call on me. And having myself made it a rule never to engage in a lottery or any other adventure of mere chance, I can, with the less candor or effect, urge it on others, however laudable or desirable its object may be. No one more sincerely wishes the spread of information among mankind than I do, and none has greater confidence in its effect towards supporting free and good government. I am sincerely rejoiced, therefore, to find that so excellent a fund has been provided for this noble purpose in Tennessee. Fifty thousand dollars placed in a safe bank, will give four thousand dollars a year, and even without other aid, must soon accomplish buildings sufficient for the object in its early stage. I consider the common plan followed in this country, but not in others, of making one large and expensive building, as unfortunately erroneous. It is infinitely better to erect a small and separate lodge for each separate professorship, with only a hall below for his class, and two chambers above for himself; joining these lodges by barracks for a certain portion of the students, opening into a covered way to give a dry communication between all the schools. The whole of these arranged around an open square of glass and trees, would make it, what it should be in fact, an academical village, instead of a large and common den of noise, of filth and of fetid air. It would afford that quiet retirement so friendly to study, and lessen the dangers of fire, infection and tumult. Every professor would be the police officer of the students adjacent to his own lodge, which would include those of his own class of preference,

---

* *The Writings of Thomas Jefferson*, Memorial Edition, XI, pp. 386-88. In Jefferson's "Thoughts on Lotteries," given in Thomas Jefferson Randolph's *Memoir, Correspondence, and Miscellanies, from the Papers of Thomas Jefferson*, IV, pp. 428-37, Jefferson gave reasons for asking the General Assembly of Virginia permission to sell his property by lottery. He lists more than sixty lotteries permitted by that body between 1784 and 1791 for the benefit of academies, the College of William and Mary, the Literary Fund of the state, a Lancasterian school, bridges, roads, navigation, counties, streets, religious groups, a paper mill, Masonic lodge, and for individuals to complete geographical and literary works. Here Jefferson also pointed out his public services of sixty-one years. See also his letter of January 20 to Joseph C. Cabell and of February 17, 1826, to James Madison on his personal need of the privilege of the lottery. This was granted by the General Assembly February 20, 1826, a few months before his death.

and might be at the head of their table, if, as I suppose, it can be reconciled with the necessary economy to dine them in smaller and separate parties, rather than in a large and common mess. These separate buildings, too, might be erected successively and occasionally, as the number of professorships and students should be increased, or the funds become competent.

I pray you to pardon me if I have stepped aside into the province of counsel; but much observation and reflection on these institutions have long convinced me that the large and crowded buildings in which youths are pent up, are equally unfriendly to health, to study, to manners, morals and order; and, believing the plan I suggest to be more promotive of these, and peculiarly adapted to the slender beginnings and progressive growth of our institutions, I hoped you would pardon the presumption, in consideration of the motive which was suggested by the difficulty expressed in your letter, of procuring funds for erecting the building. But, on whatever plan you proceed, I wish it every possible success, and to yourselves the reward of esteem, respect and gratitude due to those who devote their time and efforts to render the youths of every successive age fit governors for the next. To these accept, in addition, the assurance of mine.

Jefferson's Reply to Governor Plumer on the Dartmouth College Case, 1816 *

MONTICELLO, July 21, 1816.

I thank you, Sir, for the copy you have been so good as to send me, of your late speech to the legislature of your State, which I have read a second time with great pleasure, as I had before done in the public papers. It is replete with sound principles, and truly republican. Some articles, too, are worthy of peculiar notice. The idea that institutions established for the use of the nation cannot be touched nor modified, even to make them answer their end, because of rights gratuitously supposed in those employed to manage them in trust for the public, may perhaps be a salutary provision against the abuses of a monarch, but is most absurd against the nation itself. Yet our lawyers and priests generally inculcate this doctrine, and suppose that preceding generations held the earth more freely than we do; had a right to impose laws on us, unalterable by ourselves, and that we, in like manner, can make laws and impose burdens on future generations, which they will have no right to alter; in fine, that the earth belongs to the dead and not the living. I remark also the phenomenon of a chief magistrate recommending the reduction of his own compensation. This is a solecism of which the wisdom of our late Congress cannot be accused. I, however, place economy among the first and most important of republican virtues, and public debt as the greatest of the dangers to be feared. We see in England the consequences of the want of it, their laborers reduced to live

* A. E. Bergh (Ed.), *The Writings of Thomas Jefferson*, XV, pp. 46-47.

on a penny in the shilling of their earnings, to give up bread, and resort to oatmeal and potatoes for food; and their landholders exiling themselves to live in penury and obscurity abroad, because at home the government must have all the clear profits of their land. In fact, they see the fee simple of the island transferred to the public creditors, all its profits going to them for the interest of their debts. Our laborers and landholders must come to this also, unless they severely adhere to the economy you recommend. I salute you with entire esteem and respect.

The Catholepistemiad or University of Michigania Is Established, 1817 *

Be it enacted by the Governor and the Judges of the Territory of Michigan that there shall be in the said Territory a *catholepistemiad,* or university, denominated the *catholepistemiad,* or university, of Michigania. The *catholepistemiad,* or university, of Michigania shall be composed of thirteen *didaxiim* or professorships: first, a *didaxia,* or professorship, of *catholepistemia,* or universal science, the *didactor,* or professor, of which shall be president of the institution; second, a *didaxia,* or professorship, of *anthropoglossica,* or literature, embracing all the *epistemiim,* or sciences, relative to language; third, a *didaxia,* or professorship, of *mathematica,* or mathematics; fourth, a *didaxia,* or professorship, of *physiognostica,* or natural history; fifth, a *didaxia,* or professorship, of *physiosophica,* or natural philosophy; sixth, a *didaxia,* or professorship, of *astronomia,* or astronomy; seventh, a *didaxia,* or professorship, of *chymia,* or *iatrica,* or medical sciences; ninth, a *didaxia,* or professorship, of chemistry; eighth, a *didaxia,* or professorship, of *aeconomica,* or economical sciences; tenth, a *didaxia,* or professorship, of *ethica,* or ethical sciences; eleventh, a *didaxia,* or professorship of *polemitactica,* or military sciences; twelfth, a *didaxia,* or professorship, of *diagetica,* or historical sciences; and, thirteenth, a *didaxia* or professorship of *ennaeica,* or intellectual sciences, embracing all the *epistemiim,* or sciences, relative to the minds of animals, to the human mind, to spiritual existences, to the deity, and to religion, the *didactor,* or professor, of which shall be vice-president of the institution. The *didactors,* or professors, shall be appointed and commissioned by the Governor. There shall be paid, from the treasury of Michigan, in quarterly payments, to the president of the institution, to the vice-president, and to each *didactor,* or professor, an annual salary, to be, from time to time,

* *Laws of the Territory of Michigan,* II, pp. 105-06. Given in *Records of the University of Michigan,* 1817-1837 (Ann Arbor, Published by the University, 1935), pp. 3-5. This odd educational organization seems to show a bit of resemblance to the Regents of the University of New York, the University of France, and the grandiose Senatus Academicus of the University of Georgia, created in 1785 to have control of education in that State. See Andrew Ten-Brook, *American State Universities and the University of Michigan* (Cincinnati, 1875); and E. E. Brown, *The Origin of the American State Universities* (University of California Press, 1903).

ascertained by law. More than one *didaxia,* or professorship, may be conferred upon the same person. The president and *didactors,* or professors, or a majority of them, assembled, shall have power to regulate all the concerns of the institution, to enact laws for that purpose, to sue, to be sued, to acquire, to hold and to aliene, property, real, mixed, and personal, to make, to use, and to alter, a seal, to establish colleges, academies, schools, libraries, musaeums, athenaeums, botanic gardens, laboratories, and other useful literary and scientific institutions, consonant to the laws of the United States of America and of Michigan, and to appoint officers, instructors and instructrixes, in, among, and throughout, the various counties, cities, towns, townships, and other geographical divisions, of Michigan. Their name and stile as a corporation shall be "The *catholepiste-miad,* or university, of Michigania." To every subordinate instructor, and instructrix, appointed by the *catholepistemiad,* or university, there shall be paid, from the treasury of Michigan, in quarterly payments, an annual salary, to be, from time to time, ascertained by law. The existing public taxes are hereby increased fifteen per cent; and, from the proceeds of the present, and of all future public taxes, fifteen percent are appropriated for the benefit of the *catholepistemiad,* or university. The treasurer of Michigan shall keep a separate account of the university fund. The *catholepiste-miad,* or university, may propose and draw four successive lotteries, deducting from the prizes in the same fifteen per cent for the benefit of the institution. The proceeds of the preceding sources of revenue, and of all subsequent, shall be applied, in the first instance, to the acquisition of suitable lands and buildings, and books, libraries, and apparatus, and afterwards to such purposes as shall be, from time to time, by law directed. The *honorarium* for a course of lectures shall not exceed fifteen dollars, for classical instruction ten dollars a quarter, and for ordinary instruction six dollars a quarter. If the judges of the court of any county, or a majority of them, shall certify that the parent, or guardian, of any person has not adequate means to defray the expense of the suitable instruction, and that the same ought to be a public charge, the *honorarium* shall be paid from the Treasury of Michigan. An annual report of the state, concerns, and transactions, of the institution shall be laid before the legislative power for the time being. This law, or any part of it, may be repealed by the legislative power for the time being.

Made, adopted, and published, from the laws of seven of the original states, to wit the states of Connecticut, Massachusetts, New-Jersey, New-York, Ohio, Pennsylvania, and Virginia, as far as necessary and suitable to the circumstances of Michigan; at the City of Detroit, on Tuesday the twenty sixth day of August, in the year one thousand eight hundred seventeen.

Report of the Rockfish Gap Commission (Thomas Jefferson, Chairman)
to Locate the Site of the University of Virginia, 1818 *

The Commissioners for the University of Virginia, having met, as by law required, at the tavern, in Rockfish Gap, on the Blue Ridge, on the first day of August, of this present year, 1818; and having formed a board, proceeded on that day to the discharge of the duties assigned to them by the act of the Legislature, entitled "An act, appropriating part of the revenue of the literary fund, and for other purposes"; and having continued their proceedings by adjournment, from day to day, to Tuesday, the 4th day of August, have agreed to a report on the several matters with which they were charged, which report they now respectfully address and submit to the Legislature of the State.

The first duty enjoined on them, was to enquire and report a site, in some convenient and proper part of the State, for an university, to be called the "University of Virginia." In this enquiry, they supposed that the governing considerations should be the healthiness of the site, the fertility of the neighboring country, and its centrality to the white population of the whole State. For, although the act authorized and required them to receive any voluntary contributions, whether conditional or absolute, which might be offered through them to the President and Directors of the Literary Fund, for the benefit of the University, yet they did not consider this as establishing an auction, or as pledging the location to the highest bidder.

Three places were proposed, to wit: Lexington, in the county of Rockbridge, Staunton, in the county of Augusta, and the Central College, in the county of Albemarle. Each of these was unexceptionable as to healthiness and fertility. It was the degree of centrality to the white population of the State which alone then constituted the important point of comparison between these places; and the Board, after full enquiry, and impartial and mature consideration, are of opinion, that the central point of the white population of the State is nearer to the Central College than to either Lexington or Staunton, by great and important differences; and all other circumstances of the place in general being favorable to it, as a position for an university, they do report the Central College, in Albermarle, to be a convenient and proper part of the State for the University of Virginia.

2. The Board having thus agreed on a proper site for the University, to be reported to the Legislature, proceed to the second of the duties assigned to them—that of proposing a plan for its buildings—and they are of opinion that it should consist of distinct houses or pavilions, arranged at proper distances on each side of a lawn of a proper breadth, and of

* *Early History of the University of Virginia as Contained in the Letters of Thomas Jefferson and Joseph C. Cabell* (Richmond, J. W. Randolph, 1856), pp. 432-47. The original of this document in Jefferson's handwriting is the property of the Virginia State Library. Photocopy is in the Southern Historical Collection, the University of North Carolina.

indefinite extent, in one direction, at least; in each of which should be a lecturing room, with from two to four appartments, for the accommodation of a professor and his family; that these pavilions should be united by a range of dormitories, sufficient each for the accommodation of two students only, this provision being deemed advantageous to morals, to order, and to uninterrupted study; and that a passage of some kind, under cover from the weather, should give a communication along the whole range. It is supposed that such pavilions, on an average of the larger and smaller, will cost each about $5,000; each dormitory about $350, and hotels of a single room, for a refectory, and two rooms for the tenant, necessary for dieting the students, will cost about $3500 each. The number of these pavilions will depend on the number of professors, and that of the dormitories and hotels on the number of students to be lodged and dieted. The advantages of this plan are: greater security against fire and infection; tranquillity and comfort to the professors and their families thus insulated; retirement to the students; and the admission of enlargement to any degree to which the institution may extend in future times. It is supposed probable, that a building of somewhat more size in the middle of the grounds may be called for in time, in which may be rooms for religious worship, under such impartial regulations as the Visitors shall prescribe, for public examinations, for a library, for the schools of music, drawing, and other associated purposes.

3, 4. In proceeding to the third and fourth duties prescribed by the Legislature, of reporting "the branches of learning, which should be taught in the University, and the number and description of the professorships they will require," the Commissioners were first to consider at what point it was understood that university education should commerce? Certainly not with the alphabet, for reasons of expediency and impracticability, as well from the obvious sense of the Legislature, who, in the same act, make other provision for the primary instruction of the poor children, expecting, doubtless, that in other cases it would be provided by the parent, or become, perhaps, subject of future and further attention of the Legislature. The objects of this primary education determine its character and limits. These objects would be,

To give to every citizen the information he needs for the transaction of his own business;

To enable him to calculate for himself, and to express and preserve his ideas, his contracts and accounts, in writing;

To improve, by reading, his morals and faculties;

To understand his duties to his neighbors and country, and to discharge with competence the functions confided to him by either;

To know his rights; to exercise with order and justice those he retains; to choose with discretion the fiduciary of those he delegates; and to notice their conduct with diligence, with candor, and judgment;

And, in general, to observe with intelligence and faithfulness all the social relations under which he shall be placed.

To instruct the mass of our citizens in these, their rights, interests and duties, as men and citizens, being then the objects of education in the primary schools, whether private or public, in them should be taught reading, writing and numerical arithmetic, the elements of mensuration, (useful in so many callings,) and the outlines of geography and history. And this brings us to the point at which are to commence the higher branches of education, of which the Legislature require the development; those, for example, which are,

To form the statesmen, legislators and judges, on whom public prosperity and individual happiness are so much to depend;

To expound the principles and structure of government, the laws which regulate the intercourse of nations, those formed municipally for our own government, and a sound spirit of legislation, which, banishing all arbitrary and unnecessary restraint on individual action, shall leave us free to do whatever does not violate the equal rights of another;

To harmonize and promote the interests of agriculture, manufactures and commerce, and by well informed views of political economy to give a free scope to the public industry;

To develop the reasoning faculties of our youth, enlarge their minds, cultivate their morals, and instill into them the precepts of virtue and order;

To enlighten them with mathematical and physical sciences, which advance the arts, and administer to the health, the subsistence, and comforts of human life;

And, generally, to form them to habits of reflection and correct action, rendering them examples of virtue to others, and of happiness within themselves.

These are the objects of that higher grade of education, the benefits and blessings of which the Legislature now propose to provide for the good and ornament of their country, the gratification and happiness of their fellow-citizens, of the parent especially, and his progeny, on which all his affections are concentrated.

In entering on this field, the Commissioners are aware that they have to encounter much difference of opinion as to the extent which it is expedient that this institution should occupy. Some good men, and even of respectable information, consider the learned sciences as useless acquirements; some think that they do not better the condition of man; and others that education, like private and individual concerns, should be left to private individual effort; not reflecting that an establishment embracing all the sciences which may be useful and even necessary in the various vocations of life, with the buildings and apparatus belonging to each, are far beyond the reach of individual means, and must either derive existence from public patronage, or not exist at all. This would leave us, then, without those callings which depend on education, or send us to other countries to seek the instruction they require. But the Commissioners are happy in considering the statute under which they are assembled as proof that the Legislature is far from the abandonment of objects so interesting. They are sensible that the advantages of well-directed education, moral, political and economical, are truly above all estimate. Education generates habits of application, of order, and the love of virtue; and controls, by the force of habit, any innate obliquities in our moral organization. We should be far, too, from the discouraging persuasion that man is fixed, by the law of his nature, at a given point; that his improvement is a chimera, and the hope delusive of rendering ourselves wiser, happier or better than our forefathers were. As well might it be urged that the wild and uncultivated tree, hitherto yielding sour and bitter fruit only, can never be made to yield better; yet we know that the grafting art implants a new tree on the savage stock, producing what is most estimable both in kind and degree. Education, in like manner, engrafts a new man on the native stock, and improves what in his nature was vicious and perverse into qualities of virtue and social worth. And it cannot be but that each generation succeeding to the knowledge acquired by all those who preceded it, adding to it their own acquisitions and discoveries, and handing the mass down for successive and constant accumulation, must advance the knowledge and well-being of mankind, not *infinitely,* as some have said, but *indefinitely,* and to a term which no one can fix and foresee. Indeed, we need look back half a century, to times which many now living remember well, and see the wonderful advances in the sciences and arts which have been made within that period. Some of these have rendered the elements themselves subservient to the purposes of man, have harnessed them to the yoke of his labors, and effected the great blessings of moderating his own, of accomplishing what was beyond his feeble force, and extending the comforts of life to a much enlarged circle, to those who had before known its necessaries only. That these are not the vain dreams of sanguine hope, we have before our eyes real and living examples. What, but education, has advanced us beyond the condition of our indigenous neighbors? And what chains them to their present state of barbarism and wretchedness, but a bigotted veneration for the supposed superlative wisdom of their fathers, and the preposterous idea that they are to look backward for better things, and not forward, longing, as it should seem, to return to the days of eating acorns and roots, rather than indulge in the degeneracies of civilization? And how much more encouraging to the achievements of science and improvement is this, than the desponding view that the condition of man cannot be ameliorated, that what has been must ever be, and that to secure ourselves where we are, we must tread with awful reverence in the footsteps of our fathers. This doctrine is the genuine fruit of the alliance between Church and State; the tenants of which, finding themselves but too well in their present condition, oppose all advances which might unmask their usurpations, and monopolies of honors, wealth, and power, and fear every change, as endangering the comforts they now hold. Nor must we omit to mention, among the benefits of education, the incalculable advantage of training up able counsellors to administer the affairs of our country in all its departments, legislative, executive and judiciary, and to bear their proper share in the councils of our national government; nothing more than education advancing the prosperity, the power, and the happiness of a nation.

Encouraged, therefore, by the sentiments of the Legislature, manifested in this statute, we present the following tabular statement of the branches of learning which we think should be taught in the University, forming them into groups, each of which are within the powers of a single professor:

I. Languages, ancient:
 Latin,
 Greek,
 Hebrew.

II. Languages, modern:
 French,
 Spanish,
 Italian,
 German,
 Anglo-Saxon.

III. Mathematics, pure:
 Algebra,
 Fluxions,
 Geometry, Elementary,
  Transcendental.
 Architecture, Military,
  Naval.

IV. Physico-Mathematics:
 Mechanics,
 Statics,
 Dynamics,
 Pneumatics,
 Acoustics,
 Optics,
 Astronomy,
 Geography.

V. Physics, or Natural Philosophy:
 Chemistry,
 Mineralogy.

VI. Botany,
 Zoology.

VII. Anatomy,
 Medicine.

VIII. Government,
 Political Economy,
 Law of Nature and Nations,
 History, being interwoven with
  Politics and Law.

IX. Law, municipal.

X. Ideology,
 General Grammar,
 Ethics,
 Rhetoric,
 Belles Lettres, and the fine arts.

Some of the terms used in this table being subject to a difference of acceptation, it is proper to define the meaning and comprehension intended to be given them here:

Geometry, Elementary, is that of straight lines and of the circle.

Transcendental, is that of all other curves; it includes, of course, *Projectiles,* a leading branch of the military art.

Military Architecture includes Fortification, another branch of that art.

Statics respect matter generally, in a state of rest, and include Hydrostatics, or the laws of fluids particularly, at rest or in equilibrio.

Dynamics, used as a general term, include Dynamics proper, or the laws of *solids* in motion; and Hydrodynamics, or Hydraulics, those of *fluids* in motion.

Pneumatics teach the theory of air, its weight, motion, condensation, rarefaction, &c.

Acoustics, or Phonics, the theory of sound.

Optics, the laws of light and vision.

Physics, or Physiology, in a general sense, mean the doctrine of the physical objects of our senses.

Chemistry is meant, with its other usual branches, to comprehend the the theory of agriculture.

Mineralogy, in addition to its peculiar subjects, is here understood to embrace what is real in geology.

Ideology is the doctrine of thought.

General Grammar explains the construction of language.

Some articles in this distribution of sciences will need observation. A professor is proposed for ancient languages, the Latin, Greek, and Hebrew, particularly; but these languages being the foundation common to all the sciences, it is difficult to foresee what may be the extent of this school. At the same time, no greater obstruction to industrious study could be proposed than the presence, the intrusions and the noisy turbulence of a multitude of small boys; and if they are to be placed here for the rudiments of the languages, they may be so numerous that its character and value as an University will be merged in those of a Grammar school. It is, therefore, greatly to be wished, that preliminary schools, either on private or public establishment, could be distributed in districts through the State, as preparatory to the entrance of students into the University. The tender age at which this part of education commences, generally about the tenth year, would weigh heavily with parents in sending their sons to a school so distant as the central establishment would be from most of them. Districts of such extent as that every parent should be within a day's journey of his son at school, would be desirable in cases of sickness, and convenient for supplying their ordinary wants, and might be made to lessen sensibly the expense of this part of their education. And where a sparse population would not, within such a compass, furnish subjects sufficient to maintain a school, a competent enlargement of district must, of necessity, there be submitted to. At these district schools or colleges, boys should be rendered able to read the easier authors, Latin and Greek.

This would be useful and sufficient for many not intended for an University education. At these, too, might be taught English grammar, the higher branches of numerical arithmetic, the geometry of straight lines and of the circle, the elements of navigation, and geography to a sufficient degree, and thus afford to greater numbers the means of being qualified for the various vocations of life, needing more instruction than merely menial or praedial labor, and the same advantages to youths whose education may have been neglected until too late to lay a foundation in the learned languages. These institutions, intermediate between the primary schools and University, might then be the passage of entrance for youths into the University, where their classical learning might be critically completed, by a study of the authors of highest degree; and it is at this stage only that they should be received at the University. Giving then a portion of their time to a finished knowledge of the Latin and Greek, the rest might be appropriated to the modern languages, or to the commencement of the course of science for which they should be destined. This would generally be about the fifteenth year of their age, when they might go with more safety and contentment to that distance from their parents. Until this preparatory provision shall be made, either the University will be overwhelmed with the grammar school, or a separate establishment, under one or more ushers, for its lower classes, will be advisable, at a mile or two distant from the general one; where, too, may be exercised the stricter government necessary for young boys, but unsuitable for youths arrived at years of discretion.

The considerations which have governed the specification of languages to be taught by the professor of modern languages were, that the French is the language of general intercourse among nations, and as a depository of human science, is unsurpassed by any other language, living or dead; that the Spanish is highly interesting to us, as the language spoken by so great a portion of the inhabitants of our continents, with whom we shall probably have great intercourse ere long, and is that also in which is written the greater part of the earlier history of America. The Italian abounds with works of very superior order, valuable for their matter, and still more distinguished as models of the finest taste in style and composition. And the German now stands in a line with that of the most learned nations in richness of erudition and advance in the sciences. It is too of common descent with the language of our own country, a branch of the same original Gothic stock, and furnishes valuable illustrations for us. But in this point of view, the Anglo-Saxon is of peculiar value. We have placed it among the modern languages, because it is in fact that which we speak, in the earliest form in which we have knowledge of it. It has been undergoing, with time, those gradual changes which all languages, ancient and modern, have experienced; and even now needs only to be printed in the modern character and orthography to be intelligible, in a considerable degree, to an English reader. It has this value, too, above the Greek and Latin, that while it gives the radix of the mass of our language, they explain its innovations only. Obvious proofs of this have been presented to the modern reader in the disquisitions of Horn Tooke; and Fortescue Aland has well explained the great instruction which may be derived from it to a full understanding of our ancient common law, on which, as a stock, our whole system of law is engrafted. It will form the first link in the chain of an historical review of our language through all its successive changes to the present day, will constitute the foundation of that critical instruction in it which ought to be found in a seminary of general learning, and thus reward amply the few weeks of attention which would alone be requisite for its attainment; a language already fraught with all the eminent science of our parent country, the future vehicle of whatever we may ourselves achieve, and destined to occupy so much space on the globe, claims distinguished attention in American education.

Medicine, where fully taught, is usually subdivided into several professorships, but this cannot well be without the accessory of an hospital, where the student can have the benefit of attending clinical lectures, and of assisting at operations of surgery. With this accessory, the seat of our University is not yet prepared, either by its population or by the numbers of poor who would leave their own houses, and accept of the charities of an hospital. For the present, therefore, we propose but a single professor for both medicine and anatomy. By him the medical science may be taught, with a history and explanations of all successive theories from Hippocrates to the present day; and anatomy may be fully treated. Vegetable pharmacy will make a part of the botanical course, and mineral and chemical pharmacy of those of mineralogy and chemistry. This degree of medical information is such as the mass of scientific students would wish to possess, as enabling them in their course through life, to estimate with satisfaction the extent and limits of the aid to human life and health, which they may understandingly expect from that art; and it constitutes such a foundation for those intended for the professions, that the finishing course of practice at the bed-sides of the sick, and at the operations of surgery in a hospital, can neither be long nor expensive. To seek this finishing elsewhere, must therefore be submitted to for a while.

In conformity with the principles of our Constitution, which places all sects of religion on an equal footing, with the jealousies of the different sects in guarding that equality from encroachment and surprise, and with the sentiments of the Legislature in favor of freedom or religion, manifested on former occasions, we have proposed no professor of divinity; and the rather as the proofs of the being of a God, the creator, preserver, and supreme ruler of the universe, the author of all the relations of morality, and of the laws and obligations these infer, will be within the province of the professor of ethics; to which adding the developments of these moral obligations, of those in which all sects agree, with a knowledge of the languages, Hebrew, Greek, and Latin, a basis will be formed common to all sects. Proceeding thus far without offence to the Constitution, we have thought it proper at this point to leave every sect to provide, as they think fittest, the means of further instruction in their own peculiar tenets.

We are further of opinion, that after declaring by law that certain sciences shall be taught in the University, fixing the number of professors they require, which we think should, at present, be ten, limiting (except as to the professors who shall be first engaged in each branch,) a maximum for their salaries, (Which should be a certain but moderate subsistence, to be made up by liberal tuition fees, as an excitement to assiduity,) it will be best to leave to the discretion of the visitors, the grouping of these sciences together, according to the accidental qualifications of the professors; and the introduction also of other branches of science, when enabled by private donations, or by public provision, and called for by the increase of population, or other change of circumstances; to establish beginnings, in short, to be developed by time, as those who come after us shall find expedient. They will be more advanced than we are in science and in useful arts, and will know best what will suit the circumstances of their day.

We have proposed no formal provision for the gymnastics of the school, although a proper object of attention for every institution of youth. These exercises with ancient nations, constituted the principal part of the education of their youth. Their arms and mode of warfare rendered them severe in the extreme; ours, on the same correct principle, should be adapted to our arms and warfare; and the manual exercise, military manoeuvres, and tactics generally, should be the frequent exercises of the students, in their hours of recreation. It is at that age of aptness, docility, and emulation of the practices of manhood, that such things are soonest learnt and longest remembered. The use of tools too in the manual arts is worthy of encouragement, by facilitating to such as choose it, an admission into the neighboring workshops. To these should be added the arts which embellish life, dancing, music, and drawing; the last more especially, as an important part of military education. These innocent arts furnish amusement and happiness to those who, having time on their hands, might less inoffensively employ it. Needing, at the same time, no regular incorporation with the institution, they may be left to accessory teachers, who will be paid by the individuals employing them, the University only providing proper apartments for their exercise.

The fifth duty prescribed to the Commissioners, is to propose such general provisions as may be properly enacted by the Legislature, for the better organizing and governing the University.

In the education of youth, provision is to be made for, 1, tuition; 2, diet;

3, lodging; 4, government; and 5, honorary excitements. The first of these constitutes the proper functions of the professors; 2, the dieting of the students should be left to private boarding houses of their own choice, and at their own expense; to be regulated by the Visitors from time to time, the house only being provided by the University within its own precincts, and thereby of course subjected to the general regimen, moral or sumptuary, which they shall prescribe. 3. They should be lodged in dormitories, making a part of the general system of buildings. 4. The best mode of government for youth, in large collections, is certainly a desideratum not yet attained with us. It may be well questioned whether *fear* after a certain age, is a motive to which we should have ordinary recourse. The human character is susceptible of other incitements to correct conduct, more worthy of employ, and of better effect. Pride of character, laudable ambition, and moral dispositions are innate correctives of the indiscretions of that lively age; and when strengthened by habitual appeal and exercise, have a happier effect on future character than the degrading motive of fear. Hardening them to disgrace, to corporal punishments, and servile humiliations cannot be the best process for producing erect character. The affectionate deportment between father and son, offers in truth the best example for that of tutor and pupil; and the experience and practice of other [1] countries, in this respect, may be worthy of enquiry and consideration with us. It will then be for the wisdom and discretion of the Visitors to devise and perfect a proper system of government, which, if it be founded in reason and comity, will be more likely to nourish in the minds of our youth the combined spirit of order and self-respect, so congenial with our political institutions, and so important to be woven into the American character. 5. What qualifications shall be required to entitle to entrance into the University, the arrangement of the days and hours of lecturing for the different schools, so as to facilitate to the students the circle of attendance on them; the establishment of periodical and public examinations, the premiums to be given for distinguished merit; whether honorary degrees shall be conferred, and by what appellations; whether the title to these shall depend on the time the candidate has been at the University, or, where nature has given a greater share of understanding, attention, and application; whether he shall not be allowed the advantages resulting from these endowments, with other minor items of government, we are of opinion should be entrusted to the Visitors; and the statute under which we act having provided for the appointment of these, we think they should moreover be charged with

The erection, preservation, and repair of the buildings, the care of the

---

[1] A police exercised by the students themselves, under proper discretion, has been tried with success in some countries, and the rather as forming them for initiation into the duties and practices of civil life.

grounds and appurtenances, and of the interest of the University generally.

That they should have power to appoint a bursar, employ a proctor, and all other necessary agents.

To appoint and remove professors, two-thirds of the whole number of Visitors voting for the removal.

To prescribe their duties and the course of education, in conformity with the law.

To establish rules for the government and discipline of the students, not contrary to the laws of the land.

To regulate the tuition fees, and the rent of the dormitories they occupy.

To prescribe and control the duties and proceedings of all officers, servants, and others, with respect to the buildings, lands, appurtenances, and other property and interests of the University.

To draw from the literary fund such moneys as are by law charged on it for this institution; and in general.

To direct and do all matters and things which, not being inconsistent with the laws of the land, to them shall seem most expedient for promoting the purposes of the said institution; which several functions they should be free to exercise in the form of by-laws, rules, resolutions, orders, instructions, or otherwise, as they should deem proper.

That they should have two stated meetings in the year, and occasional meetings at such times as they should appoint, or on a special call with such notice as themselves shall prescribe by a general rule; which meetings should be at the University, a majority of them constituting a quorum for business; and that on the death or resignation of a member, or on his removal by the President and Directors of the Literary Fund, or the Executive, or such other authority as the Legislature shall think best, such President and Directors, or the Executive, or other authority, shall appoint a successor.

That the said Visitors should appoint one of their own body to be Rector, and with him be a body corporate, under the style and title of the Rector and Visitors of the University of Virginia, with the right, as such, to use a common seal; that they should have capacity to plead and be impleaded in all courts of justice, and in all cases interesting to the University, which may be the subjects of legal cognizance and jurisdiction; which pleas should not abate by the determination of their office, but should stand revived in the name of their successors, and they should be capable in law and in trust for the University, of receiving subscriptions and donations, real and personal, as well from bodies corporate, or persons associated, as from private individuals.

And that the said Rector and Visitors should, at all times, conform to such laws as the Legislature may, from time to time, think proper to enact for their government; and the said University should, in all things, and at all times, be subject to the control of the Legislature.

And lastly, the Commissioners report to the Legislature the following conditional offers to the President and Directors of the Literary Fund, for the benefit of the University:

On the condition that Lexington, or its vicinity, shall be selected as the site of the University, and that the same be permanently established there within two years from the date, John Robinson, of Rockbridge county, has executed a deed to the President and Directors of the Literary Fund, to take effect at his death, for the following tracts of land, to wit:

400 acres on the North fork of James river, known by the name of Hart's bottom, purchased of the late Gen. Bowyer.

171 acres adjoining the same, purchased of James Griggsby.

203 acres joining the last mentioned tract, purchased of William Paxton.

112 acres lying on the North river, about the lands of Arthur Glasgow, conveyed to him by William Paxton's heirs.

500 acres adjoining the lands of Arthur Glasgow, Benjamin Camden and David Edmonson.

545 acres lying in Pryor's gap, conveyed to him by the heirs of William Paxton, deceased.

260 acres lying in Childer's gap, purchased of Wm. Mitchell.

300 acres lying, also, in Childer's gap, purchased of Nicholas Jones.

500 acres lying on Buffalo, joining the lands of Jas. Johnston.

340 acres on the Cowpasture river, conveyed to him by General James Breckenridge—reserving the right of selling the two last mentioned tracts, and converting them into other lands contiguous to Hart's bottom, for the benefit of the University; also, the whole of his slaves, amounting to 57 in number; one lot of 22 acres, joining the town of Lexington, to pass immediately on the establishment of the University, together with all the personal estate of every kind, subject only to the payment of his debts and fulfillment of his contracts.

It has not escaped the attention of the Commissioners, that the deed referred to is insufficient to pass the estate in the lands intended to be conveyed, and may be otherwise defective; but, if necessary, this defect may be remedied before the meeting of the Legislature, which the Commissioners are advised will be done.

The Board of Trustees of Washington College have also proposed to transfer the whole of their funds, viz: 100 shares in the funds of the James River Company, 31 acres of land upon which their buildings stand, their philosophical apparatus, their expected interest in the funds of the Cincinnati Society, the libraries of the Graham and Washington Societies, and $3,000 in cash, on condition that a reasonable provision be made for the present professors. A subscription has also been offered by the people of Lexington and its vicinity, amounting to $17,878, all which will appear from the deed and other documents, reference thereto being had.

In this case, also, it has not escaped the attention of the Commissioners, that questions may arise as to the power of the trustees to make the above transfers.

On the condition that the Central College shall be made the site of the University, its whole property, real and personal, in possession or in action, is offered. This consists of a parcel of land of 47 acres, whereon the buildings of the college are begun, one pavilion and its appendix of dormitories being already far advanced, and with one other pavilion, and equal annexation of dormitories, being expected to be completed during the present season—of another parcel of 153 acres, near the former, and including a considerable eminence very favorable for the erection of a future observatory; of the proceeds of the sales of two glebes, amounting to $3,280 86 cents; and of a subscription of $41,248, on papers in hand, besides what is on outstanding papers of unknown amount, not yet returned —out of these sums are to be taken, however, the cost of the lands, of the buildings, and other works done, and for existing contracts. For the conditional transfer of these to the President and Directors of the Literary Fund, a regular power, signed by the subscribers and founders of the Central College generally, has been given to its Visitors and Proctor, and a deed conveying the said property accordingly to the President and Directors of the Literary Fund, has been duly executed by the said Proctor, and acknowledged for record in the office of the clerk of the county court of Albemarle.

Signed and certified by the members present, each in his proper handwriting, this 4th day of August, 1818.

TH: JEFFERSON,	HENRY E. WATKINS,
CREED TAYLOR,	JAMES MADISON,
PETER RANDOLPH,	A. T. MASON,
WM. BROCKENBROUGH,	HUGH HOLMES,
PHIL C. PENDLETON,	PHIL. SLAUGHTER,
SPENCER ROANE,	WM. H. CABELL,
JOHN M. C. TAYLOR,	NAT. H. CLAIBORNE,
J. G. JACKSON,	WM. A. C. DADE,
ARCH'D RUTHERFORD,	WILLIAM JONES,
ARCH'D STUART,	THOMAS WILSON.
JAMES BRECKENRIDGE,	

Daniel Webster Cites the North Carolina Case of 1805 to Support His Argument in the Dartmouth College Case

In *University* v. *Foy* the Supreme Court of North Carolina pronounced unconstitutional and void a law repealing a grant to the University of North Carolina: although that University was originally erected and endowed by a Statute of the State. The case was a grant of lands, and the court decided that it could not be resumed. This is a grant of the power and capacity to hold lands. Where is the difference of the cases, upon principles? *

When the court in North Carolina declared the law of the state, which repealed a grant to its university, unconstitutional and void, the legislature had the candor and the wisdom to repeal the law. This example, so honorable to the state which exhibited it, is most fit to be followed on this occasion. And there is good reason to hope that a state which has hitherto been so much distinguished for temperate councils, cautious legislation, and regard to law, will not fail to adopt a course which will accord with her highest and best interest, and, in no small degree, elevate her reputation. It was for many obvious reasons most anxiously desired that the question of the power of the legislature over this charter should have been finally decided in the state court. An earnest hope was entertained that the judges of that court might have viewed the case in a light favorable to the rights of trustees. That hope has failed. It is here that those rights are now to be maintained, or they are prostrated forever.†

The Trustees of Dartmouth College v. Woodward, 1819 ‡

The charter granted by the British Crown to the trustees of Dartmouth College, in New Hampshire, in the year 1769, is a contract within the

---

* 4 Wheaton U.S. 57.

† Stephen K. Williams, *Cases Argued and Decided in the Supreme Court of the United States, 1815-19,* Book 4, Lawyers' Edition, p. 598.

‡ 4 Wheaton U. S., 463 ff. See also Walter F. Dodd, *Cases and Other Authorities on Constitutional Law* (St. Paul, Minn., West Publishing Co., 1937), pp. 1306-16. Efforts to transform "private" colleges into institutions that would be under direct or indirect "public" control came to a head in this case. With the legal verbiage and technicalities removed, the issue here settled was that a charter was an inviolable contract within the meaning of the Constitution of the United States and decision in the case gave negative answer to the question whether, under the Constitution, a state legislature had "the power to modify or abrogate a charter legally granted in all good faith."

Meantime, efforts had been made to improve relations between Yale College and the state of Connecticut which resulted in lengthy and bitter contests when opponents of the institution proposed legislative establishment of a rival institution or a change in Yale's charter. A movement to much the same end began in the legislature of New York where King's College (later Columbia) had fallen into disfavor during the Revolution. There were anxieties over attempted legislative interference with Harvard and animus about the College in Philadelphia which had been established through efforts of Benjamin Franklin and his associates. See Albert Frank Gegenheimer, *William Smith: Educator and Churchman* (Philadelphia, University of Pennsylvania Press, 1943). Another case was that of Liberty Hall Academy in Virginia. When the legislature of that state in 1796 displaced the charter and the trustees of that academy, the Scotch-Irish Presbyterians rose up in righteous wrath, resisted the efforts of the Legislature, and struck back so mightily that that body retreated as gracefully as it could and in 1798 repealed its previous action on Liberty Hall, with the provision: "That the said academy shall hereafter be called and known as the name of Washington."

In 1796 President George Washington gave to Liberty Hall Academy one hundred shares of stock in the James River Company which had been presented to him by the General Assembly of Virginia in recognition of his services during the Revolution. Washington was reluctant to accept the gift for himself personally but agreed to do so if he could use the shares for some good cause. He presented them to Liberty Hall Academy the name of which, as already noted, was changed to Washington Academy. This grew into Washington and Lee meaning of the clause of the Constitution of the United States, which declares that no State shall make any law impairing the obligations of contract. The charter was not dissolved by the Revolution.

An act of the State legislature of New Hampshire, altering the charter, without the consent of the corporation, in a material respect, is an act impairing the obligation of the charter, and is unconstitutional and void.

Under its charter, Dartmouth College was a private and not a public corporation. That a corporation is established for purposes of general charity, or for education generally, does not *per se,* make it a public corporation, liable to the control of the legislature.

Error to the superior court of the State of New Hampshire.

This is an action of trover, brought by the Trustees of Dartmouth College against William H. Woodward, in the state court of New Hampshire, for the book of records, corporate seal, and other corporate property, to which the plaintiffs allege themselves to be entitled.

A special verdict, after setting out the rights of the parties, finds for the defendant, if certain acts of the Legislature of New Hampshire, passed on the 27th of June and on the 18th of December 1816, be valid, and binding on the trustees without their assent, and not repugnant to the Constitution of the United States; otherwise, it finds for the plaintiffs.

The superior court of judicature of New Hampshire rendered a judgment upon this verdict for the defendant, which judgment has been brought before this court by writ of error. The single question now to be considered is, do the acts to which the verdict refers violate the Constitution of the United States? . . .

This court can be insensible neither to the magnitude nor delicacy of this question. The validity of a legislative act is to be examined, and the opinion of the highest law tribunal of a state is to be revised; an opinion which carries with it intrinsic evidence of the diligence, of the ability, and the integrity with which it was formed. On more than one occasion this court has expressed the cautious circumspection with which it approaches the consideration of such questions; and has declared that, in no doubtful

University which has received an income of more than $400,000 from Washington's gift, and still has the capital fund.

Some legends have grown up around the Dartmouth College Case in which Daniel Webster was principal counsel. Among these is the often quoted statement alleged to have been made by Webster directly to Chief Justice John Marshall: "Sir, you may destroy this little institution; it is weak; it is in your hands! You may put it out; but if you do, you must carry on your work! You must extinguish, one after another, all those great lights of science, which, for more than a century, have thrown their radiance over the land! It is, sir, as I have said, a small college,—and yet there are those who love it."

There is little documentary evidence on the report of this fervid statement by Webster. What seems to have happened is that Chauncey A. Goodrich, of Yale, had gone to Washington as a sort of unofficial observer for this institution, whose fortunes could well have been involved in the decision in the Dartmouth College Case. He is said to have reported this version of Webster's peroration to Rufus Choate who dramatized and sentimentalized the incident in his memorial address on Webster in 1853, more than thirty years after Goodrich had heard Webster's speech.

case, would it pronounce a legislative act to be contrary to the constitution. But the American people have said, in the constitution of the United States, that "no state shall pass any bill of attainder, ex post facto law, or law impairing the obligation of contracts." In the same instrument they have also said, "that the judicial power shall extend to all cases in law and equity arising under this constitution." On the judges of this court, then, is imposed the high and solemn duty of protecting, from even legislative violation, those contracts which the constitution of our country has placed beyond legislative control; and, however irksome the task may be, this is a duty from which we dare not shrink. . . .

It can require no argument to prove that the circumstances of this case constitute a contract. An application is made to the crown for a charter to incorporate a religious and literary institution. In the application it is stated that large contributions have been made for the object, which will be conferred on the corporation as soon as it shall be conveyed. Surely in this transaction every ingredient of a complete and legitimate contract is to be found.

The points for consideration are, 1. Is this contract protected by the Constitution of the United States? 2. Is it impaired by the acts under which the defendant holds?

1. On the first point it has been argued that the word "contract," in its broadest sense, would comprehend the political relations between the government and its citizens, would extend to officers held within a state for state purposes, and to many of those laws concerning civil institutions, which must change with circumstances, and be modified by ordinary legislation; which deeply concern the public, and which, to preserve good government, the public judgment must control. That even marriage is a contract, and its obligations are affected by the laws respecting divorces. That the clause in the Constitution, if construed in its greatest latitude, would prohibit these laws. Taken in its broad, unlimited sense, the clause would be an unprofitable and vexatious interference with the internal concerns of a state, would unnecessarily and unwisely embarrass its legislation, and render immutable those civil institutions which are established for purposes of internal government, and which, to subserve those purposes, ought to vary with varying circumstances. That as the framers of the Constitution could never have intended to insert in that instrument a provision so unnecessary, so mischievous, and so repugnant to its general spirit, the term "contract" must be understood in a more limited sense. That it must be understood as intended to guard against a power of at least doubtful utility, the abuse of which had been extensively felt, and to restrain the legislature in future from violating the right to property. That anterior to the formation of the Constitution, a course of legislation had prevailed in many, if not in all, of the states, which weakened the confidence of man in man, and embarrassed all transactions between individuals, by dispensing

with a faithful performance of engagements. To correct this mischief, by restraining the power which produced it, the state legislatures were forbidden "to pass any law impairing the obligation of contracts," that is, of contracts respecting property, under which some individual could claim a right to something beneficial to himself; and that since the clause in the Constitution must in construction receive some limitation, it may be confined, and ought to be confined, to cases of this description; to cases within the mischief it was intended to remedy. . . .

A corporation is an artificial being, invisible, intangible, and existing only in contemplation of law. Being the mere creature of law, it possesses only those properties which the charter of its creation confers upon it, either expressly or as incidental to its very existence. These are such as are supposed best calculated to effect the object for which it was created. Among the most important are immortality, and, if the expression may be allowed, individuality; properties, by which a perpetual succession of many persons are considered as the same, and may act as a single individual. They enable a corporation to manage its own affairs, and to hold property without the perplexing intricacies, the hazardous and endless necessity, of perpetual conveyances for the purpose of transmitting it from hand to hand. It is chiefly for the purpose of clothing bodies of men in succession with these qualities and capacities that corporations were invented and are in use. conveyances for the purpose of transmitting it from hand to hand. It is chiefly for the purpose of clothing bodies of men in succession with these qualities and capacities that corporations were invented and are in use. By these means, a perpetual succession of individuals are capable of acting for the promotion of the particular object, like one immortal being. But this being does not share in the civil government of the country, unless that be the purpose for which it was created. Its immortality no more confers on it political power or a political character than immortality would confer such power or character on a natural person exercising the same powers would be. If, then, a natural person, employed, by individuals in the education of youth, or for the government of a seminary in which youth is educated, would not become a public officer, or be considered as a member of the civil government, how is it that this artificial being, created by law for the purpose of being employed by the same individuals for the same purposes, should become a part of the civil government of the country? . . .

This is plainly a contract to which the donors, the trustees, and the crown (to whose rights and obligations New Hampshire succeeds) were the original parties. It is a contract made on a valuable consideration. It is a contract for the security and disposition of property. It is a contract, on the faith of which, real and personal estate has been conveyed to the corporation. It is then a contract within the letter of the Constitution, and within its spirit also, unless the fact that the property is invested by the donors in trustees for the promotion of religion and education, for the benefit of persons who are perpetually changing, though the objects remain the same, shall create a particular exception, taking this case out of the prohibition contained in the Constitution. . . .

The opinion of the court, after mature deliberation is, that this is a contract, the obligation of which cannot be impaired without violating the Constitution of the United States. This opinion appears to us to be equally supported by reason and by the former decisions of this court. . . .

The whole power of governing the college is transferred from trustees, appointed according to the will of the founder, expressed in the charter, to the executive of New Hampshire. The management and application of the funds of this eleemosynary institution, which are placed by the donors in the hands of trustees named in the charter and empowered to perpetuate themselves, are placed by this act under the control of the government of the state. The will of the state is substituted for the will of the donors in every essential operation of the college. This is not an immaterial change. The founders of the college contracted, not merely for the perpetual application of the funds which they gave to the objects for which those funds were given; they contracted also to secure that application by the constitution of the corporation. They contracted for a system which should, as far as human foresight can provide, retain forever the government of the literary institution they had formed, in the hands of persons approved by themselves. This system is totally changed. The charter of 1769 exists no longer. It is reorganized; and reorganized in such a manner, as to convert a literary institution, moulded according to the will of its founders, and placed under the control of private literary men, into a machine entirely subservient to the will of government. This may be for the advantage of this college in particular, and may be for the advantage of literature in general; but it is not according to the will of the donors, and is subversive of that contract on the faith of which their property was given. . . .

The judgment of the state court must, therefore, be reversed.

Congressional Objections to the Proposal to Grant Public Lands for the Endowment of State Universities, 1819 *

Mr. Poindexter, from the Committee on Public Lands, to whom was referred a resolution instructing said committee to inquire into the expediency of appropriating one hundred thousand acres of land to each State, for the endowment of a university in each State, reported:

That they are fully impressed with the propriety and importance of giving every encouragement and facility to the promotion of learning, and the diffusion of knowledge over the United States, which can be done without a violation of the principle of the constitution, and the system of

* *American State Papers, Public Lands,* III, p. 363.

policy heretofore adopted for the advancement of the general welfare. The proposition under consideration is, whether it be or be not expedient to authorize a grant of one hundred thousand acres of land to each State in the Union, making in the whole two million three hundred thousand acres, to be vested in bodies corporate, created by the several States having the care and management of their respective universities. Your committee have no specific knowledge of the necessity which exists for this appropriation, in reference to any particular State whose resources may not be adequate to the support of literary institutions, as no petitions or memorials have been referred to them on the subject. In the absence of these it is fair to presume that the internal wealth and industry of the population, composing the several States, have been found sufficient to answer all the purposes of public education and instruction, so far as they have deemed it prudent and necessary to apply the means they possess to those objects. But if the aid of the General Government should, at any time, be required to enable a particular State, or every member of the Union, to carry into effect a liberal and enlarged system of education, suited to the views, capacities, and circumstances, of all classes of society; and if it should be thought wise and constitutional to extend to them the national bounty, the donation of extensive tracts of lands in the unappropriated Territories of the United States appears to your committee to be the most exceptionable form in which the requisite assistance could be granted. To invest twenty-three corporations, acting under State authority, with a fee simple estate in two million three hundred thousand acres of land, to be located in the Western States and Territories, would put it in their power to impede the settlement of that section of the Union by withholding these lands from market; to interfere with the general regulations now in force for the disposal of the public lands; to divide settlements which would otherwise be contiguous; and, consequently, to lessen the value of the lands offered for sale by the United States in the neighborhood of these large grants, which may remain unoccupied for any length of time, at the discretion of the Legislature of the State to which the donation is made. Your committee are of opinion that, besides these strong objections to the donations proposed in the resolutions submitted to their consideration, it does not comport with sound policy, or the nature of our republican institutions, to grant monopolies of large and extensive tracts of the public domain, either to individuals or bodies corporate. The lands of the United States ought, as far as practicable, to be distributed in small quantities among the great body of the people for agricultural purposes; and this principle ought in no instance to be violated, where the grantee is exempted from the payment of a valuable consideration to the Government. Your committee are sensible that it may be found necessary and useful, for the promotion of learning in this growing republic, either to endow a national university, or to extend its benevolence in a reasonable and proper proportion to individual States;

but, in either case, they are of opinion that the requisite aid should be given in money and not in the mode pointed out in the resolution referred to them. They, therefore, recommend the following resolution to the House: *Resolved,* That it is inexpedient to grant to each State one hundred thousand acres of land for the endowment of a university in each State.

A Comparison of Collegiate Rules at Harvard, the University of Virginia and the University of South Carolina, 1820's *

When Jefferson drafted the rules for the University of Virginia he is supposed to have been considerably influenced by the rules then in force at Harvard. He possessed copies not only of these but of the contemporary rules of South Carolina College. A few of the laws of the three institutions which show the greatest similarity are here brought together for convenient comparison. Others show less similarity if any. These specimens are taken from the *Enactments of the Rector and Visitors of the University of Virginia,* 1825, the *Laws of Harvard College,* 1820, and Green's *History of the University of South Carolina,* 1916.

HARVARD, VI, pp. 20-21.

"IV. To prevent those tumults and disorders which are frequent at entertainments, and to guard against extravagance and needless expenses, no undergraduate shall make any festive entertainments in the College, the town of Cambridge, or the vicinity, except at Commencement and at public Exhibitions, with the permission of the President, under a penalty, for making or being present at such, not exceeding eight dollars."

SOUTH CAROLINA, *Green,* p. 221.

"No student shall make any festival (*sic*) entertainment in the college, or in the town of Columbia or take part in anything of the kind, without liberty previously obtained of the President."

VIRGINIA, p. 8.

"No student shall make any festive entertainment within the precincts of the University, nor contribute to, or be present at them there or elsewhere but with the consent of each of the Professors whose school he attends, on pain of a minor punishment."

HARVARD, VI, p. 22.

"VII. No student shall keep a gun or pistol, or any gunpowder in the College, or town of Cambridge; nor shoot, fish, or scate over deep waters, without leave from the President, or one of the Tutors or Professors, under

* Roy J. Honeywell, *The Educational Work of Thomas Jefferson* (Cambridge, Harvard University Press, 1931), pp. 279-80.

the penalty of fifty cents. And if any scholar shall fire a gun or pistol within the College walls, yard, or near the College, or near houses, or behind fences or inclosures, in the town, he shall be fined not exceeding one dollar, or suffer other college punishments."

SOUTH CAROLINA, *Green,* pp. 220-221.

"No student may keep in his room any kind of firearms or gun powder; nor fire any in or near the College, in any manner whatever; and any student who shall violate this law, shall be liable to admonition, suspension, or expulsion.

"All the students are strictly forbidden to play on any instrument of music in the hours of study, and also on Sunday; and shall abstain from their usual diversions and exercises on those days."

VIRGINIA, p. 9.

"No student shall admit any disturbing noises in his room, or make them anywhere within the precincts of the University, or fire a gun or pistol within the same, on pain of such minor sentences as the Faculty shall decree, or approve; but the proper use of musical instruments, shall be freely allowed in their rooms, and in that appropriated for the instruction in music."

HARVARD, VI, pp. 22-23.

"The students, when required, shall give evidence respecting the breach of any laws; shall admit into their chambers any of the officers, or, when sent for by them, shall immediately attend . . . or be punished by one of the high censures. . . . If entrance into a room be refused, an executive officer may break open any study or chamber door."

SOUTH CAROLINA, *Green,* p. 221.

"If any student shall refuse to open the door of his room, when required to do it by one of the Faculty, he shall be liable to public admonition; and the Faculty, when they shall think it necessary, may break open any room in the college at the expense of those by whom they are refused admittance."

VIRGINIA, pp. 9-101

"When a Professor knocks at the door of a student's room, any person being within, and announces himself, it shall be opened on pain of a minor punishment; and the Professor may, if refused, have the door broken open; and the expenses of repair shall be levied on the student or students within."

Professor George Ticknor on Harvard, 1821 *

We are neither an University—which we call ourselves—nor a respectable high school,—which we ought to be,—and . . . with *Christo et Ecclesiae* for our motto, the morals of great numbers of young men who come to us are corrupted.

Advertisement for the Opening of Indiana State Seminary Which Developed into Indiana University, 1824 †

The trustees of this institution are authorized to inform the public that the seminary buildings are now in a state of preparation, and will be ready for the reception of students by the first Monday of April, next, at which time the first session will commence under the Superintendency of the Rev'd BAYARD HALL, whom the trustees have engaged as a teacher. Mr. Hall is a gentleman whose classical attainments are perhaps not inferior to any in the western country; and whose acquaintance with the most approved methods of instruction in some of the best Universities in the United States and whose morals, manners and address, render him in every way qualified to give dignity and character to the institution.

There will be two sessions of five months each, in the year.

The admission fee for each scholar at the commencement of every session will be two dollars and fifty cents, making the expense of tuition for a year the sum of five dollars.

Good boarding can be had in respectable families, either in town or country at convenient distances, and on moderate terms, not exceeding $1.25 cents per week.

The institution will for the present be strictly classical, and each scholar will be required to furnish himself with a supply of classical books, of which the following are recommended, and will be needed from term to term:

Rose's Latin Grammar, latest edition.
Colloquies of Corderius.
Selectae Veteri.
Selectae Profanis.
Caesar.

* Letter to a committee of the Overseers of Harvard, 1821, quoted in S. E. Morison, *Three Centuries of Harvard*, p. 230. For Ticknor's views on higher educational reforms see his *Remarks on Changes Lately Proposed or Adopted in Harvard College* (Boston, 1825). This is one of the earliest and most effective arguments for changes in the college curriculum to meet changing conditions. For Thomas Jefferson's views on the elective systems, see his letter to Ticknor in H. A. Washington's *The Writings of Thomas Jefferson*, VII, pp. 300-01. Samuel Eliot Morison says that the reforms proposed by Ticknor "would have put Harvard College a generation ahead of her American rivals, made her equal to the smaller European universities, and offered a much sounder basis for introducing new subjects into the curriculum than the atomic subdivision subsequently adopted under Eliot. But conditions were not ripe, nor were Faculty or students prepared." *Three Centuries of Harvard*, p. 233.
† *The Indiana Republican* (Madison), January 7, 1824.

Virgil, & Mair's introduction.
Valpy's Grammar, latest edition.
Testament.
Graeca Minora.

None of these books are to be accompanied with an English translation, but this remark is not intended to extend to such editions as have notes in English; which indeed for beginners are preferable.

The choice of Lexicons in either language is kept discretionary with the students: Ainsworth's in Latin and Scrurevelius' in Greek are however recommended. Other books than those specified, as progress in the languages is made, will hereafter be necessary; but these only at present need be procured. The whole number of students according to the different degrees of improvement, will be distributed into several classes in which the books just enumerated are to be employed.

The seminary buildings are erected on an elevated situation affording a handsome view of Bloomington, the county seat of Monroe County, and also a commanding prospect of the adjacent country, which is altogether pleasant and well calculated for rural retreats; and as regards the healthiness of the situation, we hazard nothing in the assertion, that it cannot be excelled by any western country.

Joshua O. Howe
John Ketcham
Jonathan Nichols
Samuel Dobbs
William Lowe
D. H. Maxwell

Bloomington, Jan. 7, 1824.

Captain Alden Partridge's Arguments for Military Education, c. 1825 *

The elementary education of youth is doubtless one of the most important subjects which can occupy the attention of an enlightened and free people. It is to the rising generation that we are to look for the future guardians and protectors of the inestimable rights and privileges transmitted to us by the heroes and patriots of the revolution; they are to be the future legislators, political economists, and defenders of our country; and on them is to depend, in a very great degree, the future destinies of our mighty republic. It certainly, then, cannot be considered of small importance, that they be prepared, by a proper course of preliminary instruction and the acquirement of virtuous habits, for the correct discharge of the

* *Miscellanies*, Vol. 5, No. 17. No date or place of publication. Partridge was an energetic advocate of military education and opened his first military school at Norwich, Vermont, in 1819. Some years later he opened a similar school in Portsmouth, Virginia.

luties incident to their exalted stations; and thereby be enabled to transmit unimpaired to their posterity, the important trust committed to their charge.

I shall define elementary education, in its most perfect state, to be the preparing a youth in the best possible manner for the correct discharge of the duties of any station in which he may be placed, and consequently, shall consider as most perfect that system which shall be found best calculated to accomplish the object in view. The system of education adopted in the United States, appears to me to be defective in many respects; and—

1stly. It is not sufficiently practical, nor properly adapted to the various duties an American citizen may be called upon to discharge. Those of our youth who are destined for a liberal education, as it is called, are usually put, at an early age, to the study of the Latin and Greek languages, combining [manuscript torn] slight attention to their own language, the elements of arithmetic, &c.; and after having devoted several years in this way, they are prepared to become members of a College or University.

Here they spend four years for the purpose of acquiring a knowledge of the higher branches of learning; after which, they receive their diplomas, and are supposed to be prepared to enter on the duties of active life. But, I would ask, is this actually the case? Are they prepared in the best possible manner to discharge correctly, the duties of any station in which fortune or inclination may place them? Have they been instructed in the science of government generally, and more especially in the principles of our excellent Constitution, and thereby prepared to sit in the legislative councils of the nation? Has their attention been sufficiently directed to those great and important branches of national industry and sources of national wealth —Agriculture, Commerce and Manufactures? Have they been taught to examine the policy of other nations, and the effect of that policy on the prosperity of their own country? Are they prepared to discharge the duties of civil or military engineers, or to endure fatigue, or to become the defenders of their country's rights, and the avengers of her wrongs, either in the ranks or at the head of her armies? It appears to me not; and if not, then, agreeably to the standard established, their education is so far defective.

2dly. Another defect in the present system, is, the entire neglect, in all our principal seminaries, of physical education, or the due cultivation and improvement of the physical powers of the students.

The great importance and even absolute necessity of a regular and systematic course of exercise for the preservation of health and confirming and rendering vigorous the constitution, I presume, must be evident to the most superficial observer. It is for want of this, that so many of our most promising youths lose their health by the time they are prepared to enter on the grant theatre of active and useful life, and either prematurely die, or linger out a comparatively useless and [manuscript torn]. That the health of the closest applicant may be preserved, when he is subjected to a regular and systematic course of exercises, I know, from practical experience; and I have no hesitation in asserting, that in nine cases out of ten, it is just as easy for a youth, however hard he may study, to attain the age of manhood, with a firm and vigorous constitution, capable of enduring exposure, hunger and fatigue, as it is to grow up puny and debilitated, incapable of either bodily or mental exertion.

3dly. A third defect in our system is, the amount of idle time allowed the students; that portion of the day during which they are actually engaged in study and recitations, under the eye of their instructers, comprises but a small portion of the whole; during the remainder, those that are disposed to study, will improve at their rooms, while those who are not so disposed, will not only, not improve, but will be very likely to engage in practices injurious to their constitutions and destructive to their morals. If this vacant time could be employed in duties and exercises, which, while they amuse and improve the mind, would at the same time invigorate the body and confirm the constitution, it would certainly be a great point gained. That this may be done, I shall attempt, in the course of these observations, to shew.

4thly. A fourth defect, is the allowing to students, especially to those of the wealthier class, too much money, thereby inducing habits of dissipation and extravagance, highly injurious to themselves, and also to the seminaries of which they are members. I have no hesitation in asserting, that far the greater portion of the irregularities and disorderly proceedings amongst the students of our seminaries, may be traced to this fatal cause. Collect together at any seminary, a large number of youths, of the ages they generally are, at our institutions, furnish them with money, and allow them a portion of idle time, and it may be viewed as a miracle, if a large portion of them do not become corrupt in morals, and instead of going forth into the world to become ornaments in society, they rather are prepared to become nuisances to the same. There is in this respect, an immense responsibility resting on parents and guardians, as well as on all others having the care and instruction of youth, of which it appears to me they are not sufficiently aware.

When youths are sent to a seminary, it is presumed they are sent for the purpose of learning something that is useful, and not to acquire bad habits, or to spend money; they should consequently be furnished with every thing necessary for their comfort, convenience and improvement, but money should in no instance be put into their hands. So certainly as they have it, just so certainly will they spend it, and this will in nine cases out of ten, be done in a manner seriously to injure them, without any corresponding advantage. It frequently draws them into vicious and dissolute company, and induces habits of immorality and vice, which ultimately prove their ruin. The overweening indulgence of parents, has been the cause of the destruction of the morals and future usefulness of many a promising youth. They may eventually discover their error, but alas, it is often too late to correct it. Much better does that person discharge the duties of a real friend to the thoughtless, unwary youth, who withholds from him the means of indulging in dissipated and vicious courses.

5thly. A fifth defect is the requiring all the students to pursue the same course of studies.

All youth have not the same inclinations, nor the same capacities; one may possess a particular inclination and capacity for the study of the classics, but little or none for the mathematics and other branches of science;—with another it may be the reverse. Now it will be in vain to attempt making a mathematician of the former, or a linguist of the latter. Consequently, all the time that is devoted in this manner, will be lost, or something worse than lost. Every youth, who has any capacity or inclination for the acquirement of knowledge, will have some favorite studies, in which he will be likely to excel. It is certainly then much better that he should be permitted to pursue those, than, that by being forced to attend to others for which he has an aversion, and in which he will never excel, or ever make common proficiency, he should finally acquire a dislike to all study. The celebrated Pascal, is a striking instance of the absurdity and folly of attempting to force a youth to attend to branches of study, for which he has an utter aversion, to the exclusion of those for which he may possess a particular attachment. Had the father of this eminent man persisted in his absurd and foolish course, France would never have seen him, what he subsequently became, one of her brightest ornaments.

6thly. A sixth defect is the prescribing the length of time for completing, as it is termed, a course of education. By these means, the good scholar is placed nearly on a level with the sluggard, for whatever may be his exertions, he can gain nothing in respect to time, and the latter has, in consequence of this, less stimulus for exertion. If any thing will induce the indolent student to exert himself, it is the desire to prevent others getting ahead of him. It would be much better to allow each one to progress as rapidly as possible, with a thorough understanding of the subject.

Having thus summarily stated what appears to me the most prominent defects in our present system of elementary education, I will next proceed to point out the remedy for the same. This I shall do by describing the organization, &c. of an institution, such as I would propose.

1st. The organization and discipline should be strictly military.

Under a military system, subordination and discipline are much more easily preserved than under any other. Whenever a youth can be impressed with the true principles and feelings of a soldier, he becomes, as a matter of course, subordinate, honorable, and manly. He disdains subterfuge and prevarication, and all that low cunning, which is but too prevalent. He acts not the part of the assassin, but if he have an enemy, he meets him openly and fairly. Others may boast that they have broken the laws and regulations of the institution of which they are, or have been, members, and have escaped detection and punishment, by mean prevarication and falsehood. Not so the real soldier. If he have broken orders and regulations, he will openly acknowledge his error, and reform; but will not boast of having been insubordinate. Those principles, if imbibed and fixed in early youth, will continue to influence his conduct and actions during life; he will be equally observant of the laws of his country, as of the academic regulations under which he has lived; and will become the more estimable citizen in consequence thereof. I shall not pretend, however, that all who wear a military garb, or live, for a time, even under a correct system of military discipline, will be influenced in their conduct by the principles above stated; but if they are not, it only proves that they have previously imbibed erroneous principles, which have become too firmly fixed to be eradicated; or that nature has not formed them with minds capable of soaring above what is low and grovelling.

2dly. Military science and instruction should constitute a part of the course of education.

The constitution of the United States has invested the military defense of the country in the great body of the people. By the wise provisions of this instrument, and of the laws made in pursuance thereof, every American citizen, from eighteen to forty-five years of age, unless specially exempted by law, is liable to be called upon for the discharge of military duty he is emphatically a citizen soldier, and it appears to me perfectly proper that he should be equally prepared by education to discharge, correctly, his duties in either capacity. If we intend to avoid a standing army, (that bane of a republic, and engine of oppression in the hands of despots,) our militia must be patronized and improved, and military information must be disseminated amongst the great mass of the people; when deposited with them, it is in safe hands, and will never be exhibited in practice, except in opposition to the enemies of the country. I am well aware there are amongst us many worthy individuals, who deem the cultivation of military science a sort of heresy, flattering themselves, and endeavoring to induce others to believe, that the time has now arrived, or is very near, when wars are to cease, and universal harmony prevail amongst mankind. But, my fellow citizens, be not deceived by the syren song of peace, peace, when, in reality, there is no peace, except in a due and constant preparation for war. If we turn our attention to Europe, what do we behold? A league of crowned despots, impiously called holy, wielding a tremendous military force of two millions of mercenaries! Ill-fated Naples, and more ill-fated Spain, have both felt the effect of *their peaceable* dispositions, and were it not for the wide-spreading Atlantic, which the God of nature in his infinite goodness has interposed between us, we also, ere this, should have had a like experience. The principles of liberty are equally obnoxious to them, whether found in Europe, Asia, Africa, or America. If rendering mankind ignorant of the art of war, (as a science) would prevent wars, then would I unite most cordially with those, usually termed peace-men, for the purpose of destroying every vestige of it. But such, I am confident, would not be the result. Wars amongst nations do not arise because they understand how to conduct them skilfully and on scientific principles; but are induced by the evil propensities and dispositions of mankind. To prevent the effect, the cause must be removed. We may render nations ignorant of the use of the musket and bayonet; we may carry them back, as respects the art of war, to a state of barbarism, or even of savageism, and still wars will exist. So long as mankind possess the dispositions which they now possess, and which they ever have posessed, so long they will fight. To prevent wars then, the disposition must be changed; no remedy short of this, will be effectual. In proportion as nations are rude and unskilled in the art of war, will their military code be barbarous and unrelenting, their battles sanguinary, and their whole system of warfare, destructive. War, therefore, in such a case, becomes a far greater evil, than it does under an improved and refined system, where battles are won more by skill than by hard fighting, and the laws of war are proportionally ameliorated. What rational man, what friend of mankind, would be willing to exchange the present humane and refined system of warfare, for that practiced by an Attila, a Jenghis Khan, a Tamerlane, or a Mahomet, when hundreds of thousands fell in a single engagement, and when conquest and extermination were synonymous terms. On the principles of humanity then, it appears to me that, so long as wars do exist, the military art should be improved and refined as much as possible; for, in proportion as this is done, battles will be less sanguinary and destructive, the whole system more humane, and war itself a far less evil. But independent of any connexion with the profession of arms, or of any of the foregoing considerations, I consider a scientific knowledge of the military art, as constituting a very important part of the education of every individual engaged in the pursuit of useful knowledge, and this for many reasons; viz.:

1st. It is of great use in the reading of history, both ancient and modern.

A large portion of history is made up of accounts of military operations, descriptions of battles, sieges, &c. How, I would ask, is the reader to understand this part, if he be ignorant of the organization of armies, of the various systems of military tactics, of the science of fortification, and of the attack and defence of fortified places, both in ancient and modern times? Without such knowledge it is evident he derives, comparatively but little information from a large portion of what he reads.

2d. It is of great importance in the writing of history. I presume it will not be denied, that in order to write well on any subject, it must be understood. How, then, can the historian give a correct and intelligible account of a campaign, battle or siege, who is not only unacquainted with the principles on which military operations are conducted, but is also ignorant of the technical language necessary for communicating his ideas intelligibly on the subject. This is the principal reason why, as it appears to me, the ancient historians were so much superior to the modern. Many of their best historical writers, were military men. Some of them accomplished commanders. The account of military operations by such writers as Xenophon, Thucydides, Polybius and Caesar, are perfectly clear and intelligible, whereas when attempted by the great body of modern historians, the most we can learn is, that a fortress was besieged and taken, or that a battle was fought and a victory won, but are left in entire ignorance of the principles on which the operations were conducted, or of the reasons why the results were as they were.

3d. It is essentially necessary for the Legislature.

The military defence of our country is doubtless one of the most important trusts which is vested by the constitution in the general government, and it is a well known fact, that more money is drawn from the people and disbursed in the military, than in any other department, of the government. Now as all must be done under the sanction of the law, I would beg leave to inquire, whether it be not of the greatest importance, that those who are to make such laws should be in every respect well prepared to legislate understandingly on the subject? That there has been, and still is, a want of information on this subject amongst the great body of the members of congress, I think will be perfectly evident to any one who is competent, and will take the trouble to examine our military legislation, since the conclusion of the revolutionary war. I feel little hesitation in asserting that from want of this information, more than from any other cause, as much money has been uselessly expended in our military department alone, as would cancel a large portion of the national debt.

4th. It is of great use to the traveller.

Suppose a young man, with the best education he can obtain at any of our colleges or universities, were to visit Europe, where the military constitutes the first class of the community, and where the fortifications constitute the most important appendages to nearly all the principal cities, how much does he observe, which he does not understand? If he attempt a description of the cities, he finds himself embarrassed for want of a knowledge of fortification. If he attempts an investigation of the principles and organization of their institutions, or of their governments, he finds the military so interwoven with them all, that they cannot be thoroughly understood without it. In fine, he will return with far less information, than with the aid of a military education he might have derived. As it respects the military exercises, I would observe, that were they of no other use than in preserving the health of students, and confirming in them a good figure and manliness of deportment, I should consider these were ample reasons for introducing them into our seminaries generally; they are better calculated than any others for counteracting the natural habits of students, and can always be attended to, at such times as would otherwise be spent in idleness or useless amusements. Having expressed my views thus fully on this subject, I will next proceed to state more specifically the other branches which I would propose to introduce into a complete course of education: and—

1st. The course of classical and scientific instruction should be extensive and perfect as at our most approved institutions. The students should be earnestly enjoined and required to derive as much of useful information from the most approved authors, as their time and circumstances would permit.

2d. A due portion of time should be devoted to practical geometrical and other scientific operations in the field. The pupils should frequently be taken on pedestrian excursions into the country, be habituated to endure fatigue, to climb mountains, and to determine their altitudes by means of the barometer as well as by trigonometry. Those excursions, while they would learn them to walk, (which I estimate an important part of education,) and render them vigorous and healthy, would also prepare them for becoming men of practical science generally, and would further confer on them a correct *coup d'oeil* so essentially necessary for military and civil engineers, for surveyors, for travellers, &c., and which can never be acquired otherwise than by practice.

3d. Another portion of their time should be devoted to practical agricultural pursuits, gardening, &c.

In a country like ours, which is emphatically agricultural, I presume it will not be doubted, that a practical scientific knowledge of agriculture would constitute an important appendage to the education of every American citizen. Indeed the most certain mode of improving the agriculture of the country will be to make it a branch of elementary education. By these means, it will not only be improved, but also a knowledge of their improvements generally disseminated amongst the great mass of the people.

4th. A further portion of time should be devoted to attending familiar explanatory lectures on the various branches of military science, on the principles and practice of agriculture, commerce and manufactures, on political economy, on the constitution of the United States, and those of the individual States, in which should be pointed out particularly the powers and duties of the general government, and the existing relations between that and the state governments, on the science of government generally. In fine, on all those branches of knowledge which are necessary to enable them to discharge, in the best possible manner, the duties they owe to themselves, to their fellow men, and to their country.

5th. To the institution should be attached a range of mechanics' shops, where those who possess an aptitude and inclination might occasionally employ a leisure hour in learning the use of tools and acquiring a knowledge of some useful mechanic art.

The division of time, each day, I would make as follows, viz.:

Eight hours to be devoted to study and recitation; eight hours allowed for sleep. Three hours for the regular meals, and such other necessary personal duties as the student may require. Two hours for the military and other exercises, fencing, &c. The remaining three hours to be devoted, in due proportion, to practical agricultural and scientific pursuits and duties, and in attending lectures on the various subjects before mentioned.

Some of the most prominent advantages of the foregoing plan, would, in my opinion, be the following; viz.:

1st. The student would, in the time usually devoted to the acquirement of elementary education, (say six years) acquire, at least, as much, and I think I may may venture to say more, of book knowledge, than he would under the present system.

2d. In addition to this, he would go into the world an accomplished soldier, a scientific and practical agriculturist, an expert mechanician, an intelligent merchant, a political economist, legislator and statesman. In fine, he could hardly be placed in any situation, the duties of which he would not be prepared to discharge with honor to himself and advantage to his fellow citizens and his country.

3d. In addition to the foregoing, he would grow up with habits of industry, economy and morality, and, what is of little less importance, a firm and vigorous constitution; with a head to conceive and an arm to execute—he would emphatically possess a sound mind in a sound body.

I have thus in a summary manner endeavored to exhibit my views on the important subject of elementary education. I am sensible of my inability to do it justice; but if what I have said should be the means of drawing to it the attention of others, abler and more experienced, and who have more leisure than myself, I shall feel that much has been gained. Having devoted about sixteen years of my life to the care and instruction of the youth of our country, and having, under all circumstances, experienced from them a most ardent and devoted friendship, it can hardly be supposed I should feel indifferent to their future welfare and prosperity. I owe them a debt which I can only discharge by continuing zealously to exert myself for their improvement in useful knowledge, and endeavoring to instill into their minds such principles and habits as will render them a blessing to their parents and friends, and an ornament to our beloved country.

The First Public High School Law in the United States, 1827 *

Be it enacted, That each town or district within this Commonwealth, containing fifty families, or householders, shall be provided with a teacher or teachers, of good morals, to instruct children in orthography, reading, writing, English grammar, geography, arithmetic, and good behavior, for such term of time as shall be equivalent to six months for one school in each year; and every town or district containing one hundred families or householders, shall be provided with such teacher or teachers, for such term of time as shall be equivalent to eighteen months, for one school in each year. In every city, town, or district, containing five hundred families, or householders shall be provided with such teacher or teachers for such term of time as shall be equivalent to twenty-four months, shall also be provided with a master of good morals, competent to instruct, in addition to the branches of learning aforesaid, in the history of the United States, bookkeeping by single entry, geometry, surveying, algebra; and shall employ such master to instruct a school in such city, town, or district, for the benefit of all the inhabitants thereof, at least ten months in each year, exclusive of vacations, in such convenient places, or alternately at such places in such city, town, or district, as said inhabitants, at their meeting in March, or April, annually, shall determine; and in every city, or town, and district, containing four thousand inhabitants, such master shall be competent in addition to all the foregoing branches, to instruct the Latin and Greek languages, history, rhetoric, and logic.

Stephen Girard Provides for a College in Philadelphia for "Poor Male White Orphans," 1830 †

And, whereas, I have been for a long time impressed with the importance of educating the poor, and of placing them, by the early cultivation of their minds and the development of their moral principles, above the many temptations to which, through poverty and ignorance, they are exposed; and I am particularly desirous to provide for such a number of poor male white orphan children, as can be trained in one institution, a

---

* *Laws of Massachusetts,* January Session, 1827, chapter XCLIII. In spite of its mandatory provisions, this legislation was not well enforced until the time of Horace Mann, who became Secretary of the State Board of Education in 1837. See B. A. Hinsdale, *Horace Mann and the Common School Revival in the United States;* also G. H. Martin, *The Evolution of the Massachusetts Public School System.*

† Items XX-XXII of the will of Stephen Girard, February 16, 1830. A copy of this will was provided by Girard College, January, 1949. For a very interesting article on this unique institution see B. G. Wittels, "Lucky Sons of Stephen Girard," *The Saturday Evening Post,* December 13, 1947. In February of 1949 the institution had an enrollment of thirteen hundred students and an endowment of approximately eighty-nine million dollars, of which the sum of seventy-three million was at that time revenue-producing, "as the College and some other properties are carried on the books at a valuation of sixteen million dollars and do not produce income." Letter of February 7, 1949, from John C. Donecker, Assistant to the President, to Edgar W. Knight.

better education, as well as a more comfortable maintenance, than they usually receive from the application of the public funds: and whereas, together with the object just adverted to, I have sincerely at heart the welfare of the City of Philadelphia, and, as a part of it, am desirous to improve the neighborhood of the river Delaware, so that the health of the citizens may be promoted and preserved, and that the eastern part of the City may be made to correspond better with the interior: Now, I do give, devise and bequeath, *all the residue and remainder of my real and personal estate of* every sort and kind wheresoever situate, (the real estate in Pennsylvania charged as aforesaid) unto "the Mayor, Aldermen and Citizens of Philadelphia, their successors and assigns, in trust, to and for the several uses, intents and purposes hereinafter mentioned and declared of and concerning the same, that is to say; so far as regards my real estate in Pennsylvania, in trust, that no part thereof shall be ever sold or alienated by the said Mayor, Aldermen and Citizens of Philadelphia, or their successors, but the same shall forever thereafter be let from time to time, to good tenants, at yearly or other rents, and upon leases in possession not exceeding five years from the commencement thereof, and that the rents, issues and profits arising therefrom, shall be applied towards keeping that part of the said real estate situate in the City and Liberties of Philadelphia constantly in good repair, (parts elsewhere situate to be kept in repair by the tenants thereof respectively) and towards improving the same, whenever necessary, by erecting new buildings; and that the net residue (after paying the several annuities herein before provided for,) be applied to the same uses and purposes as are herein declared of and concerning the residue of my personal estate: and so far as regards my real estate in Kentucky, now under the care of Messrs. Triplett & Brumley, in trust, to sell and dispose of the same, whenever it may be expedient to do so, and to apply the proceeds of such sale to the same uses and purposes as are herein declared of and concerning the residue of my personal estate.

XXI. And so far as regards the residue of my personal estate, in trust, as to *two millions of dollars,* part thereof, to apply and expend so much of that sum as may be necessary, in erecting, as soon as practicably may be, in the centre of my square of ground between High and Chestnut streets, and Eleventh and Twelfth streets, in the City of Philadelphia, (which square of ground I hereby devote for the purposes hereinafter stated, and for no other, forever,) a permanent College, with suitable out-buildings, sufficiently spacious for the residence and accommodation of at least three hundred scholars, and the requisite teachers and other persons necessary in such an institution as I direct to be established, and in supplying the said College and out-buildings with decent and suitable furniture, as well as books and all things needful to carry into effect my general design.

The said College shall be constructed with the most durable materials, and in the most permanent manner, avoiding needless ornament, and attending chiefly to the strength, convenience, and neatness of the whole: It shall be at least one hundred and ten feet east and west, and one hundred and sixty feet north and south, and shall be built on lines parallel with High and Chestnut streets, and Eleventh and Twelfth streets, provided those lines shall constitute at their junction right angles: It shall be three stories in height, each story at least fifteen feet high in the clear from the floor to the cornice: It shall be fire proof inside and outside. The floors and the roof to be formed of solid materials, on arches turned on proper centres, so that no wood may be used, except for doors, windows and shutters: Cellars shall be made under the whole building, solely for the purposes of the Institution; the doors to them from the outside shall be on the east and west of the building, and access to them from the inside shall be had by steps, descending to the cellar floor from each of the entries or halls hereinafter mentioned, and the inside cellar doors to open under the stairs on the north-east and north-west corners of the northern entry, and under the stairs on the south-east and south-west corners of the southern entry; there shall be a cellar window under and in a line with each window in the first story—they shall be built one half below, and the other half above the surface of the ground, and the ground outside each window shall be supported by stout walls; the sashes should open inside, on hinges, like doors, and there should be strong iron bars outside each window; the windows inside and outside should not be less than four feet wide in the clear: There shall be in each story four rooms, each room not less than fifty feet square in the clear; the four rooms on each floor to occupy the whole space east and west on such floor or story, and the middle of the building north and south; so that in the north of the building, and in the south thereof, there may remain a space of equal dimensions, for an entry or hall in each, for stairs and landings: In the north-east and in the north-west corners of the northern entry or hall on the first floor, stairs shall be made so as to form a double staircase, which shall be carried up through the several stories; and, in like manner, in the south-east and south-west of the southern entry or hall, stairs shall be made, on the first floor, so as to form a double staircase, to be carried up through the several stories; the steps of the stairs to be made of smooth white marble, with plain square edges, each step not to exceed nine inches in the rise, nor to be less than ten inches in the tread; the outside and inside foundation walls shall be at least ten feet high in the clear from the ground to the ceiling; the first floor shall be at least three feet above the level of the ground around the building, after that ground shall have been so regulated as that there shall be a gradual descent from the centre to the side of the square formed by High and Chestnut, Eleventh and Twelfth Streets: all the outside foundation walls, forming the cellars, shall be three feet six inches thick up to the first floor, or as high as may be necessary to fix the centres for the first floor; and the inside foundation

wall, running north and south, and the three inside foundation walls running east and west (intended to receive the interior walls for the four
rooms, each not less than fifty feet square in the clear, above mentioned,)
shall be three feet thick up to the first floor, or as high as may be necessary to fix the centres for the first floor; when carried so far up, the
outside walls shall be reduced to two feet in thickness, leaving a recess
outside of one foot, and inside of six inches—and when carried so far up
the inside foundation walls shall also be reduced six inches on each side,
to the thickness of two feet; centres shall then be fixed on the various
recesses, of six inches throughout, left for the purpose, the proper arches
shall be turned, and the first floor laid; the outside and the inside walls
shall then be carried up to the thickness of two feet throughout, as high
as may be necessary to begin the recess intended to fix the centres of the
second floor, that is, the floor of the four rooms, each not less than fifty
feet square in the clear, and for the landing in the north, and the landing
in the south of the building, where the stairs are to go up—at this stage
of the work, a chain, composed of bars of inch square iron, each bar
about ten feet long, and linked together by hooks formed of the ends of
the bars, shall be laid straightly and horizontally along the several walls,
and shall be as tightly as possible worked into the center of them throughout, and shall be secured wherever necessary, especially at all the angles,
by iron clamps solidly fastened, so as to prevent cracking or swerving in
any part; centres shall then be laid, the proper arches turned for the second floor and landings, and the second floor and landings shall be laid;
the outside and the inside walls shall then be carried up of the same thickness of two feet throughout as high as may be necessary to begin in the
recess intended to fix the centers for the third floor and landings, and,
when so far carried up, another chain, similar in all respects to that used
at the second story, shall be in like manner worked into the walls throughout, as tightly as possible, and clamped in the same way with equal care;
centres shall be formed, the proper arches turned, and the third floor and
landings shall be laid; the outside and the inside walls shall then be carried up, of the same thickness of two feet throughout, as high as may be
necessary to begin the recess intended to fix the centres of the roof; and
when so carried up, a third chain, in all respects like those used at the
second and third stories, shall in the manner before described, be worked
as tightly as possible into the walls throughout, and shall be clamped with
equal care; centres shall now be fixed in the manner best adapted for the
roof, which is to form the ceiling for the third story, the proper arches
shall be turned, and the roof shall be laid as nearly horizontally as may
be, consistently with the easy passage of water to the eaves; the outside
walls, still of the thickness of two feet throughout, shall then be carried
up about two feet above the level of the platform, and shall have marble
capping, with a strong and neat iron railing thereon. The outside walls

shall be faced with slabs or blocks of marble or granite, not less than two feet thick, and fastened together with clamps securely sunk therein,—they shall be carried up flush from the recess of one foot formed at the first floor where the foundation outside wall is reduced to two feet. The floors and landings, as well as the roof, shall be covered with marble slabs, securely laid in mortar; the slabs on the roof to be twice as thick as those on the floors: In constructing the walls, as well as in turning the arches, and laying the floors, landings, and roof, good and strong mortar and grout shall be used, so that no cavity whatever may anywhere remain. A furnace or furnaces for the generation of heated air shall be placed in the cellar, and the heated air shall be introduced in adequate quantity, wherever wanted, by means of pipes and flues inserted and made for the purpose in the walls, and as those walls shall be constructed. In case it shall be found expedient for the purposes of a library, or otherwise, to increase the number of rooms, by dividing any of those directed to be not less than fifty feet square in the clear, into parts, the partition walls to be of solid materials. A room most suitable for the purpose shall be set apart for the reception, and preservation of my books and papers, and I direct that they shall be placed there by my executors, and carefully preserved therein. There shall be two principal doors of entrance into the College, one into the entry or hall on the first floor, in the north of the building, and in the centre between the east and west walls, the other into the entry or hall in the south of the building, and in the centre between the east and west walls; the dimensions to be determined by a due regard to the size of the entire building, to that of the entry, and to the purpose of the doors. The necessity for, as well as the position and size of other doors, internal or external, and also the position and size of the windows, to be, in like manner, decided on by a consideration of the uses to which the building is to be applied, the size of the building itself, and of the several rooms, and of the advantages of light and air: there should in each instance be double doors, those opening into the rooms to be what are termed glass doors, so as to increase the quantity of light for each room, and those opening outward to be of substantial wood work well lined and secured; the windows of the second and third stories I recommended to be made in the style of those in the first and second stories of my present dwelling house, North Water Street, on the eastern front thereof; and outside each window I recommend that a substantial and neat iron balcony be placed, sufficiently wide to admit the opening of the shutters against the walls; the windows of the lower story to be in the same style, except that they are not to descend to the floor, but so far as the surbase, up to which the wall is to be carried, as is the case in the lower story of my house at my place in Passyunk Township. In minute particulars, not here noticed, utility and good taste should determine. There should be at least four out-buildings, detached from the main edifice and from each other, and in such positions as shall at once answer the purposes of the Institution, and be consistent with the symmetry of the whole establishment: each building should be, as far as practicable, devoted to a distinct purpose; in that one or more of those buildings, in which they may be most useful, I direct my executors to place my plate and furniture of every sort.

The entire square, formed by High and Chestnut streets and Eleventh and Twelfth streets, shall be enclosed with a solid wall, at least fourteen inches thick, and ten feet high, capped with marble and guarded with irons on the top, so as to prevent persons from getting over; there shall be two places of entrance into the square, one in the center of the wall facing High street, and the other in the centre of the wall facing Chestnut street, at each place of entrance there shall be two gates, one opening inward, and the other outward; those opening inward to be of iron, and in the style of the gates north and south of my Banking house; and those opening outward to be of substantial wood work, well lined and secured on the faces thereof with sheet iron. The messuages now erected on the southeast corner of High and Twelfth streets, and on Twelfth street, to be taken down and removed as soon as the College and out-buildings shall have been erected, so that the establishment may be rendered secure and private.

When the College and appurtenances shall have been constructed, and supplied with plain and suitable furniture and books, philosophical and experimental instruments and apparatus, and all other matters needful to carry my general design into execution; the income, issues and profits of so much of the said sum of two millions of dollars as shall remain unexpended, shall be applied to maintain the said College according to my directions.

1. The Institution shall be organized as soon as practicable, and to accomplish the purpose more effectually, due public notice of the intended opening of the College shall be given—so that there may be an opportunity to make selections of competent instructors, and other agents, and those who may have the charge of orphans, may be aware of the provisions intended for them.

2. A competent number of instructors, teachers, assistants, and other necessary agents shall be selected, and when needful, their places from time to time, supplied; they shall receive adequate compensation for their services: but no person shall be employed, who shall not be tried skill in his or her proper department, of established moral character, and in all cases persons shall be chosen on account of their merit, and not through favour or intrigue.

3. As many poor male white orphans, between the age of six and ten years, as the said income shall be adequate to maintain, shall be introduced into the College as soon as possible; and from time to time, as

there may be vacancies, or as increased ability from income may warrant, others shall be introduced.

4. On the application for admission, an accurate statement should be taken in a book, prepared for the purpose, of the name, birth-place, age, health, condition as to relatives, and other particulars useful to be known of each orphan.

5. No orphan should be admitted until the guardians or directors of the poor, or a proper guardian or other competent authority, shall have given by indenture, relinquishment or otherwise, adequate power to the Mayor, Aldermen and Citizens of Philadelphia, or to directors or others by them appointed, to enforce in relation to each orphan every proper restraint, and to prevent relatives or others from interfering with or withdrawing such orphan from the Institution.

6. Those orphans, for whose admission application shall first be made, shall be first introduced, all other things concurring—and at all times priority of application shall entitle the applicant to preference in admission, all other things concurring; but if there shall be at any time, more applicants than vacancies, and the applying orphans shall have been born in different places, a preference shall be given—*first* to orphans born in the City of of Philadelphia; *secondly,* to those born in any other part of Pennsylvania; *thirdly,* to those born in the City of New York (that being the first port on the continent of North American at which I arrived:) and *lastly,* to those born in the City of New Orleans, being the first port on the said continent at which I first traded, in the first instance as first officer, and subsequently as master and part owner of a vessel and cargo.

7. The orphans admitted into the College, shall be there fed with plain but wholesome food, clothed with plain but decent apparal, (no distinctive dress ever to be worn) and lodged in a plain but safe manner; Due regard shall be paid to their health, and to this end their persons and clothes shall be kept clean, and they shall have suitable and rational exercise and recreation. They shall be instructed in the various branches of a sound education: comprehending Reading, Writing, Grammar, Arithmetic, Geography, Navigation, Surveying, Practical Mathematics, Astronomy, Natural, Chemical and Experimental Philosophy, the French and Spanish languages, (I do not forbid, but I do not recommend the Greek and Latin languages,) and such other learning and science as the capacities of the several scholars may merit or warrant. I would have them taught facts and things, rather than words and signs; and especially, I desire that by every proper means a pure attachment to our republican institutions, and to the sacred rights of conscience, as guaranteed by our happy constitutions shall be formed and fostered in the minds of the scholars.

8. Should it unfortunately happen, that any of the orphans admitted into the College, shall, from malconduct, have become unfit companions

for the rest, and mild means of reformation prove abortive, they should no longer remain therein.

9. These scholars, who shall merit it shall remain in the College until they shall respectively arrive at between fourteen and eighteen years of age; they shall then be bound out by the Mayor, Aldermen and Citizens of Philadelphia, or under their direction, to suitable occupations, as those of agriculture, navigation, arts, mechanical trades, and manufactures, according to the capacities and acquirements of the scholars respectively, consulting, as far as prudence shall justify it, the inclination of the several scholars, as to the occupation, art or trade, to be learned.

In relation to the organization of the College and its appendages, I leave, necessarily, many details to the Mayor, Aldermen and Citizens of Philadelphia, and their successors; and I do so, with the more confidence, as from the nature of my bequests, and the benefit to result from them, I trust that my fellow-citizens of Philadelphia, will observe and evince especial care and anxiety in selecting members for their City Councils, and other agents.

There are, however, some restrictions, which I consider it my duty to prescribe, and to be, amongst others, conditions on which my bequest for the said College is made, and to be enjoyed, namely; *First,* I enjoin and require, that if, at the close of any year, the income of the fund devoted to the purposes of the said College shall be more than sufficient for the maintenance of the Institution during that year, then the balance of the said income, after defraying such maintenance, shall be forthwith invested in good securities, thereafter to be and remain a part of the capital; but, in no event, shall any part of the said capital be sold, disposed of, or pledged, to meet the current expenses of the said Institution, to which I devote the interest, income, and dividends thereof, exclusively: *Secondly,* I enjoin and require that *no ecclesiastic, missionary, or minister of any sect whatsoever, shall ever hold or exercise any station or duty whatever in the said College; nor shall any such person ever by admitted for any purpose, or as a visitor, within the premises appropriated to the purposes of the said College.* In making this restriction, I do not mean to cast any reflection upon any sect or person whatsoever; but, as there is such a multitude of sects, and such a diversity of opinion amongst them, I desire to keep the tender minds of the orphans, who are to derive advantage from this bequest, free from the excitement which clashing doctrines and sectarian controversy are so apt to produce; my desire is, that all the instructors and teachers in the College, shall take pains to instill into the minds of the scholars the *purest principles of morality,* so that, on their entrance into active life, they may, *from inclination and habit,* evince *benevolence towards their fellow creatures,* and *a love of truth, sobriety, and industry,* adopting at the same time such religious tenets as their *matured reason* may enable them to prefer. If the income, arising from that part of the said sum of two millions of dollars, remaining after the construction and furnishing of the College and outbuildings, shall, owing to the increase of the number of orphans applying for admission, or other cause, be inadequate to the construction of new buildings, or the maintenance and education of as many orphans as may apply for admission, then such further sum as may be necessary for the construction of new buildings and the maintenance and education of such further number of orphans, as can be maintained and instructed within such buildings as the said square of ground shall be adequate to, shall be taken from the final residuary fund hereinafter expressly referred to for the purpose, comprehending the income of my real estate in the City and County of Philadelphia, and the dividends of my stock in the Schuylkill Navigation Company—my design and desire being, that the benefits of said institution, shall be extended to as great a number of orphans, as the limits of the said square and buildings therein can accommodate.

Evidence of Interest in Manual Labor Schools, 1831 *

We have already given an account of the Manual Labor School of Germantown. It is well known that a similar plan has been for some time in operation in the Western Theological Seminary at Maryville, in the Seminary at Danville in Kentucky, in the Maine Wesleyan Seminary, and at the Oneida Institute in New York, with the most happy effect upon the physical and intellectual vigor of the students. From two to four hours each day are spent in labour, a large part of the student's board is thus paid, and yet, an obvious gain is perceived in intellectual progress.

We rejoice to perceive that institutions of this kind are multiplying in our country. Anthony Morris, Esq., whose interest in this subject was excited by a visit to Hofwyl several years since, has constantly endeavoured in various ways to excite public interest on this subject. He has recently been able to carry into execution a plan he has long had in view, of establishing a school of this kind on an estate of his own, called Bolton Farm, near Bristol, Pennsylvania. We hope it may prove useful, not only as an example of benevolent enterprise, but as a model for other institutions. We have mentioned the institution at Germantown. Another school of the kind is about to be established by Mr. Mead, in Frederick County, Virginia, in which agriculture, both in theory and practice, will be combined with a course in English studies, and Hofwyl is adopted as the model for discipline and economy. A similar school has also been founded at Elizabethtown, New Jersey, and another is proposed in Litchfield County, Connecticut.

But we are particularly gratified to see this subject taken up from *the pulpit*. In a discourse by the Rev. Mr. Tyng of Philadelphia, on "The

* Editorial, *American Annals of Education,* I (January, 1831), p. 37.

Importance of uniting Manual Labour with Intellectual Attainments, in a preparation for the Ministry," we find the value of these schools ably and warmly advocated. This discourse was addressed to the Episcopal Education Society of Pennsylvania. This body has gone forward with praiseworthy enterprise to purchase a farm near Wilmington, on the Delaware River, on which they propose to educate twenty-five young men, who shall contribute most of their own support by four hours of daily labour. We cordially wish success to every effort of this kind. We almost envy our successors in the academic course, and look forward with eager and delightful anticipation to the day when something of the vigor of our fathers shall be found among the intellectual labourers of the day, and the sallow tinge of dispepsy shall cease to be the uniform testimonial of a life of study.

The Legislature of Tennessee Opposes Appropriations to the United States Military Academy, 1833 *

Whereas, many of the good citizens of these United States have viewed with deep and manifest interest, the vast appropriations of public money for the support of the Military Academy in the State of New York; a few young men, sons of distinguished and wealthy families, through the intervention of members of Congress, are educated at this institution, at the expense of the great body of the American people, which entitled them to privileges, and elevate them above their fellow citizens who have not been so fortunate as to be educated under the patronage of this aristocratical institution: and, whereas, it is considered by this General Assembly, that such institutions are repugnant to the great and fundamental principles of our Government, by creating a demand upon the Government for a large amount of money, to support and protect an institution almost unknown to the people, and well calculated in its character to fill all the offices in the army of the United States under the patronage of the Government, to the exclusion of the meritorious and talented portion of the country, who have not received their academical education at the Government school; such a power is wholly unknown to the constitution of the United States, and at war with those principles and maxims which should ever be held sacred by a free and enlightened people. Since the year 1794, when this institution was established, and a corps of artillerists and engineers, it has gradually set up claims to Government patronage, by acts of Congress from time to time, increasing the pay, rank and emoluments of its officers, as well as the number of Cadets, until the year 1812, when and appropriation of twenty-five thousand dollars was made by Congress to erect public buildings, and procuring library, apparatus, &c. and is now

* Public Acts Passed at The First Session of the Twentieth General Assembly of the State of Tennessee, 1833, pp. 122-23.

supported by annual appropriations by the Government; all of which is viewed as an unnecessary expenditure of the public funds: therefore,

1. *Resolved by the General Assembly of the State of Tennessee,* That our Senators in Congress be instructed, and our Representatives requested, to oppose the passage of all laws making further appropriations for the support of said institution.

2. *Resolved,* that the Secretary of the State cause a copy of the foregoing preamble and resolution to be furnished each of our Senators and Representatives in Congress.

The Committee on Education of the Legislature of Pennsylvania Recommends Manual Labor Schools, 1833 *

First, That the expense of education, when connected with manual labor judiciously directed, may be reduced at least one-half.

Second, That the exercise of about three hours' manual labor, daily, contributes to the health and cheerfulness of the pupil, by strengthening and improving his physical powers, and by engaging his mind in useful pursuits.

Third, That so far from manual labor being an impediment to the progress of the pupil in intellectual studies, it has been found that in proportion as one pupil has excelled another in the amount of labor performed, the same pupil has excelled the other, in equal ratio, in his intellectual studies.

Fourth, That manual labor institutions tend to break down the distinctions between rich and poor which exist in society, inasmuch as they give an almost equal opportunity of education to the poor by labor, as is afforded to the rich by the possession of wealth.

Fifth, That pupils trained in this way are much better fitted for active life, and better qualified to act as useful citizens, than when educated in any other mode,—that they are better as regards physical energy, and better intellectually and morally.

The Founding of Oberlin College, Ohio, 1834 †

The founding: We have lately received a notice of another institution with the same general object in view, in a select colony about to be established under the name of Oberlin, in Loraine County, Ohio. It is intended, ultimately, to embrace all grades of instruction from the Infant School to the Theological Seminary, with the great object of preparing teachers and pastors for the great basin of the Mississippi. Its plan is

---

* Given in J. P. Wickersham, *A History of Education in Pennsylvania* (Lancaster, Inquirer Publishing Co., 1886), p. 306.
† *American Annals of Education,* III (September, 1833), p. 429.

founded on sound principles of education. It is also to embrace the plan of manual labor, and from the favorable circumstances of its situation and privileges, its founders feel themselves authorized to state that a donation of $150, expended in establishing the literary and manual labor departments, will secure the education of one student annually for active usefulness, without any more labor than his own welfare demands.

Report on the first year: From a recent circular we learn the following additional particulars as to Oberlin Collegiate Institute.

The system embraces instruction in every department, from the Infant School to a Collegiate and Theological course. Physical and moral education are to receive particular attention. The institution was opened in December last, and has sixty students; about forty in the academic, and twenty in the primary department. All of them, whether male or female, rich or poor, are required to labor four hours daily. Male students are to be employed in agriculture, gardening, and some of the mechanic arts; females in housekeeping, useful needle-work, the manufacture of wool, the culture of silk, certain appropriate parts of gardening, &c. The Institution has 500 acres of good land, of which, though a complete forest a year ago, about 30 acres are now cleared and sown with wheat. They have also a steam mill, and a saw mill, in operation. During the present year it is contemplated to add 50 acres to the cleared land, to erect a flouring mill, a shingle machine, turning lathe, a work shop, and an extensive boarding house (which, together with the present buildings, will accommodate about 150 students), with furniture, farming mechanic, and scientific apparatus; and begin a library.

During the winter months the young men are at liberty to engage as agents, school teachers, or in any other occupation they may select. The expenses of students in the seminary for board at the table spread only with vegetable food, are 80 cents a week, and 92 cents a week for the same with animal food twice a day. Tuition is from 15 to 35 cents a week. The avails of the students' labors have thus far varied from 1 to 8 cents an hour; the average has been 5 cents. A majority of the male students have, by their four hours daily labor, paid their board, fuel, lights, washing and mending, and some even more; and this without any interference with their progress in their studies.

J. Marion Sims Reports a Duel in South Carolina College, 1835 *

I lived in the age of dueling. I was educated to believe that duels insured the proprieties of society and protected the honor of women. I have hardly a doubt but that, while I was a student in the South Carolina College, if anything had happened to have made it necessary for me to fight

* *The Story of My Life.* Edited by H. Marion-Sims (New York, D. Appleton and Co., 1885), pp. 88-91.

a duel, I would have gone out with the utmost coolness and allowed myself to be shot down. But my views on that subject were entirely changed, a long, long time ago.

The boys got up a mock duel one day between Frank Massey and Robert Burns. Frank was in the secret but poor Burns was not. But he behaved bravely. They fired cork bullets at each other. I always thought it a hard and foolish game to play off on a good fellow like Robert Burns.

There was a real duel in South Carolina College, just after I graduated. It was between Roach, of Colleton, and Adams of Richland District. Roach was a young man about six feet high and a physical beauty. Adams was no less so, though not so tall. Both men were of fine families, and Adams was supposed to be a young man of talent and promise. It occurred in this way: They were very intimate friends; they sat opposite to each other in the Stewards' Hall, at table. When the bell rang and the door was opened, the students rushed in, and it was considered a matter of honor, when a man got hold of a dish of butter or bread, or any other dish, it was his. Unfortunately, Roach and Adams sat opposite each other, and both caught hold of a dish of trout at the same moment. Adams did not let go; Roach held on to the dish. Presently Roach let go of the dish and glared fiercely in Adams's face, and said: "Sir, I will see you after supper." They sat there all through the supper, both looking like mad bulls, I presume. Roach left the supper-room first, and Adams immediately followed him. Roach waited outside the door for Adams. There were no hard words and no fisticuffs—all was dignity and solemnity. "Sir," said Roach, "What can I do to insult you?" Adams replied "This is enough, sir, and you will hear from me." Adams immediately went to his room and sent a challenge to Roach. It was promptly accepted, and each went up town and selected seconds and advisers. And now comes the strange part of this whole affair: No less a person than General Pierce M. Butler, distinguished in the Mexican war as the colonel of the Palmetto regiment, and who became Governor of South Carolina, agreed to act as second to one of these young men. The other man had as his adviser Mr. D. J. McCord, a distinguished lawyer, a most eminent citizen, a man of great talents, whose name lives in the judicial records of the state as being the author of McCord and Nott's reports. Here were two of the most prominent citizens of South Carolina, each of them about forty years of age, aiding and abetting dueling between two young men, neither of them over twenty years of age.

They fought at Lightwood Knot Springs, ten miles from Columbia. They were both men of the coolest courage. My friend Dr. Josiah C. Nott, then of Columbia, and afterward of Mobile, Alabama, who died some eight years ago in Mobile, was the surgeon to one of the parties. They were to fight at ten paces distant. They were to fire at the word "one," raising their pistols. There are two methods of dueling: One is to hold the pistol erect, pointing heavenward, dropping it at right angles with the body at the word "Fire!" and then firing at the word one, two, or three; the other is to hold the muzzle down toward the earth, and then at the word to raise it at arm's length and fire. The latter method was adopted at the Roach-Adams duel. When the word "Fire!" was given, each started to raise his pistol; but each had on a frockcoat, and the flap of Roach's coat caught on his arm, and prevented his pistol from rising. When Adams saw that, he lowered his pistol to the ground. The word was then given a second time: "Are you ready? Fire! One!" They both shot simultaneously; Dr. Nott said it was impossible to tell which was before the other. Adams was shot through the pelvis, and he lingered a few hours and died in great agony. Roach was shot through the right hip-joint, two or three inches below where his ball entered Adams's body. He lingered for a long time, and came near dying of blood-poisoning; but after weeks and months of suffering, he was able to get up, but was lame for life. I presume he was one of the most unhappy wretches on the face of the earth. He had killed his best friend, became very dissipated, and always, when he was drunk, the murder of Adams was his theme of conversation; doubtless, when he was sober, it troubled his conscience. He studied medicine and went to Philadelphia, to the Jefferson Medical College, and there he gave himself up entirely to dissipation. He had delirium tremens and died in Philadelphia, in an attack of it; I think it was in the month of January, 1836. During the latter part of his illness he was imagining that he was in hell, and begging the author of all torments to pour molten lead down his throat to quench his thirst. This account was given to me by a young man who was an eye-witness of this death-bed scene. . . .

President Francis Wayland of Brown University on Some Aspects of the Collegiate System in the United States, 1842 *

There are generally three daily recitations or lectures to be attended by each student throughout the whole course. A recitation or lecture commonly occupies one hour, though this time may in some colleges be abridged. When a class is large, it is formed into two or three sections, each pursuing the same studies, unless, as it sometimes happens, the division is made on the principle of scholarship, and then the bettter scholars are tasked more severely. The upper classes are not so commonly divided, as their instruction is to a greater extent carried on by means of Lectures.

A year, in imitation of the English colleges, is divided into three terms, and three vacations. The vacations occupy about twelve or thirteen weeks. During this time students and officers are at liberty to employ their time as they please. One of the vacations extends to the length of six or eight

---

* *Thoughts on the Present Collegiate System in the United States* (Boston, Gould, Kendall & Lincoln, 1842), pp. 32-41.

weeks, and takes place either in the summer or winter. The former is the proper season for vacation, if the health of the faculty and students, and the interests of education are considered. The latter, however, is frequently chosen, in order to accommodate those young men who wish to be absent for the purpose of teaching schools in the country.

Examinations are held at the close of each term, or at the close of the year, or at some other specified time, of all the students, in all the studies to which they have attended. These examinations are *viva voce,* and occupy in the aggregate a considerable portion of time. As, however, in this manner only one person can be examined at a time, the scrutiny which falls upon any individual can neither be very severe nor very long continued. The examination is, I believe, always restricted to the book which has been studied; the student not being considered responsible for any thing that may not have been acquired in the recitation room.

Examinations are, so far as I know, always conducted by the instructor himself. It is of course the special duty of the visitors to be present on such occasions, but, so far as I know, this duty is almost never discharged. Sometimes they appoint a committee of examination, from their own number, and when this has been made an office of small emolument, I have known it to be discharged with punctuality; but never otherwise. Sometimes, committees are appointed from the community at large, consisting of persons who are supposed to be interested in the cause of education. This plan has sometimes succeeded, but in other cases I have known it to fail altogether. In but few districts of our country could it be relied upon as at all an efficient aid to the labors of instructors.

If, after examination, a student is found to be deficient in the studies of his class, his deficiency is sometimes publicly announced, sometimes he is required to make up this deficiency in vacation, and in some institutions, he is not allowed to become a candidate for a degree unless he have passed his examinations in all the studies of the college course.

The studies of each class occupy one year. At the close of the year those students who have incurred no disability, are advanced to the next higher class. Those who have been thus advanced through all the four classes are candidates for the degree of Bachelor of Arts; and proceed to this degree as a matter of course.

The studies of each College are appointed by its Corporation or Board of visitors. These may differ in some unimportant points, yet are in all the Northern colleges so nearly similar that students in good standing in one institution find little difficulty in being admitted to any other. In order to illustrate the nature and amount of the studies pursued in a New England college, I here abridge from one of the catalogues published within the present year, 1841-2, the statutory course prescribed for a candidate for the degree of A.B. In Latin, select portions of Livy, Tacitus, Horace, Cicero de Oratore, Juvenal;—In Greek, select portions of Xenophon's

Anabasis, Memorabilia, the Iliad, some of the tragedies of Sophocles and Eschylus, with Demosthenes' Oration for the Crown; In Mathematics, Geometry, plane and solid. Algebra, Trigonometry, plane and spherical, and its applications to practical mathematics, and Analytical Geometry; in Natural Philosophy, Mechanics, Pneumatics, Hydrostatics, Optics, and Astronomy;—In natural Science, Chemistry, Vegetable and Animal Pysiology, and Geology;—In Intellectual and Moral Science, Rhetoric, theoretical and practical, Logical Intellectual and Moral Philosophy, Political Economy, Butler's Analogy, and the American Constitution. Many of these studies, besides being pursued by means of a textbook, are illustrated by full courses of lectures and ample experiments.

I have remarked that the degree of Bachelor of Arts is conferred in course upon every pupil who has, with a reasonable degree of success, pursued the studies of the college course. I ought to mention that in some instances, of late, the course has been divided. At the option of the student, after the first year, the Modern languages and History with some branches of Physical Science may be substituted for the further prosecution of the Latin and Greek languages and the Mathematics; and students pursuing this latter course are equally entitled to a degree with the others.

The degree of Master of Arts is conferred upon every Bachelor of three years standing, who applies for it and pays the customary fee. After his graduation, the connexion of the student with the University or College ceases. In England, by paying a small annual fee, he continues a member of the University, is entitled to a seat in the *senatus academicus,* and a vote upon all questions coming before that society, and if he choose, may proceed regularly to the higher degrees in the several faculties of Law, Medicine or Divinity. With us, all degrees besides those of A.M. are honorary, and are supposed to be conferred on account of high professional attainment. Colleges confer these degrees on the graduates of each other; although, more properly, I suppose they ought to restrict themselves to their own graduates. These degrees are, as I have said, always conferred by the Board of Visitors, or as it is called, the Corporation.

It has always I believe been found necessary, in order to secure the amount of diligence desirable in a course of academical education, to provide a system of accessory stimulants in addition to those derived from the simple love of truth. The love of pleasure is commonly in young persons, too strong to be controlled by the love of knowledge, or by the remote prospect of professional success. Nay, even the principle of duty too frequently requires to be strengthened by the hope of present advantage; and hence the kind and the degree of stimulants, entering into a College course, derserves a portion of our attention. In the Universities of the continent, the difficulty of procuring situations of honor or emolument, and the impossibility of being admitted to them without good University standing, provides all the stimulus which the nature of the case requires. . . .

In most of our colleges, rank is assigned to the orators at commencement according to scholarship; but even this custom is in danger of passing into desuetude. Some of our institutions, awed by the hoarse growl of popular discontent, have feared that a distinction of this kind savored of aristocracy, and have dropped it like a polluted thing. In but one of our Colleges, to my knowledge, is there any system of premiums for excellence in scholarship. Our community is divided into state sovereignties, and society has here no centre, no heart like London, nor can it ever have. A graduate leaves his College when his course is completed, and his connexion with it and his interest in it cease. We have no centre to which talent of all kinds tends. A class, as soon as it leaves the walls of College, is scattered in a few days to every State and Territory in the union. The College or University forms no integral and necessary part of the social system. It plods on its weary way solitary and in darkness. . . .

The Colleges have but little connexion with each other. The public, when strenuously appealed to, does not deny them money. They are interested in education in general and are desirous that the means of education should be afforded to a large class of the community. But here the interest ceases. After men have bestowed money, they seem utterly indifferent as to the manner in which it is to be employed. The educational system has no necessary connexions with any thing else. In no other country is the whole plan for the instruction of the young so entirely dissevered from connexion with the business of subsequent life. At West Point Military Academy, the standing of a young man in his class, determines his place in the army. Every one must see how strong an impulse this connexion must give to diligence and good behavior. Our Colleges suffer greatly from the want of something of this kind. . . .

To Dissolve Prejudices, Northern Students Should Go South and Southern Students North, 1843 *

. . . For what State, in like circumstances, has in fact, done more in behalf of learning since the Revolution, than North Carolina? It has been her allotment to begin, as well as to achieve; and good success has been her warrant of future encouragement. To sixty-five men, the Trustees of the University, is to some extent given in charge the interests of education. They are resident in different parts of the State, and would in general adorn any community. Were Northern men of letters more fully conversant with

* *The Boston Recorder,* December 14, 1843. Reprinted in *The Fayetteville Observer,* January 31, 1844. Williamson was graduated from Brown University in 1804, studied law and was admitted to the bar, was a member of the Massachusetts State Senate until the separation of Maine from Massachusetts and then served in the State Senate of Maine. He served in Congress from 1821 to 1823. Visiting the University of North Carolina in 1843 he witnessed the examinations and commencement of that institution.

them, their literary institutions and teachers; had they mere personal acquaintance and familiar intercourse with each other, and were there more
reciprocity felt in the same exalted cause; would not the effect give to members of the American family more fraternal mutuality of sentiment and
feeling? Yes, if Northern students of slender constitutions were to pass
their winters at the University of N. Carolina, they could pursue the same
classic course, and would lose no time though they return; while they
enlarge their acquaintances and local knowledge, try the climate, and
probably improve their healths. For like reasons, Southern young men
might pass summers advantageously at the Northern Colleges; and thus
a foundation be laid in early life to dissolve prejudices and inspire a spirit
of fraternity among citizens of this Great Republic, whether they fade
under a Northern, or burn under a Southern sun.

W. D. W. [illiamson]

Program of Studies at the University of Michigan, 1843 *

Year	Term	Languages and Literatures	Mathematics and Science	Intellectual and Moral Sciences
	1	Folsom's *Livy* Xenophon's *Cyro-paedia* and *Anabasis*	Bowdon's *Algebra*	
	2	Livy finished, Horace begun	Algebra finished, Legendre's *Geometry* begun, and Botany	
I		Roman Antiquities Thucydides, Herodotus		
	3	Horace finished Homer's *Odyssey*	Geometry finished; Mensuration, Applications of Algebra to Geometry	
	1	Cicero's *de Senectute* and *de Amicitia* Lysias, Isocrates, and Demosthenes	Plane and Spherical Trigonometry	
II	2	Cicero's *de Oratore* Greek tragedy, and Antiquities Newcomb's *Rhetoric*	Davies' *Descriptive and Analytical Geometry*	
	3	Tacitus' *Vita Agricola* and *Germanii*	Analytic Geometry completed, Bridge's *Conic Sections*	
		Greek tragedy		

* *Joint Documents of the Legislature of Michigan*, 1852, p. 388.

III	1	Cicero's *de Officiis* Greek poetry	Olmstead's *Natural Philosophy,* and *Zoology*	Abercrombie's *Intellectual Power* Paley's *Natural Theology*
	2	Terence Greek poetry, general grammar	Natural Philosophy, and Chemistry	
	3	Whiteley's *Rhetoric*	Olmstead's *Astronomy,* Chemistry continued and Mineralogy	
IV	1	Lectures on the Greek and Latin languages and literatures	Calculus, and Geology	Stuart's *Intellectual Philosophy,* and Cousin's *Psychology*
	2			Whiteley's *Logic* Wayland's *Moral Science* Political Grammar
	3			Studies of the Constitution Wayland's *Political Economy* Butler's *Analogy*

**A Student in the University of North Carolina
to a Friend in Virginia, 1845 ***

UNIVERSITY OF N.C. October 3d 1845.

DEAR RICHARD

I have determined to keep you waiting no longer for an answer to your last, (to me) very acceptable letter; lest you may conclude, that my doses of opium are more frequent, than good reasons will justify. But I assure you old Fellow that a letter from none of my correspondents is received with more real pleasure than one from you. I know that many of mine must necessarily prove unentertaining to you from the staleness of their contents, and I have frequently been inclined to destroy them after they are written and to wait the flood-tide of impulse for a second trial: But knowing that you take pleasure in receiving a letter from a friend though it contain nothing more than the usual salutations and assurances, I forget their imperfections, and derive pleasure from the fact that they are directed to a friend who will appreciate them as a whole, without condensing them in part. Although I am opposed to filling a letter with apologies

* Letter to Richard Irby, Blacks & Whites P. O., Nottoway County, Virginia. The original of this letter is in possession of Mrs. F. H. Jordan, Blackstone, Virginia. Typescript copy is in the Southern Historical Collection, the University of North Carolina.

for neglect and such things, yet I am confident you will excuse my present delay, when you learn, that my time has been occupied in preparing a Senior speech for my debut on the stage. I have just finished it; my subject is "The Shade of the Past." It opens a wide field for the imagination as well as for historical illustration. There are thirty-one Seniors and some very good declaimers and writers. We expect a very large audience; the ladies both of Hillsborough and Pittsborough, (the one 12, the other 18 miles distant) have engaged rooms in the village for the occasion. We have besides 13 young ladies on the (campus) but some of them the worst I ever saw in my life. I suppose that there will be about 30 or 40 young ladies, and as many matrons. We have engaged a band of musicians, and got up a party for the benefit of the few visiters who may honor us with their presence. We have also succeeded in getting the Faculty: content to allow us to speak at candle light; so that it will occupy three evenings in the week; and such gallavanting as there will be. O! hush! I will venture to say that for the last two weeks, Chapel Hill has been the gayest place this side of the Potomac. We have had a delegation of the Pittsborough girls here on a visit, and taking them altogether they are almost ahead of any thing I ever saw. The prettiest, loveliest, liveliest, and most heart-breaking, bone-cracking and study-killing images of Female sweetness, that ever *bustled* in a crowd.

There were three parties as a token of their welcome on the part of the Villagers, and their visit was interspersed with walks, rides, et cetera. For four evenings and five young ladies had 17 visiters each morning. Now a stranger would suppose that common humanity would have groaned under such a weight, but "by Gum" they were primed, charged and as ready for another 17 the fifth evening as they were the first. They left here yesterday and seven of the students accompanyed them up to Pitts'. As such sprees occur but rarely, it is not surprising that the fellows make the most of them. I had a very pleasant trip to Raleigh three weeks ago. My sister and two of her friends from Fayetteville were on a visit at Raleigh; one of the young ladies was recently from Alabama with her brother. They all agreed to ride up here and spend one evening and return the next day, as the Young lady from Alabama also had a brother in College. It was a very agreeable surprise; Campbele (the young lady? brother's name) and myself returned with them in the carriages to Raleigh; we got there on Thursday evening and staid till Tuesday morning. On Friday we carried the girls to a Pic Nic about 7 miles from Raleigh, where we had lots of fun. Monday evening there was a large party in Raleigh and as there are very few *Gallants* there, "Chapel Hill grit" beat even "Nova Scotia". Next morning the girls started down to Fayetteville, we hired buggies and rode with them about 10 miles when we parted. We gathered about a pint of the kissing essence in the parting, and filled the jug, after we got to Raleigh with the best old double-distilled Rye in the city. I have kept the best secret for the last; *Ella Marion* was one of the three! and I reckon you can guess who I rode with and talked to all the time "most hardly". It was as much as Campbele could do, to get me back to college, But I will turn over a leaf and change the subject. Our regular Sessional Spree came off last Friday week, about 20 or 30 fellows disguised with calico coats and pants, and paper hats plumed with chicken feathers sallied out in the campus about 11 o'clock at night. They commenced ringing the bell, blowing horns, shooting pistols, and then forming a line, would charge against the trees, and piles of Rocks with a savage vengeance. The Faculty came on the ground, and one attempted to enter one of the passages; the fellows ducked him with two buckets of water, pelted him with apples and finally threw a wash basin at him which made him desist. The Spors in the campus marched round to each of the Tutor's rooms and rocked their windows; after which they dispersed. But the Faculty had concealed themselves near the entrance of the passages, and recognized the fellows as they would go in their rooms. They had up about 20, but only 5 were dismissed; the others were too slipery tongued to be caught. While there are occasional sprees here, generally very good order prevails. The institution is without doubt the best in the country.

I cannot concieve the reason of Luther's not answering my letter written more than two months ago; have you heard from him lately; I saw Sid in Raleigh, and got some wholesome talks from the old fellow on various subjects. And Miss Pad told Lomap that the reason she did not consent to marry him before, was that she loved another better! I wonder if that wasn't you Toby? But she is married thank God, and now if I can stop one other soft-pated petticoat there, I will be satisfied.

Brother Thomas left Fayetteville on Monday last for Texas! I have almost concluded to get married as soon as I graduate and follow suit. Remember me to your brother and each of the Family, to John Howard and all my old acquaintances. Tell me in your next Miss Anna Boothe's post office. Don't be frightened as I am only going to send her an "address". This letter I have been compelled to write between recitation and dinner which must be its apology.

Write soon to yours as ever,

WILLIAM K. BLAKE

Defense of the Classics and Criticisms of the Elective System, 1852 *

The early life of these colleges was the epoch of their palmy existence. They were felt to be realities. They catered to no popular prejudices, but honestly aimed at the truly useful—the development of the youthful mind. And if Connecticut and Massachusetts have held an honourable place in the history of our country, if they always had the sagacity to perceive

* *The Southern Quarterly Review*, VI, New Series (1852), pp. 474-77.

their true interests, and the manliness to maintain them, it is due mainly to the efforts of their conscientious labourers in the field of instruction, who had a living faith in the utility of those departments of knowledge which our modern philosophers would discard as inconsistent with the spirit of the age.

We have not at present the means of knowing what amount of classical studies was pursued in the early existence of these colleges. We have reason to believe that it was considerably more than at present. This is certainly true of Latin. This was the conventional language of Europe, and all college theses were maintained in that language. In the life time of President Stiles, of Yale College, who died in 1796, all official intercourse between the officers and students of the college was in Latin; it is now, we believe, used only on State occasions. A glance at the curriculum now pursued, will make it obvious that no student can be expected to converse in Latin. Besides a very moderate amount of Latin required for admission, a few books of Livy, of Tacitus, and Horace, constitute the whole course. Bad as this is, the deficiency in Greek is perhaps greater. For admission, it is sufficient to be able to translate from Dalzell's Graeca Minora, or some such elementary work; and notwithstanding that Yale perhaps excels all others in the Greek department, even here the student is supposed to have completed his course at the end of the junior year. It is not wonderful, then, that so many graduates are unable to read Greek; that they sometimes forget even the characters; nor is it strange that many of them are foremost in denouncing, as time lost, that which is spent in learning what is so speedily forgotten.

The multiplicity of professors, and the impossibility of finding work for them, has, in some colleges, given rise to what is called the elective system. In Harvard, after the Sophomore year, students may select for themselves the departments which they desire to prosecute. This is done, indeed, with the approbation and consent of parents and guardians; and the statutes of the college ordain, that when no such election is made for the student, the Faculty shall make it for him. The elective studies are Greek, Latin, German, Spanish, and the higher branches of pure mathematics. Those of obligation are ethics, rhetoric, metaphysics, natural philosophy, and astronomy. It does not appear from their annual catalogue what course they assign to those students whose course of study is referred to the discretion of the Faculty.

To this system of elective studies many objections may be urged. The students no longer stand on an equal footing with regard to each other and consequently much of that wholesome emulation which should exist in a college is lost. The attempt to introduce a partial course in the Charleston College, under Dr. Adams, had this result, and was abandoned.

But perhaps a more serious objection to the system may be found in the virtual abandonment by the Faculty of the high prerogative of abso lutely guiding the education of youth. A College Faculty should be a unit. Each member should regard every other as a collaborator in the great work which he has undertaken to perform; and this can be done, only by assigning to each a reasonable portion of their common time. As soon as preferences are shown to one over another, the sense of unity is destroyed, and the esprit du corps in danger of being annihilated.

It is urged with great plausibility, that by the introduction of the elective system, a spirit of emulation is excited in the Faculty, and each member is interested to exert himself to secure scholars for himself. Something is unquestionably due to this consideration, but the Faculty which gives way to it, abandons high ground, and exposes itself to the danger of catering, not merely to the public prejudice, but what is far worse, to the tastes and prejudices of the very persons the training of whose minds is committed to its discretion.

A college must pay some respect to the spirit of the age. The Faculty which should adhere obstinately to ancient usages, is in danger of being supplanted by one which is more pliable. But there is one ground which no college can abandon without incurring the guilt of suicide. It must maintain the right of deciding absolutely what it shall teach. Interference in this respect is not to be tolerated. Dictation from without should be regarded as an unwarrantable interference. Every student committed to its care, should be referred absolutely to its discretion; and the parent or guardian who should undertake to direct the course of instruction for his son, should be respectfully invited to remove him. A college which occupies this elevated position will wield a moral power far higher than that which, referring the course of education to the discretion of others, reduces itself to the condition of a mere usher, paid to impart instruction in certain specific branches of popular education.

The great evil under which American colleges labour, is the tender age at which youths are admitted. They are frequently required to pursue studies which their minds are incapable of grasping. The only remedy for this is to increase the difficulties of admission. The tendency of the grammar schools is always to overtake the college. Require more of the candidate for admission, and at the same time you elevate the character of the grammar school. The curriculum of American colleges occupies four years. The tendency of the schools is to reduce it to three. Whenever this becomes general, the college should instantly take a step forward, and by requiring more of the candidate, enable itself to impart a more extended course of instruction. Thus, if the candidates generally enter the Sophomore class, the college should at once advance the terms of admission to the Freshman class to that point. It would be sufficient, perhaps, to extend this rule merely to classical studies. It is important that boys should read more classics. All our text-books contain references to them, which the student is supposed to have read, but which, under existing circumstances he has no time to read.

The Legislature of Illinois Recommends that Congress Provide for Industrial Universities, 1853 *

Whereas, the spirit and progress of this age and country demand the culture of the highest order of intellectual attainment in theoretic and industrial science; and

Whereas, it is impossible that our commerce and prosperity will continue to increase without calling into requisition all the elements of internal thrift arising from the labors of the farmer, the mechanic, and the manufacturer, by every fostering effort within the reach of the government; and

Whereas, a system of Industrial Universities, liberally endowed in each state of the union, co-operative with each other, and with the Smithsonian Institute at Washington, would develop a more liberal and practical education among the people, tend to more intellectualize the rising generation and eminently conduct to the virtue, intelligence and true glory of our common country; therefore be it

Resolved, by the House of Representatives, the Senate concurring herein, That our Senators in Congress be instructed, and our Representatives be requested, to use their best exertions to procure the passage of a law of Congress donating to each state in the Union an amount of public lands not less in value than five hundred thousand dollars, for the liberal endowment of a system of Industrial Universities, one in each state in the Union, to co-operate with each other, and with the Smithsonian Institute at Washington, for the more liberal and practical education of our industrial classes and their teachers; a liberal and varied education, adapted to the manifold wants of a practical and enterprising people, and a provision for such educational facilities being in manifest concurrence with the intimations of the popular will, it urgently demands the united efforts of our strength.

* Given in Edmund J. James, *The Origin of the Land Grant Act of 1862 and Some Account of Its Author, Jonathan B. Turner* (Urbana, Illinois, University of Illinois Press, 1910), pp. 16, 17; also pp. 95, 96. James says (p. 8): "There is no desire to detract one iota from the credit due Mr. Morrill for his earnest, wise and persistent advocacy of the policy of Federal Aid to education. By his action on this subject he gained and deserved the name of statesman and his glory and reputation will wax with the passing years while that of many of his colleagues who were more prominent at the time will wane and pass away; ... All honor to him for his early work and above all for his continued support of this policy once begun. On the other hand, the credit for first having devised and formulated the original plan and of having worked up the public interest in the measure so that it could be passed belongs clearly to Professor Turner and should be accorded him." Turner was born in Massachusetts, studied at Salem Academy and Yale College, and from 1833 to 1847 was professor in Illinois College, Jacksonville, where he taught Latin and Greek, rhetoric and belles-lettres. He was one of the organizers of the Illinois Teachers' Association and worked for the free school law of 1855 in that state. He served also as principal director of the Industrial League of Illinois.

Resolved, That the Governor is hereby authorized to forward a copy of the foregoing resolutions to our Senators and Representatives in Congress, and to the Executive and Legislature of each of our sister States, inviting them to co-operate with us in this meritorious enterprise.

Henry Harrisse on the Powers and Duties
of Collegiate Trustees, 1854 *

A Trustee is generally a retired public officer, a gentleman of leisure or an influential lawyer who knows but little and cares still less about the management of a literary institution. His title was conferred as a mere compliment, or on account of his well known abilities in other pursuits. Often, however, it is simply by reason of his high-sounding name. We know of such trustees who have been figuring in college catalogues for twenty years, without ever attending a single monthly or annual meeting.

Our trustees are men of experience and activity. We do not wish a numerous board, but a few diligent members who are required and never fail to attend, all the regular examinations; thus adding by their presence, importance to a ceremony which in some colleges is rapidly degenerating into a solemn mockery.

The number of trustees is limited to ten. The President of the college is ex-officio a member, has a vote, but is ineligible to the office of chairman of the Board. He, however, with four of the trustees, can call occasional meetings whenever it appears necessary. Six members and the President of the college are the number to constitute a quorum, and to fill up, by ballot, any vacancies that may occur either in the Board or in the Faculty.

The trustees elect, and may remove from office, the President and all the officers connected with the Institution.

They prescribe and amend the course of studies to be pursued by the students. They meet regularly at the end of each term, and individually visit the college by turns at least four times in the year.

They have the exclusive right of expelling a student; and may reverse

---

* Edgar W. Knight (Ed.), *Henry Harrisse on Collegiate Education* (Chapel Hill, University of North Carolina Press, 1947), p. 30. Harrisse was born in France, was a member of the faculty of the University of North Carolina in the 1850's and while there wrote an essay "On the Organization, Regulation and Management of a Literary Institution Best Adapted to the Wants and Interests of North Carolina" in a competition for a prize of $200 offered by Normal College (which developed into Trinity College, now Duke University) for the best essay on the subject. The original of the essay is the property of the New York Public Literary. Microcopy is in the Southern Historical Collection, the University of North Carolina. The essay was edited and first published in 1947.

Harrisse is perhaps best and most favorably known for his services to American scholarship. He was a keen student, a bibliophile and devoted book-collector, a distinguished bibliographer, the author of the "monumental volume," *Bibliotheca Americana Vetustissima,* and remarkable works on Columbus, and he "produced no less than ninety-one separate titles, books, monographs, papers and articles, each one of which was a noteworthy contribution to American history." Randolph G. Adams, *Three Americanists* (Philadelphia, University of Pennsylvania Press, 1939), p. 2.

all sentences of suspension pronounced by the Faculty. All other penalties, their degree and mode of infliction, are wholly left to the Faculty. We need not add that corporeal punishments of any sort are strictly prohibited.

The Trustees confer degrees; and if anyone fails to attend the board during four state meetings in succession, it is deemed a refusal to act, and the board proceeds to appoint a successor; except of course in case of sickness or temporary absence from the State at the time.

A Senator in the Legislature of Texas Opposed the Bill for a University, 1856 *

Mr. Armstrong moved to amend the Bill by striking out the word "University" wherever it occurred in the Bill and insert *"Common Schools in the several counties of the State"* and said, I have offered the amendment to decide the question whether the masses of the people or a few shall be the recipients of the benefits of our legislation. Common schools are for the people generally. Universities are for those who are most able to pay for their education. . . .

I am no advocate of the University system. My plan is *first* Common Schools then Seminaries of learning in the counties. The Common Schools above all. Universities are the ovens to heat up and hatch all manner of vice, immorality and crime. Where the youth is removed from the presence of their parents and guardians, they run into every excess and come forth steeped in sin and reckless of all consequences. While the youth reared in the country, mingling manual labor with his studies, where their physical and mental faculties are alike strengthened, cultivated and developed. Among the first class there are some exceptions, but among the last class of students, we must look for the heroes and statesmen who shall govern and defend our beloved country. When war is the word, then you see who does the fighting and suffers the fatigues of marching. They come from the masses of the people, and not from the colleges, with few exceptions. In the country schools we find all the virtues which ennoble our race taught and practiced. I do not say that virtue is wanting in Universities, but I speak comparatively. I say let the system of education be like a pyramid beginning at the foundation. General information first among the people. Then our liberties as a free people, are safe; but let the masses be left in ignorance and superstition and the educated few will soon reduce

* H. Y. Benedict, *A Source Book of the University of Texas*, pp. 58-61. Governor Pease in his message to the legislature November 6, 1855, urged the establishment of a university in that state and a bill was introduced in the Senate to create a fund for the purpose. Sharp debate in both the House and the Senate began and continued during that session and the next, with the struggle ending in 1858 when a bill for a University was approved. Some people urged two universities, one in the eastern and one in the western part of the state; some urged only one; and there were those who were opposed to any.

them to the condition of the down-trodden nations of the Old World, who are mere property in the hands of those for whom they toil. . . .

The diffusion of useful knowledge among the people generally should be our first care—discarding all the useless reading of the age. Of what avail is it that the youth can tell you of lost languages or obsolete sciences, or that they should puzzle their brains with the visionary theories of the ancient schoolmen in trying to discover how they could travel from one place to another without passing the intermediate space? Cannot the youth of the country at the school houses travel from his spelling book to the celestial mechanics of La Place? Is it not as fit a place to learn all things for man to know the school houses as the college. I say more so, for there are too many allurements and attractions around the fashionable and crowded universities for the youth to contemplate upon the knotty questions in philosophy and mathematics; not so at the school houses. The abatement of universities will send the teachers to the schools. Schools in every neighborhood will be filled with intelligent teachers and pupils, and the people will have among them all the means of useful information, but the contrary if the sciences are favored at a few places. It is putting it out of the power of the people generally to send off their children to col-- lege. They must remain at home to aid their parents to obtain a support, while the sons and daughters of the wealthy, can enjoy the privilege and receive the benefits of the poor man's money in attending these Universities built by the State. Making the poor man contribute to educate the rich man's child while his own children labor. Making the poor man subservient to the rich, a species of legislation at variance with the principles of a democratic government. I do not speak this to draw distinctions, but I must say it is anything but republican and democratic. It is a tendency, a leaning to the remnants of exclusivism, a longing after the principles of centralism. Our government is the people, then let our institutions of learning and all privileges of free government belong to the people, and leave it to the other governments to teach the few to rule the many, the few to enjoy the blood and toil of the many. I say first common schools, afterwards, and when needed, other institutions of learning might be encouraged, but the time has not yet come for the university system to be established by the State. . . .

The Senator from Brazoria argues that erection of universities in our own State will dispense with the necessity of sending our children to the North to be educated, there to receive their impressions of the North injurious to the rights of the South, to be taught principles at variance with the South. I reply, let them have their children educated in the seminaries and schools of our State, established and to be established in our State without aid. Let them erect such institutions in our own State. Those who are able to pay for university education in the North are able to apply the same means in our State. Their State pride will prompt them without legislative incentives and assistance. As to our youth being denied intercourse with the people of the North, I differ with the Senator. It is our duty to mingle with and associate with our fellow-citizens of the North. We are citizens of one Government, one common country. We can best understand our common wants by associating together, and regarding each other as belonging to one great neighborhood. We ought to encourage by every means the most intimate and friendly relations with our brethren of the North. Let us inform the various sections of the Union of our common and separate rights—our common duty, and interest, and mutual dependence on each other, and we will be the better enabled to understand our relative rights and duties. And in no way can our friendly relations with our brethren be better prompted than by a genial intercourse encouraged by every possible means. Let us not denounce in general terms the whole North, for it is to the conservative power of the national democratic party of the North that we look for the protection of Southern rights and the maintenance of the guarantees of the constitution. We look to that party for our rights, yet we condemn and denounce the whole North. We teach doctrines of non-intercourse with the North. We would discourage all friendly connections and intercourse with the North. Yet we turn to the democratic party in all times of trouble. If we by our acts alienate the feelings of the people of the North, we may expect nothing from them and then will follow in haste the dissolution of the Union with all its disastrous consequences.

Williams College in 1856 *

Williams College in 1856 was an institution of modest pretensions. Its faculty consisted of but nine members, all of them full professors, and the four classes averaged less than sixty each. There may have been half a dozen "special" students who were taking a partial course; but almost all were candidates for the degree of bachelor of arts. The curriculum was perfectly rigid; all the work was required; the only electives were in the junior year, when we were permitted to choose betwen French and German. The classes were not divided, the instructional force did not admit of that; the whole class met, three times a day, in the recitation room; naturally a student became pretty well acquainted with all his classmates. There was some advantage in the fact that all the instruction was given by full professors; tutorial assistants had been called in, in former years, but there was none of it in my day.

The teaching was mainly by means of textbooks and oral recitations;

* Washington Gladden, *Recollections* (Boston, Houghton Mifflin Co., 1909), pp. 69-73. Used by permission. Gladden was a student in Williams when the celebrated Mark Hopkins was president of the college. For the origin of Amherst College in Massachusetts, see Noah Webster, *A Collection of Papers on Political, Literary and Moral Subjects* (New York, Webster and Clark, 1843), pp. 225-54. For Webster's part in the founding of this institution, see Harry Warfel, *Noah Webster: Schoolmaster to America* (New York, The Macmillian Co., 1936), chapter XV, "Founder of Amherst College."

lectures were few; in the last two years there were a few courses, but note-books were not much used in my time. The range of teaching was not wide. In the first two years Greek, Latin, and mathematics took up nearly all the time; in the sophomore year there was a course in Weber's *Universal History*. No English was required for entrance, and the only English work of the first two years was one or two themes each term, with an occasional declamation before the class. There was also a speaking exercise, every Wednesday afternoon at the chapel, which the entire college was required to attend, and there were two speakers from each class; seniors and juniors presented original orations, sophomores and freshmen declaimed. The president and the professor of rhetoric presided, and criticised each speaker at the close of his performance.

In the junior year there were lessened rations of Latin and Greek, and some elementary instruction in science was given, so that every graduate might have some notion of the groundwork of botany and chemistry, physics and astronomy, and mineralogy and geology; a single term was sufficient for political economy, and the tale of the themes was slightly increased. The senior year was devoted largely to mental and moral science, logic, the elements of rhetoric, and criticism, and the evidences of Christianity, with Paley's *Natural Theology* and Butler's *Analogy*. I have reproduced the curriculum wholly from memory, but I think that I have not omitted anything essential.

Something like this was, I suppose, the course of study in most of the New England colleges of that period. Compare it with the bulletins of any one of them today, and it seems a meagre provision for a liberal education. Yet there was enough in this, if rightly used, to secure a fair amount of mental discipline, and to guide inquiring minds toward the things worth knowing.

Better than the methods of instruction was the personal contact with the instructors. Every student in college was personally known by every member of the faculty, and the personal interests of the teachers in the students was as paternal as the students would permit. . . .

The conspicuous figure of the college was its President, Mark Hopkins, one of the four or five great teachers that America has produced. In 1856 he was in his prime, fifty-four years of age, tall, with a slight stoop, but stalwart, with a swinging gait. Over the great dome which crowned the broad forehead, and which was now nearly denuded of its covering, long brown locks were coaxed; and the strong chin and the Roman nose, with the eyes that glanced from under beetling brows, made up a countenance of great dignity and benignity. There was but one opinion about Dr. Hopkins in college; among the students his intellectual prowess was not disputed, and the wisdom and integrity of his character were never ques-tioned. Every man has his foibles, and those who stood nearest to President Hopkins must have known what were his; but the student body, generally quick enough to spy out inconsistencies and weaknesses, were always singularly unanimous and enthusiastic in its loyalty to the great president.

He preached, frequently, in the village church, whose galleries the students occupied; and these extemporaneous discourses, delivered with great deliberation and dignity, while they always held our attention, were not apt to awaken our enthusiasm; but the baccalaureate sermon was always an event. That was fully written; its philosophical framework was strong, its logic was convincing, and it was delivered with a power and fervor which made a lasting impression.

It was in the senior year that the students came in touch with Dr. Hopkins; a large share of the work of that year was in his hands; the seniors met him every day and sometimes twice; in philosophy and ethics, in logic and theology, he was their only teacher. The tradition of his masterful instruction was always descending; the freshmen heard of it from all above them; it was the expectation of every student that, however unsatisfactory other parts of the course might turn out to be, there would be something worth while in the senior year. The expectation was not disappointed. There was nothing sensational in Dr. Hopkins' teaching; his method was quiet and familiar; his bearing was modest and dignified; but he was a past-master in the art of questioning; he knew how by adroit suggestion to kindle the interest of his pupils in the subject under discussion, and by humor and anecdote he made dry topics vital and deep waters clear. What his best students got from him was not so much conclusions or results of investigation, as a habit of mind, a method of philosophic approach, a breadth and balance of thought, which might serve them in future study. What Garfield said (I heard him say it, at a Williams banquet at Delmonico's in New York) expresses the feeling of many other graduates of the Berkshire college: "A pine bench, with Mark Hopkins at one end of it and me at the other, is a good enough college for me". . . .

College life in that time was very simple. The college buildings were plainness itself, wholly devoid of architectural pretensions; the furniture of most of the rooms was far from luxurious; the expense of living was light. My board, in a club, the first term, cost me $2.30 a week; it never exceeded $2.75 a week. The entire expense of my college course, for three years, including clothing, was less than $900. Several of the students who boarded themselves, in their own rooms, brought the cost far within that figure.

Several Greek-letter fraternities were flourishing, and there was an anti-secret confederation which made war upon them, but was quite as clannish as they were. None of these societies had houses of their own; they were content with humble quarters, which they rented in private houses, or in lofts over village stores.

A large place in the life of the college was taken by the two rival literary societies—the Philologian and the Philotechnian—to the one or the other of which every student belonged. These societies had well-furnished rooms in one of the dormitories, with libraries of three or four thousand volumes each. Their weekly meetings were events of no little interest to the college community; the program generally included one or two original orations, a debate, sometimes a poem, an essay or two, and the report of the censor upon the performances of the previous meeting. The two societies were united in the Adelphic Union, which gave three or four debates or exhibitions annually, in the chapel or the village church.

The summer vacation was short, not more than five or six weeks, and there was a long winter vacation, beginning at Thanksgiving and continuing into January, that students who were supporting themselves might teach in the winter terms of country schools. All my winters were thus employed.

A Sketch of Woodward High School in Cincinnati, 1856 *

The System of Common Schools in Cincinnati was established in 1828-29 under a special act of the Legislature, by which a tax of $7000. was annually imposed for the building of school-houses, and a like amount, in addition to the state appropriation, for the support of schools. Under this act schoolhouses were erected, in point of location, size, and internal convenience, greatly in advance of the then generally received notions as to school architecture.

In 1834 the system was greatly extended, and in 1845 the trustees were authorized to establish schools of different grades, and in 1850 to appoint a superintendent.

In 1847 a central high school was organized, and in 1852 the Woodward Fund and the Hughes Fund, amounting to $300,000, and yielding over $5000. (the Woodward estate, in 1856, yielded $4510.), were united for the purpose of sustaining two schools of this grade.

In 1853 a building was erected for the accommodation of the Hughes High School, at an expense, including lot, of about $40,000, and in 1856, in an opposite section of the city, another building, at a cost of $50,000, for the Woodward High School. The latter, built in the Tudor style of architecture, was of brick and three stories high, with a high basement. The basement contained two Philosophical Rooms, 27⅔ x 42⅔ feet in size; and four furnaces. The first and second floors were alike and contained four classrooms each, while the third floor was given over to a Lecture Hall, 68⅔ x 83⅔ feet in size, a large platform, and two small ante rooms. The building was warmed by four hot-air furnaces, and lighted by gas.

* *American Journal of Education*, IV (1858), pp. 520-25.

The course of study and textbooks for both schools, as prescribed by the school board in January, 1856, was as follows:

FIRST YEAR

First Session

English Grammar, Brown or Pinneo, completed
English History, Goodrich or Markham, completed
Ray's Algebra, to Sec. 172

Second Session

Weld's Latin Lessons, to Part II.
Fitch's Physical Geography
Andrews' and Stoddard's Latin Grammar
Ray's Algebra, to Sec. 305
Physical Geography (3 lessons)
Reading (2 lessons)

(Five lessons in each of the above weekly)

Once a Week During the Year

Lectures, by the Principal, on Morals and Manners
Aids to Composition, completed
Composition and Declamation, by sections, each once in three weeks
Reading and Vocal Music
Penmanship, if needed

SECOND YEAR

First Session

Weld's Latin Lessons, to History
Andrews' and Stoddard's Latin Grammar
Geometry, Davies' Legendre, to Book V
Gray's Natural Philosophy, to Pneumatics

Second Session

Weld's Latin Lessons, completed
Andrews and Stoddard, completed
Geometry, Davies' Legendre, to Book IX
Gray's Natural Philosophy, completed

(Five lessons in each of the above weekly)

Once a Week During the Year

Reading, Elemental Sounds
Rhetoric and Vocal Music
Composition and Declamation, by sections

THIRD YEAR

First Session

Silliman's Chemistry, to Sec. 282
Algebra and Spherics, Ray's and Davies' Legendre completed
Andrews' Caesar or Sallust, 50 Sections (3d)
German or French (3 days)

Second Session

Silliman's Chemistry, to Vegetable Chemistry
Davies' Trigonometry, completed
Cooper's Virgil's Aeneid, 3 books (3d)
German or French (3 days)

Once a Week Throughout the Year

> Constitution of the United States
> Hedge's Logic
> Reading, Rhetoric, and Vocal Music
> Composition and Declamation, by sections

FOURTH YEAR

First Session	*Second Session*
Cutter's Physiology & Hygiene	Davies' Navigation and Surveying
McIntire's Astronomy	Weber's General History
Gray and Adams' Geology	Wayland's Mental Philosophy
Folsom's Cicero, 3 Orations (3 days)	Evidences of Christianity (1 day)
Moral Philosophy (1 day)	German or French (3 days)
German or French (3 days)	

Once a Week Throughout the Year

> Critical Readings, Vocal Music
> Compositions, by sections
> Original Addresses, by sections

COLLEGE CLASS

For those preparing to enter college, the following may be substituted for the regular studies of the fourth year,

> Virgil's Aeneid, six books
> Caesar or Sallust, completed
> Cicero's Orations, six
> Crosby's Greek Grammar
> Felton's Greek Reader

An Act to Establish the University of Texas, 1858 *

Whereas, From the earliest times, it has been the cherished design of the people of the Republic and of the State of Texas, that there shall be established, within her limits, an Institution of learning, for the instruction of the youths of the land in the higher branches of learning, and in the liberal arts and sciences, and to be so endowed, supported and maintained, as to place within the reach of our people, whether rich or poor, the opportunity of conferring upon the sons of the State, a thorough education, and as a means whereby the attachment of the young men of the State to the interest, the institution, the rights of the State, and the liberties of the people, might be encouraged and increased, and to this end, hitherto liberal appropriations of the public domain have been made; and,

Whereas, The increasing population and wealth of the State, and the

* H. P. N. Gammel (Comp.) *The Laws of Texas*, IV, pp. 1020-23.

tendency of events, indicate the fitness of now putting that cherished design in effect, therefore,

Section 1. Be it enacted by the Legislature of the State of Texas, That there is hereby established, within this State, an Institution of learning, to be styled "The University of Texas," to be located at such place and in such manner as may be determined by law.

Sec. 2. The sum of one hundred thousand dollars of the United States bonds in the Treasury not otherwise appropriated, is hereby set apart and appropriated to the establishment and maintenance of the same. The fifty leagues of land, which, by the Act of January 26, 1839, entitled "An Act appropriating certain lands for the establishment of a general system of education," were set apart and appropriated for the establishment and endowment of two Colleges or Universities, are hereby set apart and appropriated to the establishment and maintenance of the University of Texas. There is hereby set apart and appropriated to the same purpose, one section of land out of every ten sections of land which have heretofore been, or may hereafter be surveyed and reserved for the use of the State, under the provisions of the Act of January 30, 1854, entitled "An Act to encourage the construction of railroads in Texas by donations of land," and under the provisions of any general or special law heretofore passed, granting lands to railroad companies, and under the provisions of the Act of February 11, 1854, granting lands to the Galveston and Brazos Navigation Company. The Governor of the State shall select the sections hereby appropriated, so that no sections selected shall adjoin, out of the lands now surveyed, as soon as practicable, and out of the lands hereafter to be surveyed, as soon thereafter as practicable, and shall cause a record to be made, in the Land Office of the State, of the sections so selected; and, thereupon, it shall be the duty of the Commissioner of the General Land Office to designate, upon the maps, the sections so selected as University lands. The sale of these sections shall hereafter be regulated by special law.

Sec. 3. The control, management and supervision, of the University, and the care and preservation of its property, subject always to the control of the legislature, is committed to a Board of ten persons, to be styled "The Administrators of the University of Texas," which shall be composed of the Governor of the State of Texas, the Chief Justice of the Supreme Court of Texas, and eight others, who shall be appointed by the Governor, by and with the consent of the Senate, to hold office for four years, and until their successors are qualified. The Administrators shall receive no compensation for their services.

Sec. 4. The following branches of learning shall be taught at the University, viz: Ancient and Modern Languages, the different branches of Mathematics, pure and physical, Natural Philosophy, Chemistry, Mineralogy, including Geology, the principles of Agriculture, Botany, Anatomy, Surgery and Medicine, Zoology, History, Ethics, Rhetoric and Belles-

Lettres, Civil Government, Political Economy, the Law of Nature, of Nations, and Municipal Law.

Sec. 5. The religious tenet of any person shall not be made a condition of admission to any privilege or office in the University; nor shall any course of religious instruction be taught or allowed, of a sectarian character and tendency.

Sec. 6. The Administrators shall have the power to appoint the President, Faculty, Instructors, and Officers, of the University, and prescribe the course of instruction and discipline to be observed, in the University. They shall fix the salaries of the President, Faculty, Instructors, and Officers of the University. Five of the Administrators, with the Governor or the Chief Justice, lawfully convened, shall be a quorum for the transaction of business. They shall meet at least once in every year, for the transaction of business, and shall keep a record of their proceedings. They shall have a Secretary, to be elected by them. They shall have power to make all regulations, which to them, shall seem expedient for carrying into effect the design contemplated by the establishment of this University, not inconsistent with the laws of the State.

Sec. 7. The administrators shall have the right of conferring, on any person whom they think worthy thereof, all literary honors and degrees known and usually granted by any University or College in the United States or elsewhere.

Sec. 8. The Administrators shall report to the Legislature, at each session, the situation of the affairs of the University.

Sec. 9. Instruction at the University shall be free, and the Administrators shall prescribe what degree of proficiencies shall entitle students to admission.

Sec. 10. A committee, to be appointed by the Legislature at each session, shall attend the annual examinations of the students of the University, and report to the Legislature thereon.

Sec. 11. The reasonable expenses incurred by the Administrators and visiting committee, in the discharge of their duties, shall be paid out of the funds of the University.

Sec. 12. The Treasurer of the State shall be Treasurer of the University funds.

Sec. 13. So soon as the location of the University is determined upon, it shall be the duty of the Administrators to proceed to the construction of the necessary buildings, and for that purpose, shall procure the services of a competent architect, who shall superintend the work; such plan and design for the building shall be adopted, as shall be consistent with the addition of wings or other structures hereafter, without marring the architectural beauty and fitness of the whole. There shall be constructed suitable buildings for the accommodation of the Professors and their families. The contracts for the buildings shall require the performance of the work under ample security for its fitness and faithfulness.

Sec. 14. The expenditure of the University, for the construction of buildings, or otherwise, shall be made under the order of the Administrators; and when money is required for the payment of the same, it shall be drawn upon the warrant of the Governor, countersigned by the Secretary, upon the Treasurer, who shall pay the same out of the University funds. And this Act shall take effect and be in force from and after its passage.

Approved February 11, 1858.

The Veto Message of President James Buchanan on the Morrill Bill, 1859 *

WASHINGTON CITY, *February 24, 1859.*
To the House of Representatives of the United States:

I return with my objections to the House of Representatives, in which it originated, the bill entitled "An act donating public lands to the several States and Territories which may provide colleges for the benefit of agriculture and mechanic arts," presented to me on the 18th instant.

This bill makes a donation to the several States of 20,000 acres of the public lands for each Senator and Representative in the present Congress, and also an additional donation of 20,000 acres for each additional Representative to which any State may be entitled under the census of 1860.

According to a report from the Interior Department, based upon the present number of Senators and Representatives, the lands given to the States amount to 6,060,000 acres, and their value, at the minimum Government price of $1.25 per acre, to $7,575,000.

The object of this gift, as stated by the bill, is "the endowment, support, and maintenance of at least one college (in each State) where the leading object shall be, without excluding other scientific or classical studies, to teach such branches of learning as are related to agriculture and the mechanic arts, as the legislatures of the States may respectively prescribe, in order to promote the liberal and practical education of the industrial classes in the several pursuits and professions in life."

As there does not appear from the bill to be any beneficiaries in existence to which this endowment can be applied, each State is required "to provide, within five years at least, not less than one college, or the grant to said State shall cease." In that event the "said State shall be bound to pay the United States the amount received of any lands previously sold, and that the title to purchasers under the State shall be valid."

The grant in land itself is confined to such States as have public lands within their limits worth $1.25 per acre in the opinion of the governor.

* James D. Richardson, *A Compilation of the Messages and Papers of the Presidents* (Washington, Government Printing Office, 1897), V, pp. 543-50.

For the remaining States the Secretary of the Interior is directed to issue "land scrip to the amount of their distributive shares in acres under the provisions of this act, said scrip to be sold by said States, and the proceeds thereof applied to the uses and purposes prescribed in this act, and for no other use or purpose whatsoever." The lands are granted and the scrip is to be issued "in sections or subdivisions of sections of not less than one-quarter of a section."

According to an estimate from the Interior Department, the number of acres which will probably be accepted by States having public lands within their own limits will not exceed 580,000 acres (and it may be much less), leaving a balance of 5,480,000 acres to be provided for by scrip. These grants of land and land scrip to each of the thirty-three States are made upon certain conditions, the principal of which is that if the fund shall be lost or diminished on account of unfortunate investments or otherwise the deficiency shall be replaced and made good by the respective States.

I shall now proceed to state my objections to this bill. I deem it to be both inexpedient and unconstitutional.

1. This bill has been passed at a period when we can with great difficulty raise sufficient revenue to sustain the expenses of the Government. Should it become a law the Treasury will be deprived of the whole, or nearly the whole, of our income from the sale of public lands, which for the next fiscal year has been estimated at $5,000,000.

A bare statement of the case will make this evident. The minimum price at which we dispose of our lands is $1.25 per acre. At the present moment, however, the price has been reduced to those who purchase the bounty-land warrants of the old soldiers to 85 cent per acre, and of these warrants there are still outstanding and unlocated, as appears by a report (February 12, 1859) from the General Land Office, the amount of 11,990, 391 acres. This has already greatly reduced the current sales by the Government and diminished the revenue from this source. If in addition thirty-three States shall enter the market with their land scrip, the price must be greatly reduced below even 85 cents per acre, as much to the prejudice of the old soldiers who have not already parted with their land warrants as to Government. It is easy to perceive that with this glut of the market Government can sell little or no lands at $1.25 per acre, when the price of bounty-land warrants and scrip shall be reduced to half this sum. This source of revenue will be almost entirely dried up. Under the bill the States may sell their land scrip at any price it may bring. There is no limitation whatever in this respect. Indeed, they must sell for what the scrip will bring, for without this fund they can not proceed to establish their colleges within the five years to which they are limited. It is manifest, therefore, that to the extent to which this bill will prevent the sale of public lands at $1.25 per acre, to that amount it will have precisely the same effect upon the Treasury as if we should impose a tax to create a loan to endow these State colleges.

Surely the present is the most unpropitious moment which could have been selected for the passage of this bill.

2. Waiving for the present the question of constitutional power, what effect will this bill have on the relations established between the Federal and State Governments? The Constitution is a grant to Congress of a few enumerated but most important powers, relating chiefly to war, peace, foreign and domestic commerce, negotiation, and other subjects which can be best or alone exercised beneficially by the common Government. All other powers are reserved to the States and to the people. For the efficient and harmonious working of both, it is necessary that their several spheres of action should be kept distinct from each other. This alone can prevent conflict and mutual injury. Should the time ever arrive when the State governments shall look to the Federal Treasury for the means of supporting themselves and maintaining their systems of education and internal policy, the character of both Governments will be greatly deteriorated. The representatives of the States and of the people, feeling a more immediate interest in obtaining money to lighten the burdens of their constituents than for the promotion of the more distant objects intrusted to the Federal Government, will naturally incline to obtain means from the Federal Government for State purposes. If a question shall arise between an appropriation of land or money to carry into effect the objects of the Federal Government and those of the States, their feelings will be enlisted in favor of the latter. This is human nature; and hence the necessity of keeping the two Governments entirely distinct. The preponderance of this home feeling has been manifested by the passage of the present bill. The establishment of these colleges has prevailed over the pressing wants of the common Treasury. No nation ever had such an inheritance as we possess in the public lands. These ought to be managed with the utmost care, but at the same time with the liberal spirit toward actual settlers.

In the first year of a war with a powerful naval nation the revenue from customs must in a great degree cease. A resort to loans will then become necessary, and these can always be obtained, as our fathers obtained them, on advantageous terms by pledging the public lands as security. In this view of the subject it would be wiser to grant money to the States for domestic purposes than to squander away the public lands and transfer them in large bodies into the hands of speculators.

A successful struggle on the part of the State governments with the General Government for the public lands would deprive the latter of the means of performing its high duties, especially at critical and dangerous periods. Besides, it would operate with equal detriment to the best interests of the States. It would remove the most wholesome of all restraints on legislative bodies—that of being obliged to raise money by taxation from their constituents—and would lead to extravagance, if not to corruption. What is obtained easily and without responsibility will be lavishly expended.

3. This bill, should it become a law, will operate greatly to the injury of the new States. The progress of settlements and the increase of an industrious population owning an interest in the soil they cultivate are the causes which will build them up into great and flourishing commonwealths. Nothing could be more prejudicial to their interests than for wealthy individuals to acquire large tracts of the public land and hold them for speculative purposes. The low price to which this land scrip will probably be reduced will tempt speculators to buy it in large amounts and locate it on the best lands belonging to the Government. The eventual consequence must be that the men who desire to cultivate the soil will be compelled to purchase these very lands at rates much higher than the price at which they could be obtained from the Government.

4. It is extremely doubtful, to say the least, whether this bill would contribute to the advancement of agriculture and the mechanic arts— objects the dignity and value of which can not be too highly appreciated.

The Federal Government, which makes the donation, has confessedly no constitutional power to follow it into the States and enforce the application of the fund to the intended objects. As donors we shall possess no control over our own gift after it shall have passed from our hands. It is true that the State legislatures are required to stipulate that they will faithfully execute the trust in the manner prescribed by the bill. But should they fail to do this, what would be the consequence? The Federal Government has no power, and ought to have no power, to compel the execution of the trust. It would be in as helpless a condition as if, even in this, the time of great need, we were to demand any portion of the many millions of surplus revenue deposited with the States for safe-keeping under the act of 1836.

5. This bill will injuriously interfere with existing colleges in the different States, in many of which agriculture is taught as a science and in all of which it ought to be so taught. These institutions of learning have grown up with the growth of the country, under the fostering care of the States and the munificence of individuals, to meet the advancing demands for education. They have proved great blessings to the people. Many, indeed most, of them are poor and sustain themselves with difficulty. What the effect will be on these institutions of creating an indefinite number of rival colleges sustained by the endowment of the Federal Government it is not difficult to determine.

Under this bill it is provided that scientific and classical studies shall not be excluded from them. Indeed, it would be almost impossible to sustain them without such a provision, for no father would incur the expense of sending a son to one of these institutions for the sole purpose of making him a scientific farmer or mechanic. The bill itself negatives this idea, and declares that their object is "to promote the liberal and practical education of the industrial classes in the several pursuits and professions of life." This certainly ought to be the case. In this view of the subject it would be far better, if such an appropriation of land must be made to institutions of learning in the several States, to apply it directly to the establishment of professorships of agriculture and the mechanic arts in existing colleges, without the intervention of the State legislatures. It would be difficult to foresee how these legislatures will manage this fund. Each Representative in Congress for whose district the proportion of 20,000 acres has been granted will probably insist that the proceeds shall be expended within its limits. There will undoubtedly be a struggle between different localities in each State concerning the division of the gifts, which may end in disappointing the hopes of the true friends of agriculture. For this state of things we are without remedy. Not so in regard to State colleges. We might grant land to these corporations to establish agricultural and mechanical professorships, and should they fail to comply with the conditions on which they accepted the grant we might enforce specific performance of these before the ordinary courts of justice.

6. But does Congress possess the power under the Constitution to make a donation of public lands to the different States of the Union to provide colleges for the purpose of educating their own people?

I presume the general proposition is undeniable that Congress does not possess the power to appropriate money in the Treasury, raised by taxes on the people of the United States, for the purpose of educating the people of the respective States. It will not be pretended that any such power is to be found among the specific powers granted to Congress nor that "it is necessary and proper for carrying into execution" any one of these powers. Should Congress exercise such a power, this would be to break down the barriers which have been so carefully constructed in the Constitution to separate Federal from State authority. We should then not only "lay and collect taxes, duties, imposts, and excises" for Federal purposes, but for every State purpose which Congress might deem expedient or useful. This would be an actual consolidation of the Federal and State Governments so far as the great taxing and money power is concerned, and constitute a sort of partnership between the two in the Treasury of the United States, equally ruinous to both.

But it is contended that the public lands are placed upon a different footing from money raised by taxation and that the proceeds arising from their sale are not subject to the limitation of the Constitution, but may be appropriated or given away by Congress, at its own discretion, to States, corporations, or individuals for any purpose they may deem expedient.

The advocates of this bill attempt to sustain their position upon the language of the second clause of the third section of the fourth article of the Constitution, which declares that "the Congress shall have power to dispose of and make all needful rules and regulations respecting the territory or other property belonging to the United States." They contend that by a fair interpretation of the words "dispose of" in this clause Congress possesses the power to make this gift of public lands to the States for purposes of education.

It would require clear and strong evidence to induce the belief that the framers of the Constitution, after having limited the powers of Congress to certain precise and specific objects, intended by employing the words "dispose of" to give that body unlimited power over the vast public domain. It would be a strange anomaly, indeed, to have created two funds —the one by taxation, confined to the execution of the enumerated powers delegated to Congress, and the other from the public lands, applicable to all subjects, foreign and domestic, which Congress might designate; that this fund should be "disposed of," not to pay the debts of the United States, nor "to raise and support armies," nor "to provide and maintain a navy," nor to accomplish any one of the other great objects enumerated in the Constitution, but be diverted from them to pay the debts of the States, to educate their people, and to carry into effect any other measure of their domestic policy. This would be to confer upon Congress a vast and irresponsible authority, utterly at war with the well-known jealousy of Federal power which prevailed at the formation of the Constitution. The natural intendment would be that as the Constitution confined Congress to well-defined specific powers, the funds placed at their command, whether in land or money, should be appropriated to the performance of the duties corresponding with these powers. If not, a Government has been created with all its other powers carefully limited, but without any limitation in respect to the public lands.

But I can not so read the words "dispose of" as to make them embrace the idea of "giving away." The true meaning of words is always to be ascertained by the subject to which they are applied and the known general intent of the lawgiver. Congress is a trustee under the Constitution for the people of the United States to "dispose of" their public lands, and I think I may venture to assert with confidence that no case can be found in which a trustee in the position of Congress has been authorized to *dispose of* property by its owner where it has been held that these words authorized such trustee to give away the fund intrusted to his care. No trustee, when called upon to account for the disposition of the property placed under his management before any judicial tribunal, would venture to present such a plea in his defense. The true meaning of these words is clearly stated by Chief Justice Taney in delivering the opinion of the court (19 Howard, p. 436). He says in reference to this clause of the Constitution:

It begins its enumeration of powers by that of disposing; in other words, making sale of the lands or raising money from them, which, as we have already said, was the main object of the cession (from the States), and which is the first thing provided for in the article.

It is unnecessary to refer to the history of the times to establish the known fact that this statement of the Chief Justice is perfectly well founded. That it never was intended by the framers of the Constitution that these lands should be given away by Congress is manifest from the concluding portion of the same clause. By it Congress has power not only "to dispose of" the territory, but of the "other property of the United States." In the language of the Chief Justice (p. 437):

And the same power of making needful rules respecting the territory is in precisely the same language applied to the other property of the United States, associating the power over the territory in this respect with the power over movable or personal property; that is, the ships, arms, or munitions of war which then belonged in common to the State sovereignties.

The question is still clearer in regard to the public lands in the States and Territories within the Louisiana and Florida purchases. These lands were paid for out of the public Treasury from money raised by taxation. Now if Congress had no power to appropriate the money with which these lands were purchased, is it not clear that the power over the lands is equally limited? The mere conversion of this money into land could not confer upon Congress new power over the disposition of land which they had not possessed over money. If it could, then a trustee, by changing the character of the fund intrusted to his care for special objects from money into land, might give the land away or devote it to any purpose he thought proper, however foreign from the trust. The inference is irresistible that this land partakes of the very same character with the money paid for it, and can be devoted to no objects different from those to which the money could have been devoted. If this were not the case, then by the purchase of a new territory from a foreign government out of the public Treasury Congress could enlarge their own powers and appropriate the proceeds of the sales of land thus purchased, at their own discretion, to other and far different objects from what they could have applied the purchase money which had been raised by taxation.

It has been asserted truly that Congress in numerous instances have granted lands for the purposes of education. These grants have been chiefly, if not exclusively, made to the new States as they successively entered the Union, and consisted at the first of one section and afterwards of two sections of the public land in each township for the use of schools, as well as of additional sections for a State University. Such grants are not, in my opinion, a violation of the Constitution. The United States is a great landed proprietor, and from the very nature of this relation it is both the right and the duty of Congress as their trustee to manage these lands as any other prudent proprietor would manage them for his own best advantage. Now no consideration could be presented of a stronger character to induce the American people to brave the difficulties and hardships of frontier life and to settle upon these lands and to purchase them at a fair price than to give to them and to their children an assurance of the means of education. If any prudent individual had held these lands, he could not have adopted a wiser course to bring them into market and enhance their value than to give a portion of them for purposes of education. As a mere speculation he would pursue this course. No person will contend that donations of land to all the States of the Union for the erection of colleges within the limits of each can be embraced by this principle. It can not be pretended that an agricultural college in New York or Virginia would aid the settlement or facilitate the sale of public lands in Minnesota or California. This can not possibly be embraced within the authority which a prudent proprietor of land would exercise over his own possessions. I purposely avoid any attempt to define what portions of land may be granted, and for what purposes, to improve the value and promote the settlement and sale of the remainder without violating the Constitution. In this case I adopt the rule that "sufficient unto the day is the evil thereof."

JAMES BUCHANAN.

Chancellor F. A. P. Barnard Is Tried and Exonerated by the Board of Trustees of the University of Mississippi, 1860 *

At a called meeting of the Board of Trustees of the University of Mississippi, convoked by order of His Excellency J. J. Pettus, *ex-officio* President of the Board, at the town of Oxford, on the 1st day of March, 1860, there were present, of the Trustees:

Hon. James M. Howry, Secretary of the Board, Hon. J. A. Ventress, Hon. Isaac N. Davis, Hon. A. H. Pegues, Col. James Brown, Col. Geo. H. Young, Wm. F. Dowd, Esq., Hon. J. W. Clapp, Hon. Charles Clark and Hon. Alex. M. Clayton.

His Excellency, Gov. Pettus, not having arrived, on motion, the Hon. Alex. M. Clayton was elected as President *pro tempore.*

---

* *Record of the Testimony and Proceedings in the Matter of the Investigation of the Trustees of the University of Mississippi . . . of the Charges Made Against the Chancellor of the University* (Jackson, Miss., Printed at the Mississippian Office, 1860). The trial was held on March 1 and 2, 1860. The entire testimony in this interesting case runs to thirty closely printed pages, but only the most pertinent extracts are given here. This was one of numerous examples of Southern opposition to Northern educational influences in the second quarter of the nineteenth century. Criticisms of such influences became more numerous and spirited before 1860. Following John Brown's attack on Harper's Ferry in October, 1859, about two hundred Southern students left medical schools in Philadelphia and returned home. *Philadelphia Bulletin,* December 20, 1859, *Richmond Enquirer,* December 23, 1859, and *Daily Dispatch* (Richmond, Va.), December 23, 1859. Edgar W. Knight, "Southern Opposition to Northern Education," *The Educational Forum,* XIV (November, 1949). Thomas L. Patrick, *Southern Criticisms of Northern Educational Influences* (typescript doctoral dissertation, the University of North Carolina, 1951).

The following communication from Dr. F. A. P. Barnard, Chancellor of the University of Mississippi, was laid before the Board, and read:

UNIVERSITY OF MISSISSIPPI, February 29, 1860.

To the Honorable the Board of Trustees of the University of Mississippi:

GENTLEMEN: In a letter addressed to your President on the 2d instant, requesting him to assemble your honorable body in special session at the present time, I assigned, as a reason for the request, a condition of things, existing in the University, which rendered such a meeting, in my view, indispensable, at the earliest possible day. The object of this communication is to explain that state of things.

Some time during the month of January, I became aware that charges has been repeatedly and publicly made against me, by Dr. Henry R. Branham, a citizen of Oxford, the tendency of which was to undermine me in the confidence of the people of the South, and thus, by injuring me, to affect very seriously the prosperity of the University.

These charges were never made in my presence, and, so long as they seemed not to menace serious harm, I treated them with little attention. Having at length learned what they were, or, at least, what some of them were, I authorized a friend to meet them with a denial. But this only provoked a reiteration of them with angry violence, which reiteration was accompanied by a citation of the names of several of my colleagues in the Faculty, as authorities who would confirm their truth.

In regard to a certain portion of the charges and specifications, other members of the Faculty besides myself were implicated; and by one of these the subject was brought before the body in session. During a discussion which arose upon it, at a meeting held on the 2d instant, there was developed such a state of things as to satisfy me, that, without the interposition of the Board of Trustees, the ordinary business of the University cou'd no longer be harmoniously prosecuted: so that, apart from the great injury likely to accrue from the injurious charges persistently uttered against myself, and to a certain extent, against some of my colleagues, I found an urgent reason for soliciting an immediate convocation of your honorable body, in the imminent danger of a state of complete disorganization.

In order that the charges, above alluded to, might be presented for your investigation in precisely the form in which they have been publicly uttered, I have obtained, from one of the gentlemen to whom they were personally addressed, the following written statement:

(Copied from a note addressed by Col. A. H. Pegues to Prof. Wm. F. Stearnes, on the 24th of February, 1860).

"On the 1st day of this month, in Kindel & Rascoe's store, Dr. Branham, in the presence of Dr. Green, Dr. Carter, (M. D., of Oxford,) and others, made the following charges against Dr. Barnard:

"1st. That he (Barnard) was unsound upon the slavery question.

"2d. That he was in favor of, and did advocate, the taking of negro testimony against a student.

"3d. That H. (a student) was arraigned and tried upon negro testimony.

"4th. That upon the question of the expulsion of H., the vote was sectionally divided—Barnard, Boynton and Moore voting in the affirmative, and the Southern men voting in the negative.

"5th. That, pending the discussion upon the case of H., Barnard asked Richardson if he would not believe his negro man, Henry, against a student, and when Richardson said he would not, Barnard said *he would*.

"6th. That all the information in the H. case was furnished by a negro woman; and that it was proposed by the other members of the Faculty, that, if Barnard and Boynton had other sources of information and would assert positively that they *knew* H. was guilty, they (the other members) would vote accordingly.

"7th. That Barnard stated that Jane (the negro woman) afterwards recognized H., and pointed him out as the man who had assailed her.

"8th. That notwithstanding the vote of expulsion failed, Barnard wrote to the guardian of the student to take him away, which he did.

"9th. That if the Board of Trustees persisted in their refusal to arraign and try Barnard for taking negro testimony against a student, he (Branham) would publish the whole thing, in the *Mississippian,* to the people of the State, over his own signature."

Col. Pegues adds: "The above are very nearly literally the charges made on the occasion alluded to, with the exception of that part in which the woman (Jane) is introduced; and even here, although I admit the possibility of not having understood or recollected the *words,* exactly, the impression made upon my mind fully warrants, I think, the report which I have made."

Of these allegations, and of the whole matter or matters to which they relate, I invite the fullest and most searching investigation, on the part of your honorable body. I invite, further, an examination into the tenor of my past life, not only for the period of twenty-two years that I have spent in unwearied devotion to the cause of Southern education, but for that earlier period of youth when I had not yet expected ever to be a resident of a Southern State; but in regard to which I have, providentially, in my possession, testimonials by Southern men, of the most unexceptionable character.

If I entertain sentiments now, or if your investigations shall discover that I have ever entertained sentiments, which shall justify any man however captious, in pronouncing me "unsound upon the slavery question," then, gentlemen, do your duty, and remove me from a position for which I am morally disqualified.

But if, on the contrary, after the severest scrutiny of my acts and my utterances, you find that the injurious allegations by which it has been attempted to strike me down from my post of usefulness, to deprive me of my occupation, and to expose me to public opprobrium, are totally and entirely groundless and false, then I ask of you, in justice to one who has, for nearly six years, honestly, conscientiously, and faithfully consecrated to your service all the energies of his intellectual and physical being, to put the stamp of your emphatic condemnation upon an outrage, in my view without a parallel in the annals of civilization.

I remain, gentlemen, respectfully, your ob't serv't,

F. A. P. BARNARD,
Chancellor of the University of Mississippi.

Henry R. Branham, M. D., of Oxford, who was present, by permission of the Board, when the foregoing communication from Chancellor Barnard was read, submitted the following as the only charges and specifications he now had to make against Dr. Barnard:-

"1st. That Dr. Barnard offered the statement of a negro as evidence against a student of the University of Mississippi, Mr. H.

"2nd. That after the Faculty refused to sustain the charge upon the testimony adduced, Dr. Barnard without the authority of the Faculty, wrote to his guardian a letter which resulted in the withdrawal of Mr. H. from the University.

"3rd. That Dr. Barnard interposed and objected to Mr. H's re-admission into the University at the opening of the following session, and thus prevented his return.

"H. R. BRANHAM."

March 1st, 1860.

Chancellor Barnard, who was present, thereupon drew up and filed the following response to the charges submitted by Dr. Branham:-

"The charges of Dr. Branham are by no means so sweeping as I desire the investigation to be. I rejoin, and undertake to prove:-

"1. That I proceeded against H. upon entirely sufficient and satisfactory evidence, before I ever knew what the negro said: the negro being my own servant, and having been cruelly outraged and beaten.

"That I never spoke to the servant on the subject of the outrage in my life, neither before nor since the occurrence.

"That during the progress of the affair, which lasted about a week, my wife mentioned to me that the servant had told her the story, and repeated it to me without any solicitation of mine.

"That at the trial of H., I presented the evidence which had satisfied me, and during the discussion, I mentioned what my wife had said of the negro's story, and did say that I regarded the coincidence as a confirmatory circumstance.

"That the Faculty did, by resolution, declare that they were morally convinced of the guilt of H.

"That this resolution was publicly read, and elicited from the students no expression of dissent.

"That H. *did* commit the act.

"2. That H. was a student of bad character before.

"That it was perfectly competent to me, as Chancellor of the University, to desire his Guardian to withdraw him, if I thought he was doing ill and exerting a bad influence,—that I *did* think so,—that the resolution of the Faculty, declaring their conviction of his guilt, amply justified my action in desiring him to be withdrawn.

"That I often so act in analogous cases, and that it is my right and duty so to do.

"3. That I did refuse to re-admit H., because he was undesirable as a student. That such is my prerogative and right.

"That, therefore, charges 2 and 3 are totally frivolous.

"Further, as to charge 1, if it were in any sense true, I was but doing my duty as a christian master, to protect my servant from outrage; and that I am sustained in this view by the highest authorities, among whom I am permitted to offer the written opinion of the Hon. Jacob Thompson.

"That college government is a parental, and not a municipal government:

"And, finally, that the question, which concerns the Board and the public, is not, whether, on a particular occasion, I committed an error of judgment or not; but whether I do entertain the principles which it is sought by these charges to fasten upon me; and in regard to this I aver that I am as 'sound on the slavery question' as Dr. Branham, or any member of this Board.

"F. A. P. BARNARD."

Thereupon, the following resolution was adopted by the Board:-

Resolved, That the extent of our investigation be such as to embrace the charges specifically made by Dr. Branham against Dr. Barnard, upon which an issue has been made up by Dr. Barnard to the Board, relating to charges against him, which, if true, render him an unsuitable person to preside over a Southern University.

That, in conducting the examination, Dr. Branham shall have an opportunity to produce all the evidence, documentary and oral, upon which he relies to support his charges, and to examine witnesses, himself; and Dr. Barnard shall have the like opportunity;—both of the parties having also the right to cross-examine as the investigation progresses; and the Board reserves the right to each member thereof to ask any question pertinent to the matter under investigation, and to examine the parties to the issue— Dr. Branham and Dr. Barnard.

That each witness be put upon his honor as to the truth of his statement, and each one be examined separately from the others.

The Board also think it a proper and important subject of investigation, as to the manner in which the proceedings of the Faculty, in their official sessions, have been divulged, or came to the knowledge of Dr. Branham; and they think it proper that the testimony introduced, upon every material point investigated, shall be reduced to writing by some person designated for that purpose by the President of the Board. . . .

OXFORD, MISSISSIPPI, March 8, 1860.

I, Wm. F. Stearns, as official reporter in the case, do hereby certify that the foregoing is a full, true and correct transcript of the testimony given in before the Board of Trustees of the University of Mississippi, on the 1st and 2d instants, upon the investigation, at the request of Dr. F. A. P. Barnard, Chancellor of the University, of the charges than and previously preferred against him by Dr. H. R. Banham; all the oral testimony, (except my own, and that of Prof. Geo. W. Carter, which was reduced to writing by Mr. Clapp,) having been taken down by myself, and mostly read over to and approved by the witnesses in the presence of Dr. Branham.

WM. F. STEARNS, *Reporter*.

March 2nd, 1860.

His Excellency, J. J. Pettus, Governor of the State of Mississippi, and *ex officio* President of the Board of Trustees of the University, this day appeared and took his seat with the other members of the Board, who were mentioned as being present yesterday; and the testimony taken before his arrival was submitted to his examination.

The taking of the testimony being concluded after dark, Dr. Branham made a few remarks, but declined to discuss the merits of the case; when Dr. Barnard addressed the Board at some length, but purposely abstained, he said, from making any comments upon the evidence.

Dr. Branham having no desire to say anything further, he and Dr. Barnard retired and left the Board to its deliberations.

Whereupon, on motion of Mr. Clark, it was moved, as the sense of the Board, that Dr. Barnard be acquitted of all the charges against him; and, the yeas and nays being called for, the said motion was carried by the following vote:

Yeas—Messrs. Pettus, (President) Clayton, Davis, Clark, Ventress, Young, Dowd, Pegues, Brown, Clapp and Howry—11.

Nays—None.

On motion of Mr. Clarke it was then moved, as the sense of the Board, that our confidence in Dr. Barnard is increased rather than diminished in consequence of this investigation; and, the yeas and nays being called for, the said motion was carried by the same unanimous vote above stated.

A committee, consisting of Messrs. Clayton, Clapp and Pettus, was then, on motion of Judge Clayton, appointed to draw up resolutions embodying the decisions just made by the Board; and that committee, through Judge Clayton, its chairman, made the following report:—

The committee to draw up resolutions enbodying the decisions of the Board upon the charges preferred against Dr. F. A. P. Barnard, the Chancellor of the University, report the following:

Resolved, That the charges are, in their opinion, wholly unsustained by the evidence, and that the said F. A. P. Barnard stands fully and honorably acquitted of every charge brought against him.

Resolved, That after a patient hearing and investigation of all the testimony in the case, we as Trustees and as Southern men, have found our confidence in the ability and integrity of the Chancellor, and his fitness for his position, increased rather than diminished, and declare our full conviction that his labors are doing great service to the cause of education and science, and placing the reputation of the University upon an immovable basis.

The said report having been received and agreeed to, the said two resolutions were then unanimously adopted by the Board.

On motion of Judge Clayton, it was

Resolved, That the Secretary inform Prof. W. F. Stearns that he is required, as a part of his duty as reporter in this case, to furnish, at as early a day as practicable, the testimony given in this case, together with the written documents introduced by any of the witnesses, to the Secretary of the Board, to be by him filed and preserved amongst the records of this Board.

I have compared the foregoing with the record in my possession and find it correct.

J. M. HOWRY, *Sec'y of the Board.*

Governor Sam Houston's Message to the Legislature of Texas on the University and on Giving Aid to Other Institutions, 1860 *

The $2,000,000 set apart for the school fund yet remains, but the balance of the $5,000,000, received from the sale of our Santa Fe territory to the United States is exhausted, except the amount set apart for the University fund, amounting to $106,972.26 and the balance mentioned of $411,402.69, belonging to the general fund. . . .

I would also commend to your consideration the importance of extending a reasonable aid to institutions of learning, now in operation in our State, supported by private enterprise, and to encourage by a general law the establishment of others. Our citizens have already displayed much zeal and enterprise in rearing up in our midst institutions which are

* *House Journal,* Eighth Legislature, Regular Session, pp. 393, 395.

accomplishing great good, to sustain these is difficult, and as the benefits arising from these are to be felt in the general prosperity of the State, and the intelligence of its entire people, a proper encouragement at the hands of the Legislature should be extended. Surrounded by proper guards a measure of this character would be productive of great good.

The establishment of a University, is, in my opinion, a matter alone for the future. At this time it is neither expedient, nor is it good policy to provide for the sale of those lands set apart for the University fund. If, at some future period it should be deemed expedient, or in keeping with a more enlarged policy, to devote our entire energies to a more general diffusion of knowledge than a University would afford, or even if the voice of the State should demand the establishment of one of these lands will then provide the means of advancing the cause of education. When that period arrives, their value will be greatly increased. If sold now, but little will be realized from them, and before the expiration of twenty years—the time upon which over fifty thousand acres would have been sold—the lands will be worth more than three-fold the amount they would bring now, with accumulated interest.

So far as the one hundred thousand dollars of bonds, and their interest, taken from the general and applied to the University fund, by the last Legislature, are concerned, I believe the condition of the treasury and our immediate necessities demand that the act be repealed, and the money again placed subject to appropriation. We need money for the protection of our frontier, and to save us from taxation, more than for a fund which promises no immediate benefit. Our common school fund already provides for the education contemplated by the Constitution, and if this amount, thus unnecessarily withdrawn from the general fund, will reduce the burthens of taxation, the people will be better able, in the future, to bear taxation to support a University, if one should be necessary.

«« V »»

GAINING PUBLIC SUPPORT
AND CONTROL; COMPULSORY
ATTENDANCE LEGISLATION

«««»»»»»»»»»»»»»»»»»»»»»»»»»»»»»»»»»

An Associated Press dispatch from Washington August 8, 1949, reported that the American states were spending more on education than on anything else, and that in the year ending June 30, 1948, more than one-fifth of all expenditures by the states ($2,312,000,000) "went to schools." Next in line were highways ($1,989,000,000), public welfare and relief ($1,609,000,000), and hospitals for the handicapped ($581,000,000), these "four functions accounting for more than two-thirds of all state spending." The states were also spending $71,000,000 for interest on debt and $179,000,000 for retirement of debt.

All the so-called principles of American education (free, universal, non-sectarian, compulsory, public support and public control) have been bitterly fought over in this country and none of them perhaps more bitterly than public support and control and compulsory-attendance legislation. The fact that education in this country began as a local interest and activity caused long and stubborn resistance to centralized public support and control; and the belief that compulsory-attendance legislation (which extended from 1852 in Massachusetts to 1918 in Mississippi) was an invasion of the parental function and the liberty of parents delayed the development of this principle, as Secretary B. G. Northrop of the Connecticut State Board of Education pointed out so well in 1872. As late as 1892, a plank in the platform of "one of the great political parties in a Western State distinguished for its excellent educational institutions and the high and law-abiding character of its citizenship" asserted opposition "to state interference with parental rights and rights of conscience in the education of children, as an infringement of the fundamental democratic doctrine . . ." But it was not until 1925 that the Supreme Court of the United States significantly held that American children could not be compelled to attend *public* schools. While bitter controversy raged about each of the principles noted above and while not all of them are fully and practically established in every community, it may be noted that increasing faith in them has been exhibited in the long and laborious struggles which the American people have been willing to engage in that these principles might be as widely applied as possible.

Non-residents of Boston Must Pay for the Instruction of Their Children, 1711 *

Whereas the Support of the Free Schools of this Town hath been, and still is, at ye Cost & charge of the Inhabitants of ye Said Town and the Select men being informed of Several Instances, of Children Sent to ye Sd Schools, whose parents, or others who of Right ought to defray the Charge of their Education, do belong to other Townes or Precincts.

Where fore they ye Sd Select men do direct the Sd School masters to demand & receive of the persons Sending any Such children the accustomed recompence for their Schooling, and to Return unto ye Select men a List of their names, once (at ye Least) every year.

Boston Finds Its Schools Expensive, 1750 †

That the Charge of supporting the several Publick Schools amounted the last Year to more than ⅓ part of the whole Sum drawn for by the Selectmen; but altho this Charge is very Considerable, & the number of Schools is greater than the Law requires, Yet as the Education of Children is of the greatest Importance to the Community; the Committee cannot be of Opinion that any Saving can be made to Advantage on that head; except the Town should think it expedient to come into Methods to oblige such of the Inhabitants who send their Children to the Publick Schools and are able to Pay for their Education themselves, to ease the Town of the Charge by assessing some reasonable Sum upon them for that purpose.

Thomas Jefferson's Bill "For the More General Diffusion of Knowledge," Introduced into the Legislature of Virginia, 1779 ‡

Section I. Whereas § it appeareth that however certain forms of government are better calculated than others to protect individuals in the free

* *Records of the Town of Boston*, XI, p. 137 (June 18, 1711). Given in R. F. Seybolt, *The Public Schools of Colonial Boston* (Cambridge, Harvard University Press, 1935), p. 40.
† *Records of the Town of Boston*, XIV, p. 192 (March 12, 1750/51). Given in Seybolt, *op cit.*, p. 40.
‡ Philip S. Foner (Ed.), *Basic Writings of Thomas Jefferson* (New York, Willey Book Co., 1944), pp. 40-46. The bill may be found in several other editions of Jefferson's writings, including Paul Leicester Ford's *The Writings of Thomas Jefferson*, II, pp. 220-29.
§ This bill embodies the first plan for a state-wide public school system in this country.

exercise of their natural rights, and are at the same time themselves better guarded against degeneracy, yet experience hath shewn that even under the best forms those intrusted with power have, in time and by slow operations, perverted it into tyranny; and it is believed that the most effectual means of preventing this would be to illuminate, as far as practicable, the minds of the people at large, and more especially to give them knowledge of those facts which history exhibiteth, that, possessed thereby of the experience of other ages and countries, they may be enabled to know ambition under all its shapes, and prompt to exert their natural powers to defeat its purpose. And whereas it is generally true that the people will be happiest whose laws are best and are best administered, and that laws will be wisely formed and honestly administered, in proportion as those who form and administer them are wise and honest; whence it becomes expedient for promoting the publick happiness, that those persons whom nature has endowed with genius and virtue should be rendered by liberal education worthy to receive and able to guard the sacred deposit of the rights and liberties of their fellow-citizens, and that they should be called to that charge without regard to wealth, birth, or other accidental condition or circumstance; but the indigence of the greater number disabling them from so educating, at their own expence, those of their children whom nature hath fitly formed and disposed to become useful instruments for the public, it is better that such should be sought for and educated at the common expence of all, than that the happiness of all should be confined to the weak or wicked.

Section II. Be it therefore enacted by the General Assembly, that in every county within this Commonwealth, there shall be chosen annually, by the electors qualified to vote for Delegates, three of the most honest and able men of their county, to be called the Aldermen of the county; and that the election of the said Aldermen shall be held at the same time and place, before the same persons, and notified and conducted in the same manner as by law is directed, for the annual election of Delegates for the county.

Section III. The person before whom such election is holden shall certify to the court of the said county the names of the Aldermen chosen, in order that the same may be entered of record, and shall give notice of their election to the said Aldermen within a fortnight after such election.

Section IV. The said Aldermen, on the first Monday in October, if it be fair, and if not, then on the next fair day, excluding Sunday, shall meet at the court-house of their county, and proceed to divide their said county into hundreds, bounding the same by water courses, mountains, or limits to be run and marked, if they think necessary, by the county surveyor, and at the county expence, regulating the size of the said hundreds, according to the best of their discretion, so as they may contain a convenient number of children to make up a school, and be of such convenient size that all the children within each hundred may daily attend the school to be established therein, and distinguishing each hundred by a particular name; which division, with the names of the several hundreds, shall be returned to the court of the county and be entered of record, and shall remain unaltered until the increase or decrease of inhabitants shall render an alteration necessary, in the opinion of any succeeding Aldermen, and also in the opinion of the court of the county.

Section V. The electors aforesaid residing within every hundred shall meet on the third Monday in October after the first election of Aldermen, at such place, within their hundred, as the said Aldermen shall direct, notice thereof being previously given to them by such person residing within the hundred as the said Aldermen shall require who is hereby enjoined to obey such requisition on pain of being punished by amercement and imprisonment. The electors being so assembled shall choose the most convenient place within their hundred for building a schoolhouse. If two or more places, having a greater number of votes than any others, shall yet be equal between themselves, the Aldermen, or such of them as are not of the same hundred, on information thereof, shall decide between them. The said Aldermen shall forthwith proceed to have a schoolhouse built at the said place, and shall see that the same be kept in repair, and when necessary, that it be rebuilt; but whenever they shall think necessary that it be rebuilt, they shall give notice as before directed, to the electors of the hundred to meet at the said schoolhouse, on such a day as they shall appoint, to determine by vote, in the manner before directed, whether it shall be rebuilt at the same, or what other place in the hundred.

Section VI. At every of those schools shall be taught, reading, writing, and common arithmetick, and the books which shall be used therein for instructing the children to read shall be such as will at the same time make them acquainted with Graecian, Roman, English, and American history. At these schools all the free children, male and female, resident within the respective hundred, shall be entitled to receive tuition gratis, for the term of three years, and as much longer, at their private expence, as their parents, guardians, or friends shall think proper.

Section VII. Over every ten of these schools (or such other number nearest thereto, as the number of hundreds in the county shall admit, without fractional divisions) an overseer shall be appointed annually by the Aldermen at their first meeting, eminent for his learning, integrity, and fidelity to the Commonwealth, whose business and duty it shall be, from time to time, to appoint a teacher to each school, who shall give assurance of fidelity to the Commonwealth, and to remove him as he shall see cause; to visit every school once in every half year at the least; to examine the scholars; see that any general plan of reading and instruction recommended by the visiters of William and Mary College shall be observed; and to superintend the conduct of the teacher in everything relative to his school.

Section VIII. Every teacher shall receive a salary of .... by the year, which, with the expenses of building and repairing the schoolhouses, shall be provided in such manner as other county expenses are by law directed to be provided and shall also have his diet, lodging, and washing found him, to be levied in like manner, and save only that such levy shall be on the inhabitants of each hundred for the board of their own teacher only.

Section IX. And in order that grammer schools may be rendered convenient to the youth in every part of the commonwealth, be it therefore enacted, that on the first Monday in November, after the first appointment of overseers appointed for the schools in the counties of Princess Ann, Norfolk, day, excluding Sunday, after the hour of one in the afternoon, the said overseer appointed for the schools in the counties of Princess Ann, Norfolk, Nansemond and Isle of Wight, shall meet at Nansemond court-house; those for the counties of Southampton, Sussex, Surry, and Prince George, shall meet at Sussex court-house; those for the counties of Brunswick, Mecklenburg, and Lunenburg, shall meet at Lunenburg court-house; those for the counties of Dinwiddie, Amelia, and Chesterfield, shall meet at Chesterfield court-house; those for the counties of Powhatan, Cumberland, Goochland, Henrico, and Hanover, shall meet at Henrico court-house; those for the counties of Prince Edward, Charlotte, and Halifax, shall meet at Charlotte court-house; those for the counties of Henry, Pittsylvania, and Bedford, shall meeet at Pittsylvania court-house; those for the counties of Buckingham, Amherst, Albemarle, and Fluvanna, shall meet at Albemarle court-house; those for the counties of Botetourt, Rockbridge, Montgomery, Washington, and Kentucky, shall meet at Botetourt court-house; those for the counties of Augusta, Rockingham, and Greenbriar, shall meet at Augusta court-house; those for the counties of Accomack and Northampton, shall meet at Accomack court-house; those for the counties of Elizabeth City, Warwick, York, Gloucester, James City, Charles City, and New Kent, shall meet at James City court-house; those for the counties of Middlesex, Essex, King and Queen, King William, and Carolina, shall meet at King and Queen court-house; those for the counties of Lancaster, Northumberland, Richmond, and Westmoreland, shall meet at Richmond court-house; those for the counties of King George, Stafford, Spotsylvania, Prince William, and Fairfax, shall meet at Spotsylvania court-house; those for the counties of Loudoun and Fauquier, shall meet at Loudoun court-house; those for the counties of Culpeper, Orange and Louisa, shall meet at Orange court-house; those for the counties of Shenandoah and Frederick, shall meet at Frederick court-house; those for the counties of Hampshire and Berkeley, shall meet at Berkeley court-house; and those for the counties of Yohogania, Monongalia, and Ohio, shall meet at Monongalia court-house; and shall fix on such place in some one of the counties of their district as shall be most proper for situating a grammer schoolhouse, endeavoring that the situation be as central as. may be to the inhabitants of the said counties; that it be furnished with good water, convenient to plentiful supplies of provisions and fuel, and more than all things that it be healthy. And if a majority of the overseers present should not concur in their choice of any one place proposed, the method of determining shall be as follows: If two places only were proposed, and the votes be divided, they shall decide between them by fair and equal lot; if more than two places were proposed, the question shall be put on those two which on the first division had the greater number of votes; or if no two places had a greater number of votes than the others, then it shall be decided by fair and equal lot (unless it can be agreed by a majority of votes) which of the places having equal numbers shall be thrown out of the competition, so that the question shall be put on the remaining two, and if on this ultimate question the votes shall be equally divided, it shall then be decided finally by lot.

Section X. The said overseers having determined the place at which the grammer school for their district shall be built, shall forthwith (unless they can otherwise agree with the proprietors of the circumjacent lands as to location and price) make application to the clerk of the county in which the said house is to be situated, who shall thereupon issue a writ, in the nature of a writ of *ad quod damnum,* directed to the sheriff of the said county commanding him to summon and impannel twelve fit persons to meet at the place, so destined for the grammer school, on a certain day, to be named in the said writ, not less than five, nor more than ten, days from the date thereof; and also to give notice of the same to the proprietors and tenants of the lands, to be viewed if they be found within the county, and if not, then to their agents therein, if any they have. Which freeholders shall be charged by the sheriff impartially, and to the best of their skill and judgment to view the lands round about the said place, and to locate and circumscribe, by certain meets and bounds, one hundred acres thereof, having regard therein principally to the benefit and convenience of the said school, but respecting in some measure also the convenience of the said proprietors, and to value and appraise the same in so many and distinct parcels as shall be owned or held by several and distinct owners or tenants, and according to their respective interests and estates therein. And after such location and appraisement so made, the said sheriff shall forthwith return the same under the hands and seals of the said jurors, together with the writ, to the clerk's office of the said county, and the right and property of the said proprietors and tenants in the said lands so circumscribed shall be immediately divested and be transferred to the commonwealth for the use of the said grammer school, in full and absolute dominion, any want of consent or disability to consent in the said owners or tenants notwithstanding. But it shall not be lawful for the said overseers so to situate the grammer schoolhouse, nor to the said jurors so to locate the said lands, as to include the mansion-house of the proprietor of the lands, nor the offices, curtilage, or garden, thereunto immediately belonging.

Section XI. The said overseers shall forwith proceed to have a house of brick or stone, for the said grammer school, with necessary offices, built on the said lands, which grammer school-house shall contain a room for the school, a hall to dine in, four rooms for a master and usher, and ten or twelve lodging rooms for the scholars.

Section XII. To each of the said grammer schools shall be allowed out of the public treasury, the sum of .... pounds, out of which shall be paid by the treasurer, on warrant from the Auditors, to the proprietors or tenants of the lands located, the value of their several interests as fixed by the jury, and the balance thereof shall be delivered to the said overseers to defray the expense of the said building.

Section XIII. In either of these grammer schools shall be taught the Latin and Greek languages, English Grammer, geography, and the higher parts of numerical arithmetick, to-wit, vulgar and decimal fractions, and the extrication of the square and cube roots.

Section XIV. A visiter from each county constituting the district shall be appointed, by the overseers, for the county, in the month of October annually, either from their own body or from their county at large, which visiters, or the greater part of them, meeting together at the said grammer school on the first Monday in November, if fair, and if not, then on the next fair day, excluding Sunday, shall have power to choose their own Rector, who shall call and preside at future meetings, to employ from time to time a master, and if necessary, an usher, for the said school, to remove them at their will, and to settle the price of tuition to be paid by the scholars. They shall also visit the school twice in every year at the least, either together or separately at their discretion, examine the scholars, and see that any general plan of instruction recommended by the visiters of William and Mary College shall be observed. The said masters and ushers, before they enter on the execution of their office, shall give assurance of fidelity to the commonwealth.

Section XV. A steward shall be employed, and removed at will by the master, on such wages as the visiters shall direct; which steward shall see to the procuring provisions, fuel, servants for cooking, waiting, house-cleaning, washing, mending, and gardening, on the most reasonable terms; the expence of which, together with the steward's wages, shall be divided equally among all the scholars boarding either on the public or private expence. And the part of those who are on private expence, and also the price of their tuitions due to the master or usher, shall be paid quarterly by the respective scholars, their parents, or guardians, and shall be recoverable, if withheld, together with costs, on motion in any Court of Record, ten days notice thereof being previously given to the party, and a jury empannelled to try the issue joined, or enquire of the damages. The said steward shall also, under the direction of the visiters, see that the house is kept in repair, and necessary enclosures be made and repaired, the accounts of which shall, from time to time, be submitted to the Auditors, and on their warrant paid by the Treasurer.

Section XVI. Every overseer of the hundred schools shall, in the month of September annually, after the most diligent and impartial examination and inquiry, appoint from among the boys who shall have been two years at the least at some one of the schools under his superintendence, and whose parents are too poor to give them farther education, some one of the best and most promising genius and disposition, to proceed to the grammer school of his district; which appointment shall be made in the court-house of the county, and on the court day for that month, if fair, and if not, then on the next fair day, excluding Sunday, in the presence of the Aldermen, or two of them at least, assembled on the bench for that purpose, the said overseer being previously sworn by them to make such appointment, without favor or affection, according to the best of his skill and judgment, and being interrogated by the said Aldermen, either on their own motion, or on suggestions from the parents, guardians, friends, or teachers of the children, competitors or such appointment; which teachers the parents shall attend for the information of the Aldermen. On which interrogatories the said Aldermen, if they be not satisfied with the appointment proposed, shall have right to negative it; whereupon the said visiter may proceed to make a new appointment, and the said Aldermen again to interrogate and negative, and so *toties quoties* until the appointment is approved.

Section XVII. Every boy so appointed shall be authorized to proceed to the grammer school of his district, there to be educated and boarded during such time as is hereafter limited; and his quota of the expence of the house together with compensation to the master or usher for his tuition at the rate of twenty dollars by year, shall be paid by the Treasurer quarterly on warrant from the Auditors.

Section XVIII. A visitation shall be held, for the purpose of probation, annually at the said grammer school on the last Monday in September, if fair, and if not, then on the next fair day, excluding Sunday, at which one-third of the boys sent thither by appointment of the said overseers, and who shall have been there one year only, shall be discontinued as public foundationers, being those who, on the most diligent examination and enquiry, shall be thought to be the least promising genius and disposition; and of those who shall have been there two years, all shall be discontinued save one only the best in genius and disposition, who shall be at liberty to continue there four years longer on the public foundation, and shall thenceforward be deemed a senior.

Section XIX. The visiters for the districts which, or any part of which, be southward and westward of James river, as known by that name, or by the names of Fluvanna and Jackson's river, in every other year, to-wit, at the probation meetings held in the years, distinguished in the Christian computation by odd numbers, and the visiters for all the other districts, at their said meetings to be held in those years, distinguished by even numbers, after diligent examination and enquiry as before directed, shall chuse one among the said seniors, of the best learning and most hopeful genius and disposition, who shall be authorized by them to proceed to William and Mary College; there to be educated, boarded, and clothed, three years; the expence of which annually shall be paid by the Treasurer on warrant from the Auditors.

Dr. Benjamin Rush to the Legislature of Pennsylvania on a System of Public Education, 1786 *

For the purpose of diffusing knowledge through every part of the state, I beg leave to propose the following simple plan.

I. Let there be one university in the state, and let this be established in the capital. Let law, physic, divinity, the law of nature and nations, economy, &c. be taught in it by public lectures in the winter season, after the manner of the European universities, and let the professors receive such salaries from the state as will enable them to deliver their lectures at a moderate price.

II. Let there be four colleges. One in Philadelphia; one at Carlisle; a third, for the benefit of our German fellow citizens, at Lancaster; and a fourth, some years hence at Pittsburgh. In these colleges, let young men be instructed in mathematics and in the higher branches of science, in the same manner that they are now taught in our American colleges. After they have received a testimonial from one of those colleges, let them, if they can afford it, complete their studies by spending a season or two in attending the lectures in the university. I prefer four colleges in the state to one or two, for there is a certain size of colleges as there is of towns and armies, that is most favourable to morals and good government. Oxford and Cambridge in England are the seats of dissipation, while the more numerous, and less crowded universities and colleges in Scotland, are remarkable for the order, diligence, and decent behaviour of their students.

* D. D. Runes, *The Selected Writings of Benjamin Rush* (New York, Philosophical Library, Inc., 1947), pp. 98-100.

II. Let there be free schools established in every township, or in districts consisting of one hundred families. In these schools let children be taught to read and write the English and German languages, and the use of figures. Such of them as have parents that can afford to send them from home, and are disposed to extend their educations, may remove their children from the free school to one of the colleges.

By this plan the whole state will be tied together by one system of education. The university will in time furnish masters for the colleges, and the colleges will furnish masters for the free schools, while the free schools, in their turns, will supply the colleges and the university with scholars, students and pupils. The same systems of grammar, oratory and philosophy, will be taught in every part of the state, and the literary features of Pennsylvania will thus designate one great, and equally enlightened family.

But, how shall we bear the expense of these literary institutions?—I answer— These institutions will *lessen* our taxes. They will enlighten us in the great business of finance—they will teach us to increase the ability of the state to support government, by increasing the profits of agriculture, and by promoting manufactures. They will teach us all the modern improvements and advantages of inland navigation. They will defend us from hasty and expensive experiments in government, by unfolding to us the experience and folly of past ages, and thus, instead of adding to our taxes and debts, they will furnish us with the true secret of lessening and discharging both of them.

But, shall the estates of orphans, bachelors and persons who have no children, be taxed to pay for the support of schools from which they can derive no benefit? I answer in the affirmative, to the first part of the objection, and I deny the truth of the latter part of it. Every member of the community is interested in the propagation of virtue and knowledge in the state. But I will go further, and add, it will be true economy in individuals to support public schools. The bachelor will in time save his tax for this purpose, by being able to sleep with fewer bolts and locks to his doors— the estates of orphans will in time be benefited, by being protected from the ravages of unprincipled and idle boys, and the children of wealthy parents will be less tempted, by bad company, to extravagance. Fewer pillories and whipping posts, and smaller gaols, with their usual expenses and taxes, will be necessary when our youth are properly educated, than at present; I believe it could be proved, that the expenses of confining, trying and executing criminals, amount every year, in most of the counties, to more money than would be sufficient to maintain all the schools that would be necessary in each county. The confessions of these criminals generally show us, that their vices and punishments are the fatal consequences of the want of a proper education in early life.

I submit these detached hints to the consideration of the legislature and of the citizens of Pennsylvania. The plan for the free schools is taken chiefly from the plans which have long been used with success in Scotland, and in the eastern states [1] of America, where the influence of learning, in promoting religion, morals, manners and good government, has never been exceeded in any country.

The manner in which these schools should be supported and governed—the modes of determining the characters and qualifications of school-masters, and the arrangement of families in each district, so that children of the same religious sect and nation, may be educated as much as possible together, will form a proper part of a law for the establishment of schools, and therefore does not come within the limits of this plan.

Report of a Committee of the House of Representatives of Pennsylvania on a School System, 1794 *

Resolved, That schools may be established throughout the State, in such a manner that the poor may be taught gratis.

Resolved, That one-fifth part of the expense necessary to support the masters of said schools be paid out of the general funds of the State.

Resolved, That the remaining four-fifths of the said expense be paid in each county, respectively, by means of a county tax.

Resolved, That the said schools be put under the direction of trustees in each county, subject to such limitations and regulations, as to the distributions of their funds, the appointment of masters, and their general arrangements as shall be provided by law.

Resolved, That the schools thus established shall be free schools, and that at least spelling, reading, writing and arithmetic, shall be taught therein.

Resolved, That ten thousand dollars a year be appropriated out of the fund of this Commonwealth, to encourage the establishment of Academies, in which grammar, the elements of mathematics, geography and history shall be taught.

Resolved, That the said sum be apportioned amongst the city and several counties of the State in proportion to their respective population.

Resolved, That whenever a sum sufficient, with the addition of the sums proposed to be given by the public, to support an Academy for the purpose aforesaid shall have been subscribed, or contributed, the additional sum of one hundred dollars a year shall be given out of the public treasury, in aid of such Academy.

Resolved, That when the number of Academies in any county shall be

---

[1] There are 600 of these schools in the small state of Connecticut, which at this time have in them 25,000 scholars.

* Given in J. P. Wickersham, *A History of Education in Pennsylvania* (Lancaster, Inquirer Publishing Co., 1886), pp. 262-63. Wickersham says that a bill on this report was presented and passed by both houses of Legislature "but was finally lost in a Conference committee. This was a near approach to the adoption of a free school system forty years before the passage of the law of 1834." *Ibid.,* p. 263.

so great, that the sum to which such county is entitled becomes insufficient to afford one hundred dollars to each, it shall be divided by the trustees aforesaid among the whole of such Academies, in proportion to the number of masters employed, and scholars taught, and the length of time in each during which each Academy is so kept and supported.

Resolved, That whenever a sum is subscribed and contributed, sufficient, if added to the income of any of the inferior schools, to procure the instruction contemplated to be given in the Academies, such school shall become an Academy and receive the additional bounty of one hundred dollars as aforesaid, subject to a reduction in the manner aforesaid.

New York's Act for the "Encouragement of Schools, 1795 *

Be it enacted by the People of the State of New York, represented in Senate and Assembly That out of the annual revenue arising to this State from its stock and other funds, excepting so much thereof as shall be necessary for the support of government, the sum of twenty thousand pounds, shall be annually appropriated for the term of five years for the purpose of encouraging and maintaining schools in the several cities and towns in this State, in which the children of the inhabitants residing in this State shall be instructed in the English language or be taught English grammar, arithmetic, mathematics and such other branches of knowledge as are most useful and necessary to complete a good English education; which sum shall be distributed among the several counties in the manner following until a new apportionment of the representation of the legislature of this State shall be made that is to say,

The city and county of New York shall be entitled to receive the sum of one thousand eight hundred and eighty eight pounds.

The county of Kings the sum of one hundred and seventy four pounds.

The county of Queens the sum of seven hundred and forty four pounds.

The county of Suffolk the sum of eight hundred and forty pounds.

The county of Richmond the sum of one hundred and seventy four pounds.

The county of West-Chester the sum of one thousand one hundred and ninety two pounds.

The county of Dutchess the sum of two thousand two hundred pounds.

The county of Ulster the sum of one thousand four hundred and forty pounds.

The county of Orange the sum of nine hundred and forty four pounds.

The county of Columbia the sum of one thousand three hundred and ninety pounds.

* Given in Thomas E. Finegan, *Free Schools: A Documentary History of the Free School Movement in New York State* (Albany, University of the State of New York, 1921), pp. 26-32.

The county of Rensselaer the sum of one thousand one hundred and ninety two pounds.

The county of Washington the sum of one thousand one hundred and fifty two pounds.

The county of Clinton the sum of two hundred pounds.

The county of Albany the sum of one thousand five hundred and ninety pounds.

The county of Saratoga the sum of one thousand and ninety two pounds.

The county of Herkimer the sum of nine hundred and thirty pounds.

The county of Montgomery the sum of eleven hundred and ninety two pounds.

The county of Otsego the sum of eight hundred and forty four pounds.

The county of Onondaga the sum of one hundred and seventy four pounds.

The county of Tioga the sum of three hundred and forty eight pounds and

The county of Ontario the sum of three hundred pounds and the treasurer of the State is hereby required to pay the said several sums of money to the treasurers of the respective counties or their respective orders on the third Tuesday of March in every year or as soon thereafter as the said monies shall come into his hands provided nevertheless that the first of the said annual payments shall be made on the third Tuesday of March in the year one thousand seven hundred and ninety six. And if the annual revenue of the State after deducting what may be necessary for the support of government shall not be sufficient for the payment of the whole of the said sum of money in any one year, then the treasurer of the State shall pay the same out of any monies not otherwise appropriated which may be or may come into the treasury, and if the whole of the said monies not otherwise appropriated shall not be sufficient for that purpose then every such payment shall be made to each county respectively in the same proportion as the whole of the said money is hereby directed to be paid before the next apportionment of the representation on the legislature and after such next appropriation shall be made, every payment of the several counties shall be in proportion to the number of electors for members of assembly in each county. And the treasurers of the respective counties are hereby authorized to retain in their hands the sum of three pence in the pound for every pound of the monies which may come into their hands by virtue of this act as a compensation for their services in receiving and paying the same.

And whereas It will be expensive and inconvenient to enumerate the inhabitants of the several towns in every year. Therefore

Be it further enacted That it shall be the duty of the supervisors in each and every of the counties of this State, at their meeting on the last Tuesday of May or within ten days thereafter in every year to apportion the said respective sums among the several towns in their respective counties after having deducted the fees of the treasurers of their respective counties for receiving and paying the same, according to the number of taxable inhabitants which shall appear to be in several towns in each county, by the tax lists, directed to be annually returned to them by the act entitled "An act for defraying the public and necessary charge in the respective counties of this State and if at their said time of meeting no such tax list shall be returned to them, by the assessors of any one or more of the towns in any county then it shall be lawful for the supervisors to estimate the number of taxable inhabitants in any such town or towns according to the best information that they shall be able to obtain; and when such apportionment shall be completed the supervisors shall certify to each town the sum of money allotted to that town by virtue of this act; and a copy of such certificate, subscribed and sealed by them, shall be delivered to each supervisor present, who shall file the same in the office of the clerk of the town, for which he shall be supervisor, and when any one or more of the supervisors are absent, it shall be the duty of the clerk of the supervisors to transmit such certificates to the clerks of the several towns whose supervisors were not present at such annual meeting, and such clerks shall file the same in their respective offices.

And be it further enacted That the mayor, aldermen and commonalty of the city of New York in common council convened shall yearly and every year during the continuance of this act cause to be raised by a tax in the said city and county a sum equal to one half of the sum appropriated for encouraging and maintaining schools in the city and county for New York by virtue of this act in the same year to be added to and applied in the same manner with the money so appropriated as aforesaid, which said sums of money so to be raised shall be assessed levied and collected and paid according to the directions of the act entitled "An act for the more effectual collection of taxes in the city and county of New York."

And be it further enacted That the supervisors of each of the several other counties of this state shall yearly and every year during the continuance of the act cause to be raised by a tax in each town in the same county a sum equal to one half of the sum to be allotted to the same town in the same year out of the money so appropriated to the county by the State in the same year by virtue of this act to be added to and applied in the same manner with the money so to be allowed to the same town in the same year by virtue of this act which said sums of money shall be raised levied collected and paid to the treasurer of the same county together with and in the same manner as the necessary and contingent charges of the said county are to be raised collected and paid by virtue of the act entitled An act for defraying the public and necessary charge in the respective counties of this State.

And be it further enacted That it shall and may be lawful for the mayor aldermen and commonalty of the city of New York in common council convened from time to time during the continuance of this act to cause as well the money so appropriated for encouraging and maintaining schools in the city and county of New York as the money to be raised in the said city and county for the same purpose by virtue of this act to be applied as well as for the encouragement and maintaining of the several charity schools as of other schools in which children shall be instructed in the English language or taught English grammar arithmetic mathematics and such other branches of knowledge as are most useful and necessary to complete a good English education whether the children taught in such charity school shall be the children of white parents or descended from Africans or Indians in such manner as the common council shall think proper and in conformity with the intent of the act and shall on or before the first day of November in the year of our Lord one thousand seven hundred and ninety six and on or before the first day of November in every year thereafter during the continuance of this act cause an account of the application and distribution of the said monies to be filed in the office of the secretary of the State who shall deliver the same to the legislature at their next session.

And be it further enacted That on the distribution of the monies assigned to or to be raised within the city and company of New York amongst the different schools in the said city that if one or more of the said schools should refuse to receive their respective proportions of the money so assigned or raised as aforesaid then in that case the same shall be appropriated to the charity schools in the said city at the discretion of the said common council.

And be it further enacted That the supervisors of the county of Albany shall yearly and every year during the continuance of this act cause to be raised by a tax in the city of Albany a sum equal to the half sum to be appropriated for encouraging and maintaining schools in the said city by virtue of this act in the same year to be added to and applied the same manner with the monies so appropriated as aforesaid which said sum of money so to be raised shall be assessed levied and collected and paid to the treasurer of the same county together with and in the same manner as the necessary and contingent charges of the same county are to be raised collected and paid by virtue of the act entitled An act for defraying the public and necessary charge in the respective counties of this State.

And be it further enacted That it shall be lawful for the mayor aldermen and commonalty of the city of Albany in common council convened from time to time during the continuance of this act to cause as well the money so appropriated for encouraging and maintaining schools in the city of Albany as the money to be raised in the said city for the same purpose by virtue of this act to be applied for the encouragement and maintenance of the schools in which children shall be instructed in the English language or taught English grammar arithmetic mathematics and such other branches of knowledge as are most useful and necessary to complete a good English education in such manner as the common council shall think proper and most agreeable to the intent of this act on or before the first day of November in the year of our Lord one thousand seven hundred and ninety six and on or before the first day of November in every year thereafter during the continuance of this act cause an account of the application of the said monies to be filed in the office of the secretary of this State who shall deliver the same to the legislature at their then next session and the treasurer of the said county of Albany is hereby directed to pay as well the money so to be allotted to as to be raised in the said city of Albany for encouraging and maintaining schools in the said city of Albany to the order of the mayor aldermen and commonalty of the city of Albany to be by them appropriated as aforesaid.

And be it further enacted That it shall be lawful for the freeholders and inhabitants in the several towns in the State who may be qualified by law to vote at town meetings to elect at their respective annual town meetings not less than three nor more than seven persons who shall have the superintendence thereof and shall determine concerning the distribution of the monies allotted or raised in the same town for the purpose of encouraging and maintaining schools by virtue of this act in the manner hereafter directed provided that for the present year the supervisor and town clerk and assessors shall be commissioners.

And be it further enacted That the city of Hudson in the county of Columbia shall be considered as a town for all the purposes contemplated in this act: And the freemen of the said city being inhabitants thereof shall annually elect commissioners of schools in like manner as last above prescribed, and at such time in every year as they are by law directed to elect aldermen assistants, and other officers in and for the said city and the said commissioners when so elected and qualified as above prescribed shall continue in office for the like time perform the like duties, exercise the like powers and proceed in doing business in like manner as the commissioners of schools in the several towns in the State; and every certificate or other matter in writing which is hereby directed to be filed in the office of the clerk of any town, shall in and for the said city be filed in the office of the clerk of the city and that the city of Albany in the county of Albany shall be considered as a town in the distribution to be made by the supervisors of the same county of the money appropriated to the same county by this act.

And be it further enacted That for the purpose of deriving a benefit from the monies hereby appropriated it shall be lawful for the inhabitants residing in the different parts of any town to associate together for the purpose of procuring good and sufficient schoolmasters, and for erecting or maintaining schools in such and so many parts of the town where they may reside as shall be found most convenient and in which shall be taught such branches of learning as are intended to receive encouragement from the monies hereby appropriated. And all such persons as may associate together for the purposes above mentioned, shall appoint two other persons to act in their behalf as trustees of every school. *Provided nevertheless* that no person shall be appointed a trustee of any such school who may be, in any other manner authorized or empowered to carry this act into effect and the said trustees shall whenever they judge it necessary confer with the commissioners of schools for the town or ward where they may reside concerning the qualifications of the master or masters that they may have employed or may intend to employ, in their school, and concerning every other matter which may relate to the welfare of their school or to the propriety of erecting or maintaining the same, to the intent that they may obtain the determination of the said commissioners whether the said school will be entitled to a part of the moneys allotted to or raised in that town by virtue of this act and whether the abilities and moral character of the master or masters employed or intended to be employed therein are such as will meet with their approbation. And the said trustees of the said several schools shall on the third Tuesday in March in every year or within four days thereafter make a return certified under their respective hands to the commissioners of schools for the town where their respective schools may have been kept containing the name or names of the master or masters who in the year next preceding may have instructed in the school for which they were appointed trustees and the time or times when they severally began and left off instructing in the said school and the number of days they may have severally instructed therein, and the terms upon which they have severally agreed to instruct, in the same and the names of the scholars who in that year have been instructed therein and the number of days which they have severally attended the school and the time or times with which the school has been kept in that year *provided nevertheless* That the name of any child who shall be under the age of four years shall not be inserted in any such returns and if after the receipt of the said returns it shall appear to the said commissioners that there is no material error, fraud or deception in them they shall collect into one sum the whole number of days for which each and every scholar that may attended any one of the said schools shall have been instructed therein, and shall apportion the monies allotted to and raised in that town for that purpose aforesaid according to the whole number of days for which instruction shall appear to have been given in each of the said schools in such manner that the school in which the greater number of days of instruction shall appear to have been given shall have a proportionally larger sum and if it shall at any time appear to the said commissioners that the abilities or moral character of the master or masters of any school are not such that they ought to be entrusted with the education of youth or that any of the branches of learning taught in any school are not such as are intended to receive encouragement from the monies appropriated by this act the said commissioners shall notify in writing the said trustees of such notification and no longer shall any allowance be made to such school unless the same thereafter be conducted to the approbation of the said commissioners and where more masters than one shall have been employed in any school the said commissioners shall apportion the monies allotted to that school among the said several masters according to such agreement as shall have been made with them by the trustees of said school or by any other person or persons who may have procured them.

And be it further enacted That nothing herein contained shall be construed to prevent the inhabitants residing near the limits or borders of any town from associating with inhabitants residing in any adjoining town for the purposes above mentioned and in every such case the trustees of the school shall be residents of the town shall make the like distribution to such school as is hereinbefore prescribed with respect to the other schools in such town.

And be it further enacted That the said commissioners in every town shall provide a book in which they shall make an entry of every school under their superintendence the names of the trustees and the names of masters the time of application made to them by the trustees and the time of approbation of the said commissioners as well of schools already established during the continuance of this act and shall on the last Tuesday in May in every year from the return of the trustees with such vouchers as may be necessary determine the sums due to the trustees of the respective schools and shall give to the trustees of each school an order on the treasurer of the county for the sum of which they shall so determine to be due and the treasurer of the county is hereby required to pay the same.

And be it further enacted That the commissioners in the several towns within this State shall on or before the first day of July in the year one thousand seven hundred and ninety-six and in every year thereafter during the continuance of this act delivered to the treasurer of their respective counties a schedule containing the number of schools the masters names the number of scholars taught and the number of days of instruction in the school of which they were the commissioners and the treasurers of the several counties shall on or before the first day of November in every year transmit the same to the secretaries office and the secretary shall lay the same before the legislature at their next meeting.

And whereas special provisions hath already been made for the encouragement of learning in the several colleges and academies in the State. Therefore

Be it further enacted That nothing in this act contained shall be so construed as to extend to any college or academy which is or hereafter shall be incorporated under the authority of the regents of the university or by virtue of any law of the State.

And be it further enacted That this act shall be in force and take effect, from and after the first Tuesday of April one thousand seven hundred and ninety-five.

Connecticut Establishes the First Permanent Public School Fund in the United States, 1795 *

An Act appropriating the Monies which shall arise on the sale of the Western Lands, belonging to this State.

Be it enacted by the Governor and Council, and House of Representatives, in General Court assembled, That the principal sum, which shall be received on the sale of the lands belonging to this State, lying west of Pennsylvania, shall be, and remain a perpetual Fund, for the purposes hereafter mentioned in this Act, to be loaned, or otherwise improved for those purposes as the General Assembly shall direct; and the interest arising therefrom, shall be, and hereby is appropriated to the support of Schools in the several Societies constituted, or which may be constituted by law, within certain local bounds within this State, to be kept according to the provisions of law, which shall from time to time be made, and to no other use or purpose whatsoever; except in the case, and under the circumstances hereafter mentioned in this Act.

Be it further enacted, That the said interest as it shall become due from time to time, shall be paid over to the said Societies, in their capacity of School Societies, according to the list of polls and rateable Estate of such Societies respectively; which shall, when such payment shall be made, have been last perfected.

Provided nevertheless, and be it further enacted, That whenever such Society shall, pursuant to a vote of such Society passed in a legal meeting warned for that purpose only, in which vote two thirds of the legal voters present in such meeting shall concur, apply to the General Assembly requesting liberty to improve their proportion of said interest, or any part thereof, for the support of the christian Ministry or the public worship of God, the General Assembly shall have full power to grant such request during their pleasure; and in case of any such grant, the School Society shall pay over the amount so granted, to the religious Societies, Churches or Congregations, of all denominations of christians within its limits, to be proportioned to such Societies, Churches or Congregations, according to the list of their respective inhabitants or members, which shall, when such payment shall from time to time be made, have been last perfected;

* *Connecticut Acts and Laws,* 1795, pp. 487-89. For a general story of this form of public school support, see F. H. Swift, *A History of Public Permanent Common School Funds in the United States,* 1795-1905 (New York, Henry Holt & Co., Inc., 1911).

and in case there shall be in such School Society any individuals composing a part only of any such religious Society, Church or Congregation, then the proportion of such individuals shall be paid to the order of the body to which they belong, by the rule aforesaid; and the monies of such individuals shall be discounted from their ministeral taxes, or contributions, and in that way inure to their exclusive benefit; and the monies so paid over, shall be applied to the purposes of the grant, and to no other whatsoever.

Be it further enacted, That if any Society, Church or Congregation, shall apply any of the aforesaid monies to any other use or purpose, than those to which they shall, or may have a right to apply them pursuant to this Act, such Society, Church or Congregation, shall forfeit and pay a sum equal to that so misapplied, to the public Treasury of this State.

Be it further enacted, That all the inhabitants living within the limits of the located Societies, who by law have or may have a right to vote in Town meetings, shall meet sometime in the month of October annually, in the way and manner prescribed in the statute, entitled "An Act for forming, ordering, and regulating Societies," and being so met shall exercise the powers given in and by said Act, in organizing themselves, and in appointing the necessary officers, as therein directed for the year ensuing; and may transact any other business on the subject of schooling in general, and touching the monies hereby appropriated to their use, in particular, according to law; and shall have power to adjourn from time to time, as they shall think proper.

Be it further enacted, That the inhabitants or members of the several religious Societies, Churches or Congregations aforesaid, who have right by law to vote in their respective meetings, on the subject of ministry, and the public worship of God, shall assemble themselves sometime in the month of December annually, or at such other time as they shall judge convenient, and may organize themselves, and appoint the necessary officers as in said act is directed, all in the way and manner therein prescribed, with power to adjourn from time to time as they may think proper; and in any of their said meetings they shall have power to transact any business relating to the ministry and the public worship of God, according to law; but shall have no power to act on the subject of schooling; any law, usage, or custom, to the contrary notwithstanding.

Be it further enacted, That an Act passed October 1793, entitled "An Act for the establishing a Fund, for the support of the Gospel Ministry, and Schools of Education," be, and the same is hereby repealed.

Pennsylvania Makes Provision for "The Education of the Poor Gratis," 1802 *

Whereas, by the first section of the seventh article of the Constitution of this Commonwealth it is directed "That the Legislature shall as soon as conveniently may be, provide by law for the establishment of schools throughout the State, in such manner as that the poor may be taught gratis," Therefore,

Section I. Be it enacted, etc. That from and after the passing of this act the Guardians and Overseers of the poor of the City of Philadelphia, the District of Southwark and townships and Boroughs within this Commonwealth, shall ascertain the names of all those children whose parents or guardians they shall judge to be unable to pay for their schooling, to give notice in writing to such parent or guardian that provision is made by law for the education of their children or the children under their care, and that they have a full and free right to subscribe at the usual rates and send them to any school in their neighborhood, giving notice thereof as soon as may be to the Guardians or Overseers of the term for which they have subscribed, the number of scholars and the rate of tuition, and in those Townships where there are no guardians or overseers of the poor, the Supervisors of the Highways shall perform the duties herein required to be done by the Guardians or Overseers of the poor.

Section II. And be it further enacted by the authority aforesaid, That every Guardian or Overseer of the poor, or Supervisor of the Highways, as the case may be, in any township or place where any such child or children shall be sent to school as aforesaid, shall enter in a book the name or names, age and length of time such child or children shall have been so sent to school, together with the amount of schooling, school-books and stationery, and shall levy and collect in the same way and manner and under the same regulations as poor taxes or road taxes are levied and collected, a sufficient sum of money from their respective townships, boroughs, wards or districts, to discharge such expenses together with the sum of five per cent for their trouble.

Section III. And be it further enacted by the authority aforesaid, That the Guardians or Overseers of the poor for the time being, or Supervisors of the Highways as the case may be, shall use all diligence and prudence in carrying this act into effect, and shall settle their accounts in the same way and manner as by the existing laws of the State, the Guardians, Overseers of the poor, and Supervisors of the poor, and Supervisors of the Highways are authorized and required to settle their accounts.

Section IV. And be it further enacted by the authority aforesaid, That this act shall continue in force for the term of three years, and from thence to the end of the next sitting of the General Assembly and no longer.

* Given in J. P. Wickersham, *op. cit.,* pp. 263-64.

An Address to the Public in Behalf of Public Schools
in New York City, 1805 *

TO THE PUBLIC

*Address of the Trustees of the "Society for Establishing a Free
School in the City of New York, for the Education of such Poor
Children as do not Belong to, or are not Provided for by, any
Religious Society."*

While the various religious and benevolent societies in this city, with a
spirit of charity and zeal which the precepts and example of the Divine
Author of our religion could alone inspire, amply provide for the education of such poor children as belong to their respective associations, there
still remains a large number living in total neglect of religious and moral
instruction, and unacquainted with the common rudiments of learning,
essentially requisite for the due management of the ordinary business of
life. This neglect may be imputed either to the extreme indigence of the
parents of such children, their intemperance and vice, or to a blind indifference to the best interests of their offspring. The consequences must be
obvious to the most careless observer. Children thus brought up in ignorance, and amidst the contagion of bad example, are in imminent danger
of ruin; and too many of them, it is to be feared, instead of being useful
members of the community, will become the burden and pests of society.
Early instruction and fixed habits of industry, decency, and order, are the
surest safeguards of virtuous conduct; and when parents are either unable
or unwilling to bestow the necessary attention on the education of their
children, it becomes the duty of the public, and of individuals, who have
the power, to assist them in the discharge of this important obligation.
It is in vain that laws are made for the punishment of crimes, or that good
men attempt to stem the torrent of irreligion and vice, if the evil is not
checked at its source; and the means of prevention, by the salutary discipline of early education, seasonably applied. It is certainly in the power of
the opulent and charitable, by a timely and judicious interposition of their
influence and aid, if not wholly to prevent, at least to diminish, the pernicious effects resulting from the neglected education of the children of
the poor.

Influenced by these considerations, and from a sense of the necessity of
providing some remedy for an increasing and alarming evil, several individuals, actuated by similar motives, agree to form an association for the

---

* This address was published in the papers of that city in May, 1805. It is given in W. O.
Bourne, *History of the Public School Society of the City of New York* (New York, 1870).
New York had a population of about 60,000 in 1800, but its educational facilities were
limited to those provided by private and denominational efforts. In 1805 some citizens of the
city applied to the legislature of the state and received a charter for a Free School Society.
To secure funds for a school building, the address given above was made.

purpose of extending the means of education to such poor children as do not belong to, or are not provided for, by any religious society. After meetings, numerously attended, a plan of association was framed, and a Memorial prepared and addressed to the legislature, soliciting an Act of Incorporation, the better to enable them to carry into effect their benevolent design. Such a law the Legislature, at their last session, was pleased to pass; and at a meeting of the Society, under the Act of Incorporation, on the sixth instant, thirteen Trustees were elected for the ensuing year.

The particular plan of the school, and the rules for its discipline and management, will be made known previous to its commencement. Care will be exercised in the selection of teachers, and, besides the elements of learning usually taught in schools, strict attention will be bestowed on the morals of the children, and all suitable means be used to counteract the disadvantages resulting from the situation of their parents. It is proposed, also, to establish, on the first day of the week, a school, called a Sunday School, more particularly for such children as, from peculiar circumstances, are unable to attend on the other days of the week. In this, as in the Common School, it will be a primary object, without observing the peculiar forms of any religious Society, to inculcate the sublime truths of religion and morality contained in the Holy Scriptures.

This Society, as will appear from its name, interferes with no existing institution, since children already provided with the means of education, or attached to any other Society, will not come under its care. Humble gleaners in the wide field of benevolence, the members of this Association seek such objects only as are left by those who have gone before, or are fellow-laborers with them in the great work of charity. They, therefore, look with confidence for the encouragement and support of the affluent and charitable of every denomination of Christians; and when they consider that in no community is to be found a greater spirit of liberal and active benevolence than among the citizens of New York, they feel assured that adequate means for the prosecution of their plan will be easily obtained. In addition to the respectable list of original subscriptions, considerable funds will be requisite for the purchase or hire of a piece of ground, and the erection of a suitable building for the school, to pay the teachers, and to defray other charges incident to the establishment. To accomplish this design, and to place the Institution on a solid and respectable foundation, the Society depend on the voluntary bounty of those who may be charitably disposed to contribute their aid in the promotion of an object of great and universal concern.

DE WITT CLINTON, *President.*
JOHN MURRAY, JR., *Vice-President.*
LEONARD BLEEKER, *Treasurer.*
B. D. PERKINS, *Secretary.*

New York, May (5th Month) 18, 1805.

Virginia Establishes a Literary Fund for the Encouragement of Learning, 1810 *

Be it enacted, That all escheats, confiscations, fines, penalties and forfeitures, and all rights in personal property accruing to the commonwealth, as derelict, and having no rightful proprietor, be, and the same are hereby appropriated to the encouragement of learning; and that the auditor of public accounts be, and he is hereby required to open an account to be designated The Literary Fund. To which he shall carry every payment hereafter made into the treasury on account of any escheat or confiscation, which has happened or may happen, or any fine, penalty or forfeiture which has been or may be imposed, or which may accrue: Provided always, That his act shall not apply to militia fines.

And be it further enacted, That this act shall in no case, change the mode of proceeding for the recovery of any of the subjects herein mentioned, but they shall be prosecuted in the same manner as if this act had not passed.

And be it further enacted, That the fund aforesaid shall be divided and appropriated as to the next legislature shall seem best adapted to the promotion of literature: Provided always, That the aforesaid fund shall be appropriated to the sole benefit of a school or schools, to be kept in each and every county within this commonwealth, subject to such orders and regulations as the general assembly shall hereafter direct.

This act shall be in force from the passing thereof.

The State of New York Provides for Common Schools and for a State Superintendent, 1812 †

I. *Be it enacted by the People of the State of New York, represented in Senate and Assembly,* That there shall be constituted an officer within this state, known and distinguished as the superintendent of common schools, which superintendent shall be appointed by the council of appointment, and shall keep his office at the seat of government, and shall be allowed an annual salary of three hundred dollars, but not to be under pay until he shall give notice of the first distribution of the school money, payable in the same way as is provided for other officers, by the act, entitled "An act for the support of government."

II. *And be it further enacted,* That it shall be the duty of the superintendent aforesaid, to digest and prepare plans for the improvement and management of the common school fund, and for the better organization of common schools; to prepare and report estimates and expenditures of

---

* *Acts of the General Assembly of Virginia,* 1809-1810, p. 15.
† *Laws of New York,* for 1812, chapter CCXLII (Passed June 19, 1812). Given in Thomas E. Finegan, *op. cit.,* pp. 43-51.

the school monies, to superintend the collection thereof, to execute such services relative to the sale of the lands, which now are or hereafter may be appropriated, as a permanent fund for the support of common schools, as may be by law required of him; to give information to the legislature respecting all matters referred to him by either branch thereof, or which shall appertain to his office; and generally to perform all such services relative to the welfare of schools, as he shall be directed to perform, and shall, prior to his entering upon the duties of his office, take an oath or affirmation for the diligent and faithful execution of his trust.

III. *And be it further enacted,* That no distribution of the interest of the school fund shall take place amongst the common schools of this State, until it shall arise to fifty thousand dollars a year; and it shall not be lawful for the superintendent aforesaid to distribute any more thany fifty thousand dollars a year until he shall find he will be able to distribute sixty thousand, and the sum of sixty thousand until the interest shall arise to seventy thousand, and so on as often as the interest shall increase ten thousand dollars, it shall be lawful for the superintendent to add to the sum last distributed ten thousand dollars more; and in all cases when he shall find he will be enabled to add ten thousand dollars to the sum last distributed, the next year, it shall be his duty to send a notice to the county clerk, and for said county clerk to notify the several town clerks in his county previous to such increase of monies to be distributed in the same form and manner as is provided in the fifth section of this act, to be made previously to the first distribution.

IV. *And be it further enacted,* That the interest of the school funds which shall accumulate annually between the time of the first distribution of fifty thousand dollars, and sixty thousand dollars, and seventy thousand dollars, and so on from time to time, shall by the comptroller, be loaned and re-loaned in the same form and manner, and on the same security as he is now by law directed to loan the monies belonging to the common school fund of this State, and shall become principal in said funds.

V. *And be it further enacted,* That the superintendent of common schools shall, in the month of January, which will be thirteen months before the first distribution of the interest of the school fund, send a notice in writing to each of the county clerks in this state, informing them that there will be a distribution of the interest of the school fund in the month of February, which will be thirteen months after the date of said notice, stating the amount that will be assigned to each county. And it shall be the duty of the said county clerks, to send a like notice to the clerk of the board of supervisors, and to each town clerk in his county, stating the amount of money to be distributed, and the time when, which notice the town clerk shall read at the opening of the next town meeting, to the intent that the town meeting may direct by their vote the supervisor, to levy on said town, at the next meeting of the board aforesaid, the sum for the support of common schools, required by this act to entitle said town to its proportion of the interest of said fund to be distributed; and the supervisor of each town so complying, shall, on or before the first Tuesday of June after, in each year, deliver a notice in writing, of such compliance, to the clerk of the board of supervisors of the county, and said clerk shall, at the opening of the next meeting of said board, report the several notices so received to the board of supervisors aforesaid, whose duty it shall be to apportion the county's proportion of said monies amongst the several towns that shall have directed the raising of such school monies, according to the population of each town as ascertained by the census of the United States having so complied, and file a list of the names of such towns, with the several sums allotted to each of them, in the office of the county treasurer, and the said county treasurer shall pay to the school commissioners of each such town its proportion of said school money according to said list. And the board of supervisors shall cause to be added to the sum raised in each of said towns, to pay the contingent expense of the respective towns, a sum equal to the sum which such town is to receive of the school monies aforesaid, with the addition of five cents on a dollar, of said sum for collection fees, and direct the collector in his warrant to pay the same, when collected, into the hands of the school commissioners of the several towns, reserving his fees, and take their receipts therefor; which receipt shall be his voucher of having paid such sum, and the treasurer shall file the same in his office, without fee or reward: *Provided always,* That the respective towns may, at their town meetings direct as much more money to be raised than is equal to their respective proportion of the school money as they may deem proper for the purposes aforesaid, not exceeding double said sum.

VI. *And be it further enacted,* That the inhabitants living within the limits of the several towns within this state, and within the cities of Hudson and Schenectady, who by law have, or may have a right to vote in town meetings, shall, on the days of their annual town meetings, choose, by ballot, three of the inhabitants of their respective towns, commissioners, to superintend and manage the concerns of the schools within said towns respectively, and to perform all such services relative to schools as they shall be directed to perform; that said commissioners, before they enter upon the execution of their office, shall respectively take an oath or affirmation, for the diligent and faithful execution of their trust, which commissioners shall be allowed for their services so much as the inhabitants of said towns respectively shall direct, and the same shall be paid out of the monies raised for town expenses. And the inhabitants of said towns respectively, shall choose a suitable number of persons within their respective towns, not exceeding six, who, together with the commissioners aforesaid, shall be inspectors of the schools of said towns respectively; which inspectors shall examine the teachers, and the respective schools, and no person shall be employed as a teacher in any one of the schools, in any of the districts of this State, who shall not have been previously examined by the inspectors aforesaid, and have received a certificate, signed by at least two of said inspectors, importing that he is duly qualified to teach a common school, and is of good moral character. And it shall be the further duty of the inspectors to examine into the state of the schools in their respective towns, both as it respects the proficiency of the scholars, and the good order and regularity of the schools; and from time to time to give their advice and directions to the trustees, as to the government of the same.

VII. *And be it further enacted,* That the commissioners aforesaid are hereby authorized and empowered to divide their respective towns into a suitable and convenient number of districts, for keeping their schools, and to alter and regulate the same from time to time, as there may be occasion; and whenever it may be necessary and convenient to form a district out of two or more adjoining towns, such district may be formed by the commissioners from all such towns parts of which may be included in such district, and may be in like manner altered or changed at their pleasure; and every such district shall be under the superintendence of the inspectors of the town in which such school-house shall be situated, and numbered accordingly. And where it shall be convenient for any neighborhood adjoining to any other state, where such neighborhood has been in the habit of sending their children to a school in such adjoining state, it shall be lawful for said commissioners to set off such neighborhood by themselves, and such neighborhood shall be entitled to their share of the monies amongst the several districts in the town where said neighborhood shall be situate, in proportion to the number of children in such neighborhood between the ages of five to fifteen years; and it shall be lawful for such neighborhood to meet together and appoint one trustee, who shall make a report to said commissioners on or before the first day day of May in each year, containing the number of children in such neighborhood from five years to fifteen inclusive, and the number educated in said school in the preceding year; and it is hereby made the duty of the commissioners aforesaid to describe and number each district within their respective towns, and deliver the same in writing to the clerk of such town, who is hereby required to record the same in the town records. And whenever a district shall be altered, pursuant to this act, it shall be the duty of the said commissioners to make a new description corresponding with such alteration, and the same shall be recorded in manner aforesaid.

VIII. *And be it further enacted,* That whenever any town in this state shall be divided into school districts, according to the directions of this act, it shall be the duty of one of the school-commissioners of said town, within twenty days after, to make a notice in writing, describing said district, and appointing a time and place for the first district meeting, and deliver said writing to some one of the freeholders or inhabitants, liable to pay taxes, residing in said district, whose duty it shall be to notify each freeholder or inhabitant residing in said district, qualified as aforesaid, by reading such notice in the hearing of each such freeholder or inhabitant, or leaving a copy thereof at the place of his abode, at least six days before the time of such meeting; and if any such freeholder or inhabitant shall neglect or refuse to give such notice, he shall pay a fine of five dollars, to be recovered in the same manner, and for the same purpose, as is provided in the ninth section of this act. Such district meeting shall have power, when so convened, by the major vote of the persons so met, to adjourn from time to time as occasion may require, and to fix on a time and place to hold their future annual meetings, which annual meeting they are hereby authorized and required to hold, and to alter and change the time and place of holding such annual meeting as they or a majority of them, at any legal meeting, may think proper. And at such first meeting, or any future meeting, the said freeholders and inhabitants, or a majority of them so met, are hereby authorized and empowered to appoint a moderator for the time being, to designate a site for their school-house, to vote a tax on the resident inhabitants of such district as a majority present shall deem sufficient to purchase a suitable site for their school-house, and build, keep in repair, and furnish it with necessary fuel and appendages; also to choose three trustees to manage the concerns of such district, whose duty it shall be to build and keep in repair their school-house, and from time to time, as occasion may require, to agree with and employ instructors, and to pay them; also to choose one district clerk to keep the records and doings of said meeting, whose doings shall be good in law, who shall be qualified by oath or affirmation, as the several town clerks are; likewise one collector, who shall have the same power and authority, and have the same fees for collecting, and be subject to the same rules, regulations and duties, as respects the business of the district, which by law appertaineth to the collectors of towns in this state; and the said trustees, clerks, and collectors shall not be compelled to serve more than one year at any one itme; and it shall be the further duty of trustees of each district as soon as may be after the district meeting have voted a tax, to make a rate bill or tax list, which shall raise the sum voted, with five cents on a dollar for collector's fees, on all the taxable inhabitants of said district, agreeable to the levy on which the town tax was levied the preceding year, and annex to said tax list or rate bill a warrant, which warrant shall be substantially as followeth:

County of . . . . ss. To . . . . collector of the . . . . district, in the town of . . . . in the county aforesaid, greeting: In the name of the people of the state of New York, you are hereby required and commanded to collect from each of the inhabitants of said district, the several sums of money written opposite to

the name of each of said inhabitants, in the annexed tax list, and within
. . . . . . days after receiving this warrant, to pay the amount of the monies
by you collected into the hands of the trustees of said district, or some one
of them, and take their or his receipt therefor. And if any one or more of
said inhabitants shall neglect or refuse to pay the sum, you are hereby
further commanded to levy on the goods and chattels of each delinquent,
and make sale thereof according to law. Given under our hands and seals
this . . . . day of 181

[L. S.]
[L. S.] Trustees
[L. S.]

IX. *And be it further enacted,* That the trustees of each district, or a
majority of them, whenever they shall deem it expedient, may call a special
meeting of the inhabitants of said district, to transact any business which
may come regularly before them: *Provided always,* That such trustees shall
give five days notice, in writing, to the inhabitants of said district respectively.

X. *And be it further enacted,* That every person and persons, being duly
chosen and appointed as aforesaid, to serve in any of the offices aforesaid,
who shall refuse to serve therein, and to take the oath, (if any by law be
required) to said office respectively belonging, if he be able to execute the
said duties, shall pay the sum of five dollars, with costs, to be recovered
by an action of debt brought by the school commissioners of the town or
any individual, on this statute, before a justice of the peace in the county
where the defendant shall dwell, in the ordinary mode of proceeding before
magistrates; which money, when collected, after deducting the costs, shall
be subject to the order of the commissioners of the town where the defendant was so chosen and appointed to office as aforesaid, for the use of
the common schools in said town; and every such officer, duly chosen and
appointed as aforesaid, having accepted (or not declared his refusal to
accept) the office he is appointed to, and who shall neglect the performance of the trust committed to him, shall pay the sum of ten dollars, and
the same shall be recovered in manner aforesaid, with costs of prosecution,
and when collected, shall be disposed of in manner aforesaid.

XI. *And be it further enacted,* That if any person who is not duly qualified, according to this act, to vote in any town-meeting, shall vote for the
choice of officers, granting of taxes, or any other matters contemplated in
this act, such persons so offending, and being thereof convicted before any
court having competent jurisdiction, shall be fined in a sum not exceeding
five dollars, and not less than three dollars, at the discretion of the court,
and shall pay all costs and charges of prosecution; and the fine, when collected, shall be disposed of in the manner directed in the preceding section.

XII. *And be it further enacted,* That the several persons appointed within any town to any office instituted by this act, may hold their offices until the annual meeting next following such appointment, and until others shall be appointed in their places; and whenever it shall happen that the said officers, or any of them, shall be vacated, either from neglect of appointment, refusal to serve, death, or removal from the district or town, or incapacity of such as may be thus appointed, such vacancy or vacancies may be supplied in the way and manner prescribed in the sixth section of the act, entitled, "an act relative to the duties and privileges of towns," in similar cases, which officers, thus appointed, shall be regarded the same in all respects as if appointed by the inhabitants of such district or town.

XIII. *And be it further enacted,* That from and after the passing of this act, the interest of the common school fund, arising under the several acts of this state, as from time to time shall become due, shall be paid to the treasurer of this state, which, together with all such monies as are by law pledged and appropriated for the encouragement and support of common schools, shall be distributed and applied pursuant to this act, and not otherwise; and to the end that the said monies may be inviolably applied in conformity to this act, and may never be diverted to any other purpose, an account shall be kept by the treasurer of the receipts and dispositions thereof, separate and distinct from other accounts.

XIV. *And be it further enacted,* That the several towns in this state which shall conform to the provisions of this act, shall be entitled to such monies, to be distributed to them severally, according to the number of inhabitants in each town, to be ascertained by the respective census under the constitution of the United States, subject nevertheless to a distribution thereof, by said town, to the several school districts therein, pursuant to this act.

XV. *And be it further enacted,* That the several school districts within the several towns in this state which shall conform to the provisions of this act, shall be entitled to the monies deposited with the commissioners as aforesaid, to be distributed to said districts severally, according to the number of children within each district, between the ages of five and fifteen inclusive, as shall appear from the returns of the trustees aforesaid, made pursuant to this act; and it is hereby made the duty of said commissioners, annually, on or before the first day of May, to apportion the monies aforesaid to the several school districts, in manner aforesaid; but in each district, composed of more than one town, each of the several parts shall draw its proportion, according to its number of children as aforesaid, from the town in which such part shall be situate; for which purpose, it shall be the duty of the trustees of such district, not only to make a general report as is hereinafter directed, but a report of the number of children in each part, to their several town commissioners respectively, and to pay over to each of said districts its share thereof, on the order of one or more of the trustees of such district, taking a receipt therefor; which monies shall be applied and expended by said trustees in paying the wages of the teachers to be employed, and for no other purpose; and further, that the accounts of the said commissioners shall annually be audited and settled by the board appointed by law to settle accounts of overseers of the poor in the respective towns: *Provided,* That after the first year, no order shall be accepted, nor shall the commissioners aforesaid deliver the monies, directed to be delivered as aforesaid, until two of the trustees of such district shall have certified in writing, under their hands in the words following, viz.: We, the trustees of the   school district within the town of   do certify, that the school in said district hath been kept for three months at least, during the year ending on the first day of May last, by an instructor duly appointed and approved in all respects, according to law, and that all the monies by us drawn from the commissioners for said year, appropriated for schools, have been faithfully applied and expended in paying the wages of said instructor.—Dated

Trustees.

Provided always, That nothing shall be so construed as to prevent any persons attending said schools, whom the trustees aforesaid may deem proper to admit: *Provided further,* That whenever the aggregate expense of paying the instructors in schools, in any of the towns in this State, shall in any year equal or exceed the fund deposited with the commissioners as aforesaid, although any one or more of the districts in such town shall not have kept a school within the year, or not long enough to expend its proportion of such monies which otherwise would have belonged to such district, the monies thus unexpended and remaining with the commissioners aforesaid, shall be paid to and applied in the districts which have complied with the law, and which shall have expended, in paying instructors, a sum exceeding their proportion, regard being had, as far as may be, to their respective rights; but if such aggregate expense shall not equal the funds for any given year, then the monies shall remain with the commissioners aforesaid, to be added to and distributed with the monies next to be appropriated under this act.

XVI. *And be it further enacted,* That if the trustees appointed under this act shall make a false certificate, by means whereof the school monies aforesaid shall be fraudulently obtained from the commissioners, each person signing such false certificate shall forfeit the sum of twenty dollars to the commissioners of such town to which such trustees shall belong, to be recovered by action of debt on this statute, in the name of the said commissioners, who are hereby required to prosecute therefor accordingly; and the sum when recovered, shall be applied for the benefit of the common schools in said town.

XVII. *And be it further enacted,* That the trustees of the several school districts shall, annually, on the first day of May, make and transmit to the commissioners of the town wherein their respective districts are situated, a report, specifying the length of time a school hath been kept in said district; the amount of monies received; the manner the same hath been expended; and, as nearly as may be, the number of scholars taught therein, and the number of children, from five years old to fifteen inclusive, except Indian children otherwise provided for by law; whereupon the commissioners of the several towns aforesaid shall, on or before the first day of July, annually, make a town report to the clerk of the county wherein such town shall be situate, which report shall embrace the same objects as are contained in the report of the trustees as aforesaid; and the clerks of the several counties in this state shall, on or before the first day of November, annually, make a county report, in manner aforesaid, comprising the several reports received by them as aforesaid, and transmit the same to the superintendent of common schools; whereupon the said superintendent shall annually, on or before the first Tuesday in February, make a report to the legislature, embracing all the objects contemplated in this act: *Provided always,* That the several duties enjoined on the several county treasurers and county clerks, shall be done without fee or reward; and if any of the said treasurers or clerks shall refuse to do any of said duties, he or they shall forfeit and pay the same fine which is imposed, as aforesaid, on the town commissioners and trustees of districts; which fine shall be recovered in the same way, and applied to the same purpose, as the fines imposed on said commissioners and trustees.

XVIII. *And be it further enacted,* That out of the school money apportioned by the superintendent, from time to time, to the county of Albany, the city of Albany shall have its proportion, with the towns in the county, according to the population thereof, and shall be paid by the county treasurer into the hands of the trustees of the Lancaster school, in said city, who shall give their receipt therefor, to be applied to the education of such poor children, belonging to said city, which may be, in the opinion of the said trustees, entitled to gratuitous education: *Provided,* That the said trustees shall receive into said school, all the children of every poor person residing in said city, and in no wise turn away any child that shall be, for that purpose, presented to them, from time to time; and that said trustees shall account to the county treasurer of said county for the faithful application of said money, according to the true intent and meaning of this act; and shall make a true report of the state of the school, with the number of scholars educated in said school, in the year last passed, to the county clerk, on the first day of July in each year, to be incorporated into the county report to be made to the superintendent of common schools.

XIX. *And be it further enacted,* That the clerk of each town and of the cities of Hudson and Schenectady, shall, at any time after the passing of this act, on application of any six freeholders of such city or town, warn a town-meeting, giving at least eight days notice of such meeting in the

manner now provided by law, for the purpose of electing commissioners
of schools.

XX. *And be it further enacted,* That in all cases in which any new town
or towns may have been erected, or shall hereinafter be erected, from a
part of any other town or towns since the census aforesaid, it shall be the
duty of the supervisors of such towns, to meet on the day of the month,
and at the place directed by law for erecting such town, or at such other
time and place as they may agree upon, and shall then and there apportion
the money to be divided between the said towns, in the same proportion as
the poor of the town, and the money belonging to them, shall be divided.

James G. Carter on "This Wretched Mockery" of Education in Massachusetts, 1824 *

The pilgrims of Plymouth set the first example not only to our own
country, but to the civilized world, of a system of free schools, at which
were educated together, not by compulsion, but from mutual choice, all
classes of the community—the high, the low, the rich, and the poor—
a system, by which the state so far assumed the education of the youth, as
to make all property responsible for the support of common schools for
the instruction of all children. This institution was indeed the foster child,
and has justly been the pride, of Massachusetts and of New England. Its
influences were strong, and they still are strong, upon the moral and
political character of the people. . . .

If the policy of the legislature in regard to free schools for the last twenty
years be not changed, the institution which has been the glory of New
England will, in twenty years more, be extinct. If the State continue to
relieve itself of the trouble of providing for the instruction of the whole
people, and to shift the responsibility upon the towns, and the towns upon
the districts, and the districts upon individuals, each will take care of himself and his own family as he is able, and as he appreciates the blessing
of a good education. The rich will, as a class, have much better instruction
than they now have, while the poor will have much worse or none at
all. The academies and private schools will be carried to much greater
perfection than they have been, while the public free schools will become
stationary or retrograde, till at length they will be thrown for support upon
the gratuitous and of course capricious and uncertain efforts of individuals; and then, like the lower schools of the crowded cities of Europe, they
will soon degenerate into mere mechanical establishments, such as the
famous *seminaries* of London, Birmingham, and Manchester, of which we
hear so much lately, not for rational, moral, and intellectual instruction of
human beings, but for training young animals to march, sing, and draw
figures in sand—establishments in which the power of one man is so pro-

* "Essays on Popular Education." Given in *Old South Leaflets,* VI, No. 135, pp. 201, 220.

ligiously multiplied that he can overlook, direct, and control the intellectual exercises of a thousand! And this wretched mockery of education they must be right glad to accept as a charity instead of inheriting as their birthright as good instruction as the country affords.

An Early Educational "Survey," by the Faculty of the College (Now University) of South Carolina, 1825 *

To the Legislature of the State of South Carolina, the Faculty of the South-Carolina College, with all respect beg leave to Report—

That in conformity with the Resolution adopted by both houses of the Legislature, on the 20th December, 1825, requesting the Faculty to prepare a detailed System for the better regulation of PUBLIC SCHOOLS, and other Seminaries of learning in this State, and that they report the same at an early period of the next session of the Legislature, the Faculty aforesaid have given to the subjects of the said resolution their best attention. In so doing they have taken a view of the present system of free schools in this State, and of the present state of the South-Carolina College.

And first, with Respect to the Free School system adopted among us, the Faculty would briefly premise the acknowledged truths, that no society has a right to exact obedience to the laws from those members of the community, who, without any neglect on the part of their parents or themselves, have had no means of instruction so as to enable them to acquire reasonable information of what the laws are which they are required to obey. That no person can be expected to make a good citizen of a Republican Government, who is not able to read and understand the Constitution which he is required to support: and although despotism may rest satisfied with a state of ignorance among the mass of its subjects; who have nothing to do with the laws but to obey them, it is not so in a Republican Government, where the people are actual parties to the laws that are enacted. In such a government, the means of understanding these laws should be universally distributed throughout the community. In Europe, where the class

* This report was printed as a broadside on one side of a sheet about the size of newspapers of those days. Dr. Yates Snowden of the University of South Carolina located and made a manuscript copy which he found in a library which has "I am informed, gone up in flames, according to the good old southern custom of losing historical documents by fire. Doctor Snowden's manuscript copy is in the South Caroliniana Library [the University of South Carolina]. It was from this copy that I made the copy that I sent you." Letter from Dean Orin F. Crow of the School of Education, the University of South Carolina, September 10, 1948, to Edgar W. Knight. A copy of Dean Crow's copy now is in the Southern Historical Collection, the University of North Carolina. The above survey was followed by other surveys in South Carolina in the 1830's, one by Professor Stephen Elliott and James H. Thornwell of the College of South Carolina and published in 1840 under the title *Reports on the Free School System, to the General Assembly of South Carolina;* another in 1846 by R. E. W. Allston, at the request of the State Agricultural Society of South Carolina; and another the following year by a committee of which Henry Sumner was chairman. Sumner said that the results of the earlier studies were "splendid nothings," a fate that had overtaken some educational surveys in this country in recent years.

called the poor are indeed too poor to spare anything from the scanty earnings that barely supply the necessaries of life, a system of Free Schools to educate those children whose parents cannot afford the means of their education, is no more than common justice would require of every reasonable Government in that quarter of the world: but unfortunately it is rendered by none. It was amply provided for by the primary schools of Republican France, and is very imperfectly supplied by the Charity Schools and Sunday Schools of England. But with the Restoration of the Bourbon Dynasty in France, the system gradually fell into disuse. Nor does the institution of public free schools prevail in any of the monarchies of the continent of Europe.

In this country we have no class of poor similar to the same denomination in Europe, where the weight of taxation presses heavily on the lower classes. If any of our own citizens approach to this situation, except through sickness or personal disability, it is for the most part owing to a culpable want, either of industry or frugality. Poor we have, who may be so denominated comparatively; but we have no class of citizens who are unable, while in health, to earn (with reasonable industry) more than is absolutely necessary to a comfortable subsistence. But where a family presses on the daily earnings of a parent, it may very often be difficult to spare the money which an elementary education for his children may require. On this consideration it seems right that the community should afford reasonable aid, without superseding the exertions of the parent; so as to enable every child in the State, where the scattered and scanty population does not forbid it, to be instructed in the more useful and elementary branches of knowledge, and put upon the road of voluntary improvement. But the State cannot be expected to locate a free school at every man's door; the difficulties which arise from a very scattered population must be submitted to, till the gradual progress of improvement shall take them away.

Before entering on the details which may be properly considered under this head, the Faculty wish to examine the system of Free Schools at present adopted in this State, that its defects, if any, may be seen, and the remedies more easily suggested.

For several years past in South Carolina, Commissioners of free schools have been appointed in each district, with power to send the children of the poor to some teacher, to receive instruction free of expense to the parent. The Reports are annually transmitted, but they are not all transmitted, nor are the printed summaries of these reports sufficiently accurate and detailed to afford the necessary information to ascertain in what way the adopted system answers or does not answer the valuable results expected from it. They may be sufficient for a report of the committee satisfactory to the house; but more detailed information would be useful to the public.

By the return of free schools of Dec. 3, 1825, when corrected [1] (Acts of 1825, p. 113) it will appear, that

The number of schools, was	746
The number of scholars taught	9061
The average number for each school about	12
The whole expense to the State	$37,640
The average expense scholar about	$4 10-100
The average compensation to the School-master	$50

From many districts there are no returns.

It does not appear from the printed reports that the Commissioners have retained the names of the scholars, or the time of entrance and departure, and how long each scholar charged for, while he remained at school, or whether the same scholar has returned after an absence, and been charged anew with the year, or what they have been taught, or what proficiency they have made, or whether the Commissioners have employed a school master, or sent scholars to a school already established, or in what manner the books, papers, pens, ink and slates have been provided or paid for. The returns, however satisfactory to the House, are not ample enough to furnish many details necessary to an accurate examination of them, and to appreciate the present system at its just value.

It is manifest that twelve scholars to a school is not sufficient to employ a teacher the whole of his time: and that a competent teacher cannot be had for $50 a year. This is on a supposition that in all cases the teachers are employed by the Commissioners. How the fact is the Faculty have no means of ascertaining.

Under the present system, everything is left to the Commissioners; nor do we find that there is any responsibility as to the capacity of the teacher, or any mode of ascertaining whether he does his duty by the children sent to him. The parents who send the scholars, and are exonerated from the expense, feel little or no interest, it is to be feared, in the manner in which the schools are conducted. It is universally true that we never estimate highly what costs us nothing. The Commissioners do their duty by sending the scholars whose parents require it, and by paying the teacher: Nor does it seem imperative on them to take further trouble. Such a system as this does not promise to become efficient or satisfactory: and in fact, an opinion seems generally to prevail, that the sums drawn for, do not produce a benefit at all proportioned to the expense.

In some parts of the State the population is dense, private grammar

[1] The casting up of the figures is erroneous in the printed table. The number of schools assigned to Union district is set down at page 114 as 236 for 230 scholars. This is manifestly a mistake; the figure is 236, being erroneously put there—we have therefore taken it at 36 schools, and 230 scholars.

The number of schools in Abbeville are not returned, I have stated them at 46, from the average number of scholars in the rest of the table.

schools abound: in other parts the inhabitants of a district are very much separated and scattered, and grammar schools are scarce. It is not easy to devise an efficient system for a population so differently circumstanced. Nor can any system work well that is not subject to the inspection and superintendence of persons interested in its success, because they pay for it. Nor will sufficient interest be taken in the conduct of it by those who do not contribute to the expense of it. The Faculty, therefore, deeming it essential that the parents of the children sent to school should feel that they have a right to take an active interest in its government, are of the opinion that the system adopted, whatever it may be, should assist only, without superseding the right and the duty of parents to provide for and superintend the education of their children.

Moreover, the common feeling of the laborious class of citizens among us revolts at an obligation that looks like the bestowing of alms. They would rather pay a small sum to a good school frequented also by the children of the more opulent parents than send their children to a charity school. This is a feeling fit to be encouraged, for independence of spirit is the parent of existence and of good conduct.

The Faculty therefore make it an essential part of their plan that every man, however poor comparatively, should be required to pay a small sum for the education of his children, that he may more distinctly feel that he has a *right* to have them educated, and take an interest in the management of the school. This principle seems contained in the school Act of New York State, Section VI.

Each district varies so much in its local circumstances from every other, that the Faculty feel themselves incompetent to lay down a detailed plan which shall equally fit every situation and contingency. They recommend therefore that all details of the district schools should be left to the management of the Commissioners, and the parents whose children are sent.

As a general plan, they propose that the Commissioners of each district shall fix upon the number of schools, their situation and the expense of erecting and furnishing such schoolhouses as they may deem necessary and the expense of the masters to be employed in teaching. Having thus ascertained the probable expense of the free school establishment in the district, according to their own views of the exigency of the case, they shall be empowered to raise by an assessment on all the taxable inhabitants, one half of the whole proposed expense for one year, and so soon as that assessment shall be actually paid into their hands, they shall certify the same to the treasurer of the State, and shall thereupon be entitled to draw out of the State treasury, a sum equal to the assessment actually paid into their hands by the inhabitants of the district. So that the expense of free schools shall be borne in equal proportions by an assessment on the taxable inhabitants of the district for this express purpose, and by the State Treasury.

That the Commissioners for this purpose, whether the general commissioners of the district, or the school commissioners for this purpose to be annually and especially elected (as may be deemed best) shall with the aggregate sum so made up proceed to establish and furnish as many school houses, in such situations as they may think fit; and to employ as many teachers as they may deem necessary for the purpose of instruction on this plan: and receive the applications of such citizens as wish their children to be instructed at such schools, on the terms now proposed.

That every parent whose child (male or female) is sent by the Commissioners to the public school, shall pay, to the school-master, one dollar and a half per quarter; if more than one child is sent from one family, the parent shall pay a dollar per quarter for each.

That the school master shall be entitled to each also the children of such parents as can afford to pay a full price for their children, and whose children are not sent under the authority of the Commissioners. For children of this description the price of tuition shall be such as the parents and the teacher may agree upon.

That the branches of knowledge taught to the children sent under the sanction of the Commissioners shall be reading, writing, arithmetic and geography. Arithmetic shall be considered to comprehend the rule of three direct and inverse, vulgar and decimal fractions, the extraction of the square and cube roots and the mensuration of superficies and solids.

For the purpose of aiding the studies in Geography every school house shall be furnished by the Commissioners with a map of the world; a map of each quarter of the world, and a map of the United States. Among the books to be read shall be some good abridgement of the history of America, and of our Revolutionary War; the Constitution of the United States, and of our own State.

That public quarterly examinations of all the scholars sent under the sanction of the Commissioners shall be held. Which quarterly examinations shall be attended by the Commissioners as part of their duty, and by such of the parents and others as may think proper, in order that there may be an incentive to industry and proficiency both in the teacher and the scholars.

That no person shall be appointed a master of any such school who has not yet received a certificate of his qualifications for the duty after an Examination by the Faculty of the South Carolina College.

That the salary of the school master payable quarterly shall in no case be less than 350 dollars per annum, besides the payments for each scholar. The Faculty being persuaded that a salary sufficient to allow a comfortable livelihood is absolutely necessary to obtain teachers of due qualifications and to induce them to do their duty by making it their interest to do so. Every such teacher ought to be competent also to teach a grammar school, or he will not be competent to teach with accuracy Reading, writing, arithmetic and geography. This provision may render the schools more scattered but they will be much more efficient. No school master who is contented to teach a dozen scholars and no more, is likely to be qualified to teach at all.

That the school master shall be removable by the Commissioners on complaint made and duly substantiated before the Judge of the Court of Common Pleas or Chancery on his regular circuit. The reasons for applying for the removal being served on the school master a reasonable time before the Court.

That a regular account be kept of each scholar sent by the Commissioners; at what time and how long each hath staid at school.

That it shall not be competent to [for?] the Commissioners to send more than 25 scholars to any one school in the district.

The Faculty apprehend, that if there be 350 schools distributed throughout the State for the purpose of giving to the citizens who may be comparatively considered as poor, an opportunity of sending their children, it will be a reasonable assistance for the State to afford, and will not cost more than 65,000 dollars. It is not reasonable to assist those who will not assist themselves; the parents who produce a family are as much bound to contribute to their education in a reasonable degree, as to their food. On the plan now proposed it is certain that no more money will be asked for from the State than the exigence of the case requires; for those who ask it, must contribute equally.

The exertions of other States to supply education to the poor, far exceeds what is now proposed; for instance in South Carolina containing 237,440 white inhabitants, about 9,000 poor children are taught; in New York containing 1,372,812 inhabitants 425,350 children were taught in 1826. In South Carolina there were in 1825 about 700 schools; in New York in 1825 there were 7,051 school districts. In Massachusetts the proportion is nearly the same, but we have not the details.

It ought to be compulsory on the Commissioners, under a penalty, to transmit to the Legislature full Annual Returns.

In addition to these our proposals, it has been suggested by some of the Faculty, that a competent teacher of a good grammar school should be established at the Court House of each district in the State, to whose salary the State should contribute; leaving the remainder of his emoluments to depend on his own exertions. Whether the State can afford this additional expense, or whether the Legislature would be willing to incur it we know not. But their [sic] is no fact of which the Faculty are more deeply persuaded than this: the general system of education throughout the State, and the system of education at the College suffer greatly for want of a sufficient number of grammar school teachers really competent to their business, distributed throughout the State. It is a want of the first necessity daily and hourly felt during the performance of our duties at this College. There is a further question connected with this subject.

Ought the community at the public expense, to establish universities, or collegiate seminaries for the teaching of the higher branches of knowledge? Branches to which the poor cannot have access, and of which their probable avocations in future life will have no need? We have no hesitation in saying Yes. For the following reasons:

First. Knowledge is power. The higher grades of knowledge, such as higher mathematics and astronomy, chemistry, mechanical philosophy, the elements of politics, political economy, ethics, logic, the theory of language, of jurisprudence, of botany, mineralogy, anatomy, physiology and pathology are not only greatly conducive to private comfort and improvement, but they constitute the indispensable [*sic*] basis of all national power, national wealth, prosperity, reputation and happiness. The nations that possess them in the greatest degree are the most powerful. The facts are too glaring to admit of doubt. Look at Great Britain and France: it is not necessary to look farther. I refer to the discourse of Cuvier for the incalculable influence of the higher grades of science and literature on the happiness and prosperity of nations.

Secondly. These requirements are not merely accessary [necessary?] of themselves and for their own sake, and for home use, but they constitute the main difference between nations in respect to their power and their influence over each other. For the extensive application of the higher branches of knowledge, I need refer not only to the discourse of Cuvier, but to Dupin's account of the prodigious scientific power of Great Britain; to the present state of astronomy and nautical instruments; to the discoveries and applications of *chemistry:* to the steam engine; and to the other innumerable labor-saving machines guided by the higher mathematics, and the algebraical calculus, which seems to have subjected to its power the whole range of scientific fact.

Thirdly. The apparatus of every description, buildings, professors, instruments, machines, library, &c, absolutely necessary for instruction in the higher branches of knowledge, are far too expensive for any private speculations. Private persons, if they could command the necessary capital, could never command the price of tuition that would repay such an expenditure. *In no nation whatever* have these institutions been attempted, or could they have succeeded without public aid to a great amount; and from the nature of them, they cannot be set up on an efficient scale, but at the public expense. Nor is this a misappropriation of the public money for the benefit of the rich, and to the exclusion of the poor. It is not meant to benefit the rich, or the poor, or both, or either; but as an instrument of national benefit, like an army or navy for public defense. These institutions are absolutely necessary to furnish us with the same advantage derived from the possession of knowledge that our neighbors enjoy. The terms and conditions on which it is to be communicated, will vary with the condition of the society in which they are erected.

Fourthly. The higher the scale of education in the best society, the higher will be the amount of knowledge required in every other class from the highest to the lowest. If the quantity of acquired knowledge in the higher ranks of society be but moderate, how can we expect any among the lowest? Experience has fully shown that the progress and influence of good education is downward. I hope it is not necessary to dwell on this well known truth, which universal experience has so well settled.

The Legislature has declined any aid toward a Medical School connected with the College, *a practise* which *has been sanctioned in most other States* where an University or Collegiate Seminary, approaching to an University has been founded. Perhaps the medical school at Charleston may prove sufficient, (as there is reason to expect) for the granting of medical degrees to graduates of this State and its vicinity. Medical schools of good reputation are now so numerous throughout the United States, that it has become very questionable whether any practitioner ought to be allowed to practice in South Carolina, who has not graduated at some regular college or acquired fully and accurately that quantity of medical knowledge that would fairly entitle him to a degree. The time has past away when it was expedient to license persons who were not graduates. The facilities for attaining degrees are now so numerous that they ought to be insisted on. The Faculty therefore take the liberty of recommending that the powers of the medical boards of South Carolina be altered accordingly; that they may be invested with the power of granting medical degrees after strict examination into the qualifications of the candidate as respects anatomy, physiology, surgery, midwifery, medical chemistry, the materia medica, and the theory and practice of medicine, and that none but graduates in medicine be licensed to practice. The higher the evidence of attainment which our laws require from practitioners in the learned professions, the higher will be the standard of literary accomplishment, and of general information.

Unless we strive anxiously to keep up with the knowledge of the day, the efforts of our neighbors will soon leave us far behind.

The same observations will extend also to the profession of the law. It is not expedient that the lives and properties of the citizens should be implicitly confided to young half educated, half informed, unpledged practitioners; who are in haste, not to acquire knowledge, but to gain a livelihood by the mechanical practice of professions that require much study and much knowledge laboriously acquired, where at the commencement of practice there is no experience.

We complain with great reason of the practical operation of our legal system; much of that complaint arises from the too great number, and the gross incompetence of too many of the practitioners, owing to a want of liberal and continued legal education. The education of medical men and of legal men ought to be learned education. Their professional studies require not only previous learning, but a period of close attention of certainly not less than three or rather four years after leaving COLLEGE. It is not a justifiable reason to send out a half informed young man to practice on the constitutions or the properties of the citizens, that *he must earn his living*. If he cannot afford the means of obtaining the required knowledge, he ought not to pursue the profession to which it is absolutely necessary.

Hence, for the same reason as medical degrees are exacted as evidences of a certain portion of elementary knowledge in the physician, evidence arising from at least an equal length of study, and an equally rigorous and impartial examination ought to be exacted from every man who aspires to be a legal practitioner. Much of the disgraceful acts and chicanery, truly or falsely attributed to the legal profession, would have no foundation, if the previous education were required to be of a high standard. The Faculty, deeming these subjects within the scope of the Legislative Resolution directing this report, take the liberty of offering these suggestions. The details as to the legal profession will better come from the learned judges on the bench.[2]

Where an article purchased is such that with reasonable care a purchaser can prevent himself from being imposed upon, there is no reason for any precautions. Any man can sufficiently judge of a pair of shoes, or a piece of cloth, or a joint of meat. But it is not so with Physics and with Law. They are out of the common course of knowledge and observation: in their present state they are too complicated and mysterious to be sufficiently understood by those who have not devoted their time and attention exclusively to them. A citizen who applies to a lawyer or a physician, must depend entirely on his character, and must repose implicit confidence in his knowledge and ability. Life and property are at stake in such cases, and therefore we deem it right that due precautions should be taken by the Legislature that the implicit confidence thus necessarily reposed should be guarded from deception, and that public evidence of reasonable skill and attainment should be required from those whose duty it is to acquire and possess them, before they levy a contribution on their fellow citizens by pretending to have done so.

All this is respectfully submitted by the Faculty of South Carolina College, through their president, Thomas Cooper, M.D.

The Report of the School Commissioners which ought to be transmitted within the first week of every Legislative Session, under a penalty for neglect, should comprise in a tabular form, divided into columns, the following particulars:

2 In these two last proposals two of the Faculty do not coincide, deeming it right to leave physic and law open and unrestricted.

1. Number of schools in the districts, established under the authority of the Commissioners.
2. Salary paid to, or money received by, the teacher of each school, by the Commissioners.
3. Number of scholars sent by the Commissioners to each school, and their names.
4. How many scholars were taught for three months.
5. How many for six months.
6. How many for nine months.
7. How many for twelve months.
8. Disbursements for school furniture.
9. Average expense of each scholar per quarter.
10. To what schools already established have scholars been sent by the Commissioners, how many, and at what expense.
11. What portion of the school fund placed at the disposal of the Commissioners has been expended, and what remains in their hands.

An Open Letter Against Schools and Internal Improvements, 1829 *

To the members of the approaching legislature:

What need have we of additional Roads and Canals? Have we not enough of them now? Cannot a man go from place to place, withersoever he will without obstruction? and what more could he do, were the whole State cut up into roads and by-paths? * * * If a person can not find his way, as things are, let him make use of his tongue and inquire. But we must forsooth have better ways of getting our produce to market. The present accommodations suited well enough our fathers, and they became rich in their use; and it is quite doubtful if, with greater facilities, we should be any better off an hundred years hence. I trust your wisdom will be, as your wisdom has been heretofore, decidedly against innovations and alterations, under the species disguise of improvements.

You will probably be asked, Gentlemen, to render some little assistance to the University of our State. But I hope you will strenuously refuse to do this likewise. It is respectfully submitted to the wisdom above mentioned, whether our good old-field schools are not abundantly sufficient for all our necessities. Our fathers and mothers jogged along uncomplainingly without colleges; and long experience proves them to be very expensive things. The University has already cost the people not a little; and the good it has accomplished thus far is extremely doubtful; if I might not rather allege it to have been productive of mischief. College learned persons give themselves great airs, are proud, and the fewer of them we have amongst us the better. I have long been of the opinion, and trust you will

---

* "X," in *The Raleigh (North Carolina) Register*, November 9, 1829. (A satire or hoax?)

join me in it, that establishments of this kind are aristocratical in their nature, and evidently opposed to the plain, simple, honest matter-of-fact republicanism, which ought to flourish among us. The branches of learning cultivated in them are, for the most part, of a lofty arrogant and useless sort. Who wants Latin and Greek and abstruse mathematics in these times and in a country like this? Might we not as well patronize alchymy, astrology, heraldry and the black art? . . . In the third place, it is possible, but not very likely I confess, that you may be solicited to take some steps with regard to the establishment among us of common schools. Should so rediculous a measure be propounded to you, you will unquestionably, for your own interest, as well as that of your constituents, treat it with the same contemptuous neglect which it has ever met with heretofore. Common schools indeed! Money is very scarce, and the times are unusually hard. Why was such a matter never broached in better and more prosperous days? Gentlemen, it appears to me that schools are sufficiently plenty, and that the people have no desire they should be increased. Those now in operation are not all filled, and it is very doubtful if they are productive of much real benefit. Would it not redound as much to the advantage of young persons, and to the honour of the State, if they should pass their days in the cotton patch, or at the plow, or in the cornfield, instead of being mewed up in a school house, where they are earning nothing? Such an ado as is made in these times about education, surely was never heard of before. Gentlemen, I hope you do not conceive it at all necessary, that *everybody* should be able to read, write and cipher. If one is to keep a store or a school, or to be a lawyer or physician, such branches may, *perhaps,* be taught him; though I do not look upon them as by any means indispensable: but if he is to be a plain farmer, or a mechanic, they are of no manner of use, but rather a detriment. There need no arguments to make clear so self-evident a proposition. Should schools be established by law, in all parts of the State, as at the North, our taxes must be considerably increased, possibly to the amount of one per cent and six-pence on a poll; and I will ask any prudent, sane, saving man if he desires his taxes to be higher? . . .

You will doubtless be told that our State is far behind her sisters in things of this sort,—and what does this prove? Merely, that other states are before us; which is their affair, and not ours. We are able to govern ourselves without reference to other members of the confederation; and thus are we perfectly independent. We shall always have reason enough to crow over them, while we have power to say, as I hope we may ever have, that our taxes are lighter than theirs. . . .

The Workingmen of Philadelphia on Education
at Public Expense, 1830 *

It is now forty years since the adoption of the constitution of Pennsylvania, and although that instrument strongly recommends that provision be made for the education of our youth at the public expense, yet during that long period has the salutary and patriotic obligation been disregarded by our legislative authority, and thousands are now suffering the consequences of this disregard to the public welfare on the part of our rulers.

It is true, that some attempts have been made to remedy the omission in two or three districts of the state, but they have proved ineffectual. The very spirit in which these provisions have been made not only defeats the object intended, but tends also to draw still broader the line of distinction between the rich and the poor. All who receive the limited knowledge imparted by the present system of public education are looked upon as paupers, drawing from a fount which they have in no wise contributed toward creating. The spirit of independence and of feeling in which all participate, cause the honest and industrious poor to reject a proffered bounty that connects with its reception a seeming disgrace. This honest pride in relation to charity schools, however injurious its effects may be on the poor man's offspring, is nevertheless commendable, inasmuch as it is in accordance with the spirit of our free institutions, with our elevated national character—and such a narrow policy is less than they have a right to demand at the hands of their representatives.

It is in vain for the opponents of equal education to assert that the poor, if left to themselves, will use their exertions to educate their children, and that the expenses saved them by its being accomplished by public means, will be expended by the public on less important subjects; for it is a lamentable fact, that persons destitute of education are ignorant of the loss they sustain, and hence, fail to avert the evil from their offspring. The ignorance of the parent generally extends to his children's children, while the blessings of a liberal education are handed down from father to son as a legacy which poverty cannot impoverish.

We confidently anticipate the cordial co-operation of our brethren

* "Address of the City and County Convention to the Working Men of the State" of Pennsylvania, *Mechanics' Free Press* (Philadelphia), July 10, 1830. For a good treatment of the influence of the labor movement on education, see P. R. V. Curoe, *Educational Attitudes and Policies of Organized Labor in the United States* (New York, Teachers College, Columbia University, Bureau of Publications, 1926). Chapters II and III deal with the subject from the beginning of the labor movement in this country to 1860. Curoe concludes, contrary to some views of earlier writers on the subject, that "in the two decades preceding the Civil War the points of contact between our educational development and organized labor were neither many nor important." Also consult John R. Commons (Ed.), *A Documentary History of American Industrial Society* which contains a valuable collection of source materials.

throughout the state in favour of this great object, so essential to our happiness as freemen.

An Argument Against State Support of Education, 1830 *

It is an old and sound remark, that government cannot provide for the necessities of the People; that it is they who maintain the government, and not the latter the People. Education may be among their necessities; but it is one of that description which the state or national councils cannot supply, except partially and in a limited degree. They may endow public schools for the indigent, and colleges for the most comprehensive and costly scheme of instruction. To create or sustain seminaries for the tuition of all classes—to digest and regulate systems, to adjust and manage details, to render a multitude of schools effective, is beyond their province and power. Education in general must be the work of the intelligence, need, and enterprise of individuals and associations. At present, in nearly all the most populous parts of the United States, it is attainable for nearly all the inhabitants; it is comparatively cheap, and if not the best possible, it is susceptible of improvement and likely to be advanced. Its progress and wider diffusion will depend, not upon government, but upon the public spirit, information, liberality, and training of the citizens themselves, who may appreciate duly the value of the object as a national good, and as a personal benefit for their children. Some of our writers about universal public instruction and discipline seem to forget the constitution of modern society, and declaim as if our communities could receive institutions or habits like those of Sparta.

Messages of Governors of States on Education, 1831 †

We are happy to see that the governors of Maine, New York, Pennsylvania, Delaware, South Carolina, Ohio, and Illinois, in their recent messages to the Legislatures of those States, have adverted to common education: in some instances with peculiar emphasis. In addition to these, Gov. Trimble of Ohio, in his last message (Dec. 6, 1830) adverted with interest to the same subject.

The executive of Maine congratulates the members of the legislature on account of the progress and influence of "mental light and good morals among the people." Speaking of literary institutions generally, he says: "For the correct management and progressive improvement of these institutions we cannot feel too anxious, since on education depends so much of our happiness and the security of our free governments."

Gov. Throop, of New York, speaks in the most unqualified terms of the

* *Philadelphia National Gazette*, July 12, 1830.
† *American Annals of Education*, I, p. 131.

importance of general education to the happiness of a free people, and the very existence of free institutions. He rejoices that the public mind is beginning to awake on this great subject. After a recapitulation of the most important facts contained in the Superintendent's last Report, he says: "I feel confident that, under proper regulations, a vast amount of knowledge in arts and sciences, connected with agriculture and handicraft, which are simple in their principles and easily comprehended, might be taught to children during those years which are usually spent at common schools." He complains of a want of competent instructors, and of suitable books, for the purposes of the common schools.

Gov. Hamilton of South Carolina, says that the only safe and effective Agrarian system is the scheme of public education. This alone will secure to the poor their just rights; and he recommends the subject to the consideration of the legislature.

Gov. McArthur, of Ohio, insists that "intelligence alone is capable of self-government." He urges upon every member of the community, as a "solemn duty," attention to common schools.

The executive of Delaware urges in the strongest terms the claims of primary education, from various considerations, especially from the fact that an enlightened public opinion is the only safeguard of a government like ours. He thinks, however, that legislation in that State has been carried far enough; and that an attempt to give further aid to the cause, by extending the system of taxation, would defeat the object intended.

Gov. Reynolds, of Illinois, suggests the importance of having our eyes fixed on the rising generation, in all our movements. His language on this subject is strong and emphatic, and his arguments incontrovertible. He speaks, especially, of the importance of having the intellectual growth "keep pace with the physical."

Gov. Wolf, of Pennsylvania, devotes a very considerable portion of his message to the same subject, taking a very liberal and extended view of its importance.

Extracts from the Message of Governor Wolf to the Legislature of Pennsylvania, 1833 *

Universal education, if it were practical to enforce it everywhere, would operate as a powerful check upon vice, and would do more to diminish the black catalogue of crimes, so generally prevalent, than any other measure, whether for prevention or punishment, that has hitherto been devised; and in this State it is not only considered as being entirely practicable, but is enjoined by the Constitution as a solemn duty, the non-compliance with which has already stamped the stain of inexcusable negligence upon the character of the Commonwealth, which nothing short of prompt and effi-

* Given in Wickersham, *op. cit.*, pp. 308-09.

cient measures in compliance with the constitutional requirement can remove.

To provide by law "for the establishment of schools throughout the State, in such a manner that the poor may be taught gratis," is one of the public measures to which I feel it to be my duty now to call your attention, and most solemnly to press upon your consideration. Our apathy and indifference in reference to this subject becomes the more conspicuous when we reflect that whilst we are expending millions for the improvement of the physical condition of the State, we have not hitherto appropriated a single dollar that is available for the intellectual improvement of its youth, which, in a moral and political point of view, is of ten-fold more consequence, either as respects the moral influence of the State, or its political power and safety.

According to the returns of the last census, we have, in Pennsylvania, 581,180 children under the age of 15 years, and 149,080 between the ages of 15 and 20 years, forming an aggregate of 730,269 juvenile persons of both sexes, under the age of 20 years, most of them requiring more or less instruction. And yet with all this numerous youthful population growing up around us, who in a few years are to be our rulers and our lawgivers, the defenders of our country, and the pillars of the State, and upon whose education will depend in great measure the preservation of our liberties and the safety of the republic, we have neither schools established for their instruction, nor provisions made by law for establishing them as enjoined by the Constitution.

It is time, fellow citizens, that the character of our State should be redeemed from the state of supineness and indifference under which its most important interest, the education of its citizens, has so long been languishing, and that a system should be arranged that would ensure not only an adequate number of schools to be established throughout the State, but would extend its provisions so as to secure the education and instruction of a competent number of active, intelligent teachers, who will not only be prepared, but well qualified, to take upon themselves the government of the schools and to communicate instruction to the scholars.

A Melancholy Picture of Schools in New Jersey, 1835 *

It is conceded on all hands that under the existing system the great benefit indicated by the term "popular education" is not attained. The number of schools is not sufficiently large. The quality of schools existing is deplorably below the mark as to the fiscal arrangements, the subjects taught, the manner of teaching, the checks and guards upon all who manage or instruct, and the harmony, connection, and unity of the plan which should pervade the whole. The requisitions made of teachers are small

* *American Annals of Education*, V, p. 139.

and altogether unfixed. There is no stated examination of teachers. Many are declared to be incompetent. Many are known to be intemperate and otherwise grossly immoral. There is no suitable responsibility of the teacher. To go back to the causes of this lamentable state of things, there is no sufficient inducement held out to the intelligent and enterprising to become teachers. The remuneration is niggardly, and there are no facilities for training of instructors; no central supervision from whom the character and qualifications of the instructor may be certified to society at large. Hence, there are few who remain long in this employment.

The Able Speech by Thaddeus Stevens on Behalf of Free Schools in Pennsylvania, 1835 *

Mr. Speaker: I will briefly give you the reasons why I shall oppose the repeal of the school law.

This law was passed at the last session of the legislature with unexampled unanimity, but one member of this house voting against it. It has not yet come into operation, and none of its effects have been tested by experience in Pennsylvania. The passage of such a law is enjoined by the constitution; and has been recommended by every governor since its adoption. Much to his credit, it has been warmly urged by the present executive in his annual messages delivered at the opening of the legislature. To repeal it now, before its practical effects have been discovered, would argue that it contained some glaring and pernicious defect, and that the last legislature acted under some strong and fatal delusion, which blinded every man of them to the interests of the Commonwealth. I will attempt to show that the law is salutary, useful and important, and that consequently the last legislature acted wisely in passing and the present would act unwisely in repealing it; that, instead of being oppressive to the people, it will lighten their burdens, while it elevates them in the scale of human intellect.

It would seem to be humiliating to be under the necessity, in the nineteenth century, of entering into a formal argument, to prove the utility, and, to free governments, the absolute necessity of education. More than two thousand years ago the Deity, who presided over intellectual endowments, ranked highest for dignity, chastity, and virtue among the goddesses worshipped by cultivated pagans. And I will not insult this house or our constituents by supposing any course of reasoning necessary to convince them of its high importance. Such necessity would be degrading to a Christian age, a free republic.

* *Report* of the United States Commissioner of Education for 1898-1899, pp. 518-24. This speech appears also in Thomas E. Finegan (Ed.), *Free Schools: A Documentary History of the Free School Movement in New York State,* pp. 59-66. For a description of the effect of this speech on the Legislature and the press, see Samuel W. McCall, *Thaddeus Stevens* (Boston, Houghton Mifflin Co., 1899), pp. 34-45.

If then, education be of admitted importance to the people, under all forms of government, and of unquestioned necessity, when they govern themselves, it follows, of course, that its cultivation and diffusion is a matter of public concern, and a duty which every government owes to its people. In accordance with this principle, the ancient Republics, who were most renowned for their wisdom and success, considered every child born subject to their control, as the property of the State, so far as its education was concerned; and during the proper period of instruction they were withdrawn from the control of their parents and placed under the guardianship of the Commonwealth. There, all were instructed at the same school; all were placed on perfect equality, the rich and the poor man's sons; for all were deemed children of the same common parent of the Commonwealth. Indeed, where all have the means of knowledge placed within their reach, and meet at common schools on equal terms, the forms of government seem of less importance to the happiness of the people than is generally supposed; or rather, such a people are seldom in danger of having their rights invaded by their rulers. They would not long be invaded with impunity. Prussia, whose form of government is absolute monarchy, extends the blessing of free school into every corner of the kingdom—to the lowest and poorest of the people. With a population equal to our whole Union, she has not more than 20,000 children who do not enjoy its advantages. And the consequence is, that Prussia, although governed by an absolute monarch, enjoys more happiness, and the rights of the people are better respected than in any other government in Europe.

If an elective Republic is to endure for any great length of time, every elector must have sufficient information, not only to accumulate wealth and take care of his pecuniary concerns, but to direct wisely the legislature, the ambassadors, and the Executive of the nation—for some part of all these things, some agency in approving or disapproving of them, falls to every freeman. If then, the permanency of our Government depends upon such knowledge, it is the duty of government to see that the means of information be diffused to every citizen. This is a sufficient answer to those who deem education a private and not a public duty—who argue that they are willing to educate their own children, but not their neighbor's children.

But while but few are found ignorant and shameless enough to deny the advantages of general education, many are alarmed at its supposed burdensome operation. A little judicious reflection, or a single year's experience, would show that education, under the free-school system, will cost more than one-half less, and afford better and more permanent instruction than the present disgraceful plan pursued by Pennsylvania. Take a township 6 miles square and make the estimate; such townships, on an average, will contain about 200 children to be schooled. The present rate of tuition generally (in the country) is $2 per quarter. If the children attend school two quarters each year, such township would pay $800 per annum. Take the free-school system—lay the township off into districts 3 miles square; the farthest scholars would then have 1½ miles to go, which would not be too far. It would require four schools. These will be taught, I presume, as in other States, three months in the winter by male and three months in the summer by female teachers; good male teachers can be had at from $16 to $18 per month and board themselves; females at $9 per month. Take the highest price, $18, for three months would be $54, and then for females at $9 for three months, $27, each school would cost $81; or four to a township, $324. The price now paid for the same is $800; saving for each township of 6 miles square, $476 per annum.

If the instruction of 200 scholars will save by the free-school law $476, the 500,000 children in Pennsylvania will save $1,190,000! Very few men are aware of the immense amount of money which the present expensive and partial mode of education costs the people. Pennsylvania has half a million of children, who either do, or ought to go to school six months in the year. If they do go, at $2 per quarter, their schooling costs $2,000,000 per annum! If they do not go when they are able, their parents deserve to be held in disgrace. Where they are unable, if the State does not furnish the means, she is criminally negligent. But by the free-school law, that same amount of education which would now cost $2,000,000, could be supplied at less than one-third of this amount. The amendment which is now proposed as a substitute for the school law of last session, is, in my opinion, of a most hateful and degrading character. It is a reenactment of the pauper law of 1809. It proposes that the assessors shall take a census, and make a record of the poor. This shall be revised, and a new record made by the county commissioners, so that the names of those who have the misfortune to be poor men's children shall be forever preserved, as a distinct class, in the archives of the country! The teacher, too, is to keep in his school a pauper book, and register the names and attendance of poor scholars; thus pointing out and recording their poverty in the midst of their companions. Sir, hereditary distinctions of rank are sufficiently odious; but that which is founded on poverty is infinitely more so. Such a law should be entitled "An act for branding and marking the poor, so that they may be known from the rich and proud." Many complain of this tax, not so much on account of its amount, as because it is for the benefit of others and not themselves. This is a mistake; it is for their own benefit, inasmuch as it perpetuates the Government and insures the due administration of the laws under which they live, and by which their lives and property are protected. Why do they not urge the same objection against all other taxes? The industrious, thrifty, rich farmer pays a heavy county tax to support criminal courts, build jails, and pay sheriffs and jail keeprs, and yet probably he never has, and never will have, any personal use of either. He never gets the worth of his money by being tried for a crime before the court, by being allowed the privilege of the jail on conviction, or receiving an equivalent from the sheriff or his hangman officers! He cheerfully pays the tax which is necessary to support and punish convicts, but loudly complains of that which goes to prevent his fellow-being from becoming a criminal, and to obviate the necessity of those humiliating institutions.

This law is often objected to, because its benefits are shared by the children of the profligate spendthrift equally with those of the most industrious and economical habits. It ought to be remembered that the benefit is bestowed, not upon the erring parents, but the innocent children. Carry out this objection and you punish children for the crimes or misfortunes of their parents. You virtually establish castes and grades founded on no merit of the particular generation, but on the demerits of their ancestors; an aristocracy of the most odious and insolent kind—the aristocracy of wealth and pride.

It is said that its advantages will be unjustly and unequally enjoyed, because the industrious, money-making man keeps his whole family constantly employed, and has but little time for them to spend at school; while the idle man has but little employment for his family, and they will constantly attend school. I know, sir, that there are some men, whose whole souls are so completely absorbed in the accumulation of wealth, and whose avarice so increases with success, that they look upon their very children in no other light than as instruments of gain—that they, as well as the ox and the ass within their gates, are valuable only in proportion to their annual earnings. And, according to the present system, the children of such men are reduced almost to an intellectual level with their co-laborers of the brute creation. This law will be of vast advantage to the offspring of such misers. If they are compelled to pay their taxes to support schools, their very meanness will induce them to send their children to them to get the worth of their money. Thus it will extract good out of the very penuriousness of the miser. Surely a system which will work such wonders, ought to be as greedily sought for, and more highly prized, than that coveted alchemy which was to produce gold and silver out of the blood and entrails of vipers, lizards, and other filthy vermin.

Why, sir, are the colleges and literary institutions of Pennsylvania now, and ever have been, in a languishing and sickly condition? Why, with a fertile soil and genial climate, has she, in proportion to her population, scarcely one-third as many collegiate students as cold, barren New England? The answer is obvious; she has no free schools. Until she shall have you may in vain endow college after college; they will never be filled, or filled only by students from other States. In New England free schools plant the seeds and the desire of knowledge in every mind, without regard to the wealth of the parent or the texture of the pupil's garments. When the seed, thus universally sown, happens to fall on fertile soil, it springs up and is fostered by a generous public until it produces its glorious fruit. Those who have but scanty means and are pursuing a collegiate education, find it necessary to spend a portion of the year in teaching common schools; thus imparting the knowledge which they acquire, they raise the dignity of the employment to a rank which it should always hold, honorable in proportion to the high qualifications necessary for its discharge. Thus devoting a portion of their time to acquiring the means of subsistence, industrious habits are forced upon them and their minds and bodies become disciplined to a regularity and energy which is seldom the lot of the rich. It is no uncommon occurrence to see the poor man's son, thus encouraged by wise legislation far outstrip and bear off the laurels from the less industrious heirs of wealth. Some of the ablest men of the present and past days never could have been educated, except for that benevolent system. Not to mention any of the living, it is well known that that architect of an immortal name, who plucked "the lightning from heaven and the sceptre from tyrants," was the child of free schools. Why shall Pennsylvania now repudiate a system which is calculated to elevate her to that rank in the intellectual, which, by the blessing of Providence, she holds in the natural world? To be the keystone of the arch, the "very first among her equals?" I am aware, sir, how difficult it is for the great mass of people, who have never seen this system in operation, to understand its advantages. But is it not wise to let it go into full operation and learn its results from experience? Then, if it prove useless or burdensome, how easy to repeal it. I know how large a portion of the community can scarcely feel any sympathy with, or understand the necessity of the poor; or appreciate the exquisite feelings which they enjoy when they see their children receiving the boon of education, and rising in intellectual superiority above the clogs which hereditary poverty had cast upon them. It is not wonderful that he whose far acres have descended to him, from father to son in unbroken succession, should never have sought for the surest means of alleviating it. Sir, when I reflect how apt hereditary wealth, hereditary influence, and perhaps as a consequence, hereditary pride are to close the avenues and steel the heart against the wants and the rights of the poor, I am induced to thank my Creator for having from early life bestowed upon me the blessings of poverty. Sir, it is a blessing, for if there be any human sensation more ethereal and divine than all others, it is that which feelingly sympathizes with misfortune.

But we are told that this law is unpopular; that the people desire its repeal. Has it not always been so with every new reform in the condition of man? Old habits and old prejudices are hard to be removed from the mind. Every new improvement which has been gradually leading man from the savage, through the civilized, up to a highly cultivated state, has required the most strenuous, and often perilous exertions of the wise and good. But, sir, much of its unpopularity is chargeable upon the vile arts of unprincipled demagogues. Instead of attempting to restore the honest mis-apprehensions of the people, they cater to their prejudices, and take advantage of them to gain low, dirty, temporary, local triumphs. I do not charge this on any particular party. Unfortunately almost the only spot on which all parties meet in union is this ground of common infamy. I have seen the present chief magistrate of this Commonwealth violently assailed as the projector and father of this law. I am not the eulogist of that gentleman; he has been guilty of many deep political sins; but he deserves the undying gratitude of the people for the steady, untiring zeal which he has manifested in favor of common schools. I will not say that his exertions in that cause have covered all, but they have atoned for many of his errors. I trust that the people of this State will never be called on to choose between a supporter and an opposer of free schools. But if it should come to that; if that should be made the turning point on which we are to cast our suffrages; if the opponent of education were my most intimate personal and political friend, and the free-school candidate my most obnoxious enemy, I should deem it my duty as a patriot, at this moment of our intellectual crisis, to forget all other considerations, and I should place myself unhesitatingly and cordially in the ranks of Him whose banner streams in light. I would not foster nor flatter ignorance to gain political victories which, however, they might profit individuals, must prove disastrous to our country. Let it not be supposed from these remarks that because I deem this a paramount object that I think less highly than heretofore of those great important cardinal principles which for years past have controlled my political action. They are, and ever shall be, deeply cherished in my inmost heart. But I must be allowed to exercise my own judgment as to the best means of effecting that and every other object which I think beneficial to the community. And, according to that judgment, the light of general information will as surely counteract the pernicious influence of secret, oath-bound, murderous institutions as the sun in heaven dispels the darkness and damp vapors of the night.

It is said that some gentlemen here owe their election to their hostility to general education—that it was placed distinctly on that ground, and that others lost their election by being in favor of it; and that they consented to supersede the regularly nominated candidates of their own party, who had voted for this law. May be so. I believe that two highly respectable members of the last legislature, from Union county, who voted for the school law, did fail of reelection on that ground only. They were summoned before a county meeting, and requested to pledge themselves to vote for its repeal as the price of their reelection. But they were too high minded and honorable men to consent to such degradation. The people, incapable for the moment of appreciating their worth, dismissed them from their service. But I venture to predict that they have passed them by only for the moment. Those gentlemen have earned the approbation of all good and intelligent men more effectually by their retirement than they could ever have done by retaining popular favor at the expense of self-humiliation. They fell, it is true, in this great struggle between the powers of light and darkness; but they fell, as every Roman mother wished her sons to fall, facing the enemy with all their wounds in front.

True, it is, that two other gentlemen, and I believe two only, lost their election on account of their vote on that question. I refer to the late members from Berks, who were candidates for reelection; and I regret that gentlemen whom I so highly respect and whom I take pleasure in ranking among personal friends, had not possessed a little more nerve to enable them to withstand the assaults which were made upon them; or if they must be overpowered, to wrap their mantles gracefully around them and yield with dignity. But this, I am aware, requires a high degree of fortitude, and those respected gentlemen, distracted and faltering between the dictates of conscience and the clamor of the populace, at length turned and fled. But duty had detained them so long that they fled too late, and the shaft which had already been winged by ignorance overtook and pierced them from behind. I am happy to say, sir, that a more fortunate fate awaited our friends from York. Possessing a keener insight into futurity and a sharper instinct of danger, they saw the peril at a greater distance and retreated in time to escape the fury of the storm, and can now safely boast that "discretion is the better part of valor," and that "they fought and ran away, and live to fight—on t'other side."

Sir, it is to be regretted that any gentleman should have consented to place his election on hostility to general education. If honest ambition were his object, he will ere long lament that he attempted to raise his monument of glory on so muddy a foundation. But, if it be so, that they were placed to obstruct the diffusion of knowledge, it is but justice to say, that they fitly and faithfully represent the spirit which sent them here, when they attempt to sacrifice this law on the altars which, at home, among their constituents, they have raised and consecrated to intellectual darkness; and on which they are pouring out oblations to send forth their fetid and noxious odors over the 10 miles square of their ambitions! But will this legislature, will the wise guardians of the dearest interests of a great Commonwealth, consent to surrender the high advantages and brilliant prospects which this law promises, because it is desired by worthy gentlemen, who, in a moment of causeless panic and popular delusion, sailed into power on a Tartarean flood? A flood of ignorance darker, and, to the intelligent mind, more dreadful than that accursed pool at which mortals and immortals tremble! Sir, it seems to me that the liberal and enlightened proceedings of the last legislature have aroused the demon of ignorance from his slumber; and, maddened at the threatened loss of his murky empire, his discordant howlings are heard in every part of our land!

Gentlemen will hardly contend for the doctrine of cherishing and obeying the prejudices and errors of their constituents. Instead of prophesying smooth things and flattering the people with the belief of their perfection, and thus retarding the mind in its onward progress, it is the duty of faithful legislators to create and sustain such laws and institutions as shall teach us our wants, foster our cravings after knowledge, and urge us forward in the march of intellect. The barbarous and disgraceful cry which we hear abroad in some parts of our land, "that learning makes us worse—that education makes men rogues," should find no echo within these walls. Those who hold such doctrines anywhere would be the objects of bitter detestation if they were not rather the pitiable objects of commiseration, for even voluntary fools require our compassion as well as natural idiots.

Those who would repeal this law because it is obnoxious to a portion of the people would seem to found their justification on a desire of popularity. That is not an unworthy object when they seek that enduring fame which is constructed of imperishable materials. But have these gentlemen looked back and consulted the history of their race to learn on what foundation and on what materials that popularity is built which outlives its possessor, which is not buried in the same grave which covers his mortal remains? Sir, I believe that kind of fame may be acquired by deep learning, or even the love of it, by mild philanthropy or unconquerable courage. And it seems to me that, in the present state of feeling in Pennsylvania, those who will heartily and successfully support the cause of general education can acquire at least some portion of the honor of all these qualities combined, while those who oppose it will be remembered without pleasure and soon pass away with the things that perish.

In giving this law to posterity you act the part of the philanthropist, by bestowing upon the poor as well as the rich the greatest earthly boon which they are capable of receiving; you act the part of the philosopher by pointing if you do not lead them up the hill of science; you act the part of the hero if it be true as you say that popular vengeance follows close upon your footsteps. Here, then, if you wish true popularity, is a theater in which you may acquire it. What renders the name of Socrates immortal but his love of the human family exhibited under all circumstances and in contempt of every danger? But courage, even with but little benevolence may confer, lasting renown. It is this which makes us bow with involuntary respect at the name of Napoleon, of Caesar, and of Richard of the Lion Heart. But what earthly glory is there equal in luster and duration to that conferred by education? What else could have bestowed such renown upon the philosophers, the poets, the statesmen, and orators of antiquity? What else could have conferred such undisputed applause upon Aristotle, Demosthenes, and Homer; on Virgil, Horace and Cicero? And is learning less interesting and important now than it was in centuries past, when those statesmen and orators charmed and ruled empires with their eloquence?

Sir, let it not be thought that these great men acquired a higher fame than is within the reach of the present age. Pennsylvania's sons possess as high native talents as any other nation of ancient or modern time. Many of the poorest of her children possess as bright intellectual gems if they were as highly polished as did the scholars of Greece or Rome. But too long, too disgracefully long, has coward, trembling, proscrastinating legislation permitted them to lie buried in "dark, unfathomable caves."

If you wish to acquire popularity, how often have you been admonished to build not your monuments of brass or marble but make them of ever-living mind. Although the periods of yours or your children's renown can not be as long as that of the ancients, because you start from a later period, yet it may be no less brilliant. Equal attention to the same learning, equal ardor in pursuing the same arts and liberal studies, which has rescued their names from the rust of corroding time and handed them down to us untarnished from remote antiquity, would transmit the names of your children and your children's children in a green, undying fame down through the long vista of succeeding ages until time shall mingle with eternity.

Let all, therefore, who would sustain the character of the philosopher or philanthropist sustain this law. Those who would add thereto the glory of the hero, can acquire it here, for in the present state of feeling in Pennsylvania, I am willing to admit that but little less dangerous to the public man is the war club and battle-ax of savage ignorance, than to the Lion-hearted Richard was the keen scimitar of the Saracen. He who would oppose it, either through inability to comprehend the advantages of general education, or from unwillingness to bestow them on all his fellow-citizens, even to the lowest and the poorest, or from dread of popular vengeance, seems to me to want either the head of the philosopher, the heart of the philanthropist or the nerve of the hero.

All these things would be easily admitted by almost every man, were it not for the supposed cost. I have endeavored to show that it is not expensive; but, admit that it were somewhat so, why do you cling so closely to your gold? The trophies which it can purchase, the idols which it sets up, will scarcely survive their purchaser. No name, no honor can long be perpetuated by mere matter. Of this Egypt furnishes melancholy proof. Look at her stupendous pyramids, which were raised at such immense expense of toil and treasure! As mere masses of matter they seem as durable as the everlasting hills, yet the deeds and the names they were intended to perpetuate are no longer known on earth. That ingenious people attempted to give immortality to matter, by embalming their great men and monarchs. Instead of doing deeds worthy to be recorded in history, their very names are unknown, and nothing is left to posterity but their disgusting mortal frames for idle curiosity to stare at. What rational being can view such soulless, material perpetuation, with pleasure? If you can enjoy it, go, sir, to the foot of Vesuvius; to Herculaneum and Pompeii, those eternal monuments of human weakness. There, if you set such value on material monuments of riches, may you see all the glory of art, the magnificence of wealth, the gold of Ophir, and the rubies of the East, preserved in indestructible lava, along with their haughty wearers—the cold, smooth, petrified, lifeless beauties of the "Cities of the Dead."

Who would not shudder at the idea of such prolonged material identity? Who would not rather do one living deed than to have his ashes forever enshrined in ever-burnished gold? Sir, I trust that when we come to act on this question we shall all take lofty ground—look beyond the narrow space which now circumscribes our visions—beyond the passing, fleeting point of time on which we stand; and so cast our votes that the blessing of education shall be conferred on every son of Pennsylvania—shall be carried home to the poorest child of the poorest inhabitant of the meanest hut of your mountains, so that even he may be prepared to act well his part in this land of freemen, and lay on earth a broad and a solid foundation for that enduring knowledge which goes on increasing through increasing eternity.

Tennessee Creates an *Ex Officio* State Board of Education and Provides for a Chief State School Officer, 1836 *

Section 1. Be it enacted by the General Assembly of the State of Tennessee. That the Treasurer of the State, the Comptroller of the treasury, and an executive officer, to be called the Superintendant of public instruction, who shall be appointed by joint vote of both branches of this General Assembly, shall be, and they are hereby created and constituted a body politic and corporate, by the name and style of the Board of Commissioners of Common Schools for the State of Tennessee, who shall have perpetual succession, and by the name and style aforesaid, may hold and possess property of every kind in trust for the use of common schools, may sue and be sued, plead and be impleaded, answer and be answered unto, defend and be defended in all courts of record or any other place whatsoever; and also to make, have and use a common seal, and the same to break, alter and renew at their pleasure, and generally to do and execute all acts, matters and things, which a corporation or body politic in law may and can lawfully do and execute. The Superintendant of public instruction shall be president of the Board of Commissioners; and all notes, bonds, obligations, transfers, or other instruments of writing made or executed by the Board, shall be signed by him, and where necessary, sealed with the corporate seal of the Board; which Board shall be subject, nevertheless, to legislative modification, alteration or repeal.

Sec. 2. The Superintendant of public instruction shall hold his office for

* *Public Acts Passed at the First Session of the Twenty-first General Assembly of the State of Tennessee, 1835-36, pp. 110-14.*

two years, and until his succesor shall be elected and qualified, and shall be paid a salary from the public treasury of fifteen hundred dollars annually, to be paid quarterly; and shall, before entering on the discharge of his duties, enter into bond with good and sufficient security, to be approved of by, and made payable to the Governor of the State, in the sum of one hundred thousand dollars, conditioned for the faithful discharge of the duties of his office; and shall take an oath to support the constitution of the United States, the constitution of the State, and an oath of office.

Sec. 3. That branch of his duties which relates to the common schools shall be, amongst other things, to prepare and submit an annual report to the legislature, containing a full and comprehensive statement of the amount and condition, together with plans for the improvement and management of the common school fund, and such a plan for the organization of a system of common schools as he may think advisable, and such other matters relating to his office and to common schools as he shall deem expedient to communicate.

Sec. 4. The monies, notes, bonds, stocks, securities, and other property belonging to the State or common school fund, in the possession or under the control of the agents appointed to close the concerns of the bank of the State, the county common school commissioners and county bank agents shall, on demand, be delivered by the person or persons having the possession of the same, to the Superintendant of public instruction, or to the authorized agent of the Board of Common School Commissioners; and all clerks, sheriffs, collectors or other persons, companies or corporations, who may now, or at any time hereafter, have possessions of any funds or property appropriated to the use of common schools in this State, shall deliver the same in like manner unless otherwise directed by law: *Provided,* that in paying over to the Superintendant of public instruction, the monies, notes, bonds, obligations, or other securities which may be in the possession or under the control of the county common school commissioners, they shall not be required to pay, but may retain any internal improvement fund, or any individual donation which may have been made to the school funds of their counties respectively, and which shall be left under the control and management of the county school commissioners as directed by the existing laws.

Sec. 5. The late treasurer of East Tennessee is hereby directed to deliver to the Superintendant of public instruction or the authorized agent of the Board of Common School Commissioners, all the accounts, documents, books, and papers, in his office pertaining to the sale of the lands in the Hiwassee district, and the college and academy lands south of French Broad and Holston rivers; and the Superintendant of public instruction is hereby authorized and directed to make settlement with said treasurer as to his agency in conducting the affairs connected with the sale of the Hiwassee lands, and in receiving the money therefor, and also as to his agency in conducting the affairs connected with the college and academy lands and funds; and to receive from him any money or securities for money which may be in his possession, belonging or appropriated to the use of colleges, academies, or common schools.

Sec. 6. All escheated money or property in the State, shall, on demand, be delivered by the person having the possession of the same, to the said Superintendant or the agent of the Board of Common School Commissioners, and the Board is hereby authorized to dispose of any such property in such manner as they may deem best for the interest of the common school fund.

Sec. 7. The Board of Common School Commissioners shall appoint an agent in each county in the State whenever they may deem it necessary, who shall give bond and security for the faithful performance of his duties, and shall take an oath faithfully to account for all school funds which may come to his hands, and for the faithful performance of his other duties as required by law or the instructions of the Board of Common School Commissioners, shall be paid for his services annually a sum to be agreed on with the Board of Commissioners not exceeding one hundred dollars, and whose duty it shall be to make a report to the Superintendant of public instruction, containing the name of each debtor in his county to the school fund, the amount of each debt with the security therefor, specifying the date of its execution and maturity, and an account of any bank stock, turnpike stock, or property, belonging by law to the school fund.

Sec. 8. When the Superintendant of public instruction shall have received said reports, he shall cause all debts due to the common school fund on bond or otherwise, and all bank stock, road stock, and other property belonging to said fund, to be registered in books to be kept in his office, in which shall be opened an account with each debtor, showing the place of his residence, the amount of his debt and the security therefor; the registry of property belonging to said fund shall show where it is situated, its kind, quantity, and an estimate of its value.

Sec. 9. Said Superintendant shall furnish to each county agent a schedule of all accounts against the debtors of the school fund in his county, alphabetically arranged, and shall cause said agents to have the securities therefor renewed every six months, calling in ten per centum on the amount of each debt at the time of the first renewal, and each subsequent renewal, calling in twenty-five per centum on the amount of the debt due after the payment of the first instalment, so that the whole debt will then be collected in four equal semi-annual instalments, besides the interest, which shall be paid in advance on each renewal, and which process shall be repeated every six months till the whole debt shall be collected.

Sec. 10. All debts due, or which may fall due at the bank of the State at Nashville, or at the branch bank at Knoxville, not contracted with the understanding or agreement that the obligation therefor should be renewed upon the payment of the interest, and a certain call upon the principal, shall, whenever the same may be due, be forthwith collected by the Superintendant of public instruction, and all other debts or monies due to the school fund, which were not originally loans made with the understanding that the securities therefor should be renewed according to the existing laws, shall be collected in like manner.

Sec. 11. As fast as the curtailments and interest shall be paid, or any of the school fund shall be otherwise collected, it shall be paid by the county agent or the persons collecting or having possession of the same, into the hands of the Superintendent of public instruction, who shall invest the same by subscribing for stock of the Planters Bank of Tennessee, in the name of the Board of Common School Commissioners; and who shall in like manner reinvest the profits as they arise on the capital stock, or deposit the same upon the best terms and for the highest rate of interest he may be able to obtain, or he may deem most advisable.

Sec. 12. All persons paying any money, or delivering property, stock, notes, bonds, obligations or other securities to the Superintendent of public instruction, under the provisions of this act, shall take duplicate receipts therefor, one of which shall be kept by the person taking the same, and the other shall be by such person immediately forwarded to the comptroller of the treasury, who shall record the same in a book to be kept by him for that purpose, and file the original in his office.

Sec. 13. The real estate belonging to the bank of the State at Nashville, and the branch at Knoxville, shall be sold by the Superintendant of public instruction at public sale, after having given forty days notice in some public newspaper of the time, place and conditions of the sale, and shall be sold on such credit as the Board of School Commissioners may think advisable, not exceeding two years for the longest payment, and a lien shall be retained on the property until the payment of the purchase money.

Sec. 14. The Superintendant of public instruction shall ascertain and report to the next regular session of the Legislature, the amount and condition of the college and academy funds in this State, which such plans for the better management of the same, and for the organization of a general system of education, as he may deem expedient.

Sec. 15. All monies reasonably expended by the Superintendent in the execution of his duties, shall, upon due proof be allowed to him by the comptroller, and be paid out of the treasury.

Sec. 16. All notes, bonds, or other obligations, which may be taken to secure the payment of any of the school funds other than such funds as may be left under the control of the county school commissioners, shall be made payable to the Superintendent of public instruction and his successors in office.

Sec. 17. It shall be the duty of the Superintendant of public instruction to keep his office in the town of Nashville, at which he shall redeem all notes now in circulation on the Bank of the State of Tennessee, or the Branch Bank at Knoxville, whenever they may be presented for payment.

Sec. 18. The Superintendant of public instruction shall be authorized to take power of attorney from the debtors to the school fund, authorizing him to confess judgment for the amount of such debts and interest, in the same manner that the president of the Bank of the State of Tennessee was authorized to confess judgment upon debts due to that institution.

Governor Edward Everett Recommends a State Board of Education for Massachusetts, 1837 *

The abstract of the returns of the schools throughout the Commonwealth, prepared with great judgment and care, by the Secretary of State, has been already submitted to you. I am persuaded that this document will be regarded with great interest by the Legislature. The fact that a sum of money, exceeding the whole public expenditure of the Commonwealth, is raised by taxation and voluntary contribution, for the support of schools, must be deemed, in the highest degree, honorable to our citizens.

While nothing can be farther from my purpose, than to disparage the common schools as they are, and while a deep sense of personal obligation to them will ever be cherished by me, it must yet be candidly admitted, that they are susceptible of great improvements. The school houses might, in many cases, be rendered more commodious. Provision ought to be made for affording the advantages of education, throughout the whole year, to all of a proper age to receive it. Teachers well qualified to give elementary instruction in all the branches of useful knowledge, should be employed; and small school libraries, maps, globes and requisite scientific apparatus should be furnished. I submit to the Legislature, whether the creation of a board of commissioners of schools, to serve without salary, with authority to appoint a secretary, on a reasonable compensation, to be paid from the school fund, would not be of great utility. Should the Legislature take advantage of the ample means now thrown into their hands, greatly to increase the efficiency of the school fund, I cannot but think that they would entitle themselves to the gratitude of the whole People. The wealth of Massachusetts always has been, and always will be, the minds of her children; and good schools are a treasure, a thousand fold more precious, than all the gold and silver of Mexico and Peru.

Whether any extraordinary addition be made to the school fund, or it be left to its accumulation as already provided for, I beg leave respectfully to suggest the expediency of reconsidering the provisions of law which govern its distribution. Unquestioned experience elsewhere has taught, that the principle of distribution established by the Revised Statutes, goes far to render a school fund useless. On the contrary, where it is apportioned

* *Resolves of the General Court of the Commonwealth of Massachusetts, 1837, pp. 465-66.*

in the ratio of the sums raised by taxation for the support of schools, (which is the principle adopted by the great and liberal State of New York,) the fund becomes at once the stimulus and the reward of the efforts of the People.

Massachusetts Creates the First State Board of Education in the United States, 1837 *

Section 1. The board of education shall consist of the governor and lieutenant-governor, and eight persons appointed by the governor with the advice and consent of the council, each to hold office eight years from the time of his appointment, one retiring each year in the order of appointment; and the governor, with the advice and consent of the council, shall fill all vacancies in the board which may occur from death, resignation, or otherwise.

Sect. 2. The board may take and hold to it and its successors, in trust for the commonwealth, any grant or device of lands, and any donation or bequest of money or other personal property, made to it for educational purposes; and shall forthwith pay over to the treasurer of the commonwealth, for safe keeping and investment, all money and other personal property so received. The treasurer shall from time to time invest all such money in the name of the commonwealth, and shall pay to the board, on the warrant of the governor, the income or principal thereof, as it shall from time to time require; but no disposition shall be made of any devise, donation, or bequest, inconsistent with the conditions or terms thereof. For the faithful management of all property so received by the treasurer he shall be responsible upon his bond to the commonwealth, as for other funds received by him in his official capacity.

Sect. 3. The board shall prescribe the form of registers to be kept in the schools, and the form of the blanks and inquiries for the returns to be made by school committees; shall annually on or before the third Wednesday of January lay before the legislature an annual report containing a printed abstract of said returns, and a detailed report of all the doings of the board, with such observations upon the condition and efficiency of the system of popular education, and such suggestions as to the most practicable means of improving and extending it, as the experience and reflection of the board dictate.

Sect. 4. The board may appoint its own secretary, who, under its direction, shall make the abstract of school returns required by section three; collect information respecting the condition and efficiency of the public schools and other means of popular education; and diffuse as widely as possible throughout the commonwealth information of the best system of studies and method of instruction for the young, that the best education

* *The General Statutes of the Commonwealth of Massachusetts*, 1860, pp. 210-11.

which public schools can be made to impart may be secured to all children who depend upon them for instruction.

Sect. 5. The secretary shall suggest to the board and to the legislature, improvements in the present system of public schools; visit, as often as his other duties will permit, different parts of the commonwealth for the purpose of arousing and guiding public sentiment in relation to the practical interests of education; collect in his office such school-books, apparatus, maps, and charts, as can be obtained without expense to the commonwealth; receive and arrange in his office the reports and returns of the school committees; and receive, preserve, or distribute, the state documents in relation to the public school system.

Sect. 6. He shall, under the direction of the board, give sufficient notice of, and attend such meetings of teachers of public schools, members of the school committees of the several towns, and friends of education generally in any county, as may voluntarily assemble at the time and place designated by the board; and shall at such meetings devote himself to the object of collecting information of the condition of the public schools of such county, of the fulfilment of the duties of their office by members of the school committees of all the towns and cities, and of the circumstances of the several school districts in regard to teachers, pupils, books, apparatus, and methods of education, to enable him to furnish all information desired for the report of the board required in section three.

Sect. 7. He shall send the blank forms of inquiry, the school registers, the annual report of the board, and his own annual report, to the clerks of the several towns and cities as soon as may be after they are ready for distribution.

Sect. 8. He shall receive from the treasury, in quarterly payments an annual salary of two thousand dollars, and his necessary travelling expenses incurred in the performance of his official duties after they have been audited and approved by the board; and all postages and other necessary expenses arising in his office, shall be paid out of the treasury in the same manner as those of the different departments of the government.

Sect. 9. The board may appoint one or more suitable agents to visit the several towns and cities for the purpose of inquiring into the condition of the schools, conferring with teachers and committees, lecturing upon subjects connected with education, and in general of giving and receiving information upon subjects connected with education, in the same manner as the secretary might do if he were present.

Sect. 10. The incidental expenses of the board, and the expenses of the members thereof incurred in the discharge of their official duties, shall be paid out of the treasury, their accounts being first audited and allowed.

Sect. 11. The assistant librarian of the state library shall act when necessary as clerk of the board.

Horace Mann Replies to the Boston Schoolmasters, 1845 *

After acquainting myself with the different school systems in the United States, and visiting schools in a large portion of the States of our Union I went abroad. In European schools I saw many things, good, bad, and indifferent. The good I attempted to describe for imitation, and the bad for warning. Of the indifferent there is no lack of specimens in our own country. In some instances, what has been seen abroad was compared with what existed at home; but no particular teacher, or town, or class of schools, was designated for special approval or disapproval. I left the good sense of the community to make the application. Before that tribunal all good schools and good teachers would be safe; nay, would obtain commendation. . . .

The Report of my tour, being prepared under the most adverse circumstances, was very far from being what I desired. Although it contains not a single assertion which I would wish to retract, yet I would have had it in some respects more full, in others more explicit. But one thing is certain: That Report contained no special allusion to, or comparison with any class of the Boston schools. It has had, judging from the number of copies disposed of, more than a hundred thousand readers in this country, and not one of them, that I have ever heard of, out of the city of Boston, ever surmised that it contained any attack, either open or covert, upon the Boston Masters. Nay, some of the Masters did not discern it, until their vision was aided by sharper-sighted eyes; and subsequently to their having expressed a favorable opinion. From the number of copies which have been sold, and the selections made from it by the public press, it must have been deemed to contain some useful information respecting school systems and modes of instruction and discipline; and it has been acknowledged to do so in the countries to which it refers. . . .

It was this Report which the Boston Masters saw fit so virulently to assail. And what were its sins; or rather—to put the question more broadly and therefore more favorably for them—what were the supposed errors in my philosophy of instruction and discipline? On their own showing, they were four, and these only:

1. I was supposed to lean too far to the side of oral instruction, as contra-distinguished from the study of textbooks.

2. I was,—mistakenly however,—supposed to approve the intense activity and excitement of some of the Scotch schools.

* *Answer to the "Rejoinder" of Twenty-Nine Boston Schoolmasters* (Boston, 1845), pp. 10-13. Mann's famous seventh report in 1843, as Secretary of the Massachusetts State Board of Education, on European school systems annoyed thirty-one Boston schoolmasters who, in 1844, attacked the report in a printed statement of 144 pages, to which Mann replied two months later in a document of 176 pages. Twenty-nine of the schoolmasters replied in a "Rejoinder" of 54 pages to which Mann issued an "Answer" in 124 pages and the controversy came to a close. It helped mightily, however, to enhance Mann's reputation as a vigorous and convincing advocate of public support and control of education.

3. I was charged with error in advocating the method of teaching children to read, by beginning with words, instead of letters; and

4. It was numbered among my sins that I indulged the hope of seeing corporal punishment more and more disused in our schools, as its necessity might be gradually superseded, by substituting the pleasures of knowledge and high motives of action in its stead, until, at some future period (which I never attempted to fix), it might be dispensed with, except, as I was accustomed to express it, "in most extraordinary cases."

The above were proper subjects for discussion; and, in the *Common School Journal,* I had published whatever had been offered me, adverse to my own views on these points, as readily as I had published my own opinions. But, though proper subjects for discussion, they furnished no provocation for hostile attack. . . . They furnished no pretext or shadow of excuse for holding me up before the public as having been ignorant of, and indifferent to, the cause of education before my appointment as Secretary; or for attempting to array the whole State in arms against me, by the false accusation of my "great disparagement of committees, teachers, and the condition of the school system of Massachusetts"; or for assailing the Normal Schools, because I was friendly to them, or their Principals, because they were friendly to me; or for accusing me and my friends of a base collusion for most unworthy objects; or for comparing me, personally, with some of the most offensive of the English tourists who have ever visited this country; or, in fine, for the imputation of many other most dishonorable motives and actions with which the *Remarks* abound.

What exaggerated the offensiveness of these libels, and showed the spirit from which they emanated, is, that the members of the "Association" sacrificed great differences among themselves in order to combine against me.

A Subscriber to His Paper Writes Horace Greeley in Opposition to Free Schools in New York, 1849 *

CRAWFORD, ORANGE COUNTY

FRIEND GREELEY:

I have been a subscriber to, and a reader of your paper several years, and it has been my pleasure to agree with you on almost every question that has agitated the public; but on the Free School Law I fear I shall have to agree to differ. I wish to give an illustration of what I consider will be the practical workings of it. The district to which I belong, received last year, about $40.00 of public money; the new law increased it one third; we next term then, will receive, say $55.00. This not being sufficient to support the school one year, it is left to the district to say whether they will raise any more or not. The majority of taxpayers in this district have no children to send to school, and are moreover, opposed to the law and say

* G. T. F., in *New York Weekly Tribune,* October 19, 1849.

they will not vote any money to support schools. The money received will barely support the school during the summer—say six months; will not the effect be to deprive us of a school during the remainder of the year? I am a mechanic, not a taxpayer; if agreeable to you please give me your views, in your weekly, and oblige,

G. T. F.

An Editorial in Favor of Free Schools, 1849 *

VOTE FOR FREE SCHOOLS

The legal voters of the State are to determine, by their ballots on the first Tuesday of next month, whether their common schools shall or shall not be free to all children seeking instruction therein, as they are already in this city and Poughkeepsie, and as we believe, in some of the larger villages throughout the State. At present these schools are properly supported by state funds, partly by a tax on property, and partly by a tax on each scholar known as the *rate bill*. Insignificant as the sums charged in rate bills may seem, they yet bear very hard on many a poor working man with a large family of children. Five or six dollars a year are often charged in rate bills against a man whose earnings for the year, though he work hard and steadily, fall short of $200; and out of his pittance he has to pay the rent of his dwelling, and feed and clothe a family of seven or eight persons. This case is even worse with many a poor widow, left destitute with three or four children to support by needlework, at which she cannot earn thirty cents a day although she do her best.

It is all she can do to clothe her children so that she need not be ashamed to send them to school; to pay for their schooling, even partially, is beyond her ability. Now it is true that they might go, and be sneered at as paupers, if she could not and did not pay; but she cannot forget the time she held her head as high as her neighbors, and it is hard to own oneself a pauper while health and hope remain. So she keeps her children at home intending to teach them herself; but famine and rent crowd her from hour to hour, and their lessons are few. Hurried and meagre indeed, so the boys grow up untaught in the streets, exposed to every contamination, initiated in every vice, and the girls learn too little to fit them for the sphere in which their mother once moved, and too much (from her) to content themselves in an humbler; and the result is far too often their ruin.

The education of children is a duty of parents when they are able, but it is a duty of the community whether all the parents are able or not. Not for his own sake merely, but for the sake of the whole, should every child be educated. A single ignorant person is a source of evil and peril to the community. That person, properly educated, might have invented some-

* *New York Weekly Tribune,* October 24, 1849.

thing, evolved an idea for want of which the development of the race may be arrested for a whole half a century. Not only as the duty of all, but for the benefit of all, we entreat every elector who wishes well to his kind, to suffer nothing to deter him from attending the polls at the ensuing election and there depositing his ballot in favor of free schools.

The First Compulsory School Law in the United States, 1852 *

AN ACT CONCERNING THE ATTENDANCE OF CHILDREN AT SCHOOL

Be it enacted by the Senate and House of Representatives in General Court assembled, and by the authority of the same, as follows:

Sect. 1. Every person who shall have any child under his control, between the ages of eight and fourteen years, shall send such child to some public school within the town or city in which he resides, during at least twelve weeks, if the public schools within such town or city shall be so long kept, in each and every year during which such child shall be under his control, six weeks of which shall be consecutive.

Sect. 2. Every person who shall violate the provisions of the first section of this act shall forfeit, to the use of such town or city, a sum not exceeding twenty dollars, to be recovered by complaint or indictment.

Sect. 3. It shall be the duty of the school committee in the several towns or cities to inquire into all cases of violation of the first section of this act, and to ascertain of the persons violating the same, the reasons, if any, for such violation, and they shall report such cases, together with such reasons, if any, to the town or city in their annual report; but they shall not report any cases such as are provided for by the fourth section of this act.

Sect. 4. If, upon inquiry by the school committee, it shall appear, or if upon the trial of any complaint or indictment under this act it shall appear, that such child has attended some school, not in the town or city in which he resides, for the time required by this act, or has been otherwise furnished with the means of education for a like period of time, or has already acquired those branches of learning which are taught in common schools, or if it shall appear that his bodily or mental condition has been such as to prevent his attendance at school, or his acquisition of learning for such a period of time, or that the person having the control of such child, is not able, by reason of poverty, to send such child to school, or to furnish him with the means of education, then such person shall be held not to have violated the provisions of this act.

* *Acts and Resolves Passed by the General Court of Massachusetts in the Year 1852,* pp. 170-71. By an act of 1850 the General Court had given authority to cities and towns of Massachusetts "to make any needful provisions and arrangements concerning habitual truants and children not attending school, without any regular and lawful occupation, growing up in ignorance, between the ages of six and sixteen...." *Acts and Resolves Passed by the General Court of Massachusetts in the Year 1850,* pp. 468-69.

Sect. 5. It shall be the duty of the treasurer of the town or city to prosecute all violations of this act. (*Approved by the Governor,* May 18, 1852.)

Compulsory School Attendance Legislation, 1852-1918 *

Massachusetts was the first of the American states to enact legislation on compulsory-school attendance. This was in 1852. By 1890 the following states and territories had enacted such legislation:

State	Year	State	Year
Massachusetts	1852	Wyoming	1876
District of Columbia	1864	Ohio	1877
Vermont	1867	Wisconsin	1879
New Hampshire	1871	Rhode Island	1883
Michigan	1871	Illinois	1883
Washington	1871	Dakota	1883
Connecticut	1872	Montana	1883
New Mexico	1872	Minnesota	1885
Nevada	1873	Nebraska	1887
New York	1874	Idaho	1887
Kansas	1874	Colorado	1889
California	1874	Oregon	1889
Maine	1875	Utah	1890
New Jersey	1875		

Names of County Superintendents in Pennsylvania, With Their Salaries, 1854 †

Adams, David Wills	$ 300	Chester, R. Agnew Futhey	$1,000
Allegheny, James M. Pryor	1,000	Clarion, Robert W. Orr	300
Armstrong, John A. Campbell	300	Clearfield, A. T. Schryver	200
		Clinton, R. C. Allison	300
Beaver, Thomas Nicholson	350	Columbia, Joel E. Bradley	300
Bedford, T. W. B. McFadden	300	Crawford, S. S. Sears	400
Berks, Wm. A. Good	250	Cumberland, Daniel Shelly	500
Blair, Hugh A. Caldwell	400	Dauphin, S. D. Ingram	300
Bradford, Emanuel Guyer	500	Delaware, George Smith	500
Bucks, Joseph Fell	1,000	Elk, Wm. B. Gillis	75
Butler, Isaac Black	300	Erie, Wm. H. Armstrong	600
Cambria, Robert L. Johnston	400	Fayette, Joshua V. Gibbons	600
Carbon, Joseph H. Siewers	400	Forest, John O. Hays	250
Centre, Wm. J. Gibson	600	Franklin, James McDowell	600

* *Report* of the United States Commissioner of Education 1888-1889, I, p. 471. The movement for compulsory-school attendance legislation was slow in the Southern states. Initial legislation on the subject was enacted in Tennessee in 1905; in North Carolina in 1907; in Virginia in 1908; in Arkansas in 1909; in Louisiana in 1910; in South Carolina, Texas, Florida, and Alabama in 1915; in Georgia in 1916; and in Mississippi in 1918. Revisions, extensions, and improvements in this legislation have been made from time to time in most of the American states. Given here are the laws in Massachusetts, in New York, in Tennessee, and in Mississippi.

† Given in Wickersham, *op. cit.,* p. 509.

Fulton, Robert Ross . . . . . $ 100
Greene, John A. Gordon . . 262.50
Huntingdon, James S. Barr 300
Indiana, Sam. P. Bollman . . 500
Jefferson, John C. Wagaman 300
Juniata, David Laughlin . . . 200
Lancaster, J. P. Wickersham 1,500
Lawrence, Thomas Berry . . 500
Lebanon, John H. Kluge . . 760
Lehigh, Charles W. Cooper 500
Luzerne, John W. Lescher . . 500
Lycoming, J. W. Barrett . . . 500
McKean, Fordyce A. Allen 250
Mercer, Jomes C. Brown . . 400
Mifflin, Robert C. Ross 500
Monroe, Chas. S. Detrick . . 300
Montgomery, Ephraim L.
   Acker 600
Montour, Paul Leidy 350
Northampton, Valentine Hill-
   burn 625

Northumberland, J. J. Rei-
   mensnyder . . . . $ 350
Perry, Adam Height 300
Pike, Ira B. Newman 100
Potter, M. R. Gage 300
Schuylkill, J. K. Krewson . . 1,000
Somerset, Jos. J. Stutzman 400
Sullivan, Richard Bedfore . . 50
Susquehanna, Willard Rich-
   ardson 350
Tioga, J. F. Calkins 400
Union, J. S. Whitman 300
Venango, Manly C. Bebee . . 200
Warren, Theo. D. Edwards 300
Washington, John L. Gow . . 1,000
Wayne, John F. Stoddard . . 500
Westmoreland, Matthew Mc-
   Kinstry 550
Wyoming, Cornelius R. Lane 150
York, Jacob Kirk 500

Compulsory-Attendance Legislation Is Urged for New York, 1867 *

The opinion expressed by the Rev. Mr. Beecher on Sunday last, that education should be compulsory, agrees precisely with the views hitherto urged by the Sun. One of the essential requisites for good citizenship is a fair elementary education, such as is within the scope of every intellect, in all grades of society. The acquisition of this knowledge need not interfere materially with other duties, yet it is very common to find children totally neglected in this respect, either through the indifference or the avarice of parents. The early years, when the mind is plastic, and most capable of receiving the ground work of education, are in many cases allowed to pass in other occupations; or as is too often the case, in idleness and mischief. What is lost before the age of fifteen is seldom regained in later years. The necessities of life begin to make themselves felt, and between the cares of mind and physical toil, it is not easy to find time for systematic education. It would be well, therefore, if parents and guardians were compelled by law to send their children between certain ages, to the public or other schools. A law to this effect would be no hardship to those who are disposed to do their duty, but it would oblige delinquents to give their children the advantages which the State provides for all. The system has long prevailed in Prussia and the German states, and the consequence is, that education there is more universal than in any other country. Ignorance is especially inexcusable in this country, where every male citizen has a share and interest in the government under which he lives. Without some

* Editorial, *New York Sun*, April 16, 1867. Given in Finegan, *op. cit.*, p. 559.

education, men and women are wholly unfit to do their part in the civilized society of this republic, and since children of tender age have themselves no discretion or choice in the matter, it is eminently proper that their natural and legal protectors should be obliged by law to afford them every facility for obtaining a substantial and practical English education. The stability and credit of our nation depends in no small degree on the efficiency of our system of popular education, and every state should take measures to render compulsory such a share of education as is indispensable to intelligent citizens. This subject will be an appropriate one for discussion in the forthcoming constitutional convention in this State.

New York Abolishes the Rate Bill, 1867 *

Hereafter all moneys now authorized by any special acts to be collected by rate bill for the payment of teachers' wages, shall be collected by tax, and not by rate bill.

Secretary B. G. Northorp, of the Connecticut State Board of Education, Answers the Opponents of Compulsory Educational Legislation, 1872 †

Such a law would create a new crime. I reply, it ought to. To bring up children in ignorance *is* a crime and should be treated as such. As the most prolific source of criminality it should be under the ban of legal condemnation and the restraint of legal punishment. All modern civilization and legislation has made new crimes. Barbarism recognizes but few. To employ children in factories who are under 10 years of age or who have not attended school, or to employ minors under 18 years of age more than 12 hours a day, is each a new crime.

It interferes with the liberty of parents. I reply again, it ought to, when they are incapacitated by vice or other causes for the performance of essential duties as parents. Many other laws limit personal liberty. The requisition to serve on juries, or to aid the sheriff in arresting criminals, or the exactions of military service in the hour of the country's need—these and many other laws do this. If the law may prohibit the owner from practicing cruelty upon his horse or ox, it may restrain the parent from dwarfing the mind and debasing the character of his child. If the State may imprison and punish juvenile criminals, it may remove the causes of their crime and

---

* Given in Finegan, *op. cit.*, p. 555. F. H. Swift gives the following dates for the abolition of the rate bills in some of the states: Massachusetts, 1827; Delaware, 1829; Pennsylvania, 1834; Vermont, 1850; Indiana, 1851; Ohio, 1853; Iowa, 1858; New York, 1867; Rhode Island, 1868; Connecticut, 1868; Arkansas, 1868; Florida, 1869; Virginia, 1870; Utah, 1890. *A History of Public Permanent Common School Funds in the United States, 1795-1905* (New York, Henry Holt & Co., Inc., 1911), p. 27.

† *Annual Report Connecticut Board of Education*, 1872, p. 32. Given in *Bulletin*, 1914, No. 2, United States Bureau of Education, pp. 10, 11.

its consequences of loss, injury, and shame. The child has rights which not even a parent may violate. He may not rob his child of the sacred right of a good education. The law would justly punish a parent for starving his child, and more mischief is done by starving the mind than by famishing the body. The right of a parent to his children is founded on his ability and disposition to supply their wants of body and mind. When a parent is disqualified by intemperance, cruelty, or insanity, society justly assumes the control of the children. In ancient Greece the law gave almost unlimited authority to the father over his offspring. The same is true in some semibarbarous nations now. In all Christian lands the rights of the parents are held to imply certain correlative duties, and the duty to educate is as positive as to feed and clothe. Neglected children, when not orphans in fact, are virtually such, their parents ignoring their duties, and thus forfeiting their rights as parents. The State should protect the helpless, and especially these, its defenseless wards, who otherwise will be vicious as well as weak.

It arrogates new power by the Government. So do all quarantine and hygienic regulations and laws for the abatement of nuisances. Now, ignorance is as noxious as the most offensive nuisance, and more destructive than bodily contagions. Self-protection is a fundamental law of society.

It is un-American and unadapted to our free institutions. To put the question in the most offensive form, it may be asked, "Would you have policemen drag your children to school?" I answer, "Yes, if it will prevent his dragging them to jail a few years hence." But this law in our land would invoke no "dragging" and no police espionage or inquisitorial searches. With the annual enumeration and the school registers in hand, and the aid of the teachers and others most conversant with each district, school officers could easily learn who are the absentees. . . .

Compulsory education is monarchical in its origin and history. Common as is this impression it is erroneous. Connecticut may justly claim to be one of the first States in the world to establish the principle of compulsory education. On this point our earliest laws were most rigid. They need but slight modification to adapt them to the changed circumstances of the present. Before the peace of Westphalia, before Prussia existed as a kingdom, and while Frederick William was only "elector of Brandenburg," Connecticut adopted coercive education. . . .

Attendance would be just as large without the law as it is now. It may be so. But so far from being an objection, this fact is strong proof of the efficiency of that law which has itself helped create so healthful a public sentiment. Were the law to be abrogated to-morrow the individual and general interest in public education would remain. The same might have been said of Connecticut for more than 170 years after the adoption of compulsory education. During all that period a native of this State of mature age unable to read the English language would have been looked upon as a prodigy. Still, in Connecticut as well as in Germany, it was the law itself which greatly aided in awakening public interest and in fixing the habits, associations, and traditions of the people.

New York's First Compulsory School Attendance Legislation, 1874 *

The People of the State of New York, represented in Senate and Assembly, do enact as follows:

Section 1. All parents and those who have the care of children shall instruct them, or cause them to be instructed, in spelling, reading, writing, English grammar, geography and arithmetic. And every parent, guardian or other person having control and charge of any child between the ages of eight and fourteen years shall cause such child to attend some public or private day school at least fourteen weeks in each year, eight weeks at least of which attendance shall be consecutive, or to be instructed regularly at home at least fourteen weeks in each year in spelling, reading, writing, English grammar, geography and arithmetic, unless the physical or mental condition of the child is such as to render such attendance or instruction inexpedient or impracticable.

2. No child under the age of fourteen years shall be employed by any person to labor in any business whatever during the school hours of any school day of the school term of the public school in the school district or the city where such child is, unless such child shall have attended some public or private day-school where instruction was given by a teacher qualified to instruct in spelling, reading, writing, geography, English grammar and arithmetic, or shall have been regularly instructed at home in said branches, by some person qualified to instruct in the same, at least fourteen weeks of the fifty-two weeks next preceding any and every year in which such child shall be employed, and shall, at the time of such employment, deliver to the employer a certificate in writing, signed by the teacher, or a school trustee of the district or of a school, certifying to such attendance or instruction; and any person who shall employ any child contrary to the provisions of this section, shall, for each offense, forfeit and pay a penalty of fifty dollars to the treasurer or chief fiscal officer of the city or supervisor of the town in which such offense shall occur, and said sum or penalty, when so paid, to be added to the public school money of the school district in which the offense occurred.

3. It shall be the duty of the trustee or trustees of every school district, or public school, or union school, in every town and city, in the months of September and of February of each year to examine into the situation of the children employed in all manufacturing establishments in such school district; and, in case any town or city is not divided into school districts,

---

* *Laws of the State of New York, Passed at the Ninety-Seventh Session of the Legislature,* 1874, pp. 532-35.

it shall, for the purposes of the examination provided for in this section, be divided by the school authorities thereof into districts, and the said trustees notified of their respective districts, on or before the first day of January of each year; and the said trustee or trustees shall ascertain whether all the provisions of this act are duly observed, and report all violations thereof to the treasurer or chief fiscal officer of said city or supervisor of said town. On such examination, the proprietor, superintendent or manager of said establishment shall, on demand, exhibit to said examining trustee, a correct list of all children between the ages of eight and fourteen years employed in said establishment with the said certificates of attendance on school, or of instruction.

4. Every parent, guardian or other person having control and charge of any child between the ages of eight and fourteen years, who has been temporarily discharged from employment in any business, in order to be afforded an opportunity to receive instruction or schooling, shall send such child to some public or private school, or shall cause such child to be regularly instructed as aforesaid at home for the period for which such child may have been so discharged, to the extent of at least fourteen weeks in all in each year, unless the physical or mental condition of the child is such as to render such an attendance or instruction inexpedient or impracticable.

5. The trustee or trustees of any school district or public school, or the president of any union school, or in case there is no such officer, then such officer as the board of education of said city or town may designate, is hereby authorized and empowered to see that sections one, two, three, four and five of this act are enforced, and to report in writing all violations thereof, to the treasurer or chief fiscal officer of his city or to the supervisor of his town; any person who shall violate any provision of sections one, three and four of this act, shall, on written notice of such violation, from one of the school officers above named, forfeit, for the first offense, and pay to the treasurer or chief fiscal officer of the city or to the supervisor of the town in which he resides, or such offense has occurred, the sum of one dollar, and after such first offense, shall, for each succeeding offense in the same year, forfeit and pay to the treasurer of said city or supervisor of said town the sum of five dollars for each and every week, not exceeding thirteen weeks in any one year during which he, after written notice from said school officer, shall have failed to comply with any of said provisions, the said penalties, when paid, to be added to the public school money of said school district in which the offense occurred.

6. In every case arising under this act where the parent, guardian, or other person having the control of any child between the said ages of eight and fifteen years, is unable to provide such child for said fourteen weeks with the text-books required to be furnished to enable such child to attend school for said period, and shall so state in writing to the said trustee, the said trustee shall provide said text-books for said fourteen weeks at the public school for the use of such child, and the expense of the same shall be paid by the treasurer of said city or the supervisor of said town on the certificate of the said trustee, specifying the items furnished for the use of such child.

7. In case any person having the control of any child between the ages of eight and fourteen years, is unable to induce said child to attend school for the said fourteen weeks in each year and shall so state in writing to said trustee, the said child shall, from and after the date of the delivery to said trustee of said statement in writing, be deemed and dealt with as an habitual truant, and said person shall be relieved of all penalties incurred for said year after said date, under sections one, four and five of this act, as to such child.

8. The board of education or public instruction, by whatever name it may be called in each city, and the trustees of the school districts and union school in each town by an affirmative vote of a majority of said trustees at a meeting or meetings to be called for this purpose, on ten days' notice in writing to each trustee, said notice to be given by the town clerk, are for each of their respective cities and towns hereby authorized and empowered and directed on or before the first day of January, eighteen hundred and seventy-five, to make all needful provisions, arrangements, rules and regulations concerning habitual truants and children between said ages of eight and fourteen years of age, who may be found wandering about the streets or public places of such city or town during the school hours of the school day of the term of the public school of said city or town, having no lawful occupation or business, and growing up in ignorance, and said provisions, arrangements, rules and regulations shall be such as shall, in their judgment, be most conducive to the welfare of such children, and to the good order of such city or town; and shall provide suitable places for the discipline and instruction and confinement, when necessary, of such children, and may require the aid of the police of cities and constables of towns to enforce their said rules and regulations; provided, however, that such provisions, arrangements, rules and regulations, shall not go into effect as laws for said several cities and towns, until they shall have been approved, in writing, by a justice of the supreme court for the judicial district in which said city or town is situated, and when so approved he shall file the same with the clerk of the said city or town who shall print the same and furnish ten copies thereof to each trustee of each school district or public or union school of said city or town. The said trustees shall keep one copy thereof posted in a conspicuous place in or upon each school-house in his charge during the school terms each year. In like manner, the same, in each city or town may be amended or revised annually in the month of December.

9. Justices of the peace, civil justices and police justices shall have

jurisdiction, within their respective towns and cities, of all offenses and of all actions for penalties or fines described in this act, or that may be described in said provisions, arrangements, rules and regulations authorized by section eight of this act. All actions for fines and penalties under this act, shall be brought in the name of the treasurer or chief fiscal officer of the city or supervisor of the town to whom the same is payable, but shall be brought by and under the direction of the said trustee or trustees, or said officer designated by the board of education.

10. Two weeks attendance at a half time or evening school shall for all purposes of this act be counted as one week at a day school.

11. This act shall take effect on the first day of January, eighteen hundred and seventy-five.

Proposed Amendment to the Constitution of the United States Prohibiting the States from Using Public School Funds or Public Lands for the Benefit of Religious Groups, 1876 *

No state shall make any law respecting the establishment of religion or prohibiting the free exercise thereof; and no money raised by taxation in any state for the support of public schools or derived from any public fund therefor, nor any public lands devoted thereto, shall ever be under the control of any religious sect or denomination, nor shall any money so raised or lands so devoted be divided between religious sects or denominations.

This article shall not vest, enlarge, or diminish legislative power in the Congress.

Enactment of Compulsory-Attendance Laws Favored, 1897 †

Resolved, That we approve the enactment by many of the states of the Union of compulsory-attendance laws, and that we hereby give expression to our belief that state supervision is necessary to the proper enforcement of those laws.

Tennessee's Compulsory School Law, 1905 ‡

Section 1. *Be it enacted by the General Assembly of the State of Tennessee,* That every parent, guardian, or other person in counties of this

---

* *Congressional Record,* IV, Part 6 and Appendix, 44th Congress, 1st Session, p. 5190. The vote in the House was 180 yeas, 7 nays, 98 not voting (p. 5191). Two-thirds voting in the affirmative, the joint resolution was passed (p. 5192). Vote in the Senate was 28 yeas, 16 nays. Two-thirds of the Senators present not voting for the resolution, the same was not passed (p. 5595).

† Resolution by the Department of Superintendence, National Educational Association, *Journal of Proceedings and Addresses,* 1897, p. 198.

‡ *Acts of the State of Tennessee,* 1905, pp. 1040-44. This was the first state law on compulsory attendance in the South.

State having a population of not less than twelve thousand eight hundred and ninety (12,890) and not more than twelve thousand nine hundred (12,900), according to the Federal Census of 1900 or any subsequent Federal Census, "and of a population of not more than twenty-one thousand (21,000) nor of not less than twenty thousand five hundred (20,500), according to the Federal Census of 1900 or of any subsequent Federal Census," having control or charge of a child or children between the ages of eight and fourteen years, shall send such child or children to a public school or to some other school for at least fourteen weeks of each year, or in case the public school in the district in which such child resides shall be in session for less than fourteen weeks, they shall send them for the entire session, unless such attendance in whole or in part is excused by the School Directors of the district in a written exemption, showing on whose application granted.

Sec. 2. *Be it further enacted,* That no such exemption from school attendance shall be granted unless the child is in such condition physically or mentally as to prevent attendance at school, or its application to study, for the period of exemption—exception in cases of actual destitution, where the wages of the child are essential for the support of the family, the County Court shall, if it deems wise, excuse such attendance or make an appropriation to reimburse the family for the loss of wages incurred by attendance upon school.

Sec. 3. *Be it further enacted,* That the attendance of fourteen weeks required above shall begin with the notification of the parent, guardian, or other custodian, as described in Section 7 of this Act, and shall be consecutive, except for holidays, vacation, detention by sickness, or other necessary and unavoidable causes, and such intermissions of such attendance are not to be counted as part of the fourteen weeks required.

Sec. 4. *Be it further enacted,* That any failure on the part of any parent, guardian, or other person to comply with the foregoing sections of this Act, shall be a misdemeanor and shall be punishable by a fine of one ($1) dollar for each week that each child in his or her control shall fail of attendance for the required period of fourteen weeks; such fine to be collectible by suit before any Justice of the Peace in the county, in the name of the State, and to be paid to the Clerk of the School District in which such child resides, for the benefit of the public school fund of that district.

Sec. 5. *Be it further enacted,* That during the period of the year that the public schools of any School District affected by the provisions of this Act are in operation, it shall be a misdemeanor, punishable by fine, for any person, firm, or corporation to hire or use the services of any child residing in such district under the age of fourteen years during school hours, unless such child shall first have attended school during the scholastic years then current for the length of time required by this Act, or unless such child has been exempted from school attendance in the manner allowed and prescribed by this Act; and a violation of this provision shall subject the offender to a fine of two dollars and fifty cents ($2.50) for each offense, collectible by suit before any Justice of the Peace of the county, in the name of the State, and payable to the Clerk of the School District, for the use of the public schools of this district.

Sec. 6. *Be it further enacted,* That it shall be the duty of the District Clerks whose duty it is to take the school census within their respective territories to find out and report, at the time of taking the annual census of the school children of their respective districts as required by existing laws, the names of all children between the ages of eight and fourteen years residing in their districts, with the age of each, and the name and residence of the parent, guardian, or other person having care and control of each of such children. And they shall make of these statistics triplicate reports— one for the School Directors of the district, one for the County Superintendent of Public Instruction. And it shall be the duty of the State Superintendent to furnish in blank the proper forms and schedules for such reports to the County Superintendent, who shall distribute them to the District Clerks.

Sec. 7. *Be it further enacted,* That it shall be the duty of the District Directors, as soon as practicable after the completion of the school census of each year, to apportion the children of their respective districts between the ages of eight and fourteen years, as shown by the census statistics so taken, among the public schools of the district, and to furnish each principal or teacher with a list of the children so assigned to him, and the name and residence of their parent, guardian, or other person having control of them. And it shall be the duty of said principals or teachers at the opening of the school year to bring to the attention of all parents, guardians, and custodians of the children so assigned to them, respectively, the provisions and penalties of this Act, and they shall ascertain and record the names of all children between said ages, who attend schools other than public schools of the district, and shall keep a record of the actual time of attendance of all the children attending the public schools of the district, and shall from time to time, as required by the School Directors, make report to them of these matters and show in such report the extent of the delinquency of all parents, guardians, and custodians of the children assigned to them, respectively, who shall fail in any respect to comply with the provisions of this Act; *Provided,* that the attendance of any child for the required period upon any school other than the public schools, which teaches the same branches as the public schools of the district, or equivalent branches, shall be deemed a satisfactory compliance with the requirements of this Act. And a written certificate of the principal of any school stating the time or times of such attendance shall be sufficient evidence of the fact; *Provided further,* that in all cases where it is claimed that the child has attended school for the required time at some school other than the public schools, it shall be the duty of the parent, guardian, or custodian of that child to furnish such certificate of his attendance; and if by reason of their failure to furnish such certificate, proceedings are instituted against such parent, guardian, or custodian of that child to furnish such certificate of (required by) this Act, such proceedings shall be at the expense of such defendant.

Sec. 8. *Be it further enacted,* That the District Directors shall make such regulations and require of the public school teachers such reports from time to time as to the attendance and non-attendance of the children assigned to them, respectively, for supervision, as that the records of their offices shall, at all times, show the names and residences of all the persons who fail to comply with the requirements of this Act, and such records shall, at all reasonable times, be accessible to the public.

Sec. 9. *Be it further enacted,* That it shall be the duty of the said District Directors, through the District Clerk, as their agent, to enforce the payment and collection of all fines for the violation of this Act, incurred by employers of children and by parents or others within the respective districts, and for this purpose to institute all necessary suits therefor, in the name of the State, against such delinquents before some Justice of the Peace of the Civil District where the defendant may be residing at the time such suit is brought, and it shall be the duty of the District Clerk and Treasurers of School Boards to receive and receipt for such fines, and to report and account for the same from time to time to the School Directors of the district.

Sec. 10. *Be it further enacted,* That it shall be the duty of the Superintendent of Public Instruction of the county to require from the District Directors of the various School Districts having control of the public schools to make reports from time to time, as may be thought expedient, showing the enrollment of all the children within their respective School Districts between the ages of eight and fourteen years, the public schools or other substituted schools, and the extent to which such attendance on the part of any child falls short of the requirements of this Act, together with the names and residences of their parents, guardians, or other custodians of the children, who have failed in any respect to meet the requirements of this Act, and a list of the fines incurred thereunder, and the amount of such fines actually collected. It shall be the further duty of the County and State Superintendents to show, as far as possible, in their annual reports, or in their special reports, which may be made from time to time, the effect and operation of this law, and to recommend such amendments and extensions thereof, as in their judgment may be deemed wise, for the more effectual attainment of the purposes of this Act.

Sec. 11. *Be it further enacted,* That this Act take effect from and after its passage, the public welfare requiring it.

Passed April 12, 1905.

Opposition to Compulsory Educational Legislation, 1914 *

Though nearly all the States in the Union have enacted compulsory attendance laws, each State has had to overcome much opposition on the part of those who argued that such laws are un-American in principle, in that they interfere with the personal liberty of the parent. In 1891 and 1893 Gov. Pattison, of Pennsylvania, vetoed compulsory education bills on that ground. In 1895, when Gov. Hastings signed a similar bill, he did so only because he did not wish to obtrude his judgment in the matter, which was against the bill.

The plea that such laws interfere with personal liberty has, however, never been recognized by the courts, and all such laws now on the statutes of the several States are considered constitutional.

Among the arguments offered by those opposed to the enactment of compulsory attendance laws are these: (1) a new crime is created; (2) it interferes with the liberty of parents; (3) new powers are arrogated by the Government; (4) it is un-American and not adapted to our free institutions; (5) compulsory education is monarchical in its origin and history; (6) attendance is just as great without the law.

Mississippi's Initial Law on Compulsory Attendance at School, 1918 †

Section 1. Be it enacted by the Legislature of the State of Mississippi, That on and after the first day of September, 1918, every parent, guardian or other person in the state of Mississippi having control or charge of any child or children between the ages of seven and fourteen years, inclusive, shall be required to send such child or children to a public school or to a private, denominational or parochial school taught by a competent instructor, and such child or children shall attend school for at least sixty days during each and every scholastic year; provided that the county school board, or in case of a separate school district, the board of trustees shall have power to reduce the period of compulsory attendance to not less than forty days for any individual school; provided further, that the period of compulsory attendance for each school shall commence at the beginning of the school, unless otherwise ordered by the county school board or by the board of trustees of a separate school district, as the case may be.

Sec. 2. That any and all children who have completed the common school course of study or the equivalent thereof, shall be exempt from the provisions of this act, and in case there be no public school within two and one-half miles by the nearest traveled road of any person between the ages of seven and fourteen years inclusive, he or she shall not be subject to the

* W. S. Deffenbaugh, "Compulsory Attendance Laws in the United States," *Bulletin*, 1914, No. 2, United States Bureau of Education, p. 10.
† *Laws of the State of Mississippi* (Jackson, Miss., Tucker Printing House, 1918), pp. 312-15. The last of the states initially to enact legislation on the subject.

provisions of this act unless public transportation within reasonable walking distance is provided; provided further, that the teacher of any school with the approval of the trustees of the school shall have the authority, in the exercise of their discretion, to permit the temporary absence of children from the school, between the ages of seven and fourteen inclusive, in extreme cases of emergency or domestic necessity.

Sec. 3. That any and all children who are physically or mentally incapacitated for the work of the school are exempt from the provisions of this act, but the school authorities shall have the right, and they are hereby authorized, when such exemption, under the provisions of this act, is claimed by any parent, guardian or other person having control of such child or children, to require from a practicing physician a properly attested certificate that such child or children should not be required to attend school on account of some physical or mental condition which renders his attendance impractical or inexpedient.

Sec. 4. That in case where because of extreme poverty, the services of such children are necessary for their own support, or the support of their parents, as attested by an affidavit of said parents, the teacher shall, with the consent of the trustees, spare such child or children from attendance; or in case where such parent, guardian or other person having control of the child, shall show before an officer by affidavit, that the child is without necessary books and clothing for attending school and that he is unable to provide them, the said child may be excused from attendance, until through charity or other means, books and clothing have been provided, and thereafter the child shall no longer be exempt from such attendance.

Sec. 5. That it shall be the duty of the principal teacher of all schools to report to the county superintendent all cases of non-enrollment and non-attendance in accord with section 1 of this act. In all cases investigated by the county superintendent, where no valid reason for non-enrollment or non-attendance is found, it shall be the duty of the county superintendent to give written notice to the parent, guardian or other person having control of the child, which notice shall require the attendance of said child at such school within three days from date of said notice.

Sec. 6. That if within three days from date of service of such notice, the parent, guardian or other person having control of such child, does not comply with the requirements, the county superintendent may, if he deem it necessary, make affidavit against such parent, guardian or other person having control of such child, before any justice of the peace, mayor or police justice of any town or city as the case may be, in which such offense shall be committed, which court is hereby clothed with jurisdiction over all offenders with full power to hear and try all complaints, and on conviction, punish by a fine of not less than one dollar ($1.00) nor more than ten dollars ($10.00) for each offense and enforce their collection.

Sec. 7. All school officers, including those in private, denominational or parochial schools in this state, offering instruction to pupils within the compulsory attendance ages, are hereby required to make and furnish all reports that may be required by the state superintendent of education and by the county superintendent of education, or by the trustees of any municipal separate school district, with reference to the working of this act. Every teacher employed in the public schools of the state of Mississippi is hereby required to make a report to the county superintendent or principal of a municipal separate school district in which he may be employed, showing the names and addresses of all pupils who have been truant or habitually absent from school during the previous month, and stating the reason for such truancy or habitual absence, if known.

Sec. 8. That in case any pupil has become habitually truant or a menace to the best interests of the school which he is attending, or should attend, then it shall be the duty of the teacher to report such fact and condition to the parent, guardian or other person having control of such child, who shall be held liable, under the provisions of this act, for the regular attendance and good conduct of such child, unless such parent, guardian or other person having control of such child shall state in writing to the teacher that he or she is unable to control such child, whereupon said teacher shall proceed against such incorrigible pupils as a disorderly person before a court of competent jurisdiction, and said child upon conviction may be sentenced to any custodial institution that may be open to such children. If there be no available institution, then such incorrigible child shall be expelled from school.

Sec. 9. That in order that the provisions of this act may be more definitely enforced, the county superintendent of education shall, not later than ten days before the annual compulsory attendance term, furnish to each principal of a rural school and to the superintendent or principal teacher of the school or schools in any municipal separate district, a list of all the children from seven to fourteen years of age, inclusive, who should attend the school or schools under the charge of the said principal teacher of the rural school, or of the superintendent or principal of the school or schools in any municipal separate district, as the case may be, giving the name, date of birth, age, race, sex and estimated distance from the school house by the nearest traveled road, the name and address of parents, guardian or other person in parental relationship.

Sec. 9. (a) The provisions of this act shall not be applicable to any county in the state, unless and until an election shall have been held to determine whether or not the people of said county, or of any supervisors district, separate school district or consolidated school district shall vote to come in under same.

Sec. 9. (b) The board of supervisors of any county shall, upon petition signed by twenty per cent of the qualified electors of said county, or twenty per cent of the qualified electors of a supervisors district, or by twenty per cent of the qualified electors of any separate school district, or by twenty per cent of the qualified electors of any consolidated school district of said country, order an election to be held in the county at large, or in a separate school district, or in a consolidated school district, as the case may be, to determine the will of the people as to whether said county or separate school district, or consolidated school district shall come under the provisions of this act. In the event a majority of those voting in said election shall vote for compulsory school attendance, then the provisions of this act shall apply, and not otherwise.

Sec. 9. (*c*) Provided, that in any county, or supervisors district, or consolidated school district, or separate school district where a special election shall have been held and carried in favor of the provisions of this act, no subsequent election on the subject of compulsory school attendance shall be held within four scholastic years after the date of such election.

Sec. 10. That this act take effect and be in force from and after September 1, 1918.

Children of Compulsory School Age Cannot Be Compelled to Attend Public Schools, 1925 *

Pierce, Governor of Oregon, et. al. v. *Society of Sisters.*
Pierce, Governor of Oregon, et. al. v. *Hill Military Academy.*

Appeals from the District Court of the United States for the District of Oregon.

Arguments by counsel for Society of Sisters and by Hill Military Academy included the following: The fundamental theory of liberty upon which all governments of this Union rests excludes any general power of the State to standardize its children by forcing them to accept instruction from public teachers only.

The Oregon Compulsory Education Act which, with certain exemptions, requires every parent, guardian or other person having control of a child between the ages of eight and sixteen years to send him to a public school in the district where he resides, for the period during which the school is held for the current year, is an unreasonable interference with the liberty of the parents and guardians to direct the upbringing of the children, and in that respect violates the Fourteenth Amendment.

In a proper sense, it is true that corporations can not claim for themselves the liberty guaranteed by the Fourteenth Amendment, and, in general, no person in any business has such an interest in possible customers as to enable him to restrain exercise of proper power by the State upon the ground that he will be deprived of patronage.

* 268 U. S. 510-36. For other decisions of courts on educational issues, see Index.

But where corporations owning and conducting schools are threatened with destruction of their business and property through the improper and unconstitutional compulsion exercised by this statute upon parents and guardians, their interest is direct and immediate and entitles them to protection by injunction.

The Act, being intended to have general application, can not be construed in its application to such corporations as an exercise to amend their charters. *Berea College* v. *Kentucky,* 211 U.S. 45.

Where the injury threatened by an unconstitutional statute is present and real before the statute is to be effective, and will become irreparable if relief be postponed to that time, a suit to restrain future enforcement of the statute is not premature.

Appeals from decrees of the District Court granting preliminary injunctions restraining the governor, and other officials, of the State of Oregon from threatening or attempting to enforce an amendment to the school law,—an initiative measure adapted by the people November 7, 1922, to become effective in 1926—requiring parents and others having control of young children to send them to the primary schools of the State. The plaintiffs were two Oregon corporations, owning and conducting schools. . . .

It is not seriously debatable that the parental right to guide one's child intellectually and religiously is a most substantial part of the liberty and freedom of the parent.

The statute in suit trespasses, not only upon the liberty of the parents individually, but upon their liberty collectively as well. It forbids them, as a body, to support private and parochial schools and thus give to their children such education and religious training as the parents may see fit, subject to the valid regulations of the State. In that respect the enactment violates the public policy of the State of Oregon and the liberty which parents have heretofore enjoyed in that State.

The legislative power of a State in relation to education does not involve the power to prohibit or suppress private schools and colleges. The familiar statement that education is a public function means no more than that it is a function that the State may undertake, because it vitally interests and concerns the State that children shall be furnished the means of education and not left to grow up in ignorance. But the power of the State to provide public schools carries with it no power to prohibit and suppress private schools and colleges which are competent and qualified to afford what the State wants, namely, education. . . .

The present case is wholly outside the principle that, where a State may enter upon an undertaking which can be conducted profitably and satisfactorily only as a monopoly, it may prevent competition or the continuing use of competing facilities by condemning and destroying property under the power of eminent domain and just compensation. In its essence, the

Oregon law is one strangling scientific investigation in private laboratories. The social interests menaced by the suppression of private educational institutions and the denial of liberty to pursue long rooted habits and traditions among our people are peculiarly of the character that the Fourteenth Amendment was most immediately designed to protect from state political action. . . .

The statute impairs the obligation of contract embodied in the appellee's corporate charter. *Dartmouth College* case, 4. Wheat. 518.

Any restrictions upon the rights of the individual are arbitrary and oppressive unless intended to promote the public welfare and having a reasonable relation to that purpose. Where the legislative action is arbitrary and has no reasonable relation to a purpose which it is competent for the Government to effect, the legislature transcends the limits of its power in interfering with the liberty of contract. . . .

The act is not designed and intended to promote compulsory education. It adds nothing to the standard of education, it does not broaden the educational field; the changing of the ages for compulsory school attendance is in no way affected by the clause relating to private schools. . . .

Mr. Justice McReynolds delivered the opinion of the Court:

. . . No question is raised concerning the power of the State reasonably to regulate all schools, to inspect, supervise and examine them, their teachers and pupils; to require that all children of proper age attend some school, that teachers shall be of good moral character and patriotic disposition, that certain studies plainly essential to good citizenship must be taught, and that nothing be taught which is manifestly inimical to the public welfare.

The inevitable practical result of enforcing the Act under consideration would be destruction of appellees' primary schools, and perhaps all other private primary schools for normal children within the State of Oregon.

Under the doctrine of *Meyer* v. *Nebraska,* 262 U.S. 390, we think it entirely plain that the Act of 1922 unreasonably interferes with the liberty of parents and guardians to direct the upbringing and education of children under their control. . . . The fundamental theory of liberty under which all governments in this Union repose excludes any general power of the State to standardize its children by forcing them to accept instruction from public teachers only. The child is not the mere creature of the State; those who nurture him and direct his destiny have the right, coupled with the high duty, to recognize and prepare him for additional obligations.

Appellees are corporations and therefore, it is said, they cannot claim for themselves the liberty which the Fourteenth Amendment guarantees. Accepted in the proper sense, this is true. But they have business and property for which they claim protection. These are threatened with destruction through the unwarranted compulsion which appellants are exercising over present and prospective patrons of their schools. And this court has gone very far to protect against loss threatened by such action. . .

Plaintiffs ask protection against arbitrary, unreasonable and unlawful interference with their patrons and the consequent destruction of their business and property. . . .

The suits were not premature. The injury to appellees was present and very real, not a mere possibility in the remote future. If no relief had been possible prior to the effective date of the Act, the injury would have become irreparable. Prevention of impending injury by unlawful action is a well recognized function of courts of equity.

Ralph Bradford, General Manager of the Chamber of Commerce of the United States, on the Need for Closer Relations Between Business and Education, 1944 *

The need for a much closer working relationship between business and educators in planning for the public education of the future has been clearly outlined by the National Chamber's Committee on Education. Obviously business men have an interest in public education—first of all as the fathers of sons and daughters who are to be educated; and second as heads of business enterprise that has a stake both coming and going. On the one hand, expenditures for public education are a major item in local and state tax bills; on the other, business is largely dependent upon the products of public education for its operating personnel.

If education is anything at all, it is an instrumentality for preparing young people to fit themselves most productively and most happily into the life of the community. I mean the home town or city—for that is where most of the young people who attend schools there will pass their adult years. Public education as a matter of history, and I think as a matter of wisdom, has been locally controlled. It should continue to be so, in the interest of gearing education to community needs. If that is to be accomplished successfully, it can be done more readily through the cooperation of business men with educational authorities.

You will agree, I think, that our educational pattern is under sharp scrutiny today, both by educators and laymen. We want to help, working cooperatively with educational leaders, in forging an educational system that will meet the needs of all Americans. Our approach is not being made from the economy point of view, in the narrow sense, but rather from the standpoint of what is best for the whole economy, including, of course, its social aspects. Our hope is to help in the development of a broad general outline of purposeful public education to meet the expanding and changing needs of both the individual and the nation.

Education has, or must have if it is to serve its purpose, two great

* Committee on Education, The Chamber of Commerce of the United States, *Education, An Investment in People*, 1944, p. 5.

values—both necessary to American progress. From the standpoint of the individual, it equips his perceptions for greater satisfaction in the pursuit of the world's biggest business—which is the business of living. And from the standpoint of public investment, it has the responsibility of serving an expanding economy by progressively upgrading the productive skills and management aptitudes of the American people. Both these functions are of vital concern to American business, because they are integral with our country's welfare.

One bar to intelligent cooperation between educators and business men has been a lack of understanding, each of the needs of the other. There has been too much disposition on the part of business men to look on educators as impractical theorists who don't know the value of a dollar; and on the part of educators to regard business men as a bunch of penny-pinching skinflints. The way to clear up such misunderstandings as these, is to get together and talk things over.

Through its Committee on Education, the National Chamber is working to bring together in the local communities the educators and business men to discuss the basic problems of education. The head of this committee is Thomas C. Boushall, a man who is almost devoutly convinced not only of the important role of education, but of the need for better understanding between business men and educators. Our approach to the question of education is not what is it costing us, but is it doing the job? And what, in the first place, is the job? This is the challenge to all communities! Let's find out what needs to be done—and do it together!

"Alas, the Poor School Superintendent," 1946 *

After the world was made safe for democracy, the school administrator immediately interested himself in ventilating devices, cafeteria counters, the amount of window space required for a certain-sized room (called fenestration, in the profession), the number of toilet hoppers per pupil population, the best paint for damp surfaces, and the amount of air a pupil breathes per hour. And, of course, not having much time for meeting pupils, he relegated "cases" (the new word for pupils) whenever he could to a dean of boys or a "home room" teacher. His manner, appearance, and attitude were those of a corporation head. He figured supplies by car-load lot, and, turning about, evaluated courses down to an eighth of a credit; he was all system and efficiency. He was well manicured, carried a brief case long before one was popular, and joined the service clubs. He took pains to let his business companions know that he was a regular fellow and warily held back any pretensions to learning, for he realized that

---

* George H. Henry, "Alas, the Poor School Superintendent," *Harper's Magazine,* November, 1946, pp. 136-38. Used by permission. See also H. E. Buchholz, "The Pegagogues at Armageddon," *The American Mercury,* XXIX (June, 1933), pp. 129-38.

among his social set "brains" were in dispute. In truth, many principals readily realized that their position was an excellent preparation for insurance and selling. During these booming twenties he preferred to be called an educator. Better yet, he might be called a co-ordinator or integrator of the "system." He figured how to get the maximum learning per hour of instruction, per pupil, per grade—in respectful adaptation of the methods of Ford's miracle asesmbly line.

He came chiefly from the farm and the lower middle class, had college training, was tickled over his rise to a higher social level, and acted it. At this stage he departed, once and for all, from the humanist tradition, never returning to it, being generally a major in mathematics, which served him well for the mechanics of administration. And so it was that the "engineering" facet was added to the job.

The progressive movement changed the type considerably. The new emphasis on "doing" certainly loosened up the administrator and rid him of pomp. He climbed mountains with the kids, camped out with them in a pup tent, officiated at sports events, danced the new jazz, sang with them in assembly, chaperoned beach parties and hayrides. He might direct a summer camp. Since everybody was making money and everybody was happy with it, what else was there for a schoolman to do? Wasn't education, the great American dream, about fully realized? But he was due for a setback; for a few years after, when the business boom burst and people, sobering up, took stock, the school administrator lost status for the first time in the history of the noble experiment. People everywhere asked for an accounting of these new-fangled goings-on that pushed aside the dear old three R's, that went way back even to the rugged days of slate and saliva.

Average Salaries of Public School Teachers in the United States, 1946-1947 *

Rank	State	Average Salary	Rank	State	Average Salary
1	California	$3304	14	Arizona	$2368
2	New York	3302	15	Ohio	2350
3	Massachusetts	2852	16	New Mexico	2307
4	New Jersey	2837	17	Pennsylvania	2304
5	Connecticut	2790	18	Utah	2269
6	Illinois	2681	19	Wisconsin	2259
7	Michigan	2635			
8	Washington	2628		National Average	$2254
9	Oregon	2461	20	Nevada	2175
10	Maryland	2443	21	Colorado	2170
11	Indiana	2433	22	Idaho	2117
12	Delaware	2416	23	Minnesota	2050
13	Rhode Island	2414	24	New Hampshire	1981

* *North Carolina Public School Bulletin*, XIII (April, 1949), p. 7.

Rank	State	Average Salary	Rank	State	Average Salary
25	Louisiana	$1959	36	West Virginia	$1711
26	Florida	1939	38	Nebraska	1696
27	Iowa	1922	39	Vermont	1672
28	Oklahoma	1920	40	Georgia	1618
29	Texas	1915	41	Maine	1586
30	Kansas	1904	42	North Dakota	1486
31	Missouri	1871	43	Kentucky	1481
32	Virginia	1845	44	Tennessee	1480
33	Montana	1838	45	Alabama	1443
34	Wyoming	1810	46	South Carolina	1298
34	North Carolina	1810	47	Arkansas	1255
36	South Dakota	1711	48	Mississippi	984

The United States Chamber of Commerce Presents the Arguments For and Against Federal Aid to General Education, 1948 *

AFFIRMATIVE ARGUMENT

I. Federal aid for the equalization of educational opportunities is essential and justifiable.

   A. Great educational inequalities exist.

      1. Many children attend school too little each year.

         a. Four million children, aged 5 to 17, were not enrolled in school last year (two million aged 5 years).

         b. Of those enrolled, over 3 million were absent each day.

         c. State school terms vary in length from 7 months to 9 months.

         d. Our mobile population creates intense over-crowding of schools in some areas each year (West Coast population up 50% since 1940).

      2. In many areas educational facilities are deplorably inadequate.

         a. School buildings are over-crowded and ill-equipped.

         b. Books and other teaching materials are scarce or obsolete.

         c. Salaries and quality of teachers are frequently low, especially in elementary schools.

         d. Library or audio-visual aids are meager or unavailable.

         e. Vocational or avocational courses are often lacking.

         f. Guidance based on surveys, tests and measurements is almost non-existent.

* *Which Way Education?* (Washington, Committee on Education, Chamber of Commerce of the United States, December, 1948), pp. 4-14. Used by permission. After being discussed for a month behind closed doors by the House Committee on Education and Labor the federal aid bill was shelved in the early part of 1950. After the exchange of opinions between Francis Cardinal Spellman and Mrs. Eleanor Roosevelt in the summer of 1949, which assumed national proportions and was one of the significant educational events of that year, the federal aid bill became hopelessly involved in the religious issue which had made its appearance in such proposals since the Hoar Bill of 1870.

Median Salaries Paid and Their Purchasing Power, 1940-41 and 1948-49 *

Position (1)	Year (2)	Group I Over 500,000		Group II 100,000-500,000		Group III 30,000-100,000		Group IV 10,000-30,000		Group V 5,000-10,000		Group VI 2,500-5,000	
		Median (3)	Value (4)	Median (5)	Value (6)	Median (7)	Value (8)	Median (9)	Value (10)	Median (11)	Value (12)	Median (13)	Value (14)
CLASSROOM TEACHERS													
Elementary	1940-41	$2,434	$2,384	$1,901	$1,862	$1,608	$1,575	$1,432	$1,403	$1,289	$1,262	$1,149	$1,125
	1948-49	4,019	2,364	3,265	1,921	2,955	1,738	2,778	1,634	2,609	1,535	2,483	1,461
Junior-High	1940-41	2,801	2,743	2,087	2,044	1,847	1,809	1,597	1,564	1,452	1,422	1,301	1,274
	1948-49	4,092	2,407	3,537	2,081	3,280	1,929	3,014	1,773	2,874	1,691	2,677	1,575
Highschool	1940-41	3,106	3,042	2,288	2,241	2,039	1,997	1,803	1,766	1,626	1,593	1,428	1,399
	1948-49	4,689	2,758	3,793	2,231	3,444	2,026	3,269	1,923	3,017	1,775	2,877	1,692
All Types	1940-41	2,708	2,652	2,029	1,987	1,763	1,727	1,551	1,519	1,424	1,395	1,273	1,247
	1948-49	4,242	2,495	3,423	2,014	3,150	1,853	2,964	1,744	2,783	1,637	2,655	1,562
PRINCIPALS													
Supervising Elementary	1940-41	3,966	3,884	2,948	2,887	2,470	2,419	2,220	2,174	2,081	2,038	1,878	1,839
	1948-49	5,907	3,475	4,676	2,751	4,195	2,468	3,872	2,278	3,941	2,318	3,692	2,172
Junior-High	1940-41	5,134	5,028	3,761	3,684	3,175	3,110	2,598	2,545	1,992	1,951	1,596	1,563
	1948-49	6,906	4,062	5,373	3,161	4,788	2,816	4,300	2,529	3,778	2,222	3,163	1,861
Highschool	1940-41	5,412	5,301	4,183	4,097	4,000	3,918	3,303	3,235	2,596	2,543	2,136	2,092
	1948-49	7,321	4,306	6,073	3,572	5,468	3,216	4,796	2,821	4,232	2,489	3,948	2,322
ADMINISTRATION													
Superintendents	1940-41	13,200	12,929	8,237	8,068	6,116	5,990	4,693	4,596	3,780	3,702	3,219	3,153
	1948-49	16,000	9,412	11,250	6,618	8,772	5,160	6,830	4,018	5,763	3,390	5,106	3,004
Business Managers	1940-41	7,750	7,591	4,700	4,603	3,457	3,386	2,625	2,571	2,150	2,106	1,950	1,910
	1948-49	8,333	4,902	6,583	3,872	5,330	3,135	4,600	2,706	3,900	2,294	3,667	2,157

387

* N.E.A. Journal, May, 1949, p. 352. Actual dollars shown by median columns; value columns show purchasing power in 1935-1939 dollars.

    3. There is great inequality in the distribution of the educational load among communities.

        a. Regions vary to a great extent in the distribution of this load.

            (1) They vary in the nature and extent of their population.

            (2) They vary in their numbers of young dependents in proportion to the supporting adult population.

            (3) Rural and poor communities are at a special disadvantage as compared to urban and wealthier ones.

        b. There is unequal distribution of taxable wealth.

        c. In some cases poorer regions and states are making greater efforts to pay for education than some of the wealthier ones.

B. The provision of a minimum basic education is a national responsibility as well as a local and state responsibility.

    1. National and international problems press the issue.

        a. Low standards in any community are a drawback and liability to all other parts of the country.

            (1) The levels of cultural and economic literacy are evidence of the effect of inadequate standards.

            (2) The increased mobility of the people makes the deficiencies of any region of national concern.

                (*a*) Much migration is from areas in which facilities are poorest and to centers of industry, wealth and population.

                (*b*) The problems distributed by such mobility are interstate and of national extent.

        b. Education has become more and more a matter of national economic importance.

            (1) With technological advance, specialization of industry and the like, we have ceased to be self-contained and relatively independent communities.

            (2) The economic welfare and expansion of the country depends increasingly on trained youth drawn from every section.

        c. The high rejection rate of World War II revealed our shortage of able and trained men for our Nation's defense.

        d. Upon an adequately educated citizenship may eventually depend the preservation of democracy itself.

            (1) A high level of political intelligence best contributes to the safety of democracy.

            (2) Sound reasoning, evaluating, and other intellectual equipment resulting from adequate standards of education are of high import in periods of extensive propaganda and other subversive influences.

2. The provision of additional financial resources is in some areas not reasonably possible on the basis of state and local support alone.
   a. New sources of revenue are frequently lacking.
   b. Increased federal taxation is depleting the taxable resources left to communities and states.
   c. Even under a model tax plan and reforms in the educational system some communities and states would not be able to support an adequate program for their educational needs.

3. The federal government is the most adequate agency to provide for the deficiencies of educational programs and bring about the standards and equitable distribution of opportunities desired.
   a. It can most effectively bridge the inequalities between the states as well as those within them.
   b. Federal financial aid would give some responsibility to the level of government having access to the most ample tax resources.

C. The principle of federal action and appropriations for education has long been established.
  1. The federal government has shown its interest in education from its earliest beginnings and throughout its history.
  2. It is in accord with the principle of federal grants-in-aid made to many other activities affecting the national welfare.
  3. Federal participation in financial support of educational activities in the states is today considerable.
    a. Annual appropriations of millions of dollars are now being made for activities benefiting special phases of education, vocational, agricultural and the like.
    b. Other federal grants go to handicapped, to school lunch and other special programs.
    c. The GI Bill has established the need for federal aid if all young people are to be educated to the maximum of their ability through secondary and higher education.
  4. Federal aid to education is constitutionally sound.

II. A program of federal participation in education through annual grants for the equalization of educational opportunities would be feasible and beneficial.
A. Federal aid under bills now being considered (S. 472 or H.R. 2953) provide for wise and adequate administration.
  1. The U.S. Office of Education has had long experience in administering such aids.
  2. The states must maintain considerable effort (2% of income) to be eligible for the aid.

      a. The controversial "matching of federal funds" is not demanded.

   3. Complete accounting for expenditures is required each year from every state, with a plan of apportionment to be submitted each year.

   4. No control of the "what," "why," "how" or "who" of teaching is granted any federal agency.

      a. The states have complete control of the distribution and use of the aid within stated requirements (the $50 per child "floor.")

B. Federal grants to education would be effective in promoting equalization of educational opportunities to an extent not otherwise possible.

   1. Funds would supplement the state and local financial outlays for education and provide for more and better equipment and teachers.

      a. Building programs not otherwise possible to communities would be assisted (through release of local funds—S. 472 forbids use of federal aid for capital outlay.)

      b. Better teaching standards and teacher training could be promoted.

      c. More adequate educational opportunities would be extended to remote and poorer regions.

      d. Various groups of youth at present under educational handicap would be better provided for.

         (1) More adequate educational opportunity would be accorded to Negro education under federal sponsorship than when left to the states.

         (2) Shifting populations would be better provided for educationally if federal funds were available.

         (3) Children in government areas would be provided with more and better educational facilities with more justice to the communities in and near which they reside.

            (*a*) The burden of such support is not properly a responsibility of the communities.

            (*b*) In many cases the communities have not the resources to adequately take care of these additional burdens.

C. Federal grants to education would be beneficial to the national economy.

   1. It would be of economic advantage.

      a. It would lighten the increasing strain upon the taxpaying resources of communities, including the over-worked property tax.

  b. It could provide increasing numbers of vocationally skilled workers and economically literate citizens in areas most needing them.

 2. Federal interest in education would have political effects of increasing importance to the states and nation.

  a. It would free State Departments of Education from local limitations and enable them to provide better state supervision of education.

  b. An educated citizenship will better insure sound political thinking, locally and nationally.

 3. The social effects of such federal assistance would be widespread.

  a. The weakest regional societies would receive the greatest upgrading of social skill and understanding.

  b. The reduction of educational inequality would reduce racial and class tensions.

D. The fear that the establishment of federal aid for education would endanger the principle of the separation of church and state is invalid.

 1. Federal grants to private and sectarian schools is not proposed except in a relatively few states (S. 472 leaves this question to the states).

 2. The principle of the separation of church and state is widely protected by the states themselves.

 3. The states are entitled to judge for themselves what services may reasonably be extended as affecting educational welfare.

  a. They are better able to determine which schools are public.

  b. It is their province to decide what services should be provided for the children themselves irrespective of whether they are in public or private schools.

 4. A clear differentiation between aiding "schools" and aiding "children" has already been established in most state-aid plans.

 5. Present legislation in no way encourages states to modify this principle in administering federal aid.

E. Federal grants now being proposed (S. 472 and H. R. 2953) will not lead to inimical control of or interference with the educational program.

 1. Federal financial aid can exist without federal control.

  a. The policy of federal aid to land-grant colleges has been in effect a hundred years, yet they have not become federal institutions.

  b. Other federal aid administered by the U. S. Office of Education has brought no federal domination.

 2. A certain minimum of federal oversight to safeguard the proper

expending of the funds does not mean interference with the administration of the schools or the content of the educational programs.

    a. The administrative powers granted to the U. S. Office of Education merely provide minimum conditions for partaking in the aid.

    b. Congress can correct any administrative abuses which might develop.

3. Proposed legislation affords no grounds for the fear of the standardization of education or the regimenting of the minds of the people.

NEGATIVE ARGUMENT

I. It would be undesirable and unwise to institute grants by the federal government for the equalization of educational opportunities.

    A. General education is not properly a function of the federal government.

        1. From the beginning it has been regarded as a local, state, and private concern. Every State Constitution recognizes this responsibility.

        2. The Constitution grants no power to the federal government over education, except through the "general welfare" clause of the Tenth Amendment.

        3. Education is better controlled locally.

            a. It is properly a matter to be kept close to the people.

                (1) It is a matter vital to the interests of parents, local taxpayers and the local community.

                (2) There is need for its flexibility and adaptation to community and individual needs.

            b. The experimentation of numerous "local laboratories" is of great advantage to educational progress.

        4. Federal control of education, some degree of which would inevitably develop out of the provision for federal support, would be hostile to the best interests of education and democratic government.

            a. It would institute a control remote from the people.

            b. It would tend to take on impersonal, mechanized, dictated patterns.

            c. It would establish the framework in which regimentation can grow.

    B. There is not sufficient need for the proposed grants of federal funds for the support of educational programs throughout the nation.

        1. There is little need for federal aid under normal conditions.

            a. The greatest public school program in the world has been developed by responsible local and state agencies.

    b. States are assuming increasingly heavier responsibilities for educational needs and tending to promote state-wide equalization programs.

    c. As yet state expenditures on schools have involved in most states only a small proportion of their resources.

2. Arguments for federal aid for education could be applied with almost equal force to many other activities affecting the national interest (diet, clothing, housing, health, medicine, etc.).

3. The federal government has been consistently sympathetic to particular educational needs.

    a. It has contributed vast sums in the past for educational benefit.

    b. It is now giving financial aid to various activities concerned directly with special phases of education or otherwise touching the educational welfare of the nation (vocational, handicapped, school lunch, veterans, exchange teachers, etc.).

4. Equalization of educational opportunities has been proceeding rapidly under state and local impetus. Inequality of our regional economies has been reduced by 50% in the last two decades. Federal aid is less justifiable than ever before.

5. Most statistics used by proponents of federal aid are of a pre-war or war date which makes them invalid today because of great shifts in our population and the equalization of regional economies since 1940.

    a. Proponents employ many irrelevant fact suchs as that 4 million children are not in school—when *2 million of these are 5 year-olds* and another *1⅓ million are above compulsory attendance age*.

C. Increased spending by the national government at this time would be unwise.

1. It would further demoralize the federal budget at a time when federal spending and the federal debt are at an unprecedented level.

    a. Proponents of federal aid have repeatedly asserted that this first legislation (S. 472) asks only a small sum ($300 million) in order to get the principle established. They indicate that several billion dollars really are needed each year—and in addition that $10 billion are needed for buildings.

2. It would probably be conducive of waste (if not misuse) of funds.

    a. There is no assurance of economical or wise use of funds.

       (1) In various cases previous grants to states for education have been wasteful (NYA, Lanham Act).

        (2) Existing inefficiencies in educational processes at state
and local levels would in many instances absorb such
funds wastefully (lack of consolidation; bi-racial systems; political dissoluteness).

    b. Many localities would demand their share of the funds
whether needed or not (all 48 states would receive $5 per
child under present legislation).

    c. Funds would be subject to more irresponsible use by reason
of their source being remote. The "easy come-easy go" attitude would be encouraged. Audits (in S. 472) would be
accepted without any type of independent verification or
check.

D. The proposed grants for education would not bring about equalization of educational opportunities.

  1. Real equalization is not attained merely by having available
equal amounts of funds for educational use.

    a. It is not brought about without provision for adequate class-
rooms, appropriate courses of study and equipment, and
competent teachers.

        (1) Such equalization of opportunities is definitely a matter
of individual and community needs, not determined or
understandable by federal administrators.

          (*a*) The needs and interests of students must be taken
into account.

          (*b*) Adaptability to communities, prospective employ-
ments, and other satisfactions of living must be
provided for.

          (*c*) Full use of community resources should be made.

          (*d*) S. 472 evades the real school needs that define
"educational opportunity." Capital outlay is forbidden, and consolidation of school districts, certification, teacher training, etc., are ignored.

    b. Real equalization is not brought about by the distribution of
funds on some pre-determined basis.

        (1) Identical grants of federal money to each state would
wastefully provide many states with unneeded funds.

        (2) Providing states with grants on a basis proportionate to
their school population would favor some states at the
expense of others equally deserving or more so.

          (*a*) In many cases the facilities essential to one com-
munity would be wasted in another.

          (*b*) Wealthy states having centers of large population
like Illinois or New York would receive allocations
without any justifying need.

    (3) To supply financial assistance to states on a basis of their failure to support schools, would place a premium on local irresponsibility.

        (*a*) State or local responsibilities would very likely relax to the level set by federal law if federal monies were available to replace state money.

        (*b*) State educational funds might be diverted to other governmental needs and federal funds be depended on to a greater extent for education.

        (*c*) State inefficiencies would be rewarded rather than penalized by greater proportionate grants of federal funds.

    (4) All of these methods of allotting funds make for further inequalities rather than for real equalizations among the states and communities.

        (*a*) Inequalities would be perpetuated in property assessment and the general tax base for schools both within and between the states.

        (*b*) Exemption laws and state limitations on bonded indebtedness would continue.

        (*c*) Political expediency forced 3 changes in the formula of S. 472 to include more states as recipients and, finally, to include *all* the states. Half of the requested appropriation ($150 million) thus serves primarily political purposes rather than the educational intent stated in the bill.

2. There will always be some degree of inequality among communities, states and regions unless a completely federalized system of public education is created.

    a. Both moral and financial support of education from local sources will be unequal.

    b. Wealthy and/or progressive sections will probably always maintain their lead educationally.

        (1) They will always have the assets to provide more abundant and better opportunities.

        (2) Advanced and/or progressive sections more often have leaders who make better use of available facilities than more backward regions.

    c. Differentiation and diversity have always been marks of a growing civilization; standardization, a mark of a decaying society.

E. Under federal grants we would face possible dangers both to our educational processes and to our democracy.

    1. Federal grants would tend to break down one of our funda-

mental educational principles involving the separation of church and state.

a. Demands would sooner or later be made for the extension of public funds to private and sectarian schools (as is allowed in presently proposed bills).

(1) Without such aid private and sectarian schools would find it increasingly difficult to compete with financially aided public ones unless *all* states allowed them to participate in the federal monies.

(2) Such a proposal has received favorable comment from authoritative religious organizations. (Others condemn it.)

b. Several beginnings have been made contrary to this long-established principle.

(1) In some states public transportation has been extended to pupils irrespective of whether they attend public or parochial schools.

(2) The same has been advocated (and allowed in some states) for free textbooks, wider library facilities, health services and the like.

(3) A few states permit tuition payment to private or parochial schools.

c. The claim that such help is for the benefit of the children and not for the private or religious schools is a mere clouding of the issue.

(1) Such aid is a definite financial help to the schools.

(2) Once there is an opening wedge more demands will be made until the whole principle is overthrown.

2. The extensive distribution of federal money for general education would inevitably tend toward the standardization and regimentation of education.

a. A moderate degree of supervision and control would be inevitable from the outset, however much it was desired to avoid it.

(1) Proposed methods of allocating funds set up certain prerequisites and requirements.

(2) A reasonable supervision or accounting of the use of funds would be required under any sound plan of distributing them.

(3) Some degree of evidence of improvement resulting from federal funds would be requested in any administrative procedures set-up.

b. Such supervision would tend to indirect control of many aspects of state and local policy.

    (1) Local educational policies would tend to conform more and more to federal requirements in order to obtain the funds.

    (2) National influence and direction of policies would tend to grow. Administration of the Vocational Education Acts and the GI Bill (P. L. 346) demonstrates this.

  c. A widespread and injurious standardization would tend to crowd out the present system.

    (1) "Equalization of educational opportunity," not defined in present legislation, would have to be defined in order to administer the law. Administrative decisions, auditors' decisions, statisticians' decisions and court decisions would make the final "definition" which legislation evaded.

    (2) Proponents of federal aid are on the horns of a dilemma, i.e., federal aid without control means waste and defeat of the very purpose of the legislation; federal aid with controls might bring improvement but at the cost of the freedom of the teaching profession—and perhaps our national freedom.

      (*a*) The U.S. Commissioner (even under S. 472) is empowered to check up on the "progress on education" through questionnaires—from which to report to the Congress with recommendations for revisions of the law (e.g., further expenditures and more controls).

    (3) Initiative and experimentation at the local level would be discouraged.

    (4) An inelastic, bureaucratic and dictated education would eventually result.

3. It might lead to political control of our national life through the regimentation of our national thought.

  a. Control of such central education agencies was basic to the dictatorships of the 1930's and preceded the more recent downfall of Poland and Czechoslovakia.

II. The objectives sought by federal grants to education can in most instances be adequately realized without resource to federal aid.

  A. The wider equalization of educational opportunities can be attained within the states themselves.

    1. States have already increased their support of education extensively. Salaries are higher. Building programs are expanding.

    2. They are showing ever increasing interest in higher standards and wider equalizations within their boundaries.

3. Such local responsibility, close to the people, is the best guarantee of real educational welfare.

4. Every state in the nation is spending far less of its "people's" income than in 1940.

    a. If each state had increased its support of education in 1947 by an amount equal to the proposed allocation of S. 472, forty-five states would still have been spending far less of their income than in 1940—the other three about the same.

B. Increased financial resources for education can reasonably be obtained in most instances within the states.

1. The tax base could be adjusted where necessary to provide such funds.

    a. A broader tax base for school funds at both local and state levels could be provided in many states. Many states have recently started such programs.

    b. A model tax system could be adopted which would provide a better balance for the whole governmental income, local, state and federal, and assure adequate educational finances within the states.

2. The institution of wider general economies and reforms within political units would in many cases release additional funds for education.

    a. Reforms in educational administration would release funds for more essential educational needs to the advantage of the whole.

        (1) Wider consolidations of districts could be promoted.

        (2) Greater efficiencies could otherwise be instituted, as in building, purchasing, etc.

        (3) Such reforms would be fundamentally helpful; likely as valuable as the accrual of new funds.

    b. In many instances general economies in the political structure itself could be instituted with advantage and would release general funds for educational use.

3. Regional economies have equalized rapidly during the last decade.

    a. Equalization through natural economic and social pressures is a sign of normal, healthy progress. Equalization forced by central government indicates that prejudice or tradition is preventing self-correction—and signifies decay within a society.

C. The federal government could more acceptably contribute to educational progress through such channels as it has already appropriated for such aid.

1. Aid to such specialized forms of education lighten the total

educational burden of the nation with less danger to educational welfare.

    a. Appropriations given for agricultural education, vocational training and the like are an essential help to national education without constituting a corresponding danger to general educational processes and concepts.

    b. Other activities (such as those in the emergency defense program) specifically directed at the national educational welfare have provided necessary benefits which are not assured in general federal aid proposals.

    c. By returning certain tax sources to the states, the federal government could help all states to finance all needed school improvements from their own resources.

        (1) The construction or equipping of buildings, or the improvement of school transportation should give little opportunity for control of the curriculum or methods of teaching.

2. A more generous support of the U.S. Office of Education would provide a highly useful means of extending national educational welfare, without the necessity of general annual grants.

    a. By enlarged support of this Office essential educational experimentation, demonstration and research could be substantially improved and extended.

    b. The results of its findings would be available everywhere for the enriching and perfecting of the educational processes and content. State Departments of Education could be improved and expanded under such guidance.

    c. No control would be instituted but its services would be everywhere open to voluntary use.

    d. Such educational progress as would thus be brought about, might accomplish much at the same time to more adequately meet other unsolved and pressing problems of our national life.

        (1) The Office of Education would become a competent advisory agency to other government bureaus at both the federal and state levels.

    e. The concentration of administration over all types of specialized educational assistance programs in this office could lead to a coördinated and consistent federal policy in education without any over-all encroachment on state and local prerogatives.

«« VI »»

TEACHERS AND TEACHING

«««‹›»»»»»»»»»»»»»»»»»»»»»»»»»»»»»»»»»»»

In the first chapter appear several documents on teachers in the American colonies, including instructions to teachers in the Dutch possessions, the license and the contract of a teacher in Albany and in Flatbush, New York; the request of the General Assembly of Virginia for change in the method of licensing teachers in that colony; the petition of Ezekiel Cheever of New England for his position and pay; England's oath required of teachers; the contract of a school-master among the Lutherans in Pennsylvania; a license issued by the governor of Georgia; requirements in the Anglican colonies of teachers' license from the Bishop of London, and other documents which indicate something of the status of the colonial teacher. The documents presented in this section throw further light on the education, certification, salaries of teachers and on restrictions placed on them especially in times of military and economic crises.

Dr. Benjamin Rush on the Occupation of the Teacher, 1790 *

The occupation of a school-master is truly dignified. He is, next to mothers, the most important member of civil society. Why then is there so little rank connected with that occupation? Why do we treat it with so much neglect or contempt? It is because the voice of reason, in the human heart, associates with it the idea of despotism and violence. Let school-masters cease to be tyrants, and they will soon enjoy the respect and rank, which are naturally connected with their profession.

We are grossly mistaken in looking up wholly to our governments, and even to ministers of the gospel, to promote public and private order in society. Mothers and school-masters plant the seeds of nearly all the good and evil which exist in our world. Its reformation must therefore be begun in nurseries and in schools. If the habits we acquire there, were to have no influence upon our future happiness, yet the influence they have upon our governments, is a sufficient reason why we ought to introduce new modes, as well as new objects of education into our country.

James G. Carter on Teachers in Massachusetts, 1824 †

. . . To whom do we assign the business of governing and instructing our children from four to twelve years of age? Who take upon themselves the trust of forming those principles and habits which are to be strengthened and confirmed in manhood, and make our innocent littles ones through life happy or miserable in themselves, and the blessings or the curses of society? To analyze, in detail, the habits which are formed and confirmed in these first schools, to trace the abiding influence of good ones, or to

---

* D. D. Runes (Ed.), *The Selected Writings of Benjamin Rush* (New York, Philosophical Library, Inc., 1947), p. 114. For the status of teachers in the colonial schools, see "The Colonial Teacher" above. Interest in improving the qualifications and salaries of teachers developed slowly but this interest was increased through the influence of The American Institute of Instruction, organized in Boston in 1830; by state educational associations which began to be organized before 1860 and also by the National Teachers' Association which began in 1857, became the National Educational Association in 1870 and the National Education Association of the United States under charter by the Congress in 1906.

† "Essays on Popular Education." Given in *Old South Leaflets*, VI, No. 135, pp. 214-16. "The one man who did more to cast up a highway for Horace Mann than any other was Mr. James G. Carter, to whom Dr. Barnard says 'more than to any other person belongs the credit of first having attracted the attention of the leading minds of Massachusetts to the necessity of immediate and thorough improvement in the system of free or public schools, and having clearly pointed out the most direct and thorough mode of procuring that improvement by providing for the training of competent teachers for these schools.' " *Ibid.*, pp. 220-21.

describe the inveteracy of bad ones, would lead me from my present purpose. But are these interesting years of life and these important branches of education committed to those who understand their importance or their influence upon the future character? Are they committed to those who would know what to do to discharge their high trust successfully if they did, indeed, understand their importance? I think not. And I am persuaded that all who have reflected but for a moment upon the age, the acquirements, and the experience of those who assume to conduct this branch of education must have come to the same conclusion.

The teachers of the primary summer schools have rarely had any education beyond what they have acquired in the very schools where they begin to teach. Their attainments, therefore, to say the least, are usually *very moderate.* But this is not the worst of it. They are often very young, they are constantly changing their employment, and consequently can have but little experience; and, what is worse than all, they never have had any direct preparation for their profession. This is the only service in which we venture to employ young and, often, ignorant persons, without some previous instruction in their appropriate duties. We require experience in all those whom we employ to perform the slightest mechanical labor for us. We would not buy a coat or a hat of one who should undertake to make them without a previous apprenticeship; nor would any one have the hardihood to offer to us the result of his first essay in manufacturing either of these articles. We do not even send an old shoe to be mended, except it be to a workman of whose skill we have had ample proof. Yet we commit our children to be educated to those who know nothing, absolutely nothing, of the complicated and difficult duties assigned to them. Shall we trust the development of the delicate bodies, the susceptible hearts, and the tender minds of our little children to those who have no knowledge of their nature? Can they, can these rude hands, finish the workmanship of the Almighty? No language can express the astonishment which a moment's reflection of this subject excites in me.

But I must return to the examination of the qualifications of the female teachers of the primary summer schools, from which purposes I have unconsciously a little departed to indulge in a general remark. They are a class of teachers unknown in our laws regulating the schools, unless it be by some latitude of construction. No standard of attainments is fixed, at which they must arrive before they assume the business of instruction; so that any one *keeps school,* which is a very different thing from *teaching school,* who wishes to do it, and can persuade, by herself or her friends, a small district to employ her. And this is not a very difficult matter, especially when the remuneration for the employment is so very trifling. The farce of an examination and a certificate from the minister of the town (for it is a perfect farce) amounts to no efficient check upon the obtrusions of ignorance and inexperience. As no standard is fixed by law, each minister makes a standard for himself, and alters it as often as the peculiar circumstances of the case require; and there will always be enough of peculiar circumstances to render a refusal inexpedient.

Let those who are conversant with the manner in which these schools are managed say whether this description of them undervalues their character and efficacy. Let those who conduct them pause and consider whether all is well, and whether there are not abuses and perversions in them, which call loudly for attention and reformation. Compare the acquirements, the experience, the knowledge of teaching possessed by these instructors, not one with another—for the standard is much too low—but with what they might be, under more favorable circumstances and with proper preparation. Compare the improvement made in these little nurseries of piety and religion, of knowledge and rational liberty, not one with another—for the progress in all of them is much too slow—but with what the infant mind and heart are capable of, at this early age, under the most favorable auspices. And there can be no doubt that all will arrive at the same conclusions—a dissatisfaction with the condition of these schools, and an astonishment that the public have been so long contented with so small results from means which all will acknowledge capable of doing so much. . . .

A Teacher's Contract in Texas, 1825 *

Natchidosche, *Articles of an English School* to be taught in this place by Thomas Jefferson Garner. We the under subscribers do obligate ourselves to find said T. J. Garner a Suficient House to Teach in, his Board Such as Common diet and Lodging-Firewood and fuel for the Benefit of the School and one dollar & fifty Cents a month for Each Scholar two thirds of which may be discharged in young Cattle, (Bulls Excepted) at Market price the balance of one third will be discharged in Cash—the Said Garner by his Father will continue the School the full term of twelve Months. Every Saturday & Sunday Excepted and Said T. J. Garner, by his father will keep good order in his School with & by the assistance of the Parents and Guardians of the Said Children who is committed to his charge, the School to Commence as soon as the Said Thomas Jefferson Garner may or can Arrive in this place from the U.S. of America—& the Said Garner by his Father Jas. Garner will use the utmost of his Abilities to Teach their Children in Spelling, Reading writing & Arithmetic as his abilities admit & they capable to Receive in Testimony whereof we the under Subscribers have Set our different hands with the number of Scholars annexed hereto Any widow in indigent circumstances—under good Report of her Neighbors—her child or Children Shall and will be taught grattis—

* Given in Frederick Eby, *Education in Texas: Source Materials,* University of Texas Bulletin, No. 1824 (April 25, 1918), p. 94.

whereof we have Interchangeably Set our Different hands this 29th Day of Nov. 1825.

JAMES GARNER on the part
of his son. T. J. GARNER.

N.B. If at the end of one quarter of a year the Employers shall not approve of the conduct of Said T. J. Garner, the School will be dismissed after paying Said Garner for his time.

Superintendent A. G. Flagg of the Common Schools of New York on Lack of Good Salaries of Teachers, 1828 *

One of the principal reasons why the standard of education in the common schools has not been more elevated is to be found in the unwillingness on the part of the school districts to make adequate compensation to teachers of approved talents and qualifications. How else does it happen, when at a time when the merchant is overstocked with clerks, and the professions of law and medicine are thronged with students there is such a lamentable deficiency in the number of those who have the inclination and the ability to engage in the business of instruction?

Samuel Read Hall on "The Requisite Qualifications of an Instructor," 1829 †

Having adverted in the preceding lecture, to certain existing evils, unfriendly to the character and usefulness of common schools, I shall, in this, call your attention to the *requisite qualifications of an instructer.* The subject is one of high importance. It is not every one of those, even, who possesses the requisite literary attainments, who is qualified to assume the direction of a school. Many entirely fail of usefulness, though possessed of highly cultivated minds. Other ingredients enter into the composition of a good schoolmaster. Among these *common sense* is the first. This is a qualification exceedingly important, as in teaching school one has constant occasion for its exercise. Many, by no means deficient in intellect, are not persons of common sense. I mean by the term, that faculty by which things are seen as they are. It implies judgment and discrimination, and a proper sense of propriety in regard to the common affairs of life. It leads us to form judicious plans of action, and to be governed by our circumstances,

---

* "Improvement of Common Education," *American Journal of Education,* III, p. 436.
† Arthur D. Wright and George E. Gardner (Eds.), *Hall's Lectures on School-Keeping* (Hanover, N. H., Dartmouth Press, 1929), pp. 65-68. This is an exact reproduction of the first edition of Hall's work, the first treatise in English in this country on the subject of teaching (Boston, Richardson, Lord and Holbrook, 1829). The pioneer writer on the subject of education in this country was Christopher Dock who published in German his *Schulordnung* in 1770. See 'Martin G. Brumbaugh, *The Life and Works of Christopher Dock* (Philadelphia, J. B. Lippincott Co., 1908).

in such a way as men in general will approve. It is the exercise of reason, uninfluenced by passion or prejudice. It is in man nearly what instinct is in brutes. It is very different from genius or talent, as they are commonly defined, but is better than either. It never blazes forth with the splendour of noon, but shines with a constant and useful light.

2. *Uniformity of temper* is another important trait in the character of an instructer. Where this is wanting, it is hardly possible to govern or teach with success. He, whose temper is constantly varying, can never be uniform in his estimation of things around him. Objects change in their appearance as passions change. What appears right in any given hour may seem wrong in the next. What appears desirable to-day, may be held with aversion to-morrow. An uneven temper, in any situation of life, subjects one to many inconveniences. But when placed in a situation where his every action is observed, and where his authority must be in constant exercise, the man who labours under this malady is especially unfortunate. It is impossible for him to gain and preserve respect among his pupils. No one who comes under the rule of a person of uneven temper, can know what to expect or how to act.

3. A capacity to *understand and discriminate character,* is highly important in him who engages in schoolkeeping. The dispositions of children are so various, the treatment and government of parents so dissimilar, that the most diversified modes of governing and teaching need to be employed. The instructer who is not able to discriminate, but considers all alike, and treats all alike, does injury to many. The least expression of disapprobation to one, is often more than the severest reproof to another; a word of encouragement will be sufficient to excite attention in some, while another will require to be urged, by every motive that can be placed before him. All the varying shades of disposition and capacity should be quickly learned by the instructer, that he may benefit all and do injustice to none. Without this, well meant efforts may prove hurtful, because ill-directed, and the desired object may be defeated, by the very means used to obtain it.

4. It is desirable that teachers should possess much *decision of character*. In every situation of life this trait is important, but in none more so than in that of which I am treating. The little world, by which he is surrounded, is the miniature of the older community. Children have their aversions and partialities, their hopes and fears, their plans, schemes, propensities and desires. These are often in collision with each other, and not unfrequently in collision with the laws of the school, and in opposition to their own best interest. Amidst all these, the instructer should be able to pursue a uniform course. He ought not to be easily swayed from what he considers right. If he be easily led from his purpose, or induced to vary from established rules, his school must become a scene of disorder. Without decision, the teacher loses the confidence and respect of his pupils.

I would not say, that, if convinced of having committed an error, or of having given a wrong judgment, you should persist in the wrong. But I would say, that it should be known as one of your first principles in school-keeping, that what is required must be complied with in every case, unless cause can be shown why the rule ought, in a given instance, to be dispensed with. There should *then* be a frank confession of error. In a word, without decision of purpose in a teacher, his scholars can never be brought under that discipline, which is requisite for his own ease and convenience, or for their improvement in knowledge.

5. A schoolmaster ought to be *affectionate*. The human heart is so constituted, that it cannot resist the influence of kindness. When affectionate intercourse is the offspring of those kind feelings which arise from true benevolence, it will have an influence on all around. It leads to ease in behaviour, and genuine politeness of manners. It is especially desirable in those who are surrounded by the young. Affectionate parents usually see their children exhibit similar feelings. Instructers, who cultivate this state of temper, will generally excite the same in their scholars. No object is more important than to gain the love and good will of those who are to teach. In no way is this more easily accomplished than by a kind interest manifested in their welfare; an interest which is exhibited by actions as well as words. This cannot fail of being attended with desirable results.

6. A just *moral discernment,* is of pre-eminent importance in the character of an instructer. Unless governed by a consideration of his moral obligation, he is but poorly qualified to discharge the duties which devolve upon him, when placed at the head of a school. He is himself, a moral agent, and accountable to himself, to his employers, to his country and to his God, for the faithful discharge of duty. If he have no moral sensibility, no fear of disobeying the laws of God, no regard for the institutions of our holy religion, how can he be expected to lead his pupils in the way that they should go? The cultivation of virtuous propensities is more important to children than even their intellectual culture. The *virtuous* man, though illiterate, will be happy, while the learned, if *vicious,* must be miserable in proportion to his attainments. The remark of the ancient philosopher, that "boys ought to be taught that which they will most need to practise when they come to be men," is most true. To cultivate virtuous habits, and awaken virtuous principles;—to excite a sense of duty to God, and of dependence on Him, should be the first objects of the teacher. If he permits his scholars to indulge in vicious habits—if he regard nothing as sin, but that which is a transgression of the laws of the school, if he suffer lying, profaneness, or other crimes, to pass unnoticed and unpunished, he is doing an injury for which he can in no way make amends. An instructer without moral feeling, not only brings ruin to the children placed under his care, but does injury to their parents, to the neighbourhood, to the town, and, doubtless, to other generations. The moral character of instructers should

be considered a subject of very high importance; and let every one, who knows himself to be immoral, renounce at once the thought of such an employment, while he continues to disregard the laws of God, and the happiness of his fellow men. Genuine piety is highly desirable in every one entrusted with the care and instruction of the young; but morality, at least, should be *required,* in every candidate for that important trust.

The Origin and Early Years of the American Institute of Instruction, 1830 *

The American Institute of Instruction was well born in the Massachusetts State House, August 19, 1830, with President Francis Wayland, of Brown University, as president.

The changes in the educational world since then are incredible. Prior to 1830 there had been no educational association, barring one or two temporary gatherings, notably one at Brooklyn, Conn., in 1827. Today there are city organizations that will have an audience of 2,000, counties that can gather 3,000 teachers, sectional state meetings with 4,000, state associations with 5,000, while the National Educational Association has reached 40,000 paid memberships in a year. There are more than a third of a million teachers gathered in conventions annually, and yet there are hundreds of members of the National Educational Association who were born before there was any educational association. It is well, therefore, to pause in our admiration of the educational association spirit and grandeur of today and worship at the shrine of the mother of them all.

In order to appreciate what it signified to have an association of educators in those days we must consider the conditions. There was no public-school teaching force from which to draw. There was not a state, county, or city superintendent in the country; not a state or city normal school; not six free public high schools; no public libraries; no state university or state college; no textbook publishing houses or agents; no makers of school furniture, of school furnaces, of ventilating appliances, fire escapes, school apparatus, lead pencils, steel pens, blackboards, crayons, maps, charts, of kindergarten materials, or of teachers' books or teachers' journals. No one had ever earned a dollar as an educational lecturer. Eliminate all the classes and interests herein suggested, and who can conceive of an educational convention today?

It is well, also, to consider the difficulties under which this first meeting was held. There were no electric lines, no steamships, no railroads. President Wayland had to go forty miles by stage to reach the meetings, which were held in Boston for the first seven years. It was the only place to which all stage lines ran. William B. Calhoun, of Springfield, who was president

---

* Albert E. Winship, "The American Institute of Instruction," National Education Association, *Fiftieth Anniversary Volume,* 1857-1906, pp. 457-61.

for six of the first nine years, made the stage ride of a hundred miles each way to be at the meetings. The more one studies the conditions, the more he wonders at the achievements of those days. . . .

Great men stood forth with more grandeur in those days than at present. Every man stood for something clear and distinct and was fighting for it in a statesmanlike way. "Wire pulling"—I use the term with no disrespect —was unthought of then. Opinion must be fortified with fact, philosophy, and logic in order to win. This association furnished the forum for great exploitation of schemes for public care of the insane and feeble-minded, and public education of the deaf and blind. Here William B. Fowler exploited phrenology for years; Dio Lewis, physical culture; Lewis B. Monroe demonstrated elocutionary possibilities; and other men of historic importance pleaded eloquently for various causes. Here may be said to have been born Greenleaf's notable *Arithmetics,* Greene's famous *Analysis,* Harkness' Latin series, Newman's *Rhetoric,* Fowler's textbooks, George S. Hillards' *Readers,* Mason's *Music Series,* Wayland's *Philosophies,* Bradbury-Eaton's *Arithmetic,* and a host of other books of high merit and great popularity.

Students of American education know full well the significance of the names of men who were in frequent attendance: Mann, Howe, Theodore Parker, Samuel J. May, Gallaudet, Henry Barnard, Ralph Waldo Emerson, Cyrus Pierce, Asa Gray, Benjamin Greenleaf, James G. Carter, David P. Page, Gideon F. Thayer, Thomas Sherwin, Wm. C. Woodbridge, Barnas Sears, George S. Boutwell, Charles Northend, William Russell, William H. Wells, John D. Philbrick, George B. Emerson, Edward Beecher, William D. Ticknor, Wm. C. Fowler, C. C. Felton, Ariel Parish, Daniel Huntington, John Pierpont, A. Bronson Alcott, and Elizabeth Peabody.

The American Institute of Instruction was largely responsible for giving Horace Mann to the educational leadership of America. If it had done nothing more, this alone is all-sufficient reward for its existence. Mr. Mann was in the legislature, but his plans were political and his purposes philanthropic. He was interested in the defective and dependent classes and was working for the insane, the blind, the deaf, and the feeble-minded. He was a good lawyer, a brilliant public speaker, and an intense leader of any conscience cause. Even up to the moment when he accepted the secretaryship of the Massachusetts State Board of Education his closest friends never thought of him as an educator. He was in 1830 a member of the Massachusetts legislature, and Francis Wayland, president of his *alma mater,* was presiding over the American Institute of Instruction in the Massachusetts State House. Of course, Mr. Mann was there and was intensely interested in what was being planned, and this inspiration was largely influential in leading him into educational work for life.

The chief glory of the American Institute of Instruction is that it was a cause and not an effect. Had it come ten years later we should have had several causes to assign for its coming, but in 1830 there is really no adequate suggestion as to the cause, with many resultant effects apparent. . . .

For seven years all the meetings were held in Boston. They were always well attended, the membership dues were promptly paid, and all expenses were readily met.

Local jealousy, or a missionary spirit, got in its work at the end of seven years, and it began its migratory life. It would be interesting to know the line of argument that controlled affairs in 1837. Perhaps President Calhoun had wearied of that stage ride from Springfield; but, be that as it may, Mr. Mann got the Massachusetts legislature to appropriate $300 a year toward the expenses; and the next seven meetings were held in Worcester, Lowell, Springfield, Providence, Boston, New Bedford, and Pittsfield. This appropriation, increased in 1866 to $500, was continued until 1873.

Despite the legislative subsidy, the Institute was not in as good financial condition for forty years after as it was in the first seven years.

The American Institute of Instruction fostered the public-school sentiment and developed it into a scheme which more nearly approximated a "system" than was to be found elsewhere in the United States; but this great service was not appreciated by the beneficiaries of its labors. No grammar-school men took any part in its official life for sixteen years. The management was in the hands of the classical men and educational statesmen.

While public-school positions were multiplied and salaries increased because of the association, the public-school people shunned the meetings, and proceeded to organize state associations in Massachusetts (1845) and Connecticut (1846) in which no one was admitted to membership who was not actually engaged in teaching, and they had a teachers' program and published a teachers' monthly. It is assumed that they meant well, that they sincerely believed that professional class consciousness would be advantageous; but this we do know, that they dealt a serious blow to the American Institute of Instruction, and to the cause of education.

The men at whom the act of elimination was aimed were Horace Mann, Dr. S. G. Howe, Gallaudet, Charles Sumner, Edward Everett, Josiah Quincy, Edmund Dwight, Gardner Brewer, and their distinguished associates, who proceeded to eliminate themselves from all responsibility, organized various other associations for the exploitation of their philanthropic purposes, and the public school felt the loss of these influences. It is never an easy matter to think in large units, or in extensive units, and these men surely failed, so others have failed, in seeing the danger in the narrowing influence of professional class consciousness. The state association took up its specific work, and these same men came into control of the Institute of Instruction and ran it along broader lines than the state association, but on narrower lines than those of its early years.

While the meetings were interesting and important the finances were a constant source of trouble from 1845 to 1875, when a new order of things prevailed. It is commonly spoken of as "the coming of the reign of Rhode Island." For eight years thereafter there was not a Massachusetts man in the presidency, and eight years out of ten there was no Massachusetts man in the secretaryship. Prior to that time there had never been a secretary who was not from Massachusetts. This was in no sense intentional or the result of a conspiracy. The Massachusetts men had wearied of the burden, and some of them desired its abandonment for the advantage they thought would come to the state association. It is a sad fact, that, left to the Bay State men, the historic and glorious American Institute of Instruction would probably have departed this life before it was fifty years old. To Rhode Islanders is largely due its new life and prosperity. True, they commercialized it, but the stimulant was indispensable to its life. These men put the American Institute of Instruction on a new tack, leading the world in the idea of making the reduced railroad rate dependent upon membership in the association. . . .

Wages of Teachers in Connecticut, 1832 *

The average compensation, in addition to board, is about $11 a month for male teachers, and $1 a week for females. Many females, however, of considerable experience, teach at $0.75; and some whose experience is less, at $0.62½ or even $0.50. Many board themselves and teach for $1, as it is very generally supposed that a female instructor can earn enough at some other employment, during the intervals between school hours, to pay for her board. It seems scarcely understood by parents, or even by some teachers, that duty requires them to devote any greater part of their time to their school than the 6 hours usually allotted for this purpose. It is even regarded as a matter of surprise to see an instructor, as occasionally happens, devoting his whole time to the interests of his school. We have indeed known one teacher of unusual qualifications who, for the sum of $100 a year and board, devoted himself wholly to the duties of a large school; and in one instance at even a smaller price. . . . The compensation for teaching is so small that few are employed as teachers, except those who happen for a short time to be destitute of any regular employment. As soon as constant employment with increased wages is offered them they usually abandon school keeping. Thus it happens that few teachers of tried experience are to be found. The profession is generally filled by young persons from 16 to 25 years of age, and many of them strangers in the town where they are employed. As they are not expecting to gain their reputation or livelihood by teaching, there is little motive for exertion or improvement.

* *American Annals of Education.* II, p. 202.

The Committee on Education of the Legislature of Pennsylvania on Teachers in the Common Schools, 1833 *

In this country, the schoolmaster, as he is termed, does not enjoy that consideration which the services required of him and the talents necessary to perform these services ought to confer on him. The men who are intrusted to form the minds of the youth of this country, and to direct their expanding energies, should be classed as a profession of the highest order. Their labors are great, their services are valuable, and therefore their reward should be so liberal as to attract the best talents. It is a melancholy truth, that in most parts of the country, even in New England, the occupation of a schoolmaster yields less profit than that derived from the humblest mechanical labor. In many places the schools are taught by those who accept ten or twelve dollars a month for their services. Can any rational man think that the talents and acquirements that ought to be imparted, can be obtained for such wages? If a system of education is to be established, let the scale of expenditure be liberal; let it form an important department of the Government; let every man connected with its administration, from the head of the department to the humblest teacher, be considered as a highly valuable public servant, and as such enjoy a liberal reward. Let this be done, and though the public schools will yield no revenue, they will annually contribute to the republic something more valuable—a body of virtuous and enlightened citizens.

Phillips Andover Academy (Massachusetts) Undertakes the Education of Teachers, 1834 †

We have insisted upon no point more earnestly, or with more confidence, than the *necessity of a professional education for teachers,* as indispensable to the permanent improvement of our schools. We are rejoiced to learn that the Trustees of Phillips' Academy have resolved to place the Seminary at Andover on a broader and more permanent basis for the accomplishment of this object. They have been urged to this measure by the success of the plan thus far, and the numerous calls for teachers from the destitute portions of our country. In addition to the large building and apparatus already used for this purpose, a farm for manual labor, lodging houses, and a hall for boarding have been provided as a means of diminishing the expenses of students. It is confidently believed that many young men, well qualified for the office, are ready to devote themselves to the business of teaching as a profession, provided they can receive a little aid in addition to the means of support now offered.

* Given on J. P. Wickersham, *A History of Education in Pennsylvania* (Lancaster, Inquirer Publishing Co., 1886), p. 305.
† *American Annals of Education,* June, 1834, p. 288.

Henry Barnard on Teachers in the German Schools, 1835 *

The success of the school systems of Germany is universally attributed by her own educators to the above features of her school law—especially those which relate to the teacher. These provisions respecting teachers may be summed up as follows:—

1. The recognition of the true dignity and importance of the office of teacher in a system of public instruction.

2. The establishment of a sufficient number of Teachers' Seminaries, or Normal Schools, to educate, in a special course of instruction and practice, all persons who apply or propose to teach in any public primary school, with aids to self and professional improvement through life.

3. A system of examination and inspection, by which incompetent persons are prevented from obtaining situations as teachers, or are excluded and degraded from the ranks of the profession, by unworthy or criminal conduct.

4. A system of promotion, by which faithful teachers can rise in a scale of lucrative and desirable situations.

5. Permanent employment through the year, and for life, with a social position and a compensation which compare favorably with the wages paid to educated labor in other departments of business.

6. Preparatory schools, in which those who wish eventually to become teachers, may test their natural qualities and adaptation for school teaching before applying for admission to a Normal School.

7. Frequent conferences and associations for mutual improvement, by an interchange of opinion and sharing the benefit of each others' experience.

8. Exemption from military service in time of peace, and recognition, in social and civil life, as public functionaries.

9. A pecuniary allowance when sick, and provision for years of infirmity and old age, and for their families in case of death.

10. Books and periodicals, by which the obscure teacher is made partaker in all the improvements of the most experienced and distinguished members of the profession in his own and other countries.

Calvin E. Stowe Says Women Should Be Employed in the Elementary Schools, 1837 †

. . . Indeed, such is the state of things in this country, that we cannot expect to find male teachers for all our schools. The business of educating,

---

* Henry Barnard, *National Education in Europe* (New York, Charles B. Norton, 1854), second edition, p. 33. Barnard had made his observations of European schools in 1835-1836. Reports by several Americans on education in Europe before 1860 are believed to have had much effect on education in this country. See Edgar W. Knight, *Reports on European Education* (New York, McGraw-Hill Book Co., Inc., 1930).

† Given in Knight, *op. cit.*, p. 311.

especially young children, must fall, to a great extent on female teachers. There is not the same variety of tempting employment for females as for men, they can be supported cheaper, and the Creator has given peculiar qualifications for the education of the young. Females, then, ought to be employed extensively in all our elementary schools, and they should be encouraged and aided in obtaining the qualifications necessary for this work. There is no country in the world where woman holds so high a rank, or exerts so great an influence, as here; wherefore, her responsibilities are the greater, and she is under obligations to render herself the more actively useful. I think our fair countrywomen, notwithstanding the exhortations of Harriet Martineau, Fanny Wright, and some other *ladies* and *gentlemen,* will never seek distinction in our public assemblies for public discussion, or in our halls of legislation; but in their appropriate work of educating the young, of forming the opening mind to all that is good and great, the more they distinguish themselves the better. . . .

Horace Mann Reports Private Gift of $10,000 to Promote Instruction in Normal Schools in Massachusetts, 1838 *

To the President of the Senate, and the Speaker of the House of Representatives.

GENTLEMEN,

Private munificence has placed conditionally at my disposal, the sum of Ten Thousand Dollars, to promote the cause of Popular Education in Massachusetts.

The condition is, that the Commonwealth will contribute the same amount from unappropriated funds, in aid of the same cause;—both sums to be drawn upon equally, as needed, and to be disbursed under the direction of the Board of Education, in qualifying Teachers of our Common Schools.

As the proposal contemplates that the State, in its collective capacity, shall do no more than is here proffered to be done by private means, and as, with a high and enlightened disregard of all local, party and sectional views, it comprehends the whole of the rising generation in its philanthropic plan, I cannot refrain from earnestly soliciting for it the favorable regards of the Legislature.

Very respectfully

HORACE MANN

Secretary of the Board of Education

BOSTON, March 12th, 1838.

* *Common School Journal,* February 1, 1839. The gift, made by Edmund Dwight, Boston merchant and a member of the newly created state board of education of Massachusetts, was accepted by the Legislature as the resolves below show. After careful consideration the state board of education decided to provide for three normal schools. The first of these was opened at Lexington, July 3, 1839; another at Barre, September 4 of that year; and the third at Bridgewater, September 9, 1840. These were the first state normal schools in the United States.

The Legislature of Massachusetts Accepts the Gift and Resolves to Provide for the Education of Teachers, 1838 *

Whereas, by letter from the Honorable Horace Mann, Secretary of the Board of Education, addressed, on the 12th of March current, to the President of the Senate, and the Speaker of the House of Representatives, it appears, that private munificence has placed at his disposal the sum of ten thousand dollars, to promote the cause of popular education in Massachusetts, on condition that the Commonwealth will contribute from unappropriated funds, the same amount in aid of the same cause, the two sums to be drawn upon equally from time to time, as needed, and to be disbursed under the direction of the Board of Education in qualifying teachers for our Common Schools; therefore,

Resolved, That his Excellency, the Governor, be, and he is hereby authorized and requested, by and with the advice and consent of the Council, to draw his warrant upon the Treasurer of the Commonwealth in favor of the Board of Education, for the sum of $10,000, in such installments and at such times, as said Board may request: *provided,* said Board, in their request, shall certify, that the Secretary of said Board has placed at their disposal an amount equal to that for which such application may by them be made; both sums to be expended, under the direction of said Board, in qualifying teachers for the Common Schools in Massachusetts.

Resolved, That the Board of Education shall render an annual account of the manner in which said moneys have been by them expended.

Admission Requirements and Course of Study in the Early Normal Schools of Massachusetts, 1839 †

As a prerequisite to admission, candidates must declare it to be their intention to qualify themselves to become school teachers. If they belong to the State, or have an intention and a reasonable expectation of keeping school in the State, tuition is gratis. Otherwise, a tuition-fee is charged, which is intended to be about the same as is usually charged at good academies in the same neighborhood. . . .

If males, pupils must have attained the age of seventeen years com-

---

* *Ibid.* This and the preceding document may be found also in *Tenth Annual Report of the Massachusetts State Board of Education,* 1846.

† *Tenth Annual Report of the Massachusetts State Board of Education,* 1846. New York was using academies for the education of teachers before Massachusetts set up normal schools. Some states followed the pattern in New York; but by 1860 seven other states had followed the Massachusetts plan and set up normal schools: Connecticut and Michigan in 1849, Rhode Island in 1852, Iowa in 1855, Illinois in 1857, Minnesota in 1858, and Pennsylvania in 1859. By 1900 all the states had made some provision for the training of teachers but it was not until 1910 that all had established normal schools. See Edgar W. Knight, "A Century of Teacher-Education," *The Educational Forum,* IX (1945), pp. 149-61.

plete, and of sixteen, if females; and they must be free from any disease or infirmity, which would unfit them for the office of school teachers.

They must undergo an examination, and prove themselves to be well versed in orthography, reading, writing, English grammar, geography, and arithmetic.

They must furnish satisfactory evidence of good intellectual capacity and of high moral character and principles.

Examinations for admission take place at the commencement of each term, of which there are three in a year.

Term of study.

... The minimum of the term of study is one year, and this must be in consecutive terms of the schools. ...

Course of study.

The studies first to be attended to in the State Normal Schools are those which the law requires to be taught in the district schools, namely, orthography, reading, writing, English grammar, geography, and arithmetic. When these are mastered, those of a higher order will be progressively taken.

For those who wish to remain at the school more than one year, and for all belonging to the school, so far as their previous attainments will permit, the following course is arranged:

1. Orthography, reading, grammar, composition, rhetoric, and logic.
2. Writing and drawing.
3. Arithmetic, mental and written, algebra, geometry, bookkeeping, navigation, surveying.
4. Geography, ancient and modern, with chronology, statistics and general history.
5. Human Physiology, and hygiene or the Laws of Health.
6. Mental Philosophy.
7. Music.
8. Constitution and History of Massachusetts and of the United States.
9. Natural Philosophy and Astronomy.
10. Natural History.
11. The principles of piety and morality, common to all sects of Christians.
12. The science and art of teaching, with reference to all the above-named studies.

Religious exercises.

A portion of the Scriptures shall be read daily, in every State Normal School.

Henry Barnard on the Heavy "Turnover" Among Teachers in Connecticut, 1839 *

Most of the teachers employed the past winter, have not taught the same schools two successive seasons. . . . In this single fact is found an explanation of many of the acknowledged defects in our schools.

In the first place, nearly one month of the school is practically lost in the time consumed by the teacher in getting acquainted with the temper, wants, dispositions, and previous progress of his various pupils, with a view to their proper classification, and to the adaptation of his own peculiar modes of government and instruction. By the time the school is in good progress, the scholars begin to drop away, the school money is exhausted, and the school dismissed. After a vacation of unnecessary length, as far as the recreation and relief of the children are concerned, the summer school commences with reduced numbers, under a less vigilant supervision, with a poorly compensated teacher, to go through the same course as before; and so on from year to year. The loss of time consequent on the change of teachers, and the long intermission between the two seasons of schooling, not only retards the progress of the school, but leads to the breaking up of regular habits of study, which will be felt in the whole future life.

In the second place, it leads to the perpetual and expensive change of school books, so much complained of, and so justly complained of, by parents. Every teacher has his favorite text books, and is naturally desirous of introducing them wherever he goes. And as there is no system adopted in relation to this subject in any society, he usually succeeds in introducing more or less of them into every school. The money now expended in the purchase of new books, caused by the change of teachers, would go far to continue the same teacher another month in the same school. Thus the district might practically gain, without any additional expense, two months schooling each year by employing the same teacher year after year.

In the third place, this practice excludes from our common schools nearly all those who have decided to make teaching a profession and drives them, almost as a matter of course, into private schools or academies.

Henry Barnard on Women as Teachers, 1839 †

The average rate of wages for male teachers is $15.48 per month, exclusive of board; for female teachers, $8.33. This includes the very liberal salaries paid in some of our large cities and districts, for teachers

---

* *First Annual Report,* as Secretary of the Board of Commissioners of Common Schools in Connecticut, pp. 37-38.

† *Ibid.,* pp. 38-39.

permanently engaged. Leaving them out of the estimate, the average rate
will be somewhat reduced.

It is time for every friend of improvement in our common schools to
protest against the inadequate and disproportionate compensation paid to
female teachers. I have no hesitation in saying, that in the schools which
I have visited, the female teachers were as well qualified, as devoted to
their duties, and really advanced their pupils as far as the same number
of male teachers. Let but a more generous appreciation of the value of
their services as teachers, especially in the primary departments, prevail—
let the system be so far modified as to admit of their being employed more
extensively than now, not only in the summer, but the winter schools, and,
as far as possible for the year round, and a new and happy impulse would
not only be felt, in the more thorough intellectual training of youth, but
in the improved manners and morals of society. As it is now, that class
of females best qualified, by having enjoyed the advantages of superior and
expensive schools, cannot be induced to enter the common schools as
teachers, on account of the inadequate compensation, and the unnecessary difficulties and inconveniences connected with the employment. If
the State would but furnish an opportunity for a numerous and most
deserving class of young females, who are forced by their necessities into
the corrupted atmosphere and unhealthy employments of our workshops
and factories, to prepare themselves for teaching, and then remove the obstacles in the way of their being employed to the best advantage, an untold
amount of female talent and usefulness, now in part wasted, or if employed
even at better compensation, at least to a far less useful purpose, would
be enlisted in the so much needed work of molding the childhood and
youth of this State and nation.

This is a field in which practical and immediate improvement can be
made. Fitted by nature, education, and the circumstances of society with
us, for teachers, our law should be framed, so as to encourage and admit
of their more general and permanent employment. Schools of a higher
grade than the common district school as it exists, should be established,
as well for other purposes, but especially with a view of adapting the
studies there to the better education of females than can now be given.
This is one of the most serious deficiencies of common school instruction.
It is not adapted to form and cultivate a sufficiently high standard of
female character. This want can be supplied, and is in some measure supplied, to the daughters of the wealthy, by our many excellent, but expensive female seminaries. But these are practically closed to two thirds
of the community.

Superintendent Francis R. Shunk of Pennsylvania on the Need for
Improved Methods of Teaching and Managing Schools, 1841 *

It is also hoped that some competent individual, abounding in practical knowledge upon the subject, will prepare and publish a manual †
for the teachers of our primary schools, in which the best means, which
experience in this and other countries furnishes, for imparting instruction
in the branches taught in these schools, will be systematized. If all that is
known upon this interesting subject were thus embodied by a master hand,
the work would be of incalculable value. There are many men who possess
the adequate knowledge for teachers who are defective in the art of communicating it. These would be greatly benefited by the wisdom and experience of the best teachers of the age.

Connected with the art of teaching scholars is that of governing a
school; this, like that of governing communities, is a science, the principles
of which, if properly arranged by the light of experience and philosophy,
would add an inestimable item to the knowledge of our teachers. The
barbarous system of governing the mind by the infliction of stripes upon
the body, would, like the penal code of other times, soon be ameliorated
by a correct illustration of this science; and the schoolroom, under a
proper system of government, adapted to this enlightened age, would be
the delight, instead of being, as it now too often is, the terror of our
children.

On the Need for the Education of Teachers in Texas, 1846 ‡

Several colleges have been incorporated by the Texas congress, but
most of them exist only on the statute books. Only three, so far as my
information extends, have either suitable buildings or a regular organization
namely, Rutersville College, San Augustine University and the Wesleyan
College at San Augustine. These institutions commend themselves to the
friends of learning and the public generally. They have planted the germ
of knowledge and virtue in many minds, which, if nourished, will grow
and flourish in vernal beauty and vigor. Their advantages are accessible to
all classes of the community, and should be enjoyed by all.

---

* Given in J. P. Wickersham, *op. cit.*, pp. 358-59.

† Christopher Dock, of Pennsylvania, published in German his *Schulordnung* in 1770,
the first treatise on the subject in this country. Samuel Read Hall published in 1829 his
Lectures on School-Keeping, the first treatise on the subject in English in this country.
Among other books on teaching were Jacob Abbott's *The Teacher; or Moral Influences
Employed in the Instruction and Government of the Young* (1833) and David Page's
Theory and Practice of Teaching (1847). See Stuart G. Noble, "From 'Lectures on School-
keeping' (1829) to 'Introduction to Education' (1925)," *School and Society*, XXIII (June
26, 1926).

‡ Rev. Chauncey Richardson, President of Rutersville College; Address on education,
given before the educational convention of Texas, at Houston, January, 1846. Quoted in
Frederick Eby, *op. cit.*, pp. 198-99.

A period has arrived in our history when the importance of a good education should be viewed in its proper light. Our wisest and ablest men should direct their attention and the public mind to this great subject. It is worthy the efforts of the noblest patriots, the wisest philanthropists, and the purest Christians. The grand obligation and business of this generation is to educate the succeeding generation for a higher level of action. We must go on in this work till the cloud of mental and moral darkness, which now hangs over us, is rolled away, and the light of science and religion shall shine in meridian splendor. Then shall our "sons be as plants grown up in their youth, and our daughters as corner-stones polished after the similitude of a palace. . . ."

But how shall correct education be secured to all the youth of Texas? Most assuredly by the establishment of a good system of education, in connection with the institutions of a high order. To effect this object, well-taught, able, and Christian teachers are wanted. They are essential to good schools. They should be formed after the right model; their principles and characters developed in due proportions, themselves examples of human excellence. Teachers must be prepared in our own institutions, as they will never come from abroad in sufficient numbers to supply our wants. They must be raised up and qualified on the spot, to go forth to the work of elevating this empire of mind and heart. A teachers' department should be established immediately in the colleges now in operation in Texas, where they shall be prepared for their task, not only by a course of instruction designed for their personal improvement, but by teaching them how to instruct and to educate. A permanent class of instructors must be formed. The office of instruction ought to be coveted by persons of the best talents, and sufficiently rewarded to secure such in the profession. It is of the highest importance that those who cultivate the germ of thought, and form the habits of thinking and feeling of the rising generation, should be well qualified for their delicate and responsible work. They must be apt to teach; to be able to lay an idea in a child's mind just as it lies in their own minds. Teachers must know how to govern. They must possess firmness, kindness, and gentleness. A teacher must be, in the truest sense of the term, a gentleman. True politeness is gentleness and good will to mankind reduced to practice. He must be emphatically a good man, as he is a leader to go before and lead out or call forth the child to the perfection of his nature. He is the young child's spiritual architect. The office of teachers is a high and responsible one, because they are the builders up of a new generation. Albert Gallatin, while engaged in teaching, was more truly deserving of honor than when managing the fiscal concerns of the United States; and Louis Philippe, while teaching a little handful of pupils in Pittsburg was by far a greater benefactor to mankind than while sitting on the throne of France, surrounded by thirty millions of loyal subjects.

Advice of David P. Page to Prospective Teachers, 1847 *

Those who are beginning the study of education should be reminded that the field of inquiry is a vast one, and that if they would attain the highest professional standing, they must pursue this subject in its three main phases—the practical, the scientific, and the historical. If the time for preparation is short, a beginning should be made in becoming acquainted with the best current methods of organizing, governing, and instructing a school. Then should follow a study of the science of education, to the end that the teacher may interpret the lessons of daily experience, and thus be helped to grow into higher and higher degrees of competence; and, finally, for giving breadth of view, for taking full advantage of all past experience and experiments, and for gaining that inspiration which comes from re-tracing the long line of an illustrious professional ancestry, there should be a study of the history of education.

All who propose to teach need to recollect that the very basis of fitness for teaching, so far as it can be gained from study, is a broad and accurate scholarship. To be a teacher, one must first of all be a scholar. So much stress is now placed on method, and the theory of teaching, that there is great danger of forgetting the supreme importance of scholarship and culture. For these there is no substitute; and any scheme of professional study that is pursued at the expense of scholarship and culture, is essentially bad. To be open-minded, magnanimous, and manly; to have a love for the scholarly vocation, and a wide and easy range of intellectual vision, are of infinitely greater worth to the teacher than any authorized set of technical rules and principles. Well would it be for both teachers and taught, if all who read this book were to be inspired by Plato's ideal of the cultured man: "A lover, not of a part of wisdom, but of the whole; who has a taste for every sort of knowledge and is curious to learn, and is never satis-fied; who has magnificence of mind, and is the spectator of all time and all existence; who is harmoniously constituted; of a well-proportioned and gracious mind, whose own nature will move spontaneously towards the true being of every thing; who has a good memory, and is quick to learn, noble, gracious, the friend of truth, justice, courage, temperance."

Fifty Students at the University of Virginia Are Educated at the Expense of the State on Condition That They Teach Two Years, 1857 †

The revenue of the University of Virginia is derived from an endowment by the State of an annual sum of fifteen thousand dollars, and from the proceeds of the tuition-fees of the students. Fifty pupils are annually

* David P. Page, *Theory and Practice of Teaching*, Payne edition, pp. 22-24.
† *De Bow's Review*, Vol. XXII—Third series, Vol. II (1857), p. 68.

educated at the expense of the State, on the sole condition of their teaching two years in some public or private school within its limits.

President James B. Angell Recommends Courses in Pedagogy at the University of Michigan, 1874 *

It cannot be doubted that some instruction in Pedagogics would be very helpful to our Senior class. Many of them are called directly from the University to the management of large schools, some of them to the superintendency of the schools of a town. The whole work of organizing schools, the management of primary and grammar schools, the art of teaching and governing a school,—of all this it is desirable that they know something before they go to their new duties. Experience alone can thoroughly train them. But some familiar lectures on these topics would be of essential service to them.

The University of Michigan Establishes a Chair of the "History, Theory, and Art of Education," 1879 †

The University of Michigan is one of the most progressive as well as efficient of our great schools of learning, and adapts itself with singular facility to the situation in a rapidly developing country. It was, we believe, the first of our larger universities to adopt the elective system of study, and its spirit has been always hospitable and generous. The most striking fact in its recent annals is the establishment of a chair of the history, theory,

* Report to the Board of Regents, 1874. Given in B. A. Hinsdale, *History of the University of Michigan* (Ann Arbor, Published by the University, 1906), p. 83. Four years later President Angell again recommended courses in education, suggesting that for a time perhaps "a non-resident lecturer occupying a part of the year might meet the wants of our students." In 1879 the faculty endorsed the recommendation and the Regents created and filled a chair of "the Science and the Art of Teaching." An official circular sent out in August of 1879 stated the objects of the new chair: To fit students of the University of Michigan "for higher positions in the public school service"; to promote the study of educational science; to teach educational history and theory and comparative education; to "secure to teaching the rights, prerogatives, and advantages of a professional"; and to give "a more perfect unity to our state educational system by bringing the secondary schools into closer relations with the University." The next year President Angell said in his report that he was "not aware that there was at that time a chair exclusively for this work in any other American College."

† "Teaching How to Teach," an editorial in *Harper's Weekly*, July 26, 1879, p. 583. In addition to his services in public schools, William H. Payne (1836-1907) was for a time President of the Michigan Teachers' Association and editor of its organ, *The Michigan Teacher*. His address on "The Relation between the University and our High Schools," given the first year he was at Adrian and published in 1871 strongly advocated a coördinated school system in Michigan and the training of prospective teachers in the science and the art of teaching. This address is said to have attracted the attention of President James B. Angell of the University of Michigan who invited Payne to the new chair to which the editorial above refers. In 1887 Payne became Chancellor of the University of Nashville and President of Peabody Normal School. Among his many educational books were his edition of David P. Page's *Theory and Practice of Teaching* (1885); *Contributions to the Science of Education* (1886); a translation from the French of Gabriel Compayré's *History of Pedagogy* (1886); *Elements of Psychology* (1890); *Psychology Applied to Education* (1893); and a translation of Rousseau's *Emile* (1893).

and art of education. The value of such a chair is seen at once from the fact that the public schools of Michigan generally fall under the control of the graduates of the university. The State Normal School is engaged in the same general work, but upon another plane. In a society like ours, whose security depends upon educated intelligence, there is no more important function and service than that of teaching the teachers. The art of the teacher is that of effectively communicating knowledge. But this can be taught, like every art and science, only by those who are especially fitted for the work; and the University of Michigan is fortunate in finding for its new chair apparently the very man to fill it.

The authorities of the university have invited to the new professorship the late Superintendent of the Public Schools of Adrian, Professor Payne. He has been twenty-one years continuously in the public school service of the State, and his admirable influence has been gladly and generally acknowledged. But his efficient administration has only deepened his interest in the philosophic principles of his profession, and his views were fully set forth in a course of lectures delivered last year in the Normal Department of Adrian College, which have commanded the interested attention of "educators" as an admirable exposition of the subject. He is now called to the first chair of the kind established in this country, and the University of Michigan again justifies its position as the head of the educational system of the State.

This action will promote the highest interests of education, not only by tempting future teachers to the training of the university, but by apprising the public that teaching is itself an art, and that the knowledge how to teach may make all the difference between school money well or uselessly spent in the community. Both the educational and charitable systems of Michigan have an enviable reputation, and the good example again set by its university will be doubtless heeded and followed elsewhere.

The National Educational Association Commends the Practice of the Study of Pedagogy in Colleges and Universities, 1880 *

Resolved: That this Association commends the practice of establishing chairs of Pedagogics in Universities and Colleges, under such arrangements as will put the study of the Science of Education on the same footing as other sciences, in the course of study of these institutions.

William James on "Psychology and the Teaching Art," 1892 †

In the general activity and uprising of ideal interests which every one with an eye for fact can discern all about us in American life, there is

---

* *Addresses and Proceedings of the National Educational Association*, 1880, p. 157.
† *Talks to Teachers on Psychology*, New Edition, with an introduction by John Dewey

perhaps no more promising feature than the fermentation which for a dozen years or more has been going on among the teachers. In whatever sphere of education their functions may lie, there is to be seen among them a really inspiring amount of searching of the heart about the highest concerns of their profession. The renovation of nations begins always at the top, among the reflective members of the State, and spreads slowly outward and downward. The teachers of this country, one may say, have its future in their hands. The earnestness which they at present show in striving to enlighten and strengthen themselves is an index of the nation's probabilities of advance in all ideal directions. The outward organization of education which we have in our United States is perhaps, on the whole, the best organization that exists in any country. The State school systems give a diversity and flexibility, an opportunity for experiment and keenness of competition, nowhere else to be found on such an important scale. The independence of so many of the colleges and universities; the give and take of students and instructors between them all; their emulation, and their happy organic relations to the lower schools; the traditions of instruction in them, evolved from the older American recitation-method (and so avoiding on the one hand the pure lecture-system prevalent in Germany and Scotland, which considers too little the individual student, and yet not involving the sacrifice of the instructor to the individual student, which the English tutorial system would seem too often to entail,)—all these things (to say nothing of that coeducation of the sexes in whose benefits so many of us heartily believe), all these things, I say, are most happy features of our scholastic life, and from them the most sanguine auguries may be drawn.

Having so favorable an organization, all we need is to impregnate it with geniuses, to get superior men and women working more and more abundantly in it and for it and at it, and in a generation or two America may well lead the education of the world. I must say that I look forward with no little confidence to the day when that shall be an accomplished fact.

No one has profited more by the fermentation of which I speak, in pedagogical circles, than we psychologists. The desire of the schoolteachers for a completer professional training, and their aspiration toward the 'professional' spirit in their work, have led them more and more to turn to us for light on fundamental principles. And in these few hours which we are to spend together you look to me, I am sure, for information concerning

and William H. Kilpatrick (New York, Henry Holt & Co., Inc., 1939), pp. 3-14. In 1892 William James, professor in Harvard University and pioneer American writer on psychology, was asked by the Harvard Corporation to give some public lectures on psychology to the teachers in Cambridge, Massachusetts. His views on what psychology can and cannot be expected to do for teaching are set out here. His commonsense advice to teachers on the degree to which they should attempt to be psychologists is still timely. The entire lecture, here reproduced by permission of the publishers, is still significant and pertinent more than half a century after it was given and is an important historical document.

the mind's operations, which may enable you to labor more easily and effectively in the several schoolrooms over which you preside.

Far be it from me to disclaim for psychology all title to such hopes. Psychology ought certainly to give the teacher radical help. And yet I confess that, acquainted as I am with the height of some of your expectations, I feel a little anxious lest, at the end of these simple talks of mine, not a few of you may experience some disappointment at the net results. In other words, I am not sure that you may not be indulging fancies that are just a shade exaggerated. That would not be altogether astonishing, for we have been having something like a 'boom' in psychology in this country. Laboratories and professorships have been founded, and reviews established. The air has been full of rumors. The editors of educational journals and the arrangers of conventions have had to show themselves enterprising and on a level with the novelties of the day. Some of the professors have not been unwilling to co-operate, and I am not sure even that the publishers have been entirely inert. 'The new psychology' has thus become a term to conjure up portentous ideas withal; and you teachers, docile and receptive and aspiring as many of you are, have been plunged in an atmosphere of vague talk about our science, which to a great extent has been more mystifying than enlightening. Altogether it does seem as if there were a certain fatality of mystification laid upon the teachers of our day. The matter of their profession, compact enough in itself, has to be frothed up for them in journals and institutes, till its outlines often threaten to be lost in a kind of vast uncertainty. Where the disciples are not independent and critical-minded enough (and I think that, if you teachers in the earlier grades have any defect—the slightest touch of a defect in the world—it is that you are a mite too docile), we are pretty sure to miss accuracy and balance and measure in those who get a license to lay down the law to them from above.

As regards this subject of psychology, now, I wish at the very threshold to do what I can to dispel the mystification. So I say at once that in my humble opinion there *is* no 'new psychology' worthy of the name. There is nothing but the old psychology which began in Locke's time, plus a little physiology of the brain and senses and theory of evolution, and a few refinements of introspective detail, for the most part without adaptation to the teacher's use. It is only the fundamental conceptions of psychology which are of real value to the teacher; and they, apart from the aforesaid theory of evolution, are very far from being new. I trust that you will see better what I mean by this at the end of all these talks.

I say moreover that you make a great, a very great mistake, if you think that psychology, being the science of the mind's laws, is something from which you can deduce definite programmes and schemes and methods of instruction for immediate schoolroom use. Psychology is a science, and teaching is an art; and sciences never generate arts directly out of themselves. An intermediary inventive mind must make the application, by using its originality.

The science of logic never made a man reason rightly, and the science of ethics (if there be such a thing) never made a man behave rightly. The most such sciences can do is to help us to catch ourselves up and check ourselves, if we start to reason or to behave wrongly; and to criticise ourselves more articulately after we have made mistakes. A science only lays down lines within which the rules of the art must fall, laws which the follower of the art must not transgress; but what particular things he shall positively do within those lines is left exclusively to his own genius. One genius will do his work well and succeed in one way, while another succeeds as well quite differently; yet neither will transgress the lines.

The art of teaching grew up in the schoolroom, out of inventiveness and sympathetic concrete observation. Even where (is in the case of Herbart) the advancer of the art was also a psychologist, the pedagogics and the psychology ran side by side, and the former was not derived in any sense from the latter. The two were congruent, but neither was subordinate. And so everywhere the teaching must *agree* with the psychology, but need not necessarily be the only kind of teaching that would so agree; for many diverse methods of teaching may equally well agree with psychological laws.

To know psychology, therefore, is absolutely no guarantee that we shall be good teachers. To advance to that result, we must have an additional endowment altogether, a happy tact and ingenuity to tell us what definite things to say and do when the pupil is before us. That ingenuity in meeting and pursuing the pupil, that tact for the concrete situation, though they are the alpha and omega of the teacher's art, are things to which psychology cannot help us in the least.

The science of psychology, and whatever science of general pedagogics may be based on it, are in fact much like the science of war. Nothing is simpler or more definite than the principles of either. In war, all you have to do is to work your enemy into a position from which the natural obstacles prevent him from escaping if he tries to; then to fall on him in numbers superior to his own, at a moment when you have led him to think you far away; and so, with a minimum of exposure of your own troops, to hack his force to pieces, and take the remainder prisoners. Just so, in teaching, you must simply work your pupil into such a state of interest in what you are going to teach him that every other object of attention is banished from his mind; then reveal it to him so impressively that he will remember the occasion to his dying day; and finally fill him with devouring curiosity to know what the next steps in connection with the subject are. The principles being so plain, there would be nothing but victories for the masters of the science, either on the battlefield or in the schoolroom, if they did not both have to make their application to an incalculable quantity in the shape of the mind of their opponent. The mind of your own enemy, the pupil, is working away from you as keenly and eagerly as is the mind of the commander on the other side from the scientific general. Just what the respective enemies want and think, and what they know and do not know, are as hard things for the teacher as for the general to find out. Divination and perception, not psychological pedagogics or theoretic strategy, are the only helpers here.

But, if the use of psychological principles thus be negative rather than positive, it does not follow that it may not be a great use, all the same. It certainly narrows the path for experiments and trials. We know in advance, if we are psychologists, that certain methods will be wrong, so our psychology saves us from mistakes. It makes us, moreover, more clear as at what we are about. We gain confidence in respect to any method which we are using as soon as we believe that it has theory as well as practice at its back. Most of all, it fructifies our independence, and it reanimates our interest, to see our subject at two different angles—to get a stereoscopic view, so to speak, of the youthful organism who is our enemy, and, while handling him with all our concrete tact and divination, to be able, at the same time, to represent to ourselves the curious inner elements of his mental machine. Such a complete knowledge as this of the pupil, at once intuitive and analytic, is surely the knowledge at which every teacher ought to aim.

Fortunately for you teachers, the elements of the mental machine can be clearly apprehended, and their workings easily grasped. And, as the most general elements and workings are just those parts of psychology which the teacher finds most directly useful, it follows that the amount of this science which is necessary to all teachers need not be very great. Those who find themselves loving the subject may go as far as they please, and become possibly none the worse teachers for the fact, even though in some of them one might apprehend a little loss of balance from the tendency observable in all of us to overemphasize certain special parts of a subject when we are studying it intensely and abstractly. But for the great majority of you a general view is enough, provided it be a true one; and such a general view, one may say, might almost be written on the palm of one's hand.

Least of all need you, merely *as teachers,* deem it part of your duty to become contributors to psychological science or to make psychological observations in a methodical or responsible manner. I fear that some of the enthusiasts for child-study have thrown a certain burden on you in this way. By all means let child-study go on—it is refreshing all our sense of the child's life. There are teachers who take a spontaneous delight in filling syllabuses, inscribing observations, compiling statistics, and computing the per cent. Child-study will certainly enrich their lives. And, if its results, as treated statistically, would seem on the whole to have but trifling value, yet the anecdotes and observations of which it in part consist do certainly acquaint us more intimately with our pupils. Our eyes and ears grow quickened to discern in the child before us processes similar to those we have read of as noted in the children—processes of which we might otherwise have remained inobservant. But, for Heaven's sake, let the rank and file of teachers be passive readers if they so prefer, and feel free not to contribute to the accumulation. Let not the prosecution of it be preached as an imperative duty or imposed by regulation on those to whom it proves an exterminating bore, or who in any way whatever miss in themselves the appropriate vocation for it. I cannot too strongly agree with my colleague, Professor Münsterberg, when he says that the teacher's attitude toward the child, being concrete and ethical, is positively opposed to the psychological observer's, which is abstract and analytic. Although some of us may conjoin the attitudes successfully, in most of us they must conflict.

The worst thing that can happen to a good teacher is to get a bad conscience about her profession because she feels herself hopeless as a psychologist. Our teachers are overworked already. Every one who adds a jot or tittle of unnecessary weight to their burden is a foe of education. A bad conscience increases the weight of every other burden; yet I know that child-study, and other pieces of psychology as well, have been productive of bad conscience in many a really innocent pedagogic breast. I should indeed be glad if this passing word from me might tend to dispel such a bad conscience, if any of you have it; for it is certainly one of those fruits of more or less systematic mystification of which I have already complained. The best teacher may be the poorest contributor of child-study material, and the best contributor may be the poorest teacher. No fact is more palpable than this.

So much for what seems the most reasonable general attitude of the teacher toward the subject which is to occupy our attention.

The Committee of Ten on Teachers and Teaching, 1893 *

Every reader of this report and of the reports of the nine Conferences will be satisfied that to carry out the improvements proposed more highly trained teachers will be needed than are now ordinarily to be found for the service of the elementary and secondary schools. The Committee of Ten desire to point out some of the means of procuring these better trained teachers. For the further instruction of teachers in actual service, three agencies already in existence may be much better utilized than they now are. The Summer Schools which many universities now maintain might be resorted to by much larger number of teachers, particularly if some aid, such as the payment of tuition fees and travelling expenses, should be given

* *Report of the Committee of Ten on Secondary School Studies* (Washington, United States Bureau of Education, 1893), pp. 53-55.

to teachers who are willing to devote half of their vacations to study, by the cities and towns which these teachers serve. Secondly, in all the towns and cities in which colleges and universities are planted, these colleges or universities may usefully give stated courses of instruction in the main subjects used in the elementary and secondary schools to teachers employed in those towns and cities. This is a reasonable service which the colleges and universities may render to their own communities. Thirdly, a superintendent who has himself become familiar with the best mode of teaching any one of the subjects which enter into the school course can always be a very useful instructor for the whole body of teachers under his charge. A real master of any one subject will always have many suggestions to make to teachers of other subjects. The same is true of the principal of a high school, or other leading teacher in a town or city. In every considerable city school system the best teacher in each department of instruction should be enabled to give part of his time to helping the other teachers by inspecting and criticising their work, and showing them, both by precept and example, how to do it better.

In regard to preparing young men and women for the business of teaching, the country has a right to expect much more than it has yet obtained from the colleges and normal schools. The common expectation of attainment for pupils of the normal schools has been altogether too low the country over. The normal schools, as a class, themselves need better apparatus, libraries, programmes, and teachers. As to the colleges, it is quite as much an enlargement of sympathies as an improvement of apparatus or of teaching that they need. They ought to take more interest than they have heretofore done, not only in the secondary, but in the elementary schools; and they ought to take pains to fit men well for the duties of a school superintendent. They already train a considerable number of the best principals of high schools and academies; but this is not sufficient. They should take an active interest, through their presidents, professors, and other teachers, in improving the schools in their respective localities, and in contributing to the thorough discussion of all questions affecting the welfare of both the elementary and the secondary schools.

Finally, the Committee venture to suggest, in the interest of secondary schools, that uniform dates—such as the last Thursday, Friday, and ¹urday, or the third Monday, Tuesday, and Wednesday of June and mber—be established for the admission examinations of colleges ˀentific schools throughout the United States. It is a serious incon- for secondary schools which habitually prepare candidates for ˀrent colleges or scientific schools that the admission examina- ˀnt institutions are apt to occur on different dates, sometimes ˀparated.

also wish to call attention to the service which Schools ˀngineering, and Technology, whether connected with universities or not, can render to secondary education by arranging their requirements for admission, as regards selection and range of subjects, in conformity with the courses of study recommended by the Committee. By bringing their entrance requirements into close relation with any or all of the programmes recommended for secondary schools, these professional schools can give valuable support to high schools, academies, and preparatory schools.

CHARLES W. ELIOT,
WILLIAM T. HARRIS,
JAMES B. ANGELL,
JOHN TETLOW,
JAMES M. TAYLOR,
OSCAR D. ROBINSON,
JAMES H. BAKER,
RICHARD H. JESSE,
JAMES C. MACKENZIE,
HENRY C. KING.

The Committee of Fifteen on the Training of Secondary School Teachers, 1895 *

Perhaps one-sixth of the great body of public school teachers in the United States are engaged in secondary work and in supervision. These are the leading teachers. They give educational tone to communities, as well as inspiration to the body of teachers.

It is of great importance that they be imbued with the professional spirit springing from sound professional culture. The very difficult and responsible positions that they fill demand ripe scholarship, more than ordinary ability, and an intimate knowledge of the period of adolescence, which Rousseau so aptly styles the second birth.

The elementary schools provide for the education of the masses. Our secondary schools educate our social and business leaders. The careers of our college graduates who mainly fill the important places in professional and political life are determined largely by the years of secondary training. The college or university gives expansion and finish, the secondary school gives character and direction.

It should not be forgotten that the superintendents of public schools are largely taken from the ranks of secondary teachers, and that the scholarship, qualities, and training required for the one class are nearly equivalent to that demanded for the other.

Our high schools, too, are the source of supply for teachers in elementary schools. Hence the pedagogic influences exerted in the high school should lead to excellence in elementary teaching.

* *Educational Review*, IX (March, 1895), pp. 224-29.

The superintendent who with long foresight looks to the improvement of his schools will labor earnestly to improve and especially to professionalize the teaching in his high school. The management which makes the high school an independent portion of the school system, merely attached and loftily superior, which limits the supervision and influence of the superintendent to the primary and grammar grades, is short-sighted and destructive.

There ought also to be a place and a plan for the training of teachers for normal schools. The great body of normal and training schools in the United States are secondary schools. Those who are to teach in these schools need broad scholarship, thorough understanding of educational problems, and trained experience. To put into these schools teachers whose scholarship is that of the secondary school and whose training is that of the elementary is to narrow and depress rather than broaden and elevate.

If college graduates are put directly into teaching without special study and training, they will teach as they have been taught. The methods of college professors are not in all cases the best, and, if they were, high school pupils are not to be taught nor disciplined as college students are. High school teaching and discipline can be that neither of the grammar school nor of the college, but is *sui generis*. To recognize this truth and the special differences is vital to success. This recognition comes only from much experience at great loss and partial failure, or by happy intuition not usually to be expected, or by definite instruction and directed practice. Success in teaching depends upon conformity to principles, and these principles are not a part of the mental equipment of every educated person.

These considerations and others are the occasion of a growing conviction, widespread in this land, that secondary teachers should be trained for their work even more carefully than elementary teachers are trained. This conviction is manifested in the efforts to secure normal schools adapted to training teachers for secondary schools, notably in Massachusetts and New York, and in the numerous professorships of pedagogy established in rapidly increasing numbers in our colleges and universities.

The training of teachers for secondary schools is in several essential respects the same as that for teachers of elementary schools. Both demand scholarship, theory, and practice. The degree of scholarship required for secondary teachers is by common consent fixed at a collegiate education. No one—with rare exceptions—should be employed to teach in a high school who has not this fundamental preparation.

It is not necessary to enter in detail into the work of theoretical instruction for secondary teachers. The able men at the head of institutions and departments designed for such work neither need nor desire advice upon this matter. And yet for the purposes of this report it may be allowable to point out a plan for the organization of a secondary training school.

Let it be supposed that two essentials have been found in one locality,

(1) a college or university having a department of pedagogy and a department of post-graduate work; (2) a high school, academy, or preparatory school whose managers are willing to employ and pay a number of graduate students to teach under direction for a portion of each day. These two conditions being met, we will suppose that pedagogy is offered as an elective to the college seniors.

Two years of instruction in the science and art of teaching are to be provided; one, mostly theory with some practice, elective during the senior year; the other, mostly practice with some theory, elective for one year as post-graduate work.

During the senior year is to be studied:

THE SCIENCE OF TEACHING

The elements of this science are:

I. Psychology in its physiological, apperceptive, and experimental features. The period of adolescence here assumed the prominence that childhood has in the psychological study preparatory to teaching in lower schools. This is the period of beginnings, the beginning of a more ambitious and generous life, a life having the future wrapped up in it; a transition period, of mental storm and stress, in which egoism gives way to altruism, romance has charm, and the social, moral, and religious feelings bud and bloom. To guide youth at this formative stage, in which an active fermentation occurs that may give wine or vinegar according to conditions, requires a deep and sympathetic nature, and that knowledge of the changing life which supplies guidance wise and adequate.

II. Methodology: a discussion of the principles of education and of the methods of teaching the studies of the secondary schools.

III. School Economy should be studied in a much wider and more thorough way than is required for elementary teachers. The school systems of Germany, France, England, and the leading systems of the United States should also be studied.

IV. History of education, the tracing of modern doctrine back to its sources; those streams of influence now flowing and those that have disappeared in the sands of the centuries.

V. The philosophy of education as a division of an all-involving philosophy of life and thought in which unity is found.

THE ART OF TEACHING

This includes observation and practice. The observation should include the work of different grades and of different localities, with minute and searching comparison and reports upon special topics. How does excellent primary work differ from excellent grammar-grade work? How do the standards of excellence differ between grammar grades and high-school grades? between high-school and college work? What are the arguments for and against coeducation in secondary schools as determined by experience? What are the upper and lower limits of secondary education as determined by the nature of the pupil's effort?

In the college class in pedagogy much more than in the elementary normal school can the class itself be made to afford a means of practice to its members. Quizzes may be conducted by students upon the chapters of the books read or the lectures of the professors. These exercises may have for their object review, or improved statement, or enlarged inference and application, and they afford an ample opportunity to cultivate the art of questioning, skill in which is the teacher's most essential accomplishment.

The head of the department of pedagogy will of course present the essential methods of teaching, and the heads of other departments may lecture on methods pertaining to their subject of study; or secondary teachers of known success may still better present the methods now approved in the several departments of secondary work.

Post-Graduate Year

To those graduates who have elected pedagogy in their senior year may be offered the opportunity of further study in this department, with such other post-graduate work as taste and opportunity permit. From those selecting advanced work in pedagogy the board in charge of the affiliated secondary school should elect as many teachers for its school as are needed, employing them for two-thirds time at one-half the usual pay for teachers without experience. Under the professor of pedagogy of the college, the principal, and the heads of departments of the school these student-teachers should do their work, receiving advice, criticism, and illustration as occasion requires. The time for which they are employed would provide for two hours of class work and about one hour of clerical work or study while in charge of a schoolroom. These student-teachers should be given abundant opportunity for the charge of pupils while reciting or studying, at recess and dismissals, and should have all the responsibilities of members of the faculty of this school. Their work should be inspected as frequently as may be by the heads of the departments in which they teach, by the principal of the school, and by the professor of pedagogy. These appointments would be virtually fellowships with an opportunity for most profitable experience.

In the afternoon of each day these students should attend to college work and especially to instruction from the professor in pedagogy, who could meet them occasionally with the heads of the departments under whose direction they are working.

On Saturdays a seminary of two hours' duration might be held, conducted by the professor of pedagogy and attended by the student-teachers and the more ambitious teachers of experience in the vicinity. These seminaries would doubtless be of great profit to both classes of participants and the greater to each because of the other. (Such a training school for secondary teachers in connection with Brown University and the Providence High School is contemplated for the coming year.)

It will not be needful to specify further the advantages to the student-teachers. The arrangement likewise affords advantage to the affiliated school, especially in the breadth of view this work would afford to the heads of departments, the intense desire it would beget in them for professional skill, the number of perplexing problems which it would force them to attempt the solution of.

The visits of the professor of pedagogy, and the constant comparison he would make between actual and ideal conditions, would lead him to seek the improvement not only of the students in practice but of the school as a whole.

When several earnest and capable people unite in a mutual effort to improve themselves and their work all the essential conditions of progress are present.

Average Monthly Salaries of Rural Teachers in Thirty-four States, 1897 *

The question of the support afforded teachers is one great hindrance in the way of improving the rural school. The following table, showing the average monthly salaries paid teachers in rural schools, has been compiled from answers to circulars sent out to state superintendents. It is unfortunate that in most states the statistics make no distinction between city and rural

	Males	Females		Males	Females
Alabama	$25	$20	Missouri	$40	$34
Arkansas	33	30	Montana	60	45
California [1]	67	56	Nebraska	35	30
Colorado [2]	50	45	Nevada	85	60
Connecticut	30	30	New Hampshire	30	30
Delaware	35	33	New York [4]	37	37
Illinois	30	25	Ohio	35	29
Indiana	40	35	Pennsylvania [5]	42	33
Iowa	35	30	Rhode Island	40	36
Kansas	40	32	South Carolina	30	27
Kentucky	36	34	South Dakota	36	31
Louisiana	40	33	Utah	53	37
Maine	35	22	Vermont	39	27
Maryland	29	29	Virginia	28	25
Massachusetts [3]	32	26	West Virginia	36	36
Michigan	29	25	Wisconsin	46	30
Minnesota	40	31	Wyoming	45	40

[1] Includes schools of not more than two teachers.
[2] Includes the schools in the agricultural sections only.
[3] Based on fifty-two male teachers and 143 female teachers in towns under $500,000 valuation.
[4] $9.26 a week, counting thirty-three and one-third weeks in a year.
[5] Not including the city of Philadelphia.

* Report of the Committee of Twelve on Rural Schools, *Journal of Proceedings and Addresses, National Educational Association,* 1897, pp. 393-94.

school-teachers. Consequently many of the returns are estimated. They are valuable, however, for purposes of comparison and general information.

Defects and Remedies in the Certification of Teachers, 1906 *

In the study we have made of present conditions, perhaps the two most significant weaknesses revealed in our systems of certification were the low standards and the great lack of uniformity. To raise and to standardize our certification requirements ought to be the main lines of future progress.

The amount of common knowledge which we as a people have is increasing so rapidly, our elementary-school curriculum is being enriched so fast, and the general intelligence of our people is becoming of such a standard that the teacher with a meagre intellectual equipment should no longer have a place in our educational system. Yet Table III in Chapter iii shows clearly that, for the twenty-eight states tabulated, it is possible to secure a third-grade teacher's certificate in 90 per cent of the number with no educational test beyond the common-school branches; and for the thirty-seven states tabulated it is possible to secure a first-grade certificate, in two-thirds of these states, without giving evidence of knowing anything about a single high-school subject except algebra, and in two-fifths of the states without knowing even this. These low-standard certificates are wholly out of place to-day, and ought to be eliminated at the earliest possible moment.

The great diversity in our requirements and our unwillingness to recognize equivalents are two of our marked educational characteristics. So great is the diversity that a good teacher today is unnecessarily hampered in his ability to move about, not only from state to state, but also from county to county, and often from county to city and from one city to another. Many of these restrictions are not warranted by any educational standards, but are more of the nature of a protective tariff levied on foreign capacity and in favor of home production. This makes the local examination system, with its accompanying barriers, in the nature of a protected industry, and this is not in the interests of good education. The strict county system too often perpetuates the rule of the weak by shielding them from the competition of the strong. All barriers to competency are wrong.

That these barriers exist has been pointed out frequently in previous chapters, and need only be summarized here. In fourteen states there is no admission to the teaching profession except on examination. In eleven of these states forty or more subjects are required to secure the highest certificate granted, and all must be secured on examination. In fourteen states no recognition is given to diplomas from normal schools or other institutions of learning within the state. The graduates of such institutions are

* E. P. Cubberley, "The Certification of Teachers," *Fifth Yearbook of the National Society for the Scientific Study of Education*, 1906, Part II, pp. 73-77.

placed on a par with the "graduates" of the country school. In nineteen states absolutely no recognition is given to any form of credential from another state. Only eleven states recognize normal-school diplomas from other states; seventeen recognize college or university diplomas from outside the state; and eighteen recognize a life-diploma or state professional certificate from elsewhere. In a number of our states there is no recognition of certificates from one county to another within the state. Many of these barriers are indefensible, while the defense of others can be eliminated with ease by raising and standardizing requirements. . . .

Each state must, of course, be allowed to set its own standards, and it cannot be expected to accept certificates or diplomas from states having a distinctly lower standard. This should be recognized and accepted, and reciprocity should not be expected. Instead of being "uppish" about it and striking back by way or retaliation, as certain states do because their credentials are not accredited by some more progressive state, they should on the contrary welcome a teacher from such a state because of his better training and what he may bring. . . .

In almost every state, too, these low-standard certificates are good for teaching in any part of the school system in which the holder can secure employment. This should not be allowed to continue, but separate certificates should be erected for special fields of work. In the case of high-school teachers this is especially important. Teachers in all branches of the service should be required to know more than they are expected to teach, and the importance of this for high-school teachers cannot be overemphasized.

In the field of supervision we have scarcely made a beginning in the preparation and selection of a body of educational leaders, and we are tied to present practices by a political string. In our lack of leadership we partake of a common weakness of democracy—that of emphasizing the importance of the masses and forgetting the leader who must lead and direct them. The soldier, the lawyer, the doctor, and the engineer have cast aside the apprenticeship and the successful-practitioner methods, but the educator has not as yet evolved that far in his thinking. Our pedagogical departments and the organized body of our pedagogical knowledge are too recent to have reached the point of general use and application. We are in education where the army and the navy were before the establishment of West Point and Annapolis, and where the engineer, the doctor, and the lawyer were a generation ago, before the development of modern professional schools for the training of leaders in these fields. Yet leaders must be trained for work in education, as in these other professional fields, if we are to make any great and worthy progress in the future.

In the matter of examinations there is great need of our decreasing the emphasis we now place on the written test. We could greatly improve our certificating systems by erecting certain educational prerequisites and accepting evidence of education in lieu of at least part of the examinations.

As fast as can be done, the periodical written examination ought to be diminished in importance as a means of recruiting our teaching force. We ought to insist more and more on securing the educated and trained teacher instead of the new recruit. Not only should the number of examinations be decreased, but teachers of training or of long and satisfactory experience ought to be relieved of the necessity of frequent tests. There is no valid excuse, for example, for compelling a graduate of a state normal school to pass a county examination before she can teach. If her normal-school diploma does not stand for better education and better professional preparation than the county examination represents, and if she is not superior to the untrained product of the county examination method, then it is time either to renovate the normal schools of the state and put in a corps of teachers who can produce a better output, or to abolish them entirely and save an unnecessary expense.

The securing of the educated and trained teacher instead of the raw recruit is, however, an economic problem as well as an educational one, though this economic problem has an educational aspect as well. There never can be high educational standards for teachers in states which are organized on the district system, and which apportion their money on the very objectionable census basis and which raise but a small general tax, until there is a radical reform in the methods of raising school revenue and of apportioning funds after they have been raised. In the ultimate analysis there are but three primary problems in education. The first is how properly to finance a school system. The second is how to secure a trained teaching force for it. The third is how to supervise it and to produce leaders for its management and improvement. The financial problem always underlies the other two.

Normal Schools Are Transformed into Colleges, 1912 *

How great a part personal and institutional ambition has played in the development of educational politics it would be difficult to say, but the results of it can be seen in every state where the divided institution exists. These appear usually in two forms: first, the endeavor of each institution to cover the whole field of education and the consequent duplications which ensue; secondly, the widespread tendency to drop the legitimate work for which the institution was founded in order to take up some other work, which appeals to the ambitions of its president, or of its board of trustees, or of its faculty or alumni.

Examples of the first sort have just been alluded to. Other examples in the educational history of Iowa, Colorado, Michigan, and various other states will readily occur to the reader.

* Henry S. Pritchett, in *Seventh Annual Report of the Carnegie Foundation for the Advancement of Teaching*, 1912, pp. 149-52.

Where three or four state institutions exist, this rivalry has inevitably led to much commerce with the legislature, to overlapping institutions, and in nearly all cases to a strenuous struggle for students. The three-cornered rivalry between the university, the agricultural and mechanical college, and the normal school in the states like Iowa and Kansas are typical instances of the results of such a régime.

A singular outcome of this situation in recent years has been the effort of the normal school in many states to transform itself into an arts college. The normal school is at best a singular institution, seldom related logically to the educational system of its state. Its weakness from the educational point of view lies in the fact that it undertakes to make a teacher of a man or woman whose education is so limited as to afford slender basis for a teacher's training. From the time of Horace Mann, however, it has been the agency upon which our states have come more and more to depend for the training of teachers for the elementary schools, and particularly for the rural elementary schools, since the larger cities have in many cases provided agencies to train teachers for their own schools. Notwithstanding its educational isolation, some such agency as the normal school seems necessary at the present stage of our educational organization, and probably will be necessary for many years to come. When one considers that in many of the middle western states not more than ten per cent of all the public school teachers have had the equivalent of a high school education, one realizes that in order to obtain the necessary teachers for the common schools of the country, some agency must for a long time prepare a large number as best it may. One may well hope that the low standards of training for rural teachers now in use in many states may be raised, and that the necessary number of teachers may be forthcoming at a continually higher level, and that school teachers may soon be themselves fairly educated men and women. In any case the function of the normal school in our present situation is definite, clear, and of immense importance. It is therefore little less than astounding to find normal schools in so many states ready to turn aside from this definite and important work, in the effort to transform themselves into weak colleges, and this, too, in states where the number of such colleges is already larger than the ability of the population to sustain. This movement has arisen in some cases out of the ambitions of the heads of these institutions and of their faculties, who somehow have the mistaken feeling that the work of the college is more honorable and more desirable. In some cases it has been undertaken with the honest belief that the two institutions, college and normal school, would grow side by side, a result which would be against all our educational experience; but from whatever motive undertaken, it has inevitably involved these schools in politics.

An illustration of such legislation is found in the measure passed by the last session of the Wisconsin legislature to the following effect: "The Board of Normal School regents may extend the course of instruction in any normal school so that any course, the admission to which is based upon graduation from an accredited high school or its equivalent, may include the substantial equivalent of the instruction given in the first two years of a college course. Such course of instruction shall not be extended further than the substantial equivalent of the instruction given in such college course without the consent of the legislature."

This language is capable of at least two interpretations. It might mean the extension of the normal school course for two years along normal school and pedagogical lines equivalent in intellectual demand to the corresponding years in college, thereby training a better teacher, or it might mean the superimposing on the normal school of two years of ordinary college work. Apparently both of these ideas were in the minds of those interested in the legislation. As a matter of fact, however, the normal schools have immediately translated this legislation into the authority for establishing the first two years of an arts college.

It requires no prophet to see whither this movement leads. Under the arrangement college students and normal school students are in the same classes. It will not be long before there is an attempt to so extend the curriculum that the equivalent of four college years will be given. Already the normal schools are introducing technical studies and asking for credit for the first half of curricula in agriculture and engineering. There are in Wisconsin eight state normal schools, and more are in prospect. This movement means the transformation of these schools from institutions primarily designed for the training of teachers to colleges having the ordinary college atmosphere with all the distractions which differentiate the American college from the professional school. It may be wise for these professional schools to be transformed into colleges, but if this is to be done, it should come only after a fair and full discussion of the whole matter from the educational point of view. There are those who contend that the atmosphere and spirit of the present day college can be successfully grafted upon the professional school. Perhaps this is true, although the evidence would seem to be against it. The result of such a mixture is likely to be an institution lacking the best qualities of both. But in any case, such legislation should not be enacted until those responsible for it have had a full discussion of the whole matter by men familiar with educational problems and who are not directly interested in the problems either of the Wisconsin normal schools or the Wisconsin endowed colleges. Wisconsin has in many respects led the way among American commonwealths in the intelligent use of experts in the solution of legislative problems. This question is one which ought not to be legislated upon without the light of expert and unbiased educational judgment. To legislate on such a technical question in the absence of an expert survey of the problem is to legislate in the dark.

Teachers in High Schools Deficient in English, 1913 *

All candidates for high-school teaching positions should have work in English extending thru at least two years, with emphasis upon oral and written composition. The committee is impelled to make this recommendation because of the deficiencies in English that so frequently characterize high-school teachers. The committee recognizes, however, that even the best technical training in English composition will not alone suffice to accomplish the desired results. In addition to this, every effort should be made in all classes to develop adequate habits of clear and concise expression, and to encourage effective standards of diction, syntax, and logical organization. We recommend that the conference urge upon college and university authorities the importance of emphasizing this phase of education in all classes in which intending high-school teachers are enrolled.

(The last recommendation is an interesting confirmation of the necessity of coöperation in English, even in the college.)

The Need for Professionally Prepared Teachers, 1914 †

Last year there were enrolled in the public schools of this nation more than eighteen million children. This army is officered by nearly five hundred fifty thousand teachers and is maintained at an annual expense of almost a half billion of dollars. It must also be remembered that this vast expenditure does not include interest on an investment of approximately a billion and a half.

Notwithstanding this enormous enrolment and this vast expenditure of money, the nation has far from ideal results. One-fourth of the pupils enrolled were absent every day. The enrolment, large as it is, includes but little more than half of the population between the ages of five and eighteen. So far as the public schools are concerned, the average child of school age is receiving but ninety days of schooling each year. If this is the record shown by the average child for the thirteen years lying between five and eighteen, it would mean that the completion of the sixth grade of the elementary school is what we are to rely upon in the way of a common scholarship in perpetuating the institutions of which we are so proud and which have been established by so immense an expenditure of blood and treasure and toil.

I do not forget that I am dealing with that anomalous creature that never had a concrete existence—the average child. Nor do I forget the incalculable value of an educated leadership which will continue to emerge from our higher institutions of learning. But I insist that there is another thing

* Resolution of the Conference of High Schools with the University of Illinois, 1913. *Journal of Proceedngs and Addresses,* National Education Association, 1913, p. 480.

† President John W. Cook, State Normal School, De Kalb, Illinois. *Journal or Proceedings and Addresses,* National Education Association, 1914. pp. 113-15.

that should not be forgotten, and that is the theory of the nature and destiny of man upon which our system of government is broadly grounded. This is not a theory of the average man but of the individual man, and what we are learning about the average man in these startling statistics points to the more startling fact that as there are vast numbers above the average, so there are vaster numbers below the average, because of the small contribution of their limited education. Moreover, these statistics do not seem disposed to change. It is evident that these conditions must change and change radically or we must rely upon some other agency than popular education for the perpetuity of our civilization.

But this is not all that lies on the shadow side of the picture. There are indeed five hundred thousand teachers, which will afford one to every twenty-four of the children that are at school every day. If they were all thoroly skilled in their task, the favored twenty-four would be well cared for during the brief time of their attendance at school. Certainly, since the children are to be there for so short a period, every consideration would seem to demand that the teachers should possess the highest attainable capacity so that no part of this precious fragment of opportunity should run to waste. Conservation of resources is the watchword of our modern industrial life. Save everything that will yield a profitable atom is the essence of our economic theory. The pride of the manufacturer bears an inverse ratio to the size of his scrap-heap. But what of this human scrap-heap and what it suggests of all the other consequent scrap-heaps if the teaching shall lack in effectiveness because of the poor qualifications of the teachers? "As is the teacher so is the school" is as trite as the multiplication table and also as true. If there shall be a negligible scrap-heap at the factory, it will mean that thoroly trained operatives are doing the work. In some way they have learned the technic of their calling. There should not be even a negligible scrap-heap at the school; every worker should be a master of technic in the multiform relations of a teacher to a child. . . .

Turn from the capable artisan to the teacher and what do we find? Society dignifies his occupation by including him within the professional class, a class that is supposed to be differentiated from other workers by a clear consciousness of the scientific principles which determine its procedures. It goes without saying that in every profession there is an art side, possibly an artisan side, but no calling has warrant to be designated as a profession if it lack this regulative scientific knowledge. Teaching is unquestionably an art, but if it is not more then it must be denied the privilege of ranking with the professions. All of us have seen the "natural" teacher with her wonderful "knack," doing wretchedly bad things in a wonderfully skilful way. She was left to her own devices. She learned as the apprentice would learn if he had no master. As he would consign spoiled material to the scrap-heap by his educational blunders, so she will consign precious material to the spiritual scrap-heap as the price of her education.

And what shall we say of our five hundred thousand teachers? I shall certainly be among the last to deny the existence of a class of workers in this vast organization who are as clearly entitled to professional honors as any men and women in the great complex of our civilization. They have reached their eminence by the traditional method of producing a professional class—thru a thorogoing study of the underlying scientific principles and their rational application in practice. Unfortunately the greater part may not thus be regarded. Success has come to them thru a wasteful experience; thru a violation of this principle of conservation that is the battle-cry of the time; thru the sacrifice of the richest resource of any people.

Allowing six years for the average life of a teacher, and the estimate is liberal, more than eighty thousand new teachers annually find employment in the elementary grades of the public schools. The public normal schools graduate some twenty thousand; sixty thousand untrained teachers annually begin to find their way to skill by their experiments with the defenseless children; sixty thousand more have been struggling with their problem for a year; and another sixty thousand are beginning to feel somewhat comfortably at home after an experience of two years, if they have been so favorably conditioned as to be under intelligent supervision. If they have not, the chances are that their latter state is as bad as their first and possibly worse.

The case is clear. The supreme need of the school is a body of carefully trained teachers. To this end the professional schools for their preparation must be multiplied until there shall be a real profession of teaching and no one shall be admitted within its portals who lacks the password.

The Need of Loyalty Oaths for Teachers, 1920 *

Of the three so-called Lusk bills in the Legislature against the Socialists, the Teacher's Loyalty bill has been passed by both houses. It requires public school teachers to obtain from the Board of Regents a certificate of loyalty to the State and Federal Constitutions and the laws and institutions of the United States. Such certification is sorely needed. There has been only too much evidence of the success of the Socialists in imparting their fatal doctrines to young and ductile minds. It is incredible that the State should allow schools or teachers whose teaching is for the express purpose of destroying the State. The danger is not that any loyal teacher will be disqualified, but that disloyal teachers will profess loyalty.

Governor Alfred E. Smith Vetoes Teachers' Oath Bill in New York, 1920 †

The test established is not what the teacher teaches, but what the teacher believes. This bill must be judged by what can be done under its provisions.

* *The New York Times*, April 22, 1920.
† *The New York Times*, May 20, 1920.

It permits one man (the State Commissioner of Education) to place upon any teacher the stigma of disloyalty, and this even without hearing or trial. The bill unjustly discriminates against teachers as a class. It deprives teachers of their right to freedom of thought. It limits the teaching staff of the public schools to those only who lack the courage or the mind to exercise their legal right to just criticism of existing institutions.

Governor Dixon of Montana Vetoes Measure for Loyalty Oath, 1921 *

On the ground that the bill requiring teachers in Montana schools and colleges to take an oath of allegiance to the United States was unconstitutional and would cause a fertile field of "political heresy hunting," Governor Dixon vetoed the measure today.

Governor Franklin D. Roosevelt Warns of Excess Supply of Teachers, 1930 †

. . . It is, perhaps, a tendency of mothers and fathers to think when their daughters start to grow up that the finest thing they can do is to become teachers, that the whole world will be opened up to them that way. But today there are 5,000 women teachers, qualified to teach in the State [New York], out of jobs. That is the other side of the picture. . . .

We must not forget the law of supply and demand in this field also. That is why we must stop and consider before adding anything to the present capacity of our normal schools for turning out new teachers or before building new schools.

This does not mean, of course, that we must stop adding facilities to our present institutions to improve them. . . .

How Much Schooling Did American Teachers Have in 1930-31? ‡

Approximately 1 out of every 20 elementary teachers in the United States in 1930-31 had no schooling beyond the high school. . . . The rural schools had the largest percentage of their teachers in this group, but on

---

* *The New York Times,* February 6, 1921.

† Franklin D. Roosevelt, address on "Supply of Teachers" at Oswego Normal School, *The New York Times,* August 29, 1930. 3:3.

‡ *National Survey of the Education of Teachers,* Vol. VI, Bulletin 1933, No. 10 (Washington, Government Printing Office, 1935), pp. 37-40. This was a three-year study made by funds provided by Congress and the results were published in six volumes. The final volume, "Summary and Interpretations," showed how inadequate in "amount" and "time" was the education of teachers when the data were collected. In 1938 the American Council on Education projected through its Commission on Teacher Education a comprehensive cooperative study on the subject. Eight volumes came out of this effort, six prepared by members of the staff and two by the Commission itself: *Teachers for Our Time,* a statement of the Commission's own views, and *The Improvement of Teacher Education* which summarized the work of the Commission and listed its findings and recommendations. From *The Improvement of Teacher Education,* the Commission's final report, are drawn and given below some of the more significant statements.

the other hand, the cities, and even the largest cities, had 3 or more percent of their teachers with this inexcusably meager preparation—inexcusable because, even though many of them were older teachers who entered teaching 20 or more years ago when standards were lower, they should not have been permitted to remain in teaching during that time without adding to their educational preparation. . . .

One-fifth of the elementary teachers of the United States who had completed high school reported 1 year or less in college as the highest level of their training. . . .

The situation just presented is both unjustifiable and challenging. Something should be done to remedy it, and done immediately. . . .

The answer to the third question concerning the number of teachers who barely meet the minimum standard of educational preparation is that in 1930-31 approximately half of the elementary teachers belonged in that group. About half (46.2 percent) of the elementary teachers had had 2 years' work above high school in a normal school, teachers college, junior college, college, or university. The size of this group affords a basis for encouragement if one looks backward a few years, but the encouragement should disappear when it is realized that nearly three-fourths of our elementary teachers (72.4 percent) had no more than the minimum educational preparation when that minimum was as low as only 2 years above high school. The number of teachers in the 2 years of college-work group may help justify the impression that many persons now teaching took no more pre-service education than was required for admission to teaching. For many of those persons the only sure way to increase their education would be to raise the minimum standard by regulation, since it is unlikely that they will do it voluntarily. . . .

The answer to the fifth question—the number with 1 or more years of graduate work affords little comfort to those who believe that teaching should be comparable with the so-called "learned professions" in the educational equipment of its members or to those who believe that teachers in the elementary schools should be as well educated as the teachers in the high schools. Not 1 in every 200 rural school teachers had done a year's graduate work when the data were collected in 1930-31 and even in the largest cities where competition for placement is keenest and tenure longest only 1 elementary teacher in each 20 reported a year or more of graduate work. To be sure, small as these percentages are, they are better than nothing especially if they show the beginning of a movement toward adequate education of elementary teachers. They are relatively very small when compared with those for high-school teachers in this country or for either elementary or high-school teachers in some European countries. . . .

California's Teachers' Oath, 1931 *

Section 12009. Except as provided in this section, no credential shall be granted to any person unless and until he has subscribed to the following oath or affirmation:

"I solemnly swear (or affirm) that I will support the constitution of the United States of America, the constitution of the State of California, and the laws of the United States and the State of California, and will by precept and example, promote respect for the flag and the statutes of the United States and of the State of California, reverence for law and order, and undivided allegiance to the government of the United States of America."

The oath or affirmation shall be subscribed before any person authorized to administer oaths or before any member of a board of trustees or any board of education of the state and filed with the state board of education. Any person who is a citizen or subject of any country other than the United States, and who is employed in any capacity in any of the public schools of the state shall, before entering upon the discharge of his duties, subscribe to an oath to support the institutions and policies of the United States during the period of his sojourn within the state. Upon the violation of any of the terms of the oath or affirmation, the state board of education shall suspend or revoke the credential which has been issued.

New York's Teachers' Oath, 1934 †

Section 709. After October first, nineteen hundred thirty-four, it shall be unlawful for any citizen of the United States to serve as teacher, instructor or professor in any school or institution in the public school system of the state or in any school, college, university or other educational institution in this state, whose real property or any part of it is exempt from taxation, under section four of the tax law unless and until he or she shall have taken and subscribed the following oath or affirmation:

"I do solemnly swear (or affirm) that I will support the constitution of the United States of America and the constitution of the state of New York, and that I will faithfully discharge, according to the best of my ability, the duties of the position of . . . .
(title of position and name or designation of school, college, university or institution to be here inserted), to which I am now assigned."

The oath required by this section shall be administered by the president

---

* *California Laws,* 1943, chapter 71, section 12009. For an academic "cold war" between the faculties of the University of California and its Regents in 1950, see *The New York Times* for April 9, of that year. Fortunately, the critical issue was finally compromised by a substitute for the drastic oath to which the faculties had so bitterly objected.

† *New York Education Law,* section 709.

or other head of such school, college, university or institution, or by the officer or person, or in the case of a board or body by a member of the board or body, having authority to employ such person as a teacher, instructor or professor in such school, college, university or institution, and each is hereby authorized to administer it. The officer, person or member administering such oath shall cause a record or notation of the fact to be made in the books or records of the school, college, university or institution, and forthwith transmit the oath as taken and subscribed to the commissioner of education, who shall file it in his office, where it shall be subject to public inspection. It shall be unlawful for an officer, person or board having control of the employment, dismissal or suspension of teachers, instructors or professors in such a school, college, university or institution, to permit a person to serve in any such capacity therein in violation of the provisions of this section. This section shall not be construed to require a person to take such oath more than once during the time he or she is employed in the same school, college, university or institution, though there be a change in the title or duties of the position.

The provisions of section thirty of the civil service law shall not apply to a person who is required to take the oath prescribed by this section.

Congress Enacts Legislation for "Loyalty Oath" for Teachers in the District of Columbia, 1935 *

The children of officers and men of the United States Army, Navy, and Marine Corps, and children of other employees of the United States stationed outside the District of Columbia shall be admitted to the public schools without payment of tuition: *Provided,* That hereafter no part of any appropriation for the public schools shall be available for the payment of the salary of any person teaching or advocating Communism.

Some Arguments For and Against Teachers' Oaths, 1935 †

Arguments advocates of teachers' oaths gave:
1. Why shouldn't teachers take an oath? Many public officials are required to do so.
2. Any teacher who would not agree to support the Federal and State Constitutions and laws is unfit to train future citizens.
3. Many educators and teachers are communistic. Oaths of allegiance would exclude communists from public schools.
4. Teachers have great influence in molding public opinion and should be 100% Americans.

* *United States Statutes at Large.* Vol. 49, Part I, p. 356.
† *School Life,* Vol. 20 (June, 1935), p. 234.

5. Teachers should not be permitted to use their positions to promote propaganda or prejudiced views.

Arguments against teachers' oaths:

1. The duties of teaching differ from those of Government officials.
2. Most of the existing patriotism in the United States has been instilled by the great army of teachers, past and present.
3. No proof exists that teachers as a class are disloyal or communistic.
4. Teachers' oaths may become instruments for restricting the freedom of teaching. There is no agreement on what constitutes violation of oaths.
5. School Boards now have adequate authority to deal with any teacher when it is shown that he uses his position to disseminate political propaganda or prejudicial opinions, or for attempts to overthrow the government.
6. Education includes not only a process of imparting truth but also a search for truth as well, and teachers and students should be free to examine the merits and demerits of old and new theories pertaining to political, economic, religious, or natural philosophy.
7. Others who mold public opinion such as politicians, newspapermen, and authors are not subject to an oath of allegiance, and compelling teachers to take oaths singles them out as disloyal.

Teachers' Oath in Massachusetts, 1935 *

Section 30. Oath or Affirmation Required of Certain Professors, Instructors and Teachers. Every citizen of the United States, entering service, on or after October first, nineteen hundred and thirty-five, as professor, instructor or teacher at any college, university, teachers' college, or public or private school, in the commonwealth shall, before entering upon the discharge of his duties, take and subscribe to, before an officer authorized by law to administer oaths, or, in case of a public school teacher, before the superintendent of schools or a member of the school committee of the city or town in whose school he is appointed to serve, each of whom is hereby authorized to administer oaths and affirmations under this section, the following oath or affirmation:

"I do solemnly swear (or affirm) that I will support the Constitution of the United States and the Constitution of the Commonwealth of Massachusetts, and that I will faithfully discharge the duties of the position of (insert name of position) according to the best of my ability."

Such oath or affirmation shall be so taken and subscribed to by him in duplicate. One of such documents shall be filed with such superintendent of schools or principal officer of such college, university or school in the

* *Annotated Laws of Massachusetts,* chapter 71, section 30A.

commonwealth and shall be transmitted by him to the commissioner of education, and the other shall be delivered by the subscriber to the board, institution or person employing him. No professor, instructor or teacher who is a citizen of the United States shall be permitted to enter upon his duties within the commonwealth unless and until such oath or affirmation shall have been so subscribed and one copy thereof so filed and the other so delivered.

Nothing herein contained shall be construed to interfere in any way with the basic principle of the constitution which assures every citizen freedom of thought and speech and the right to advocate changes and improvements in both the state and federal constitutions.

Carl Becker of Cornell University on Loyalty Oaths for Teachers, 1935 *

ITHACA, NEW YORK, December 15

In compliance with the Ives law, an official of Cornell University recently requested me to sign the following statement: "I do solemnly swear (or affirm) that I will support the Constitution of the United States of America and the Constitution of the State of New York, and that I will faithfully discharge, according to the best of my ability, the duties of the position to which I am now assigned."

After reading this statement carefully, I signed it, willingly and without resentment. I always wish to conform to the laws, and in this instance there was no difficulty in doing so, since this law, so far as I could see, neither deprived me of any rights that I formerly had nor imposed upon me any duties not already imposed. There was even a certain advantage in having the statement presented for my signature: it made me think about the obligation of citizens to support the Constitution and the laws. I asked this question: are citizens not obliged to support the Constitution and the laws unless they take an oath to do so? Applying a well-known rule for interpreting legal documents, one might infer that formerly no citizens of New York, except public officials taking such an oath, were so obliged, and that now no citizens except public officials and teachers are so obliged. That was a new and intriguing idea. I had taken it for granted that all citizens are obligated to support the laws; and with the best will in the world I still fail to see what meaning any law can have if it has not the one meaning without which it would not be a law—namely, that all citizens are obligated to conform to its provisions. What, then, does the Ives law mean? So far as I can see, nothing except this: that teachers in New York State are obliged to acknowledge in writing that they are obligated by the obligations imposed upon them by the duties they have assumed, and by the obliga-

---

* "In Support of the Constitution," *The Nation*, Vol. 140 (January 2, 1935), pp. 13-14.

tions imposed upon all citizens by the Constitution of the United States and the Constitution of the State of New York.

Having reached this conclusion, I asked another question: Does the New York Legislature think that a subordinate authority can make an obligation imposed by a superior authority any more obligatory than it already is? The Constitution of the United States, so I have at least been told, is the supreme law of the land. The Constitution of the State of New York is, within limits defined by the Constitution of the United States, the supreme law of New York State. The New York Legislature is a subordinate authority, its jurisdiction being defined by provisions in both constitutions. It has no authority to modify either constitution, nor can it create any rights or duties not explicitly or implicitly authorized by one or the other of the two constitutions. I can make nothing of the Ives law as a legal document except that it is a redundancy, unless it be also an impertinence: by enacting it, the New York Legislature presumes to reimpose obligations already imposed by the supreme law of the land.

All this laborious thinking led me to ask a third question: Have I up to now "supported" the Constitution of the United States and the Constitution of the State of New York, and have I faithfully "discharged" the duties of "the position to which I am assigned"? Taking the first point first (in literary discourse it is well to be systematic), I feel sure that I have always supported the Constitution of the United States, and that I have supported the Constitution of the State of New York during the seventeen years that I have resided in that State. I intend to go on supporting both constitutions, and as a down payment on that promised intention I hereby declare that the Ives law, in my opinion, was unnecessary and unwise: unnecessary, because it imposes on teachers no obligations that did not already exist, except the formal one of signing the statement quoted above; unwise, because the obligation to sign the statement will irritate many teachers all of the time, without making any of them at any time support the constitution more loyally, or discharge their duties more faithfully, than they did before.

In making this explicit statement about the Ives law, I am clearly "discharging" the duties "of the position to which I am now assigned," and I am "supporting" both the Constitution of the United States and the Constitution of the State of New York. To take the second point first (in literary discourse one should aim at variety), both constitutions rest upon the principle that laws should be enacted by representatives freely chosen by the citizens, and that it is not only the right but the duty of citizens to express, either orally or in print, their approval or disapproval of the conduct of their representatives, and of the laws enacted by them. Both constitutions, unless I am mistaken, contain provisions which guarantee citizens against any infringement, by statute or otherwise, of that right. Happily (returning now to the first point), the "duties of the position to which I am now assigned" do not, so far as I can learn, conflict in any way with my obligation to support the Constitution of the United States and the Constitution of the State of New York. I am a teacher of history. The duty of a teacher of history, as I understand it, is to learn, and encourage his pupils to learn, what has actually happened in some period of human history, and to discuss with the utmost freedom before his pupils any opinion, judgment, or theory that may be formed about the cause or the effect or the importance of what has happened. The Ives law is something that has happened, and so far as that law is concerned I can "discharge the duties of the position to which I am assigned" only by declaring that it would have been better, in my opinion, if the Governor and Assembly of New York had prevented it from happening. I have now discharged that duty in writing, and I intend, when ever occasion seems fitting, to discharge it orally.

In closing I wish it clearly understood that this expression of an adverse opinion on the Ives law does not exhaust my capacity to support the Constitution of the United States and the Constitution of the State of New York. I reserve the right, for the future, to support these admirable high authorities by freely expressing my opinion about any social or political question that may arise. If at any time it should seem to me highly desirable to amend or to abolish the Constitution of the United States or the Constitution of New York State, I shall, availing myself of the principle that "all just governments rest upon the consent of the governed," support both constitutions, and at the same time "faithfully discharge the duties of the position to which I am now assigned," saying so. At present I am not in favor of abolishing either constitution, nor have I any amendments to propose to either. In times past there have been people who believed that men could be made wise and good by proper laws and constitutions. I have never been convinced of this, but I am open to conviction. When anyone devises a constitution that will make legislators wise enough to know that people cannot be made loyal to the constitution, or faithful in the discharge of their duties, by passing laws requiring them to be so, I will support that constitution as faithfully and loyally as I am now supporting the Constitution of the United States and the Constitution of the State of New York.

The American Association of University Professors Opposes Loyalty Oaths for Teachers, 1937 *

Whereas loyalty oath laws for teachers are futile in effecting the legitimate aims of such laws, that is an understanding of and loyalty towards American ideals; and whereas these laws can easily be used as an instrument to promote intolerance, restrict our civil liberties and the

* Bulletin of the American Association of University Professors, Vol. 23 (January, 1937), p. 7.

freedom of teaching, and to accentuate propaganda against democratic ideals; and whereas, these laws cast an undeserved aspersion on the integrity and loyalty of the teaching profession. Be it resolved, therefore, that our chapters and all citizens are urged to oppose the enactment of such laws, and to work for their repeal in states where such laws are already on the statute books.

Congress Repeals the Provision Relating to the Teaching or Advocating of Communism, 1937 *

Be it enacted by the Senate and House of Representatives of the United States of America in Congress assembled, That the proviso appearing in the fourteenth paragraph under the subheading "Miscellaneous" under the heading "Public Schools" in the District of Columbia Appropriation Act for the fiscal year ending June 30, 1936, approved June 14, 1935 (49 Stat. 356), and reading as follows: *"Provided,* That hereafter no part of any appropriation for the public schools shall be available for the payment of the salary of any person teaching or advocating communism", is hereby repealed: *Provided, however,* That nothing herein shall be construed as permitting the advocating of communism.

Illness of Teachers Causes the Annual Loss of Two Million School Days, 1938 †

Health is essential to efficiency of the highest attainable level in almost any line of work. It is peculiarly important for teachers, not only because of the strenuous demands of the classroom on their strength and energies but also because teacher health is the cornerstone of any effective school health program. The Ninth Yearbook Committee has made a distinctive contribution, therefore, by analyzing the health problems of teachers and by bringing together an invaluable series of constructive and practical suggestions with respect to the conservation and promotion of teacher health. Few subjects of greater timeliness could have been selected for study by a national committee of classroom teachers than that so ably treated in this volume, *Fit To Teach.*

The health of the teacher is far more than an individual problem, affecting the success and happiness of the person concerned. It is a matter of first importance to the general public because of its direct and indirect influences on the health of children. This study of teacher health, therefore, should find its way not only to the teachers of America but to all those who share responsibility with them for the maintenance of health

---

* *United States Statutes at Large,* Vol. 50, Part I, p. 211.
† *Fit to Teach,* Ninth Yearbook, Department of Classroom Teachers, National Education Association of the United States, 1938. Foreword, and pp. 1, 2.

among teachers. It has a vital message for the leaders of teachers' professional organizations, for those engaged in teacher education, and for school administrators and schoolboard members who must act for their respective communities. . . .

Today, tomorrow, and every *average* school day during the year more than 300,000 pupils will be taught by substitute teachers because their regular teachers are confined at home with personal illness. School work will be seriously interrupted of course, for a substitute teacher, however efficient, seldom can carry on as the regular teacher would do. In many classes regular work will be laid aside until the teacher returns and the children will be given busy work—"just to keep them quiet!" In addition to this serious educational loss, there is an unfortunate economic one. Many of the 12,000 teachers whose places are being filled each day by substitutes will lose either the whole day's wages, or whatever part of that amount must be paid to the substitute teacher. In other cases there will be no personal loss of salary to the teachers who are ill, but the school districts will pay the substitutes. In either event, the sickness is costly, even without including doctor and hospital bills. During one school year some 285,000 teachers are absent one or more days because of illness; they lose time totaling no less than 2,000,000 days.

If ill health among teachers were responsible for nothing more than the absences and losses mentioned above, an urgent need for better teacher health would be obvious. Other unfortunate results, however, scarcely less serious than these—if somewhat less apparent—must be attributed to teachers' illnesses.

Especially significant are the damaging effects of health disorders which lower vitality, reduce efficiency, and cause irritability without keeping teachers away from their classrooms. Health is more than freedom from serious disorders; it is an abundance of life. Health and fitness mean sufficient vitality and power for the excellent performance of the tasks one is doing, or those which may be demanded of him—not simply enough to be acceptable to oneself, but enough to be acceptable to the world. Because of this fact, the most careful self-appraisal is warranted.

Have *you* as much of health, of fitness, as you can get and maintain by intelligent, conscientious effort? If not, you are wasteful of opportunity and spendthrift in the use, or neglect, of resources of superlative value to you and to society. Many of the conditions which lower the health and fitness of teachers are beyond their powers of personal control. Yet the gain in fitness and morale within the control of the teachers themselves, would, if demonstrated, make an astounding showing. An impressive majority of teachers are living well below the level of health and fitness attainable by them. Where do *you* stand? Are you one of the nation's truly fit teachers? Perhaps—but the chances are several to one that you are missing a real margin of possible success and satisfaction because you are not living nearer to the peak of your own optimum health level.

Physical fitness is not everything. It is not the main goal of life or of education. It is not always immediately essential to that which is finest in mind, personality, and character. Some of the great men and women of history have accomplished deeds of immortal distinction in spite of pain and physical disability. However, nothing in such lives can be interpreted in defense or praise of weakness, or unfitness. It must be conceded that fitness of health is fundamental for completeness and the best of life.

The situation which has been described should not be taken to mean that teachers are subject to an unusual number of health disorders. On the contrary, they are absent from duty less often because of illness than is true of workers in most other occupations and professions. Neither is there any evidence that teachers, more than others, fail to attain fully their own best health possibilities. This favorable comparison with other groups, however, does not in any way lessen the need for better teacher health.

Improvement of teacher health is a problem that requires both a positive and a negative approach. Any sound program of teacher health must be concerned with (1) conserving and developing more fully the good health which teachers enjoy, and (2) reducing the amount of ill health among teachers. It is with this dual program that the present volume deals. Clearer understanding of the specific problems involved and of the essential point of view maintained thruout this volume should come from a brief consideration of the meaning of the term "health."

Abraham Flexner on the Importance of Humor in Teachers and Teaching, 1938 *

As a matter of principle I have long since made it a rule not to write forewords, for having once made an exception it may become extremely embarrassing subsequently to decline. Though the risks are great I cannot resist the temptation to say a word that may disarm hostility to and arouse interest in Professor Simon's book entitled *Preface to Teaching.*

Books on teaching are proverbially dull. They are usually written without spirit and in a jargon which my late chief, Dr. Wallace Buttrick, President of the General Education Board, was in the habit of calling "pedigese." Professor Simon's book is not dull—it is, in fact, decidedly interesting, and it is written in English—excellent English—clear, non-technical, vigorous, and understandable. Moreover, his views upon the function and scope of teaching are so sane that every effort should be made to disseminate them, not only through the teaching profession but through Parents' and Teachers' Associations, which have an important interest in

* In Foreword to Henry Simon's *Preface to Teaching* (New York, Oxford University Press, 1938). Used by permission.

what happens in schools. Professor Simon is a teacher—a born teacher—and he is a master of the art of discussing his task and his experience.

In recent years professors of education have frequently taken themselves far too seriously. Aware of the fact that the world is changing—by the way, it has always been changing—they have assumed that, having in charge the younger generation, it is their business to change the world according to their conception of what it should be. Though I cannot pretend to an exhaustive knowledge of recent educational literature, Professor Simon represents a quite different standpoint. He recognizes frankly that the schools are of this world and that, though within a limited range they can do something to mould character and instil ideas, the outlook of children will nevertheless be mainly determined by the families to which they belong and the companions with whom they associate, not to mention a thousand other factors, the influence of which may or may not be considerable.

In addition to a sound view of the scope of the school and the potentialities of the teacher Professor Simon is equally sensible in suggestions which he makes to the teacher himself or herself regarding the conduct of his or her classics. Nothing could be better than his discussion of such terrifying problems, in so far as the new teacher is concerned, as interest and discipline about both of which much nonsense has been written and more nonsense has been practised.

His book can therefore be commended to all those who naturally shrink from orthodox educational literature, and it should also be pressed upon the attention of those who wallow in this literature under the impression that the more unintelligible an educational discussion is, the more scientific it becomes.

I have but one major point of difference with Professor Simon. I read his book rapidly and of course I may be mistaken, but I cannot recall that the word "humour" occurs in its pages. If it does, it is certainly insufficiently stressed. As one who has been a teacher and interested in teaching for more years than I care to confess even to myself, I should say that, while Professor Simon is correct in the emphasis which he places upon knowledge of subject matter, the importance of humour in the conduct of a class or of an educational institution comes very close to the importance of knowing what one is trying to teach. Teachers are apt to fall into grooves. They lead very regular, very systematic, and very long lives. They tend, therefore, quite unconsciously, to aridity. A school principal endowed with a lively sense of humour, even to the point of practical joking, is a blessing in any school, as indeed he is in any educational institution. He keeps teachers human, alive; and nothing goes so far towards preserving a modest view as to what they can hope to accomplish as a lively sense of humour which permeates the whole institution. Within the classroom humour is of even greater importance. Most subjects are inherently dull to most pupils. The interest of most pupils can very rarely be secured for fundamental subjects such as spelling, arithmetic, algebra, in themselves, and it is even easy to squeeze all possible interest out of inherently interesting subjects like history, literature, science; but pupils are, with all their shrewdness, in some respects unsuspecting beings, and a teacher who is endowed with a sense of humour, even to the point of practical joking at irregular intervals, can often keep his class so keen and alive that the members think they are interested in the subject and act as though they are, when, as a matter of fact, they are really only fond of their teacher and his sprightly ways. Of course, there are teachers who are devoid of a sense of humour and who would be grotesque figures if they endeavoured to simulate it. In these cases I should advise that they take to another vocation.

When Professor Simon's second edition appears, as it undoubtedly will, I hope he will supply an explicit and elaborate statement regarding the part that humour can play in teaching, for humour makes the life of the teacher tolerable and sugarcoats many an unpleasant dose that has to be swallowed by the pupil.

"Leading Issues and Promising Trends" in Teacher Education, 1946 *

The leading issues in teacher education have been repeatedly dealt with in this and other reports of and to the Commission. In those same volumes there have been repeatedly set forth the conclusions of the Commission and of its staff respecting directions of movement likely to lead to improvement. It seems proper, however, in drawing this final statement to a close to sum up briefly with respect to these matters. The purpose will be to suggest points at which continuing attacks should be aimed, and reforms that in the Commission's opinion deserve particular emphasis.

THE CONDITIONS OF TEACHING

It must be observed at the outset that the improvement of teacher education depends fundamentally upon an increase in the attractiveness of the teaching profession. The ablest young people cannot be recruited to teaching—or if they are persuaded to prepare for the profession, will not enter and remain in it—unless the conditions surrounding their work are satisfying. Moreover, unless this is the case teachers on the job will not be able or encouraged to make the most of their powers, or likely to behave in such fashion as steadily to increase their competence.

Salaries are, of course, of basic importance. The worth apparently placed on teaching by the American people (the *average* salary they provided for

---

* *The Improvement of Teacher Education,* final report of the Commission on Teacher Education (Washington, American Council on Education, 1946), pp. 262-67. Used by permission of the American Council on Education.

classroom teachers, supervisors, and principals in 1944-45 was less than $1,800) does small credit to their presumable regard for the welfare of their children and of their society. Salaries must be increased. And since many states are financially unable to raise teachers' salary to respectable levels through their own efforts alone, federal aid to education is indispensable.

Occupational security is another matter to which much more attention must be given. Too many promising prospects have been kept from entering upon teaching, and too many promising teachers have been prevented from realizing their full potentialities, by the insecurities that frequently beset the profession. Competent teachers must be assured of tenure. Arrangements with respect to sickness and the like must be at least as enlightened as those provided for industrial workers. And pension systems, or comparable guarantees of income after retirement, must be further instituted.

The right to live a normal life must be granted to teachers, Too many communities make unreasonable demands on members of the profession so far as their out-of-school hours and private lives are concerned. It is justifiable to expect that teachers should be good specimens of the culture, and it is desirable that they should play the part of good citizens in the general life of the community. But to insist upon a hypocritical simulation of a standard that the lay community itself does not live up to is a destructive procedure. Such a practice can only breed rebellion and reduce teaching effectiveness. It is equally indefensible to forbid teaching by married women including mothers. This not only represents a discrimination that has lost any sanction in other feminine occupations, but it excludes from the schools women with a type of experience that is likely to enhance their competence.

Democratic administrative leadership greatly increases the satisfactions felt by teachers, enables them to work up to the limits of their existing abilities, and encourages them to engage in activities that result in professional growth. The best preparation in the world will not produce a teacher who can do a good job in an atmosphere of suspicion, disdain, or tyranny. The Commission's experience has demonstrated how favorable administrative attitudes and practices make for the improvement of teaching in service.

An in-service program of teacher education, centered in the school system, can further enhance the satisfactions of teachers and consequently the attractions of the profession. Teachers like other human beings enjoy learning to do a better job. When they are helped to do so by methods such as those described in this and other Commission-sponsored reports they appreciate the values of the experience.

RECRUITMENT AND SELECTION OF TEACHERS

There can be no doubt that many young men and women capable of becoming superior teachers never even consider entering the profession. This is partly because its rewards are never sufficiently called to their attention, partly because they cannot afford the preparation required. It is also regrettably true that no small number of individuals are permitted to complete preparation for teaching, and subsequently to become teachers, who are not adequately suited to the work. It is important that steps be taken to correct these situations.

Recruitment is a responsibility that should be shared by the faculties of both high schools and colleges, and that may receive helpful support from state departments of education. The basic approach should be through developing firstrate programs of general vocational guidance. The task of helping young people to select a life work wisely is one that educational institutions should take very seriously. The ultimate responsibility of choice should be reserved to the individual, and he should be encouraged and helped to weigh alternatives. But if the advantages of the teaching profession—its social worth and personal satisfactions—are adequately set forth there can be little doubt that more able persons will be attracted to it.

Colleges that prepare teachers have an opportunity not only to help high school students understand what becoming and being a teacher means, but they are also ordinarily in a position to engage in effective recruitment on their own campuses. Incidentally it should be recognized that individual faculty members often exercise a negative influence, so far as recruitment for teaching is concerned, by reason of their prejudice against work in the schools and sometimes against colleages who specialize in teacher preparation. Finding ways to bring such persons into closer contact with school situations and school people, and to gain their participation in local planning for the improvement of teacher education, has been found helpful in desirably modifying their attitudes.

More financial aid for firstrate students who are eager to become teachers is undoubtedly needed. The fully attested fact that as many able young Americans never go to college as do so is disturbing evidence that our educational system falls far short of serving the public weal to the degree it ought. Measures designed to provide equal educational opportunity regardless of occupational intention are demanded by American ideals. The introduction of such measures is no doubt likely to come piecemeal in relation to particular social needs. The shortage of young scientists and the prestige of science resulting from the war have given rise to a strong demand that special provision be made to facilitate college training in this field. But in the world that science has been shaping, better education for all citizens through the public schools has certainly become a primary need. The provision of such education requires better teachers, better prepared. Society cannot afford not to provide the means whereby these teachers may be produced.

Selection must, of course, be made from among those who propose to become teachers: all such cannot be presumed to possess adequate ability and promise. During the war the critical shortage of teachers inevitably resulted in a relaxation of selective procedures. But conditions now developing promise to become favorable to a resumption of efforts along these lines. Institutions where teachers are prepared ought, consequently, to renew their efforts to develop effective techniques of selection and to apply them with increasing vigor. Selection should normally be a continuous process, cumulating evidence being used as a basis for periodical reconsideration of earlier decisions. Furthermore, the students themselves should be given some responsibility in the selective process; they should be helped to interpret the evidence bearing upon the question of their suitability for the teaching profession; and joint rather than unilateral decisions should be sought.

PREPARATORY PROGRAMS

Reform of programs for the pre-service education of teachers requires continuous attention. The Commission knows of no program now existing that could be considered wholly satisfactory. It assumes that none ever will exist. In other words, it believes that as certain problems in teacher education are for the time being satisfactorily solved, others take their place. For teacher education is a dynamic business. The needs of children and society, the needs of the schools, change. Hence the demands on teacher preparation change. Meantime the institutions where preparation takes place, the persons responsible for guiding that preparation, and the knowledge and beliefs by which they themselves are guided, change as well. . . .

Average Annual Salaries of Teachers, Principals and Other
Instructional Personnel in Public Elementary and
Secondary Schools, 1948 *

Rank	State	Average Salary	Rank	State	Average Salary
1	California	$3690	24	Colorado	$2540
2	New York	3476	25	Minnesota	2482
3	Washington	3325	26	West Virginia	2364
4	Maryland	3321	27	New Hampshire	2355
5	Connecticut	3249	28	Oklahoma	2277
6	Arizona	3136	29	Idaho	2239
7	Rhode Island	3105	30	Louisiana	2236
8	Massachusetts	3103	31	Kansas	2191
9	New Jersey	3102	32	Wyoming	2187
10	Indiana	3073	33	North Carolina	2114
11	Michigan	3020	34	Missouri	2099
12	Illinois	3016	35	Iowa	2088
13	Nevada	2988	36	Vermont	2066
14	Utah	2968	37	Virginia	2062
15	Oregon	2941	38	Alabama	1957
16	Ohio	2847	39	Nebraska	1919
17	New Mexico	2741	40	Tennessee	1901
18	Delaware	2642	41	Kentucky	1884
19	Florida	2641	42	South Dakota	1883
			43	Maine	1767
National Average		$2639	44	South Carolina	1742
			45	Georgia	1724
			46	North Dakota	1665
20	Pennsylvania	$2597	47	Arkansas	1545
21	Texas	2585	48	Mississippi	1256
22	Montana	2582			
23	Wisconsin	2560			

New York Requires Loyalty Oath for Teachers, 1949 †

*The People of the State of New York, represented in Senate
and Assembly, do enact as follows:*

Section 1. The legislature hereby finds and declares that there is common report that members of subversive groups, and particularly of the
communist party and certain of its affiliated organizations, have infiltrated
into public employment in the public schools of the state. This has occurred
and continues despite the existence of statutes designed to prevent the
appointment to or the retention in employment in public office and particularly in the public schools of the state of members of any organization
which teaches or advocates that the government of the United States or
of any state or of any political subdivision thereof shall be overthrown by

---

* *NEA Journal,* March, 1950, p. 174. Comparable figures on salaries as other educational
statistics for the country at large are generally out of date before the data can be assembled
and verified. The *NEA Journal* said in March of 1950 that the average salary of teachers
in the United States "should within a generation reach at least $5,000."

† *Laws of New York,* 1949, chapter 360. This was declared unconstitutional in November,
1949.

force or violence or by any unlawful means. The consequence of any such infiltration into the public schools is that subversive propaganda can be disseminated among children of tender years by those who teach them and to whom the children look for guidance, authority and leadership. The legislature finds that members of such groups frequently use their office or position to advocate and teach subversive doctrines. The legislature finds that members of such groups are frequently bound by oath, agreement, pledge or understanding to follow, advocate and teach a prescribed party line or group dogma or doctrine without regard to truth or free inquiry. The legislature finds that such dissemination of propaganda may be and frequently is sufficiently subtle to escape detection in the classroom. It is difficult, therefore, to measure the menace of such infiltration in the schools by conduct in the classroom. The legislature further finds and declares that in order to protect the children in our state from such subversive influence it is essential that the laws prohibiting persons who are members of subversive groups, such as the communist party and its affiliated organizations, from obtaining or retaining employment in the public schools, be rigorously enforced. The legislature deplores the failure heretofore to prevent such infiltration which threatens dangerously to become a commonplace in our schools. To this end, the board of regents, which is charged primarily with the responsibility of supervising the public school systems in the state, should be admonished and directed to take affirmative action to meet this grave menace and to report thereon regularly to the state legislature. . . .

1. The board of regents shall adopt, promulgate, and enforce rules and regulations for the disqualification or removal of superintendents of schools, teachers or employees in the public schools in any city or school district of the state who violate the provisions of section three thousand twenty-one of this article or who are ineligible for appointment to or retention in any office or position in such public schools on any of the grounds set forth in section twelve-a of the civil service law and shall provide therein appropriate methods and procedure for the enforcement of such sections of this article and the civil service law.

2. The board of regents shall, after inquiry, and after such notice and hearing as may be appropriate, make a listing of organizations which it finds to be subversive in that they advocate, advise, teach or embrace the doctrine that the government of the United States or of any state or of any political subdivision thereof shall be overthrown or overturned by force, violence or any unlawful means, or that they advocate, advise, teach or embrace the duty, necessity or propriety of adopting any such doctrine, as set forth in section twelve-a of the civil service law. Such listings may be amended and revised from time to time. The board, in making such inquiry, may utilize any similar listings or designations promulgated by any federal agency or authority authorized by federal law, regulation or

executive order, and for the purposes of such inquiry, the board may request and receive from such federal agencies or authorities any supporting material or evidence that may be made available to it. The board of regents shall provide in the rules and regulations required by subdivision one hereof that membership in any such organization included in such listing made by it shall constitute prima facie evidence of disqualification for appointment to or retention in any office or position in the public schools of the state.

3. The board of regents shall annually, on or before the fifteenth day of February, by separate report, render to the legislature, a full statement of measures taken by it for the enforcement of such provisions of law and to require compliance therewith. Such reports shall contain a description of surveys made by the board of regents, from time to time, as may be appropriate, to ascertain the extent to which such provisions of law have been enforced in the city and school districts of the state. . . .

The University of California Requires Loyalty Oath of Its Faculty, 1949 *

I do not believe in and am not a member of, nor do I support any party or organization that believes in, advocates or teaches the overthrow of the United States government by force or by any illegal, unconstitutional methods.

The National Education Association Opposes Members of the Communist Party as Teachers in American Schools, 1949 †

The National Education Association affirms that the foundations of our American system of government are built in our free public schools. The Association strongly asserts that all schools have an obligation to teach the rights, privileges, and the responsibilities of living in a democracy.

The responsibility of the schools is to teach the superiority of the American way of life, founded as it is on the dignity and worth of the individual; therefore, our youth should know it, believe in it, and live it continuously.

* Associated Press dispatch from Berkeley, California, June 12, 1949. "We don't like the idea of oaths; nobody does," Dr. George Pettitt, assistant to President R. G. Sproul, was quoted as saying. "But in the face of the 'cold war hysteria' we now are experiencing, something had to be done." A half dozen or more members of the faculty, who opposed a bill earlier introduced into the Legislature of California requiring a teachers' oath, were quoted as saying: "It is a confession of little faith to argue that after 150 years of existence American institutions now can be preserved only by resort to suppression and persecution." In the early part of 1950 the issue over the oath became very acute in the faculties of this institution, President R. G. Sproul himself dissenting from the action of the Board of Regents to require the taking of the oath. As noted above, the controversy was finally compromised.

† *Report of the Committee on Resolutions of the Representative Assembly of the National Education Association of the United States*, Boston, July 8, 1949. The American Association of School Administrators at its meeting in February of 1950 resolved against loyalty oaths for teachers and against employing Communists as teachers in the schools.

As a measure of defense against our most potent threat, American schools should teach about communism and all forms of totalitarianism, including the principles and practices of the Soviet Union and the Communist Party in the United States. Teaching about communism does not mean advocacy of communism. Such advocacy should not be permitted in American schools.

Members of the Communist Party shall not be employed in the American schools. Such membership involves adherence to doctrines and discipline completely inconsistent with the principles of freedom on which American education depends. Such membership and the accompanying surrender of intellectual integrity render an individual unfit to discharge the duties of a teacher in this country.

At the same time we condemn the careless, incorrect, and unjust use of such words as "Red" and "Communist" to attack teachers and other persons who in point of fact are not Communists, but who merely have views different from those of their accusers. The whole spirit of free American education will be subverted unless teachers are free to think for themselves. It is because members of the Communist Party are required to surrender this right, as a consequence of becoming part of a movement characterized by conspiracy and calculated deceit, that they shall be excluded from employment as teachers and from membership in the National Education Association.

The Association charges the teaching profession with the obligation of providing the best defense of democracy through full participation in making democracy really live and work.

The National Education Association Resolves on Professional Standards for Teachers, 1949 *

a. The minimum educational qualifications for all teachers shall be a bachelor's degree with an inservice educational requirement for additional work toward a master's degree or its equivalent.

b. Minimum salaries with adequate annual increments shall be established which recognize the services and responsibilities of the teacher and compensate for thorough professional education, inservice growth, and years of experience. It is recommended that only evidence of professional education and successful experience shall be used for the determination of salaries.

c. Teacher-education programs shall be developed that meet high minimum standards that are acceptable in all states.

d. Certification standards shall be raised and reciprocal certification between states shall be established. Emergency certificates shall be eliminated.

e. Existing retirement systems shall be strengthened for all whom they

* Resolution of the Representative Assembly of the N.E.A., July 8, 1949.

serve by extending benefits on a sound actuarial statewide basis with reciprocity among states; such systems shall be developed in all areas where they do not already exist. All school-district employees shall continue to be omitted from Federal social security.

Phi Beta Kappa on Freedom of Teaching, 1949 *

As a Society committed since 1776 to the promotion of liberal studies and the ideal of freedom in education, Phi Beta Kappa is firmly opposed to efforts, from either the extreme right or the extreme left, to restrict within our institutions of learning the impartial analysis and evaluations of any and all literary, political, economic, social or religious tenets.

The never-ending search for truth by the open and inquiring mind is a basic necessity for the survival of the democratic way of life. To the fundamental concepts of our democratic tradition, including the freedom to teach or publish the results of honest and competent inquiry, the overwhelming majority of college teachers are deeply devoted. To impose upon them loyalty tests not required of other professions, or for outside non-professional bodies to investigate their professional competence or integrity, affects adversely the morale of both college teachers and their students. In institutions where such practices obtain, teachers are being intimidated and students are being led to believe that colleges dare no longer engage in the disinterested pursuit of truth, but must become instruments of propaganda. Phi Beta Kappa is bound to be concerned whenever conditions prevail in our schools and colleges which threaten in such ways the American principle of freedom of teaching.

The Committee on Qualifications is required by the Society's constitution to inform itself regarding the status and practices of institutions sheltering chapters of Phi Beta Kappa which may jeopardize the Society's ideals and to report such practices to the Society for appropriate action.

The Committee feels that at this time it is especially important to call upon all the institutions with which its chapters are associated to withstand the emotional pressure, from whatever quarter, to substitute dogma for critical analysis.

The American Association of School Administrators Oppose Loyalty Oaths for Teachers and Communists as Teachers, 1950 †

We oppose state laws requiring special oaths for teachers.

We believe that members of the Communist party of the United States should not be employed as teachers.

* *The Key Reporter*, XIV, No. 4 (Autumn, 1949), p. 1.
† Resolutions of the Association in Atlantic City, 1950.

« VII »

SOME EDUCATIONAL PRACTICES

«««««« ««««««««««««««««««««««««««««««<>»»»»»»»»»»»»»»»»»»»»»»»»»»»

Documents illustrative of the general character of American education in the early days appear in earlier chapters, especially "The Colonial Climate" and "Teachers and Teaching." There it may be observed that a very prominent characteristic of education in the early days was the domination of religious purpose. Apparently in elementary and secondary education this was the chief purpose, which was present also in philanthropic activities and to some extent even in apprenticeship practices. Another striking characteristic until toward the end of the nineteenth century was localism in educational administration and support which had led to the random establishment of schools. Collegiate practices ran to a somewhat fixed pattern in the institutions that were founded before the Revolutionary War and even later. Collegiate rules were generally harsh and wore the color of Calvinism. Theology was the center of intellectual gravity and educational discipline was severe. Materials of education—elementary, secondary, and higher—continued meager until far after 1860 and methods of teaching were generally wasteful, when measured by modern standards. Until far into the nineteenth century education was looked upon as a function of the family and the church and not of the state. Then as now educational practices strongly proved the principle in social history that education reflects life outside the schools. Schoolhouses were as crude, equipment was as meager, and teachers were as poorly prepared, respected, and rewarded as the standards of the time required.

Boston Requests the Selectmen to Recommend "Suitable Persons" for Masters in "The Grammar School at ye North," 1712 *

The Sel. man pursurant to the Town vote and the directions in the Law have advised abt a Master for the Grammar School at ye North, and Accordingly have Treated with Mr Recompense Wadsworth as judging him to be a Suitable person for that Service, and do accordingly Recommend him to the Town, and do propose that Sixty pounds p. annum be allowed him for ye Sd Service.

The Ministers of Boston Are Consulted About a Master for the North Grammar School, 1718 †

Whereas the Revd Ministers of this Town have already (most of them) Signified under their hands, their approbation of the Select mens choyce of mr Thoms. Robie to Succeed as master of the North Grammar School.

Voted. That the Town Clerk be directed in the Name of the Sel. men by the first opportunity to Give the Sd Mr Robie an Invitation to under take that charge as master of the Sd School, and to desire him (as soon as may be) to Signify to them his Mind and Inclination Relating thereto.

Rowland Jones, Schoolmaster in Pennsylvania, Gives an Account of His Method of Teaching, 1730 ‡

SIR, you required an account of my method of instruction in school. I endeavor, for beginners, to get Primers with syllables, viz., from one to 2, 3, 4, 5, 6, 7 or 8. I take them several times over them till they are perfect, by way of repeating according as I find occasion, and then to some place forward according to their capacity and commonly every two or three leaves. I make them repeat perhaps two or three times over, and when they get the Primer pretty well I serve them so in the Psalter, and we have some Psalters with the proverbs at the latter end. I give them that to learn, the which I take to be very agreeable, and still follow repetitions till

---

* *Records of the Town of Boston,* XI 178 (February 12, 1712), p. 178. Given in Robert F. Seybolt, *The Public Schools of Colonial Boston, 1635-1775* (Cambridge, Harvard University Press, 1935), p. 29.

† *Records of the Town of Boston,* XIII (February 10, 1718/19), p. 49. Given in Seybolt, *op. cit.,* p. 30.

‡ Given in J. P. Wickersham, *A History of Education in Pennsylvania* (Lancaster, Inquirer Publishing Co., 1886), p. 214.

I find they are masters of such places. Then I move them into such places as I judge they are fit for, either in the New or Old Testament, and as I find they advance I move them not regarding the beginning nor ending of the Bible, but moving them where I think they may have benefit by. So making of them perfect in the vowels, consonants and dipthongs, and when they go on in their reading clean without any noising, singing or stumbling, with deliberate way, then I set them to begin the Bible in order to go throughout. And when I begin writing I follow them in the letters till they come to cut pretty clean letters and then one syllable and so to 2, 3, 4, and to the longest words, and when they join handsomely I give them some sweet pleasing verses, some perhaps on their business, some on behaviour, and some on their duty to parents, etc., of such I seldom want them to command, and when they come to manage double copies readily I give them some delightful sentences or Proverbs or some places in the Psalms or any part of the Bible as they are of forwardness and also to other fancies that may be for their benefit. And when I set them cyphering I keep them to my old fancy of repeating and shall go over every rule till they are in a case to move forward and so on. And I find no way that goes beyond that of repeating both in spelling, reading, writing and cyphering, and several gentlemen, viz., Ministers and others have commended it and some schoolmasters take to it, and though I speak it I have met with no children of the standing or time of mine, could come up with them on all accounts or hardly upon any; I also give them tasks, when able, to learn out of books according to their ability, but one girl exceeded all. She had a great many parts in the Bible by heart and had the whole book of St. John and hardly would miss a word. I put them to spell twice a week and likewise to Catechism, and likewise I catechise every Saturday and often on Thursdays. Sometimes I set them to sing Psalms.

Curriculum Is Announced for Franklin's Academy of Philadelphia, 1750 *

NOTICE is hereby given, That the Trustees of the ACADEMY of Philadelphia, intend (God willing) to open the same on the first Monday of January next; wherein Youth will be taught the Latin, Greek, English, French, and German Languages, together with History, Geography, Chronology, Logic, and Rhetoric; also Writing, Arithmetic, Merchants Accounts, Geometry, Algebra, Surveying, Gauging, Navigation, Astronomy, Drawing in Perspective, and other mathematical Sciences; with natural and mechanical Philosophy, &c. agreeable to the Constitutions heretofore published, at the Rate of Four Pounds per annum, and Twenty Shillings entrance.

* *Pennsylvania Gazette,* December 18, 1750. Given in Seybolt, *op. cit.,* pp. 98, 99.

The Selectmen of Boston Induct a Master of the North Writing School, 1761 *

On Wednesday the 2d. of this Inst. April The Selectmen in Body visited the North Writing School, and introduced Mr. John Tileston as Master of that School. Their Chairman Mr. Cushing in the Name of the whole, inculcated upon the new Master, not only the common and more ordinary dutys of a good Schoolmaster, but also recommended to him such a conduct and behaviour, as the peculiar Circumstances of his School more especially demanded, and having expressed their hopes that the Just expectation of the Town from his appointment would be answer'd. The Chairman then addressed the Scholars, exhorting them to behave with all duty and Respect to their new Master—to improve with diligence and chearfulness, the happy advantages they were under for gaining usefull knowledge; and above all to avoid and shun those Vices and follys which the Youth of the present Day are too prone to indulge themselves in, and to cultivate and practice those Virtues, upon which not only their own happiness, but the future prosperity of the Community so greatly depended.

An Account of School Life at Phillips Andover Academy, 1780 †

School begins at eight o'clock with devotional exercises; a psalm is read and sung. Then a class consisting of four scholars repeat memoriter two pages in Greek Grammar, after which a class of thirty persons repeats a page and a half of Latin Grammar; then follows the "Accidence tribe," ‡ who repeat two, three, four, five and ten pages each. To this may be added three who are studying arithmetic; one is in the Rule of Three, another in Fellowship, and the third is in Practice. School is closed at night by reading Dr. Doddridge's Family Expositor, accompanied by rehearsals, questions, remarks and reflections, and by the singing of a hymn and a prayer.

---

* *Records of the Town of Boston*, XIX (April 15, 1761), p. 145. Given in Seybolt, *op. cit.*, p. 31.

† A letter from the first principal, Eliphalet Pearson, to the trustees in 1780. Given in M. E. Brown and H. G. Brown, *The Story of John Adams, A New England Schoolmaster* (New York, Charles Scribner's Sons, 1900), pp. 47, 48.

‡ This refers to one of the oldest school books of New England. "Cheever's Accidence," or "A Short Introduction to the Latin Tongue," was written by Master Ezekiel Cheever of New Haven, and eighteen editions appeared before the Revolution. Cheever was born in London in 1614, came to Boston in the 1630's, and taught in grammar schools in New Haven, Ipswich and Charlestown, Massachusetts. In 1670 he became master of the Boston Latin School where he taught for nearly forty years. The first known edition of his celebrated *Accidence* was published in Boston in 1709. Upon his death Reverend Cotton Mather, one of Cheever's pupils, wrote:
"He died on Saturday morning, August 27, 1708, in the ninety-fourth year of his age; after he had been a skillful, painful schoolmaster for seventy years; and had the singular favour of Heaven, that though he had usefully spent his life among children, yet he had not become twice a child; but held his abilities, with his usefulness, in an unusual degree to the very last."

On Monday the scholars recite what they can remember of the sermons heard on the Lord's Day previous; on Saturday the bills are presented and punishments administered.

Jedidiah Morse, Pioneer American Geographer, on Imperfections in Geographies Dealing with America, 1789 *

So imperfect are all the accounts of America hitherto published, even by those who once exclusively professed the best means of information, that from them very little knowledge of this country can be acquired. Europeans have been the sole writers of American Geography, and have too often suffered fancy to supply the place of facts, and thus have led their readers into errors, while they professed to aim at removing their ignorance. But since the United States have become an independent nation, and have risen into Empire, it would be reproachful for them to suffer this ignorance to continue; and the rest of the world have a right now to expect authentic information. To furnish this has been the design of the author of the following work; but he does not pretend that this design is completed, nor will the judicious and candid expect it, when they consider that he has trodden, comparatively, an unbeaten path—that he has had to collect a vast variety of materials—that these have been widely scattered—and that he could derive but little assistance from books already published. Four years have been employed in this work, during which period, the Author has visited the several states in the Union, and maintained an extensive correspondence with men of Science; and in every instance has endeavored to derive his information from the most authentic sources; he has also submitted his manuscripts to the inspection of Gentlemen in the states which they particularly described, for their correction. It is possible, notwithstanding, and indeed very probable, that inaccuracies may have crept in; but he hopes there are none of any great importance, and that such as may be observed, will not be made the subject of severe censure,

* Preface to *The American Geography; or, a View of the Present State of All the Empires, Kingdoms, States, and Republics of the Known World, and of the United States of America in Particular* second edition (London, Printed for John Stockdale, Piccadilly, 1792). An Englishman, by name Winterbotham, wrote or compiled a geography while serving a sentence in Newgate on political charges and in doing so "lifted" verbatim much of Morse's book. Winterbotham's book was reprinted in New York. Morse refused to ignore the offense and brought suit under the copyright law enacted by Congress in 1790, largely as the result of the energetic efforts of Noah Webster, "father" of copyright in this country. Prior to national legislation authors lacked adequate legal protection from literary pirates except the little afforded by state legislation. In his action against Winterbotham, Morse had Alexander Hamilton and James Kent, afterwards Chancellor of New York. The case, decided in April, 1798, to the full satisfaction of Morse, was one of the earliest involving copyright in this country and came to be recognized as a precedent. Hamilton wrote Morse from New York January, 1795: "You will confer a favour upon me to allow me to render you a little service which may be in my power on the present occasion, and without compensation. Be assured it will give me real pleasure, and let that be my recompense. Mr. Kent and I have conferred on your affair. It is necessary for us to see the book in question, in order to a safe opinion. . . ."

but ascribed to some pardonable cause. He flatters himself, however, that the work now offered to the public, will be found to be as accurate, complete and impartial as the present state of American Geography and History could furnish. After all, like the Nation of which it treats, it is but an infant, and as such solicits the fostering care of the country it describes; it will grow and improve as the nation advances towards maturity, and the Author will gratefully acknowledge every friendly communication which will tend to make it perfect.

In the prosecution of the work, he has aimed at utility rather than originality, and of course, when he has met with publications suited to his purpose, he has made a free use of them; and he thinks it proper here to observe, that, to avoid unnecessary trouble, he has frequently used the words as well as the ideas of the writers, although the reader has not been particularly apprized of it. . . .

Dr. Benjamin Rush on Proper Amusements and Punishments for Schools, 1790 *

. . . I would propose that the amusements of our youth, at school, should consist of such exercises as will be most subservient to their future employments in life. These are: 1. agriculture; 2. mechanical occupations; and 3. the business of the learned professions.

I. There is a variety in the employments of agriculture which may readily be suited to the genius, taste, and strength of young people. An experiment has been made of the efficacy of these employments, as amusements, in the Methodist College of Abington, in Maryland; and, I have been informed, with the happiest effects. A large lot is divided between the scholars, and premiums are adjudged to those of them who produce the most vegetables from their grounds, or who keep them in the best order.

II. As the employments of agriculture cannot afford amusement at all seasons of the year, or in cities I would propose, that children should be allured to seek amusements in such of the mechanical arts as are suited to their strength and capacities. Where is the boy who does not delight in the use of a hammer—a chisel—or a saw? and who has not enjoyed a high degree of pleasure in his youth, in constructing a miniature house?

III. To train the youth who are intended for the learned profession or for merchandize, to the duties of their future employments, by means of useful amusements, which are *related* to those employments, will be impracticable; but their amusements may be derived from cultivating a spot of ground; for where is the lawyer, the physician, the divine, or the merchant, who has not indulged or felt a passion, in some part of his life, for rural improvements?—Indeed I conceive the seeds of knowledge in

* D. D. Runes (Ed.), *The Selected Writings of Benjamin Rush* (New York, Philosophical Library, Inc., 1947), pp. 106-14.

agriculture will be most productive, when they are planted in the minds of this class of scholars.

I have only to add under this head, that the common amusements of children have no connection with their future occupations. Many of them injure their clothes, some of them waste their strength, and impair their health, and all of them prove more or less, the means of producing noise, or of exciting angry passions, both of which are calculated to beget vulgar manners. The Methodists have wisely banished every species of play from their college. Even the healthy and pleasurable exercise of swimming, is not permitted to their scholars, except in the presence of one of their masters.

Do not think me too strict if I here exclude *gunning* from the amusements of young men. My objections to it are as follows:

1. It hardens the heart, by inflicting unnecessary pain and death upon animals.

2. It is unnecessary in civilized society, where animal food may be obtained from domestic animals, with greater facility.

3. It consumes a great deal of time, and thus creates habits of idleness.

4. It frequently leads young men into low, and bad company.

5. By imposing long abstinence from food, it leads to intemperance in eating, which naturally leads to intemperance in drinking.

6. It exposes to fevers, and accidents. The newspapers are occasionally filled with melancholy accounts of the latter, and every physician must have met with frequent and dangerous instances of the former, in the course of his practice.

I know the early use of a gun is recommended in our country, to teach our young men the use of firearms, and thereby to prepare them for war and battle. But why should we inspire our youth, by such exercises, with hostile ideas towards their fellow creatures?—Let us rather instill into their minds sentiments of universal benevolence to men of all nations and colours. Wars originate in error and vice. Let us eradicate these, by proper modes of education, and wars will cease to be necessary in our country. The divine author and lover of peace "will then suffer no man to do us wrong; yea, he will reprove kings for our sake, saying, touch not my anointed and do my people no harm." Should the nations with whom war is a trade, approach our coasts, they will retire from us, as Satan did from our Saviour, when he came to assault him; and for the same reason, because they will "find nothing in us" congenial to their malignant dispositions; for the flames of war can be spread from one nation to another, only by the conducting mediums of vice and error.

I have hinted at the injury which is done to the health of young people by some of their amusements; but there is a practice common in all our schools, which does more harm to their bodies than all the amusements that can be named, and that is obliging them to sit too long in *one place,* or crowding too many of them together in *one room*. By means of the former, the growth and shape of the body have been impaired; and by means of the latter, the seeds of fevers have often been engenderd in schools. In the course of my business, I have been called to many hundred children who have been seized with indispositions in school, which evidently arose from the action of morbid effluvia, produced by the confined breath and perspiration of too great a number of children in one room. To obviate these evils, children should be permitted, after they have said their lessons, to amuse themselves in the open air, in some of the useful and agreeable exercises which have been mentioned. Their minds will be strengthened, as well as their bodies relieved by them. To oblige a sprightly boy to sit *seven* hours in a day, with his little arms pinioned to his sides, and his neck unnaturally bent towards his book; and for *no crime!*—what cruelty and folly are manifested, by such an absurd mode of instructing or governing young people!

. . . The innocent infirmities of human nature are no longer proscribed, and punished by the church. Discipline, consisting in the vigilance of officers, has lessened the supposed necessity of military executions; and husbands—fathers—and masters now blush at the history of the times, when wives, children, and servants, were governed only by force. But unfortunately this spirit of humanity and civilization has not reached our schools. The rod is yet the principal instrument of governing them, and a school-master remains the only despot now known in free countries. Perhaps it is because the little subjects of their arbitrary and capricious power have not been in a condition to complain. I shall endeavour therefore to plead their cause, and to prove that corporal punishments (except to children under four or five years of age) are never necessary, and always hurtful, in schools,—The following arguments I hope will be sufficient to establish this proposition.

1. Children are seldom sent to school before they are capable of feeling the force of rational or moral obligation. They may therefore be deterred from committing offences, by motives less disgraceful than the fear of corporal punishments.

2. By correcting children for ignorance and negligence in school, their ideas of *improper* and *immoral* actions are confounded, and hence the moral faculty becomes weakened in after life. It would not be more cruel or absurd to inflict the punishment of the whipping-post upon a man, for not dressing fashionably or neatly, than it is to ferule a boy for blotting his copy book, or mis-spelling a word.

3. If the natural affection of a parent is sometimes insufficient, to restrain the violent effects of a sudden gust of anger upon a child, how dangerous must the power of correcting children be when lodged in the hands of a school-master, in whose anger there is no mixture or parental affection! Perhaps those parents act most wisely, who never trust them-

selves to inflict corporal punishments upon their children, after they are four or five years old, but endeavour to punish, and reclaim them, by confinement, or by abridging them of some of their usual gratifications, in dress, food or amusements.

4. Injuries are sometimes done to the bodies, and sometimes to the intellects of children, by corporal punishments. I recollect, when a boy, to have lost a school-mate, who was said to have died in consequence of a severe whipping he received in school. At that time I did not believe it possible, but from what I now know of the disproportion between the violent emotions of the mind, and the strength of the body in children, I am disposed to believe, that not only sickness, but that even *death* may be induced, by the convulsions of a youthful mind, worked up to a high sense of shame and resentment.

The effects of thumping the head, boxing the ears, and pulling the hair, in impairing the intellects, by means of injuries done to the brain, are too obvious to be mentioned.

5. Where there is *shame,* says Dr. Johnson, there may be *virtue.* But corporal punishments, inflicted at school, have a tendency to destroy the sense of shame, and thereby to destroy all moral sensibility. The boy that has been often publicly whipped at school, is under great obligations to his maker, and his parents, if he afterwards escape the whipping-post or the gallows.

6. Corporal punishments, inflicted at school, tend to beget a spirit of violence in boys towards each other, which often follows them through life; but they more certainly beget a spirit of hatred, or revenge, towards their masters, which too often becomes a ferment of the same baneful passions towards other people. The celebrated Dr. afterwards Baron Haller declared, that he never saw, without horror, during the remaining part of his life, a school-master, who had treated him with unmerited severity, when he was only ten years old. A similar anecdote is related of the famous M. de Condamine. I think I have known several instances of this vindictive, or indignant spirit, to continue towards a cruel and tyrannical school-master, in persons who were advanced in life, and who were otherwise of gentle and forgiving dispositions.

7. Corporal punishments, inflicted at schools, beget a hatred to instruction in young people. I have sometimes suspected that the Devil, who knows how great an enemy knowledge is to his kingdom, has had the address to make the world believe that *feruling, pulling* and *boxing ears, cudgelling, horsing,* &c. and, in boarding-schools, a *little starving,* are all absolutely necessary for the government of young people, on purpose that he might make both schools, and school-masters odious, and thereby keep our world in ignorance; for ignorance is the best means the Devil ever contrived, to keep up the number of his subjects in our world.

8. Corporal punishments are not only hurtful, but altogether unneces-

sary, in schools. Some of the most celebrated and successful school-masters, that I have known, never made use of them.

9. The fear of corporal punishments, by debilitating the body, produces a corresponding debility in the mind, which contracts its capacity of acquiring knowledge. This capacity is enlarged by the tone which the mind acquires from the action of hope, love, and confidence upon it; and all these passions might easily be cherished, by a prudent and enlightened schoolmaster.

10. As there should always be a certain ratio between the strength of a remedy, and the excitability of the body in diseases, so there should be a similar ratio between the force employed in the government of a school, and the capacities and tempers of children. A kind rebuke, like fresh air in a fainting fit, is calculated to act upon a young mind with more effect, than stimulants of the greatest power; but corporal punishments level all capacities and tempers, as quack-medicines do, all constitutions and diseases. They dishonour and degrade our species; for they suppose a total absence of all moral and intellectual feeling from the mind. Have we not often seen dull children suddenly improve, by changing their schools? The reason is obvious. The successful teacher only accommodated his manner and discipline to the capacities of his scholars.

11. I conceive corporal punishments, inflicted in an arbitrary manner, to be contrary to the spirit of liberty, and that they should not be tolerated in a free government. Why should not children be protected from violence and injuries, as well as white and black servants?—Had I influence enough in our legislature to obtain only a single law, it should be to make the punishment for striking a school boy, the same as for assaulting and beating an adult member of society. . . .

The following method of governing a school, I apprehend, would be attended with much better effects, than that which I have endeavoured to show to be contrary to reason, humanity, religion, liberty, and the experience of the wisest and best teachers in the world.

Let a school-master endeavour, in the first place, to acquire the confidence of his scholars, by a prudent deportment. Let him learn to command his passions and temper, at all times, in his school,—Let him treat the name of the Supreme Being with reverence, as often as it occurs in books, or in conversation with his scholars.—Let him exact a respectful behaviour towards himself, in his school; but in the intervals of school hours, let him treat his scholars with gentleness and familiarity. If he should even join in their amusements, he would not lose, by his condescension, any part of his authority over them. But to secure their affection and respect more perfectly, let him, once or twice a year, lay out a small sum of money in pen-knives, and books, and distribute them among his scholars, as rewards for proficiency in learning, and for good behaviour.

If these prudent and popular measures should fail of preventing offences at school, then let the following modes of punishment be adopted.

1. *Private* admonition. By this mode of rebuking, we imitate the conduct of the divine Being towards his offending creatures, for his *first* punishment is always inflicted *privately*, by means of the *still* voice of conscience.

2. Confinement after school-hours are ended; but with the knowledge of the parents of the children.

3. Holding a small sign of disgrace, of any kind, in the middle of the floor, in the presence of a whole school.

If these punishments fail of reclaiming a bad boy, he should be dismissed from school, to prevent his corrupting his schoolmates. It is the business of parents, and not of school-masters, to use the last means for eradicating idleness and vice from their children.

The world was created in love. It is sustained by love. Nations and families that are happy, are made so only by love. Let us extend this divine principle, to those little communities which we call schools. Children are capable of loving in a high degree. They may therefore be governed by love. . . .

How the Day in School in Middlesex County, Connecticut, Was Spent, 1799 *

I. *General.* Instructors and scholars, shall punctually attend their schools, in due season, and the appointed number of hours.

The whole time of instructors and scholars shall be entirely devoted to the proper business and duties of the school.

Every scholar shall be furnished with necessary books for his instruction. In winter, effectual provision ought to be made for warming the schoolhouse, in season, otherwise the forenoon is almost lost.

The Bible—in selected portions—or the New Testament, ought, in Christian schools, to be read by those classes who are capable of reading decently, at the opening of the school before the morning prayer. If this mode of reading be adopted, it will remove every objection of irreverence, and answer all the purposes of morality, devotion, and reading. Some questions may be very properly proposed and answered by the master or scholars; and five minutes, thus spent, would be very profitable exercise of moral and other instruction.

Proper lessons, and fully within the scholar's power to learn, ought to be given to every class, each part of the day. These daily lessons ought to be faithfully learned and recited to the master, or his approved monitors.

One lesson in two or more days may be a review of the preceding lessons of those days, and one lesson in each week a review of the studies of that week. The sum of this review, fairly written or noted in the book studied,

---

* Visitors and Overseers of Schools, *Code of Regulations*, May 7, 1799. Given in *American Annals of Education*, VII (January, 1837), pp. 17-20.

may be carried by the scholars, each Saturday, to their respective parents or guardians.

Scholars equal in knowledge ought to be classed together. Those whose progress merits advancement should rise to a higher class, and those who decline by negligence should be degraded.

2. *School hours and work.* The hours of school ought, as much as possible, to be appropriated in the following, or a similar manner, viz:

IN THE MORNING, the Bible may be delivered to the head of each class, and by them to the scholars capable of reading decently or looking over. This reading, with some short remarks, or questions, with the morning prayer, may occupy the *first half hour*. The *second,* may be employed in hearing the morning lessons, while the younger classes are preparing to spell and read. The *third half hour* in attention to the writers. The *fourth* in hearing the under classes read and spell. The *fifth* in looking over and assisting the writers and cipherers. The *sixth* in hearing the under classes spell and read the second time; and in receiving and depositing pens, writing and reading books.

In all exercises of reading the teacher ought to pronounce a part of the lessons, giving the scholars a correct example of accent and emphasis, pauses, tones, and cadence. In all studies, the scholars ought to be frequently and critically observed. The teacher's eye on all his school is a great preservative of dilligence and order.

IN THE AFTERNOON, the *first* half hour may be employed in spelling together, repeating grammar, rules of arithmetic, and useful tables, with a clear, and full, but soft voice, while the instructor prepares pens, writing books, &c. The *second* and *third* half hours in hearing the under classes and assisting the writers and cipherers. The *fourth* in hearing the upper classes read. The *fifth* in hearing the under classes read, and spell the second time. The *sixth* in receiving and depositing the books &c, as above.

That the school be closed with an evening prayer, previous to which the scholars shall repeat a psalm or hymn—and also the Lord's prayer.

Saturday may be wholly employed in an orderly review of the studies of the week, excepting one hour appropriated to instruction in the first principles of religion and morality; and in repeating, together, the ten commandments. That the Catechism usually taught in schools be divided, by the master, into four sections, one of which shall be repeated successively on each Saturday.

"Peter Parley" (Samuel G. Goodrich) Describes a Typical Rural School in New England Around 1800 *

The surroundings of the schoolhouse to which he went as a child were ... bleak and desolate. Loose, squat stone walls, with innumerable

* Clifton Johnson, *Old-Time Schools and School-Books* (New York, The Macmillan Co., 1904), pp. 116-17. Used by permission.

breaches, inclosed the adjacent fields. A few tufts of elder, with here and there a patch of briers and pokeweed, flourished in the gravelly soil. Not a tree, however, remained, save an aged chestnut. This, certainly, had not been spared for shade or ornament, but probably because it would have cost too much labor to cut it down; for it was of ample girth.

The schoolhouse chimney was of stone, and the fireplace was six feet wide and four deep. The flue was so ample and so perpendicular that the rain, sleet, and snow fell directly to the hearth. In winter the battle for life with green fizzling fuel, which was brought in lengths and cut up by the scholars, was a stern one. Not infrequently the wood, gushing with sap as it was, chanced to let the fire go out, and as there was no living without fire, the school was dismissed, whereat all the scholars rejoiced.

I was about six years old when I first went to school. My teacher was "Aunt Delight," a maiden lady of fifty, short and bent, of sallow complexion and solemn aspect. We were all seated upon benches made of slabs —boards having the exterior or rounded part of the log on one side. As they were useless for other purposes, they were converted into school benches, the rounded part down. They had each four supports, consisting of straddling wooden legs set into auger holes.

The children were called up one by one to Aunt Delight, who sat on a low chair, and required each, as a preliminary, "to make his manners," which consisted of a small, sudden nod. She then placed the spelling-book before the pupil, and with a pen-knife pointed, one by one, to the letters of the alphabet, saying "What's that?"

I believe I achieved the alphabet that summer. Two years later I went to the winter school at the same place kept by Lewis Olmstead—a man who made a business of ploughing, mowing, carting manure, etc., in the summer, and of teaching school in the winter. He was a celebrity in ciphering, and Squire Seymour declared that he was the greatest "arithmeticker" in Fairfield County. There was not a grammar, a geography, or a history of any kind in the school. Reading, writing, and arithmetic were the only things taught, and these very indifferently—not wholly from the stupidity of the teacher, but because he had forty scholars, and the custom of the age required no more than he performed.

**Some Fly-Leaf Scribblings of Children in the
School-Books in the Early Days ***

Steal not this Book
For fear of Shame
For hear you read
The owners name
Asa Stebbins Book

* *Ibid.*, pp. 153-57. Used by permission.

If this book should chance to roam
Box its ears and send it home.

Steal not this book, for if you do
Tom Harris will be after you.

Steal not this book for fear of strife
For the owner carries a big jacknife.

Steal not this book my honest friend
for fear the gallos will be your end
The gallos is high, the rope is strong,
To steal this book you know is wrong.

Let every lerking thief be taught,
This maxim always sure,
That learning is much better bought
Than stolen from the poor.
Then steal not this book.

Whoever steals this
Book away may
Think on that great
judgement day when
Jesus Christ shall
come and say
Where is that book you
Stole away,
Then you will say
I do not know
and Christ will say
go down below.

Francis Barton
is my name america
is my nation
pitsfield is my
dwelling place
and christ is my
salvation when
i am dead and
in my grave and
all my bones are
rotton its youl
remember me or else
i will be forgotten.

If there should be another flood,
Then to this book I'd fly;
If all the earth should be submerged
This book would still be dry.

J. Marion Sims, Famous American Surgeon and Gynecologist, Tells of His Early Education in South Carolina, 1819 *

My father, feeling the want of an education himself, was determined to educate his children, and so he began with me at a very early age. He then had a little store about a mile north of the Hanging-Rock Creek, on the road leading to Lancaster. This was in 1818. Mr. Blackburn, a Scotchman, had just opened a school in an old field, very near the ford of the creek. Mr. Buck Caston lived a mile north of us, and his children were obliged to pass our door to get to Mr. Blackburn's school. His eldest daughter, Betsey, knowing that my father was anxious to have me go to school, volunteered to call on going by every day and take me to school with them; promising to protect me against all dangers and imposition from other boys in the school. I don't remember much about it, except that the teacher flogged the boys occasionally, very severely, and stood some of them up in the corner with a fool's cap on. I here learned my letters, and to spell in two syllables by the end of the term. The school was only for the summer term.

The next year, 1819, when I was six years old, my father sent me to a boarding-school, some six or eight miles from home. The teacher here was an Irishman, Mr. Quigley, a man about fifty-five years old, and a rigid disciplinarian; altogether very tyrannical, and sometimes cruel. He was badly pock-marked, and had lost an eye by small-pox—otherwise a handsome man. I was very unhappy at his house. He had two grown daughters; one of the daughters was very unkind to me, the other was sympathetic. But my impressions then and my convictions now are that the best place for a child under ten years of age is with his mother. A very curious custom prevailed in this school, which was that the boy who arrived earliest in the morning was at the head of his class during the day, and was considered the first-honor boy. The one who arrived second took the second place, and so on. There was great rivalry among some half-dozen of the most ambitious of the boys. James Graham was about ten years old. He was almost always first in the morning. Although I was so very young, only six, I occasionally made efforts to get there earlier than he did. I suppose the schoolhouse was not more than three quarters of a mile from the teacher's residence, where I boarded; but it seemed to me, at the time, that it was very much farther than that. However, the boy that got ahead of James Graham had to rise very early in the morning. I remember getting up one morning long before daybreak. The dread of my young life was mad dogs and "runaway niggers." I started off for the school-house on a trot, an hour

* J. Marion Sims, *The Story of My Life*. Edited by H. Marion-Sims (New York, D. Appleton and Co., 1885), pp. 54-63. This is a remarkable and engaging story. Students enjoy it and also the article on Sims in *The Dictionary of American Biography*, XVII, pp. 186-88. For Sims's account of a duel in South Carolina College where he received his undergradute education, see above, pp. 258-260.

before day, looking anxiously from side to side, and before and behind, fearing all the time those two great bugbears of my young life, viz., mad dogs and runaway niggers, with which the minds of the young were so often demoralized by negro stories. When I arrived at the school-house the wind was blowing very severely. It was in the autumn; the acorns were falling on the clap-boards covering the log-cabin, and I didn't feel very comfortable, and was most anxious for James Graham to come. At last he arrived, greatly to my relief. This was my first and last first-honor day. I was content after this to resign this post to James Graham.

This teacher had one remarkable peculiarity in regard to the admission of small boys to his school. It made no odds whether a boy was good or bad, he invariably got a flogging on the first day. The teacher always sought some pretext to make a flogging necessary, and when he began he seldom stopped until the youngster vomited or wet his breeches. I remember, as if it were yesterday, when a little boy, James Smith, about seven years old, came with his two older brothers to school.

He did not come as a pupil. His mother wished to go to a camp-meeting for a day or two, and sent him with his brothers to school, because she did not wish to leave him at home alone with the negroes. He was a pretty little blue-eyed, flaxen-haired boy, and wore a red Morocco-leather Bumbalo cap, and red Morocco shoes, a checked jacket, and nankeen pants, fitting tight round the ankles and tied with red ribbons. And his shoulders were covered with a broad white linen collar, neatly ruffled. He was as pretty as a picture, the envy of all the little boys, and admiration of all the little girls in the school. Old Quigley had that one eye on him all morning. I wondered if James would be initiated in the usual way, with all that finery on. If so, I felt sorry for his vanity and his Sunday clothes. It was about eleven o'clock. James had been on his good behavior all morning. The teacher would soon go out for his usual morning leg-stretching; when, unfortunately for James, he started to run across the school-room. This was against the rules. In running, he tripped and fell sprawling in the middle of the floor. Old Quigley lit on him with a keen, new hickory-switch, and began to initiate him in his usual way into the mysteries of pedagogism. The little fellow yelled and kicked, and screamed that he would tell his pa. This was of no use. Old Cockeye whipped the harder. He was not afraid of any boy's pa. I felt so sorry for the dear little boy. I had passed along that road. I knew too well what had to come, and I thought to myself: "Poor little fellow. If you only knew what I do, you would throw up that breakfast, even to the milk and peaches, or you would spoil them breeches." At last my mind was relieved when I saw the nankeens change color. Thereupon old Quigley immediately stopped whipping.

He made it a rule to whip, when he once began, till the remedy worked either up or down, when he immediately arrested his whipping. This was at a time when it was the custom for the boys to turn out the master a day or two before the term of school ended. Schools were seldom taken up for a longer period than from three to six months. The first quarter of Mr. Quigley's school was about to terminate, and the big boys agreed to turn him out and make him treat before the beginning of the second quarter. It was the teacher's habit, every day, to take a walk of fifteen or twenty minutes, about eleven o'clock in the morning, calling to his desk some of the larger boys to keep order during his absence. No sooner had he descended the foot of the hill leading toward the spring than the three larger boys in the school began barricading the door. There was only one door to the cabin, and by taking up the benches, which were ten or fifteen feet long, and crossing them diagonally, one to the right and another to the left, in the door, the benches projecting as much outside as inside the house, a complete barricade was formed which could easily be defended against assault from without. When the old gentleman saw what had been done he became perfectly furious. He was so violent that he easily intimidated the ringleaders. He swore that he would not give up, and would not treat, and that he was coming into the house whether or no. At last he commenced to climb on the roof of the house, and to throw a part of it off. It was covered with boards held on by poles. The ringleaders, seeing that he was sure to effect an entrance anyway, became intimidated, and agreed to remove the barricade if he would promise not to whip them. After parleying a little while, he promised that he would not flog the ringleaders. He was a man of most violent temper, and, although fifty-five years of age, he was very strong and active. The ringleader of the gang was young Bob Stafford. He was tall, slender, and very strong; but was evidently afraid of the teacher, and showed the white feather decidedly. As Mr. Quigley came in he walked up to young Stafford, who stood trembling in the middle of the room, and said: "Sir," as he drew his big fist back, "I have a great mind to run my fist right through your body!" I had always thought Mr. Quigley would do whatever he said he would do, and I remembered with what horror I looked at Stafford, expecting every minute to see the old gentleman's fist come out through his back.

My father came to see me but once during the six months I was in this school. My mother came to see me about once a month. I was dying to tell her of the bad treatment I received from the teacher and from one of his daughters. The old gentleman was very obstinate, and not only punished me unnecessarily at school, but he would not let me have what I wanted to eat, and would compel me to eat things absolutely distasteful to me. I wished to tell my mother of all this, of how Miss Nelly used to box my ears and pull my hair, and how old Quigley used to punish me, but I was too closely watched. I could never get her to one side, never see her alone. At last I became desperate. And right in the presence of the whole family I told the whole truth of the severe treatment that I had endured ever since

I had been there, and that she must take me home; if she didn't, I would run away and leave the place even if I were captured by runaway niggers and devoured by mad dogs. I would have run away long before, but for the dread of mad dogs and "runaway niggers." . . .

The next school that I attended was taught by Mr. John E. Sanderson, an Irishman. I was now seven years old. He taught school alternately in the Waxhaws and Hanging-Rock neighborhoods. The Waxhaws were in the northern part of the county, and the Hanging-Rock neighborhood in the southern. He was a fine teacher for arithmetic and writing. But he was very cruel, and whipped the boys often without any provocation at all. He thrashed them even when they were nearly grown, although he was a small man. But he was so violent in his temper and in the government of his school that the larger boys were afraid of him. There was only one day in the week when the school was happy, and that was Monday. He always got drunk on Saturday night, remained so all day Sunday, and came to school Morning morning as full as he could be, and then was always jolly and good-tempered. He would then pinch the girls' arms, and say witty things to the boys, and he never whipped anybody on Monday, so we were always happy on that day. But when Tuesday arrived he reverted to his old ways of severity. We had one poor fellow named Ike Tillman in the school. He was an orphan, and was for many years under the tuition of Mr. Sanderson, and wherever he located a school, whether in one part of the county or the other, Ike Tillman always followed him. He was a bad boy without being very bad. He was very indolent, but not stupid. Mr. Sanderson had begun to whip him when he was seven or eight years old, and the boy had got so used to it that he expected to be flogged every day, even when he was eighteen years old and nearly six feet high. And he was seldom disappointed. At last one or two of the boys, about his own age, said to him, one day, "Ike, you're too big to be flogged; if I were you, I would show fight next time."

"Well," he said, "boys if you'll stand by me I will do it; but if you don't I can't afford it."

They agreed to stand by him. Ike had a slate about twelve by ten inches, and the wooden frame had been broken and lost. The next day Mr. Sanderson called up Ike for a thrashing. Ike came up, with his slate in his hand, leaning it against his bosom, and he said:

"Mr. Sanderson, you have been whipping me, sir, ever since I was a little boy. I am now a man. I will be d—d if I'll stand it any longer! If you come a step nearer to me, I will split you d—d old head open with this slate!"

Mr. Sanderson was surprised, and he changed his tactics immediately, and said:

"Why, Ikey, why, you would not strike me with that slate, would you?"

Ike said: "You come one step toward me and I'll split you open, clean down from your head to your backbone, and," said he, "these boys have promised to see me through the fight!"

"Well, Ikey," said Mr. Sanderson, "we have lived together a long time, but I don't think we can afford to be enemies; and, if you are willing, we'll let by-gones be by-gones, and we'll enter from this day on into a new relationship." The old man saw that the game was up and too strong for him; and, sure enough, so far as Ike Tillman and the larger boys were concerned, the old man was taught a lesson that he never forgot afterward. . . .

Regulations for the Schools of Providence, Rhode Island, 1820 *

The Publick Schools are established for the general benefit of the community; And all children, of both sexes, having attained the age of six years, shall be received therein and faithfully instructed, without preference or partiality.

The Instruction shall be uniform in the several schools, and shall consist of spelling, Reading, the use of Capital letters and Punctuation, Writing, English Grammar & Arithmetick.

The Pronunciation shall be uniform in the several schools & the standard shall be the *Critical Pronouncing Dictionary* of John Walker.

The following Books, and none others, shall be used in the several schools, viz: *Alden's Spelling Book,* first & second part, *New Testament, American Preceptor,* Murray's *Sequel to the English Reader,* Murray's *Abridgement of English Grammar* and Dabols *Arithmetick.*

The scholars shall be put in separate classes according to their several improvements, each sex by itself.

The Schools are statedly to begin and end as follows: From the first Monday in October to the first Monday in May to begin at 9 o'clock A.M. and end at 12 ock.M.: and half past one ock P.M. & end at half past four ock. P.M. From the first Monday in May to the first Monday in October, to begin at 8 ock. A.M. & end at 11 ock A.M.; And at 2 ock. P.M. and end at 5 ock P.M.

The Scholars shall be excused from attending the schools on Saturdays, on Christmas day, on the 4th day of July, on public Fasts and Thanksgiving, on the last Monday in April, on the day of Regimental Training; on the day succeeding each quarterly visitation and during the whole of Commencement Week. But on no other days shall the Preceptors dismiss the Schools without permission obtained from the Town Council.

As Discipline and Good Government are absolutely necessary to improvement it is indispensible that the scholars should implicitly obey the Regulations of the Schools.

---

* Report of a committee appointed to revise the regulations for the schools. Given in *Centennial Report of the School Committee,* 1899-1900, pp. 42-43.

The good morals of the Youth being essential to their own comfort & to their progress in useful knowledge, they are strictly enjoined to avoid idleness and profaneness, falsehood and deceitfulness, and every other wicked & disgraceful practice; and to conduct themselves in a sober, orderly & decent manner both in & out of school. If any scholar should prove disobedient & refractory, after all reasonable means used by the Preceptor to bring him or her to a just sense of duty, such offender shall be suspended from attendance & instruction in any School, until the next visitation of the committee. Each Scholar shall be punctual in attendance at the appointed hour and be as constant as possible in daily attendance and all excuses for absence shall be by note, from the Parent or Guardian of the scholar.

It shall be the duty of the Preceptors to report at each quarterly visitation the names of those scholars who have been grossly negligent in attending School or inattentive to their Studies.

It is recommended to the Preceptors, as far as practicable, to exclude corporal punishment from the schools, and particularly that they never permit it to be inflicted by their ushers in their presence, or at any time by a scholar.

That they inculcate upon the scholars the necessity of good behaviour during their absence from school. That they endeavor to convince the children by their treatment that they feel a parental affection for them, and never make dismission from school at an early hour a reward for good conduct or diligence, but endeavor to teach the scholars to consider being at school as a privilege & dismission from it as a punishment.

That they endeavor to impress on the minds of the scholars a sense of the Being & Providence of God & their obligations to love & reverence Him,—their duty to their parents & preceptors, the beauty & excellency of truth, justice & mutual love, tenderness to brute creatures, the happy tendency of self government and obedience to the dictates of reason & religion; the observance of the Sabbath as a sacred institution, the duty which they owe to their country & the necessity of a strict obedience to its Laws, and that they caution them against the prevailing vices.

Rules and Contract for Governing a School in South Carolina, 1820 *

Rule 1st. Every scholar Shall attend School With his or her face and hands Cleanly Washed thar hair Neatly comeed And Shall not Waist thar time Coming to or Going from Scholl and Shall pass all persons Met by them With respect by bowing & Speaking to them.————

* Typescript copy furnished by Superintendent J. G. Richards, Jr., Camden City Schools, and verified by Mr. H. L. Watson, Greenwood. The rules were found among the papers of Mr. Watson's great-grandfather, Elihu Watson. The document forms a sort of contract between G. S. Warren and John N. Golding and Elihu Watson on the management of the school.

Rule 2nd. Each and Every Scholar Shall pay due respect to thar teacher as he is Thar omediate head and teacher they are also to pay respect to all persons Who Shall at any time come to Said School as a visit. by rising & modestly Bowing thar bodies & Emediately return to thar Steadies and Stick close to the Same During his her or that Stay & at thar departure they Shall all arise & Again modestly bowing thar bodies————

JOHN N. GOLDING

Rule 3rd. No Scholar Shall Indulge tham Selves in Wrestling Climbing Trees rioting fighting telling lies Swearing Calling Nick names but Shall prudently calling every person by thar proper names

Rule 4th. No Scollar Shall be permitted to carry Disagreeable news from School Such As Will produce Strife Amongst any party of School.

Rule 5th. If any person not under the Jurisdiction of parents of Gardeens Shall Subscribe to said School and Will not conform to thees rules laid Down by me Shall be expeld from said School and Pay All the Subscription Money &c————

Rule 6th. And Last Any Purson or Scholar Violating Said rules Shall receive such Corporal punishment as the Teacher may deem Fit. &c &c

Feb. 16th day 1820   ELIHUE WATSON

My Most worthy friend I have Give thees rules to you as I have them But I Charge you Not to fail in one point from the first Day if you want to have Satisfaction never fail at the Start but Fulfill your rules and after they find out out you are as Good as your Word they will mind you and it will be an easy life to you & onor I wish may follow you and Success My Friend E. Watson

G. S. WARREN

JOHN N. GOLDING

North District) Articles of Agreement made and concluded on by Elihue Watson of the one part and the under Subscribers of the other part ————Witnesseth, I, the Said E. Watson do propose the Teaching of A School Five days in Each Week for the Space of Six Months which will consist of Reading Writing and Arithmetic We the under subscribers for his Service & Good performance Do promise to pay to the Said E. Watson for Each Scholar Annexed to our Names Six Dollars to be paid In hand the last day of the School. I, the Said E. Watson, do promise to pay due Respect to Each and Every Scholar Without Partiality & To forward them in the fore mentioned Sciences of learning as fast as thar talents Will Admit of. I, the Said E. Watson, Promises to keep Good rule & order in School Attend at Sd School At all Regular School hours & make up all my lost Time only holidies Excepted.

This the 9th Day of   1820 A.D.

Horace Greeley on "Turning Out" the Teacher
in New England About 1820 *

At the close of the morning session of the first of January, and perhaps on some other day that the big boys chose to consider or make a holiday, the moment the master left the house in quest of his dinner, the little ones were started homeward, the doors and windows suddenly and securely barricaded, and the older pupils, thus fortified against intrusion, proceeded to spend the afternoon in play and hilarity. I have known a master to make a desperate struggle for admission, but the odds were too great. If he appealed to the neighboring fathers, they were apt to advise him to desist, and let matters take their course. I recollect one instance, however, where a youth was shut out who, procuring a piece of board, mounted from a fence to the roof of the schoolhouse and covered the top of the chimney nicely with his board. Ten minutes thereafter, the house was filled with smoke, and its inmates, opening the doors and windows, were glad to make terms with the outsider.

Pestalozzian Department in a Kentucky School, 1830 †

In this department, the younger students will have the foundation laid, by constant and appropriate *practice,* of valuable habits such as *observation, analysis, induction,* &c. For the attainment of this, the most important of the two great ends of education, the principles laid down by that revered philanthropist, with whose name we have honoured this branch of our school, are admirably calculated. The following are some of them.

I. "The instruction given should be adapted to the age and capacity of the pupil, so that he will comprehend it easily and perfectly.

II. "A regular and easy progression should be observed, beginning with that which is simple and plain, and proceeding by easy and gradual steps, to that which is complicated and difficult.

III. "In this progress, nothing should be passed, till it is perfectly understood and familiarized, so that it will be retained, both as a useful

---

* Clifton Johnson, *Old-Time Schools and School-Books* (New York, The Macmillan Co., 1904), pp. 123-26. Used by permission. For an account of the "turn out" of a teacher in Georgia about 1800, see A. B. Longstreet's *Georgia Scenes* (New York, Harper & Bros., 1850), pp. 73-81. For similar account in North Carolina about 1847, see Calvin H. Wiley's *Alamance; or, The Great and Final Experiment* (New York, Harper & Bros., 1847), pp. 19-21.
† *Prospectus of the Rev. Mr. Peers's School* . . . (Lexington, Kentucky, printed by Joseph G. Norwood, 1830), p. 15. The four principles given above are practically identical with those set out by Dr. Joseph Buchanan in *Western Spy and Literary Cadet,* March 3, 1821, and given in N. H. Sonne's *Liberal Kentucky, 1780-1828* (New York, Columbia University Press, 1939), p. 96. Buchanan was born in Virginia, was a graduate of Transylvania University, a physician, educator and writer and exponent of liberalism. He studied with Joseph Neef at the latter's school near Philadelphia and was an energetic advocate of the Pestalozzian methods of teaching. Rev. Mr. Peers may have taken the principles from the source indicated above.

acquisition in itself, and as a facility to the acquisition of other matters connected with and depending upon it.

IV. "A plan of discipline and excitement should be employed which will produce great ardor and industry of pursuit, and supersede the necessity of coercion by an appeal to force or fear."

Among other things in which our pupils will be *practiced* in conformity with these principles, are elementary Mathematical exercises relating both to number and form, *exact copies of which as used in Pestalozzi's school,* we have been fortunate enough to obtain (together with many valuable directions), from a Swiss gentleman who aided in organizing his institution.

How to Prevent the Evils of Whispering Among Pupils and Their Leaving Their Seats, 1833 *

Whispering and leaving seats. In regard to this subject, there are very different methods, now in practice in different schools. In some, especially in very small schools, the teacher allows the pupils to act according to their own discretion. They whisper and leave their seats whenever they think it necessary. This plan may possibly be admissible in a very small school; that is, one of ten or twelve pupils. I am convinced, however, that it is very bad here. No vigilant watch, which it is possible for any teacher to exert, will prevent a vast amount of mere talk, entirely foreign to the business of the school. I tried this plan very thoroughly, with high ideas of the dependence which might be placed upon conscience and a sense of duty, if these principles are properly brought out to action in an effort to sustain the system. I was told by distinguished teachers, that it would not be found to answer. But predictions of failure in such cases only prompt to greater exertions, and I persevered. But I was forced at last to give up the point, and adopt another plan. My pupils would make resolutions enough; they understood their duty well enough. They were allowed to leave their seats and whisper to their companions, whenever, *in their honest judgment, it was necessary for the prosecution of their studies.* I knew that it sometimes would be necessary, and I was desirous to adopt this plan to save myself the constant interruption of hearing and replying to requests. But it would not do. Whenever, from time to time, I called them to account, I found that a large majority, according to their own confession, were in the habit of holding daily and deliberate communication with each other, on subjects entirely foreign to the business of the school. A more experienced teacher would have predicted this result, but I had very high ideas of the power of cultivated conscience; and in fact, still have. But then, like almost all other persons who become possessed of a good idea, I could not be satisfied without carrying it to an extreme.

* Jacob Abbott, *The Teacher; or Moral Influences Employed in the Instruction and Government of the Young* (Boston, Peirce and Parker, 1833), pp. 34-38.

Still it is necessary to give pupils, sometimes, the opportunity to whisper and leave seats. Cases occur where this is unavoidable. It cannot therefore be forbidden altogether. How then, you will ask, can the teacher regulate this practice, so as to prevent the evils which will otherwise flow from it, without being continually interrupted by the request for permission?

By a very simple method. *Appropriate particular times at which all this business is to be done,* and *forbid it altogether* at every other time. It is well on other accounts to give the pupils of a school a little respite, at least every hour:—and if this is done, an intermission of study for two minutes each time, will be sufficient. During this time, *general* permission should be given to speak or to leave seats provided they do nothing at such a time to disturb the studies of others. This has been my plan for two or three years, and no arrangement which I have ever made, has operated for so long a time, and so uninterruptedly, as entirely to my satisfaction as this. It of course will require some little time, and no little firmness, to establish the new order of things, where a school has been accustomed to another course; but where this is once done, I know no one plan so simple and so easily put into execution, which will do so much towards relieving the teacher of the distraction and perplexity of his pursuits.

In making the change however, it is of fundamental importance that the pupils should themselves be interested in it. Their co-operation, or rather the co-operation of the majority, which it is very easy to obtain, is absolutely essential to success. I say this is very easily obtained. Let us suppose that some teacher, who has been accustomed to require his pupils to ask and obtain permission, every time they wish to speak to a companion, is induced by these remarks to introduce this plan. He says accordingly to his school:

"You know that you are now accustomed to ask me whenever you wish to obtain permission to whisper to a companion, or to leave your seats. Now I have been thinking of a plan which will be better for both you and me. By our present plan, you are sometimes obliged to wait before I can attend to your request. Sometimes I think it is unnecessary, and deny you, when perhaps I was mistaken, and it was really necessary. At other times, I think it very probable, that when it is quite desirable for you to leave your seat, you do not ask, because you think you may not obtain permission, and you do not wish to ask and be refused. Do you, or not, experience these inconveniences from our present plan?"

The boys would undoubtedly answer in the affirmative.

"I experience great inconvenience, too. I am very frequently interrupted when busily engaged, and it also occupies a great portion of my time and attention. It requires as much mental effort to consider and decide sometimes whether I ought to allow a pupil to leave his seat, as it would to decide a much more important question. Therefore I do not like our plan, and I have another to propose."

	No. of Counties
New York Expositor	6
Johnson's	1

Reading Books.

		No. of Counties
New York	Reader	59
National	"	6
United States	"	13
Juvenile	"	10
Hall's Western	"	1
Young's	"	1
Southern	"	1
Cobb's	"	7
Angel	"	5

Grammars.

	No. of Counties
Murray's	43
Exercise and Key to do	10
Kirkham's	21
Smith's	15
Parley's	1
Olney's	1
Greenleaf's	2

Geographies.

	No. of Counties
Olney's	40
Adams's	16
Parley's	30
Woodbridge's	7
Smith's	9
Mitchell's	8
Cumming's	4
Smiley's	1
Murray's	1

Science.

	No. of Counties
Bonnycastle's Mensuration	1
Swift's Philosophy	1
Blair's Rhetoric	1
Gibson's Surveyor	1
Gummer's do.	1
Playfair's Geometry	1
Colburn's Algebra	2
Comstock's Philosophy	1
Phelps's do	1

Latin Classics

		No. of Counties
Virgil		1
Class	Reader	4
Little	"	1
Electic	"	4

		No. of Counties
Primary	"	1
M'Guffey's	"	1
Elementary English	"	1
English	"	52
Introduction to Murray's		30
Sequel to English Reader		8
Bible and Testament		103
Blair's Reading Exercise		3
Emerson's Class Books		2
Parley's Works		11
Cobb's Sequel		1
Pleasing Companion		1
Young Ladies' Class Books		1
Scholar's Guide		1
American Preceptor		8
Moral Instructor		5
Popular Lessons		4
Columbian Orator		2
Scott's Lessons		2
Family Story Book		1
United States Constitution		1
Book of Commerce		1
Parent's Cabinet		1
Cabinet Library		1
Robinson Crusoe's Journal		1

Biographies.

		No. of Counties
Life of Washington		5
	Marion	3
	Franklin	1
Memoirs of S. Dale		1

Histories.

		No. of Counties
United States [author not named]		18
United States, by Grimshaw		20
Do.	by Jesse	1
Do.	by Adams	1
Do.	by Hale	2
Do.	by Goodrich	1
Do.	by Webster	1
History of America [author not named]		2
Rome, principally Grimshaw's		15
Greece, principally Grimshaw's		12
England, do.		17
1st Book of History		1
2d. do.		1
Frost's United States		3
History of Ancient Persia		1

	No. of Counties			No. of Counties
Tucker's History	1		Jesse's	13
Whelpley's Compend and History	1		Parke's	6
			Smiley's	5
Ecclesiastical History	1		Emerson's	6
Worcester's do.	1		Fowler's	2
History of Europe	1		Adams's	1
Natural History	2		Walsh's	2
Olney's "	1		Ray's	3
Parley's History	12		Davie's	1
Goldsmith's do.	1		Slocumb's	1
Tytler's do.	1		Mercantile	1
Parley's Bible History	2		Dobold's	1
			Colburn's	4
Arithmetics.			Western Calculator	2
Pike's	76		Electic	1
Smith's	19			

Horace Mann on the Value of Written Examinations in the Schools, 1845 *

(Many circumstances conspire to place these Reports † of the committees among the most remarkable, as well as the most instructive and admonitory of all our school documents. The high character of the committees who conducted the examination; the mode of examination, at once thorough, and perfectly fair and impartial, the labor and care expended in reducing the results of the examination to a tabular form, so that the common eye can compare them, and determine at a glance the relative standing of each school; the astounding character of the results themselves, and the consequences, in regard to a change of teachers, to which they have already conduced, together with the admirable suggestions and doctrines, laid down in their pages, on many of the most important topics that pertain to our schools;—all these, and other considerations, combine to give an extraordinary degree of importance to these Reports, and to commend them to the attentive perusal, not only of those parents immediately interested in the city schools, but of the whole people of the State.—Ed.)

Having now completed our extracts from the Report of the Committee on the Grammar Schools, and also our abstract of the Tables, we find the whole subject too deeply freighted with interest and instruction to allow us to pass it unnoticed. In order that our remarks may stand in immediate connection with the subject to which they refer, we postpone, until another

* *The Common School Journal* (Massachusetts), October 1, 1845.
† Reports of examinations in the schools of Boston in 1845, which seems to have been the first place in this country to have written examinations. See O. W. Caldwell and S. A. Courtis, *Then and Now in Education*, 1845-1923 (Yonkers, N. Y., World Book Co., 1924). This book reproduces the examination questions and a full report on the results.

pupil or a class to a test-question—to a point that will reveal their condition as to ignorance or knowledge—the teacher bolts out with some suggestion or leading question that defeats the whole purpose at a breath. We would look with all possible lenity upon teachers who take such a course; for we perceive the vehemence of the temptation under which they labor. When the pupils of their favorite class, and perhaps in their favorite study, are in danger of being sunk in the abysses of their own ignorance, how natural it is for a kind-hearted and quick-feeling teacher to wish to throw them a rope. But such interference is unjust, not to say ungentlemanly. The case supposed is the very juncture where the teacher should abstain from intermeddling, though he should be obliged to thrust his pocket-handkerchief into his mouth, or put his head out of the window. Of what use to examine a school, if each boy and girl is to be like Punch and Judy in the puppet-show, and to be told by another the things they are to say? While, then, we respect the feelings which prompt the teacher to interfere with the course of the examination, we consider it a great point gained, to prevent the mischief of their indulgence. Now where a school is examined by written or printed questions, distributed on the instant, by the examining committee, questions of which the teachers themselves are as ignorant as the pupils—they must, perforce, look on at their leisure. Though they writhe in anxiety, yet their ill-judged kindness can do no harm; their improper suggestions are excluded. They are obliged to reflect that the day of probation has passed; the time for trial and judgment has come.

5. And, what is not inferior in value to either of the preceding considerations, it does determine, beyond appeal or gainsaying, whether the pupils have been faithfully and competently taught.

All pupils of average ability, who have been properly taught, should have a command, not merely of the particular fact, or the general statement of a truth or principle, but also of its connections, relations and applications; and every faithful examiner will strive to know whether they possess the latter as well as the former species of information. Text books contain a much greater proportion of isolated facts, and of abstract principles, than of relations and applications. This is the circumstance which gives pertinency and significancy to their distinctive appellation,—text books. They are books containing texts. These texts the teacher is to expound. Each one of them should be the foundation of a discourse, or of a series of discourses. This is teaching. Hearing recitations from a book, is not teaching. It has no claim to be called by this dignified and expressive name. It is the exposition of the principle contained in the book; showing its connection with life, with action, with duty; making it the nucleus around which to gather all related facts and all collateral principles:— it is this, and this only, which can be appropriately called teaching. All short of this is mere journey-work, rude mechanical labor and drudgery.

Now the method of examination lately adopted by the Boston School

Committee, settles the question as definitely, what kind or quality of instruction has been given by the masters, as it does what amount or extent of proficiency has been made by the pupils. A pupil may most faithfully commit the whole of one of our grammars to memory, and yet know nothing more of the science of English Grammar, than a parrot, who has been taught to say "Pretty Poll," knows of the power and copiousness of the English language; or he may con Geography and Atlas, till he can repeat every line in the one and remember every island speck in the other, and yet have no distinct conception of anything beyond the visible horizon. A child may know,—as any child unless it be an idiotic one does,—that water will run down hill, and yet never be led to embrace the truth, that it is mountain ridges and table lands that give descent and direction to the course of rivers. Nay, because he has faithfully learned the fact that the upper part of a map represents the north, he may conscientiously deny that the waters of Lake Erie run into Lake Ontario, because as he holds his map before him, it looks as though they must, for that purpose, run up hill. A child may know how to spell from a spelling-book, and yet, when put to the twofold operation of writing and spelling, he may bring vowels and consonants into very strange juxtapositions. Or he may be introduced to ten thousand English words, and not know the real meaning and use of more than five hundred of them.

We repeat, then, that this method of examination tests, in a most admirable manner, the competency or sufficiency of the teaching which the pupils have received; for, as a workman is not taught any art or handicraft, until he can execute it, so a child is not taught any principle until he can explain it, or apply it. Where children of ordinary abilities have been continuously and for a long time under instruction, any deficiencies, of the kinds above specified, are not to be laid to their charge, but to that of their instructors. How should pupils know what lies beyond the text books, or what is necessary in order to understand the text book, unless they have been taught it? The case is different, we acknowledge, with regard to children who attend school irregularly, or for short periods only. In such cases, it would be unjust to hold the instructor responsible for their deficiencies.

6. There is another point, in which every faithful committee man has a deep interest, which is not merely subserved, but secured by the mode under consideration. It takes away all possibility of favoritism, and all ground for the suspicion of favoritism. Almost unpleasant, and generally, we doubt not, an unfounded accusation, is sometimes brought against examiners;—namely, that they are guilty of partiality in putting out questions; that they visit the iniquities of fathers upon children, by selecting difficult questions for the child of an adversary or opponent, and reserving the easy ones for the children of friends. Now, in its practical mischiefs, the next worst thing to their committing so unjust an act, is the suspicion

Description of a School in New York State, 1847 *

Now, my friends, let me take you back fifty-two years to a little log school-house a few miles from Antwerp, in Jefferson county, near the line of St. Lawrence county, where I was engaged in teaching my first school. My wages were fourteen dollars a month, and I was to board around.

This boarding around was jolly fun if one enjoyed it; but I confess I did not enjoy it as well as perhaps some others would. For instance, the schoolmaster was a very distinguished individual; he must have the best the house afforded, and at bed time he was ushered into the spare room off the parlor, with a zero atmosphere. We had good board and a plenty, consisting largely of rye-and-Indian bread, good butter, potatoes, pork or mutton, boiled cider apple sauce, and delicious mince pies.

The school-house was comfortable. Wherever the chinking between the logs had become loose mud-mortar had been used to plaster it up, and every crevice had been closed. A large open fireplace graced one side of the room. Pegs had been driven into the logs; and slabs reversed, reaching around three sides of the room, served as desks. Slabs with pegs driven in for legs made pretty good seats and, of course, the pupils sat facing the wall, an advantage to the teacher that the modern school-room does not afford.

We had plenty of good hard wood and lots of back-logs. The wood was cut four feet long, and in preparing it from the tree a length would often be found so knotty that it would not split easily and it was saved for a back-log. A log four feet long and from ten to fifteen inches in diameter was something of an affair to handle. But the teacher with the help of the boys could usually manage it, and the log was placed at the back of the fire-place, where it would last in cold weather about a week. The fire was built in front of the log, and the wood was held in place by large andirons.

Now for the school. I found myself surrounded on Monday morning by forty or forty-five as bright, as intelligent-looking a class of boys and girls as I have ever met in school.

I thought those young women, some of them as old as their master, dressed in their homemade plaids, were perfectly beautiful, and I have never had reason to change my mind.

I am unable to find a full list of the books in use. I find the Old English reader, Daboll's arithmetic, Webster's speller, and Kirkham's grammar. I do not remember to have used any geography. Our writing books were composed of several sheets of fools-cap paper folded and sewn together by the mother or sister, and the master was expected to set the copies and mend the goose-quill pens. I think there was no chart or map of any

* J. W. Hooper, *Three Score and Ten in Retrospect* (Syracuse, N. Y., C. W. Bardeen, 1900).

description in the school-room. All from seven years old up were expected to read, write, spell, and cipher from the same text-book.

The school was organized and ready for work. I think I never felt more proud than when standing at my little home-made table in about the centre of the room, surrounded by that class of boys and girls. And, think of it, they called me master! And I was their teacher.

David P. Page on Public Examinations, 1847 *

It is now the usage in all our schools to have public examinations,—generally at the close of the term, or a portion of a term,—in order to test, in some measure, the industry and skill of the teacher, and the proficiency of the pupils. I am hardly prepared to oppose this usage, because I am inclined to believe examinations are of some utility as a means of awakening an interest in the parents of the children: perhaps they do something to stimulate school-officers, and also to excite to greater effort during the term both the teacher and the pupils. Still, public examinations, as frequently conducted, are not without *serious objections*. 1. They certainly cannot be looked upon as criterions of the faithfulness or success of teachers. A man *with* tact, and *without* honesty, may make his school appear to far greater advantage than a better man can make a better school appear. This has often happened. It is not the most faithful and thorough teaching that makes the show and attracts the applause at a public exhibition. It is the superficial, mechanical, *memoriter* exercise that is most imposing. Who has not seen a class, that recited by rote and *in concert* at a celebration, win the largest approbation, when many of the individuals knew not the import of the *words* they uttered. *Names* in geography have been thus "said or sung," when the things signified were to the children as really *terrae incognitae* as the fairy lands of Sinbad the Sailor.

2. Nor can such exhibitions be claimed justly to indicate the proficiency of the pupils. Every experienced teacher knows that the best scholars often fail at a public examination, and the most indolent and superficial often distinguish themselves. The spectators, not unfrequently, in pointing out the *talent* of the school, makes the teacher smile at their blunders.

3. They present a strong temptation to dishonesty on the part of the teacher. Since so much stress is laid upon the examination, and particularly, in some regions, upon the *Celebration*, where several schools are brought together to make a show for a few hours, it must be rather an uncommon man who will have sufficient principle to exhibit his school *as it is*, and refuse to make those efforts so very common to have it appear *what it is not*. The wish, expressed or implied, of the parents, and the ambition of the children, all conspire to make the teacher yield to a usage so common. Consequently, several weeks will be spent to *prepare* the

* *Theory and Practice of Teaching* (Payne edition, 1885), pp. 290-95.

averaging the year. Such a course would be favorable for both mind and body.

4. Some time before and after school and perhaps a portion of the noon time should be devoted to drilling exercises, such as sounds of letters, laws of orthoepy, etc., etc.

5. Commencement, recess, closing and recitation should always be at a specified time, and at a signal given by the hand bell or something equally appropriate.

6. Not more than one scholar should leave the house at the same time, some mark of absence should then be left and a speedy return required.

7. No scholar should be permitted to stay out of the house in school time. Each scholar, large or small, should have a seat and be required to stay at it in time of school.

8. Teachers should not indulge in the plays and sports of the scholars, for by such course moral influence is greatly weakened if not lost.

9. The practice of "turning out teachers" is full of mischief, and should be "hooted" from civilized society.

II. Manner of Teaching

1. Schools should be strictly silent; none being allowed to speak aloud but the teacher and those who are speaking or reciting to him.

2. Books should be uniform, and scholars should be regularly and thoroughly classed.

3. Specified lessons should be given on all subjects and recitations exacted. Allowing scholars their own time to learn lessons as well as permitting them to pursue studies upon which they do not recite are pernicious practices.

4. As soon as children have learned the letters of the alphabet or while learning them, they should be taught the sounds which these represent. This will best be done by writing the letters on the blackboard and practicing the learners separately and in concert.

5. Pronunciation should be learned by rule, because it would be more accurate and of easier acquisition; the present mode being uncertain, interminable, and without system.

6. In spelling, polysyllables the learner should pronounce from the first upon each syllable.

7. Orthoephy and orthography (i.e., pronouncing and spelling), with and without the book, should be learned in connection and as nearly as possible at the same time.

8. In connection with spelling, the meaning and use of words should also be learned.

9. As soon as children can pronounce monosyllables, they should be taught to read them in easy sentences, proceeding in the same manner with

two syllables, three, etc. In Webster's speller everything should be learned as the child advances.

10. Spelling should never be discontinued in common schools, but the spelling book should be used only by those who study it; whatever book the learner is using will always afford proper spelling and defining exercises.

11. Great care should be taken that children *learn* to read correctly; if they were correctly taught in regard to stops, tones, etc., from the first, wrong habits would be avoided and proper ones easily formed.

12. Writing should be commenced at an early period and assiduously practiced until a neat and accurate penmanship is acquired.

III. Course of Instruction

A regular system is of the utmost consequence both to accuracy and success; and no small amount of time is now lost in our common schools for want of a regular course. We believe the following subjects and classification adapted to the cultivation of the mind and the wants of the people.

1. Spelling and reading. While the child is learning these, it may be allowed to write on the slate during a small portion of each day; it will also be profited by studying Holbrook's apparatus of solids, figures, minerals, maps, etc. The spelling book should not be relinquished until any combination of letters can be pronounced, and all the rules of orthoepy can be accurately given.

2. Reading, writing on paper, the first principles of oral arithmetic, primary lessons in geography, exercises on the rules of orthography.

3. Reading, writing short sentences, oral and written arithmetic, and primary geography,—scholars should write after a copy until they learn to shape their letters correctly.

4. Reading, writing, composition, arithmetic, and geography.

5. Composition, arithmetic, geography, and English grammar.

6. Arithmetic, English grammar, United States history, and astronomy.

7. English grammar, book keeping, and mensuration.

8. Algebra, natural philosophy, and English poetry.

9. Geometry, chemistry, and physiology.

The old books may be retained where it is not practicable to buy new ones, but uniformity should at once be secured if possible.

IV. Punishment

1. All punishments that mortify, that is, such expedients as punish by mortification they inflict, should be totally abandoned; this will exclude dunce-blocks, leather spectacles, carrying rules, standing up to be pointed at, and all such practices.

2. Privations, such as keeping the offender from play at recess, noon, etc., may be used advantageously; but the great instrument of school order

him, when he called at Means's on Monday morning to draw the pittance of pay that was due him.

He had expected a petition for a holiday on Christmas day. Such holidays are deducted from the teacher's time, and it is customary for the boys to "turn out" the teacher who refuses to grant them, by barring him out of the school-house on Christmas and New York's morning. Ralph had intended to grant a holiday if it should be asked, but it was not asked. Hank Banta was the ringleader in the disaffection, and he had managed to draw the surly Bud, who was present this morning, into it. It is but fair to say that Bud was in favor of making a request before resorting to extreme measures, but he was overruled. He gave it as his solemn opinion that the master was mighty peart, and they would be beat anyhow some way, but he would lick the master fer two cents ef he warn't so slim that he'd feel like he was fighting a baby.

And all that day things looked black. Ralph's countenance was cold and hard as stone, and Shocky trembled where he sat. Betsey Short tittered rather more than usual. A riot or a murder would have seemed amusing to her.

School was dismissed, and Ralph, instead of returning to the Squire's, set out for the village of Clifty, a few miles away. No one knew what he went for, and some suggested that he had "sloped."

But Bud said "he warn't that air kind. He was one of them air sort as died in their tracks, was Mr. Hartsook. They'd find him on the ground nex morning, and he 'lowed the master war made of that air sort of stuff as would burn the dog-on'd ole school-house to ashes, or blow it into splinters, but what he'd beat. Howsumdever he'd said he was a-goin' to help, and help he would; but all the sinno in Golier wouldn't be no account again the cuty they was in the head of the master."

But Bud, discouraged as he was with the fear of Ralph's "cute," went like a martyr to the stake and took his place with the rest in the school-house at nine o'clock at night. It may have been Ralph's intention to preoccupy the school-house, for at ten o'clock Hank Banta was set shaking from head to foot at seeing a face that looked like the master's at the window. He waked up Bud and told him about it.

"Well, what are you a-tremblin' about, you coward?" growled Bud. He won't shoot you; but he'll beat you at this game, I'll bet a hoss, and me, too, and make us both as 'shamed of ourselves as dogs with tin-kittles to their tails. You don't know the master, though he did duck you. But he'll larn you a good lesson this time, and me too, like as not." And Bud soon snored again, but Hank shook with fear every time he looked at the blackness outside the windows. He was sure he heard foot-falls. He would have given anything to have been at home.

When morning came, the pupils began to gather early. A few boys who were likely to prove of service in the coming siege were admitted through the window, and then everything was made fast, and a "snack" was eaten.

"How do you 'low he'll get in?" said Hank, trying to hide his fear.

"How do I 'low?" said Bud. "I don't 'low nothin' about it. You might as well ax me where I 'low the nex' shootin' star is a-goin' to drap. Mr. Hartsook's mighty onsartin. But he'll git in, though, and tan your hide fer you, you see ef he dont. *Ef* he don't blow up the school-house with gunpowder!" This last was thrown in by way of alleviating the fears of the cowardly Hank, for whom Bud had a great contempt.

The time for school had almost come. The boys inside were demoralized by waiting. They began to hope that the master had "sloped." They dreaded to see him coming.

"I don't believe he'll come," said Hank, with a cold shiver. "It's past school-time."

"Yes, he will come, too," said Bud. "And he 'lows to come in here mighty quick. I don't know how. But he'll be a-standin' at that air desk when it's nine o'clock. I'll bet a thousand dollars on that. *Ef* he don't take it into his head to blow us up!" Hank was now white.

Some of the parents came along, accidentally of course, and stopped to see the fun, sure that Bud would thrash the master if he tried to break in. Small, on the way to see a patient perhaps, reined up in front of the door. Still no Ralph. It was just five minutes before nine. A rumor now gained currency that he had been seen going to Clifty the evening before, and that he had not come back, though in fact Ralph had come back, and had slept at Squire Hawkins's.

"There's the master," cried Betsey Short, who stood out in the road shivering and giggling alternately. For Ralph at that moment emerged from the sugar-camp by the school-house, carrying a board.

"Ho! ho!" laughed Hank, "he thinks he'll smoke us out. I guess he'll find us ready." The boys had let the fire burn down, and there was now nothing but hot hickory coals on the hearth.

"I tell you he'll come in. He didn't go to Clifty fer nothin'," said Bud, who sat still on one of the benches which leaned against the door. "I don't know how, but they's lots of ways of killing a cat besides chokin' her with butter. He'll come in—*ef* he don't blow us all sky-high!"

Ralph's voice was now heard, demanding that the door be opened.

"Let's open her," said Hank, turning livid with fear at the firm, confident tone of the master.

Bud straightened himself up. "Hank, you're a coward. I've got a mind to kick you. You got me into this blamed mess, and now you want to crawfish. You jest tech one of these 'ere fastenin's, and I'll lay you out flat of your back afore you can say Jack Robinson."

The teacher was climbing to the roof with the board in hand.

"That air won't win," laughed Pete Jones outside. He saw that there was no smoke. Even Bud began to hope that Ralph would fail for once.

Plymouth, known for the Pilgrim Father's landing,
By Cape Cod Bay, in Massachusetts standing.
And Worcester, that's near the Bay State's center,
As a great thoroughfare, we next will enter.

MASSACHUSETTS

Called the Bay State. Noted for its wealth, and the active part it took in
the great struggle for the liberty and independence of our country.
The eastern part is uneven, and the western mountainous. Mount Tom,
Mount Holyoke, Saddle Mount and Wachusett, are celebrated peaks.
Boston is noted as the capital, and as the largest town in New England.
Charlestown for the Bunker Hill Monument.
Cambridge for its university.
Lynn for the manufacture of shoes.
Marblehead for its cod-fisheries.
Salem for its wealth, obtained in the India trade.
Gloucester for cod and mackerel-fisheries.
Newburyport, the most northern town in the State, for commerce.
Lowell, as the first town in manufacturing in the United States.
New Bedford and Nantucket for whale fisheries.
Plymouth for the landing of Pilgrim Fathers, 1620.

CONNECTICUT

And Hartford, Middletown, and Say-brook bide,
Fast by Connecticut's unfailing tide.
New London, Bridgeport, Fairfield and New Haven,
With Norwalk by Long Island Sound are graven.
And Stonington, southeast of all, we hail,
That with New London, fish for seal and whale.

CONNECTICUT

Noted for the ingenious character of its inhabitants, and for its schools.
The common school fund, in this state, is over two millions of dollars.
It has been distinguished for its men of genius and learning.
Hartford and New Haven are the capitals.

NEW YORK

In New York State, where Hudson meets the brine,
New York and Brooklyn in their trade combine.
On the same tide, West Point and Newburg stay:
Poughkeepsie, Hudson, Troy, and Albany.
Schenectady, with Utica and Rome,
Upon the Erie Channel find a home.
Here Syracuse and Rochester, we see—
The last is on the River Genessee.
Then Brockport comes, with lockport in the score;
As Buffalo is found on Erie's shore.
From Buffalo east, takes Attica her fare;
In Genessee, Batavia has a share.

Then Canandaigua in Ontario view;
As stands Geneva east, with Waterloo.
Auburn is seated by Owasco tide.
South of Cayuga, Ithaca is spied.
Oxford and Norwich in Chenango trace;
In Courtland County, Courtland has a place.
Bath in Steuben, Elmira in Chemung;
Owego next, then Binghampton in Broome.
   Near Saratoga, Ballston makes her quarters,
And both are noted for their mineral waters.
Salem in Washington, with Sandy Hill;
Whitehall is where Champlain's dark waves distil.
Ticonderoga lives by Lake Champlain.
Where stands Crown Point, and Plattsburg holds her reign.
   Oswego sits beside Ontario's border;
While on the eastern coast is Sackett's Harbor.
A place to Watertown, Black River warrants;
As Ogdensburgh is found upon St. Lawrence.

New York

Called the Empire State. Noted for its canals, railroads, extensive commerce, and its great political influence.

Its population is greater than any other state in the union.

The route from New York to Buffalo, is one of the greatest thoroughfares in the world.

The scenery on the Hudson is of a sublime and imposing character.

The steamboats on this river are celebrated for speed and grandeur.

Albany, on the Hudson, is noted as the capital.

New York, at the mouth of the Hudson, as being the largest, most commercial, and important town in America.

West Point for its military academy.

Sing Sing and Auburn for State prisons.

Utica for the State Lunatic Asylum.

Schenectady for Union College.

Syracuse for its salt works.

Rochester for its flouring mills.

Lockport for its costly and expensive canal locks.

Buffalo as one of the most commercial towns in the United States on the lines of two of the greatest thoroughfares in America—the Erie Canal, and Niagara and Lake Ontario routes.

Ballston and Saratoga for mineral waters.

Oswego as the principal port on Lake Ontario.

Sacketts Harbor for a battle fought during the last war with Great Britain.

Watertown for its neatness and manufactures.

Ogdensburgh as lying adjacent to Canada East.

The population is a multifarious mass of Europeans and Americans. The former are characterised for their industry and temperate habits; the latter for superior intelligence and enterprise.

Madison, between Third and Fourth lakes, is the capital.

Milwaukee, the largest town in the State, is noted for its rapid advancements in wealth, population and importance.

OREGON

This territory lies north of California, and between the Rocky Mountains and the Pacific Ocean. It is noted for being the great Western division of the United States; as well as for the enormous growth of its pines, which are sometimes found 250 feet high.

The soil, west of the Cascade Range, is represented as extremely productive.

Oregon City stands in a fertile valley near the falls of Willamette river; it contains upwards of 500 inhabitants.

Astoria is near the mouth of Columbia river.

CALIFORNIA

This country was once claimed by Mexico, but was ceded to the United States by treaty, in 1848. It lies between the Rocky Mountains on the east, and the Pacific Ocean on the west.

It is noted for the vast quantity of gold found within its borders. The gold is dug from the mountains and rocks, and from the sand in the beds of the rivers.

Herbert Quick on the Influence of McGuffey's Readers, c. 1870 *

To two farmer boys born, one in Washington County, Pennsylvania, and the other in Ohio, I owe my first taste of good literature. They were William and Alexander McGuffey, the authors respectively of the First and Fifth Eclectic Readers, and the Fifth Reader of the edition of 1844. These were the standard school readers of my day; except that the 1844 Fifth Reader, or McGuffey's Rhetorical Guide, had been found too difficult, not only for the pupils but for the teachers of the community. My copy of it was an old dog's-eared volume left by my brother Orison when he left for Pike's Peak. These text-books constitute the most influential volumes ever published in America. They were our most popular reading books for generations—and for anything I know in their present form—they may be still. They had a spirit of their own, compilations as they were. And it was, in spite of much that was British in selections and illustrations, the spirit of America at its best. . . .

I have just looked at a copy of a twenty-year-old edition of the McGuffey's First Reader. It has not a single lesson that was in the one I took in my trembling hand when Maggie Livingstone called me to her to begin

* *One Man's Life: An Autobiography* (Indianapolis, Bobbs-Merrill Co., 1925), pp. 156-59. Used by permission of the publishers.

learning my letters. Mine had a green cover; but it was hidden by the muslin which my mother had stitched over it to save the wear on a book that cost thirty cents. It was filled with illustrations which I now know were of British origin; for all the men wore knee breeches, the girls had on fluffy pantalets and sugar-scoop bonnets, and the ladies huge many-flounced skirts. One boy had a cricket bat in his hand; and the ruling passions of the youngsters seemed to be to shoot with the bow and to roll the hoop. "Can you hop, Tom? See, I can hop! Tom, hop to me." How easily does the English language lend itself to early lessons of such simplicity!

These books were intensely moral, soundly religious, and addicted to the inculcation of habits of industry, mercy and most of the virtues. Lucy was exorted to rise because the sun was up. "Mary was up at six," she was assured; and then was added the immortal line, "Up, up, Lucy, and go out to Mary"; which scoffers perverted to "Double-up, Lucy." Most of the words were of one syllable; but "How doth the little busy bee" was in it, I am certain; and "I like to see a little dog and pat him on the head." It was an easy book, and if it fell short of the power in the moral and religious fields of the more advanced volumes,—why, so did its students in the practice of the vices and the need for reproof or warning.

My mastery of the First and Second Readers—just the opening of the marvels of the printed page—was a poignant delight. The reading of anything gave me a sort of ecstasy. These books did not, however, set in operation the germinant powers of actual literary treasure-hunting. They did give to the mind of the writer and to the world some things of universal knowledge. We learned that George Washington could not tell a lie about the cherry tree; and that his father proved to him the existence of God by the device of sewing lettuce in a trench which spelled George's name. "It might have grown so by chance," said the elder Washington in this Second Reader lesson; but George saw clearly that it could not have come by chance. Some one sowed those seeds in that way. And his father assured him that this world of wonderful adaptations could not have come as it has by chance. There were many fables, and lessons about insects, birds and beasts. Most of the scenes were British. Our habits, our morals and our faith were carefully kept in mind; and we grew to know Mary's Lamb by heart. . . .

The Committee of Fifteen on the Correlation of Studies in Elementary Education, 1895 *

Your Committee understands by correlation of studies:

1. Logical order of topics and branches

First, the arrangement of topics in proper sequence in the course of study, in such a manner that each branch develops in an order suited to

* *Educational Review*, IX (March, 1895), pp. 230-31. Interest in the correlation of studies was another influence of Herbartianism which swept American schools in the 1880's and 1890's.

and to bring college and high school into intimate relations of mutual dependence, have our cordial approval and sympathy.

We urge more attention to the study of the history and principles of
education in colleges and universities, not alone that their graduates may
be the better prepared for the work of teaching, but in order that there
may be sent out into the community an increasing number of educated
citizens, who have some knowledge of educational conditions and precedents, and who will thus be able to contribute a prompt and intelligent
support to the work of the public school.

We ask the attention of the executive and legislative departments of the
government to the valuable work of the Bureau of Education and to the
pressing need of adequate appropriations for its support. The salary of
the commissioner is pitifully small, and is beneath the dignity of the office
and of this nation. On behalf of the teachers of the country we ask for its
increase, and also for the provision of funds to enable educational investigations and experiments to be undertaken and extended.

The association has contributed to the current discussion of educational
problems three reports of the highest importance, perpared after laborious
and long-continued study and investigation: one on secondary education,
one on elementary education, and one on the conduct and support of the
rural school. We earnestly commend these reports, the work of trained
specialists, not only to teachers, but also to legislatures, to members of
school boards, to the press, and to intelligent citizens generally. They
offer a safe guide for future progress.

To all officers, associations, and individuals who have contributed to
the success of this meeting; to the press of Milwaukee and Chicago, which
has reported our proceedings with accuracy and unexampled fullness, and
to the retiring President, Charles R. Skinner, for his vigorous, intelligent,
and progressive administration, the thanks of this association are due, and
are most cordially tendered.

(Signed)

NICHOLAS MURRAY, of New York, *Chairman,*
JAMES H. CANFIELD, of Ohio,
CHARLES H. KEYES, of California,
DAVID K. GOSS, of Indiana,
J. R. PRESTON, of Mississippi.

The Carnegie Foundation's Definition of Educational "Units," 1906 *

The terms college and university have, as yet, no fixed meaning on this
continent. It is not uncommon to find flourishing high schools which bear

* *First Annual Report of the President and Treasurer,* of The Carnegie Foundation for
the Advancement of Teaching, pp. 38-39. "Thus the unit triumphed, both in the examining
and in the certificating colleges. . . . It may not be entirely an accident that the automobile
and the unit system were invented at about the same time and were perfected and popularized
almost simultaneously." R. L. Duffus, *Democracy Enters College: A Study of the Rise and
Decline of the Academic Lockstep* (New York, Charles Scribner's Sons, 1936), p. 51.

one or the other of these titles. To recognize institutions of learning without some regard to this fact would be to throw away whatsoever opportunity the Foundation has for the exertion of educational influence.

The trustees have, therefore, adopted for the present an arbitrary definition of what constitutes a college, one framed very closely after that adopted in the revised ordinances of the State of New York. This definition is expressed in the rules of the Foundation as follows:

"An institution to be ranked as a college, must have at least six (6) professors giving their entire time to college and university work, a course of four full years in liberal arts and sciences, and should require for admission, not less than the usual four years of academic or high school preparation, or its equivalent, in addition to the preacademic or grammar school studies."

In order to judge what constitutes "four years of academic or high-school preparation" the officers of the Foundation have made use of a plan commonly adopted by college entrance examination boards. By this plan college entrance requirements are designated in terms of units, a unit being a course of five periods weekly throughout an academic year of the preparatory school. For the purposes of the Foundation the units in each branch of academic study have also been quantitatively defined, the aim being to assign values to the subjects in accordance with the time usually required to prepare adequately upon them for college entrance. Thus, plane geometry, which is usually studied five periods weekly throughout an academic year of the preparatory school, is estimated as one unit. In other words, the value of the unit is based upon the actual amount of work required and not upon the time specified for the preparation of the work.

A difficulty, however, arises in estimating by this method the entrance requirements of the various colleges and universities. The large majority of institutions accept the certificates of "approved" preparatory schools and academies. In the courses of these "approved" schools it frequently happens that there is a marked discrepancy between the amount of work required and the time specified for the preparation of the work, when judged by the definitions of the units as adopted by the officers of the Foundation. For example, plane geometry may be accepted as an entrance requirement by an institution, although that subject has been studied in the preparatory school for only two periods weekly throughout an academic year. In such cases the officers of the Foundation will credit the institution with plane geometry solely upon the basis of the time given to the preparation of the subject. Thus, plane geometry, studied two periods weekly throughout an academic year, would be counted as two-fifths of a unit and not as one unit. Or, if the time given to the preparation of the academic course is generally below the standard, the officers of the Foundation reserve the right to consider such work as altogether unsatisfactory unless adequate explanation is offered.

Fourteen units constitute the minimum amount of preparation which may be interpreted as "four years of academic or high-school preparation." The definitions of the units, given in the following pages, are in close accordance with the requirements of the College Entrance Examination Board.

A District Superintendent of Schools of Brooklyn, New York, on Sex Hygiene in the Schools, 1914 *

My first strong conviction on this subject is that no superintendent or board of superintendents or board of education has any right to add to the curriculum of any public school talks or lessons or lectures on the more intimate phases of sex hygiene without the approval of the taxpayers supporting such school.

My second strong conviction is that no lectures should be delivered to pupils, which, if written or printed and sent thru the mails to the parents of those pupils, would cause the arrest of the sender.

My reasons for these convictions are: (1) pupils are forced by law to attend these schools; (2) the schools are erected and maintained, and the teachers and superintendents are paid, by the taxpayers.

Another strong conviction of mine is that the dangers and the evils resulting from class- or group-teaching of this subject are greater than those resulting from no teaching of it.

Now I do not claim that ignorance is synonymous with innocence; but I do deny that knowledge is purity. Some of the most vicious among both sexes know all that there is to be known both as to human relations and as to the physical dangers often resulting therefrom; yet they use their knowledge, not to the end of living purer lives themselves or leading others to live purer lives, but simply to save themselves from certain undesired results of impure living. And some of the purest lives are lived by those who know nothing either of such relations or of the mental and physical decay resulting therefrom; but who, knowing only that certain things are wrong, have sufficient will power and sufficient loyalty to an ideal to do the right and avoid the wrong.

And here let me say that such will to do right must be our hope, rather than the fear of contracting the loathsome diseases, the whole history and nature of which some extremists would have us spread before our children. Miss Blake, referring to this, pointed out that seven murders occurred among the spectators of the last public hanging on Holborn Hill.

What then shall be our "twentieth-century ideal" and how shall we attain it?

Our ideal should be a young man and a young woman equally pure in

---

* Grace E. Strachan, "Wanted: A Twentieth-Century Ideal," *Journal of Proceedings and Addresses,* National Education Association, 1914, pp. 317-18.

body, mind, and soul—each preserving and revering the body always as the temple of the future race, and each determined that no fault of his or hers shall mar or lessen the usefulness of the body, mind, or soul of the child who may be born of him or her.

How attain this ideal?

In babyhood and childhood, parents, teachers, and preachers should teach purity and modesty of thought, word, and act without sounding the depths of all it may mean. Parents should encourage their children to give them their fullest confidence. When troubled or doubtful in special cases, they should consult a physician. Teachers should watch zealously and, when any child's actions or appearance seem to demand special consideration, should consult with the principal and the parents. Where it is evident that the parents cannot be depended on for the assistance needed, the physician—home or school—or the school nurse may be called on. But this instruction and this advice should always be given "one by one." For Mary Brown may have a very bad, depraved mind, and be guilty of very bad practices, but she will be very careful not to let all the girls and the boys in her school know how bad she is. She may be watching and waiting select one here and there to drag into her net; but let her sit in a room with three hundred others and listen with them to a talk on these hidden subjects, and the barriers are at once washed away, the guardians of reserve and modesty are routed, and she feels free to discuss and to instruct in her own dangerous way. I believe there is no greater danger threatening the modesty and the sanctity of the home than the man or the woman who advocates teaching all the intimate facts of human relations to little children and young boys and girls "just as they would teach arithmetic."

Superintendent Thomas A. Mott, Seymour, Indiana, on Sex Hygiene in the Schools, 1914 *

...It is something for the child to know at the right time some of the important facts relating to his development into manhood; it is something for the child to know the chief dangers that confront him during the unfolding of his sexual powers; but this movement in the schools must mean more than this. The problem includes the development of right attitudes of mind, of high ideals and ethical standards of life, of respect for the social standards and conventions of society, of an appreciation of the sanctity of the home, the sacredness of motherhood, and the love of little children. Everything in the school curriculum that leads in this direction is a part of the teaching of race hygiene.

Physiology and hygiene are required subjects in most schools. In grades above the sixth, the boys should be separated from the girls. The boys

* *Ibid.*, p. 324.

should have a male teacher, preferably a father. The girls should have a woman teacher. In our city, the boys' classes are taught by a man of high ideals, a teacher of fine experience, a father of boys. The teacher of the girls' classes in physiology is a college-trained woman, a woman of dignity, and with a rich experience as a teacher. In these classes, nothing need be held back which the students should know. The real questions of the laws of reproduction the schools should leave to the home. But such knowledge of sex hygiene as the pupils should know may be taught by the teacher as the occasion demands. . . .

National Manufacturers' Association on the Plight of the Public Schools, 1914 *

There are about two million boys and girls between fourteen and eighteen in the United States out of school and, for the most part, at work. This marks our common school as so hopelessly, wickedly inefficient and damaging as to call for instant and tremendous consideration and readjustment.

Charles W. Eliot on Educational Defects in the United States, 1919 †

The United States Bureau of Education has printed for wide distribution as a Teacher's Leaflet President Eliot's outspoken and emphatic statement of "certain defects in American education and the remedies for them," originally written for the fourth commencement of Reed College and published in the Reed College Record.

"The war with Germany," says President Eliot, "has presented to the American people much new evidence concerning the grave defects in their own physical and mental condition and, therefore, presumably, in their training and education during at least two generations past. To study the remedies for the defects disclosed by our attempts to recruit quickly a great Army and a great Navy, and simultaneously to man our war industries with as large a number of competent mechanics and operatives, is the most urgent duty of all institutions and persons who possess any of the elements of educational leadership. Especially is it the duty of American universities, college, technical institutes, school boards, and normal schools to study the changes in the elementary and secondary schools of the country needed in order to remedy in the rising generations the physical and mental defects from which their predecessors have suffered. That study should lead, first, to a clear understanding of those defects, and, second, to an intelligent prescription of the appropriate remedies. To

* Given in *Journal of Proceedings and Addresses*, National Education Association, 1914, p. 313.
† Editorial, "President Eliot on Our Educational Defects," *Educational Review*, LVII (January-May, 1919), pp. 179-80.

apply the remedies is the duty of legislatures, school boards, and educational administrators all over the country."

The writer discusses in turn physical defects in school children and drafted men; bad diet; the lack of systematic physical training; infant mortality; tuberculosis; alcoholism; venereal diseases; and the mental defects of illiteracy; the lack of manual skill and training of the senses, and the general and habitual absence of accuracy of observation or statement in the American people. The remedies in each instance are plainly suggested. The pamphlet is not one easy to quote from or to summarize. It should be read by a wide public.

Hamlin Garland Describes "Friday Exercises" at the Seminary Which He Attended in the Middle West, 1923 *

The school was in truth a very primitive institution, hardly more than a high school, but it served its purpose. It gave farmers' boys like myself the opportunity of meeting those who were older, finer, more learned than they, and every day was to me like turning a fresh and delightful page in a story book, not merely because it brought new friends, new experiences, but because it symbolized freedom from the hay fork and the hoe. Learning was easy for me. In all but mathematics I kept among the highest of my class without much effort, but it was in the "Friday Exercises" that I earliest distinguished myself.

It was the custom at the close of every week's work to bring a section of the pupils upon the platform as essayists or orators, and these "exercises" formed the most interesting and the most passionately dreaded feature of the entire school. No pupil who took part in it ever forgot his first appearance. It was at once a pillory and a burning. It called for self-possession, memory, grace and gesture and a voice!

My case is typical. For three or four days before my first ordeal, I could not eat. A mysterious uneasiness developed in my solar plexus, a pain which never left me—except possibly in the morning before I had time to think. Day by day I drilled and drilled and drilled, out in the fields at the edge of the town or at home when mother was away, in the barn while milking—at every opportunity I went through my selection with most impassioned voice and lofty gestures, sustained by the legends of Webster and Demosthenes, resolved upon a blazing victory. I did everything but mumble a smooth pebble—realizing that most of the boys in my section were going through precisely the same struggle. Each of us knew exactly how the others felt, and yet I cannot say that we displayed acute sympathy one with another; on the contrary, those in the free section con-

---

* Hamlin Garland, *A Son of the Middle Border* (New York, The Macmillan Co., 1923), pp. 197-200. Used by permission.

sidered the antics of the suffering section a very amusing spectacle and we were continually being "joshed" about our lack of appetite.

The test was, in truth, rigorous. To ask a bashful boy or shy girl fresh from the kitchen to walk out upon a platform and face that crowd of mocking students was a kind of torture. No desk was permitted. Each victim stood bleakly exposed to the pitiless gaze of three hundred eyes, and as most of us were poorly dressed, in coats that never fitted and trousers that climbed our boottops, we suffered the miseries of the damned. The girls wore gowns which they themselves had made, and were, of course, equally self-conscious. The knowledge that their sleeves did not fit was of more concern to them than the thought of breaking down—but the fear of forgetting their lines also contributed to their dread and terror.

While the names which preceded mine were called off that first afternoon, I grew colder and colder till at last I shook with a nervous chill, and when, in his smooth, pleasant tenor, Prof. Bush called out "Hamlin Garland" I rose in my seat with a spring like Jack from his box. My limbs were numb, so numb that I could scarcely feel the floor beneath my feet and the windows were only faint gray glares of light. My head oscillated like a toy balloon, seemed indeed to be floating in the air, and my heart was pounding like a drum.

However, I had pondered upon this scene so long and had figured my course so exactly that I made all the turns with moderate degree of grace and succeeded finally in facing my audience without falling up the steps (as several others had done) and so looked down upon my fellows like Tennyson's eagle on the sea. In that instant a singular calm fell over me. I became strangely master of myself. From somewhere above me a new and amazing power fell upon me and in that instant I perceived on the faces of my classmates a certain expression of surprise and serious respect. My subconscious oratorical self had taken charge.

I do not at present recall what my recitation was, but it was probably *Catiline's Defense* or some other of the turgid declamatory pieces of classic literature with which all our readers were filled. It was bombastic stuff, but my blind, boyish belief in it gave it dignity. As I went on my voice cleared. The window sashes regained their outlines. I saw every form before me, and the look of surprise and pleasure on the smiling face of my principal exalted me.

Closing amid hearty applause, I stepped down with a feeling that I had won a place among the orators of the school, a belief which did no harm to others and gave me a good deal of satisfaction. As I had neither money nor clothes, and was not of figure to win admiration, why should I not express the pride I felt in my power to move an audience? Besides I was only sixteen!

The principal spoke to me afterwords, both praising and criticising my method. The praise I accepted, the criticism I naturally resented. I realized some of my faults of course, but I was not ready to have even Prof. Bush tell me of them. I hated "elocution" drill in class. I relied on "inspiration." I believed that orators were born, not made. . . .

Hamlin Garland Testifies to the Influence of the McGuffey's Readers, 1923 *

One night as we were all seated around the kerosene lamp my father said, "Well, Belle, I suppose we'll have to take these young ones down to town and fit 'em out for school." These words so calmly uttered filled our minds with visions of new boots, new caps and new books, and though we went obediently to bed we hardly slept, so excited were we, and at breakfast next morning, not one of us could think of food. All our desires converged upon the wondrous expedition—our first visit to town. . . .

Then came our new books, a McGuffey reader, a Mitchell geography, a Ray's arithmetic, and a slate. The books had a delightful new smell also, and there was singular charm in the smooth surface of the unmarked slates. I was eager to carve my name in the frame. At last with our treasures under the seat (so near that we could feel them), with our slates and books in our laps we jolted home, dreaming of school and snow. To wade in the drifts with our fine high-topped boots was now our desire. . . .

The school-house which was to be the center of our social life stood on the bare prairie about a mile to the southwest and like thousands of other similar buildings in the west, had not a leaf to shade it in summer nor a branch to break the winds of savage winter. "There's been a good deal of talk about setting out a wind-break," neighbor Button explained to us, "but nothing has as yet been done." It was merely a square pin box painted a glaring white on the outside and a desolate drab within; at least drab was the original color, but the benches were mainly so greasy and hacked that original intentions were obscured. It had two doors on the eastern end and three windows on each side.

A long square stove (standing on slender legs in a puddle of bricks), a wooden chair, and a rude table in one corner, for the use of the teacher, completed the movable furniture. The walls were roughly plastered and the windows had no curtains.

It was a barren temple of the arts even to the residents of Dry Run, and Harriet and I, stealing across the prairie one Sunday morning to look in, came away vaguely depressed. We were fond of school and never missed a day if we could help it, but this neighborhood center seemed small and bleak and poor.

With what fear, what excitement we approached the door on that first day, I can only faintly indicate. All the scholars were strange to me except

* Hamlin Garland, *A Son of the Middle Border* (New York, The Macmillan Co., 1923), pp. 90, 92, 95, 96, 112. Used by permission.

Albert and Cyrus Button, and I was prepared for rough treatment. However, the experience was not so harsh as I had feared. True, Rangely Field did throw me down and wash my face in snow, and Jack Sweet tripped me up once or twice, but I bore these indignities with such grace and could command, and soon made a place for myself among the boys.

Burton Babcock was my seat-mate, and at once became my chum. You will hear much of him in his chronicle. He was two years older than I and though pale and slim was unusually swift and strong for his age. He was a silent lad, curiously timid in his classes and not at ease with his teachers.

I cannot recover much of that first winter of school. It was not an experience to remember for its charm. Not one line of grace, not one touch of color relieved the room's bare walls or softened its harsh windows. Perhaps this very barrenness gave to the poetry in our readers an appeal that seems magical, certainly it threw over the faces of Frances Babcock and Mary Abbie Gammons a lovelier halo.—They were "the big girls" of the school, that is to say, they were seventeen or eighteen years old,—and Frances was the special terror of the teacher, a pale and studious pigeon-toed young man who was preparing for college. . . .

Our readers were almost the only counterchecks to the current of vulgarity and baseness which ran through the talk of the older boys, and I wish to acknowledge my deep obligation to Professor McGuffey, whoever he may have been, for the dignity and literary grace of his selections. From the pages of his readers I learned to know and love the poems of Scott, Byron, Southey, Wordsworth and a long line of the English masters. I got my first taste of Shakespeare from the selected scenes which I read in these books. . . .

A Statement of the Principles of Progressive Education, 1924 *

I. Freedom to Develop Naturally.

The conduct of the pupil should be governed by himself according to the social needs of his community, rather than by arbitrary laws. Full opportunity for initiative and self-expression should be provided, together with an environment rich in interesting material that is available for the free use of every pupil.

II. Interest, the Motive of All Work.

Interest should be satisfied and developed through: (1) Direct and indirect contact with the world and its activities, and the use of the experience thus gained. (2) Application of knowledge gained, and correlation between different subjects. (3) The consciousness of achievement.

III. The Teacher a Guide, Not a Task-Master.

It is essential that teachers should believe in the aims and general prin-

* Progressive Education: A Quarterly Review of the Newer Tendencies in Education, I, No. I (April, 1924), p. 2.

ciples of Progressive Education and that they should have latitude for the development of initiative and originality.

Progressive teachers will encourage the use of all the senses, training the pupils in both observation and judgment; and instead of hearing recitations only, will spend most of the time teaching how to use various sources of information, including life activities as well as books; how to reason about the information thus acquired; and how to express forcefully and logically the conclusions reached.

Ideal teaching conditions demand that classes be small, especially in the elementary school years.

IV. Scientific Study of Pupil Development.

School records should not be confined to the marks given by the teachers to show the advancement of the pupils in their study of subjects, but should also include both objective and subjective reports on those physical, mental, moral and social characteristics which affect both school and adult life, and which can be influenced by the school and the home. Such records should be used as a guide for the treatment of each pupil, and should also serve to focus the attention of the teacher on the all-important work of development rather than on simply teaching subject matter.

V. Greater Attention to All that Affects the Child's Physical Development.

One of the first considerations of Progressive Education is the health of the pupils. Much more room in which to move about, better light and air, clean and well ventilated buildings, easier access to the out-of-doors and greater use of it, are all necessary. There should be frequent use of adequate playgrounds. The teachers should observe closely the physical condition of each pupil and, in co-operation with the home, make abounding health the first objective of childhood.

VI. Co-operation Between School and Home to Meet the Needs of Child-Life.

The school should provide, with the home, as much as is possible of all that the natural interests and activities of the child demand, especially during the elementary school years. These conditions can come about only through intelligent co-operation between parents and teachers.

VII. The Progressive School a Leader in Educational Movements.

The Progressive School should be a leader in educational movements. It should be a laboratory where new ideas, if worthy, meet encouragement; where tradition alone does not rule, but the best of the past is leavened with the discoveries of today, and the result is freely added to the sum of educational knowledge.

Charles W. Eliot Congratulates *Progressive Education*
on its First Issue, 1924 *

I congratulate you on the very interesting contents of the first number
of the quarterly magazine to be published by the Progressive Education
Association.

The Progressive Schools are increasing rapidly in number and in influence and the educational public is becoming more and more awake to
their merits. They are to be the schools of the future in both America and
Europe.

The Status of Latin and Greek in the American
Schools, 1923-1924 †

The total enrolment in Latin in the secondary schools of the country
for the year 1923-1924 is estimated by the United States Bureau of Education at 940,000, slightly in excess of the combined enrolment in all other
foreign languages. It is approximately 27.5% of the total enrolment of
pupils in all secondary schools, including the seventh and eighth grades of
junior high schools, or 30% if these grades are not included. The enrolment in Greek is only about 11,000, but shows some signs of increase. In
the public high schools nearly one-half of the Latin enrolment is in the
ninth grade or below, while only one-fifteenth is in the twelfth grade. About
one-half of this decrease is due to the corresponding decrease in total
enrolment.[1] About 83% of the 20,500 secondary schools of the country
offer instruction in one or more foreign languages. Of this number 94%
offer Latin, a slightly larger percentage than in the case of all other foreign
languages combined. The number offering four years of Latin is more than
double the number offering three years of French, four years being the
ordinary maximum time given to Latin and three years the ordinary maximum time given to French.

There are approximately 22,500 teachers of Latin in the secondary
schools of the country. More than 25% of these teachers have had less
than eight years of schooling beyond the elementary grades, almost exactly
25% have not studied Latin beyond the secondary-school stage and only
slightly over 25% have studied Greek,—half of this number not beyond
the secondary-school stage.

The Latin enrolment in the colleges of the country in 1923-1924 was
approximately 40,000 and the Greek enrolment about 16,000. There are

---

* *Ibid.,* p. 3. The Progressive Education Association had been organized in 1918 and Eliot
was its first president.
 † *The Classical Investigation.* Conducted by the advisory committee of the American
Classical League (Princeton, Princeton University Press, 1924), pp. 16-18. This study was
made by a grant from the General Education Board.
 [1] This makes no allowance for the appreciable number of pupils who begin Latin in the
second year or later.

many signs in the colleges of an increasing interest in both Latin and Greek. Recent extensive studies show that there is a strong voluntary tendency to offer Latin for college entrance and that although "the largest specific (foreign) language requirement is in Latin," the average offerings of Latin presented by candidates for college entrance amount to "more than three times the prescription." [2]

Of the 609 colleges in the United States listed in 1922-1923, by the United States Bureau of Education, 234 offer courses in beginning Latin, 470 in beginning Greek, 237 give teacher-training courses in Latin and 214 require two to four years of Latin for admission to the A. B. course.

Apparently only five states have a definite requirement that one must have studied Latin (or Greek) in college in order to teach the subject in the public high schools of the state, and only one state requires any previous teachers' training work in the language.

Thirty-nine of the forty-eight state superintendents of public instruction state that their attitude toward Latin is sympathetic or distinctly friendly. Seven express themselves as neutral and two as unsympathetic or distinctly unfriendly. As regards Greek, eight are sympathetic or distinctly friendly, twenty-four are neutral and sixteen are unsympathetic or distinctly unfriendly.

Pope Pius XI Opposes "Progressive Education," 1929 *

Every method of education founded, wholly or in part, on the denial or forgetfulness of original sin and grace, and relying on the sole powers of human nature, is unsound. Such, generally speaking, are those modern systems bearing various names which appeal to a pretended self-government and unrestrained freedom on the part of the child, and which diminish or even suppress the teacher's authority and action, attributing to the child an exclusive primacy of initiative, and an activity independent of any higher law, natural or divine, in the work of his education. . . .

A Plea for Common Sense in Education, 1932 †

It is now more than ten years since my cousin, Stanwood Cobb, of Washngton, D. C., came to my house, full of dreams for a new type of education. Long into the night we talked, on subjects we had often discussed before, going over the possibilities of an organization to carry out plans he had been forming with a group of progressive thinkers in Washington, and discussing personalities who might serve in the cause.

[2] Report of Clyde Furst, Association of American Colleges, 111 Fifth Avenue, New York, Vol. X, No. 3 (Bulletin of May, 1924), pp. 200, 201.

* Encyclical Letter on the Christian Education of Youth. *Current History* XXXI (March, 1930), p. 1099.

† Ernest Cobb, *One Foot on the Ground: A Plea for Common Sense in Education* (New York, G. P. Putnam's Sons, 1932), Introduction, pp. 9-13. Used by permission of the author and publishers.

The next morning he called President Emeritus Eliot, of Harvard, by telephone, and was promised an interview that same day. Before he left I gave him a small check to cover what my membership dues and initiation might be in the new association he was planning; so, apart from the founders, I believe I was the first member of the association to be known as the Progressive Education Association. That evening he called back to say that President Eliot heartily approved of the plans, declared his belief in the need for a more liberal philosophy and a freer technique in education, and had agreed to be our first president.

There were many wealthy and influential people who stood ready to help those engaged in such a work, and the opportunity did indeed seem ripe. The public schools had before this time become conscious of their limitations, and were eager to find ways for improvement and a much more liberal field of activity.

At that day I had what I thought were clear and definite aims for such an association, and looked eagerly forward to a unified group through which such aims could be fulfilled. My idea was in general that, accepting the usual problems of public education as a standard, we should organize schools and classes where experiments could safely be tried, and where we could show those working in the ordinary conditions of public school life how their problems might be solved in happier and more successful ways.

Greatly to my astonishment, however, I found that these ideas were not going to be at all the ideas of many people active and influential in pushing forward the doctrines to be known as those of Progressive Education. The gap immediately formed has been impossible for me to cross, because, while I accepted the common burdens and problems of public education as a normal and desirable field of work, this new group seemed eager to scrap the whole body of educational practice hitherto in use, and substitute most radical educational adventures, which, while not impossible in their small, wealthy schools, have proved of little value, even there, and quite beyond the power or desire of the public schools to follow.

I have treasured the college entrance examinations as the one salvation of our public school system. To me they have been the symbol of that standard of efficiency absolutely needed in such a field of mental endeavor. Without them I believe the output of our public education would have fallen far, far short of the value it has today. As a matter of fact, I believe the college entrance examinations have set the only important standard of efficiency by which our schools might judge their work.

Yet, almost from the first, the Progressives have damned the colleges and their entrance examinations. As they came to realize that their methods would not prepare pupils to pass these tests, their condemnation has become more sweeping. Instead of a careful inspection of their own work, they have heaped the burden on the colleges.

I have said nothing and written nothing regarding Progressive education, because I could not agree, and saw no chance for helpful criticism; but I have tried to keep in touch with the work in their schools and in their writing. I have kept up my membership in good standing, because I felt sure that a time would come when the cooler heads would realize that an inventory must be taken and our mistakes honestly admitted.

That time seems at hand. The editor of the Progressive Education magazine has written me, asking if I would write a critique of Progressive education, saying: "Progressive education very much needs severe self-criticism and appraisal." I could not possibly say anything important on this subject in a magazine article, so I am putting before you in this book my own opinions, and what I know to be the opinions of many practical school men on this subject.

Of course a book written from the *I* point of view must be personal, and not free from conceit. The fact is that people who tell frankly what they think and believe themselves always interest me more than those who speak impersonally, and hide their own beliefs, if any, behind a professional mask. Most other people seem to prefer personal confessions also, and that gives me courage.

So this book will be mostly just between us. I shall quote few authorities, merely putting before you those subjects that Progressive people have made important, saying what I think, giving the general opinion of those hundreds of school executives and teachers with whom I talk, and will ask you to look into your own mind as you read, so that you may see how your own experience compares with ours.

W. J. Cameron on the *McGuffey Readers,* 1935 *

At Greenfield—the early American village which Mr. Ford has assembled at Dearborn—two log cabins may be seen side by side. They are preserved, not merely to illustrate pioneer conditions, but because of their association with a great man. One of them is the birthplace of William Holmes McGuffey, the other is a schoolhouse such as he attended as a child.

McGuffey was a schoolmaster. His schoolroom was the length and breadth of the United States; his scholars were three generations of Americans. Through the medium of six humble school readers he was able to revolutionize education and formulate a national standard of character on which the new America molded itself for fifty years. These books head the list of American best sellers. Except the Bible and the dictionary no

---

* W. J. Cameron. A talk given in the Ford Sunday Evening Hour, March 17, 1935, over a nation-wide network of the Columbia Broadcasting System from Detroit. For additional material on these famous books, see Henry H. Vail, *A History of the McGuffey Readers* (Cleveland, Ohio, The Burrows Brothers, 1911); Mark Sullivan, *Our Times,* II, pp. 10-16; H. C. Minnich, *William Holmes McGuffey and His Readers* and *Old Favorites from the McGuffey Readers* (New York, American Book Co., 1936).

books have ever sold so many millions of copies. Year after year a million and a half McGuffey's Readers were printed, and about 1880 they reached nearly two millions a year. There is no record like it. Thousands of the stanchest citizen-builders of this nation were graduated into active life out of McGuffey's old Second Reader. The American people were made articulate, their moral ideals were elevated, their thought deepened and broadened through the influence of these tens of millions of unpretending little schoolbooks. Even today they are read or remembered with affectionate reverence by multitudes of our people.

McGuffey is the father of graded school studies. He evolved this by seating children of various ages on a log, reading to them, and noting what was best received by each age. He was the first American to dispel the gloom of schoolbooks by giving play in them to humor and irony. Earlier elementary education in this country reeked dolefully of the graveyard and epitaphs and future punishment. McGuffey took the moral life and made it a strong and free and beautiful thing. He not only disciplined the mind to think, he fortified the character of his pupils with ideals of reverence and rectitude. Truthfulness, industry, consideration for the weak, kindness, respect of conscience, a firm reliance on the right to justify itself always and everywhere—this was the tonic iron he distilled for the soul of young America. He made principles live in such characters as the hare and the tortoise, and Meddlesome Mattie, and in such sayings as "Try, try again" and "No excellency without great labor." It was not books he taught, but life; not words, but qualities.

Mr. Ford's interest in McGuffey was revived by a simple incident. One afternoon as the school children danced and shouted past the Ford home, Mrs. Ford remembered some verses she had learned from McGuffey's Readers in her school days—

> "Hear the children gaily shout
> 'Half past four and school is out!'"

Search was made for her old schoolbooks, but the First Reader, in which the verses were, was not to be found. Mr. and Mrs. Ford telephoned their friends, but none had the book. For a long time after that Mr. Ford haunted the old bookshops of many cities in search of McGuffey's Readers. The result was one of the finest collections of these Readers in the country. Miami University, at Oxford, Ohio, which possesses many McGuffey relics, made him a replica of the great schoolmaster's study table. McGuffey manuscripts and letters appeared at Dearborn. The farm on which he was born, near Claysville, in the hills of Pennsylvania, was purchased as a memorial. And then one sunny afternoon last September, on that farm, in the presence of 15,000 people and presidents and professors of universities and colleges with which McGuffey in his lifetime had been associated, Mr. Ford's monument in honor of the author of the Readers was dedicated. It stands on the exact spot where the chimney of McGuffey's childhood home reared its squat and sturdy mass. And Mr. Ford made a speech that day. True, it was a very short speech, but even that is extraordinary. He doesn't believe that much is accomplished by talk. But that McGuffey Day in Pennsylvania was an occasion! Mr. Ford is probably prouder of his knowledge of the six McGuffey Readers than of any other volumes in his extensive library.

William Holmes McGuffey belongs in the calendar of our national prophets. He is honored at Dearborn because moral principles became educational essentials under his system. Many wish that our present public education might be made the means of character formation that it was in McGuffey's day. We are trying to restore that type of teaching at Greenfield Village.

John Dewey States the Aims of "Progressives," 1938 *

If one attempts to formulate the philosophy of education implicit in the practices of the newer education, we may, I think, discover certain common principles amid the variety of progressive schools now existing.

To imposition from above is opposed expression and cultivation of individuality; to external discipline is opposed free activity; to learning from texts and teachers, learning through experience; to acquisition of isolated skills and techniques by drill, is opposed acquisition of them as means of attaining ends which make direct vital appeal; to preparation for a more or less remote future is opposed making the most of the opportunities of present life; to static aims and materials is opposed acquaintance with a changing world.

There is always the danger in a new movement that in rejecting the aims and methods of that which it would supplant, it may develop its principles negatively rather than positively and constructively. Then it takes its clue in practice from that which is rejected instead of from the constructive development of its own philosophy.

EFFECTIVE AUTHORITY SOUGHT

When external authority is rejected, it does not follow that all authority should be rejected, but rather that there is need to search for a more effective source of authority. Because the older education imposed the knowledge, methods and the rules of conduct of the mature person upon the young, it does not follow that the knowledge and skill of the mature person has no directive value for the experience of the immature. On the contrary, basing education upon personal experience may mean multiplied and more intimate contacts between the mature than ever existed in the traditional school, and consequently more, rather than less; guidance by others.

Just because traditional education was a matter of routine in which the

* *The New York Times,* June 3, 1938. Used by permission.

plans and programs were handed down from the past, it does not follow that progressive education is a matter of planless improvisation.

It is, accordingly, a much more difficult task to work out the kinds of materials, of methods and of social relationships that are appropriate to the new education, than is the case with traditional education. I think many of the difficulties experienced in the conduct of progressive schools and many of the criticisms leveled against them arise from this source. The difficulties are aggravated and the criticisms are increased when it is supposed that the new education is somehow easier than the old.

BUSINESS OF THE TEACHER

Traditional education tended to ignore the importance of personal impulse and desire as moving springs. But this is no reason why progressive education should identify impulse and desire with purpose and thereby pass lightly over the need for careful observation, for wide range of information and for judgment if students are to share in the formation of the purposes which activate them.

In any educational scheme the occurrence of a desire and impulse is not the final end. It is an occasion and a demand for the formation of a plan and method of activity. Such a plan, to repeat, can be formed only by study of conditions and by securing all relevant information.

The teacher's business is to see that the occasion is taken advantage of. Since freedom resides in the operations of intelligent observation and judgment by which a purpose is developed, guidance given by the teacher to the exercise of the pupils' intelligence is an aid to freedom, not a restriction upon it.

Sometimes teachers seem to be afraid even to make suggestions to the members of a group as to what they should do. I have heard of cases in which children are surrounded with objects and materials and then left entirely to themselves, the teacher being loath to suggest even what might be done with the materials lest freedom be infringed upon. Why, then, even supply materials, since they are a source of some suggestion or other?

But what is more important is that the suggestion upon which pupils act must in any case come from somewhere. It is impossible to understand why a suggestion from one who has a larger experience and a wider horizon should not be at least as valid as a suggestion arising from some more or less accidental source.

PLAN STRESSES COOPERATION

It is possible of course to abuse the office, and to force the activity of the young into channels which express the teacher's purpose rather than that of the pupils. But the way to avoid this danger is not for the adult to withdraw entirely. The way is, first, for the teacher to be intelligently aware of the capacities, needs and past experience of those under instruction, and, secondly, to allow the suggestion made to develop into a plan and project by means of the further suggestions contributed and organized into a whole by the members of the group. The plan, in other words, is a cooperative enterprise, not a dictation.

Visitors to some progressive schools are shocked by the lack of manners they come across. One who knows the situation better is aware that to some extent the absence is due to the eager interest of children to go on with what they are doing. In their eagerness they may, for example, bump into each other and into visitors with no word of apology.

One might say that this condition is better than a display of merely external punctillio accompanying intellectual and emotional lack of interest in school work. But it also represents a failure in education, a failure to learn one of the most important lessons of life, that of mutual accommodation and adaptation. Education is going on in a one-sided way, for attitudes and habits are in process of formation that stand in the way of future learning that springs from easy and ready contact and communications with others.

A primary responsibility of educators is that they not only be aware of the general principle of the shaping of actual experience by environing conditions, but that they recognize in the concrete what surroundings are conducive to having experiences that lead to growth. Above all, they should know how to utilize the surroundings, physical and social, that exist so as to extract from them all that they have to contribute to building up experiences that are worth while.

Infant as an Illustration

Let me illustrate from the case of an infant. The needs of a baby for food, rest and activity are certainly primary and decisive in one respect. Nourishment must be provided; provision must be made for comfortable sleep, and so on. But these facts do not mean that a parent shall feed that baby at any time when the baby is cross or irritable, that there shall not be a program of regular hours of feeding and sleeping, etc.

The wise mother takes account of the needs of the infant, but not in a way which dispenses with her own responsibility for regulating the objective conditions under which the needs are satisfied. And if she is a wise mother in this respect, she draws upon past experiences of experts as well as her own, for the light that these shed upon what experiences are most conducive to the normal development of infants. Instead of these conditions being subordinated to the immediate internal condition of the baby, they are definitely ordered so that a particular kind of interaction with these immediate internal states may be brought about.

The trouble with traditional education was not that educators took upon themselves the responsibility for providing an environment. The trouble was that they did not consider the other factor in creating an experience; namely, the powers and purposes of those taught. It was assumed that a certain set of conditions was intrinsically desirable, apart from their ability to evoke a certain quality of response in individuals.

This lack of mutual adaptation made the process of teaching and learning accidental. Those to whom the provided conditions were suitable managed to learn. Others got on as best they could.

Perhaps the greatest of all pedagogical fallacies is the notion that a person learns only the particular thing he is studying at the time. Collateral learning in the way of formation of enduring attitudes, of likes and dislikes, may be and often is much more important than the spelling lesson or lesson in geography or history that is learned. For these attitudes are fundamentally what count in the future.

PUTS DESIRE TO LEARN FIRST

The most important attitude that can be formed is that of desire to go on learning. If impetus in this direction is weakened instead of being intensified, something much more than mere lack of preparation takes place. The pupil is actually robbed of native capacities which otherwise would enable him to cope with the circumstances that he meets in the course of his life.

We often see persons who have had little schooling and in whose case the absence of set schooling proves to be a positive asset. They have at least retained their native common sense and power of judgment, and its exercise in the actual conditions of living has given them the precious gift of ability to learn from the experiences they have.

What avail is it to win prescribed amounts of information about geography and history, to win ability to read and write if in the process the individual loses his own soul; loses appreciation of things worth while, of the values to which these things are relative; if he loses desire to apply what he has learned and, above all, loses the ability to extract meaning from his future experiences as they occur?

«« VIII »»

EXTENDING THE SCHOOLS
UPWARD AFTER 1860

«««««««« ««««««««««««««««««««««««««««««««««««»»»»»»»»»»»»»»»»»»»»»»»»»»»»»»»»»»»

It was noted in Chapter IV that of the more than five hundred colleges established in sixteen American states before 1860 only 104 survived and became "permanent," nine of these being the colonial colleges. Competition, one of the causes of this high mortality rate, has continued. In 1900 there were about 600 colleges with about 240,000 students; in 1950 the United States Office of Education reported 1808 higher educational institutions with enrollments of 2,400,000 students. Between 1930 and 1950 more than 150 additions were made to the list recognized by that Office. The President's Commission on Higher Education in 1947 proposed for 1960 an enrollment of 4,600,000 students; and there was rather common agreement in 1950 that at least 3,000,000 would be enrolled by the middle of that decade. Although there were only about 4,000,000 college graduates in 1940 it was predicted in 1949 that by the 1960's "we can expect at least 10 million people with college diplomas. . . ." *The New York Times* published an article January 2, 1949, under the title "Millions of B.A.'s, But No Jobs," by Seymour E. Harris who says in *Market for College Graduates* (Harvard University Press, 1950) that by 1969 there will be two or three college graduates for every job they are prepared to fill.

In 1900 collegiate endowments were reported at about 170 million dollars. In 1938 these had reached 1,600 million. Forty-nine higher educational institutions received gifts between 1920 and 1937 amounting to 780 million. Higher education had become a very big part of the immense social undertaking known generally as education. Some of the same conditions that promoted this tremendous development were those that stimulated expansion of secondary education. Among these were the great increase in economic wealth, the findings of the laboratories of the experimental psychologists, whose studies tended to overthrow the dogma of "faculty psychology" and to deny the validity of the doctrine of formal mental discipline and of the transfer of training, and the attacks upon the assumption of disciplinary values in secondary edu-

539

cational curricula. And after the report of the Committee on College Entrance Requirements in 1899, requirements for admission to college became more flexible. See R. L. Duffus, *Democracy Enters College* (New York, Charles Scribner's Sons, 1936); John R. Tunis, *Was College Worth While?* (New York, Harcourt, Brace & Co., Inc., 1936); C. E. Lovejoy, *So You're Going to College* (New York, Simon and Schuster, Inc., 1940); *Lovejoy's Complete Guide to American Colleges and Universities,* by the same author and publisher, 1948; and A. J. Brumbaugh (Ed.), *American Universities and Colleges* (Washington, American Council on Education, 1948).

《《《《《《《《《《《《《《《《《《《《《《《《《《《《《《《《《《《《》》》》》》》》》》》》》》》》》》》》》》》》》》》》》》》》》》》

The Morrill (Land-Grant College) Act, 1862 *

An Act donating Public Lands to the several States and Territories which may provide Colleges for the Benefit of Agriculture and the Mechanic Arts.†

Be it enacted by the Senate and House of Representatives of the United States of America in Congress assembled, That there be granted to the several States, for the purposes hereinafter mentioned, an amount of public land, to be apportioned to each State a quantity equal to thirty thousand acres for each senator and representative in Congress to which the States are respectively entitled by the apportionment under the census of eighteen hundrd and sixty: *Provided,* That no mineral lands shall be selected or purchased under the provisions of this act.

Sec. 2. And be it further enacted, That the land aforesaid, after being surveyed, shall be apportioned to the several States in sections or subdivisions of sections, not less than one quarter of a section; and whenever there are public lands in a State subject to sale at private entry at one dollar and twenty-five cents per acre, the quantity to which said State shall be entitled shall be selected from such lands within the limits of such State, and the Secretary of the Interior is hereby directed to issue to each of the States in which there is not the quantity of public lands subject to sale at private entry at one dollar and twenty-five cents per acre, to which said State may be entitled under the provisions of this act, land scrip to the amount in acres for the deficiency of its distributive share; said scrip to be

---

* *The Statutes at Large of the United States,* XII (1863), pp. 503-05. Many agricultural and scientific societies had sprung up in this country before 1860. In an address before an educational convention in Virginia in 1857 Governor Henry Wise urged provisions for instruction in "all the applied sciences of agriculture" and said that ignorance of agriculture had ruined more men in Virginia than "any other cause known to me except brandy, fox-hounds, and horse-racing." Generally throughout the country there was rising interest in the subject of agriculture. In the early 1840's many memorials had been presented to Congress asking for the establishment of colleges of agriculture, mechanics, highway engineering, and architecture. In 1847 a Legislative Committee of New York recommended such a school for that state; the Constitution of Michigan in 1850 provided that as soon as practicable an agricultural college should be established in that state; Congress ordered an investigation and study in 1856 of agricultural conditions throughout the country and three years later a bill sponsored by Justin S. Morrill of Vermont passed Congress which provided a grant of public lands in each state for the support of a College of Agriculture and Mechanical Arts. The legislation was vetoed by President James Buchanan but it was signed in 1862 by President Lincoln.

† One of the reasons which President Buchanan gave for his veto of this bill in 1859 (see pp. 282-89 above) was that it "will injuriously interfere with existing colleges...." He thought that such competition would be unfair.

sold by said States and the proceeds thereof applied to the uses and purposes prescribed in this act, and for no other use or purpose whatsoever: *Provided,* That in no case shall any State to which land scrip may thus be issued be allowed to locate the same within the limits of any other State, or of any Territory of the United States, but their assignees may thus locate said land scrip upon any of the unappropriated lands of the United States subject to sale at private entry at one dollar and twenty-five cents, or less, per acre: *And provided, further,* That not more than one million acres shall be located by such assignees in any one of the States: *And provided, further,* That no such location shall be made before one year from the passage of this act.

Sec. 3. And be it further enacted, That all the expenses of management, superintendence, and taxes from date of selection of said lands, previous to their sales, and all expenses incurred in the management and disbursement of the moneys which may be received therefrom, shall be paid by the States to which they may belong, out of the treasury of said States, so that the entire proceeds of the sale of said lands shall be applied without any diminution whatever to the purposes hereinafter mentioned.

Sec. 4. And be it further enacted, That all moneys derived from the sale of the lands aforesaid by the States to which the lands are apportioned, and from the sales of land scrip hereinbefore provided for, shall be invested in stocks of the United States, or of the States, or some other safe stocks, yielding not less than five per centum upon the par value of said stocks; and that the moneys so invested shall constitute a perpetual fund, the capital of which shall remain forever undiminished, (except so far as may be provided in section fifth of this act,) and the interest of which shall be inviolably appropriated, by each State which may take and claim the benefit of this act, to the endowment, support, and maintenance of at least one college where the leading object shall be, without excluding other scientific and classical studies, and including military tactics, to teach such branches of learning as are related to agriculture and the mechanic arts, in such manner as the legislatures of the States may respectively prescribe, in order to promote the liberal and practical education of the industrial classes in the several pursuits and professions in life.

Sec. 5. And be it further enacted, That the grant of land and land scrip hereby authorized shall be made on the following conditions, to which, as well as the provisions hereinbefore contained, the previous assent of the several States shall be signified by legislative acts:

First. If any portion of the fund invested, as provided by the foregoing section, or any portion of the interest thereon, shall, by any action or contingency, be diminished or lost, it shall be replaced by the State to which it belongs, so that the capital of the fund shall remain forever undiminished; and the annual interest shall be regularly applied without diminution to the purposes mentioned in the fourth section of this act, except that a sum, not exceeding ten per centum upon the amount received by any State under the provisions of this act, may be expended for the purchase of lands for sites or experimental farms, whenever authorized by the respective legislatures of said States.

Second. No portion of said fund, nor the interest thereon, shall be applied, directly or indirectly, under any pretence whatever, to the purchase, erection, preservation, or repair of any building or buildings.

Third. Any State which may take and claim the benefit of the provisions of this act shall provide, within five years, at least not less than one college, as described in the fourth section of this act, or the grant to such State shall cease; and said State shall be bound to pay the United States the amount received of any lands previously sold, and that the title to purchasers under the State shall be valid.

Fourth. An annual report shall be made regarding the progress of each college, recording any improvements and experiments made, with their cost and results, and such other matters, including State industrial and economical statistics, as may be supposed useful; one copy of which shall be transmitted by mail free, by each, to all the other colleges which may be endowed under the provisions of this act, and also one copy to the Secretary of the Interior.

Fifth. When lands shall be selected from those which have been raised to double the minimum price, in consequence of railroad grants, they shall be computed to the States at the maximum price, and the number of acres proportionately diminished.

Sixth. No State while in a condition of rebellion or insurrection against the government of the United States shall be entitled to the benefit of this act.

Seventh. No State shall be entitled to the benefits of this act unless it shall express its acceptance thereof by its legislature within two years from the date of its approval by the President.

Sec. 6. And be it further enacted, That land scrip issued under the provisions of this act shall not be subject to location until after the first day of January, one thousand eight hundred and sixty-three.

Sec. 7. And be it further enacted, That the land officers shall receive the same fees for locating land scrip issued under the provisions of this act as is now allowed for the location of military bounty land warrants under existing laws; *Provided,* their maximum compensation shall not be thereby increased.

Sec. 8. And be it further enacted, That the Governors of the several States to which scrip shall be issued under this act shall be required to report annually to Congress all sales made of such scrip until the whole shall be disposed of, the amount received for the same, and what appropriation has been made of the proceeds.

APPROVED, July 2, 1862.

The Supreme Court of Michigan Establishes the Legality
of Taxes for Secondary Education, 1874 *

Bill to enjoin collection of school taxes: High school: Superintendent. The decree below, dismissing the bill filed in this case to restrain the collection of such portion of the school taxes assessed against the complainants for the year 1872 as have been voted for the support of the high school in the village of Kalamazoo and for the payment of the salary of the superintendent, is affirmed.

COOLEY, J.:

The bill in this case is filed to restrain the collection of such portion of the school taxes assessed against complainants for the year 1872, as have been voted for the support of the high school in that village, and for the payment of the salary of the superintendent. While, nominally, this is the end sought to be attained by the bill, the real purpose of the suit is wider and vastly more comprehensive than this brief statement would indicate, inasmuch as it seeks a judicial determination of the right of school authorities, in what are called union school districts of the state, to levy taxes upon the general public for the support of what in this state are known as high schools, and to make free by such taxation the instruction of children in other languages than the English. The bill is consequently, of no small interest to all the people of the state; and to a large number of very flourishing schools, it is of the very highest interest, as their prosperity and usefulness, in a large degree, depend upon the method in which they are supported, so that a blow at this method seems a blow at the schools themselves. The suit, however, is not to be regarded as a blow purposely aimed at the schools. It can never be unimportant to know that taxation, even for the most useful or indispensable purposes, is warranted by the strict letter of the law; and whoever doubts its being so in any particular case, may well be justified by his doubt in asking a legal investigation, that, if errors or defects in the law are found to exist, there may be a review of the subject in legislation, and the whole matter be settled on legal grounds, in such manner and on such principles as the public will may indicate, and as the legislature may prescribe.

The complainants rely upon two objections to the taxes in question, one of which is general, and the other applies only to the authority or action of this particular district. The general objection has already been indicated; the particular objection is that, even conceding that other districts in the

---

* 30 *Michigan Reports* (1874-75), 69-84. This very important case was heard July 10 and 15 and decision in it was given July 21, 1874. There was no appeal to the Supreme Court of the United States. The Michigan Court at that time was composed of Chief Justice Benjamin F. Graves and Associate Justices Thomas M. Cooley, James V. Campbell and Isaac P. Christiancy. The decision by Mr. Justice Cooley is given in full because it presents some very important aspects of American educational history.

state may have authority under special charters or laws, or by the adoption of general statutes, to levy taxes for the support of high schools in which foreign and dead languages shall be taught, yet this district has no such power, because the special legislation for its benefit, which was had in 1859, was invalid for want of compliance with the constitution in the forms of enactment, and it has never adopted the general law (*Comp. L.,* § 3742), by taking a vote of the district to establish a union school in accordance with its provisions, though ever since that law was enacted the district has sustained such a school, and proceeded in its action apparently on the assumption that the statutes in all respects were constitutional enactments, and had been complied with.

Whether this particular objection would have been worthy of serious consideration had it been made sooner, we must, after this lapse of time, wholly decline to consider. This district existed *de facto,* and we suppose *de jure,* also, for we are not informed to the contrary, when the legislation of 1859 was had, and from that time to the present it has assumed to possess and exercise all the franchises which are now brought in question, and there has since been a steady concurrence of action on the part of its people in the election of officers, in the levy of large taxes, and in the employment of teachers for the support of a high school. The state has aquiesced in this assumption of authority, and it has never, so far as we are advised, been questioned by any one until, after thirteen years user, three individual tax payers, out of some thousands, in a suit instituted on their own behalf, and to which the public authorities give no countenance, come forward in this collateral manner and ask us to annul the franchises. To require a municipal corporation, after so long an acquiescence, to defend, in a merely private suit, the irregularity, not only of its own action, but even of the legislation that permitted such action to be had, could not be justified by the principles of law, much less by those of public policy. We may justly take cognizance in these cases, of the notorious fact that municipal action is often exceedingly informal and irregular, when, after all, no wrong or illegality has been intended, and the real purpose of the law has been had in view and been accomplished; so that it may be said the spirit of the law has been kept while the letter has been disregarded. We may also find in the statutes many instances of careless legislation, under which municipalities have acted for many years, until important interests have sprung up, which might be crippled or destroyed, if then for the first time matters of form in legislative action were suffered to be questioned. If every municipality must be subject to be called into court at any time to defend its original organization and its franchises at the will of any dissatisfied citizen who may feel disposed to question them, and subject to dissolution, perhaps, or to be crippled in authority and powers if defects appear, however complete and formal may have been the recognition of its rights and privileges, on the part alike of the state and of its citizens, it may very justly be said that few of our municipalities can be entirely certain of the ground they stand upon, and that any single person, however honestly inclined, if disposed to be litigious, or over technical and precise, may have it in his power in many cases to cause infinite trouble, embarrassment and mischief.

It was remarked by Mr. Justice Campbell in *People* v. *Maynard,* 15 Mich. 470, that "in public affairs where the people have organized themselves under color of law into the ordinary municipal bodies, and have gone on year after year raising taxes, making improvements, and exercising their usual franchises, their rights are properly regarded as depending quite as much on the acquiescence as on the regularity of their origin, and no *ex post facto* inquiry can be permitted to undo their corporate existence. Whatever may be the rights of the individuals before such general acquiescence, the corporate standing of the community can no longer be open to question." To this doctrine were cited *Rumsey* v. *People,* 19 N.Y. 41, and *Lanning* v. *Carpenter,* 20 N.Y. 447. The cases of *State* v. *Bunker,* 59 Me. 366; *People* v. *Salomon,* 54 Ill. 41, and *People* v. *Lothrop,* 24 Mich. 235, are in the same direction. The legislature has recognized this principle with special reference to school districts, and has not only deemed it important that their power should not be questioned after any considerable lapse of time, but has even established what is in effect a very short act of limitation for the purpose in declaring that "Every school district shall, in all cases, be presumed to have been legally organized, when it shall have exercised the franchises and privileges of a district for the term of two years": *Comp. L.* 1871, § 3591. This is wise legislation, and short as the period is, we have held that even a less period is sufficient to justify us in refusing to interfere except on the application of the state itself: *School District* v. *Joint Board, etc.,* 27 Mich. 3.

It may be said that this doctrine is not applicable to this case because here the corporate organization is not questioned, but only the authority which the district asserts to establish a high school and levy taxes therefor. But we think that, though the statute may not in terms apply, in principle it is strictly applicable. The district claims and has long exercised powers which take it out of the class of ordinary school districts, and place it in another class altogether, whose organization is greatly different and whose authority is much greater. So far as the externals of corporate action are concerned, the two classes are quite distinct, and the one subserves purposes of a higher order than the other, and is permitted to levy much greater burdens. It is not very clear that the case is not strictly within the law; for the organization here claimed is that of a union school district, and nothing else, and it seems little less than an absurdity to say it may be presumed from its user of corporate power to be a school district, but not such a district as the user indicates, and as it has for so long a period claimed to be. But however that may be, we are clear that even if we might be allowed by the law to listen to the objection after the two years, we cannot in reason consent to do so after thirteen. It cannot be permitted that communities can be suffered to be annoyed, embarrassed and unsettled by having agitated in the courts after such a lapse of time questions which every consideration of fairness to the people concerned and of public policy require should be raised and disposed of immediately or never raised at all.

The more general question which the record presents we shall endeavor to state in our own language, but so as to make it stand out distinctly as a naked question of law, disconnected from all considerations of policy or expediency; in which light alone are we at liberty to consider it. It is, as we understand it, that there is no authority in this state to make the high schools free by taxation levied on the people at large. The argument is that while there may be no constitutional provision expressly prohibiting such taxation, the general course of legislation in the state and the general understanding of the people have been such as to require us to regard the instruction in the classics and in living modern languages in these schools as in the nature not of practical and therefore necessary instruction for the benefit of the people at large, but rather as accomplishments for the few, to be sought after in the main by those best able to pay for them, and to be paid for by those who seek them, and not be general tax. And not only has this been the general state policy, but this higher learning of itself, when supplied by the state, is so far a matter of private concern to those who receive it that the courts ought to declare it incompetent to supply it wholly at the public expense. This is in substance, as we understand it, the position of the complainants in this suit.

When this doctrine was broached to us, we must confess to no little surprise that the legislation and policy of our state were appealed to against the right of the state to furnish a liberal education to the youth of the state in schools brought within the reach of all classes. We supposed it had always been understood in this state that education, not merely in the rudiments, but in an enlarged sense, was regarded as an important practical advantage to be supplied at their option to rich and poor alike, and not as something pertaining merely to culture and accomplishment to be brought as such within the reach of those whose accumulated wealth enabled them to pay for it. As this, however, is now so seriously disputed, it may be necessary, perhaps, to take a brief survey of the legislation and general course, not only of the state, but of the antecedent territory, on the subject.

It is not disputed that the dissemination of knowledge by means of schools has been a prominent object from the first, and we allude to the provision of the ordinance of 1787 on that subject, and to the donation of lands by congress for the purpose, only as preliminary to what we may have to say regarding the action of the territorial authorities in the premises. Those authorities accepted in the most liberal spirit the requirement of the ordinance that "schools and the means of education shall forever be encouraged," and endeavored to make early provision therefor on a scale which shows they were fully up to the most advanced ideas that then prevailed on the subject. The earliest territorial legislation regarding education, though somewhat eccentric in form, was framed in this spirit. It was "an act to establish the Catholepistemiad, or University of Michigania," adopted August 26, 1817, which not only incorporated the institution named in the title, with its president and thirteen professors, appointed by the governor, but it provided that its board of instruction should have power "to regulate all the concerns of the institution, to enact laws for that purpose," "to establish colleges, academies, schools, libraries, museums, atheneums, botanic gardens, laboratories and other useful literary and scientific institutions, consonant to the laws of the United States of America, and of Michigan, and to appoint officers and instructors and instructrices, in, among, and throughout the various counties, cities, towns, townships and other geographical divisions of Michigan." To provide for the expense thereof the existing public taxes were increased fifteen per cent., and from the proceeds of all future taxes fifteen per cent. was appropriated for the benefit of this corporation: *Territorial Laws, Vol. 2, p.* 104; *Sherman's School Laws, p.* 4. The act goes but little into details, as was to be expected of a law which proposed to put the whole educational system of the commonwealth into the hands and under the control of a body of learned men, created and made territorial officers for the purpose of planning and carrying it out; but the general purpose was apparent that throughout the territory a system of most liberal education should be supported at the public expense for the benefit of the whole people. The system indicated was prophetic of that which exists to-day, and is remarkable in this connection mainly, as being the very first law on the subject enacted in the territory, and as announcing a policy regarding liberal instruction which, though perhaps impracticable in view of the then limited and scattered population of the territory, has been steadily kept in view from that day to the present.

This act continued in force until 1821, when it was repealed to make way for one "for the establishment of an university," with more limited powers, and authorized only "to establish colleges, academies and schools depending upon the said university," and which, according to the general understanding at the time and afterwards, were to be schools intermediate the university and such common schools as might exist or be provided for: *Code of 1820, p.* 443; *Code of 1827, p.* 445. In 1827 the educational system was supplemented by "an act for the establishment of common schools," which is also worthy of special attention and reflection, as indicating what was understood at that day by the common schools which were proposed to be established.

The first section of that act provided "that every township within this territory, containing fifty families or householders, shall be provided with a good schoolmaster or schoolmasters, of good morals, to teach children to read and write, and to instruct them in the English or French language, as well as in arithmetic, orthography, and decent behavior, for such term of time as shall be equivalent to six months for one school in each year. And every township containing one hundred families or householders, shall be provided with such schoolmaster or teacher, for such term of time, as shall be equivalent to twelve months for one school in each year. And every township containing one hundred and fifty families or householders shall be provided with such schoolmaster or teacher for such term of time as shall be equivalent to six months in each year, and shall, in addition thereto, be provided with a schoolmaster or teacher, as above described, to instruct children in the English language for such term of time as shall be equivalent to twelve months for one school in each year. And every township containing two hundred families or householders shall be provided with a grammar schoolmaster, of good morals, *well instructed in the Latin, French and English languages,* and shall, in addition thereto, be provided with a schoolmaster or teacher, as above described, to instruct children in the English language, for such term of time as shall be equivalent to twelve months for each of said schools in each year." And the townships respectively were required under a heavy penalty, to be levied in case of default on the inhabitants generally, to keep and maintain the schools so provided for: *Code of 1827,* p. 448; *Territorial Laws,* Vol. 2, p. 472.

Here, then, was a general law, which, under the name of common schools, required not only schools for elementary instruction, but also grammar schools to be maintained. The qualifications required in teachers of grammar schools were such as to leave it open to no doubt that grammar schools in the sense understood in England and the Eastern States were intended, in which instruction in the classics should be given, as well, as in such higher branches of learning as would not usually be taught in the schools of lowest grade. How is it possible, then, to say, as the exigencies of complainants' case require them to do, that the term common or primary schools, as made use of in our legislation, has a known and definite meaning which limits it to the ordinary district schools, and that consequently the legislative authority to levy taxes for the primary schools cannot be held to embrace taxation for the schools supported by village and city districts in which a higher grade of learning is imparted.

It is probable that this act, like that of 1817, was found in advance of the demands of the people of the territory, or of their ability to support high schools, and it was repealed in 1833, and another passed which did not expressly require the establishment or support of schools of secondary grade, but which provided only for school directors, who must maintain a district school at least three months in each year: *Code of 1833,* p. 129. The act contains no express limitations upon their powers, but it is not important now to consider whether or not they extended to the establishment of grammar schools as district schools, where, in their judgment, they might be required. Such schools would certainly not be out of harmony with any territorial policy that as yet had been developed or indicated.

Thus stood the law when the constitution of 1835 was adopted. The article on education in that instrument contained the following provisions:

"2. The legislature shall encourage by all suitable means the promotion of intellectual, scientific and agricultural improvement. The proceeds of all lands that have been, or hereafter may be, granted by the United States to this state for the support of schools, which shall hereafter be sold or disposed of, shall be and remain a perpetual fund, the interest of which, together with the rents of all such unsold lands, shall be inviolably appropriated to the support of schools throughout the state.

"3. The legislature shall provide for a system of common schools, by which a school shall be kept up and supported in each school district at least three months in every year; and any school district neglecting to keep up and support such a school may be deprived of its equal proportion of the interest of the public fund."

The fifth section provided for the support of the university, "with such branches as the public convenience may hereafter demand for the promotion of literature, the arts and sciences," etc. Two things are specially noticeable in these provisions: *first,* that they contemplated provision by the state for a complete system of instruction, beginning with that of the primary school and ending with that of the university; *second,* that while the legislature was required to make provisions for district schools for at least three months in each year, no restriction was imposed upon its power to establish schools intermediate the common district school and the university, and we find nothing to indicate an intent to limit their discretion as to the class or grade of schools to which the proceeds of school lands might be devoted, or as to the range of studies or grade of instruction which might be provided for in the district schools.

In the very first executive message after the constitution went into effect, the governor, in view of the fact that "our institutions have leveled the artificial distinctions existing in the societies of other countries, and have left open to every one the avenues to distinction and honor," admonished the legislature that it was their "imperious duty to secure to the state a general diffusion of knowledge," and that "this can in no wise be so certainly effected as by the perfect organization of a uniform and liberal system of common schools." Their "attention was therefore called to the effectuation of a perfect school system, open to all classes, as the surest basis of public happiness and prosperity." In his second message he repeated his admonitions, advising that provision be made for ample compensation to teachers, that those of the highest character, both moral and intellectual, might be secured, and urging that the "youth be taught the first principles in morals, in science, and in government, commencing their studies in the primary schools, elevating its grades as you approach the district seminary, and continue its progress till you arrive at the university." This message indicated no plan, but referred the legislature to the report of the superintendent, who would recommend a general system.

The system reported by superintendent Pierce contemplated a university, with branches in different parts of the state as preparatory schools, and district schools. This is the parent of our present system, and though its author did not find the legislature prepared to accept all his views, the result has demonstrated that he was only a few years in advance of his generation, and that the changes in our school system which have since been adopted have been in the direction of the views which he then held and urged upon the public. And an examination of his official report for 1837 will show that the free schools he then favored were schools which taught something more than the rudiments of a common education; which were to give to the poor the advantages of the rich, and enable both alike to obtain within the state an education broad and liberal, as well as practical.

It would be instructive to make liberal extracts from this report did time and space permit. The superintendent would have teachers thoroughly trained, and he would have the great object of common schools "to furnish good instruction in all the elementary and common branches of knowledge, for all classes of community, *as good, indeed, for the poorest boy of the state as the rich man can furnish for his children with all his wealth.*" The context shows that he had the systems of Prussia and of New England in view, and that he proposed by a free school system to fit the children of the poor as well as of the rich for the highest spheres of activity and influence.

It might also be useful in this connection to show that the Prussian system and that "of the Puritans," of which he speaks in such terms of praise, resemble in their main features, so far as bringing within the reach of all a regular gradation of schools is concerned, the system of public instruction as it prevails in this state to-day. But it is not necessary for the purposes of the present case to enter upon this subject. It must suffice to say that the law of 1827, which provided for grammar schools as a grade of common schools, was adopted from laws which from a very early period had been in existence in Massachusetts, and which in like manner, under heavy penalties, compelled the support of these grammar schools in every considerable town: See *Mass. Laws,* 1789, p. 39; compare *General Stat.,* 1860, p. 215, § 2.

The system adopted by the legislature, and which embraced a university and branches, and a common or primary school in every school district of the state, was put into successful operation, and so continued, with one important exception, until the adoption of the constitution of 1850. The exception relates to the branches of the university, which the funds of the university did not warrant keeping up, and which were consequently abandoned. Private schools to some extent took their place; but when the convention met to frame a constitution in 1850, there were already in existence, in a number of the leading towns, schools belonging to the general public system, which were furnishing instruction which fitted young men for the university. These schools for the most part had been organized under special laws, which, while leaving the primary school laws in general applicable, gave the districts a larger board of officers and larger powers of taxation for buildings and the payment of teachers. As the establishment and support of such schools were optional with the people, they encountered in some localities considerable opposition, which, however, is believed to have been always overcome, and the authority of the districts to provide instruction in the languages in these union schools was not, so far as we are aware, seriously contested. The superintendent of public instruction devotes a considerable portion of his annual report for 1848 to these schools, and in that of 1849 he says: "This class of institutions, which may be made to constitute a connecting link between the ordinary common school and the state university, is fast gaining upon the confidence of the public. Those already established have generally surpassed the expectations of their founders. Some of them have already attained a standing rarely equaled by the academical institutions of the older states. Large, commodious, and beautiful edifices have been erected in quite a number of villages for the accommodation of these schools. These school-houses frequently occupy the most eligible sites in the villages where they are located. I am happy in being able to state in this connection that the late capitol of our state, having been fitted up at much expense, was, in June last, opened as a *common school-house;* and that in that house is maintained a free school which constitutes the pride and ornament of the city of the straits." This *common* free school was a union school equivalent in its instruction to the ordinary high school in most matters, and the report furnishes very clear evidence that the superintendent believed schools of that grade to be entirely competent under the primary school law.

It now becomes important to see whether the constitutional convention and the people, in 1850, did any thing to undo what previously had been accomplished towards furnishing high schools as a part of the primary school system. The convention certainly did nothing to that end. On the contrary, they demonstrated in the most unmistakable manner that they cherished no such desire or purpose. The article on education as originally reported, while providing for free schools to be kept in each district at least three months in every year, added that "the English language and no other shall be taught in such schools." Attention was called to this provision, and it was amended so as to read that instruction should be "conducted in the English language." The reason for the change was fully given, that as it was reported it might be understood to prohibit the teaching of other languages than the English in the primary schools; a result that was not desired. Judge Whipple stated in the convention that, in the section from which he came, French and German were taught, and "it is a most valuable improvement of the common school system." The late superintendent Pierce said that in some schools Latin was taught, and that he himself had taught Latin in a common school. He would not adopt any provision by which any knowledge would be excluded. "All that we ought to do is this: we should say the legislature shall establish primary schools." This, in his opinion, would give full power, and the details could be left to legislation: See *Debates of the Convention,* 269, 549.

The instrument submitted by the convention to the people and adopted by them provided for the establishment of free schools in every school district for at least three months in each year, and for the university. By the aid of these we have every reason to believe the people expected a complete collegiate education might be obtained. The branches of the university had ceased to exist; the university had no preparatory department, and it must either have been understood that young men were to be prepared for the university in the common schools, or else that they should go abroad for the purpose, or be prepared in private schools. Private schools adapted to the purpose were almost unknown in the state, and comparatively a very few persons were at that time of sufficient pecuniary ability to educate their children abroad. The inference seems irresistible that the people expected the tendency towards the establishment of high schools in the primary school districts would continue until every locality capable of supporting one was supplied. And this inference is strengthened by the fact that a considerable number of our union schools date their establishment from the year 1850 and the two or three years following.

If these facts do not demonstrate clearly and conclusively a general state policy, beginning in 1817 and continuing until after the adoption of the present constitution, in the direction of free schools in which education, and at their option the elements of classical education, might be brought within the reach of all the children of the state, then, as it seems to us, nothing can demonstrate it. We might follow the subject further, and show that the subsequent legislation has all concurred with this policy, but it would be a waste of time and labor. We content ourselves with the statement that neither in our state policy, in our constitution, or in our laws, do we find the primary school districts restricted in the branches of knowledge which their officers may cause to be taught, or the grade of instruction that may be given, if their voters consent in regular form to bear the expense and raise the taxes for the purpose.

Having reached this conclusion, we shall spend no time upon the objection that the district in question had no authority to appoint a superintendent of schools, and that the duties of superintendency should be performed by the district board. We think the power to make the appointment was incident to the full control which by law the board had over the schools of the district, and that the board and the people of the district have been wisely left by the legislature to follow their own judgment in the premises.

It follows that the decree dismissing the bill was right, and should be affirmed.

The other justices concurred.

Editorial Protest Against the Ph.D. as an Honorary Degree, 1892 *

A number of protests have reached the *Educational Review* against the practice of many colleges in conferring the degree of Doctor of Philosophy as an honorary degree. This pernicious and demoralizing practice was more marked at the last Commencement season than ever before. Scores of these degrees were given without any warrant whatever. It cannot be too strongly insisted upon that no college is justified in giving this degree at all, and no university should confer it except for advanced study and research carried on in residence. The suggestion has been made that the *Educational Review* should make a list of the colleges that persist in this abuse and publish it from time to time. It might be more efficacious to print a list of the persons who receive and accept such a degree.

Charles W. Super of Ohio University (Athens) on "So-Called Honorary Degrees," 1892 †

The point made in the *Educational Review* (IV: 208) against conferring the degree of Ph.D. as a mere honor, is well taken. I believe that a large majority, certainly a large proportion, of the college faculties in this country share your views. But what are they to do when boards of trustees take the matter in hand and grant the degree without consulting them? Cases have occurred where these bodies have not only acted without the sanction of the faculties whose masters they were, but against their vigorous protest. There are men, some of them prominent in educational circles, whose influence can be bought with such a low price. And there are boards of trustees short-sighted enough to suppose that the influence of such men will be of more value to an institution authorized to confer degrees, than a reputation for care in the bestowal of its honors. On the other hand, the mere requirement of post-graduate study and a thesis does not much mend matters. I have read a number of these productions, a few by Ameri-

---

* *Educational Review*, IV (September, 1892), p. 208. The editors of this magazine at that time were Nicholas Murray Butler, E. H. Cook, William H. Maxwell, and Addison B. Poland. See below for approval of this editorial by Charles W. Super, Ohio University. In spite of many protests, the practice of conferring the Ph.D. as an honorary degree continued into the present century.

† *Ibid.*, November, 1892, pp. 388-89.

can students in Germany, that are mere compilations, and evidently the work of persons who did not know what is meant by independent research. Yet they were published as dissertations for which the degree of Doctor of Philosophy had been given. The degree business in this country is a huge farce, and has long been so. Degree-conferring institutions are usually liberal in the inverse ratio to their importance. These things will never be otherwise until the intelligence of the governing boards of our colleges and universities rises far above the present average. Nor is it wise to assume that all college faculties are above reproach herein.

The Committee of Ten Proposes a Program for Secondary Schools, 1893 *

Year	Classical.		Latin-Scientific.	
	Three foreign languages (one modern).		Two foreign languages (one modern).	
I.	Latin	5p.	Latin	5p.
	English	4p.	English	4p.
	Algebra	4p.	Algebra	4p.
	History	4p.	History	4p.
	Physical Geography	3p.	Physical Geography	3p.
		20p.		20p.
II.	Latin	5p.	Latin	5p.
	English	2p.	English	2p.
	[1] German (or French) begun	4p.	German (or French) begun	4p.
	Geometry	3p.	Geometry	3p.
	Physics	3p.	Physics	3p.
	History	3p.	Botany or Zoology	3p.
		20p.		20p.
III.	Latin	4p.	Latin	4p.
	[1] Greek	5p.	English	3p.
	English	3p.	German (or French)	4p.
	German (or French)	4p.	Mathematics {Algebra 2, Geometry 2}	4p.
	Mathematics {Algebra 2, Geometry 2}	4p.	Astronomy ½ yr. & Meteorology ½ yr.	3p.
		20p.	History	2p.
				20p.
	Latin	4p.	Latin	4p.
	Greek	5p.	English {as in Classical 2, additional 2}	4p.
	English	2p.		
	German (or French)	3p.	German (or French)	3p.

* *Report of the Committee of Ten on Secondary School Studies* (Washington, United States Bureau of Education, 1893), pp. 46, 47.

[1] In any school in which Greek can be better taught than a modern language, or in which local public opinion or the history of the school makes it desirable to teach Greek in an ample way, Greek may be substituted for German or French in the second year of the Classical programme.

Year

IV. Chemistry .... 3p.
Trigonometry & Higher
Algebra
           or
History   3p.
                                ―――
                                20p.

Chemistry .... 3p.
Trigonometry & Higher
Algebra
           or
History   3p.
Geology or Physiography
    ½ yr.   and
Anatomy, Physiology, &
Hygiene ½ yr............. 3p.
                            ―――
                            20p.

Modern Languages.
Two foreign languages
(both modern).

English.
One foreign language
(ancient or modern).

French (*or* German) begun .. 5p.
English .... 4p.
I. Algebra .... 4p.
History .... 4p.
Physical Geography .... 3p.
                          ―――
                          20p.

Latin, or German, or French 5p.
English .... 4p.
Algebra .... 4p.
History .... 4p.
Physical Geography .... 3p.
                          ―――
                          20p.

French (*or* German)........ 4p.
English .... 2p.
II. German (*or* French) begun .. 5p.
Geometry .... 3p.
Physics .... 3p.
Botany or Zoology......... 3p.
                          ―――
                          20p.

Latin, or German, or
   French ....5 or 4p.
English ....3 or 4p.
Geometry .... 3p.
Physics .... 3p.
History .... 3p.
Botany or Zoology......... 3p.
                          ―――
                          20p.

French (*or* German)...... 4p.
English .... 3p.
German (*or* French)....... 4p.
III. Mathematics {Algebra 2 } 4p.
                 {Geometry 2 }
Astronomy ½ yr. &
Meteorology ½ yr. .... 3p.
History .... 2p.
                          ―――
                          20p.

Latin, or German, or French .. 4p.
English {as in others 3 }
        {additional 2   } ..... 5p.
Mathematics {Algebra 2 } 4p.
            {Geometry 2 }
Astronomy ½ yr. &
Meterology ½ yr. .... 3p.
        {as in the Latin-}
History { Scientific 2   } .. 4p.
        {additional 2   }
                          ―――
                          20p.

French (*or* German)....... 3p.
English {as in Classical 2}
        {additional 2   } 4p.
German (*or* French)....... 4p.
Chemistry .... 3p.
Trigonometry & Higher
Algebra
IV.   *or*
History   3p.
Geology or Physiography
    ½ yr.   and
Anatomy, Physiology, &
Hygiene ½ yr. .... 3p.
                          ―――
                          20p.

Latin, or German, or French .. 4p.
English {as in Classical 2}
        {additional 2   } .. 4p.
Chemistry .... 3p.
Trigonometry & Higher Algebra 3p.
History .... 3p.
Geology or Physiography
    ½ yr.   and
Anatomy, Physiology, &
Hygiene ½ yr............. 3p.
                          ―――
                          20p.

The Committee of Ten on Requirements for Admission to College, 1893 *

One of the subjects which the Committee of Ten were directed to consider was requirements for admission to college; and particularly they were expected to report on uniform requirements for admission to colleges, as well as on a uniform secondary school programme. Almost all the Conferences have something to say about the best mode of testing the attainments of candidates at college admission examinations; and some of them, notably the Conferences on History and Geography, make very explicit declarations concerning the nature of college examinations. The improvements in the secondary schools the various subjects which enter into the course will be found clearly described under each subject in the several Conference reports; but there is a general principle concerning the relation of the secondary schools to colleges which the Committee of Ten, inspired and guided by the Conferences, feel it their duty to set forth with all possible distinctness.

The secondary schools of the United States, taken as a whole, do not exist for the purpose of preparing boys and girls for colleges. Only an insignificant percentage of the graduates of these schools go to colleges or scientific schools. Their main function is to prepare for the duties of life that small proportion of all the children in the country—a proportion small in number, but very important to the welfare of the nation—who show themselves able to profit by an education prolonged to the eighteenth year, and whose parents are able to support them while they remain so long at school. There are, to be sure, a few private or endowed secondary schools in the country, which make it their principal object to prepare students for the colleges and universities; but the number of these schools is relatively small. A secondary school programme intended for national use must therefore be made for those children whose education is not to be pursued beyond the secondary school. The preparation of a few pupils for college or scientific school should in the ordinary secondary school be the incidental, and not the principal object. At the same time, it is obviously desirable that the colleges and scientific schools should be accessible to all boys or girls, who have completed creditably the secondary school course. Their parents often do not decide for them, four years before the college age, that they shall go to college, and they themselves may not, perhaps, feel the desire to continue their education until near the end of their school course. In order that any successful graduate of a good secondary school should be free to present himself at the gates of the college or scientific school of his choice, it is necessary that the colleges and scientific schools of the country should accept for admission to appropriate courses of their instruction the attainments of any youth who has passed creditably through

* *Ibid.*, pp. 51-53.

a good secondary school course, no matter to what group of subjects he may have mainly devoted himself in the secondary school. As secondary school courses are now too often arranged, this is not a reasonable request to prefer to the colleges and scientific schools; because the pupil may now go through a secondary school course of a very feeble and scrappy nature —studying a little of many subjects and not much of any one, getting, perhaps, a little information in a variety of fields, but nothing which can be called a thorough training. Now the recommendations of the nine Conferences, if well carried out, might fairly be held to make all the main subjects taught in the secondary schools of equal rank for the purposes of admission to college or scientific school. They would all be taught consecutively and thoroughly, and would all be carried on in the same spirit; they would all be used for training the powers of observation, memory, expression, and reasoning; and they would all be good to that end, although differing among themselves in quality and substance. In preparing the programmes of Table IV., the Committee had in mind that the requirements for admission to colleges might, for schools which adopted a programme derived from that table, be simplified to a considerable extent, though not reduced. A college might say,—We will accept for admission any groups of studies taken from the secondary school programme, provided that the sum of the studies in each of the four years amounts to sixteen, or eighteen, or twenty periods a week,—as may be thought best,—and provided, further, that in each year at least four of the subjects presented shall have been pursued at least three periods a week, and that at least three of the subjects shall have been pursued three years or more. For the purposes of this reckoning, natural history, geography, meteorology, and astronomy might be grouped together as one subject. Every youth who entered college would have spent four years in studying a few subjects thoroughly; and, on the theory that all the subjects are to be considered equivalent in educational rank for the purposes of admission to college, it would make no difference which subjects he had chosen from the programme—he would have had four years of strong and effective mental training. The Conferences on Geography and Modern Languages make the most explicit statement to the effect that college requirements for admission should coincide with high-school requirements for graduation. The Conference on English is of opinion "that no student should be admitted to college who shows in his English examination and his other examinations that he is very deficient in ability to write good English." This recommendation suggests that an ample English course in the secondary school should be required of all persons who intend to enter college. It would of course be possible for any college to require for admission any one subject, or any group of subjects, in the table, and the requirements of different colleges, while all kept within the table, might differ in many respects; but the Committee are of opinion that the satisfactory completion of any one of the four years' courses of study embodied in the foregoing programmes should admit to corresponding courses in colleges and scientific schools. They believe that this close articulation between the secondary schools and the higher institutions would be advantageous alike for the schools, the colleges, and the country.

The Committee on College Entrance Requirements Approves the Elective System in High Schools, 1899 *

The following resolutions adopted by the committee serve to put in concrete form the leading principles that guided the committee itself in its consideration of the special reports, and which in its judgment are to be considered as first principles in the adjustment of relations between secondary and higher schools. These resolutions, embodying such principles, are what the committee offers in lieu of any ideal program or curriculum. The resolutions that follow are to be considered as covering, not every principle that the committee might wish to see recognized, but only those which could be discussed and agreed to in the limited time at the committee's disposal.

I. *Resolved,* That the principle of election be recognized in secondary schools.

II. *Resolved,* That the requirements for admission to technical schools should be as extended and thoro as the requirements for admission to college.

III. *Resolved,* That the teachers in the secondary schools should be college graduates, or have the equivalent of a college education.

IV. *Resolved,* That we favor a unified six-year high-school course of study beginning with the seventh grade.

V. *Resolved,* That in the interpretation of the recommendations of this committee concerning the subjects to be included in the secondary-school program and the requirements for admission to college, for which credit should be given, it is distinctly understood that all secondary schools will not offer opportunities for the pursuit of all these subjects, and that the colleges will select those only which they deem wise and appropriate.

* National Educational Association, *Journal of Proceedings and Addresses,* 1899, pp. 655-68. Following the discussion of a paper on "What action ought to be taken by universities and secondary schools to promote the introduction of the programs recommended by the Committee of Ten?" by William Carey Jones of the University of California, at the meeting of the National Educational Association in Denver in 1895, the following resolution was adopted:

"Whereas, The most pressing need for higher education in this country is a better understanding between the secondary schools and the colleges and universities in regard to requirements for admission; therefore

"*Resolved,* That the Department of Secondary Education appoint a committee of five, of which the present president shall be one, and request the appointment of a similar committee by the Department of Higher Education, the two to compose a committee of conference, whose duty it shall be to report at the next annual meeting a plan for the accomplishment of this end, so urgently demanded by the interests of higher education." *Ibid.,* 633. After long work and study the joint committee came out with the resolutions given above.

VI. *Resolved,* That, while the committee recognizes as suitable for recommendation by the colleges for admission the several studies enumerated in this report, and while it also recognizes the principle of large liberty to the students in secondary schools, it does not believe in unlimited election, but especially emphasizes the importance of a certain number of constants in all secondary schools and in all requirements for admission to college.

Resolved, That the committee recommends that the number of constants be recognized in the following proportion, namely: four units in foreign languages (no language accepted in less than two units), two units in mathematics, two in English, one in history, and one in science.

VII. *Resolved,* That the colleges will aid the secondary schools by allowing credit toward a degree for work done in secondary schools, beyond the amount required for entrance, when equal in amount and thoroness to work done in the same subjects in college.

VIII. *Resolved,* That for students who have met a definite requirement in any science, and who continue the subject in college, it seems to us desirable that there be provided a suitable sequel to the school course in continuation of the study; such students being in no case placed in the same class with beginners.

IX. *Resolved,* That we approve of encouraging gifted students to complete the preparatory course in less time than is required by most students.

X. *Resolved,* That in general we recognize in schools the admissibility of a second year in advanced work in the same subject, instead of a second year in a related subject; for example, two years in biology, instead of one year in biology and one year in chemistry, where local conditions favor such an arrangement.

XI. *Resolved,* That is is desirable that colleges should accept, in addition to the year of United States history and civil government already recommended, at least one-half year of intensive study of some period of history, especially of the United States.

XII. *Resolved,* That we recommend that any piece of work comprehended within the studies included in this report that has covered at least one year of four periods a week in a well-equipped secondary school, under competent instruction, should be considered worthy to count toward admission to college.

XIII. *Resolved,* That it is desirable that our colleges and universities should accept as a unit for admission a year's work in economics, including under this head a course in elementary political economy, supplemented by adequate instruction in commercial geography and industrial history.

XIV. *Resolved,* That we recommend an increase in the school day in secondary schools, to permit a larger amount of study in school under supervision.

The Association of American Universities Is Formed, 1900 *

I. NAME

This organization is called THE ASSOCIATION OF AMERICAN UNIVERSITIES.

II. PURPOSE

It is founded for the purpose of considering matters of common interest relating to graduate study.

III. MEMBERSHIP

1. *Qualifications.*—It is composed of institutions on the North American continent engaged in giving advanced or graduate instruction.

2. *Initial Membership.*—Its initial membership consists of the following institutions:

University of California.
Catholic University of America.
The University of Chicago.
Clark University.
Columbia University.
Cornell University.
Harvard University.
The Johns Hopkins University.
The Leland Stanford, Jr., University.
University of Michigan.
University of Pennsylvania.
Princeton University.
University of Wisconsin.
Yale University.

3. *Election of New Members.*—Other institutions may be admitted, at the annual conference, on the invitation of the Executive Committee, indorsed by a three-fourths vote of the members of the Association.

IV. MEETINGS

The Association shall hold an annual conference at such time and place as the Executive Committee may direct.

V. PROGRAM

The Executive Committee shall prepare a program for each meeting.

VI. OFFICERS

The officers of the Association shall be President, Vice-President, and Secretary.

* The Association of American Universities, *Journal of Proceedings and of the First and Second Annual Conferences*, 1900, 1901, pp. 7, 8, 11. The membership in the Association in 1949 numbered thirty-four institutions. In addition to the original members the following have been admitted to membership: University of Virginia, 1904; University of Illinois, 1908; University of Minnesota, 1908; University of Missouri, 1908; Indiana University, 1909; State University of Iowa, 1909; University of Kansas, 1909; University of Nebraska, 1909; Ohio State University, 1916; Northwestern University, 1917; University of North Carolina, 1922; Washington University, 1923; McGill University, 1926; University of Toronto, 1926; University of Texas, 1929; Brown University, 1933; California Institute of Technology, 1934; Massachusetts Institute of Technology, 1934; Duke University, 1938; University of Rochester, 1941.

These three, with two others elected by the Association, shall constitute the Executive Committee.

VII. VOTING POWER

In each conference, each university may have any number of representatives, but each university shall have a single vote.

VIII. LIMITATION OF POWERS

No act of the Association shall be held to control the policy or line of action of any institution belonging to it.

THE CALL

The presidents of Harvard University, Columbia University, the Johns Hopkins University, the University of Chicago, and the University of California issued an invitation to sister-institutions to a conference to be held in Chicago in February, 1900, for the consideration of problems connected with graduate work.

The following paragraphs embody important points in the invitation:

We beg to suggest that the time has arrived when the leading American universities may properly consider the means of representing to foreign universities the importance of revising their regulations governing the admission of American students to the examinations for the higher degrees.

This invitation is prompted by a desire to secure in foreign universities, where it is not already given, such credit as is legitimately due to the advanced work done in our own universities of high standing, and to protect the dignity of our Doctor's degrees. It seems to us, for instance, that European universities should be discouraged from conferring the degree of Doctor of Philosophy on American students who are not prepared to take the degree from our own best universities, and from granting degrees to Americans on lower terms than to their native students.

There is reason to believe that among other things the deliberations of such a conference as has been proposed will (1) result in a greater uniformity of the conditions under which students may become candidates for higher degrees in different American universities, thereby solving the questions of migration, which has become an important issue with the Federation of Graduate Clubs; (2) raise the opinion entertained abroad of our own Doctor's degree; (3) raise the standard of our own weaker institutions.

This invitation is extended to the University of California, the Catholic University of America, the University of Chicago, Clark University, Columbia University, Cornell University, Harvard University, the Johns Hopkins University, University of Michigan, University of Pennsylvania, Princeton University, the Leland Stanford, Jr., University, University of Wisconsin, and Yale University. The United States Commissioner of Education has been invited to take part in the conference. The Federation of Graduate Clubs has likewise been invited to send a delegate.

In accordance with the above call, there was held at the University of Chicago, February 27 and 28, 1900, a conference of representatives of certain institutions.

After careful discussion of the subject, a permanent organization was effected under the name of THE ASSOCIATION OF AMERICAN UNIVERSITIES. The publication of the minutes and proceedings of the several conferences of the Association and of the meetings of its Executive Committee was authorized by vote of the Association at the second session of the Second Annual Conference, taken February 27, 1901.

William James on the Ph.D. Octopus, 1903 *

Some years ago we had at our Harvard Graduate School a very brilliant student of philosophy, who, after leaving us and supporting himself by literary labor for three years, received an appointment to teach English literature at a sister institution of learning. The governors of this institution, however, had no sooner communicated the appointment than they made the awful discovery that they had enrolled upon their staff a person who was unprovided with the Ph.D. degree. The man in question had been satisfied to work at philosophy for her own sweet (or bitter) sake, and had disdained to consider that an academic bauble should be his reward.

His appointment had thus been made under a misunderstanding. He was not the proper man; and there was nothing to do but to inform him of the fact. It was notified to him by his new President that his appointment must be revoked, or that a Harvard doctor's degree must forthwith be procured.

Although it was already the spring of the year, our subject, being a man of spirit, took up the challenge, turned his back upon literature (which in view of his approaching duties might have seemed his more urgent concern) and spent the weeks that were left him, in writing a metaphysical thesis and grinding his psychology, logic and history of philosophy up again, so as to pass our formidable ideals.

When the thesis came to be read by our committee, we could not pass it. Brilliancy and originality by themselves won't save a thesis for the doctorate; it must also exhibit a heavy technical apparatus of learning; and this our candidate had neglected to bring to bear. So, telling him that he was temporarily rejected, we advised him to pad out the thesis properly, and return with it next year, at the same time informing his new President

* "The Ph.D. Octopus," *Harvard Monthly*, March, 1903. This was reprinted in *Educational Review*, LV (February, 1918), pp. 149-57. The editor of that magazine (Nicholas Murray Butler) said that the conditions which the article described in 1903 "have been but slightly altered, if at all, in the intervening years." For a later treatment of the same subject, see Jacques Barzun, *Teacher in America* (Boston, Little, Brown & Co., 1945), pp. 195-200, 203-08.

that this signified nothing as to his merits, that he was of ultra Ph.D. quality, and one of the strongest men with whom we had ever had to deal.

To our surprise we were given to understand in reply that the quality *per se* of the man signified nothing in this connection, and that three magical letters were the thing seriously required. The College had always gloried in a list of faculty members who bore the doctor's title, and to make a gap in the galaxy, and admit a common fox without a tail, would be a degradation impossible to be thought of. We wrote again, pointing out that a Ph.D. in philosophy would prove little anyhow as to one's ability to teach literature; we sent separate letters in which we outdid each other in eulogy of our candidate's powers, for indeed they were great; and at last, *mirabile dictu,* our eloquence prevailed. He was allowed to retain his appointment provisionally, on condition that at one year later at the farthest his miserably naked name should be prolonged by the sacred appendage, the lack of which had given so much trouble to all concerned.

Accordingly he came up here the following spring with an adequate thesis (known since in print as a most brilliant contribution to metaphysics), past a first rate examination, wiped out the stain, and brought his college into proper relations with the world again. Whether his teaching, during that first year, of English Literature was made any better by the impending examination in a different subject, is a question which I will not try to solve.

I have related this incident at such length because it is so characteristic of American academic conditions at the present day. Graduate schools still are something of a novelty, and higher diplomas something of a rarity. The latter, therefore, carry a vague sense of preciousness and honor, and have a particularly "up-to-date" appearance, and it is no wonder if smaller institutions, unable to attract professors already eminent, and forced usually to recruit their faculties from the relatively young, should hope to compensate for the obscurity of the names of their officers of instruction by the abundance of decorative titles by which those names are followed on the pages of the catalogs where they appear. The dazzled reader of the lost, the parent or student, says to himself, "this must be a terribly distinguished crowd—their titles shine like the stars in the firmament, Ph.D.'s, S.D.'s, and Litt.D.'s, bespangle the page as if they were sprinkled over it from a pepper caster."

Human nature is once for all so childish that every reality becomes a sham somewhere, and in the minds of Presidents and Trustees the Ph.D. degree is in point of fact already looked upon as a mere advertising resource, a manner of throwing dust in the Public's eyes. "No instructor who is not a Doctor" has become a maxim in the smaller institutions which represent demand; and in each of the larger ones which represent supply, the same belief in decorated scholarship expresses itself in two antagonistic passions, one for multiplying as much as possible the annual output of doctors, the other for raising the standard of difficulty in passing, so that the Ph.D. of the special institution shall carry a higher blaze of distinction than it does elsewhere. Thus we at Harvard are proud of the number of candidates whom we reject, and of the inability of men who are not *distingués* in intellect to pass our tests.

America is thus as a nation rapidly drifting toward a state of things in which no man of science or letters will be accounted respectable unless some kind of badge or diploma is stamped upon him, and in which bare personality will be a mark of outcast estate. It seems to me high time to rouse ourselves to consciousness, and to cast a critical eye upon this grotesque tendency. Other nations suffer terribly from the Mandarin disease. Are we doomed to suffer like the rest?

Our higher degrees were instituted for the laudable purpose of stimulating scholarship, especially in the form of "original research." Experience has proved that great as the love of truth may be among men, it can be made still greater by adventitious rewards. The winning of a diploma certifying mastery and marking a barrier successfully past, acts as a challenge to the ambitious; and if the diploma will help to gain bread-winning positions also, its power as a stimulus to work is tremendously increased. So far, we are on innocent ground; it is well for a country to have research in abundance, and our graduate schools do but apply a normal psychological spur. But the institutionizing on a large scale of any natural combination of need and motive always tends to run into technicality and to develop a tyrannical machine with unforeseen powers of exclusion and corruption. Observation of the workings of our Harvard system for twenty years past has brought some of these drawbacks home to my consciousness, and I should like to call the attention of the readers of the *Monthly* to this disadvantageous aspect of the picture, and to make a couple of remedial suggestions, if I may.

In the first place, it would seem that to stimulate study, and to increase the *gelehrtes Publikum,* the class of highly educated men in our country, is the only positive good, and consequently the sole direct end at which our graduate schools, with their diploma-giving powers, should aim. If other results have developed they should be deemed secondary incidents, and if not desirable in themselves, they should be carefully guarded against.

To interfere with the free development of talent, to obstruct the natural play of supply and demand in the teaching profession, to foster academic snobbery by the *prestige* of certain privileged institutions, to transfer accredited value from essential manhood to an outward badge, to blight hopes and promote invidious sentiments, to divert the attention of aspiring youth from direct dealings with truth to the passing of examinations—such consequences, if they exist, ought surely to be regarded as drawbacks to the system, and an enlightened public consciousness ought to be keenly alive to the importance of reducing their amount. Candidates themselves do seem to be keenly conscious of some of these evils, but outside of their ranks or in the general public no such consciousness, so far as I can see, exists; or if it does exist, it fails to express itself aloud. Schools, Colleges and Universities, appear enthusiastic over the entire system, just as it stands and unanimously applaud all its developments.

I beg the reader to consider some of the secondary evils which I have enumerated. First of all, is not our growing tendency to appoint no instructors who are not also doctors an instance of pure sham? Will anyone pretend for a moment that the doctor's degree is a guarantee that its possessor will be a successful teacher? Notoriously his moral, social and personal characteristics may utterly disqualify him for success in the classroom; and of these characteristics his doctor's examination is unable to take any account whatever. Certain bare human beings will always be better candidates for a given place than all the doctor-applicants on hand; and to exclude the former by a rigid rule, and in the end to have to sift the latter by private inquiry into their personal peculiarities among those who know them, just as if they were not doctors at all, is to stultify one's own procedure. You may say that at least you guard against ignorance of the subject by considering only the candidates who are doctors; but how then about making doctors in one subject teach a different subject? This happened in the instance by which I introduced this article, and it happens daily and hourly in all our colleges. The truth is that the Doctor-Monopoly in teaching, which is becoming so rooted an American custom, can show no serious grounds whatsoever for itself in reason. As it actually prevails and grows in vogue among us, it is due to childish motives exclusively. In reality it is but a sham, a bauble, a dodge whereby to decorate the catalogs of schools and colleges.

Next, let us turn from the general promotion of a spirit of academic snobbery to the particular damage done to individuals by the system.

There are plenty of individuals so well endowed by nature that they pass with ease all the ordeals with which life confronts them. Such persons are born for professional success. Examinations have no terrors for them, and interfere in no way with their spiritual or worldly interests. There are others, not so gifted, who nevertheless rise to the challenge, get a stimulus from the difficulty, and become doctors, not without some baleful nervous wear and tear and retardation of their purely inner life, but on the whole successfully and with advantage. These two classes form the natural Ph.D.'s for whom the degree is legitimately instituted. To be sure, the degree is of no consequence one way or the other for the first sort of man, for in him the personal worth obviously outshines the title. To the second set of persons, however, the doctor-ideal may contribute a touch of energy and solidarity of scholarship which otherwise they might have lacked, and were our candidates all drawn from these classes, no oppression would result from the institution.

But there is a third class of persons who are genuinely, and in the most pathetic sense, the institution's victims. For this type of character the academic life may become, after a certain point, a virulent poison. Men without marked originality or native force, but fond of truth and especially of books and study, ambitious of reward and recognition, poor often, and needing a degree to get a teaching position, weak in the eyes of their examiners—among these we find the veritable *chair à canon* of the wars of learning, the unfit in the academic struggle for existence. There are individuals of this sort for whom to pass one degree after another seems the limit of earthly aspirations. Your private advice does not discourage them. They will fail, and go away to recuperate, and then present themselves for another ordeal, and sometimes prolong the process into middle life. Or else, if they are less heroic morally they will accept the failure as a sentence of doom that they are not fit, and are broken-spirited men thereafter.

We of the university faculties are responsible for deliberately creating this new class of American social failures, and heavy is the responsibility. We advertise our "schools" and send out our degree requirements, knowing well that aspirants of all sorts will be attracted, and at the same time we set a standard which intends to pass no man who has not native intellectual distinction. We know that there is no test, however absurd, by which, if a title or decoration, a public badge or mark, were to be won by it, some weekly suggestible or hauntable persons would not feel challenged and remain unhappy if they went without it. We dangle our three magic letters before the eyes of these predestined victims, and they swarm to us like moths to an electric light. They come at a time of life when failure can no longer be repaired easily and when the wounds it leaves are permanent; and we say deliberately that mere work faithfully performed, as they perform it, will not by itself save them, they must in addition put in evidence the one thing they have not got, namely this quality of intellectual distinction. Occasionally, out of sheer human pity, we ignore our high and mighty standard and pass them. Usually, however, the standard, and not the candidate, commands our fidelity. The result is caprice, majorities of one on the jury, and on the whole, a confession that our pretensions about the degree can not be lived up to consistently. Thus, partiality in the favored cases; in the unfavored, blood on our hands; and in both a bad conscience—are the results of our administration.

The more widespread becomes the belief that our diplomas are indispensable hall-marks to show the sterling metal of their holders, the more widespread these corruptions will become. We ought to look to the future carefully, for it takes generations for a national custom, once rooted, to be grown away from. All the European countries are seeking to diminish the check upon individual spontaneity which state examinations with their tyrannous growth have brought in their train. We have had to institute state examinations too; and it will perhaps be fortunate if some day hereafter our descendants, comparing machine with machine, do not sigh with regret for old times and American freedom, and wish that the régime of the dear old bosses might be reinstalled, with plain human nature, the glad hand and the marble heart, liking and disliking, and man-to-man relations grown possible again. Meanwhile, whatever evolution our state examinations are destined to undergo, our universities at least should never cease to regard themselves as the jealous custodians of personal and spiritual spontaneity. They are, indeed, its only organized and recognized custodians in America today. They ought to guard against contributing to the increase of official-ism and snobbery and insincerity as against a pestilence. They ought to keep truth and disinterested labor always in the foreground, treat degrees as secondary incidents, and in season and out of season make it plain that what they live for is to help men's souls, and not to decorate their persons with diplomas.

There seems to be three obvious ways in which the increasing hold of the Ph.D. Octopus upon American life can be kept in check.

The first way lies with the universities. They can lower their fantastic standards (which here at Harvard we are so proud of) and give the doc-torate as a matter of course, just as they give the bachelor's degree, for a due amount of time spent in patient labor in a special department of learning, whether the man be a brilliantly gifted individual or not. Surely native distinction needs no official stamp, and should disdain to ask for one. On the other hand, faithful labor, however commonplace, and years devoted to a subject, always deserve to be acknowledged and requited.

The second way lies with both the universities and the colleges. Let them give up their unspeakably silly ambition to bespangle their lists of officers with these doctorial titles. Let them look more to substance and less to vanity and sham.

The third way lies with the individual student, and with his personal advisers in the faculties. Every man of native power, who might take a higher degree, and refuses to do so, because examinations interfere with the free following out of his more immediate intellectual aims, deserves well of his country, and in a rightly organized community, would not be made to suffer for his independence. With many men the passing of these extraneous tests is a very grevious interference indeed. Private letters of recommendation from their instructors, which in any event are ultimately needful, ought, in these cases, completely to off-set the lack of the bread-winning degree; and instructors ought to be ready to advise students against it upon occasions, and to pledge themselves to back them later personally in the market-struggle which they have to face.

It is indeed odd to see this love of titles—and such titles—growing up in a country of which the recognition of individuality and bare manhood have so long been supposed to be the very soul. The independence of the State, in which most of our colleges stand, relieves us of those more odious forms of academic politics which continental European countries present. Anything like the elaborate university machine of France, with its throttling influences upon individuals, is unknown here. The spectacle of the *Rath* distinction in its innumerable spheres and grades, with which all Germany is crawling today, is displeasing to American eyes; and displeasing also in some respects is the institution of knighthood in England, which, aping as it does an aristocratic title, enables one's wife as well as one's self so easily to dazzle the servants at the house of one's friends. But are we Americans ourselves destined after all to hunger after similar vanities on an infinitely more contemptible scale? And is individuality with us also going to count for nothing unless stamped and licensed and authenticated by some title-giving machine? Let us pray that our ancient national genius may long preserve vitality enough to guard us from a future so unmanly and so unbeautiful!

Charter of General Education Board, 1903 *

Be it enacted by the Senate and House of Representatives of the United States of America in Congress assembled, That William H. Baldwin, Junior, Jabez L. M. Curry, Frederick T. Gates, Daniel C. Gilman, Morris K. Jesup, Robert C. Ogden, Walter H. Page, George Foster Peabody, and Albert Shaw, and their successors, be, and they hereby are, constituted a body corporate of the District of Columbia; that the name of such body corporate shall be GENERAL EDUCATION BOARD, and that by such name the said persons and their successors shall have perpetual succession.

Sec. 2. That the object of the said corporation shall be the promotion of education within the United States of America, without distinction of race, sex, or creed.

Sec. 3. That for the promotion of such object the said corporation shall have power to build, improve, enlarge, or equip, or to aid others to build, improve, enlarge, or equip, buildings for elementary or primary schools, industrial schools, technical schools, normal schools, training schools for teachers, or schools of any grade, or for higher institutions of learning, or, in connection therewith, libraries, workshops, gardens, kitchens, or other educational accessories; to establish, maintain, or endow, or aid others to establish, maintain, or endow, elementary or primary schools, industrial schools, technical schools, normal schools, training schools for teachers, or schools of any grade, or higher institutions of learning; to employ or aid others to employ teachers and lecturers; to aid, coöperate with, or endow associations or other corporations engaged in educational work within the United States of America, or to donate to any such association or corporation any property or moneys which shall at any time be held by the said corporation hereby constituted; to collect educational statistics and infor-

* General Education Board, *Charter and By-Laws* (New York, 1938), pp. 1-5.

mation, and to publish and distribute documents and reports containing the same, and in general to do and perform all things necessary or convenient for the promotion of the object of the corporation.

Sec. 4. That the said corporation shall further have power to have and use a common seal and to alter and change the same at its pleasure; to sue or be sued in any court of the United States or other court of competent jurisdiction; to make by-laws for the admission or exclusion of its members, for the election of its trustees, officers, and agents, and otherwise; for the casting of votes by its members or trustees by proxy; for the purchase, management, sale, or transfer of its property, the investment and control of its funds, and the general transaction of its business; to take or receive, whether by gift, grant, devise, bequest, or purchase, any real or personal estate, or to hold, grant, convey, hire, or lease the same for the purposes of its incorporation; to accept and administer any trust of money or of real or personal estate for any educational purpose within the object of the corporation as aforesaid; to prescribe by by-laws or otherwise the terms and conditions upon which money, real estate, or personal estate shall be acquired, or received by the said corporation, and for the grant, transfer, assignment, or donation of any or all property of the said corporation, real or personal, to any society or corporation for any of the said purposes for which the said corporation is hereby incorporated, and otherwise generally for the management cf the property and the transaction of the business of the corporation.

Sec. 5. That the members of the corporation shall be not less than nine in number and not more than seventeen, as may be prescribed by the by-laws of the corporation: Provided, however, That if and when the number of members shall be less than nine, the members remaining shall have power to add and shall add to their number until the number shall be not less than nine: And provided, That no act of the corporation shall be void because at the time such act shall be done the number of the members of the corporation shall be less than nine; that all the members of the corporation shall be its trustees; that no member of the said association shall, by reason of such membership or his trusteeship, be personally liable for any of its debts or obligations; that each member of the corporation shall hold his membership for a term of three years and until his successor shall be chosen; Provided, however, That the members shall be at all times divided into three classes numerically, as nearly as may be, and that the original members shall, at their first meeting, or as soon thereafter as shall be convenient, be divided into three classes, the members of the first class to hold their membership and office until the expiration of one year from the first day of January next after the enactment of this law, the members of the second class until the expiration of two years thereafter, and the members of the third class until the expiration of three years thereafter, and that in every case the member shall hold office after the expiration of his term until his successor shall be chosen: And provided, further, That in case any member shall, by death, resignation, incapacity to act, or otherwise, cease to be a member during his term, his successor shall be chosen to serve for the remainder of such term and until his successor shall be chosen; and that the principal office of the said corporation shall be in the City of Washington, District of Columbia: Provided, That meetings may be held elsewhere within the United States as may be determined by the members or provided by the by-laws.

Sec. 6. That all real property of the corporation within the District of Columbia which shall be used by the corporation for the educational or other purposes of the corporation as aforesaid, other than the purpose of producing income, and all personal property and funds of the corporation held, used, or invested for educational purposes as aforesaid, or to produce income to be used for such purposes, shall be exempt from taxation: Provided, however, That this exemption shall not apply to any property of the corporation which shall not be used for, or the income of which shall not be applied to, the educational purposes of the corporation: And provided further, That the corporation shall annually file with the Secretary of the Interior of the United States a report in writing stating in detail the property, real and personal, held by the corporation, and the expenditure or other use or disposition of the same or the income thereof during the preceding year.

Sec. 7. That this charter shall be subject to alteration, amendment, or repeal at the pleasure of the Congress of the United States.
Approved, January 12, 1903.

The Right Honorable James Bryce, M. P., on Higher Education in The United States, 1905 *

There has been within these last thirty-five years a development of the higher education in the United States perhaps without a parallel in the world. Previously the Eastern States had but a very few universities whose best teachers were on a level with the teachers in the universities of western Europe. There were a great many institutions bearing the name of university over the Northern and Middle States and the West, and a smaller number in the South, but they gave an instruction which, though in some

* "America Revisited: The Changes of a Quarter-Century," *The Outlook,* Vol. 79 (March 25, 1905), pp. 736-39. Mr. Bryce was universally regarded in the United States "as the foremost expositor and critic of American institutions, manners and traits." He was asked by *The Outlook* "to set down on paper some of the changes which have struck me on revisiting that country. Thirty-four years have passed since I first saw it, and twenty-one years since I spent in it a time long enough to form impressions. . . ." Mr. Bryce's *The American Commonwealth,* which appeared in 1888, was one of the most thorough and penetrating studies which had been attempted of this country and still occupies an unquestioned position in the field. Mr. Bryce was the British Ambassador to the United States from 1907 to 1913. For comments on other aspects of American life, see the same magazine for April 1, 1905, pp. 846-55.

places (and especially in New England) it was sound and thorough as far as it went, was really the instruction rather of a secondary school than of a university in the proper sense. In the West and South the teaching, often ambitious when it figured in the programme, was apt to be superficial and flimsy, giving the appearance without the solid reality of knowledge. The scientific side was generally even weaker than the literary. These universities or colleges had their value, for their very existence was a recognition of the need for an education above that which the school is intended to supply. I ventured even then to hazard the opinion that the reformers who wished to extinguish the bulk of them or to turn them into schools, reserving the degree-granting power to a selected few only, were mistaken, because improvement and development might be expected. But I did not expect that the development would come so fast and go so far. No doubt there are still a great many whose standard of teaching and examination is that of a school not of a true university. But there are also many which have risen to the European level, and many others which are moving rapidly towards it. Roughly speaking—for it is impossible to speak with exactness—America has now not less than fifteen or perhaps even twenty seats of learning fit to be ranked beside the universities of Germany, France, and England as respects the completeness of the instruction which may provide and the thoroughness at which they aim. Only a few have a professorial staff containing names equal to those which adorn the Faculties of Berlin and Leipzig and Vienna, of Oxford, Cambridge, Edinburgh, and Glasgow. Men of brilliant gifts are scarce in all countries, and in America there has hardly been time to produce a supply equal to the immense demand for the highest instruction which has lately shown itself. It is the advance in the standard aimed at, and in the efforts to attain that standard, that is so remarkable. Even more noticeable is the amplitude of the provision now made for the study of the natural sciences, and of those arts in which science is applied to practical ends. In this respect the United States has gone ahead of Great Britain, aided no doubt by the greater pecuniary resources which not a few of her universities possess, and which they owe to the wise liberality of private benefactors. In England nothing is so hard as to get money from private persons for any educational purpose. Mr. Carnegie's splendid gift to the universities of Scotland stands almost alone. In America nothing is so easy. There is, indeed, no better indication of the prosperity of the country and of its intelligence than the annual record of the endowments bestowed on the universities by successful business men, some of whom have never themselves had more than a common-school education. Only in one respect does that poverty which Europe has long associated with learning reappear in America. The salaries of presidents and professors remain low as compared with the average incomes of persons in the same social rank, and as compared with the cost of living. That so many men of an energy and ability sufficient to win success and wealth in a business career do nevertheless devote themselves to a career of teaching and research is a remarkable evidence of the intellectual zeal which pervades the people.[1]

The improvement in the range and quality of university teaching is a change scarcely more remarkable than the increased afflux of students. It seems (for I have not worked the matter out in figures, as I am giving impressions and not statistics) to have grown much faster than population has grown, and to betoken an increased desire among parents and young men to obtain a complete intellectual equipment for life. The number of undergraduates at Harvard is much larger than is the number who resort to Oxford; the number at Yale is larger than the number at Cambridge (England). Five leading universities of the Eastern States—Harvard, Yale, Columbia, Princeton, Pennsylvania—count as many students as do all the universities of England (omitting in both cases those who attend evening classes only), although there are twice as many universities in England now as there were forty years ago, and although the English students have much more than doubled in number. And whereas in England the vast majority of students go to prepare themselves for some profession—law, journalism, medicine, engineering, or the ministry of the Established Church—there is in America a considerable proportion (in one institution I heard it reckoned at a third or more) who intend to choose a business career, such as manufactures, or banking, or commerce, or railroading. In England nearly every youth belonging to the middle or upper class who takes to business goes into a commercial office or a workshop not later than seventeen. In the United States, if he graduates at a university, he continues his general liberal education till he is twenty-one or twenty-two. This practical people does not deem these three years lost time. They believe that the young man is all the more likely to succeed in business if he goes to it with a mind widely and thoroughly trained. To say that the proportion of college graduates to the whole population is larger in America than in any European country would not mean much, because graduation from a good many of the colleges means very little. But if we take only those colleges which approach or equal the West European standard, I think the proportion will be as high as it is in Germany or Switzerland or Scotland, and higher than it is in England.

This feature of recent American development has an important bearing on the National life. It is a counterpoise to the passion, growing always more intense, for material progress, to the eagerness to seize every chance, to save every moment, to get the most out of every enterprise. It tends to diffuse a taste for scientific and literary knowledge among a class to most of whom, in other countries, few opportunities have been opened for acquiring such a taste. It adds to the number of those who may find some

---

[1] Many subjects are taught to large classes at the best Eastern universities for the study of which hardly any students can be secured in England.

occasion in their business life for turning a knowledge of natural science to practical account, and so benefiting the country as well as themselves. Nor is its social influence to be overlooked. One is frequently impressed in America by the attachment of the graduates to the place of their education, by their interest in its fortunes, by their willingness to respond when it asks them for money. In the great cities there are always University Clubs, and in some cities these clubs become centers for social and political action for good public ends. Not unfrequently they take the lead to municipal reform movements.

When I pass from the places set apart for the cultivation of letters and learning to the general state of letters and learning in the community, it is much more difficult to formulate any positive impressions. One feels a change in the spirit of the books produced, and a change in the taste of the reading public, but one cannot say exactly in what the alteration consists, nor how it has come, nor whether it will last. Having no sufficient materials for a theory on the subject, I can venture only on a few scattered remarks. Literary criticism, formerly at a low ebb, seems to have sensibly improved, whereas in England many people doubt if it is as acute, as judicious, and as delicate as it was in the sixties. The love of poetry and the love of art are more widely diffused in America than ever before; one finds, for instance, a far greater number of good pictures in private houses than could have been seen thirty years ago, and the building up of public art galleries has occupied much of the thought and skill of leading citizens as well as required the expenditure of vast sums. Great ardor is shown in the investigation of dry subjects such as questions of local history. The interest taken in constitutional topics and economic questions, indeed in everything that belongs to the sphere of political science, is as great as it is in Germany or France, and greater than in Britain. This interest is, indeed, confined to one class, which chiefly consists of university teachers, but it is a new and a noteworthy phenomenon. Few people thought or wrote on these matters thirty years ago.

On the other hand, it is said, and that by some who have the best special opportunities for knowing, that serious books, *i.e.,* books other than fiction and the lighter forms of *belles-lettres,* find no larger sale now, when readers are more numerous and richer, than they did in the seventies. No one can fail to observe the increasing number and popularity of the magazines; and it seems likely that they are now more read, in proportion to books, than they used to be. The same thing is happening in England. It is a natural consequence of the low prices at which, owing to the vast market, magazines containing good matter and abundant illustrations can be sold. It may also be due to that sense of hurry which makes the ordinary American little disposed to sit down to work his way through a book. Both these factors are more potent in the United States than they were ever before, or than they are in Europe.

If in America as well as in England the growth of population has not been accompanied by a growing demand for books (other than fiction), let us remember and allow for the results of another change which has passed upon both countries. It is a change which is all the more noticeable in America because it is there quite recent. It is the passion for looking on at and reading about athletic sports. The love of playing and watching games which require strength and skill is as old as mankind, and needs no explanation. So the desire not to play but to look on at chariot races and gladiatorial combats was a passion among the people of Rome for many centuries. The circus factions at Constantinople have their place in history, and a bad place it is. But this taste is in America a thing almost of yesterday. It has now grown to vast proportions. It occupies the minds not only of the youth at the universities, but also of their parents and of the general public. Baseball matches and football matches excite an interest greater than any other public events except the Presidential election, and that comes only once in four years. The curse of betting which dogs football as well as horse-racing in England seems to be less prevalent in America; nor do the cities support professional football clubs like those which exist in the towns of northern England and even of Scotland. But the interest in one of the great contests, such as those which draw forty thousand spectators to the great "Stadium" recently erected at Cambridge, Massachusetts, appears to pervade nearly all classes more than does any "sporting event" in Great Britain. The American love of excitement and love of competition has seized upon these games, but the fashion, like that of playing golf and that of playing bridge, seems to have come from England. It is a curious instance of the more intimate social relations between the two countries that speak the same language that fashions of this kind pass so quickly from the one to the other and do not pass from either to Continental Europe. There has been no development of the devotion to athletic sports in Germany or in France coincident with that which is so marked a feature of modern England and so novel a feature in America.

Andrew Carnegie Establishes the Carnegie Foundation for the Advancement of Teaching, 1905 *

NEW YORK, April 16, 1905.

GENTLEMEN:

I have reached the conclusion that the least rewarded of all the professions is that of the teacher in our higher educational institutions. New York City generously, and very wisely, provides retiring pensions for teachers in her public schools and also for her policemen. Very few indeed of our colleges are able to do so. The consequences are grievous. Able men hesi-

* The Carnegie Foundation for the Advancement of Teaching, *First Annual Report of the President and Treasurer*, 1906, pp. 7, 8.

tate to adopt teaching as a career, and many old professors whose places should be occupied by younger men, cannot be retired.

I have, therefore, transferred to you and your successors, as Trustees, $10,000,000.00, 5% First Mortgage Bonds of the United States Steel Corporation, the revenue from which is to provide retiring pensions for the teachers of Universities, Colleges, and Technical Schools in our country, Canada and Newfoundland under such conditions as you may adopt from time to time. Expert calculation shows that the revenue will be ample for the purpose.

The fund applies to the three classes of institutions named, without regard to race, sex, creed or color. We have, however, to recognize that State and Colonial Governments which have established or mainly supported Universities, Colleges or Schools may prefer that their relations shall remain exclusively with the State. I cannot, therefore, presume to include them.

There is another class which states do not aid, their constitution in some cases even forbidding it, viz., Sectarian Institutions. Many of these established long ago, were truly sectarian, but today are free to all men of all creeds or of none—such are not to be considered sectarian now. Only such as are under the control of a sect or require Trustees (or a majority thereof), Officers, Faculty or Students, to belong to any specified sect, or which impose any theological test, are to be excluded.

* Trustees shall hold office for five years and be eligible for re-election. The first Trustees shall draw lots for one, two, three, four or five year terms, so that one-fifth shall retire each year. Each institution participating in the Fund shall cast one vote for Trustees.

The trustees are hereby given full powers to manage the Trust in every respect, to fill vacancies of non-ex-officio members; appoint executive committees; employ agents; change securities, and, generally speaking, to do all things necessary, in their judgment, to secure the most beneficial administration of the Funds.

By a two-thirds vote they may from time to time apply the revenue in a different manner and for a different, though similar purpose to that specified, should coming days bring such changes as to render this necessary in their judgment to produce the best results possible for the teachers and for education.

No Trustee shall incur any legal liability flowing from his Trusteeship. All travelling and hotel expenses incurred by Trustees in the performance of their duties shall be paid from the Fund. The expenses of a wife or daughter accompanying the Trustees to the Annual meeting are included.

I hope this Fund may do much for the cause of higher education and

* In view of the desirability of a permanent, self-perpetuating governing board, the provisions of this paragraph were, upon the advice and with the consent of Mr. Carnegie, omitted from the Act of Incorporation which forms the present charter of the Foundation.

to remove a source of deep and constant anxiety to the poorest paid and yet one of the highest of all professions.

Gratefully yours,

ANDREW CARNEGIE

A Committee of the N.E.A. Advises "Economy of Time in Education," 1913 *

If the previous contentions with regard to elementary and collegiate education are established, the period of secondary education will begin with the twelfth year. The question then arises, When shall it end? As at present, at the end of the eighteenth year? Or later, so as to include the freshman and sophomore years of college, thus abolishing the tertiary or collegiate division of liberal training? These are questions difficult to answer, because they raise the problem of articulation our three types of schools for general education with each other and with schools for vocational education. They involve, too, the need to know the valid distinctions which can separate a continuous system for cultural education into three distinct institutional units.

The secondary school has tended to extend its limits upward to include the first two years of college, as well as downward to include the last two years of the elementary school. But the former tendency is comparatively slight. The mass of experience seems to favor the latter, as has already been suggested; and the theoretic considerations corroborate actual practice in this direction. The inclusion of the two collegiate years in the high-school unit is opposed by arguments of a sort difficult to overcome. The largest gap in our school system exists between high school and college. The most advanced teaching of a cultural type is very closely dependent upon the research of the university in replenishing its stock from advancing knowledge. The equipments required by college and university are more nearly coincident than those of college and high school. Endowed institutions constitute a larger proportion of the schools for higher education than they do for secondary education. An upward extension of the high school is so difficult as to seem inexpedient, while a downward extension seems logically to be a line of least resistance. On these grounds it is probable that, in the generality of cases, high school education will plan to include the period from the twelfth to the eighteenth year.

The objections which have been urged against the inclusion of the collegiate years by the high school hold largely against any proposal that the college should attach to itself the upper two years of high school. Such a proposal is not seriously made. If it were, all our current tendency would be against it. Even the smaller colleges are tending to drop the preparatory

---

* *Report of the Committee of the National Education Association on Economy of Time in Education*, Bulletin No. 38, 1913, United States Bureau of Education, pp. 25-27.

academies or high schools which have so frequently been associated with them. The larger institutions did so long ago. The discussion of any such proposal to extend the college downward would, therefore, be largely academic.

Charter of The Rockefeller Foundation, 1913 *

The People of the State of New York, represented in Senate and Assembly, do enact as follows:

Section 1. John D. Rockefeller, John D. Rockefeller, Junior, Frederick T. Gates, Harry Pratt Judson, Simon Flexner, Starr J. Murphy, Jerome D. Greene, Wickliffe Rose, and Charles O. Heydt, together with such persons as they may associate with themselves, and their successors, are hereby constituted a body corporate by the name of The Rockefeller Foundation, for the purpose of receiving and maintaining a fund or funds, and applying the income and principal thereof to promote the well-being of mankind throughout the world. It shall be within the purposes of said corporation to use, as means to that end, research, publication, the establishment and maintenance of charitable, benevolent, religious, missionary, and public educational activities, agencies, and institutions, and the aid of any such activities, agencies, and institutions already established and any other means and agencies which from time to time shall seem expedient to its members or trustees.

2. The corporation hereby formed shall have power to take and hold by bequest, devise, gift, purchase, or lease, either absolutely or in trust, for any of its purposes, any property, real or personal, without limitation as to amount or value, except such limitations, if any, as the legislature shall hereafter specifically impose; to convey such property and to invest and reinvest any principal; and to deal with and expend the income and principal of the corporation in such manner as in the judgment of the trustees will best promote its objects. It shall have all the power and be subject to all the restrictions which now pertain by law to membership corporations created by special law so far as the same are applicable thereto and are not inconsistent with the provisions of this act. The persons named in the first section of this act, or a majority of them, shall hold a meeting and organize the corporation and adopt a constitution and by-laws not inconsistent with the constitution and laws of this state. The constitution shall prescribe the manner of selection of members, the number of members who shall constitute a quorum for the transaction of business at meetings of the corporation, the number of trustees by whom the business and affairs of the corporation shall be managed, the qualifications, powers, and the manner of selection of the trustees and officers of the corporation, the manner of amending the constitution and by-laws of the corporation, and any other

* *Laws of the State of New York,* 1913, Chapter 488. Approved May 14, 1913.

provisions for the management and disposition of the property and regulation of the affairs of the corporation which may be deemed expedient.

3. No officer, member, or employee of this corporation shall receive or be lawfully entitled to receive any pecuniary profit from the operations thereof except reasonable compensation for services in effecting one or more of its purposes, or as a proper beneficiary of its strictly charitable purposes.

4. This act shall take effect immediately.

Call for Meeting for the Organization of the American Association of University Professors, 1914 *

The scientific and specialized interests of members of American university faculties are well cared for by various learned societies. No organization exists, however, which at once represents the common interests of the teaching staffs and deals with the general problems of university policy. Believing that a society, comparable to the American Bar Association and the American Medical Association in kindred professions, could be of substantial service to the ends for which universities exist, members of the faculties of a number of institutions have undertaken to bring about the formation of a national Association of University Professors. The general purposes of such an Association would be to facilitate a more effective coöperation among the members of the profession in the discharge of their special responsibilities as custodians of the interests of higher education and research in America; to promote a more general and methodical discussion of problems relating to education in higher institutions of learning; to create means for the authoritative expression of the public opinion of college and university teachers; to make collective action possible; and to maintain and advance the standards and ideals of the profession. The specific activities in which these general purposes may best find expression will, of course, become fully evident only through experience. There is, however, already manifest among university teachers an interest in such matters as the proper organization of departments, and their relation to one another; the relations of instruction and research, both in colleges and graduate schools; the adjustment of graduate to undergraduate instruction, and of professional studies to both; the possibility of coöperation between universities to prevent unnecessary duplication of effort; the effectiveness of the manner in which the university teaching profession is now recruited; the problem of graduate fellowships and scholarships; the desirability and practicability of an increased migration of graduate students; the suitable recognition of intellectual eminence, and the manner of awarding honorary degrees; the proper conditions of the tenure of the professorial office; methods of appointment and promotion,

* Bulletin of the American Association of University Professors, II, pp. 11-13.

and the character of the qualifications to be considered in either case; the function of faculties in university government; the relations of faculties to trustees; the impartial determination of the facts in cases in which serious violations of academic freedom are alleged. It may be expected that the Association will from time to time take up the consideration of subjects of this character, will create committees for the purpose of ascertaining the experience and the existing practice of the American universities in such matters, and will, at its annual meetings, discuss the committees' reports and make recommendations upon the questions which these reports may raise. It would also appear desirable that the Association should, as soon as its financial condition makes this possible, establish an annual, semi-annual or quarterly periodical, devoted to the discussion of similar questions and to the interchange of information respecting the policies and activities of the different universities.

Those concerned in the organization of the Association do not, however, desire in any way to determine its programme in advance. What seems to them essential is that, in the working out of a national policy of higher education and research, the general body of university teachers shall exercise an effectual influence; that in the determination of the future of the profession, the profession itself shall have a voice; that issues hereafter arising which may seriously affect the work of the universities, or the usefulness, dignity, or standards of the professorate, shall be dealt with only after careful consideration and wide discussion. These essentials appear unlikely to be realized, unless there exist some organization fairly representative of the ideals, the interests and the point of view of the profession as such.

President Alexander Meiklejohn of Amherst College on the Purpose of the Liberal College, 1914 *

There are many different interpretations of the purpose of the liberal college. They are all partially true but most of them are false as accounts of the primary aim of liberal education. The liberal college is not simply a quiet retreat shut off from the conflicts of real life. Such men as Kant and Darwin, in the quiet of the study and the laboratory, were molding and shaping the entire social scheme of the nineteenth and twentieth centuries. The warfare of ideas may be quiet, but it is not shut off from the affairs of life; it is fundamental to them all. The liberal college is not a place where boys may seek "culture" in some sense which shall make them consciously superior to their fellows. Genuine culture is always a by-product. It comes not by seeking, but by doing something worth while. The liberal college is not concerned merely with the classics, if by that is meant a study of the past. No people were ever more modern in spirit than the

* *Journal of Proceedings and Addresses*, National Education Association, 1914, pp. 102-03.

Greeks. Their language and literature, their art and philosophy are well worthy of our study. But perhaps the best lesson they have to give us is that of the vital necessity of knowledge of our own time and our own people. The liberal college is not an institution which has lost its mission. It is sometimes said that since the college was founded to train ministers and since that work is now done by the theological schools, it has no longer any justification for existence. But the old college had something to give, not only to ministers, but also to doctors, lawyers, teachers, and business men. And the new liberal college has the same mission for men whatever their calling is to be. It is sometimes said that the task of the liberal college is simply to train boys to think, to give them intellectual method, and that hence it makes very little difference what they think about, what courses they take, during the college years. But if thinking is worth doing, those four years should not be wasted. There are certain essential and fundamental interests to which any liberally educated man should give attention; and no man is liberally educated unless he has in some way or other dealt with them in his own experience. Finally, the liberal college is not merely an institution for training "scholars," men who are to be by profession "investigators" in some field of learning. In a democratic society the liberal college is seeking, not merely the intellectual boy, but also the average American boy, and it proposes to train him for life whatever his profession or calling may be.

The fundamental principle of the liberal college, like that of all advanced education, technical or professional, rests on the opposition of action by custom and action by intelligence. All schools alike believe that activities guided by ideas are, in the long run, more successful than activities determined by habit and hearsay. The liberal college has, therefore, selected one group of activities for study. Just as the bridge builder studies mathematics and applied mechanics, just as the physician studies chemistry and biology, so the teacher in the liberal college studies those activities which are common to all men. We believe that human living can be made more successful if men understand it. We set our boys, or should set them, to the study of the religious life, the moral problems, the social and economic institutions, the world of physical and natural phenomena, the records of literature and history. Here are features of human living common to all men. To understand them, to be acquainted with them, is to be liberally educated.

There are men who would prefer that their sons be not educated with regard to religion, morals, social and economic problems. These men want all the new appliances in farming, all the newest devices and inventions in transportation and engineering, but they would prefer that the fundamental things of life be left to habit, tradition, and instinct. As against such men the liberal college is up in arms. There never was a time when men needed light on the great human affairs, the things we have in common, more than we need it now. Intelligence has improved our roads and bridges; it will improve ourselves, our living. The task of the liberal college is just as definite as that of any technical school. Its day is not ending; it is just beginning to dawn.

Stephen Leacock on the American System of Graduate Instruction, 1916 *

. . . Now our American system . . . breaks up the field of knowledge into many departments, subdivides these into special branches and sections, and calls upon the scholar to devote himself to a microscopic activity in some part of a section of a branch of a department of the general field of learning. This specialised system of education that we pursue does not of course begin at once. Any system of training must naturally first devote itself to the acquiring of a rudimentary knowledge of such elementary things as reading, spelling, and the humbler aspects of mathematics. But the further the American student proceeds the more this tendency to specialisation asserts itself. When he enters upon what are called post-graduate studies, he is expected to become altogether a specialist, devoting his whole mind to the study of the left foot of the garden frog, or to the use of the ablative in Tacitus, or to the history of the first half hour of the Reformation. As he continues on his upward way, the air about him gets rarer and rarer, his path becomes more and more solitary until he reaches, and encamps upon, his own little pinnacle of refined knowledge staring at his feet and ignorant of the world about him, the past behind him, and the future before him. At the end of his labours he publishes a useless little pamphlet called his thesis which is new in the sense that nobody ever wrote it before, and erudite in the sense that nobody will ever read it. Meantime the American student's ignorance of all things except his own part of his own subject has grown colossal. The unused parts of his intellect have ossified. His interest in general literature, his power of original thought, indeed his wish to think at all, is far less than it was in the second year of his undergraduate course. More than all that, his interestingness to other people has completely departed. Even with his fellow scholars so-called he can find no common ground of intellectual intercourse. If three men sit down together and one is a philologist, the second a numismatist, and the third a subsection of a conchologist, what can they find to talk about?

I have had occasion in various capacities to see something of the working of this system of the higher learning. Some years ago I resided for a month or two with a group of men who were specialists of the type described, most of them in pursuit of their degree of Doctor of Philosophy, some of them—easily distinguished by their air of complete vacuity—already in possession of it. The first night I dined with them, I addressed

* *Essays and Literary Studies* (New York, John Lane Co., 1916), pp. 76-88.

to the man opposite me some harmless question about a recent book that I thought of general interest. "I don't know anything about that," he answered, "I'm in sociology." There was nothing to do but to beg his pardon and to apologise for not having noticed it.

Another of these same men was studying classics on the same plan. He was engaged in composing a doctor's thesis on the genitive of value in Plautus. For eighteen months past he had read nothing but Plautus. The manner of his reading was as follows: first he read Plautus all through and picked out all the verbs of estimating followed by the genitive, then he read it again and picked out the verb of reckoning, then the verbs of wishing, praying, cursing, and so on. Of all these he made lists and grouped them into little things called Tables of Relative Frequency, which, when completed, were about as interesting, about as useful, and about as easy to compile as the list of wholesale prices of sugar at New Orleans. Yet this man's thesis was admittedly the best in his year, and it was considered by his instructors that had he not died immediately after graduation, he would have lived to publish some of the most daring speculations on the genitive of value in Plautus that the world has ever seen.

I do not here mean to imply that all our scholars of this type die, or even that they ought to die, immediately after graduation. Many of them remain alive for years, though their utility has of course largely departed after their thesis is complete. Still they do and can remain alive. If kept in a dry atmosphere and not exposed to the light, they may remain in an almost perfect state of preservation for years after finishing their doctor's thesis. I remember once seeing a specimen of this kind enter into a country post-office store, get his letters, and make a few purchases, closely scrutinised by the rural occupants. When he had gone out the postmaster turned to a friend with the triumphant air of a man who has information in reserve and said, "Now wouldn't you think, to look at him, that man was a d——d fool?" "Certainly would," said the friend, slowly nodding his head. "Well, he isn't," said the postmaster emphatically; "he's a Doctor of Philosophy." But the distinction was too subtle for most of the auditors.

In passing these strictures upon our American system of higher education, I do not wish to be misunderstood. One must of course admit a certain amount of specialisation in study. It is quite reasonable that a young man with a particular aptitude or inclination towards modern languages, or classical literature, or political economy, should devote himself particularly to that field. But what I protest against is the idea that each of these studies is apt with us to be regarded as wholly exclusive of the others, and that the moment a man becomes a student of German literature he should lose all interest in general history and philosophy, and be content to remain as ignorant of political economy or jurisprudence as a plumber. The price of liberty, it has been finely said, is eternal vigilance, and I think one may say that the price of real intellectual progress is eternal alertness, an increasing and growing interest in all great branches of human knowledge. Art is notoriously long and life is infamously short. We cannot know everything. But we can at least pursue the ideal of knowing the greatest things in all branches of knowledge, something at least of the great masters of literature, something of the best of the world's philosophy, and something of its political conduct and structure. It is but little that the student can ever know, but we can at least see that the little is wisely distributed.

And here perhaps it is necessary to make a further qualification to this antagonism of the principle of specialisation. I quite admit its force and purpose as applied to such things as natural science and medicine. These are branches capable of isolation from the humanities in general, and in them progress is not dependent on the width of general culture. Here it is necessary that a certain portion of the learned world should isolate themselves from mankind, immure themselves in laboratories, testing, dissecting, weighing, probing, boiling, mixing, and cooking to their heart's content. It is necessary for the world's work that they should do so. In any case this is real research work done by real specialists *after* their education and not *as* their education. Of this work the so-called researches of the graduate student, who spends three years in writing a thesis on John Milton's god-mother, is a mere parody.

Nor is it to be thought that this post-graduate work upon the preparation of a thesis, this so-called original scholarship is difficult. It is pretentious, plausible, esoteric, cryptographic, occult, if you will, but difficult it is not. It is of course laborious. It takes time. But the amount of intellect called for in the majority of these elaborate compilations is about the same, or rather less, than that involved in posting the day book in a village grocery. The larger part of it is on a level with the ordinary routine clerical duties performed by a young lady stenographer for ten dollars a week. One must also quite readily admit that just as there is false and real research, so too is there such a thing as a false and make-believe general education. Education, I allow, can be made so broad that it gets thin, so extensive that it must be shallow. The educated mind of this type becomes so wide that it appears quite flat. Such is the education of the drawing-room conversationalist. Thus a man may acquire no little reputation as a classical scholar by constant and casual reference to Plato or Diodorus Siculus without in reality having studied anything more arduous than the Home Study Circle of his weekly paper. Yet even such a man, pitiable though he is, may perhaps be viewed with a more indulgent eye than the ossified specialist.

It is of course not to be denied that there is even in the field of the humanities a certain amount of investigation to be done—of research work, if one will—of a highly specialized character. But this is work that best be done not by way of an educational training—for its effect is usually the reverse of educational, but as a special labour performed for its own

sake as the life work of a trained scholar, not as the examination requirement of a prospective candidate. The pretentious claim made by so many
of our universities that the thesis presented for the doctor's degree must
represent a distinct contribution to human knowledge will not stand examination. Distinct contributions to human knowledge are not so easily nor
so mechanically achieved. Nor should it be thought either that, even where
an elaborate and painstaking piece of research has been carried on by a
trained scholar, such an achievement should carry with it any recognition
of a very high order. It is useful and meritorious no doubt, but the esteem
in which it is held in the academic world in America indicates an entirely
distorted point of view. Our American process of research has led to an
absurd admiration of the mere collection of facts, extremely useful things
in their way but in point of literary eminence standing in the same class as
the Twelfth Census of the United States or the Statistical Abstract of the
United Kingdom. So it has come to pass that the bulk of our college-made
books are little more than collections of material out of which in the hands
of a properly gifted person a book might be made. In our book-making in
America—our serious book-making, I mean—the whole are of presentation, the thing that ought to be the very essence of literature, is sadly
neglected. "A fact," as Lord Bryce once said in addressing the assembled
historians of America, "is an excellent thing and you must have facts to
write about; but you should realise that even a fact before it is ready for
presentation must be cut and polished like a diamond." "You need not be
afraid to be flippant," said the same eminent authority, "but you ought to
have a horror of being dull." Unfortunately our American college-bred
authors cannot be flippant if they try: it is at best but the lumbering play-
fulness of the elephant, humping his heavy posteriors in the air and wig-
gling his little tail in the vain attempt to be a lamb.

The head and front of the indictment thus presented against American
scholarship is seen in its results. It is not making scholars in the highest
sense of the term. It is not encouraging a true culture. It is not aiding in the
creation of a real literature. The whole bias of it is contrary to the development of the highest intellectual power; it sets a man of genius to a drudg-
ing task suitable to the capacities of third-class clerk, substitutes the
machine-made pedant for the man of letters, puts a premium on painstaking dulness and breaks down genius, inspiration, and originality in the
grinding routine of the college tread-mill. Here and there, as is only
natural, conspicuous exceptions appear in the academic world of America.
A New England professor has invested the dry subject of government with
a charm that is only equalled by the masterly comprehensiveness of his
treatment: a Massachusetts philosopher held for a lifetime the ear of the
educated world, and an American professor has proved that even so
abstruse a subject as the history of political philosophy can be presented
in a form at once powerful and fascinating.

But even the existence of these brilliant exceptions to the general rule cannot invalidate the proposition that the effect of our American method upon the cycle of higher studies is depressing in the extreme. History is dwindling into fact lore and is becoming the science of the almanac; economics is being buried alive in statistics and is degenerating into the science of the census; literature is stifled by philology, and is little better than the science of the lexicographer. . . .

The Seven Cardinal Principles of Secondary Education, 1918 *

Secondary education should be determined by the needs of the society to be served, the character of the individuals to be educated, and the knowledge of educational theory and practice available. These factors are by no means static. Society is always in process of development; the character of the secondary-school population undergoes modification; and the sciences on which educational theory and practice depend constantly furnish new information. Secondary education, however, like any other established agency of society, is conservative and tends to resist modification. Failure to make adjustments when the need arises leads to the necessity for

* *Cardinal Principles of Secondary Education* (Washington, Government Printing Office, 1918), Bulletin No. 35, 1918, Department of the Interior, Bureau of Education. A report of the commission on the reorganization of secondary education. Pp. 7-11. More than 130,000 copies of the report were distributed, and the seven cardinal principles flourished in educational conventions, teachers' meetings, and in other places of pedagogical discussions, resounding from one end of the country to the other. Some of these principles or "Objectives" had appeared in 1859 in Herbert Spencer's "What Knowledge is of Most Worth?" but by 1938 it had become increasingly clear that education could not be made as effective by slogans and mottoes as some of these had promised to be. In that year the Educational Policies Commission of the National Education Association and the American Association of School Administrators published *The Purposes of Education in American Democracy* and came out with four large objectives: (1) self-realization; (2) human relationship; (3) economic efficiency; and (4) civic responsibility; but stated that each of these was "capable of further subdivision." For example, under the first objective, "self-realization," the Commission sub-divides as follows:
The Inquiring Mind. The educated person has an appetite for learning.
Speech. The educated person can speak the mother tongue clearly.
Reading. The educated person reads the mother tongue efficiently.
Writing. The educated person writes the mother tongue effectively.
Number. The educated person solves his problems of counting and calculating.
Sight Hearing. The educated person is skilled in listening and observing.
Health Knowledge. The educated person understands the basic facts concerning health and disease.
Health Habits. The educated person protects his own health and that of his dependents.
Public Health. The educated person works to improve the health of the community.
Recreation. The educated person is participant and spectator in many sports and other pastimes.
Intellectual Interests. The educated person has mental resources for the use of leisure.
Esthetic Interests. The educated person appreciates beauty.
Character. The educated person gives responsible direction to his own life.
Confusion in "aims" or "objectives" or "purposes" of education, very numerous nowadays, is a conspicuous characteristic of American education. More than fifteen hundred social aims of English, three hundred aims of arithmetic, eight hundred generalized aims of the social studies have been listed here and there in courses of study and in special studies of the curriculum, often to the dismay of teachers. See H. L. Caswell and D. S. Campbell, *Curriculum Development* (New York, American Book Co., 1935), pp. 119, 120.

extensive reorganization at irregular intervals. The evidence is strong that such a comprehensive reorganization of secondary education is imperative at the present time.

1. *Changes in society.*—Within the past few decades changes have taken place in American life profoundly affecting the activities of the individual. As a citizen, he must to a greater extent and in a more direct way cope with problems of community life, State and National Governments, and international relationships. As a worker, he must adjust himself to a more complex economic order. As a relatively independent personality, he has more leisure. The problems arising from these three dominant phases of life are closely interrelated and call for a degree of intelligence and efficiency on the part of every citizen that can not be secured through elementary education alone, or even through secondary education unless the scope of that education is broadened.

The responsibility of the secondary school is still further increased because many social agencies other than the school afford less stimulus for education than heretofore. In many vocations there have come such significant changes as the substitution of the factory system for the domestic system of industry; the use of machinery in place of manual labor; the high specialization of processes with a corresponding subdivision of labor; and the break-down of the apprentice system. In connection with home and family life have frequently come lessened responsibility on the part of the children; the withdrawal of the father and sometimes the mother from home occupations to the factory or store; and increased urbanization, resulting in less unified family life. Similarly, many important changes have taken place in community life, in the church, in the State, and in other institutions. These changes in American life call for extensive modifications in secondary education.

2. *Changes in the secondary-school population.*—In the past 25 years there have been marked changes in the secondary-school population of the United States. The number of pupils has increased, according to Federal returns, from one for every 210 of the total population in 1889-90, to one for every 121 in 1899-1900, to one for every 89 in 1909-10, and to one for every 73 of the estimated total population in 1914-15. The character of the secondary-school population has been modified by the entrance of large numbers of pupils of widely varying capacities, aptitudes, social heredity, and destinies in life. Further, the broadening of the scope of secondary education has brought to the school many pupils who do not complete the full course but leave at various stages of advancement. The needs of these pupils can not be neglected, nor can we expect in the near future that all pupils will be able to complete the secondary school as full-time students.

At present only about one-third of the pupils who enter the first year of the elementary school reach the four-year high school, and only about one in nine is graduated. Of those who enter the seventh school year, only one-half to two-thirds reach the first year of the four-year high school. Of those who enter the four-year high school about one-third leave before the beginning of the second year, about one-half are gone before the beginning of the third year, and fewer than one-third are graduated. These facts can no longer be safely ignored.

3. *Changes in educational theory.*—The sciences on which educational theory depends have within recent years made significant contributions. In particular, educational psychology emphasizes the following factors:

(*a*) *Individual differences in capacities and aptitudes among secondary-school pupils.* Already recognized to some extent, this factor merits fuller attention.

(*b*) *The reëxamination and reinterpretation of subject values and the teaching methods with reference to "general discipline."*—While the final verdict of modern psychology has not as yet been rendered, it is clear that former conceptions of "general values" must be thoroughly revised.

(*c*) *Importance of applying knowledge.*—Subject values and teaching methods must be tested in terms of the laws of learning and the application of knowledge to the activities of life, rather than primarily in terms of the demands of any subject as a logically organized science.

(*d*) *Continuity in the development of children.*—It has long been held that psychological changes at certain stages are so pronounced as to overshadow the continuity of development. On this basis secondary education has been sharply separated from elementary education. Modern psychology, however, goes to show that the development of the individual is in most respects a continuous process and that, therefore, any sudden or abrupt break between the elementary and the secondary school or between any two successive stages of education is undesirable.

The foregoing changes in society, in the character of the secondary-school population, and in educational theory, together with many other considerations, call for extensive modifications of secondary education. Such modifications have already begun in part. The present need is for the formulation of a comprehensive program of reorganization, and its adoption, with suitable adjustments, in all the secondary schools in the Nation. Hence it is appropriate for a representative body like the National Education Association to outline such a program. This is the task entrusted by that association to the Commission on the Reorganization of Secondary Education.

Education in the United States should be guided by a clear conception of the meaning of democracy. It is the ideal of democracy that the individual and society may find fulfillment each in the other. Democracy sanctions neither the exploitation of the individual by society, nor the disregard of the interests of society by the individual. More explicitly—

The purpose of democracy is so to organize society that each member may develop his personality primarily through activities designed for the well-being of his fellow members and of society as a whole.

This ideal demands that human activities be placed upon a high level of efficiency; that to this efficiency be added and appreciation of the significance of these activities and loyalty to the best ideals involved; and that the individual choose that vocation and those forms of social service in which his personality may develop and become most effective. For the achievement of these ends democracy must place chief reliance upon education.

Consequently, education in a democracy, both within and without the school, should develop in each individual the knowledge, interests, ideals, habits, and powers whereby he will find his place and use that place to shape both himself and society toward ever nobler ends.

In order to determine the main objectives that should guide education in a democracy it is necessary to analyze the activities of the individual. Normally he is a member of a family, of a vocational group, and of various civic groups, and by virtue of these relationships he is called upon to engage in activities that enrich the family life, to render important vocational services to his fellows, and to promote the common welfare. It follows, therefore, that worthy home-membership, vocation, and citizenship, demand attention as three of the leading objectives.

Aside from the immediate discharge of these specific duties, every individual should have a margin of time for the cultivation of personal and social interests. This leisure, if worthily used, will recreate his powers and enlarge and enrich life, thereby making him better able to meet his responsibilities. The unworthy use of leisure impairs health, disrupts home life, lessens vocational efficiency, and destroys civic-mindedness. The tendency in industrial life, aided by legislation, is to decrease the working hours of large groups of people. While shortened hours tend to lessen the harmful reactions that arise from prolonged strain, they increase, if possible, the importance of preparation for leisure. In view of these considerations, education for the worthy use of leisure is of increasing importance as an objective.

To discharge the duties of life and to benefit from leisure, one must have good health. The health of the individual is essential also to the vitality of the race and to the defense of the Nation. Health education is, therefore, fundamental.

There are various processes, such as reading, writing, arithmetical computations, and oral and written expression, that are needed as tools in the affairs of life. Consequently, command of these fundamental processes, while not an end in itself, is nevertheless an indispensable objective.

And, finally, the realization of the objectives already named is dependent upon ethical character, that is, upon conduct founded upon right principles, clearly perceived and loyally adhered to. Good citizenship, vocational excellence, and the worthy use of leisure go hand in hand with ethical character; they are at once the fruits of sterling character and the channels through which such character is developed and made manifest. On the one hand, character is meaningless apart from the will to discharge the duties of life, and, on the other hand, there is no guarantee that these duties will be rightly discharged unless principles are substituted for impulses, however well-intentioned such impulses may be. Consequently ethical character is at once involved in all the other objectives and at the same time requires specific consideration in any program of national education.

This commission, therefore, regards the following as the main objectives of education: 1. Health. 2. Command of fundamental processes. 3. Worthy home-membership. 4. Vocation. 5. Citizenship. 6. Worthy use of leisure. 7. Ethical character.

The naming of the above objectives is not intended to imply that the process of education can be divided into separated fields. This can not be, since the pupil is indivisible. Nor is the analysis all-inclusive. Nevertheless, we believe that distinguishing and naming these objectives will aid in directing efforts; and we hold that they should constitute the principal aims in education.

Thorstein Veblen on Academic Administration and Policy, 1918 *

Men dilate on the high necessity of a businesslike organization and control of the university, its equipment, personnel and routine. What is had in mind in this insistence on an efficient system is that these corporations of learning shall set their affairs in order after the pattern of a well-conducted business concern. In this view the university is conceived as a business house dealing in merchantable knowledge, placed under the governing hand of a captain of erudition, whose office it is to turn the means in hand to account in the largest feasible output. It is a corporation with large funds, and for men biased by their workday training in business affairs it comes as a matter of course to rate the university in terms of investment and turnover. Hence the insistence on business capacity in the executive heads of the universities, and hence also the extensive range of businesslike duties and powers that devolve on them.

Yet when all these sophistications of practical wisdom are duly allowed for, the fact remains that the university is, in usage, precedent, and commonsense preconception, an establishment for the conservation and advancement of the higher learning, devoted to a disinterested pursuit of knowledge. As such, it consists of a body of scholars and scientists, each and several of whom necessarily goes to his work on his own initiative and pursues it in his own way. This work necessarily follows an orderly sequence and procedure, and so takes on a systematic form, of an organic

* *The Higher Learning in America* (New York, B. W. Huebsch, 1918), pp. 85-92.

kind. But the system and order that so govern the work, and that come into view in its procedure and results, are the logical system and order of intellectual enterprise, not the mechanical or statistical systematization that goes into effect in the management of an industrial plant or the financiering of a business corporation.

Those items of human intelligence and initiative that go to make up the pursuit of knowledge, and that are embodied in systematic form in its conclusions, do not lend themselves to quantitative statement, and can not be made to appear on a balance-sheet. Neither can that intellectual initiative and proclivity that goes in as the indispensable motive force in the pursuit of learning be reduced to any known terms of subordination, obedience, or authoritative direction. No scholar or scientist can become an employe in respect of his scholarly or scientific work. Mechanical systematization and authoritative control can in these premises not reach beyond the material circumstances that condition the work in hand, nor can it in these external matters with good effect go farther than is necessary to supply the material ways and means requisite to the work, and to adapt them to the peculiar needs of any given line of inquiry or group of scholars. In order to their best efficiency, and indeed in the degree in which efficiency in this field of activity is to be attained at all, the executive officers of the university must stand in the relation of assistants serving the needs and catering to the idiosyncrasies of the body of scholars and scientists that make up the university; in the degree in which the converse relation is allowed to take effect, the unavoidable consequence is wasteful defeat. A free hand is the first and abiding requisite of scholarly and scientific work.

Now, in accepting office as executive head of a university, the incumbent necessarily accepts all the conditions that attach to the administration of his office, whether by usage and commonsense expectation, by express arrangement, or by patent understanding with the board to which he owes his elevation to this post of dignity and command. By usage and precedent it is incumbent on him to govern the academic personnel and equipment with an eye single to the pursuit of knowledge, and so to conduct its affairs as will most effectually compass that end. That is to say he must so administer his office as best to serve the scholarly needs of the academic staff, due regard being scrupulously had to the idiosyncrasies, and even to the vagaries, of the men whose work he is called on to further. But by patent understanding, if not by explicit stipulation, from the side of the governing board, fortified by the preconceptions of the laity at large to the same effect, he is held to such a conspicuously efficient employment of the means in hand as will gratify those who look for a voluminous turnover. To this end he must keep the academic administration and its activity constantly in the public eye, with such "pomp and circumstance" of untiring urgency and expedition as will carry the conviction abroad that the university under his management is a highly successful going concern, and he must be able to show by itemized accounts that the volume of output is such as to warrant the investment. So the equipment and personnel must be organized into a facile and orderly working force, held under the directive control of the captain of erudition at every point, and so articulated and standardized that its rate of speed and the volume of its current output can be exhibited to full statistical effect as it runs.

The university is to make good both as a corporation of learning and as a business concern dealing in standardized erudition, and the executive head necessarily assumes the responsibility of making it count wholly and unreservedly in each of these divergent, if not incompatible lines. Humanly speaking, it follows by necessary consequence that he will first and always take care of those duties that are most jealously insisted on by the powers to whom he is accountable, and the due performance of which will at the same time yield some sufficiently tangible evidence of his efficiency. That other, more recondite side of the university's work that has substantially to do with the higher learning is not readily set out in the form of statistical exhibits, at the best, and can ordinarily come to appraisal and popular appreciation only in the long run. The need of a businesslike showing is instant and imperative, particularly in a business era of large turnover and quick returns, and to meet this need the uneventful scholastic life that counts toward the higher learning in the long run is of little use; so it can wait, and it readily becomes a habit with the busy executive to let it wait.

It should be kept in mind also that the incumbent of executive office is presumably a man of businesslike qualifications, rather than of scholarly insight,—the method of selecting the executive heads under the present régime makes that nearly a matter of course. As such he will in his own right more readily appreciate those results of his own management that show up with something of the glare of publicity, as contrasted with the slow-moving and often obscure working of inquiry that lies (commonly) somewhat beyond his intellectual horizon. So that with slight misgiving, if any, he takes to the methods of organization and control that have commended themselves in that current business enterprise to which it is his ambition to assimilate the corporation of learning.

These precedents of business practice that are to afford guidance to the captain of erudition are, of course, the precedents of competitive business. It is one of the unwritten, and commonly unspoken, commonplaces lying at the root of modern academic policy that the various universities are competitors for the traffic in merchantable instruction, in much the same fashion as rival establishments in the retail trade compete for custom. Indeed, the modern department store offers a felicitous analogy, that has already been found serviceable in illustration of the American university's position in this respect, by those who speak for the present régime as well as by its critics. The fact that the universities are assumed to be irreconcilable competitors, both in the popular apprehension and as evidenced by the manoeuvres of their several directors, is too notorious to be denied by any but the interested parties. Now and again it is formally denied by one and another among the competing captains of erudition, but the reason for such denial is the need of it.

Now, the duties of the executive head of a competitive business concern are of a strategic nature, the object of his management being to get the better of rival concerns and to engross the trade. To this end it is indispensable that he should be a "strong man" and should have a free hand, though perhaps under the general and tolerant surveillance of his board of directors. Any wise board of directors, and in the degree in which they are endowed with the requisite wisdom, will be careful to give their general manager full discretion, and not to hamper him with too close an accounting of the details of his administration, so long as he shows gratifying results. He must be a strong man; that is to say, a capable man of affairs, tenacious and resourceful in turning the means at hand to account for this purpose, and easily content to let the end justify the means. He must be a man of scrupulous integrity, so far as may conduce to his success, but with a shrewd eye to the limits within which honesty is the best policy, for the purpose in hand. He must have full command of the means entrusted to him and full control of the force of employes and subordinates who are to work under his direction, and he must be able to rely on the instant and unwavering loyalty of his staff in any line of policy on which he may decide to enter. He must therefore have free power to appoint and dismiss, and to reward and punish, limited only by the formal ratification of his decisions by the board of directors who will be careful not to interfere or inquire unduly in these matters,—so long as their strong man shows results.

The details and objective of his strategy need not be known to the members of the staff; indeed, all that does not concern them except in the most general way. They are his creatures, and are responsible only to him and only for the due performance of the tasks assigned them; and they need know only so much as will enable them to give ready and intel-ligent support to the moves made by their chief from day to day. The members of the staff are his employes, and their first duty is a loyal obedience; and for the competitive good of the concern they must utter no expression of criticism or unfavourable comment on the policy, actions or personal characteristics of their chief, so long as they are in his employ. They have eaten his bread, and it is for them to do his bidding.

Such is the object-lesson afforded by business practice as it bears on the duties incumbent on the academic head and on the powers of office delegated to him. It is needless to remark on what is a fact of common notoriety, that this rule drawn from the conduct of competitive business is commonly applied without substantial abatement in the conduct of academic affairs.

Under this rule the academic staff becomes a body of graded subalterns, who share the confidence of the chief in varying degrees, but who have no decisive voice in the policy or the conduct of affairs of the concern in whose pay they are held. The faculty is conceived as a body of employes, hired to render certain services and turn out certain scheduled vendible results.

The chief may take advice; and, as is commonly the practice in analogous circumstances in commercial business, he will be likely to draw about him from among the faculty a conveniently small number of advisers who are in sympathy with his own ambitions, and who will in this way form an unofficial council, or cabinet, or "junta," to whom he can turn for informal, anonymous and irresponsible, advice and moral support at any juncture. He will also, in compliance with charter stipulations and parliamentary usage, have certain officially recognized advisers,—the various deans, advisory committees, Academic Council, University Senate, and the like,—with whom he shares responsibility, particularly for measures of doubtful popularity, and whose advice he formally takes *coram publico;* but he can not well share discretion with these, except on administrative matters of inconsequential detail. For reasons of practical efficiency, discretion must be undivided in any competitive enterprise. There is much fine-spun strategy to be taken care of under cover of night and cloud. . . .

Thorstein Veblen on the Influence of Business Upon Higher Education, 1918 *

Under compulsion of such precedents, drawn from the conduct of competitive business, publicity and "good-will" have come to take a foremost place in the solicitude of the academic directorate. Not that this notoriety and prestige, or the efforts that go to their cultivation, conduce in any appreciable degree to any ostensible purpose avowed, or avowable, by any university. These things, that is to say, rather hinder than help the cause of learning in that they divert attention and effort from scholarly workmanship to statistics and salesmanship. All that is beyond cavil. The gain which so accrues to any university from such an accession of popular illusions is a differential gain in competition with rival seats of learning, not a gain to the republic of learning or to the academic community at large; and it is a gain in marketable illusions, not in serviceability for the ends of learning or for any other avowed or avowable end sought by the universities. But as competitors for the good-will of the unlettered patrons of learning the university directorates are constrained to keep this need of a reputable notoriety constantly in mind, however little it may all appeal to their own scholarly tastes.

* *Ibid.,* 137-43. For a discussion of the social and economic composition of governing boards of thirty leading American universities, see H. P. Beck, *Men Who Control Our Universities* (New York, King's Crown Press, 1947).

It is in very large part, if not chiefly, as touches the acquirement of prestige, that the academic work and equipment are amenable to business principles,—not overlooking the pervasive system of standardization and accountancy that affects both the work and the equipment, and that serves other purposes as well as those of publicity; so that "business principles" in academic policy comes to mean, chiefly, the principles of reputable publicity. It means this more frequently and more consistently than anything else, so far as regards the academic administration as distinguished from the fiscal management of the corporation.

Of course, the standards, ideals, principles and procedure of business traffic enter into the scheme of university policy in other relations also, as has already appeared and as will be shown more at large presently; but after all due qualification is had, it remains true that this business of publicity necessarily, or at least commonly, accounts for a disproportionately large share of the business to be taken care of in conducting a university, as contrasted with such an enterprise, e.g., as a bank, a steel works, or a railway company, on a capital of about the same volume. This follows from the nature of the case. The common run of business concerns are occupied with industrial enterprise of some kind, and with transactions in credit,—with a running sequence of bargains from which the gains of the concern constantly looks. Such concerns have to meet their competitors in buying, selling, and effecting contracts of all kinds, from which their gains are to come. A university, on the other hand, can look to no such gains in the work which is its sole ostensible interest and occupation; and the pecuniary transactions and arrangements which it enters into on the basis of its accumulated prestige are a relatively very trivial matter. There is, in short, no appreciable pecuniary gain to be looked for from any traffic resting on the acquired prestige, and therefore there is no relation of equivalence or discrepancy between any outlay incurred in this behalf and the volume of gainful business to be transacted on the strength of it; with the result that the academic directorate applies itself to this pursuit without *arrière pensée*. So far as the acquired prestige is designed to serve a pecuniary end it can only be useful in the way of impressing potential donors, —a highly speculative line of enterprise, offering a suggestive parallel to the drawings of a lottery.

Outlay for the purpose of publicity is not confined to the employment of field-agents and the circulation of creditable gossip and reassuring printed matter. The greater share of it comes in as incidental to the installation of plant and equipment and the routine of academic life and ceremony. As regards the material equipment, the demands of a creditable appearance are pervading and rigorous; and their consequences in the way of elaborate and premeditated incidentals are, perhaps, here seen at their best. To the laity a "university" has come to mean, in the first place and indispensably, an aggregation of buildings and other improved real-estate. This material equipment strikes the lay attention directly and convincingly; while the pursuit of learning is a relatively obscure matter, the motions of which can not well be followed by the unlettered, even with the help of the newspapers and the circular literature that issues from the university's publicity bureau. The academic work is, after all, unseen, and it stays in the background. Current expenditure for the prosecution of this work, therefore offers the enterprise in advertisement a less advantageous field for the convincing use of funds than the material equipment, especially the larger items,—laboratory and library buildings, assembly halls, curious museum exhibits, grounds for athletic contests, and the like. There is consequently a steady drift of provocation towards expenditure on conspicuous extensions of the "plant," and a correlative constant temptation to parsimony in the more obscure matter of necessary supplies and service, and similar running-expenses without which the plant can not effectually be turned to account for its ostensible use; with the result, not infrequently, that the usefulness of an imposing plant is seriously impaired for want of what may be called "working capital."

Indeed, instances might be cited where funds that were much needed to help out in meeting running expenses have been turned to use for conspicuous extensions of the plant in the way of buildings, in excess not only of what was needed for their alleged purpose but in excess of what could conveniently be made use of. More particularly is there a marked proclivity to extend the plant and the school organization into new fields of scholastic enterprise, often irrelevant or quite foreign to the province of the university as a seminary of learning; and to push these alien ramifications, to the neglect of the urgent needs of the academic work already in hand, in the way of equipment, maintenance, supplies, service and instruction.

The running-expenses are always the most urgent items of the budget, as seen from the standpoint of the academic work; and they are ordinarily the item that is most parsimoniously provided for. A scanty provision at this point unequivocally means a disproportionate curtailment of the usefulness of the equipment as well as of the personnel,—as, e.g., the extremely common and extremely unfortunate practice of keeping the allowance for maintenance and service in the university libraries so low as seriously to impair their serviceability. But the exigencies of prestige will easily make it seem more to the point, in the eyes of a businesslike executive, to project a new extension of the plant; which will then be half-employed, on a scanty allowance, in work which lies on the outer fringe or beyond the university's legitimate province.[1]

---

[1] This is a nearly universal infirmity of American university policy, but it is doubtless not to be set down solely to the account of the penchant for a large publicity on the part of the several academic executives. It is in all likelihood due as much to the equally ubiquitous inability of the governing boards to appreciate or to perceive what the current needs of the academic works are, or even what they are like. Men trained in the conduct of business

In so discriminating against the working capacity of the university, and in favour of its real-estate, this pursuit of reputable publicity further decides that the exterior of the buildings and the grounds should have the first and largest attention. It is true, the initial purpose of this material equipment, it is ostensibly believed, is to serve as housing and appliances for the work of inquiry and instruction. Such, of course, continues to be avowed its main purpose, in a perfunctorily ostensible way. This means a provision of libraries, laboratories, and lecture rooms. The last of these is the least exacting, and it is the one most commonly well supplied. It is also, on the whole, the more conspicuous in proportion to the outlay. But all these are matters chiefly of interior arrangement, appliances and materials, and they are all of a relatively inconspicuous character. Except as detailed in printed statistics they do not ordinarily lend themselves with appreciable effect to the art of advertising. In meeting all these material requirements of the work in hand a very large expenditure of funds might advantageously be made—advantageously to the academic use which they are to serve—without much visible effect as seen in perspective from the outside. And so far as bears on this academic use, the exterior of the buildings is a matter of altogether minor consequence, as are also the decorative appointments of the interior.

In practice, under compulsion of the business principles of publicity, it will be found, however, that the exterior and the decorative appointments are the chief object of the designer's attention; the interior arrangement and working appointments will not infrequently become a matter of rude approximation to the requirements of the work, care being first taken that these arrangements shall not interfere with the decorative or spectacular intent of the outside. But even with the best-advised management of its publicity value, it is always appreciably more difficult to secure appropriations for the material equipment of a laboratory or library than for the shell of the edifice, and still more so for the maintenance of an adequate corps of caretakers and attendants. . . .

On Competition in the Colleges, 1920 *

. . . And so, Mr. President, the colleges of the Commonwealth salute you today. If they bow beneath their responsibility, it is but the better to fit

---

enterprise, as the governing boards are, will have great difficulty in persuading themselves that expenditures which yield neither increased dividends nor such a durable physical product as can be invoiced and added to the capitalization, can be other than a frivolous waste of good money; so that what is withheld from current academic expenditure is felt to be saved, while that expenditure which leaves a tangible residue of (perhaps useless) real estate is, by force of ingrained habit, rated as new investment.

* William Louis Poteat, "The Colleges of the State," extract from his greetings to President Harry W. Chase at his inauguration at the University of North Carolina, 1920. *The State University and the New South* (Chapel Hill, University of North Carolina Press, 1920), pp. 71-72.

themselves to its weight. If resources are inadequate, consecration is deep and enthusiasm boundless. They welcome you as a helper, guide, inspirer. They proclaim anew their fellowship with this great institution in building the saner, juster society of tomorrow, the humaner, fairer, happier North Carolina. Our joint obligation does not end on our State boundaries. Together we must labor so to settle in the national mind the spirit of international justice and brotherhood as to make it impossible for a handful of obscurantists ever again to set our great country in a shameful isolation with Mexico against the organized enlightenment and conscience of mankind. We shall need to be on guard lest institutional loyalty betray us into the practical fallacy of regarding our institutions as ends in themselves rather than as apparatus and means for the education of all the people. The common task is too sacred and too large for jealousies and the rancor of competition. Competition? A lady standing on the beach quite ready for the surf explained why she did not go in by saying, "Another lady is using the ocean."

Some "Defects and Excesses of Present-Day Athletic Contests," 1929 *

. . . The preceding pages have dealt with a complicated situation of which organized athletics are but one factor. It remains to summarize the particular defects and excesses of present-day athletic contests as set forth in detail in the chapters of this report. The game of football looms large in any account of the growth of professionalism in college games. This does not mean that other sports are untouched by the influences that have converted football into a professional vocation.

The unfavorable results upon students through the athletic development may be briefly stated in the following terms:

1. The extreme development of competitive games in the colleges has reacted upon the secondary schools. The college athlete begins his athletic career before he gets to college.[1]

2. Once in college the student who goes in for competitive sports, and in particular for football, finds himself under a pressure, hard to resist to give his whole time and thought to his athletic career. No college boy training for a major team can have much time for thought or study.

---

* Henry S. Pritchett, in Howard J. Savage (Ed.), *American College Athletics,* Bulletin Number Twenty-Three (New York, The Carnegie Foundation for the Advancement of Teaching, 1929), Preface, pp. xiv-xvii. For the varying views on the subject of athletics in American education, see W. C. Ryan (Ed.), *The Literature of American School and College Athletics,* Bulletin Number Twenty-Four (New York, The Carnegie Foundation for the Advancement of Teaching, 1929). See also Pritchett's proposal to substitute inter-collegiate horse racing for inter-collegiate football, given below.

[1] "The predominance of sports in schools, in the national life, in the press, not only crowds out what is, or should be, more important, but it creates an atmosphere in which these important things are made to appear superfluous." Abbé Dimnet, *The Art of Thinking,* page 61.

3. The college athlete, often a boy from a modest home, finds himself suddenly a most important man in the college life. He begins to live on a scale never before imagined. A special table is provided. Sport clothes and expensive trips are furnished him out of the athletic chest. He jumps at one bound to a plane of living of which he never before knew, all at the expense of some fund of which he knows little. When he drops back to a scale of living such as his own means can afford, the result is sometimes disastrous.

4. He works (for it is work, not play) under paid professional coaches whose business it is to develop the boy to be an effective unit in a team. The coach of to-day is no doubt a more cultivated man than the coach of twenty years ago. But any father who has listened to the professional coaching a college team will have some misgivings as to the cultural value of the process.

5. Inter-college athletics are highly competitive. Every college or university longs for a winning team in its group. The coach is on the alert to bring the most promising athletes in the secondary schools to his college team. A system of recruiting and subsidizing has grown up, under which boys are offered pecuniary and other inducements to enter a particular college. The system is demoralizing and corrupt, alike for the boy who takes the money and for the agent who arranges it, and for the whole group of college and secondary school boys who know about it.

6. Much discussion has been had as to the part the college graduate should have in the government of his college. In the matter of competitive athletics the college alumnus has, in the main, played a sorry role. It is one thing for an "old grad" to go back and coach the boys of his college as at Oxford or Cambridge, where there are no professional coaches and no gate receipts. It is quite another thing for an American college graduate to pay money to high school boys, either directly or indirectly, in order to enlist their services for a college team. The process is not only unsportsmanlike, it is immoral to the last degree. The great body of college graduates are wholly innocent in this matter. Most college men wish their college to win. Those who seek to compass that end by recruiting and subsidizing constitute a small, but active, minority, working oftentimes without the knowledge of the college authorities. This constitutes the most disgraceful phase of recent inter-college athletics.

7. The relation of organized sports to the health of college students is not a simple question. The information to deal with it completely is not yet at hand. A chapter of the report is devoted to this subject. In general it may be said that the relation of college organized sports to the health of the individual student is one dependent on the good sense exhibited by the college boy in participating in such sports, and to the quality of the advice he receives from the college medical officer.

8. For many games the strict organization and the tendency to commer-

cialize the sport has taken the joy out of the game. In football, for example, great numbers of boys do not play football, as in English schools and colleges, for the fun of it. A few play intensely. The great body of students are onlookers.

9. Finally, it is to be said that the blaze of publicity in which the college athlete lives is a demoralizing influence for the boy himself and no less so for his college.

It goes without saying that fifty thousand people (not an unusual attendance) could not be gathered to witness a football game, through the mere pull of college loyalty or interest in the sport. The bulk of the spectators do not understand the game. They are drawn to this spectacle through wide spread and continuous publicity. The relation of the press to the inter-college sports is described in detail in a chapter devoted to that subject. It is sufficient here to add a brief statement.

The American daily, or weekly, paper lives on its advertising, not on the subscriptions paid by its readers. The news policy of the paper is determined by this fundamental fact. It desires to print the things that will be eagerly read by the great body of everyday men and women who shop in the stores. The working woman likes to read of the fine clothes of the society belle, her husband delights in the startling accounts of fights or the details of the professional baseball games. The paper, being human, supplies the kind of news the advertisers like. It prints much for those of wider interests, but it follows the desires of its great advertising constituency all the time.

This has led to a form of personal news-telling unknown in any other country. In no other nation of the world will a college boy find his photograph in the metropolitan paper because he plays on a college team. All this is part of the newspaper effort to reach the advertiser. The situation is regrettable alike for journalism and for the public good. But it exists.

Into this game of publicity the university of the present day enters eagerly. It desires for itself the publicity that the newspapers can supply. It wants students, it wants popularity, but above all it wants money and always more money.

The athlete is the most available publicity material the college has. A great scientific discovery will make good press material for a few days, but nothing to compare to that of the performance of a first-class athlete. Thousands are interested in the athlete all the time, while the scientist is at best only a passing show.

And so it happens that the athlete lives in the white light of publicity and his photograph adorns the front pages of metropolitan (which means New York, Boston, Chicago, San Francisco, Los Angeles, New Orleans, and a hundred other) dailies. It must be an unusual boy who can keep his perspective under such circumstances. Why should the college boy be subjected to this régime merely to enable some thousands of attractive young reporters to make a living?

Inter-Collegiate Horse-Racing Is Proposed for Inter-Collegiate Football, 1932 *

In its twenty-third bulletin, issued in 1929, the Carnegie Foundation published a detailed study of athletics as practised in American colleges. The report made clear the fact that in the colleges of our country organized athletics, and particularly football, had ceased to be games played for sport's sake, and had been transformed into shows for the public, through which the colleges received huge sums in gate receipts, comparable in some cases to the income from tuition fees.

This report aroused varied emotions in the breasts of those responsible for the conduct of college athletics. There were some quick denials, but the facts in detail were always made available, and in the end the accuracy of the report was generally admitted. Some colleges proceeded to "clean up," but in general this process, even when the intentions were of the best, has not been easy.

In the words of the sermon to the fishes,—

> The sermon now ended,
> Each turned and descended;
> The eels kept on eeling,
> The pikes kept on stealing.
> Much delighted were they,
> But preferred the old way.

The truth is that trying to keep college football pure and undefiled, and at the same time make it pay large sums into the college treasury, is very much like the effort to enforce the Volstead Act—it runs counter to the qualities of human nature. When the football player sees his college gather in a million dollars in one year in gate receipts and considers how hard he has been worked to achieve that result, he is strongly inclined to feel that he is entitled to some of the swag. To be sure, this money is supposed to be used to maintain the general athletic programme; but for the football player athletics means reporting for duty in August, and working hard till after Thanksgiving, only to resume practice early in the spring. He has begun his football in the secondary school (sometimes for pay), and when he sees his college taking in all this easy money he sees no reason why he should not receive something for the hard work which brings so much money into the college till. At this point comes the bootlegging alumnus,

---

* Henry S. Pritchett, "A Substitute for Football," *The Atlantic Monthly*, Vol. 150 (October, 1932), pp. 446-48. The author was for many years President of The Carnegie Foundation for the Advancement of Teaching.

filled with ardor for the success of Alma Mater, ready to subsidize the young athlete by dark and devious methods.

This makes a situation in which our poor human nature is sorely tried. College officers may do their best, but under the most virtuous of deans it is difficult to keep the young athlete from taking pay if his college is cashing in on the game to the tune of hundreds of thousands. It is the Eighteenth Amendment complex transferred to college athletics.

The situation might be dealt with in several ways.

The colleges might, conceivably, take action to denature football as a money-making enterprise. They might cut out the professional coach, give up gate receipts, and put football back to the status of a game as it is conducted by the undergraduates of Oxford and Cambridge. This would be admirable, but is there any probability that it will be done in any reasonable time? Would, for example, great football institutions like Harvard and Notre Dame, or Chicago and the University of Southern California, forgo games in which some hundreds of thousands of dollars are realized at a single gathering? Perhaps they will in time, but the time may be in the long future. If one of the good old colleges had the courage to do this, it would reap a reward beyond its wildest expectations. A little virtue in a naughty world is so resplendent.

There is another method which does not impose so severe a test of academic virtue, but which may accomplish much. That is, to substitute some other sport for football that will bring just as much revenue into the college chest while not exacting the toll in young lives and lowered college ideals for which football is now, in large measure, responsible. For the cost of commercialized football is to be reckoned, not only in the present, but in the future lives of young men whose ideals of the intellectual life have been shaped under its influence. Boys start in the secondary school as candidates for football glory. They are steered into a football career in college, where they are worked to the full limit of their physical powers, showered with demoralizing publicity, and are able to catch but a faint vision of the intellectual life for which the college is supposed to stand (and sometimes does). The practical problem is to rescue these boys from the football régime and substitute something else which will bring the college just as much money.

The substitute must provide at least three things: it must be a great spectacle which will attract crowds of paying sight-seers, it must invoke at least the semblance of college rivalry, and it must be so ordered that graduates and undergraduates can easily bet their money on the result. It ought, of course, to be simple enough for the spectators—men, women, and children—to understand. But experience has shown that this is not indispensable if the ballyhoo is sufficiently vigorous. Many a spectator at a football game does not know what it is all about. He sees only the struggling figures, and if he has good luck may catch sight of some warrior carried out on his shield—sometimes wounded, perhaps slain—to make a Roman holiday.

There is one sport that fulfills all these conditions, an ancient sport beloved of men from time immemorial—horse racing. Instead of a football fight with its enormous draft on the energies of its devotees and its toll of young life, let us introduce in the colleges the humane and noble sport of horse racing!

The suggestion may seem a trifle bizarre at first glance, but a little reflection will show that horse racing has had a close relation to the intellectual life from the earliest times. In all sacred and profane literature the horse has been the intimate friend of man, and it has been his mission to take upon his broad shoulders the load that had become too heavy for his master. The sun itself traveled in a chariot drawn by the most beautiful and the swiftest horses.

It will be at once recognized that a horse race has all the advantages of a football bout and lacks many of its objectionable qualities.

In the first place, it is a better money-maker than a football show. Secondly, it is the sort of event on which the old grads and the undergrads can bet in more ways than they can even in football. In the third place, it has the great advantage that the whole audience, including the feminine part, can understand it.

This last point may have its practical advantages. True, many thousands of dollars are spent every year in paying the admission to football games for those who have only the faintest notion of what the game means or how it is played. But in this very fact there is a danger. It may be that people will grow weary of paying good money to watch a show they do not comprehend. But horse racing is as old as civilization and promises to live to the end of time. It has a universal human appeal. It is more conservative to tie up to horse racing as a steady income than to football, which has indeed proved a paying investment in recent years, but which may go bad in the market at any moment, like many other investments that seemed so fair only three years ago. Think what a pot of money a Harvard-Yale horse race would take in!

Of course there are simple-minded people who still inquire what need a university has to make money out of a football team, particularly when the boys who earn the money have to work so hard that they have very little time for the intellectual life which is assumed to be the purpose of the university. Such people point to the fact that no great university of the Old World—not Oxford, nor Paris, nor Berlin, nor Bologna—has ever made a cent out of football. But this is all beside the point. Our universities did not grow into universities as did those of Europe. They assumed the name just as a good man in Kentucky acquires the title of Colonel. They are in a large measure made up of undergraduate colleges, schools of business, correspondence schools, music schools, and all the other things that serve to attract students. This state of affairs is likely to continue for a long time, and these institutions will desire to obtain large sums of money to maintain an athletic régime so that their boys may be induced to play games which apparently they would not otherwise play. Hence the need for football or some equally good money-getter.

It is from this consideration that horse racing commends itself so admirably as a substitute for football. It will bring in just as much money— perhaps more. It will give the boys time to study. It will save the lives of a number of boys every year. It will bring the youth into acquaintance with that noble servant of man, the horse. Here is the solution of the problem of how the colleges can make enough money out of one sport to support an elaborate programme of athletics while at the same time protecting their students from the commercializing tendencies of the process. Horse racing is the answer. Once more let that noble animal lift from the shoulders of mankind a load which becomes year by year more difficult to carry.

Alfred E. Smith Receives an Honorary Degree from Harvard, 1933 *

HIS HARVARD SHEEPSKIN

Andrew Jackson got his LL.D. at Harvard a hundred years ago and the surviving Federalists howled in wrath. The General wasn't doctored on his merits alone. In accordance with tradition he was honored as a visiting President. Yesterday Governor Smith became a son-in-law of Harvard, as Mr. Evarts used to speak of himself. He may be said to have passed after examination. His four terms as Governor were behind him. He had been defeated as a nominee for President and again as a candidate for the nomination. He was a great private citizen. The irritations and resentments of politics had subsided.

It was a good time for the university to remember the faithful servant of the people, the man who had the laws of New York at his finger ends, the admirable figure in the Constitutional Convention, the skilled Executive, the reorganizer of the State government, the brave and generous leader who was never afraid to take the losing side. He is in good company on that list of holders of honorary degrees. Educated in a better and rougher school, who would have him other than he is? Exposed to a college, might not his character and personality have lost something of their salience, his wit of its edge, his humor of its gayety? To such a man a college offers its laurels with a sort of apology. Unfortunate enough not to breed him, it has the grace and the sense to adopt him.

If Harvard is an old Massachusetts institution, Al is the most beloved

* Editorial in *The New York Times*, June 23, 1933.

of all Massachusetts institutions. That State grudges him to New York; would like to kidnap him; make him permanent ruler of a realm composed of Massachusetts, Rhode Island and, perhaps, Connecticut. Probably the insurance people would like to have him settle in Massachusetts or keep away altogether, since he is in danger of being crushed by the multitudes every time he goes there.

We congratulate President Lowell. He has done justice to a fellow-student and illustrious practitioner of the art of government. We likewise congratulate Mr. Caleb Cheeshahteaumuck, now or formerly of Martha's Vineyard and the class of 1665. He is no longer lonely. Henceforth Harvard will have on her catalogue two little Injun boys—Caleb and Sachem Smith.

Bliss Perry on Complicated Educational Administration, 1935 *

I was too preoccupied with my own classes to know much about what was going on in the University. Fortunately I had little committee work, and was quite out of touch with the complicated machinery of administration which was housed in University Hall.† I fear I was jealous of University Hall, for it had developed the habit of robbing the English Department of some of our best men—Briggs, Hurlbut, Greenough, Murdock, and, for one year, Lowes—in order to utilize them as Deans. It is, I am told, an honor to become a Dean, but it is one dearly purchased if it means the temporary or permanent end of a scholar's productivity. The whole tendency of American institutions is to breed ten administrators to one real teacher. I used to pass University Hall with something of the small boy's dread of passing a cemetery: for teachers lay buried there under their roll-topped desks. Only once did I get a cheerful picture of it, and that was during a holiday in Florence in 1928. George W. Cram, the Recorder of the University, was likewise in Florence, and one day we tramped out to a hill-town beyond the Certosa to see the frescoes in the ancient church and incidentally to try a cup of the mulled wine for which the local restaurant was famous. In that one excursion I heard more amusing gossip about the machinery of University Hall than I had picked up in twenty years at Cambridge.

Stephen Leacock on Higher Education, 1935 ‡

The colleges have got far away from their original mission. They began as places of piety and learning. They did not teach people how to make money. In those days people of gentlemanly birth did not make

* Bliss Perry, *And Gladly Teach: Reminiscences* (Boston, Houghton Mifflin Co., 1935), p. 257. Used by permission.
† At Harvard.
‡ *The McGill News*, Spring, 1935.

money—when they wanted it, they took it! The college did not teach men a career—that was done with an axe! But the colleges were supposed to fit men to die; there are no courses in this subject now.

In the place of the older learning, the colleges have embarked on a wilderness of functions. They are gay from noon to night with student activities—they sing, they dance, they act. They run mimic newspapers and mock parliaments and make-believe elections. They put their athletics over with a hoot and a roar that costs more in one season that the old college spent in a decade. In this tumult of activity the "midnight oil" of the pale student of half a century ago is replaced by the two A.M. gasoline of his burly successor.

All this was grand in boom times when life was pitched in that tempo, and when we all grew richer on paper every day. Now the crash has come and the college, like the rest of the world, must get back to facts. Girls and boys of 19 and 20 have no right to perpetual distraction, to unending "activity," and make-believe autonomy.

Back to the Latin grammar with them. Make them learn the passive subjunctive of a dependent verb. Then, they will be ready to die, and thus, . . . worthy to live.

Robert M. Hutchins on Higher Education, 1938 *

Most American parents want to send their children to college. And their children, for the most part, are anxious to go. It is an American tradition that there is something about a college that transforms an ordinary infant into a superior adult. Men and women who have been to college sometimes suspect that this is not the case, but they seldom say so. They are alumni, and, as such, it is their life work to maintain the tradition that college—their college anyway—is the greatest place in the world.

College is the greatest place in the world for those who ought to go to college and who go for the right reasons. For those who ought not to go to college or who go for the wrong reasons, college is a waste of time and money.

Who should go to college? In order to answer this question, we might well begin by deciding who should not. My experience with college, as student, teacher and commencement orator, convinces me that the following persons should not go to college:

Children whose parents have no other reason for sending them than that they can afford to.

Children whose parents have no other reason for sending them than to get them off their hands for four years.

* "Why Go to College?" *The Saturday Evening Post*, January 22, 1938. Used by permission.

Children whose characters are bad and whose parents believe that college will change them for the better.

Children who have had no other reason for going to college than to avoid work or have a good time for four years.

Children who have no other reason for going to college than to have a stadium in which to demonstrate their athletic ability.

Children who have no other reason for going to college than the notion that it will help them achieve social or financial success in later life.

These children should be kept at home, or they should be sent to a country club, a trade school, or a body-building institute. There is, or should be, no place for them in an institution whose only excuse for existing is the training of the mind.

If we may then proceed to the original question—"Who should go to college?"—I submit the following answer:

Anyone should go to college who has demonstrated both an aptitude and a desire for more education than he has been able to get in elementary and high school. And I may add that to deprive any such person of a college education because his parents cannot afford to give him one is to commit an offense not only against the individual but also against society at large. . . .

Some three hundred college and university presidents recently answered a questionnaire in which they were asked to list, in the order of importance, what they regarded as the purposes of their institutions. Mental discipline, which ranked first sixty years ago, according to a recent analysis of the college catalogues of that day, now ranks twenty-second among the twenty-five avowed purposes of our institutions of higher learning. It is preceded by such objects of higher education as good manners. "Good manners" have no place in the program of higher education. "Personality" has no place in the program of higher education. "Character" has no place in the program of higher education. College develops character by giving young people the habits of hard work and honest analysis. If it tries to teach character directly, it succeeds only in being boring.

An expensively dressed lady once approached the head of a school where I was a teacher and said, "My boy is eighteen years old, and I'm afraid he has been spoiled. I want you to take him and make a man out of him." The head of the school, who was one of the nation's wiser educators, lifted a line from the classics by way of reply: "Late, late, too late—ye cannot enter now."

Why, then, go to college? If the social graces and athletic proficiency can be obtained elsewhere and for less money, if it is too late to alter profoundly the character of a boy or girl of eighteen, perhaps the reason for going to college is to learn how to get into the higher income tax brackets. . . .

President F. P. Keppel of Carnegie Corporation of New York
on the "Preposterous" Increase in the Creation
of Academic Degrees, 1939 *

Education in the United States is a giant industry, providing a living for more than a million individuals and in its processes controlling the time and energies of thirty million others. It has not only its professional sanctions, but its folklore and its stereotypes, its vested interests and its political ties. As a going concern, it has acquired great momentum, but it is one of the prices we still gladly pay for a democracy that this momentum cannot be centrally directed.

Obviously no one is trying either to give or to get a bad education, but our ideas as to what is good and what is bad are as many and as varied as the stars in the heavens. As Professor Hildebrand of the University of California has pointed out, "the gap between American faith in education and satisfaction in its results is sufficiently great to give rise to a continual stream of diagnoses and cures." Society's demands upon education, never very clear or constant, shift with such changes in our community life as the disappearance of the backyard, of farm chores, of the old relations between the master and the apprentice, and with the changing place of the church in society. Education needs money, and those responsible for providing it are faced with actual want in many places and with uncertainty everywhere.

Meanwhile, the new knowledge is piling up more rapidly than education can analyze and digest it and revise its curricula accordingly. Some of the new knowledge bears directly upon education's own processes, as in psychology and in physical and mental hygiene, and indirectly as it suggests new tools of instruction in adaptations of radio and photography.

The prevailing confusion is revealed when one turns to the most conspicuous of the outward and visible signs of educational achievement. Academic degrees for the bachelor, the master, and the doctor were devised to meet the needs of medieval life in theology, in law, in medicine, and in the arts. For centuries there was little or no change. In the eighteenth century, for better or for worse, German universities set the example of a separate doctorate of philosophy as a primary degree, and in the nineteenth century the general pattern was broadened to make provision for such new branches as engineering. Since then, the creation of academic degrees has increased to a preposterous point in the United States. In 1935-36, for instance, our colleges and universities awarded 163 different kinds of degrees in course, creating 143,000 bachelors, 18,000 masters, and 2,700 doctors. As frosting for the cake, honorary degrees of 51 varieties were awarded to 1,350 persons.

* Carnegie Corporation of New York, *Report of the President and of the Treasurer*, 1939, pp. 35-37.

Only in a few strong professions, notably medicine and law, and the older branches of engineering, can it be said that the possession of a degree today necessarily means anything. Elsewhere, all too often, a degree as such may mean literally nothing. All over the country teaching and other vacancies are being filled by degrees, not by men or women, the appointing bodies accepting the diploma as a substitute for the tiresome process of really finding out something as to the professional and personal qualifications of individual human beings. Sometimes the situation presents curious anomalies, as in the fine arts, where the possession of a Ph.D., however much it may imply as to scholarly knowledge, all too often reflects the absence of creative interest and capacity on the part of the possessor.

Extracts from the "G.I. Bill of Rights," the Education of Veterans, 1944 *

1. Any person who served in the active military or naval service on or after September 16, 1940, and prior to the termination of the present war,[1] and who shall have been discharged or released therefrom under conditions other than dishonorable, and who either shall have served ninety days or more, exclusive of any period he was assigned for a course of education or training under the Army specialized training program or the Navy college training program, which course was a continuation of his civilian course and was pursued to completion, or as a cadet or midshipman at one of the service academies, or shall have been discharged or released from active service by reason of an actual service-incurred injury or disability, shall be eligible for and entitled to receive education or training under this part: *Provided,* That such course shall be initiated not later than four years after either the date of his discharge or the termination of the present war,[1] whichever is the later: *Provided further,* That no such education or training shall be afforded beyond nine years after the termination of the present war. [1]

2. Any such eligible person shall be entitled to education or training at an approved educational or training institution for a period of one year plus the time such person was in the active service on or after September 16, 1940, and before the termination of the war,[1] exclusive of any period he was assigned for a course of education or training under the Army specialized training program or the Navy college training program, which

* House Committee Print No. 371, 80th Congress, 2d Session (Washington, Government Printing Office, 1948), pp. 7-10. The number of veterans who received education or training under the "G.I. Bill of Rights" to February 28, 1949, was 5,827,000. The number who received G.I. unemployment allowances to January 31, 1949, was 7,711,500. The number who received G.I. self-employment allowances to January 31, 1949, was 668,250. The number of veterans who received G.I. guaranteed loans to February 25, 1949, was 1,572,538. Letter from A. W. Woolford, Director Information Service, Veterans Administration, to Edgar W. Knight, April 20, 1949.

[1] Termination of the war fixed at July 25, 1947, by Public Law 239, 80th Cong., July 25, 1947.

course was a continuation of his civilian course and was pursued to completion, or as a cadet or midshipman at one of the service academies, but in no event shall the total period of education or training exceed four years: *Provided,* That his work continues to be satisfactory throughout the period, according to the regularly prescribed standards and practices of the institution: *Provided further,* That wherever the period of eligibility ends during a quarter or semester and after a major part of such quarter or semester has expired, such period shall be extended to the termination of such unexpired quarter or semester.

3. (*a*) Such person shall be eligible for and entitled to such course of education or training, full time or the equivalent thereof in part-time training, as he may elect, and at any approved educational or training institution at which he chooses to enroll, whether or not located in the State in which he resides, which will accept or retain him as a student or trainee in any field or branch of knowledge which such institution finds him qualified to undertake or pursue: *Provided,* That, for reasons satisfactory to the Administrator, he may change a course of instruction: *And provided further,* That any such course of education or training may be discontinued at any time, if it is found by the Administrator that, according to the regularly prescribed standards and practices of the institution, the conduct or progress of such person is unsatisfactory.

(*b*) Any such eligible person may apply for a short, intensive postgraduate, or training course of less than thirty weeks: *Provided,* That the Administrator shall have the authority to contract with approved institutions for such courses if he finds that the agreed cost of such courses is reasonable and fair: *Provided further,* That (1) the limitation of paragraph 5 shall not prevent the payment of such agreed rates, but there shall be charged against the veteran's period of eligibility the proportion of an ordinary school year which the cost of the course bears to $500, and (2) not in excess of $500 shall be paid for any such course.

(*c*) Any such eligible person may apply for a course of instruction by correspondence without any subsistence allowance: *Provided,* That the Administrator shall have authority to contract with approved institutions for such courses if he finds that the agreed cost of such courses is reasonable and fair: *Provided further,* (1) That the provisions of paragraph 5 shall not apply to correspondence courses; (2) that one-fourth of the elapsed time in following such course shall be charged against the veteran's period of eligibility; and (3) that the total amount payable for a correspondence course or courses for any veteran shall not exceed $500; *And provided further,* That nothing herein shall be construed to preclude the use of approved correspondence courses as a part of institutional or job training, subject to regulations prescribed by the Administrator.

4. From time to time the Administrator shall secure from the appropriate agency of each State a list of the educational and training institu-

tions (including industrial establishments), within such jurisdiction, which are qualified and equipped to furnish education or training (including apprenticeship, refresher or retraining and institutional on-farm training), which institutions, together with such additional ones as may be recognized and approved by the Administrator, shall be deemed qualified and approved to furnish education or training to such persons as shall enroll under this part: *Provided,* That wherever there are established State apprenticeship agencies expressly charged by State laws to administer apprentice training, whenever possible, the Administrator shall utilize such existing facilities and services in training on the job when such training is of one year's duration or more.

5. The Administrator shall pay to the educational or training institution (including the institution offering institutional on-farm training), for each person enrolled in full time or part time course of education or training, the customary cost of tuition, and such laboratory, library, health, infirmary, and other similar fees as are customarily charged, and may pay for books, supplies, equipment, and other necessary expenses, exclusive of board, lodging, other living expenses, and travel, as are generally required for the successful pursuit and completion of the course by other students in the institution: *Provided,* That in no event shall such payments, with respect to any person, exceed $500 for an ordinary school year unless the veteran elects to have such customary charges paid in excess of such limitation, in which event there shall be charged against his period of eligibility the proportion of an ordinary school year which such excess bears to $500: *Provided further,* That no payments shall be made to institutions, business or other establishments furnishing apprentice training on the job: *And provided further,* That any institution may apply to the Administrator for an adjustment of tuition and the Administrator, if he finds that the customary tuition charges are insufficient to permit the institution to furnish education or training to eligible veterans, or inadequate compensation therefor, may provide for the payment of such fair and reasonable compensation as will not exceed the estimated cost of teaching personnel and supplies for instruction; and may in like manner readjust such payments from time to time.

6. While enrolled in and pursuing a course under this part, (including an institutional on-farm training course (such person, upon application to the Administrator, shall be paid a subsistence allowance of $65 per month, if without a dependent or dependents, or $90 per month, if he has a dependent or dependents, including regular holidays and leave not exceeding thirty days in a calendar year: Except, That (1) while so enrolled and pursuing a course of full-time institutional training, such person, shall be paid a subsistence allowance of $75 per month, if without a dependent or dependents, or $105 per month if he has one dependent or $120 per month if he has more than one dependent, and (2) while so

enrolled and pursuing a course of part-time institutional training, including a course of institutional on-farm training, or other combination course, such person shall be paid, subject to the limitations of this paragraph, additional subsistence allowance in an amount bearing the same relation to the difference between the basic rates and the increased rates provided in (1) hereof as the institutional training part of such course bears to a course of full-time institutional training. Such person attending a course on a part-time basis, and such person receiving compensation for productive labor whether performed as part of his apprentice or other training on the job at institutions, business or other establishments, or otherwise, shall be entitled to receive such lesser sums, if any, as subsistence or dependency allowances as may be determined by the Administrator: *Provided,* That in no event shall the rate of such allowance plus the compensation received exceed $210 per month for a veteran without a dependent, or $270 per month for a veteran with one dependent, or $290 for a veteran with two or more dependents: *Provided further,* That only so much of the compensation as is derived from productive labor based on the standard workweek for the particular trade or industry, exclusive of overtime, shall be considered in computing the rate of allowances payable under this paragraph.[2]

7. Any such person eligible for the benefits of this part, who is also eligible for the benefit of part VII, may elect either benefit or may be provided an approved combination of such courses: *Provided,* That the total period of any such combined courses shall not exceed the maximum period or limitations under the part affording the greater period of eligibility. . . .

The President's Commission on Higher Education Recommends National Scholarship and Fellowship Programs, 1947 *

The inadequacy of existing funds for scholarships and fellowships makes a national program imperative if higher education is to fulfill its responsibility to the individual, to the Nation, and to the world. In view of the imperative need for highly trained personnel and in the light of the vast expenditure now being made by the Federal Government for the education and training only of veterans, this is a reasonable proposal. The program for veterans has already justified itself as a splendid contribution to postwar progress for the individual and for society. Surely the continuance and extension of such a program to the youth of the future is equally justified.

Unless present legislation is amended, all veterans discharged prior to July 1, 1947, must have completed their education under the GI bill by

---

2 Sec. 3 of Public Law 512, 80th Cong., provides that this Act shall take effect April 1, 1948.
* The President's Commission on Higher Education, *Higher Education for American Democracy* (Washington, 1947), II, pp. 51-56.

July 1, 1956. The diminishing of the number of new veteran enrollees will gradually enable the normal flow of secondary school graduates into college to be resumed at a rate higher than the prewar level. This increased flow of high school graduates will result from many factors, including population increases. It is thus advisable that new provisions to equalize opportunities be initiated in 1948-49.

Confronted by this larger demand and recognizing the economic difficulties which will preclude many qualified students from entering college, this Commission recommends that a national program of Federal scholarships in the form of grants-in-aid be provided for at least 20 percent of all undergraduate, nonveteran students. The Commission is convinced that the basis of individual need coupled with the requisite qualifications of total personal abilities and interests should be the controlling factor in the selection of the recipients of such aid.

In the following elaboration of this recommendation, the Commission emphasizes that it is more concerned with the establishment of a broad approach to method than with rigid insistence on the wisdom of all details, many of which would necessarily evolve at the administrative stage of operation.

In point of timing, this Commission makes its recommendation in two parts—one specifying a progressively increasing 5-year program of Federal appropriations for scholarship grants, and the other suggesting alternative possibilities for the period from 1953 through 1960.

The fiscal recommendations are of this dual character, not because it might not be justifiable to propose a program of Federal appropriations on a scale which would eventually equal the amounts required in the GI Bill. *It seems obvious that, in the national interest, we as a nation can well afford to invest in the education of needy nonveterans amounts approaching those which we are now investing in the education and training of qualified veterans.* But this Commission prefers to take account of a number of qualifying, if incalculable, factors in offering recommendations of total amounts for grants-in-aid for the immediate future. Among these factors are, for example, the possibility of State universities substantially lowering their fees in the near future; the likelihood of the general level of wages and salaries remaining at a level as high as at present; the possibility of an increasing number who may be able to go to community colleges and live at home; the possibility of the States themselves adding or extending programs of substantial State grants-in-aid to many more high school graduates; and finally, the size of the gross national product in the years ahead.

The primary purpose of a Federal scholarship program is to equalize educational opportunity by eliminating, at least in part, the economic factor in determining college attendance. The amount of the scholarship would vary with the financial need of the individual, depending on the actual amount required to make it possible for him to attend and continue in college. The amount of the scholarship might reach a proposed maximum of $800 for an academic year. For purposes of estimating the first year's cost, an average scholarship of $400 may be assumed. This leads to an initial recommendation for 1948-49 of approximately $120,000,000 for Federal scholarships which would give assistance to some 300,000 students. This is, in the Commission's view, a conservative and wholly defensible recommendation, especially in the light of the extent of economic handicaps set forth earlier in this volume. And it constitutes a beginning which will enable administrative and selective procedures to be set up and be tested prior to the possible expansion of the program.

Since the Commission recommends that scholarships be available to a minimum of 20 percent of all non-veteran students, this program in dollar amounts should be augmented each year, as the GI appropriation needs recede. It is therefore recommended that in each fiscal year after 1948-49 and continuing through 1952-53, an amount be appropriated over and above $120,000,000.

The computation and the total amount suggested here, are not necessarily regarded by this Commission as either ideally desirable or adequate to meet what our analysis reveals to be the known inadequacies. But, at this level of expenditure a start can be made. The continuing needs will demonstrate themselves, and will result in a more informed and adequate authorization of Federal expenditure in the years after 1953.

In these years, several options may be suggested as to the amounts of Federal appropriation to be wisely advocated. At the present time the veterans' tuition and subsistence requirements for post high school education cost over $1,000,000,000 per year of Federal money. There are those who would say that to equal this amount for annual nonveteran grants-in-aid by the year 1960 would not represent an extravagant or unjustifiable outlay for this important educational purpose. If the figure $1,000,000,000 is taken as the amount to earmark out of Federal funds for this purpose by 1960, it becomes readily possible to construct a program of progressively increasing numbers of grants from 1953 to 1960, which would build up to this figure or to any agreed fractional part of it. Obviously, Federal funds are voted on the basis of public conviction of public need and value. And this Commission is convinced that with a preliminary trial period of a few years, the Congress will appropriate funds on a scale commensurate with what an informed public opinion will by that time come to identity as an urgent national need.

In general terms, the procedure recommended in connection with this grant-in-aid program is as follows:

Each applicant would select the college or university which he or she desired to attend and would assure his or her admission to it in the regular way.

Each State would establish a representative scholarship commission to administer funds granted to it for this purpose by the Federal Government.[1]

In suitable State legislation it should be provided that this scholarship commission would include representatives of public and private secondary schools where appropriate, or public and private colleges and universities where appropriate, of the chief State school officer and of public-spirited citizens at large within each State. This Commission would be charged to act upon requests for individual grants-in-aid made to it by those secondary school students who are residents of the State and who had been accepted for admission by an approved college or university of their own choice in any State. The Commission would also be responsible for the annual renewal of such grants on the basis of an established procedure of renewal certificates as issued by the college or university for satisfactory completion of the previous year's work.

A maximum of seven annual grants to one student should be specified. This will permit the use of such grants for graduate or professional study. The maximum amount allowed for any one grant would be $800 per year.

This grant-in-aid provision would be available to students in approved 2-year and 4-year colleges, public and private, and for graduate study including professional schools for a maximum of 3 years. Individual exceptions might be made in professional fields requiring more than 7 years of preparation.

The primary basis for determining the award of the scholarship to an individual student should be his financial need. The award would further depend upon the applicant's ability, character, sense of responsibility, and such other factors as may be adjudged pertinent within the announced purposes of the appropriation.

The broad basis for determining those applicants who would give definite promise of profiting from a college education should be set forth in regulations by the Federal agency responsible for the administration of the total fund, which should be the one primarily concerned with higher education. The conduct of any examinations, interviews and the like would be left to suitable provision to be made by each State's scholarship commission in harmony with the basic Federal regulations.

The proportion of the total Federal appropriation which would be available annually to each State's scholarship commission should be determined by taking equal account of two factors:

[1] Statement of dissent:

I dissent from the proposal for State administration of scholarships. Since the purpose of such scholarships is exclusively to enable more students to obtain a higher education, and not to influence the distribution of students as between regions or between private and public institutions, I believe that Federal scholarships should be prorated among colleges and universities and administered by them on the basis of individual student need and ability. Under the National Youth Administration program our colleges and universities proved their capacity to redeem such a responsibility.

MILTON S. EISENHOWER.

(1) 50 percent of the weight would be given to the number of high-school graduates in each State, each year, in relation to the total number of high-school graduates in the United States; and

(2) 50 percent of the weight would be determined on the proportion of young people in the 18-21 year age group, resident within the State, to the total 18-21 year old youth in the total population.

The following example illustrates the application of the principles. If 5 percent of the high-school graduates of the country are in one State and 3 percent of the 18-21 year old age group in the United States reside in that same State, 4 percent of the total Federal appropriation would be available to assist youth of college age who are residents of that State.

This Commission recognizes the complex problems involved in any national program of grants-in-aid, but believes that the difficulties can be resolved through careful and continuing appraisal of the effectiveness of its operation.

The scholarship commission in each State, acting in close conjunction with the agency in that State responsible for higher education, should be the instrumentality for channeling the funds from the Federal Government to the individual students from each State.

If there should be any unused balance of the total amount allocated to any State, this would revert to the Federal Treasury at the end of each fiscal year.

This Commission recognizes also that at present this proposal would, to some extent, work against those States in which secondary school education is inadequate. But the availability of grants, plus the use of the suggested formula, should provide a stimulus to the improvement of secondary education. In certain States where this improvement is dependent clearly upon access to Federal equalizing funds, consideration might well be given to the establishment of provisions for drawing upon part of these resources for a grant-in-aid program to secondary school students, at least during their last 2 years in high school.

In order to provide appropriate and adequate encouragement of graduate study beyond the baccalaureate degree and to assure the nation of an adequate supply of highly trained personnel, this Commission recommends a program of fellowships for graduate study.

The genuine need for an expanded program of advanced and professional study is emphasized by the fact that in the academic year 1946-47, approximately 40,000 graduate degrees were granted in all the colleges and universities of the country, of which number only 3,787 represented the learned doctoral degrees.

There has been clear and widespread recognition of the importance of such a program in terms of research developments; new contributions to knowledge; and as pointed out in the volume of this Commission's report entitled "Staffing Higher Education," of attracting able young people into study which would eventually qualify them for college teaching and administration.

This Commission, therefore, recommends that Federal funds be appropriated to provide for the establishment of a program of Federal fellowships. The amount of each fellowship should be $1,500 a year and the number of such fellowships be 10,000 in the year 1948-49; 20,000 in 1949-50; and 30,000 in 1950-51 through 1952-53.

Recipients should be selected on the basis of a national competitive examination.

Each fellowship would continue for a maximum of 3 years if the student maintains acceptable academic standards of attainment, with explicit renewal each year to qualifying students.

The holder of each fellowship would be allowed to select his own field of graduate study and to pursue it at an institution of his own choice, if the university selected offers appropriate courses in his chosen field.

The program here recommended would entail a Federal appropriation of $15,000,000 for the academic year 1948-49; $30,000,000 for 1949-50; and $45,000,000 for 1950-51 and for the two succeeding years. This appropriation is in addition to that proposed for the Federal scholarship program and in addition to funds provided for other fellowships already made available in specialized fields.

The Rôle of the Federal Government in Higher Education, 1947 *

The time has come for America to develop a sound pattern of continuing Federal support for higher education. The analyses presented in the preceding chapter show that the Federal Government must assume a large and important role in financing higher education.

The following basic principles are those which this Commission believes should guide the development and expansion of Federal financial relationship with higher education.

1. In its relationships to higher education, the Federal Government should recognize the national importance of a well-rounded and well-integrated program of education for all citizens, regardless of age, sex, race, creed, or economic and social status. . . .

2. Federal funds for the general support of institutions of higher education should be distributed among the States on an equalization basis. . . .

3. Federal appropriations for the general support of higher education should clearly recognize the responsibility of the States for the administration and control of the education programs. . . .

4. Adequate safeguards should be established by the Federal Government to assure the full realization of the purposes for which aid is to be granted. . . .

* *Ibid.,* V, pp. 54-61.

5. Federal funds for the general support of current educational activities and for general capital outlay purposes should be appropriated for use only in institutions under public control. . . .

6. Federal funds provided for scholarships or grants-in-aid for the purpose of helping individuals of ability and fellowships for those of special talent to obtain equality of opportunity in education should be paid directly to the qualifying individuals. . . .

7. As is deemed necessary, the Federal Government should make contracts with individual institutions, publicly or privately controlled, for specific services authorized by national legislation. . . .

Although the urgent needs for higher education in America fully justify and demand that immediate steps be taken toward the realization of the complete program recommended by the President's Commission, the Commission is well aware of certain practical problems involved in attaining the goals. These problems demand that the approach to the proposed program be gradual and that appropriate account be taken of the needs of education at all levels.

More of the Nation's youth must find it possible and profitable to remain in high school through graduation. Elementary and secondary schools must be improved and greater equality of educational opportunity provided at these levels. Frequent studies have shown convincingly that Federal financial assistance is necessary in accomplishing these objectives. Such assistance should be provided at these levels concurrently with any assistance at the higher-education level.

Appropriate and readily accessible programs of higher education must be developed. Adequate physical facilities must be constructed. Greater awareness on the part of youth and adults of the importance of further education will need to develop. These things will take time—sufficient time to allow for sound planning and development.

Nevertheless, there should be no delay in moving immediately toward the ultimate attainment of the proposed program. Planning and development should begin at once. With this in mind, the President's Commission recommends that the following program of Federal aid for higher education be adopted and put into action in the fiscal year 1948-49.

To establish greater equality of educational opportunity for those able and interested in continuing their education beyond high school, the Federal Government, as previously stated, should appropriate for the fiscal year 1948-49 the sum of $120,000,000 for a national program of scholarships to be administered by the States in accordance with general standards established by the Federal Government. This appropriation should be increased annually through 1952-53 in an amount sufficient to provide scholarships for 20 per cent of the nonveteran enrollment. This appropriation is in addition to the programs already established by the Federal Government for scholarships in special fields. It is recommended that all

Federally financed scholarships and fellowships be unified into one generally available program.

To develop and encourage youth of special talent to rise to the top level in the professions, research, and instruction the Federal Government should provide 10,000 fellowships in 1948-49, 20,000 in 1949-50, and 30,000 in 1950-51, 1951-52, and 1952-53. This program calls for an appropriation of $15,000,000 in 1948-49, $30,000,000 in 1949-50, and 45,000,000 each year thereafter through 1952-53. These amounts should be in addition to those now available from the Federal Government in special fields. . . .

Federal aid to the States for educational expenditures by publicly controlled institutions of higher education should be initiated with an appropriation for the fiscal year 1948-49. This should be an amount equal to one-twelfth of the $638,000,000 possible deficit in realizing the complete program of higher education recommended by this Commission for 1960. This appropriation should be increased each year thereafter by one-twelfth of the original amount until 1952-53 when the program should be re-examined in terms of the progress made by that time toward realizing the goals proposed for 1960. This means that the appropriations should be as follows:

1948-49	$53,000,000
1949-50	106,000,000
1950-51	159,000,000
1951-52	212,000,000
1952-53	265,000,000

It is recommended that all States share in the appropriations for educational and general aid, and that this aid be apportioned among the States on an equalization basis, each State's share being determined in accordance with an objective formula designed to measure the State's relative need for higher education and its relative ability to finance an adequate program. The development and application of such a formula involves the use of technical measurements. It should be formulated and frequently reviewed on the basis of studies made of the cost of various levels and types of an adequate program of higher education, of the relative needs of the population for higher education at the various levels, of the relative abilities of the States to support education, and of the fair share of the burden of cost which should be borne by State and local governments.

The total additional amounts needed by publicly controlled institutions to expand their physical plant to the recommended size by 1960 is $7,758,-000,000. *Under the plan envisioned by this Commission, the Federal Government would provide one-third of the total amount of the expansion. The remaining two-thirds would then be provided by the States, with whatever assistance local governments can give.*

This building program should be initiated as soon as possible, and proceed at a rapid pace toward completion. Only if the physical facilities are available can expanded educational opportunity exist for the youth of this Nation. Yet, there are good reasons for not advocating an extensive building program in the immediate future. The scarcity of labor and materials in the building industries, the desperate national need for more housing, and the high prevailing costs are among these reasons.

It is to be understood, that a building program of the size recommended cannot be undertaken and completed in a short time, and, because of its magnitude, must be integrated with other building programs of national importance. To start the program, therefore, it is recommended that in 1948-49 there be appropriated a sum equal to one-twelfth of the total amount this Commission deems suitable for Federal participation, or $216,000,000. In the years from then through 1952-53, it is suggested that at least that same amount be appropriated annually. After 1952-53, the program should be reviewed with the idea of establishing a flexible pattern of appropriations consistent with the needs as they appear at that time and in the light of potential developments beyond that date.

It is recommended that Federal aid for capital outlay be apportioned among the States on an equalization basis, similar to that proposed for general aid. The allocation should be determined through the use of an objective formula based on building needs in the States, variations in building costs, and the relative abilities of the States to finance necessary construction. Provision should be made for frequent review of the formula in the light of fluctuating costs and changing educational needs. . . .

Two Members of the President's Commission on Higher Education Dissent from Its Recommendations on Financing Higher Education, 1947 *

This statement of dissent is concerned primarily with the unqualified recommendation of the Commission that Federal funds for current expenditures and capital outlay be appropriated for use in publicly controlled institutions of higher education only. A careful review of the Commission's report as a whole has convinced us that this particular recommendation is inconsistent with other policies and proposals advocated by the Commission. Furthermore, the reasons proposed by the majority of the Commission in support of this recommendation are really nothing more than declarations that public colleges and universities must have a priority for Federal funds and that private institutions would be subjected to governmental control if they should accept Federal funds. These declarations do not furnish any valid support for the statement of a principle that, under no circumstances and regardless of State policies and practices, may Fed-

* *Ibid.*, pp. 65-68.

eral funds for current expenditures and capital outlay be provided to privately controlled institutions of higher education as such. Nowhere in the report are any sound reasons given on the basis of which privately controlled colleges and universities, which have had long and distinguished records of service to our Nation in peace and war, should be disqualified from the benefits of a Federal-aid program.

Before presenting in detail the reasons for our position, we wish to stress the point that our dissent is not a mere personal plea for the special interests of private education. A recent poll conducted by the American Council on Education revealed that 241 members, about half of those replying to the Council's questionnaire, voted in favor of the proposition that Federal funds be made available "to nonprofit private as well as to public education," including, therefore, privately and publicly controlled institutions of higher learning. And these votes, we have every reason to believe, were cast in the best interests of the general welfare. In light of this fact, we, as members of the Commission, are convinced that it is our duty to state to the President of the United States and to the American public that this drastic recommendation to bar private colleges and universities from receiving Federal funds does not reflect the thinking of the most representative cross section of American college and university leaders and will certainly have dangerous implications for the future welfare of both public and private higher education.

This recommendation, as we understand it, is based on a theory of educational finance which asserts that "public control" rather than "service to the public" shall be the sole criterion of a school's eligibility to receive public funds. Underlying this theory is the assumption that American democracy will be best served by a mighty system of public higher education to be financed by local, State, and Federal taxes, and to be controlled, managed, and supervised by governmental agencies. Accordingly, the Commission's report predicts—and without regrets—the gradual elimination of those private colleges and universities which are unable to keep pace with their publicly endowed competitors. The report also envisions the development of a Nation-wide system of higher education in which private colleges and universities will play an increasingly minor role.

We believe it is timely in this connection to call attention to the dangers of a higher educational system largely or completely dominated by the State. Exclusive control of education, more than any other factor, made the dictatorships of Germany, Italy, and Japan acceptable to an ever-increasing number of their populations. The question immediately comes to mind whether American education can continue to withstand the modern social trend toward governmental domination of the educational process. We confess definite misgivings on this point, now that the Commission has so decisively recommended a monopoly of tax funds for publicly controlled colleges and universities. We fear that legislation implementing the Commission's recommendation would go a long way toward establishing an administrative structure for higher education whereby Government in the United States might easily use the Nation's public colleges and universities to promote its political purposes.

With respect to the report itself, we are unable to determine why the Commission recommended in such an unqualified fashion that no Federal funds for current expenditures and capital outlay be given to private institutions of higher learning. Throughout the report there are frequent references to the quasi-public functions performed by private colleges and universities, and repeatedly these institutions are praised for their achievements in serving the public welfare. We note also that the Commission had no hesitancy in recommending that private institutions should lower their fees, adopt certain personnel practices, accept contracts from the Government for specialized research, admit students who receive national scholarships and fellowships, and follow a policy of nondiscrimination in admitting members of minority groups. In the Commission's own words:

". . . It is becoming generally acknowledged that, despite a large measure of private control and private support, these institutions are vitally affected with the public interest. Not only is this reflected in the privilege of tax exemption which they are accorded, but also in the process of State accreditation in certain States, and in the recognition that they constitute part of a program of higher education dedicated to the Nation's welfare. They are thus genuinely vested with a public interest and as such are morally obligated to abandon all restrictive policies. . . ."

The Commission accordingly has decided that, although private institutions must render the same public service as do public schools, they shall receive none of the funds appropriated by Government as compensation for the public service rendered. This decision would appear to us as arbitrary, to say the least.

In making this recommendation, the Commission apparently lost sight of its primary purpose which was to propose ways and means of equalizing educational opportunity for higher education on a much broader basis than ever before in history and to provide for the expansion and development of educational facilities at the higher levels to meet the needs of a vastly increased number of students. In the light of this purpose, nothing could be more untimely, nothing more futilely doctrinaire than for this Commission to adopt a recommendation which would, in effect, destroy the happy balance and cordial relations which now exist in higher education, and which would cause many of our great private institutions to curtail expansion of facilities at a time when such expansion is absolutely necessary in terms of the general welfare.

We now turn our attention to the specific reasons allegedly supporting the recommendation to which we object. In our opinion, these reasons are either gratuitous or specious. The report declares that Government has "a prime responsibility" to provide opportunities for higher education and has a "fundamental obligation . . . to establish a sound system of public education and to support it to the fullest extent possible." The report also states that the discharge of this responsibility "does not deny in any way" the right of individuals to have and to support their own schools. We fail to see how it follows from these "reasons" that private institutions which are, as a matter of fact, cooperating with the Government by providing a "high quality" education for thousands of young men and women should be disqualified from receiving Federal aid.

We are not impressed by the Commission's admonition that the acceptance of Federal funds would expose private education to Federal control. The very same admonition might be directed to publicly controlled colleges and universities. As the report clearly indicates, it is the policy of the Commission that Federal aid to education must not impose upon the institutions assisted any form of Federal control over their academic or personnel practices. Furthermore, it is the considered judgment of the Commission that publicly controlled colleges and universities may accept Federal aid without submitting to any Federal dictation on their academic policies. There appears to be no reason why Federal aid to privately controlled institutions would entail a greater risk of Federal control than would similar aid to publicly controlled institutions. In practice, the amount of Federal aid to any institution would not be large enough to expose the institution to Federal control as ordinarily understood.

We submit that the criterion of a school's eligibility to receive Federal funds should be its "service to the public" and not "public control." Our position is based upon our conviction that American democracy will be best served if higher education in the future, as in the past, will continue to be regarded as a responsibility to be shared by public and private colleges and universities. This American tradition of democratic school administration suggests that the Government should be disposed to aid any qualified college or university, regardless of whether it is administered by a quasi-public body, like a board of trustees appointed by the State officials or elected by the people, or whether it is managed by a private nonprofit corporation. In no case should Government be conceded the right to measure its financial aid to an institution by the degree of control which it exercises over its administration. In the matter of control, the Government must be neutral. Its standard is "service to the public" and this standard squares with the American tradition of democracy in education.

That private colleges and universities do perform a public service is a fact beyond dispute. We see no reason why they should not continue and be helped to continue this service.

Msgr. FREDERICK G. HOCHWALT
MARTIN R. P. McGUIRE

Harold J. Laski on the Graduate System of Education
in The United States, 1948 *

... The publication in 1883, of the first series of the Johns Hopkins *Studies in Historical and Political Science* was a landmark in the academic history of the United States. Within a decade the doctorate in philosophy had become the well-nigh indispensable passport to the right to teach in an American university.

The popularity of the system grew by leaps and bounds. A university soon became an institution which could take pride in its ability to attract graduate students. Research achieved a status equal with teaching in importance; the tradition became established that there was little or no hope of a permanent university position without the degree of doctor of philosophy. Teachers were appointed in the belief that, where they went, research students would follow; it even became increasingly necessary for the teacher to publish in order that his name might be continually in the minds of students who were uncertain what university to choose for their graduate work. Or, if he did not publish, he needed the kind of influence with his colleagues in other universities which enabled him to secure posts for the students who were registered under his supervision. Once, moreover, the doctorate had become a passport to a college post, it began to be a distinction universally sought. The members of the faculty of a normal school desired it as a means to promotion. A teacher in a high school would regard it as the key which unlocked the door to a principalship. It became necessary to invent ways and means of helping along the young men and women in quest, in ever-increasing numbers, of their Ph.D. Not everyone could be given a scholarship, still less a travelling scholarship. But there could be teaching fellows, who combined some form or other of class work, quarter-time or half-time, with their research; there could be university assistants, who paid their way through college by taking off the professor's hands the laborious work of holding the "quiz" or a class or reading his examination papers for him; or there could be the research assistant to the professor, who hunted down references for him in the library, made notes at his indication of significant material he desired to use but had not the time to go through for himself, read his proofs for printers' errors, and compiled the index to his book. I have even known research assistants who read and digested for their professors books in languages the professors could not read, so that, on publication, they could not be accused of overlooking important foreign work they ought to have known. And in between the performance of such labours the assistant went on with his own researches. First, as a rule, he took the master's degree, an examination in a field of studies connected with the subject on which he

* *The American Democracy* (New York, Viking Press, Inc., 1948), pp. 374-80. Used by permission of the author and publisher.

thought of specializing. Then he prepared for and took his general examination, an oral examination in which a group of professors "grilled" him, much in the manner of continental Europe, to be sure that his background knowledge was adequate for the work on which he proposed to embark. After this, he would begin preparing his thesis, which might take him anywhere from two to five or six years, according to the time at his disposal and his habits of work.

The range of academic studies, moreover, which now shelter themselves under the wings of a university institution has increased at an almost terrifying speed. There is the vast area of commerce, both territorial and functional; there is the complex called "home economics," which may include the analysis of family budgets or the examination of the machinery most suitable for dish-washing in small restaurants. There is the immense area called "education," on which one student may be working at the history of the methods of teaching elementary arithmetic, another on professional solidarity among teachers in England, a third on tendencies towards centralization in the state educational system of Illinois, and a fourth on what French critics think of the American educational system. The study of Romance philology may take one man to the examination of what Dante has to say about each species of the animal kingdom mentioned in his works, and another to an analysis of the use in French of the infinite, instead of the finite, verb. A group of students may take the problems of reconstruction in the South after the Civil War, and each give attention to their impact upon a particular state. Another group may study the drift to administrative centralization in one or a number of states. As each new specialism pushes its way to university recognition, it is hardly unfair to say that its teachers feel they have won for it its full status when one of their students has received his doctorate in the subject.

The writing of a thesis goes through a physiological rhythm almost as regular as the circulation of the blood. The student chooses his "topic" in consultation with the professor who is to supervise his work. It is curiously rare for a student to know what it is he wants to write about. Far more usually, he accepts the professor's suggestion, and he then decides upon a theme from a list of possible subjects which the wise professor keeps, as it were, in stock; or he works upon some project the material of which may ultimately be the basis of a chapter, or a paragraph, or a footnote in the *magnum opus* the professor is writing. The subject once chosen, the student compiles a bibliography of whatever exists about his subject, with special reference to manuscript material or to remote sources, like old newspapers, not previously used in work upon his theme. He goes through all the obvious material conscientiously, taking careful notes as he reads; if the manuscripts are in Europe, in the British Museum, for example, or the Bibliothèque Nationale, he tries to get a scholarship to London or Paris, or to get a loan against his future, to consult them; or he may be fortunate enough to persuade a wealthy university to have photostatic copies made that he can peruse at leisure in its library. After more note-taking, he begins to arrive at a scheme of work which he will probably amend somewhat in the light of discussion with his supervisor. He then begins the heavy work of writing his thesis, consulting at intervals his supervisor or other professors from whom he may get ideas or counsel. As he writes, he will support each statement he makes with a footnote showing the source from which it is taken, until, not seldom, the text itself seems like a small island, surrounded by a veritable ocean of references. And when the last chapter is done, he will conscientiously add the most comprehensive bibliography he can compile, perhaps classified with a minute precision that would evoke a smile of approval from the shade of that ingenious librarian who invented the Dewey decimal system. The thesis submitted, he is examined upon it by a small committee of professors to whose hands is entrusted the fate of the research and its author.

Not even in Germany has so massive a system been evolved, so intricate and so terrifying, in order to help a young man or woman learn how to write a book. It has evoked an endless stream of protests, of which, perhaps, the acid essay of William James is the most famous.* But no criticism has yet proved powerful enough to stay its torrential movement; it has been said that in the year before the outbreak of the Second World War more than three thousand doctorates were granted in the United States. I have myself calculated that in one Midwestern university alone, and that by no means the largest of its area, over six hundred doctorates were conferred from 1919 to 1939. Sometimes the university requires that the theme be printed; most of them today more mercifully ask no more than the submission of several typewritten copies, one of which will remain on file in its library. But few of them are published in the ordinary way; only a minute percentage, when published, ever reach the dignity of a second edition. Out of 459 numbers in the Johns Hopkins' series, which represents the best work of all its graduate students in the social sciences for sixty years, only fifty-four are out of print; and the demand for these is apparently not ample enough to justify reprinting. Out of 380 numbers in the well-known Columbia University *Studies in History and Economics and Public Law,* published between 1893 and 1903, only nine appear to be out of print, and only one volume seems to have gone into a second edition. Much the same is true of similar series published under the auspices of Harvard and Yale Universities.

Obviously enough, statistics of this character tell but a small part of the significance of any volume. Few people would, or could, rightly expect that a learned and heavily documented book could normally expect to have a wide sale. Its author is almost certain to be unknown; his theme is likely

* See above.

to be narrow; nor is he likely to have made any exciting discoveries or put forward any important generalizations. Yet, when all this is granted, the picture remains a disturbing one. A student writes a book not because he feels called to write that particular book, but because he is bound to write a book in order, broadly speaking, to have a certificate of competence which entitles him to begin or to continue teaching in a university. He rarely conceives of the subject he takes as the preliminary study for some great book he has at least the ambition one day to write. He rarely even seeks to approach it in an original way. It is often thorough, often useful, now and again it may shed some new ray of light of real significance upon its subject. It is but seldom that its author finds inspiration or even stimulus in doing it. It is a task that must be got through; it is a means to opening a gate, a possible road to promotion. Rarely, indeed, does he see the bridge between his particular field of study and the next field. Rarely, either, does he inquire whether what he does is important in itself or likely to be the basis upon which some later scholar may build more important work. His anxiety is to get the work done so that he may enter the stage of work where he has become his own master.

I do not want for an instant to paint a picture that is out of perspective. Everyone knows that remarkable books have been written for the doctorate, and that some of them rank as indispensable in their field. But that is not because they are written for the doctorate; it is because they were written by remarkable men and women. The system as a whole holds hundreds of students in bondage every year to an idea that is wholly illusory. Some of them are fundamentally incapable of writing a good book. Others are not yet mature enough to write one. Others, again, have no desire to write a book and learn little or nothing from their effort to write it. And the system develops habits of its own. It begets what the French call the *fureur de l'inédit*. It begets the obligation not to write upon a topic, however important, upon which someone else is known to be writing; hence the publication every year, in the learned American journals, of long lists of subjects already pre-empted. It begets the passion for footnotes, the conviction that no statement will be believed unless it can be referred to an earlier writer or document, and it gets, perhaps above all, what can only be termed bibliographical elephantiasis. No doubt there are supervisors work with whom is an illumination the light from which will give vision to the student for the rest of his days; no one who worked with Frederick J. Turner, or with Carl Becker, but must have felt the excitement of seeing how the great artist hews from the rough stone a portrait which comes to life, just as no one can have submitted an idea for critical examination to William James, or to Morris Cohen, without the joy of seeing how a great swordsman can cut it to pieces. Quite obviously, a man who is born for thought or learning, whether in the humanities or in the sciences, will find the Ph.D. a hurdle he can take in his stride; and there will always be some for whom the system leads to association out of which solid work, even occasionally inspired work, will emerge.

Yet, granted all this, the system has now become a vast machine which kills the very purposes it was intended to serve. It leads to premature and excessive specialization. It leads to the production of a fantastic mass of minute researches of which but a small part has any special significance either for the author or for the public they are intended to reach. In the social sciences especially, it breeds a race of researchers who cannot see the woods for the trees. But its worst effect is, I think, that in all save the really exceptional scholar, it becomes a form of escapism which makes for unreal thinking and ineffective teaching. It makes for the first because the intense concentration on a small theme seems to breed a type which becomes afraid either of large generalizations or considering issues which reach beyond its boundaries. He becomes unaccustomed to the co-ordination of his specialism with the larger problems of which it is a part. There even comes a time when he resents being asked either to let his mind play freely over a large realm of ideas or to show an awareness that the need to arrive is not less important than the preparation for the journey. And he becomes, only too often, an ineffective teacher, because his training inhibits him from realizing that the one thing his students want to know is how the subject helps to explain the kind of world in which they live. He thinks that the more he detaches himself from such an explanation, the more scholarly his treatment ought to be regarded. He begins by taking no risks because he is uncertain; he ends by taking no risks because he has ceased, by use and wont, to have any convictions at all. He becomes a purveyor of information, most of which is easily available in books, which he retails afresh every year in much the same way as an automobile dealer sells his cars.

It would be an immense boon to American education if the Ph.D., together with the immense administrative apparatus it has come to involve, were got rid of altogether. Most of the labour it involves is not in any real sense, educational. Most of the men and women who have something real to say in their chosen field of study would say it anyhow, whether there were a degree or no; and its existence leads a multitude of people to try to say something when they are uneasily conscious either that they have nothing to say or that what they are asked to examine is not in fact worth, as a problem, the immense effort they have to spend upon it. I think it is reasonable to insist that most of the creative minds in American universities are aware that this is the case; but they shrink from the effort involved in a sustained attack upon what has now become an immense vested interest in the university. Not least among the evils is the fact that it tends to destroy the reflective mind, the mind that broods over a large range of facts until, by a flash of insight, a relation is seen between them from which they come to have a new meaning. In place of the thinker, it puts the card

index; in place of the play of ideas, it puts the footnote and the bibliography. Nothing invented since the Inquisition has had so sterilizing an effect
upon that habit of free speculation and eager debate of first principles out
of which the scholar is most likely to transform information into wisdom.

Two other features of the university system deserve a word. The first
derives directly, the other indirectly, from the institution of the doctorate.
The first is the use of volume of production as one of the main indices to
promotion. Unless a teacher makes his mark early, either by a promising
piece of work or by the quality of his personality, there is a constant drive
to publish, especially in a large university, lest his claim to promotion be
overlooked. The result is that the learned journals of the United States are
full of what can only be called machine-made research in which the habits
of the aspirant to a Ph.D. are prolonged year after year until the teacher
is satisfied he can climb no higher. He is afraid of being labelled as "un-
productive," so that, year after year, he will devote his leisure to grinding
out articles which are only too often dead even before they have reached
the printed page. And because most of the scholars who edit the journals
are aware that the articles are insignificant, the question of whether to
publish them or not tends to become either the presence of some unpublished document or the tabulation of some material, the first of which will
only very rarely have importance, and the second of which will give a
precision, the labour of which is out of all proportion to its value, to some
simple platitude which everyone knew before. It may be a letter, say, of
Robert Southey saying that he has received a parcel of books for which he
had asked, or it may be a table to prove that in a New England village there
are more Packards above the railroad tracks per family than there are
below them. The point I am concerned to make is that the whole academic
atmosphere tends to lead to the insistent cult of the insignificant, and those
who are driven to the practice of this cult are bound themselves, before
long, to become insignificant too.

The other feature which needs emphasizing is the cult of the textbook.
This depends upon a number of factors. The need for a doctorate tends to
make the achievement of a permanent university post something that few
teachers will reach before their thirties. By this time they may well be
married and have family responsibilities. They find it difficult to live in any
real comfort on their salaries. They know that the author of a successful
textbook will certainly earn a far greater reward than he is likely to do in
the normal way if he gives his time to serious research. His needs are great;
the publisher's offer is tempting. He knows that it is, of course, a gamble,
but if it is a successful gamble he can buy a new car, or take his family
away for the summer vacation instead of spending hot and tiring days in
New York City or Chicago, or get someone in "to do the chores or look
after the children" so that his wife may have some time in which to call
her soul her own. The result can be seen in the catalogue of any educational

publisher in the United States. Each has his history of America, his government of America, his geography of America, his principles of economics, his textbook of statistical method, or of accountancy, or of ancient history, or of medieval history, or of modern history. Once there is a large potential audience to whom teachers can address textbooks, they will be published almost beyond computation; and since the appetite grows by what it feeds on, one success is only too likely to lead to another venture, in the hope that it may be repeated. These books vary very little from one another. They usually crowd such a mass of information into their six to eight hundred pages that the student loses himself in their midst. And, worst of all, the need to get the book used in as large a range of colleges as possible leads to the suppression of any ideas that have colour or vitality or a bias that might offend. Nor must it be forgotten that one of the inevitable results on the student is that he expects to find in the textbook all he needs to know about the subject, and he tends to regard with horror the notion that he may reasonably be asked to read the original authorities out of which the subject gained its existing contours. . . .

Trends in Costs of Higher Education, 1948 *

One of the most important current problems in higher education in America is that of cost trends. The future of these trends has been a subject of extensive speculation and forecasting, and it hinges on many other factors, both assumed and real, in the complete picture. If it is assumed that our nation is to undergo another critical period in domestic and international affairs, any projection of past or present trends into the future becomes an impossibility. On the other hand, if it is assumed that our nation is to continue on a peace time economy, then the value of an investigation of past and present cost trends is extremely great.

"Research in educational finance has shown that the quantity and quality of the educational program are closely related to the level of expenditure." [1] The trend of costs is, therefore, very important and must be examined from the standpoint of overall costs, as well as from the viewpoint of the specifics involved in the segmented costs included in the total picture. Expenditures must be classified in order to understand developments as they have occurred. Cost factors of an internal nature must be studied in conjunction with the external factors affecting costs. Measures of trends, of types of costs, and of total costs must be attempted for the short run period and for the longer intervals of time, if those involved in educational pursuits are to realize and be informed on the problems that lie ahead.

* W. Lyle Wilhite, "Cost Trends in Higher Education," in *Current Trends in Higher Education* (Washington, Department of Higher Education, N.E.A., June, 1948), pp. 7, 12.
[1] "Financing Higher Education," *Higher Education for American Democracy*, Vol. V (Washington, D. C., Government Printing Office, December 1947, p. 10.

The direction of the trend of overall costs during the past several years has been upward.[2] Part of this rise has been due to an increasing price level, and part has been caused by the need for expanded facilities to carry on the educational program. The predictions of the number of students who will attend institutions of higher education in the future years vary somewhat, but only with some knowledge of recent cost trends will colleges and universities be able to predicate future action as situations change. . . .

It is imperative that each educational institution study both its short run and long run programs in view of the cost problems which may arise. Higher education has been and is such a vital part of our whole American system that it is necessary that it be maintained on a high plane. There must be a continued investment in the maintenance of present educational facilities and the creation of new ones. Adequate educational facilities and competent personnel must be available when needed if progress is to continue. The very life of the nation depends upon constant advancement through the training of the younger generation.

Historically, higher education has been conducted on a fairly low cost level. As a consequence of this fact, the rising trend, especially during recent years, has been felt more severely than it has been felt in industry and business where prices could be varied and income increased more easily. The increased costs must be met, even if they continue to rise, in order that our system of higher education may continue to progress toward the goals to which it aspires.

Can the Private Schools Survive? 1948 *

. . . What then is to be the future of the independent schools? It is no answer to say that some should be spared and some disposed of. The private schools are in this together (they have lately discovered), for their reputation is a group one.

---

[2] The average cost per student in 1940 for the entire United States amounted to approximately $375. In 1947 the average cost was approximately $470.

* Russell Lynes, "Can the Private School Survive?" *Harper's Magazine,* Vol. 196, No. 1172 (January, 1948), pp. 47-48. Used by permission of author and publisher. On the same day in early February of 1950 the presidents of two eminent universities dealt with the question of the future of higher education under private support and control. President A. Hollis Edens of Duke University, which had on a campaign to raise twelve million dollars, said that the private institutions had to be preserved. "It would be a sad day in the United States if private education were squeezed out of business. The United States probably has more privately endowed institutions than it will be able to preserve. Some of them must die. It is our duty to see a sufficient number maintained to do the job ahead." At the same time President Charles Seymour of Yale University warned that the private institutions would surely disappear unless they matched the sense of responsibility state universities had assumed for the welfare of the community. These provided "a challenging example of service for the privately-owned universities. It is important to note that their contributions to the higher learning are of the first order and their influence in the educational world is steadily increasing. Private universities have their own peculiar values, the disappearance of which would be the nation's loss. We must be careful to put them at the nation's service. . . . If we prove our worth, our freedom will not disappear. The price of freedom is service."

Anyone who has discussed private schools with public school educators has been challenged to answer a question which goes beyond matters of independence and gets to the root of the system of private education. If there were no private schools, they ask, and the parents who now expend their interest, influence, and money on them were forced to patronize the public schools, wouldn't all public education benefit? Wouldn't these mothers and fathers be more interested in the quality of public education? Wouldn't they bring pressure to bear to make public education more effective, and wouldn't this improve the educational opportunities of all American children?

These are reasonable and important questions. It seems to me that the level of public education would be raised in those communities where any appreciable number of children now go to local private schools or are sent away to school. There is almost nothing, educationally, that the public schools in such places could not do if they had the financial support and intelligent backing of the whole community. But few communities (especially the small ones) could afford to have special schools, or even special classes, for the ablest boys and girls. It would be the wealthy suburbs that would benefit first if there were no private schools, and some city school districts in which well-to-do families live. But this raises a counter question: would not special schools, or better schools in a limited number of wealthy communities, constitute a social problem just such as that which the private schools now create—one of special educational privilege based on wealth?

There is often confusion, I think, between the ideas of equal education for everyone and equal educational *opportunity* for everyone. Obviously not all children are suited for the same kind of education, and it is ridiculous to suppose that they are. There is great peril in any educational system that tends toward intellectual leveling off, and it is a mistake to think that leveling off of this sort is democratic. We need a variety of *kinds* of schools as a means of stimulating, not merely intellectual growth, but also inventiveness and the kind of intellectual independence that is basic to our society. Numerically insignificant as they are, the independent schools can provide an important element in this variety.

Dr. Frank Aydelotte, who retired a few months ago as director of the Institute of Advanced Study at Princeton, recently said that the level of education can be raised only from the top. If this is so, then there is a place for schools, free of political and other pressures, that have the resources with which to experiment, teachers who are well paid, and the advantages of a high degree of selectivity among their pupils. The problem is to make the independent schools as good as they claim to be (and this they can do only for themselves); to make them available to those who most deserve them and who will benefit most; and to make them responsible, not only to their own closed group, but for the betterment of public education as well.

How to make the independent schools available is suggested (merely suggested) by the kind of program that the GI Bill now provides for veterans. If there were ever government support of education without government interference in educational programs, this is it. In effect the government is supplying scholarships for deserving young men and women, and it is not unlikely that this may establish a pattern for the support of education in America that will outlive the GI Bill. I do not mean that the government is going to supply especially promising boys and girls with the wherewithal to send them to St. Marks or Exeter or Shipley or Brearley; but there may eventually be some provision, perhaps locally organized; perhaps organized by foundations, to enable talented boys and girls to seek out the best schools. This is a long way off, I am sure, and the private schools can benefit from it only when they have convinced the public (if they ever can) that they are not institutions of special privilege for the rich, but the very best schools that are available to any American boy or girl.

Ten years ago the Educational Policies Commission said in a report: "Once created and systematized, any program of educational thought and practice takes on professional and institutional stereotypes, and tends to outlast even profound changes in the society in which it assumed its original shape." This is what has happened to the independent schools. "Profound changes in society" since the days of their prime have made them seem as much of an anachronism as the governess in her black frilled cap. The schools are too close to their own problems to see how tradition-bound they appear from the outside, not merely to those who have regarded them with suspicion for years but to many who would like to patronize them but who distrust the imprint which they leave. They are too used to their comforts and luxuries, their often elaborate buildings, or their trappings that emanate decaying refinement, to see that these things have little to do with education and a great deal to do with the spirit that could be their undoing.

There is nothing the matter with their basic aims and ideals, with the variety of kinds of education they offer. But there is a great deal that many Americans dislike in the concept of special education for the well-to-do, especially at a time when public education needs all the support it can muster. If they are to justify themselves, the private schools must use their independence not merely as a barricade against the pressures they mistrust but as a weapon in the service of the entire community.

Charter of the Regional Council for Education, 1948 *

WHEREAS, The Governors and educators of the States of Maryland, Florida, Georgia, Louisiana, Alabama, Mississippi, West Virginia, Ten-

---

* *The Regional Council for Education* (Atlanta, 1948), Appendix. See Benjamin Fine, "Regional System Is Seen as a Great Advance in Higher Education in the South," *The New York Times,* July 24, 1949.

nessee, Arkansas, North Carolina, South Carolina, Texas, Oklahoma and Virginia have, for many years, conducted studies looking to the establishment and maintenance of jointly operated regional educational institutions for graduate, professional, technological, scientific and literary training at the higher levels; and

WHEREAS, the aforesaid states have entered into a Compact providing for the planning and establishment of regional educational facilities, such Compact to become effective upon the giving by the Congress of the United States of its consent and the legislative approval of the several states; and

WHEREAS, pending the time when the aforesaid Compact may be approved by the Congress and by the Legislatures, it is desirable that a non-profit corporation be established to conduct a survey of higher education within the several states; to accept funds and disburse the same for that purpose and to do such other and further things as may be consistent with the purposes of the Compact above referred to.

1. The name of this non-profit corporation shall be the Regional Council for Education and its present permanent address shall be: The Executive Office, The Capitol, Tallahassee, Florida.

2. The General purpose of the corporation shall be to conduct a survey of facilities for higher education within the states hereinabove named to accept and disburse funds in furtherance of the duties hereunder, and to do such other and further things as may be consistent with the purposes of the Compact heretofore entered into by the Governors of the states so named.

3. The membership of this corporation shall consist of the Governor and two citizens of each signatory state, who shall be appointed by the Governor thereof. Each Governor shall continue as a member of this corporation during his tenure of office as Governor and the members appointed by the Governor shall hold membership at his pleasure.

4. This corporation shall have perpetual existence.

5. The officers of the corporation shall be a President, a Vice President, a Secretary-Treasurer and such additional officials as shall be created by the corporation from time to time. The members of the corporation shall meet annually or at such other times as may be required and the officers shall be elected to hold office until the next annual meeting. For the purposes of this incorporation the first officers shall be Millard F. Caldwell, President, Clyde Erwin, Vice President, H. C. Byrd, Secretary-Treasurer.

6. The names and residences of the subscribers hereto are as follows:

James N. McCord	Nashville, Tennessee
Raymond R. Paty	Atlanta, Georgia
Doak S. Campbell	Tallahassee, Florida
Joseph Hillis Miller	Gainesville, Florida
Millard F. Caldwell	Tallahassee, Florida

7. The members shall formulate, establish, alter or rescind by-laws not inconsistent with law and provide for a Board of Directors, an executive committee, a study committee and such other committees as may be found desirable with such powers and authority as may be lawfully delegated to them from time to time.

8. The corporation shall be limited in its authority to contract indebtedness and liability to two-thirds of the amount specified below and to purchase and hold real property in the aggregate amount of funds pledged or subscribed from time to time for the furtherance of the aims of the corporation, in no event to exceed $100,000.00 in value.

9. This corporation shall have all the general duties and powers of other non-profit corporations and all duties and powers reasonably necessary for the complete accomplishment of all the objectives of the corporation as set forth herein.

General Conclusions of the Temporary Commission on the Need for a State University in New York, 1948 *

The State of New York is confronted with a serious problem in the field of higher education, the implications of which reach far into the future. The great upsurge of demand for opportunities for higher education, though of relatively recent origin, according to all indications is likely to continue unabated. This demand is not being adequately taken care of today, and will be even less well met in the future under the State's existing facilities and type of organization.

The action taken by the State in this critical situation may affect the whole course of development of our higher educational system, the happiness of youth, and the prosperity of our population for many years to come.

The State has a large number and a great variety of colleges and universities. Some are supported by the State and others by New York City, but the large majority are privately supported and operated, under charters granted by the State. Geographically, they are widely distributed. Several of them are recognized as among the leading colleges and universities of the United States and of the world.

These institutions until recently served with reasonable adequacy a student population—full- and part-time—of some 200,000 but even then a substantial proportion of the youth of this State was denied the opportunities for higher education by economic and other barriers, including discrimination on account of race, creed, color, or national origin.

The increasing complexity of modern life, the rise in standards of living, and the rapid technological advances prompt youth to reach out for higher education as a means for better understanding of the problems of society,

* *Report of the Temporary Commission on the Need for a State University*, 1948, pp. 14-18.

enjoyment of the better things of life, and more effective preparation for appropriate trades and professions. It is imperative to an expanding democratic society to make sure that their quest is satisfied. The war and postwar periods have especially demonstrated the need of the Nation for more college and university trained personnel.

Under the existing organization of higher education a substantial number of youth are debarred from attending college by lack of resources with which to pay tuition or living expenses while attending school. Thus, less than half of New York's high school graduates whose records place them among the highest fourth of their classes go on to college. Most of the others in this quartile, as well as many other students qualified to benefit by college education, do not have funds sufficient to enable them to attend college.

The necessarily high tuition fees of the private colleges and universities keep many students from enroling. An even greater barrier to the student living away from home is the extra cost of room and board. Temporarily, the Federal Government through the G.I. Bill of Rights has opened the opportunity for higher education to large numbers of young veterans who could not otherwise afford college training. But when these benefits run out, the economic exclusions will again operate unless public action is taken.

In addition, some members of New York's large minority groups have had difficulty in securing access to educational facilities on an equal basis with other students. This is true not only on the college level but on the professional and graduate school levels as well. This discrimination is repellent to the American spirit and must be eliminated.

Under the pressure of the veteran enrolment as well as of increased applications from nonveterans for admission, the enrolment (full-time, part-time and extension) in the institutions of higher education of this State has expanded to 310,000, or 50 per cent above the prewar figure.

The veteran registration will continue to be significant through 1955, and may continue to be a factor affecting enrolment until 1960, while the nonveteran enrolment, as indicated by the trends in the number of students graduating from high school and in the percentage of graduates interested in college education, will continue to increase rapidly both in absolute numbers and in relative importance. Clearly, on the basis of student demand, the pressures now felt will grow rather than diminish.

The Associated Colleges of Upper New York with their three emergency colleges are temporarily satisfying a part of the need to accommodate this increase in enrolment. While two of the member colleges, Sampson and Champlain, have certain potentialities for future use, either as community colleges or as small four-year institutions, the charter of the three colleges expires in 1949. Moreover, the properties belong to the Federal Government.

If, therefore, this demand is to be satisfied in the future, publicly supported low-cost facilities, as well as other aids to students which will remove the economic barriers standing in the way of their attendance, must be considerably expanded. There must also be measures to remove discrimination against members of minority groups.

At this time when costs are high and large additional expenditures of funds are required, private colleges and universities are unable fully to meet the needs of the students. Tuition charges have already been advanced and the rate of return from endowment funds is low; and because of high taxes there is less assurance than formerly of sustained support from private sources. The result is that New York State, which has come to depend so largely upon private philanthropy for the financing of higher education, is likely to suffer serious deterioration in its program of education unless tax funds are used to provide additional facilities and financial support.

To the extent that existing institutions are not equipped to meet the present and prospective needs, the state and local governments must stand ready to help.

This expansion of the public provision for higher education, which is greatly needed, will be in line with a long established trend in this State. Over the years, New York has extended its concern for higher education, introducing scholarships and establishing a number of institutions of its own in various specialized fields. This extension has been particularly rapid in the past seven or eight years, as is shown by the rise in the State's appropriations for higher education from $7.2 million in 1940-41 to $20.3 million in 1947-48.

New York City has been expanding its own municipal colleges until they now serve almost 29,000 full-time students and almost 40,000 part-time students at a cost to the City of $12.4 million in 1947-48. Thus the combined state and local support for higher education today aggregates almost $33 million.

The full scope of the State's program can be seen from the detailed picture. Of the $20 million state appropriation, $3.2 million is for scholarships to 8,500 students, while $17 million goes to the support of 32 institutions with a total enrolment of 28,500 students (almost all full-time).

Nine institutions are operated for the State, under contract, by private institutions. Six of these are professional colleges of which four (agriculture, home economics, veterinary medicine, and industrial relations) are operated by Cornell University. The four have an aggregate enrolment of 2,563 students, and cost the State $4.8 million annually. The College of Forestry, with 865 students and an appropriation of $738,000, is operated by Syracuse University. The College of Ceramics, with 377 students and an appropriation of $280,000, is operated by Alfred University. The remaining three institutions at Sampson, Mohawk, and Champlain are in the liberal arts field. They are the emergency colleges, enroling 8,256 students and have cost the State $2.4 million in operations to date.

Of the remaining 23 state institutions, 11 are teachers colleges, with a total enrolment of 10,552 students and appropriations of $4.1 million in 1947-48; and one is the Maritime Academy, with 358 students and an appropriation of $490,000. Finally, there are 11 institutes providing two-year terminal technical, and in some cases agricultural, education for 5,518 students at a cost to the State of $2.2 million.

Thus the State has established extensive facilities in several fields of specialized higher education, but has not as yet provided a complete state university program of its own.

The conditions of the times require a broadening of the public provisions for higher education on all fronts. They require also more effective assurance of equality of educational opportunity to all qualified youth. These ends can best be served by a long-range program comprised of the following measures:

1. Immediate establishment of a State University as a corporate entity.
2. Appointment by the Governor for the initial development of this State University of a temporary Board of Trustees for a six-year term and operating under the general supervision of the Board of Regents. By or before the end of this period, this Board shall present, together with a report of its activities, recommendations for the permanent operation of governance of the University within the higher educational system of the State as established under the Board of Regents.
3. The State University should place prime emphasis upon the development of widely distributed and greatly expanded facilites throughout the State and may include as a part of the distributed facilities on a single campus a university program comprising undergraduate, graduate, and professional work, either by taking over an existing institution or by building a new one. The University, in conjunction with private and local public institutions, will provide a balanced and adequate program of higher education for the State.
4. The establishment of full four-year college programs in certain sections of the State not adequately served by any university or college, either by taking over and expanding existing institutions or by building new ones, or by state aid.
5. Establishment of two medical centers by the State, including schools of medicine, dentistry, nursing, and public health, one upstate and one in the New York metropolitan area. This program may be achieved either by taking over and expanding existing private institutions or by building new ones, or by state aid.
6. Establishment of an additional state-supported school of veterinary medicine at one of the medical centers.

7. Consideration of financial assistance to private medical schools where special need exists.

8. Broadening of the programs of the state teachers colleges to include training of preschool, elementary school, and secondary school teachers and to provide in-service training as well as to authorize these colleges to grant graduate degrees in appropriate fields; and establishment of two centers, one upstate and one in the New York metropolitan area, to train teachers for technical institutes and community colleges.

9. Provision of state aid for teacher education in the four municipal colleges of New York City, on the basis of the relation of the number of teachers in New York City to the number upstate. On the basis of current upstate support, the immediate state aid to New York City would approximate $2.9 million, and more in the future.

10. Establishment, with state aid, of locally administered public community colleges, offering two-year terminal general and technical education, thus providing for an important unmet need in the educational system of New York State. The capital costs of these colleges should be shared equally by the localities and by the State. One-third of the current costs should be financed by local contributions, one-third by student fees, and one-third by state aid under a long-range master plan prepared by the Trustees of the State University, and approved by the Board of Regents, and by the Governor. The existing state institutes should be converted into local community colleges where feasible.

11. The establishment of an expanded scholarship program involving scholarships without stipends and an increased number of scholarships with stipends, for both general education and graduate and professional work.

12. Development of a comprehensive system of counseling service in the educational institutions of the State under the leadership of the State Education Department.

13. Charging the Board of Regents with responsibility for insuring admission to colleges and universities without regard to race, color, creed, or national origin, with power to enforce its orders.

Some of these measures can be effected immediately; others will require steady effort over many years. These measures comprehend a long-range program which will serve the State as a guide in the development of higher education.

In giving its support to such a broad program, the State would be in accord with the American ideal of providing education at low cost to students at the undergraduate, graduate, and professional levels. In a free society the public welfare, the good of the individual, and the promotion of the democratic process require that equal educational opportunity be provided to all qualified persons if adequate civic, technical, and professional leadership is to be developed.

Governor Thomas E. Dewey Approves the Bill About Complaints Against Educational Institutions for Alleged Discrimination of Applicants, 1948 *

This bill is a further step by New York State to reduce obnoxious and undemocratic barriers based on religious belief or the accident of birth. Discrimination is already unlawful in our public schools. This bill adds to already existing provisions on the subject a clear and extensive prohibition of discrimination in admissions against any person because of race, religion, creed, color or national origin by any school of higher education. It carefully preserves, however, religious freedom and the right of religious groups to establish and control schools in furtherance of their religion.

It is the product of two years' study, debate and deliberation by the Commission on a State University. The Commission found that such discrimination existed in certain instances. This new law presents the Commission's final agreement upon a procedure to bring such discrimination to an end.

As a nation, perhaps more than any other in the world, we are proud of and devoted to the education of our children. College and university education has become the goal of an ever increasing number of parents. Nothing can be more ugly or agonizing to any parent than the realization that his child is to be denied his full opportunity for learning and contribution merely because of his parentage. Such restraints are foreign to a country of growth, a country of progress, a country of moral leadership and a country born and preserved by the sacrifice of those who thought they were fighting for freedom.

Education and particularly higher education is a quest for the truth; baseless distinctions have no place in that quest. Education controls the opportunity for professional careers; careers should depend only upon ability to serve. Education flourishes in the controversy of divergent groups, in conflicting ideas and ideals; intellectual inbreeding has always proved disastrous.

This new law is another demonstration of the solid progress to be made upon the basis of full discussion, mutual education, persuasion and agreement.

The bill is approved.

(Signed)   THOMAS E. DEWEY

* *Ibid.*, p. 52.

An Act in Relation to Complaints Against Educational Institutions for Alleged Discrimination in the Admission of Applicants, 1948 *

The People of the State of New York, represented in Senate and Assembly, do enact as follows:

Section 1. Chapter twenty-one of the laws of nineteen hundred nine, entitled "An act relating to education, constituting chapter sixteen of the consolidated laws," as amended and recodified by chapter eight hundred twenty of the laws of nineteen hundred forty-seven, is hereby amended by adding thereto a new section, to be section three hundred thirteen, to read as follows:

§ 313. (1) Declaration of policy. It is hereby declared to be the policy of the state that the American ideal of equality of opportunity requires that students, otherwise qualified, be admitted to educational institutions without regard to race, color, religion, creed or national origin, except that, with regard to religious or denominational educational institutions, students, otherwise qualified, shall have the equal opportunity to attend therein without discrimination because of race, color or national origin. It is a fundamental American right for members of various religious faiths to establish and maintain educational institutions exclusively or primarily for students of their own religious faith or to effectuate the religious principles in furtherance of which they are maintained. Nothing herein contained shall impair or abridge that right.

(2) Definitions. (*a*) Educational institution means any educational institution of post-secondary grade subject to the visitation, examination or inspection by the state board of regents or the state commissioner of education.

(*b*) Religious or denominational educational institution means an educational institution which is operated, supervised or controlled by a religious or denominational organization and which has certified to the state commissioner of education that it is a religious or denominational educational institution.

(3) Unfair educational practices. It shall be an unfair educational practice for an educational institution after September fifteenth, nineteen hundred forty-eight:

(*a*) To exclude or limit or otherwise discriminate against any person or persons seeking admission as students to such institution because of race, religion, creed, color, or national origin; except that nothing in this section shall be deemed to affect, in any way, the right of a religious or denominational educational institution to select its students exclusively or primarily from members of such religion or denomination or from giving preference in such selection to such members or to make such selection of its students

* *Laws of the State of New York*, 1948, Chapter 753.

as is calculated by such institution to promote the religious principles for which it is established or maintained.

(b) To penalize any individual because he has initiated, testified, participated or assisted in any proceedings under this section.

(c) It shall not be an unfair educational practice for any educational institution to use criteria other than race, religion, creed, color or national origin in the admission of students.

(4) Certification of religious and denominational institutions. An educational institution operated, supervised or controlled by a religious or denominational organization may, through its chief executive officer, certify in writing to the commissioner that it is so operated, controlled or supervised and that it elects to be considered a religious or denominational educational institution, and it thereupon shall be deemed such an institution for the purposes of this section.

(5) Procedure. (a) Any person seeking admission as a student who claims to be aggrieved by an alleged unfair educational practice, hereinafter referred to as the petitioner, may himself, or by his parent or guardian, make, sign and file with the commissioner of education a verified petition which shall set forth the particulars thereof and contain such other information as may be required by the commissioner. The commissioner shall thereupon cause an investigation to be made in connection therewith and after such investigation if he shall determine that probable cause exists for crediting the allegations of the petition, he shall attempt by informal methods of persuasion, conciliation or mediation to induce the elimination of such alleged unfair educational practice.

(b) Where the commissioner has reason to believe that an applicant or applicants have been discriminated against, except that preferential selection by religious or denominational institutions of students of their own religion or denomination shall not be considered an act of discrimination, he may initiate an investigation on his own motion.

(c) The commissioner shall not disclose what takes place during such informal efforts at persuasion, conciliation or mediation nor shall he offer in evidence in any proceeding the facts adduced in such informal efforts.

(d) A petition pursuant to this section must be filed with the commissioner within one year after the alleged unfair educational practice was committed.

(e) If such informal methods fail to induce the elimination of the alleged unfair educational practice, the commissioner shall have power to refer the matter to the board of regents which shall issue and cause to be served upon such institution, hereinafter called the respondent, a complaint setting forth the alleged unfair educational practice charged and a notice of hearing before the board of regents, at a place therein fixed to be held not less than twenty days after the service of said complaint.

Any complaint issued pursuant to this section must be issued within two years after the alleged unfair educational practice was committed.

(*f*) The respondent shall have the right to answer the original and any amended complaint and to appear at such hearing by counsel, present evidence and examine and cross-examine witnesses.

(*g*) The commissioner and the board of regents shall have the power to subpoena witnesses, compel their attendance, administer oaths, take testimony under oath and require the production of evidence relating to the matter in question before it or them. The testimony taken at the hearing, which shall be public shall be under oath and shall be reduced to writing and filed with the board of regents.

(*h*) After the hearing is completed the board of regents shall file an intermediate report which shall contain its findings of fact and conclusions upon the issues in the proceeding. A copy of such report shall be served on the parties to the proceeding. Any such party within twenty days thereafter, may file with the regents exceptions to the findings of fact and conclusions, with a brief in support thereof, or may file a brief in support of such findings of fact and conclusions.

(*i*) If, upon all the evidence, the regents shall determine that the respondent has engaged in an unfair educational practice, the regents shall state their findings of fact and conclusions and shall issue and cause to be served upon such respondent a copy of such findings and conclusions and an order requiring the respondent to cease and desist from such unfair educational practice, or such other order as they deem just and proper.

(*j*) If, upon all the evidence, the regents shall find that a respondent has not engaged in any unfair educational practice, the regents shall state their findings of fact and conclusions and shall issue and cause to be served on the petitioner and respondent, a copy of such findings and conclusions, and an order dismissing the complaint as to such respondent.

(6) Judicial review and enforcement. (*a*) Whenever the board of regents has issued an order as provided in this section it may apply to the supreme court for the enforcement of such order by a proceeding brought in the supreme court within the third judicial district. The board of regents shall file with the court a transcript of the record of its hearing, and the court shall have jurisdiction of the proceeding and of the questions determined therein, and shall have power to make an order annulling or confirming, wholly or in part, or modifying the determination reviewed. The order of the supreme court shall be subject to review by the appellate division of the supreme court and the court of appeals, upon the appeal of any party to the proceeding, in the same manner and with the same effect as provided on an appeal from a final judgment made by the court without a jury.

(*b*) Any party to the proceeding, aggrieved by a final order of the board of regents, may obtain a judicial review thereof by a proceeding under article seventy-eight of the civil practice act, which shall be brought in the appellate division of the supreme court for the third judicial department.

(7) Regents empowered to promulgate rules and regulations. The regents from time to time may adopt, promulgate, amend or rescind rules and regulations to effectuate the purposes and provisions of this section.

(8) The commissioner shall include in his annual report to the legislature (1) a resume of the nature and substance of the cases disposed of through public hearings, and (2) recommendations for further action to eliminate discrimination in education if such is needed.

§ 2. This act shall take effect July first, nineteen hundred forty-eight.

Some Standards of the New England Association of Colleges and Secondary Schools, 1949 *

This organization shall be called "The New England Association of Colleges and Secondary Schools."

Its object † shall be the advancement of the cause of education in the colleges and secondary schools of New England.

Minimum requirements for an acceptable senior college, university, or other institution of higher education granting the baccalaureate or higher degree . . . (Amended December 5, 1941).

An institution of higher education shall have clearly defined educational objectives. Its application for membership in the Association will be judged by:

---

* Taken from the official printed rules and standards of the association, in force in 1949.

† Wide diversity in entrance requirements to the colleges in the latter part of the past century caused much unrest, uncertainty, and confusion in higher as well as in secondary education all over the United States. Several conditions caused this confusion. The immense increase in economic wealth of the American people enabled more young people than formerly to go to and remain in school; from the laboratories of the experimental psychologists came evidence that tended to deny the validity of the doctrine of formal mental discipline and the transfer of training, with the result that the ancient dogma of disciplinary values in the curricula of secondary education was beginning to fall under suspicion and attack. Also, psychological studies on individual differences and of the social backgrounds of pupils and their choice of careers were appearing, the significance of the period of adolescence was emphasized by G. Stanley Hall and John Dewey was promoting the general thesis that education is life and not preparation for life. Moreover, the implication of the report of the Committee on Secondary School Studies (The Committee of Ten) in 1893 was that one subject was as good as another when taught for the same length of time. Out of these conditions developed the regional standardizing educational associations, beginning in New England in 1885, followed by the Middle States and Maryland in 1892, the North Central in 1895, the Southern in 1895, and the Northwestern in 1918. Each of these six associations was the invention of educational necessity. See I. L. Kandel, *History of Secondary Education* (Boston, Houghton Mifflin Co., 1930), pp. 466-98; Edgar W. Knight, "The Southern Association: Retrospect and Prospect," *The Georgia Review*, I (Spring, 1947); R. L. Duffus, *Democracy Enters College* (New York, Charles Scribner's Sons, 1936). The standardizing associations were concerned in the early years with quantitative standards. In recent times these associations seem to show some concern for qualitative standards. In addition to the standards of the New England Association only those of the North Central Association (and only for secondary schools) are here given. For the most part the standards of all these regional standardizing agencies are somewhat similar.

A. The effectiveness of its various curricula in realizing its objectives
B. The preparation and experience of its faculty
C. The administrative leadership it affords
D. Its provisions for admitting students who are well qualified to benefit from its offerings
E. The adequacy of its physical plant
F. Its financial ability to carry out the purposes it has set

The minimum requirements outlined below are meant to serve as a guide to the institution applying for membership in the Association and as an aid to the committee of the Association in determining the adequacy of the total arrangements within the given institution to realize its avowed purposes. The decision will be influenced more by evidence that the institution is functioning as a whole in fulfilling its objectives than by its ability to meet each specific standard.

Institutions in the third group should be able to submit evidence that their educational standards are on the same high level as those in the senior colleges and universities of New England in all points mentioned above.

The information blank is comprehensive, in order that the institution may present the total arrangements and practices for realizing its avowed purposes.

As a general rule the application of any institution for membership in the New England Association of Colleges and Secondary Schools will not be considered until a period of at least two years has elapsed after the graduation of its first class.

GENERAL CONTROL

The general control of an institution of higher education should be the function of a board of trustees, and the institution should not be privately owned and/or operated for profit.

FACULTY

In senior colleges, universities, and other institutions there should be a large percentage of faculty members teaching full-time within the institution.

In senior colleges and universities members of the faculty of professorial rank should have at least two years of study in their respective fields in a recognized graduate school. In general, heads of departments should have a doctor's degree or a corresponding professional or technical education or attainment. Members of the faculty doing research should have an adequate background of training and experience in their respective fields, judged on the basis of the highest standards. Instructors or other members of the faculty below professorial rank should show evidence of adequate preparation, especially in their own subjects, as well as successful experience and teaching efficiency.

In other institutions of higher education granting the baccalaureate or higher degree there should be evidence that a high percentage of members of the faculty teaching the strictly academic subjects have a background of preparation and teaching experience comparable to that of members of the faculty of senior colleges and universities doing work of the same kind and on the same level. Members of the faculty teaching technical or other courses in a highly specialized field requiring a high degree of skill or creative ability should have a background of training and experience which will be readily recognized as equivalent to the academic preparation of faculty members of a senior college or university teaching academic subjects.

The ratio of the number of students to the number of faculty members above the grade of assistant should not exceed fifteen to one.

The teaching schedule of each member of the faculty should be so arranged that the total load per week shall vary according to the subject taught, but in no case should this load exceed eighteen classroom hours or their equivalent per week. Extension work, late-afternoon or evening classes, work in other institutions, regularly assigned weekly conference hours, and administrative duties constitute the equivalent of classroom work and should be taken into consideration in determining the total weekly load.

The number of students in a laboratory class should not exceed the number for which adequate facilities are on hand nor, when judged by the nature of the subject matter, the number that an instructor can handle effectively.

Program of Studies

A senior college should offer instruction in at least eight major fields of liberal arts and sciences, in each of which at least one teacher of professorial rank should devote his whole time to instruction in that field.

Each curriculum in the program of studies of each undergraduate college in a university should include a sufficient number of courses to provide an adequate cultural or general background and a degree of concentration and continuity of subject matter to fulfill the avowed purpose of the curriculum. In each major field of instruction there should be one or more teachers of professorial rank who devote their entire time to instruction in that field.

In other institutions of higher education granting the baccalaureate or higher degree each curriculum in the program of studies should include a sufficient number of courses to provide an adequate cultural or general background and a degree of concentration and continuity of subject matter to fulfill the avowed purpose of the curriculum. In each major field of instruction there should be one or more teachers of professorial rank who devote their time to instruction in that field.

REQUIREMENTS FOR ADMISSION

As a general practice an institution of higher education should demand for admission the satisfactory completion of a course in a secondary school approved by a recognized accrediting agency, or the equivalent of such a course. In school systems organized on the 6-3-3 plan the course may be three years in length; otherwise, the usual four-year course should be the basis for admission. The major portion of the secondary school course accepted for admission should provide an adequate foundation for the curriculum to which the student is admitted.

REQUIREMENTS FOR GRADUATION

A senior college, university, or other institution of higher education granting the baccalaureate or higher degree should require for graduation from the undergraduate curricula the equivalent of one hundred twenty semester hours, that is, four years of college work as evaluated at present, with such further scholastic qualitative requirements as are necessary to the attainment of its objectives.

RECOGNITION BY OTHER INSTITUTIONS

A senior college, university, or other institution of higher education granting the baccalaureate or higher degree should be able to present evidence that its graduates are prepared to enter recognized graduate schools in other colleges or universities as candidates for advanced degrees.

GUIDANCE PROGRAM

A senior college, university, or other institution of higher education granting the baccalaureate or higher degree should have a definite program for determining the intellectual capacity of all of its students. It is desirable that provision should be made for studying abilities of the students as a basis for educational and vocational guidance.

ACTIVITIES PROGRAM

A senior college, university, or other institution of higher education granting the baccalaureate or higher degree should provide opportunities for a well-regulated program of such student activities as are necessary to meet the cultural, social, and physical needs of its students.

LIBRARY

A senior college or university should have a professionally administered library, adequate to the effective realization of its stated educational objectives. The library should contain at least eight thousand volumes, exclusive of public documents, so distributed that the various curricula under the stated objectives are each provided with adequate reference material. One of more full-time professionally trained librarians should be employed, and at least one should have full faculty ranking.

Other institutions of higher education granting the baccalaureate or higher degree should have professionally administered libraries, adequate to the effective realization of their stated objectives. In those institutions offering a program in a highly specialized field or fields, where the various laboratories themselves serve the need for reference material to a greater extent than in a liberal arts program, the number of volumes may be less than in a senior college or university, but in no case should the number of volumes, exclusive of public documents, be less than five thousand. The volumes should be so distributed that the various curricula under the stated objectives are each provided with adequate reference material. One or more full-time professionally trained librarians should be employed, and it is desirable that one should have full faculty ranking.

The extent to which the library is actually used by both students and faculty; the number, the variety, the recency of publication, and suitability of the books; the sufficiency of space set aside for quiet study and leisure-time reading; the accessibility of other library materials, such as periodicals and newspapers; and the amount of the annual appropriation for new books are among the factors which will be considered in judging the adequacy of the library.

Student Health

Each institution should be able to present evidence that adequate provision has been made for medical attention, nurse service, infirmary accommodations, and other precautionary measures to insure the physical health and care of its students.

Physical Plant

The material equipment and upkeep of the institution, including its lands, buildings, classrooms, libraries, laboratories, and apparatus for the teaching of all laboratory subjects should be sufficient to insure efficient operation. The physical plant should be adequate to provide safe, sanitary, and healthful conditions, as judged by modern standards.

Finance

Each institution should be able to submit evidence of sound financial structure and operation over a period of at least three years.

Standards for Independent Secondary Schools
(Amended December 6, 1946)*

1. A school applying should have been in existence for at least five years as a college preparatory school with an integrated course of studies,

* *Ibid.*

with the majority of the students enrolled for at least two consecutive years, and with an overall program having regard to the spiritual, social, and physical welfare of the students. No school which is wholly or in the main a tutoring school shall be eligible for admission.

2. The school applying must have at least one third of its students college candidates and a satisfactory ratio of faculty to students.

3. The school applying must submit the following credentials:

   a. A satisfactory summary of its course of study; the qualifications of its faculty; the nature of its plant and equipment; and a summary of its college entrance record in terms of the questionnaire issued by the Committee on Admissions.

   b. Five confidential letters from heads of institutions which are members of the Association, of which not more than three shall be from either schools or colleges. . . .

4. The school applying must be inspected either by members of the Committee on Admissions or by deputies appointed by the Chairman.

5. All applications should be made and data presented prior to October 15 of any year. Final action can take place only through ratification of the recommendations of the Admissions Committee by the Annual Meeting of the Association each December.

Standards for Public Secondary Schools
(Adopted December 6, 1946)*

1. The function of a secondary school is to develop in each of its pupils in accordance with his ability the knowledge, power, interests, habits and skills which will make him a useful member of society, and enable him to realize his highest personal potentialities. Preparation for study in higher institutions is an important part of this function, but no less important is the training of the pupils whose formal education will end with the secondary school.

2. A well balanced program of studies, competent administration and instruction, and a high moral tone in the school are essential factors to the fulfillment of its function. The results of such fulfillment will be shown in the pupils by mastery of subject matter, the acquisition of correct habits of thought and study, right social and civil attitudes and by successful careers after leaving school. A school unable to conform in one or more respects to the following standards should justify this failure by clear evidence of satisfactory results.

3. The requirement *for graduation* from a secondary school shall be the completion of at least fifteen units, following the completion of eight years of elementary school work or the equivalent. Fractional units may be counted toward this total. In systems differently organized, for example a

* *Ibid.*

ninth grade. A unit is defined as a year's work in one subject, representing approximately one-fourth of a full year of school work for a pupil of normal 6-3-3 or a 6-6 system, four of the fifteen units may be completed in the ability. To count as a unit, the recitation periods must aggregate at least 120 sixty-minute hours of class work. It is recommended that unprepared work count one-half as much time as prepared work. The Association recommends a school year of at least 180 actual school days, a school day of at least five hours exclusive of intermissions, and school periods of at least forty minutes in length.

4. Guidance procedures should be sufficiently adequate to provide each pupil with the data necessary for making wise educational and vocational plans, and to cause him to consider his school experiences in the light of his probable future activities.

5. Within the framework of these standards the school should ensure that each pupil receive instruction in those courses necessary to secure admission to the institution of higher learning which he has chosen.

6. A system of records should be maintained to provide adequate information about each pupil. Such records should include data about the academic progress, health, results of standardized achievement and intelligence tests, attendance, extra-curricular activities, and the necessary personal and family data for each pupil.

7. At least four teachers, including the principal, should be employed on full time in a four-year secondary school. The principal's schedule should allow time for his duties of administration and supervision. A clerical force should be employed sufficient to allow teachers and principal to attend chiefly to instruction and guidance. The number of pupils per teacher, based on average membership, should not exceed twenty-five.

8. Teachers of academic subjects should have completed at least four years of study in institutions of collegiate grade, including professional training equivalent to twelve semester hours. Teachers of non-academic subjects should have completed at least two years of study beyond the secondary school, including courses in the subjects taught. Successful teaching or work experience may be accepted in partial fulfillment of this requirement.

9. No teachers should give class instruction for more than five periods or more than 150 pupil-periods daily. The Association recommends 125 pupil-periods per teacher as a satisfactory daily average, and that the size of classes should ordinarily be limited to thirty as a maximum.

10. The construction and care of school buildings should be such as to ensure hygenic and safety conditions for both pupils and teachers. Periodic inspections of the plant should be a regular part of administrative routine.

11. Laboratory and library facilities should be adequate for all subjects taught. Systematic instruction in the use of the library should be given.

The equipment of the school should include a suitable gymnasium and an adequate plot for out-of-door games.

12. Provisions should be made for teacher work rooms and rest rooms, and for adequate facilities for duplicating instructional materials.

13. Each pupil should receive instruction in the essentials of personal and community health; and, unless excused for cause, he should take part in regular physical exercise under trained instructors.

14. Provision should be made for the services of a school nurse and school doctor who will conduct thorough physical examinations of all pupils at least once a year and maintain records of such examinations.

Policies, Regulations, and Criteria of the North Central Association for the Approval of Secondary Schools, 1949 *

The aims of the North Central Association of Colleges and Secondary Schools are, first, to bring about a better acquaintance, a keener sympathy and a heartier cooperation between the colleges and secondary schools of this territory; second, to consider common educational problems and to devise the best ways and means of solving them; and third, to promote the physical, intellectual and moral well-being of students by urging proper sanitary conditions of school buildings, adequate library and laboratory facilities, and higher standards of scholarship.

The Association aims to approve only those schools which possess organization, teaching force, standards of scholarship, equipment, and *esprit de corps,* of such character as will unhesitatingly commend them to any educator, college or university in the territory of the North Central Association. The Association believes, furthermore, that the policies and regulations adopted and the criteria used as bases for the approval of secondary schools should be evaluative in character and should serve to encourage a maximum of growth and development on the part of its member schools.

GUIDING PRINCIPLES

1. An institution should be judged upon the basis of the total pattern it presents as an institution of its type. While it seems necessary that institutions be judged in terms of particular characteristics, it should be recognized that wide variations will appear in the degree of success achieved.

2. It should be accepted as a principle of procedure that deficiency in

* From official printed statements of the association, 1949. For practices of this association in accrediting higher educational institutions, see its *Revised Manual of Accrediting,* 1941, pp. 1-2. "You will note that we do not employ 'standards' as such. In 1934 the North Central Association gave up specific minimum requirements for the accreditation of colleges and universities. Our evaluation is based on evidence concerning the quality of the total program of an institution in relation to the quality of similar institutions." Letter from Manning M. Pattillo, Jr., Assistant Secretary, Commission on Colleges and Universities, to Edgar W. Knight May 5, 1949.

one field may be compensated for by strength in other fields—no school should be denied accreditation because it fails to meet a specific standard if its total pattern of achievement is good.

3. A school should be judged, in so far as is possible, in terms of its own philosophy and the purpose which it serves in its own community.

4. Criteria should be flexible, and of a type that can readily adjust themselves to changing conditions. The fact should be recognized that individual differences exist among schools and among communities.

5. Objective criteria should be based upon a sufficient amount of research and experimentation to establish their validity as measuring instruments.

6. While it seems desirable that criteria regard as basic certain characteristics, such as faculty preparation, the intellectual and moral tone of a school, the nature of the school plant, the adequacy of equipment and supplies, the quality of the school library and library service, the condition of the records, the policies of the board of education, the financial status, the teaching load, and the educational program, it should be recognized that considerable divergence from normal standards may occur in one of these characteristics without greatly detracting from the educational merits of an institution. Uniformity in every detail stifles educational experimentation and is not only unnecessary but undesirable.

7. Criteria, to be of maximum value, must be stimulating and conducive to educational growth; they should provide the facilities for continuous self evaluation and the incentive to strive endlessly toward higher goals of achievement.

POLICIES OF THE COMMISSION ON SECONDARY SCHOOLS

Policy 1.

A school which has submitted its annual report to the State Committee, which is in the highest class of schools as officially listed by the properly constituted educational authorities of the state and which has been approved continuously for five years shall not be dropped without a year's warning except by a three-fourths vote of the members of the Commission present. A school which has not been approved continuously for five years may be dropped without warning.

Policy 2.

It is the policy of the Commission to recommend the removal from the approved list of the Association any school which after a year's warning continues to violate the same Regulation or Criterion for approval which was violated the previous year. Upon the recommendation of the State Committee, this policy, however, may be waived by a three-fourths vote of the Commission members present.

State Committees are encouraged to advise a school which has been warned for violation of a Regulation or a Criterion to submit to an evaluation, using the *Evaluative Criteria*. This evaluation is to be carried out when, in the opinion of the State Committee, it will assist in improving the condition for which the school was warned, or in explaining the extenuating circumstances which may justify a second warning, or even the discontinuance of the warning.

Policy 3.

Secondary schools are approved for an indefinite period. All schools on the approved list, however, shall submit such reports as the Commission may require. The certificate showing that a school is approved by the Association is valid as long as the school meets the conditions for approval as defined by the Commission on Secondary Schools and approved by the Association.

Policy 4.

Credits acquired through summer session work, extension courses, correspondence courses, or state examinations will be accepted by the Association as counting toward the preparation of the teacher, if such credits are accepted by an approved institution of higher education.

The Association recognizes that credit established in accordance with the recommendations in *A Guide to the Evaluation of Educational Experiences in the Armed Services* is sound. Such credit may be counted as a part of the preparation of the teacher, when accepted by an approved institution of higher education.

Policy 5.

The Chairman of the State Committee is the official agent of communication between the approved schools of the state and the Secretary of the Commission on Secondary Schools. He is responsible to the Commission for the distribution, collection and filing of all reports, and for such other duties as the Association may direct. In those states having an inspector of schools or other person with similar duties appointed by the state university, such person shall be the Chairman of the State Committee. In those states where there is no such official appointed by the state university, the inspector of schools or other person having similar duties appointed by the state superintendent of public instruction or state commissioner of education shall be the Chairman of the State Committee. In all other states, the Chairman of the State Committee is elected by the Association for an indefinite term on nomination of the Executive Committee.

Policy 6.

The interim authority for interpreting Policies, Regulations, and Criteria for the Approval of Secondary Schools is the Secretary of the Commission on Secondary Schools.

Policy 7.

It is the policy of the Association to warn high schools for violation of the conditions for eligibility to the approved list of the Association and to drop from this list any high school which violates the same Regulation or Criterion during consecutive years. High schools also may be warned or dropped whenever it becomes evident that they frequently violate conditions for eligibility to the approved list. In the case of a minor violation, the Association may instruct the State Committee to advise the school concerned. It is the policy of the Association not to take an action which is different from that recommended by the State Committee without first notifying the committee of the state concerned.

State Committees are encouraged to advise a school which has been warned for violation of a Regulation or a Criterion to submit to an evaluation, using the *Evaluative Criteria.* (See Policy 2)

Policy 8.

In the case of individual schools of any state, reasonable deviations from Regulations and Criteria may be accepted by the Commission and approved by the Association when recommended by the State Committee. Such recommendations must be supported by substantial evidence showing that these deviations are justifiable.

No school should be denied approval if it fails to meet fully all Criteria and Regulations, provided its total educational pattern is good, as revealed by the results of a competent survey or other evidence. Policy 8 also applies to new schools seeking admission. State Committees and Reviewing Committees are justified in expecting closer adherence to published Regulations and Criteria in the case of new schools. Special attention, however, shall be given to the reports of State Committees which have used the Evaluative Criteria as one of the steps to be taken by new schools in making their applications for admission. It is recommended that State Committees ask each prospective new school to carry out at least a self evaluation using the *Evaluative Criteria.* Such schools should be encouraged to use the full Cooperative Study procedure, supplemented by a review of the self evaluation by a visiting committee or by the State Committee. . . .

An International University Is Proposed in Congress, 1949 *

A BILL

To create and establish an international university for the purpose of promoting universal understanding, justice, and permanent peace, to provide for the course of study, management, and operation of the University, and for other purposes.

* H.R. 3393, 81st Congress, 1st Session, March 9, 1949. This bill was referred to the Committee on Foreign Affairs.

Be it enacted by the Senate and House of Representatives of the United States of America in Congress assembled, That for the purpose of maintaining, and encouraging, and promoting international understanding, justice, decency, friendship, and lasting peace among all nations and all people, there is hereby established an international educational institution, to be known as the University for Universal Peace (hereinafter referred to as the "University"). The University shall be located in the central part of the United States.

Sec. 2. The management of the University shall be vested in a Board of Control (hereinafter referred to as the "Board"). The Board shall determine the site for the location of the University, shall without regard to the civil-service laws employ the faculty and such other officers, employees, and agents as it deems proper and necessary for the purposes of this Act, and shall have authority to prescribe such rules and regulations as may be necessary to carry out the purposes of this Act.

Sec. 3. (*a*) The Board shall consist of one member from each State to be elected by the legislature thereof on a nonpartisan basis. After their election, the members of the Board shall meet and organize in the city of Minneapolis, State of Minnesota, at a date and place designated by the President of the United States. They shall elect from among their own number a chairman, a vice chairman, a secretary, and a treasurer, and shall define the duties of each.

(*b*) After the Board is organized it shall by lot divide its members into three classes so that one-third of such members shall hold office for a term of two years, one-third for a term of four years, and one-third for a term of six years. Thereafter the term for which the members of the Board are elected shall be for a term of six years, except that in the case of a vacancy the governor of the State from which the vacancy occurs may appoint a member to serve until the next legislature meets. Each member of the Board shall hold office until his successor is elected and qualified.

(*c*) The members of the Board of Control other than the secretary and the treasurer shall serve without compensation but shall receive their actual travel and subsistence expenses while away from their places of residence in the performance of their duty. The secretary and the treasurer shall receive a salary of not less than $12,000 per annum and an allowance at the rate of 10 cents per mile for necessary travel expenses.

Sec. 4. (*a*) The faculty of the University shall consist of a president, vice president, and such deans, professors, associate professors, librarians, chaplains, and instructors as are necessary for the proper instruction of the students in universal justice and decency and foreign understanding. In case of death, resignation, or disability of the president to act, the vice president shall act and perform his duties.

(*b*) The faculty of the University by majority vote of all its members shall promulgate, and from time to time amend and repeal, such bylaws, rules, and regulations as it deems fit and necessary for the proper conduct of the University.

(c) The term of the contracts and salaries to be paid to the members of the faculty shall be determined by the Board without regard to the Classification Act of 1923, as amended. The salary of the president shall not be less than $20,000 a year.

(d) The Board shall select the first president, deans, and heads of departments of the faculty of the University from among the leading and outstanding educators of the world and of the Nation. Thereafter, the president, deans, and heads of departments shall nominate the faculty of the University, subject to approval or rejection by the Board. Two-thirds of the faculty shall at all times be natural-born citizens of the United States.

Sec. 5. (a) The course of study of the University shall extend over a period of at least nine months each year for five years, and one year of post graduate study, and only those students who have finished their high-school education, or its equivalent, and who, under the rules and regulations promulgated by the faculty, pass a satisfactory examination showing ability and adaptability to carry on the courses of study described in subsection (b) of this section shall be eligible for admission.

(b) The courses of study shall include, but not be limited to, geography, forms of government, political and governmental theories, international law and international cooperation, international business and trade practices, the foreign and domestic diplomacies of the various nations, governments, and states of the world, racial and religious prejudices and their eradication, and such other subjects taught in universities and colleges in the United States as may be prescribed by the rules and regulations of the faculty.

(c) The University is authorized to confer an appropriate degree of bachelor of justice and peace upon its graduates, and the degree of master of justice and peace upon one additional year of post graduate study, and other appropriate degrees.

Sec. 6. The student body shall consist of (a) not more than thirty students each year from the District of Columbia, and each State, Territory, and possession of the United States, to be selected by the ranking official of education of such District, State, Territory, or possession, who can qualify as to ability and adaptability under the rules and regulations promulgated by the faculty of the University, and (b) not more than thirty students in any one year from any one foreign state, nation, or people which students are qualified as to ability and adaptability and are eligible under the rules and regulations promulgated by the faculty. No student shall be admitted who has passed his thirtieth birthday.

Sec. 7. (a) The expenses for students from the District of Columbia, and the States, Territories, and possessions of the United States, shall be allowed and paid by such District, States, Territories, and possessions. The expenses of students of foreign nations, states, or people, shall be provided for by their respective governments or people.

(*b*) It is the purpose of this Act that all foreign graduates, upon the completion of their course of education at the University, promptly return to their native state, nation, or people to devote their time to affairs of state and to bring about a better understanding among the people of all nations.

(*c*) It is the purpose of this Act that all graduates of the United States shall devote their time and energy to international affairs and foreign service with a view of bringing about a more friendly and lasting relation among all nations.

Sec. 8. The Board is authorized to encourage and accept, on behalf of the University, donations of money, endowments, and other gifts of any and all kinds, from any State or foreign government and/or from any political subdivision of such State or foreign government and/or from any corporation foreign or domestic, and/or from any and all persons of any State or foreign government, and to accept the donation of a site for its location.

Sec. 9. There is hereby authorized to be appropriated $25,000,000, and such other amounts as may be necessary, from time to time, to carry out the provisions of this Act.

The Indiana Association of Church Related Independent Colleges Opposes Federal Aid to Higher Education, 1949 *

We, the members of the Indiana Association of Church Related and Independent Colleges, consisting of twenty-six colleges and universities throughout the State, reaffirm our belief in the present American system of education, consisting of State supported, church related, and privately endowed elementary and secondary schools, colleges, and universities, each complementary to the other with their diversity and competition maintaining the freedom which is the chief ornament of all.

We hold that this freedom would be threatened by any general Federal subvention of higher education, which would involve a great immediate financial burden, and, we believe, ultimate regimentation and control.

We, therefore, unite in supporting the following specific propositions:

1. We advocate adequate financing of State owned colleges and universities through State taxes.
2. In general, we oppose Federal aid to all institutions of higher learning. Any financial support of education from the Federal Govern-

* Resolution passed January, 1949. Furnished by President O. P. Kretzmann of Valparaiso University, May 23, 1949.

ment should be for specific purposes, for individual scholarships, or granted on an outright single gift basis.

Properly administered, this would not involve regimentation or control.

3. We believe that private institutions of higher learning should continue to look to churches, foundations, individuals, business corporations, and other non-governmental sources for financial support.

« IX »

UP FROM SLAVERY: EDUCATIONAL
AND OTHER RIGHTS OF NEGROES

«««‹›»»»»»»»»»»»»»»»»»»»»»»»»»»»»»»»»»»»»

Systematic efforts to establish and maintain schools for Negroes were not made in this country prior to 1861, but the history of "the various educational processes to which the Negroes in America have been subjected is interwoven with the history of the United States from the year 1619, when the first slaves were landed, to the present moment. The story of the development of the African slave, with his easy-going barbarism, to the present condition of the American Negro is full of interest and instruction . . ." (*Negro Education: A Study of the Private and Higher Schools for Colored People in the United States* [Washington, Government Printing Office, 1917], Bulletin No. 38, 1916, I, p. 243). When the slaves were emancipated in 1863 the number of people of African descent in this country had grown to about four million. Prior to 1830 few thoughtful people in the South were opposed to the education of their slaves. The need of teaching reading as a means of becoming familiar with the Bible and the principles of Christianity was recognized; and for practical reasons it was necessary that some of the slaves on large plantations should know to read and write. Moreover, some house servants were depended on for help with the master's children in their lessons. The most drastic laws in the slave-holding states against teaching Negroes were passed between 1830 and 1835 as results of uprising of slaves, especially the disturbances led by Denmark Vesey in South Carolina and the more terrifying disturbance led by Nat Turner in Virginia in 1831, and the fear of such uprisings. After 1860 numerous missionary and "aid" societies in the North sent teachers to the South for the care and teaching of the freedmen. (See Henry L. Swint, *The Northern Teacher in the South, 1862-1870* [Nashville, Tenn., Vanderbilt University Press, 1941]; Edgar W. Knight, "The 'Messianic' Invasion of the South after 1865," *School and Society,* LVII [1943], pp. 645-51; also LVIII [1943], pp. 107-09.) The Freedmen's Bureau, established in the War Department about a month before the surrender of General Robert E. Lee, was charged with "the control of all subjects relating to refugees and freedmen." Under these and other auspices elementary schools for Negroes were opened; and in some of these missionary efforts appear the origins of some higher educational institutions for Negroes in the South. C. G. Woodson says that by 1860 about 10 per cent of the adult Negroes in this country had acquired the rudiments of education, but he adds that the proportion of those who had such rudiments was less at the outbreak of the war than it had been about 1825 (*The Education of the Negro Prior to 1861* [New York, G. P. Putnam's Sons, 1915], p. 228). The National Educational Association at its meeting in 1865, a few months after Appomattox, looked upon the South as a vast field for educational and missionary effort. Later some philanthropic foundations were established, such as the Slater Fund, the Jeanes Fund, and the Phelps-Stokes Fund, primarily to aid the education of Negroes in the South. The Peabody Fund, set up in 1867, also gave aid to that cause; and by 1916 eight philanthropic funds were devoting "part or all of their income for the improvement of Negro schools." Between 1938 and 1950 the Supreme Court of the United States handed down some significant decisions on equal rights for Negroes.

South Carolina Prohibits the Teaching of Slaves to Write, 1740 *

And *whereas,* the having of slaves taught to write, or suffering them to be employed in writing, may be attended with great inconveniences; *Be it therefore enacted* by the authority aforesaid, That all and every person or persons whatsoever, who shall hereafter teach, or cause any slave or slaves to be taught, to write, or shall use or employ any slave as a scribe in any manner of writing whatsoever, hereafter taught to write, every such person or persons, shall, for every such offense, forfeit the sum of one hundred pounds current money.

The Presbytery of Lexington (Virginia) Licenses John Chavis as Preacher, 1800 †

Presbyn. had an interloquitur to consider the popular discourse of Mr. Chevis & after some deliberation thereon agreed to sustain it as a satisfactory part of trial & to licence him to preach the Gospel. Mr. Chevis was accordingly licensed & record thereof was ordered to be made in the following words, viz. at Timber Ridge Meetinghouse, the 19th. day of November, 1800, the Presbn. of Lexington having received sufficient testimonials in favor of Mr. John Chevis, of his being of good moral character, of his being in full communion with the church & his having made some progress in literature, proceeded to take him through a course of trials for licensure & he having given satisfaction as to his experimental acquaintance with religion & proficiency in divinity, Presbn. did & hereby do express their approbation of these parts of trial & he having adopted the Confession of Faith of this church & satisfactorily answered the questions appointed to be put to candidates to be licensed the Presby. did & hereby do license him the said Jno. Chevis to preach the Gospel of Christ as a probationer for the holy ministry within the bounds of this Presby. or wherever he shall be orderly called, hoping as he is a man of colour he may be peculiarly useful to those of his own complexion. Ordered that Mr. Chevis receive an attested copy of the above minutes.

* David J. McCord, *The Statutes at Large of South Carolina,* VII, p. 413.
† *Minutes,* November 19, 1800.

John Chavis, Negro, Is Engaged as Missionary by the General Assembly of the Presbyterian Church, 1801 *

That . . . Mr. John Chavis, a black man of prudence and piety, who has been educated and licensed to preach by the Presbytery of Lexington in Virginia, be employed as a missionary among people of his own colour, until the meeting of the next General Assembly; and that for his better direction in the discharge of duties which are attended with many circumstances of delicacy and difficulty, some prudential instructions be issued to him by the assembly, governing himself by which, the knowledge of religion among that people may be made more and more to strengthen the order of society: And the Rev. Messrs. Hoge, Alexander, Logan, and Stephenson, were appointed a committee to draught instructions to said John Chavis, and prescribe his route.

The Court of Quarter Sessions of Rockbridge County, Virginia, Certifies to the Freedom of John Chavis, 1802 †

On the motion of Rev. John Chavis, a black man, It is ordered that the clerk of this court certify that the said Chavis has been known to the court for several years last past and that he has always, since known to the court, been considered as a freeman and they believe him to be such, and that he has always while in this county conducted himself in a decent orderly and respectable manner, and also that he has been a student at Washington Academy where they believe he went through a regular course of Academical Studies.

---

* *Acts and Proceedings*, 1801, p. 7. It has commonly been said that this remarkable man was a full-blooded, free-born Negro, that he was educated at Princeton, had an unusual mastery of the classics, was a very effective teacher and Presbyterian preacher, and that he was received as an equal socially and was asked to table by the most respectable white people in the neighborhoods in which he lived in North Carolina in the early part of the nineteenth century. He had a school in Raleigh in which he taught white boys and the sons of prominent families were among his students. Most of the earlier writers on Chavis said that he went to Princeton, and a letter from V. Lansing Collins, Secretary of that institution, to Edgar W. Knight, September 14, 1929, said that although there were no known official records to verify Chavis's attendance at Princeton, the tradition or belief that he was a student there was so strong that Chavis was listed among the non-graduates of the institution. As the court record below shows, it was believed that Chavis attended Washington Academy which developed into Washington and Lee University. For a partial bibliography on this man, see Edgar W. Knight, "Notes on John Chavis," *The North Carolina Historical Review*, VII (July, 1930), pp. 326-45, and his "A Negro Teacher of Southern Whites," *The Baltimore Sun*, December 8, 1929. Chavis had to discontinue preaching in North Carolina as result of a statute of 1832 forbidding slaves and free Negroes to preach or exhort in public. It has been said that Chavis himself owned slaves. Many Negroes did. See *Popular Science Monthly*, LXXXI (November, 1912), pp. 483-94.

† Order Book No. 6, p. 10. See also J. C. Ballach, *A History of Slavery in Virginia*, p. 110.

Joseph Gales, Whig Editor of a Raleigh Newspaper, Praises Chavis and His School, 1830 *

On Friday last, we attended an examination of the free children of color, attached to the school conducted by *John Chavis,* also colored, but a regularly educated Presbyterian minister, and we have seldom received more gratification from any exhibition of a similar character. To witness a well regulated school, composed of this class of persons—to see them setting an example both in behavior and scholarship, which their *white* superiors might take pride in imitating, was a cheering spectacle to a philanthropist. The exercises throughout, evinced a degree of attention and assiduous care on the part of the instructor, highly creditable, and of attainment on the part of his scholars almost incredible. We were also much pleased with the sensible address which closed the examination. The object of the respectable teacher, was to impress on the scholars, the fact, that they occupied an inferior and subordinate station in society, and were possessed but of limited privileges; but that even *they* might become useful in their particular sphere by making a proper improvement of the advantages afforded them.

The Importation of Slaves Is Prohibited, 1808 †

Be it enacted by the Senate and House of Representatives of the United States of America in Congress assembled, That from and after the first day of January, one thousand eight hundred and eight, it shall not be lawful to import or bring into the United States or the territories thereof from any foreign kingdom, place, or country, any negro, mulatto, or person of colour, with intent to hold, sell, or dispose of such negro, mulatto, or person of colour, as a slave, or to be held to service or labour.

Sec. 2. And be it further enacted, That no citizen or citizens of the United States, or any other person, shall, from and after the first day of January, in the year of our Lord one thousand eight hundred and eight, for himself, or themselves, or any other person whatsoever, either as master, factor, or owner, build, fit, equip, load or otherwise prepare any ship or vessel, in any port or place within the jurisdiction of the United States, nor shall cause any ship or vessel to sail from any port or place within the same, for the purpose of procuring any negro, mulatto, or person of colour, from any foreign kingdom, place, or country, to be transported to any port or place whatsoever, within the jurisdiction of the United States, to be held, sold, or disposed of as slaves, or to be held to service or labour; and if any ship or vessel shall be so fitted out for the purpose aforesaid, or shall be caused to sail so as aforesaid, every such ship or vessel, her tackle,

---

* *The Raleigh Register,* April 22, 1830.
† *U. S. Statutes at Large,* II, p. 426.

apparel, and furniture, shall be forfeited to the United States, and shall be liable to be seized, prosecuted, and condemned in any of the circuit courts or district courts, for the district where the said ship or vessel may be found or seized.

A Methodist Minister of Charleston Is "Pumped" for Teaching Negroes, 1823 *

I well remember the morning, 23 years ago, and the conversation, when Mr. Asbury was about to leave Charleston, and Mr. Dougherty in charge of the society. In allusion to the large number of colored Members: I leave you, said he, a flower garden and a kitchen garden, to cultivate; and, following out the similie, he pointed to him the importance of attention to the blacks. The greater pleasure would be derived from an attention to the masters; the greater advantage from attention to the slaves. Mr. Dougherty was not satisfied with laboring for the adult slaves only; he established a school for the black children. In a letter to Mr. Asbury, he observes, I do not only suffer the reproach common to Methodist Preachers, but I have rendered myself still more vile, as "the negro schoolmaster." His success was too great to be endured by the jealous authorities; the alarm was spread among the populace; but, as the schoolmaster would take no hint to abandon his sable pupils, the mob assembled, in great numbers on a Sunday evening, in Cumberland street, before the church. The Preacher was forcibly hurried from the pulpit into the midst of the mob, who seem not to have made their arrangement how to dispose of their victim. A pause ensued, and while several proposals were making, a voice was heard above the rest, *"to the pump"*—to the pump was now the general cry. The pump stood in Church street, near the corner of Cumberland street, not many yards distant from the church. Mr. Dougherty was hurried on towards it, by the multitude, and thrown down so as to receive its whole contents, until the phrenzy of the mob began to abate; he was then suffered to return to his lodgings, without any serious injury—and, I believe, unruffled with any unholy emotion of heart. He used to relate the event with the utmost composure, and occasional pleasantry.

The General Assembly of Virginia Prohibits the Teaching of Slaves, Free Negroes, or Mulattoes to Read or Write, 1831 †

4. *Be it further enacted,* That all meetings of free negroes or mulattoes, at any school-house, church, meeting-house or other place for teaching them reading or writing, either in the day or night, under whatsoever pretext, shall be deemed and considered as an unlawful assembly; and any

* *The Wesleyan Repository,* Vol. III (1823), pp. 162-163. Given in Addie Grace Wardle, *History of the Sunday School Movement in the Methodist Episcopal Church,* p. 48.
† *Supplement to the Revised Code of the Laws of Virginia, Richmond,* 1833, chapter 186.

justice of the county or corporation, wherein such assemblage shall be, either from his own knowledge, or on the information of others, of such unlawful assemblage or meeting, shall issue his warrant, directed to any sworn officer or officers, authorizing him or them, to enter the house or houses where such unlawful assemblage or meeting may be, for the purpose of apprehending or dispersing such free negroes or mulattoes, and to inflict corporal punishment on the offender or offenders, at the discretion of any justice of the peace, not exceeding twenty lashes.

5. *Be it further enacted,* That if any white person or persons assemble with free negroes or mulattoes, at any schoolhouse, church, meeting-house, or other place for the purpose of instructing such free negroes or mulattoes to read or write, such person or persons shall, on conviction thereof, be fined in a sum not exceeding fifty dollars, and moreover may be imprisoned at the discretion of a jury, not exceeding two months.

6. *Be it further enacted,* That if any white person for pay or compensation, shall assemble with any slaves for the purpose of teaching, and shall teach any slave to read or write, such person, or any white person or persons contracting with such teacher so to act, who shall offend as aforesaid, shall, for each offence, be fined at the discretion of a jury, in a sum of not less than ten, nor exceeding one hundred dollars, to be recovered on an information or indictment.

7. The judges of the superior courts of law, and the attorneys prosecuting for the commonwealth, in the county and corporation courts, are hereby required to give this act in charge to their several grand juries.

8. This act shall be in force from the first day of June next.

North Carolina Forbids Slaves or Free Negroes to Preach, 1831 *

An act for the better regulation of the conduct of negroes, slaves and free persons of color.

That it shall not be lawful under any pretence for any free negro, slave or free person of color to preach or exhort in public, or in any manner to officiate as a preacher or teacher in any prayer meeting or other association for worship where slaves of different families are collected together; and if any free negro or free person of color shall be thereof duly convicted on indictment before any court having jurisdiction thereof, he shall for each offense receive not exceeding thirty-nine lashes on his bare back; and where any slave shall be guilty of a violation of this act, he shall on conviction before a single magistrate receive not exceeding thirty-nine lashes on his bare back.

II. That it shall not be lawful for any slave to go at large as a freeman, exercising his or her own discretion in the employment of his or her time; nor shall it be lawful for any slave to keep house to him or herself as a free

* *Laws of North Carolina,* 1831-1832, chapter IV.

person, exercising the like discretion in the employment of his or her time; and in case the owner of any slave shall consent or connive at the commission of such offence, he or she so offending shall be subject to indictment, and on conviction be fined in the discretion of the Court not exceeding one hundred dollars: *Provided,* that nothing herein shall be construed to prevent any person permitting his or her slave or slaves to live or keep house upon his or her land for the purpose of attending to the business of his or her master or mistress.

Alabama Forbids the Teaching of Slaves to Read or Write, 1832 *

Sec. 10. And be it further enacted, That any person or persons who shall endeavor or attempt to teach any free person of color, or slave to spell, read, or write, shall upon conviction thereof by indictment, be fined in a sum not less than two hundred and fifty dollars nor more than five hundred dollars.

The Religious Instruction of Slaves in South Carolina, 1834 †

A report has been made to the Presbyterian Synod of South Carolina and Georgia on the subject of the religious instruction of the colored population, which advocates in strong terms, not merely its safety but its importance. They urge that there will be a better understanding of the relation of masters and servants, which will lead to more kindness on the one hand, and more faithfulness on the other; that it will cultivate principles and feelings which will soften the character of the slave, will banish his superstition, and promote the love of peace and industry; that it will promote the morality and religion of the white population, by diminishing and removing those vices which infect all who witness them, while it will furnish the slave with that light and hope, which it is the highest duty of Christians to furnish them. It is with peculiar pleasure that we see such a report, drawn up by men familiar with slaves in the states where their numbers are greatest, and meeting with boldness and triumphant argument the objections which are brought. May their plea be heard!

The General Assembly of South Carolina Prohibits Slaves from Being Taught to Read or Write, 1834 ‡

Be it enacted by the Honorable the Senate and House of Representatives, now met and sitting in General Assembly, and by the authority of

* *Acts Passed at the Thirteenth Annual Session of the General Assembly of the State of Alabama,* 1831-32, p. 16.
  † *American Annals of Education and Instruction,* August, 1834, p. 386.
  ‡ *Acts and Resolutions of the General Assembly of South Carolina Passed in December, 1834,* chapter 5.

the same, If any person shall hereafter teach any slave to read or write, or shall aid or assist in teaching any slave to read or write or cause or procure any slave to be taught to read or write; such person, if a free white person, upon conviction thereof, shall, for each and every offence against this act, be fined not exceeding one hundred dollars, and imprisoned not more than six months; or if a free person of color, shall be whipped not exceeding fifty lashes, and fined not exceeding fifty dollars, at the discretion of the court of magistrates, and free holders before which such free person of color is tried; and if a slave, shall be whipped at the discretion of the court, not exceeding fifty lashes: the informer to be entitled to one half of the fine, and to be a competent witness; and if any free person of color or slave, shall keep any school or other place of instruction, for teaching any slave or free person of color to read or write, such a free person of color or slave, shall be liable to the same fine, imprisonment and corporal punishment, as are by this section, imposed and inflicted on free persons of color and slaves, for teaching slaves to read or write.

Provision for Schools for Colored Children in New York, 1841 *

A school for colored children may be established in any city or town of this state, with approbation of the commissioners or town superintendent of such city or town, which shall be under the charge of the trustees of the district in which such school shall be kept; and in places where no school districts exist, or where from any cause it may be expedient, such school may be placed in charge of trustees to be appointed by the commissioners or town superintendent of common schools of the town or city, and if there be none, to be appointed by the state superintendent. Returns shall be made by the trustees of such schools to the town superintendent at the same time and in the same manner as now provided by law in relation to districts; and they shall particularly specify the number of colored children over five and under sixteen years of age, attending such school from different districts, naming such districts respectively, and the number from each. The town superintendent shall apportion and pay over to the trustees of such schools, a portion of the money received by them annually, in the same manner as now provided by law in respect to school districts, allowing to such schools the proper proportion for each child over five and under sixteen years of age, who shall have been instructed in such school at least four months by a teacher duly licensed, and shall deduct such proportion from the amount that would have been apportioned to the district to which such child belongs; and in his report to the state superintendent, the town superintendent shall specially designate the schools for colored children in his town or city.

* *Statutes at Large of the State of New York,* III, pp. 446-47.

The Legislature of Virginia Provides for a Young Slave
To Be Taught, 1842 *

Whereas, it appearing to the general assembly that Henry Juett Gray, of the county of Rockingham, a blind youth of reputable character and exemplary deportment, who has made considerable progress in scientific attainments, is desirous of qualifying himself to become a teacher of the blind; and that in order to his comfort and extensive usefulness, it is necessary that he should have the services of a servant capable of reading and writing, which object cannot be permanently secured otherwise than by the education of a young slave named Randolph, the property of said Henry Juett: and it further appearing that Robert Gray, the father of said Henry Juett, is willing to indemnify the public against any possible injury which might be apprehended from the misconduct of said slave:

1. *Be it therefore enacted,* That it shall be lawful for the said Henry Juett Gray, or any friend for him, to employ from time to time any competent white person or persons to teach the said slave Randolph reading and writing, and for such white persons or persons so to teach said slave without incurring any of the penalties prescribed by law in such cases: *Provided, however,* that this act shall be of no force or effect until the said Robert Gray, or some other responsible person, shall execute before the county court of Rockingham county bond with two or more sufficient sureties, payable to the sitting justices thereof, and their successors, in a penalty to be fixed by said court, but not less than double the value of said slave at mature age, and conditioned for indemnifying the commonwealth and the citizens thereof against any improper use of said slave of the art of reading and writing, and for the sale and removal of said slave by said Henry Juett Gray, or any future proprietor thereof, beyond the limits of this commonwealth, in the event of his conviction of any crime, unless the judgment of conviction shall have the effect of preventing such sale or removal; which bond may be sued on and prosecuted from time to time, in the names of said justices, for the use of the commonwealth, or any citizen thereof aggrieved, for the recovery of any damages which may be sustained by reason of any breach of the condition thereof: *And provided also,* That to give effect to this act, the county court of Rockingham county shall be satisfied and cause it to be certified of record, that the said slave is a boy of good moral character and correct deportment: *And provided moreover,* That the general assembly reserves to itself full power to alter, modify or repeal this act at any time hereafter, and to require the sale and removal of said slave beyond the limits of this commonwealth.

2. This act shall be in force from the passing thereof.

* *Acts of Virginia,* 1841-42, p. 164.

Religious Instruction of Negroes in South Carolina, 1847 *

A large and respectable meeting was held at the Second Presbyterian Church, on Sabbath morning, May 9th, after a discourse by Rev. J. B. Adger and an address by Rev. C. C. Jones, D.D. on the best mode of securing, in an efficient and proper manner, the religious instruction of the colored people. After the reading of the resolutions adopted by the Session of the Church.

On motion of W. C. Dukes, Esq. the Hon. R. B. Gilchrist took the Chair, and introduced the subject with some most appropriate remarks, expressive of the importance and interest of the occasion. Mr. William Miller was requested to act as Secretary.

The following resolutions were then introduced in a very full and able speech by Hon. F. H. Elmore, and seconded, with some additional remarks, by Alexander Black, Esq.:

Resolved, That, in the opinion of this meeting, the proper religious instruction of the colored population is a duty pressed upon us by considerations of sound policy, as well as Christian obligation.

Resolved, That we concur entirely in the opinions expressed by the Session of this Church and by the Presbytery of Charleston, that, in order that such instruction should be given efficiently, and, at the same time, with proper safe-guards, it must be afforded by thoroughly educated ministers, of sound principles, who are devoted to the welfare of that people, and who understand our institutions.

Resolved, That the offer of the Rev. John B. Adger, to devote himself gratuitously to this work of piety and usefulness, embodying, as he does, in himself, all the qualifications desirable for this delicate and responsible office, should be accepted, and the funds be immediately subscribed for the erection of a Church for a colored congregation under his ministry.

Resolved, That a subscription for this object be now opened to raise the funds necessary, to be received by the committee appointed by the Session, and expended under their management.

Mrs. Margaret Douglass Is Arrested, Tried, and Convicted of Teaching Negro Children to Read in Norfolk, Virginia, 1853 †

A Southern lady living with a daughter in Norfolk, Virginia, sixty-six years ago and being greatly interested in the religious and moral instruc-

---

* *The Charleston Courier,* May 13, 1847.

† For full account of the trial, see John D. Lawson (Ed.), *American State Trials: A Collection of the Important and Interesting Criminal Trials Which Have Taken Place in the United States, from the Beginning of Our Government to the Present Day* (St. Louis, F. H. Thomas Law Book Co., 1917), VII, pp. 45-60. For her own account of the case, see *The Personal Narrative of Mrs. Margaret Douglass, A Southern Woman, Who Was Imprisoned for One Month in the Common Jail, Under the Laws of Virginia, for the Crime of Teaching Free Colored Children to Read* (Boston, John P. Jewett and Company, 1854). A copy of this book is in the Duke University Library; microcopy in the Southern Histori-

tion of colored children and finding that the Sunday school where they were allowed to attend was not sufficient, invited them to come to her house, where in a back room upstairs she and her daughter taught them to read and write. She knew that it was against the law to teach slaves, and so she was careful to take none in her school but free colored children. One day a couple of city constables entered with a warrant and marched the two teachers and the children to the Mayor's office, where she was charged with teaching them to read, contrary to law. She explained that none of the children were slaves and that she had no idea that a child could not be taught to read simply because it was black. But the Mayor told her that this was the law, but as she had acted in good faith he would dismiss the case. But the Grand Jury heard of it and indicted her, and at the next term of court she was tried for a violation of the Virginia code which provided that every assemblage of negroes for the purpose of religious worship, where it was conducted by a negro, and every assemblage of negroes for instruction in reading and writing, or in the night time, for any purpose, was unlawful, and if a white person assembled with negroes to instruct them to read and write, he should be fined and imprisoned. She refused the services of a lawyer and defended herself, and though she called several witnesses to show that the same thing had been done for years in the Sunday schools in the city, the jury convicted her, but placed the penalty at a fine of only one dollar. But this was overruled by the judge who sentenced her to be imprisoned for a month, which sentence was duly carried out. . . .*

Hinton Rowan Helper on the Baneful Influences of Slavery, 1857 †

In one way or another we are more or less subservient to the North every day of our lives. In infancy we are swaddled in Northern muslin; in childhood we are humored with Northern gewgaws; in youth we are in-

---

cal Collection, the University of North Carolina. For the brutal treatment of Prudence Crandall, a well-educated young white woman who admitted Negro girls to her boarding school in Connecticut in the early 1830's, see Carter G. Woodson, *The Education of the Negro Prior to 1861*, pp. 171-75.

* Mrs. Douglass was born in Washington, D. C., but removed while quite young to Charleston, South Carolina, where she was married and resided until 1845, when at the death of her son, she went with her daughter, Rosa, to Norfolk, Va., to reside. Though a slave-owner herself and the daughter of slaveholders, she took an interest in giving religious instruction to Negro children.

† Hinton Rowan Helper, *The Impending Crisis of the South: How to Meet It*, pp. 22-23; 184; 398-99; 406-08. Helper was born in Davie County, North Carolina, and was graduated from Mocksville Academy near his home in 1848, having been taught by "the renowned Peter S. Ney (supposedly the field marshal of Napoleon), and by the Reverend Baxter Clegg." Although he had been a Whig he identified himself with the newly formed Republican party. His *Impending Crisis* was rejected by several reputable publishers, including Harper's, Scribner's and Appleton's, and was finally published in 1857 after the youthful author had guaranteed a New York book agent against financial loss. "This book was probably the most caustic, scathing, and vituperative criticism of slavery and slaveholders ever written. No volume was ever more thoroughly condemned or more heartily

structed out of Northern books; at the age of maturity we sow our "wild oats" on Northern soil; in middle-life we exhaust our wealth, energies and talents in the dishonorable vocation of entailing our dependence on our children and on our children's children, and, to the neglect of our own interests and the interests of those around us, in giving aid and succor to every department of Northern power; in the decline of life we remedy our eye-sight with Northern spectacles, and support our infirmities with Northern canes; in old age we are drugged with Northern physic; and, finally, when we die, our inanimate bodies, shrouded in Northern cambric, are stretched upon the bier, borne to the grave in a Northern carriage, entombed with a Northern spade, and memorized with a Northern slab! . . . Slavery is a shame, a crime, and a curse—a great moral, social, civil, and political evil—an oppressive burden to the blacks, and an incalculable injury to the whites—a stumbling block to the nation, an impediment to progress, a damper on all the nobler instincts, principles, aspirations and enterprises of man, and a dire enemy to every true interests. . . .

But more than this—where a system of enforced servitude prevails, a fearful degree of ignorance prevails also, as its necessary accompaniment. The enslaved masses are, of course, thrust back from the fountains of knowledge by the strong arm of law, while the poor non-slaveholding classes are almost as effectually excluded from the institutions of learning by their poverty—the sparse population of slaveholding districts being unfavorable to the maintenance of free schools, and the exigencies of their condition forbidding them to avail themselves of any more costly educational privileges. . . .

It is true, these States [slave States] have their educated men,—the majority of whom owe their literary culture to the colleges of the North. Not that there are no Southern colleges—for there are institutions, so called, in a majority of the Slave States.—Some of them, too, are not deficient in the appointments requisite to our higher educational institutions; but as a general thing, Southern colleges are colleges only in *name,* and will scarcely take rank with a third-rate Northern academy, while our academies, with a few exceptions, are immeasurably inferior to the public schools of New-York, Philadelphia, and Boston. The truth is, there is a vast inert mass of stupidity and ignorance, too dense for individual effort to enlighten or remove, in all communities cursed with the institution of slavery. Disguise the unwelcome truth as we may, slavery is the parent of

---

praised. It probably had the greatest circulation of any book of non-fiction ever published in the United States, unless it was Harvey's *Coin's Financial School* near the close of the last century. With the possible exception of *Uncle Tom's Cabin* it created a greater political furore than any volume ever published in America, and it had a tremendous bearing on Lincoln's election in 1860 and on the sectional conflict which followed. . . . To own a copy was against good taste and traitorous to the South. Worse than that, it was a penal offense to own or circulate a copy. Three men were hanged in Arkansas for owning copies. . . ."
Hugh T. Lefler, *Hinton Rowan Helper: Advocate of A White America* (Charlottesville, Va., The Historical Publishing Co., 1935), pp. 6, 7.

ignorance, and ignorance begets a whole brood of follies and of vices, and every one of these is inevitably hostile to literary culture. The masses, if they think of literature at all, think of it only as a costly luxury, to be monopolized by the few.

The proportion of white adults over twenty years of age in each State, who cannot read and write, to the *whole* white population, is as follows:

Connecticut,	1 to every 568	Louisiana,	1 to every 38½
Vermont,	1 " 473	Maryland,	1 " 27
New Hampshire,	1 " 310	Mississippi,	1 " 20
Massachusetts,	1 " 166	Delaware,	1 " 18
Maine,	1 " 108	South Carolina,	1 " 17
Michigan,	1 " 97	Missouri,	1 " 16
Rhode Island,	1 " 67	Alabama,	1 " 15
New Jersey,	1 " 58	Kentucky,	1 " 13½
New York,	1 " 56	Georgia,	1 " 13
Pennsylvania,	1 " 50	Virginia,	1 " 12½
Ohio,	1 " 43	Arkansas,	1 " 11½
Indiana,	1 " 18	Tennessee,	1 " 11
Illinois,	1 " 17	North Carolina,	1 " 7

In this table, Illinois and Indiana are the only Free States which, in point of education, are surpassed by any of the Slave States; and this disgraceful fact is owing, principally, to the influx of foreigners, and to immigrants from the Slave States. New-York, Rhode Island, and Pennsylvania have also a large foreign element in their population, that swells very considerably this percentage of ignorance. For instance, New-York shows, by the last census, a population of 98,722 who cannot read and write, and of this number 68,052 are foreigners; Rhode Island, 3,607, of whom 2,359 are foreigners; Pennsylvania, 76,272, of whom 24,989 are foreigners. On the other hand, the ignorance of the Slave States is principally *native* ignorance, but comparatively few emigrants from Europe seeking a home upon a soil cursed with "the peculiar institution." North Carolina has a foreign population of only 340, South Carolina only 104, Arkansas only 27, Tennessee only 505, and Virginia only 1,137, who cannot read and write; while the aggregate of *native* ignorance in these five States (exclusive of the *slaves,* who are debarred all education by *law*) is 278,948! No longer ago than 1837, Governor Clarke, of Kentucky, in his message to the Legislature of that State, declared that "by the computation of those most familiar with the subject, *one-third of the adult population of the State are unable to write their names;*" and Governor Campbell, of Virginia, reported to the Legislature, that "from the returns of ninety-eight clerks, it appeared that of 4,614 applications for marriage licenses in 1837, no less than 1,047 were made by men unable to write."

In the Slave States the proportion of free white children between the ages of five and twenty, who are found at any school or college, is not quite *one-fifth* of the whole; in the Free States, the proportion is more than *three-fifths*. . . .

"Southerner at School with Negroes!" 1859 *

There has been much ill-feeling among the citizens of Benton, Ala., against Mr. Greenwood, a merchant of that place, for sending his daughter to Connecticut to be educated in a school where negroes are allowed to attend. We have no fancy for such a piece of *green-wood*. Nor do we think, *any* Southern man is acting right who sends his sons or daughters to the Northern schools to be educated—thereby ignoring those of his own section, and feeding fat those who are not his supporters. There are enough good schools and teachers too in the South to educate *all* her children by all her own people.

The Emancipation Proclamation, 1863 †

By the President of the United States of America:

A Proclamation.

Whereas on the 22d day of September, A.D. 1862, a proclamation was issued by the President of the United States, containing, among other things, the following, to wit:

"That on the 1st day of January A.D. 1863, all persons held as slaves within any State or designated part of a State the people whereof shall then be in rebellion against the United States shall be then, thenceforward, and forever free; and the executive government of the United States, including the military and naval authority thereof, will recognize and maintain the freedom of such persons and will do no act or acts to repress such persons, or any of them, in any efforts they may make for their actual freedom.

"That the executive will on the 1st day of January aforesaid, by proclamation, designate the States and parts of States, if any, in which the people thereof, respectively, shall then be in rebellion against the United States; and the fact that any State or the people thereof shall on that day be in good faith represented in the Congress of the United States by members chosen thereto at elections wherein a majority of the qualified voters of such States shall have participated shall, in the absence of strong countervailing testimony, be deemed conclusive evidence that such State and the people thereof are not then in rebellion against the United States."

Now, therefore, I, Abraham Lincoln, President of the United States, by virtue of the power in me vested as Commander-in-Chief of the Army and Navy of the United States in time of actual armed rebellion against the authority and government of the United States, and as a fit and necessary war measure for surpressing said rebellion, do, on this 1st day of January,

* *The Southern Advocate* (Huntsville, Alabama), December 7, 1859.
† *U.S. Statutes at Large*, XII, pp. 1268-69.

A.D. 1863, and in accordance with my purpose so to do, publicly proclaim for the full period of one hundred days from the first day above mentioned, order and designate as the States and parts of States wherein the people thereof, respectively, are this day in rebellion against the United States the following, to wit:

Arkansas, Texas, Louisiana (except the parishes of St. Bernard, Plaquemines, Jefferson, St. John, St. Charles, St. James, Ascension, Assumption, Terrebonne, Lafourche, St. Mary, St. Martin, and Orleans, including the city of New Orleans), Mississippi, Alabama, Florida, Georgia, South Carolina, North Carolina, and Virginia (except the forty-eight counties designated as West Virginia, and also the counties of Berkeley, Accomac, Northhampton, Elizabeth City, York, Princess Anne, and Norfolk, including the cities of Norfolk and Portsmouth), and which excepted parts are for the present left precisely as if this proclamation were not issued.

And by virtue of the power and for the purpose aforesaid, I do order and declare that all persons held as slaves within said designated States and parts of States are, and henceforward shall be, free; and that the Executive Government of the United States, including the military and naval authorities thereof, will recognize and maintain the freedom of said persons.

And I do hereby enjoin upon the people so declared to be free to abstain from all violence, unless in necessary self-defense; and I recommend to them that, in all cases when allowed, they labor faithfully for reasonable wages.

And I further declare and make known that such persons of suitable condition will be received into the armed service of the United States to garrison forts, positions, stations, and other places, and to man vessels of all sorts in said service.

And upon this act, sincerely believed to be an act of justice, warranted by the Constitution upon military necessity, I invoke the considerate judgment of mankind and the gracious favor of Almighty God.

The Freedmen's Bureau Is Established, 1865 *

*An Act to establish a Bureau for the Relief of Freedmen
and Refugees.*

Be it enacted, That there is hereby established in the War Department, to continue during the present war of rebellion, and for one year thereafter, a bureau of refugees, freedmen, and abandoned lands, to which shall be committed, as hereinafter provided, the supervision and management of all

---

* *U.S. Statutes at Large,* XIII, pp. 507 ff. This Bureau was set up to care for the freedmen and for abandoned lands in the Southern states and was to continue for one year, but on February 19, 1866, the act was extended for a year under a bill which President Johnson vetoed. In July of that year a supplementary freedmen's bureau act was passed over his veto.

abandoned lands, and the control of all subjects relating to refugees and freedmen from rebel states, or from any district of country within the territory embraced in the operations of the army, under such rules and regulations as may be prescribed by the head of the bureau and approved by the President. The said bureau shall be under the management and control of a commissioner to be appointed by the President, by and with the advice and consent of the Senate. . . .

Sec. 2. That the Secretary of War may direct such issues of provisions, clothing, and fuel, as he may deem needful for the immediate and temporary shelter and supply of destitute and suffering refugees and freedmen and their wives and children, under such rules and regulations as he may direct.

Sec. 3. That the President may, by and with the advice and consent of the Senate, appoint an assistant commissioner for each of the states declared to be in insurrection, not exceeding ten in number, who shall, under the direction of the commissioner, aid in the execution of the provisions of this act; . . . And any military officer may be detailed and assigned to duty under this act without increase of pay or allowances. . . .

Sec. 4. That the commissioner, under the direction of the President, shall have authority to set apart, for the use of loyal refugees and freedmen, such tracts of land within the insurrectionary states as shall have been abandoned, or to which the United States shall have acquired title by confiscation or sale, or otherwise, and to every male citizen, whether refugee or freedmen, as aforesaid, there shall be assigned not more than forty acres of such land, and the person to whom it was so assigned shall be protected in the use and enjoyment of the land for the term of three years at an annual rent not exceeding six per centum upon the value of such land, as it was appraised by the state authorities in the year eighteen hundred and sixty, for the purpose of taxation, and in case no such appraisal can be found, then the rental shall be based upon the estimated value of the land in said year, to be ascertained in such manner as the commissioner may by regulation prescribe. At the end of said term, or at any time during said term, the occupants of any parcels so assigned may purchase the land and receive such title thereto as the United States can convey, upon paying therefore the value of the land, as ascertained and fixed for the purpose of determining the annual rent aforesaid. . . .

The Capacity of the Negro for Education, 1865 *

Their behalf that reading and writing are to bring with them inestimable advantages, seems, in its universality and intensity, like a mysterious instinct. All who have been among them bear witness to this fact. As

* *Report* of the New England Freedmen's Aid Society, 1865. Given in Walter L. Fleming, *Documentary History of Reconstruction.* II, pp. 174-75.

respects aptitude to learn, there is similar unanimity of testimony. It cannot be expected that a man or woman whose only school-training heretofore has been that of the plantation-school, or that children whose ancestors have been slaves for generations back, should show the same quickness that the children of New-England parents manifest. The negro adult or child, before he enters the Freedmen's school, has been at a very bad preparatory school. Slave-masters are not good schoolmasters: still,—due allowance made for parentage and training—it is not too much to say, that the aptitude at acquiring the elements of knowledge is, by the testimony of all our teachers, marvelous under the circumstances. They do not write as if they found calls for more patience than is demanded in our ordinary Northern schools. And it is a most significant fact, that the most enthusiastic are not the new teachers, but those who have been at their posts from the beginning. It may be of interest to some, to know that they do not find any difference, in respect to intellect, between those of pure blood and those of mixed blood.

The importance of the work of educating the freedmen, can hardly be exaggerated. Its results will reach into the future. . . . The great mass of white men, who are now disloyal, will remain, for some time to come, disaffected. Black men who are now friendly will remain so. And to them must the country look in a large degree, as a counteracting influence against the evil councils and designs of the white freemen.

The Northern Teacher in the South after 1865 *

During the last years of the Civil War and throughout the period of reconstruction several thousand Northern teachers, selected and supported by aid societies and educational associations, entered the South and established schools for Negroes and whites. Abolitionist in sentiment and equalitarian in practice, these men and women represented a philosophy which was anathema to the Southern whites, and the program which they introduced met with hearty and active opposition.

* Henry L. Swint, *The Northern Teacher in the South,* 1862-1870 (Nashville, Tenn., Vanderbilt University Press, 1941). Preface. The documents that follow in this section are drawn largely from this work with the permission of the author and publisher.

Swint estimates that the expenditure for Northern teachers in the South from 1862 to 1870 was between five million and six million dollars. In freedmen's schools in the South in 1869, two years after the beginning of Congressional Reconstruction, there were 9,500 teachers, most of them from Northern States. Among the organizations that were active in relief, religious and educational work in the South during the years following the end of the war were the American Union Commission; New England Freedmen's Aid Society; Pennsylvania Freedmen's Relief Association; National Freedmen's Relief Association of New York; Western Freedmen's Aid Society; American Freedmen's Union Commission; American Missionary Society; Freedmen's Aid Society of the Methodist Episcopal Church; Boston Educational Commission; Indiana Freedmen's Aid Commission; Indiana Yearly Meeting of Friends; Friends' Association of Philadelphia for the Relief of Colored Freedmen, all of which seem to have cooperated with the Bureau of Refugees, Freedmen, and Abandoned Lands (Freedmen's Bureau), created in the War Department, March 3, 1865.

Immediately after the collapse of the Confederacy many Southern leaders advocated the education of the freedmen, but they insisted that such education be carried out by the Southerner rather than by the "Yankee schoolmarm." As the political controversy progressed from bitterness to violence the Northern teacher became the object of social ostracism, persecution, and physical assault. . . .

A Virginia Editor Objects to Northern Teachers, 1866 *

They are gone or going.—The only joy of our existence in Norfolk has deserted us. The "negro school-marms" are either gone, going, or to go, and we don't much care which, whereto, or how—whether it be to the more frigid regions of the Northern zone, or to a still more torrid climate; indeed, we may say that we care very little what land they are borne to, so not again to "our'n," even though it be that bourn whence no traveler returns. Our grief at their departure is, however, lightened somewhat by the recollection of the fact that we will get rid of an abominable nuisance.

Our only fear is that their departure will not be eternal, and like other birds of prey they may return to us in season, and again take shelter, with their brood of black birds, under the protecting wings of that gobbling and foulest of old fowls, the well known buzzard yclept Freedmen's Bureau.

In all seriousness, however, we congratulate our citizens upon a "good riddance of bad baggage" in the reported departure of these impudent missionaries. Of all the insults to which the Southern people have been subjected, this was the heaviest to bear . . . to have sent among us a lot of ignorant, narrow-minded, bigoted fanatics, ostensibly for the purpose of propagating the gospel among the heathen, and teaching our little negroes and big negroes, and all kinds of negroes, to read the Bible and show them the road to salvation . . . but whose real object was to disorganize and demoralize still more our peasantry and laboring population. . . .

We hail with satisfaction the departure of these female disorganizers, and trust no favoring gale will ever return them to our shores, and that their *bureau* and other furniture may soon follow in their wake.

The Ku Klux Klan Warns a Northern Teacher, 1868 †

You are a dern aberlition puppy and scoundrel if We hear of your name in the papers again we will burn your hellish house over your head cut your entrals out.

The K K s are on your track and you will be in hell in four days if you

---

* *Norfolk Virginian*, July 2, 1866. Swint, *op. cit.*, pp. 105-06.

† *Freedmen's Record*, IV (May, 1868), pp. 80-81. Swint, *op. cit.*, p. 108. Swint says that "G.W.A." referred "to G. W. Ashburn, prominent Radical politician in Georgia, who was murdered in Jonesboro, Georgia."

don't mind yourself, mind that you don't go the same way that G.W.A. went some night
Yours in hell

K K K

The Civil Rights Act, 1875 *

Whereas it is essential to just government we recognize the equality of all men before the law, and hold that it is the duty of government in its dealings with the people to mete out equal and exact justice to all, of whatever nativity, race, color, or persuasion, religious or political; and it being the appropriate object of legislation to enact great fundamental principles into law: Therefore,

Be it enacted, That all persons within the jurisdiction of the United States shall be entitled to the full and equal enjoyment of the accommodations, advantages, facilities, and privileges of inns, public conveyances on land or water, theaters, and other places of public amusement; subject only to the conditions and limitations established by law, and applicable alike to citizens of every race and color, regardless of any previous condition of servitude.

Sec. 2. That any person who shall violate the foregoing section by denying to any citizen, except for reasons by law applicable to citizens of every race and color, and regardless of any previous condition of servitude, the full enjoyment of any of the accommodations, advantages, facilities, or privileges in said section enumerated, or by aiding or inciting such denial, shall, for every such offense, forfeit and pay the sum of five hundred dollars to the person aggrieved thereby, . . . and shall also, for every such offense, be deemed guilty of a misdemeanor, and, upon conviction thereof, shall be fined not less than five hundred nor more than one thousand dollars, or shall be imprisoned not less than thirty days nor more than one year. . . .

Sec. 3. That the district and circuit courts of the United States shall have, exclusively of the courts of the several States, cognizance of all crimes and offenses against, and violations of, the provisions of this act. . . .

Sec. 4. That no citizen possessing all other qualifications which are or may be prescribed by law shall be disqualified for service as grand or petit juror in any court of the United States, or of any State, on account of race, color, or previous condition of servitude; and any officer or other person charged with any duty in the selection or summoning of jurors who shall exclude or fail to summon any citizen for the cause aforesaid shall, on conviction thereof, be deemed guilty of a misdemeanor, and be fined not more than five thousand dollars.

Sec. 5. That all cases arising under the provisions of this act . . . shall be renewable by the Supreme Court of the United States, without regard to the sum in controversy. . . .

* *U. S. Statutes at Large,* XVIII, pp. 335 ff.

Threat to a White Teacher of a Negro School in
Pike County, Alabama, 1875 *

September 20th 1875

Mr. Banks we thought we would give you a chance to save yourself one of the worst scourings that a man ever got and you can do so by reading this note and acting upon its contents. You have set up a nigger school in the settlement which we will not allow you to teach if you was a full blooded negro we would have nothing to say but a white skin negro is a little more than we can stand you can dismiss the school imediately or prepar yourself to travail we will give you a chance to save yourself and you had better move instanter.

Our little band calls themselves The Writing Straitners and if you dont leave this settlement with your negro children we will straten you.

Booker T. Washington Receives an Honorary Master's
Degree from Harvard, 1896 †

More than once I have been asked what was the greatest surprise that ever came to me. I have little hesitation in answering that question. It was the following letter, which came to me one Sunday morning when I was sitting on the veranda of my home at Tuskegee, surrounded by my wife and three children:—

HARVARD UNIVERSITY, CAMBRIDGE, May 28, 1896
PRESIDENT BOOKER T. WASHINGTON,
MY DEAR SIR: Harvard University desires to confer on you at the approaching Commencement an honorary degree; but it is our custom to confer degrees only on gentlemen who are present. Our Commencement occurs this year on June 24, and your presence would be desirable from about noon till about five o'clock in the afternoon. Would it be possible for you to be in Cambridge on that day?
Believe me, with great regard,

Very truly yours,
CHARLES W. ELIOT

This was a recognition that had never in the slightest manner entered into my mind, and it was hard for me to realize that I was to be honoured by a degree from the oldest and most renowned university in America. As I sat upon my veranda, with this letter in my hand, tears came into my eyes. My whole former life—my life as a slave on the plantation, my work

---

* *State Journal,* October 4, 1875. Given in Walter L. Fleming's *Documentary History of Reconstruction.* II, p. 206. The notice was dated September 20, 1875. Fleming says that "Such notices were sent to obnoxious teachers, especially in the white districts after 1870."
† Booker T. Washington, *Up from Slavery* (New York, Doubleday, Doran and Co., 1938), pp. 295-302. For Washington's views on the education of the Negro, see his *The Future of the American Negro* (Boston, Small, Maynard and Company, 1899), pp. 18, 23-24, 25-26, 32-34, 41, 68-69, 73, 77, 79, 93, 106-08, 137, 153, 173, 181, 182-83, 195, 205-06, 240, 243-44.

in the coal-mine, the times when I was without food and clothing, when I made my bed under a sidewalk, my struggles for an education, the trying days I had had at Tuskegee, days when I did not know where to turn for a dollar to continue the work there, the ostracism and sometimes oppression of my race,—all this passed before me and nearly overcame me. . . .

At nine o'clock, on the morning of June 24, I met President Eliot, the Board of Overseers of Harvard University, and the other guests, at the designated place on the university grounds, for the purpose of being escorted to Sanders Theatre, where the Commencement exercises were to be held and degrees conferred. Among others invited to be present for the purpose of receiving a degree at this time were General Nelson A. Miles, Dr. Bell, the inventor of the Bell telephone, Bishop Vincent, and the Rev. Minot J. Savage. We were placed in line immediately behind the President and the Board of Overseers, and directly afterward the Governor of Massachusetts, escorted by the Lancers, arrived and took his place in the line of march by the side of President Eliot. In the line there were also various other officers and professors, clad in cap and gown. In this order we marched to Sanders Theatre, where, after the usual Commencement exercises, came the conferring of the honorary degrees. . . .

When my name was called, I rose, and President Eliot, in beautiful and strong English, conferred upon me the degree of Master of Arts. After these exercises were over, those who had received honorary degrees were invited to lunch with the President. After the lunch we were formed in line again, and were escorted by the Marshal of the day, who that year happened to be Bishop William Lawrence, through the grounds, where, at different points, those who had been honoured were called by name and received the Harvard yell. This march ended at Memorial Hall, where the alumni dinner was served. . . .

Among the speakers after dinner were President Eliot, Governor Roger Wolcott, General Miles, Dr. Minot Savage, the Hon. Henry Cabot Lodge, and myself. When I was called upon, I said, among other things:—

It would in some measure relieve my embarrassment if I could, even in a slight degree, feel myself worthy of the great honour which you do me to-day. Why you have called me from the Black Belt of the South, from among my humble people, to share in the honours of this occasion, is not for me to explain; and yet it may not be inappropriate for me to suggest that it seems to me that one of the most vital questions that touch our American life is how to bring the strong, wealthy, and learned into helpful touch with the poorest, most ignorant, and humblest, and at the same time make one appreciate the vitalizing, strengthening influence of the other. How shall we make the mansions on yon Beacon Street feel and see the need of the spirits in the lowliest cabin in Alabama cotton-fields or Louisiana sugar-bottoms? This problem Harvard University is solving, not by bringing itself down, but by bringing the masses up.

If my life in the past has meant anything in the lifting up of my people and the bringing about of better relations between your race and mine, I assure you from this day it will mean doubly more. In the economy of God there is but one standard by which an individual can succeed—there is but one for a race. This country demands that every race shall measure itself by the American standard. By it a race must rise or fall, succeed or fail, and in the last analysis mere sentiment counts for little. During the next half-century and more, my race must continue passing through the severe American crucible. We are to be tested in our patience, our forbearance, our perseverance, our power to endure wrong, to withstand temptations, to economize, to acquire and use skill; in our ability to compete, to succeed in commerce, to disregard the superficial for the real, the appearance for the substance, to be great and yet small, learned and yet simple, high and yet the servant of all.

As this was the first time that a New England university had conferred an honorary degree upon a Negro, it was the occasion of much newspaper comment throughout the country. A correspondent of a New York paper said:—

When the name of Booker T. Washington was called, and he arose to acknowledge and accept, there was such an outburst of applause as greeted no other name except that of the popular soldier patriot, General Miles. The applause was not studied and stiff, sympathetic and condoling; it was enthusiasm and admiration. Every part of the audience from pit to gallery joined in, and a glow covered the cheeks of those around me, proving sincere appreciation of the rising struggle of an ex-slave and the work he has accomplished for his race.

A Boston paper said, editorially:—

In conferring the honorary degree of Master of Arts upon the Principal of Tuskegee Institute, Harvard University has honoured itself as well as the object of this distinction. The work which Professor Booker T. Washington has accomplished for the education, good citizenship and popular enlightenment in his chosen field of labour in the South entitles him to rank with our national benefactors. The university which can claim him on its list of sons, whether in regular course or *honoris causa,* may be proud. . . .

Another Boston paper said:—

It is Harvard which, first among New England colleges, confers an honorary degree upon a black man. No one who has followed the history of Tuskegee and its work can fail to admire the courage, persistence, and splendid common sense of Booker T. Washington. Well may Harvard honour the ex-slave, the value of whose services, alike to his race and country, only the future can estimate.

The correspondent of the New York *Times* wrote:—

All the speeches were enthusiastically received, but the coloured man carried off the oratorical honours, and the applause which broke out when he had finished was vociferous and long-continued. . . .

John Spencer Bassett of Trinity College Describes Booker T. Washington the Greatest Man Born in the South in a Century, with the Exception of Robert E. Lee, and Starts Violent Controversy, 1903 *

. . . The development of the negro since the war has been calculated to intensify this natural race feeling. Singularly enough both his progress and his regression under the regime of freedom have brought down on him the hostility of the whites. His regression might well do this because it has stood for his lapse into a lower state after the removal of the supporting hand of the white man. This lapse has not occurred in all sections of the race—perhaps it has not occurred with a majority of the race—but there can be no denial that some negroes today are more worthless than any negroes in slavery. The master was always a restraining hand on the negro, holding back at both extremes. He kept the slave man from going into the higher fields of intellectual development; he confirmed his lack of high moral purpose and he weighed down his self-respect and his individuality,

* "Stirring up the Fires of Race Antipathy," *The South Atlantic Quarterly,* II (October, 1903), 298-99. In this article Bassett tried to give a calm and sane discussion of the "Negro Problem" but in doing so presented some views that sharply clashed with those commonly held in the South and led to considerable excitement. Most of the press condemned Bassett, editor of the magazine, and also President Kilgo and Trinity College; while favorable editorials appeared in papers in Boston, New York, and Omaha which gave the little college more than a local reputation. *The Omaha Daily Bee* (December 6, 1903) called the outcome of the case "A Victory for Free Speech," *The Independent* (December 10, 1903) called it "A Southern Victory," and *The Brooklyn Daily Eagle* (December 3, 1903) gave to its editorial the title "Free Speech in the South," *The Boston Herald* to its "Free Speech in the Universities," and *The New York Evening Post* "College Freedom, South and North." Josephus Daniels, editor of *The News and Observer* (Raleigh) spelled Bassett's name "bASSett." The trustees of Trinity College met from 7 P.M. to 3 A.M., heard the case of Bassett's resignation, voted 18 to 7 not to accept it, and then witnessed or soon read about the burning of the editor of *The News and Observer* in effigy by the students of the college who generally stood up for their very scholarly and popular teacher. When Kilgo appeared before the trustees and made a powerful plea for academic freedom he had in his possession his own resignation and the resignations of the members of the faculty; and if Bassett's resignation had been accepted Trinity College (now Duke University) would have been without a president or a faculty. See Paul N. Garber, *John Carlisle Kilgo: President of Trinity College, 1894-1910* (Durham, N. C., Duke University Press, 1937), pp. 239-86; Virginius Dabney, *Liberalism in the South* (Chapel Hill, University of North Carolina Press, 1932), pp. 339-41. This was the first time *The South Atlantic Quarterly* had discussed racial issues. In the same issue of the magazine President Kilgo had an article on "Our Duty to the Negro." (The statement in high praise of Booker T. Washington, which set off the controversy, was not in the original draft of the article. Bassett inserted it in the proof after wide and somewhat wild newspaper accounts of the serving of breakfast, by a hotel of the Seaboard Air Line Railway in Hamlet, North Carolina, to a group of Negro business men including Washington.) For further discussion of cases involving freedom of speech in the South see Dabney, *op. cit.;* and for cases involving conflicts between religious orthodoxy and heterodoxy, fundamentalism and modernism, science and theology, and over Darwinism see Arthur M. Schlesinger, "A Critical Period in American Religion," *Proceedings of the Massachusetts Historical Society,* LXIV, pp. 523-48.

all of which were checks on the best negroes. On the other hand the master was a check on the lowest tendencies of the negro. He restrained his dissipations; he sought to save him from disease; he tried to make him honest and peaceable; and he was very careful that he should not be an idler. The removal of the master's authority has produced a marked change on each of these extremes. The upper class negro has seized with surprising readiness his new opportunity. No sensible man in the North or in the South who is not blinded by passion will deny that the better negroes of the country have made a remarkable record since the days of emancipation. In the same way the lower class have also made a rapid progress. Among them idleness and shiftlessness have increased; petty crimes and quarrels have increased; coarse ideas have found greater sway; and viciousness has augmented. These good and these bad habits are the fruits of his freedom.

Neither of these two classes, the upper and the lower, are all the negroes; and in forgetting this fact some well intentioned people have fallen into serious error. A man whose mind runs away into baseless optimism is apt to point to Booker T. Washington as a product of the negro race. Now Washington is a great and good man, a Christian statesman, and take him all in all the greatest man, save General Lee, born in the South in a hundred years; but he is not a typical negro. He does not even represent the better class of negroes. He is an exceptional man; and, endowed as he is, it is probable that he would have remained uneducated but for the philanthropic intervention of white men. The race, even the best of them, are so far behind him that we cannot in reason look for his reproduction in the present generation. It is, therefore, too much to hope, for a continued appearance of such men in the near future. It is also too much to set his development up as a standard for his race. To expect it is to insure disappointment. . . .

President Kilgo Resigns in Defense of Bassett, 1903 *

To the Board of Trustees of Trinity College

Honorable Sirs:—

With due respect, and I trust with becoming dignity, I herewith hand you my resignation as President of Trinity College. This action is taken in the full light and sacred appreciation of cordial relations which have existed between us during the entire period of my occupancy of the administrative office of Trinity College,—a period now far into the tenth year. It is not worth while to recount any of the successes of these years. The record is before the eyes of men. However, it is becoming of me to express my thanks for all courtesies and confidences received from your honorable

* Paul N. Garber, *John Carlisle Kilgo: President of Trinity College, 1894-1910* (Durham, N. C., Duke University Press, 1937), pp. 274-75.

Board. It is also due you as well as myself to place on record the reasons which have influenced me to present you my resignation.

First, as an American citizen, striving to cherish a genuine love of his nation, and having an abiding faith in the principles of freedom, I cannot consistently, for the sake of punishing a foolish and needless act in a fellow-citizen, do violence to my faith in and love of my country's principles, which were born out of the holiest and intensest wish to found in the earth a nation resting on the spirit of human tolerance.

Second, having been born in the South, I openly confess a love of Southern life and the deepest sympathies with its traditions, and therefore cannot approve, and do not approve, any rash disregard of the feelings which belong to true Southern character. This spirit of loyalty to the South makes it impossible for me to consent to co-operate with any idea which seems to say that Southern people have nothing of a forgiving tolerance and a patient courage. The record of the noblest Southern spirits established just the opposite.

Third, from childhood I was taught the doctrines which belong to Methodism, a Church seemingly ordained to proclaim the doctrine of human tolerance and freedom, at a time when ecclesiastical, civic, and social intolerance was arrogant and tyrannical, and I cannot have any part in an act which in the slightest way seems to repudiate the Church whose doctrines and principles I came, as a child, to believe and love.

Fourth, conscious of parental duties to those of my own home, and to the generations to come, I am unwilling for the sake of personal comfort, or any other temporal consideration, to make a record which may cause doubt of my faith in my country's ideals, and the noblest virtues of the Christian religion.

Fifth, with a claim to a modest love of learning, I stand pledged for the defense of academic freedom. I assert, with due emphasis, and positiveness, that academic freedom is not set for the defense of academic folly. However, I cannot believe that academic folly should be punished with banishment and exile. It is nobler to forgive academic folly than it is to banish men for it. I cannot consent to have the most foreign connection with any act which enslaves thought, shuts any gate to truth and virtue, and intimidates the mind in its efforts to gain helpful knowledge.

Sixth, amid all the struggle of history, the chief struggle has been the incoming of an eternal kingdom founded upon truth and right and tolerance and love and freedom. This kingdom was born of blood; it is acquainted with the severest persecutions; but as the centuries have multiplied it has grown. Having an unshaken faith in it, I am bound to its principles, and prefer to suffer in adherence to its spirit of tolerance than to escape any pain by the slightest denials of the spirit of the Christian religion.

In conclusion, I ask you to regard this act as being born out of those impulses which carry in them permanent destiny.

Assuring you of love, I am,

Yours sincerely,

JNO. C. KILGO

The Legislature of Kentucky Prohibits Mixed Schools, 1904 *

That it shall be unlawful for any person, corporation or association of persons to maintain or operate any college, school or institution where persons of the white and negro races are both received as pupils for instruction; and any person or corporation who shall operate or maintain any such college, school or institution shall be fined one thousand dollars, and any person or corporation who may be convicted of violating the provisions of this act, shall be fined one hundred dollars for each day they may operate said school, college or institution, after such conviction.

That any instructor who shall teach in any school, college or institution where members of the said two races are received as pupils for instruction shall be guilty of operating and maintaining same and fined as provided in the first section hereof.

It shall be unlawful for any white person to attend any school or institution where negroes are received as pupils or receive instruction, and it shall be unlawful for any negro or colored person to attend any school or institution where white persons are received as pupils or receive instruction. Any person so offending shall be fined fifty dollars for each day he attends such institution or school.

Nothing in this act shall be construed to prevent any private school, college or institution of learning from maintaining a separate and distinct branch thereof, in a different locality, not less than twenty-five miles distant, for the education exclusively of one race or color.

Berea College v. Commonwealth of Kentucky, 1908 †

MR. JUSTICE BREWER . . . delivered the opinion of the court.

There is no dispute as to the facts. That the act does not violate the constitution of Kentucky is settled by the decision of its highest court, and

* Acts of the General Assembly of the Commonwealth of Kentucky, 1904, pp. 181-82. It was under this law, passed March 22, 1904, to go into effect a few months later, that the indictment was brought against Berea College. See below, "Berea College v. Commonwealth of Kentucky."

† Berea College v. Commonwealth of Kentucky, 211 U.S. 53-58. Berea College admitted both white and Negro students until the enactment of the statute given above. Early in 1950, after nearly a half century, the legislature of Kentucky by a vote of twenty-three to three in the senate and fifty to sixteen in the house did away with the "Day Law" of 1904 and thus made it possible for Berea College to admit Negroes. The new law said that Negroes may attend schools offering classes above the high school level provided (1) that the trustees approve and (2) that comparable courses are not available at Kentucky State College for Negroes at Frankfort. See Time, April 24, 1950, p. 91, and The Berea Alumnus, April, 1950, pp. 202-03, 223.

the single question for our consideration is whether it conflicts with the Federal Constitution. The Court of Appeals discussed at some length the general power of the State in respect to the separation of the two races. It also ruled that "the right to teach white and negro children in a private school at the same time and place is not a property right. Besides, appellant as a corporation created by this State has no natural right to teach at all. Its right to teach is such as the State sees fit to give to it. The State may withhold it altogether, or qualify it." *Allgeyer* v. *Louisiana,* 165 U.S. 578.

Upon this we remark that when a state court decides a case upon two grounds, one Federal and the other non-Federal, this court will not disturb the judgment if the non-Federal ground, fairly construed, sustains the decision. *Murdock* v. *City of Memphis,* 20 Wall. 590, 636; *Eustis* v. *Bolles,* 150 U.S. 361; *Giles* v. *Teasley,* 193 U.S. 146, 160; *Allen* v. *Arguimbau,* 198 U.S. 149.

Again, the decision by a state court of the extent and limitation of the powers conferred by the State upon one of its own corporations is of a purely local nature. In creating a corporation a State may withhold powers which may be exercised by and cannot be denied to an individual. It is under no obligation to treat both alike. In granting corporate powers the legislature may deem that the best interests of the State would be subserved by some restriction, and the corporation may not plead that in spite of the restriction it has more or greater powers because the citizen has. "The granting of such right or privilege [the right or privilege to be a corporation] rests entirely in the discretion of the State, and, of course, when granted, may be accompanied with such conditions as its legislature may judge most befitting to its interests and policy." *Home Ins. Co.* v. *New York,* 134 U.S. 594, 600; *Perine* v. *Chesapeake & Delaware Canal Co.,* 9 How. 172, 184; *Horn Silver Mining Co.* v. *New York,* 143 U.S. 305-312. The act of 1904 forbids "any person, corporation or association of persons to maintain or operate any college," etc. Such a statute may conflict with the Federal Constitution in denying to individuals powers which they may rightfully exercise, and yet, at the same time, be valid as to a corporation created by the State.

It may be said that the Court of Appeals sustained the validity of this section of the statute, both against individuals and corporations. It ruled that the legislation was within the power of the State, and that the State might rightfully thus restrain all individuals, corporations and associations. But it is unnecessary for us to consider anything more than the question of its validity as applied to corporations.

The statute is clearly separable and may be valid as to one class while invalid as to another. Even if it were conceded that its assertion of power over individuals cannot be sustained, still it must be upheld so far as it restrains corporations.

There is no force in the suggestion that the statute, although clearly separable, must stand or fall as an entirety on the ground the legislature would not have enacted one part unless it could reach all. That the legislature of Kentucky desired to separate the teaching of white and colored children may be conceded, but it by no means follows that it would not have enforced the separation so far as it could do so, even though it could not make it effective under all circumstances. In other words, it is not at all unreasonable to believe that the legislature, although advised beforehand of the constitutional question, might have prohibited all organizations and corporations under its control from teaching white and colored children together, and thus made at least uniform official action. The rule of construction in questions of this nature is stated by Chief Justice Shaw in *Warren* v. *Mayor of Charlestown,* 2 Gray 84, quoted approvingly by this court in *Allen* v. *Louisiana,* 103 U.S. 80-84.

"But if they are so mutually connected with and dependent on each other, as conditions, considerations or compensations for each other as to warrant a belief that the legislature intended them as a whole, and that if all could not be carried into effect, the legislature would not pass the residue independently, and some parts are unconstitutional, all the provisions which are thus dependent, conditional or connected, must fall with them."

See also *Loeb* v. *Township Trustees,* 179 U.S. 472, 490, in which this court said:

"As one section of a statute may be repugnant to the Constitution without rendering the whole act void, so, one provision of a section may be invalid by reason of its not conforming to the Constitution, while all the other provisions may be subject to no constitutional infirmity. One part may stand, while another will fall, unless the two are so connected or dependent on each other in subject-matter, meaning or purpose, that the good cannot remain without the bad. The point is, not whether the parts are contained in the same section, for, the distribution into sections is purely artificial; but whether they are essentially and inseparably connected in substance—whether the provisions are so interdependent that one cannot operate without the other."

Further, inasmuch as the Court of Appeals considered the act separable, and while sustaining it as an entirety gave an independent reason which applies only to corporations, it is obvious that it recognized the force of the suggestions we have made. And when a state statute is so interpreted this court should hesitate before it holds that the Supreme Court of the State did not know what was the thought of the legislature in its enactment. *Missouri, Kansas & Texas Railway* v. *McCann,* 174 U.S. 580, 586; *Tullis* v. *Lake Erie & Western Railroad,* 175 U.S. 348, 353.

While the terms of the present charter are not given in the record, yet it was admitted on the trial that the defendant was a corporation organized and incorporated under the general statutes of the State of Kentucky, and of course the state courts, as well as this court on appeal, take judicial notice of those statutes. Further, in the brief of counsel for the defendant is given a history of the incorporation proceedings, together with the charters. From that it appears that Berea College was organized under the authority of an act for the incorporation of voluntary associations, approved March 9, 1854 (2 Stanton Rev. Stat. Ky. 553), which act was amended by an act of March 10, 1856 (2 Stanton, 555), and which in terms reserved to the General Assembly "the right to alter or repeal the charter of any associations formed under the provisions of this act, and the act to which this act is an amendment, at any time hereafter." After the constitution of 1891 was adopted by the State of Kentucky and on June 10, 1899, the college was reincorporated under the provisions of chap. 32, art. 8, Ky. Stat. (Carroll's Ky. Stat. 1903, p. 459), the charter defining its business in these words: "Its object is the education of all persons who may attend its institution of learning at Berea, and, in the language of the original articles, 'to promote the cause of Christ.' " The constitution of 1891 provided in § 3 of the bill of rights that "Every grant of a franchise, privilege or exemption shall remain, subject to revocation, alteration or amendment." Carroll's Ky. Stat. 1903, p. 86. So that the full power of amendment was reserved to the legislature.

It is undoubtedly true that the reserved power to alter or amend is subject to some limitations, and that under the guise of an amendment a new contract may not always be enforcible upon the corporation or the stockholders; but it is settled "that a power reserved to the legislature to alter, amend or repeal a charter authorizes it to make any alteration or amendment of a charter granted subject to it, which will not defeat or substantially impair the object of the grant, or any rights vested under it, and which the legislature may deem necessary to secure either that object or any public right. *Commissioners on Inland Fisheries* v. *Holyoke Water Power Co.,* 104 Massachusetts, 446, 451; *Holyoke Co.* v. *Lyman,* 15 Wall. 500, 522;" *Close* v. *Glenwood Cemetery,* 107 U.S. 466, 476.

Construing the statute, the Court of Appeals held that "if the same school taught the different races at different times, though at the same place or at different places at the same time it would not be unlawful." Now, an amendment to the original charter, which does not destroy the power of the college to furnish education to all persons, but which simply separates them by time or place of instruction, cannot be said to "defeat or substantially impair the object of the grant." The language of the statute is not in terms an amendment, yet its effect is an amendment, and it would be resting too much on mere form to hold that a statute which in effect works a change in the terms of the charter is not to be considered as an amendment, because not so designated. The act itself, being separable, is to be read as though it in one section prohibited any person, in another section any corporation, and in a third any association of persons to do the acts named. Reading the statute as containing a separate prohibition on all corporations, at least, all state corporations, it substantially declares that any authority given by previous charters to instruct the two races at the same time and in the same place is forbidden, and that prohibition being a departure from the terms of the original charter in this case may properly be adjudged an amendment.

Again, it is insisted that the Court of Appeals did not regard the legislation as making an amendment, because another prosecution instituted against the same corporation under the fourth section of the act, which makes it a misdemeanor to teach pupils of the two races in the same institution, even although one race is taught in one branch and another in another branch, provided the two branches are within twenty-five miles of each other, was held could not be sustained, the court saying: "This last section, we think, violates the limitations upon the police power: it is unreasonable and oppressive." But while so ruling it also held that this section could be ignored and that the remainder of the act was complete not withstanding. Whether the reasoning of the court concerning the fourth section be satisfactory or not is immaterial, for no question of its validity is presented, and the Court of Appeals, while striking it down, sustained the balance of the act. We need concern ourselves only with the inquiry whether the first section can be upheld as coming within the power of a State over its own corporate creatures.

We are of opinion, for reasons stated, that it does come within that power, and on this ground the judgment of the Court of Appeals of Kentucky is

Affirmed.

Mr. Justice Harlan, dissenting.

Court Cases Face Tests in Southern Universities, 1935 *

Two years ago a Negro student, who had graduated at the North Carolina College for Negroes, applied for admission to the pharmacy school of the University of North Carolina.

When his application was refused he sought court aid to require the University to show cause why a citizen of the State, qualified in all respects except that he was a Negro, should not be admitted to a tax-supported institution which offered the only course in pharmacy in North Carolina. The immediate question was solved when the General Assembly appropriated funds for Negro students to continue graduate and professional studies in Northern institutions. But the basic question is unanswered.

A similar case is already in the courts in Maryland, where a Negro graduate of Amherst College is seeking to enter the University of Maryland

* Lenoir Chambers, in *The New York Times,* September 1, 1935, IV, 6:2.

Law School; and the question will probably be raised in Missouri and perhaps elsewhere.

The University of Virginia has taken no action yet. Since the graduate department has considerable leeway in the admission of students, and since the institution from which the applicant graduated is not on the accredited list of the Association of American Universities, to which the University of Virginia belongs, technical reasons may be found for denying the application.

Virginia, whose State constitution says that "white and colored children shall not be taught in the same schools," is one of eighteen States which have drawn this racial line. For grammar school, high school and collegiate education, separate schools and colleges are maintained.

But the point to the present efforts, and the protest they express, is that neither Virginia nor many other States provide graduate and professional educational facilities for Negroes.

No effort is made to deny the validity of the protest from the legal point of view. But almost without exception those newspapers discussing the case, including several which have been conspicuous in urging the removal of many discriminations against Negroes, have pointed out what one of them calls "the ponderous weight of social custom" and have called into question the wisdom of rectifying "the injustice in a manner that ignores the deep-lying and still-operative forces that have compelled a separation of the races in the South's educational establishments."

Negro Teachers in Maryland Seek Salaries Equal to Those Paid White Teachers, 1937 *

Montgomery County school officials have until February 6 to show cause why Negro teachers should not be paid the same salary scale as that of white teachers.

William B. Gibson, Jr., teacher and assistant principal in the Rockville Negro Elementary School, filed a mandamus suit in Circuit Court here yesterday asking that the Negro teachers receive the same rate of pay as white teachers. Judge Charles Woodward signed an order giving the defendants until February 6 to show cause why the petition should not be granted.

Edwin W. Broome, County School Superintendent, said he understood the action was filed as a test case to have the State Court of Appeals rule on a law separating the white and Negro schools.

* *The New York Times,* January 2, 1937, 15:2.

Missouri's Position on the Teaching of Negroes from 1847 to 1865 Is Reported, 1938 *

... St. Louis public schools, beginning with their graduation exercises this month, are celebrating their centennial. Throughout the year they will commemorate in various ways the day in 1838 when the first school in the city opened with two teachers for its 175 children. . . .

Negroes were not admitted until 1866, when separate schools were founded for them, a system which still persists. From 1847 to 1865 it was a crime punishable in Missouri by fine and imprisonment to teach a Negro anything.

Missouri ex rel. Gaines v. Canada, Registrar of the University of Missouri, et al., 1938 †

Argued November 9, 1938.—Decided December 12, 1938.

1. The State of Missouri provides separate schools and universities for whites and negroes. At the state university, attended by whites, there is a course in law; at the Lincoln University, attended by negroes, there is as yet none, but it is the duty of the curators of that institution to establish one there whenever in their opinion this shall be necessary and practicable, and pending such development, they are authorized to arrange for legal education of Missouri negroes, and to pay the tuition charges therefor, at law schools in adjacent States where negroes are accepted and where the training is equal to that obtainable at the Missouri State University. Pursuant to the State's policy of separating the races in its educational institutions, the curators of the state university refused to admit a negro as a student in the law school there because of his race; whereupon he sought a mandamus, in the state courts, which was denied. *Held:*

(1) That inasmuch as the curators of the state university represented the State, in carrying out its policy, their action in denying the negro admission to the law school was state action, within the meaning of the Fourteenth Amendment. P. 343.

(2) The action of the State in furnishing legal education within the State to whites while not furnishing legal education within the State to negroes, was a discrimination repugnant to the Fourteenth Amendment. P. 344.

If a State furnishes higher education to white residents, it is bound to furnish substantially equal advantages to negro residents, though not necessarily in the same schools.

(3) The unconstitutional discrimination is not avoided by the purpose of the State to establish a law school for negroes whenever necessary and

* *The New York Times,* January 16, 1938, II, 5:5.
† 305 U.S. 337-54. For three very significant decisions of the Court, June 5, 1950, see below.

practicable in the opinion of the curators of the University provided for negroes. P. 346.

(4) Nor are the requirements of the equal protection clause satisfied by the opportunities afforded by Missouri to its negro citizens for legal education in other States. P. 348.

The basic consideration here is not as to what sort of opportunities other States provide, or whether they are as good as those in Missouri, but as to what opportunities Missouri itself furnishes to white students and denies to negroes solely upon the ground of color. The admissibility of laws separating the races in the enjoyment of privileges afforded by the State rests wholly upon the equality of the privileges which the laws give to the separated groups within the State. By the operation of the laws of Missouri a privilege has been created for white law students which is denied to negroes by reason of their race. The white resident is afforded legal education within the State; the negro resident having the same qualifications is refused it there and must go outside the State to obtain it. That is a denial of the equality of the legal right to the enjoyment of the privilege which the State has set up, and the provision for the payment of tuition fees in another State does not remove the discrimination. P. 348.

(5) The obligation of the State to give the protection of equal laws can be performed only where its laws operate, that is, within its own jurisdiction. It is there that the equality of legal right must be maintained. That obligation is imposed by the Constitution upon the States severally as governmental entities—each responsible for its own laws establishing the rights and duties of persons within its borders. P. 350.

(6) The fact that there is but a limited demand in Missouri for the legal education of negroes does not excuse the discrimination in favor of whites. P. 350.

(7) Inasmuch as the discrimination may last indefinitely—so long as the curators find it unnecessary and impracticable to provide facilities for the legal education of negroes within the State, the alternative of attendance at law schools in other States being provided meanwhile—it can not be excused as a temporary discrimination. P. 351.

2. The state court decided this case upon the merits of the federal question, and not upon the propriety of remedy by mandamus. P. 352.

342 Mo. 121; 113 S.W. 2d 783, reversed.

MR. CHIEF JUSTICE HUGHES delivered the opinion of the Court. . . .

The judgment of the Supreme Court of Missouri is reversed and the cause is remanded for further proceedings not inconsistent with this opinion.

Reversed.

Separate opinion of MR. JUSTICE MCREYNOLDS . . .

MR. JUSTICE BUTLER concurs in the above views.

A Newspaper Account of "The Gaines Decision," 1938 *

In a six-to-two decision, the Supreme Court to-day ruled in effect that Lloyd Gaines, a St. Louis Negro, must either be admitted to the Law School of the University of Missouri or a school of law must be established at Lincoln University maintained by Missouri for the higher education of Negroes, to which he can be admitted. . . .

The Hughes (Chief Justice Hughes) finding, reversing the Missouri Supreme Court, held that Mr. Gaines was entitled under the Fourteenth Amendment of the Constitution to a legal education equivalent to that provided for white students and that he had not received "equal protection" of the laws by the offer of Missouri to pay his tuition in an adjacent State where there was no discrimination against Negro students.

Mr. Gaines, a graduate of Lincoln University at Jefferson City had asked for admission to the law school at the university. After his application was refused, he sought a writ of mandamus to compel the registrar and the board of curators to admit him. The Missouri courts denied the application for mandamus, whereupon Mr. Gaines brought the case to Washington.

Justice Hughes said the high court was of the opinion "that petitioner was entitled to be admitted to the law school of the State University in the absence of other and proper provisions for his legal training within the state."

The Chief Justice, in his opinion, observed that it was admitted at the trial that Mr. Gaines's work and credits at Lincoln University would qualify him for admission to the University Law School, if he were found otherwise eligible.

"He was refused admission," said Justice Hughes, "upon the ground that it was 'contrary to the constitution, laws and public policy of the State to admit a Negro as a student in the University of Missouri.' It appears that there are schools of law in connection with the State universities of four adjacent states, Kansas, Nebraska, Iowa, and Illinois, where non-resident Negroes are admitted."

. . . "The question here," the opinion later said, "is not of a duty of the State to supply legal training, or of the quality of the training which it does supply, but of its duty when it provides such training to furnish it to the residents of the State upon the basis of an equality of right.

"By the operation of the laws of Missouri a privilege has been created for white law students which is denied to Negroes by reason of their race. The white resident is afforded legal education within the State; the Negro resident having the same qualifications is refused it there and must go outside the State to obtain it. That is a denial of the equality of legal right to the enjoyment of privilege which the State has set up, and the provision

* *The New York Times*, December 13, 1938, 1:2.

for the payment of tuition fees in another State does not remove that discrimination.". . .

Editorial Comment on "The Gaines Decision," 1938 *

Once more the Supreme Court has spoken out in defense of equality of human rights. It has held that as long as the State of Missouri chooses to provide training for law students it must not deny to Negroes, as it has done, a privilege that it extends to white law students.

We do not think that the critics who so often denounce the Supreme Court for "obstructing the will of the people as expressed through their Legislatures" will object strongly to this decision. They will recognize in this case that the court was acting in accordance with the provision of the Constitution.

The decision cannot be ascribed to the effects of the president's court enlargement campaign. The court's record on this type of decision goes too far back for that . . . of those critics who argue that the Supreme Court merely defends the "plutocracy" and the "corporations," it is charitable to assume that they have had memories.

Sixteen States Are Affected by "The Gaines Case," 1938 †

Charles Houston, counsel for Lloyd L. Gaines, said to-night that the Supreme Court decision probably would increase higher education facilities for Negroes in sixteen states which now bar them from State professional schools.

Mr. Houston, who directed the case from the time Mr. Gaines, 25, was refused admission to the Missouri Law School in 1935, said that he was certain legal proceedings would be started in other States to bring about provisions for establishment of Negro professional schools or for admission of Negroes to established schools.

The decision, he believed, "completely knocked out as a permanent policy" the practice of paying Negro students' tuition in other States in place of giving them schooling in their home States.

Seven states now provide such grants, he said: Missouri, Virginia, West Virginia, Kentucky, Tennessee, Oklahoma and Maryland. Maryland also provided that Negroes may attend its State university if the subjects they want are not taught in Negro schools.

Mr. Houston said the following States excluded Negroes from their universities and made no other provision for graduate training: Alabama, Arkansas, Delaware, Florida, Georgia, Louisiana, Mississippi, North Carolina, South Carolina, and Texas. . . .

* *The New York Times,* December 13, 1938, 24:1.
† *The New York Times,* December 13, 1938, 10:3.

*Alston et al. v. School Board of the City of Norfolk
(Virginia) et al., 1940 ***

Circuit Court of Appeals, Fourth Circuit. June 18, 1940.

Fixing salaries of Negro teachers in public schools at a lower rate than that paid to white teachers of equal qualifications and experience, and performing the same duties on the sole basis of race and color, is violative of the "due process" and "equal protection" clauses of the Fourteenth Amendment.

The action was dismissed in the District Court of the United States for the Eastern District of Virginia, at Norfolk; Luther B. May, Judge Plaintiffs appealed.

Taken before Circuit Judges Parker, Soper, and Dobie and reversed.

JUDGE PARKER:

Melvin O. Alston and the Norfolk Teachers' Association, composed of the Negro school teachers of that city, against the school board and the superintendent of schools of Norfolk. The purpose of the action was to obtain a declaratory judgment, to the effect that the policy of the defendants in maintaining a salary schedule which fixes the salaries of Negro teachers at a lower rate than that paid to white teachers of equal qualifications and experience, and performing the same duties and services, on the sole basis of race and color, is violative of the due process and equal protective clauses of the Fourteenth Amendment, and also to obtain an injunction restraining defendants from making any distinction on the ground of race and color in fixing the salaries of public school teachers in Norfolk. The case was dismissed by the lower court on the ground that Alston and the School Board were the only necessary parties to the cause and that Alston had waived such constitutional rights as he was seeking to enforce by having entered into a written contract with the School Board to teach for a year at the price fixed in the contract.

On the appeal presented by plaintiffs three questions arose: (1) Whether upon the face of the complaint an unconstitutional discrimination was shown in the fixing of the salaries of school teachers by the defendants; (2) Whether the rights of the plaintiffs were infringed by such discrimination; and (3) Whether plaintiffs waived their right to complain of the discrimination by entering into contracts with the School Board for the current year.

The Circuit Court of Appeals held that

* *Federal Reporter*, Second Series. Vol. 112, F.2d, pp. 992-97. U. S. Supreme Court refused to hear the case. Denied certiorari. North Carolina, in which no litigation on equal salaries was brought, in 1944 equalized salaries of Negroes and whites, the first Southern state to do so, as a moral and legal obligation of the state and in fulfilling a pledge earlier made to the Negroes of that commonwealth. State officials and representative Negroes chose to achieve equalization by agreement rather than by litigation. In 1950 several of the Southern states were moving toward equalized salaries.

1. Unconstitutional.
2. Rights of plaintiffs were infringed.
3. The fact that the plaintiffs had entered into contract with the School Board to teach for a certain salary for the current year does not preclude them from asking relief.

The order appealed from was reversed and the cause "remanded for further proceedings not inconsistent herewith."

The University of Texas Must Admit Negroes, 1950 *

MR. CHIEF JUSTICE VINSON delivered the opinion of the Court. . . .

In the instant case, petitioner filed an application for admission to the University of Texas Law School for the February, 1946 term. His application was rejected solely because he is a Negro. Petitioner thereupon brought this suit for mandamus against the appropriate school officials, respondents here, to compel his admission. At that time, there was no law school in Texas which admitted Negroes.

The State trial court recognized that the action of the State in denying petitioner the opportunity to gain a legal education while granting it to others deprived him of the equal protection of the laws guaranteed by the Fourteenth Amendment. The court did not grant the relief requested, however, but continued the case for six months to allow the State to supply substantially equal facilities. At the expiration of the six months, in December, 1946, the court denied the writ on the showing that the authorized university officials had adopted an order calling for the opening of a law school for Negroes the following February. While petitioner's appeal was pending, such a school was made available, but petitioner refused to register therein. The Texas Court of Civil Appeals set aside the trial court's judgment and ordered the cause "remanded generally to the trial court for further proceedings without prejudice to the right of any party to this suit.". . .

The University of Texas Law School, from which petitioner was excluded, was staffed by a faculty of sixteen full-time and three part-time professors, some of whom are nationally recognized authorities in their field. Its student body numbered 850. The library contained over 65,000 volumes. Among the other facilities available to the students were a law review, moot court facilities, scholarship funds, and Order of the Coif affiliation. The school's alumni occupy the most distinguished positions in the private practice of the law and in the public life of the State. It may properly be considered one of the nation's ranking law schools.

The law school for Negroes which was to have opened in February, 1947, would have had no independent faculty or library. The teaching was

---
* The United States Law Week, June 6, 1950, pp. 4405-07.

to be carried on by four members of the University of Texas Law School faculty, who were to maintain their offices at the University of Texas while teaching at both institutions. Few of the 10,000 volumes ordered for the library had arrived; nor was there any full-time librarian. The school lacked accreditation.

Since the trial of this case, respondents report the opening of a law school at the Texas State University for Negroes. It is apparently on the road to full accreditation. It has a faculty of five full-time professors; a student body of 23; a library of some 16,500 volumes serviced by a full-time staff; a practice court and legal aid association; and one alumnus who has become a member of the Texas Bar.

Whether the University of Texas Law School is compared with the original or the new law school for Negroes, we cannot find substantial equality in the educational opportunities offered white and Negro law students by the State. In terms of number of the faculty, variety of courses and opportunity for specialization, size of the student body, scope of the library, availability of law review and similar activities, the University of Texas Law School is superior. What is more important, the University of Texas Law School possesses to a far greater degree those qualities which are incapable of objective measurement but which made for greatness in a law school. Such qualities, to name but a few, include reputation of the faculty, experience of the administration, position and influence of the alumni, standing in the community, traditions and prestige. It is difficult to believe that one who had a free choice between these law schools would consider the question close. . . .

In accordance with these cases, petitioner may claim his full constitutional right: legal education equivalent to that offered by the State to students of other races. Such education is not available to him in a separate law school as offered by the State. We cannot, therefore, agree with respondents that the doctrine of *Plessy* v. *Ferguson,* 163 U.S. 537 (1896), requires affirmance of the judgment below. Nor need we reach petitioner's contention that *Plessy* v. *Ferguson* should be reexamined in the light of contemporary knowledge respecting the purposes of the Fourteenth Amendment and the effects of racial segregation. . . .

We hold that the Equal Protection Clause of the Fourteenth Amendment requires that petitioner be admitted to the University of Texas Law School. The judgment is reversed and the cause is remanded for proceedings not inconsistent with this opinion.

Reversed.

The University of Oklahoma Must Not Segregate White
and Negro Students, 1950 *

MR. CHIEF JUSTICE VINSON delivered the opinion of the Court.

In this case, we are faced with the question whether a state may, after admitting a student to graduate instruction in its state university, afford him different treatment from other students solely because of his race. . . .

Appellant is a Negro citizen of Oklahoma. Possessing a Master's Degree, he applied for admission to the University of Oklahoma in order to pursue studies and courses leading to a Doctorate in Education. At that time, his application was denied, solely because of his race. The school authorities were required to exclude him by the Oklahoma statutes, . . . which made it a misdemeanor to maintain or operate, teach or attend a school at which both whites and Negroes are enrolled or taught. Appellant filed a complaint requesting injunctive relief, alleging that the action of the school authorities and the statutes upon which their action was based were unconstitutional and deprived him of the equal protection of the laws. . . .

A statutory three-judge District Court held that the State had a constitutional duty to provide him with the education he sought as soon as it provided that education for applicants of any other group. It further held that to the extent the Oklahoma statutes denied him admission they were unconstitutional and void. On the assumption, however, that the State would follow the constitutional mandate, the court refused to grant the injunction, retaining jurisdiction of the cause with full power to issue any necessary and proper orders to secure McLaurin the equal protection of the laws.

Following this decision, the Oklahoma legislature amended these statutes to permit the admission of Negroes to institutions of higher learning attended by white students, in cases where such institutions offered courses not available in the Negro schools. The amendment provided, however, that in such cases the program of instruction "shall be given at such colleges or institutions of higher education upon a segregated basis." Appellant was thereupon admitted to the University of Oklahoma Graduate School. In apparent conformity with the amendment, his admission was made subject to "such rules and regulations as to segregation as the President of the University shall consider to afford Mr. G. W. McLaurin substantially equal educational opportunities as are afforded to other persons seeking the same education at the Graduate College," a condition which does not appear to have been withdrawn. Thus he was required to sit apart at a designated desk in an anteroom adjoining the classroom; to sit at a designated desk on the mezzanine floor of the library, but not to use the desks in the

---

* *Ibid.*, pp. 4407-50. For the Court's decision, June 5, 1950, in the Elmer W. Henderson case against the Southern Railway Company see the same reference, pp. 4352-55. The combined effect of the three decisions given in June of 1950 made it plain that "separate facilities must truly be equal."

regular reading room; and to sit at a designated table and to eat at a different time from the other students in the school cafeteria.

To remove these conditions, appellant filed a motion to modify the order and judgment of the District Court. That court held that such treatment did not violate the provisions of the Fourteenth Amendment and denied the motion. This appeal followed.

In the interval between the decision of the court below and the hearing in this Court, the treatment afforded appellant was altered. For some time, the section of the classroom in which appellant sat was surrounded by a rail on which there was a sign stating, "Reserved For Colored," but these have been removed. He is now assigned to a seat in the classroom in a row specified for colored students; he is assigned to a table in the library on the main floor; and he is permitted to eat at the same time in the cafeteria as other students although here again he is assigned to a special table.

It is said that the separations imposed by the State in this case are in form merely nominal. McLaurin uses the same classroom, library and cafeteria as students of other races; there is no indication that the seats to which he is assigned in these rooms have any disadvantage of location. He may wait in line in the cafeteria and there stand and talk with his fellow students, but while he eats he must remain apart.

These restrictions were obviously imposed in order to comply, as nearly as could be, with the statutory requirements of Oklahoma. But they signify that the State, in administering the facilities it affords for professional and graduate study, sets McLaurin apart from the other students. The result is that appellant is handicapped in his pursuit of effective graduate instruction. Such restrictions impair and inhibit his ability to study, to engage in discussions and exchange views with other students, and, in general, to learn his profession.

Our society grows increasingly complex, and our need for trained leaders increases correspondingly. Appellant's case represents, perhaps, the epitome of that need, for he is attempting to obtain an advanced degree in education, to become, by definition, a leader and trainer of others. Those who will come under his guidance and influence must be directly affected by the education he receives. Their own education and development will necessarily suffer to the extent that his training is unequal to that of his classmates. State-imposed restrictions which produce such inequalities cannot be sustained.

It may be argued that appellant will be in no better position when these restrictions are removed, for he may still be set apart by his fellow students. This we think irrelevant. There is a vast difference—a Constitutional difference—between restrictions imposed by the state which prohibit the intellectual commingling of students, and the refusal of individuals to commingle where the state presents no such bar. . . .

The removal of the state restrictions will not necessarily abate individual and group predilections, prejudices and choices. But at the very least, the state will not be depriving appellant of the opportunity to secure acceptance by his fellow students on his own merits.

We conclude that the conditions under which this appellant is required to receive his education deprive him of his personal and present right to the equal protection of the laws. See *Sweatt* v. *Painter,* 339 U.S. We hold that under these circumstances the Fourteenth Amendment precludes differences in treatment by the state based upon race. Appellant, having been admitted to a state-supported graduate school, must receive the same treatment at the hands of the state as students of other races. The judgment is

Reversed.

«« X »»

EDUCATIONAL AND OTHER RIGHTS
OF WOMEN; CO-EDUCATION

«««‹›»»»

The long delay in attention to the education of women is one of the extraordinary chapters in American educational history, although causes for indifference and even hostility to their education are not difficult to find. To the poets, philosophers, and prophets of the past woman seemed an enigma. In church she was said to be a saint, abroad an angel, and a devil at home. To Vergil she was "fickle and changeful," to Milton a "fair defect," to Francis Galton "capricious and coy," to pessimistic Nietzsche "God's *second* mistake," and Rousseau's views on her education were in the tradition of the "lords of creation" of his time. There is some evidence also that Christian theology failed for a long time vigorously to promote the idea of the education and other rights for women. St. Paul advised young Timothy: "Let a woman learn in quietness, with all subjection, but I permit not a woman to teach, nor to have dominion over man, but to be in quietness." According to this apostle, wives should submit themselves unto their husbands as "unto the Lord." St. Peter referred to woman as "the weaker vessel."

As late as 1850 American women were under heavy civil, social, political, economic, and educational disabilities. Those few spokesmen for the rights of women believed that their retarded educational condition was due not so much to their inferior intellectual abilities as to their lack of opportunities. But the climate of opinion was heavy against the education of women. After discussing the subject at length, the members of a lyceum in Massachusetts in the 1830's voted that it would be undesirable to confer academic and literary degrees on women. It was looked upon as inconsistent with the retiring delicacy of female character for women to take part in public exercises. The professions were long closed to women. When the first medical degree was conferred upon a woman about a century ago, most people said she was either bad or mad. But changes in the status of women in this country during the past century rank high among the most conspicuous phenomena in its social and educational history, and in all these phenomena the improved position in their education is perhaps the most significant. See Thomas Woody, *A History of Women's Education in the United States* (New York and Lancaster, Pa., Science Press, 1929).

Mary Wollstonecraft on Education and Other Rights of Women, 1792 *

I have already animadverted on the bad habits which females acquire when they are shut up together; and I think that the observation may fairly be extended to the other sex, till the natural inference is drawn which I have had in view throughout—that to improve both sexes they ought, not only in private families, but in public schools, to be educated together.

If marriage be the cement of society, mankind should all be educated after the same model, or the intercourse of the sexes will never deserve the name of fellowship, nor will women ever fulfil the peculiar duties of their sex, till they become enlightened citizens, till they become free by being enabled to earn their own subsistance, independent of men; in the same manner, I mean, to prevent misconstruction, as one man is independent of another. Nay, marriage will never be held sacred till women, by being brought up with men, are prepared to be their companions rather than their mistresses; for the mean doublings of cunning will ever render them contemptible, whilst oppression renders them timid. So convinced am I of this truth, that I will venture to predict that virtue will never prevail in society till the virtues of both sexes are founded on reason; and, till the affections common to both are allowed to gain their due strength by the discharge of mutual duties.

Were boys and girls permitted to pursue the same studies together, those graceful decencies might early be inculcated which produce modesty without those sexual distinctions that taint the mind. Lessons of politeness, and that formulary of decorum, which treads on the heels of falsehood, would be rendered useless by habitual propriety of behaviour. Not indeed put on for visitors, like the courtly robe of politeness, but the sober effect of cleanliness of mind. Would not this simple elegance of sincerity be a chaste homage paid to domestic affections, far surpassing the meretricious com-

* Mary Wollstonecraft, *A Vindication of the Rights of Woman*, with an introduction by Elizabeth Robins Pennell (London, Walter Scott, Paternoster Row, 1891). The book was first published in England in 1792 and republished in Philadelphia in 1794. The extracts above are taken from the English edition of 1891, pp. 237-53. "Mary Wollstonecraft's startling challenge to masculine supremacy, published in 1792 was as portentous in one sphere as Rousseau's social contract in another." Charles and Mary Beard, *The Rise of American Civilization.* I, p. 464. Wollstonecraft wrote on the rights of women nearly a century after the appearance of Daniel Defoe's *Essay on Projects* which would have placed no limitations on the education of women. "One of the most barbarous customs in the world," wrote Defoe, "considering us a civilized and a Christian country is that we deny the advantages of learning to women."

pliments that shine with false lustre in the heartless intercourse of fashionable life? But till more understanding preponderates in society, there will ever be a want of heart and taste, and the harlot's *rouge* will supply the place of that celestial suffusion which only virtuous affections can give to the face. . . .

When therefore I call women slaves, I mean in a political and civil sense; for indirectly they obtain too much power, and are debased by their exertions to obtain illicit sway.

Let an enlightened nation then try what effect reason would have to bring them back to nature, and their duty; and allowing them to share the advantages of education and government with man, see whether they will become better, as they grow wiser and become free. They cannot be injured by the experiment, for it is not in the power of man to render them more insignificant than they are at present.

To render this practicable, day schools for particular ages should be established by Government, in which boys and girls might be educated together. The school for the younger children, from five to nine years of age, ought to be absolutely free and open to all classes. A sufficient number of masters should also be chosen by a select committee in each parish, to whom any complaint of negligence, &c., might be made, if signed by six of the children's parents.

Ushers would then be unnecessary; for I believe experience will ever prove that this kind of subordinate authority is particularly injurious to the morals of youth. What, indeed, can tend to deprave the character more than outward submission and inward contempt? Yet how can boys be expected to treat an usher with respect, when the master seems to consider him in the light of a servant, and almost to countenance the ridicule which becomes the chief amusement of the boys during the play hours?

But nothing of this kind could occur in an elementary day school, where boys and girls, the rich and poor, should meet together. And to prevent any of the distinctions of vanity, they should be dressed alike, and all obliged to submit to the same discipline, or leave the school. The schoolroom ought to be surrounded by a large piece of ground, in which the children might be usefully exercised, for at this age they should not be confined to any sedentary employment for more than an hour at a time. But these relaxations might all be rendered a part of elementary education, for many things improve and amuse the senses, when introduced as a kind of show, to the principles of which, dryly laid down, children would turn a deaf ear. For instance, botany, mechanics, and astronomy; reading, writing, arithmetic, natural history, and some simple experiments in natural philosophy, might fill up the day; but these pursuits should never encroach on gymnastic plays in the open air. The elements of religion, history, the history of man, and politics, might also be taught by conversations in the Socratic form.

After the age of nine, girls and boys, intended for domestic employments, or mechanical trades, ought to be removed to other schools, and receive instruction in some measure appropriated to the destination of each individual, the two sexes being still together in the morning; but in the afternoon the girls should attend a school, where plain work, mantua-making, millinery, &c., would be their employment.

The young people of superior abilities, or fortune, might now be taught, in another school, the dead and living languages, the elements of science, and continue the study of history and politics, on a more extensive scale, which would not exclude polite literature.

Girls and boys still together? I hear some readers ask. Yes. And I should not fear any other consequence than that some early attachment might take place; which, whilst it had the best effect on the moral character of the young people, might not perfectly agree with the views of the parents, for it will be a long time, I fear, before the world will be so far enlightened that parents, only anxious to render their children virtuous, shall allow them to choose companions for life themselves. . . .

In this plan of education the constitution of boys would not be ruined by the early debaucheries, which now make men so selfish, or girls rendered weak and vain, by indolence, and frivolous pursuits. But, I presuppose, that such a degree of equality should be established between the sexes as would shut out gallantry and coquetry, yet allow friendship and love to temper the heart for the discharge of higher duties. . . .

I have already inveighed against the custom of confining girls to their needle, and shutting them out from all political and civil employments; for by thus narrowing their minds they are rendered unfit to fulfil the peculiar duties which nature has assigned them. . . .

Make them free, and they will quickly become wise and virtuous, as men become more so, for the improvement must be mutual, or the injustice which one-half of the human race are obliged to submit to retorting on their oppressors, the virtue of man will be worm-eaten by the insect whom he keeps under his feet.

Let men take their choice. Man and woman were made for each other, though not to become one being; and if they will not improve women, they will deprave them. . . .

Dr. Benjamin Rush on the Education of Women, 1798 *

I beg pardon for having delayed so long to say any thing of the separate and peculiar mode of education proper for women in a republic. I am sensible that they must concur in all our plans of education for young men, or no laws will ever render them effectual. To qualify our women for this

---

* "On the Mode of Education Proper in A Republic." Given in D. D. Runes (Ed.), *The Selected Writings of Benjamin Rush* (New York, Philosophical Library, Inc., 1947), pp. 95-96.

purpose, they should not only be instructed in the usual branches of female education, but they should be taught the principles of liberty and government; and the obligations of patriotism should be inculcated upon them. The opinions and conduct of men are often regulated by the women in the most arduous enterprizes of life; and their approbation is frequently the principal reward of the hero's dangers, and the patriot's toils. Besides, the first impressions upon the minds of children are generally derived from the women. Of how much consequence, therefore, is it in a republic, that they should think justly upon the great subject of liberty and government.

Thomas Jefferson on the Education of Women, 1818 *

MONTICELLO, March 14, 1818.

DEAR SIR,

Your letter of February 17th found me suffering under an attack of rheumatism, which has but now left me at sufficient ease to attend to the letters I have received. A plan of female education has never been a subject of systematic contemplation with me. It has occupied my attention so far only as the education of my own daughters occasionally required. Considering that they would be placed in a country situation, where little aid could be obtained from abroad, I thought it essential to give them a solid education, which might enable them, when become mothers, to educate their own daughters, and even to direct the course for sons, should their fathers be lost, or incapable, or inattentive. My surviving daughter accordingly, the mother of many daughters as well as sons, has made their education the object of her life, and being a better judge of the practical part than myself, it is with her aid and that of her élèves that I shall subjoin a catalogue of the books for such a course of reading as we have practiced.

A great obstacle to good education is the inordinate passion prevalent for novels, and the time lost in that reading which should be instructively employed. When this poison infects the mind, it destroys its tone and revolts it against wholesome reading. Reason and fact, plain and unadorned, are rejected. Nothing can engage attention unless dressed in all the figments of fancy, and nothing so bedecked comes amiss. The result is a bloated imagination, sickly judgment, and disgust toward all the real businesses of life. This mass of trash, however, is not without some distinction; some few modelling their narratives, although fictitious, on the incidents of real life, have been able to make them interesting and useful vehicles of a sound morality. Such, I think, are Marmontel's new moral tales, but not his old ones, which are really immoral. Such are the writings of Miss Edgeworth, and some of those of Madame Genlis. For a like reason, too, much poetry should not be indulged. Some is useful for form-

---

* Letter to Nathaniel Burwell, March 14, 1818. Given in Paul Leicester Ford, *The Writings of Thomas Jefferson*, X, pp. 104-6.

ing style and taste. Pope, Dryden, Thompson, Shakspeare, and of the French, Molière, Racine, the Corneilles, may be read with pleasure and improvement.

The French language, become that of the general intercourse of nations, and from their extraordinary advances, now the depository of all science, is an indispensable part of education for both sexes. In the subjoined catalogue, therefore, I have placed the books of both languages indifferently, according as the one or the other offers what is best.

The ornaments too, and the amusements of life, are entitled to their portion of attention. These, for a female, are dancing, drawing, and music. The first is a healthy exercise, elegant and very attractive for young people. Every affectionate parent would be pleased to see his daughter qualified to participate with her companions, and without awkwardness at least, in the circles of festivity, of which she occasionally becomes a part. It is a necessary accomplishment, therefore, although of short use, for the French rule is wise, that no lady dances after marriage. This is founded in sound physical reasons, gestation and nursing leaving little time to a married lady when this exercise can be safe or innocent. Drawing is thought less of in this country than in Europe. It is an innocent and engaging amusement, often useful, and a qualification not to be neglected in one who is to become a mother and instructor. Music is invaluable where a person has an ear. Where they have not, it should not be attempted. It furnishes a delightful recreation for the hours of respite from the cares of the day, and lasts us through life. The taste of this country, too, calls for this accomplishment more strongly than for either of the others.

I need say nothing of household economy, in which the mothers of our country are generally skilled, and generally careful to instruct their daughters. We all know its value, and that diligence and dexterity in all its processes are inestimable treasures. The order and economy of a house are as honorable to the mistress as those of the farm to the master, and if either be neglected, ruin follows, and children destitute of the means of living.

This, Sir, is offered as a summary sketch on a subject on which I have not thought much. It probably contains nothing but what has already occurred to yourself, and claims your acceptance on no other ground than as a testimony of my respect for your wishes, and of my great esteem and respect.

Mary Lyon on the Purposes of Mount Holyoke Seminary, 1835 *

The character of the young ladies, who shall become members of this Seminary the first year, will be of great importance to the prosperity of the Institution itself, and to the cause of female education. Those, who use

* Given in *Old South Leaflets*, VI, No. 145, pp. 425-28.

their influence in making out the number, will sustain no unimportant responsibility. It is very desirable, that the friends of this cause should carefully consider the real design of founding this Institution, before they use their influence to induce any of their friends and acquaintances to avail themselves of its privileges.

This institution is to be founded by the combined liberality of an enlarged benevolence, which seeks the greatest good on an extensive scale. Some minds seem to be cast in that peculiar mould, that the heart can be drawn forth only by individual want. Others seem best fitted for promoting public good. None can value too much the angel of mercy, that can fly as on the wings of the wind to the individual cry for help as it comes over in tender and melting strains. But who does not venerate those great souls—great by nature—great by education—or great by grace—or by all combined, whose plans and works of mercy are like a broad river swallowing up a thousand little rivulets. How do we stand in awe, when we look down, as on a map, upon their broad and noble plans, destined to give untold blessings to the great community in which they dwell—to their nation—to the world. As we see them urging their way forward, intent on advancing as fast as possible, the renovation of the whole human family—and on hastening the accomplishment of the glorious promises found on the page of inspiration, we are sometimes tempted to draw back their hand, and extend it forth in behalf of some traveller by the wayside, who seems to be overlooked. But we look again, and we behold the dearest personal interests of the traveller by the wayside, and those of a thousand other individuals included in their large and warm embrace.

This is the class of benevolent men who will aid in founding this Seminary; these the men who are now contributing of their time and money to carry forward this enterprise.

It is ever considered a principle of sacred justice in the management of funds, to regard the wishes of the donors. The great object of those, who are enlisting in this cause, and contributing to it, as to the sacred treasury of the Lord, cannot be misunderstood. It is to meet public and not private wants. They value not individual good less, but the public good more. They have not been prompted to engage in this momentous work by a desire to provide for the wants of a few of the daughters of our land for their own sakes as individuals, but by a desire to provide for the urgent necessities of our country, and of the world, by enlisting in the great work of benevolence, the talents of many of our daughters of fairest promise. This Institution is expected to draw forth the talents of such, to give them a new direction, and to enlist them permanently in the cause of benevolence. We consider it as no more than a due regard to justice, to desire and pray, that a kind Providence may send as scholars to this Seminary, those who shall go forth, and by their deeds, do honor to the Institution, and to the wisdom and benevolence of its founders. The love of justice will also lead us to desire and pray, that the same kind Providence may turn away the feet of those, who may in after life dishonor the Institution, or be simply harmless cumberers of the ground, though they should be our dearest friends, and those who for their own personal benefit, need its privileges more than almost any others.

The ground features of this Institution are to be an elevated standard of science, literature, and refinement, and a moderate standard of expense; all to be guided and modified by the spirit of the gospel. Here we trust will be found a delightful spot for those, "whose heart has stirred them up" to use all their talents in the great work of serving their generation, and of advancing the Redeemer's kingdom.

In the same manner, we doubt not, that the atmosphere will be rendered uncongenial to those who are wrapped up in self, preparing simply to please, and to be pleased, whose highest ambition is, to be qualified to amuse a friend in a vacant hour.

The age of the scholars will aid in giving to the Institution a choice selection of pupils. This Seminary is to be for adult young ladies; at an age when they are called upon by their parents to judge for themselves to a very great degree and when they can select a spot congenial to their taste. The great and ruling principle—an ardent desire to do the greatest possible good, will we hope, be the presiding spirit in many hearts, bringing together congenial souls. Like many institutions of charity, this does not hold out the prospect of providing for the personal relief of individual sufferers, nor for the direct instruction of the ignorant and degraded. But it does expect to collect, as in a focus, the sparks of benevolence, which are scattered in the hearts of many of our daughters, and after having multiplied them many fold and having kindled them to a flame, and given them a right direction, to send them out to warm and to cheer the world. Some of them may be the daughters of wealth, and the offering will be no less acceptable, because they have something besides themselves to offer to the great work. Others, may be the daughters of mere competency, having been fitted for the service by an answer to Agur's petition. Others, again may struggle under the pressure of more moderate means, being called to surmount the greatest obstacles by persevering effort, and the aid of friends. But provided they have kindled spirits on the great essential principles, all can go forward together without a discordant note.

It has been stated, that the literary standard of this Institution will be high. This is a very indefinite term. There is no acknowledged standard of female education, by which an institution can be measured. A long list of branches to be taught, can be no standard at all. For if so, a contemplated manual labor school to be established in one of the less improved of the western states, whose prospectus we chanced to notice some two or three years since, would stand higher than most of our New-England colleges. Whether the institution was ever established we know not, nor do we remember its name or exact location. But the list of branches to be taught as they appeared on paper, we do remember, as for the time, it served as a happy illustration of a general principle, relating to some of our attempts to advance the cause of education among us. In a seminary for females, we cannot as in the standard of education for the other sex, refer to established institutions, whose course of study and standard of mental discipline are known to every literary man in the land. But it is believed, that our statement cannot be made more intelligible to the enlightened community, than by simply saying, that the course of study, and standard of mental culture will be the same as that of the Hartford Female Seminary—of the Ipswich Female Seminary—or of the Troy Female Seminary—or of some other institution that has stood as long, and ranked as high as these seminaries. Suffice it to say, that it is expected, that the Mount Holyoke Female Seminary will take the Ipswich Female Seminary for its literary standard. Of course there will be room for a continued advancement; as that institution has been raising its own standard from year to year. But at the commencement, the standard is to be as high as the present standard of that seminary. It is to adopt the same high standard of mental discipline—the same slow, thorough, and patient manner of study; the same systematic and extensive course of solid branches. Though this explanation will not be universally understood, yet it is believed that it will be understood by a great many in New England, and by many out of New England—by those, who have long been intimately acquainted with the character of that seminary, or who have witnessed its fruits in the lives of those whom it has sent forth to exert a power over society, which cannot be exerted by mere goodness without intellectual strength. "By their fruits ye shall know them."

A College for Women in Kentucky, 1835 *

College for Ladies.—The Kentucky Legislature has conferred upon Messrs. Van Doren's Institute for Young Ladies, in Lexington, the chartered rights and standing of a College, by the name of Van Doren's College for young Ladies. By the power granted by the Board of Trustees and the Faculty of the College, we understand from the Daily Reporter, that a Diploma and the honorary degree of M.P.L. (Mistress of Polite Literature) will be conferred upon those young ladies who complete the prescribed course of studies; and that the same honor may be conferred upon other distinguished ladies in our country; and also, that the honorary degree of M.M. (Mistress of Music,) and M.I. (Mistress of Instruction,) may be conferred by this College upon suitable candidates.

Female Degrees.—Yesterday we gave some accounts of the degrees conferred in the Young Ladies College in Kentucky.—In addition to those, we would recommend the following, which we think will be of more use—

* *Republican and Journal* (Springfield, Massachusetts), March 14, 1835.

namely—M.P.M. (Mistress of Pudding Making,) M.D.N. (Mistress of the Darning Needle,) M.S.B. (Mistress of the Scrubbing Brush,) and especially M.C.S. (Mistress of Common Sense.) But, in order to fit the girls for those degrees, it will be necessary to organize a new department—and we recommend to the faculty of the institute to apply to the Legislature immediately for an enlargement of its powers, to enable it to confer these new and more useful degrees—and we furthermore recommend to them to procure some well qualified Professors, from among the farmers' wives, and especially from some of the best regulated kitchens, to teach the young ladies the useful art of house-wifery. When they have done this in the proper manner to fit them for taking charge of the family, and making their husband's fireside comfortable, then let the degrees we have recommended, be conferred, in course; and then, in due season, if they succeed according to their merits, they will attain to the honorary degree, to which, we dare say, they are all looking forward, namely, that of R.W. (the Respectable Wife) H.H. (Of a Happy Husband;) and M.W.R.F. (Mother of a Well Regulated Family.)

Some Activities at Wesleyan College, Macon, Georgia, 1837 *

After a solemn prayer, ninety young ladies came forward and registered their names as candidates for admission. It was an occasion of deep and thrilling excitement. A large and respectable number of the citizens of Macon were assembled in the college chapel to witness the opening scene. The hopes and fears of its friends, the predictions of its enemies, and the eager delight of the congregated pupils all conspired to invest the service with an interest additional to its intrinsic importance.

Before the termination of the first term the number of pupils had increased to 168.

At sunrise the girls who boarded in the college were summoned by a bell to meet in the chapel for family prayer, conducted by the president. Attendance was compulsory. From then until breakfast they studied, then had recreation in autumn and winter until nine; in spring and summer, until eight.

Next, all pupils boarding and day scholars, assembled for morning prayer. Recitations followed until eleven, study hour until twelve, boarders in their rooms and day students in the chapel under the supervision of a

* *The Wesleyan Alumnae Magazine,* May, 1940. When George F. Pierce, the first president of this institution (believed to be the first college in this country to confer academic degrees on women) was trying to raise funds for it, first known as Georgia Female College, he met many arguments against the higher education of women. Among them was that "man loves a learned scholar, but not a learned wife"; "all that a woman needs to know is how to read the New Testament and spin and weave clothing for her family. . . . I shall not have one of your graduates for a wife, and I will not give you a cent for any other object." Another argument was that "if and after a woman marries," her higher education is wasted. A foreign traveller after visiting Wellesley College is reported to have said: "This is all very fine, but . . . how does it affect their chances for marriage?"

teacher. From twelve until two came dinner and recreation; then study until four when all classes recited again. At five there was prayer and dismissal. Supper and recreation followed until seven, study until nine, and afterwards retire and sleep at will.

The yard immediately around the college has been graded to a level, extending over a lot of four acres. The whole enclosure is well adapted for tasteful adornment, and affords the young ladies ample space for exercise and recreation.

In fair weather, free and regular exercise in the open air will be encouraged. The merry laugh, the cheerful sport, will not be considered indecorous, but encouraged as the best means of giving elasticity and energy both to the mental and physical powers.

I rise to perform my last duty connected with my official relation to you. The work of instruction is done; its cares, its longings are in the past.

In my humble opinion, a grievous error has been incorporated into the organization of society, and is recognized as truth and supported upon system. Woman's influence has been underrated as to its nature and capabilities, fettered and circumscribed as to its operations, and even when acknowledged has been appropriated to ends, though worthy perhaps, yet far beneath the actual reach of her power. Woman's empire is the heart, the poets say, and they say truly; but they have restricted their meaning to taste and sentiment and sensibility, and to the bland virtues of domestic life. Female influence has softened our rough nature and made us polite when we might have been clowns. This is the sphere assigned to women.

These are insignificant achievements, lever power to move an infant's burden. Woman can do more. It is her province, her right, her duty. Minds, morals, character come within the range of her responsibilities, and her action upon these ought to be cheered, encouraged, upheld by public sentiment.

Identify yourselves with the refined, the intellectual, the benevolent, and thus take the proud position to which your circumstances and claims entitle you, and which a discerning public will not fail to award you. The sphere of woman is constantly enlarging as education fits her for loftier duties and Christian philanthropy multiplies her means of doing good. If every successive year do not witness the augmentation of female influence upon the interests of mankind—if the dawning glories of the day that science and commerce and religion are rolling onward to the zenith do not wake a most generous ambition—then will the guilt of a most culpable neglect lie at your door.

Oh, come forth and live! Tear off the bandages of a vitiated taste, compress no more the organs of breathing, bounding thought, let your understandings swell out in the fullness of their native dimensions and walk abroad majestic in thought, radiant with light, and marching onward to achievements so glorious that the past and the present shall be to the future as the glimmering light of an isolated moonbeam to the full-orbed glories of noon.

The First Convention on the Rights of Women Declares
Its Sentiments and Resolutions, 1848 *

When, in the course of human events, it becomes necessary for one portion of the family of man to assume among the people of the earth a position different from that which they have hitherto occupied, but one to which the laws of nature and of nature's God entitle them, a decent respect to the opinions of mankind requires that they should declare the causes that impel them to such a course.

We hold these truths to be self-evident: that all men and women are created equal; that they are endowed by their Creator with certain inalienable rights; that among these are life, liberty, and the pursuit of happiness; that to secure these rights governments are instituted, deriving their just powers from the consent of the governed. Whenever any form of government becomes destructive of these ends, it is the right of those who suffer from it to refuse allegiance to it, and to insist upon the institution of a new government, laying its foundation on such principles, and organizing its powers in such form, as to them shall seem most likely to effect their safety and happiness. Prudence, indeed, will dictate that governments long established should not be changed for light and transient causes; and accordingly all experience hath shown that mankind are more disposed to suffer, while evils are sufferable, than to right themselves by abolishing the forms to which they were accustomed. But when a long train of abuses and usurpations, pursuing invariably the same object evinces a design to reduce them under absolute despotism, it is their duty to throw off such government, and to provide new guards for their future security. Such has been the patient sufferance of the women under this government, and such is now the necessity which constrains them to demand the equal station to which they are entitled.

The history of mankind is a history of repeated injuries and usurpations on the part of man toward woman, having in direct object the establishment of an absolute tyranny over her. To prove this, let facts be submitted to a candid world.

He has never permitted her to exercise her inalienable right to the elective franchise.

* Elizabeth Stanton, Susan B. Anthony, and Matilda Gage (Eds.), *History of Woman Suffrage,* second edition (Rochester, N. Y., Charles Mann, 1889), I, pp. 70-73. This convention, at Seneca Falls, N. Y., was the result of the refusal of the World Antislavery Convention in London in 1840 to seat a group of American women delegates and their determination that women as well as slaves required emancipation. According to announcement in the *Seneca County Courier* of July 14, 1848, the first day was given over exclusively for women. "The public generally are invited to be present on the second day, when Lucretia Mott, of Philadelphia, and other ladies and gentlemen, will address the convention."

He has compelled her to submit to laws, in the formation of which she had no voice.

He has withheld from her rights which are given to the most ignorant and degraded men—both natives and foreigners.

Having deprived her of this first right of a citizen, the elective franchise, thereby leaving her without representation in the halls of legislation, he has oppressed her on all sides.

He has made her, if married, in the eye of the law, civilly dead.

He has taken from her all right in property, even to the wages she earns.

He has made her, morally, an irresponsible being, as she can commit many crimes with impunity, provided they be done in the presence of her husband. In the covenant of marriage, she is compelled to promise obedience to her husband, he becoming, to all intents and purposes, her master—the law giving him power to deprive her of her liberty, and to administer chastisement.

He has so framed the laws of divorce, as to what shall be the proper causes, and in case of separation, to whom the guardianship of the children shall be given, as to be wholly regardless of the happiness of women—the law, in all cases, going upon a false supposition of the supremacy of man, and giving all power into his hands.

After depriving her of all rights as a married woman, if single, and the owner of property, he has taxed her to support a government which recognizes her only when her property can be made profitable to it.

He has monopolized nearly all the profitable employments, and from those she is permitted to follow, she receives but a scanty remuneration. He closes against her all the avenues to wealth and distinction which he considers most honorable to himself. As a teacher of theology, medicine, or law, she is not known.

He has denied her the facilities for obtaining a thorough education, all colleges being closed against her.

He allows her in Church, as well as State, but a subordinate position, claiming Apostolic authority for her exclusion from the ministry, and, with some exceptions, from any public participation in the affairs of the Church.

He has created a false public sentiment by giving to the world a different code of morals for men and women, by which moral delinquencies which exclude women from society, are not only tolerated, but deemed of little account in man.

He has usurped the prerogative of Jehovah himself, claiming it as his right to assign for her a sphere of action, when that belongs to her conscience and to her God.

He has endeavored, in every way that he could, to destroy her confidence in her own powers, to lessen her self-respect, and to make her willing to lead a dependent and abject life.

Now, in view of this entire disfranchisement of one-half the people of this country, their social and religious degradation—in view of the unjust laws above mentioned, and because women do feel themselves aggrieved, oppressed, and fraudulently deprived of their most sacred rights, we insist that they have immediate admission to all the rights and privileges which belong to them as citizens of the United States.

In entering upon the great work before us, we anticipate no small amount of misconception, misrepresentation, and ridicule; but we shall use every instrumentality within our power to effect our object. We shall employ agents, circulate tracts, petition the State and National legislatures, and endeavor to enlist the pulpit and the press in our behalf. We hope this Convention will be followed by a series of Conventions embracing every part of the country.

The following resolutions were discussed by Lucretia Mott, Thomas and Mary Ann McClintock, Amy Post, Catharine A. F. Stebbins, and others, and were adopted:

WHEREAS, The great precept of nature is conceded to be, that "man shall pursue his own true and substantial happiness." Blackstone in his Commentaries remarks, that this law of Nature being coeval with mankind, and dictated by God himself, is of course superior in obligation to any other. It is binding over all the globe, in all countries and at all times; no human laws are of any validity if contrary to this, and such of them as are valid, derive all their force, and all their validity, and all their authority, mediately and immediately, from this original; therefore,

Resolved, That such laws as conflict, in any way, with the true and substantial happiness of woman, are contrary to the great precept of nature and of no validity, for this is "superior in obligation to any other."

Resolved, That all laws which prevent woman from occupying such a station in society as her conscience shall dictate, or which place her in a position inferior to that of man, are contrary to the great precept of nature, and therefore of no force or authority.

Resolved, That woman is man's equal—was intended to be so by the Creator, and the highest good of the race demands that she should be recognized as such.

Resolved, That the women of this country ought to be enlightened in regard to the laws under which they live, that they may no longer publish their degradation by declaring themselves satisfied with their present position, nor their ignorance, by asserting that they have all the rights they want.

Resolved, That inasmuch as man, while claiming for himself intellectual superiority, does accord to woman moral superiority, it is pre-eminently his duty to encourage her to speak and teach, as she has an opportunity, in all religious assemblies.

Resolved, That the same amount of virtue, delicacy, and refinement of behavior that is required of woman in the social state, should also be required of man, and the same transgressions should be visited with equal severity on both man and woman.

Resolved, That the objection of indelicacy and impropriety, which is so often brought against woman when she addresses a public audience, comes with a very ill-grace from those who encourage, by their attendance, her appearance on the stage, in the concert, or in feats of the circus.

Resolved, That woman has too long rested satisfied in the circumscribed limits which corrupt customs and a perverted application of the Scriptures have marked out for her, and that it is time she should move in the enlarged sphere which her great Creator has assigned her.

Resolved, That it is the duty of the women of this country to secure to themselves their sacred right to the elective franchise.

Resolved, That the equality of human rights results necessarily from the fact of the identity of the race in capabilities and responsibilities.

Resolved, therefore, That, being invested by the Creator with the same capabilities, and the same consciousness of responsibility for their exercise, it is demonstrably the right and duty of woman, equally with man, to promote every righteous cause by every righteous means; and especially in regard to the great subjects of morals and religion, it is self-evidently her right to participate with her brother in teaching them, both in private and in public, by writing and by speaking, by any instrumentalities proper to be used, and in any assemblies proper to be held; and this being a self-evident truth growing out of the divinely implanted principles of human nature, any custom or authority adverse to it, whether modern or wearing the hoary sanction of antiquity, is to be regarded as a self-evident falsehood, and at war with mankind.

At the last session Lucretia Mott offered and spoke to the following resolution:

Resolved, That the speedy success of our cause depends upon the zealous and untiring efforts of both men and women, for the overthrow of the monopoly of the pulpit, and for the securing to woman an equal participation with men in the various trades, professions, and commerce.

The only resolution that was not unanimously adopted was the ninth, urging the women of the country to secure to themselves the elective franchise. Those who took part in the debate feared a demand for the right to vote would defeat others they deemed more rational, and make the whole movement ridiculous.

But Mrs. Stanton and Frederick Douglass seeing that the power to choose rulers and make laws, was the right by which all others could be secured, persistently advocated the resolution, and at last carried it by a small majority. . . .

Placing a Daughter at School, 1853 *

I have brought my daughter to you to be taught everything.
　　Dear Madam, I've called for the purpose
　　　　Of placing my daughter at school;
　　She's only thirteen, I assure you,
　　　　And remarkably easy to rule.
　　I'd have her learn painting and music,
　　　　Gymnastics and dancing, pray do,
　　Philosophy, grammar and logic,
　　　　You'll teach her to read, of course, too.

　　I wish her to learn every study
　　　　Mathematics are down on my plan,
　　But of figures she scarce has an inkling
　　　　Pray instruct her in those, if you can.
　　I'd have her taught Spanish and Latin,
　　　　Including the language of France;
　　Never mind her very bad English,
　　　　Teach her that when you find a good chance.

　　On the harp she must be a proficient,
　　　　And play the guitar pretty soon,
　　And sing the last opera music
　　　　Even though she can't turn a right tune.

　　You must see that her manners are finished,
　　　　That she moves with a Hebe-like grace;
　　For, though she is lame and one-sided,
　　　　That's nothing to do with the case.

　　Now to you I resign this young jewel,
　　　　And my words I would have you obey;
　　In six months return her, dear madam,
　　　　Shining bright as an unclouded day.
　　She's no aptness, I grant you, for learning
　　　　And her memory oft seems to halt;
　　But, remember, if she's not accomplished　,
　　　　It will certainly be your fault.

Interest in the South in the Education of Women, 1857 †

...Strange it is, but true, that, with us, there is a much more lively interest felt in the cause of female education, than in the education of

---

* *Godey's Lady Book*, XLVI (May, 1853), p. 457.
† Letter from A. W. Richardson, of Selma, Alabama, to Henry Barnard, March 23, 1847. The original of this letter is the property of the library of New York University and is here used by its permission. Photocopy in Southern Historical Collection, the University of North Carolina.

young men. Is not this an effort in the *right direction?* Educate the *girls*—*thoroughly educate them*—and the *boys* in order to render themselves *respectable in their eyes,* will find means *to educate themselves.* Let the *future mothers* be *educated,* and the chances are that *their children* will not be neglected. . . .

President Charles W. Eliot of Harvard University on the Subject, 1869 *

The attitude of the University in the prevailing discussions touching the education and fit employments of women demands brief explanation. America is the natural arena for these debates; for here the female sex has a better past and a better present than elsewhere. Americans, as a rule, hate disabilities of all sorts, whether religious, political, or social. Equality between the sexes, without privilege or oppression on either side, is the happy custom of American homes. While this great discussion is going on, it is the duty of the University to maintain a cautious and expectant policy. The Corporation will not receive women as students into the College proper, nor into any school whose discipline requires residence near the school. The difficulties involved in a common residence of hundreds of young men and women of immature character and marriageable age are very grave. The necessary police regulations are exceedingly burdensome. The Corporation are not influenced to this decision, however, by any notions about the innate capacities of women. The world knows next to nothing about the natural mental capacities of the female sex.

Rules at Mount Holyoke in the Eighteen Seventies †

Mount Holyoke students in the eighteen seventies had no weekly *News* in which to print opinions, carping or humorous, on local conditions, but their progressive spirits found literary expression in humorous writing which in part has been handed down in manuscript under the heading "Seminary Literature: Blue Laws and Fire Laws," burlesques of rules and requirements of the time.

The *Harvard Crimson* got hold of these burlesques of fifty years ago and in the issue of December 13, 1927, printed a few of them, along with some official laws of the Harvard code of 1734, saying that they were more or less observed at Mount Holyoke considerably less than a century ago. The rules imposed on Harvard students of two hundred years ago paralleled the burlesques written by Mount Holyoke students one hundred

---

* Inaugural address, 1869. Given in S. E. Morison, *The Development of Harvard University* (Cambridge, Harvard University Press, 1930), p. lxx. Also in Edgar W. Knight, *What College Presidents Say* (Chapel Hill, University of North Carolina Press, 1940), pp. 300-01.
† Bertha E. Blakely, in *Mount Holyoke Alumnae Quarterly,* April, 1928, pp. 32-34.

and forty years later. Both sets were copied in part the next day by the *Boston Herald*. The *Boston Post* printed more than the *Herald* and commented more at length. The "rules" of a woman's college seem to give more kick to the journalists than the old restrictions of Harvard, if one may judge by the three forms of this story sent by two (probably three) syndicates to newspapers all over the country. Our Press Bureau has received clippings from forty-nine papers in twenty-two states. Twenty-four supplied by the United Press omit mention of Harvard except to say that Harvard University archives furnished these Mount Holyoke rules of 1734. Only one paper changed the date to 1834, The National News Service story, dated Cambridge, Mass., returned from seven states, begins "Pity if you will the poor co-ed of A.D. 1734." A third form of the story is headed "Ancient Feminine Conduct" and assigns the rules to 1834. Various college and university papers have printed the "rules" without comment.

Only one newspaper of the forty-nine, the Manchester, N. H., *Leader,* discovered an anachronism in putting the *Atlantic Monthly* (founded in 1857) on the censored list and noted that Scott's death was more than a century later than 1734. Does this suggest a slight lack in historical perspective and in a sense of humor in newspaper offices and among college editors or the editors' estimate of what the public will consume? We imagine that the *Harvard Crimson* copied some yellowed manuscript with tongue in cheek, but perhaps did not expect to spread the hoax quite so widely. The greatest surprise to us was the gullibility of the *New York Sun* which had a serious editorial January 30 on "Stern Days at Holyoke," tracing appreciatively the development of the education of women in this country, and finding in these prescriptions (that is, the supposed original rules at Mount Holyoke, "which Mary Lyon opened as a seminary in 1837"), which "poor young girls with a thirst for knowledge" "did not find unattractive," "the germs of much history of the rise of women's colleges." This was copied by the *Schenectady Union Star* as "Yesterday's Best Editorial."

At Harvard, "Laws, Liberties, and Orders," confirmed by the overseers and president of the college in the years 1642-46 forbade students "to buy or sell anything without the permission of parents, guardians, or tutors, (or) to speak in any language but the Latin, unless required to do so in their public exercises." "No freshman shall wear his hat in the college yard unless it rains, hails or snows, provided he be on foot and have not both hands full."

The rules of the revised Harvard code of 1734 which were quoted in the *Harvard Crimson* are:

"Sec. VI. All the Scholars shall, at Sunset in the evening preceding the Lord's Day, retire to their chambers, and not unnecessarily leave them; and all disorders on said evenings shall be punished as violations of the Sabbath are. And every Scholar, on the Lord's Day, shall carefully apply himself to the Duties of Religion and Piety. And whosoever shall profane said Day by unnecessary Business or Visiting, Walking on the Common, or in the Streets or Fields in the town of Cambridge, or by any sort of Diversion before sunset—shall be fined 10 shillings.

"Sec. IX. Undergraduates shall repeat at least the main heads of the forenoon and afternoon sermons on Lord's Day evenings in the Hall, and such as are Delinquent shall be punished—not exceeding three shillings."

At Harvard and at Yale tutors were expected to visit students' rooms in study hours, and especially after nine in the evening, to see that all were in their chambers and applying themselves to their studies.

The burlesque fire laws of Mount Holyoke were printed a few years ago by the Philadelphia Alumnae Association. Some of the blue laws are given below through the courtesy of Mrs. Mary (Kimball) Cummings, of the class of 1880, who loaned her manuscript copy to the library:

"Admission. No young lady shall become a member of this institution who cannot kindle a fire, wash potatoes, repeat the multiplication table, and at least two-thirds of the shorter catechism.

"Outfit. Every candidate for admission must be provided with a pair of rubber boots, one pair of cowhides, a copy of 'Ladies Students' Manual,' subdued hoops (or hopes) and a clothes line, orthodox length.

"Exercise. Every young lady of the school shall walk at least a mile each day unless an earthquake, freshet or some other calamity prevents. The bounds on the north are indicated by stakes, also on the southwest. If any young lady shall wilfully go beyond said bounds she shall wash dishes and mop floors two weeks as penalty.

"Reading. No student shall devote more than two hours each week to miscellaneous reading. The *Atlantic Monthly,* 'Shakespeare,' 'Scott's Novels,' 'Robinson Crusoe' and other immoral works are strictly forbidden. The *Boston Recorder, Missionary Herald,* 'Doddridge's Rise and Progress,' also 'Washington's Farewell Address' are earnestly recommended as light reading.

"Dress. No young lady connected with this institution shall adorn herself with any gay flowers or any other vanity; and no color of an exceedingly gay nature will be tolerated. Subdued yellow, dignified mouse or puritan grey recommended.

"Company. No member of this school is expected to have any intimate gentleman acquaintances unless they be returned missionaries or agents of some benevolent society.

"Essays. No young lady shall at any time write compositions except on the following subjects: Friendship, Hope, Time, Flowers, Beauties of Nature and Benevolence; those designing to be 'old maids' may add that of Love.

"Time at the mirror. No young lady shall spend more than three consecutive minutes at the mirror.

"Every young lady shall rise at three and retire at eight o'clock.

"No letters must be sent out without first submitting them to a council of teachers who will revise, amend or alter as the case may be.

"Sabbath Rules. No young lady who is a member of this school shall laugh or look out of the window on the Sabbath. Failure in the observance of these rules shall be attended with severe punishment.

"Every young lady shall learn the various 250 rules of the institution by heart and recite them in Parlor A, Sunday evening. No young lady shall purchase at any time any eatables whatever, unless with express permission, which will only be granted to buy 4 cents worth of peppermints or lemondrops once a term. Photographs and plaster busts are strictly prohibited. 'Thou shalt worship no image.' "

President F. A. P. Barnard of Columbia University on the Subject, 1878 *

Whatever may be the fate of the present suggestion [to open Columbia College to women], the undersigned cannot permit himself to doubt that the time will yet come when the propriety and wisdom of this measure will be fully recognized; and, as he believes that Columbia College is destined in the coming centuries to become so comprehensive in the scope of her teaching as to be able to furnish to all inquirers after truth the instruction they may desire in whatever branch of human knowledge, he believes also that she will become so catholic in her liberality as to open widely her doors to all inquirers without distinction either of class or of sex.

The National Educational Association Resolves on the Higher Education of Women, 1879 †

Resolved, That it is the sense of this Association that the general government should, at an early period, look to the feasibility of donating a portion of the public domain for the endowment and maintenance of at least one institution in each State and Territory for the higher education of women.

* *Report* for 1878-79, p. 68.
† *The Addresses and Journal of the Proceedings,* 1879, p. 98. When Ella Flagg Young, brilliant superintendent of schools in Chicago, became in 1910 the first woman president of the National Education Association, it was recalled that earlier upon attendance at a meeting of this organization she was required to sit in the gallery and listen to but not participate in the discussions carried on by men. See Mildred S. Fenner, "The National Education Association, 1892-1942" (typescript doctoral dissertation, George Washington University, 1945), p. 32.

President James B. Angell of the University of Michigan on the Subject, 1883 *

Women graduates are doing their full part in winning a reputation for Michigan University, and are justifying the wisdom of the Regents who opened to them the opportunities for a thorough classical training.

President Nicholas Murray Butler of Columbia University Says Co-Education Is a Dead Issue, 1902 †

Co-education is a dead issue. The American people have settled the matter. . . . Why discuss the matter further?

President G. Stanley Hall of Clark University on the Subject, 1904 ‡

It is now well established that higher education in this country reduces the rate of both marriage and offspring. . . . I think it established that mental strain in early womanhood is a cause of imperfect mammary function which is the first stage of the slow evolution of sterility. . . . A boy forced to see too much of girls is sure to lose something, either by excess or defect, from the raw material of his manhood.

The higher education of women involves all the difficulties of that of men, with many new problems of its own. The girls' colleges think it wisest to train for self-support, and hold that if marriage comes it can best take care of itself. I urge the precise reverse.

President John F. Goucher of Baltimore Woman's College on the Subject, 1904 §

The high grade, thoroughly equipped colleges for women, established at great expense during the past two or three decades, have more applicants knocking at their doors than they can accommodate. This is a demonstration of dissatisfaction with the coeducational experiment.

* *Education*, September, 1883.
† *Journal of Education*, November 13, 1902.
‡ *Journal of Proceedings and Addresses*, National Educational Association, 1904, pp. 538, 540, 542. Under the heading "Serenity," *Time* of June 12, 1950, noted that of thirty-three Phi Beta Kappas graduated at Barnard College that week fourteen were already married, and one of them explained that serenity was the secret of their scholarship. "There's nothing to worry about on the emotional side after you're married, so I did better work at college. That's what all the girls say."
§ *Papers and Addresses* of the Association of Colleges and Preparatory Schools of the Southern States, 1904.

President M. Carey Thomas of Bryn Mawr College
on the Subject, 1908 *

There is, however, one grave peril which must be averted from women's education at all hazards. Most of the universities of the west and many eastern universities, like Cornell, Columbia and Pennsylvania, are boring through their academic college course at a hundred places with professional courses. In many colleges everything that is desirable for a human being to learn to do counts towards a bachelor's degree—ladder work in the gymnasium (why not going upstairs?), swimming in the tank (why not one's morning bath?), cataloging in the library (why not one's letter home?).

President Emeritus C. A. Richmond of Union College
on the Subject, 1934 †

Many believe that the new found liberty which women have achieved but not fully understood has lowered the tone of our women's colleges both in manners and in morals.

* *Educational Review*, January, 1908, p. 76.
† *Bulletin of the Association of American Colleges*, December, 1934, p. 468. The higher education of women has developed rapidly during the past two or three decades. In the 1940's Harvard enlisted on the side of co-education, after more than three centuries of high masculine tradition and prestige. In the fall of 1950 the Harvard Law School was made available to qualified women and with that action all branches of higher scholarship in America's oldest and most eminent higher educational institution became open to them. See J. Anthony Lewis, "Harvard Goes Co-ed, But Incognito," *The New York Times Magazine*, May 1, 1949. In that year women received 118,534 of the 422,754 collegiate degrees awarded in this country, more than 102,000 of the 366,000 bachelor's, more than 15,000 of the 50,000 master's and 522 of the 5,200 doctorates.

«« XI »»
SOME LATER EDUCATIONAL
DEVELOPMENTS

«««<O>»»»»»»»»»»»»»»»»»»»»»»»»»»»»»»»»»»

Among the forces that have had effect on education since 1860 are the prodigious material development of the United States and its swift scientific and industrial growth; remarkable increase in wealth and in population; the accumulation of huge fortunes which made possible the establishment of philanthropic foundations the like of which the world has never known; the increase in the comfort and ease of life for the workingman as well as for others and the extraordinary absence of pauperism as compared with other countries; immigration; changes in rural life and in the character of home life in this country under the industrial and electrical revolutions. These and other changes are not only obvious to those who have been and still are on the scene but have been vividly pointed out by foreign visitors. (See James Bryce, "America Revisited: The Changes of a Quarter-Century," *Outlook*, Vol. 79 (March 25 and April 1, 1905), pp. 733-40, 846-55). Some of the educational changes in the latter part of the past century came through the work and influence of Europeans,—Pestalozzi, Herbart, Froebel, Wundt, Montessori; while other changes came through the writings and teachings in this country of Americans, including William James, G. Stanley Hall, William T. Harris, Francis W. Parker, John Dewey, Edward L. Thorndike, and hosts of those whom these men taught and inspired. The period since the First World War has witnessed increased efforts to get federal educational aid; the development of the junior high school and the junior college; movements for adult educational activities; restrictions against teachers through "loyalty" oaths (Chapter VI); suits at law on requirements that pupils salute the United States flag and other suits that involved the issue of religious instruction in public schools; charges and counter-charges on the American tradition of the separation of church and state and the alleged increase in secularism in American education.

Henry Huxley Rebukes Bishop Wilberforce Over Darwinism, 1860 *

In connection with the recent meeting at Nottingham of the British Association for the Advancement of Science, a writer in *The London News Chronicle* revives the story of the famous encounter in 1860 of Huxley and Bishop Wilberforce.

The Bishop had previously written that "the principle of natural selection is absolutely incompatible with the word of God," and he came to the meeting of the British Association to crush the "hodge-podge" of philosophers with his authority.

He attacked Darwin violently and in the course of his speech asked Huxley whether it was on his grandfather's or on his grandmother's side that he claimed descent from a monkey.

Huxley heard the question, whispered to his neighbor "The Lord hath delivered him into mine hands" and then rose to reply.

After stating the scientific arguments for evolution, he looked toward the Bishop and said:

"A man has no reason to be ashamed of having an ape for his grandfather. If there were an ancestor whom I should feel shame in recalling, it would rather be a man who plunges into scientific questions with which he has no real acquaintance, only to obscure them with an aimless rhetoric and distract the attention of his hearers from the real point at issue by eloquent digressions and skilled appeals to religious prejudice."

The British Association gasped, says *The New Chronicle Writer*. Half the room burst into cheers; half waited aghast for fire from heaven to punish such rudeness to a Bishop. The Bishop himself took it very well. One lady fainted and had to be taken out. The copious newspaper reports of Huxley's retort did more to laugh down prejudice against Darwinism than any number of learned treatises.

---

* *The New York Times,* October 24, 1937. Experimental science, including the Darwinian theory of evolution which sought to give explanation to the riddle of the universe different from that which theology, so long the queen of the sciences, had given, led to battles between the theological fundamentalists and modernists. The period from 1870 to 1900 has been described as "critical" in religion in this country. (See Arthur M. Schlesinger, "A Critical Period in American Religion," *Proceedings of the Massachusetts Historical Society*, LXIV, 523, p. 48.) The conflict between science and theology had wide effect on American educational theories and practices. In that conflict some ministers lost their pulpits and some teachers their chairs. The issue became heated again in the 1920's when attempts were made to restrict freedom of teaching. Several state legislatures attempted and a few succeeded in passing laws and resolutions that prohibited the teaching of the Darwinian hypothesis.

The Hoar Bill to Provide for a System of National Education, 1870 *

Mr. Hoar, on leave, introduced the following bill: To establish a system of national education.

Whereas the Constitution of the United States as recently amended more completely to carry into effect the great principles for which it was ordained, has recognized the right of large numbers of the people, heretofore excluded, to take part in the government, by whose votes the most important and vital public questions may be determined; and, whereas the education of all the citizens, so as to fit them, as far as possible, for an intelligent participation in public affairs, becomes, therefore, an object of national interest and concern, and indispensable to the general welfare; and, whereas an adequate provision for the education of the people is one of the first and most important duties of government: Therefore, Be it enacted by the Senate and House of Representatives of the United States of America in Congress assembled, that these shall be appointed by the President by and with the advice and consent of the Senate, within and for each State, a State superintendent of national schools, who shall receive a salary of   , and who shall hold office for the term of four years from the date of his appointment, unless sooner removed by the president.

Sec. 2. And be it further enacted, that the State superintendent shall divide his State into as many divisions of convenient size as the number of representatives in Congress to which said State is entitled, with divisions shall be the same as the districts into which said State shall be divided for the choice of representatives, unless for special reasons it shall seem advisable other wise to divide the State. The Secretary of the Interior shall appoint for each of said divisions a division inspector of national schools, who shall reside within said division, and who shall hold his office until removed by the Secretary of the Interior and who shall receive a salary of

Sec. 3. And be it further enacted, that said divisions shall be divided by the State superintendent into school districts of convenient size having reference to the number of children dwelling therein, and their convenience in attending school. The Secretary of the Interior shall appoint some suitable

---

* H.R. 1326, February 25, 1870. Microfilm of this bill is in the Southern Historical Collection, University of North Carolina. Among the arguments used against this bill: that it was unconstitutional; would tend to break down the principle of the separation of church and state; would destroy local interest and initiative; would bring about centralization and bureaucratic thought control by the party in power; would be cumbersome and unworkable; would be an insult to white Southerners and inflame racial issues; would be very expensive; and that the many federal offices created by the bill would tend to make education a "political football" to be used mainly for purposes of patronage. Some of these arguments resemble some of those used in recent years in opposition to federal aid for education. For an excellent discussion of the Hoar Bill, the Perce Bill, the Burnside Bill and the Blair Bills between 1870 and 1890 see G. C. Lee, *The Struggle for Federal Aid: First Phase* (New York, Bureau of Publications, Teachers College, Columbia University, 1949).

person to be local superintendent of national school within each school district. The compensation of said local superintendents shall be fixed by the Secretary of the Interior by such general regulations as he shall prescribe. But no local superintendent shall receive more than at the rate of

The divisions and districts shall be distinguished by such numbers or other names as the Secretary of the Interior shall prescribe. Whenever, in the opinion of the State superintendent, any portion of the territory embraced within any division is so sparsely settled that it is impracticable to establish permanent schools there in, such portion of territory need not be included in any school district.

Sec. 4. And be it further enacted that such number of schools shall be kept in each district as the State superintendent shall direct, Provided, that there shall be opportunity afforded to every child dwelling therein between the ages of   and of   to attend school for at least six months in each year subject to such regulations and restrictions as shall be necessary for the discipline of the schools.

Sec. 5. And be it further enacted, that it shall be the duty of every local Superintendent to select the place for the schoolhouse within his district, which he shall purchase or hire in the name of the United States. No contract for such purchase or hire shall be concluded without the written approbation of the State superintendent. In case no suitable place can be obtained with the consent of the owner the division inspector may appropriate a tract for such purpose, by filing a description of the same, by metes and bounds, in the clerk's office of the district court of the United States wherein the same is situated, together with an estimate of the damages caused to any person by taking the same, which appropriation and estimate shall be first approved by the State superintendent, and shall then be recorded by said clerk in a book to be kept for that purpose. From the date of said filing the title of said tract of land shall vest in the United States. Said division inspector shall cause notice to be given of said appropriation and estimate to all persons known to be interested in the tract appropriated, and shall also cause a copy of said notice to be posted upon said tract, within thirty days from the filing of said appropriation and estimate as aforesaid. Any person interested in said estate, aggrieved by the estimate of his damages, may apply by petition to the district court where in said land is situated, setting forth a description of the land, and the fact that he is so aggrieved; and the judge of said court shall thereupon cause due notice to be given by the petitioner to the State superintendent; and if it shall appear to said court that the petitioner is interested in the land so taken, it shall appoint three disinterested and discreet men to be commissioners to revise the estimate of the damages occasioned to the petitioner as aforesaid, the report of whom, or the majority of whom returned into said court and accepted thereby, shall be final and conclusive between the parties to the matter of said damages. The court may for good cause shown, set aside the report of said commissioners, and recommit the matter to them, or to new commissioners, at its discretion.

Sec. 6. And be it further enacted, that the schoolbooks to be used in all the national schools shall be such as are prescribed by the said superintendent, under the direction of the Commissioner of Education. They shall be furnished by State superintendent to the division inspector, and by the latter to the local superintendent, for the children within his district, and by him distributed to them at cost; Provided, that if any child is unable to pay the cost of the books needed and used by it the same shall be furnished gratuitously.

Sec. 7. And be it further enacted, that it shall be the duty of the local superintendent to provide for the care and protection and repairing of the school houses, and to procure fuel therefor, where necessary. If it shall be necessary to erect a school house in any district, the local superintendent shall contract for the same, the contract therefor to receive the approbation of the State superintendent before it shall be binding.

Sec. 8. And be it further enacted, that the local superintendent shall select and contract with a teacher or teachers for the schools within his district, at a rate and for a period of time to be approved by the State Superintendent.

Sec. 9. And be it further enacted, that the Commissioner of Education shall prescribe forms of registers of the attendance, conduct, age, and other particulars respecting the pupils in each school, and shall furnish blanks for the same. The same shall be kept by the teachers in accordance with the rules prescribed by the Commissioners, and shall be returned to the State superintendent. The State superintendent shall make abstracts of said returns, and return them annually to the Commissioner of Education, at such time as the latter shall prescribe, and shall also make a report stating the condition and means of Education in his State with such suggestions as will seem to him important. In the performance of all the duties provided by this act, the local superintendent shall be subject to the direction of the division inspector, the division inspector to those of the State superintendent, and the State superintendent shall be subject to the directions of the Commissioner of Education.

Sec. 10. And be it further enacted that no books shall be used in any of the national schools, nor shall any instruction be given therein calculated to favor the peculiar tenets of any religious sect.

Sec. 11. And be it further enacted, that it shall be the duty of all instructors of youth to exert their best endeavors to impress on the minds of children and youth committed to their care and instruction, the principles of piety and justice, and a sacred regard for truth, love of their country, of liberty, humanity and universal benevolence, sobriety, industry and frugality, chastity, moderation, and temperance, and those other virtues which are the ornaments of human society and the basis upon which a republican

Constitution is founded; and it shall be the duty of such instructors to endeavor to lead their pupils, as their ages and capacities will admit, into a clear understanding of the tendency of the above named virtues, to preserve and perfect a republican Constitution and secure the blessings of liberty, as well as to promote their future happiness, and also to point out to them the evil tendency of the opposite vices.

Sec. 12. And be it further enacted, that it shall be the duty of the division inspector to visit as often as once a year each school in his district, to keep himself informed, as far as may be, of the condition of the schools therein, and exercise a general care and oversight of the same, and to make report of the condition of all schools within his division annually, to the State superintendent.

Sec. 13. And be it further enacted that the Commissioner of Education shall annually report to Congress the condition of the national schools in each State together with such suggestions concerning the same as he shall deem important. He shall also, from time to time, prescribe such rules as he shall think fit for the government of the State and local superintendents and division inspectors in accomplishing the purpose of this act.

Sec. 14. And be it further enacted, that the Secretary of the Treasury shall prescribe such rules, in conformity to law, as shall in his judgment be necessary to provide for the payment of teachers, for land, school houses, and other objects herein provided for; and may require such vouchers from any of the officers herein provided for as may be necessary to insure security in the application of moneys so paid.

Sec. 15. And be it further enacted, that a direct tax of   million dollars is hereby laid upon the United States, and the same shall be apportioned among the States, respectively in the manner following:

Sec. 16. And be it further enacted, that said tax shall be assessed and collected in the mode prescribed for the collection of the direct tax in the forty-fifth chapter of the acts of the first session of the thirty-seventh Congress and the acts in addition thereto; Provided, that the assessors and collectors who are now, or may hereafter be, charged by law with the duty of assessing or collecting the internal revenue shall assess and collect the tax herein provided, and the collection districts for the assessment and collection of the direct tax shall be the same as are now or may hereafter be, established for the assessment and collection of said revenue. The dwelling house and lot of land on which the same stands constituting the homestead of any householder having a family and actually owned by him or her shall be exempted from such tax to the value of one thousand dollars.

Sec. 17. And be it further enacted, that all sums of money assessed and raised in each State by virtue of this act shall be expended therein for the purposes of education, as in this act declared.

Sec. 18. And be it further enacted, that any state may lawfully assume, collect, assess, and pay into the treasury of the United States the direct tax, or its quota thereof, imposed by this act upon such State, according to the provisions of said forty-fifth chapter of the acts of the first session of the thirty-seventh Congress.

Sec. 19. And be it further enacted, that this act shall take effect on the first day of   , eighteen hundred and seventy.   . Any state may at its election in lieu of the tax provided for by this act, provide for all the children within its borders between the ages of   and   suitable instruction in reading, writing, orthography, arithmetic, geography, and the history of the United States. If any state shall, before said last named day by a resolve of its legislature, approved by the governor, engage to make such provision, and shall notify the President of the United States thereof, all future proceeding for appointing the officers provided for herein, or for the assessment or collection of aforesaid tax within such State, shall be suspended for twelve months from said date. If, at the expiration of said twelve months, it shall be proved to the satisfaction of the President of the United States that there is established in said State a system of common schools which provides reasonably, for all the children therein who dwell where the population is sufficiently dense to enable schools to be maintained, suitable instruction in the aforesaid branches no further steps shall be taken for the appointment of officers or the assessing of the tax therein; otherwise, he shall proceed to cause said tax to be assessed and said schools to be established within such State forthwith thereafter.

The Blair Bill to Aid in the Establishment and Temporary Support of Common Schools, 1881 *

Be it enacted by the Senate and House of Representatives of the United States of America in Congress assembled, That for ten years next after the passage of this act there shall be annually appropriated from the money in the Treasury the following sums, to wit: The first year the sum of $15,000,000, the second year the sum of $14,000,000, the third year the sum of $13,000,000, and thereafter a sum diminished $1,000,000 yearly from the sum last appropriated until ten annual appropriations shall have been made, when all appropriations under this act shall cease; which several sums shall be expended to secure the benefits of common-school education to all the children living in the United States.

Sec. 2. That the instruction in the common schools wherein these moneys shall be expended shall include the art of reading, writing, and speaking the English language, arithmetic, geography, history of the United States, and such other branches of useful knowledge as may be taught under local laws, and may include, whenever practicable, instruction in the

---

* *Congressional Record*, 49 Cong., 1st Sess., VII, Part 2, pp. 1282-83. This bill or one very similar to it passed the Senate April 7, 1884, by a vote of 33 yeas and 11 nays.

arts of industry; which instruction shall be free to all, without distinction of race, nativity, or condition in life: *Provided,* That nothing herein shall deprive children of different races, living in the same community but attending separate schools, from receiving the benefits of this act the same as though the attendance therein were without distinction of race.

Sec. 3. That such money shall annually be divided among and paid out in the several States and Territories in that proportion which the whole number of persons in each who, being of the age of ten years and over, can not read and write bears to the whole number of such persons in the United States; and until otherwise provided such computation shall be made according to the official returns of the census of 1880.

Sec. 4. That such moneys shall be expended in each State by the concurrent action, each having a negative upon the other, of the Secretary of the Interior, on the part of the United States, and of the superintendent of public schools, board of education, or other body in which the administration of the public-school laws shall be vested, on the part of the several States wherein the expenditures are respectively to be made; and whenever the authorities of the United States and of the State fail to agree as to the distribution, use, and application of the money hereby provided for, or any part thereof, payment thereof, or such part thereof, shall be suspended, and if such disagreement continue throughout the fiscal year for which the same was appropriated, it shall be covered into the Treasury and shall be added to the general appropriation for the next year, provided for in the first section of this act.

All sums of money appropriated under the provisions of this act to the use of any Territory shall be applied to the use of schools therein by the Secretary of the Interior, through the commissioner of common schools, whose appointment is hereinafter provided for.

Sec. 5. That the moneys distributed under the provisions of this act shall be used in the school districts of the several States and Territories in such way as to provide for the equalization of school privileges to all the children throughout the State or Territory wherein the expenditure shall be made, thereby giving to each child an opportunity for common-school education; and to this end existing public schools not sectarian in character may be aided, and new ones may be established, as may be deemed best in the several localities.

Sec. 6. That a part of the money apportioned to each State or Territory, not exceeding one-tenth thereof, may yearly be applied to the education of teachers for the common schools therein, which sum may be expended in maintaining institutes or temporary training schools or in extending opportunities for normal or other instruction to intelligent and suitable persons, of any color, who are without necessary means, and who shall agree, in writing, to qualify themselves and teach in the common schools of such State or Territory at least one year.

Sec. 7. That the design of this act not being to establish an independent system of schools, but rather to aid for the time being in the development and maintenance of the school systems established by local power, and which must eventually be wholly maintained by the States and Territories wherein they exist, it is hereby provided that no part of the money appropriated under this act shall be paid out in any State or Territory which shall not during the first five years of the operation of this act annually expend for the maintenance of common schools, free to all, at least one-third of the sum which shall be allotted to it under the provisions hereof, and during the second five years of its operation a sum at least equal to the whole it shall be entitled to receive under this act; and if such expenditure shall not be shown to the Secretary of the Interior at the end of each fiscal year by each State or Territory, respectively, or by such other evidence as shall be satisfactory to him, then the allotment under this act for each subsequent year so long as there shall be a deficiency of such expenditure by the State or Territory from the proceeds of local funds, whether derived from taxation or otherwise, shall be expended for the support of common schools therein wholly in the discretion of the Secretary, who shall apply the same to the support of existing or to the establishment of new schools in such way as he shall deem best.

Sec. 8. That no part of the money herein provided for shall be used for the erection of school-houses or school-buildings of any description, nor for rent of the same: *Provided, however,* That whenever it shall appear to the Secretary that otherwise any given locality will remain wholly without reasonable common-school advantages, he may, in his discretion, from the general fund allotted to the State or Territory, provide schools and for their temporary accommodations, by rent or otherwise, in the most economical manner possible: *And provided further,* That in no case shall more than 5 per cent. of such allotment be set apart for or be expended under the provisions of this section.

Sec. 9. That there shall be appointed by the President, by and with the advice and consent of the Senate, a commissioner of common schools in each State and Territory, who shall be a citizen thereof and shall reside therein, and shall perform all such duties as may be assigned to him by the Secretary of the Interior, and who shall be specially charged with all the details of the execution of this act within his jurisdiction, and in co-operation with the State authorities. In the Territories he shall also be charged with the general supervision and control of public education, and shall possess all the powers now vested in Territorial superintendents and boards of education, or by whatever Territorial officers the same may have been hitherto exercised. He shall be paid a salary of not less than three nor more than five thousand dollars, in the discretion of the Secretary of the Interior. He shall annually make full reports of all matters connected with schools in his jurisdiction to the Secretary of the Interior, and particular reports when called upon by the Secretary, and especially of all details in the administration of this act. In addition to his other duties he shall devote himself to the promotion of the general interests of public education in the State or Territory for which he is appointed.

Sec. 10. That any State, in which the number of persons ten years of age and upward who can not read is not over 5 per cent. of the whole population, signifying its desire that the amount allotted to it under the provisions of this act shall be appropriated in any other way for the promotion of common-school education, in its own borders or elsewhere, its allotment shall be paid to such State to be thus appropriated: *Provided,* That its Legislature shall have first considered the question of its appropriation to the general fund for use under the provisions of this act in States and Territories where the proportion of illiterate persons is more than 5 per cent. of the whole population.

Sec. 11. That any State whose illiterate is greater than 5 per cent. of its whole population failing to accept the provisions of this act and to comply with its provisions, so as to be entitled to its allotment from year to year, the sum allotted to such State, subject to the discretionary action of the Secretary of the Interior under the sixth and seventh sections of this act, shall become a part of the fund to be distributed among the States which shall be entitled to their respective allotments, and to the Territories. And any State not accepting the provisions of this act, nor acquiring the right to dispose of its allotment as provided in the preceding section, the same shall become a part of the general fund for like distribution.

Sec. 12. That the District of Columbia shall be entitled to the privileges of a Territory under the provisions of this act, but there shall be no commissioner of common schools appointed for said District, nor shall its existing laws and school authorities be interfered with. The Commissioner of Education shall be charged with the duty of superintending the distribution of its allotment, and shall make full report of his doings to the Secretary of the Interior.

Sec. 13. That the Secretary of the Interior shall be charged with the practical administration of this law through the Bureau of Education, and all moneys paid under its provisions shall be made by Treasury warrant to the individual performing the service to whom indebtedness shall be due, and who shall be personally entitled to receive the money, or to his agent, duly authorized by him, upon vouchers approved by the State authorities, when under the provisions of this act their approval is necessary, and by the commissioner of common schools for the State or Territory wherein the expenditure shall be made, and by the Secretary of the Interior.

Sentiment on the Blair Bill Changes, 1886 *

In the debate which had been going on for some days the opponents of the bill had decidedly the best of the argument, but many Senators were committed upon it by their votes in a former Congress, when it was not so fully considered. There will be no such obstacle to independent judgment in the House. . . . There has been a great change of sentiment on the subject since it was first broached, and the feeling seems to be spreading that the Southern States, where illiteracy is most prevalent, will be able to provide for the education of their own people, and will be more likely to do so if left to themselves.

Federal Aid for Education in the South is Urged, 1887 †

That we reaffirm our conviction of the urgent necessity of temporary Federal aid in the education of the illiterate masses of the South.

The Culture-Epoch Theory in Education, 1899 ‡

The doctrine of recapitulation might recommend itself to the educator thru several considerations of various degrees of importance: by satisfactory evidences, by weight of authority, by a record of practical utility in school matters, or by signs of marked promise for the future. But a detailed examination of these claims would of course require a volume and much special knowledge. The object of the present paper is merely to look at the doctrine in a general way, with intent to discover what attitude toward it on the part of the practical teacher is likely to be most fruitful of good and least productive of harm.

The first question will naturally be: Can we accept the doctrine as a fact? In seeking light on this preliminary inquiry, we must at once distinguish the theory from the notion of an undefined general correspondence between the course of the race and that of the individual. The latter view, taken in the loose, vague way, appears almost axiomatic. The race and the child begin with a comparatively simple and go on to a comparatively complex life. What the race has attained is, in a general way, the end set before the individual, and, in passing from analogous starting-points to analogous goals, it would seem to follow, from the existence of one world and one general kind of process called mind, that the race and the individual must gather up and organize experience in somewhat the same

* Editorial in *The New York Times* as given in *The Nation*, XLII (March 11, 1886), p. 208.

† Resolution of the National Educational Association. *Journal of Proceedings and Addresses*, 1887, p. 47. This organization favored the Blair Bills and many times resolved in favor of federal aid to education.

‡ Louise Morris Hannum, State Normal School, Greeley, Colorado. *Journal of Proceedings and Addresses of the National Educational Association*, 1899, pp. 576-82.

fashion—must get from the starting-point to the goal by somewhat the same path. In this form the idea of recapitulation is more congenial to the poet and the mystic than to the teacher; it has abundant uses in speculation and imaginative expression, but no definite relation to methods and school curricula. The more precise—or, rather, the least nebulous—conception of the doctrine assumes that the development both of the race and of the individual can be described as a progress thru certain stages; and that, with some relatively calculable variations, these stages correspond in the two series. The inference is then drawn that, since the history of the child is writ large in that of the race, we can see more clearly in the race than in the child what is the true order of development. To this is often added the idea that, since the race has preserved the products of its activity in the most important stages, we have ready to hand the true food on which the child must be nourished as he goes thru the several zones of progress from infancy to manhood. It seems needless to say that the admission of the undefined general correspondence just mentioned, in which all are doubtless agreed, does not imply acceptance of the more precise doctrine of recapitulation. Nor can the latter be foisted upon us as a corollary of the doctrine of evolution. It is true that the biological argument for the culture-epoch theory would be less tenable without the doctrine of evolution; but it does not follow, because our species is believed to be the result of successive variations from less complex organisms, that therefore the youth of the species should pass thru the successive variations from primitive man. If a theory of recapitulation definite enough to deserve practical consideration is to stand at all, it must do so by force of independent proof. . . .

Altogether, a glance over the evidence for the culture-epoch theory, from the layman's point of view, tends to emphasize the judgment: unproved. That there is a high degree of general probability for some form of parallelism between the development of the individual and that of the race would probably, we repeat, be conceded by all. But the terms of the parallelism are undecided, the epochs indefinite, the evidence of corresponding stages full of gaps and ambiguities.

How, then, shall we look at the weight of authority which heralds the doctrine from many quarters and from thinkers as diverse as Goethe, Kant, Pestalozzi? The truth seems to be that the prominent men who refer to the theory or use it in their educational schemes have simply seized upon the conception in a loose, constructive fashion, without careful research or critical examination of evidence. An authority is not one whose dictum is to be taken without convincing reasons, but one who has demonstrated his ability to give such reasons. In this sense, no one of the older philosophers and educators is an authority on culture epochs. Some of the most famous whose names are quoted, as Goethe and Darwin, have but casually discussed or questioned the doctrine, while others, as Ziller and Hartmann, have been occupied in accurately dividing the years of childhood among the culture epochs rather than in finding a warrant for doing so. Some authorities, again, have apparently cherished the theory because it was to their minds the vehicle of a stronger conviction that the faculties of children ought to be developed according to some order. It seems, indeed, to be true that valuable conceptions have been reached thru the culture-epoch theory which might have been delayed without it, tho their truth is quite independent of it. But that is, of course, no more an argument for the doctrine than the facts discovered by the Chaldaeans about eclipses are an argument for astrology. If authority is to count at all in our attitude toward recapitulation as a tenable theory, it must be simply to strengthen the undefined analogy between race and child which no one is disposed to question. . . .

Herbart supposed that the doctrine should be applied to the matter of instruction in history, literature, and language, and reached the somewhat amusing conclusion that Greek and Latin should be taught before French and Italian, and that Roman history—perhaps the least congenial of records to children—should precede modern historical tales. Herbart's dominant belief that the child should assimilate in order the traces of moral culture in the race was developed by Ziller, who, after a happy course in the *Odyssey* and *Robinson Crusoe,* led the children from the heroic and individual epoch thru the various stages of relation to the community represented by the patriarchs, judges, kings, the life of Christ, and the history of the apostles, ending in the Reformation and the catechism. Vogt took something from the Procrustean caste of the system by avoiding the attempt of Herbart, Ziller, and Hartmann to assign a particular year to each epoch, and Beyer broadened the conception by attempting to apply it to nature study—a field which Herbart had believed to be quite outside the principle; but otherwise the general features of the Herbartian scheme were retained, with, however, one important element of progress. This is the tendency to transfer the emphasis from the selection of proper culture products to study of the progressive movement of the mental life. Vogt made extensive studies in child nature in order to determine the characteristic phases of child development during the first fourteen years of life. But this new attempt, it is plain, has its value quite distinct from any question of recapitulation. So also Rein, caring little for the mere material imparted in comparison with the quality of action and desire aroused, offers principles of guidance which are really based on study of the child in his relation to the ends of education, not in his relation to the development of the race. And, in general, it is impossible to review the history of the culture-epoch theory without discovering that, other things being equal, the theorists have contributed to pedagogical wisdom just in proportion as they have given over the attempt to get at the child thru the race and have addressed themselves to the slow and difficult task of getting knowledge about children at first hand. It is doubtful whether from Herbart to Baldwin all the schemes constructed according to the principle of recapitulation are worth, either in substance or in stimulus, one careful study of some phase of the child mind; and it is certain that the best thing about the culture-epoch theory is that it forgets itself and outgrows itself in single-minded study of children.

And, after all, the usefulness of the culture-epoch generalization in the field of concrete, practical investigation to which it has helped to lead is only what we should expect. There is no royal road to definite gains in education. Wide-embracing hypotheses like evolution and recapitulation enlarge our grasp, gratify our reason, strengthen our sympathies, give meaning to life; but they do not rectify our civilization nor provide us with school curricula. It is, indeed, easily possible, putting aside practical claims, to exaggerate the extent to which the reason may be comforted by the explanation which the theory of recapitulation is supposed to give of the mysteries of childhood. . . .

The hypothesis of culture epochs is not, then, one from which, even if admitted, we could reason deductively; it is not yet defined with sufficient sharpness nor interpreted with sufficient certainty. We cannot teach or withhold anything at any period of the child's development simply because the race learned or did not learn it at a supposed corresponding period. The end of education is supplied in part by the demands of the civilization of which the child is to become a part; his own needs, the order of his development, and the subject-matter suited to its various phases can in the last resort be determined only by child study and by experimental psychology. The impression seems to be growing among us that the threefold root of the principle of sufficient reason for everything pedagogical is biology, sociology, and psychology. If this means that the three are equally closely related to the problems of education, we must demur. Sociology may help to determine the end and the subject-matter as a whole; biology may clear up what psychology is of itself unable to explain; but the standard of reference is always the child, and the final arbiter and interpreter of data from whatever source, as well as the organon of knowledge about the mental elements and the laws that govern their connection, is psychology pursued under experimental conditions. . . .

Since, however, a general correspondence between race and individual development is admitted by all, we cannot reproach those who cling to the theory as suggestive and stimulating, provided they are not seduced by the charm of wide generalizations into admitting it as a guiding principle. If it be conceded that the doctrine cannot in ever so slight a degree take the place of experimental psychology, cannot be reasoned from deductively or used as a working hypothesis in practical pedagogy, we may welcome it as a point of view for all the value it may have in widening our conceptions or in teaching patience with the imperfect stages of child-growth.

The Kindergarten Should Be an Integral Part of the
Public School System, 1913 *

It is a well-known fact that all organized bodies are conservative, that to introduce a new feature it is necessary that the idea be completely worked thru a series of evolutions, beginning with specialists on the subject. Froebel was the great discoverer of infancy as a phase of life worth considering, as the beginning of the moral, aesthetic, and educational tastes of life. He was the pioneer specialist in kindergarten work and his life was spent in trying to convince the German nation of one fact, that early childhood is an important period in the formation of tendencies or the creation of attitudes in life. He died without seeing any tangible results, but since 1836 he has been the authority which modern thought has followed. The gradual growth of his ideas, the try-out of his plans by organizing kindergartens in the slums among the poor and uneducated class, has taken over half a century.

The kindergarten, like every other new movement, has had to be fostered by individuals and associations especially interested. Organized institutions do not undertake new interests. Ideas must first be worked out and their practical worth proven before they are adopted by public institutions.

Upon the answers to three questions must depend the answer to the question whether the kindergarten should now be adopted as an integral part of the public-school systems of states and cities:

1. Is all education a function of the state?
2. Should there be formal education provided for children before the age of six?
3. Is the kindergarten program an effective one?

My answer to each of these is in the affirmative, and therefore do I believe that the kindergarten should be adopted as an integral part of our system of education.

When this is done, great care will be necessary to prevent the kindergarten work becoming over-formal and losing its most essential characteristics. To prevent this there must be no attempt to grade children on their attainments or take out definite and fixed courses of study, nor must we suppose that because the children are small, teachers do not need a high degree of education. Women of the best education and training must be selected for teachers of the kindergarten classes. Personality counts more here than anywhere else.

* United States Commissioner of Education P. P. Claxton. *Journal of Proceedings and Addresses,* National Education Association, 1913, p. 426.

Discussion of the Report of the Committee on Tests and Standards
of Efficiency of the National Council of Education, 1913 *

EDWARD C. ELLIOTT, University of Wisconsin, Madison, Wis.—The ultimate problem of this committee is not that of establishing procedure or defining tests; rather it is that of creating a new kind of confidence on the part of the public in the work of the public schools. This confidence constitutes the capital with which the efficient school system must develop its dividends and activities. Many recent educational events have contributed to a weakening of that bond of trust that must ever obtain between the community and its fundamental institutions.

In devising tests and formulating standards, this committee must constantly have in mind the intelligent and public-minded portion of our citizenship. These tests and standards, however technical in character and object, must not have their significance clouded by esoteric verbiage. Our people of today want to understand what their educational system is, and what it is supposed to do. The ultimate worth of the efficiency principles and devices must be measured by the extent to which they are brought within the comprehension of the typical layman. Our aim must be the bulwarking of the cause of public education by a new common confidence in the performance of schools. This new confidence cannot be sustained upon vague theory nor upon standards that are established in defiance either of scientific procedure or of common-sense. If our schools are to have credit for work, this new confidence must obtain; if our school systems are entitled to the new confidence, they must have these new tests and standards. . . .

C. N. KENDALL, state commissioner of education, Trenton, N. J.—The Council has done well to appoint this committee to attempt an inventory of the factors which measure school efficiency.

I venture the opinon that any serious discussion of standards and tests will have a salutary influence upon the public, upon school boards, upon teachers, and upon superintendents. I believe the day is past when any system of schools, municipal or state, can safely ignore analysis of its results. . . .

In conclusion, I wish to advance five propositions:

1. A system of schools should have, under the leadership of the superintendent, its own local machinery for testing and investigating. A trained educational statistician might well be on the superintendent's office staff, or available for his use. A committee of laymen, citizens appointed by the board of education upon the recommendation of the superintendent, might, with the co-operation of the superintendent, present a survey of value. The

* *Journal of Proceedings and Addresses*, National Education Association, 1913, pp. 398-404.

report of such a local body, it is true, would probably take on local color or prejudice, but it could make some contribution. I do not wish to convey the impression that it could do as effective work as an outside body, but it might be a sort of clearing-house between the superintendent and public opinion which would strengthen the hands of the superintendent.

2. The survey should take into account purely local conditions which have affected school efficiency; for example, rapid growth in population, the character of the foreign-born population, lack of public funds to establish and maintain vocational training.

3. The report should not fail to recognize the achievements of the schools. This is due to the public, to the superintendent, to principals, and to teachers. Nothing will bring educational surveys into disrepute more surely than a survey which summarizes the work of the schools in the words of a college professor who recently passed judgment upon schools in such a discriminating statement as this: "The schools are absolutely rotten."

4. The survey should clearly indicate whether the general movement of the schools in spirit and results is in the direction of increased efficiency. The element of comparison should not be left out. Comparison with other cities? Yes. Comparison with previous conditions in the same city? By all means, yes.

5. The investigation should preferably be made by at least three persons. An adverse report will carry farther, in my judgment, and be received with more confidence, if it is the combined opinion of a group of persons than if it is the opinion of one man, however capable and conscientious he may be. . . .

BEN BLEWETT, superintendent of instruction, St. Louis, Mo.—The membership of the committee submitting this report represents the scholarship and practical experience competent to consider this question of surpassing importance. . . .

The report is, however, disappointing in at least one of its conclusions and certainly in some of the things it omits saying.

If I may venture to summarize the conclusions, they are:

1. That any school or school system may be justly measured in the functioning of its several activities.

2. That one standard of measure that can test its efficiency as a whole is impossible.

3. That the measures applied must be standards in the several and respective activities.

4. That these standards must be established by some bureau, committee, or group of experts selected because of ripe scholarship and broad experience in administration.

5. That varying conditions in social groups are factors in the results.

6. That an unrelated money value cost unit is a meaningless and mis-

chievous standard of measure of results in any of the activities of a school system, even in those activities having to do with such material things as cost of buildings and supplies.

7. That the community shares with the schoolmaster in the responsibility for the efficiency or inefficiency of the system of schools.

The report is disappointing in its second conclusion. While it is true as far as it goes, it is misleading in not going far enough. Not one test can prove that the piece of metal I have on my laboratory table is gold, but there is one test by which I can prove that it is not gold.

If it will not resist the drop of acid, I know that it is base, not pure. Tho we cannot be assured that a school system is efficient because it stands the test in any one, two, or more of its departments, or in some of the subjects of its curriculum work, its failure to show one dominant purpose or aim for its whole work is conclusive evidence that it is inefficient. Nor is the conclusiveness of the evidence vitiated by any question concerning the adequacy of the purpose or aim of any part of the work. . . .

J. M. GREEN, principal of State Normal School, Trenton, N. J.—We of our country are energetic and often very emotional. We are quite given to rushing new acquaintances, new ideas, and sometimes, I am afraid, new terms without much relating of ideas. It is easy to pick from the files of newspapers and magazines names of men upon whom the eyes of the nation were focused, and whose praises were on every tongue for a brief season. How many of us could now readily recite the names of even the select few who have been chosen to the Hall of Fame?

Recall the favor in politics of such expressions as "taxation without representation," "the little log cabin," "Tippecanoe and Tyler too," "the full dinner pail," "the open door," "imperialism," "conservation," "progressive," and, in education, of such expressions as "object teaching," "coordination," "correlation," "concentration," "Herbartianism," etc.

There is a saving grace in our rushing. We are not likely to allow it to carry us clear off our feet, and our fads often leave a residuum of real and lasting value. Just now we are rushing the term *efficiency*. I do not know exactly what the term means. It is like some other expressions that we try to define—not by any specific language—but by talking much around and about them. . . .

For this committee the National Council is asked to make a liberal appropriation and prepare itself to make further endowment in order to make possible the increase in the efficiency of our system of public education and the establishment of our teaching profession. . . .

There are to my mind three strong reasons why the National Council of Education should not undertake the proposition:

First, the Council is not wise enough to select such a committee.

Second, there are no men wise enough to constitute such a committee.

Thiıd, the National Education Association has not money enough to spare to meet the necessary expenses of such a committee.

There should be no objection to any superintendent of public instruction, any president of a college, or any board of education seeking any advice from anyone, but the National Council of Education should not designate that one. . . .

J. M. RICE, formerly editor, *The Forum,* Mt. Vernon, N. Y.—To express my views on educational standards and tests of efficiency as briefly as possible, I shall state them in the form of two fundamental propositions, which, from my viewpoint, are of equal importance. They are:

1. That standards and tests of efficiency are capable of development on a scientific basis in education.

2. That such development has its limitations.

These two propositions will suffice to indicate that, in my opinion, we are here confronted by a problem that presents two elements, a knowable and an unknowable one. Now, if the new movement may be expected to be rewarded by the advent of a real science of education, it will be necessary for our educators to recognize that unless they confine their attention in the development of standards to those elements that are knowable, and for this reason are subject to standardization, the whole movement is liable to go awry. . . .

Leonard P. Ayres on the History and Present Status of Educational Measurements, 1918 *

Measurements in education are fifty years old if we count from the oldest beginnings of which we have record. They are twenty-five years old if we reckon from the time that Dr. Rice, the pioneer and pathmaker among American scientific students of education, began his work in this field. They are ten years old if we begin our count with the earliest efforts of Professor Thorndike, who is the father of the present movement.

We are indebted to Professor Thorndike for having discovered what is apparently the earliest record of work in the field of educational measurements as we now use that term. As early as 1864 a school master in England, the Rev. George Fisher, of the Greenwich Hospital School, had seen the need and possibilities of standards, and with prophetic foresight an-

* "History and Present Status of Educational Measurements," *The Seventeenth Yearbook of the National Society for the Study of Education* (Bloomington, Ill., Public School Publishing Co., 1918), Part II: "The Measurement of educational Products, pp. 9-15. Students interested in the subject should read J. M. Rice's "The Futility of the Spelling Grind," which provoked derision from the N.E.A. These articles may be found in *The Forum,* XXXIII, pp.163-72 and 409-19, following his "Obstacles to National Educational Reform" which had appeared in the same magazine in December, 1896, pp. 385-95. Similar studies by Rice were later published in *The Forum* as follows: on arithmetic, XXXIV, pp. 281-97, 437-52; on languages, XXXIV, pp. 269-93, 440-57. He concludes his articles on spelling: "Consequently our efforts should be primarily directed toward supplying our schools with competent teachers."

ticipated present-day achievements. His practice was as follows: "A book called the 'Scale-Book' has been established, which contains the numbers assigned to each degree of proficiency in the various subjects of examination: for instance, if it be required to determine the numerical equivalent corresponding to any specimen of 'writing,' a comparison is made with the various standard specimens, which are arranged in this book in order of merit; the highest being represented by the number 1, and the lowest by 5, and the intermediate values by affixing to these numbers the fractions ¼, ½, or ¾. So long as these standard specimens are preserved in the institution, so long will instant numerical values for proficiency in 'writing' be maintained. And since fac-similes can be multiplied without limit, the same principle might be generally adopted.

"The numerical values for 'spelling' follow the same order and are made to depend upon the percentage of mistakes in writing from dictation sentences from works selected for the purpose, examples of which are contained in the 'Scale-Book,' in order to preserve the same standard of difficulty.

"By a similar process values are assigned for proficiency in mathematics, navigation, Scripture, knowledge, grammar and composition, French, general history, drawing, and practical science, respectively. Questions in each of these subjects are contained in the 'Scale-Book,' to serve as types, not only of the difficulty, but of the nature of the questions, for the sake of future reference; observing that the same numerals are used in the same order as before, viz., number 1 denotes the highest, and number 5 the lowest amount of attainment.

"In respect to the numerical values of 'reading,' as regards accuracy, taste or judgment, it is obvious that no other standard of measurement can be applied, beyond the interpretation of the terms 'good,' 'bad,' 'indifferent,' etc., existing at the period of examination. And the same observation will apply to the estimation of numbers of 'characters' and 'natural abilities,' as determined by the united testimony of the respective masters.

"Having stated this much with regard to the plan pursued in this school, I may well add that the advantage derived from this numerical mode of valuation, as applied to educational subjects, is not confined to its being a concise method of registration, combined with a useful approximation to a *fixed standard* of estimation, applicable to each boy; but it affords also a means of determining the *sum total,* and therefrom the means or average condition or value of any given number of results." [1]

Mr. Fisher's efforts seem to have produced no lasting results. Progress in the scientific study of education was not possible until people could be brought to realize that human behavior was susceptible of quantitative

[1] Reported by E. B. Chadwick in the *Museum, A Quarterly Magazine of Education, Literature and Science,* Vol. III, 1864. See also *Journal of Educational Psychology,* Vol. 4, p. 551.

study, and until they had statistical methods with which to carry on their investigations. Both of these were contributed in large measure by Sir Francis Galton. As early as 1875 he published scientific studies of the traits of twins, of number-forms, of color-blindness, and of the efficacy of prayer. Out of his work came much of experimental and educational psychology, and indirectly, educational measurements. It was he who developed the statistical methods necessary for the quantitative study of material which seemed at the outset entirely qualitative and not at all numerical in nature.

In America the real inventor of the comparative test was Dr. J. M. Rice. Dr. Rice studied in Germany and came under the influence of the German psychologists at Jena and Leipsic. Returning to this country, he became interested in education and one day in 1894 the new idea was born. Of this invention Dr. Rice says: "In truth, however, I came to recognize that this (the claims of school men following different courses of study) was all talk,—that no one really knew the facts, because there were no standards to serve as guides. Then one day, the idea flashed through my mind that the way to settle the question was to try it out. For a beginning I decided to take spelling, and on that very day I made up a list of 50 words with the view of giving them as a test to the pupils of the schools as I went on my tour from town to town. I have no record of the date of the inspiration, but I think it was some time in October, 1894."

Dr. Rice's work, however, did not meet with the approval of the educators of the day. One of his earlier reports in this field indicated that children who had spent thirty minutes a day for eight years in the study of spelling did not at the end of that time spell any better than the children in another school system who had spent only fifteen minutes a day for eight years in the same study. The presentation of these results brought upon the investigator almost unlimited attack. The educators who discussed his findings and those who reviewed them in the educational press united in denouncing as foolish, reprehensible, and from every point of view indefensible, the effort to discover anything about the value of the teaching of spelling by finding out whether or not the children could spell. They claimed that the object of such work was not to teach children to spell, but to develop their minds! It was the issue between the investigator and the formalist in education, and the conflict that is still under way is the conflict that was then for the first time clearly defined.

Little by little the more thoughtful men in the field of education appreciated the suggestive value of Dr. Rice's work and some few of them, notably Professor Hanus of Harvard, dared to come to his support. Slowly the tide turned in his favor, until by common consent the general validity of his conclusions was tentatively accepted. His methods, however, were not generally adopted, and for more than ten years but little progress was made beyond the work of the pioneer himself.

If Dr. Rice is to be called the inventor of education measurement, Professor E. L. Thorndike should be called the father of the movement. In 1895, Professor Thorndike was a student at Columbia, struggling with statistical methods in a course on measurements under Boas, and "finding it new and very hard for me to learn." [2] His interests were in the field of psychology and the work of Rice made a deep and lasting impression. Gradually his experimental work came more and more into the educational field. He began to preach the need of measurement and to experiment with tests and scales. The Stone Arithmetic Tests were published in 1908. The Thorndike Scale for the measurement of merit in handwriting was presented before Section L of the American Association for the Advancement of Science at its Boston meeting, in December, 1909, and was published in the *Teachers College Record* the following March. The construction of this scale, based on the equal difference theorem formulated by Cattell, marks the real beginning of the scientific measurement of educational products.

During the past ten years the growth of the scientific movement in education has been continuous and rapid. It has been closely related to the survey movement which had its real inception in 1907 in a great social study of the city of Pittsburgh, which was termed "A Survey." Three years later two college professors, Hanus of Harvard and Moore of Yale, conducted studies of the school systems of Montclair and East Orange in New Jersey. These studies differed from earlier investigations of school systems in that their purpose was to tell the public about their public schools, and each investigator, borrowing the term from the contemporary social movement, used the word "survey" to designate a section of his report. In the years that have followed, scores of surveys of city, state and county school systems have been conducted, and in ever increasing degree they have utilized, as perhaps the most important of their methods, the scales and tests used in the measurement of educational processes and products.

The two movements were represented in the New York school inquiry of 1911-12. For the first time in a formal educational investigation tests were used as an aid in evaluating the results of public-school work. These were the Courtis arithmetic tests, which had by that time attracted a good deal of attention. Their successful use in the New York survey not only settled all doubts as to the availability of the tests themselves for the measurement of educational attainment, but also firmly established the principle that in conducting school surveys scientific tests must be utilized where they are available.

One of the recommendations of the survey committee in New York City was that a Bureau of Research be established to conduct a continuous survey, from within the school system itself and for its benefit. This recommendation was immediately adopted and the Bureau organized in Septem-

[2] Quotation from a personal letter.

ber, 1913. Previous to this time, there had been in various cities committees and other organizations, which had made studies of various phases of administrative and instructional work, but to New York City probably belongs the credit of first establishing a formal organization having for its purpose the continuous critical study of its own activities by scientific methods.

By this time, Boston, Detroit, and many other cities, were experimenting with measurement and obtaining results of value. Other bureaus were soon established. The Division of Education of the Russell Sage Foundation had turned its attention to work of this type as early as 1907, the Boston Bureau was organized in 1913, and similar organizations in Detroit, Kansas City, and Oakland soon followed. During these same years faith and interest in measurements had been greatly stimulated by the development of the Binet-Simon tests and by the wide-spread attention given to the study of retardation and elimination in school systems. A demand for men trained for the work was created. Superintendents and teachers also were clamoring for technical knowledge of methods and for explanations of the results obtained. For ten years graduates of Teachers College, Columbia University, and of the School of Education of Chicago University had had impressed upon them that measurement and scientific experimentation were highly desirable in education and they had been at least partly prepared for such work. Next, this training was expanded into formal courses in educational measurement. Soon courses in measurement appeared in all the great universities and the movement began to gain full momentum.

The meetings of the Department of Superintendence of the National Education Association afford an excellent index of the progress of the movement. Dr. Rice's report in 1897 was received with derision. The Philadelphia meeting in 1912, after a heated discussion, voted against measurement by a small majority, but two years later a committee on Tests and Standards made a favorable report which was adopted by a considerable majority.

Today tests and scales are used throughout this country and around the world. In England, Germany, and France, before the war, beginnings had been made. Scales for the measurement of Chinese writing and composition are now in process of construction. In Australia and New Zealand, in India and Hawaii, and throughout the length and breadth of the United States and Canada, tests and scales are in daily service, proving valuable tools in the hands of those who know how to use them.

The scientific method is at base analytic scrutiny, exact measuring, careful recording, and judgment on the basis of observed fact. Science in education is not a body of information, but a method, and its object is to find out and to learn how. By its aid, education is becoming a profession. Courses of study are being adapted to the needs of children; teaching effort and supervisory control are becoming more efficient. The center of interest in education has become the child, rather than the teacher, and efforts to improve the quality of instruction begin by finding out what the children can do, rather than by discussing the methods by which the teacher proceeds.

Educational measurement has been accepted by the American public. This Yearbook is in itself a proof of that. That the methods of today are still crude and imperfect must be admitted by even the most enthusiastic supporters of the movement. They deal most effectively with only the simple mechanical skills, and even here they are still far from perfect. Nevertheless, they are extending each year their range of availability and their field of application.

The importance of the movement lies not only in its past and present achievements, but in the hope of the future. Knowledge is replacing opinion, and evidence is supplanting guess-work in education as in every other field of human activity. This is the supreme fact to which this Yearbook bears witness. The future depends upon the skill, the wisdom, and the sagacity of the school men and women of America. It is well that they should set about the task of enlarging, perfecting, and carrying forward the scientific movement in education, for the great war has marked the end of the age of haphazard, and the developments of coming years will show that this is true in education as in every other organized field of human endeavor.

A Bill to Create a Department of Education and for Federal Aid to Education, 1918 *

Be it enacted by the Senate and House of Representatives of the United States of America in Congress Assembled, That there is hereby created an executive department in the Government, to be called the Department of Education, with a Secretary of Education, who is to be the head thereof, to be appointed by the President, by and with the advice and consent of the Senate, who shall receive a salary of $12,000 per annum, and whose tenure of office shall be like that of the heads of other executive departments; and section one hundred and fifty-eight of the Revised Statutes is hereby amended to include such department, and the provisions of title four of the Revised Statutes, including all amendments thereto, are hereby made applicable to said department. The said Secretary shall cause a seal of office to be made for such department of such device as the President shall approve, and judicial notice shall be taken of the said seal.

Sec. 2. That there shall be in said department at least three Assistant Secretaries of Education, to be appointed by the President, each of whom

* S. 4987, 65th Congress, 2nd Session. This bill was introduced October 10, 1918, by Senator Smith of Georgia. A similar bill was introduced into the House by Representative Towner May 19, 1919, and was known as H.R. 7.

shall receive a salary of $10,000 per annum. Each Assistant Secretary of Education shall perform such duties as may be prescribed by the Secretary or by law. There shall be appointed, as is prescribed by law for the other executive departments, such chiefs of bureaus, branches, or divisions, and such educational attachés to American Embassies in foreign countries and such clerks, clerical assistants, auditors, inspectors, and special agents or representatives as may from time to time be provided for by Congress.

Sec. 3. That there be transferred to the Department of Education the Bureau of Education and such educational war-emergency commissions or boards or educational activities already established by Act of Congress as in the judgment of the President should be transferred to the Department of Education.

The President of the United States is hereby empowered in his discretion to transfer to the Department of Education such offices, bureaus, divisions, boards, or branches of the Government connected with or attached to any of the executive departments, or organized independently of any department, devoted to educational matters which concern the United States as a whole or the educational system of any State or States of the Union, which in his judgment should be controlled by, or the functions of which should be exercised by, the Department of Education.

Sec. 4. That the office records and papers now on file in and pertaining exclusively to the business of any bureau, office, division, board, or branch of the public service transferred by this Act to the Department of Education, together with the furniture now in use in such bureau, office, division, board, or branch of the public service, shall be, and are hereby, transferred to the Department of Education.

Sec. 5. That the Secretary of Education shall have charge, in the buildings or premises occupied by or assigned to the Department of Education, of the library, furniture, fixtures, records, and other property pertaining to it, or hereafter acquired for use in its business; he shall be allowed to expand for periodicals and the purposes of the library and for rental of appropriate quarters for the accommodation of the Department of Education within the District of Columbia, and for all other incidental expenses, such sums as Congress may provide from time to time: *Provided, however,* That where any office, bureau, division, board, or branch of the public service transferred to the Department of Education by this Act, or by the President, as provided in this Act, is occupying rented buildings or premises, it may still continue to do so until other suitable quarters are provided for its use: *Provided further,* That all officers, clerks, and employees now employed in or by any bureau, office, division, board, or branch of public service by this Act transferred to the Department of Education are each and all hereby transferred to the said Department of Education at their present grades and salaries, except where otherwise provided in this Act: *And provided further,* That all laws prescribing the work and defining the duties of the several bureaus, offices, divisions, boards, or branches of public service by this Act transferred to and made part of the Department of Education shall, so far as the same are not in conflict with the provisions of this Act, remain in full force and effect, to be executed under the direction of the Secretary of Education, to whom is hereby granted definite authority to readjust the work of any of the said bureaus, offices, boards, or branches of public service so transferred in such way as in his judgment will best accomplish the purposes of this Act.

Sec. 6. That there shall be a Solicitor in the Department of Justice for the Department of Education, whose salary shall be $5,000 per annum.

Sec. 7. That all duties performed, and all power and authority now possessed or exercised by the head of any executive department in and over any bureau, office, officer, board, division, or branch of public service transferred by this Act to the Department of Education, or any business arising therefrom or pertaining thereto, or in relation to the duties performed by it and authority conferred by law upon such bureau, office, officer, board, division, or branch of public service, whether of an appellate or revisory character or otherwise, shall hereafter be vested in and exercised by the Secretary of Education.

Sec. 8. That the Secretary of Education shall annually at the close of each fiscal year make a report in writing to Congress, giving an account of all moneys received and disbursed by him and his department, and describing the work done by the department. He shall also make other reports as hereinafter provided. He shall also, from time to time, make such special investigations and reports as he may be required to do by the President, or by Congress, or as he himself may deem necessary.

Sec. 9. That it shall be the specific duty of the Department of Education to cooperate with the States in the development of public educational facilities, including public-health education, within the respective States.

In order that the cooperation with the States in the promotion of education may be carried out for the best interests of education and public health in the respective States, the Secretary of Education, subject to the approval of the President, is authorized to reorganize such bureaus, offices, boards, divisions, or branches of public service as are transferred to the Department of Education. In this reorganization he shall consider—

(1) The encouragement of the study and investigation of problems relating to the educational purposes set forth in this Act and to such other educational problems as may, in the judgment of the Secretary of Education, require attention and study. Research shall be undertaken directly by the Department of Education in the fields of (a) illiteracy; (b) immigrant education; (c) public-school education, and especially rural education; (d) public-health education and recreation; (e) the preparation and supply of competent teachers for the public schools; and (f) such other fields as come within the provisions of this Act or as may come within the pro-

visions of other Acts of Congress relating to the Department of Education.

(2) The encouragement of higher and professional education and the encouragement of learned societies, including the appointment of such commissions as the Secretary of Education may deem necessary.

(3) The encouragement of physical and health education and recreation, these terms to be inclusive of all public health questions relating to school children and to adults, and of social and recreational problems which relate not only to the native born but also and especially to the foreign-born population.

In order to carry out the provisions of this section the Secretary of Education is authorized to make such appointments or recommendations of appointments, in the same manner as provided for appointments in other departments, of such educational attachés to foreign embassies, and such investigators and representatives as may be needed, subject, however, to the appropriations that have been made or may be made to any bureau, office, board, division, or branch of public service which is transferred by this Act or may be transferred; and where appropriations have not been made, the appropriation provided for in section ten of this Act shall be available. All provisions of Congress for cooperating with the States in the promotion of education, unless otherwise provided by law, shall be supervised through and by this department. The Secretary of Education is hereby authorized to assign to each assistant secretary such duties as in his judgment seem best in order to carry out the provisions of this Act.

Sec. 10. That there is hereby appropriated to the Department of Education the sum of $500,000 annually, to be available from and after the passage of this Act, for the purpose of paying salaries and conducting investigations and of paying all incidental expenses, including traveling expenses, and rent where necessary, and for the purpose of allowing the Department of Education to inaugurate a system of attachés to American embassies abroad to deal with educational matters. But this section is not to be construed as in any way interfering with any appropriation which has hitherto been made and which may hereafter be made to any bureau, office, division, board, or branch of public service, which is by this Act transferred to and made a part of the Department of Education, or which may hereunder be transferred by the President; and said appropriations are hereby continued in full force, to be administered by the Secretary of Education in such manner as is prescribed by law.

Sec. 11. That in order to cooperate with the States in the promotion of education, as hereinafter specified, there is hereby appropriated, out of any money in the Treasury not otherwise appropriated, the following sums: For the fiscal year ending June thirtieth, nineteen hundred and twenty, and annually thereafter, $100,000,000.

Sec. 12. That in order to cooperate with the States in the abolition of illiteracy, three-fortieths of the sum annually appropriated by section eleven of this Act shall be used for the instruction of illiterates ten years of age and over. Such instruction shall deal with the common-school branches and the duties of citizenship, and when necessary shall prepare for some definite occupation. Said sum shall be apportioned to the States in the proportion which their respective illiterate populations of ten years of age and over (not including foreign-born illiterates) bear to such total illiterate population of the United States, not including outlying possessions, according to the last preceding census of the United States.

Sec. 13. That in order to cooperate with the States in the Americanization of immigrants, three-fortieths of the sum annually appropriated by section eleven of this Act shall be used to teach immigrants ten years of age and over to speak and read the English language and the duties of citizenship, and to develop among them an appreciation of and respect for the civic and social institutions of the United States. The said sum shall be apportioned to the States in the proportions which their respective foreign-born populations bear to the total foreign-born population of the United States, not including outlying possessions, according to the last preceding census of the United States.

Sec. 14. That in order to cooperate with the States in the efforts to equalize educational opportunities, five-tenths of the sum annually appropriated by section eleven of this Act shall be used for the improvement of public schools of less than college grade, with the definite aim of extending school terms and of stimulating State and local interest in improving, through better instruction and gradation and through consolidation and supervision, the rural schools and schools in sparsely settled localities. The said sum shall be apportioned to the States in the proportions which the numbers of teachers in the public schools of the respective States bear to the total number of public-school teachers in the United States, not including outlying possessions, said apportionment to be based upon figures collected by the Department of Education: *Provided, however,* That no State shall share in the apportionment provided by this section of this Act unless such State shall require every public-school district to maintain a legal school for at least twenty-four weeks in each year, and unless such State shall have enacted and enforced an adequate compulsory school-attendance law, and unless such State shall have enacted and enforced laws requiring that the basic language of instruction in the common-school branches in all schools, public and private, shall be the English language only.

Sec. 15. That in order to cooperate with the States in the promotion of physical and health education and recreation two-tenths of the sum annually appropriated by section eleven of this Act shall be used for physical education and recreation, the medical and dental examination of children of school age, the determination of mental and physical defects in such children, the employment of school nurses, the establishment and maintenance of school dental clinics, and the instruction of the people in the principles of health and sanitation. The said sum shall be apportioned to the States in the proportions which their respective entire populations bear to the total population of the United States, not including outlying possessions, according to the last preceding census of the United States.

Sec. 16. That in order to cooperate with the States in preparing teachers for the schools, particularly rural schools, three-twentieths of the sum annually appropriated to the States by section eleven of this Act shall be used to prepare teachers, to encourage a more nearly universal preparation of prospective teachers, to extend the facilities for the improvement of teachers already in service, to encourage through the establishment of scholarships and otherwise a greater number of talented young people to make adequate preparation for public-school service, and otherwise to provide an increased number of trained and competent teachers. The said sum shall be apportioned to the States in the proportion which the numbers of teachers in the public schools of the respective States bear to the total number of public-school teachers in the United States, not including outlying possessions, said apportionment to be based on figures collected by the Department of Education.

Sec. 17. That in the event the allotments under sections twelve, thirteen, fourteen, fifteen, and sixteen to any State aggregate less than $20,000 per annum and said State is willing to meet all the conditions of this Act and to provide $1 for each dollar of Federal money, either from State or local sources, or both, to the sum of $20,000 per annum, the Secretary of Education is authorized to make said allotment; and in order to guarantee to any State a minimum of not less than $20,000, provided said State meets the conditions of this Act as herein specified, an additional sum of $500,000, or as much thereof as may be needed, is hereby appropriated annually.

Sec. 18. That in order to secure the benefits of the appropriation made in section eleven of this Act and of all or any of apportionments made in sections twelve, thirteen, fourteen, fifteen, sixteen, or seventeen of this Act any State may, through the legislative authority thereof, accept the provisions of this Act and designate its chief State educational authority, whether a State board of education or a State superintendent of public instruction, with all necessary power to cooperate as herein provided with the Department of Education in the administration of this Act in so far as it relates to the aiding of the States in the promotion of education. In any State in which the legislature does not meet in nineteen hundred and nineteen, if the governor of that State, so far as he is authorized to do so, shall accept the provisions of this Act and designate the State board of education, the State superintendent of public instruction, or other chief State educational authority to act in cooperation with the Department of Education, the said Department of Education shall recognize such designation by the governor for the purposes of this Act until the legislature of such State meets in due course and has been in session sixty days. Any State may accept the provisions of any one or more of the respective apportionments herein authorized and may defer the acceptance of any one or more of said apportionments: *Provided, however,* That no State that does not have, or establish within two years after this Act becomes effective, a satisfactory system of preparing teachers shall be allowed to participate in any of said apportionments, except those referring to the education of illiterates in section twelve and to the education of immigrants in section thirteen, until it maintains such a system for the preparation of teachers. In the acceptance of the provisions of this Act the legislature shall designate and appoint as custodian for all funds received as apportionments under the provisions of this Act its State treasurer, who shall receive and provide for the proper custody and disbursement of all money paid to the State from such apportionments, said disbursements to be made from warrants duly drawn by the State board of education, State superintendent of public instruction, or other chief State educational authority designated to cooperate with the Department of Education as provided in this section of this Act.

Sec. 19. That the Secretary of Education is authorized to frame rules and regulations for carrying out the provisions of this Act and is furthermore authorized to prescribe a plan of keeping accounts of educational expenditures for use in the several States in so far as such expenditures relate to the provisions of this Act. The Secretary may prescribe or approve the forms to be used in keeping such school accounts and the making of such school records as in his judgment are required to insure the proper administration of the provisions of this Act. He shall appoint an auditor to have charge of such accounting in the several States and of the examination of such accounts, and he shall appoint such assistant auditors as may be necessary to aid in examining and verifying said accounts showing expenditure of moneys by the States for the purpose of meeting the provisions of this Act and of examining such other educational records as may be required.

Sec. 20. That in order to secure the benefits of the appropriations made in sections eleven and seventeen of this Act and of all or any of the apportionments made in sections twelve, thirteen, fourteen, fifteen, or sixteen of this Act the State board of education, the State superintendent of public instruction, or other chief State educational authority which may be duly designated to cooperate with the Department of Education, as provided in section eighteen of this Act, shall present to the Secretary of Education plans and regulations for carrying out the provisions of this Act in said State, which plans shall be approved by the said Secretary of Education before any allotment or apportionment of funds is made to said State. The plans of the said State board of education, State superintendent of public instruction, or other chief State educational authority designated to co-operate with the Department of Education shall specifically show courses of study and the standards for teacher-training preparation to be maintained. When said plans are approved the said Secretary of Education shall apportion to the said State such fund or funds as said State may be entitled to under this Act: *Provided, however,* That no money appropriated shall be paid from any fund in any year to any State, unless a sum equally as large has been provided by said State, or by local authorities, or by both, for the abolition of illiteracy, for the Americanization of immigrants, for the improvement of public schools, for physical education, for teacher training, or such other purpose as the case may be: *And provided further,* That no such sum shall be used by any State, county, district, or local authority, directly or indirectly, for the purchase, rental, erection, preservation, or repair of any building or equipment, or for the purchase or rental of land, or for the support of any religious or privately endowed, owned, or conducted school or college, but only for schools entirely owned and controlled and conducted by the State or county or district, or local authority, as may be provided for under the laws controlling and regulating the public-school system of said State.

Sec. 21. That the Secretary of the Treasury is hereby instructed to pay quarterly, on the first day of July, October, January, and April, to the treasurer of any State entitled to any apportionment, such apportionment as is properly certified to him by the Secretary of Education. Wherever any part of the fund apportioned annually to any State for any of the purposes named in sections twelve, thirteen, fourteen, fifteen, or sixteen of this Act has not been expended for said purpose, a sum equal to such unexpended part shall be deducted from the next succeeding annual apportionment made to said State for said purpose. The Secretary of Education may withhold the apportionment of moneys to any State whenever it shall be determined that such moneys are not being expended for the purposes and under the conditions of this Act. If any portion of the moneys received by the treasurer of a State under this Act for any of the purposes herein provided shall, by action or contingency, be diminished or lost, it shall be replaced by such State, and until so replaced no subsequent apportionment for such purpose shall be paid to such State.

Sec. 22. That every State accepting the provisions of this Act shall, not later than September first of each year, make a report to the Secretary of Education, showing in such detail as he may prescribe the work done in said State in carrying out the purposes and provisions of this Act, and the receipt and expenditure of moneys paid to said State under the conditions of this Act. If any State fails to make said report within the time prescribed the Secretary of Education may, in his discretion, discontinue immediately the payment of any moneys which have been apportioned under the terms of this Act to said State. The Secretary of Education, not later than

December first of each year, shall make a report to Congress on the administration of sections eleven, twelve, thirteen, fourteen, fifteen, sixteen, seventeen, eighteen, nineteen, twenty, and twenty-one of this Act, and shall include in said report a summary of the reports made to him by the several States. The Secretary of Education shall, at the same time, make such recommendations to define further the purposes and plans for Federal cooperation with the States in education as will, in his judgment, improve the administration of the moneys appropriated under sections eleven, twelve, thirteen, fourteen, fifteen, sixteen, and seventeen of this Act.

Sec. 23. That this Act shall take effect March fourth, nineteen hundred and nineteen, and all Acts and parts of Acts inconsistent with this Act are hereby repealed.

Pope Pius XI Opposes Sex Education and Co-education, 1929 *

Another very grave danger is that naturalism which nowadays invades the field of education in that most delicate matter of purity of morals. Far too common is the error of those who with dangerous assurance and under an ugly term propagate a so-called sex-education, falsely imagining they can forearm youths against the dangers of sensuality by means purely natural, such as a foolhardy initiation and precautionary instruction for all indiscriminately, even in public; and, worse still, by exposing them at an early age to the occasions, in order to accustom them, so it is argued, and as it were to harden them against such dangers.

Such persons grievously err in refusing to recognize the inborn weakness of human nature, and the law of which the Apostle speaks, fighting against the law of the mind; and also in ignoring the experience of facts, from which it is clear that, particularly in young people, evil practices are the effect not so much of ignorance of intellect as of weakness of a will exposed to dangerous occasions, and unsupported by the means of grace.

In this extremely delicate matter, if, all things considered, some private instruction is found necessary and opportune, from those who hold from God the commission to teach and who have the grace of state, every precaution must be taken. Such precautions are well known in traditional Christian education. . . .

False also and harmful to Christian education is the so-called method of "co-education." This too, by many of its supporters, is founded upon naturalism and the denial of original sin; but by all, upon a deplorable confusion of ideas that mistakes a levelling promiscuity and equality, for the legitimate association of the sexes. . . .

* *Current History,* XXXI (March, 1930), p. 1099.

A New Educational Program for the State of New York, 1938 *

The State of New York wants and needs a new educational program to meet the requirements of the rising generation in this changing world. In proceeding to develop such a new program to fulfill New York's educational objectives, it would be a mistake to discard any element of the old program which is still thoroughly sound and effective. It would also be an error to start off enthusiastically on yet untried theories on a large-scale basis. Therefore the New Program presented herewith is based squarely upon that which we now have in the State of New York. Virtually every new policy suggested has been tried, in one form or another, successfully by some school system in the State. Inasmuch as thousands of school administrators, teachers, laymen, state officials, board members, and other school officers and authorities have generously participated in this Inquiry, this program may be regarded not as the invention of a few men, but rather as the harvest of the best current thinking and experience on school problems of the State as a whole.

In order that the broad outlines of the New Program may be seen clearly, together with the more important departures from existing procedures, there are presented in this chapter in quick review the nine major elements involved. Each of the important suggestions which have to do with broad educational policies, with immediate administrative changes, and with finance is discussed more fully in this volume, since this report is intended primarily for the layman and for those who determine policy. Those suggestions which deal specifically with the content and techniques of education and which necessarily require extensive treatment, are presented in detail in the supporting studies of the Inquiry.

In presenting this New Program the directors of the Inquiry have endeavored to be very specific even as to the immediate practical steps to be taken. For a decade committees, commissions, and educational statesmen have been formulating and presenting splendid statements and fine principles. We feel that the time has come for one state, at least, to say in specific terms exactly what are the first steps to be taken toward these objectives.

OUTLINE OF NEW EDUCATIONAL PROGRAM

1. *Secondary Education*

The secondary schools should recognize the needs of youth today by offering in addition to the college preparatory program, which has been

* *Education for American Life,* The Regents' Inquiry (New York, McGraw-Hill Book Co., Inc., 1938), pp. 45-51. The Regents' Inquiry into the Character and Cost of Public Education in the State of New York was one of the most extensive educational "surveys" ever made in this country. The Inquiry was organized in 1935 with Owen D. Young as chairman of the Special Committee and many experts and specialists participated in the study which was published in several volumes. The material immediately above was drawn from the concluding volume.

so much overemphasized, more specific courses and work to fit boys and girls for useful citizenship, for self-support, and for a growing individual life. This is to be accomplished in such ways as the following:

Begin the secondary school program with the seventh grade in all school districts.

Make general education the central objective of the secondary school program by devoting the greater part of the time up to the end of the twelfth grade to the study of general science, human relations, community life, world history, general mathematics, and the arts—subjects which touch many now divided academic topics, and which cover matters of direct value and interest to the average American citizen. Present these broad fields of knowledge in the ways in which they are generally encountered in life and work, and not as semester hours for college entrance. Introduce more "review" in basic skills, such as reading and writing, particularly for those whose elementary school work is deficient.

Recognize that the school has a distinct responsibility for character education, not by multiplying rules and discipline, but by establishing student activities, developing a knowledge of the great ethical literature and standards of mankind, and above all, by furnishing inspiring leadership in school. Make understanding and enthusiasm for the democratic system part of character education.

Make all high schools large enough, but not too large (300- to 1,200-pupil capacity if possible), so that there can be electives without too small classes, and so that pupils may really experience student government, intramural sports, group music, and clubs—activities which should be greatly expanded as part of the school program. Make possible easier cooperation among school systems to handle the more specialized subjects economically.

Establish a guidance service in each school system equipped to give educational and vocational help to boys and girls in high school and to those who have finished but have not found a satisfactory first job.

Permit a pupil to leave school at sixteen years of age, if he has a real job. If he is unemployed and is not attending an educational institution, require him to continue under the supervision of the school and to pursue the kind of educational program thus worked out until he is eighteen, unless he gets a job in the meantime. This program may be in school or not, as the boy and his advisers may determine. Discontinue continuation schools.

Include general vocational education in the program of every comprehensive high school. In high school vocational courses lay chief emphasis on broad vocational training and not on the development of specialized skills.

Gradually add to the secondary school program beyond the twelfth grade new cultural courses and new subprofessional courses which will prepare boys and girls to enter the technical and semi-professional occupations—surveying, laboratory work, junior engineering occupations and the like —wherever such courses are not now available. These new high school courses beyond the twelfth grade should qualify for state aid only on the approval of the local expanded educational plan by the State.

Base high school graduation on readiness to leave school, as judged by local school officers in accordance with rules and regulations to be approved by the State Education Department, and discontinue the Regents' Diploma. The local diploma should specify the work done and the competence achieved.

End the Regents' Examinations as graduation tests, and transform them into examinations designed to discover the weak spots in curriculum or teaching. Make available to the schools a variety of examinations through which the schools themselves can measure pupils' achievement.

Emphasize in the school health and physical education program mental, emotional, as well as physical health. Protect pupils and teachers against persons within the school exercising a destructive emotional influence. Expand sports and activities in which all can join which have adult carry-over values; abandon the perfunctory but expensive annual "physical examination" now required by law and have in its place one examination on school entrance, one on entering seventh grade, one on entering ninth grade, and one at the end of twelfth grade.

Give more attention specifically to gifted youth and to handicapped youth, not only for their sake and the future of society, but also as a means of improving instruction for the average group of students.

Improve libraries and increase reference, research, field work, and report-writing assignments; increase emphasis on English expression and broad reading.

The school authorities cannot undertake the whole responsibility within each community for the development of an intelligent handling of the problems of youth, but the school authorities should join with other interested groups in seeing that the work of all local agencies which deal with youth in the area is coordinated and is in some way meeting each of the basic problems of youth.

2. *The Elementary School*

The educational needs of children up to the beginning of adolescence require a more definite and appropriate elementary school program. This is to be achieved in such ways as the following:

Begin the elementary school with children of about the age of five, except where the difficulty of transporting young children makes this impossible. Preprimary, or kindergarten work as it is popularly called, should be a part of the regular school program and should be entitled to state aid on the same basis as the rest of the elementary program.

End the elementary school throughout the State with the sixth grade or at about the pupil's twelfth birthday.

Every elementary school should be part of a system maintaining a complete secondary school program, and promotion within the elementary school and from the elementary to the secondary school should be determined locally in terms of the good of the child and in general accord with standards to be approved by the State but without the use of uniform Regents' Examinations.

Make every elementary school large enough, but not too large (desirable limits are 180 to 600 pupils), so that classes may be of economical size, the educational facilities may be more adequate, some specialized teaching may be introduced, and the pupils may engage in group activities.

Make character development a central aim of the school program by providing inspiring teachers, introducing meaningful experiences into the curriculum, bringing parents actively into school affairs, introducing the pupil to outstanding ethical literature and standards, and coordinating the school program and that of the other community agencies concerned with the child.

Emphasize the importance of the basic mental tools—reading, writing, speech, and arithmetic—and expect every normal pupil to have a mastery of them by the end of the sixth grade. See to it that these skills are learned through their use in carefully selected experiences in which the learner can see how they function in daily life. See to it that the contents of the course of study are better geared to the psychological development of the child, especially in the fields of arithmetic, language, and the social studies. Greatly enrich the work in literature and reading.

Revise the elementary school curriculum. Try to reduce the number of isolated, piecemeal elements of the curriculum, discontinue the present practice of adding new bodies of content by specific legal enactment and repeal such existing legal requirements. Integrate the curriculum more fully by bringing out the relationships among the major fields of human experience which should form the basis of its structure.

Organize instruction so as to provide more adequately for differences in the abilities of children. Provide more fully for the education of the gifted and talented children of the community. Take steps to reduce the high percentage of nonpromotion found in many of the schools of the State. Study more fully the factors both in and out of school that may be conditioning the educational product unfavorably. Establish local or regional educational guidance clinics to provide the expert assistance needed to make such a program a success.

Strengthen the educational provisions for mentally and physically handicapped children, and, subject to state regulations, require adjoining districts to cooperate in the maintenance of such services.

Take steps to make available for teachers more adequate and up-to-date instructional supplies, materials, and equipment. Make more extensive use of modern means of instruction, such as the radio, motion pictures, and other visual aids. Make certain that all schools have good library facilities and that the curriculum makes use of them. Introduce the wider use of field trips, excursions, visits to museums and to art galleries, and other trips, with the aid of school buses. Amend the law to require the provision of free textbooks and essential supplies to all children in public schools.

Organize a planned cooperative state and local program of research and experimentation dealing with all aspects of the educational process, including organization, curriculum, teaching procedures, appraisal, materials of instruction, and personnel.

Evaluation of the Contributions of the National Youth Administration, 1939 *

The various programs of the National Youth Administration have been discussed in some detail in the preceding chapters of this study. In this chapter an effort will be made to evaluate the contributions of the youth administration and its programs to (1) the solution of the relief problem; (2) the establishment, development, and extension of educational concepts and policies; (3) the solution of urgent problems of youth; (4) cooperative activity in local communities; and (5) Federal administrative policy.

THE RELIEF PROBLEM

Adequate statistics from which to determine the extent to which the National Youth Administration has contributed to the solution of the relief problem are not available. Only a rough estimate is possible. Of all persons registered in the unemployment census of November 1937, approximately 1,100,000 persons 16 to 19 years of age and about 1,300,000 persons 20 to 24 years of age were reported as either "totally unemployed" (but not necessarily on relief) or employed as "emergency workers" (necessarily on relief). "Emergency workers" alone constituted about one-fifth of the total within the age group 15 to 24. If it may be assumed that of the 15 to 19 year age group reported in the unemployment census roughly two-thirds are 18 to 19 years of age, it may be estimated that there were approximately 2,000,000 persons 18 to 24 years of age in the "totally unemployed or employed on emergency work" category, of whom approximately 400,000 were in "emergency work."

But in that same month, November 1937, the National Youth Administration employed approximately 122,000 youth aged 18 to 24 on (emergency) work projects. It thus provided for at least one-twentieth of all

---

* The Advisory Committee on Education. *The National Youth Administration* (Washington, Government Printing Office, 1939), pp. 86-91.

youth aged 18 to 24 who were totally unemployed or on emergency work, and about one-fourth of those on emergency (relief) work.

To what extent beyond the conservative measure here determined it is reasonable to go by the inclusion of youth aided on the student aid program it is impossible to estimate. Relief is not the only criterion of eligibility for student aid as it is for employment on work projects. It is obvious, however, that the estimates of the proportion of unemployed youth aided by the National Youth Administration are definitely conservative.

In view of the fact that the hourly wages of youth employed on the work projects are directly proportional to those paid to adult workers on the works program, and that the latter in turn are determined in accord with prevailing standard rates for employment in private industry, it not infrequently happens that work project youth receive hourly wages higher than the average available locally to youth in private industry.[1] To this extent the National Youth Administration operates in conformity with the established Federal principle of security wage employment.

By adhering to accepted desirable policies relating to the minimum age for the participation of youth in gainful employment, it is probable that the National Youth Administration has helped to raise the level of wages and to lengthen the period of formal educational experience. By employing youth on public projects, the youth administration has helped to reduce pressure on the labor market and competition for jobs among adult workers. At the same time, it has provided youth with guidance, experience, and training against the time that they will join the ranks of adult applicants for employment.

EDUCATIONAL CONCEPTS AND POLICIES

As an emergency agency, flexible in its administration and with relatively large available funds, the National Youth Administration has been able to experiment in educational programs which, under ordinary circumstances, would have received little consideration by regular agencies of Government, and which even today are not fully recognized by the majority of educators.

Through the extension of educational opportunities to the underprivileged, the Youth Administration has uncovered a reservoir of competent youth desirous of continued education for whom almost no provision has been made in the past. It has demonstrated the possibility of providing educational opportunities at small cost which have proved of considerable advantage to the youth and to the institutions involved. And, by providing merely the essentials for the maintenance of youth, it has increased school and college enrollments by 300,000 to 400,000 without sacrificing quality to quantity.

---

[1] It should be noted, however, that youth employed on youth work projects are employed only on a part-time basis and at a maximum wage of $25 per month.

Experimentation which grew out of the necessity for combining work with schooling has demonstrated possibilities of profound educational significance. Especially noteworthy in this connection are those work projects, sponsored by educational institutions, in which youth are maintained in residence at the institutions and undergo a course of training related to their employment on work of benefit to the institutions themselves. To the extent that the National Youth Administration has been successful in this combining work and schooling, the more pointedly by contrast does it emphasize the inadequacies of the conventional current curriculum and guidance policies at both high school and college levels.

Although the nominal aim of the National Youth Administration has been to serve as a relief agency, it has actually fulfilled an educational function as well. Because relief was the primary objective, the educational policy of the Youth Administration has of necessity been of a temporizing and exigent nature. Had the educational function been considered as of primary rather than of secondary importance, it is not unlikely that the policies and programs here reported would have been considerably altered. To the conflicting practices inevitably resultant from this confusion concerning the relative importance of the functions of relief and education may in large measure be attributed many of the apparent discrepancies and inconsistencies in the present program.

URGENT PROBLEMS OF YOUTH

If there is today a "lost generation" of youth lacking work experience, lacking guidance, abandoned by the school, and disowned by industry, and if, as is often claimed, the new social and economic status of youth resultant from changes in the age composition of the population calls for national leadership in meeting the problems of youth, then it must be conceded that in large measure the National Youth Administration has contributed significantly toward the solution of these problems.

Without doubt the depression adversely affected the morale of youth. But by providing youth with an articulate agency for the expression of their needs and a focal point of direct action in meeting them, the National Youth Administration has helped to restore their morale. The indictment that actual achievement has failed to measure up to the demand for service becomes, therefore, a criticism not of inadequacy in function so much as of limitations in application. Through each of its major programs the National Youth Administration has provided youth with facilities for continued education, work experience, practical guidance, and, so far as possible, placement in employment in private industry. There is much to indicate that the morale and health of youth participating in student aid and work projects employment have improved.

By experimenting with youth of unrevealed potentialities in unusual situations, the National Youth Administration has drawn attention to many inadequacies in the current provisions for vocational guidance. Many unemployed youth, poorly educated and untrained, are to all appearances fit for nothing but unskilled or semiskilled work; nevertheless, time and again, reports are received concerning the surprising extent of their achievements when given the right environment, an encouraging and skillful supervisor or foreman, and the chance to do constructive work.

BENEFITS TO LOCAL COMMUNITIES

Liberal funds and a definite program have made it possible for the National Youth Administration to draw together in effective cooperation the frequently dissident and often individually impotent local agencies which exist in many communities. Under the leadership of the National Youth Administration and its advisory committees, of which these agencies are now constituent members, many communities have learned the advantage of united effort. It is not unreasonable to assume that some of the progress thus achieved will endure. Nor is the achievement limited to local communities. The coordination of interested agencies, both public and private, has been of such a nature that it may well be said that the youth program of today is limited to no geographical or political boundaries but is a part of the national life.

In demonstrating what concerted action can accomplish on behalf of youth the National Youth Administration has convinced many local communities that it is possible for them to employ, train, and direct their youth, and that, given proper direction and wise planning, the contributions made by the youth thus engaged are often of real and lasting value. In several instances, at their own expense, communities have taken over the responsibility and administration of programs initiated by the National Youth Administration.

FEDERAL ADMINISTRATIVE POLICY

The National Youth Administration has cooperated successfully with private as well as public agencies, in groups and individually. Its success in conducting a Nation-wide enterprise through a system of decentralized control probably has had significant bearing on the relationship between Federal and State Governments in educational matters. By extending aid to individuals rather than to institutions or agencies it has avoided the implications of interference with the authority of local units. At the same time it has demonstrated not only that cooperative programs between agencies at different levels of control can be effective, but also that such programs offer possibilities of substantial economies in administration.

Children May Be Expelled from School for Refusing
to Salute the National Flag, 1940 *

*Board of Education of Minersville (Pennsylvania) School District et al.
v. Gobitis et al.*

Argued April 25, 1940.—Decided June 3, 1940.

1. A state regulation requiring that pupils in the public schools, on pain of expulsion, participate in a daily ceremony of saluting the national flag, whilst reciting in unison a pledge of allegiance to it "and to the Republic for which it stands; one Nation indivisible, with liberty and justice for all" —*held* within the scope of legislative power, and consistent with the Fourteenth Amendment, as applied to children brought up in, and entertaining, a conscientious religious belief that such obeisance to the flag is forbidden by the Bible and that the Bible, as the Word of God, is the supreme authority. P. 591.

2. Religious convictions do not relieve the individual from obedience to an otherwise valid general law not aimed at the promotion or restriction of religious beliefs. P. 594.

3. So far as the Federal Constitution is concerned, it is within the province of the legislatures and school authorities of the several States to adopt appropriate means to evoke and foster a sentiment of national unity among the children in the public schools. P. 597.

4. This Court can not exercise censorship over the conviction of legislatures that a particular program or exercise will best promote in the minds of children who attend the common schools an attachment to the institutions of their country, nor overrule the local judgment against granting exemptions from observance of such a program. P. 598.

108 F. 2d 683, reversed.

MR. JUSTICE FRANKFURTER delivered the opinion of the Court.

Reversed.

A grave responsibility confronts this Court whenever in courts of litigation it must reconcile the conflicting claims of liberty and authority. But when the liberty invoked is liberty of conscience, and the authority is

* 310 U.S. 586-607. This decision was reversed in the Barnette case (West Virginia) in 1943. 319 U.S. 624 ff. For interesting treatments of religion and the state and of religious education in the public schools, see *Law and Contemporary Problems*, Durham, N. C.: Duke University School of Law, XIV (Winter, 1949); and "The Status of Religious Education in the Public Schools," Research Division, National Education Association, June, 1949. Among other important court decisions given in this volume are the famous Dartmouth College case, the Kalamazoo case, the Berea (Kentucky) case, the Missouri or Gaines case, the Oregon Decision, the New Jersey Bus case, and the much publicized McCollum case, on religious instruction in the schools. For legal cases involving higher education see Edward C. Elliott and M. M. Chambers, *The Colleges and the Courts* (New York, The Carnegie Foundation for the Advancement of Teaching, 1936); M. M. Chambers, *The Colleges and the Courts, 1941-1945* (same place and publisher, 1946). See also Newton Edwards, *The Courts and the Public Schools* (Chicago, University of Chicago Press, 1933).

authority to safeguard the nation's fellowship, judicial conscience is put to its severest test. Of such a nature is the present controversy.

Lillian Gobitis, aged twelve, and her brother William, aged ten, were expelled from the public schools of Minersville, Pennsylvania, for refusing to salute the national flag as part of a daily school exercise. The local Board of Education required both teachers and pupils to participate in this ceremony. The ceremony is a familiar one. The right hand is placed on the breast and the following pledge recited in unison: "I pledge allegiance to my flag, and to the Republic for which it stands; one nation indivisible, with liberty and justice for all." While the words are spoken, teachers and pupils extend their right hands in salue to the flag. The Gobitis family are affiliated with "Jehovah's Witnesses," for whom the Bible as the Word of God is the supreme authority. The children had been brought up conscientiously to believe that such a gesture of respect for the flag was forbidden by command of Scripture.[1]

The Gobitis children were of an age for which Pennsylvania makes school attendance compulsory. Thus they were denied a free education, and their parents had to put them into private schools. To be relieved of the financial burden thereby entailed, their father, on behalf of the children and in his own behalf, brought this suit. He sought to enjoin the authorities from continuing to exact participation in the flag-salute ceremony as a condition of his children's attendance at the Minersville school. After trial of the issues, Judge Maris gave relief in the District Court, ... on the basis of a thoughtful opinion at a preliminary stage of the litigation; ... his decree was affirmed by the Circuit Court of Appeals. ... Since this decision ran counter to several *per curiam* dispositions of this Court, we granted *certiorari* to give the matter full reconsideration. ... By their able submissions, the Committee on the Bill of Rights of the American Bar Association and the American Civil Liberties Union, as friends of the Court, have helped us to our conclusion. ...

MR. JUSTICE McREYNOLDS concurs in the result.

MR. JUSTICE STONE dissenting.

New Jersey Provides for the Transportation of Children to Non-Public Schools, 1941 *

Whenever in any district there are children living remote from any school-house, the board of education of the district may make rules and contracts for the transportation of such children to and from school, includ-

---

[1] Reliance is especially placed on the following verses from Chapter 20 of Exodus:
"3. Thou shalt have no other gods before me.
"4. Thou shalt not make unto thee any graven image, or any likeness of any thing that is in heaven above, or that is in the earth beneath, or that is in the water under the earth:
"5. Thou shalt not bow down thyself to them, nor serve them: ..."

* *Acts of the One Hundred and Sixty-fifth Legislature of the State of New Jersey*, p. 581.

ing the transportation of school children to and from school other than a public school as is operated for profit in whole or in part.

When any school district provides any transportation for public school children to and from school, transportation from any point in such established school route to any other point in such established school route shall be supplied to school children residing in such school district in going to and from school other than a public school, except such school as is operated for profit in whole or in part.

Nothing in this section shall be so construed as to prohibit a board of education from making contracts for the transportation of children to a school in an adjoining district when such children are transferred to the district by order of the county superintendent of schools, or when any children shall attend school in a district other than that in which they shall reside by virtue of an agreement made by the respective boards of education.

This act shall take effect July first, one thousand nine hundred and forty-one.

Approved June 9, 1941.

Children May Not Be Expelled from School for Refusing to Salute the National Flag, 1943 *

West Virginia State Board of Education et al. v. *Barnette et al.*
Argued March 11, 1943.—Decided June 14, 1943.

1. State action against which the Fourteenth Amendment protects includes action by a state board of education. P. 637.

2. The action of a State in making it compulsory for children in the public schools to salute the flag and pledge allegiance—by extending the right arm, palm upward, and declaring, "I pledge allegiance to the flag of the United States of America and to the Republic for which it stands; one Nation, indivisible, with liberty and justice for all"—violates the First and Fourteenth Amendments. P. 642.

So *held* as applied to children who were expelled for refusal to comply, and whose absence thereby became "unlawful," subjecting them and their parents or guardians to punishment.

3. That those who refused compliance did so on religious grounds does not control the decision of this question; and it is unnecessary to inquire into the sincerity of their views. P. 634.

4. Under the Federal Constitution, compulsion as here employed is not a permissible means of achieving "national unity." P. 640.

Appeal from a decree of a District Court of three judges enjoining the enforcement of a regulation of the West Virginia State Board of Education requiring children in the public schools to salute the American flag.

* 319 U.S. 624 ff.

MR. JUSTICE JACKSON delivered the opinion of the Court.

Following the decision by this Court on June 3, 1940, in *Minersville School District* v. *Gobitis,* 310 U.S. 586, the West Virginia legislature amended its statutes to require all schools therein to conduct courses of instruction in history, civics, and in the Constitution of the United States and of the State "for the purpose of teaching, fostering and perpetuating the ideals, principles and spirit of Americanism, and increasing the knowledge of the organization and machinery of the government." Appellant Board of Education was directed, with advice of the State Superintendent of Schools, to "prescribe the courses of study covering these subjects" for public schools. The Act made it the duty of private, parochial and denominational schools to prescribe courses of study "similar to those required for the public schools."

The Board of Education on January 9, 1942, adopted a resolution containing recitals taken largely from the Court's *Gobitis* opinion and ordering that the salute to the flag become "a regular part of the program of activities in the public schools," that all teachers and pupils "shall be required to participate in the salute honoring the Nation represented by the Flag; provided, however, that refusal to salute the Flag be regarded as an act of insubordination, and shall be dealt with accordingly."

Failure to conform is "insubordination" dealt with by expulsion. Readmission is denied by statute until compliance. Meanwhile the expelled child is "unlawfully absent" and may be proceeded against as a delinquent. His parents or guardians are liable to prosecution, and if convicted are subject to fine not exceeding $50 and jail term not exceeding thirty days.

Appellees, citizens of the United States and of West Virginia, brought suit in the United States District Court for themselves and others similarly situated asking its injunction to restrain enforcement of these laws and regulations against Jehovah's Witnesses. The Witnesses are an unincorporated body teaching that the obligation imposed by law of God is superior to that of laws enacted by temporal government. Their religious beliefs include a literal version of Exodus, Chapter 20, verses 4 and 5, which says: "Thou shalt not make unto thee any graven image, or any likeness of anything that is in heaven above, or that is in the earth beneath, or that is in the water under the earth; thou shalt not bow down thyself to them nor serve them." They consider that the flag is an "image" within this command. For this reason they refuse to salute it.

Children of this faith have been expelled from school and are threatened with exclusion for no other cause. Officials threaten to send them to reformatories maintained for criminally inclined juveniles. Parents of such children have been prosecuted and are threatened with prosecutions for causing delinquency.

The Board of Education moved to dismiss the complaint setting forth these facts and alleging that the law and regulations are an unconstitutional denial of religious freedom, and freedom of speech, and are invalid under the "due process" and "equal protection" clauses of the Fourteenth Amendment to the Federal Constitution. The cause was submitted on the pleadings to a District Court of three judges. It restrained enforcement as to the plaintiffs and those of that class. The Board of Education brought the case here by direct appeal.

This case calls upon us to reconsidering a precedent decision, as the Court throughout its history often has been required to do. Before turning to the *Gobitis* case, however, it is desirable to notice certain characteristics by which this controversy is distinguished.

The freedom asserted by these appellees does not bring them into collision with rights asserted by any other individual. It is such conflicts which most frequently require intervention of the State to determine where the rights of one end and those of another begin. But the refusal of these persons to participate in the ceremony does not interfere with or deny rights of others to do so. Nor is there any question in this case that their behavior is peaceable and orderly. The sole conflict is between authority and rights of the individual. The State asserts power to condition access to public education on making a prescribed sign and profession and at the same time to coerce attendance by punishing both parent and child. The latter stand on a right of self-determination in matters that touch individual opinion and personal attitude. . . .

If there is any fixed star in our constitutional constellation, it is that no official, high or petty, can prescribe what shall be orthodox in politics, nationalism, religion, or other matters of opinion or force citizens to confess by word or act their faith therein. If there are any circumstances which permit an exception, they do not now occur to us.

We think the action of the local authorities in compelling the flag salute and pledge transcends constitutional limitations on their power and invades the sphere of intellect and spirit which it is the purpose of the First Amendment to our Constitution to reserve from all official control.

The decision of this Court in *Minersville School District* v. *Gobitis* and the holdings of those few *per curiam* decisions which preceded and foreshadowed it are overruled, and the judgment enjoining enforcement of the West Virginia Regulation is

Affirmed.

MR. JUSTICE ROBERTS and MR. JUSTICE REED adhere to the views expressed by the Court in *Minersville School District* v. *Gobitis,* 310 U.S. 586, and are of the opinion that the judgment below should be reversed.

MR. JUSTICE BLACK and MR. JUSTICE DOUGLAS, concurring . . .

MR. JUSTICE MURPHY, concurring . . .

MR. JUSTICE FRANKFURTER, dissenting . . .

The Supreme Court Sustains the Practice of Public Transportation
of Non-Public School Children, 1947 *

Pursuant to a New Jersey statute authorizing district boards of education to make rules and contracts for the transportation of children to and from schools other than private schools operated for profit, a board of education by resolution authorized the reimbursement of parents for fares paid for the transportation by public carrier of children attending public and Catholic schools. The Catholic schools operated under the superintendency of a Catholic priest and, in addition to secular education, gave religious instruction in the Catholic Faith. A district taxpayer challenged the validity under the Federal Constitution of the statute and resolutions, so far as they authorized reimbursement to parents for the transportation of children attending sectarian schools. No question was raised as to whether the exclusion of private schools operated for profit denied equal protection of the laws; nor did the record show that there were any children in the district who attended, or would have attended but for the cost of transportation, any but public or Catholic schools. *Held:*

1. The expenditure of tax-raised funds thus authorized was for a public purpose, and did not violate the due process clause of the Fourteenth Amendment.

2. The statute and resolution did not violate the provision of the First Amendment (made applicable to the states by the Fourteenth Amendment) prohibiting any "law respecting an establishment of religion."

In a suit by a taxpayer, the New Jersey Supreme Court held that the state legislature was without power under the state constitution to authorize reimbursement to parents of bus fares paid for transporting their children to schools other than public schools. The New Jersey Court of Errors and Appeals reversed, holding that neither the statute nor a resolution passed pursuant to it violated the state constitution or the provisions of the Federal Constitution in issue. . . .

A New Jersey statute authorizes its local school districts to make rules and contracts for the transportation of children to and from schools. The appellee, a township board of education, acting pursuant to this statute, authorized reimbursement to parents of money expended by them for the bus transportation of their children on regular busses operated by the public transportation system. Part of this money was for the payment of transportation of some children in the community to Catholic parochial schools. These church schools give their students, in addition to secular education, regular religious instruction conforming to the religious tenets and modes of worship of the Catholic Faith. The superintendent of these schools is a Catholic priest.

The appellant, in his capacity as a district taxpayer, filed suit in a state

* 330 U.S. 1-74.

court challenging the right of the Board to reimburse parents of parochial school students. He contended that the statute and the resolution passed pursuant to it violated both the State and the Federal Constitutions. That court held that the legislature was without power to authorize such payment under the state constitution. The New Jersey Court of Errors and Appeals reversed, holding that neither the statute nor the resolution passed pursuant to it was in conflict with the State constitution or the provisions of the Federal Constitution in issue. . . .

We must consider the New Jersey statute in accordance with the foregoing limitations imposed by the First Amendment. But we must not strike that state statute down if it is within the State's constitutional power even though it approaches the verge of that power. See *Interstate Ry.* v. *Massachusetts,* Holmes, J., *supra* at 85, 88. New Jersey cannot consistently with the "establishment of religion" clause of the First Amendment contribute tax-raised funds to the support of an institution which teaches the tenets and faith of any church. On the other hand, other language of the amendment commands that New Jersey cannot hamper its citizens in the free exercise of their own religion. Consequently, it cannot exclude individual Catholics, Lutherans, Mohammedans, Baptists, Jews, Methodists, Nonbelievers, Presbyterians, or the members of any other faith, *because of their faith, or lack of it,* from receiving the benefits of public welfare legislation. While we do not mean to intimate that a state could not provide transportation only to children attending public schools, we must be careful, in protecting the citizens of New Jersey against state-established churches, to be sure that we do not inadvertently prohibit New Jersey from extending its general state law benefits to all its citizens without regard to their religious belief.

Measured by these standards, we cannot say that the First Amendment prohibits New Jersey from spending tax-raised funds to pay the bus fares of Parochial school pupils as a part of a general program under which it pays the fares of pupils attending public and other schools. It is undoubtedly true that children are helped to get to church schools. There is even a possibility that some of the children might not be sent to the church schools if the parents were compelled to pay their children's bus fares out of their own pockets when transportation to a public school would have been paid for by the State. The same possibility exists where the state requires a local transit company to provide reduced fares to school children including those attending parochial schools, or where a municipally owned transportation system undertakes to carry all school children free of charge. Moreover, state-paid policemen, detailed to protect children going to and from church schools from the very real hazards of traffic, would serve much the same purpose and accomplish much the same result as state provisions intended to guarantee free transportation of a kind which the state deems to be best for the school children's welfare. And parents might refuse to risk their children to the serious danger of traffic accidents going to and from parochial schools, the approaches to which were not protected by policemen. Similarly, parents might be reluctant to permit their children to attend schools which the state had cut off from such general government services as ordinary police and fire protection, connections for sewage disposal, public highways and sidewalks. Of course, cutting off church schools from these services, so separate and so indisputably marked off from the religious function, would make it far more difficult for the schools to operate. But such is obviously not the purpose of the First Amendment. That Amendment requires the state to be a neutral in its relations with groups of religious believers and non-believers; it does not require the state to be their adversary. State power is no more to be used so as to handicap religions than it is to favor them.

This Court has said that parents may, in the discharge of their duty under state compulsory education laws, send their children to a religious rather than a public school if the school meets the secular educational requirements which the state has power to impose. See *Pierce* v. *Society of Sisters*, 268 U.S. 510. It appears that these parochial schools meet New Jersey's requirements. The State contributes no money to the schools. It does not support them. Its legislation, as applied, does no more than provide a general program to help parents get their children, regardless of their religion, safely and expeditiously to and from accredited schools.

The First Amendment has erected a wall between church and state. That wall must be kept high and impregnable. We could not approve the slightest breach. New Jersey has not breached it here.

Extracts from the Constitution of the United Nations Educational, Scientific and Cultural Organization, 1948 *

The governments of the States parties to this Constitution on behalf of their peoples declare:

that since wars begin in the minds of men, it is in the minds of men that the defences of peace must be constructed;

that ignorance of each other's ways and lives has been a common cause, throughout the history of mankind, of that suspicion and mistrust between the peoples of the world through which their differences have all too often broken into war;

that the great and terrible war which has now ended was a war made possible by the denial of the democratic principles of the dignity, equality and mutual respect of men, and by the propagation, in their place, through ignorance and prejudice, of the doctrine of the inequality of men and races;

that the wide diffusion of culture, and the education of humanity for

* UNESCO and the National Commission-Basic Documents. Department of State, Publication 3082, pp. 1-3. See also other publications on this significant undertaking, especially *First Session of the General Conference of UNESCO,* Paris, November 19-December 10, 1946; *Second Session of the General Conference of UNESCO,* Mexico City, November 6-December 3, 1947 (Washington, Government Printing Office, 1947 and 1948).

justice and liberty and peace are indispensable to the dignity of man and constitute a sacred duty which all the nations must fulfill in a spirit of mutual assistance and concern;

that a peace based exclusively upon the political and economic arrangements of governments would not be a peace which could secure the unanimous, lasting and sincere support of the peoples of the world, and that the peace must therefore be founded, if it is not to fail, upon the intellectual and moral solidarity of mankind.

For These Reasons, the States parties to this Constitution, believing in full and equal opportunities for education for all, in the unrestricted pursuit of objective truth, and in the free exchange of ideas and knowledge, are agreed and determined to develop and to increase the means of communication between their peoples and to employ these means for the purposes of mutual understanding and a truer and more perfect knowledge of each other's lives;

In Consequence Whereof they do hereby create the United Nations Educational, Scientific and Cultural Organisation for the purpose of advancing, through the educational and scientific and cultural relations of the peoples of the world, the objectives of international peace and of the common welfare of mankind for which the United Nations Organisation was established and which its Charter proclaims.

ARTICLE I. PURPOSES AND FUNCTIONS

1. The purpose of the Organisation is to contribute to peace and security by promoting collaboration among the nations through education, science and culture in order to further universal respect for justice, for the rule of law and for the human rights and fundamental freedoms which are affirmed for the peoples of the world, without distinction of race, sex, language or religion, by the Charter of the United Nations.

2. To realise this purpose the Organisation will:

(*a*) collaborate in the work of advancing the mutual knowledge and understanding of peoples, through all means of mass communication and to that end recommend such international agreements as may be necessary to promote the free flow of ideas by word and image;

(*b*) give fresh impulse to popular education and to the spread of culture;

by collaborating with Members, at their request, in the development of educational activities;

by instituting collaboration among the nations to advance the ideal of equality of educational opportunity without regard to race, sex or any distinctions economic or social;

by suggesting educational methods best suited to prepare the children of the world for the responsibilities of freedom;

(*c*) maintain, increase and diffuse knowledge;

by assuring the conservation and protection of the world's inheritance of books, works of art and monuments of history and science, and recommending to the nations concerned the necessary international conventions;

by encouraging cooperation among the nations in all branches of intellectual activity, including the international exchange of persons active in the fields of education, science and culture and the exchange of publications, objects of artistic and scientific interest and other materials of information;

by initiating methods of international cooperation calculated to give the people of all countries access to the printed and published materials produced by any of them.

3. With a view to preserving the independence, integrity and fruitful diversity of the cultures and educational systems of the States Members of this Organisation, the Organisation is prohibited from intervening in matters which are essentially within their domestic jurisdiction. . . .

The Supreme Court Holds that Religious Instruction Cannot Be Given in Public School Buildings, 1948 *

With the permission of a board of education, granted under its general supervisory powers over the use of public school buildings, religious teachers, employed subject to the approval and supervision of the superintendent of schools by a private religious group including representatives of the Catholic, Protestant and Jewish faiths, gave religious instruction in public school buildings once each week. Pupils whose parents so requested were excused from their secular classes during the periods of religious instruction and were required to attend the religious classes; but other pupils were not released from their public school duties, which were compulsory under state law. A resident and taxpayer of the school district whose child was enrolled in the public schools sued in a state court for a writ of mandamus requiring the board of education to terminate this practice. *Held:*

1. A judgment of the State Supreme Court sustaining denial of the writ of mandamus on the ground that the state statutes granted the board of education authority to establish such a program drew into question "the validity of a statute" of the State within the meaning of § 237 of the Judicial Code, and was appealable to this Court.

2. As a resident and taxpayer of the school district and the parent of a child required by state law to attend the school, appellant had standing to maintain the suit.

3. Both state courts having ruled expressly on appellant's claim that the state program violated the Federal Constitution, a motion to dismiss the appeal on the ground that appellant failed properly to present that question in the State Supreme Court cannot be sustained.

4. This utilization of the State's tax-supported public school system and

* 333 U.S. 203-56.

its machinery for compulsory public school attendance to enable sectarian groups to give religious instruction to public school pupils in public school buildings violates the First Amendment of the Constitution, made applicable to the states by the Fourteenth Amendment. . . .

This case relates to the power of a state to utilize its tax-supported public school system in aid of religious instruction insofar as that power may be restricted by the First and Fourteenth Amendments to the Federal Constitution.

The appellant, Vashti McCollum, began this action for mandamus against the Champaign Board of Education in the Circuit Court of Champaign County, Illinois. Her asserted interest was that of a resident and taxpayer of Champaign and of a parent whose child was then enrolled in the Champaign public schools. Illinois has a compulsory education law which, with exceptions, requires parents to send their children, aged seven to sixteen, to its tax-supported public schools where the children are to remain in attendance during the hours when the schools are regularly in session. Parents who violate this law commit a misdemeanor punishable by fine unless the children attend private or parochial schools which meet educational standards fixed by the State. District boards of education are given general supervisory powers over the use of the public school buildings within the school districts. Ill. Rev. Stat. ch. 122, § § 123, 301 (1943).

Appellant's petition for mandamus alleged that religious teachers, employed by private religious groups, were permitted to come weekly into the school buildings during the regular hours set apart for secular teaching, and then and there for a period of thirty minutes substitute their religious teaching for the secular education provided under the compulsory education law. The petitioner charged that this joint public-school religious group program violated the First and Fourteenth Amendments to the United States Constitution. The prayer of her petition was that the Board of Education be ordered to "adopt and enforce rules and regulations prohibiting all instruction in and teaching of religious education in all public schools in Champaign School District Number 71, . . . and in all public school houses and buildings in said district when occupied by public schools. . . ."

The foregoing facts, without reference to others that appear in the record, show the use of tax-supported property for religious instruction and the close cooperation between the school authorities and the religious council in promoting religious education. The operation of the State's compulsory education system thus assists and is integrated with the program of religious instruction carried on by separate religious sects. Pupils compelled by law to go to school for secular education are released in part from their legal duty upon the condition that they attend the religious classes. This is beyond all question a utilization of the tax-established and tax-supported public school system to aid religious groups to spread their faith. And it falls squarely under the ban of the First Amendment (made applicable to the States by the Fourteenth) as we interpreted it in *Everson* v. *Board of Education,* 330 U.S. 1. There we said: "Neither a state nor the Federal Government can set up a church. Neither can pass laws which aid one religion, aid all religions, or prefer one religion over another. Neither can force or influence a person to go to or to remain away from church against his will or force him to profess a belief or disbelief in any religion. No person can be punished for entertaining or professing religious beliefs or disbeliefs, for church attendance or non-attendance. No tax in any amount, large or small, can be levied to support any religious activities or institutions, whatever they may be called, or whatever form they may adopt to teach or practice religion. Neither a state nor the Federal Government can, openly or secretly, participate in the affairs of any religious organizations or groups and *vice versa.* In the words of Jefferson, the clause against establishment of religion by law was intended to erect 'a wall of separation between church and State.' " *Id.* at 15-16. The majority in the *Everson* case, and the minority as shown by quotations from the dissenting views in our notes 6 and 7, agreed that the First Amendment's language, properly interpreted, had erected a wall of separation between Church and State. They disagreed as to the facts shown by the record and as to the proper application of the First Amendment's language to those facts.

Recognizing that the Illinois program is barred by the First and Fourteenth Amendments if we adhere to the views expressed both by the majority and the minority in the *Everson* case, counsel for the respondents challenge those views as dicta and urge that we reconsider and repudiate them. They argue that historically the First Amendment was intended to forbid only government preference of one religion over another, not an impartial governmental assistance of all religions. In addition they ask that we distinguish or overrule our holding in the *Everson* case that the Fourteenth Amendment made the "establishment of religion" clause of the First Amendment applicable as a prohibition against the States. After giving full consideration to the arguments presented we are unable to accept either of these contentions.

To hold that a state cannot consistently with the First and Fourteenth Amendments utilize its public school system to aid any or all religious faiths or sects in the dissemination of their doctrines and ideals does not, as counsel urge, manifest a governmental hostility to religion or religious teachings. A manifestation of such hostility would be at war with our national tradition as embodied in the First Amendment's guaranty of the free exercise of religion. For the First Amendment rests upon the premise that both religion and government can best work to achieve their lofty aims if each is left free from the other within its respective sphere. Or, as we said in the *Everson* case, the First Amendment has erected a wall between Church and State which must be kept high and impregnable.

Here not only are the State's tax-supported public school buildings used for the dissemination of religious doctrines. The State also affords sectarian groups an invaluable aid in that it helps to provide pupils for their religious classes through use of the State's compulsory public school machinery. This is not separation of Church and State.

The cause is reversed and remanded to the State Supreme Court for proceeding not inconsistent with this opinion.

Practice and Usage in Aid to Sectarian Schools and Sectarianism in Public Schools, 1949 *

States	Rental of church-owned buildings for public-school purposes	Free textbooks furnished parochial-school pupils	Transportation of parochial-school pupils at public expense	Bible-reading in public schools	Excusing pupils for attendance at "week-day church" schools	Religious instruction by church teachers inside public schools during school hours	Use of public schools by religious groups after school hours	Employment of public-school teachers wearing religious garb
1	2	3	4	5	6	7	8	9
Alabama.	Yes	No	No	Required	Yes	Yes	Yes	Yes
Alaska............	Yes	No	No	No answer	Yes	No	No	No
Arizona..........	Yes	No	No	No	No	No	Yes	No
Arkansas..........	Yes	No	No	Required	Yes	No	Yes	Yes
California........	Yes	No	Yes	No	Yes	No	No	No
Colorado..........	Yes	No	Yes	Permitted	Yes	No	Yes	Yes
Connecticut.......	Yes	No	Yes	Permitted	Yes	No*	Yes	No
Delaware..........	b	No	No	Required	No	No	No*	b
District of Columbia	No	No	No	Required	No	No	No	No
Florida...........	No	No	No	Required	Yes	No	Yes	No
Georgia.	b	No	No	Required	Yes	No	Yes	No
Hawaii............	Yes	No	Yes	Permitted	Yes	Yes	Yes	Yes
Idaho.............	Yes	No	No	Required	Yes	No	Yes	No
Illinois..........	b	No'	Yes	No	Yes	No	Yes	No
Indiana...........	No	No	Yes^d	Permitted	Yes	No	Yes	Yes
Iowa..............	No	No	No	Permitted	No	No	Yes	No
Kansas............	Yes	No	No	Permitted	Yes	No	Yes	No
Kentucky..........	Yes	No	Yes	Required	Yes	No	Yes	Yes
Louisiana.........	Yes	Yes	Yes	No	Yes	Yes	Yes	b
Maine.............	b	No	No	Required	Yes	Yes	Yes	No
Maryland..........	b	No	Yes	Permitted	Yes	No	No	Yes
Massachusetts.....	b	No	Yes	Required	Yes	No	No*	No
Michigan..........	Yes	No	Yes	Permitted	Yes	No	Yes	b
Minnesota.........	Yes	No	No	b	Yes	f	Yes	Yes
Mississippi.......	b	No	Yes	Permitted	Yes	No	Yes	No
Missouri..........	Yes	....	No	Permitted	Yes	No	Yes	No
Montana...........	...	No	....	....	Yes	No	Yes	Yes
Nebraska..........	Yes	No	No	Permitted	No	....	....	....
Nevada............	...	....	....	....	No	No	No	No
New Hampshire....	b	No	Yes	Permitted	No	....	....	....
New Jersey........	b	No	Yes	Required	Yes	No	Yes	b
New Mexico........	Yes	Yes	Yes	Yes	Yes	No	Yes	b
New York.........	No	No	Yes	No	No	No	Yes	Yes
North Carolina....	e	No	No	Permitted	Yes	No	No	No
North Dakota.....	Yes	No	No	Permitted	No	Yes	No	No
Ohio..............	Yes	No	No	Permitted	No	No	Yes	Yes
Oklahoma..........	Yes	No	Yes	Permitted	Yes	Yes	Yes	Yes
Oregon............	Yes	Yes	Yes	Permitted	Yes	Yes	Yes	Yes
Pennsylvania......	Yes	No	No	Required	Yes	Yes	Yes	No
Rhode Island......	b	No	Yes	Permitted	Yes	No	No	No
South Carolina.....	Yes	No	No	Permitted	Yes	No	Yes	b
South Dakota......	Yes	No	No	No	Yes	No	Yes	No
Tennessee.........	Yes	No	No	Required	Yes	No	No	Yes
Texas.............	b	No	No	Permitted	No	No	b	Yes
Utah..............	Yes	No	No	Permitted	No	Yes	No*	Yes
Vermont..........	b	No	No	Permitted	Yes	No	Yes	b
Virginia..........	Yes	No	No	Permitted	Yes	Yes	b	b
Washington.......	Yes	No	No	Permitted	Yes	Yes	Yes	b
West Virginia.....	Yes	Yes	No	No	No	No	Yes	No
Wisconsin.........	f	No	No	Permitted	Yes	No	Yes	No
Wyoming..........	Yes	No	Yes	Permitted	No	No	Yes	b

a Was tried out and found unsuccessful and so discontinued.
b Law silent; state superintendent did not comment on practice.
c Except when church burned.
d If no extra expense is entailed.
e Except for church festivals.
f No answer.
g "No parochial schools in state," reported state superintendent.

* "The Status of Religious Education in the Public Schools" (Washington, Research Division, National Education Association, 1949), p. 23.

President Truman on the Rôle of Education and Research in Our Democratic Society, 1950 *

If education and research are to play their full role in strengthening our democratic society, we must expand our basic research, we must devise types of education that will prepare youth more effectively for participation in modern society, and we must provide better educational opportunities for more of our people.

It is predominantly a responsibility of all government—local, state and Federal—to provide for the education of our citizens. The Federal Government for many years has given financial aid to special aspects of education, such as vocational education, and to institutions for special groups, such as Howard University.

It has become increasingly evident that Federal support of a more general character is needed if satisfactory educational opportunities are to be made available for all.

The nation cannot afford to waste human potentialities, as we are now doing, by failing to provide adequate elementary and secondary education for millions of children and by failing to help hundreds of thousands of young people who could benefit from higher education.

The importance of this need requires that we provide substantial Federal assistance to states for general educational purposes and for certain other important programs in this field.

To progress toward these objectives, this budget includes expenditures for education and general research (not including large amounts in veterans, national defense and other categories) of 434 million dollars in the fiscal year 1951, compared with 125 million dollars in 1950. More than three-fourths is for grants to states.

The increase is entirely accounted for by the additional expenditures in 1951 resulting from the new legislation I am recommending. This legislation will entail a further moderate increase in later years.

MORE TEACHERS WANTED

Promotion of education—Elementary and secondary.—The high mobility that characterizes our people means that no state is immune to the effects of ignorance and illiteracy in other states. The welfare of the nation as a whole demands that the present educational inequalities be reduced. Educational inequalities are primarily due to differences in the financial resources of states and localities. Income per capita in some states is less than half as great as in others. The states with the lowest incomes have the greatest proportion of school-age children and are unable to finance a fair educational opportunity even with greater effort in terms of tax burden.

School enrollments in practically every state have risen recently and will

* From President Truman's Budget Message, 1950.

continue to rise owing to the increased birth rate. Millions of our children are now taught in over-crowded classrooms. For others education is provided only on a part-time basis.

At the very time when we need more and better teachers, schools must still employ tens of thousands whose qualifications do not meet the standards necessary to provide a satisfactory quality of teaching. Because salaries are generally inadequate, too few capable young people are preparing to enter the teaching profession.

For these reasons I urge the Congress to complete legislative action to permit the Federal Government to aid the states in support of the maintenance and operation costs of a basic minimum program of elementary and secondary education. The budget provides for beginning this aid in the fiscal year 1951.

There is a shortage of school buildings in many parts of the country due to the wartime deferment of construction and the increase in the school-age population. In many localities the need for facilities results from the sudden and substantial impact of Federal activities.

I recommend that the Congress enact legislation providing for grants to states for surveys of their need for facilities and their resources, and grants for the construction of buildings in those particular areas where Federal activities have been responsible for increased enrollments.

For a number of years several Federal agencies, under separate authorizations, have been helping to finance the education of children living on Federal property and in communities affected by Federal activities. I recommend that the Congress enact general legislation to establish a single program for all Federal agencies.

Promotion of education—Higher education.—Large numbers of young people and adults wish to continue their education beyond high school in order to prepare for entrance to professional schools, to receive additional technical or vocational training or to round out their general education.

For many of our people, post-secondary education on a part-time or full-time basis, provided in institutions located within commuting distance of home, would meet their needs at low cost. Several of the states are now developing community institutions for this purpose.

I have asked the Federal Security Administrator to make a comprehensive study of this development in order to determine whether the Federal Government might appropriately take any action to encourage the states and localities to establish and expand "community colleges."

Primarily because of low family incomes and of the high costs involved, more than half of our young people who could benefit from a college education are now unable to attend. This failure to develop to the fullest extent the capacities of our young people is a matter of national concern. As a step toward correcting this situation, I shall transmit to the Congress a legislative proposal to authorize a limited Federal program to assist capable youth who could not otherwise do so to pursue their desired fields of study at the institutions of their choice.

This budget includes 1 million dollars as a tentative estimate of appropriations needed in the fiscal year 1951 to establish the required organization and to initiate the program. Assistance to students would begin in the fiscal year 1952.

National Science Foundation.—The Government is investing hundreds of millions of dollars in research—primarily in applied research in the military, atomic energy, and health fields.

We must consider, however, not only the ways in which the great reservoir of scientific knowledge already at our disposal can best be utilized, but also the best paths to follow for the discovery of further basic knowledge.

To this end, we urgently need a National Science Foundation to stimulate basic research and to assure an effective balance among the Federal research programs. By developing a national research policy and by formulating a truly national research budget it should be possible to relate the activities of public and private institutions in a concerted effort to advance the frontiers of knowledge.

The budget provides 500 thousand dollars for the initial administrative expenses of the proposed National Science Foundation, in the expectation that the Congress will enact legislation, already passed by the Senate, to establish it.

Index

Abbott, Jacob, *The Teacher*, 420n, 488n

Academic administration and policy, Thorstein Veblen on, 590-594; Bliss Perry on, 605; Stephen Leacock on, 605-606

Academic degrees, "preposterous" increase of, 608, 609

Academic freedom, first case involving, in the United States (1653), 64-65

Academy and College of Philadelphia, 1

Academies in England advertise in Virginia newspaper, 44

Academy of Arts and Sciences in Richmond, Virginia, Quesnay de Beaurepaire's, 127-132; Sara Bache to Benjamin Franklin on, 127-128; announcement of, 128; official approval of, 129; prospectus of, 129-132

"A Critical Period in American Religion" (Arthur M. Schlesinger), 682n; 727n

Act to establish the University of Texas, 279-282

Adams, H. B., *Thomas Jefferson and the University of Virginia,* 127n

Adams, R. G., *Three Americanists,* 271n

Address in behalf of schools in New York City (1805), 319-320

Admission requirements for admission to early normal schools in Massachusetts, 416, 417

A Documentary History of Education in the South Before 1860 (Edgar W. Knight), I, 8n, 21n, 41n, 45n, 58n; II, 90

Advertisements of schools, teachers, and tutors, 1, 41-44

Agricultural schools, recommended, 186-200; urged by Governor Henry Wise of Virginia, 541n; by legislative committee of New York, 541n

A History of Education in Pennsylvania (J. P. Wickersham), 30n, 69n

A History of Harvard University (Benjamin Pierce), 72n

A History of Higher Education in America (C. F. Thwing), 186n

A History of Public Permanent Common School Funds in the United States (F. H. Swift), 316n

A History of Quaker Government in Pennsylvania (Isaac Sharpless), 38n

A History of Women's Education in the United States (Thomas Woody), 702

Aid to sectarian schools, practices in, 778

Alabama, prohibits the teaching of slaves to read and write, 666

"Alas, the Poor School Superintendent" (G. H. Henry), 384, 385

Alston against School Board of Norfolk, Virginia, 695

American Antiquarian Society, possesses papers of Joseph Lancaster, 134

American Association of University Professors, opposes loyalty oaths for teachers, 451, 452; call for organization of, 579, 580

American Association of School Administrators, opposes Communists as teachers, 462, 463; loyalty oaths for teachers, 464

American College Athletics (H. S. Pritchett and H. J. Savage), 598n

American Colleges and Universities (D. G. Tewksbury), 180; 186n

American colonies, education in, inheritance from Europe, 1

American Institute of Instruction, origin and early years of, 409-412; Francis Wayland, president of, 409; frequent participants in, 410

American Journal of Education, 151n

American State Universities and the University of Michigan (Andrew Ten-Brook), 214n

American state university, origin in the South, 193n

American Universities and Colleges (A. J. Brumbaugh), 540

Amusements and punishments in the schools, Benjamin Rush on proper, 471-476

Amsterdam, Classis of gives instructions to schoolmasters, 16

Anderson, James S. M., *History of the Church of England in the Colonies,* 21n

Angell, President James B., recommends chair of pedagogy in University of Michigan (1874), 423; on the education of women, 722

Announcement of opening of King's College (Columbia), 1754, 81-83; of lottery for, 83

Apprenticeship theories and practices, 1, 8-15; legislation on, in Virginia, 9; in Massachusetts, 10; indentures on, in Virginia, 10-12; in New England, 12-13; in New York, 13-14; Andrew Johnson bound out, 14-15

Argument against state support of education, 343

Arithmetic taught by singing, 510n

Arkansas, books used in the schools of (1846), 499; history of education in (Stephen B. Weeks), 499n

A Source Book of the University of Texas (H. Y. Benedict), 272n

Athletic contests, defects and excesses of, 598-601; inter-collegiate horse-racing proposed for, 601-604

Attendance of children at school, first law on, 365, 366

Average salaries of teachers (1948), 460

Ayres, L. P., on educational measurements, 744-749

Bannister, J., Jr., Thomas Jefferson to, on education in Europe, 91, 92

Barnard, F. A. P., 180; exonerated by trustees of the University of Mississippi, 289-295; on the education of women, 721

Barnard, Henry, 133; letters to, 173-176; letters of, 173n; W. H. Stiles to, 173-175; Ashbel Smith to, 175, 176; on influence of the lyceum, 176, 177; on teachers in German schools, 414; on heavy turnover among teachers, 418; on women as teachers, 418, 419; on "boarding around" the teacher, 491

Barnett (flag-saluting) Case, 768-770

Basic Writings of Thomas Jefferson (Philip S. Foner), 91n

Bassett, John S., praises Booker T. Washington and starts violent controversy, 682-685; President Kilgo of Trinity College (Duke University) resigns in defense of, 683-685

Becker, Carl, on loyalty oaths for teachers, 449-451

Beecher, Henry Ward, advocate of the lyceum, 151n

Bell, Alexander, advocate of monitorial schools, 133

Benedict, H. Y., *A Source Book of the University of Texas,* 272n

Benjamin Franklin and the University of Pennsylvania (F. N. Thorpe), 31n

Bennett, Joshua, 38n; fine remitted for violating loyalty oath (1779), 40

Berea College Case, 685-689; 766n

Berkeley, William, reports on Virginia (1671), 68, 69

Bethesda Orphan House in Georgia, 58n

Bevis, A. M., *Diets and Riots,* 186n

Blair Bills, for national educational aid, 728n; 732-735; change in sentiment on, 736

Blake, W. B., to Richard Irby, about life in the University of North Carolina, 265-267

Blewett, Ben, on tests of efficiency, 742, 743

Blodget, William, *Economica: A Statistical Manual of the United States,* 98; account of a conversation with George Washington about a national university, 98, 99

"Boarding around" the teacher, Henry Barnard on, 491; account of, 506, 507

Boogher, E. W. G., *Secondary Education in Georgia, 1732-1858,* 41n; 181n

Books used in the schools of Virginia (1844), 491-493; of Arkansas (1846), 499

Boston, non-residents must pay school fees, 299; finds its schools expensive, 299; schoolmasters of in controversy with Horace Mann, 362n; request of for suitable persons as teachers, 467; ministers of consulted about a teacher; selectmen of induct a teacher, 469

Booth, Reverend B., of Liverpool, England, advertises his academy in Virginia, 44

Bowker, R. R., *Copyright: Its History and Its Law,* 120n

Bradford, Ralph, on business and education, 383, 384

British and Foreign School Society, Joseph Lancaster falls out with, 134

Brown, E. E., *The Making of Our Middle Schools,* 31n; *The Origin of the American State Universities,* 214n

Brown, John, attacks Harper's Ferry, 289n

Brown University, 1

Brumbaugh, A. J., *American Universities and Colleges,* 540

Brumbaugh, Martin G., *The Life and Works of Christopher Dock,* 31n

Bryce, James, on higher education in the United States, 571-575; 726

Buchanan, President James, vetoes Morrill (Land-grant College) Bill, 1859, 282-289

Buchholz, H. E., "The Pedagogues at Armageddon," 384n

Budd, Thomas, views on educational needs in Pennsylvania (1685), 69, 70

Burnside Bill, for national educational aid, 728n

Business and education, closer relations between needed, 383-384

Business education, in Philadelphia (1751), 42, 43

Butler, Nicholas Murray, on the education of women, 722

Buttrick, Wallace, 454

Butts, R. F., *The College Charts Its Course,* 186n

Cabell, Joseph C., to Joseph Lancaster, 137-138

Caldwell, Joseph, advocates Lancasterian schools, 134

Caldwell, O. W. and S. A. Courtis, *Then and Now in Education,* 493n

Calhoun, John C., to Joseph Lancaster, 141, 142

California, loyalty oath for teachers in, 445, 446

Cameron, W. J., on *McGuffey's Readers,* 533-535

Can the private schools survive? 631-633

Carnegie, Andrew, establishes the Carnegie Foundation for the Advancement of Teaching, 575-577

Carter, James G., 133; on "wretched mockery" of education in Massachusetts, 330, 331; on teachers in Massachusetts, 403-405

Carter, Robert, master of Nomini Hall, Virginia, 45n

Cases and Other Authorities on Constitutional Law (W. F. Dodd), 229n

Catholepistemaid (University of Michigan), charter of, 214, 215

Chamber of Commerce of the United States on business and education, 383, 384; arguments for and against federal aid, 386-399

Chambers, M. M., *The Colleges and the Courts,* 766n

Charter of the General Education Board, 569-571; of the Rockefeller Foundation, 578, 579; of Regional Council for Education, 633-635

Chase, H. W., 597n

Chautauqua Movement, succeeds the lyceum, 151n

Chavis, John, Negro, licensed as Presbyterian preacher, 661; engaged as missionary, 662; educated at Washington Academy, 662; taught white boys, 662n; school of praised, 663

Cheever, Ezekiel, asks to keep his position and pay as schoolmaster, 20-21; 469n

Children, cannot be compelled to attend public school, 380-383; may be expelled from school for refusal to salute the national flag, 766, 767; may not be expelled for refusal, 768-770

Choate, Rufus, 230n

Church and state, early movement for separation of, 107-112

Civil Rights Act (1875), 678

Classics, defense of, 267-270

Classis of Amsterdam gives instruction to schoolmasters, 16

Clinton, Governor DeWitt, of New York, advocate of Lancasterian schools, 134

Cobb, Ernest, makes plea for common sense in education, 531-533

Co-education, Pope Pius XI opposes, 757

Cokesbury College (Maryland), rules of, 201, 202

College entrance requirements, Committee of Ten on, 557, 559

College of Geneva, proposal to remove to Virginia, 90; Washington to John Adams on, 101

College of New Jersey, 1

College of South Carolina, faculty of makes educational survey, 331-340

College of William and Mary, awards honorary masters' degree to Benjamin Franklin, 84; Thomas Jefferson on conditions at, 87; bill to amend constitution of, 186-191

Colleges, number and endowments of, 539; competition in, 597, 598

Collegiate, degrees conferred in 1802, at Columbia, Harvard, Dartmouth, Yale, Princeton, North Carolina, 205, 206; rules at Harvard, University of Virginia, University of South Carolina, 235, 236; system of the United States, Francis Wayland on, 260-263

Colonists in Bondage (A. E. Smith), 8n

Columbia College, degrees conferred by (1802), 205

Commission on Teacher Education, excerpts from report of, 456-459

Committee on College Entrance Requirements, on elective system in secondary
schools, 559, 560
Committee of Fifteen, on teachers, 431-
435; on correlation of studies, 517, 518
Committee of Ten, on teachers, 429, 431;
proposes program for secondary
schools, 555, 556; on requirements for
admission to college, 557-559; 644n
Committee on Tests and Standards, discussion of report of, 741-744
Compulsory attendance legislation, B. G.
Northrop on, 297; Supreme Court on,
297, 380-383; first (Massachusetts),
365-366; extends from 1852 to 1918,
297, 366; urged in New York, 367,
368; opposition to, 368-370; New
York's first, 370-373; Tennessee's first,
373-376; Mississippi's first, 377-380
Conant, President James B., 64n
Connecticut, separates church and state,
107n; first copyright law in, 120-122;
establishes first permanent public
school endowment, 316-318; wages of
teachers in (1832), 412; heavy turnover of teachers in, 418
Contract, with Dutch schoolmaster in
New York, 17-19; with teachers in
Pennsylvania (1747), 30
Convention, educational, in Michigan,
153-155; J. D. Pierce addresses, 154
Copyright: Its History and Its Law (R. R.
Bowker), 120n; early laws on, 120-
126; in Connecticut, 120-122; in Mary-
land, New Jersey, New Hampshire,
Rhode Island, Pennsylvania, South
Carolina, Virginia, North Carolina,
Georgia, New York, 120n; in Massa-
chusetts, 122-123; by Congress, 123-
126; first litigation under, 120n
Cornbury, Governor Edward of New
York, grants James Jeffray license to
teach, 21
Corporal punishment at Harvard (1656),
67
Correlation of studies, Committee of Fif-
teen on, 517, 518
Coon, Charles L., North Carolina Schools
and Academies, 41n, 181n
Cooley, Thomas M., writes decision in
Kalamazoo Case, 544-554
Court Cases, involving the education of
Negroes, 691-700
Courtis, S. A. and O. W. Caldwell, Then
and Now in Education, 493n
Crane, Ichabod, 16n
Craven, Braxton, on proper practices in
the school, 503-506
Culture-epoch theory, 736-739

Curoe, P. R. V., Educational Attitudes
and Policies of Organized Labor in the
United States, 342n

Dabney, Virginius, Liberalism in the
South, 682n
Dartmouth College, 1; degrees conferred
by (1802), 205
Dartmouth College Case, 180, 200n; Jefferson to Governor Plumer on, 213,
214; Daniel Webster cites North Carolina case in, 228, 229; 229-233; 766n
Darwinism, fight in the United States
over, 682n; Bishop Samuel Wilberforce
rebukes Henry Huxley over, 727
Davis, John, tutor from England, inter-
views a planter in South Carolina, 54-
57; employed in the College of Charleston and in Virginia, 54n; his Travels of
Four Years and A Half in the United
States of America, 54n
Debating in the Colonial Chartered Colleges (David Potter), 72n
Delaware, early constitutional provisions
for schools, 117
Democracy Enters College (R. L. Duf-
fus), 540; 644n
Department of Education, bill to estab-
lish, 749-757
Dewey, John, 424n; states the aims of the
"Progressives," 535-538; 644n; 726
Dewey, Governor Thomas E., approves
bill against discrimination in higher
education in New York, 640
Dexter, Franklin B. (Documentary His-
tory of Yale University), 71n
Diets and Riots (A. M. Bevis), 186n
Discrimination in higher education in
New York, act against, 641-644
District of Columbia, loyalty oath for
teachers in, 447; repealed, 452
Dix, Dorothea, memorializes legislature
of Massachusetts, 155, 156
Dock, Christopher, tells of proper treat-
ment of children in school, 31-35; his
Schulordnung, 31n, 406n, 420n
"Documentary History of Education in
South Carolina" (Gertrude Foster),
27n
Documentary History of Yale University
(Franklin B. Dexter), 71n
Dodd, W. F., Cases and Other Authori-
ties on Constitutional Law, 229n
Douglass, Mrs. Margaret, convicted of
teaching Negroes in Norfolk, Virginia,
669, 670n
Duel, in South Carolina College, 258-260
Duffus, R. L., Democracy Enters Col-
lege, 540, 644n

Dunster, President Henry of Harvard, dismissed because of his views on infant baptism, 64-65; petition of, 65, 66

"Dust and Ashes," letter from, to Virginia Company, 4-5

Dutch schoolmaster, contract with, in New York, 17-19

Early Constitutional provisions for schools, in Pennsylvania, 113, 117; in North Carolina, 113, 114; in Georgia, 114, 117; in Vermont, 114; in Massachusetts, 114-116; in New Hampshire, 116; in Northwest Ordinance, 116; in Vermont, 116; in Delaware, 117; in Ohio, 117, 118; in Indiana, 118, 119

Early History of the University of Virginia as Contained in the Letters of Thomas Jefferson and Joseph C. Cabell, 216n

East India School, 1

Economica: A Statistical Manual of the United States (Samuel Blodget), 98

"Economy of time," urged by the National Education Association, 577, 578

Edens, A. Hollis, on the future of higher education, 631n

Editorial by Horace Greeley in favor of free schools, 364, 365

Education, in American Colonies, 1; in Europe, Thomas Jefferson on, 91, 92; Noah Webster on, 93-96; George Washington on, 97

Education for American Life, 758n

Educational activities of the Society for the Propagation of the Gospel in Foreign Parts, 21-29

Educational Attitudes and Policies of Organized Labor in the United States (P. R. V. Curoe), 342n

Educational, defects, Charles W. Eliot on, 524, 525

Educational laws, initial, in Massachusetts, 62, 63

Educational measurements, L. P. Ayres on, 744-749

Educational practices, 466-538

Educational units, defined by the Carnegie Foundation, 520-522

Edwards, Newton, 133

Eggleston, Edward, on "turning out" the teacher in Indiana, 507-510; The Hoosier Schoolmaster, 507n

Eisenhower, M. S., dissents from recommendations of the President's Commission on Higher Education, 615n

Elective system, criticisms of, 267-270

Eliot, President Charles W. of Harvard, opposes national university, 98n; on educational defects, 524, 525; congratulates Progressive Education on its first issue, 530; on the education of women, 718

Elliott, E. C., The Colleges and the Courts, 766n; on tests of efficiency, 741

Elsbree, Willard S., The American Teacher, 16n

Emancipation Proclamation, 673, 674

Emerson, R. W., advocate of the lyceum, 151n

English Act of 1601 (apprenticeship), 8

Established Church, membership in required of teacher in Charleston, S.C., 29; in New Bern, N. C., 36; Presbyterian teacher in South Carolina promises to conform to rites of, 29-30

Everett, Edward, advocate of the lyceum, 151n

Evils of whispering, how to prevent, 488-491

Examinations, Horace Mann on value of written, 493-499; David Page on public, 501-503

Extracts from Constitution of UNESCO, 773-775

Farish, Hunter Dickinson, Journal and Letters of Philip Vickers Fithian), 45n

Federal aid to education, arguments for and against, 386-399; Hoar Bill for, 386n; exchange of opinion on by Francis Cardinal Spellman and Mrs. Eleanor Roosevelt, 386n; to higher education opposed by Indiana Association of Church Related Colleges, 657, 658; bills for, 728-736; 749-757

Finegan, Thomas E., Free Schools: A Documentary History of the Free School Movement in New York State, 16n

First American State university to be chartered (Georgia), 192, 193n; first to open (North Carolina), 192, 193n

First public high school law (Massachusetts), 247

Fitzgerald, J. G., The Diaries of George Washington, 182n

Fitzpatrick, John C., The Writings of George Washington, 97n

Fithian, Philip, diary of, 1; tutor in Carter family in Virginia, 45n; letter to John Peck, his successor, 45-53

Flag-saluting cases, 766; 767; 768-770

Flexner, Abraham, on humor in teachers and teaching, 454-456

Fly-leaf scribblings on school-books, 478, 479

Foner, Philip S., *Basic Writings of Thomas Jefferson*, 91n

Ford, Henry, interest in *McGuffey's Readers*, 533-535

Ford, P. L., *The Writings of Thomas Jefferson*, 108n, 186n

Ford, Worthington C., 105, 106

Foster, Gertrude, "Documentary History of Education in South Carolina," 27n

Francke, August Hermann, 58n

Franklin, Benjamin, his academy to prepare teachers, 31; "Proposals Relating to the Education of Youth in Pensilvania" (1749), 75-80; on the value of history, 78, 79; receives honorary master's degree from the College of William and Mary, 84; satirical letter to "Messrs. Weems and Gant," 110-112; academy of, 181n

Freedom of the press, early case involving (John Peter Zenger, 1734), 72

Freedom of teaching, Phi Beta Kappa on, 464

Freedmen's Bureau, established, 659; 674, 675

Free Negroes, cannot be taught to read and write in Virginia, 664, 665; cannot preach in North Carolina, 665, 666

Free Schools: A Documentary History of the Free School Movement in New York State (Thomas E. Finegan), 16n

"Friday exercises," Hamlin Garland describes, 525-527

Gaines Decision, 691, 692; newspaper account of, 693, 694; States affected by, 694, 766n

Gaines, President Francis P. of Washington and Lee University, 103n

Gales, Joseph, praises school of John Chavis, Negro, 663

Gallaudet, Thomas H., advocate of the lyceum, 151n

Gardner, George E. and Arthur D. Wright, *Hall's Lectures on School-Keeping*, 406n

Garland, Hamlin, describes "Friday exercises" in the schools, 525-527; on the influence of *McGuffey's Readers*, 527, 528

Gegenheimer, A. F., *William Smith: Educator and Churchman*, 229n

General Education Board, charter of, 569-571

Geography taught by singing, 510-516

Geographies, Jedidiah Morse on imperfections of textbooks on, 470, 471

Georgia, legislature of makes aliens of

Georgians who study in Europe, 93; early constitutional provisions for schools, 114, 117; early copyright law in, 120n; first state to charter a state university, 192, 193n

"G.I. Bill of Rights," extracts from, 609-612

Girard College, endowment of, 247n

Girard, Stephen, provides for Lancasterian school in Philadelphia, 150; will of, 150n; provides for college in Philadelphia, 247-255; "Lucky sons of," 247n

Gladden, Washington, *Recollections*, 274n

Gobitis (flag-saluting) Case, 766, 767; decision in reversed, 766n

Government and Labor in Early America (R. B. Morris), 8n

Governors, messages of, on education, 343-345

Goucher, John F., on the education of women, 722

Graduate instruction, William James on the "Ph.D. Octopus," 563-569; Stephen Leacock on, 582-586; H. J. Laski on, 624-630

Greeley, Horace, advocate of the lyceum, 151n; a subscriber of opposes free schools, 363; Greeley replies, 364, 365; on turning out the teacher in New England (1820), 487

Green, J. M., on tests of efficiency, 743, 744

Gooch, R. B., to Horace Mann, 157, 158; Mann's reply to, 158-160

Goodrich, C. A., 230n

Goodrich, Samuel G. ("Peter Parley"), describes typical day in New England rural school, 477, 478

Grimké, Thomas S., advocate of the lyceum, 151n

Griscom, John, advocate of the lyceum, 151n

Habersham, James, 58n

Hadley, President Arthur T., of Yale University, quoted, 71n

Hall, G. Stanley, 644n, 726; on the education of women, 722

Hall, Samuel R., *Lectures on School-Keeping*, 31n, 406n, 420n; on requisite qualifications of teachers, 406-409

Hamilton, Alexander, 120n

Harris, Seymour E., on market for college graduates, 539

Harris, W. T., 726

Harrisse, Henry, on collegiate trustees, 271, 272

Harvard College, 1; rules of (1642-1646), 60-62; fines and corporal punishment in, 67; subjects discussed for master's degrees at (1743), 72-74; list of fines at (1750), 80-81; overseers of remonstrate against another college in Massachusetts (1762), 85-87; awards LL.D. to George Washington, 87, 88; degrees conferred by (1802), 205; rules of in 1820's, 235, 236; George Ticknor on, 237; confers honorary degree on Booker T. Washington, 679-682; "Goes Co-ed, But Incognito," 723n

Hawkins, Ernest, *Historical Notices of the Missions of the Church of England,* 21n

Hayes, Cecil B., *The American Lyceum,* 151n

Helper, Hinton Rowan, *The Impending Crisis of the South: How to Meet It,* 670n; on baneful influences of slavery, 670-672

Henrico College and East India School, 1; R. H. Land on, 2, 7; Treasurer of Virginia Company reports on, 3; letter from "Dust and Ashes" on, 4-5; passengers and crew of Royal James contribute to, 5; Indian Massacre destroys prospects of, 5-7; Virginia Company ready to assist, 7

Henry, G. H., "Alas the Poor School Superintendent," 384, 385

Henry Harrisse on Collegiate Education (Edgar W. Knight), 271n

High school, first law on, 247

Higher education, Thorstein Veblen on, 590-594; Bliss Perry on, 605; Stephen Leacock on, 605, 606; Robert M. Hutchins on, 606, 607; F. P. Keppel on, 608, 609; rôle of Federal government in, 617-620; trends in cost of, 630, 631; A. Hollis Edens on the future of, 631n; Charles Seymour on the future of, 631n; Regional Council for in the South, 633-635; need for state university in New York, 635-640

Hill, James W., "The Movement to Establish a National University Prior to 1860," 98n

Historical Notices of the Missions of the Church of England (Ernest Hawkins), 21n

History, Benjamin Franklin on the value of, 78, 79

History of the Church of England in the Colonies (James S. M. Anderson), 21n

History of Secondary Education (I. L. Kandel), 644n

Hoar Bill for federal aid to education, 386n, 728-732

Hochwalt, F. G., dissents from recommendations of the President's Commission on Higher Education, 620-623

Holbrook, Josiah, proposes constitution for lyceum, 145, 146, 151n

Holmes, Oliver Wendell, advocate of the lyceum, 151n

Horse-racing, proposed for inter-collegiate football, 601-604

Houston, Governor Sam of Texas, recommends aid to non-public institutions, 295, 296

How to prevent whispering among pupils and their leaving their seats, 488-491

Howe, John de la, provides for first manual labor school, 196n

Humor, importance of in teachers and teaching, 454-456

Hutchins, R. M., on higher education, 606, 607

Huxley, Henry, rebuked by Bishop Samuel Wilberforce on Darwinism, 727

Indian Affairs, Office of, to Horace Mann, 167, 168

Indian Massacre (1622), report of, 5-7

Indiana, early constitutional provisions for schools, 118, 119; account of turning out teacher in, 507-510; Association of Church Related Colleges of opposes Federal aid to higher education, 657, 658

Indiana State Seminary, opening of, 237, 238

Industrial universities, legislature of Illinois recommends, 270, 271

Illinois, legislature of recommends industrial universities, 270, 271

Instructions to clergy of the S.P.G., 21-25; to schoolmasters, employed by the Society, 26-27

Insurrection, Nat Turner, 8n, 659; Denmark Vesey, 659

Inter-collegiate horse-racing proposed for football, 601-604

International University is proposed, 654-657

Issues and trends in the education of teachers (1946), 456-459

James, William, on "Psychology and the Teaching Art," 425-429; on the "Ph.D. Octopus," 563-569; 726

Jeans Fund, 660

Jefferson, Thomas, to John Page about conditions at the College of William

Jefferson, Thomas (*contd.*)
and Mary College, 87; on education in Europe, 91, 92; to Congress on national university, 103, 104; "A Bill for the More General Diffusion of Knowledge" and "A Bill for Establishing Religious Freedom," 108n; bill for religious freedom in Virginia, 108-110; bill to amend constitution of the College of William and Mary, 186-191; given permission to sell his property by lottery, 212n; declines to sell lottery tickets, 212, 213; to Governor Plumer on Dartmouth College Case, 213, 214; chairman Rockfish Gap Commission, 216; educational bill (1779) for Virginia, 299-306; on the education of women, 706, 707

Jeffray, James, licensed to teach in New York, 21

Jehovah's Witnesses, refuse to salute national flag, 766, 767; 768-770

Jernegan, M. W., *Laboring and Dependent Classes in Colonial America,* 8n

John Peter Zenger, His Press, His Trial and A Bibliography of Zenger Reprints (Livingston Rutherford), 72n

Johnson, Andrew, bound out to a tailor, 14-15

Johnson, Clifton, *Old-Time Schools and School-Books,* 506n

Jones, Rowland, Pennsylvania teacher, gives account of his method of teaching, 467, 468

Journal and Letters of Philip Vickers Fithian (Hunter Dickinson Farish), 45n

Kalamazoo decision, 544-554; 766n

Kandel, I. L., *History of Secondary Education,* 644n

Kendall, C. M., on tests of efficiency, 741, 742

Kent, Chancellor James of New York, 120n

Kentucky, prohibits mixed schools, 685; Berea College Case in, 685-689; satire on college for women in, 710, 711

Keppel, F. P., on "preposterous" increase in academic degrees, 608, 609

Kilgo, President John C., of Trinity College (Duke University), resigns in defense of John S. Bassett, 683-685

Kilpatrick, W. H., 425n

Kindergarten, should be part of school system, 740

Kingsbury, Susan Myra, edits *Records of the Virginia Company,* 2

King's College (Columbia), 1; announcement of opening (1754), 81-83; lottery for (1754), 83

Knight, Edgar W., *Documentary History of Education in the South Before 1860,* I, 8n, 21n, 41n, 45n, 58n; II, 90; "More Evidence of Horace Mann's Influence in the South," 157n; "Some Evidence of Henry Barnard's Influence in the South," 173n; "North Carolina's 'Dartmouth College Case,'" 209n; *Henry Harrisse on Collegiate Education,* 271n; "Southern Opposition to Northern Education," 289n

Ku Klux Klan, warns a Northern teacher, 677, 678

Laboring and Dependent Classes in America (M. W. Jernegan), 8n

Lancaster, Joseph, 133; falls out with British and Foreign School Society, 134; James Stevenson to, 136, 137; Joseph C. Cabell to, 137, 138; to his daughter, 139-141; John C. Calhoun to, 141, 142

Lancasterian schools, advocates of, 133, 134; in North Carolina, 135; in Philadelphia, 135, 136; Board of Regents of New York may charter, 142, 143; Stephen Girard provides for, 150

Land, R. H., on Henrico College, 2; quoted, 7n

Land-grant college (Morrill) bill, vetoed by President Buchanan, 282-289; act, 541-543

Land grants for state universities, congressional objections to, 233, 234

Laski, H. J., on graduate instruction in the United States, 624-630

Latin and Greek, status of in the schools (1924), 530, 531

Leacock, Stephen, on graduate instruction, 582-586; on higher education, 605, 606

Lectures on School-Keeping (Samuel R. Hall), 31n, 406n, 520n

Lee, General Robert E., 659

Lefler, Hugh T., *Hinton Rowan Helper: Advocate of A White America,* 671n

Letter of "Dust and Ashes" to Virginia Company, 4-5

Lewis, J. Anthony, "Harvard Goes Co-ed, But Incognito," 723n

Liberalism in the South (Virginius Dabney), 682n

Liberty Hall Academy (Virginia) receives gift from George Washington, 103n, 229, 230n; name changed to Washington College and then to Washington and Lee University, 103n

Liberty Hall Academy (North Carolina), charter of, 182-185

Lincoln, Abraham, advocate of the lyceum, 151n; Emancipation Proclamation by, 673, 674

Lindsley, Philip, advocate of the lyceum, 151n, 180

Literary funds, Connecticut establishes, 316-318, Virginia establishes, 321

Literary property, early protection of, 120-126

Lotteries, for King's College (Columbia), 83; in Virginia, 212n; Thomas Jefferson's views on, 212

Lovejoy, C. E., *So You're Going to College*, 540

Loyalty oaths for teachers, in Massachusetts (1776), 36; C. H. Van Tyne on during the American Revolution, 36n; in New Jersey (1777), 37; in Pennsylvania (1778), 37, 38; early protest against (1779), 38-40; fine remitted for violation of, 40; need of for teachers, 443; Governor Dixon of Montana vetoes measure for, 443, 444; in California, 445, 446; in New York, 446, 447; act of Congress on, 447; arguments for and against, 447, 448; in Massachusetts, 448; Alfred E. Smith vetoes in New York, 443; Carl Becker on, 449-451; American Association of University Professors opposes, 451, 452; Congress repeals act on, in District of Columbia, 452; in New York, 460-462; in University of California, 462; American Association of School Administrators opposes, 464

"Lucky Sons of Stephen Girard" (B. G. Wittels), 247n

Luxury tax, proposed for support of the University of Virginia (1805), 206-208

Lyceum, Josiah Holbrook proposes constitution for, 145, 146; American is organized, 151, 152; advocates of 151n; succeeded by Chautauqua, 151n; leaders in, 151n; constitution of, 152; subjects discussed by, 153; Henry Barnard on influence of, 176, 177

Lynes, Russell, "Can the Private Schools Survive?" 631-633

Lyon, Mary, on purposes of Mount Holyoke Seminary, 707-710

Mann, Horace, 133; letters to, 157-163; H. R. West to, 160; Odd Fellows of North Carolina to, 161, 162; on free school system, 163-165; extracts from tenth report of, 163n; on relation between education and prosperity, 165, 166; extracts from twelfth report of, 165n; Masonic Lodge of Alabama to, 166, 167; Office of Indian Affairs asks advice of, 167, 168; J. B. Minor to, 169-172; replies to Boston Schoolmasters, 362, 363; reports gift to promote normal schools in Massachusetts, 415; legislature accepts, 416; on the value of written examinations, 493-499

Manual labor school recommended, 186-200; John de la Howe provides for first, 196n; interest in, 255, 256; recommended by Legislature of Pennsylvania, 257

Marshall, Chief Justice John, 230n

Maryland, early copyright law in, 120n; establishes Lancasterian schools, 134; Negro teachers in seek salaries equal to those paid white teachers, 690

Masonic Lodge of Alabama to Horace Mann, 166, 167

Massachusetts, enacts loyalty oath for teachers (1776), 36; initial educational law in (1647), 62, 63; bill of rights in, 110; establishes religious freedom, 112; early constitutional provisions for schools in, 114-116; early copyright law in, 122-123; Dorothea Dix memorializes legislature of, 155, 156; argument against poll tax for voting in, 172; enacts first public high school law, 247; first state to enact a compulsory school law (1852), 297; J. G. Carter on "wretched mockery" of education in, 330, 331; creates first state board of education, 360, 361; James G. Carter on teachers in, 403-405; Horace Mann reports gift to promote normal schools in, 415; legislature of accepts gift for normal schools in, 416; loyalty oath for teachers in, 36, 448

Massachusetts Historical Society, 157n

Massacre, Indian, in Virginia (1622), report of, 5-7

Master's degrees, subjects discussed for, at Harvard (1743), 72-74

Medill, W., of Office of Indian Affairs, to Horace Mann, 167, 168

Meiklejohn, Alexander, on the purpose of a liberal college, 580-582

"Messrs. Weems and Gant," Benjamin Franklin's satirical letter to, 110-112

Methodist minister of Charleston, South Carolina, is "pumped" for teaching Negroes, 664

Michigan, educational convention in, 153-155; supreme court of establishes loyalty of secondary schools (Kalamazoo decision), 544-554

Middlesex County (Connecticut), a school day in, 476, 477

Military education, arguments for, 238-246

Military school, at Norwich, Vermont, 238n; at Portsmouth, Virginia, 238n

"Millions of B.A.'s, But no Jobs" (Seymour E. Harris), 539

Mills, Caleb, 133

Mississippi, last state to enact a compulsory school law (1918), 297

Missouri, Gaines Decision in, 691, 692

Montana, Governor Dixon vetoes loyalty oath for teachers in, 443, 444

Morison, Samuel Eliot, quoted, 64n; *Three Centuries of Harvard,* 64n

Morrill, J. S., 541n

Morrill (Land-Grant College) Act, 541-543

Morrill (Land-Grant College) Bill, vetoed by President James Buchanan, 282-289

Morris, R. B., *Government and Labor in Early America,* 8n

Morrison, A. J., edits John Davis's *Travels of Four Years and A Half in the United States of America,* 54n

Morse, Jedidiah, sues William Winterbotham under the first national copyright law, 120n; 470n; on imperfections of geographies, 470, 471

Mott, Thomas A., on sex hygiene in the schools, 523, 524

Mount Holyoke Seminary, purposes of, 707-710; rules of, 718-721

Murphey, Archibald D., advocate of Lancasterian schools, 134

McClure, William, brings Joseph Neef to United States, 138n

McCollum Case, 766n

McConaughy, J. L., on collegiate chapel and food, 186n

McGuffey Readers, Herbert Quick on influence of, 516, 517; Hamlin Garland on influence of, 527, 528; W. J. Cameron on, 533-535; Henry Ford's interest in, 533-535

McGuire, R. P., dissents from recommendations of the President's Commission on Higher Education, 620-623

National Education Association commends the study of pedagogy in the universities, 424; resolutions of (1897),

519, 520; advises "economy of time," 577, 578; views the South as a vast missionary field, 660; on the education of women, 721

National Manufacturers' Association, on the plight of the schools, 524

National Survey of the Education of Teachers, 444n

National University, early proposals for, 98-106; arguments for and against, 98n; President Andrew D. White of Cornell favors, 98n; President Charles W. Eliot of Harvard opposes, 98n; Samuel Blodget on, 98, 99; Edgar B. Wesley on, 98n; James W. Hill on, 98n; George Washington on, 100, 101; to Congress on, 102, 103, gives stock for, 103; Jefferson on, 103, 104; bill to establish (1816), 104, 105; report on Washington's gift for, 105, 106

National Youth Administration, contributions of, 762-765

Neef, Joseph, comes to United States, 138n

Negroes, educational and other rights of, 659-700; uprisings led by Denmark Vesey and Nat Turner, 659; funds established for the education of, 660; Methodist minister is "pumped" for teaching, 664; religious instruction provided for in South Carolina, 666, 669; New York provides schools for, 667; Mrs. Margaret Douglass convicted of teaching, 669, 670n; capacity of for education, 675, 676; court cases involving education of, 691-700; University of Texas must admit, 696, 697; University of Oklahoma must not segregate, 698-700

New England Association of Colleges and Secondary Schools, standards of, 644-651

Newark Academy, opening of, 181, 182

New Hampshire, separates church and state, 107n; early constitutional provisions for schools, 116; early copyright law in, 120n

New Haven, remonstrance against locating collegiate school in (1717), 71

New Jersey, schoolmasters in must hold license from Bishop of London, 35; qualifications of teachers in, 35, 36; early copyright law in, 120n; melancholy picture of education in, 345, 346; provides for transportation of nonpublic school children, 767, 768; Supreme Court sustains, 771-773

New Jersey Archives, 35n

New Jersey Bus Case, 766n, 771-773

New York, John Shutte, licensed to teach in, 17; John Walton offers to teach many subjects in, 41; early copyright law in, 120n; act for the encouragement of schools (1795), 309-316; provides for common schools and a chief state school officer, 321-330; first compulsory school law, 370-373; A. G. Flagg on lack of good teachers in, 406; description of school in (1847), 500, 501; need for state university in, 635-640; legislation against discrimination in higher education in, 641-644; provides schools for Negro children, 667; new educational program for, 758, 762; *New York Mercury,* 35n

Normal College (North Carolina) offers prize for best essay on plans for a collegiate institution, 271n

Normal Schools, Horace Mann reports gift to promote in Massachusetts, 415; requirements for admission to, in Massachusetts, 416-417; set up in various states, 416n; transferred into colleges, 438-440

North Carolina, early constitutional provisions for schools, 113, 114; early copyright law in, 120n; first to open a state university, 193n; provision for support of by escheats, 200, 201; support withdrawn, 204; open letter against schools in, 340-341; prohibits slaves and free Negroes to preach, 665, 666

North Carolina Schools and Academies (Charles L. Coon), 41n, 181n

North Carolina's "Dartmouth College Case," 209-211

North Central Association of Colleges and Secondary Schools, standards of, 651-654

Northern teachers in the South after 1865, 676-678; objections to, 677; Northern students should go South and Southern students North to dissolve sectional prejudices, 263, 264

Northwest Ordinance, provision for schools in, 116

Northrop, B. G., on compulsory attendance laws, 297; answers opponents of compulsory education, 368-370

Oath required of teachers by England, 29

Oberlin College, the founding of, 257, 258

Objections to land-grants for state universities, 233-235

Odd Fellows, Grand Lodge of North Carolina to Horace Mann, 161, 162

Ohio, early constitutional provisions for schools, 117, 118

Oklahoma, University of must not segregate Negro and white students, 698-700

Old-Time Schools and School-Books (Clifton Johnson), 506n

Olmsted, Denison, advocate of the lyceum, 151n

Opposition to European educational influences, 89-119 by Thomas Jefferson, 91, 92; by Legislature of Georgia, 93; by Noah Webster, 93-96; by Legislature of Virginia, 96, 97; by George Washington, 97

Oregon Case, 380-383, 766n

Organized labor, educational attitudes of, 342n

Ould, Robert, 139n

Our Times: United States, 1900-1925 (Mark Sullivan), 510n

Overseers of Harvard remonstrate against another college in Massachusetts (1762), 85-87

Page, David, *Theory and Practice of Teaching,* 420n advice to prospective teachers, 422, 423n, 501n

Parker, F. W., 726

Pascoe, C. F., *Two Hundred Years of the S.P.G.,* 21n

Patrick, Thomas L., *Southern Criticisms of Northern Educational Influences,* 289n

Partridge, Captain Alden, on military education, 238-246; opens military school at Norwich, Vermont, and Portsmouth, Virginia, 238n

Payne, W. H., professor of pedagogy in University of Michigan, 423n

Peabody Fund, 660

Peck, John, succeeds Philip Fithian as tutor in Carter family in Virginia, 45n; Fithian's letter to, 45-53

Pennsylvania, educational needs in (1685), 69, 70; Benjamin Franklin's educational proposals for youth in (1749), 78-80; early constitutional provisions for schools, 113, 117; early copyright law in, 120n; Legislature of recommends manual labor schools, 257; report of a committee on a school system (1794), 308, 309; message of Governor Wolf on education, 344, 345; famous speech of Thaddeus Stevens on education in, 346-355; county superintendents and their salaries in, 366, 367; on teachers in schools of, 413; on need for improved methods of teaching and managing schools in, 420

Pennsylvania Society for the Promotion of Public Schools declares its purposes, 143-145

Pennypacker, Governor Samuel of Pennsylvania, 31n

Permanent public school fund, Connecticut establishes first, 316-318; F. H. Swift on, 316n

Perry Bliss, on complicated educational administration, 605

Pestalozzian department in a Kentucky school (1830), 487, 488

"Peter Parley" (Samuel G. Goodrich), describes typical day in New England rural school, 477, 478

Phelps-Stokes Fund, 660

Ph.D., protest against as honorary degree, 554; Charles W. Super on, 554; William James on "Ph.D. Octopus," 563-569

Phi Beta Kappa, on freedom of teaching, 464

Philanthropic societies, in American colonies, 1

Phillips Andover Academy chartered, 192; undertakes to prepare teachers, 413; account of school life in, 469, 470

Phillips, Wendell, advocate of the lyceum, 151n

Pierce, Benjamin, A History of Harvard University (1833), 72n

Pierce Bill, for national educational aid, 728n

Piertersen, Evert, schoolmaster, instructions to, 16

Platform of Working Men's Party of Boston, 147, 148

Plight of the schools, National Manufacturers' Association on, 524

Plumer, Governor of New Hampshire, Jefferson to, on Dartmouth College Case, 213, 214

Poll tax, argument against for voting in Massachusetts, 172

"Poor male white orphans," Stephen Girard provides college for, 247-255

Poore, B. F., The Federal and State Constitutions, 113n

Pope Pius XI, on progressive education, 531; Encyclical Letter on the Christian Education of Youth, 531n; opposes sex education and co-education, 757

Poteat, W. L., on competition in the colleges, 597, 598

Potter, David, Debating in the Colonial Chartered Colleges, 72n

Practices, educational, 466-538

Preface to Teaching (Henry Simon), commented on by Abraham Flexner, 454-456

Presbyterian schoolmaster in South Carolina promises to conform to Established Church, 29-30

President's Commission on Higher Education, recommends scholarships and fellowships, 612-620; Milton S. Eisenhower dissents from, 615n; F. G. Hochwalt and R. P. McGuire dissent from, 620-623

Princeton College, 1; degrees conferred by (1802), 205

Principles of progressive education, statement of, 528-530; Pope Pius XI on, 531; John Dewey gives aims of, 535-538

Pritchett, H. S. and H. J. Savage, American College Athletics, 598n; proposes inter-collegiate horse-racing for football, 601-604

Progressive education, statement of principles of (1924), 528-530; Pope Pius XI on, 531; John Dewey on, 535-538

Proposal to move the College of Geneva to Virginia, 90, 101; to prevent the use of public funds for benefit of religious groups, 373

"Proposals Relating to the Education of Youth in Pensilvania" (Benjamin Franklin, 1749), 75-80

Proposed: The University of the United States (Edgar B. Wesley), 98n

Protest against Ph.D. as honorary degree, 554

Public school support, Thaddeus Stevens makes famous speech for, 346-355

Public schools, not a province of government, 148, 149; argument against, 149

Purchasing power of teachers' salaries, 1941 and 1949, 387

Purpose of a liberal college, Alexander Meiklejohn on, 580-582

Qualifications required of schoolmasters of the S.P.G., 27-29

Queen's College (North Carolina), chartered, 182n; George Washington on, 182n

Quesnay de Beaurepaire, Chevalier, establishes Academy of Arts and Sciences in Richmond, Virginia, 127-132

Questions to political candidates by working men of Philadelphia, 146, 147

Quick, Herbert, on influence of McGuffey's Readers, 516, 517

Quincy, Josiah, The History of Harvard University, 1840, 60n

Records of the Company of Massachusetts Bay, 62n

Records of the University of Michigan, 214n

Recollections (Washington Gladden), 274n

Regional Council for Education, charter of, 633-635

Regional standardizing educational associations, formation of, 644n

Regulations of schools in Providence, Rhode Island (1820), 484-485; of a school in South Carolina (1820), 485, 486; Braxton Craven on, 503-506

Religious freedom, early movement for, 107-112; constitutional provisions on, in North Carolina, 107, 108; Jefferson's bill for, in Virginia, 108-110; Massachusetts establishes, 112

Religious groups, proposal to prevent public funds for use of, 373

Religious instruction, cannot be given in public school buildings, 775-778

Religious tests abolished, 107n

Remonstrance against locating collegiate school at New Haven (1717), 71

Research and education, President H. S. Truman on, 779-781

Resolutions of National Education Association (1897), 519-520

Reward for return of Andrew Johnson, apprentice, 15

Rhode Island, early copyright law in, 120n

Rice, J. M., on tests of efficiency, 744; "The Futility of the Spelling Grind," 744n

Richey, Herman G., 133

Richmond, C. A., on the education of women, 723

Rockfish Gap Commission, report of, 216-228; members of, 228

Roosevelt, Franklin D., warns against excess supply of teachers, 444

Roosevelt, Mrs. Eleanor, exchanges opinions with Francis Cardinal Spellman on federal aid to education, 386n

Royal James, passengers and crew of make contributions to Henrico College, 5

Rules of Colonial Colleges, 1, 60-62, 63-64; of Cokesbury College (Maryland), 201, 202

Runes, D. D., *The Selected Writings of Benjamin Rush,* 306n, 403n

Rush, Benjamin, to legislature of Pennsylvania on public education, 306-308; on the occupation of teacher, 403; on proper amusements and punishments in the schools, 471-476; on the education of women, 705, 706

Rural teachers, salaries of (1897), 435, 436

Rustication, 87n

Rutgers College, 1

Rutherford, Livingston (*John Peter Zenger, His Press, His Trial and A Bibliography of Zenger Reprints,* 1904), 72n

Salaries of teachers (1947), 385, 386; of rural (1897), 435, 436; purchasing power of in 1941 and 1949, 387

Satire on college for women in Kentucky, 710-711

Schlesinger, Arthur M., "A Critical Period in American Religion," 682n, 727n

Schmidt, G. P., *The Old Time College President,* 186n

Schools, advertisements of, 1; early constitutional provisions for, 113-119; open letter against, 340-341

Schoolmasters, indentured for disposal in Baltimore, 15; instructions to, by classis of Amsterdam, 16; change in method of licensing in Virginia, 19-20; qualifications of required by S.P.G., 27-29; must hold license in New Jersey from Bishop of London, 35

Schulordnung (Christoper Dock), first professional book on education and teaching in this country, 31n

Secondary education, seven cardinal principles of, 586-590

Secondary Education in Georgia (E. W. G. Boogher), 41n, 181n

Secondary schools, program proposed for by Committee of Ten, 555, 556; Committee on College Entrance Requirements proposes electives for, 559, 560; Can the private school survive? 631-633

Sectarian schools, practices in public aid to, 778

Senatus Academicus reports educational plan for the University of Georgia, 202-204

Separation of church and state, early movement for, 107-112

Seven cardinal principles of secondary education, 586-590

Sex hygiene, district superintendent of schools in Brooklyn on, 522, 523; Superintendent Thomas A. Mott, of Indiana on, 523, 524; Pope Pius XI opposes, 757

Seybolt, Robert F., *Source Studies in American Colonial Education,* 13n; *The Private Schools of Colonial Boston,* 41n

Seymour, Charles, on the future of higher education, 631n

Sharpless, Isaac, *A History of the Quaker Government in Pennsylvania,* 38n

Shaughnessy, Donald D., "Teachers' Loyalty-Oath Laws and Joshua Bennett," 40n

Shunk, Francis R., on new and improved methods of teaching and managing schools in Pennsylvania, 420

Shutte, John, licensed to teach in New York, 17

Simon, Henry, *Preface to Teaching,* 454n

Sims, J. Marion, on a duel in South Carolina College, 258-260; on his early education in South Carolina, 480-484

Singing, geography taught by, 510-516; arithmetic taught by, 510n

Slater Fund, 660

Slaves, South Carolina prohibits teaching to write, 661; to read and write, 666, 667; importation of prohibited, 663, 664; Virginia prohibits teaching of, 664, 665; must not preach in North Carolina, 665, 666; Methodist minister is "pumped" for teaching, 664; cannot be taught to read and write in Alabama, 666; religious instruction of in South Carolina, 666, 669; emancipated, 673, 674

Smith, Alfred E., vetoes loyalty oath law in New York, 443; receives honorary degree from Harvard, 604, 605

Smith, Ashbel, to Henry Barnard, 175, 176

Society for the Propagation of the Gospel in Foreign Parts, educational activities of, 21-29

Source Studies in American Colonial Education (Robert F. Seybolt), 13n

South Carolina, many school subjects offered in (1733, 1744), 41, 42; early copyright law in, 120n; early educational survey in, 331-340; prohibits the teaching of slaves to write, 661; to read and write, 666, 667; religious instruction of Negroes in, 666, 669

South Carolina College, duel in, 258-260

Southern Criticisms of Northern Educational Influences (Thomas L. Patrick), 289n

Southern Historical Collection, 134, 157n, 173n

"Southerner at school with Negroes," 673

"Southern Opposition to Northern Education" (Edgar W. Knight), 289n

Southern students, should go North and Northern students South to dissolve prejudices, 263, 264; leave Northern institutions after John Brown's raid, 289n

So You're Going to College (C. E. Lovejoy), 540

Sparks, Jared, *The Works of Benjamin Franklin,* 58n; 74n

Spellman, Francis Cardinal, exchanges opinions with Mrs. Roosevelt on federal aid to education, 386n

Sproul, President R. G., dissents from action of the Board of Regents of the University of California on loyalty oath for its faculty, 462n

State board of education, Tennessee creates *ex officio* body, 355-359; Governor Edward Everett recommends for Massachusetts, 359, 360; Massachusetts creates first board, 360, 361

State and Church, early movement for separation of, 107-112

State superintendent of schools, New York provides for, 321-330; Tennessee creates *ex-officio* office of, 355-359

State University in New York, need for, 635-640; Governor Thomas E. Dewey approves bill against discrimination of applicants, 640; act on the subject, 641-644

Stevens, Thaddeus, famous speech for public school support, 346-355

Stevenson, James, to Joseph Lancaster, 136, 137

Stiles, W. H., to Henry Barnard, 173-175

Stowe, Calvin E., on women as teachers, 415

Subjects discussed by candidates for the master's degree at Harvard (1743), 72-74; for debating in the colonial colleges, 72n

Sullivan, Mark, *Our Times: United States, 1900-1925,* 510n

Sunday schools, convention to promote interest in, 150, 151

Supreme Court of the United States, holds that a charter is a contract (Dartmouth College Decision), 180, 200n, 229-233; that children cannot be forced to attend public school (Oregon Decision) 380-383; that Negroes must be provided educational facilities equal to those provided for white people, 691-700; that children can be expelled from school for failure to salute the national flag, 766, 767; that they cannot be expelled for such refusal, 768-770; that non-public school children can be transported to school at public expense, 771-773; that religious instruction cannot be given in public-school buildings, 775-778

Swift, F. H., *A History of Public Permanent Common School Funds in the United States*, 316n

Swint, H. L., *The Northern Teacher in the South*, 659

Syms, Benjamin, will of, in Virginia, 58-60; school provided by, 58n

Tappan, Henry, 180

Teachers and tutors, advertisements of, 1; oath required of by England, 29; one purpose of Benjamin Franklin's academy, 31; qualifications required of in New Jersey, 35, 36; loyalty oath required of in Massachusetts (1776), 36; in New Jersey (1777), 37; in Pennsylvania (1778), 37, 38; salaries of (1947), 385, 386; purchasing power of salaries in 1941 and 1949, 387; contract of in Texas, 405-406; Samuel R. Hall on requisite qualifications of, 406-409; wages of in Connecticut (1832), 412; in Pennsylvania, 413; Phillips Andover Academy undertakes to prepare, 413; Henry Barnard on in Germany, 414; Calvin E. Stowe on women as, 415; academies used for training, 416n; on need for the education of in Texas, 420, 421; David Page to prospective, 422; prepared at the University of Virginia, 422, 423; the University of Michigan established a chair of pedagogy (1879), 423, 424; Committee of Ten on, 429-431; Committee of Fifteen on, 431-435; defects in certification of, 436-438; deficient in English in high schools, 441; need for professionally trained, 441-443; need of loyalty oaths for, 443; Franklin D. Roosevelt warns against excess supply of, 444; amount of schooling of (1930), 444, 445; annual cost of illness of, 452-454; Abraham Flexner on importance of humor in, 454-456; issues and trends in education of, 456-459; salaries of (1948), 460; National Education Association opposes communists as, 462, 463; on professional standards for, 463, 464; Phi Beta Kappa on freedom of, 464

"Teachers' Loyalty Oath Laws and Joshua Bennett" (Donald F. Shaughnessy), 40n

Ten-Brook, Andrew, *American State Universities and the University of Michigan*, 214n

Tennessee, legislature of opposes appropriations to the United States Military Academy, 256, 257; creates *ex-officio* state board of education and state superintendent of schools, 355-359

Texas, a senator in the legislature opposes a university, 272-274; a teacher's contract in (1825), 405, 406; need for the education of teachers in, 420, 421

Tewksbury, D. G., *American Colleges and Universities Before the Civil War*, 180, 186n

The American Lyceum (Cecil B. Hayes), 151n

The American Teacher (Willard S. Elsbree), 16n

The Association of American Universities, established (1900), 561-563

The Carnegie Foundation for the Advancement of Teaching, defines educational "units," 520-522

The College Charts Its Course (R. F. Butts), 186n

The Colleges and the Courts (E. C. Elliott and M. M. Chambers), 766n

The Diaries of George Washington (J. G. Fitzgerald), 182n

The Education of the Negro Prior to 1861 (C. G. Woodson), 660

The Federal and State Constitutions (B. F. Poore), 113n

"The Futility of the Spelling Grind" (J. M. Rice), 744n

The History of Harvard University (Josiah Quincy), 60n

The Hoosier Schoolmaster (Edward Eggleston), 507n

The Impending Crisis of the South: How to Meet It (H. R. Helper), 670n

Then and Now in Education (O. W. Caldwell and S. A. Courtis), 493n

Theory and Practice of Teaching (David Page), 501n

The Improvement of Teacher Education, excerpts from, 456-459

Three Americanists (R. G. Adams), 271n

Three Centuries of Harvard (Samuel Eliot Morison), 64n

The Life and Works of Christopher Dock (Martin G. Brumbaugh), 31n

The Making of Our Middle Schools (E. E. Brown), 31n

"The Movement to Establish a National University" (James W. Hill), 98n

The Northern Teacher in the South (H. L. Swint), 650

The Old Time College President (G. P. Schmidt), 186n

"The Pedagogues at Armageddon" (H. E. Buchholz), 384n

The Private Schools of Colonial Boston (Robert F. Seybolt), 41n

The Rockefeller Foundation, charter of, 578, 579

The Selected Writings of Benjamin Rush (D. D. Runes), 306n

The Teacher (Jacob Abbott), 488n

Thorpe, F. N., *Benjamin Franklin and the University of Pennsylvania,* 31n

The Writings of George Washington (John C. Fitzpatrick), 97n

The Writings of Thomas Jefferson (P. L. Ford), 118n; 186n

Thomas, M. Carey, on the education of women, 723

Thomas Jefferson and the University of Virginia (H. B. Adams), 127n

The Works of Benjamin Franklin (Jared Sparks), 58n; 74n

Thorndike, Edward L., 726; "father" of the measurement-movement, 747

Thwing, Charles F., *A History of Higher Education in America,* 186n

Ticknor, George, on Harvard, 237; S. E. Morison on reforms of, 237n

Transportation of non-public school children provided (New Jersey), 767, 768; Supreme Court sustains, 771-773

Travels of Four Years and A Half in the United States of America (John Davis), 54n

Trends in costs of higher education, 630, 631

Truman, President H. S., on education and research, 779-781

Two Hundred Years of the S. P. G. (C. F. Pascoe), 21n

Tunis, John R., *Was College Worth While?* 540

Turner, Nat, uprising of Negroes led by, 8n; 659

Tutorial practices, 45-47

Tutors and teachers, advertisements of, 1

"Turning out" the teacher, Horace Greeley on (1820), 487; account of in Indiana, 507-510

UNESCO, extracts from constitution of, 773-775

United States Military Academy, appropriations to opposed, 256, 257

University of California, loyalty oath for professors in, 462; President R. G. Sproul dissents from action of the Board of Regents on, 462n

University of Georgia, charter of, 192-196

University of Michigania (Catholepistemiad), charter of, 214, 215; program of studies in, 264, 265; establishes chair of pedagogy (1879), 423, 424

University of Mississippi, trustees of exonerate President F. A. P. Barnard, 289-295

University of North Carolina, degrees conferred (1802), 205; suit *vs.* Foy and Bishop, 209n; Daniel Webster cites, 228, 229; description of social life at, 265-267

University of Oklahoma must not segregate Negro and white students, 698-700

University of South Carolina, rules at, in 1820's, 235, 236

University of Texas, establishment of opposed, 272-274; act to establish, 279-282; required to admit Negroes, 696, 697

University of Virginia, proposal to establish by subscription, lottery and luxury tax, 206-209; rules at, in 1820's, 235, 236; educates fifty students for teaching (1857), 422, 423

Van Tyne, C. H., on loyalty oaths during the American Revolution, 36n

Veblen, Thorstein, on academic administration and policy, 590-594; on the influence of business on, 594-597

Vermont, early constitutional provisions for schools, 114, 116

Vesey, Denmark, uprising of Negroes led by, 659

Veterans provision for the education of, 609-612

Virginia, early educational efforts in, 3-7; early apprenticeship practices in, 9-12; changes method of licensing schoolmasters, 19-20; need for college in (1660-1662), 67, 68; William Berkeley's report on, 68, 69; legislature of resolves against the education of American youth in Europe, 96, 97; early copyright law in, 120n; Pestalozzian school in, 138n; Jefferson's bill for education in, 299-306; establishes literary fund, 321; books used in the schools of (1844), 491-493; prohibits teaching of slaves, free Negroes and mulattoes to read and write, 664, 665; provides for the teaching of a young slave to read and write, 668

Virginia Company of London, 2

Walton, John, offers to teach many subjects in New York (1723), 41

Was College Worth While? (John R. Tunis), 540

Washington, Booker T., receives honorary degree from Harvard, 679-82; description of as great move starts controversy, 682-685

Washington, George, receives LL.D. from Harvard, 1, 87, 88; deplores the education of Americans in Europe, 97; Samuel Blodget's account of conversation with, 98, 99; vests navigation stock in legislature of Virginia, 99, 100; on national university, 100, 101; to John Adams on removal of College of Geneva to Virginia, 101; to Congress on national university, 102; gives navigation stock for national university, 103; will of, 103n; gift to Liberty Hall Academy, 229, 230n

Washington & Lee University, beneficiary of gift of George Washington, 103n

Wayland, Francis, on the collegiate system of the United States, 260-263; 409

Webster, Daniel, in Dartmouth College Case, 228-233

Webster, Noah, criticizes the education of Americans in Europe, 93-96; "father" of copyright, 120n

Weeks, Stephen B., *History of Public School Education in Arkansas,* 499n

Wesley, Edgar B., *Proposed: The University of the United States,* 98n

Wesley, Reverend John, 58n

Wesleyan College (Georgia) some activities of (1837), 711-713

West, H. R., to Horace Mann, 160

White, President Andrew D., of Cornell favors national university, 98n

Whitefield, Reverend George, 58n

Wickersham, J. P., *A History of Education in Pennsylvania,* 30n, 69n, 430n

Wiley, Calvin, 133

Wilberforce, Bishop Samuel, rebukes Henry Huxley over Darwinism, 727

William and Mary College. See College of William and Mary

William and Mary College Quarterly Historical Papers, 84n

William Smith: Educator and Churchman (A. F. Gegenheimer), 229n

Williams College, in 1856, 274-277

Williamson, W. D., says Northern students should go South and Southern students North to dissolve prejudices, 263, 264

Wills, educational provisions in, 1

Winterbotham, William, sued by Jedidiah Morse under first national copyright, 120n, 470n

Winyaw Indigo Society in South Carolina, 58n

Witherspoon, President John of Princeton, 45n

Wittels, G. B., "Lucky Sons of Stephen Girard," 247n

Wolf, Governor, message to legislature on education, 344, 345

Wollstonecraft, Mary, on the education and other rights of women, 703-705

Women, educational and other rights of, 701-723; long delay in education of, 701; Mary Wollstonecraft on, 703-705; Benjamin Rush on, 705, 706; Thomas Jefferson on, 706, 707; satire on college for Kentucky, 710, 711; first convention on rights of, 713-716; satire on placing a daughter at school, 717; interest in the South in the education of, 717, 718; Charles W. Eliot on, 718; F. A. P. Barnard on, 721; National Education Association on, 721; James B. Angell on, 722; Nicholas Murray Butler on, 722; G. Stanley Hall on, 722; John F. Goucher on, 722; M. Carey Thomason, 723; C. A. Richmond on, 723

Woodbridge, W. C., advocate of the lyceum, 151n

Woodson, C. G., *The Education of the Negro Prior to 1861,* 660

Woodward High School in Cincinnati in 1856, sketch of, 277-279

Woody, Thomas, *A History of Women's Education in the United States,* 702

Working men of Philadelphia, questions to political candidates by, 146; 147; on public education, 342

Workingmen's Party of Boston, platform of, 147, 128

Wright, Arthur D. and George E. Gardner, *Hall's Lectures on School-Keeping,* 406n

Written examinations, Horace Mann on value of, 493-499

Yale College, 1; degrees conferred (1802), 205

Zenger, John Peter, early case involving freedom of the press, 72